TEACHER'S EDITION

Houghton
Mifflin
Harcourt

collections

GRADE 8

Program Consultants:

Kylene Beers

Martha Hougen

Carol Jago

William L. McBride

Erik Palmer

Lydia Stack

HISTORY

bio.

Cover, Title Page Photo Credits: © Tek Image/Getty Images

Printed in the U.S.A.

ISBN 978-0-544-08706-4

2 3 4 5 6 7 8 9 10 0914 22 21 20 19 18 17 16 15 14 13

4500431992   A B C D E F G

Houghton
Mifflin
Harcourt

collections

Teacher's Edition Table of Contents

Kylene Beers Nationally known lecturer and author on Reading and Literacy; 2011 recipient of the Conference on English Leadership Exemplary Leader Award; coauthor of *Notice and Note: Strategies for Close Reading*; former President of the National Council of Teachers of English. Dr. Beers is the nationally known author of *When Kids Can't Read: What Teachers Can Do* and coeditor of *Adolescent Literacy: Turning Promise into Practice*, as well as articles in the *Journal of Adolescent and Adult Literacy*. Former editor of *Voices from the Middle*, she is the 2001 recipient of NCTE's Richard W. Halley Award, given for outstanding contributions to middle-school literacy. She recently served as Senior Reading Researcher at the Comer School Development Program at Yale University as well as Senior Reading Advisor to Secondary Schools for the Reading and Writing Project at Teachers College.

Martha Hougen National consultant, presenter, researcher, and author. Areas of expertise include differentiating instruction for students with learning difficulties, including those with learning disabilities and dyslexia; and teacher and leader preparation improvement. Dr. Hougen has taught at the middle school through graduate levels. Recently her focus has been on working with teacher educators to enhance teacher and leader preparation to better meet the needs of all students. Currently she is working with the University of Florida at the Collaboration for Effective Educator Development, Accountability, and Reform Center (CEEDAR Center) to improve the achievement of students with disabilities by reforming teacher and leader licensure, evaluation, and preparation. She has led similar efforts in Texas with the Higher Education Collaborative and the College & Career Readiness Initiative Faculty Collaboratives. In addition to peer-reviewed articles, curricular documents, and presentations, Dr. Hougen has published two college textbooks: *The Fundamentals of Literacy Assessment and Instruction Pre-K–6* (2012) and *The Fundamentals of Literacy Assessment and Instruction 6–12* (2014).

Carol Jago Teacher of English with 32 years of experience at Santa Monica High School in California; author and nationally known lecturer; and past President of the National Council of Teachers of English. Currently serves as Associate Director of the California Reading and Literature Project at UCLA. With expertise in standards assessment and secondary education, Ms. Jago is the author of numerous books on education, including *With Rigor for All* and *Papers, Papers, Papers*, and is active with the California Association of Teachers of English, editing its scholarly journal *California English* since 1996. Ms. Jago also served on the planning committee for the 2009 NAEP Framework and the 2011 NAEP Writing Framework.

William L. McBride Curriculum Specialist. Dr. McBride is a nationally known speaker, educator, and author who now trains teachers in instructional methodologies. He is coauthor of *What's Happening*, an innovative, high-interest text for middle-grade readers, and author of *If They Can Argue Well, They Can Write Well*. A former reading specialist, English teacher, and social studies teacher, he holds a masters in reading and a doctorate in curriculum and instruction from the University of North Carolina at Chapel Hill. Dr. McBride has contributed to the development of textbook series in language arts, social studies, science, and vocabulary. He is also known for his novel *Entertaining an Elephant*, which tells the story of a veteran teacher who becomes reinspired with both his profession and his life.

Erik Palmer Veteran teacher and education consultant based in Denver, Colorado. Author of *Well Spoken: Teaching Speaking to All Students* and *Digitally Speaking: How to Improve Student Presentations*. His areas of focus include improving oral communication, promoting technology in classroom presentations, and updating instruction through the use of digital tools. He holds a bachelor's degree from Oberlin College and a master's degree in curriculum and instruction from the University of Colorado.

Lydia Stack International ESL consultant. Director of the Screening and Assessment Center in the San Francisco Unified School District. Her areas of expertise are English language teaching strategies, ESL standards for students and teachers, and curriculum writing. Her teaching experience includes 25 years as an elementary and high school ESL teacher. She is past president of TESOL. Her awards include the James E. Alatis Award for Service to TESOL and the San Francisco STAR Teacher Award. Her publications include *On Our Way to English*; *Wordways*; *Games for Language Learning*; and *Visions: Language, Literature, Content*.

Additional thanks to the following Program Reviewers

Rosemary Asquino	Carol M. Gibby	Linda Beck Pieplow
Sylvia B. Bennett	Angie Gill	Molly Pieplow
Yvonne Bradley	Mary K. Goff	Mary-Sarah Proctor
Leslie Brown	Saira Haas	Jessica A. Stith
Haley Carroll	Lisa M. Janeway	Peter Swartley
Caitlin Chalmers	Robert V. Kidd Jr.	Pamela Thomas
Emily Colley-King	Kim Lilley	Linda A. Tobias
Stacy Collins	John C. Lowe	Rachel Ukleja
Denise DeBonis	Taryn Curtis MacGee	Lauren Vint
Courtney Dickerson	Meredith S. Maddox	Heather Lynn York
Sarah Easley	Cynthia Martin	Leigh Ann Zerr
Phyllis J. Everette	Kelli M. McDonough	
Peter J. Foy Sr.	Megan Pankiewicz	

Blended classroom?   Flipped?   Traditional approach?

Collections offers maximum **flexibility** for planning instruction.

Teacher Dashboard

Log onto the Teacher Dashboard and *my*SmartPlanner. Use these **versatile** and fully **searchable** tools to **customize** lessons that engage students and achieve your instructional goals.

Text Complexity Rubrics

help you identify dimensions of complex text.

Measures — Lexile: 1260L

Qualitative Measures

Levels of Meaning/Purpose
more than one purpose; implied, easily identified from context

Structure
organization of main ideas and details complex but mostly explicit

Language Conventionality and Clarity
some unfamiliar, academic, or domain-specific words

Knowledge Demands
extensive knowledge of history required

COLLECTION 1 INSTRUCTIONAL OVERVIEW

PLAN

Collection 1 Lessons		COMMON CORE Key Learning Objective	Performance Task	Vocabulary Strategy	Language and Style	Student Instructional Support	CLOSE READER Selection
ANCHOR TEXT Argument by Anna Quindlen "A Quilt of a Country," p. 000	Lexile 1260	The student will be able to... analyze an author's claim and delineate and evaluate an argument	Writing Activity: Argument	Patterns of Word Changes	Noun Clauses	**Scaffolding for ELL Students:** Understand Cultural References **When Students Struggle:** Summarize (label not in TE)	Blog by Eboo Patel "Making the Future Better, Together" p. 000 Lexile 0000
ANCHOR TEXT Short Story by Nadine Gordimer "Once Upon a Time," p. 000	Lexile 1390	The student will be able to... analyze author's choices concerning the structure of a text and determine and make inferences about the theme of a work of fiction.	Speaking Activity: Fairy Tale	Words from Latin	Prepositional Phrases	**Scaffolding for ELL Students:** Language: Dialect **When Students Struggle:** • Theme • Words from Latin **To Challenge Students:** Write from Author's Perspective	Short Story by Lisa Fugard "Night Calls" p. 000 Lexile 0000
Essay by Kimberly M. Blaeser from "Rituals of Memory," p. 000	Lexile 1380	The student will be able to... determine a central idea and analyze its development over the course of a text	Speaking Activity: Discussion	Denotations and Connotations		**Scaffolding for ELL Students:** Analyze Language **When Students Struggle:** Main Idea and Supporting Details	
Speech by Abraham Lincoln "The Gettysburg Address," p. 000	Lexile 1170	The student will be able to... analyze an author's purpose and the use of rhetorical devices in a seminal U.S. document	Speaking Activity: Presentation	Multiple-Meaning Words	Parallel Structure	**Scaffolding for ELL Students:** Analyze Language **When Students Struggle:** Comprehension **To Challenge Students:** Tone and Structure	Speech by Bill Clinton "Oklahoma Bombing Memorial Address," p. 000 Lexile 0000
Photo Essay "Views of the Wall," p. 000 Poem by Alberto Rios "The Vietnam Wall," p. 000		The student will be able to... analyze the representation of a subject in two separate mediums	Media Activity: Reflection			**Scaffolding for ELL Students:** Build Background **When Students Struggle:** Compare Text and Photos	

COLLECTION 1 DIGITAL OVERVIEW

mySmartPlanner | eBook | myNotebook | myWriteSmart | fyi

Collection 1 Lessons	Media	Teach and Practice		Assess	
Student Edition | eBook	▶ Video Links	**Close Reading and Evidence Tracking**		**Performance Task**	Online Assessment
ANCHOR TEXT Argument by Anna Quindlen "A Quilt of a Country"	🔊 Audio "A Quilt of a Country"	**Close Read Screencasts** • Modeled Discussion 1 (lines 22-28) • Modeled Discussion 2 (lines 72-79) • Close Read application pdf (lines 00-000)	**Strategies for Annotation** • Delineate and Evaluate an Argument • Patterns of Word Change	Writing Activity: Argument	Selection Test
CLOSE READER Blog by Eboo Patel "Making the Future Better, Together"	🔊 Audio "Making the Future Better, Together"				
ANCHOR TEXT Short Story by Nadine Gordimer "Once Upon a Time"	🔊 Audio "Once Upon a Time"	**Close Read Screencasts** • Modeled Discussion 1 (lines 1-10) • Modeled Discussion 2 (lines 121-130) • Close Read application pdf (lines 000-000)	**Strategies for Annotation** • Analyze Author's Choices: Text Structure	Speaking Activity: Fairy Tale	Selection Test
CLOSE READER Short Story by Lisa Fugard "Night Calls"	🔊 Audio "Night Calls"				
Essay by Kimberly M. Blaeser from "Rituals of Memory"	🔊 Audio from "Rituals of Memory"		**Strategies for Annotation** • Determine Central Idea • Denotation and Connotation	Speaking Activity: Discussion	Selection Test
Speech by Abraham Lincoln "The Gettysburg Address"	▶ Video HISTORY "The Gettysburg Address: A New Declaration of Independence" 🔊 Audio "The Gettysburg Address"		**Strategies for Annotation** • Analyze Seminal U.S. Documents	Speaking Activity: Presentation	Selection Test
CLOSE READER Speech by Bill Clinton "Oklahoma Bombing Memorial Address"	🔊 Audio "Oklahoma Bombing Memorial Address"				
Photo Essay Views of the Wall Poem by Alberto Rios "The Vietnam Wall"	▶ Video HISTORY "Remembering Fallen Friends" 🔊 Audio "The Vietnam Wall"		**Strategies for Annotation** • Analyze Representations in Different Mediums	Media Activity: Reflection	Selection Test
Collection 1 Performance Tasks: A Preparing a Speech B Writing an Analytical Essay	fyi hmhfyi.com	**Interactive Lessons** A Writing Arguments A Giving a Presentation	B Writing Informative Texts B Using Textual Evidence	A Preparing a Speech B Writing an Analytical Essay	Collection Test

For Systematic Coverage of Writing and Speaking & Listening Standards	**Interactive Lessons** Writing as a Process Participating in Collaborative Discussions	**Lesson Assessments** Writing as a Process Participating in Collaborative Discussions

---

Print planning

pages show the integrated Table of Contents and all assets in the **Student Edition** and the **Close Reader.**

Digital natives?   Media enthusiasts?   Writers?

Collections engages learners with today's digital tools.

Voices and images

from **A&E®**, **bio.®**, and **HISTORY®** transport students to different times and places.

Online Tools

allow students to annotate critical passages for discussion and writing, by using **highlighting, underlining,** and **notes.**

*my*Notebook

stores students' annotations and notes for use in **Performance Tasks.**

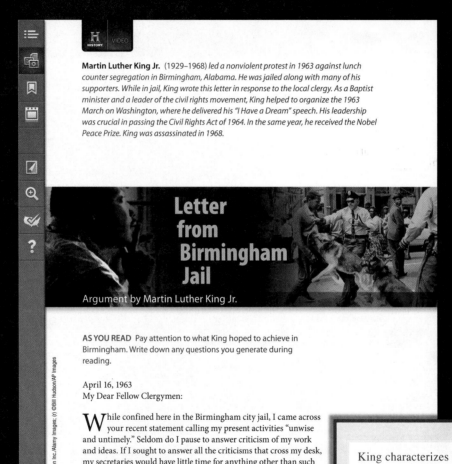

Martin Luther King Jr. (1929–1968) *led a nonviolent protest in 1963 against lunch counter segregation in Birmingham, Alabama. He was jailed along with many of his supporters. While in jail, King wrote this letter in response to the local clergy. As a Baptist minister and a leader of the civil rights movement, King helped to organize the 1963 March on Washington, where he delivered his "I Have a Dream" speech. His leadership was crucial in passing the Civil Rights Act of 1964. In the same year, he received the Nobel Peace Prize. King was assassinated in 1968.*

Letter from Birmingham Jail

Argument by Martin Luther King Jr.

AS YOU READ Pay attention to what King hoped to achieve in Birmingham. Write down any questions you generate during reading.

April 16, 1963
My Dear Fellow Clergymen:

While confined here in the Birmingham city jail, I came across your recent statement calling my present activities "unwise and untimely." Seldom do I pause to answer criticism of my work and ideas. If I sought to answer all the criticisms that cross my desk, my secretaries would have little time for anything other than such correspondence in the course of the day, and I would have no time for constructive work. But since I feel that you are men of genuine good will and that your criticisms are sincerely set forth, I want to try to answer your statement in what I hope will be patient and reasonable terms.

I think I should indicate why I am here in Birmingham, since you have been influenced by the view which argues against "outsiders coming in." I have the honor of serving as president of the Southern Christian Leadership Conference, an organization

Letter from Birmingham Jail **319**

Student Note ✖

King characterizes his critics as "men of good-will" to suggest that an understanding can be reached with them.

✔ Save to Notebook   Delete   Save

*my*Notebook

King characterizes his critics as "men of good-will" to suggest that an understanding can be reached with them.

Credits: (l) ©CSU Archives/Everett Collection Inc./Alamy Images; (r) ©Bill Hudson/AP Images

Informational text

on **fyi** is linked to each collection topic and is **curated** and **updated** monthly.

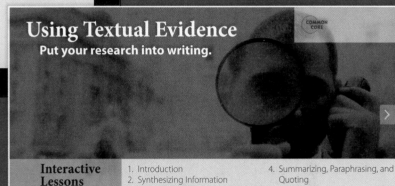

Available in Your eBook

Digital Collections

for **writing, speaking,** and **listening** provide opportunities for in-depth instruction and practice in key 21st-century skills.

Available in Your eBook

Media Lessons

prompt students to read **news reports, literary adaptations, ads,** and **websites** as complex texts.

Collections prepares students for rigorous expectations.

Background *The Hmong (hmông) are an ethnic group from southern China, Laos, Vietnam, and Thailand. In the 1970s, war and conflict caused many of the Hmong people in Laos to flee to refugee camps in Thailand. Author* **Kao Kalia Yang** *(b. 1980) was born in one of these camps. She moved with her family, including her older sister Dawb, to Minnesota in 1987. Four other siblings were born in the United States, where all the Yang children received their educations.*

from
The Latehomecomer

Memoir by Kao Kalia Yang

SETTING A PURPOSE As you read, notice the challenges and the opportunities that life in a new country presents Kao Kalia Yang. How does Yang react to her situation?

We had been in America for almost ten years. I was nearly fifteen, and Dawb had just gotten her driver's license. The children were growing up. We needed a new home—the apartment was too small. There was hardly room to breathe when the scent of jasmine rice and fish steamed with ginger mingled heavily with the scent of freshly baked pepperoni pizza—Dawb's favorite food. We had been looking for a new house for nearly six months.

It was in a poor neighborhood with houses that were
10 ready to collapse—wooden planks fallin
away, sloping porches—and huge, old tr
realty sign in the front yard, a small patc
of the white house. It was one story, with
and a single wide window framed by bla
black door. There was a short driveway

(c) ©Houghton Mifflin Harcourt; (tr) ©Der Yang

Anchor Texts
drive each collection and have related selections in the **Close Reader.**

Close Reading Screencasts
provide **modeled conversations** about text at point of use in your **eBook.**

I was feeling a strong push to reinvent myself. Without my realizing, by the time high school began, I had a feeling in the pit of my stomach that I had been on simmer for too long. I wanted to bubble over the top and douse the confusing fire that burned in my belly. Or else I wanted to turn the

These images give the impression the narrator is uncomfortable.

Background *A member of the Standing Rock Sioux,* **Susan Power** *was born in 1961 and grew up in Chicago. She spent her childhood listening to her mother tell stories about their American Indian heritage. These stories later served as inspiration for Power's writing. As a young girl, Power made frequent visits with her mother to local museums—trips that inspired her memoir "Museum Indians."*

Museum Indians

Memoir by Susan Power

Close Reader

allows students to apply standards and practice close reading strategies in a consumable **print** or **digital** format.

CLOSE READ
Notes

1. **READ ▶** As you read lines 1–16, begin to cite text evidence.

- Underline a metaphor in the first paragraph that describes the mother's braid.
- Underline a metaphor in the second paragraph that describes the mother's braid differently.
- In the margin, note the adjectives the narrator uses to describe the braid.

A snake coils in my mother's dresser drawer; it is thick and black, glossy as sequins. My mother cut her hair several years ago, before I was born, but she kept one heavy braid. It is the <u>three-foot snake</u> I lift from its nest and handle as if it were alive.

"Mom, why did you cut your hair?" I ask. I am a little girl lifting a <u>sleek black river</u> into the light that streams through the kitchen window. Mom turns to me.

"It gave me headaches. Now put that away and wash your hands for lunch."

10   "You won't cut *my* hair, will you?" I'm sure this is a whine.

"No, just a little trim now and then to even the e

I return the dark snake to its nest among

arranging it so that its thin tail hides

thick
black
glossy

Independence?　Confidence?　Achievement?

Collections scaffolds assessment demands in the classroom.

Performance Tasks

create opportunities for students to respond **analytically** and **creatively** to complex texts.

*my*WriteSmart

provides a **collaborative** tool to revise and edit **Performance Tasks** with peers and teachers.

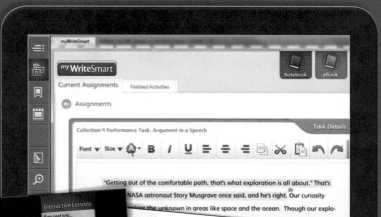

COLLECTION 1
PERFORMANCE TASK

Interactive Lessons
If you need help...
• Writing Arguments
• Using Textual Evidence

Write an Argument

This collection focuses on how and why Europeans came to the Americas and what happened as they settled in unfamiliar environments. In turn, Relocating to the Americas dramatically changed settlers' lives. In turn, the settlers changed the Americas through their interaction with its land and its native populations. Look back at the anchor text, "Of Plymouth Plantation," and at other texts you have read in this collection. Synthesize your ideas about them by writing an argument. Your argument should persuade readers to agree with your claim about how immigration changed America, and how America changes those who come here.

COMMON CORE

W 1a–e Write arguments to support claims in an analysis of substantive topics or texts, using valid reasoning and relevant and sufficient evidence.

W 9 Draw evidence form literary or informational texts to support analysis, reflection, and research.

An effective argument

- identifies a central issue or question
- states a precise claim in response to the question
- develops the claim with valid reasons and relevant evidence, such as examples and quotations from the texts
- anticipates opposing claims and counters them with well-supported counterclaims
- establishes clear, logical connections among claims, counterclaims, reasons, and evidence
- includes an introduction, a logically structured body including transitions, and a conclusion
- maintains an appropriate tone based on its audience and context
- follows the conventions of written English

*my*Notebook

PLAN

Analyze the Text Think about the following questions as they relate to the anchor text, "Of Plymouth Plantation":

- Why did European settlers come to the New World?
- When settlers came to explore and settle the Americas, how did it change their lives?
- What changes did these settlers bring to the Americas?

Choose one question to address in your argument. Then, select three texts from this collection—including "Of Plymouth Plantation"—that provide evidence for your position. These texts might present similar or different views from each other.

ACADEMIC VOCABULARY

As you share your ideas about the role of immigration in American society, be sure to use these words.

adapt
coherent
device
displace
dynamic

Collection Performance Task **103**

COLLECTION 6　TASK A
ARGUMENT

	Ideas and Evidence	Organization	Language
ADVANCED	• The introduction is memorable and persuasive; the claim clearly states a position on a substantive topic. • Valid reasons and relevant evidence from the texts convincingly support the writer's claim. • Counterclaims are anticipated and effectively addressed with counterarguments. • The concluding section effectively summarizes the claim.	• The reasons and textual evidence are organized consistently and logically throughout the argument. • Varied transitions logically connect reasons and textual evidence to the writer's claim.	• The writing reflects a formal style and an objective, or controlled, tone. • Sentence beginnings, lengths, and structures vary and have a rhythmic flow. • Spelling, capitalization, and punctuation are correct. • Grammar and usage are correct.
COMPETENT	• The introduction could do more to capture the reader's attention; the claim states a position on an issue. • Most reasons and evidence from the texts support the writer's claim, but they could be more convincing. • Counterclaims are anticipated, but the counterarguments need to be developed more. • The concluding section restates the claim.	• The organization of reasons and textual evidence is confusing in a few places. • A few more transitions are needed to connect reasons and textual evidence to the writer's claim.	• The style is informal in a few places, and the tone is defensive at times. • Sentence beginnings, lengths, and structures vary somewhat. • Several spelling and capitalization mistakes occur, and punctuation is inconsistent. • Some grammatical and usage errors are repeated in the argument.
	• The introduction is ordinary; the claim identifies an issue, but the writer's position is not clearly stated. • The reasons and evidence from the texts are not always logical or relevant. • Counterclaims are anticipated but not addressed logically. • The concluding section includes an incomplete summary of the claim.	• The organization of reasons and textual evidence is logical in some places, but it often doesn't follow a pattern. • Many more transitions are needed to connect reasons and textual evidence to the writer's position.	• The style becomes informal in many places, and the tone is often dismissive of other viewpoints. • Sentence structures barely vary, and some fragments or run-on sentences are present. • Spelling, capitalization, and punctuation are often incorrect but do not make reading the argument difficult. • Grammar and usage are incorrect in many places, but the writer's ideas are still clear.
	• The introduction is missing. • Significant supporting reasons and evidence from the texts are missing. • Counterclaims are neither anticipated nor addressed. • The concluding section is missing.	• An organizational strategy is not used; reasons and textual evidence are presented randomly. • Transitions are not used, making the argument difficult to understand.	• The style is inappropriate, and the tone is disrespectful. • Repetitive sentence structure, fragments, and run-on sentences make the writing monotonous and hard to follow. • Spelling and capitalization are often incorrect, and punctuation is missing. • Many grammatical and usage errors change the meaning of the writer's ideas.

Common Core Assessment

print and **online** resources provide instruction in three steps: **Analyze the Model, Practice the Task,** and **Perform the Task.**

STEP **2** — **PRACTICE THE TASK**

Should a business have the right to ban teenagers?

You will read:
▶ A NEWSPAPER AD
Munchy's Promise

▶ A BUSINESS ANALYSIS
Munchy's Patrons in July–October

▶ A STUDENT BLOG
Munchy's Bans Students!

▶ A NEWSPAPER EDITORIAL
A Smart Idea Can Save a Business

You will write:
▶ AN ARGUMENTATIVE ESSAY
Should a business have the right to ban teenagers?

Mr. Jones,
Here is the analysis of
July vs. October data.
Your Accountant,
Hector Ramirez, CPA

Munchy's Patrons in October

- minors
- adults

73%

Monthly Sales

- minors
- adults

September   October

studies on sleep deprivation have
only thing that might improve. An
ositively affect a student's mood
says that when he was in school,
and were better rested. With
hers and students would get along

agers should take affirmative
otherwise adjust to the reality of
m to research done in the 1990s,
nd wake patterns in adolescents
xperts talked, and California
tened. She introduced House
, the "ZZZ's to A's Act," to
earlier than 8:30 A.M.

g again. It's 7:00 A.M. You say to
nd I've got plenty of time to get
e a huge difference in your mood

You use an effective
transition to create cohesion
and signal the introduction
of another reason. Your
language is formal and non-
combative. You remain
focused on your purpose.

You anticipated and
addressed an opposing claim
that is likely to occur to
your audience. Your answer
to the opposing claim is
well-supported with valid
evidence.

Smooth flow from beginning
to end. Clear conclusion
restates your claim. Your
evidence is convincing.
Excellent use of conventions
of English. Good job!

hart.
wn in the graph?
wo forms of data.

ol should start later? If so, which data was the most

Unit 1: Argumentative Essay **9**

Unit 1: Argumentative Essay **11**

Unit 1: Argumentative Essay **7**

Graphics

enhance instruction, making **Common Core Assessment** unique and effective.

CC? **Common Core Enrichment App**

provides instant feedback for **close reading practice** with appeal for today's students.

COLLECTION 1
Culture and Belonging

Collection Overviews

Each collection suggests different starting points, as well as overviews of digital resources and instructional topics for selections.

COLLECTION PERFORMANCE TASKS

Annotated Student Edition Table of Contents

Topical Organization

Each collection reflects an engaging topic that connects selections for discussion and analysis, so students can explore several dimensions of the topic.

COMMON CORE

COLLECTION 1
Culture and Belonging

ANCHOR TEXT	**SHORT STORY** My Favorite Chaperone	Jean Davies Okimoto		3
	PERSONAL ESSAY Bonne Année	Jean-Pierre Benoît	▶	31
	RESEARCH STUDY A Place to Call Home	Scott Bittle and Jonathan Rochkind		41
ANCHOR TEXT	**MEMOIR** *from* The Latehomecomer	Kao Kalia Yang	▶	53
MEDIA ANALYSIS	**DOCUMENTARY** New Immigrants Share Their Stories	Lisa Gossels		71
	POEM The Powwow at the End of the World	Sherman Alexie		75

COLLECTION PERFORMANCE TASKS

Write an Expository Essay	79
Write a Personal Narrative	83

Close Reader

SHORT STORY
Golden Glass   Alma Luz Villanueva

ESSAY
What to Bring   Naisha Jackson

MEMOIR
Museum Indians   Susan Power

KEY LEARNING OBJECTIVES	Make inferences. Analyze plot. Analyze characterization. Analyze allusion. Analyze imagery. Analyze central idea and details.	Identify and analyze elements of a memoir. Analyze elements of a personal essay. Analyze use of text features and graphic aids. Determine use of figurative language. Analyze and evaluate elements of a documentary.

eBook *Explore It!*

  Video Links  | eBook *Read On!* Novel list and additional selections | Visit **hmhfyi.com** for current articles and informational texts.

Image credits: ©Debra Hughes/Shutterstock

Common Core State Standards

Each collection addresses a range of **Common Core State Standards,** ensuring coverage of the Reading Literature and Reading Informational Texts standards.

Close Reader

The **Close Reader** provides selections related to the collection topic for additional practice and application of close reading skills and annotation strategies.

COLLECTION 2
The Thrill of Horror

Student Edition + Close Reader

In each collection, the collection topic is explored in both the **Student Edition** and **Close Reader** selections. This page shows how the two components are integrated.

Annotated Student Edition Table of Contents

Anchor Texts

Complex and challenging, the anchor texts provide a cornerstone for exploring the collection topic, while also being integral to the Collection Performance Task. Close Reader selections relate to the Student Edition anchor texts.

Compare Text and Media

To underscore that textual analysis applies to media as well as print, a rich variety of media is compared to other texts for close reading and analysis.

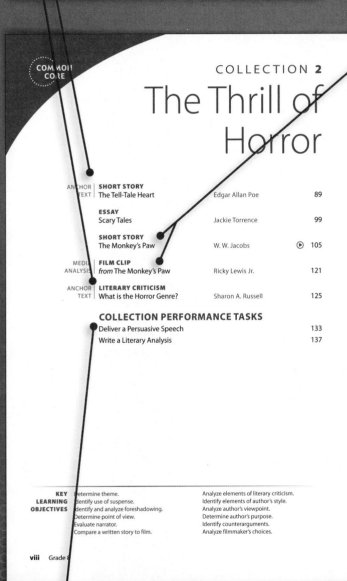

COMMON CORE

COLLECTION 2

The Thrill of Horror

Close Reader

KEY LEARNING OBJECTIVES

Determine theme.
Identify use of suspense.
Identify and analyze foreshadowing.
Determine point of view.
Evaluate narrator.
Compare a written story to film.

Analyze elements of literary criticism.
Identify elements of author's style.
Analyze author's viewpoint.
Determine author's purpose.
Identify counterarguments.
Analyze filmmaker's choices.

Image credits: ©Andreas Gradin/Shutterstock

eBook *Explore It!*

 Video Links

 eBook *Read On!*
Novel list and additional selections

fyi Visit **hmhfyi.com** for current articles and informational texts.

Collection Performance Tasks

One or two Collection Performance Tasks present a cumulative task in which students draw on their reading and analysis of the collection's selections, as well as additional research.

COLLECTION 3
The Move Toward Freedom

Classic and Contemporary Texts

From great writers of the nineteenth century to respected contemporary authors, students encounter a range of literature. Canonical texts help to provide a context for more recent selections.

COLLECTION PERFORMANCE TASKS

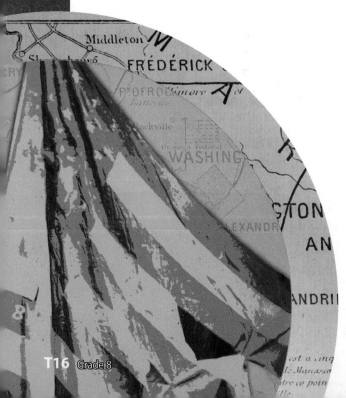

Complex Texts

With rich themes, distinctive language, stylistic elements, and high knowledge demands, complex texts from all genres challenge students to grow as readers and thinkers.

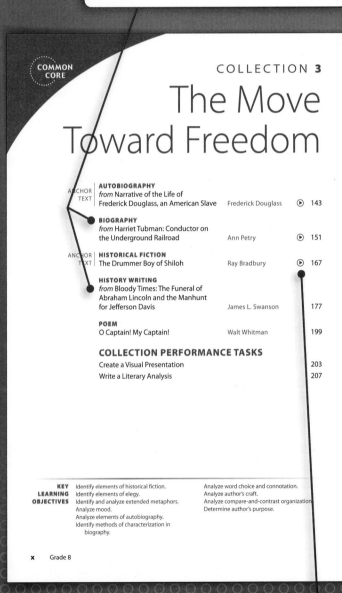

COMMON CORE

COLLECTION **3**

The Move Toward Freedom

KEY LEARNING OBJECTIVES	Identify elements of historical fiction.	Analyze word choice and connotation.
	Identify elements of elegy.	Analyze author's craft.
	Identify and analyze extended metaphors.	Analyze compare-and-contrast organization
	Analyze mood.	Determine author's purpose.
	Analyze elements of autobiography.	
	Identify methods of characterization in biography.	

Close Reader

BIOGRAPHY
My Friend Douglass   Russell Freedman

SHORT STORY
A Mystery of Heroism   Stephen Crane

JOURNAL ENTRIES
Civil War Journal   Louisa May Alcott

Image credits: ©Corbis; (bg) ©Antonio Abrignani/Shutterstock

eBook *Explore It!*

▶ Video Links		**eBook** *Read On!* Novel list and additional selections	**fyi** hmhfyi.com **Visit hmhfyi.com** for current articles and informational texts.

  HISTORY® and A&E®

Adding the images and voices that make selections and historical periods come alive, these video assets are available at point of use in the eBook.

eBook

The eBook, both Student Edition and Teacher's Edition, is your entryway to a full complement of digital resources.

COLLECTION 4
Approaching Adulthood

Focus on Argument

Through a range of informational texts, students analyze claims and supporting evidence.

COLLECTION PERFORMANCE TASKS

Annotated Student Edition Table of Contents

Compare Texts

To enrich the analysis and discussion of each text, students compare and contrast selections, exploring elements such as authors' choices, themes, and the structure of arguments.

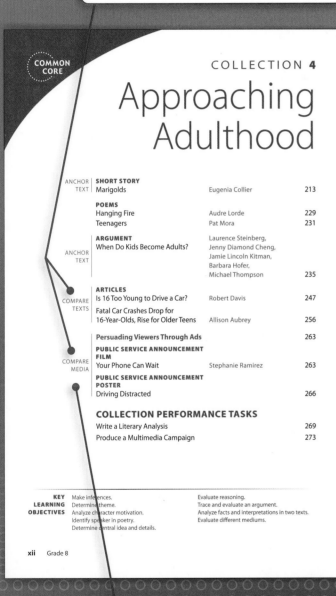

COMMON CORE

COLLECTION 4

Approaching Adulthood

Close Reader

KEY LEARNING OBJECTIVES
Make inferences.
Determine theme.
Analyze character motivation.
Identify speaker in poetry.
Determine central idea and details.

Evaluate reasoning.
Trace and evaluate an argument.
Analyze facts and interpretations in two texts.
Evaluate different mediums.

Image credits: ©jumpingsack/Shutterstock

eBook *Explore It!*

▶ Video Links | eBook *Read On!* Novel list and additional selections 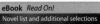 | Visit **hmhfyi.com** for current articles and informational texts.

Media Analysis

Lessons based on media provide opportunities for students to apply analysis and techniques of close reading to other kinds of texts.

Digital Resources

From video links to additional selections and informational texts, a range of digital resources in the eBook complements and enriches students' reading.

COLLECTION 5
Anne Frank's Legacy

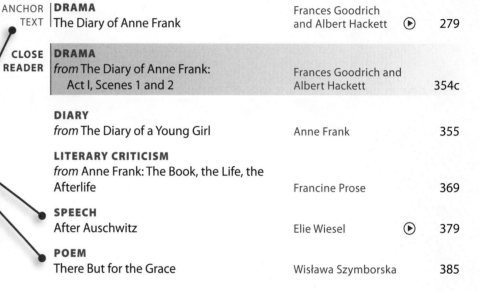

Prize-Winning Writers

Selections by acclaimed writers expose students to the very best in literary and nonfiction texts.

COLLECTION PERFORMANCE TASK

Image Credit: ©Tim DeWaele/Corbis

Annotated Student Edition Table of Contents

Variety of Genres

Both the Student Edition and the Close Reader include a variety of genres of literary texts, informational texts, and media. The genre of each selection is clearly labeled.

COMMON CORE

COLLECTION 5

Anne Frank's Legacy

Close Reader

KEY LEARNING OBJECTIVES
Identify and analyze elements of drama.
Analyze flashback.
Analyze sound devices in poetry.
Make inferences.
Identify and analyze elements of a diary.
Analyze impact of word choice on tone.
Analyze persuasive techniques.
Determine use of rhetorical devices.
Determine author's viewpoint.

Image credits: ©Tim De Waele/Corbis

eBook *Explore It!*

▶ Video Links | HISTORY | A&E | **eBook** *Read On!* Novel list and additional selections | fyi hmhfyi.com **Visit hmhfyi.com** for current articles and informational texts.

Text-Dependent Questions

Both the Student Edition and the Close Reader include text-dependent questions that require students to re-enter the text and cite text evidence to support their claims.

INTEGRATED PROGRAM CONTENTS

Cultural Diversity
To enrich students' perspectives, writers from diverse cultures are featured.

Image Credit: ©Debra Hughes/Shutterstock

Annotated Student Edition Table of Contents

KEY LEARNING OBJECTIVES
Analyze point of view and narrator.
Determine and analyze style.
Determine use of figurative language.
Analyze rhyme scheme and meter.
Compare and contrast poetic structure.
Draw conclusions.
Analyze imagery.
Delineate and evaluate an argument.

eBook *Explore It!*

 Video Links 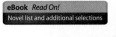 eBook *Read On!* Novel list and additional selections **Visit hmhfyi.com** for current articles and informational texts.

Image credits: ©Debra Hughes/Shutterstock

Collection Performance Tasks

Collection Performance Tasks require students to develop a variety of writing and speaking products, working through the process of planning, producing, revising, and presenting for each task.

fyi

The fyi website at hmhfyi.com provides additional contemporary informational texts to enhance each collection. Updated regularly, this site expands background knowledge, discussion, and research.

Student Resources

Information, Please

When students have questions, they can turn to Student Resources for answers. This section includes information about Performance Tasks, the nature of argument, vocabulary and spelling, and grammar, usage, and mechanics.

Word Knowledge

The Glossaries provide definitions for selection, academic, and domain-specific vocabulary, conveniently compiled in a single location.

DIGITAL OVERVIEW

Connecting to Your World

Every time you read something, view something, write to someone, or react to what you've read or seen, you're participating in a world of ideas. You do this every day, inside the classroom and out. These skills will serve you not only at home and at school, but eventually (if you can think that far ahead!), in your career.

The digital tools in this program will tap into the skills you already use and help you sharpen those skills for the future.

Start your exploration at my.hrw.com

Start with the Dashboard

Get one-stop access to the complete digital program for *Collections* as well as management and assessment tools.

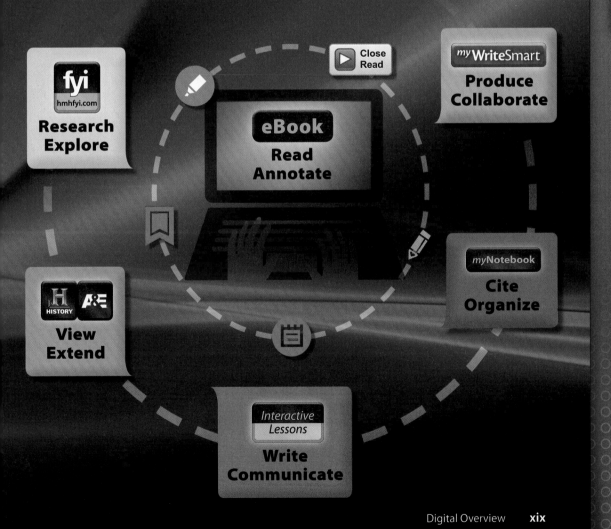

Research Explore — fyi hmhfyi.com

Close Read

my **WriteSmart** — **Produce Collaborate**

eBook Read Annotate

my Notebook — **Cite Organize**

HISTORY A&E — **View Extend**

Interactive Lessons — **Write Communicate**

Digital Overview **xix**

COMMON CORE

DIGITAL COLLECTIONS

Writing and Speaking & Listening

Communication in today's world requires quite a variety of skills. To express yourself and win people over, you have to be able to write for print, for online media, and for spoken presentations. To collaborate, you have to work with people who might be sitting right next to you or at the other end of an Internet connection.

Comprehensive Standards Coverage

Twelve digital collections provide thorough coverage of all Writing and Speaking and Listening Common Core State Standards.

Available Only in Your eBook

Interactive Lessons

The interactive lessons in these collections will help you master the skills needed to become an expert communicator.

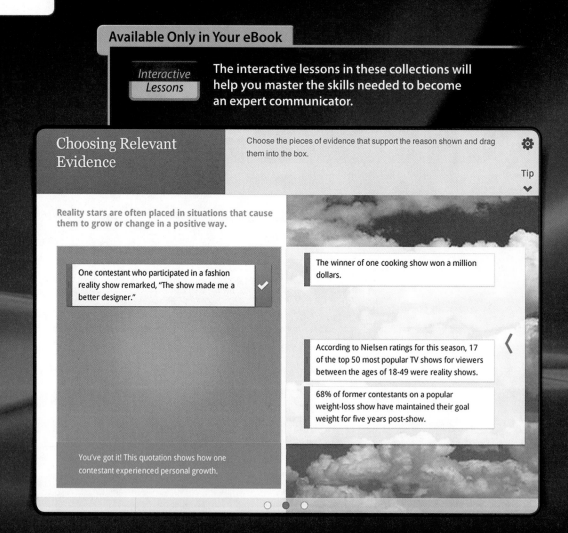

Choosing Relevant Evidence

Choose the pieces of evidence that support the reason shown and drag them into the box.

Tip

Reality stars are often placed in situations that cause them to grow or change in a positive way.

One contestant who participated in a fashion reality show remarked, "The show made me a better designer." ✓

The winner of one cooking show won a million dollars.

According to Nielsen ratings for this season, 17 of the top 50 most popular TV shows for viewers between the ages of 18-49 were reality shows.

68% of former contestants on a popular weight-loss show have maintained their goal weight for five years post-show.

You've got it! This quotation shows how one contestant experienced personal growth.

Writing Arguments
Learn how to build a strong argument.

COMMON CORE — W 1, W 10

Interactive Lessons

1. Introduction
2. What Is a Claim?
3. Support: Reasons and Evidence
4. Building Effective Support
5. Creating a Coherent Argument
6. Persuasive Techniques
7. Formal Style
8. Concluding Your Argument

Student-Directed Lessons

Though primarily intended for individual student use, these interactive lessons also offer opportunities for whole-class and small-group instruction and practice.

Writing Informative Texts
Shed light on complex ideas and topics.

COMMON CORE — W 2, W 10

Interactive Lessons

1. Introduction
2. Developing a Topic
3. Organizing Ideas
4. Introductions and Conclusions
5. Elaboration
6. Using Graphics and Multimedia
7. Precise Language and Vocabulary
8. Formal Style

Writing Narratives
A good storyteller can always capture an audience.

COMMON CORE — W 3, W 10

Interactive Lessons

1. Introduction
2. Narrative Context
3. Point of View and Characters
4. Narrative Structure
5. Narrative Techniques
6. The Language of Narrative

Writing as a Process

Get from the first twinkle of an idea to a sparkling final draft.

COMMON CORE W 4, W 5, W 10

Interactive Lessons

1. Introduction
2. Task, Purpose, and Audience
3. Planning and Drafting
4. Revising and Editing
5. Trying a New Approach

Teacher Support

Each collection in your teacher eBook includes

- support for English language learners and less-proficient writers
- instructional and management tips for every screen
- a rubric
- additional writing applications

Producing and Publishing with Technology

Learn how to write for an online audience.

COMMON CORE W 6

Interactive Lessons

1. Introduction
2. Writing for the Internet
3. Interacting with Your Online Audience
4. Using Technology to Collaborate

Conducting Research

There's a world of information out there. How do you find it?

COMMON CORE W 6, W 7, W 8

Interactive Lessons

1. Introduction
2. Starting Your Research
3. Types of Sources
4. Using the Library for Research
5. Conducting Field Research
6. Using the Internet for Research
7. Taking Notes
8. Refocusing Your Inquiry

xxii Grade 8

Evaluating Sources
Don't believe everything you read!

COMMON CORE **W 8**

Interactive Lessons

1. Introduction
2. Evaluating Sources for Usefulness
3. Evaluating Sources for Reliability

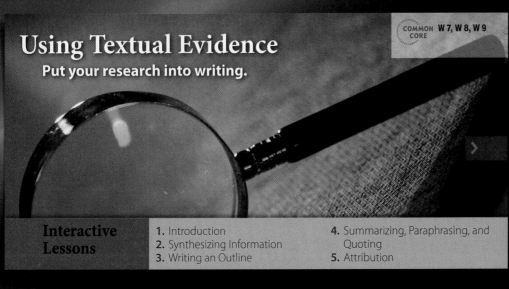

Using Textual Evidence
Put your research into writing.

COMMON CORE **W 7, W 8, W 9**

Interactive Lessons

1. Introduction
2. Synthesizing Information
3. Writing an Outline
4. Summarizing, Paraphrasing, and Quoting
5. Attribution

Participating in Collaborative Discussions
There's power in putting your heads together.

COMMON CORE **SL 1**

Interactive Lessons

1. Introduction
2. Preparing for Discussion
3. Establishing and Following Procedure
4. Speaking Constructively
5. Listening and Responding
6. Wrapping Up Your Discussion

Authentic Practice of 21st-Century Skills

Students have ample opportunities to evaluate real websites, engage in digital collaboration, conduct Web research, and critique student discussions.

Analyzing and Evaluating Presentations

COMMON CORE SL 2, SL 3, SL 6

**Media-makers all want your attention.
What are they trying to tell you?**

Interactive Lessons	1. Introduction	4. Tracing a Speaker's Argument
	2. Analyzing a Presentation	5. Rhetoric and Delivery
	3. Evaluating a Speaker's Reliability	6. Synthesizing Media Sources

Giving a Presentation

COMMON CORE SL 4, SL 6

**Learn how to talk to a
roomful of people.**

Interactive Lessons	1. Introduction	3. The Content of Your Presentation
	2. Knowing Your Audience	4. Style in Presentation
		5. Delivering Your Presentation

Using Media in a Presentation

COMMON CORE SL 5

**If a picture is worth a thousand words,
just think what you can do with a video.**

Interactive Lessons	1. Introduction	3. Using Presentation Software
	2. Types of Media: Audio, Video, and Images	4. Practicing Your Presentation

Assessments in *my*WriteSmart

Test students' mastery of the standards covered in each digital collection by assigning the accompanying assessment in *my*WriteSmart.

| eBook | *my*Notebook | **fyi**
hmhfyi.com | *my*WriteSmart |

Supporting Close Reading, Research, and Writing

Understanding complex texts is hard work, even for experienced readers. It often takes multiple close readings to understand and write about an author's choices and meanings. The dynamic digital tools in this program will give you opportunities to learn and practice this critical skill of close reading—and help you integrate the text evidence you find into your writing.

Integrated Digital Suite

The digital resources and tools in *Collections* are designed to support students in grappling with complex text and formulating interpretations from text evidence.

Learn How to Do a Close Read

An effective close read is all about the details; you have to examine the language and ideas a writer includes. See how it's done by accessing the **Close Read Screencasts** in your eBook. Hear modeled conversations about anchor texts.

Close Read Screencasts

For each anchor text, students can access modeled conversations in which readers analyze and annotate key passages.

of the birds, how they soared and glided overhead. He pointed out the slow, graceful sweep of their wings as they beat the air steadily, without fluttering. Soon Icarus was sure that he, too, could fly and, raising his arms up and down, skirted over the white sand and even out over the waves, letting his feet touch the snowy foam as the water thundered and broke over the sharp rocks. Daedalus watched him proudly but

Soon Icarus was sure that he, too, could fly and, raising his arms up and down, skirted over the white sand and even out over the waves, letting his feet touch the snowy foam as the water thundered and broke over the sharp rocks.

There might be a sense of danger here.

Daedalus watched him proudly but with misgivings. He called Icarus to his side and, putting his arm round the boy's shoulders, said, 'Icarus, my son, we are about to make our flight. No human being has ever traveled through the air before, and I want you to listen carefully to my instructions.

Annotate the Texts

Practice close reading by utilizing the powerful annotation tools in your eBook. Mark up key ideas and observations using highlighters and sticky notes.

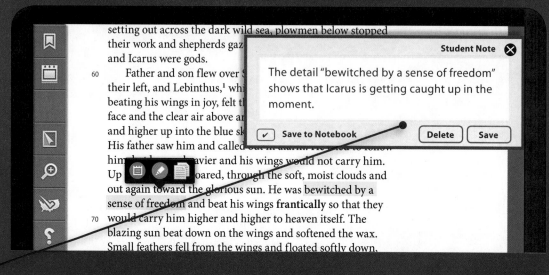

Digital Tools for Close Reading

Annotation tools allow students to note central ideas and details about an author's craft. Students can save their annotations to *my*Notebook, tagging them to particular performance tasks.

Collect Text Evidence

Save your annotations to your notebook. Gathering and organizing this text evidence will help you complete performance tasks and other writing assignments.

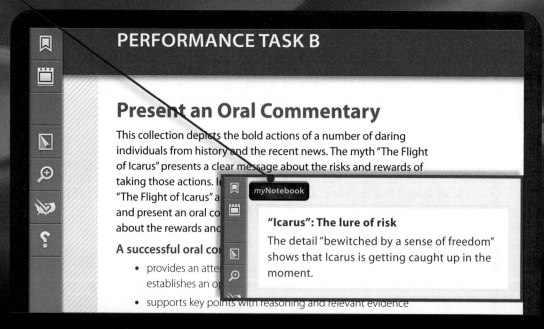

Find More Text Evidence on the Web

Tap into the *FYI* website for links to high-interest informational texts about collection topics. Capture text evidence from any Web source by including it in your notebook.

High-Interest Informational Text

Updated monthly, *FYI* features links to reputable sources of informational text.

Integrate Text Evidence into Your Writing

Use the evidence you've gathered to formulate interpretations, draw conclusions, and offer insights. Integrate the best of your text evidence into your writing.

Tools for Writing

Assign and manage performance tasks in *my*WriteSmart. Students can use the annotations they've gathered and tools for writing and collaboration to complete each task.

Digital Spotlight **xxvii**

Correlation of *Collections*, Grade 8, to the English Language Arts Common Core State Standards

The grade 8 standards on the following pages define what students should understand and be able to do by the end of the grade. They correspond to the College and Career Readiness (CCR) anchor standards below by number. The CCR and grade-specific standards are necessary complements—the former providing broad standards, the latter providing additional specificity—that together define the skills and understandings that all students must demonstrate.

College and Career Readiness Anchor Standards for Reading

Common Core State Standards

KEY IDEAS AND DETAILS

1. Read closely to determine what the text says explicitly and to make logical inferences from it; cite specific textual evidence when writing or speaking to support conclusions drawn from the text.

2. Determine central ideas or themes of a text and analyze their development; summarize the key supporting details and ideas.

3. Analyze how and why individuals, events, and ideas develop and interact over the course of a text.

CRAFT AND STRUCTURE

4. Interpret words and phrases as they are used in a text, including determining technical, connotative, and figurative meanings, and analyze how specific word choices shape meaning or tone.

5. Analyze the structure of texts, including how specific sentences, paragraphs, and larger portions of the text (e.g., a section, chapter, scene, or stanza) relate to each other and the whole.

6. Assess how point of view or purpose shapes the content and style of a text.

INTEGRATION OF KNOWLEDGE AND IDEAS

7. Integrate and evaluate content presented in diverse formats and media, including visually and quantitatively, as well as in words.

8. Delineate and evaluate the argument and specific claims in a text, including the validity of the reasoning as well as the relevance and sufficiency of the evidence.

9. Analyze how two or more texts address similar themes or topics in order to build knowledge or to compare the approaches the authors take.

RANGE OF READING AND LEVEL OF COMPLEXITY

10. Read and comprehend complex literary and informational texts independently and proficiently.

Reading Standards for Literature

Common Core State Standard	Student Edition/Teacher's Edition
KEY IDEAS AND DETAILS	
1. Cite the textual evidence that most strongly supports an analysis of what the text says explicitly as well as inferences drawn from the text.	**Student Edition** 27, 28, 77, 78, 96, 118, 174, 202, 207–210, 226, 232, 233, 269–272, 324, 354, 388, 402, 430, 432, 434, 436 **Teacher's Edition** 3, 4, 5, 6, 8, 9, 11, 12, 13, 14, 15, 16, 17, 18, 20, 21, 22, 23, 24, 26, 27, 28, 30a, 75, 76, 77, 78, 91, 92, 93, 95, 96, 105, 106, 108, 109, 110, 111, 114, 115, 117, 118, 167, 168, 169, 170, 174, 176a, 200, 202, 207, 213, 214, 215, 216, 218, 220, 221, 222, 223, 224, 226, 228a, 230, 232, 269, 279, 280, 281, 282, 283, 284, 286, 287, 288, 290, 291, 295, 297, 298, 300, 302, 308, 309, 310, 312, 313, 314, 317, 320, 323, 325, 331, 332, 335, 344, 345, 347, 351, 354, 354a, 388, 388a, 397, 398, 399, 400, 402, 428, 430, 431, 432, 433, 434, 436, 436a
2. Determine a theme or central idea of a text and analyze its development over the course of the text, including its relationship to the characters, setting, and plot; provide an objective summary of the text.	**Student Edition** 28, 117, 118, 124, 173, 174, 225, 226, 232, 233, 269–272, 388, 402, 432, 434, 436 **Teacher's Edition** 28, 30a, 107, 108, 109, 112, 116, 117, 118, 120a, 124, 167, 173, 174, 176a, 213, 214, 218, 223, 224, 225, 226, 230, 232, 234a, 269, 388, 388a, 402, 404a, 431, 432, 434, 436
3. Analyze how particular lines of dialogue or incidents in a story or drama propel the action, reveal aspects of a character, or provoke a decision.	**Student Edition** 27, 28, 96, 117, 118, 173, 174, 225, 226, 324, 353, 354, 402 **Teacher's Edition** 3, 5, 6, 8, 9, 11, 13, 14, 15, 17, 19, 20, 21, 22, 23, 24, 25, 26, 27, 28, 30a, 96, 98a, 105, 106, 108, 110, 111, 112, 115, 117, 118, 169, 173, 174, 215, 217, 221, 222, 225, 226, 228, 282, 283, 284, 286, 288, 289, 290, 294, 295, 296, 298, 300, 308, 310, 313, 320, 323, 326, 327, 328, 329, 331, 332, 335, 336, 341, 344, 345, 349, 353, 354, 354a, 402
CRAFT AND STRUCTURE	
4. Determine the meaning of words and phrases as they are used in a text, including figurative and connotative meanings; analyze the impact of specific word choices on meaning and tone, including analogies or allusions to other texts.	**Student Edition** 28, 77, 78, 96, 173, 174, 201, 202, 225, 226, 233, 387, 388, 401, 402, 430, 434, 436 **Teacher's Edition** 7, 16, 18, 19, 28, 70a, 75, 76, 77, 78a, 78b, 90, 94, 96, 105, 110, 115, 162, 168, 169, 170, 171, 172, 173, 174, 200, 201, 202, 202a, 214, 219, 221, 225, 226, 230, 234a, 283, 285, 287, 288, 289, 294, 297, 299, 301, 302, 306, 312, 315, 316, 323, 328, 334, 337, 342, 348, 387, 388, 396, 398, 399, 400, 401, 402, 428, 429, 430, 434, 436, 436a

Common Core State Standard	Student Edition/Teacher's Edition
5. Compare and contrast the structure of two or more texts and analyze how the differing structure of each text contributes to its meaning and style.	**Student Edition** 201, 202, 233, 432, 434, 435, 436 **Teacher's Edition** 162, 200, 201, 202, 202a, 368a, 431, 432, 433, 434, 435, 436
6. Analyze how differences in the points of view of the characters and the audience or reader (e.g., created through the use of dramatic irony) create such effects as suspense or humor.	**Student Edition** 95, 96, 118, 401, 402 **Teacher's Edition** 89, 90, 92, 93, 95, 96, 98a, 118, 328, 395, 396, 397, 398, 401, 402, 404a
INTEGRATION OF KNOWLEDGE AND IDEAS	
7. Analyze the extent to which a filmed or live production of a story or drama stays faithful to or departs from the text or script, evaluating the choices made by the director or actors.	**Student Edition** 123, 124 **Teacher's Edition** 122, 123, 124, 124a
8. (Not applicable to literature)	
9. Analyze how a modern work of fiction draws on themes, patterns of events, or character types from myths, traditional stories, or religious works such as the Bible, including describing how the material is rendered new.	**Student Edition** 77, 78, 117, 118 **Teacher's Edition** 77, 78, 78a, 78b, 108, 109, 112, 117, 118, 120a
RANGE OF READING AND LEVEL OF TEXT COMPLEXITY	
10. By the end of the year, read and comprehend literature, including stories, dramas, and poems, at the high end of grades 6–8 text complexity band independently and proficiently.	**Student Edition** 199–202, 213–226, 279–354, 395–402, 427–434 **Teacher's Edition** 199A, 213A, 279A, 395A, 427A

Reading Standards for Informational Text

Common Core State Standard	Student Edition/Teacher's Edition

KEY IDEAS AND DETAILS

1. Cite the textual evidence that most strongly supports an analysis of what the text says explicitly as well as inferences drawn from the text.

Student Edition
38, 51, 68, 74, 103, 130, 137–140, 149, 164, 196, 244, 255, 258, 260, 273–276, 366, 367, 376, 384, 415, 416, 425, 441–444, R22–R28

Teacher's Edition
32, 34, 35, 36, 38, 41, 42, 44, 45, 46, 48, 51, 53, 54, 59, 61, 62, 63, 65, 68, 74, 100, 103, 125, 127, 128, 130, 137, 144, 145, 149, 153, 155, 156, 157, 158, 159, 160, 161, 164, 166a, 178, 179, 180, 182, 183, 185, 188, 190, 191, 193, 196, 244, 247, 248, 249, 251, 253, 254, 255, 256, 257, 258, 260, 273, 356, 357, 358, 359, 362, 363, 364, 365, 366, 367, 376, 384, 405, 407, 408, 409, 410, 411, 412, 413, 415, 416, 418a, 420, 422, 425, R22, R23

2. Determine a central idea of a text and analyze its development over the course of the text, including its relationship to supporting ideas; provide an objective summary of the text.

Student Edition
37, 38, 68, 74, 103, 129, 130, 255, 260, 367, 376, 384, 416, 425, R16–R21, R22–R28

Teacher's Edition
32, 37, 38, 40a, 51, 68, 74, 103, 125, 126, 127, 128, 129, 130, 132a, 146, 149 , 246a, 247, 248, 249, 251, 253, 254, 255, 256, 260, 262a, 367, 376, 384, 416, 425, R16, R17, R21, R22

3. Analyze how a text makes connections among and distinctions between individuals, ideas, or events (e.g., through comparisons, analogies, or categories).

Student Edition
37, 38, 50, 51, 67, 68, 74, 103, 129, 130, 148, 149, 163, 164, 195, 196, 244, 255, 258, 260, 366, 367, 376, 416, R16–R21

Teacher's Edition
31, 34, 37, 38, 43, 46, 49, 50, 51, 52a, 56, 58, 59, 62, 64, 66, 67, 68, 74, 103, 125, 127, 128, 129, 130, 132a, 144, 145, 146, 147, 148, 149, 150a, 151, 152, 153, 155, 157, 158, 159, 160, 161, 163, 164, 166a, 178, 179, 180, 185, 188, 190, 195, 196, 198a, 244, 248, 249, 251, 254, 255, 256, 257, 258, 260, 355, 357, 361, 362, 365, 366, 367, 368a, 376, 416, R16, R18, R21, R25

CRAFT AND STRUCTURE

4. Determine the meaning of words and phrases as they are used in a text, including figurative, connotative, and technical meanings; analyze the impact of specific word choices on meaning and tone, including analogies or allusions to other texts.

Student Edition
38, 51, 67, 68, 102, 103, 130, 149, 163, 164, 195, 196, 244, 258, 367, 375, 376, 383, 384, 415, 416, 425

Teacher's Edition
33, 38, 48, 51, 53, 55, 56, 57, 58, 59, 61, 63, 65, 67, 68, 70a, 99, 100, 102, 103, 127, 130, 143, 149, 153, 154, 155, 156, 158, 159, 161, 163, 164, 179, 183, 184, 186, 189, 191, 192, 193, 196, 238, 243, 244, 251, 252, 258, 360, 361, 367, 371, 373, 375, 376, 380, 381, 382, 383, 384, 384a, 386, 405, 408, 409, 410, 412, 413, 414, 415, 416, 425

Common Core State Standard	Student Edition/Teacher's Edition
5. Analyze in detail the structure of a specific paragraph in a text, including the role of particular sentences in developing and refining a key concept.	**Student Edition** 37, 38, 68, 148, 149, 163, 164, 195, 196, 243, 255, 260, 367, 384, 424, R16–R21 **Teacher's Edition** 34, 37, 38, 68, 146, 148, 149, 150a, 151, 152, 153, 154, 155, 156, 158, 159, 161, 163, 164, 166a, 178, 179, 180, 185, 188, 195, 196, 198a, 236, 239, 243, 247, 249, 253, 255, 260, 367, 380, 382, 384, 384a, 406, 418a, 420, 421, 422, 424, R16, R17, R20, R21, R25
6. Determine an author's point of view or purpose in a text and analyze how the author acknowledges and responds to conflicting evidence or viewpoints.	**Student Edition** 74, 102, 103, 129, 130, 148, 149, 243, 244, 366, 367, 375, 376, 384, 416, 425, R16–R21, R22–R28 **Teacher's Edition** 35, 37, 40a, 47, 74, 101, 102, 103, 104, 125, 127, 128, 129, 130, 132a, 143, 144, 147, 148, 149, 150a, 182, 235, 236, 237, 238, 239, 240, 241, 242, 243, 244, 246a, 357, 359, 361, 365, 366, 367, 368a, 369, 370, 372, 374, 375, 376, 384, 416, 420, 425, R16, R22

INTEGRATION OF KNOWLEDGE AND IDEAS

7. Evaluate the advantages and disadvantages of using different mediums (e.g., print or digital text, video, multimedia) to present a particular topic or idea.	**Student Edition** 73, 74, 123, 124, 258, 268 **Teacher's Edition** 73, 74, 74a, 122, 123, 124
8. Delineate and evaluate the argument and specific claims in a text, assessing whether the reasoning is sound and the evidence is relevant and sufficient; recognize when irrelevant evidence is introduced.	**Student Edition** 243, 244, 258, 260, 376, 424, 425, R22–R28 **Teacher's Edition** 24, 25, 26, 27, 30, 186, 187, 188, 189, 190, 192a, 193, 194, 195, 196, 197, 198, 238, 316a, R23, R24, R26, R28, R29
9. Analyze a case in which two or more texts provide conflicting information on the same topic and identify where the texts disagree on matters of fact or interpretation.	**Student Edition** 30, 279, 280 **Teacher's Edition** 70a, 236, 237, 238, 239, 240, 241, 242, 243, 244, 246a, 256, 257, 258, 260, 376, 384, 419, 421, 422, 423, 424, 425, 426a, R22, R27, R28

RANGE OF READING AND LEVEL OF TEXT COMPLEXITY

10. By the end of the year, read and comprehend literary nonfiction at the high end of the grades 6–8 text complexity band independently and proficiently.	**Student Edition** 41–51, 125–130, 247–258, 405–416, 419–425 **Teacher's Edition** 41A, 125A, 247A, 405A, 419A

College and Career Readiness Anchor Standards for Writing

Common Core State Standards

TEXT TYPES AND PURPOSES

1. Write arguments to support claims in an analysis of substantive topics or texts, using valid reasoning and relevant and sufficient evidence.

2. Write informative/explanatory texts to examine and convey complex ideas and information clearly and accurately through the effective selection, organization, and analysis of content.

3. Write narratives to develop real or imagined experiences or events using effective technique, well-chosen details, and well-structured event sequences.

PRODUCTION AND DISTRIBUTION OF WRITING

4. Produce clear and coherent writing in which the development, organization, and style are appropriate to task, purpose, and audience.

5. Develop and strengthen writing as needed by planning, revising, editing, rewriting, or trying a new approach.

6. Use technology, including the Internet, to produce and publish writing and to interact and collaborate with others.

RESEARCH TO BUILD AND PRESENT KNOWLEDGE

7. Conduct short as well as more sustained research projects based on focused questions, demonstrating understanding of the subject under investigation.

8. Gather relevant information from multiple print and digital sources, assess the credibility and accuracy of each source, and integrate the information while avoiding plagiarism.

9. Draw evidence from literary or informational texts to support analysis, reflection, and research.

RANGE OF WRITING

10. Write routinely over extended time frames (time for research, reflection, and revision) and shorter time frames (a single sitting or a day or two) for a range of tasks, purposes, and audiences.

Writing Standards

Common Core State Standard	Student Edition/Teacher's Edition	Digital Collection/Lesson
TEXT TYPES AND PURPOSES		
1. Write arguments to support claims with clear reasons and relevant evidence.	**Student Edition** 133–136, 260, 268, 273–276, 388, 441–444, R2–R3 **Teacher's Edition** 133–136, 273–276, 441–444, R2	**Writing Arguments** • Introduction • What Is a Claim? • Support: Reasons and Evidence • Building Effective Support • Creating a Coherent Argument • Persuasive Techniques • Formal Style • Concluding Your Argument

Common Core State Standard	Student Edition/Teacher's Edition	Digital Collection/Lesson
a. Introduce claim(s), acknowledge alternate or opposing claims, and organize the reasons and evidence logically.	**Student Edition** 133–136, 260, 268, 273–276, 388, 441–444, R2–R3 **Teacher's Edition** 133–136, 273–276, 388, 441–444, R2	**Writing Arguments** • What Is a Claim? • Creating a Coherent Argument
b. Support claim(s) with logical reasoning and relevant evidence, using accurate, credible sources and demonstrating an understanding of the topic or text.	**Student Edition** 133–136, 260, 268, 273–276, 388, 441–444, R2–R3 **Teacher's Edition** 133–136, 273–276, 388, 441–444, R2	**Writing Arguments** • Support: Reasons and Evidence • Building Effective Support
c. Use words, phrases, and clauses to create cohesion and clarify the relationships among claim(s), reasons, and evidence.	**Student Edition** 133–136, 273–276, 388, 441–444, R2–R3 **Teacher's Edition** 133–136, 273–276, 388, 441–444, R2	**Writing Arguments** • Creating a Coherent Argument
d. Establish and maintain a formal style.	**Student Edition** 133–136, 273–276, 388, 441–444, R2–R3 **Teacher's Edition** 133–136, 273–276, 388, 441–444, R2	**Writing Arguments** • Formal Style
e. Provide a concluding statement or section that follows from and supports the argument presented.	**Student Edition** 133–136, 273–276, 388, 441–444, R2–R3 **Teacher's Edition** 133–136, 273–276, 388, 441–444, R2	**Writing Arguments** • Concluding Your Argument
2. Write informative/explanatory texts to examine a topic and convey ideas, concepts, and information through the selection, organization, and analysis of relevant content.	**Student Edition** 28, 68, 79–82, 96, 118, 137–140, 196, 207–210, 226, 269–272, 389–392, R4–R5 **Teacher's Edition** 50, 131–134, 179–182, 190, 214, 230, 248, 259–262, 337–340, 341–344, R4	**Writing Informative Texts** • Introduction • Developing a Topic • Organizing Ideas • Introductions and Conclusions • Elaboration • Using Graphics and Multimedia • Precise Language and Vocabulary • Formal Style **Using Textual Evidence** • Writing an Outline

Common Core State Standard	Student Edition/Teacher's Edition	Digital Collection/Lesson
a. Introduce a topic clearly, previewing what is to follow; organize ideas, concepts, and information, using strategies such as definition, classification, comparison/contrast, and cause/effect; include formatting (e.g., headings), graphics (e.g., charts, tables), and multimedia when useful to aiding comprehension.	**Student Edition** 79–82, 137–140, 149, 207–210, 269–272, 389–392, R4–R5 **Teacher's Edition** 79–82, 137–140, 207–210, 269–272, 389–392, R4	**Writing Informative Texts** • Developing a Topic • Organizing Ideas • Introductions and Conclusions • Using Graphics and Multimedia
b. Develop the topic with relevant facts, definitions, concrete details, quotations, or other information and examples.	**Student Edition** 79–82, 96, 118, 137–140, 149, 207–210, 269–272, 389–392, R4–R5 **Teacher's Edition** 79–82, 118, 137–140, 149, 207–210, 269–272, 389–392, R4	**Writing Informative Texts** • Elaboration
c. Use appropriate transitions to create cohesion and clarify the relationships among ideas and concepts.	**Student Edition** 79–82, 137–140, 207–210, 269–272, 389–392, R4–R5 **Teacher's Edition** 79–82, 137–140, 207–210, 269–272, 389–392, R4	**Writing Informative Texts** • Organizing Ideas
d. Use precise language and domain-specific vocabulary to inform about or explain the topic.	**Student Edition** 79–82, 137–140, 207–210, 269–272, 389–392, R4–R5 **Teacher's Edition** 79–82, 137–140, 207–210, 269–272, 389–392, R4	**Writing Informative Texts** • Precise Language and Vocabulary
e. Establish and maintain a formal style.	**Student Edition** 79–82, 137–140, 207–210, 269–272, 389–392, R4–R5 **Teacher's Edition** 79–82, 137–140, 207–210, 269–272, 389–392, R4	**Writing Informative Texts** • Formal Style
f. Provide a concluding statement or section that follows from and supports the information or explanation presented.	**Student Edition** 79–82, 137–140, 207–210, 269–272, 389–392, R4–R5 **Teacher's Edition** 137–140, 207–210, 269–272, 389–392, R4	**Writing Informative Texts** • Introductions and Conclusions

Common Core State Standard	Student Edition/Teacher's Edition	Digital Collection/Lesson
3. Write narratives to develop real or imagined experiences or events using effective technique, relevant descriptive details, and well-structured event sequences.	**Student Edition** 79–82, 83–86, R6–R7 **Teacher's Edition** 79–82, 83–86, R6	**Writing Narratives** • Introductions • Narrative Context • Point of View and Characters • Narrative Structure • Narrative Techniques • The Language of Narrative
a. Engage and orient the reader by establishing a context and point of view and introducing a narrator and/or characters; organize an event sequence that unfolds naturally and logically.	**Student Edition** 83–86, 437–440, R6–R7 **Teacher's Edition** 83–86, 437–440, R6	**Writing Narratives** • Narrative Context • Point of View and Characters • Narrative Structure
b. Use narrative techniques, such as dialogue, pacing, and description, to develop experiences, events, and/or characters.	**Student Edition** 83–86, 437–440, R6–R7 **Teacher's Edition** 83, R6	**Writing Narratives** • Narrative Structure • Narrative Techniques • The Language of Narrative
c. Use a variety of transition words, phrases, and clauses to convey sequence, signal shifts from one time frame or setting to another, and show the relationships among experiences and events.	**Student Edition** 53–56, 175–178, R6–R7 **Teacher's Edition** 53–56, 175–178, R6	**Writing Narratives** • Narrative Structure
d. Use precise words and phrases, relevant descriptive details, and sensory language to capture the action and convey experiences and events.	**Student Edition** 83–86, 437–440, R6–R7 **Teacher's Edition** 83–86, 437–440, R6	**Writing Narratives** • The Language of Narrative
e. Provide a conclusion that follows from and reflects on the narrated experiences or events.	**Student Edition** 83–86, 437–440, R6–R7 **Teacher's Edition** 83–86, 437–440, R6	**Writing Narratives** • Narrative Structure

PRODUCTION AND DISTRIBUTION OF WRITING

Common Core State Standard	Student Edition/Teacher's Edition	Digital Collection/Lesson
4. Produce clear and coherent writing in which the development, organization, and style are appropriate to task, purpose, and audience. (Grade-specific expectations for writing types are defined in standards 1–3 above.)	**Student Edition** 79–82, 83–86, 133–136, 203–206, 226, 233, 260, 354, 376, 388, 389–392, 402, 436, 437–440, 441–444, R2–R3, R4–R5, R6–R7 **Teacher's Edition** 28, 79, 83, 96, 133, 203, 226, 233, 260, 262a, 354, 376, 388, 402, 436, R2, R6	**Writing as a Process** • Task, Purpose, and Audience

Common Core State Standard	Student Edition/Teacher's Edition	Digital Collection/Lesson
5. With some guidance and support from peers and adults, develop and strengthen writing as needed by planning, revising, editing, rewriting, or trying a new approach, focusing on how well purpose and audience have been addressed. (Editing for conventions should demonstrate command of Language standards 1–3 up to and including grade 8.)	**Student Edition** 79–82, 83–86, 133–136, 137–140, 207–210, 269–272, 273–276, 389–392, 437–440, 441–444 **Teacher's Edition** 79, 83, 133, 137, 273	**Writing as a Process** • Introduction • Planning and Drafting • Revising and Editing • Trying a New Approach
6. Use technology, including the Internet, to produce and publish writing and present the relationships between information and ideas efficiently as well as to interact and collaborate with others.	**Student Edition** 203–206, 273–276, 444 **Teacher's Edition** 203, 269, 273	**Producing and Publishing with Technology** • Introduction • Writing for the Internet • Interacting with Your Online Audience • Using Technology to Collaborate

RESEARCH TO BUILD AND PRESENT KNOWLEDGE

7. Conduct short research projects to answer a question (including a self-generated question), drawing on several sources and generating additional related, focused questions that allow for multiple avenues of exploration.	**Student Edition** 38, 51, 68, 74, 78, 118, 164, 196, 203–206, 207–210, 244, 268, 384, 389–392, 425, R8–R11 **Teacher's Edition** 38, 51, 68, 74, 78, 118, 164, 174, 196, 198a, 203, 244, 384, R8	**Conducting Research** • Introduction • Starting Your Research • Types of Sources • Using the Library for Research • Conducting Field Research • Using the Internet for Research • Refocusing Your Inquiry **Using Textual Evidence** • Synthesizing Information
8. Gather relevant information from multiple print and digital sources, using search terms effectively; assess the credibility and accuracy of each source; and quote or paraphrase the data and conclusions of others while avoiding plagiarism and following a standard format for citation.	**Student Edition** 51, 68, 79–82, 118, 133–136, 196, 273–276, 384, 441–444, R8–R11 **Teacher's Edition** 51, 68, 70a, 118, 133, 174, 196, 273, 384, R8	**Conducting Research** • Types of Sources • Using the Library for Research • Using the Internet for Research **Evaluating Sources** • Introduction • Evaluating Sources for Usefulness • Evaluating Sources for Reliability **Using Textual Evidence** • Summarizing, Paraphrasing, and Quoting • Attribution
9. Draw evidence from literary or informational texts to support analysis, reflection, and research.	**Student Edition** 78, 96, 118, 137–140, 149, 164, 196, 207–210, 226, 233, 260, 269–272, 273–276, 354, 376, 384, 388, 389–392, 402, 436, 441–444 **Teacher's Edition** 78, 79, 149, 260, 269	**Writing Informative Texts** • Elaboration **Conducting Research** • Taking Notes **Using Textual Evidence** • Introduction • Synthesizing Information • Summarizing, Paraphrasing, and Quoting

Common Core State Standard	Student Edition/Teacher's Edition	Digital Collection/Lesson
a. Apply *grade 8 Reading standards* to literature (e.g., "Analyze how a modern work of fiction draws on themes, patterns of events, or character types from myths, traditional stories, or religious works such as the Bible, including describing how the material is rendered new").	**Student Edition** 96, 118, 137–140, 207–210, 226, 233, 269–272, 354, 388, 402, 436 **Teacher's Edition** 28, 96, 118, 137, 207, 226, 233, 269, 354, 388, 402, 436	
b. Apply *grade 8 Reading standards* to literary nonfiction (e.g., "Delineate and evaluate the argument and specific claims in a text, assessing whether the reasoning is sound and the evidence is relevant and sufficient; recognize when irrelevant evidence is introduced").	**Student Edition** 149, 164, 196, 260, 273–276, 376, 384, 389–392, 441–444 **Teacher's Edition** 164, 196, 273, 376	

RANGE OF WRITING

10. Write routinely over extended time frames (time for research, reflection, and revision) and shorter time frames (a single sitting or a day or two) for a range of discipline-specific tasks, purposes, and audiences.	**Student Edition** 83–86, 137–140, 226, 233, 260, 269–272, 354, 376, 388, 389–392, 402, 436, 437–440, 441–444 **Teacher's Edition** 28, 83, 96, 137, 226, 233, 260, 269, 354, 376, 388, 402, 436	**Writing as a Process** • Task, Purpose, and Audience **Writing Arguments** **Writing Informative Texts** **Writing Narratives** **Using Textual Evidence**

College and Career Readiness Anchor Standards for Speaking and Listening

Common Core State Standards
COMPREHENSION AND COLLABORATION
1. Prepare for and participate effectively in a range of conversations and collaborations with diverse partners, building on others' ideas and expressing their own clearly and persuasively.
2. Integrate and evaluate information presented in diverse media and formats, including visually, quantitatively, and orally.
3. Evaluate a speaker's point of view, reasoning, and use of evidence and rhetoric.
PRESENTATION OF KNOWLEDGE AND IDEAS
4. Present information, findings, and supporting evidence such that listeners can follow the line of reasoning and the organization, development, and style are appropriate to task, purpose, and audience.
5. Make strategic use of digital media and visual displays of data to express information and enhance understanding of presentations.
6. Adapt speech to a variety of contexts and communicative tasks, demonstrating command of formal English when indicated or appropriate.

Speaking and Listening Standards

Common Core State Standard	Student Edition/Teacher's Edition	Digital Collection/Lesson
COMPREHENSION AND COLLABORATION		
1. Engage effectively in a range of collaborative discussions (one-on-one, in groups, and teacher led) with diverse partners on *grade 8 topics, texts, and issues*, building on others' ideas and expressing their own clearly.	**Student Edition** 38, 96, 103, 130, 149, 164, 174, 202, 207–210, 233, 354, 367, 376, 384, 416, R12–R13 **Teacher's Edition** 104a, 130, 174, 202, 207–210, 354, R12	**Participating in Collaborative Discussions** • Introduction • Preparing for Discussion • Establishing and Following Procedure • Speaking Constructively • Listening and Responding • Wrapping Up Your Discussion
a. Come to discussions prepared, having read or researched material under study; explicitly draw on that preparation by referring to evidence on the topic, text, or issue to probe and reflect on ideas under discussion.	**Student Edition** 38, 96, 103, 130, 149, 164, 207–210, 233, 354, 367, 376, 384, 416, R12–R13 **Teacher's Edition** 38, 96, 103, 150a, 164, 207–210, 233, 367, 376, 384, 416, R12	**Participating in Collaborative Discussions** • Preparing for Discussion
b. Follow rules for collegial discussions, track progress toward specific goals and deadlines, and define individual roles as needed.	**Student Edition** 367, 376, 384, 416, R12–R13 **Teacher's Edition** 150a, 367, 376, 384, 416, R12	**Participating in Collaborative Discussions** • Establishing and Following Procedure
c. Pose questions that connect the ideas of several speakers and respond to others' questions and comments with relevant evidence, observations, and ideas.	**Student Edition** 103, R12–R13 **Teacher's Edition** 103, 150a, R12	**Participating in Collaborative Discussions** • Speaking Constructively • Listening and Responding
d. Acknowledge new information expressed by others and, when warranted, qualify or justify their own views in light of the evidence presented.	**Student Edition** 376, R12–R13 **Teacher's Edition** 150a, R12	**Participating in Collaborative Discussions** • Wrapping Up Your Discussion
2. Analyze the purpose of information presented in diverse media and formats (e.g., visually, quantitatively, orally) and evaluate the motives (e.g., social, commercial, political) behind its presentation.	**Student Edition** 73, 74, 123, 124, 174, 265, 267, 268 **Teacher's Edition** 72, 73, 74a, 122, 123, 124, 124a, 174, 264, 265	**Analyzing and Evaluating Presentations** • Introduction • Analyzing a Presentation
3. Delineate a speaker's argument and specific claims, evaluating the soundness of the reasoning and relevance and sufficiency of the evidence and identifying when irrelevant evidence is introduced.	**Student Edition** 103, 244, R14–R15 **Teacher's Edition** 103, 104, 244, 354, R14	**Analyzing and Evaluating Presentations** • Identifying a Speaker's Claim • Tracing a Speaker's Argument

Common Core State Standard	Student Edition/Teacher's Edition	Digital Collection/Lesson
PRESENTATION OF KNOWLEDGE AND IDEAS		
4. Present claims and findings, emphasizing salient points in a focused, coherent manner with pertinent descriptions, facts, details, and examples; use appropriate eye contact, adequate volume, and clear pronunciation.	**Student Edition** 96, 103, 124, 130, 133–136, 149, 164, 174, 244, 273–276, 425, R14–R15 **Teacher's Edition** 74a, 96, 103, 104, 124, 130, 133–136, 164, 174, 244, 273, 426a, R14	**Giving a Presentation** • Introduction • The Content of Your Presentation • Style in Presentation • Delivering Your Presentation
5. Integrate multimedia and visual displays into presentations to clarify information, strengthen claims and evidence, and add interest.	**Student Edition** 74, 124, 133–136, 203–206, 244, 268, 273–276, 425 **Teacher's Edition** 74a, 75, 124, 133–136, 203–206, 244, 273	**Using Media in a Presentation** • Introduction • Types of Media: Audio, Video, and Images • Using Presentation Software • Building and Practicing Your Presentation
6. Adapt speech to a variety of contexts and tasks, demonstrating command of formal English when indicated or appropriate. (See grade 8 Language standards 1 and 3 for specific expectations.)	**Student Edition** 96, 133–136, 202, 233, 244, 354, 425 **Teacher's Edition** 96, 133–136, 202, 233, 244	**Participating in Collaborative Discussions** • Speaking Constructively **Giving a Presentation** • Style in Presentation

College and Career Readiness Anchor Standards for Language

Common Core State Standards
CONVENTIONS OF STANDARD ENGLISH
1. Demonstrate command of the conventions of standard English grammar and usage when writing or speaking.
2. Demonstrate command of the conventions of standard English capitalization, punctuation, and spelling when writing.
KNOWLEDGE OF LANGUAGE
3. Apply knowledge of language to understand how language functions in different contexts, to make effective choices for meaning or style, and to comprehend more fully when reading or listening.
VOCABULARY ACQUISITION AND USE
4. Determine or clarify the meaning of unknown and multiple-meaning words and phrases by using context clues, analyzing meaningful word parts, and consulting general and specialized reference materials, as appropriate.
5. Demonstrate understanding of figurative language, word relationships and nuances in word meanings.
6. Acquire and use accurately a range of general academic and domain-specific words and phrases sufficient for reading, writing, speaking, and listening at the college and career readiness level; demonstrate independence in gathering vocabulary knowledge when considering a word or phrase important to comprehension or expression.

Language Standards

Common Core State Standard	Student Edition/Teacher's Edition
CONVENTIONS OF STANDARD ENGLISH	
1. Demonstrate command of the conventions of standard English grammar and usage when writing or speaking.	**Student Edition** 30, 40, 70, 104, 120, 166, 176, 198, 228, 246, 262, 404, 418, R29–R52 **Teacher's Edition** 104, 105a, 262, 418, R29, R37, R39, R41, R48, R43, R52
a. Explain the function of verbals (gerunds, participles, infinitives) in general and their function in particular sentences.	**Student Edition** 40, 198, 228, R29, R45–R46 **Teacher's Edition** 40, 198, 228, R29, R46
b. Form and use verbs in the active and passive voice.	**Student Edition** 70, R29, R41 **Teacher's Edition** 70, R29, R41
c. Form and use verbs in the indicative, imperative, interrogative, conditional, and subjunctive mood.	**Student Edition** 30, 120, 166, 176, 404 **Teacher's Edition** 30, 120, 166, 176, R29
d. Recognize and correct inappropriate shifts in verb voice and mood.	**Student Edition** 246, R40–R41 **Teacher's Edition** 246, R29
2. Demonstrate command of the conventions of standard English capitalization, punctuation, and spelling when writing.	**Student Edition** 98, 132, 234, 378, 418, R29, R32–R35, R53, R59–R63 **Teacher's Edition** 98, 418, R29
a. Use punctuation (commas, ellipsis, dash) to indicate a pause or break.	**Student Edition** 98,132, 378, R29, R32–R34 **Teacher's Edition** 98, 132, 378, R29
b. Use an ellipsis to indicate an omission.	**Student Edition** 378, R34 **Teacher's Edition** 378

Common Core State Standard	Student Edition/Teacher's Edition
c. Spell correctly.	**Student Edition** 234, R53, R59–R63 **Teacher's Edition** 234, R53

KNOWLEDGE OF LANGUAGE

Common Core State Standard	Student Edition/Teacher's Edition
3. Use knowledge of language and its conventions when writing, speaking, reading, or listening.	**Student Edition** 70, 120, R29–R52 **Teacher's Edition** 70, 120, R29
a. Use verbs in the active and passive voice and in the conditional and subjunctive mood to achieve particular effects (e.g., emphasizing the actor or the action; expressing uncertainty or describing a state contrary to fact).	**Student Edition** 70, 120, 166, R29, R41 **Teacher's Edition** 70, 120, 166, R29

VOCABULARY ACQUISITION AND USE

Common Core State Standard	Student Edition/Teacher's Edition
4. Determine or clarify the meaning of unknown and multiple-meaning words and phrases based on *grade 8 reading and content*, choosing flexibly from a range of strategies.	**Student Edition** 29, 39, 52, 69, 97, 119, 131, 150, 175, 197, 227, 245, 261, 368, 377, 417, 426, R53–R59 **Teacher's Edition** 150, 197, 260, 368, R53
a. Use context (e.g., the overall meaning of a sentence or paragraph; a word's position or function in a sentence) as a clue to the meaning of a word or phrase.	**Student Edition** 29, 119, 150, 175, 197, 261, 368, R53 **Teacher's Edition** 29, 119, 150, 175, 197, 260, 368, R53
b. Use common, grade-appropriate Greek or Latin affixes and roots as clues to the meaning of a word (e.g., *precede, recede, secede*).	**Student Edition** 52, 69, 119, 131, 150, 227, 245, 377, 426, R53, R54, R56 **Teacher's Edition** 52, 69, 119, 131, 150, 227, 245, 377, 426, R53
c. Consult general and specialized reference materials (e.g., dictionaries, glossaries, thesauruses), both print and digital, to find the pronunciation of a word or determine or clarify its precise meaning or its part of speech.	**Student Edition** 39, 97, 119, 417, R53, R58–R59 **Teacher's Edition** 39, 97, 119, 417, R53
d. Verify the preliminary determination of the meaning of a word or phrase (e.g., by checking the inferred meaning in context or in a dictionary).	**Student Edition** 29, 69, 119, 150, 197, 227, 245, 368, 377, 417, 426, R53, R58 **Teacher's Edition** 29, 69, 119, 150, 197, 227, 245, 246, 368, 377, 417, 426

Common Core State Standard	Student Edition/Teacher's Edition
5. Demonstrate understanding of figurative language, word relationships, and nuances in word meanings.	**Student Edition** 165, 175, 195, 368, 403, R53, R56–58 **Teacher's Edition** 165, 175, 195, 368, 403, R53, R56
a. Interpret figures of speech (e.g., verbal irony, puns) in context.	**Student Edition** 175, 403, R53 **Teacher's Edition** 165, 316, 334, 403
b. Use the relationship between particular words to better understand each of the words.	**Student Edition** 165, R53, R56–R58 **Teacher's Edition** 165, R53, R56
c. Distinguish among the connotations (associations) of words with similar denotations (definitions) (e.g., *bullheaded, willful, firm, persistent, resolute*).	**Student Edition** 195, 368, R53, R57 **Teacher's Edition** 178, 186, 192, 368
6. Acquire and use accurately grade-appropriate general academic and domain-specific words and phrases; gather vocabulary knowledge when considering a word or phrase important to comprehension or expression.	**Student Edition** 2, 29, 52, 69, 79, 83, 88, 119, 133, 137, 142, 175, 203, 207, 212, 227, 261, 269, 273, 278, 389, 393, 394, 437, 441, R53–R59 **Teacher's Edition** 2, 52, 69, 88, 142, 175, 212, 227, 260, R53

Complex Text:
What It Is and What It Isn't . . . or Don't Let a Good Poem Get You Down

By Carol Jago

Do you sometimes think that what your teacher asks you to read is too hard? Let me tell you a secret. Those poems and passages can be tough for your teacher as well. Just because a text isn't easy doesn't mean there is something wrong with it or something wrong with the reader. It means you need to do more than skim across the words on the page. Reading complex text takes effort and focused attention. Do you sometimes wish writers would just say what they have to say simply? I assure you that writers don't use long sentences and unfamiliar words to annoy their readers or make readers feel dumb. They employ complex syntax and rich language in order to express complex ideas.

Excellent literature and nonfiction—the kind you will be reading over the course of the year—challenges readers in various ways. Sometimes the background of a story or the content of an essay is so unfamiliar that it is difficult to understand why characters are behaving as they do or to follow the argument a writer is making. By persevering, reading like a detective, and following clues in the text, you will find that your store of background knowledge grows. As a result, the next time you read about this subject, the text won't seem nearly as hard. The more you read, the better a reader you will become.

Good readers aren't put off by challenging text. When the going gets rough, they know what to do. Let's take vocabulary, a common measure of text complexity, as an example. Learning new words is the business of a lifetime. Rather than shutting down when you meet a word you don't know, take a moment to think about the word. Is any part of the word familiar to you? Is there something in the context of the sentence or paragraph that can help you figure out its meaning? Is there someone or something that can provide you with a definition? When reading literature or nonfiction from a time period other than our own, the text is often full of words we don't know. Each time you meet those words in succeeding readings you will be adding to your understanding of the word and its use. Your brain is a natural word-learning machine. The more you feed it complex text, the larger a vocabulary you'll have.

Have you ever been reading a long, complicated sentence and discovered that by the time you reached the end you had forgotten the beginning? Unlike the sentences we speak or dash off in a note to a friend, complex text is often full of sentences that are not only lengthy but also constructed in intricate ways. Such sentences require readers to slow down and figure out how phrases relate to one another as well as who is doing what to whom. Remember, rereading isn't cheating. It is exactly what experienced readers know to do when they meet dense text on the page. On the pages that follow you will find stories and articles that challenge you at the sentence level. Don't be intimidated. With careful attention to how those sentences are constructed, their meaning will unfold right before your eyes.

> **"Your brain is a natural word-learning machine. The more you feed it complex text, the larger a vocabulary you'll have."**

Another way text can be complex involves the density of the ideas in a passage. Sometimes a writer piles on so much information that you think your head might explode if you read one more detail or one more qualification. At times like this talking with a friend can really help. Sharing questions and ideas, exploring a difficult passage together, can help you tease out the meaning of even the most difficult text. Poetry is often particularly dense and for that reason it poses particular challenges. A seemingly simple poem in terms of vocabulary and length may express extremely complex feelings and insights. Poets also love to use mythological and Biblical allusions which contemporary readers are not always familiar with. The only way to read text this complex is to read it again and again.

You are going to notice a range of complexity within each collection of readings. This spectrum reflects the range of texts that surround us: some easy, some hard, some seemingly easy but in fact hard, some seemingly hard but actually easy. Whatever their complexity, I think you will enjoy these readings tremendously. Remember, read for your life!

Understanding the Common Core State Standards

What are the English Language Arts Common Core State Standards?

The Common Core State Standards for English Language Arts indicate what you should know and be able to do by the end of your grade level. These understandings and skills will help you be better prepared for future classes, college courses, and a career. For this reason, the standards for each strand in English Language Arts (such as Reading Informational Text or Writing) directly relate to the College and Career Readiness Anchor Standards for each strand. The Anchor Standards broadly outline the understandings and skills you should master by the end of high school so that you are well-prepared for college or for a career.

How do I learn the English Language Arts Common Core State Standards?

Your textbook is closely aligned to the English Language Arts Common Core State Standards. Every time you learn a concept or practice a skill, you are working on mastering one of the standards. Each collection, each selection, and each performance task in your textbook connects to one or more of the standards for English Language Arts listed on the following pages.

The English Language Arts Common Core State Standards are divided into five strands: Reading Literature, Reading Informational Text, Writing, Speaking and Listening, and Language.

©Blend/Getty Images

Strand	What It Means to You
Reading Literature (RL)	This strand concerns the literary texts you will read at this grade level: stories, drama, and poetry. The Common Core State Standards stress that you should read a range of texts of increasing complexity as you progress through high school.
Reading Informational Text (RI)	Informational text encompasses a broad range of literary nonfiction, including exposition, argument, and functional text, in such genres as personal essays, speeches, opinion pieces, memoirs, and historical and technical accounts. The Common Core State Standards stress that you will read a range of informational texts of increasing complexity as you progress from grade to grade.
Writing (W)	For the Writing strand you will focus on generating three types of texts—arguments, informative or explanatory texts, and narratives—while using the writing process and technology to develop and share your writing. The Common Core State Standards also emphasize research and specify that you should write routinely for both short and extended time frames.
Speaking and Listening (SL)	The Common Core State Standards focus on comprehending information presented in a variety of media and formats, on participating in collaborative discussions, and on presenting knowledge and ideas clearly.
Language (L)	The standards in the Language strand address the conventions of standard English grammar, usage, and mechanics; knowledge of language; and vocabulary acquisition and use.

Common Core Code Decoder

The codes you find on the pages of your textbook identify the specific knowledge or skill for the standard addressed in the text.

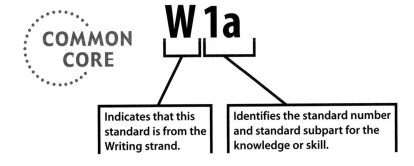

COMMON CORE

W 1a

Indicates that this standard is from the Writing strand.

Identifies the standard number and standard subpart for the knowledge or skill.

English Language Arts
Common Core State Standards

Listed below are the English Language Arts Common Core State Standards that you are required to master by the end of grade 8. To help you understand what is required of you, we have provided a summary of the concepts you will learn on your way to mastering each standard.

College and Career Readiness Anchor Standards for Reading

Common Core State Standards

KEY IDEAS AND DETAILS

1. Read closely to determine what the text says explicitly and to make logical inferences from it; cite specific textual evidence when writing or speaking to support conclusions drawn from the text.

2. Determine central ideas or themes of a text and analyze their development; summarize the key supporting details and ideas.

3. Analyze how and why individuals, events, and ideas develop and interact over the course of a text.

CRAFT AND STRUCTURE

4. Interpret words and phrases as they are used in a text, including determining technical, connotative, and figurative meanings, and analyze how specific word choices shape meaning or tone.

5. Analyze the structure of texts, including how specific sentences, paragraphs, and larger portions of the text (e.g., a section, chapter, scene, or stanza) relate to each other and the whole.

6. Assess how point of view or purpose shapes the content and style of a text.

INTEGRATION OF KNOWLEDGE AND IDEAS

7. Integrate and evaluate content presented in diverse formats and media, including visually and quantitatively, as well as in words.

8. Delineate and evaluate the argument and specific claims in a text, including the validity of the reasoning as well as the relevance and sufficiency of the evidence.

9. Analyze how two or more texts address similar themes or topics in order to build knowledge or to compare the approaches the authors take.

RANGE OF READING AND LEVEL OF TEXT COMPLEXITY

10. Read and comprehend complex literary and informational texts independently and proficiently.

Reading Standards for Literature, Grade 8 Students

The College and Career Readiness Anchor Standards for Reading apply to both literature and informational text.

Common Core State Standards	What It Means to You
KEY IDEAS AND DETAILS	
1. Cite the textual evidence that most strongly supports an analysis of what the text says explicitly as well as inferences drawn from the text.	You will use information from the text to support its main ideas—both those that are stated directly and those that are suggested.
2. Determine a theme or central idea of a text and analyze its development over the course of the text, including its relationship to the characters, setting, and plot; provide an objective summary of the text.	You will define a text's theme or main idea by analyzing its relationship to the characters, setting, and plot, as well as how it unfolds throughout the text. You will also summarize the main idea of the text without adding your own ideas or opinions.
3. Analyze how particular lines of dialogue or incidents in a story or drama propel the action, reveal aspects of a character, or provoke a decision.	You will analyze how specific events or lines of dialogue in a story or drama move the action forward or show you things about the characters.
CRAFT AND STRUCTURE	
4. Determine the meaning of words and phrases as they are used in a text, including figurative and connotative meanings; analyze the impact of specific word choices on meaning and tone, including analogies or allusions to other texts.	You will analyze specific words, phrases, and patterns of sound in the text to determine what they mean and how they contribute to the text's larger meaning.
5. Compare and contrast the structure of two or more texts and analyze how the differing structure of each text contributes to its meaning and style.	You will compare and contrast the forms of two or more texts and analyze how those forms contribute to meaning and style.
6. Analyze how differences in the points of view of the characters and the audience or reader (e.g., created through the use of dramatic irony) create such effects as suspense or humor.	You will analyze how differences between the points of view of characters and readers create effects like suspense or humor.

Common Core State Standards	What It Means to You
INTEGRATION OF KNOWLEDGE AND IDEAS	
7. Analyze the extent to which a filmed or live production of a story or drama stays faithful to or departs from the text or script, evaluating the choices made by the director or actors.	You will compare and contrast how events and information are presented in a text and a filmed or live production of the text.
8. (Not applicable to literature)	
9. Analyze how a modern work of fiction draws on themes, patterns of events, or character types from myths, traditional stories, or religious works such as the Bible, including describing how the material is rendered new.	You will recognize and analyze how an author draws from and uses historical source material.
RANGE OF READING AND LEVEL OF TEXT COMPLEXITY	
10. By the end of the year, read and comprehend literature, including stories, dramas, and poems, at the high end of grades 6–8 text complexity band independently and proficiently.	You will read and understand grade-level appropriate literary texts by the end of grade 8.

Reading Standards for Informational Text, Grade 8 Students

Common Core State Standards	What It Means to You
KEY IDEAS AND DETAILS	
1. Cite the textual evidence that most strongly supports an analysis of what the text says explicitly as well as inferences drawn from the text.	You will cite information from the text to support its main ideas—both those that are stated directly and those that are suggested.
2. Determine a central idea of a text and analyze its development over the course of the text, including its relationship to supporting ideas; provide an objective summary of the text.	You will determine a text's main idea by analyzing its relationship to supporting details as well as how it progresses throughout the text. You will also summarize the text as a whole without adding your own ideas or opinions.

Common Core State Standards	What It Means to You
3. Analyze how a text makes connections among and distinctions between individuals, ideas, or events (e.g., through comparisons, analogies, or categories).	You will analyze the ways in which a text groups together or separates individuals, events, and ideas.

CRAFT AND STRUCTURE

Common Core State Standards	What It Means to You
4. Determine the meaning of words and phrases as they are used in a text, including figurative, connotative, and technical meanings; analyze the impact of specific word choices on meaning and tone, including analogies or allusions to other texts.	You will analyze specific words and phrases in the text to determine both what they mean and how they affect the text's tone and meaning as a whole.
5. Analyze in detail the structure of a specific paragraph in a text, including the role of particular sentences in developing and refining a key concept.	You will examine individual paragraphs in a text and analyze how particular sentences contribute to the whole.
6. Determine an author's point of view or purpose in a text and analyze how the author acknowledges and responds to conflicting evidence or viewpoints.	You will understand the author's point of view and analyze how the author sets his or her position apart from others.

INTEGRATION OF KNOWLEDGE AND IDEAS

Common Core State Standards	What It Means to You
7. Evaluate the advantages and disadvantages of using different mediums (e.g., print or digital text, video, multimedia) to present a particular topic or idea.	You will evaluate the benefits and drawbacks of using visual and non-visual mediums to present information.
8. Delineate and evaluate the argument and specific claims in a text, assessing whether the reasoning is sound and the evidence is relevant and sufficient; recognize when irrelevant evidence is introduced.	You will evaluate the strength of the author's claims and reasoning and identify any faults or weaknesses in them.
9. Analyze a case in which two or more texts provide conflicting information on the same topic and identify where the texts disagree on matters of fact or interpretation.	You will compare and contrast at least two different authors' treatments of the same subject and show where they disagree on matters of fact or opinion.

Common Core State Standards	What It Means to You

RANGE OF READING AND LEVEL OF TEXT COMPLEXITY

10. By the end of the year, read and comprehend literary nonfiction at the high end of the grades 6–8 text complexity band independently and proficiently.	You will demonstrate the ability to read and understand grade-level appropriate literary nonfiction texts by the end of grade 8.

College and Career Readiness Anchor Standards for Writing

Common Core State Standards

TEXT TYPES AND PURPOSES

1. Write arguments to support claims in an analysis of substantive topics or texts, using valid reasoning and relevant and sufficient evidence.

2. Write informative/explanatory texts to examine and convey complex ideas and information clearly and accurately through the effective selection, organization, and analysis of content.

3. Write narratives to develop real or imagined experiences or events using effective technique, well chosen details, and well-structured event sequences.

PRODUCTION AND DISTRIBUTION OF WRITING

4. Produce clear and coherent writing in which the development, organization, and style are appropriate to task, purpose, and audience.

5. Develop and strengthen writing as needed by planning, revising, editing, rewriting, or trying a new approach.

6. Use technology, including the Internet, to produce and publish writing and to interact and collaborate with others.

RESEARCH TO BUILD AND PRESENT KNOWLEDGE

7. Conduct short as well as more sustained research projects based on focused questions, demonstrating understanding of the subject under investigation.

8. Gather relevant information from multiple print and digital sources, assess the credibility and accuracy of each source, and integrate the information while avoiding plagiarism.

9. Draw evidence from literary or informational texts to support analysis, reflection, and research.

RANGE OF WRITING

10. Write routinely over extended time frames (time for research, reflection, and revision) and shorter time frames (a single sitting or a day or two) for a range of tasks, purposes, and audiences.

Writing Standards, Grade 8 Students

Common Core State Standards	What It Means to You
TEXT TYPES AND PURPOSES	
1. Write arguments to support claims with clear reasons and relevant evidence.	You will write and develop arguments with clear reasons and strong evidence that include
a. Introduce claim(s), acknowledge and distinguish the claim(s) from alternate or opposing claims, and organize the reasons and evidence logically.	a clear organization of claims and counterclaims
b. Support claim(s) with logical reasoning and relevant evidence, using accurate, credible sources and demonstrating an understanding of the topic or text.	strong, accurate support for claims
c. Use words, phrases, and clauses to create cohesion and clarify the relationships among claim(s), counterclaims, reasons, and evidence.	use of cohesive words, phrases, and clauses to link information
d. Establish and maintain a formal style.	a formal style
e. Provide a concluding statement or section that follows from and supports the argument presented.	a strong concluding statement that summarizes the argument
2. Write informative/explanatory texts to examine a topic and convey ideas, concepts, and information through the selection, organization, and analysis of relevant content.	You will write clear, well-organized, and thoughtful informative and explanatory texts with
a. Introduce a topic clearly, previewing what is to follow; organize ideas, concepts, and information into broader categories; include formatting (e.g., headings), graphics (e.g., charts, tables), and multimedia when useful to aiding comprehension.	a clear introduction and organization, including headings and graphic organizers (when appropriate)
b. Develop the topic with relevant, well-chosen facts, definitions, concrete details, quotations, or other information and examples.	sufficient supporting details and background information
c. Use appropriate and varied transitions to create cohesion and clarify the relationships among ideas and concepts.	cohesive transitions to link ideas
d. Use precise language and domain-specific vocabulary to inform about or explain the topic.	precise language and relevant vocabulary

Common Core State Standards	What It Means to You
e. Establish and maintain a formal style.	a formal style
f. Provide a concluding statement or section that follows from and supports the information or explanation presented.	a strong conclusion that restates the importance or relevance of the topic
3. Write narratives to develop real or imagined experiences or events using effective technique, relevant descriptive details, and well-structured event sequences.	You will write clear, well-structured, detailed narrative texts that
a. Engage and orient the reader by establishing a context and point of view and introducing a narrator and/or characters; organize an event sequence that unfolds naturally and logically.	draw your readers in with a clear topic that unfolds logically
b. Use narrative techniques, such as dialogue, pacing, description, and reflection, to develop experiences, events, and/or characters.	use narrative techniques to develop and expand on events and/or characters
c. Use a variety of transition words, phrases, and clauses to convey sequence, signal shifts from one time frame or setting to another, and show the relationships among experiences and events.	use a variety of transition words to clearly signal shifts between time frames or settings
d. Use precise words and phrases, relevant descriptive details, and sensory language to capture the action and convey experiences and events.	use precise words and sensory details that keep readers interested
e. Provide a conclusion that follows from and reflects on the narrated experiences or events.	have a strong conclusion that reflects on the topic

PRODUCTION AND DISTRIBUTION OF WRITING

4. Produce clear and coherent writing in which the development, organization, and style are appropriate to task, purpose, and audience. (Grade-specific expectations for writing types are defined in standards 1–3 above.)	You will produce writing that is appropriate to the task, purpose, and audience for whom you are writing.
5. With some guidance and support from peers and adults, develop and strengthen writing as needed by planning, revising, editing, rewriting, or trying a new approach, focusing on how well purpose and audience have been addressed.	With help from peers and adults, you will revise and refine your writing to address what is most important for your purpose and audience.

Common Core State Standards	What It Means to You
6. Use technology, including the Internet, to produce and publish writing and present the relationships between information and ideas efficiently as well as to interact and collaborate with others.	You will use technology to share your writing and to provide links to other relevant information.

RESEARCH TO BUILD AND PRESENT KNOWLEDGE

Common Core State Standards	What It Means to You
7. Conduct short research projects to answer a question (including a self-generated question), drawing on several sources and generating additional related, focused questions that allow for multiple avenues of exploration.	You will conduct short research projects to answer a question using multiple sources and generating topics for further research.
8. Gather relevant information from multiple print and digital sources, using search terms effectively; assess the credibility and accuracy of each source; and quote or paraphrase the data and conclusions of others while avoiding plagiarism and following a standard format for citation.	You will effectively conduct searches to gather information from different sources and assess the strength of each source, following a standard format for citation.
9. Draw evidence from literary or informational texts to support analysis, reflection, and research. a. Apply *grade 8 Reading standards* to literature (e.g., "Analyze how a modern work of fiction draws on themes, patterns of events, or character types from myths, traditional stories, or religious works such as the Bible, including describing how the material is rendered new"). b. Apply *grade 8 Reading standards* to literary nonfiction (e.g., "Delineate and evaluate the argument and specific claims in a text, assessing whether the reasoning is sound and the evidence is relevant and sufficient; recognize when irrelevant evidence is introduced").	You will paraphrase, summarize, quote, and cite primary and secondary sources to support your analysis, reflection, and research.

RANGE OF WRITING

Common Core State Standards	What It Means to You
10. Write routinely over extended time frames (time for research, reflection, and revision) and shorter time frames (a single sitting or a day or two) for a range of discipline-specific tasks, purposes, and audiences.	You will write for many different purposes and audiences both over short and extended periods of time.

College and Career Readiness Anchor Standards for Speaking and Listening

Common Core State Standards
COMPREHENSION AND COLLABORATION
1. Prepare for and participate effectively in a range of conversations and collaborations with diverse partners, building on others' ideas and expressing their own clearly and persuasively.
2. Integrate and evaluate information presented in diverse media and formats, including visually, quantitatively, and orally.
3. Evaluate a speaker's point of view, reasoning, and use of evidence and rhetoric.
PRESENTATION OF KNOWLEDGE AND IDEAS
4. Present information, findings, and supporting evidence such that listeners can follow the line of reasoning and the organization, development, and style are appropriate to task, purpose, and audience.
5. Make strategic use of digital media and visual displays of data to express information and enhance understanding of presentations.
6. Adapt speech to a variety of contexts and communicative tasks, demonstrating command of formal English when indicated or appropriate.

Speaking and Listening Standards, Grade 8 Students

Common Core State Standards	What It Means to You
COMPREHENSION AND COLLABORATION	
1. Engage effectively in a range of collaborative discussions (one-on-one, in groups, and teacher-led) with diverse partners on *grade 8 topics, texts, and issues,* building on others' ideas and expressing their own clearly.	You will actively participate in a variety of discussions in which you
a. Come to discussions prepared, having read or researched material under study; explicitly draw on that preparation by referring to evidence on the topic, text, or issue to probe and reflect on ideas under discussion.	have read any relevant material beforehand and have come to the discussion prepared
b. Follow rules for collegial discussions and decision-making, track progress toward specific goals and deadlines, and define individual roles as needed.	work with others to establish goals and processes within the group
c. Pose questions that connect the ideas of several speakers and respond to others' questions and comments with relevant evidence, observations, and ideas.	ask questions that connect the ideas of several speakers and give relevant responses to the questions of others

Common Core State Standards	What It Means to You
d. Acknowledge new information expressed by others and, when warranted, qualify or justify their own views in light of the evidence presented.	recognize different perspectives and adjust your own views if necessary
2. Analyze the purpose of information presented in diverse media and formats (e.g., visually, quantitatively, orally) and evaluate the motives (e.g., social, commercial, political) behind its presentation.	You will analyze the purposes of and reasons for presenting information in different media and formats.
3. Delineate a speaker's argument and specific claims, evaluating the soundness of the reasoning and relevance and sufficiency of the evidence and identifying when irrelevant evidence is introduced.	You will evaluate a speaker's argument and identify any false reasoning or evidence.

PRESENTATION OF KNOWLEDGE AND IDEAS

Common Core State Standards	What It Means to You
4. Present claims and findings, emphasizing salient points in a focused, coherent manner with relevant evidence, sound valid reasoning, and well-chosen details; use appropriate eye contact, adequate volume, and clear pronunciation.	You will organize and present information to your listeners in a logical sequence and engaging style that is appropriate to your task and audience.
5. Integrate multimedia and visual displays into presentations to clarify information, strengthen claims and evidence, and add interest.	You will use digital media to enhance and add interest to presentations.
6. Adapt speech to a variety of contexts and tasks, demonstrating command of formal English when indicated or appropriate.	You will adapt the formality of your speech appropriately.

College and Career Readiness Anchor Standards for Language

Common Core State Standards

CONVENTIONS OF STANDARD ENGLISH

1. Demonstrate command of the conventions of standard English grammar and usage when writing or speaking.

2. Demonstrate command of the conventions of standard English capitalization, punctuation, and spelling when writing.

KNOWLEDGE OF LANGUAGE

3. Apply knowledge of language to understand how language functions in different contexts, to make effective choices for meaning or style, and to comprehend more fully when reading or listening.

Common Core State Standards

VOCABULARY ACQUISITION AND USE

4. Determine or clarify the meaning of unknown and multiple-meaning words and phrases by using context clues, analyzing meaningful word parts, and consulting general and specialized reference materials, as appropriate.

5. Demonstrate understanding of word relationships and nuances in word meanings.

6. Acquire and use accurately a range of general academic and domain-specific words and phrases sufficient for reading, writing, speaking, and listening at the college and career readiness level; demonstrate independence in gathering vocabulary knowledge when considering a word or phrase important to comprehension or expression.

Language Standards, Grade 8 Students

Common Core State Standards	What It Means to You
CONVENTIONS OF STANDARD ENGLISH	
1. Demonstrate command of the conventions of standard English grammar and usage when writing or speaking.	You will correctly understand and use the conventions of English grammar and usage, including
a. Explain the function of verbals (gerunds, participles, infinitives) in general and their function in particular sentences.	explaining the function of verbals
b. Form and use verbs in the active and passive voice.	using verbs in both active and passive voice
c. Form and use verbs in the indicative, imperative, interrogative, conditional, and subjunctive mood.	using verbs in the indicative, imperative, interrogative, conditional, and subjunctive mood
d. Recognize and correct inappropriate shifts in verb voice and mood.	recognizing and correcting shifts in verb voice and mood
2. Demonstrate command of the conventions of standard English capitalization, punctuation, and spelling when writing.	You will correctly use the conventions of English capitalization, punctuation, and spelling, including
a. Use punctuation (commas, ellipsis, dash) to indicate a pause or break.	using different punctuation to indicate a pause or break

Common Core State Standards	What It Means to You
b. Use an ellipsis to indicate an omission.	using ellipsis to indicate when text has been left out
c. Spell correctly.	spelling correctly

KNOWLEDGE OF LANGUAGE

Common Core State Standards	What It Means to You
3. Use knowledge of language and its conventions when writing, speaking, reading, or listening.	You will apply your knowledge of language in different contexts by
a. Use verbs in the active and passive voice and in the conditional and subjunctive mood to achieve particular effects (e.g., emphasizing the actor or the action; expressing uncertainty or describing a state contrary to fact).	choosing appropriate verb voice and mood to create different effects

VOCABULARY ACQUISITION AND USE

Common Core State Standards	What It Means to You
4. Determine or clarify the meaning of unknown and multiple-meaning words and phrases based on *grade 8 reading and content,* choosing flexibly from a range of strategies.	You will understand the meaning of grade-level appropriate words and phrases by
a. Use context (e.g., the overall meaning of a sentence or paragraph; a word's position or function in a sentence) as a clue to the meaning of a word or phrase.	using context clues
b. Use common, grade-appropriate Greek or Latin affixes and roots as clues to the meaning of a word (e.g., *precede, recede, secede*).	using Greek or Latin roots
c. Consult general and specialized reference materials (e.g., dictionaries, glossaries, thesauruses), both print and digital, to find the pronunciation of a word or determine or clarify its precise meaning or its part of speech.	using reference materials
d. Verify the preliminary determination of the meaning of a word or phrase (e.g., by checking the inferred meaning in context or in a dictionary).	inferring and verifying the meanings of words in context

Common Core State Standards	What It Means to You
5. Demonstrate understanding of figurative language, word relationships, and nuances in word meanings.	You will understand figurative language, word relationships, and slight differences in word meanings by
a. Interpret figures of speech (e.g., verbal irony, puns) in context.	interpreting figures of speech in context
b. Use the relationship between particular words to better understand each of the words.	analyzing relationships between words
c. Distinguish among the connotations (associations) of words with similar denotations (definitions) (e.g., *bullheaded, willful, firm, persistent, resolute*).	distinguishing among words with similar definitions
6. Acquire and use accurately grade-appropriate general academic and domain-specific words and phrases; gather vocabulary knowledge when considering a word or phrase important to comprehension or expression.	You will learn and use grade-appropriate vocabulary.

Culture and Belonging

❝ Culture is the widening of the mind and of the spirit. **❞**

—Jawaharlal Nehru

1

PLAN

CONNECTING WORD AND IMAGE

ASK STUDENTS to discuss how the collection opener image and the collection quotation work together to create a connection.

PERFORMANCE TASK PREVIEW

Point out to students that they will complete two performance tasks at the end of the collection. The performance tasks will require them to further analyze the selections in the collection and to synthesize ideas about these analyses. They will present their findings in a variety of products.

ACADEMIC VOCABULARY

View It!

Professional Development Podcast:
Academic Vocabulary

Students can acquire facility with the academic vocabulary words through frequent, repeated exposure as they analyze and discuss the selections in the collection. Academic vocabulary can be used in the following instructional contexts to enable students to incorporate the academic vocabulary words into their working vocabulary.

- Collaborative Discussion at the end of each selection
- Analyzing the Text questions for each selection
- Selection-level Performance Task
- Vocabulary instruction (for Critical Vocabulary and/or for Vocabulary Strategy)
- Language Conventions
- End-of-collection Performance Task for all selections in the collection

ASK STUDENTS to review the Academic Vocabulary word list for this collection. You may wish to pronounce each word aloud, so students hear the correct pronunciation. Then, discuss the definitions and the related forms for each word. Remind students that they will encounter these five academic vocabulary words throughout the collection.

Culture and Belonging

In this collection, you will explore how people develop their own identity within a new culture.

hmhfyi.com

COLLECTION
PERFORMANCE TASK Preview

At the end of this collection, you will have the opportunity to complete two performance tasks:

- In one, you will conduct research and write an expository essay on the best ways for newcomers to adjust to living in the United States.

- In the second, you will write a personal narrative about adjusting to a new situation or fitting in with different groups.

ACADEMIC VOCABULARY

Study the words and their definitions in the chart below. You will use these words as you discuss and write about the texts in this collection.

Word	Definition	Related Forms
contribute (kən-trĭb´yōōt) v.	to give or supply for a common purpose	contribution, contributor, contributing
immigrate (ĭm´ĭ-grāt´) v.	to enter and settle in a new country	immigrant, immigration, migrate, migratory
reaction (rē-ăk´shən) n.	a response to something	react, reactionary
relocate (rē-lō´kāt) v.	to move to a new place	relocated, relocation
shifting (shĭft´ĭng) adj.	changing attitudes, judgments, or emphasis	shift, shifted

2

USING COLLECTIONS YOUR WAY

Use the following information, along with the charts on the following pages, to help you decide how you want to introduce the collection. Based on your teaching style, your students' interests, or your instructional goals, you may want to structure this collection in various ways. You may choose different entry points each time you teach the collection.

"I love to concentrate on contemporary literature."

This short story focuses on an immigrant family and the adjustments they face in contemporary America.

Background *In addition to being the author of more than a dozen novels for young adults, Jean Davies Okimoto (b. 1942) is a therapist. Perhaps that is why she has such insight into the characters that she portrays. Okimoto typically writes about the everyday problems and challenges faced by teenagers like Maya, the main character in "My Favorite Chaperone." Maya and her family have come to the United States from Kazakhstan, a country in Central Asia that used to be part of the Soviet Union.*

My Favorite Chaperone

Short Story by Jean Davies Okimoto

SETTING A PURPOSE As you read, pay attention to Maya's interactions with her family and her friends. How do these interactions help you to understand the challenges of being an immigrant in a new country?

In homeroom when Mr. Horswill handed out the permission slip for the Spring Fling, the all-school dance, I almost didn't take one. Why should I bother when I was sure the answer would be the same? Even though I'm in ninth grade now, it would still be the same. No. *Nyet* is what they say, and I don't want to hear this again. But I took a permission slip anyway. I don't know why I didn't just shake my head when this very popular girl Marcia Egness was handing them out. And even after I took one, I don't know why I didn't throw it away. Maybe I just couldn't give up hope. It's like that in America. It's a place where things can change for people, and many people always seem to have hope. At least that's how it seems to me. Maybe I was beginning to think this way, too, although my hope was very small.

My Favorite Chaperone **3**

Background *A collaboration between two very different New York schools is at the heart of the Building Bridges project. Newcomers High School in Queens, New York, is dedicated to teaching recent immigrants, while St. Luke's is a private middle school in Manhattan where students have many advantages.*

MEDIA ANALYSIS

New Immigrants Share Their Stories

Documentary directed by Lisa Gossels

SETTING A PURPOSE Through letter writing, video diaries, and interviews, the English learners from Newcomers tell their personal immigration stories with support and encouragement from their St. Luke's "buddies." Together the students hope to change stereotyped ideas about immigrants, highlight their reasons for coming to America, and share their goals and dreams for the future. The documentary *New Immigrants Share Their Stories* chronicles the students' project.

As you view the film, pay attention to the interviews between the immigrant students and their "buddies." Listen to the questions asked and the answers given. Also watch the facial expressions and gestures of the individuals. Think about what you learn about the two groups from these conversations. Write down any questions you have as you view.

New Immigrants Share Their Stories **71**

"I like to use digital products as a starting point."

This documentary film highlights the immigration experiences of students who attend Newcomers High School in Queens, New York.

"I require my students to do a lot of research."

Data from a long-term research study sheds new light on the often-sensitive topic of immigration.

Background *Public Agenda is a non-profit organization that does research to find out people's opinions on important issues. It hopes that by making people's opinions heard, government leaders will be better able to find good solutions to some of our nation's biggest problems. Public Agenda has done research on a variety of topics, including immigration, education, healthcare, and the economy.*

A Place to Call Home:

What Immigrants Say Now About Life in America

Research Study by Scott Bittle and Jonathan Rochkind

SETTING A PURPOSE As you read, pay attention to the immigrants' attitudes about their decisions to come to the United States. What do you find surprising about the information presented?

Introduction

It's a cliché to say that America is a nation of immigrants, but like most clichés, this one began as a statement of simple truth. Another truth is that if we're going to overhaul immigration policy, it only makes sense to listen to the people who will be most affected by it: immigrants. To craft a just and practical policy, we need to see America through the immigrant's eyes. That's true whether you favor an open door or a higher fence. You can't hope to implement sound strategies unless you understand what brings people to the United States and what they think about the nation once they get here.

That's what Public Agenda hopes to accomplish with A PLACE TO CALL HOME: WHAT IMMIGRANTS SAY NOW ABOUT LIFE IN AMERICA, the follow-up to our pioneering 2002 survey of immigrants, NOW THAT I'M HERE.

A Place to Call Home **41**

mySmartPlanner | **eBook** | **my**Notebook | **my**WriteSmart | **fyi** hmhfyi.com

Collection 1 Lessons	Media	Teach and Practice	
Student Edition | eBook	▶ **Video Links** HISTORY A&E	**Close Reading and Evidence Tracking**	
ANCHOR TEXT Short Story by Jean Davies Okimoto "My Favorite Chaperone"	◀ **Audio** "My Favorite Chaperone"	**Close Read Screencasts** • Modeled Discussion 1 (lines 58–67) • Modeled Discussion 2 (lines 315–332) • Close Read Application (lines 549–559)	**Strategies for Annotation** • Analyze Stories: Character • Analyze Language • Using Context Clues
CLOSE READER Short Story by Alma Luz Villanueva "Golden Glass"	◀ **Audio** "Golden Glass"		
Personal Essay by Jean-Pierre Benoit "Bonne Année"	◀ **Audio** "Bonne Année"		**Strategies for Annotation** • Determine Central Idea and Details • Using a Glossary
Research Study by Scott Bittle and Jonathan Rochkind "A Place to Call Home"	▶ **Video HISTORY** *Immigrating* ◀ **Audio** "A Place to Call Home"		**Strategies for Annotation** • Cite Evidence • Analyze Nonfiction Elements • Using Greek Prefixes
CLOSE READER Essay by Naisha Jackson "What to Bring"	◀ **Audio** "What to Bring"		
ANCHOR TEXT Memoir by Kao Kalia Yang from *The Latehomecomer*	▶ **Video HISTORY** *Laos* ◀ **Audio** from *The Latehomecomer*	**Close Read Screencasts** • Modeled Discussion 1 (lines 124–131) • Modeled Discussion 2 (lines 272–280) • Close Read Application (lines 447–462)	**Strategies for Annotation** • Analyze Text: Memoir • Analyze the Meanings of Words and Phrases • Using Latin Prefixes
CLOSE READER Memoir by Susan Power "Museum Indians"	◀ **Audio** "Museum Indians"		
Documentary directed by Lisa Gossels *New Immigrants Share Their Stories*			
Poem by Sherman Alexie "Powwow at the End of the World"	◀ **Audio** "Powwow at the End of the World"		**Strategies for Annotation** • Determine Meaning of Words and Phrases
Collection 1 Performance Tasks: **A** Write an Expository Essay **B** Write a Personal Narrative	**fyi** hmhfyi.com	**Interactive Lessons** **A** Writing Informative Texts **A** Writing as a Process	**B** Writing Narratives

For Systematic Coverage of Writing and Speaking & Listening Standards	**Interactive Lessons** Writing as a Process Participating in Collaborative Discussions	

Assess		Extend	Reteach
Performance Task	**Online Assessment**	**Teacher eBook**	**Teacher eBook**
Writing Activity: Summary	Selection Test	**Write a Summary > Interactive Graphic Organizers >** Sequence Chart	**Analyze Stories: Plot > Level Up Tutorial >** Plot Stages
Media Activity: Poster	Selection Test	**Determine Author's Purpose > Interactive Whiteboard Lesson >** Author's Purpose and Perspective	**Determine Central Idea and Details > Level Up Tutorial >** Main Idea and Supporting Details
Writing Activity: Explanation	Selection Test	**Integrating Information from Text and Graphic Aids > Level Up Tutorial >** Reading Graphic Aids	**Text Features > Interactive Whiteboard Lesson >** Reading Informational Text
Writing Activity: Report	Selection Test	**Evaluating Sources > Interactive Lessons >** Evaluating Sources	**Figurative Language > Level Up Tutorial >** Figurative Language and Imagery
Media Activity: Video	Selection Test	**Creating a Video > Interactive Lessons >** Using Media in a Presentation	**Evaluate a Documentary**
Speaking Activity: Discussion	Selection Test	**Analyze Modern Fiction > Interactive Whiteboard Lesson >** Comparing Texts **Analyze Lyric Poems > Level Up Tutorial >** Narrator and Speaker **Analyze Poetry: Line Length**	**Determine Meaning of Words and Phrases: Allusion**
A Write an Expository Essay **B** Write a Personal Narrative	Collection Test		

Lesson Assessments
Writing as a Process
Participating in Collaborative Discussions

Collection 1 Lessons	COMMON CORE Key Learning Objective	Performance Task
ANCHOR TEXT **Short Story by Jean Davies Okimoto** **"My Favorite Chaperone," p. 3A** **Lexile 830L**	**The student will be able to . . .** recognize and analyze the elements of a story's plot and the author's methods of characterization.	Writing Activity: Summary
Personal Essay by Jean-Pierre Benoît **"Bonne Année," p. 31A** **Lexile 700L**	**The student will be able to . . .** analyze elements of a personal essay, including its purpose, structure, central idea, and supporting details.	Media Activity: Poster
Research Study by Scott Bittle and **Jonathan Rochkind** **"A Place to Call Home," p. 41A** **Lexile 1220L**	**The student will be able to . . .** use text features and graphic aids to analyze and understand a nonfiction text.	Writing Activity: Explanation
ANCHOR TEXT **Memoir by Kao Kalia Yang** **from *The Latehomecomer,* p. 53A** **Lexile 1030L**	**The student will be able to . . .** analyze imagery and figurative language to better understand a memoir.	Writing Activity: Report
Documentary directed by Lisa Gossels ***New Immigrants Share Their Stories,* p. 71A**	**The student will be able to . . .** recognize elements used in a documentary and understand and evaluate the purpose of each one.	Media Activity: Video
Poem by Sherman Alexie **"Powwow at the End of the World," p. 75A**	**The student will be able to . . .** use imagery and allusion to make inferences about the deeper meaning of a poem.	Speaking Activity: Discussion

Collection 1 Performance Tasks:
A Write an Expository Essay
B Write a Personal Narrative

Vocabulary Strategy	Language and Style	Student Instructional Support	CLOSE READER Selection
Context Clues	Imperative Mood	**Scaffolding for ELL Students:** Analyze Language: Conjunctions **When Students Struggle:** • Use of Foreign Words • Track Story Events **To Challenge Students:** Analyze Character Choices	Short Story by Alma Luz Villanueva "Golden Glass," p. 30b **Lexile 1010L**
Using a Glossary	Participles	**Scaffolding for ELL Students:** Analyze Language: Idiomatic Expressions **When Students Struggle:** Recognize Supporting Details	
Using Greek Prefixes		**Scaffolding for ELL Students:** Analyze Language: Idiomatic Expressions **When Students Struggle:** Use Subheadings	Essay by Naisha Jackson "What to Bring," p. 52b **Lexile 1010L**
Using Latin Prefixes	Active and Passive Voice	**Scaffolding for ELL Students:** Analyze Language: Synonyms **When Students Struggle:** Analyze Causes and Effects **To Challenge Students:** Analyze the Impact of Perspective	Memoir by Susan Powers "Museum Indians," p. 70b **Lexile 850L**
		Scaffolding for ELL Students: Compound Words **When Students Struggle:** Viewing with a Partner	
		Scaffolding for ELL Students: Analyze Language: Syntax	

*my*SmartPlanner   Create lesson plans and access resources online.

ANCHOR TEXT My Favorite Chaperone

Short Story by Jean Davies Okimoto

Why This Text?

As students become more accomplished readers, they are better able to analyze the elements that develop a story's plot and characters. This lesson focuses on plot and character development, helping students connect to the characters and their conflicts.

▶ **View It!**

Professional Development Podcast:

Text-Dependent Analysis

Key Learning Objective: The student will be able to recognize and analyze the elements of a story's plot and the author's methods of characterization.

For practice and application:

Worktext selection:
"Golden Glass,"
a short story by Alma Luz Villanueva

COMMON CORE Common Core Standards

RL 1 Cite textual evidence.
RL 2 Determine a theme or central idea; summarize.
RL 3 Analyze how dialogue propels action and reveals character.
RL 4 Analyze the impact of specific word choices on meaning and tone.
W 2 Write informative/explanatory text to examine a topic.
W 4 Produce clear and coherent writing.
W 9a Apply grade 8 Reading standards to literature.
W 10 Write routinely over extended and shorter time frames.
L 1c Form and use verbs in the imperative mood.
L 4a Use context as a clue to the meaning of a word or phrase.
L 4d Verify word meanings in a dictionary.

◢ Text Complexity Rubric

Quantitative Measures	**My Favorite Chaperone** Lexile: 830L
Qualitative Measures	**Levels of Meaning/Purpose** multiple levels of meaning (multiple themes)
	Structure less familiar story concepts
	Language Conventionality and Clarity less straightforward sentence structure
	Knowledge Demands experience contains unfamiliar aspects
Reader/Task Considerations	Teacher determined Vary by individual reader and type of text

CLOSE READ

Background Have students read the background and information about the author. Tell students that when Kazakhstan was part of the Soviet Union, people from outside the region were encouraged to go there to farm. These non-native people eventually outnumbered the natives. When Kazakhstan became an independent country in 1991, the government's policies began to favor native Kazakhs, leading many non-natives to immigrate to other countries.

SETTING A PURPOSE Direct students to use the Setting a Purpose question to focus their reading. Tell students to generate questions as they read.

Analyze Stories: Character (LINES 1–14)

COMMON CORE RL 1, RL 3

Point out that the narrator is a character in the story, and that she begins the story by presenting her thoughts and actions in a particular situation.

A **ASK STUDENTS** to reread lines 1–14 to analyze what this first paragraph reveals about the narrator. What can you infer about the narrator? *(The narrator is a student who wants to be able to go to a school dance but thinks it is unlikely she can get permission. The use of the word* nyet *and the reference to life in America suggest that the narrator may be an immigrant to the United States.)* Draw attention to the narrator's decision to take the permission slip even though she is sure she will not be allowed to attend the dance. What does this action reveal about her? *(Possible answer: She is hopeful.)*

Background *In addition to being the author of more than a dozen novels for young adults,* **Jean Davies Okimoto** *(b. 1942) is a therapist. Perhaps that is why she has such insight into the characters that she portrays. Okimoto typically writes about the everyday problems and challenges faced by teenagers like Maya, the main character in "My Favorite Chaperone." Maya and her family have come to the United States from Kazakhstan, a country in Central Asia that used to be part of the Soviet Union.*

My Favorite Chaperone

Short Story by Jean Davies Okimoto

SETTING A PURPOSE As you read, pay attention to Maya's interactions with her family and her friends. How do these interactions help you to understand the challenges of being an immigrant in a new country?

A In homeroom when Mr. Horswill handed out the permission slip for the Spring Fling, the all-school dance, I almost didn't take one. Why should I bother when I was sure the answer would be the same? Even though I'm in ninth grade now, it would still be the same. No. *Nyet* is what they say, and I don't want to hear this again. But I took a permission slip anyway. I don't know why I didn't just shake my head when this very popular girl Marcia Egness was handing them out. And even after I took one, I don't know why I didn't throw it away. Maybe I just couldn't give up hope. It's like that in America. It's a place where things can change for people, and many people always seem to have hope. At least that's how it seems to me. Maybe I was beginning to think this way, too, although my hope was very small.

©D. Barton/Shutterstock; (bg) ©Elena Schweitzer/Shutterstock; (tr) ©Roger Davies

10

Close Read Screencasts ▶ *View It!*

Modeled Discussions

Have students click the *Close Read* icons in their eBooks to access two screencasts in which readers discuss and annotate the following key passages:

- the adjustment Maya's parents must make to provide for the family when they move to America (lines 58–67)
- Maya's carefully worded "translation" of the principal's description of her brother's fight. (lines 315–332)

As a class, view and discuss at least one of these videos. Then have students pair up to do an independent close read of an additional passage—Maya's daydream about how different her life would be if she ran away to the Lui's house (lines 549–559).

CLOSE READ

Analyze Stories: Plot

COMMON CORE **RL 1**

(LINES 15–56)

Tell students that beginning on line 15, the narrator is describing events from the past that brought her family to America. Review that most stories begin by introducing **characters,** the people involved in the story, and the **setting,** the time and place of the story. Early in a story, the author also introduces a **conflict,** or problem that has to be solved.

B **CITE TEXT EVIDENCE** Lines 15–56 reveal background on and aspects of the story's characters, setting, and conflict. What details explain how an international dating magazine brought the narrator's family to America? *(The story is set in Kazakhstan and then in America. The narrator introduces Aunt Madina, Mama, and Papa. Their initial conflict involves lack of money. Aunt Madina met her American husband and moved after placing her picture in a dating magazine. "Things got very hard" in Kazakhstan. The narrator's parents "lost their teaching jobs" and had to sell family possessions to survive. Aunt Madina asked the narrator's family to join her in America and they agreed.)*

CRITICAL VOCABULARY

sponsor: The narrator is explaining the circumstances that led to her family's move to America.

ASK STUDENTS what is suggested by Aunt Madina's needing to sponsor the narrator's family. *(There is likely to be a law or requirement that someone already living in America must vouch for, or support, any immigrant who wants to come here.)*

SCAFFOLDING FOR ELL STUDENTS

Analyze Language The compound and complex sentences in the text may present a challenge for some students. Guide them to highlight conjunctions and clauses to help them better understand these sentences.

- Highlight in yellow coordinating conjunctions such as *and, or,* and *but.*

- Highlight in blue phrases or clauses that begin with subordinating conjunctions or words such as *who, when,* or *where.*

ASK STUDENTS to demonstrate understanding by answering basic questions about each part of the sentences containing highlights.

B We came to America through an international dating magazine. I don't mean that our whole family was in the magazine looking for dates, just Madina Zhamejakova, my aunt. Aunt Madina came after Kazakhstan broke away from the Soviet Union and things got very hard. Everyone's pay
20 was cut and the *tenge,* our money, was worth less and less. Then my grandmother died. That was the worst part. She was the head of our family, and without her everything fell apart. That's when Aunt Madina started reading international dating magazines.

The next thing we knew, she had a beautiful photo taken of herself wearing her best outfit, a black dress with a scoop neck and a red silk band around the neck. Aunt Madina is very pretty. Mama says she looks like an old American movie star we saw on TV named Natalie Wood, except Aunt Madina
30 looks more Kazakh with her dark, beautiful Asian eyes. She sent the photo to one of these magazines, and in a very short time a man from Seattle saw her picture. He started calling her, and they would talk on the phone for hours. I guess he had plenty of money for these calls, which Aunt Madina thought was a good sign. After about six months, he asked her to marry him.

His name was Bob Campbell and he'd been in the navy. He told Aunt Madina he never had a chance to meet anyone because he traveled so much. Maybe that was true, but Mama
40 was worried.

"Madina, something must be wrong with this man if he has to find a wife through a magazine."

Mama was afraid for her, but Aunt Madina went to America anyway and married Mr. Bob Campbell. She phoned us a lot from America, and Mama admitted she sounded okay. Madina said Bob was a lot older and had less hair than in the picture he had sent her. He was also fatter than in the picture, but he was very nice. She sounded so good, Mama stopped worrying about Aunt Madina, but then things got so bad in
50 Kazakhstan that she worried all the time about us. Papa and Mama lost their teaching jobs because the government was running out of money. Mama had to go to the market and sell many of our things: clothes, dishes, even some furniture. When Aunt Madina asked us to come to America for the hundredth time, we were running out of things to sell and my parents finally agreed. Aunt Madina **sponsored** us, and not

sponsor
(spŏn´ sər) *v.* If you *sponsor* someone, you support his or her admission into a group.

He started calling her, and they would talk on the phone for hours. I guess he had plenty of money for these calls, which Aunt Madina thought was a good sign.

long after we got here, Papa got a job driving a cab, and Mama worked cleaning people's houses. It was hard for them not to have the respect they were used to from holding government teaching jobs, but they had high regard for the food they could now easily buy at the store.

Six months after we got here, the Boeing Company moved to Chicago and Mr. Bob Campbell got transferred there. When Aunt Madina left with him, it broke Mama's heart. Aunt Madina was the only person we knew from Kazakhstan, and it felt like our family just huddled together on a tiny island in the middle of a great American sea.

I looked at the permission slip, wishing there were some special words I could say to get Mama and Papa to sign it. Around me, everyone in my homeroom was talking excitedly about the Spring Fling. Mama says she thinks the school is strange to have parties and events after school when students should be doing their homework. Ever since I've been at Beacon Junior High, the only slip they signed was for the gymnastics team. Papa loves sports. (I think he told Mama that giving permission for this activity was important for my education.) I can't find words to say how grateful I was he signed that slip. The gymnastics team is a fine, good thing in my life. I compete in all the events: vault, beam, floor exercise, and my favorite: the uneven bars. I love to swing up and up, higher and higher, and as I fly through the air, a wonderful thing happens and suddenly I have no worries and no responsibilities. I'm free!

But there's another reason why I love gymnastics. Shannon Lui is on the team. We became friends when she was a teaching assistant in my ESL class. We're the same age, but she says I'm like her little sister. Her grandparents came from China, and her parents speak perfect English. Everything about Shannon's family is very American. Her mother has a red coat with gold buttons from Nordstrom, and her father cooks and sometimes even washes dishes! (I couldn't believe this when I first saw it; no Kazakh man would do kitchen work.) Shannon encouraged me to try out for the gymnastics team, and the team has meant even more to me this year since I got put in the mainstream and had to leave ESL. Since I left ESL, I often feel like I'm in the middle of a game where I don't know the players, the rules, or even the object of the game.

CLOSE READ

Analyze Stories: Plot
COMMON CORE RL 1, RL 3

(LINES 68–78)

Tell students that in line 68, the story returns to the present and reveals more about the narrator's conflict related to the permission slip.

C **ASK STUDENTS** to reread lines 68–78 to identify the story's conflict. What does the conflict reveal about the narrator's parents? *(The conflict is the narrator's desire to go to the Spring Fling, though she is sure her parents will not give their permission for her to do so. The narrator's parents seem traditional and conservative, and think school activities should focus on education rather than social activities: Mama thinks it is "strange to have parties and events after school when students should be doing their homework.")*

Analyze Stories: Character
COMMON CORE RL 1, RL 3

(LINES 78–97)

Point out that readers learn more about the narrator as she shares her thoughts about being a member of the gymnastics team.

D **CITE TEXT EVIDENCE** Have students reread lines 78–97 to identify the reasons why the gymnastics team "is a fine, good thing." What do those reasons reveal about the narrator? *(The narrator says, "as I fly through the air, a wonderful thing happens . . . no worries and no responsibilities. I'm free!" and "Shannon Lui is on the team. We became friends . . . Shannon's family is very American." The reasons reveal the narrator's struggles to mesh her Kazakh life and responsibilities with what she sees of American life and culture.)*

Analyze Stories: Character (LINES 111–125)

 COMMON CORE RL 1, RL 3

Tell students that **dialogue** is the written conversation between two or more people in a story. Explain that readers learn new information about the narrator, Maya, through the dialogue in lines 111–125.

Ⓔ CITE TEXT EVIDENCE Ask students to reread lines 111–125 to find the words and phrases that reveal Maya's reaction to being called to the office. What does the way she speaks to Mr. Walsh reveal about her feelings? *(Maya's "voice came out as a whisper." She says she "felt such terror" that she "could barely speak." Her strong reaction suggests that she has a great fear of the consequences if she causes trouble.)*

CRITICAL VOCABULARY

stun: The narrator is describing her feelings as she is singled out by her school's vice-principal.

ASK STUDENTS to infer why the narrator would feel stunned, based on what they know about her so far. *(The narrator has said that gymnastics makes her feel free, with "no responsibilities." Also, she has mentioned two different permission slips, which implies she usually follows the rules. Readers can infer that she's generally well behaved in school and that having the vice-principal speak to her is very unusual.)*

In my next class, Language Arts, even though I knew it was foolish, I was dreaming of the Spring Fling. I really like
100 Language Arts. Ms. Coe, our teacher, is also the gymnastics coach, and there's a guy in the class, Daniel Klein, who was my partner for a research project last semester. He encouraged me to talk and listened to what I had to say (he's also a very handsome guy), and I always look forward to this class so I can see him. I was trying to think of some ideas to convince Mama and Papa to give permission (and also sneaking glances at Daniel Klein) when Mr. Walsh, the vice-principal, came into our class. He whispered something to Ms. Coe and she nodded. And then I was **stunned** because she nodded and
110 pointed to me!

"Maya, you're wanted in the office," Ms. Coe said. "You can go now with Mr. Walsh."

My fingers tingled with fear. What was wrong? What had I done? Mr. Walsh only comes for people when there's trouble.

Like a robot, I gathered my books and followed Mr. Walsh. As he closed the classroom door behind us, my heart began to bang and I felt like I needed to go to the bathroom. In the hallway he told me Ms. Johnson, the school counselor, wanted to speak with me.

120 "What is wrong?" My voice came out as a whisper. I felt such terror I could barely speak.

"What's that?" Mr. Walsh couldn't hear my whisper.

"What is wrong?" I tried to speak more loudly.

"She didn't say. She just asked me to find you since I was heading down the hall anyway."

I suddenly remembered Sunstar Sysavath, who was in my ESL class last year. Her family came from Cambodia, and on her first day at Beacon she was in the wrong line in the lunchroom. Mr. Walsh went to help her, and he tapped her on
130 her shoulder to get her attention. When she felt the tap and saw him, she lifted her hands in the air as if she were being arrested and about to be shot. People who saw this in the lunchroom laughed, but it wasn't a joke. Sunstar was filled with terror.

I knew I wouldn't be shot, but walking with Mr. Walsh to the office seemed like one of the longest walks of my life. I often fill my mind with nice things, such as imagining myself at the Olympics winning a gold medal for the U.S.A.— especially on days like today, when we have a gymnastics meet

stun
(stŭn) *v.* To *stun* someone is to make him or her feel shocked or dazed.

APPLYING ACADEMIC VOCABULARY

contribute	shifting

As you discuss the short story, incorporate the following Collection 1 academic vocabulary words: *contribute* and *shifting*. Discuss the descriptions and actions that **contribute** to students' understanding of Maya as a character. Encourage them to watch for evidence that her mindset is **shifting** from the culture of Kazakhstan to her new American culture.

140 after school. But now my mind was filled with nothing. It was empty, like a dry riverbed where there is only cracked, baked earth and nothing lives.

I walked into the main office, where Ms. Johnson was waiting for me. "Come with me, Maya." Ms. Johnson smiled at Mr. Walsh. "Thanks, Tom."

Like a person made from wood, a puppet, I followed Ms. Johnson through the main office down the hall to her office across from the principal's. She showed me in and closed the door behind us.

©Diverse Images/Getty Images

150 "Sit down, dear."

I sat in a chair across from her desk and clutched my books to my chest. I'd never been in her office before. She had many nice green plants in front of the window and a small fish tank in one corner. I stared at the brightly colored fish swimming back and forth, back and forth. Then Ms. Johnson spoke.

"I received a call from Mr. Shanaman, the principal at Evergreen Elementary, and your brother's been suspended for fighting."

"Nurzhan?"

160 "Yes. Nurzhan Alazova." She read his name from a pink message slip. "They haven't been able to locate your mother, so they called over here to see if you could help."

My Favorite Chaperone **7**

CLOSE READ

Analyze Language

COMMON CORE RL 4

(LINES 140–149)

Tell students that a **simile** is a comparison using the words *like* or *as*. Explain that authors often use such comparisons to help readers create a vivid picture of a scene in their minds.

F ASK STUDENTS to reread lines 140–149 to identify the comparisons that help them imagine the scene as Maya arrives at the office. What is the effect of the author's comparisons? *(The author says that Maya's mind "was empty, like a dry riverbed where there is only cracked, baked earth and nothing lives." Maya moves "like a person made from wood, a puppet." The comparison creates a feeling of stiffness, or a lack of life. It reinforces the idea that Maya is terrified in this situation.)*

Analyze Stories: Plot

COMMON CORE RL 1, RL 3

(LINES 163–180)

Explain that in a story's **rising action,** characters encounter issues and complications as they try to resolve a story's conflict.

G **ASK STUDENTS** to reread lines 163–180 to identify why Maya has become involved in the events surrounding her brother's suspension from school. What does her involvement suggest about her role in the family? *(Maya has become involved because school officials want her to help locate her parents; she has been asked to act as their translator. Maya's involvement suggests that she is often placed in situations "at the store, at the doctor" where she must be adult-like as she speaks for her parents.)*

CRITICAL VOCABULARY

dispatcher: The narrator is describing the steps she must take to contact her father.

ASK STUDENTS to explain why having to go through the dispatcher to reach her father adds to Maya's stress. *(Going through the dispatcher adds to Maya's waiting time, and she realizes that she may miss her gymnastics meet.)*

"Is Nurzhan all right?"

"Yes. And I believe the other boy wasn't seriously hurt."

G "Who did Nurzhan fight?" It was a foolish question— I was sure of the answer. Ms. Johnson hesitated, so I just said, "Ossie Nishizono," and she nodded.

"What must I do?" I asked.

170 "The school policy on suspension requires that the parent or guardian must have a conference at school within twenty-four hours of the suspension. Can you help us locate your mother or your father?"

"Yes. I can do that."

"Do your parents speak English, Maya?"

"Just a little."

"Then perhaps you could attend the meeting and translate for them."

"Yes. I must always do this for my parents—at the store, at the doctor, things like that."

180 "Here's the phone. I'll step out to give you some privacy."

Ms. Johnson left the office, quietly closing the door behind her. I looked at the nameplate on her desk. CATHERINE JOHNSON, it said. Outside her window, the sky was gray and it had started to rain. I stared at the phone, wishing I didn't have to be the messenger with this bad news. Then I called the Northwest Cab Company and asked them to contact my father.

"Aibek Alazova. Cab 191. I'm his daughter, and there is a family problem I must speak with him about."

190 I stayed on the line while the **dispatcher** radioed Papa. I looked at the clock and felt my heart grow heavy. In a minute the bell would ring, school would be out, and the gymnastics meet would begin.

"Maya!" Papa's voice was alarmed. "What is wrong?"

"Nurzhan has been in a fight with another boy." Then I explained in Russian what had happened, and Papa said he had to drop his passenger at the Four Seasons Hotel downtown and then he'd come straight to Nurzhan's school. He'd be there about three-thirty.

200 Ms. Johnson came back into the office as I hung up the phone. "Did you get your mother?"

"I don't have the number where she works today, but I got my father. He will come to the school."

"Good."

dispatcher
(dĭs-pǎch´ ər) *n.* A *dispatcher* is a person who sends out vehicles according to a schedule.

"Ms. Johnson?"

"Yes?"

"I will leave now for Evergreen. Will you tell Ms. Coe I have a family problem and I cannot attend the gymnastics meet?"

210 "Of course. And I'll call Mr. Shanaman at Evergreen now and let him know that you and your father will be there."

I went to my locker, got my coat, then walked quickly down the hall to the south door that opens onto the play field that joins our school with Evergreen. Poor Nurzhan, getting in such big trouble. I couldn't fault him for fighting with Ossie Nishizono. Such a mean boy—he'd been teasing Nurzhan without mercy for not speaking well and mispronouncing things. I hoped Nurzhan had given him a hard punch. But why did he have to make this fight today! I felt angry that I 220 had to miss the meet because of Nurzhan. Would Ms. Coe still want me on the team? Would she think I wasn't reliable?

But as I neared Nurzhan's school—my old school—I only worried about Papa. Even though he didn't shout at me on the phone, that didn't mean he wasn't angry. He had a person in his cab and the dispatcher might have been hearing us. Probably the dispatcher didn't know Russian, but Papa wouldn't show his anger in the cab anyway. But Papa could be very, very angry—not just with Nurzhan but with me, too. He and Mama think it's my duty to watch out for Nurzhan and 230 keep him out of trouble.

As I walked up to the front door, Mr. Zabornik, the custodian, waved to me. He was picking up papers and litter around the bushes next to the front walk. It was still raining lightly, and Mr. Zabornik's wet gray hair was pasted against his forehead.

"Hi, Maya."

"Hello, Mr. Zabornik."

"Here about your brother, I suppose."

"How did you know?"

240 "I was fixing the drainpipe when it happened." He pointed to the corner of the building by the edge of the play field. "That kid Ossie Nishizono was teasing Nurzhan something fierce. Telling him he could never be a real American, making fun of the way he talked." He bent down and picked up a candy wrapper. "Reminded me of how this bully used to treat me when my family came after the revolution."

My Favorite Chaperone **9**

CLOSE READ

Analyze Stories: Character (LINES 212–230)

COMMON CORE **RL 1, RL 3**

Explain that readers gain additional insights into Maya's character as she describes her thoughts and reactions to the news of her brother's fight.

H **CITE TEXT EVIDENCE** Have students reread lines 212–230 to make note of the ways in which Nurzhan's fight will impact Maya. What does her reaction suggest about her? *(Maya feels bad for her brother, but she is upset that his actions will cause problems for her: "I couldn't fault him for fighting . . . I felt angry that I had to miss the meet because of Nurzhan." She knows that her parents will hold her responsible for the fight: "He and Mama think it's my duty . . . to keep him out of trouble." Her reaction suggests that she has dealt with comparable situations and knows what to expect of each of her family members.)*

Remind students that authors use dialogue to reveal information about characters. In this passage, the dialogue between Mr. Zabornik and Maya supports Maya's earlier thoughts (in lines 215–218) about what drove her brother to fight.

I **CITE TEXT EVIDENCE** Ask students to reread lines 231–246 to find out what led to Nurzhan's fight. What does the conversation reveal about Nurzhan? *(Mr. Zabornik says, "That kid . . . was teasing Nurzhan something fierce. Telling him he could never be a real American, making fun of the way he talked." The conversation shows the challenges Nurzhan is facing as an immigrant in America and implies that he has put up with a lot before losing his temper.)*

CRITICAL VOCABULARY

scuffle: Mr. Zabornik is explaining to Maya that he witnessed Nurzhan's fight.

ASK STUDENTS what the phrase "this was no scuffle" suggests about the fight. *(Since* scuffle *usually describes a minor disturbance or fight, the phrase suggests that the fight was fairly serious and could have led to injuries.)*

"Oh." I think Mr. Zabornik could tell I didn't know what revolution this was.

250 "The Hungarian revolution, in 1956." He looked out over the play field and folded his arms across his chest. "Guess some things never change."

"Nurzhan's going to be suspended."

"Sorry to hear that. 'Course, the school can't allow fights, and this was no **scuffle**. But I can sure see how your brother lost his temper." Then he went back to picking up the litter. "Good luck."

scuffle
(skŭf´əl) *n.* A *scuffle* is a disorderly fight.

"Thank you, Mr. Zabornik."

I went to the front office, where Ms. Illo, the head secretary, spoke to me in a very kind way. "Maya, Mr.
260 Shanaman is waiting for you in his office. You can go right in."

Mr. Shanaman was behind his big desk, and Nurzhan was sitting on a chair in the corner. He looked like a rabbit caught in a trap. He had scrapes on his hands and on his cheek, and his eyes were puffed up. I couldn't tell if that was from crying or being hit.

"I understand your father will be coming. Is that right, Maya?"

I nodded.

270 "Just take a seat by your brother. Ms. Illo will bring your father in when he gets here."

Then Mr. Shanaman read some papers on his desk and I sat down next to Nurzhan and spoke quietly to him in Russian.

"*Neechevo, Nurzhan. Ya vas ne veenu.*" It's okay, Nurzhan. I don't blame you, is what I said.

Nurzhan's eyes were wet with tears as he nodded to me.

I stared out the principal's window. Across the street, the bare branches of the trees were black against the cement gray
280 sky. The rain came down in a steady drizzle, and after a few minutes, I saw Papa's cab turn the corner. His cab is green, the color of a lime, and he always washes and shines it. I watched Papa park and get out of the cab. His shoulders are very broad underneath his brown leather jacket, and Papa has a powerful walk, like a large, strong horse that plows fields. He walked briskly, and as he came up the steps of the school, he removed his driver cap.

10   Collection 1

WHEN STUDENTS STRUGGLE . . .

Point out the italicized words in line 275. Explain that authors often use a different kind of type when words from a foreign language—in this case, Russian—are included in a story. Guide students to use the context of the surrounding sentences to locate the translation of the Russian words.

Students may find it helpful to record the meanings of any foreign words or phrases they encounter as they continue reading.

Foreign Words	English Translation
Nyet (line 5)	*No*
tenge (line 20)	*our money*
Neechevo, Nurzhan. Ya vas ne veenu. (line 275)	*It's okay, Nurzhan. I don't blame you.*

It seemed like one thousand years, but it was only a minute before Ms. Illo brought Papa into the office. Nurzhan and I stood up when he entered, but he didn't look at us, only at Mr. Shanaman, who shook hands with him and motioned for him to have a seat.

Papa sat across the desk from Mr. Shanaman and placed his driver cap in his lap.

"We have asked Maya to translate, Mr. Alazova."

"Yes." Papa nodded. When he heard my name, he understood what Mr. Shanaman meant.

"Your son, Nurzhan, was involved in quite a nasty fight."

Papa looked at me, and I said to him in Russian, "Nurzhan was in little fight."

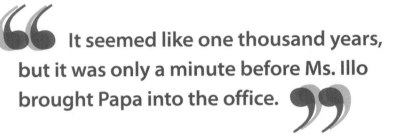

> ## It seemed like one thousand years, but it was only a minute before Ms. Illo brought Papa into the office.

Mr. Shanaman continued. "The other boy, Ossie Nishizono, needed two stitches at the hospital."

"The other boy, Ossie Nishizono, was a little hurt," I told Papa.

Nurzhan's eyes became wide as he listened to my translation.

"We have a policy that anyone who fights must be suspended from school. Both boys will receive a two-day suspension."

"The other boy, who is very bad," I translated for Papa, "is not allowed to come to school for two days and his parents must punish him. Nurzhan must stay home, too. But he should not be punished so much."

Papa nodded.

Then Mr. Shanaman said, "We've been told the other boy was teasing your son. We'd like you to help Nurzhan find ways to handle this situation without resorting to violence. We're working with the other boy to help him show respect for all students."

CLOSE READ

Analyze Stories: Character (LINES 293–314)

COMMON CORE RL 1, RL 3

Remind students that authors use dialogue to reveal what characters are like. Draw students' attention to Maya's translation of what Mr. Shanaman says.

J ASK STUDENTS to reread lines 293–314 to note the differences between what Mr. Shanaman says and what Maya translates. Point out that while Papa says very little, Maya's translation tells readers what he is like. What does her translation suggest about Papa? (*Maya's translation suggests that Papa can be volatile or quick to anger. Her translation minimizes the seriousness of the fight: "involved in quite a nasty fight" vs. "in a little fight;" "The other boy . . . needed two stitches" vs. "The other boy . . . was a little hurt.")*

Analyze Stories: Plot

COMMON CORE RL 1

(LINES 338–358)

Tell students that as the rising action continues, Maya has to deal with the aftermath of her decision to modify Mr. Shanaman's words.

Ⓚ **ASK STUDENTS** to reread lines 338–358. Why does Maya believe her actions are justified? (*While Maya admits that her actions were "sort of like telling lies" she justifies them by saying that "some lies are okay." She says that she was "scared to death of what Papa might have done."*)

320 I looked at Papa and translated: "The other boy was teasing Nurzhan in a violent manner. This boy will be punished and must learn to respect all students. We understand how Nurzhan became so angry, and we ask that you punish him by not allowing him to watch television."

"Yes, I will punish my son as you suggest," Papa said in Russian.

I looked at Mr. Shanaman. "My father says he will teach Nurzhan not to fight by giving him a very serious punishment."

330 "We are glad you understand the serious nature of this situation," Mr. Shanaman said. Then I told Papa in Russian the exact words of Mr. Shanaman.

Mr. Shanaman held out a form on a clipboard. "We require you to sign this to show that we've discussed the suspension and you'll keep Nurzhan at home until Monday."

Again, I told Papa exactly what Mr. Shanaman said, and Papa signed the form.

We said nothing as we left the school and followed Papa to his cab. Nurzhan and I sat in the back, not daring to speak.

340 There was a small rip in the leather of the seat and I poked my finger in it. The cab smelled of perfume; maybe Papa's last ride was a lady who wore a lot of it. It smelled like some kind of flower, but I couldn't name it. I wished so much I was in a beautiful meadow right then, surrounded by sweet-smelling flowers, lying in the soft grass, looking up at the clouds. I tried to calm myself by thinking about this meadow, but I just kept feeling scared—scared Papa might somehow find out I'd changed what Mr. Shanaman said.

Maybe I should've felt bad about changing Mr. Shanaman's

350 words, but I didn't. I only felt afraid. I don't mean that I think changing words like that is okay; I have to admit it's sort of like telling lies. But I think maybe some lies are okay, like in the play we read last semester about Anne Frank and how the people who were hiding her family lied and said no one was in the attic when they really were. They lied to save Anne's family from the Nazis. Maybe I wasn't saving Nurzhan from death, but I was sure scared to death of what Papa might have done if I hadn't changed the words. I stared at the back of Papa's thick neck. It was very red, and he drove in silence until

360 he pulled up in front of our building. Papa shut off the engine. Then he put his arm across the top of the seat and turned his face to us, craning his neck.

His dark eyes narrowed and his voice was severe. "I am ashamed of this! To come to this school and find you in trouble, Nurzhan! This does not seem like much punishment to me, this no watching television. You will go to bed tonight without dinner." He clenched his teeth. "I have lost money today because of you. And Maya, you must keep your brother out of trouble!" Then he waved us away furiously, like shooing away bugs. "Go now! Go!"

We went in the house, and Nurzhan marched straight to the table in the kitchen with his books. He seemed to be in such a hurry to do his work, he didn't even take off his jacket.

"Take off your jacket and hang it up, Nurzhan."

"Okay."

I began peeling potatoes for dinner, while Nurzhan hung up his jacket. Then he sat back down at the table.

"Maya, I—"

"Don't talk. Do your work."

"But I—"

"I missed the gymnastics meet because of you!"

"Watch the knife!" Nurzhan looked scared.

I glanced at my hand. I was holding the knife and I'd been waving it without realizing it.

"I wasn't going to stab you, stupid boy."

"I was only going to say thank you." Nurzhan looked glumly at his book.

I went back to peeling the potatoes. I'd had enough of him and his troubles.

"For changing what Mr. Shanaman said when you told Papa," he said in a timid voice, like a little chick peeping.

"It's okay, Nurzhan." I sighed. "Just do your work."

A few minutes before six, we heard Mama get home. She came straight to the kitchen, and when she saw Nurzhan sitting there doing his work, a smile came over her tired face.

"Oh, what a good boy, doing his work."

"Not so good, Mama. Nurzhan got in trouble." I didn't mind having to tell her this bad news too much (not like when I had to call Papa). Then I explained about the fight and how Papa had to come to the school.

"Oh, my poor little one!" Mama rushed to Nurzhan and examined his hands. Tenderly, she touched his face where it had been cut. Then she turned sharply toward me.

"Maya! How could you let this happen?"

CLOSE READ

Analyze Stories: Character (LINES 371–392)

COMMON CORE RL 1, RL 3

Point out that like their interaction in lines 272–277, the dialogue between Maya and Nurzhan in lines 371–392 gives information about the characters and their relationship.

CITE TEXT EVIDENCE Have students reread lines 371–392 to analyze what the dialogue reveals about the brother and sister. What is Maya's role in Nurzhan's life? *(Maya is responsible for taking care of her brother. With both parents working, she takes on the role of an adult in his life: "Take off your jacket and hang it up," "Do your work." The dialogue also shows that while she was protective of him during the crisis in the principal's office, she now wants him to realize that she missed an important event because of him: "I missed the gymnastics meet because of you!")*

Analyze Stories: Character (LINES 405–413)

COMMON CORE RL 1, RL 3

Explain that while the dialogue in lines 405–413 reveals Mama's view of her children, it also shows a conflict that the family must deal with as immigrants.

 **CITE TEXT EVIDENCE** Have students reread lines 405–413 to identify the difference in customs between Kazakhstan and America that causes a problem. How do you know that Maya and Nurzhan understand this difference better than their mother? *(Mama blames Maya for not doing more to defend her brother: "In Kazakhstan, if someone insults you, they have insulted everyone in the family. And everyone must respond." Maya and Nurzhan understand, "It's different here, Mama.")*

"Me! I wasn't even there."

"On the bus, when this boy is so bad to Nurzhan. You must make this boy stop."

"No, Mama," Nurzhan explained. "He would tease me more if my sister spoke for me."

410 "I don't understand this. In Kazakhstan, if someone insults you, they have insulted everyone in the family. And everyone must respond."

"It's different here, Mama."

Mama looked sad. She sighed deeply. Then the phone rang and she told me to answer it. Mama always wants me to answer because she is shy about speaking English. When her work calls, I always speak on the phone to the women whose houses she cleans and then translate for Mama. (I translate their exact words, not like with Mr. Shanaman.)

420 But it wasn't for Mama. It was Shannon, and her voice was filled with worry.

"Maya, why weren't you at the meet? Is everything all right?"

"Everything's okay. It was just Nurzhan." Then I explained to her about what had happened. "I hope I can still be on the team."

"Ms. Coe is cool. Don't worry, it won't mess anything up."

Shannon was right. The next day at practice Ms. Coe was
very understanding. Practice was so much fun I forgot all
about Nurzhan, and Shannon and I were very excited because
430　Ms. Coe said we were going to get new team leotards.

After practice we were waiting for the activity bus, talking
about the kind of leotards we wanted, when two guys from
the wrestling team joined us. One was David Pfeiffer, a guy
who Shannon talked about all the time. She always said he was
so cute, that he was "awesome" and "incredible" and things
like that. She was often laughing and talking to him after our
practice, and I think she really liked him. And today he was
with Daniel Klein!

"Hey, Maya! How was practice?"

440　"Hi." I smiled at Daniel, but then I glanced away,
pretending to look for the bus because talking to guys outside
class always made me feel embarrassed and shy.

The guys came right up to us. David smiled at Shannon.
"Wrestling practice was great! We worked on takedowns and
escapes, and then lifted weights. How was your practice?"

"Fun! We spent most of it on the beam."

"I'm still pumped from weight training!" David grinned
and picked up a metal trash can by the gym door. He paraded
around with the can, then set it down with a bang right next
450　to Shannon. Everyone was laughing, and then David bent
his knees and bounced up and down on his heels and said,
"Check this out, Daniel! Am I strong or what?" The next thing
we knew, David had one arm under Shannon's knees and one
arm under her back and he scooped her up. Shannon squealed
and laughed, and I was laughing watching them, when all of a
sudden Daniel scooped me up too!

"Chort!" I shouted, as he lifted me. I grabbed him around
his neck to hang on, and my head was squished against his
shoulder. He strutted around in a circle before he let me down.
460　I could feel that my face was the color of borscht, and I flamed
with excitement and embarrassment and couldn't stop
laughing from both joy and nervousness.

"That's nothing, man." David crouched like a weight lifter
while he was still holding Shannon and lifted her as high as
his shoulders.

It was exciting and crazy: Daniel and David showing each
other how strong they were, first picking up Shannon and
me, then putting us down, then picking us up and lifting us

My Favorite Chaperone　**15**

CLOSE READ

Analyze Stories: Character (LINES 427–462)

COMMON CORE　RL 1

Remind students that a character's actions help
readers to understand what the character is like.

CITE TEXT EVIDENCE Have students reread lines
427–462. In what ways is Maya like a typical middle
school student? In what ways is she different? *(Maya
enjoys sports and is interested in clothes and in boys
like many middle school girls; her excitement about
gymnastics practice and the new team leotards allows
her to forget her troubles for a while. She seems a bit
more shy or uncomfortable around boys than most
middle school girls.)*

Strategies for Annotation 　🖊 📋 *Annotate it!*

Analyze Stories: Character 　COMMON CORE　RL 1, RL 3

Have students locate lines 427–461. Encourage them to do the following:

- Highlight in blue the descriptions of things a typical American
  middle school student would do or say.
- Highlight in green the descriptions of things a typical middle school
  student might not do or say.

After practice we were waiting for the activity bus, talking
about the kind of leotards we wanted, when two guys from the
wrestling team joined us . . . I smiled at Daniel, but then glanced
away, pretending to look for the bus because talking to guys outside
class always made me feel embarrassed and shy.

Analyze Language: Simile (LINES 490–503)

COMMON CORE RL 1, RL 4

Remind students that a simile is a comparison using the word *like* or *as*. Tell students that such comparisons can help readers make a connection to characters' emotions.

 CITE TEXT EVIDENCE Have students reread lines 490–503 to identify the comparisons that show Maya's view of the situation after her father arrives. What is the effect of the author's comparisons? *(The author says that, "Papa stood like a huge bull in his dark leather jacket," Maya was "whimpering and trembling inside like a dog caught stealing a chicken," and Papa's silence filled the cab "like a dark cloud." The comparisons emphasize Papa's strength and power, while showing how defenseless Maya feels.)*

CRITICAL VOCABULARY

whimper: Maya is describing her reaction when her father observes Daniel lifting her in the air.

ASK STUDENTS what her whimper reveals about Maya's emotions. *(She is shocked and frightened and is probably about to cry.)*

---

higher, as if Shannon and I were weights. After a few times, whenever Daniel picked me up, I was easily putting my arms around his neck, and I loved being his pretend weight, even though Shannon and I were both yelling for them to put us down. (We didn't really mean it. Shannon is a strong girl, and if she didn't like being lifted up and held by David, there was no way it would be happening.) I couldn't believe it, but I began to relax in Daniel's arms, and I laughed each time as he slowly turned in a circle.

Then Shannon and I tried to pick them up, and it was hilarious. Every time we tried to grab them, they did wrestling moves on us and we ended up on the grass in a big heap, like a litter of playful puppies. I couldn't remember a time in my life that had been so fun and so exciting. We lay on the grass laughing, and then David and Daniel jumped up and picked Shannon and me up again.

But this time when we turned, as my face was pressed against Daniel's shoulder, I saw something coming toward the school that made me tremble with fear.

"Daniel, please. Put me down!" My voice cracked as my breath caught in my throat.

But Daniel didn't hear. Everyone was shouting and laughing, and he lifted me up even more as the lime green cab came to a halt in front of the school. The door slammed. Papa stood like a huge bull in his dark leather jacket and flung open the back door of the cab.

"MAYA ALAZOVA!" His voice roared across the parking lot. He pointed at me the way one might identify a criminal. "*EDEE SUDA!*" he shouted in Russian. COME HERE!

Daniel dropped me and I ran to the cab, **whimpering** and trembling inside like a dog caught stealing a chicken.

Papa didn't speak. His silence filled every corner of the cab like a dark cloud, slowly suffocating me with its poisonous rage. Papa's neck was deep red, and the skin on the back of my hands tingled with fear. I lay my head back against the seat and closed my eyes, squeezing them shut, and took myself far away until I was safe on the bars at a beautiful gymnastics meet in the sky. I swung back and forth, higher and higher, and then I released and flew to the next bar through fluffy white clouds as soft as goose feathers, while the air around me was sweet and warm, and my teammates cheered for me, their voices filled with love.

whimper
(hwĭm'pər) *v.* To *whimper* is to sob or let out a soft cry.

We screeched to a stop in front of our building. My head slammed back against the seat. When I struggled from the taxi, it was as though I had fallen from the bars, crashing down onto the street, where I splintered into a million pieces. And as hard as I tried, I couldn't get back on the bars any more than I could stop the hot tears that spilled from my eyes. Papa roared in front of me, and as he charged toward the door in his glistening dark leather jacket, he again seemed transformed to a creature that was half man and half bull.

520 "Gulnara!" He flung open the door, shouting for Mama, his voice filled with anger and blame.

"Why are you here? What has happened, Aibek?" Mama came from the kitchen as Nurzhan darted to the doorway and peeked around like a little squirrel.

I closed the front door and leaned against it with my wet palms flat against the wood, like a prisoner about to be shot.

"Is this how you raise your daughter! Is this what you teach her? Lessons to be a toy for American boys!" Papa spat out the words.

530 The color rose in Mama's face like a flame turned up on the stove, and she spun toward me, her eyes flashing. "What have you done?"

"Your daughter was in the arms of an American boy."

Mama looked shocked. "When? H-how can this be?" she stammered.

"Outside the school as I drove by, I found them at this. Don't you teach her anything?"

"Who let her stay after school? Who gives permission for all these things? You are the one, Aibek. If you left it to 540 me, she would come home every day. She would not have this permission!"

Mama and Papa didn't notice that I went to the bathroom and locked the door. I huddled by the sink and heard their angry voices rise and fall like the pounding of thunder, and then I heard a bang, so fierce that the light bulb hanging from the ceiling swayed with its force. Papa slamming the front door. Then I heard the engine of the cab and a sharp squeal of tires as he sped away.

I imagined running away. I would run like the wind, 550 behind the mini-mart, sailing past the E-Z Dry Cleaner, past the bus stop in an easy gallop through the crosswalk. As I ran, each traffic light I came to would turn green, until there would

My Favorite Chaperone   **17**

CLOSE READ

Analyze Stories: Plot

COMMON CORE RL 1, RL 3

(LINES 520–541)

Remind students that Maya's conflict at the beginning of the story focuses on wanting her parents to sign a permission slip so that she can attend the Spring Fling dance. Discuss how the events in this part of the plot may affect the possibility of resolving that conflict.

CITE TEXT EVIDENCE Have students reread lines 520–541 to find evidence of Maya's parents' reaction to finding her with Daniel. What does their reaction suggest about Maya's chance of being allowed to go to the dance? *(Students should note that Maya's parents blame each other: Papa says, "Is this how you raise your daughter! Is this what you teach her?" Mama says, "Who let her stay after school? Who gives permission for these things . . . If you left it to me, she would come home every day." Since they see non-school activities as a problem, it seems unlikely that they will sign the permission slip for Maya to go to the dance.)*

APPLYING ACADEMIC VOCABULARY

contribute	immigrate

As you discuss the short story, incorporate the following Collection 1 academic vocabulary words: *contribute* and *immigrate*. Discuss how the family's decision to **immigrate** to America **contributes** to the conflict Maya is facing. Encourage them to note evidence of how the culture of Kazakhstan influences Maya's parents.

Analyze Stories: Character (LINES 563–575)

 COMMON CORE RL 1, RL 4

Point out that the dialogue in lines 563–575 emphasizes Mama's traditional views.

Q **ASK STUDENTS** to reread lines 563–575. What does Mama mean when she says, "You have brought shame to your father and to this family"? *(Mama's comment suggests it is embarrassing to her parents for Maya to interact with a boy in any way, but especially if she is in physical contact with him.)*

be a string of green lights glowing like a necklace of emeralds strung all down the street. And then I would be at the Luis' house. Mrs. Lui would greet me in her red Nordstrom coat with the gold buttons. She would hug me and hold me close. Then Mr. Lui would say, "Hi, honey," and make hamburgers. "Want to use the phone, Maya?" Mrs. Lui would say. "Talk as long as you want—we have an extra line for the kids."

560 "Oh, by the way," Mr. Lui would say, "Shannon is having David and some other kids over Friday night for pizza and videos. It's fine if there's a guy you want to invite, too."

"Maya! Open this door. Do you want more trouble?" Mama rattled the doorknob so hard I thought she'd rip it off.

"I'm coming." My voice caught in my throat. I felt dizzy as I unlocked the door and held my stomach, afraid I would be sick.

"You have brought shame to your father and to this family." Mama glared at me.

570 "Mama, it was just kids joking. Guys from the wrestling team pretending some of us were weights."

"I don't know this weights."

"It was nothing, Mama!"

"Do not tell me 'nothing' when your father saw you!" she screamed.

The next morning Papa was gone when I woke up. And even though Mama hadn't yet left for work, it was like she was gone, too. She didn't speak to me and didn't even look at me, except once when she came in the kitchen. I was getting *kasha*, and

580 she stared at me like I was a stranger to her. Then she turned and left. Not only was Mama not speaking to me, but she didn't speak to Nurzhan, either. This never happens. Even when he was punished for the fight with Ossie Nishizono and had to stay home, Mama still spoke to him. But as I was getting dressed in my room, I heard Nurzhan try to talk to her. I put my ear to the door to listen.

"It's different here, Mama. I'm sure Maya and those guys were playing. Joking, like in a game."

"Quiet, boy! You know nothing of these things!"

590 I was shocked. Mama hardly ever says a harsh word to her precious boy. Then I heard her rush by, and then *bam*! The door slammed. The *kamcha* that hung by the door trembled with the force. We brought our *kamcha* when we came to

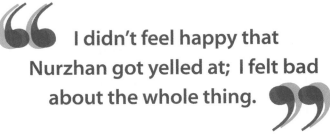

America. It looks like a riding crop with a carved wooden handle and a leather cord, decorated with some horsehair. It's an old Kazakh tradition to put the *kamcha* inside the house next to the door because it's believed to bring good fortune and happiness. But our *kamcha* was not bringing us good fortune today. Mama left without a word of goodbye to either one of us.

> ## I didn't feel happy that Nurzhan got yelled at; I felt bad about the whole thing.

I came out of my room and Nurzhan and I just looked at each other. I didn't feel happy that Nurzhan got yelled at; I felt bad about the whole thing.

"Did you hear?"

I nodded.

"She won't listen."

"Thank you for trying, Nurzhan."

"It did no good," he said with sadness. "They don't know about things here, only their own ways. They are like stone."

I wondered how long this tension and anger would stay in our home. I was afraid it might be a long time, because Mama and Papa were so upset. But gradually, in the way that winter becomes spring, there was a slight thaw each day. Perhaps because we huddled together like a tiny Kazakh island in the middle of the great American sea, we couldn't allow our winter to go on and on, and by the next week, things in my family were almost calm.

But it was not to last. On Wednesday afternoon of the following week, Mama was waiting to talk to me when I got home from school. I was afraid when I saw her. Her ankle was taped up, and she sat on the couch with her leg up on a chair. Next to it was a pair of crutches!

"Mama, what happened?"

CLOSE READ

Analyze Stories: Character (LINES 587–609)

COMMON CORE **RL 3**

Remind students that authors present a character's thoughts, speech, and actions to help readers learn what the character is like.

R ASK STUDENTS to reread lines 587–609 to focus on Nurzhan. What does Nurzhan do, and what does it reveal about him? *(Nurzhan is attempting to ease things for Maya and help his mother understand that Maya's actions have a different meaning in America than they would have at home. Nurzhan's intervention reveals that he cares about his family and feels a bond with Maya because they both are having trouble adjusting to their new home.)*

Analyze Language (LINES 612–617)

COMMON CORE **RL 4**

Explain that the author uses a comparison to describe how Maya's family gets past the crisis brought on by her encounter with Daniel.

S ASK STUDENTS to reread lines 612–617 to identify the comparison the author uses to describe the family's situation. What does the comparison suggest about what life is like for recent immigrants to the United States? *(The author says that they are "like a tiny Kazakh island in the middle of the great American sea." The comparison suggests that as new immigrants, Maya and her family are somewhat isolated. She implies that their isolation requires them to rely more on each other, and so the family members cannot remain angry at one another.)*

Analyze Stories: Plot

COMMON CORE RL 1

(LINES 624–654)

Focus attention on the ways in which Mama's injury leads to changes in Maya's life.

T **CITE TEXT EVIDENCE** Have students reread lines 624–654 to identify the ways in which Maya's life changes as a result of Mama's injury. How does Mama's injury both simplify and complicate Maya's life? *(Students should note the following evidence from the text: "It was decided that I'd take Mama's jobs for her," "I wouldn't go to gymnastics practice," "as soon as I got home I had to make dinner for everyone," "Each day I got more tired." While Maya is too busy to do the one thing she enjoys—gymnastics—she is also so focused on the tasks she must do that it is easy for her to avoid getting into trouble with her parents.)*

T "I fell at work. Mrs. Hormann took me to the emergency room. I can't work for six weeks until it heals. I must keep my foot up as much as possible."

"I'll start dinner." My eyes filled with tears, I felt so bad for her. And I felt bad that I'd made them so upset when my father saw me and Daniel. Even though I knew I hadn't done
630 anything wrong, it still bothered me that I'd been the cause of such trouble in our house.

It was decided that I'd take Mama's jobs for her while she couldn't work. I wouldn't go to gymnastics practice; instead, right after school I'd go straight to the houses Mama cleaned. The people Mama worked for agreed to this, and I worked at each house from three-thirty until six-thirty, when Papa came to pick me up. I wasn't able to clean their entire houses in this amount of time, but they told me which rooms were the most important, and I was able to clean those. Bathrooms were on
640 the list at every house.

I didn't mind doing Mama's jobs. Although I did get very tired, and I was scared sometimes that I might break something when I dusted (especially at Mrs. Hathaway's house, because she had a lot of glass vases and some small glass birds), but I didn't mind vacuuming, mopping, dusting, cleaning cupboards, counters, stoves, and refrigerators. I didn't even mind cleaning toilets. It was as if all the work I did at Mama's jobs was to make up for the problems I'd caused. And besides, our family needed the money.
650 When I finished working for Mama, as soon as I got home I had to make dinner for everyone. Each day I got more tired, and on Friday, when I was peeling potatoes, I cut my finger. I thought it was just a little cut, so I washed it off and continued to peel.

Nurzhan looked up from the table, where he was doing his work. "What's wrong with the potatoes?"

"Nothing," I said automatically, with my eyes half-closed.

"They're red!"

"What?"
660 "The potatoes, Maya. They look like you painted them with red streaks."

I looked down and saw my finger bleeding on the potatoes, and it scared me to be so tired that I hadn't seen this. "It's just blood, Nurzhan. I cut myself. It'll wash off."

"Oh, yuck."

Strategies for Annotation

✐ 🖥 *Annotate it!*

Analyze Language

COMMON CORE RL 1, RL 3

Have students use their eBook annotation tools to analyze the text. Ask them to do the following:

- Highlight in green the tasks that Maya is expected to do.
- Highlight in blue the words that describe Maya's feelings about the tasks.

I didn't mind doing Mama's jobs. Although I did get very tired, and I was scared sometimes that I might break something…

I didn't mind vacuuming, mopping, dusting, cleaning cupboards, counters, stoves, and refrigerators. . . .

It was as if all the work I did at Mama's jobs was to make up for the problems I'd caused. . . .

"Quiet, boy! I said I would wash it off."

That night at dinner, Nurzhan refused to eat the potatoes, even though there was no sign of blood on them, and I wanted to take the whole dish and dump them on his head.

670 The next week I was so tired after going to school and cleaning Mrs. Hathaway's house that I burned the chicken. After I put it in the oven, I sat at the table with Nurzhan to do my homework. I rested my head on my book for just a minute, and the next thing I knew, Nurzhan was pounding on my arm.

"Maya! The oven!" he shouted.

I woke to see smoke seeping from the oven. "Oh, no!"

I leaped up and grabbed a dishtowel and pulled the pan from the oven. The chicken was very dark but not black, although all the juice at the bottom of the pan had burned and 680 was smoking. "It's okay, Nurzhan. We can still eat it."

"Good."

Nurzhan didn't mind the almost-burned chicken that night, but Papa did.

"This tastes like my shoe!" Papa grumbled.

"Aibek, I have to keep my foot up, and Maya is doing the best she can. It is not easy. She must go to school, then do my work, then cook for us. She is just a young girl."

I looked at Mama and felt tears in my eyes. I couldn't remember another time when Mama spoke on my behalf, and 690 my tears were the kind you have when you know someone is on your side.

The next evening as dinner was cooking, I sat with Nurzhan at the kitchen table and helped him with his spelling words. While I waited for him to think how to spell *admire*, I took the permission slip for the Spring Fling from my notebook and stared at it. I'd never thrown it away.

"A-D-M-I-E-R."

"Almost, Nurzhan. It's this," I said as I wrote the correct spelling on the top of the permission slip and turned it for him 700 to see.

"A-D-M-I-R-E," he spelled. Then he looked closely at the slip. "What's this for?"

"It's a permission slip for the Spring Fling, the all-school dance, but it is only good for scratch paper to help you with spelling. Papa will never let me go. I don't know why I trouble myself to keep such a thing."

Nurzhan took the slip and put it in his notebook.

CLOSE READ

Analyze Stories: Character (LINES 682–691)

COMMON CORE RL 1, RL 3

Explain that the dialogue in lines 682–691 marks a change in Maya's relationship with Mama. As needed, review earlier evidence of what their relationship was like in lines 401–413 and in lines 563–575.

Ⓤ CITE TEXT EVIDENCE Have students reread lines 682–691 to identify what Mama says and Maya's reaction to it. What is the impact of Mama's statement on Maya? *(Mama says, "Maya is doing the best she can. It is not easy . . . she is just a young girl." Maya is both shocked and grateful.)*

Analyze Stories: Plot

COMMON CORE RL 1, RL 3

(LINES 711–749)

Tell students the **climax** of a story is the point of greatest tension, when the conflict begins to be resolved. Guide students to recall all of the complications that have prevented Maya from even asking her parents to sign the permission slip for the Spring Fling dance.

Ⓥ **CITE TEXT EVIDENCE** Have students reread lines 711–749 to identify Maya's reaction to Nurzhan's suggestion that he can convince Papa to sign the permission slip. How does Nurzhan's plan provoke a decision that pleases everyone? *(Students should note the following evidence of Maya's reaction from the text: "could only smile a sad smile," "afraid to really hope," "stared at the slip in disbelief," "Thank you, Mama. Thank you, Papa." Nurzhan's plan to be a chaperone keeps her in the company of a trusted family member while attending the dance. Maya is allowed to attend the dance in a way that respects her parents' rules and traditions. Both Maya and her parents get what they want.)*

WHEN STUDENTS STRUGGLE . . .

Some students may find it challenging to keep track of events in a longer story such as "My Favorite Chaperone." Students may find it helpful to record key events on a graphic organizer such as a flow chart.

"What are you doing with it?"

"Let me try."

710 "Try what?"

"Let me try to get permission for you from Papa."

I laughed. "Oh, Nurzhan. Don't be foolish. You waste your time. Papa will never change his thinking because of you."

"I will try anyway. When he comes home tonight, I will speak to him myself. I have a plan."

I could only smile a sad smile at the idea of little Nurzhan trying to change the mind of Papa, who is a man like a boulder.

After dinner I went to my room to study, leaving Nurzhan
720 to talk with Mama and Papa. I was afraid to really hope that any good thing could come from Nurzhan's plan. To hope and then be disappointed seemed to be worse. It was better not to hope and to live my dreams through Shannon. I could at least hear every little detail of her experience at the dance and be happy for her, giving up the idea that I'd ever be the one who goes to the dance, too.

But I comforted myself thinking about the dream in my life that really had come true—the gymnastics team. I still had that, and I was warming my heart with thoughts of the team
730 when Nurzhan burst into the room.

"Maya! You can go!" Nurzhan jumped up and down like a little monkey, and I stared at him in disbelief.

"Don't joke with me about such a thing, boy!" I snapped.

"No! It's true. Look!" He waved the permission slip in front of my face.

I stared at the slip, still in disbelief. *Aibek Alazova . . .* Papa's name and Papa's writing. *It was true!* I was still staring at the slip, still afraid to completely believe that such a thing could be true, when Mama and Papa came in.

740 "We give permission for this, Maya, because Nurzhan will go, too," Mama said.

"He will not leave your side," Papa announced in a most serious tone. "He is your *capravazhdieuushee*."

"Chaperone." I said the English word. I knew this word because the parents who help the teachers supervise the kids at school activities are called this. But I hadn't heard of a little boy being a chaperone.

"Thank you, Mama. Thank you, Papa."

"It is Nurzhan you must thank," Mama said.

Maya receives a permission slip for the Spring Fling dance.

▼

Maya is distracted from the dance when her brother is suspended for fighting.

▼

Maya is distracted again when her father sees her encounter with Daniel.

750   I thanked Nurzhan, too, and Mama and Papa left our room. Then I heard the front door close and I knew Papa had left for work.

    That night Nurzhan and I whispered in our beds after Mama had gone to sleep.

    "Nurzhan, what will I tell my friends when you come to the dance?"

    "Don't worry. I thought about that problem. You will tell them you must baby-sit for me."

    "But at a dance?"

760   "I think it will work. At least it is better than to say I am your chaperone."

    "That is true."

    I watched the orange light of the mini-mart sign blink on and off, and I heard Nurzhan's slow breathing as he fell asleep.

    "Thank you, Nurzhan," I whispered as I began to dream of the dance.

    The morning of the dance, Mama came into the kitchen while Nurzhan and I were eating *kasha*. Mama still had a wrap on her ankle, but she was walking without her crutches now.
770 She was happier, and I could tell she felt better. It was better for me, too. When Mama was happier, I didn't feel so worried about her.

    "Maya, I have something for you." Mama came to the table and put a small package wrapped in tissue paper in front of me. "Open." She pointed at the package.

    I looked up at her, my face full of surprise.

    "Open."

    Carefully, I unfolded the tissue paper and let out a gasp when I saw a small gold bracelet lying on the folds of the
780 thin paper.

    "You wear this to the dance." Mama patted my shoulder.

    "Oh, Mama." I wanted to hug her like we hug on the gymnastics team, but I was too shy. We don't hug in our family.

    "I forget sometimes when there is so much work that you are just a young girl. This bracelet my mother gave to me when I was sixteen. Girls and boys dance younger here, Maya. So you wear this now."

CLOSE READ

Analyze Stories: Character (LINES 753–766)

COMMON CORE   RL 1, RL 3

Point out that this dialogue between Maya and Nurzhan gives evidence of the way he has grown since the beginning of the story.

W   **CITE TEXT EVIDENCE** Have students reread lines 753–766 to note the details of Nurzhan's plan to chaperone Maya at the dance. What does his plan reveal about him? *(When Maya expresses concern about what her friends will think about her having a chaperone, Nurzhan says, "I thought about that problem. You will tell them you must babysit for me." The fact that Nurzhan thought about potential problems in advance and came up with a way to address them shows that he is becoming more grown-up. His solution again reveals his understanding of both American and Kazakh cultures.)*

CLOSE READ

Analyze Stories:

Character (LINES 773–792)

 COMMON CORE **RL 1, RL 3**

Discuss what the author reveals about Mama through the dialogue in lines 773–792. Point out that this dialogue also marks a change in Mama.

Ⓧ CITE TEXT EVIDENCE Have students reread lines 773–792 to note why Mama's gift for Maya is important to both of them. Why does the bracelet represent a change in Mama? *(Mama received the bracelet from her mother when she was sixteen. In giving the bracelet to Maya to wear at the dance, Mama is acknowledging that "girls and boys dance younger" in America. Story events have helped her begin to understand the differences between Kazakh and American cultures.)*

 790

"Thank you, Mama. I will be careful with it."

"I know. You're a good girl. And Nurzhan will be right there. Always by your side."

"Yes, Mama." Nurzhan nodded.

Shannon and I met in the bathroom after school, and she loaned me her peach lip-gloss. I can't remember ever being so excited about anything, and so nervous, too.

Nurzhan was waiting by the gym door when we got out of the bathroom. Shannon and I said hi to him, and he followed us into the gym. Nurzhan found a chair next to the door and waved to us while we joined Leslie Shattuck and her sister Tina and Faith Reeves from the gymnastics team. The gym got more and more crowded, and everywhere you looked there were flocks of boys and flocks of girls, but no boys and girls together, as if they were birds that only stayed with their own kind.

Then a few ninth-grade guys and girls danced together. They were very cool and everyone watched them, except some seventh-grade boys who were pushing each other around in an empty garbage can.

800

Shannon and I were laughing at those silly boys when
810 Daniel and David came up to us. I was so happy to see Daniel,
even though I was embarrassed about my face, which I knew
was once again the deepest red, like borscht. But the next
thing I knew, Daniel had asked me to dance, and Shannon was
dancing with David!

Daniel held my hand and put his arm around my
waist, and I put my hand on his shoulder just the way
Shannon and I had practiced so many times. It was a slow
dance, and Mama's bracelet gleamed on my wrist as it lay on
Daniel's shoulder.

820   "My little brother's here. I had to baby-sit."
"Want to check on him?" Daniel asked.
"Sure."

We danced over near Nurzhan, who sat on the chair like a
tiny mouse in the corner, and I introduced him to Daniel.
"Are you doing okay?" I asked Nurzhan.
"Yes. It's a little boring though."
"I'm sorry you have to be here."
"It's not that bad. The boys in the garbage can are fun to
watch. I would enjoy doing that if I came to this dance."

830   Then we danced away and danced even more slowly, and
Daniel moved a little closer to me. I looked over, afraid that
Nurzhan was watching, but all I saw was an empty chair. And
then we danced closer.

Daniel and I danced four more times that afternoon
(two fast and two *very* slow), and each time Nurzhan's chair
was empty and he seemed to have disappeared. I didn't think
too much about Nurzhan during the rest of the dance, and
on the bus going home, while Shannon and I talked and
talked, reliving every wonderful moment, I almost forgot he
840 was there.

But that night when Nurzhan and I were going to sleep
and I was thinking about how that day had been the best day
of my life, I thanked him for making it possible for me to go to
the dance.

"There's just one thing I wondered about," I whispered as
the mini-mart sign blinked on and off.
"What's that?"
"Where did you go when I danced with Daniel?"
"To the bathroom."
850   "The bathroom?"

CLOSE READ

Analyze Stories: Plot

COMMON CORE **RL 3**

(LINES 815–850)

Explain that during the **falling action** of a story the effects of the climax become clear. In this part of the plot, Maya is attending the dance that she has dreamed about.

Ⓨ ASK STUDENTS to reread lines 815–850 to compare Maya's experience at the dance to Nurzhan's. How does Nurzhan fulfill his role as chaperone while still allowing Maya to enjoy the dance? *(Nurzhan watches Maya from a corner of the room but chooses to go to the bathroom each time Maya dances with Daniel. He does what he promised his parents he would do, but he doesn't prevent Maya from having a good time.)*

TEACH

CLOSE READ

Analyze Stories: Plot

COMMON CORE RL 1, RL 3

(LINES 856–863)

Explain that the **resolution** of a story shows how its problem or conflict is solved. Discuss how Maya's desire to attend the dance ultimately helped her whole family make adjustments to their new lives in America.

 ASK STUDENTS to reread lines 856–863 to note Maya's thoughts about the dance. Why does Maya think that the bracelet represents a change in her family? *(Maya is "struck by how much things had changed." She now owns a bracelet that her mother once wore. It indicates a willingness in Maya's mother to be more mindful of the differences between their traditional culture and the modern America Maya will grow up in. The bracelet is a step toward more flexibility and understanding between Maya and her parents. It also is a way for Maya to carry her mother's traditions with her.)*

COLLABORATIVE DISCUSSION Have student partners list examples that reflect each character's experiences as he or she adjusts to life in the United States. As partners discuss their opinions about which character faces the greatest challenge, remind them to cite evidence from the text to support their choice.

ASK STUDENTS to share any questions they generated in the course of reading and discussing the selection.

"Yes."

"You are an excellent chaperone."

Nurzhan and I giggled so loud that Mama came in and told us to be quiet. "Shhh, Nurzhan, Maya. Go to sleep!" She spoke sharply to both of us.

After she left, Nurzhan fell asleep right away like he usually does. But I lay awake for a while and I looked over at Nurzhan and was struck by how much things had changed. I looked at the table by my bed and saw the gold bracelet

860 shining in the blinking light of the mini-mart sign, and I imagined Mama wearing it when she was sixteen, and I treasured what she'd said as much as the bracelet: "Girls and boys dance younger here, Maya. So you wear this now."

And I thought of Daniel, who I think is quite a special boy with a good heart. *Kak horosho.* How wonderful. Thinking of him made me smile inside. Then I closed my eyes, hoping very much that Nurzhan would like to chaperone at the next dance.

COLLABORATIVE DISCUSSION Do you think life in the United States is more challenging for Maya, for her brother, or for their parents? With a partner, discuss the story events that support your answer.

TO CHALLENGE STUDENTS . . .

Analyze Character Choices Both Maya and Nurzhan do things to deceive their parents as they try to adjust to life in the United States. For example:

- Maya purposely translates the principal's statements incorrectly.
- Nurzhan says he will act as Maya's chaperone, but he leaves the area any time she is dancing with Daniel.

ASK STUDENTS to discuss the choices each young person made to determine if they seem justified or appropriate for the circumstances. Ask each group to suggest alternatives that might have achieved the same goals without deception.

Analyze Stories: Plot

COMMON CORE RL 1, RL 3

From simple fairy tales to complex novels, most stories contain a **plot,** a series of events that occur in stages of development. Most plots focus on a **conflict,** or problem faced by the main character. The five stages of plot development are

- **exposition,** in which the characters, setting, and conflict are introduced
- **rising action,** in which the character takes steps to solve the problem even while complications might be introduced
- **climax,** or point of greatest tension in the story, in which the conflict begins to be resolved
- **falling action,** in which the effects of the climax become clear
- **resolution,** in which the end of the story reveals the final outcome

To analyze a plot, examine the way events and actions in each stage increase or help to resolve the conflict.

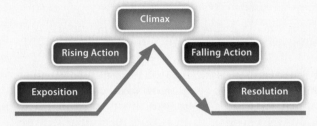

Identify the conflict Maya faces in "My Favorite Chaperone." What is the turning point that begins to resolve her conflict?

Analyze Stories: Character

COMMON CORE RL 1, RL 3

Characters are the people, animals, or imaginary creatures who take part in the action of a story. **Characterization** is the way an author reveals the traits and personality of the characters. An author may choose to reveal a character by

- describing what a character looks like
- having a narrator make direct comments about him or her
- presenting the character's thoughts, speech, and actions
- presenting other characters' thoughts, speech, and actions

Characters' speech is revealed in **dialogue,** the written conversation between two or more people in a story. Look back at Maya's dialogue with Ms. Johnson in lines 150–180. What do you learn about Maya from this conversation?

CLOSE READ

Analyze Stories: Plot

COMMON CORE RL 1, RL 3

Use the pyramid diagram to focus students' attention on the stages of plot development. Prompt students to discuss each stage, asking them to provide an example from the selection. (*Students should note that the turning point of the story comes in lines 711–732, when Nurzhan comes up with a plan to convince his parents to allow Maya to go to the school dance.*)

Analyze Stories: Character

COMMON CORE RL 1, RL 3

Guide students to discuss each method of characterization shown in the bulleted list, providing examples of each one from "My Favorite Chaperone" or from other familiar stories. (*Students should note that the conversation with Ms. Johnson reveals Maya's concern for her brother, her awareness of the problems he has been having with a bully, and the responsible role she has of regularly acting as translator for her parents.*)

Strategies for Annotation   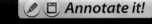 Annotate it!

Analyze Stories: Character

COMMON CORE RL 1, RL 3

Share these strategies for guided or independent analysis:

- Highlight in yellow what Maya says.
- Highlight in blue what Maya thinks.
- Use a note to explain what each highlighted example reveals about Maya.

"Is Nurzhan all right?"

"Yes. And I believe the other boy wasn't seriously hurt."

"Who did Nurzhan fight?" It was a foolish question—I was sure of the answer. Ms. Johnson hesitated, so I Nishozono," and she nodded.

"What must I do?" I asked.

> The text "It was a foolish question—I was sure of the answer" suggests that Maya knew that her brother had problems with another boy at school.

Analyzing the Text COMMON CORE RL 1, RL 2, RL 3, RL 4

Possible answers:

1. *Maya is a ninth-grade student. She loves being in America because it gives her hope. Her conflict is that she really wants to go to the Spring Fling but doesn't think her parents will sign the permission slip.*

2. *The story shows that immigrants may be affected by harsh experiences in their past. Maya has not had the same experiences Sunstar had, but she is still afraid and nervous about being called to the principal's office.*

3. *Maya's changes make the fight sound less severe ("nasty fight" vs. "little fight") and place the blame on the other boy ("teasing" vs. "teasing in a violent manner"). She changes the principal's words to protect her brother from her father's reaction.*

4. *The mother feels protective of Nurzhan and blames Maya for not protecting him or preventing the fight. These lines show that the mother sticks up for Nurzhan and blames Maya.*

5. *Maya's brother gets in trouble, her mother hurts her ankle and cannot work, and her parents become angry with her when they see her socializing with boys.*

6. *Maya's reaction shows that she would like to be free, especially from her parents' restrictions. She would like her parents to be like Mr. and Mrs. Lui, who dress well, serve hamburgers, and let their kids use the phone and hang out with other kids.*

7. *Nurzhan plays a pivotal role in resolving the conflict. He understands his parents' concerns, but he also understands Maya's wish to go the Spring Fling. The plan he devises to act as Maya's chaperone solves the problem perfectly. Maya's father gives her permission to go because Nurzhan offers to go to the dance and "chaperone" Maya.*

eBook *Annotate It!*

Analyzing the Text COMMON CORE RL 1, RL 2, RL 3, RL 4, W 2

Cite Text Evidence   Support your responses with evidence from the story.

1. **Identify** What do you learn about Maya and the conflict she faces in lines 1–14?

2. **Infer** In lines 126–136, Maya tells a story about a student who immigrates to the United States from Cambodia. How does this story advance, or add details to, the plot's rising action?

3. **Draw Conclusions** Reread lines 295–337. Complete a chart like this one to show how Maya's translation changes the meaning of what the principal says. Why does she make these changes?

Principal's Words	Maya's Translation	Effect

4. **Compare** Reread the dialogue involving Maya, her mother, and Nurzhan in lines 396–414. What does this dialogue reveal about how the mother's relationship with Maya differs from her relationship with Nurzhan?

5. **Analyze** What complications does Maya face as she attempts to resolve her conflict? List at least two.

6. **Interpret** Reread lines 527–541, in which Maya's parents are arguing about her. What does Maya's reaction tell you about what she wants?

7. **Analyze** What role does Nurzhan play in resolving the conflict?

PERFORMANCE TASK

Writing Activity: Summary Write a summary of "My Favorite Chaperone." To summarize, briefly retell the plot of the story in your own words.

- Introduce the major characters and state the conflict.

- Summarize the major events in the rising action of the story.
- Identify and describe the climax of the story.
- Describe how the conflict is resolved.

Assign this performance task.

PERFORMANCE TASK COMMON CORE RL 2, W 2, W 4, W 9a, W 10

Writing Activity: Summary Tell students to complete a graphic organizer or an outline to prepare to write their summaries. You may wish to have them highlight or otherwise indicate the five stages of plot development before they begin writing. See page 30a for additional support for writing a summary.

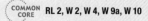

Critical Vocabulary

 L 4a, L 4d

sponsor	stun	dispatcher	scuffle	whimper

Practice and Apply Use your understanding of the Vocabulary words to answer each question.

1. If someone agreed to **sponsor** you, would you be annoyed or grateful? Why?

2. Would getting a homework assignment or getting a special award be more likely to **stun** you? Why?

3. If you were a **dispatcher**, would you need to speak to people or write to them? Why?

4. Would people be more likely to have a **scuffle** if they were angry, or if they were lost? Why?

5. If you heard someone **whimper**, would you think he or she was feeling lucky, or scared? Why?

Vocabulary Strategy: Context Clues

The **context** of a word is made up of the punctuation marks, words, sentences, and paragraphs that surround the word. When you encounter an unfamiliar word, its context may provide you with clues that can help you understand its meaning. Look at the following example:

> Mr. Walsh, the vice-principal, came into our class. He whispered something to Mrs. Coe and she nodded. And then I was <u>stunned</u> because she nodded and pointed at me!

From the context clues, you can figure out that *stunned* describes how Maya felt. The exclamation point at the end of the sentence suggests that she did not expect the principal would call her out of class. Feeling stunned probably means "to feel surprised or shocked."

Practice and Apply Review "My Favorite Chaperone" to find the following words. Complete a chart like the one shown.

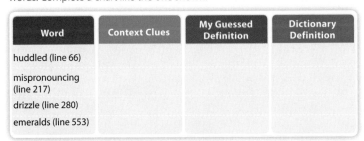

Word	Context Clues	My Guessed Definition	Dictionary Definition
huddled (line 66)			
mispronouncing (line 217)			
drizzle (line 280)			
emeralds (line 553)			

PRACTICE & APPLY

Critical Vocabulary

 L 4a, L 4d

Possible answers:

1. *Grateful; because the person supported you to join a group*

2. *A special award; because homework is a common occurrence but awards are often a surprise*

3. *Speak to people; because a dispatcher tells taxi drivers where to pick up people*

4. *Angry; because a scuffle is a fight*

5. *Scared; because a whimper is a cry or a sob*

Vocabulary Strategy: Context Clues

Word	Context Clues	My Guessed Definition	Dictionary Definition
huddled	"only person we knew... together on a tiny island"	*be close together*	*gathered tightly together*
mispronouncing	"not speaking well"	*saying words incorrectly*	*to say something incorrectly*
drizzle	"rain came down"	*a form of rain*	*light rain*
emeralds	"green lights glowing like a necklace"	*a green jewel*	*a precious stone that is colored green*

Strategies for Annotation 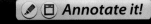 **Annotate it!**

Using Context Clues

 L 4a, L 4d

Have students locate the sentences containing *huddled, mispronouncing, drizzle,* and *emeralds* in the story. Encourage them to use their eBook annotation tools to do the following:

- Highlight each word.
- Reread the surrounding sentences, looking for clues to the word's meaning. Underline any clues you find, such as comparisons, contrasts, or definitions.
- Review your annotations and try to infer the word's meaning.

> bare branches of the trees were black against the <u>cement gray sky</u>. <u>The rain came down in a steady</u> drizzle, and after a few minutes.

PRACTICE & APPLY

Language Conventions: Imperative Mood COMMON CORE L 1c

Tell students that the way an idea is expressed suggests how a reader or listener should respond. For example, an idea expressed as a question suggests that a reader or listener should reply. Tell students that statements in the imperative mood suggest that readers or listeners should follow a command or comply with a request.

Answers:

1. *Do not ask her about the permission slip again.*

2. *Call my father and tell him what happened.*

3. *Stop teasing my brother.*

4. *Punish your son so that he never fights like this again.*

5. *Sit at the kitchen table and do your homework.*

6. *Tell your parents that they must sign this form.*

7. *Quit asking me if you can go.*

8. *Help your mother do her work.*

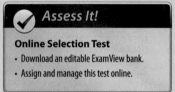

Assess It!

Online Selection Test
• Download an editable ExamView bank.
• Assign and manage this test online.

Language Conventions: Imperative Mood COMMON CORE L 1c

The **mood of a verb** refers to the manner in which the action or state of being is expressed. A verb is in the **imperative mood** when it is part of a command or request. In an imperative sentence, the subject is always implied or understood to be *you*. These sentences from "My Favorite Chaperone" are in the imperative mood.

> "Take off your jacket and hang it up, Nurzhan."

> "Let me try to get permission for you from Papa."

In the first sentence, Maya is giving her brother a command. In the second sentence, Nurzhan is requesting something from his sister, Maya. Note that the subject of both sentences (you) is not stated, but is understood.

Imperative Mood	Understood Subject	Command or Request?
Do your homework.	(You) do your homework.	command
Please help me get this done.	(You) please help me get this done.	request

Practice and Apply   Rewrite each sentence so that it is in the imperative mood. Label each sentence as a command or a request.

1. I do not want you to ask her about the permission slip again.

2. You should call my father and tell him what happened.

3. I think you should stop teasing my brother.

4. You should punish your son so that he never fights like this again.

5. I'm telling you to sit at the kitchen table and do your homework.

6. Will you please tell your parents that they must sign this form?

7. I want you to quit asking me if you can go.

8. I would like it if you would help your mother do her work.

Write a Summary

COMMON CORE

RL 2,
RL 3

TEACH

Tell students that a **summary** is a brief retelling of the most important events in a story's plot in one's own words. Emphasize that a summary is much shorter than the actual story and need not include minor details, characters, or events. Explain that a summary should include:

- the story title and its author
- the main characters and the conflict they face
- the key events that propel the action as the characters try to resolve the conflict
- the climax or turning point in the story
- the resolution of the conflict and the ending of the story

Point out that if students are not sure about whether to include an event, they should ask, "Is this event connected to the resolution of the conflict?" Explain that events that do not lead to the resolution of the conflict should probably not be included.

PRACTICE AND APPLY

Have students prepare to write a summary of "My Favorite Chaperone" by completing a graphic organizer, such as a flow chart or a story map.

 INTERACTIVE GRAPHIC ORGANIZER Have students use these interactive graphic organizers: **Sequence Chart, Flow Chart.**

When students have completed the graphic organizers, have them identify each element of a summary listed above. Then have them use the graphic organizers to write their summaries. Ask volunteers to share their written summaries with the class.

Analyze Stories: Plot

COMMON CORE

RL 1,
RL 3

RETEACH

Retell, or have students work together to retell, a simple story, such as *Cinderella* or *Jack and the Beanstalk*. Discuss the following plot stages as you guide students to identify each one in the story you choose:

- **Exposition**: Characters, setting, and a problem or conflict are introduced.
- **Rising Action**: Characters try to solve the problem as complications are introduced.
- **Climax**: The story reaches a turning point at which the conflict begins to be resolved.
- **Falling Action**: The effects of the climax become clear.
- **Resolution**: The story reaches an ending that reveals the final outcome.

Reinforce the concept that each main plot event propels the action of the story forward.

 LEVEL UP TUTORIALS Assign the following *Level Up* tutorials: **Plot Stages.**

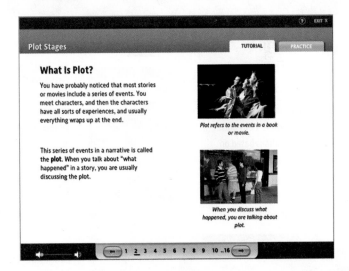

CLOSE READING APPLICATION

Have student partners work together to identify the five stages of the plot in a story they have read recently. Remind them to cite evidence in the text to describe each of the stages.

Golden Glass

Short Story by Alma Luz Villanueva

Why This Text

Students sometimes have difficulty understanding stories in which the characters are described indirectly, through suggestion and implication, rather than directly, through statements made by the author. "Golden Glass" is a two-character story, and the intensity of the drama is only accentuated by the author's decision to stay out of it as much as possible: Instead, Villanueva gives us access to the characters' inner lives by reflecting on what they say and do. With the help of the close-reading questions, students will make inferences about the characters and their motivations, thus making it easier to follow the characters' development during the course of the story.

Background Have students read the background and information about the author. Introduce the selection by pointing out that Alma Luz Villanueva is a poet as well as a writer of short fiction. Point out that this "poetic sensibility" is part of what makes her brand of storytelling so compelling: that not everything is spelled out for the reader. Point out, however, that although there is room for interpretation, there is ample evidence in the text for readers to draw on—if they are careful enough to pick up on the clues.

SETTING A PURPOSE Ask students to pay attention to the ways in which the characters' feelings and actions advance the plot. Do Ted's actions make sense in light of the information provided?

 Common Core Support

- cite textual evidence
- draw inferences about characters' traits and motivations based on clues in the text
- analyze how dialogue or story incidents reveal aspects of a character

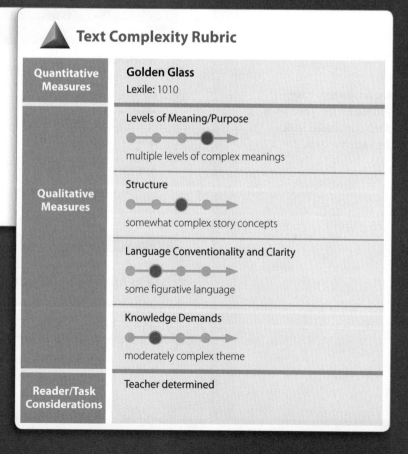

Text Complexity Rubric

Quantitative Measures	**Golden Glass** Lexile: 1010
Qualitative Measures	Levels of Meaning/Purpose — multiple levels of complex meanings
	Structure — somewhat complex story concepts
	Language Conventionality and Clarity — some figurative language
	Knowledge Demands — moderately complex theme
Reader/Task Considerations	Teacher determined

Analyze Stories: Character

Students should read this story carefully all the way through. Close-reading questions at the bottom of the page will help them focus on the characters and their motivations. As they read, students should jot down comments or questions about the text in the margins.

WHEN STUDENTS STRUGGLE . . .

To help students draw inferences about the characters in "Golden Glass," have them work in small groups to fill out a chart like the one shown below.

CITE TEXT EVIDENCE For practice in making inferences that help them understand character traits and motivations, ask students to cite text evidence for each point in the chart.

Text Example	Inference
"He seemed always to be at the center of his own universe, so it was no surprise to his mother to hear Ted say. . ." (lines 6–7)	Vida has a deep and intuitive understanding of her son.
"She trusted him to build well and not ruin things, but of course she had to know where." (lines 17–18)	Vida respects and trusts her son but knows he is not fully grown and needs her guidance.
"His eyes flashed, but he said, 'Okay.' " (line 38)	Ted is trying to cover up his strong reaction to what he perceives as his mother's nonchalance about his decision to live outside.
"Ted woke up to see the stained glass full of light. The little sun was a golden moon and the inside glass sky and the outside sky matched." (lines 144–146)	Ted understands that his need for independence and his love for his mother can exist simultaneously; that one doesn't necessarily eclipse the other.

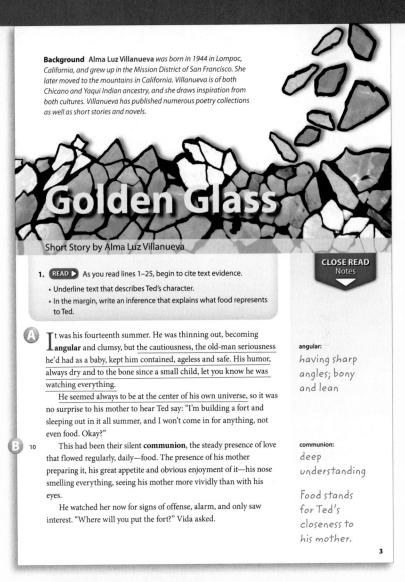

Background Alma Luz Villanueva *was born in 1944 in Lompoc, California, and grew up in the Mission District of San Francisco. She later moved to the mountains in California. Villanueva is of both Chicano and Yaqui Indian ancestry, and she draws inspiration from both cultures. Villanueva has published numerous poetry collections as well as short stories and novels.*

Golden Glass

Short Story by Alma Luz Villanueva

CLOSE READ
Notes

1. **READ ▶** As you read lines 1–25, begin to cite text evidence.
- Underline text that describes Ted's character.
- In the margin, write an inference that explains what food represents to Ted.

Ⓐ It was his fourteenth summer. He was thinning out, becoming **angular** and clumsy, but the cautiousness, the old-man seriousness he'd had as a baby, kept him contained, ageless and safe. His humor, always dry and to the bone since a small child, let you know he was watching everything.

He seemed always to be at the center of his own universe, so it was no surprise to his mother to hear Ted say: "I'm building a fort and sleeping out in it all summer, and I won't come in for anything, not even food. Okay?"

Ⓑ 10 This had been their silent **communion**, the steady presence of love that flowed regularly, daily—food. The presence of his mother preparing it, his great appetite and obvious enjoyment of it—his nose smelling everything, seeing his mother more vividly than with his eyes.

He watched her now for signs of offense, alarm, and only saw interest. "Where will you put the fort?" Vida asked.

angular:
having sharp angles; bony and lean

communion:
deep understanding

Food stands for Ted's closeness to his mother.

3

1. **READ AND CITE TEXT EVIDENCE** Explain that although this is essentially Ted's story the author maintains a neutral tone, giving away no more information than is necessary. The reader must make inferences about characters' thoughts and feelings based on what they say and do.

Ⓐ **ASK STUDENTS** to make inferences about Vida's feelings about her son by citing specific textual evidence in lines 1–25. *Responses may include text in which Vida reminisces about their physical closeness in lines 22–25.*

Critical Vocabulary: angular (line 2) Ask students to share their definitions of *angular*. Why might a teenager be described this way? *Teenagers going through a "growth spurt" can be long-limbed and bony.*

Critical Vocabulary: communion (line 10) Ask students to share their definitions of *communion*. Tell them that the base word, *commune*, can be both a noun and a verb. Have them use both forms.

The close and loving relationship between Ted and his mother, Vida, is beginning to become more strained as Ted gets older.

Vida is understanding, but still makes rules for Ted.

Ted is still obedient to his mother.

She trusted him to build well and not ruin things, but of course she had to know where. She looked at his dark, contained face and her eyes turned in and saw him when he was small, with curly golden hair, when he wrapped his arms around her neck. Their quiet times—undemanding—he could be let down, and a small toy could delight him for hours. She thought of the year he began kissing her elbow in passing, the way he preferred. Vida would touch his hair, his forehead, his shoulders—the body breathing out at the touch, his stillness. Then the explosion out the door told her he needed her touch, still.

"I'll build it by the redwoods, in the cypress trees. Okay?"

"Make sure you keep your nails together and don't dig into the trees. I'll be checking. If the trees get damaged, it'll have to come down."

"Jason already said he'd bring my food and stuff."

"Where do you plan to shower and go to the bathroom?" Vida wondered.

"With the hose when it's hot and I'll dig holes behind the barn," Ted said so quietly as to seem unspoken. He knew how to slither under her, smoothly, like silk.

"Sounds interesting, but it better stay clean—this place isn't that big. Also, on your dinner night, you can cook outdoors."

His eyes flashed, but he said, "Okay."

He began to gather wood from various stacks, drying it patiently from the long rains. He kept in his room one of the hammers and a supply of nails that he'd bought. It was early June and the seasonal creek was still running. It was pretty dark out there and he wondered if he'd meant what he'd said.

Ted hadn't seen his father in nearly four years, and he didn't miss him like you should a regular father, he thought. His father's image blurred with the memory of a football hitting him too hard, pointed (a bullet), right in the stomach, and the punishment for the penny candies—a test his father had set up for him to fail. His stomach hardened at the thought of his father, and he found he didn't miss him at all.

He began to look at the shapes of the trees, where the limbs were solid, where a space was provided (he knew his mother really would make him tear down the fort if he hurt the trees). The cypress was right next to the redwoods, making it seem very remote. Redwoods do that—they suck up sound and time and smell like another place. So he counted the footsteps, when no one was looking, from the fort to the house. He couldn't believe it was so close; it seemed so separate, alone—especially in the dark, when the only safe way of travel seemed flight (invisible at best).

Ted had seen his mother walk out to the bridge at night with a glass of wine, looking into the water, listening to it. He knew she loved to see the moon's reflection in the water. She'd pointed it out to him once by a river where they camped, her face full of longing—too naked somehow, he thought. Then, she swam out into the water, at night, as though trying to touch the moon. He wouldn't look at her. He sat and glared at the fire and roasted another marshmallow the way he liked it: bubbly, soft and brown (maybe six if he could get away with it). Then she'd be back, chilled and bright, and he was glad she went. Maybe I like the moon too, he thought, involuntarily, as though the thought weren't his own—but it was.

He built the ground floor directly on the earth, with a cover of old plywood, then scattered remnant rugs that he'd asked Vida to get for him. He **concocted** a latch and a door, with his hand ax over it, just in case. He brought his sleeping bag, some pillows, a transistor radio, some clothes, and moved in for the summer. The first week he slept with his buck knife open in his hand and his pellet gun loaded on the same side, his right. The second week Ted sheathed the knife and put it under his head, but kept the pellet gun loaded at all times. He

Ted was uncomfortable when his mother swam off, but was glad for her.

concocted
made; devised; created

---

2. ◀ REREAD Reread lines 1–25. In the margin, write an inference about Ted's relationship with his mother, Vida.

3. READ ▶ As you read lines 26–59, underline text that suggests that Ted may change his mind about the fort.

4. ◀ REREAD Reread lines 26–38. In the margin, write what you learn about Ted and Vida's relationship from the dialogue.

5. READ ▶ As you read lines 60–92, continue to cite textual evidence.

• Circle text that tells something Ted and Vida might have in common.

• In the margin, explain how the plot advances in each paragraph.

---

2. **REREAD AND CITE TEXT EVIDENCE** The author often reveals the characters' motivations indirectly, through inference, suggestion, nuance, and word choice.

B **ASK STUDENTS** to make inferences about the mother and son from what they say to each other in lines 15–16.

3. **READ AND CITE TEXT EVIDENCE** Explain that subtle changes in a character's physical demeanor allows you to make inferences about his or her state of mind.

C **ASK STUDENTS** to cite text in which Ted's confusion is conveyed through subtle changes in his behavior, rather than what the author tells you directly. *Students should cite the text in lines 34 and 38.*

FOR ELL STUDENTS Review the suffix –ly by pointing at some examples: *smoothly, patiently, nearly, really, involuntarily*. Explain that this suffix is used to to convert adjectives into adverbs. Ask volunteers to name the related adjective (*smooth, patient, near*).

4. **REREAD AND CITE TEXT EVIDENCE** The dialogue gives you a sense of Vida's parenting style.

D **ASK STUDENTS** to cite evidence that Vida is determined not to stand in the way of her son's independence. *Students should cite lines 27, 31, and 36–37.*

5. **READ AND CITE TEXT EVIDENCE** We can infer how Ted changes through what he does.

E **ASK STUDENTS** to cite evidence that Ted is becoming less afraid of sleeping outdoors. *Students should cite lines 75–78.*

Critical Vocabulary: concocted (line 73) Have students share their definitions of *concocted*. What can they infer about the way the fort was built? *Students might infer that the fort has been hurriedly and roughly put together.*

Ted first feels afraid and lonely at night, but he feels better as time goes by.

Ted had been afraid in the past and his mother had made him feel better.

Ted is brave enough to sleep without the dog now.

80 missed no one in the house but the dog, so he brought him into the cramped little space, enduring dog breath and farts because he missed *someone*.

F   Ted thought of when his father left, when they lived in the city, with forty kids on one side of the block and forty on the other. He remembered that one little kid with the funny sores on his body who chose an apple over candy every time. He worried they would starve or something worse. That time he woke up screaming in his room (he forgot why), and his sister began crying at the same time, "Someone's in here," as though they were having the same terrible dream. Vida 90 ran in with a chair in one hand and a kitchen knife in the other, which frightened them even more. But when their mother realized it was only their hysteria, she became angry and left. Later they all laughed about this till they cried, including Vida, and things felt safer.

G   He began to build the top floor now but he had to prune some limbs out of the way. Well, that was okay as long as he was careful. So he stacked them to one side for kindling and began to brace things in place. It felt weird going up into the tree, not as safe as his small, contained place on the ground. He began to build it, thinking of light. He could bring his comic books, new ones, sit up straight, and eat snacks in the daytime. He would put in a side window facing the 100 house to watch them, if he wanted, and a tunnel from the bottom floor to the top. Also, a ladder he'd found and repaired—he could pull it up and place it on hooks, out of reach. A hatch at the top of the ceiling for leaving or entering, tied down inside with a rope. He began to sleep up here, without the dog, with the tunnel closed off.

    Vida noticed Ted had become cheerful and would stand next to her, to her left side, talking sometimes. But she realized she mustn't face him or he'd become silent and wander away. So she stood

---

6. **◀ REREAD AND DISCUSS** Reread lines 82–92. With a small group, discuss how Ted feels about his father leaving.

7. **READ ▶** As you read lines 93–135, continue to cite textual evidence.

  • Underline text that shows that Ted has changed.

  • In the margin, summarize how Ted has changed.

  • In the margin, write something you learn about Ted when Vida compares him to wild pheasants in lines 107–112.

6

---

listening, in the same even breath and heartbeat she kept when she spotted the wild pheasants with their long, lush tails trailing the grape 110 arbor, picking delicately and greedily at the unpicked grapes in the early autumn light. So sharp, so perfect, so rare to see a wild thing at peace.

    She knew he ate well—his brother brought out a half gallon of milk that never came back, waiting to be asked to join him, but never daring to ask. His sister made him an extra piece of ham for his four eggs; most always he ate cold cereal and fruit or got a hot chocolate on the way to summer school. They treated Ted somewhat like a stranger, because he was.

H   Ted was taking a makeup course and one in stained glass. There, 120 he talked and acted relaxed, like a boy; no one expected any more or less. The colors of the stained glass were deep and beautiful, and special—you couldn't waste this glass. The sides were sharp, the cuts were slow and **meticulous** with a steady pressure. The design's plan had to be absolutely followed or the beautiful glass would go to waste, and he'd curse himself.

    It was late August and Ted hadn't gone inside the house once. He liked waking up, hearing nothing but birds—not his mother's voice or his sister's or his brother's. He could tell the various bird calls and liked the soft brown quail call the best. He imagined their taste and 130 wondered if their flesh was as soft as their song. Quail would've been okay to kill, as long as he ate it, his mother said. Instead, he killed jays because they irritated him so much with their shrill cries. Besides, a neighbor paid Ted per bird because he didn't want them in his garden. But that was last summer and he didn't do that anymore, and the quail were proud and plump and swift, and Ted was glad.

Ted is still skittish with his mother, but he is happy.

meticulous: *extremely careful and precise*

---

8. **◀ REREAD** Reread lines 119–125. Explain what Ted's attitude toward working with stained glass reveals about his character.

Ted cares about the glass and its colors. He is very careful in his work with the glass, and he is hard on himself when his work is not perfect.

9. **READ ▶** As you read lines 136–147, cite textual evidence.

  • Underline text that describes the stained glass.

  • In the margin, write an inference about why Ted "wouldn't mind at all" being inside again.

7

---

6. **REREAD AND DISCUSS USING TEXT EVIDENCE**

F **ASK STUDENTS** to discuss the effects of Ted's father's disappearance on his self-confidence. What might this have to do with his need for independence? What does all this have to do with a fort? *Ted needs to prove himself; he wants to show that he can survive without a father. The fort is a defense.*

7. **READ AND CITE TEXT EVIDENCE** In lines 93–104 there is a detailed description of how Ted builds his fort, followed by some of Vida's reflections in lines 105–112.

G **ASK STUDENTS** why they think the author included this information. What does it say about Ted's determination? *It shows that he is serious about making a fort he can live in—one in which he feels safe.* Cite evidence that Vida knows and respects what he is trying to do. *Students should cite lines 111–112.*

8. **REREAD AND CITE TEXT EVIDENCE** Working with stained glass does a lot to lift Ted's spirits.

H **ASK STUDENTS** to cite evidence showing why this kind of work takes the pressure off Ted. *Students should cite lines 119–122.*

9. **READ AND CITE TEXT EVIDENCE** When the stained glass is finished, Ted puts it in his fort facing the back fields.

I **ASK STUDENTS** to cite the effect his stained glass creates. *Students should cite lines 138–140.*

Critical Vocabulary: meticulous (line 123) Have students share their definitions of *meticulous*. Why is it important to be meticulous when working with stained glass? *You could cut yourself; glass could be wasted.*

Ted is more confident. He has proven himself, so he is more comfortable being in his home, and especially with his mother.

I The stained glass was finished and he decided to place it in his fort facing the back fields. In fact, it looked like the back fields—trees and the sun in a dark sky. During the day the glass sun shimmered a beautiful yellow, the blue a much better color than the sky outside:

140 deeper, like night.

J He was so used to sleeping outside now he didn't wake up during the night, just like in the house. One night, toward the end when he'd have to move back with everyone (school was starting, frost was coming and the rains), Ted woke up to see the stained glass full of light. The little sun was a golden moon and the inside glass sky and the outside sky matched.

In a few days he'd be inside, and he wouldn't mind at all.

10. ◀ **REREAD AND DISCUSS** Reread lines 136–147. With a small group, discuss what the stained glass means to Ted. Cite specific text evidence from the story in your discussion.

SHORT RESPONSE

Cite Text Evidence How does Ted change over the course of the summer? How does his relationship with his mother change? Review your reading notes, and be sure to **cite text evidence** from the story in your response.

At the beginning of the story, Ted is afraid at night. But he becomes more confident as the story moves along. At first, he seems like he is testing his need for his mother by saying he will stay in the fort, and "won't come in for anything, not even food." He questions himself when he thinks that they both like the moon. By the end of the story, Ted is confident sleeping alone at night. He works hard on a stained glass window that shows the moon. He is more comfortable with having something in common with his mother at the end of the story, and he is ready to live inside again.

8

---

10. **REREAD AND DISCUSS USING TEXT EVIDENCE** In lines 136–147 the "inside glass sky and the outside sky matched."

J **ASK STUDENTS** to look in these lines for another example of where "inside" matches "outside." Why does the author draw this parallel? *Students should cite lines 141–142 and 147. The author shows that Ted is coming to terms with his need for order (the stained glass) and his need for independence (the fort).*

SHORT RESPONSE

Cite Text Evidence Students' responses will vary but should use text evidence to support their positions. Students should:

- describe the way Ted changes over the course of the story.
- explain why Ted builds the fort and the effect this has on his mother.
- cite evidence to show why Ted is "ready to live at home again."

TO CHALLENGE STUDENTS . . .

In "Golden Glass," Ted finds working with stained glass rewarding. Tell students that people have been making colored glass since ancient times—there are numerous examples from ancient Rome and Egypt. Stained glass windows, like the one Ted made, have been made for about fifteen hundred years.

ASK STUDENTS to find images of stained glass windows from medieval times to the present. (They can do their research in libraries or online.) Remind students of the effect the completed stained glass window had on Ted: in one way it was like a window as it provided an ideal image that related to the sky outside, but in another way it was more like an illuminated painting.

Have students write a brief essay explaining their response to one or more of the stained glass windows they have researched; alternatively, they might write about the effect that stained glass has on them.

DIG DEEPER

1. With the class, return to Question 2, Reread. Have students share their responses to the question.

   ASK STUDENTS to make inferences about the characters' traits and motivations from information the author provides.

   • In lines 15–16, the author tells us that Ted watched his mother "for signs of offense" but "only saw interest." What is the author suggesting here? Did Ted *want* his mother to be offended? How did he feel when he realized she wasn't? What can students infer about Ted from this evidence?

   • Ask students about the shift that occurs when Vida speaks (line 16). Have students draw conclusions about Vida's reaction to her son's announcement. How does she react? Why do students think she responds this way? What might she be feeling?

2. With the class, return to Question 6, Reread and Discuss. Have students share the results of their discussion.

   ASK STUDENTS to discuss the effect of Ted's father's disappearance on the way Ted's character develops during the course of the story.

   • Have students think about how Ted's father's presence in the household might have changed the relationship between Ted and Vida. Do students think Ted would have had the same need for independence? Why might his connection to Vida have made the action he took necessary?

   • Have groups support their point of view using text evidence. Groups should cite evidence showing how small, scared, and undefended Ted felt after his father left, when he "woke up screaming in his room," and Vida was the one to come to the rescue.

   • Have groups analyze other factors that were involved in Ted's decision to build the fort. Ask why he thought it was necessary to cut himself off from the world he'd known.

   • Have students consider how Ted changes during the course of the story. Have them chart his progress from "boyhood" to "manhood" as reflected in his words and actions: his building of the fort, his growing confidence, his work with stained glass, and ultimately to his emergence as an independent person.

   • Have groups discuss the significance of Ted's decision to place the glass inside his fort. *Perhaps in trying to merge the inside and the outside he was attempting to bring together the disparate parts of himself.*

   ASK STUDENTS to return to their Short Response answer and revise it based on the class discussion.

CLOSE READING NOTES

Bonne Année

Personal Essay by Jean-Pierre Benoît

Why This Text?

Students regularly learn about the personal experiences of others through daily conversation, through the media, and from their own reading. This lesson guides students in exploring the message and structure of an essay that describes the impact of real-world events on the author's life.

Key Learning Objective: The student will be able to analyze elements of a personal essay, including its purpose, structure, central idea, and supporting details.

COMMON CORE Common Core Standards

RI 1 Cite textual evidence.

RI 2 Determine a central idea and analyze its development, including its relationship to supporting ideas.

RI 3 Analyze how a text makes connections among ideas or events.

RI 4 Determine the meaning of words and phrases.

RI 5 Analyze structure.

RI 6 Determine an author's point of view or purpose.

SL 1a Come to discussions prepared, having read or researched material under study.

W 7 Conduct short research projects.

L 1a Explain the function of verbals (participles).

L 4c Consult general and specialized reference materials (glossaries), both print and digital.

▲ Text Complexity Rubric

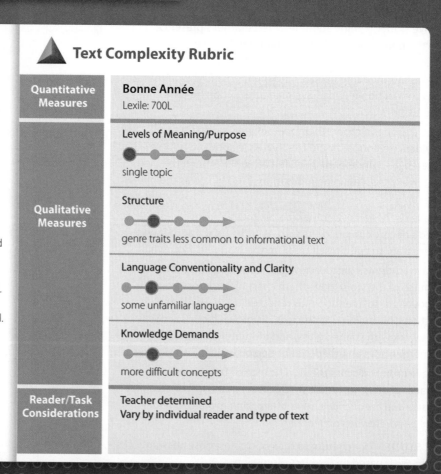

	Bonne Année
Quantitative Measures	Lexile: 700L
Qualitative Measures	**Levels of Meaning/Purpose** single topic
	Structure genre traits less common to informational text
	Language Conventionality and Clarity some unfamiliar language
	Knowledge Demands more difficult concepts
Reader/Task Considerations	Teacher determined Vary by individual reader and type of text

TEACH

CLOSE READ

Background Have students read the background information about Haiti and the author. Tell students that "Papa Doc" Duvalier began his rule of Haiti in 1957 and proclaimed himself "President for Life" in 1964. When he died in 1971, his son "Baby Doc" succeeded him, though he was only 19 years old at the time. Most Haitian immigrants came to the United States after 1970, and one of the largest Haitian-American communities in the country formed in and around New York City.

SETTING A PURPOSE Direct students to use the Setting a Purpose information to focus their reading.

Analyze Text: Personal Essay (LINES 1–12)

COMMON CORE **RI 3**

Tell students that a **personal essay** is a nonfiction essay in which an author expresses an opinion or provides some insight based on personal experiences. Point out that in this essay the author is making connections between events in his own life and historical events in Haiti.

Ⓐ ASK STUDENTS to reread lines 1–12. What is the connection between the people gathered in New York and the events occurring in Haiti? *(Students should note that the people gathered in New York are likely to be Haitian immigrants who are closely following events in Haiti. They believe Papa Doc will soon be gone, which seems important to them.)*

CRITICAL VOCABULARY

predominate: Benoît identifies the languages he hears spoken at a New Year's Day gathering in the 1960s.

ASK STUDENTS to explain why *Kreyòl* is the language that predominates in the conversations the author overhears. Why doesn't he understand this language? *(The adults are speaking* Kreyòl *because it is the main language they spoke when living in Haiti. The author was probably a baby when he left Haiti and had not learned to speak.)*

Background *Haiti is a small country located on the island of Hispaniola in the Caribbean Sea. In the late 1950s, the ruthless dictator François "Papa Doc" Duvalier took control of the country. Haitians like author **Jean-Pierre Benoît** (b.1957) and his parents began to immigrate to the United States to escape the tyrannical government. This immigration increased in the 1970s during the brutal rule of Duvalier's son, Jean-Claude "Baby Doc" Duvalier. By the 2000s, hundreds of thousands of Haitians were living in the United States.*

BONNE ANNÉE

Personal Essay by Jean-Pierre Benoît

SETTING A PURPOSE *Bonne Année* is a French phrase that means "Happy New Year." As you read, pay attention to how the author feels about the country in which he was born and the country in which he lives now. Write down any questions you have during reading.

Ⓐ It is the 1960s, a cold New Year's day in New York. The men are huddled but it is not for warmth; if anything, the Queens apartment is overheated. Important matters are to be discussed. The women are off to the side, where they will not interfere. The location of the children is unimportant; they are ignored. I am in the last category, ignored but overhearing. French, English, and *Kreyòl* commingle. French, I understand. My English is indistinguishable from that of an American child. *Kreyòl*, the language of my birthplace, is a mystery. *Kreyòl* **predominates**, but enough is said in French and English for me to follow. He is leaving. Any day. Father Doctor. Papa Doc. Apparently he is the reason we are

10

predominate
(prĭ-dŏmʹə-nāt´) *v.*
If ideas or things
predominate, they are
the most common.

SCAFFOLDING FOR ELL STUDENTS

Analyze Language Highlight in yellow multiple-meaning words and idiomatic expressions and ask students to explain what each expression means. Guide them to use the surrounding words to understand what each word or phrase means here.

> Someone has inside information. It is a matter of months, weeks, maybe days, before Duvalier falls. . . . My father is adamant, Duvalier's days are numbered.

Determine Central Idea and Details (LINES 24–38)

COMMON CORE RI 1, RI 2

Point out that the author describes another New Year's Day, beginning in line 24. Explain that the **central idea** of an essay is the main point or message an author wants to communicate. Point out that facts and opinions are two kinds of **supporting details** writers use to make a point.

B CITE TEXT EVIDENCE Have students reread lines 24–38 and identify supporting details the author provides to explain his reference to "January first." What fact tells why January first is important to Haitians? *("January first is the celebration of Haitian independence.")* What opinions does the author use to describe the day? *("A glorious day in world history, even if someone seems to have forgotten to tell the rest of the world.")* What do these details suggest about the central idea of the paragraph? *(Possible answer: the details suggest that January first is on an important day to Haitians, and thus to the author.)*

CRITICAL VOCABULARY

coup: Benoît imagines how the dictator Duvalier might be removed from power.

ASK STUDENTS to describe Benoît's vision of how a coup might take place. *(Benoît imagines that Haitians who left Haiti will return to their island country in boats and assassinate Duvalier.)*

WHEN STUDENTS STRUGGLE . . .

To help guide students' understanding of central idea and supporting details, have them work in pairs to complete an idea support map like the one shown. Explain that completing a graphic organizer like this one will help them see how details in the essay relate to the central idea.

Ask partners to write the central idea in the top box and supporting details below. For example, as students read about each January first, they might note details about the author's thoughts and feelings.

---

in New York, not Port-au-Prince.[1] And now he is leaving. And this will make all the difference. My father is clear. We are returning to Haiti. As soon as this man leaves. No need to await the end of the school year, although my schooling is otherwise so important.

20   I have no memory of Haiti. No memory of my crib in Port-au-Prince, no memory of the neighbors' children or the house in which we lived. My friends are in New York. My teachers are in New York. The Mets[2] are in New York. I do not know Papa Doc, but our destinies are linked. If he leaves, I leave. I do not want him to leave.

   B Another January first, another gathering. If it is the beginning of a new year, that is at best incidental. January first is the celebration of Haitian independence. A glorious day in world history, even if someone seems to have forgotten to tell the rest of the world. But it is not bygone glory that is of the moment. A new independence is dawning. It is more than 30 just a rumor this time. Someone has inside information. It is a matter of months, weeks, maybe days, before Duvalier falls. I am one year older now, and I understand who Duvalier is. An evil man. A thief and a murderer. A monster who holds a nation prisoner. A man who tried to have my father killed. A man who will soon get his justice. My father is adamant, Duvalier's days are numbered. And then we will return. Do I want to leave? I am old enough to realize that the question is unimportant.

   Go he must, but somehow he persists. A new year and he 40 is still in power. But not for long. This time it is true. The signs are unmistakable, the gods have finally awoken. Or have they? After so many years, the debates intensify. Voices raised in excitement, in agitation, in Haitian cadences. Inevitably, hope triumphs over history. Or ancient history triumphs over recent history. Perhaps there will be a **coup**, Haitian exiles landing on the shores with plans and weapons, a well-timed assassination.

   We are not meant to be in this country. We did not want to come. We were forced to flee or die. Americans perceive

coup
(ko͞o) *n.* A *coup* is the sudden overthrow of a government by a group of people.

---

[1] **Port-au-Prince** (pôrt′ ō-prĭns′): the capital of Haiti.
[2] **The Mets:** a professional baseball team in New York City.

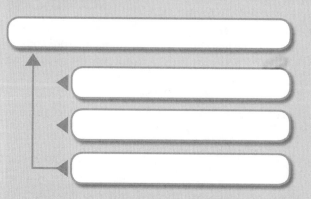

desperate brown masses swarming at their golden shores, wildly inventing claims of **persecution** for the opportunity to flourish in this prosperous land. The view from beneath the bridge is somewhat different: reluctant refugees with an aching love of their forsaken homeland, of a homeland that has forsaken them, refugees who desire nothing more than to be home again.

Then there are the children. Despite having been raised in the United States, I have no special love for this country. Despite the searing example of my elders. I am not even sure what it means to love a country. Clearly, it is not the government that one is to love. Is it then the land, the dirt and the grass, the rocks and the hills? The people? Are one people any better than another? I have no special love for this country, but neither do I desire a return to a birthplace that will, in fact, be no real return at all. If nothing else, the United States is the country that I know, English is my daily language. Another New Year, but I am not worried; we will not be back in Port-au-Prince anytime soon. With their crooked ruler the adults can no longer draw a straight line, but I can still connect the dots and see that they lead nowhere.

> " *We are not meant to be in this country. We did not want to come. We were forced to flee or die.* "

II

The Haitian sun has made the cross-Atlantic journey to shine on her **dispossessed** children. This time it is not just wispy speculation, something has changed. It is spring 1971 and there is death to celebrate. The revolutionaries have not landed on the coast, the assassin's poison has not found its blood. Nonetheless, Duvalier is dead. Unnaturally, he has died

persecution

(pûr´ sĭ-kyōō´shən) *n.* *Persecution* is the harsh treatment of others, often due to race or religion.

dispossess

(dĭs´ pə-zĕs´) *v.* To *dispossess* someone is to deny him or her ownership of something.

CLOSE READ

Analyze Language
COMMON CORE RI 4

(LINES 56–65)

Point out that **repetition,** the use of the same word or group of words more than once, is often used to emphasize a particular idea.

C ASK STUDENTS to reread lines 56–65 to identify a repeated statement. *(I have no special love for this country.)* What does the author mean by the phrase "no special love"? *(Possible answer: He does not feel a strong connection to the United States.)* What is the impact of the repetition of the phrase on the tone of the essay? *The repetition stresses that the author does not want to remain in the United States because of his love for this country.)*

CRITICAL VOCABULARY

persecution: Benoît thinks Americans do not believe the stories of immigrants who describe the terrible situation in Haiti.

ASK STUDENTS what kind of persecution Duvalier often inflicted on his opponents. *(The author says they "were forced to flee or die." Duvalier would have had them killed.)*

dispossess: Benoît describes an important political event that gives the refugees new hope.

ASK STUDENTS to explain what the Haitian refugees have been dispossessed of and why they now have a reason to be hopeful. *(The refugees have been dispossessed of their country. Since Papa Doc has now died, the exiles hope to be able to return to Haiti soon because they think his son will not remain in power long.)*

Analyze Text: Personal Essay (LINES 72–81)

COMMON CORE RI 1, RI 3, RI 5

Tell students that events in a personal essay are often told in **chronological order,** the order in which they happened, and that time clues in the text help make the sequence of events clear.

D CITE TEXT EVIDENCE Have students identify the time clues in lines 72–81 that explain when Papa Doc's rule ended and how long he and his son remained in power. *(spring 1971; The father lasted fourteen years, the son will last fifteen.)*

Remind students that in a personal essay, the author often expresses opinions or offers some insight on a topic.

E CITE TEXT EVIDENCE Have students reread lines 89–98 of the essay. Ask them what insight the author provides regarding the nature of the Haitian people. *("Haitians hope even when there is no hope.")*

D of natural causes. Only his laughable son remains. *Bébé*[3] Doc, Jean-Claude Duvalier. Everyone agrees that *Bébé* Doc will not be in power long enough to have his diapers changed.

80 Laughable *Bébé* Doc may be, but it turns out to be a long joke, and a cruel one. The father lasted fourteen years, the son will last fifteen. Twenty-nine years is a brief time in the life of a country, but a long time in the life of its people. Twenty-nine years is a very long time in the life of an exile waiting to go home.

Three years into *Bébé* Doc's terrible reign there is news of a different sort. For the first time, Haiti has qualified for the World Cup. The inaugural game is against eternal powerhouse Italy. In 1974 there are not yet any soccer moms, there is no ESPN all-sports network. Americans do not know anything

E 90 of soccer, and this World Cup match will not be televised. Yet America remains a land of immigrants. For an admission fee, the game will be shown at Madison Square Garden on four huge screens suspended in a boxlike arrangement high above the basketball floor. I go with my younger brother. In goal, Italy has the legendary Dino Zoff. Together they have not been scored upon in two years. The poor Haitians have no hope. And yet, Haitians hope even when there is no hope. The trisyllable cry of "HA-I-TI" fills the air. It meets a response, "I-TA-LIA," twice as loud but destined to be

100 replaced by an even louder HA-I-TI, followed by IT-A-LIA and again HA-I-TI in a spiraling crescendo. The game has not even started.

My brother and I join in the cheer; every time Haiti touches the ball is cause for excitement. The first half ends scoreless. The Italian fans are nervous, but the Haitian fans are feeling buoyed. After all, Haiti could hardly be expected to score a goal, not when the Germans and the English and the Brazilians before them have failed to penetrate the Italian defense. At the same time, the unheralded Haitian defenders

110 have held. The second half begins. Less than a minute has gone by and Emanuel Sanon, the left-winger for Haiti, has the ball. Less than twenty-four hours earlier he had foolhardily predicted that he will score. Zoff is fully aware of him. Sanon shoots. There is a split second of silence and then madness.

---

[3] *Bébé* (bə-bāʹ): French word that means "baby."

APPLYING ACADEMIC VOCABULARY

| reaction | contribute |

As you discuss the essay, incorporate the following Collection 1 academic vocabulary words: *reaction* and *contribute*. Have students discuss the author's **reaction** to the soccer game. Ask them to explain what factors **contribute** to his feelings of pride.

Madison Square Garden is an indoor arena in New York City where games, concerts, boxing matches, and other sports and entertainment activities take place. It is shown here with the Haitian flag.

The ball is in the back of the net, Sanon has beaten Zoff. The Italians are in shock. The world is in shock. Haiti leads 1–0.

"HA-I-TI, HA-I-TI." Half of Madison Square Garden is delirious, half is uncomprehending. The Haitians are beating the Italians. Haiti is winning. Haiti is winning. For 120 six minutes. Then the Italians come back to tie the score, 1–1. The Italians score again. And then again. The Haitians cannot respond. Italy wins 3–1.

Still. Still, for six minutes Haiti is doing the impossible, Haiti is beating Italy. Italy, which twice has won the World

---

Determine Author's Purpose (LINES 117–122)

COMMON CORE RI 1, RI 6

Explain that an **author's purpose** is his or her reason for writing. Point out that the reason for writing may be to inform, to entertain, to persuade, or to express feelings.

F **CITE TEXT EVIDENCE** Have students reread lines 117–122. Ask: *What is the author's purpose for including the story about Haiti's appearance in the soccer tournament? How do you know? (The author's purpose is to express a feeling. He says, "Half of Madison Square Garden is delirious." Though the author has no memory of life in Haiti, he still shares a sense of pride in the team's accomplishment.)*

CLOSE READ

Determine Central Idea and Details (LINES 129–134)

Help students identify facts and examples the author includes as supporting details.

G **CITE TEXT EVIDENCE** Have students reread lines 129–134. Ask: *What details in this paragraph show the important connection Haitian immigrants still have to their homeland? (Despite the fact that there is a blizzard in New York, the immigrants celebrate the end of the Duvalier regime outside. They wave Haitian flags, honk horns, and pour champagne.)*

> **CRITICAL VOCABULARY**
>
> **natal:** Benoît describes his reaction to Haiti's brief lead over Italy in a World Cup soccer match.
>
> **ASK STUDENTS** why the author concludes that the "natal pull" is stronger than he realized. *(Even though Benoît has never wanted to return to Haiti, his birthplace, the brief success of the Haitian soccer team meant more to him than any victory by his favorite American team, the Mets.)*

COLLABORATIVE DISCUSSION Have partners identify references in the text that reveal Benoît's feelings about the country of his birth, Haiti, as well as his adopted country, the United States. Ask them to discuss specific circumstances that make a country feel like home. Finally, have pairs share their conclusions with the class, inviting students who have immigrated to the United States to tell about their own experiences.

ASK STUDENTS to share any questions they generated in the course of reading and discussing the selection.

Cup. Six minutes. Perhaps the **natal** pull is stronger than it seems. For that one goal, that brief lead, those six minutes, mean more to me than all the victories of my favorite baseball team.

natal
(nāt´l) *adj.* If something is *natal*, it relates to birth.

III

February 7, 1986, amid massive protests in Haiti, Jean-Claude
130 flees the country. There is a blizzard in New York, but this does not prevent jubilant Haitians from taking to the snowy streets, waving flags, honking horns, pouring champagne. Restaurants in Brooklyn serve up free food and drink. The Duvalier regime has finally come to an end. The New Year's prediction has finally come true. If he leaves, I leave. In July, I fulfill my destiny, more or less. I return to Haiti, on an American passport, for a two-week visit.

In October the Mets win their second World Series. The city celebrates with a tickertape parade attended by over two
140 million people. A pale celebration indeed, compared to the celebrating that took place earlier in the year.

COLLABORATIVE DISCUSSION With a partner, discuss whether a person's homeland is the country where he or she is born, or the country where he or she is raised. Cite evidence from the text to support your ideas.

Determine Central Idea and Details

COMMON CORE RI 2, RI 6

The **central idea** of an essay is the main point that the author wants to communicate to readers. Sometimes an author may directly state his or her central idea. Often, however, readers must figure it out based on what the author has written. To determine what the central idea is, ask:

- Who or what does the author tell most about?
- What does the author seem to think about that person or thing?
- What overall idea do the details in the selection support?

Supporting details are the facts, opinions, examples, and anecdotes that the author provides to make his or her point. Look at these examples from "Bonne Année":

Fact	Opinion	Anecdote
"My friends are in New York. My teachers are in New York. The Mets are in New York." (lines 20–21)	"Despite having been raised in the United States, I have no special love for this country." (lines 56–57)	The author describes watching the World Cup soccer match between Haiti and Italy. (lines 85–128)

What is the central idea of "Bonne Année"? Identify at least one additional detail that supports this idea.

Analyze Text: Personal Essay

COMMON CORE RI 3, RI 5

A **personal essay** is a short work of nonfiction in which an author expresses an opinion or provides insight based on personal experiences. By connecting a topic to his or her own life, authors can make others more aware of it.

An author may use **chronological order,** or describe a sequence of events in time order. Telling things in chronological order is an easy way to help readers understand how the ideas in an essay are connected. In "Bonne Année," the author explains how things change from one New Year's Day to another:

> Another January first, another gathering. If it is the beginning of a new year, that is at best incidental. January first is the celebration of Haitian independence.

The author also uses time clues, such as dates, to make the order of events clear. Look back at the selection and find two other time clues that help you understand when the events in this selection take place.

CLOSE READ

Determine Central Idea and Details

COMMON CORE RI 2

Discuss with students the three questions in the bulleted list. Help them use the questions to determine the central idea of the essay. *(Possible answer: When you move to a new country at a young age, neither place seems entirely like home.)*

Review the types of supporting details shown.

- Ask volunteers to find other details in the essay that are facts, opinions, and anecdotes.
- Have students identify one or more additional details that support the central idea of the essay. *(Possible answer: "For that one goal, that brief lead, those six minutes, mean more to me than all the victories of my favorite baseball team.")*

Analyze Text: Personal Essay

COMMON CORE RI 3, RI 5

Guide students in a discussion of how the author uses his own experiences to discuss important issues and insights. Ask what the author says about

- what connects people to the country of their birth
- the difficulties people face in a new country

Ask students for examples of time clues used to make the chronology clear. *(Possible answers: Another New Year; Three years into Bébé Doc's terrible reign)*

Strategies for Annotation

Annotate it!

Determine Central Idea and Details

COMMON CORE RI 2

Have students use their eBook annotation tools to analyze the text. Ask them to do the following:

- Highlight in yellow examples of details that are facts.
- Highlight in blue examples of details that are personal feelings.

> Despite having been raised in the United States, I have no special love for this country.

Analyzing the Text

COMMON CORE RI 1, RI 2, RI 3, RI 4, RI 5

Answers:

1. *The family left Haiti to escape the brutality of its ruler, Papa Doc Duvalier. When Papa Doc leaves, the family will be able to return to Haiti.*

2. *The author was so young when he left Haiti that he doesn't remember it. His friends, teachers, and his favorite baseball team are in New York.*

3. *The older people wait impatiently for a return to Haiti, are not realistic about the prospects of returning, and love the country. The author is reluctant to leave New York, eventually understands that they are unlikely to return, and does not know what it means to love a country.*

4. *Haiti plays soccer powerhouse Italy in a World Cup match shown on screens at Madison Square Garden, where fans from both countries watch. Haiti scores early in the second half to lead 1–0, but Italy eventually wins 3–1. The author expresses pride over Haiti's lead, saying it means "more to me than all the victories of my favorite baseball team."*

5. *1960s: the author is told that Duvalier will leave Haiti at any moment or that a coup will depose him; the author begins to understand who Duvalier is; 1971: Duvalier dies but his son takes power; 1974: Haiti plays Italy in World Cup soccer; the author feels intense pride; 1986: Bébé Doc flees Haiti; the author returns to Haiti but only for a two-week visit. The author realizes that he has a strong connection to Haiti, but he has a stronger connection to America.*

6. *After years of waiting, when the Duvalier regime ends, the author visits Haiti for only two weeks.*

7. *Possible answer: When the author says the celebration of the Mets' World Series victory was minor compared to the Haitian community's celebration of Jean-Claude's fleeing Haiti, he is suggesting that his heart is divided. He has a soft spot for Haiti despite having grown up in the United States.*

---

 eBook *Annotate It!*

Analyzing the Text

COMMON CORE RI 1, RI 2, RI 3, RI 4, RI 5, W 7, SL 1a

Cite Text Evidence   Support your responses with evidence from the essay.

1. **Cause/Effect** When discussing Papa Doc in lines 18–23, the author says "our destinies are linked." What does his statement mean?

2. **Infer and Cite Evidence** Reread lines 1–23. What details from the text explain why it is New York rather than Haiti that feels like home?

3. **Compare** How do the author's feelings about Haiti differ from the feelings of the older generation, including his father's?

4. **Draw Conclusions** In your own words, describe the author's account of the World Cup soccer match between Italy and Haiti, and explain his reaction to this event.

5. **Compare** Using a timeline like the one shown, identify main events in the essay in chronological order. Compare the narrator's shifting hopes for returning to Haiti as each new year arrives and his understanding grows.

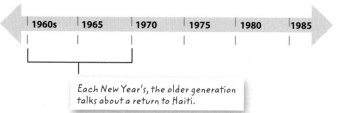

Each New Year's, the older generation talks about a return to Haiti.

6. **Analyze** Situational **irony** is a contrast between what a reader, character, or person expects and what actually happens. What is ironic about the situation the author describes in lines 129–137?

7. **Analyze and Synthesize** How does the last paragraph of the selection relate to the central idea? Consider the details about sports and celebrations that appeared earlier in the essay.

PERFORMANCE TASK

Media Activity: Poster Research Haiti's history from the 1950s to the 1980s. Create a poster in which you do the following:

- Describe the governments of Papa Doc Duvalier and his son.

- Explain some of their policies and how they affected the people of Haiti.

- Identify events and conditions that led people to leave Haiti.

Assign this performance task.

PERFORMANCE TASK

COMMON CORE W 7, SL 1a

Media Activity: Poster Have students work in pairs.

- Help partners locate appropriate print and digital resources.

- Have students present their completed posters to a small group, identifying key information they found about the Duvaliers and the impact of their policies on the people of Haiti.

- Finally, have students share their thoughts in a discussion with the class.

Critical Vocabulary

COMMON CORE L 4c

predominate	coup	persecution	dispossess	natal

Practice and Apply Explain which vocabulary word is most closely related to another word you know.

1. Which Vocabulary word goes with *relocate*? Why?

2. Which Vocabulary word goes with *baby*? Why?

3. Which Vocabulary word goes with *government*? Why?

4. Which Vocabulary word goes with *bullying*? Why?

5. Which Vocabulary word goes with *outweigh*? Why?

Vocabulary Strategy: Using a Glossary

A **glossary** is a list of specialized terms and their definitions. A text may have more than one glossary if it refers to multiple types of specialized terms.

- When a printed book contains a glossary, words are listed in the back of the book in alphabetical order.
- An electronic glossary allows readers to click on a word in the text to see its definition and hear its pronunciation.

Notice the parts of this glossary entry for the word *natal*.

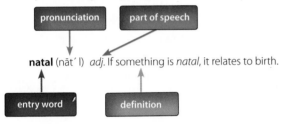

natal (nāt´ l) *adj.* If something is *natal*, it relates to birth.

Practice and Apply This literature program contains multiple glossaries. Use the table of contents and the glossaries to answer the following questions.

1. In which glossary would you expect to find a listing for the Critical Vocabulary words that are highlighted in each selection?

2. Which glossary would you use to learn definitions for the literary terms that are used in the instruction?

3. Use the glossaries to look up *predominate* and *chronological order*. What differences do you notice between the two entries?

4. According to the glossary, what is the part of speech for the word *persecution*?

Bonne Année **39**

Critical Vocabulary

COMMON CORE L 4c

Answers:

1. *dispossess: both words refer to a change or loss of a home*

2. *natal: both words refer to birth*

3. *coup: a coup is a change in governments*

4. *persecution: both words describe harsh, unfair treatment*

5. *predominate: both words refer to strength or winning*

Vocabulary Strategy: Using a Glossary

Answers:

1. *Glossary of Critical Vocabulary*

2. *Glossary of Literary and Informational Terms*

3. *For* predominate, *the glossary provides a pronunciation, a part of speech, and a sentence that explains its meaning. The entry for* chronological order *only explains its meaning.*

4. *noun*

Strategies for Annotation Annotate it!

Using a Glossary

COMMON CORE L 4c

Have students locate the glossary entry for *persecution*. Encourage them to use their eBook annotation tools to do the following:

- Highlight in yellow the entry word and its meaning.
- Highlight in blue the pronunciation.
- Highlight in green the part of speech.

persecution (pûr´ sĭ-kyōo´ shən) *n. Persecution* is the harsh treatment of others, often due to race or religion.

Language Conventions: Participles

 COMMON CORE L 1a

Explain to students that the same word can be used as different parts of speech depending upon its function in a sentence. Write these sentences:

- The athlete was <u>smiling</u>.
- The <u>smiling</u> athlete had just scored a goal.

Point out that in the first sentence, *smiling* is a verb that shows action. In the second sentence, it is an adjective (a participle) that describes *athlete*.

Answers:

1. *aching, love; forsaken, homeland*

2. *searing, example*

3. *dispossessed, children*

4. *spiraling, crescendo*

5. *unheralded, defenders*

 Assess It!

Online Selection Test
- Download an editable ExamView bank.
- Assign and manage this test online.

Language Conventions: Participles

 COMMON CORE L 1a

A verb usually shows action. A **verbal** is a word that is formed from a verb but is used as a noun, an adjective, or an adverb. A **participle** is one kind of verbal. A participle is a verb form that is used as an adjective, which modifies a noun. Writers use participles to help create vivid descriptions.

- A present participle ends in *-ing*. A past participle can have different endings, such as *-d*, *-ed*, or *-en*.

  Present participle: **The deafening cheers shook the stadium.**

  Past participle: **The disgraced regime comes to an end.**

- A participle can come before or after the noun or pronoun that it modifies, or describes.

  Before the noun it modifies: **The fallen dictator flees the country.**

  After the noun it modifies: **Haitians, smiling, celebrated in New York.**

Practice and Apply Read these sentences from "Bonne Année." Identify each participle and the noun that it modifies.

1. The view from beneath the bridge is somewhat different: reluctant refugees with an aching love of their forsaken homeland.

2. Despite the searing example of my elders, I am not even sure what it means to love a country.

3. The Haitian sun has made the cross-Atlantic journey to shine on her dispossessed children.

4. It meets a response, "I-TA-LIA," twice as loud but destined to be replaced by an even louder HA-I-TI, followed by IT-A-LIA and again HA-I-TI in a spiraling crescendo.

5. At the same time, the unheralded Haitian defenders have held.

INTERACTIVE WHITEBOARD LESSON
Determine Author's Purpose

COMMON CORE
RI 6

Tips for Identifying Author's Purpose

Choose a text you have recently read in class and use it to complete these sentence frames.

In the text titled _____, the author focuses on the topic _____.

The author's main purpose is _____ _____.

I can tell because of the following clues in the writing: _____ _____.

The audience for the text is likely _____ _____.

TEACH

Use the Interactive Whiteboard "Author's Purpose and Perspective" to teach this skill. Tell students that authors generally write for one or more of the purposes, or reasons, shown in the chart. Explain that after noting the title and topic, they can look for clues in the text to help them determine the author's purpose.

Purpose	Clues
to inform	facts and statistics
to persuade	opinions, evidence, appeals to emotion, calls to action
to entertain	amusing situations or characters; humorous details
to express thoughts or feelings	personal feelings, descriptions, or observations

PRACTICE AND APPLY

Work with students to identify the author's purpose for the passages found in the Practice & Apply section of the whiteboard lessons. Then ask partners to apply the skill further by identifying Jean-Pierre Benoît's purpose for writing the essay "Bonne Année."

Determine Central Idea and Details

COMMON CORE
RI 2

RETEACH

Review the terms *central idea* and *supporting details*. Explain that sometimes the central idea is also called the *main idea*. Point out that the **central idea** is the most important point that an author wants to make. Give an example of a central idea, such as challenges people find when moving to a new country.

Review that **supporting details** are the facts, opinions, examples, and anecdotes an author uses to make a point. Ask students to suggest supporting details for your central idea, for example:

- having to learn a new language
- feeling or looking different from other students
- being far away from friends and family members

Discuss how each detail supports the central idea.

LEVEL UP TUTORIALS Assign the following *Level Up* tutorials: **Reading for Details** and **Main Idea and Supporting Details**

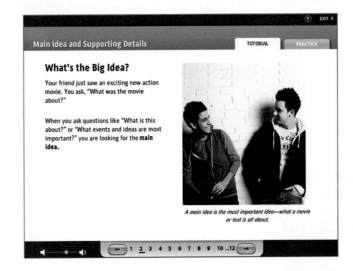

CLOSE READING APPLICATION

Student partners can work together to apply the skill to another selection in Collection 1 or to a recent magazine article.

INTERACTIVE GRAPHIC ORGANIZER Have students use one of the **Interactive Graphic Organizers** for main ideas and supporting details to record their ideas.

A Place to Call Home: What Immigrants Say Now About Life in America

Research Study by Scott Bittle and Jonathan Rochkind

Why This Text?

Immigration policy is one of the biggest challenges facing the United States today, with much of the debate on the issue fueled by emotion. This text presents the results of objective research on the topic. It is the type of text that students must read and analyze if they are to become critical thinkers and informed citizens.

▶ **View It!**

Professional Development Podcast:
Text Complexity Analysis

Key Learning Objective: The student will be able to use text features and graphic aids to analyze and understand a nonfiction text.

For practice and application:

Background *The United States has always been a land of immigrants. During the 1600s and 1700s, fewer than one million people immigrated to the new country. Today, almost one million people immigrate to the United States each year, and those immigrants tend to be younger than the general population. They generally settle in areas where there are people with similar backgrounds. (This has always been true of immigrants to the United States.) Most immigrants today settle in one of seven states: California, New York, Florida, Texas, Pennsylvania, New Jersey, and Illinois.*

What to Bring

Essay by Naisha Jackson

Close Reader selection
"What to Bring,"
Essay by Naisha Jackson

⬡ COMMON CORE Common Core Standards

RI 1 Cite textual evidence that supports inferences.
RI 3 Analyze how a text makes connections.
RI 4 Determine meanings of words and phrases.
RI 6 Determine an author's point of view and purpose.
W 7 Conduct short research projects.
W 8 Gather information from multiple print and digital sources.
L 4b Use Greek or Latin affixes and roots.
L 6 Acquire and use general academic and domain-specific words and phrases.

▲ Text Complexity Rubric

Quantitative Measures	**A Place to Call Home** Lexile: 1220L
Qualitative Measures	**Levels of Meaning/Purpose** more than one purpose; implied but easy to infer
	Structure sophisticated graphics, essential to understanding the text; may also provide information not otherwise conveyed in the text
	Language Conventionality and Clarity more complex sentence structure
	Knowledge Demands somewhat complex structure
Reader/Task Considerations	Teacher determined Vary by individual reader and type of text

TEACH

CLOSE READ

Background Have students read the background information about Public Agenda. Explain that this organization used two research techniques—surveys and focus groups—to collect information. From the surveys, they obtained statistical information from large groups of people. This data is shown on graphs in the study. In focus groups, they talked directly with smaller groups of people; quotes from those discussions are also included in the text.

SETTING A PURPOSE Direct students to use the Setting a Purpose question to focus their reading. Remind them to generate their own questions as they read.

Analyze Nonfiction Elements

COMMON CORE RI 1

(TITLE, SUBTITLE, AND SUBHEAD)

Explain that most nonfiction writing includes features that show how the author has organized the text. Point out the **heading** or title of the text and the **subtitle** that gives more information about the topic.

Ⓐ CITE TEXT EVIDENCE Have students identify the subtitle. Ask them to explain what information it provides. *(The subtitle "What Immigrants Say Now About Life in America" indicates that the text will give the opinions of immigrants, in their own words, about life in America.)*

Background *Public Agenda is a non-profit organization that does research to find out people's opinions on important issues. It hopes that by making people's opinions heard, government leaders will be better able to find good solutions to some of our nation's biggest problems. Public Agenda has done research on a variety of topics, including immigration, education, healthcare, and the economy.*

Ⓐ

A Place to Call Home:

What Immigrants Say Now About Life in America

Research Study by Scott Bittle and Jonathan Rochkind

SETTING A PURPOSE As you read, pay attention to the immigrants' attitudes about their decisions to come to the United States. What do you find surprising about the information presented?

Introduction

It's a cliché to say that America is a nation of immigrants, but like most clichés, this one began as a statement of simple truth. Another truth is that if we're going to overhaul immigration policy, it only makes sense to listen to the people who will be most affected by it: immigrants. To craft a just and practical policy, we need to see America through the immigrant's eyes. That's true whether you favor an open door or a higher fence. You can't hope to implement sound strategies unless you understand what brings people to the United States and what
10 they think about the nation once they get here.

That's what Public Agenda hopes to accomplish with A PLACE TO CALL HOME: WHAT IMMIGRANTS SAY NOW ABOUT LIFE IN AMERICA, the follow-up to our pioneering 2002 survey of immigrants, NOW THAT I'M HERE.

©Pushkin/Shutterstock

A Place to Call Home **41**

SCAFFOLDING FOR ELL STUDENTS

Analyze Language Draw attention to these expressions in line 7: *open door* and *higher fence*. Explain that these expressions have meanings that are different from the meanings of their individual words. Model these steps for determining the meanings:

- Use context to understand the meaning.
- Analyze the image suggested by the expression.

ASK STUDENTS to identify the general topic of lines 1–10. *(immigration)* Ask students what they think when they see an open door. *(that people are welcome to enter)* Then ask why someone would build a higher fence. *(to keep someone or something out)* Guide students to discuss what kind of immigration policy each expression suggests. Tell students to follow a similar process with other idiomatic expressions in the text.

CLOSE READ

 For more content and historical background, students can view the video "Immigrating" in their eBooks.

Analyze Nonfiction Elements (LINES 15–34)

 COMMON CORE RI 1

Explain that **subheadings** are headings within the text that introduce a new topic or section. Draw attention to the subheading "Part 1: The Right Move."

B CITE TEXT EVIDENCE Have students reread lines 15–34. Ask students to identify the subheading and explain what "The Right Move" refers to, citing evidence from the text. *("The Right Move" refers to the fact that, according to this study, the majority of immigrants believe they made the right decision in moving to the United States: "By that standard, immigrants in America are clearly happy with their choice. More than 7 in 10 (71 percent) report that if they could do it all over again, they'd still come to the United States.")*

CRITICAL VOCABULARY

tumult: The authors are explaining the impact of the overall economy on immigrants' perceptions of life in the United States.

ASK STUDENTS to suggest what might be part of an economic tumult. *(Possible answers: unemployment and lower wages)*

pernicious: According to the text, people have differing views of the idea that the United States is unique.

ASK STUDENTS why some people might find this idea pernicious. *(It might cause people to overlook the country's real faults and to be less likely to want to cooperate with other nations.)*

B

Part 1: The Right Move

Overall, immigrants say they're quite satisfied with life in the United States, for themselves and their children. Discrimination against immigrants doesn't seem to be part of their daily lives. Although majorities say it exists, majorities also say they haven't personally experienced much of it. Right
20 now, the biggest concern for immigrants is much the same as for native-born Americans: the economy and their own financial well-being. The economic **tumult** in our society may be shaping some of their perceptions—and motivations.

For any decision in life, whether it involves a job accepted or lost, a marriage made or ended, a school selected or a vote cast, the evaluation comes down to one question: Would you do it all over again? There may be regrets or dissatisfactions; that's part of the human condition. But if life came with a time machine or a reset button, would you make the same choice?
30 By that standard, immigrants in America are clearly happy with their choice. More than 7 in 10 (71 percent) report that if they could do it all over again, they'd still come to the United States. Nor are they likely to give up and go home; indeed, equally large numbers (70 percent) say that they intend to make the United States their permanent home.

That goes for their children as well. About three-quarters of immigrant parents (74 percent) say it's unlikely their children will want to live in their birth country, with a strong 58 percent saying it's "very unlikely."
40 The reasons for this seem straightforward: Immigrants buy in to American society. There's always been a fierce debate among pundits and political scientists about "American exceptionalism," the idea that the United States is unique among nations. Some find this idea ennobling, others **pernicious**. Maybe it's no surprise, since immigrants have volunteered to build their lives here, but the people we surveyed have very little doubt: 76 percent say the United States is "a unique country that stands for something special in the world." Only 20 percent disagree, saying that the United
50 States is "just another country that is no better or worse than any other."

tumult
(tōō′mŭlt´) *n.* A *tumult* is a disorderly disturbance.

pernicious
(pər-nĭsh′əs) *adj.* If something is pernicious, it is very harmful or destructive.

WHEN STUDENTS STRUGGLE . . .

Guide students to use the subheadings to determine the central ideas in the selection. Have them reread the first subheading and lines 15–23. Discuss how the first subheading could be stated as a central idea. *(Most immigrants believe they made the right move in coming to the United States.)* Have students record the central idea in a graphic organizer like the one shown, adding evidence that supports the central idea as they continue reading. Repeat with the subheading for Part 2.

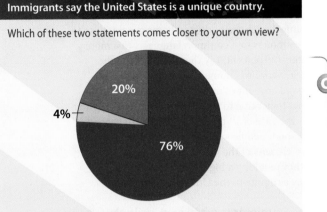

Immigrants say the United States is a unique country.

Which of these two statements comes closer to your own view?

20%

4%

76%

76%   The United States is a unique country that stands for something special in the world.

20%   The United States is just another country that is no better or worse than any other.

4%   Don't know/refused

PART 2: Fitting In

Most immigrants say that they have become comfortable in the United States quickly, yet ties to their birth countries have become stronger since 2002, particularly among recent immigrants. Most of the immigrants we surveyed either were citizens already or were in the process of being **naturalized**. For most of them, citizenship is a practical step. So is learning to speak English, with most immigrants reporting that it is difficult to get ahead or keep a job without language skills.

60   Immigrants clearly buy into American values, but how long does it take them to feel comfortable in American society? Although immigrants embrace what the United States stands for, this is no guarantee that they are able to fit in on a day-to-day basis.

The immigrants we surveyed don't seem to feel that fitting in is a major barrier and in fact say the process moved quickly. More than three-quarters (77 percent) say that it takes fewer than five years to "feel comfortable here and part of the

naturalize
(năch´ ər-ə-līz´) *v.*
When governments *naturalize* people, they grant them full citizenship.

CLOSE READ

Analyze Nonfiction Elements (CIRCLE GRAPH)

COMMON CORE   **RI 3**

Explain that graphs provide visual support for the data and conclusions in the text. Review the information provided in the circle graph.

C **ASK STUDENTS** to analyze and explain the connection between the circle graph and the authors' conclusion in lines 40–41 that "Immigrants buy in to American society." *(The text says: "76 percent say the United States is 'a unique country that stands for something special in the world.'" The graph shows visually that a large part of the whole shares this view, which supports the authors' conclusion.)*

> **CRITICAL VOCABULARY**
>
> **naturalize:** The authors explain that most immigrants choose to become naturalized.
>
> **ASK STUDENTS** why becoming naturalized might be "practical" for immigrants. *(As citizens, they have more rights in American society; for example, they are able to vote, travel with a US passport, and bring other family members to the United States.)*

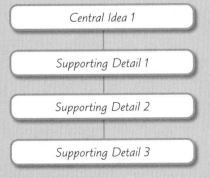

Central Idea 1

Supporting Detail 1

Supporting Detail 2

Supporting Detail 3

Analyze Nonfiction Elements (LINES 82–87)

COMMON CORE RI 1

Explain that this selection has another type of text feature that can help readers understand the text. Point out the lines in large type after line 81. Explain that this statement summarizes the information that follows it.

D **CITE TEXT EVIDENCE** Have students reread lines 82–87 and cite evidence that supports the statement in large type. *("one of the consistent themes was of immigrants being surprised by how much work it takes to succeed in the United States.")*

Point out another feature of this text: the direct quotations, indented and shown in italics, from focus group participants.

E **ASK STUDENTS** to reread lines 88–92. Ask what conclusion students can draw from this quotation and whether it supports the summary statement above. *(Conclusion: it takes much more work to make a living in the United States than immigrants expected. This supports the statement that life here is not what they thought it would be.)*

---

community," and nearly half (47 percent) say it took fewer
70 than two.

Such easy comfort with their adopted home generally isn't being propelled by money or a common language. Just more than three-quarters (76 percent) say that they came to the United States with "very little money," and only 20 percent say they had "a good amount of money to get started." Some 45 percent say that they came to this country not speaking any English at all, an increase of 10 points since 2002. In general, we aren't talking about people who move freely between nations, so-called citizens of the world. We're talking about
80 people who say they're taking a big financial and cultural gamble when they emigrate to the United States.

D **In focus groups, immigrants often said life in the United States was not what they thought it would be.**

In the focus groups we conducted as part of this study, one of the consistent themes was of immigrants being surprised by how much work it takes to succeed in the United States. Even with all of its advantages over their birth countries, the reality for many immigrants is that it can be difficult to live in the United States and achieve a good standard of living.

E *"There's the assumption that when you come here you will become wealthy very fast and very easily. I have to work*
90 *12, 16 hours a day to make a living. [In my birth country] . . . they work, like, from nine until two and then go home."*
— A woman in the Detroit, Michigan, focus group

Her sentiment is partly borne out by the survey, which also asked how often immigrants found themselves living "paycheck to paycheck." Some 70 percent of immigrants reported doing so "always," "most of the time" or "sometimes." When Newsweek asked the same question of the general public in January 2009, only 59 percent said they lived paycheck to paycheck.
100 Among our focus groups, there was a general sense that America has no better publicist than Hollywood on this

point—although movies and television often broadcast a misleading picture.

"All the movies [are] just great propaganda . . . like it's a lot of fun and [you have] a lot of money and all that. You don't think about, like, you have to pay [the] mortgage. You don't know."
—A man in New York

"When I came here, the first thing I imagined was I want to live la vida loca, the great life. When I recently arrived here, I wound up in an area that was very bad, in a two-bedroom apartment where 12 people were living. They were sharing their rent, and I said, 'What have I gotten myself into?' With time, I wound up renting another apartment. I didn't imagine it would be like this."
—A woman in the Los Angeles focus group

110

Immigrants report closer ties to their birth country than they did seven years ago. They spend more time with people from their birth country and are more likely to call home and send money.

There's some suggestion, however, that when it comes to being "comfortable" in communities, other immigrants play a critical role. Compared with results from 2002, more immigrants say that they spend time with people from their
120 birth country and have closer ties there.

Half of the immigrants we surveyed (51 percent) say they spend "a lot" of time with people from their birth country, a jump of 14 points from 2002. Other kinds of birth-country ties have strengthened as well. One is the simple act of telephoning. The number of immigrants who tell us that they call home at least once a week rose 12 points (40 percent from 28 percent). Granted, this may be partly because **telecommunications** is better and cheaper than even a few years ago. Cell phones are common, international calling
130 is less expensive and innovations like Skype and instant messaging make it easier to keep in touch.

telecommunications
(tĕl´ĭ-kə-myō͞o´ nĭ-kā´shəns) *n.*
Telecommunications are the electronic systems that telephones and other electronic devices use to send information.

CLOSE READ

Cite Evidence (LINES 116–127)   **RI 1**

Explain that readers often draw conclusions as they read. Explain that to **draw conclusions,** readers make judgments based on evidence in a text, along with their own experience and reasoning. Draw attention to the blue summary statement below line 115.

E **CITE TEXT EVIDENCE** Ask students what evidence in the text that follows this statement shows that it is a valid conclusion. *(The more recent study shows that immigrants have closer ties to their birth country than they did seven years ago. Evidence: "Compared with results from 2002, more immigrants say that they spend time with people from their birth country"; "The number of immigrants who tell us that they call home at least once a week rose 12 points.")*

CRITICAL VOCABULARY

telecommunications: The authors explain that improved telecommunications have benefited immigrants.

ASK STUDENTS to describe some examples of telecommunications that make it easier for immigrants to stay in touch with their birth country. *(Cell phones, as well as innovations like video conferencing and instant messaging, allow immigrants to stay in touch with family back home. This increase in communication has resulted in recent immigrants having stronger ties to their birth country than those in the past.)*

Strategies for Annotation   🖉 🗂 *Annotate it!*

Cite Evidence   **RI 1**

Have students locate lines 116–120. Encourage students to use their eBook annotation tools to do the following:

- Highlight in yellow the conclusion the author draws about what makes immigrants feel "comfortable."
- Underline evidence in the text that supports the conclusion.

There's some suggestion, however, that when it comes to being "comfortable" in communities, other immigrants play a critical role. Compared with results from 2002, more immigrants say that they spend time with people from their birth country and have closer ties there.

Analyze Nonfiction Elements (LINES 139–155)

COMMON CORE RI 1, RI 3

Draw attention to the bulleted list. Explain that a **bulleted list** is a list of related and equally important points in a text. As needed, point out the dark circle that precedes each item and explain that it is called a bullet.

G **CITE TEXT EVIDENCE** Have students reread lines 139–155. Ask students to analyze the connections among the bulleted items and note evidence from the text that supports their thoughts. *(All items in the list are examples of how recent immigrants have weaker ties to the United States than those in the past; the text that introduces the bulleted list states, "their ties to the United States aren't as strong. For example:")*

These strengthened ties are not merely emotional, either; they're financial. While there's been no real change in the number of immigrants who say they send money to their birth country regularly, the number who say they do so "once in a while" increased 14 points, to 44 percent. And the number who say they never send money fell from 55 percent to 37 percent.

About one-quarter of our sample was made up of more recent immigrants, those who arrived since 2001. On the whole, their ties to the United States aren't as strong. For example:

140

G

- One-third say they will go back to live in their birth country someday.

- Three in ten (32 percent) say it is likely that their children will one day want to live in their birth country (compared with 18 percent of those here before 2001).

- One-third (34 percent) say that if they had it to do over, they would either stay where they were born (26 percent) or pick a different country (8 percent).

150

- Six in ten (61 percent) say that they spend a lot of time with people from their birth country, compared with 47 percent of immigrants here before 2001.

- More than twice as many (66 percent compared with 29 percent) telephone home at least once a week.

The recent immigrants in A PLACE TO CALL HOME do seem to have different attitudes on these points than those who were recent arrivals in our 2002 study, NOW THAT I'M HERE—in other words, those who were new and still adjusting to American life in the 1990s as opposed to the 2000s. When we compare immigrants who arrived between 2001 and 2009 with those from the 2002 study who arrived between 1990 and 2001, we find:

160

- The 2001–2009 group are more likely to spend a lot of time with people from their birth country (61 percent versus 35 percent in the 2002 survey).

APPLYING ACADEMIC VOCABULARY

immigrate	shifting

As you discuss the information in the research study, incorporate the following Collection 1 academic vocabulary words: *immigrate* and *shifting*. Ask students what they learned from this study about the attitudes and experiences of people who have chosen to **immigrate** to the United States. Explain that this report is a follow-up to an earlier study, and discuss what the results reveal about **shifting** trends in immigrants' attitudes.

- They're also more likely to call their birth country at least once a week (66 percent compared with 38 percent).

170 - And, of those who came to the United States knowing little or no English, they're more likely to say they speak their native language most of the time at home (86 percent compared with 55 percent).

At least as far as perceptions go, a majority of the immigrants we surveyed in 2009 (57 percent) suggest that recent immigrants "have the same respect for American laws and customs as immigrants like you." About a third (32 percent) say that recent immigrants have less respect, though only 15 percent of immigrants who have arrived after 180 2001 agree.

Among our focus groups, there was a strong sense that American culture is a difficult force to resist. Many immigrants mentioned the materialism often associated with America as a drawback, although how they responded to it depended greatly on their personal beliefs.

Significant numbers of immigrants came to the United States without being able to speak English, and more than half still consider their language skills fair or poor. However, they consider speaking English important for getting ahead, and most say they've taken classes to improve their ability.

One of the **perpetual** flashpoints in the immigration debate has been over language: to what extent immigrants speak English and to what extent the nation should accommodate those who don't. As mentioned above, a sizable 190 number of immigrants (45 percent) come to the United States with no knowledge of English. Overall, about half of them (52 percent) report that they can read a book or newspaper "a little" or "not at all." Even more of them, 63 percent, consider their ability to speak English to be "fair" or "poor." This is a barrier, and immigrants know it. More than half of immigrants (52 percent) say it is "very hard" to get a job

perpetual
(pər-pĕch´oo-əl) *adj.*
If something is *perpetual*, it lasts for a very long time.

CLOSE READ

Determining Author's Purpose (LINES 174–180)

COMMON CORE **RI 6**

Point out that an **author's purpose** is his or her reason for writing. Explain that authors choose details and information to support his or her purpose.

H **ASK STUDENTS** to reread lines 174–180. Ask: *What do the details about immigrants' respect for American laws and customs suggest about the authors' purpose? Why might the authors have included this information? (Possible answer: The authors want to share information that shows the majority of immigrants respect the law. The authors may have wanted to acknowledge the conflicting viewpoint that many immigrants break the law.)*

CRITICAL VOCABULARY

perpetual: The authors say that the issue of language has been a "perpetual flashpoint" in the immigration debate.

ASK STUDENTS to suggest why the debate over language is perpetual. *(Possible answers: The debate continues because there is a constant flow of new immigrants. Each new wave of immigrants needs to learn English, but it can be difficult for adults, especially those who do not interact often with other English speakers. Some English speakers who hear immigrants speaking a different language may believe that the immigrants are refusing to learn English.)*

Analyze Language (LINE 195) COMMON CORE **RI 4**

Draw students' attention to the authors' conclusion about the need to speak English.

① **ASK STUDENTS** to explain why the inability to speak English is called "a barrier." *(Possible answer: A barrier is anything that prevents someone from moving where he or she wants to go. Not being able to speak English prevents immigrants from getting jobs and possibly from having relationships with others, both of which are needed to succeed in the United States.)*

Cite Evidence (LINES 195–210) COMMON CORE **RI 1**

Review that drawing a conclusion involves making a judgment based on evidence, experience, and reasoning. Remind students that this research study presents evidence drawn from surveys and focus groups. Explain that the authors have used this evidence along with experience and reasoning to draw conclusions about immigrants' attitudes.

① **CITE TEXT EVIDENCE** Have students reread lines 195–210. Ask what conclusion they can draw from this evidence about immigrants' attitudes toward language. *(Possible answer: Immigrants recognize the importance of speaking English, for themselves and their children, in order to succeed in the United States. They note that "it is 'very hard' to get a job without knowing English" and that "it is more important for schools to teach immigrant children English as quickly as possible than it is to teach them other subjects.")*

 without knowing English (although, interestingly, that's a 10-point decline from 2002), and more than half (56 percent) say that the United States should expect all immigrants to 200 learn English.

Immigrants are willing to take practical steps to address this. Seven in ten of those who came to this country knowing very little or no English at all say that they've taken classes to improve their English, a jump of 23 percent from 2002. Nearly three-quarters (74 percent) of immigrants overall say that it is more important for schools to teach immigrant children English as quickly as possible than it is to teach them other subjects in their native language. Some 88 percent of those with school-age children consider their child's English to be 210 "excellent" or "good."

Despite this, English isn't the primary language in many immigrant homes. Nearly two-thirds (64 percent) of those who came to the United States speaking little or no English say that they mostly speak their native language at home, a 25-point increase from 2002.

There's also a significant difference based on when immigrants came here and how much money they have. Ninety percent of those who still don't speak English well came to the country with very little money. Recent 220 immigrants (since 2001) are more likely to have arrived already knowing how to speak English (30 percent compared with 22 percent), but the recent immigrants who did not are also much more likely to speak their native language in the home (86 percent compared with 55 percent). These immigrants are also more doubtful about their skills, with 75 percent reporting that their English is "fair" or "poor," compared with 58 percent of immigrants who have been here a while.

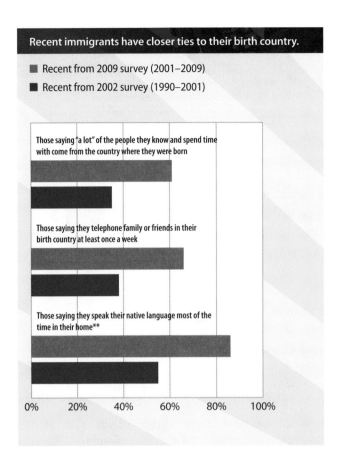

Recent immigrants have closer ties to their birth country.

- Recent from 2009 survey (2001–2009)
- Recent from 2002 survey (1990–2001)

Those saying "a lot" of the people they know and spend time with come from the country where they were born

Those saying they telephone family or friends in their birth country at least once a week

Those saying they speak their native language most of the time in their home**

0%   20%   40%   60%   80%   100%

COLLABORATIVE DISCUSSION How do the immigrants surveyed for this study feel about the United States? Compare and contrast their attitude about living in the United States to your own.

CLOSE READ

Analyze Nonfiction Elements (BAR GRAPH)

COMMON CORE   RI 3

Tell students that the text has provided several comparisons between a 2002 survey and one taken in 2009. Explain that a **bar graph,** such as the one shown on this page, is one way to show how things change over time. Point out the key at the top of the graph, and explain that it shows what each color bar represents. Draw attention to the percentages at the bottom of the graph, and explain that they indicate the percentage of respondents in each group who agreed with each statement.

K ASK STUDENTS to study the bar graph closely to identify what each color bar represents. *(Red represents recent immigrants from the 2009 survey. Blue represents recent immigrants from the 2002 survey.) How does the graph connect to the conclusion stated at the top of the graph? (Each of the three statements indicates a closer tie to the birth country. For each statement, the red line is longer than the blue, supporting the authors' conclusion by showing that more 2009 respondents than 2002 respondents agreed with the statement.)*

COLLABORATIVE DISCUSSION Have small groups of students discuss the responses of the immigrants surveyed and compare them to their own attitudes about life in the United States. Ask the groups to also discuss anything that surprises them about the results of the survey.

ASK STUDENTS to share any questions of their own they generated during the course of reading and discussing the selection.

CLOSE READ

Analyze Nonfiction Elements RI 3

Help students understand the definitions and examples shown for the different types of text features. After students have reviewed the text to identify all the subheadings, discuss the type of information provided in each section. *(The Introduction gives the purpose of the study and a general explanation of what will follow. "Part 1: The Right Move" suggests a focus on why immigrants moved to the United States and how they felt about it. "Part 2: Fitting In" suggests a focus on how immigrants have adjusted to life in their new country.)*

Review the definitions of the types of graphics presented and guide students to respond to the related questions. *(circle graph: Respondents were asked, "Which of these two statements comes closer to your own view?: 'The United States is a unique country that stands for something special in the world.' or 'The United States is just another country that is no better or worse than any other.'" The most common answer (76%) was the first one; bar graph: The bar graph in the selection compares recent immigrants from the 2009 survey with those from the 2002 survey.)*

Prompt students to explain how each graphic clarifies or makes connections to information in the text. *(Possible answer: The graphics show information in a visual way that is understandable at a glance; the graphics show information that takes several paragraphs of text to explain.)*

Analyze Nonfiction Elements RI 3

Text features are design elements such as headings, subheadings, and graphs that authors use to organize information, identify key ideas, and help guide readers through a text. Various types of text features are used for different purposes:

- The **heading** is the title of a text. A **subtitle,** or an additional part of a title, may tell more about what the piece is about.

> ### A Place to Call Home: ← heading
> **What Immigrants Say Now About Life in America** ← subtitle

- **Subheadings** are headings within the text that introduce a new topic or section. They are usually larger, darker, or more colorful than regular text.

> **Part 1: The Right Move** ← subheading

- A **bulleted list** (like the one you're reading now) is a list of related and equally important points or ideas.

Review the text and identify all the subheadings. What does each subheading suggest about the kind of information in that section?

Information can also be transmitted visually through **graphic aids,** which include graphs, charts, diagrams, photographs, and other visuals. **Graphs** are used to illustrate statistical information, and they are helpful in showing numerical relationships. Various types of graphs are used for different purposes:

- A **circle graph** is a circular shape that shows how the parts of something compare to the whole. The parts of the circle represent percentages of the whole.
- A **bar graph** is a graph that uses dark or colored bars to display amounts or percentages. Bar graphs are helpful when showing how things change over time. They often include keys, or explanations of how to read the graph.

Find the circle graph in this selection. Identify what question the respondents, or the people who participated in the study, were asked. What was the most common answer? Find the bar graph in this selection. What is being compared?

Strategies for Annotation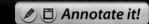

Analyze Nonfiction Elements

Share these strategies for guided or independent analysis:

- Highlight in yellow each subheading in the text.
- Underline supporting evidence in the text under the subheading.
- In notes, record any conclusions you can draw based on the evidence.

> Part 1: The Right Move
>
> Overall, immigrants say they're quite satisfied with life in the
> United States, for themselves and their children. Discrimination

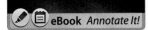
Analyzing the Text

COMMON CORE RI 1, RI 3, RI 4, W 2, W 7, W 8

Cite Text Evidence   Support your responses with evidence from the text.

1. **Infer** What does the use of the word *now* in the selection's subtitle suggest about the information provided in the text?

2. **Interpret** In lines 1–14, what does it mean "to see America through the immigrant's eyes"? Explain why the authors believe that this is important.

3. **Summarize** Are people generally happy or unhappy once they immigrate to the United States? Support your answer by explaining in your own words the information in lines 15–51.

4. **Draw Conclusions** To **draw conclusions** is to make a judgment based on evidence, experience, and reasoning. Study the circle graph that shows immigrants' views about the United States. What conclusion can you draw about the immigrants' choice to come to the United States from the evidence shown here and the information provided in the text?

5. **Cause/Effect** Reread lines 100–110. What contributes to immigrants' false impressions of what life in the United States will be like?

6. **Compare** How do the attitudes of the immigrants who have arrived here recently compare to those who arrived earlier? In a chart like the one shown, gather information from the bulleted list and bar graphs in Part 2. Then explain how immigrants' thoughts about their country of birth and their relationships with others from their birth country are shifting.

	Immigrants Surveyed in 2002	Immigrants Surveyed in 2009
Thoughts about Country of Birth		
Relationships with Others from Birth Country		

PERFORMANCE TASK

 WriteSmart

Writing Activity: Explanation Do research to discover where recent immigrants to the United States came from.

- Choose one or more years to research.
- Identify the number of immigrants who settled in the United States as

well as their birth countries.

- Compare the number of immigrants who came from various countries.
- Create a bar graph or a circle graph to show your findings.
- Explain why you chose to use the graphic aid you did.

PRACTICE & APPLY

Analyzing the Text

COMMON CORE RI 1, RI 3, RI 4

Possible answers:

1. *The use of the word* now *suggests that the information in the text is current and is being compared to earlier information.*

2. *It means "to see something from another's perspective." The authors say an effective immigration policy should reflect understanding of what brings people to the United States and what they think about it once they get here.*

3. *Immigrants are generally happy. They experience little discrimination and would make the move again given the choice. Immigrants say it is unlikely that they or their children would move back to their birth country. Most think that the United States is a unique country.*

4. *Most immigrants (76%) say the United States is a unique place that stands for something special in the world. A possible conclusion is that the immigrants came to the United States rather than another country for that reason.*

5. *Many immigrants have the idea that it will be easy to achieve a good standard of living. American movies and television programs give misleading ideas about how hard Americans work.*

6. *Thirty-two percent say it is likely that their children will one day want to live in their birth country (compared with 18 percent of those here before 2001). Fifty-one percent say they spend "a lot" of time with people from their birth country, a jump of 14 points from 2002. This suggests that newer immigrants feel more connected to their home countries.*

PERFORMANCE TASK

COMMON CORE W 7, W 8

Assign this performance task.  **WriteSmart**

Research Activity: Explanation Have pairs of students select a year or span of years and conduct their research together. You might suggest they use the following website:

http://www.dhs.gov/yearbook-immigration-statistics-2011-1

- Tell students to review the definitions of bar graphs and circle graphs before selecting the one they want to use.
- Have pairs present their findings to the class.

- Challenge students to create a new graph comparing immigration patterns in the different years that their classmates researched.

PRACTICE & APPLY

Critical Vocabulary

COMMON CORE L4 b, L 6

Possible Answers:

1. *a hurricane blew into town*

2. *they encourage people to do things that are unhealthy or unsafe*

3. *he or she wants to become a citizen*

4. *see his brother in another country as he speaks to him on the phone*

5. *finding a new home*

Vocabulary Strategy: Using Greek Prefixes

Answers:

Word	Word Meaning
teleconference	*a conference held over a distance among people in different locations*
telemarketer	*someone who sells items during phone calls*
televise	*to broadcast something on television*
telescope	*a device for looking at distant objects*
telephoto	*a device for producing a large image of a distant object*

Critical Vocabulary

COMMON CORE L 4b, L 6

tumult   pernicious   naturalize   telecommunications   perpetual

Practice and Apply Complete each sentence in a way that shows the meaning of the Vocabulary word.

1. There was **tumult** in the neighborhood when . . .

2. Advertisements can be **pernicious** if . . .

3. A government may **naturalize** an immigrant if . . .

4. Advanced **telecommunications** systems make it possible for Armando to . . .

5. One **perpetual** challenge people have when they relocate is . . .

Vocabulary Strategy: Using Greek Prefixes

Many English words are made from word parts that come from the Greek language. A **prefix** is a word part that is added to the beginning of a base word or a word root. Knowing the meaning of a prefix can often help you figure out the meaning of a new word. Look at this example from "A Place to Call Home":

> **Granted, this may be partly because <u>telecommunications</u> is better and cheaper than even a few years ago.**

If you know that the Greek prefix *tele-* means "distance," it will help you understand that *telecommunications* is "electronic communication over a distance."

Practice and Apply Use the meaning of the prefix *tele-* to help you complete a chart like the one shown.

Word	Word Meaning
teleconference	
telemarketer	
televise	
telescope	
telephoto	

Strategies for Annotation ✎ 🗐 *Annotate it!*

Using Greek Prefixes

Have students locate the sentences that begin on line 124 and end on line 126. Encourage them to use their eBook annotation tools to do the following:

- Underline the word that contains prefix *tele-*.
- Highlight the prefix in yellow.
- Highlight any clues to the word's meaning in blue.
- In a note, write the meaning of the word.
- Consult a resource, such as a dictionary, to confirm the answer.

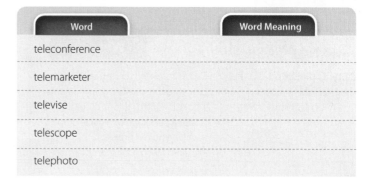

One is the simple act of <u>telephoning</u>. The number of immigrants who tell us that they call home at least once a week rose 12 points (40 percent from 28 percent). Granted, this may be partly because telecommunications is better and cheaper than even a a

"to call on the telephone"

Integrating Information from Text and Graphic Aids

TEACH

Explain that some nonfiction texts, like the research study "A Place to Call Home," contain a lot of data, such as percentages and quantities. Nonfiction writers use **graphic aids,** such as graphs and charts, to help make this information clear. To get a full understanding of a text, readers need to **integrate,** or combine, information from both the text and the graphic aids. Often, the graphic aids provide evidence to support conclusions that the author draws in the text.

- Have students reread lines 40–51. Ask what conclusion the authors draw. *("Immigrants buy in to American society.")*
- Now have students study the circle graph above the Part 2 subheading. Ask how the graph supports the authors' conclusion. *(It shows that a large majority of the immigrants surveyed, 76 percent, believe that the United States is a unique country that stands for something special.)*
- Repeat with lines 156–173 and the bar graph at the end of the selection. Discuss how integrating both types of information supports understanding.

PRACTICE AND APPLY

Remind students to keep in mind what they have learned about graphic aids as they create their graphs for the Performance Task. Suggest that they ask themselves, "What conclusions about immigration does the data in this graph support?"

 LEVEL UP TUTORIALS For additional practice, assign the following *Level Up* tutorial: **Reading Graphic Elements**

 INTERACTIVE WHITEBOARD LESSON
Text Features

READING INFORMATIONAL TEXT

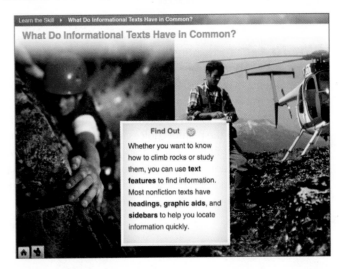

RETEACH

Review the definitions and examples of **heading, subtitle, subheadings,** and **bulleted list.** Use the Interactive Whiteboard Lesson to help students better understand how to use these features when they read informational text. Share and discuss the following:

- First, preview the text features to get a sense of the topic of the informational text.
- Use subheadings to help identify and analyze central ideas.
- Take notes or use a graphic organizer to help keep track of central ideas and the details that support them.

CLOSE READING APPLICATION

Students can apply the skill to another nonfiction text of their own choosing. Have them work independently to identify the title, subtitle (if any), and subheadings. Remind students that the subheadings can help them identify central ideas, and that using a graphic organizer can help them understand the central ideas and supporting details.

What to Bring

Essay by Naisha Jackson

Why This Text

Some students may have difficulty fully comprehending texts that deal with events outside of their own experiences. The essay "What to Bring" is such a text. In it, the author uses specific objects to illustrate the painful choices immigrants often must make. With the help of the close-reading questions, students will analyze the possessions immigrants chose to bring with them to the United States and thus develop a deep understanding of the immigrant experience.

Background Have students read the background information about immigrants to the United States. Point out who today's immigrants are and where they tend to settle. Explain that some immigrants come to the United States because it is unsafe for them to stay in their own countries; such immigrants are called refugees. The word *refugee* means "one who flees a dangerous situation."

SETTING A PURPOSE Ask students to pay attention to the objects immigrants bring with them; the nature of these objects can inform what immigrants may be feeling.

 COMMON CORE Common Core Support

- cite strong and thorough textual evidence
- draw inferences from the text
- analyze how a text makes connections among and distinctions between individuals, ideas, or events

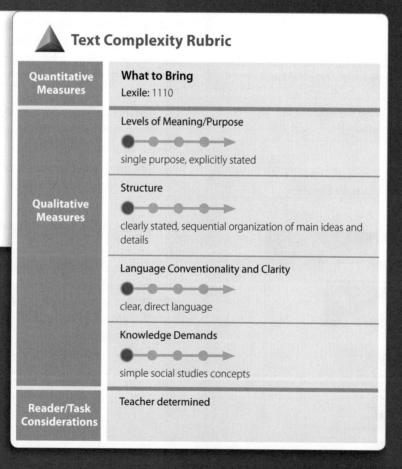

▲ **Text Complexity Rubric**

Quantitative Measures	**What to Bring** Lexile: 1110
Qualitative Measures	**Levels of Meaning/Purpose** single purpose, explicitly stated
	Structure clearly stated, sequential organization of main ideas and details
	Language Conventionality and Clarity clear, direct language
	Knowledge Demands simple social studies concepts
Reader/Task Considerations	Teacher determined

Analyze Nonfiction Elements

Students should read this essay carefully all the way through. Close-reading questions at the bottom of the page will help them to use text features as a guide to understanding the text. As they read, students should jot down comments or questions about the text in the margins.

WHEN STUDENTS STRUGGLE . . .

To help students use text features in "What to Bring," have them work in small groups to fill out a chart like the one shown below.

CITE TEXT EVIDENCE For practice in using text features, ask students to tell what information the subheads and the bulleted list gives them.

Subheads	Information
Traveling Light (p. 9)	It tells me that the text will be about immigrants traveling without taking much with them.
Precious Possessions (p. 10)	It tells me that the text will be about what possessions mean the most to immigrants.
Sentimental Journeys (p. 12)	It tells me that the text will be about something emotional that is connected with the experience of immigrants.
Bulleted List (p. 11)	It gives me examples of possessions that immigrants have brought with them.

Background *The United States has always been a land of immigrants. During the 1600s and 1700s, fewer than one million people immigrated to the new country. Today, almost one million people immigrate to the United States each year, and those immigrants tend to be younger than the general population. They generally settle in areas where there are people with similar backgrounds. (This has always been true of immigrants to the United States.) Most immigrants today settle in one of seven states: California, New York, Florida, Texas, Pennsylvania, New Jersey, and Illinois.*

What to Bring

Essay by Naisha Jackson

CLOSE READ
Notes

1. **READ ▶** As you read lines 1–24, begin to cite text evidence.
- Circle the first subhead.
- Underline the reasons people immigrate to the United States.
- In the margin, list the items that immigrants have brought with them.

(Traveling Light)

A **F** A hundred years ago, most immigrants to the United States arrived by ship and were allowed only one suitcase for the long voyage. They left almost all of their belongings behind. Recent immigrants have a much faster journey, but many of them still bring very few items with them.

Some modern immigrants move to the United States to find a better future, owning very little in their countries of origin. One immigrant from Central Africa arrived at Kennedy Airport in 2002 with twenty cents—he worked in a car wash as he earned his college
10　degree in finance. A man who emigrated from Honduras brought a ceramic Zorro pencil sharpener, which is now a treasured family possession.

Other immigrants are refugees, escaping **oppression** in their homelands. Many refugees are likely to have very few possessions, and are often unable to leave their countries with those belongings they do

twenty cents

Zorro pencil sharpener

oppression:
keeping people down by force

9

---

1. **READ AND CITE TEXT EVIDENCE** Remind students that nonfiction writers often compare and contrast a set of characteristics for emphasis.

A **ASK STUDENTS** to find the things the author compares and contrasts in the opening paragraph. How are these things alike and different? What can you conclude is the point the author wants to emphasize? *The author points out that many immigrants are similar in their need to travel light.*

Critical Vocabulary: oppression (line 13) The text says that oppression is something that refugees are trying to escape. Ask students, based on how the word is used in context, to share their definitions of *oppression*.

B have. A man who was imprisoned for nine years in a Soviet political labor camp immigrated to the United States with the help of the International Organization for Migration. He arrived with only a small flight bag. One of the few items he had with him was a
20 toothbrush he had kept in the labor camp, carved down so it could be hidden in his pocket from the guards. The thousands of children who left Cuba in 1960 were allowed to leave with only five dollars **C** and a small suitcase. One child's suitcase held his bilingual edition of Shakespeare's *Hamlet*.

toothbrush

five dollars

Hamlet

Precious Possessions

Are there any **principles** that guide what belongings an immigrant brings? There are requirements—legal documents such as passports and birth certificates—and there are items of choice. Some items you might expect, while others might come as a surprise to you.

Perhaps the two most common kinds of immigrants' belongings
30 are religious items and photographs. Immigrants may have photographs of friends and relatives they are leaving and places they used to live. New arrivals have arrived with the following religious items in their luggage:

principles:
rules

legal
documents

religious items

photographs

- a prayer book
- a Bible
- a Koran[1]
- a statue of Buddha[2]
- religious medals
- candlesticks for Sabbath candles

D 40 Immigrants often also bring things that will remind them of their homelands. A Chinese family brought ashes from the wood-burning stove they used to cook their last meal at home; a Greek woman brought a night-blooming jasmine plant. Gifts from friends also occupy space in their bags: a refugee family from violence in Ghana brought beaded necklaces they had been given. Along with a few **E** documents, some photographs, and an x-ray proving that the father had been screened for tuberculosis, these were their only possessions.

Some people bring useful objects. A man who had worked casting metal escaped past armed Iron Curtain guards in Hungary with
50 a small tool of his trade in his pocket. He started his own foundry in the United States, and still uses the tool—and he won't let anyone else use it! The husband of the woman with the night-blooming jasmine brought his barber's scissors with him, and started his shop at the local railway station. Many immigrant families bring cooking utensils—woks, rolling pins, stainless-steel bowls—and favorite knives.

gifts from
home and
items that
remind
immigrants
of home

tools and
useful items

[1] **Koran:** the sacred book of Islam that contains the revelations of God to Mohammad.
[2] **Buddha:** (563? – 483? B.C.), the founder of the religion of Buddhism.

---

2. ◀ **REREAD** Reread lines 1–24. How does the subhead hint at the information in this section? Support your answer with explicit textual evidence.

The subhead indicates that the section is about the few belongings many immigrants bring when they come to the United States. The text explains that this was the case 100 years ago, and it is still the case. The text goes on to give examples of the items immigrants packed.

---

3. **READ ▶** As you read lines 25–56, continue to cite textual evidence.
- Underline the items that immigrants have brought with them.
- In the margin, note the categories the items fall into.

10

---

4. ◀ **REREAD** Reread lines 29–39. Why might immigrants bring religious items and photographs with them? What does the bulleted list of items reveal about the variety of religious items brought? Support your answer with explicit textual evidence.

The religious items help them preserve their faith. Photographs remind them of their past. The bulleted list tells you that people from different backgrounds come to the United States.

---

5. **READ ▶** As you read lines 57–71, continue to cite textual evidence.
- Underline the items that immigrants have brought with them.
- In the margin, note the types of items mentioned in each paragraph.

11

---

2. **REREAD AND CITE TEXT EVIDENCE** In lines 16–24, the author does not directly say why the man chose to bring the old toothbrush.

B **ASK STUDENTS** to cite text evidence that helps them infer why the man brought his old toothbrush with him. *Students may cite his having had the toothbrush in a labor camp (lines 16–17); and his having carved the toothbrush so he could hide it (lines 20–21).*

3. **READ AND CITE TEXT EVIDENCE**

C **ASK STUDENTS** what they can infer about the child from Cuba who chose to bring a bilingual edition of Shakespeare's *Hamlet* (lines 23–24). *Students may infer that the play meant something very special to the boy, and he could not part with it.*

Critical Vocabulary: principles (line 25) Ask students what kinds of things guide them in their daily lives. Then ask students to share their definitions of *principles*.

4. **REREAD AND CITE TEXT EVIDENCE** Have students draw conclusions about why immigrants would choose to bring items that remind them of home.

D **ASK STUDENTS** to cite additional text evidence in lines 40–47 that helps them conclude why certain, even unexpected, items remind immigrants of home. *In lines 41–42 the Chinese family brings the ashes from their last meal; in lines 42–43 a Greek woman brings a night-blooming jasmine plant; and in lines 44–45 refugees from violence in Ghana bring beaded necklaces.*

5. **READ AND CITE TEXT EVIDENCE**

E **ASK STUDENTS** to cite text evidence in lines 48–56 that help them to draw conclusions about the immigrants who brought useful items. *In lines 48–52, a Hungarian man brought the small tool of his trade in his pocket, started his own foundry, and still won't let anyone else use his tool; in lines 52–54 a man brought his own barber's scissors and later started his own local shop.*

items based on mistaken beliefs about the U.S.

Immigrants do not always know a lot about United States life; a Ukrainian family of refugees had four large duffel bags with them, packed tightly with bedding, which they had heard was expensive and
60   inferior in America.

Sentimental Journeys

Remembrances of old lives take up immigrant suitcase space, too. Things that have been in the family for a long time help new arrivals feel more at home, or at least less alone. Parents' or grandparents' wedding rings are seldom neglected. Other items may not seem so valuable. A man who was a doctor in Myanmar brought his diploma, even though he cannot practice medicine in the United States. A girl from China brought her bright yellow metronome, simply because it was special—none of her friends had one—and she now finds that, unlike when she was in China, she enjoys practicing the piano.
70   And of course, young children (and some not so young) can be counted on to bring a favorite teddy bear.

items with sentimental value

6. ◀ **REREAD AND DISCUSS** Reread lines 1–71. With a small group, discuss the structure of the article. How might a circle graph or a bar graph add to the information given in the article?

SHORT RESPONSE

Cite Text Evidence What conclusions can you draw about the items immigrants chose to bring with them to the United States? **Cite text evidence** from the article in your response.

Most of the items help immigrants bring parts of their old lives with them to their new home. Some remind them of home (photographs and family keepsakes), and some help them continue familiar ways of life (religious items and useful tools). Whatever the item, its role is to make an immigrant feel less alone and more at home in a new land.

12

TO CHALLENGE STUDENTS . . .

Ellis Island, which opened on January 1, 1892, in upper New York Bay, was the gateway for more than 12 million immigrants who entered the United States from 1892 to 1924. More than 40 percent of current Americans can trace their family history back to Ellis Island.

ASK STUDENTS to research Ellis Island to develop a deeper understanding of the immigrant experience. Have students research and explore the trip from Europe to the United States, the steps immigrants had to go through once they reached Ellis Island, and what awaited immigrants once they passed their inspections and left Ellis Island.

DIG DEEPER

With the class, return to Question 2, Reread. Have students share their responses.

ASK STUDENTS to cite the text evidence that led to their inferences about why the man brought the toothbrush with him.

- Have students explain their inferences about the man's attachment to his toothbrush. Point out that there is nothing directly stated, but that the fact he survived a Soviet political labor camp and managed to keep the contraband toothbrush hidden might explain its importance. It is perhaps as a symbol of his own survival.

ASK STUDENTS to return their answers to Question 2 and revise them based on their discussion.

---

6. **REREAD AND DISCUSS USING TEXT EVIDENCE**

F ASK STUDENTS to assign a reporter for each group to present its response. Were immigrants overwhelmed with loss when they left their homes? Were they filled with hope at the possibility of a new life? Or did they feel a mix of loss and hope?

FOR ELL STUDENTS Explain that a metronome is a device that musicians use to help them keep a steady beat.

SHORT RESPONSE

Cite Text Evidence   Students should:

- explain what feelings or characteristics might be revealed by the immigrants who chose to bring sentimental items.
- explain what feelings or characteristics might be revealed by the immigrants who chose to bring useful items.
- use text evidence to compare and contrast how groups of immigrants might respond to the experience of immigrating.

from *The Latehomecomer*

*my*SmartPlanner Create lesson plans and access resources online.

Memoir by Kao Kalia Yang

Why This Text?

As students encounter a greater variety of nonfiction texts, they will also encounter more complex descriptive language. This lesson guides students to recognize and study the impact of imagery and figurative language.

Key Learning Objective: The student will be able to analyze imagery and figurative language to better understand a memoir.

For practice and application:

Close Reader selection
"Museum Indians,"
Memoir by Susan Power

COMMON CORE — Common Core Standards

RL 4 Determine the meaning of words and phrases.

RI 1 Cite textual evidence.

RI 2 Determine central idea; summarize.

RI 3 Analyze how a text makes connections through comparisons.

RI 4 Determine the meaning of figurative language; analyze the impact of allusions.

RI 5 Analyze structure.

RI 8 Evaluate claims in a text.

W 2 Write informative/explanatory text to examine a topic.

W 7 Conduct short research projects.

W 8 Gather information from print and digital sources.

L 1b Form and use verbs in the active and passive voice.

L 3a Use verbs in the active and passive voice.

L 4b Determine or clarify meaning using common Latin affixes.

L 4d Verify word meanings in a dictionary.

L 6 Acquire and use grade-appropriate general academic vocabulary.

Text Complexity Rubric

Quantitative Measures

from *The Latehomecomer*
Lexile: 1030L

Qualitative Measures

Levels of Meaning/Purpose

multiple levels of complex meaning

Structure

one consistent point of view

Language Conventionality and Clarity

figurative, less accessible language

Knowledge Demands

complex or sophisticated theme

Reader/Task Considerations

Teacher determined
Vary by individual reader and type of text

CLOSE READ

Background Have students read the background and information about the author. Tell students that the word *latehomecomer* comes from a German word used to describe the Jews who returned from World War II concentration camps to homes that were no longer there. Yang felt the Hmong people were in a similar situation as refugees from China, Laos, and Thailand who hoped they had finally found a home in the United States.

SETTING A PURPOSE Direct students to use the Setting a Purpose question to focus their reading. Tell students to generate questions as they read.

Analyze the Meanings of Words and Phrases

COMMON CORE — RI 1, RI 4

(LINES 9–15)

Point out that authors use vivid language and imagery to help readers picture a scene. Explain that **imagery** is a description that appeals to the senses of sight, sound, smell, feeling, or touch. These sensory images make a setting or scene more memorable for readers.

Ⓐ **CITE TEXT EVIDENCE** Tell students to reread lines 9–15 and identify the sense or senses Yang's description appeals to. What is the effect of her description? *(The description appeals to the sense of sight: colors chipping, sloping porches, a small patch of green. The description emphasizes the family's economic situation: They have been looking for a house for six months, yet a house in this condition appeals to them.)*

Background *The Hmong (hmông) are an ethnic group from southern China, Laos, Vietnam, and Thailand. In the 1970s, war and conflict caused many of the Hmong people in Laos to flee to refugee camps in Thailand. Author **Kao Kalia Yang** (b. 1980) was born in one of these camps. She moved with her family, including her older sister Dawb, to Minnesota in 1987. Four other siblings were born in the United States, where all the Yang children received their educations.*

from

The Latehomecomer

Memoir by Kao Kalia Yang

SETTING A PURPOSE As you read, notice the challenges and the opportunities that life in a new country presents Kao Kalia Yang and her family. How does Yang react to her situation?

W̲e had been in America for almost ten years. I was nearly fifteen, and Dawb had just gotten her driver's license. The children were growing up. We needed a new home—the apartment was too small. There was hardly room to breathe when the scent of jasmine rice and fish steamed with ginger mingled heavily with the scent of freshly baked pepperoni pizza—Dawb's favorite food. We had been looking for a new house for nearly six months.

It was in a poor neighborhood with houses that were
10 ready to collapse—wooden planks falling off, colors chipping away, sloping porches—and huge, old trees. There was a realty sign in the front yard, a small patch of green in front of the white house. It was one story, with a small open patio and a single wide window framed by black panels beside a black door. There was a short driveway that climbed up a

Ⓐ

(c) ©Houghton Mifflin Harcourt; (tr) ©Der Yang

The Latehomecomer **53**

Close Read Screencasts ▶ *View It!*

Modeled Discussions

Have students click the *Close Read* icons in their eBooks to access two screencasts in which readers discuss and annotate the following key passages:

- Yang's growing awareness that she is changing (lines 124–131)
- issues surrounding the need for members of Yang's family to become American citizens (lines 272–280)

As a class, view and discuss at least one of these videos. Then have students pair up to do an independent close read of an additional passage—Yang's recovery from her illness (lines 447–462).

Analyze Text: Memoir

COMMON CORE **RI 1, RI 3**

(LINES 16–25)

Explain that Yang's **memoir** is the true story of her life with a focus on her personal experiences and observations about people or events. To help readers relate or understand, Yang often compares her life to familiar situations. Tell students that an **allusion** is an indirect reference to a famous person, place, event, or literary work. As needed, explain that Laura and Mary Ingalls were characters in *The Little House in the Big Woods*, a classic story about an American pioneer family.

B CITE TEXT EVIDENCE Have students reread lines 16–25 to examine Yang's comparison of her family's situation to that of a pioneer family. What does the comparison reveal about her? *(She is excited about living in a house "that belonged to storybooks." Yang is probably an avid reader.)*

SCAFFOLDING FOR ELL STUDENTS

Analyze Language Using a whiteboard, project Yang's description of her family's search for a home. Invite volunteers to mark up lines 35–45.

- Highlight in yellow words that are synonyms for *home*.
- Highlight in blue words that are synonyms for *big*.
- Highlight in green synonyms for *street*.

ASK STUDENTS what Yang reveals about the family's search for a house with this description. *(The description suggests that the search has been extensive.)*

B little hill. No garage. It looked out of place in the east side of St. Paul. In fact, it looked out of time. The house should have been on the prairie, in the early days of Minnesota. It looked like it belonged to Laura and Mary Ingalls and a time
20 when girls wore cotton skirts with little flowers and bonnets to keep the sun away and carried pails with their sandwiches inside. The team of two old trees in the front yard dwarfed the house. From the car, my imagination took flight. I never thought I would get a chance to live in a house that belonged to storybooks.

I asked my mom, "Are you sure this is only $36,500?"

"It was really $37,000 on the paper, but Dawb asked the man to lower the price for us, and he agreed."

"It looks like at least $70,000 to me."
30 I couldn't wait to get out of the car. We had been looking for houses a long time—some we had liked well enough; most we couldn't afford. Now, this one that looked like a real antique, was only $36,500. The deal was incredible. It felt like a miracle.

Together, we had scoured the city looking for a suitable home. My mother, father, and Dawb in the front, and the rest of us in the back, all our knees touching. We had looked all summer long, driving up and down the avenues, the corridors, the smaller streets, and the busy thoroughfares of St. Paul.
40 On days of fruitless hunting, my father would drive us past the mansions on Summit Avenue for inspiration. We were awed and discussed the merits of owning the structures before us, humongous and intimidating, haunting and invincible. We marveled at the bricks and the green lawns and the ivy climbing up the walls and windows.

Dawb and I posed creative arguments for why owning such behemoths would never work for our family. These were the homes that we saw on television, the ones with the ghosts and the gun dramas, the ones with the 1980s movie stars and
50 their loose-fitting suits. These were the homes with the secret drug addicts and the eating disorders. We'd much rather live in places where men carried beverages in brown bags and walked lopsided up and down the sidewalks and a child could kick an empty beer bottle just as conveniently as a rock. We had fun with our talk, but sometimes Mom and Dad got annoyed. These houses were supposed to inspire us to work extra hard in school.

We had looked all summer long, driving up and down the avenues, the corridors, the smaller streets, and the busy thoroughfares of St. Paul. On days of fruitless hunting, my father would drive us past the mansions on Summit Avenue for inspiration. We were awed and discussed the merits of owning the structures before us, humongous and intimidating, haunting and invincible.

The small house before us would work. It would be our first piece of America, the first home we would buy with the money our parents earned. We were full of eagerness. Some of our cousins had purchased houses already; others were looking, just like us. It felt like we were joining the future with the past, our dreams and our lives coming together. This would be the home that the children would dream about for years to come.

Up close, we could see that the wood of the house was falling apart in places. White paint had been applied to the parts where the old paint had chipped. The floor of the porch was rotting. The black panels on either side of the window made it look bigger than it was. But that afternoon there was a feeling like the house was special, like it would be ours for a long time. I walked through the front door, into a space that was small, like an elevator. Then I made a left and entered our first home in America: 437 East York Avenue.

The house had the simplest design I had ever encountered. After the elevator-sized reception area, there were three bigger rooms all connected, each with a small bedroom to the right. There was a single bathroom in between the second and third bedrooms. The first room was a designated living room. The second was an "anything-you-need-me-to-be" room (that would be used to full capacity as bedroom, playroom, study room, and eating room). The third was a kitchen with enough room in the center for a round dining table (a remnant of the old owners). Off the kitchen there was a door leading to an enclosed porch area that my father liked because there was an old pencil sharpener nailed into the wall. The realtor had said that the sharpener still worked. Also off the kitchen there was a small room with just enough space for a washing and drying machine and the **requisite** heavy-duty sink. The total area of the house was 950 square feet, and it was built in 1895. It was called a two-and-a-half bedroom house because the middle room had no closet. The entire structure smelled old, like the thrift shops we were frequenting less and less.

My mother and father were in disagreement over the house. My mother kept on hoping for better. My father's position was that we had to make do with what was before us. But they both felt that they could not afford better for us.

My father said, "We can hide from the rain and the snow in here."

requisite
(rĕk´ wĭ-zĭt) *adj.*
Something that is *requisite* is needed or essential.

C

D

CLOSE READ

Analyze the Meanings of Words and Phrases   COMMON CORE RI 4

(LINES 66–74)

Explain that a **simile** is a comparison of two unlike things using the words *like* or *as*. As Yang continues to describe the house, she uses a familiar comparison to give readers a sense of its size.

C **ASK STUDENTS** to reread lines 66–74 to identify the simile Yang uses to give a first view inside the house. What is the effect of her comparison? *(Yang says that the entrance to the house "was small, like an elevator." It suggests a confined or claustrophobic feeling, especially in light of the "humongous" homes mentioned in line 43.)*

Yang uses another simile in lines 92–93 to complete her description of the house.

D **ASK STUDENTS** to reread lines 92–93 to identify the simile Yang uses to give readers a final impression of the house. What does this comparison suggest about the house? *(Yang says that the house "smells old, like the thrift shops." The comparison reinforces the idea that the house is rundown, used, and perhaps cheap.)*

CRITICAL VOCABULARY

requisite: Yang's description of the house takes readers from room to room and reveals what she finds most important in the house.

ASK STUDENTS to explain why a heavy-duty sink would be a requisite part of a laundry area. *(The sink might be used to soak heavily soiled items before washing, or to drain water from the washing machine.)*

Analyze the Meanings of Words and Phrases

  COMMON CORE **RI 4**

(LINES 101–107)

Point out that **repetition,** the use of the same word or phrase more than once, is often used to emphasize specific ideas.

E **ASK STUDENTS** to reread lines 101–107 to identify a repeated word or phrase. What idea or feeling does the repetition emphasize? *(someday; The repetition creates a hopeful feeling: the family is moving to a rundown house in a poor neighborhood, but they have hope that their lives will improve "someday.")*

Analyze Text: Memoir

  COMMON CORE **RI 3**

(LINES 124–133)

Draw attention to Yang's efforts to fit into the world around her despite the inner turmoil she is feeling.

F **ASK STUDENTS** what Yang means when she says that she "pushed against the skin that contained" her. *(Possible answer: She is growing and changing, while still trying to maintain the life and relationships she has always known.)*

---

100   "Ah-huh," we answered in various octaves.

"Someday maybe we can do better."

E We all knew he was referring to education. Someday when Dawb and I became educated, and the kids grew up and did well in school too, and my mother and father no longer had to work so hard just to get enough food and pay the heating bill. That is the someday my father was waiting for. It was the someday we were all waiting for.

We moved into the house in the fall, my first year of high school. Dawb was already attending Harding High

110   School, an inner-city school where nearly fifty percent of the student body was multicultural—many of whom were Hmong. Naturally, I would attend Harding with her. She had helped me choose my classes; I would take all the International Baccalaureate classes that I could get into, and where I couldn't, I'd take the advanced placement or college prep courses. I had gone to a small junior high school, a math and science magnet, in a white neighborhood with few Hmong kids. There I had done well in my classes; I discovered a formula I thought quite sacred: do the homework, go to class

120   every day, and when in class, follow the teacher with your eyes. I was still whispering in school, but the teachers took it in stride. I felt ready for the life changes that high school would bring my way.

F I was feeling a strong push to reinvent myself. Without my realizing, by the time high school began, I had a feeling in the pit of my stomach that I had been on simmer for too long. I wanted to bubble over the top and douse the confusing fire that burned in my belly. Or else I wanted to turn the stove off. I wanted to sit cool on the burners of life, lid on, and

130   steady. I was ready for change, but there was so little in my life that I could adjust. So life took a blurry seat.

I knew that the parameters of our life would continue, but I pushed against the skin that contained me. There would be school or work during the day and then a return to the children and babysitting. The drama of a changing body had taken me by surprise but had taken care of itself smoothly. … Dawb drove around the block, often with me beside her in the passenger seat. We were both growing up, we were big sisters, and we took care of the children, and my mother and

140   father were convinced of our status as good daughters with good grades. High school was important because it meant

56   Collection 1

APPLYING ACADEMIC VOCABULARY

reaction	relocate

As you discuss the memoir, incorporate the following Collection 1 academic vocabulary words: *reaction* and *relocate*. Invite students to discuss what it will mean to the family to **relocate** to a new home. Discuss Yang's **reaction** to the house, as well as that of her parents.

that we were closer to college. It did not **resonate** in my family that high school was a time to be young or to be old or that it was a time to sneak peeks into different worlds. Such ideas hit against the closed lids of my consciousness.

resonate
(rĕz´ ə-nāt´) *v.* When ideas *resonate*, they have a great effect or impact.

Dawb and I had decided long before that when the time came, we would strive for the University of Minnesota. We were hearing of Hmong doctors and lawyers, both men and women, all excelling in America, building successful lives
150 for themselves, their mothers and fathers, grandmothers and grandfathers. I had never actually met a Hmong doctor or lawyer, but they had clan names I recognized as clearly as I did my own: Vue, Thao, Vang, Xiong, Lee, Lor, Moua, Cha, Hang, Chang, Khang, Her, Chue, Pha, Kong, and Khue. Dawb and I wanted to add to the success of our clan in this growing list of Hmong people who had made lives for themselves and their families in America. We wanted to make the life journeys of our family worth something. Our ambitions had grown: we contemplated changing not simply our own lives but the lives
160 of poor children all over the world. And the key, we believed, was in school. But how far we could strive in school was unknown. We didn't tell anyone about our secret dreams.

Dawb had teachers who supported her all the way through. She had the kind of intelligence that a teacher could

©PhotoLink/Photodisc/Getty Images

CLOSE READ

Analyze the Meanings of Words and Phrases

 COMMON CORE **RI 4**

(LINES 154–162)

Guide students to notice Yang's hopes for the future in lines 154–162.

G **ASK STUDENTS** to reread lines 154–158. What does Yang's statement that she and her sister "wanted to make the life journeys of our family worth something" suggest about their views of their roles in the Hmong community? *(Possible answer: They believe their success will reflect well on the entire Hmong community, and make their family's struggles worthwhile.)*

CRITICAL VOCABULARY

resonate: Yang is explaining her family's view of the high school years in comparison to what many adolescents experience.

ASK STUDENTS why an idea that does not resonate in Yang's family would have a great impact on her. *(For many, adolescence is a time to experiment or test limits. For Yang, it is simply a step closer to college.)*

Analyze Text: Memoir

 COMMON CORE RI 3

(LINES 163–172)

Tell students that in a memoir, authors often compare themselves to others. While Yang has always compared herself to her older sister Dawb, she begins to recognize her connection to a high school English teacher.

H **ASK STUDENTS** what Yang means when she says that in comparison to her sister she "was lost." *(Dawb is a good student who understands how to use what she learns, while Yang has difficulty expressing herself and connecting what she learns in school to real life.)*

Analyze the Meanings of Words and Phrases

 COMMON CORE RI 4

(LINES 171–193)

Guide students to recall the author's earlier allusion to *The Little House in the Big Woods*. Point out that the author makes a second reference to works of literature in lines 174–175.

I **ASK STUDENTS** what the fact that Yang connects key events in her life to works of literature suggests about her. *(Possible answer: It suggests that literature had a great impact on her as she was growing up.)*

H see (she looked every part the interested learner), could hear (her English had no accent), and could support (she soaked up information and processed it into her world for her use). I was lost, perpetually biting my lower lip: I didn't speak well or easily, and the link between what we were learning from books
170 and living in life was harder for my mind to grasp.

I In high school, this changed. I met a teacher who changed the way I saw myself in education. Her name was Mrs. Gallentin, and she opened up a possibility that I was special. She taught ninth-grade English, where we read *Romeo and Juliet* and *Nectar in the Sieve*, as well as other literary classics. I sat near the front of the class and absorbed the books. Mrs. Gallentin had a red face and a dry sense of humor. She had little patience for kids who giggled or were fussy in their seats—students who didn't pay close attention to lessons
180 and did not do their assignments on time. I had overly curvy, confident handwriting that was hard to read, and I did not have a computer, so reviewing my work was a slow process. She may have noticed me initially because of this, and her interest was compounded by both my silence and my serious approach to literature.

Mrs. Gallentin became impressed with me because I could tell the important parts of a book. I knew how to anticipate the questions on her tests. At first, I was convinced I could read her mind. But after a few thought experiments in class,
190 I realized I was picking up understanding from the books, not from her. It was in this class that I wrote my first real essay in response to the question: Is the story of Romeo and Juliet a story of love or lust?

It took me all night long to think about the essay. I had no personal experience with love, or lust. Some of my friends said that they were in love, but I was not convinced. The phone conversations they had with their boyfriends were mostly just listening to each other's breathing. After many false beginnings, I wrote about what mattered to me. I wrote about
200 the love I felt I knew: Love is the reason why my mother and father stick together in a hard life when they might each have an easier one apart; love is the reason why you choose a life with someone, and you don't turn back although your heart cries sometimes and your children see you cry and you wish out loud that things were easier. Love is getting up each day and fighting the same fight only to sleep that night in the same

---

Strategies for Annotation ✏️ 🖥 *Annotate it!*

Analyze Text: Memoir **COMMON CORE** RI 3

Have students locate lines 167–174. Encourage them to do the following:

- Highlight in blue the words that describe what Yang was like before she started high school.
- Highlight in green the words that describe the ways in which Yang changed after she began high school.

Guide students to continue the annotation process as they read more about the teacher's impact on Yang's life.

> I was lost, perpetually biting my lower lip: I didn't speak well or easily, and the link between what we were learning from books and living in life was harder for my mind to grasp.
>
> In high school, this changed. I met a teacher who changed the way I saw myself in education. Her name was Mrs. Gallentin, and she opened up a possibility that I was special.

bed beside the same person because long ago, when you were younger and you did not see so clearly, you had chosen them.

I wrote that we'll never know if Romeo and Juliet really loved because they never had the chance. I asserted that love only happened in life, not in literature, because life is more complex. As soon as I wrote the essay, I started worrying about it—what if she didn't like it, what if she didn't agree, what if I had it all wrong. That was my first understanding of how writing worked, how it mattered to the writer, personally and profoundly.

I had written the essay out by hand first. I stayed up all night typing the essay on our gray typewriter at the dining table (it was the only surface in our house that was steady enough for us to really spread out our books and papers), slowly, with my index fingers (mistakes were costly). The sound of slow keys being clicked, first the right and then the left, eyes looking from keyboard to the page. Flexing careful fingers every few minutes. Trying to find a rhythm and a beat in the clicking of the keys, the mechanical whirl at the end of each line, the changing of paper. It took me a long time to think it through and follow the letters to the words, but the writing calmed something inside of me, it cooled my head: like water over a small burn in the pit of my mind. I watched eagerly as the third then fourth then fifth page filled with typed letters.

My mother and father came home early in the morning. They had changed their work schedules entirely to the graveyard shift (the **nominal** increase in their wages was necessary to maintain the new house). They saw my eyes closing over my work and became convinced that I was their hardest working daughter. My heavy eyes followed the way they walked so tired around the kitchen, and I grew confident that I really did know love—that I had always known it. By morning, the exhausting work of writing was done. I turned it in to Mrs. Gallentin.

Mrs. Gallentin caught me in the hall later that day and said that my essay was beautiful. She said that I wrote more than an answer to the question; I was telling her the ways in which questions come from life and end in life. I had never thought of myself as a good writer. I liked stories, and in elementary school I had written gory tales about intestines coming out. I thought I was good at math and science (what my junior high

nominal

(nŏm´ ə-nəl) *adj.*
Something that is *nominal* is small or insignificant.

CLOSE READ

Analyze Text: Memoir

 COMMON CORE RI 1, RI 3

(LINES 199–216)

Point out that in this part of the memoir, Yang compares Shakespeare's classic love story to her own experiences and observations.

J CITE TEXT EVIDENCE Have students reread lines 199–216 to find language that shows her parents persevering through hardships. Why does Yang believe that her parents are a better example of love than Romeo and Juliet? *(Possible answers: "might each have an easier one apart," "your children see you cry," "because long ago, when you were younger and you did not see so clearly, you had chosen them." Her parents stayed together even when their lives became difficult, something Romeo and Juliet "never had the chance" to do.)*

CRITICAL VOCABULARY

nominal: Yang is explaining why her parents are working a nighttime, or graveyard, shift.

ASK STUDENTS what it reveals about the family's economic situation that the parents would work through the night for a nominal increase in their wages. *(The family is struggling; even a small additional amount of money will help them make ends meet.)*

TEACH

For more content and historical background, students can view the video "Laos" in their eBooks.

Analyze the Meanings of Words and Phrases

 RI 4

(LINES 275–285)

Draw attention to the explanatory footnote that follows line 285. Guide students to connect the Hmong's role in the Vietnam conflict to their subsequent lives as refugees.

K **ASK STUDENTS** to reread lines 275–285. What is the impact of Yang's metaphor about the lives lost during the Vietnam War? *(The metaphor shows the suffering of the living as well as their sorrow for those who died.)*

CRITICAL VOCABULARY

recap: Yang wants to share her experiences with her grandmother.

ASK STUDENTS what the need to recap her understanding of recent events for her grandmother reveals about Yang and her family. *(Yang believes her immediate family's success reflects on her entire family, and that her grandmother will be proud. It may also suggest that there is not much communication with the grandmother in between visits.)*

---

school had been good at), but Mrs. Gallentin said that I had talent for literature. I didn't see it, but it pleased me to hear her say this. In the course of a semester, she opened up a real possibility that I could excel in high school and college because they were all about good reading and good writing.

I began to see a truth that my father had been asserting for a long time, long before America. In Ban Vinai Refugee Camp, I had sat on my father's shoulders, my hands secured in his hair, and I listened to him talk about how we might have a brother, how we would become educated, and how our lives would go places far beyond the horizons we saw—in America. I looked at our lives, and how could I not believe? Beyond all the spoken wishes, a dream had even come true: eight years into America and we owned a house of our own. I wanted to **recap** this journey with Grandma. I waited enthusiastically for her summer visit.

She didn't come.

In 1996, welfare reform was in the news. The program was ending. Families living on welfare had to learn how to work "within the system." This meant that my uncles in California could no longer farm on the side and raise their families with the help of the government. This meant that my grandma's sons were in danger. What's more, she herself could be at risk. She was not a citizen; there was no way she could pass the citizenship test or speak enough English to prove her loyalty, to pledge, "I will fight for America if it were ever in danger." It was fighting that all the Hmong in America had done with the lives that had fallen to the jungle floor, the spirits that had flown high into the clouds again, that had fled life and refused to return—despite all the urgings, the pleas, the crying. But we were refugees in this country, not citizens. It was not our home, only an asylum. All this came crashing down.

In American history we learned of the Vietnam War. We read about guerilla warfare and the Vietcong. The Ho Chi Minh Trail and communism and democracy and Americans and Vietnamese. There were no Hmong—as if we hadn't existed at all in America's eyes.[1]

recap
(rē-kăp´) *v.* To *recap* an event is to retell or summarize it.

---

[1] **In American history . . . in America's eyes:** When the United States' war with Vietnam spread to neighboring Laos, Laotian Hmong people fought with the United States. After the war, Hmong people had to flee from the governments of Vietnam and Laos. These governments saw them as enemies.

WHEN STUDENTS STRUGGLE . . .

Point out the change in tone that begins on line 266, where Yang moves beyond events in her own life to historical events that have a wider impact. Guide students to notice that Yang is describing the effects of changes in laws, and draw attention to phrases such as "this meant" in lines 268 and 270.

Students may find it helpful to create a cause-and-effect graphic organizer to help them keep track of the new law's effect on Yang and her family.

And yet Hmong were all over America. An exodus from California began. Minnesota was softer in the process of change. Welfare programs would not be terminated as quickly. Measures would be taken to ensure that old people received their benefits. A bill was being considered that would allow veterans of the Vietnam War, Hmong with documents, to apply for citizenship, and take the examination in Hmong. There was crazy studying everywhere. Aunt and Uncle Chue hovered over pages that he read with his French accent as she tried to make out the letters of the alphabet one at a time, through her thick reading glasses.

My own mother and father questioned themselves out loud, "What if we try to become Americans and fail?"

On the phone, Grandma said, "Lasting change cannot be forced, only inspired."

For the Hmong, inspiration came in those that were born in this country, the ready-made Americans in our arms, the little faces of boys and girls who spoke Hmong with American stiffness.

We could not remain just Hmong any longer. For our children, we could not fail. We had to try, no matter what. Even if it meant moving. Thousands of Hmong families moved from the farming lands of California to the job

The Latehomecomer **61**

CLOSE READ

Analyze the Meanings of Words and Phrases
COMMON CORE RI 1, RI 4

(LINES 293–296)

As needed, explain that immigrants wishing to become citizens of the United States must take a test. They must demonstrate the ability to read, write, and speak English, as well as have an understanding of important events in U.S. history. In some cases, the immigrants are granted a waiver to take the test in a language other than English.

L **CITE TEXT EVIDENCE** Have students reread lines 293–296 to note the imagery Yang uses to describe her aunt and uncle's studying. What impression of them does Yang create? *(Yang uses words such as "hovered," "French accent," and "thick reading glasses" to describe the sights and sounds of their studying process. The image she creates shows the intensity and urgency of their studying.)*

Cause: → EFFECT

→ EFFECT

→ EFFECT

Analyze Text: Memoir

COMMON CORE RI 1, RI 3

(LINES 338–350)

Point out that in this part of the memoir, Yang compares her father's reaction to their situation to the feelings she has about their lives.

M **CITE TEXT EVIDENCE** Tell students to reread lines 338–350 to identify the difference in Yang's father's response and her own. How is Yang's reaction also different from her earlier feelings about their house? *(Yang's father expresses his sadness through his poetry and music: "carried love songs about the falling apart of a country" and "made music of the loneliness." Yang directs her anger at their living conditions: "could not see poetry in the mold that grew wild" and "our house, so cute on the outside, rotted on the inside." Earlier she saw the house as a sign of their success in America, while now it is just another element of their struggle.)*

CRITICAL VOCABULARY

repatriate: Yang describes why becoming American citizens is so important to her family: they have no other options.

ASK STUDENTS to explain why Yang's family does not wish to be repatriated to Laos. *(The conditions in Laos are still dangerous for Hmong people. People who returned to Laos "went missing," and children were killed.)*

chide: Yang is frustrated that she cannot do more to help her family's situation.

ASK STUDENTS what they learn about Yang's father when he chides her impatience. *(Her father believes their situation will improve if they are patient.)*

---

possibilities in Minnesota companies and factories. Aunt and Uncle Chue, despite their lack of English, studied for the citizenship exam, took it, failed, despaired, studied some more, and tried again. Eventually they succeeded, and they inspired my parents to try for citizenship, too. We had no more lands to return to. After nearly fifteen years, my family knew this. The camps in Thailand had closed. Hmong people there were **repatriated**, sometimes without knowledge, back into Laos. Families went missing in the process. Lives were lost. Children were killed. Ours were only beginning to raise their eyes to a country of peace, where guns at least were hidden and death did not occur in the scalding of grass or rains that drizzled death. We could not handle any more death. In wanting to live, we were willing to try becoming Hmong Americans.

A new chapter of our lives unfolded as we strived to become Americans. We sank our roots deep into the land, took stake in the ground, and prayed to the moon that one day the wind would carry us away from our old moldy house, into a new stronger home that could not be taken away, that would not fall down on us, that would hold us safe and warm.

Grandma and the uncles from California came to live with us in Minnesota. I felt caught in the larger context of being Hmong. We were only one family in the over two hundred thousand that lived in America. We all came from the same history. I burned for our stories, our poverty, and our cause. I was only in high school, and there was very little I could do. My father **chided** my impatient heart.

He said, "Patience is the slow road to success."

My father was a poet, and had a poet's heart. He carried love songs about the falling apart of a country. He made music of the loneliness in Thailand. He sang traditional song poetry about the earth grumbling and the sky crumbling, the leaves of the human heart fluttering all the while. I was his daughter, and I could not see poetry in the mold that grew wild on our walls—no matter how much my mother, Dawb, or I scrubbed, it never stopped, no matter how many layers of paint we applied. I couldn't understand why the Hmong people had to run for their children, how their children had to make lives, again and again, in different soils, to know belonging. Why it was that our house, so cute on the outside, rotted on the inside.

repatriate
(rē-pā′ trē-āt′) *v.* To *repatriate* people is to return them to the country in which they were born.

chide
(chīd) *v.* To *chide* is to scold or correct in some way.

Why couldn't Grandma live with us now that we were all in one state? Why couldn't she live with any of her sons permanently? Because their homes were small. Because at one home, her heart yearned for another, and because all their homes together could never be like the country of her home in Laos, in the imagination and the stories she told all of us. In the world we lived in, our grandma carried her bags from one house to the next, sharing all our beds.

All this made me sick. My stomach cramped, and I could 360 no longer eat. My bones hurt. I was tired. In the night, my heart squeezed itself, and I woke up incapable of crying the pain away. I remember one night, falling asleep looking at how the car lights from the street reflected on my wall. I could hear the pounding of my heart in my ears, very loud and deep, like a hollow cry from my chest. I felt like needles were twisting their way into my chest. I remember thinking that the pain was teasing me but realizing soon that it wasn't a joke. The air in my lungs caught in my throat. I struggled for escape, my hands reaching for my heart, beating frantically 370 within me. I remember trying to cry out but finding a lack of air, a thickening tongue. I kicked desperately on the hard wall. First one, then a sad two, a final three: thinking in red: Mom and Dad, help me, I'm dying. I'm Hmong and I'm your daughter and I'm dying in the room beside yours. The thoughts were on repeat. Sweat. I could feel it breaking out on my forehead. Skin: I could feel the cold settling in. Heaving inside of myself. My eyes growing tight in the darkness, light streaming in. The door opened, slamming with force against the wall. My mom and dad rushed to my side, and I remember 380 seeing myself twisting and turning, all out of color and out of breath, but still moving with nervous life. My father tried to hold me and I could hear my mom's voice panicking and Dawb running for the phone, and then I felt **expiration** come. I stilled. Air flowed in. My vision cleared. It was slowly over.

No ambulance was called. It was too fast. What seemed like forever was little more than five minutes on a dark Minnesota night. No one knew what happened. In the doctor's office, days later, I said: perhaps it was a heart attack. The doctor didn't think so: I was too young for a heart attack. 390 My mom and dad were eager to believe the doctor. We didn't want to pursue the idea, and so we came home happy that it was all over.

expiration
(ĕk´spə-rā´shən) *n.*
Expiration is the act of exhaling or breathing out.

CLOSE READ

Analyze the Meanings of Words and Phrases

COMMON CORE   RI 1, RI 4

(LINES 359–384)

Focus students' attention on Yang's vivid description of the onset of her illness.

N CITE TEXT EVIDENCE Have students reread lines 359–384 to identify words and phrases that help them to imagine what Yang is experiencing. What is the impact of similes such as "felt like needles were twisting their way into my chest"? (*Students may note phrases such as "incapable of crying the pain away," "eyes growing tight in the darkness" and "all out of color and out of breath." Yang's words help readers imagine her pain and her desperation.*)

CRITICAL VOCABULARY

expiration: While in this context, Yang uses *expiration* to refer to breathing out, the word is more often used to describe an ending or conclusion, or even death.

ASK STUDENTS how both meanings of *expiration* are appropriate to Yang's situation. (*She is describing the effects of an illness that is making it difficult for her to breathe, but she is also describing a crisis that could have led to her death.*)

Analyze Text: Memoir

COMMON CORE RI 3

(LINES 428–430)

Tell students that Yang is comparing her illness to the history of the Hmong people.

 ASK STUDENTS what Yang's use of the word *murky* in line 429 suggests about the origins of the Hmong people. *(It suggests that the origins of the Hmong people are unclear, that like Yang's illness, it is not known exactly where they began.)*

CRITICAL VOCABULARY

despondent: Grandma's efforts to make Yang well again have been unsuccessful.

ASK STUDENTS whether Grandma is overreacting to Yang's illness. Why or why not? *(She is not overreacting. Neither traditional Hmong cures nor modern medicine are helping Yang. It is natural that she feels discouraged or helpless.)*

In the month that followed, I lost twenty pounds. The doctors didn't know what was wrong. My mother and father hovered over me. My siblings watched me grow pale and weak; the bones on my hips jutted out, and the bags under my eyes took permanent residence.

Was I making myself sick? Looking for fundamental changes in my life? I loved the children, and I was happy to

400 take care of them after school. All this time, I had been feeling like I was pushing against my skin: was it possible that I was pushing against my very own heart? The idea was a little preposterous. I didn't really believe it, but it nudged at me. But if indeed my heart did need changing, then what part of it? There was a clear division: the Hmong heart (the part that held the hands of my mom and dad and grandma protectively every time we encountered the outside world, the part that cried because Hmong people didn't have a home, the part that listened to Hmong songs and fluttered about looking for

410 clean air and crisp mountains in flat St. Paul, the part that quickly and effectively forgot all my school friends in the heat of summer) or the American heart (the part that was lonely for the outside world, that stood by and watched the fluency of other parents with their boys and girls—children who lingered in the clubs and sports teams after school waiting to be picked up later by parents who could—the part that wondered if forgetting my best friends to life was normal and necessary). My body was surely whole. The doctors said so. What was broken in me must be something doctors couldn't see.

420 I worried. The more I thought about it, the sicker I became: how does one change what one is becoming?

My grandma worried over me. She tried calling my spirit home. My rebellious, independent spirit hated the moldy house and refused to return. She tried her healing herbs. Their smell and taste took my soul far away to Thailand, to other times and places, but could not locate me in the present. Grandma grew **despondent**.

Something was wrong inside me, and its location was murky, like the origins of the Hmong home long, long ago and

430 far, far away.

despondent
(dĭ-spŏn´ dənt) *adj.*
Someone who is
despondent feels
a loss of hope or
confidence.

CLOSE READ

One day, I lay on the sofa—another day absent from school (my grades were dropping slowly)— looking up at the wall. Grandma and Dawb had gone shopping. My mother was in the kitchen preparing rice porridge for me. I heard the key in the lock. I heard them come in. I turned and saw that my grandmother had a gift for me.

There was something glittery in her hands. Her uneven gait came closer. She presented a thin silver bracelet made of elephants, bigger mother ones and smaller baby ones, circling
440 together, tusks entwined. It was the most beautiful gift anyone had ever gotten me. She told me that the man at the store had taken off a few of the elephants to fit my small wrist. Grandma put the bracelet on me and said, "Elephants protect their babies by forming a circle around them. You are sick, and I cannot protect you. I bought this for you so that the power of the elephants will protect you and make you well again."

I wore the bracelet every day. I started to eat a little bit of food and took the medicines the doctors gave me (after all of the tests and retests, the doctors said that baby lupus
450 would explain my symptoms). I wore the bracelet and grew stronger in its hold. The idea of a divided heart slowly lost merit: if there was no resolution that I could willingly and happily pick, then why not just live with it? Isn't this how all

Analyze the Meanings of Words and Phrases

COMMON CORE RI 1, RI 4

(LINES 437–451)

Tell students that a **symbol** is an object that stands for something beyond itself. Explain that the bracelet Grandma gives Yang becomes a symbol of the protection and healing that Grandma has not been able to provide.

P CITE TEXT EVIDENCE Tell students to reread lines 437–451 to note Grandma's explanation of why she chose the elephant bracelet. How does Yang emphasize her own weakness in comparison to the powerful protection of the elephants? *("Elephants protect their babies by forming a circle around them. You are sick, and I cannot protect you. … the power of the elephants will protect you and make you well again." Yang notes that the bracelet had to be made smaller to fit her wrist.)*

Strategies for Annotation   ✏️ 🖥️ *Annotate it!*

Analyze the Meanings of Words and Phrases

COMMON CORE RI 4

Have students locate lines 437–451. Encourage them to do the following:

- Highlight in yellow the words that describe the bracelet.
- Highlight in blue the words that describe the bracelet's purpose.
- Highlight in green the words that describe the elephants.

There was something glittery in her hands. Her uneven gait came closer. She presented a thin silver bracelet made of elephants, bigger mother ones and smaller baby ones, circling together, tusks entwined. It was the most beautiful gift anyone had ever gotten me.

Analyze Text: Memoir

 COMMON CORE RI 3

(LINES 463–467)

Point out that Yang compares her improving health to the weakening and eventual breaking of her bracelet.

Q ASK STUDENTS how they know that the bracelet continues to be a symbol to Yang, even after she begins to feel better. *(She keeps the bracelet even after it breaks, and she promises herself that she will have it repaired or recreated.)*

COLLABORATIVE DISCUSSION Have student partners list the experiences Yang describes in her memoir. As they discuss their opinions about which of those experiences had the greatest impact on her, remind them to cite evidence from the text to support their choice.

ASK STUDENTS to share any questions they generated in the course of reading and discussing the selection.

---

of life happens anyway? I looked at the glittering bracelet on my wrist and decided that a divided heart can be a good thing. One side can help the other. Why couldn't my chest expand to hold my heart? My father was always telling me that I needed to stiffen the walls of my heart, so it would not waver after the passage of people and places in my life. Maybe the 460 softness of my heart, which I thought would cushion whatever may come, had been my biggest weakness. I had the help of elephants. I wore the bracelet every day and felt better.

Q One day, the tusks of two elephants lost their hold on each other. I placed the bracelet in a small bag, and I promised myself that I would eventually put the tusks back together again. Or, if that was impossible, I would have another one made, just like it.

I grew well again, but I understood that my body, like every other body in the world, could die. It could be healthy or 470 not. If it carried life, then it could lose it. I was a child of war, and I should have known that we have no choice about when and where we die. When we do, we simply comply as bravely as we can. Getting up in the morning became harder than it had been. But each day, I did get up. That was the point. That had always been the point in the Hmong life, and even the American one. I grew satisfied with myself. Slowly, the sickness eased away.

COLLABORATIVE DISCUSSION Which of the author's experiences seems to have had the greatest effect on her? With a partner, discuss the reasons for your response. Cite specific evidence from the text to support your ideas.

TO CHALLENGE STUDENTS . . .

Analyze the Impact of Perspective Have students form small groups to discuss how the memoir might have been different if Yang had written about the events at the time they were happening rather than as an adult.

ASK STUDENTS to review the main events Yang describes. Which would a young person describe differently? In what ways would they be different?

Analyze the Meanings of Words and Phrases

COMMON CORE RI 4

Kao Kalia Yang conveys her family's situation by using language that creates striking images or suggests strong emotions. Her writing includes

- **imagery,** descriptions that appeal to the senses of sight, sound, smell, feeling, or taste to create an effect or evoke emotion
- **figurative language,** words and phrases that suggest meaning beyond the literal meanings of words themselves. Certain types of figurative language, such as similes and metaphors, can create comparisons between ideas that are otherwise unconnected.

	Definition	Example	Effect
imagery	vivid descriptions that appeal to one or more of readers' five senses	"... the scent of jasmine rice and fish steamed with ginger mingled heavily with the scent of freshly baked pepperoni pizza."	The scents suggest the mixing of Hmong and American cultures.
simile	a comparison of two unlike things using the words *like*, *as*, or *as if*	"I could hear the pounding of my heart in my ears, very loud and deep, like a hollow cry from my chest."	The comparison suggests the author's pain and implies a warning that it is serious.
metaphor	a comparison between two unlike things without the use of the words *like* or *as*	"We sank our roots deep into the land, took stake in the ground..."	Comparing the family to plants shows their strong desire to be part of America.

Find an example of each use of language in *The Latehomecomer*.

Analyze Text: Memoir

COMMON CORE RI 3

The Latehomecomer is a **memoir,** a true story of a person's life that focuses on personal experiences and observations about people or events. Memoirs often give readers insight into the impact of historical events on people's lives.

Yang shares her insights by making comparisons between the people or things she knows best and new ideas or feelings. For example, in lines 290–304, Yang reveals the frustrations of Hmong refugees seeking citizenship by comparing them to the Hmong children—like her own siblings—born in the United States.

What other comparisons does Yang make?

TEACH

CLOSE READ

Analyze the Meanings of Words and Phrases

COMMON CORE RI 4

Use the chart to focus students' attention on the terms presented in the lesson. *(Students may note the following examples from the selection: imagery: the team of two old trees in the front yard dwarfed the house (lines 22–23); simile: looked like a real antique (lines 32–33); metaphor: I had been on simmer for too long (lines 126–127).)*

Prompt students to discuss and define each term, asking them to provide additional examples of each from the selection and from their own experiences.

Analyze Text: Memoir

COMMON CORE RI 3

As needed, review that a comparison focuses on the ways in which two or more things are alike. Point out that comparisons may also imply the ways in which things are different. *(Students may note that Yang compares herself to her sister Dawb, or that she compares her parents' relationship to that of the title characters in Romeo and Juliet.)*

Strategies for Annotation 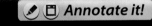 *Annotate it!*

Analyze the Meanings of Words and Phrases

COMMON CORE RI 4

Share these strategies for guided or independent analysis:

- Highlight in yellow examples of imagery.
- Highlight in blue examples of similes.
- Highlight in green examples of metaphors.
- Use a note to explain the effect of each example.

I could hear the pounding of my heart in my ears, very loud and deep, like a hollow cry from my chest.

> The metaphor "the pounding of my heart" compares the sound he hears to his own heart beating.

Analyzing the Text

 COMMON CORE — RI 1, RI 2, RI 3, RI 4, RI 5

Possible answers:

1. Yang has begun to see herself as an American. She feels a growing permanent connection to America and its culture, yet moving into a house that is old, small, and in disrepair suggests that it is not an end in itself. Yang will have to work hard to be successful.

2. Yang compares herself to a pot of boiling water to show that she's reached a turning point where something needs to change, either through a major shift (boiling over) or by accepting that she will stay the same (cooling off).

3. Yang uses the simile to acknowledge her strong need to write. Writing fulfills a need in her so intense she can almost feel it physically.

4. "I could feel the cold settling in" conveys the idea that Yang is near death, or believes she is dying.

5. The essay on Romeo and Juliet teaches Yang to write "about what mattered to me." It is "my first understanding of how writing worked, how it mattered to the writer, personally and profoundly."

6. Yang feels that she may be sick because her heart cannot accommodate both her Hmong heritage and her American feelings. As she begins to recover from her illness, she realizes that she cannot choose to be either Hmong or American because she is both: "The idea of a divided heart slowly lost merit: if there was no resolution that I could willingly and happily pick, then why not just live with it?"

7. Yang says, "I grew well again, but I understood that my body, like every other body in the world, could die." "Getting up in the morning became harder than it had been . . . I did get up. That was the point . . . in the Hmong life, and even the American one. I grew satisfied with myself."

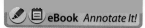 eBook *Annotate It!*

Analyzing the Text

COMMON CORE — RI 1, RI 2, RI 3, RI 4, RI 5, W 2, W 7, W 8

Cite Text Evidence   Support your responses with evidence from the text.

1. **Interpret** In lines 17–22, Yang uses an **allusion,** a reference to a famous person, place, event, or literary work. What does the reference to the characters from *The Little House on the Prairie,* a classic American children's book, suggest about how Yang has begun to see herself? How does the family's first house contribute to that self-image?

2. **Draw Conclusions** To what does the author compare herself in the metaphor in lines 124–131? Explain what the comparison shows about Yang's shifting feelings at this point in her life.

3. **Infer** The author says that writing "cooled my head: like water over a small burn in the pit of my mind." What does this simile explain about why Yang became a writer?

4. **Draw Conclusions** Read lines 359–384 to review the imagery the author uses to describe the onset of her illness. What idea or feeling does "I could feel the cold settling in" convey?

5. **Analyze** In the memoir, the author bases her essay on *Romeo and Juliet* on her own life experiences. What does this insight teach her about herself as a writer?

6. **Compare** In lines 398–421, what conflict does the author feel she is facing? How does she resolve that conflict?

7. **Analyze** How does the author's recovery from her illness change her?

PERFORMANCE TASK

 WriteSmart

Writing Activity: Report Research the Laotian Hmong's involvement in the Vietnam War, and explain how the relationship between the United States and the Hmong led families like the Yangs to immigrate to the United States.

- Use print or digital sources for your research.
- Identify why the United States recruited Hmong people for the war.
- Explain how and where the Hmong people lived after the war.
- Write a short report and share it with the class.

PERFORMANCE TASK

COMMON CORE — W 2, W 7, W 8

 Assign this performance task. WriteSmart

Writing Activity: Report Have students work in pairs to conduct their research. See page 70a for instruction in evaluating sources in research. Prompt students to locate the following information:

- Laotian Hmong were recruited to disrupt the Ho Chi Mihn Trail, a supply line in Laos.
- Many Laotian Hmong villages were bombed or burned, leaving the Hmong refugees.
- Refugee camps in Thailand were overcrowded and had no running water or electricity.
- The best-educated Hmong were allowed to immigrate to the United States first, and more immigrated as time passed.

Critical Vocabulary

requisite	resonate	nominal	recap
repatriate	chide	expiration	despondent

Practice and Apply Use what you know about the Vocabulary words to answer the following questions.

1. When might you explain that you have the **requisite** skills for a task?

2. If a new idea **resonates** with you, how might you react?

3. Does a new car cost a **nominal** amount of money? Explain.

4. Why might you **recap** an event for a friend?

5. Could you **repatriate** to another country? Why or why not?

6. How do you react to having a teacher **chide** you about your behavior?

7. What could you do to help someone who has difficulty with **expiration**?

8. What might you say or do for someone who is **despondent**?

Vocabulary Strategy: Using Latin Prefixes

Prefixes—word parts added to the beginning of a root or base word—often provide clues about the meaning of a word. For example, in the following sentence from *The Latehomecomer*, knowing that the Latin prefix *re-* usually means "again" or "back" helps you to understand the word *reinvent*. Yang wants to invent herself again, or have a new beginning.

> "I was feeling a strong push to <u>reinvent</u> myself."

When you encounter an unfamiliar word, follow these steps:
- Look for familiar word parts, such as prefixes.
- Identify the meaning of the prefix.
- Apply the meaning to define the word.

Practice and Apply Identify the *re-* word or words in the following sentences. Use the prefix meaning to define the word. Check a dictionary to confirm your definition.

1. Every Monday, my friends and I recap the weekend's events.

2. After the war, some Hmong people were repatriated back into Laos.

3. The family had to relocate after a fire destroyed their home.

4. Most students find it helpful to review a chapter before a test.

5. Getting new information can help to reform or rethink an opinion.

PRACTICE & APPLY

Critical Vocabulary

Possible answers:

1. *to prove that you should be accepted or allowed to do the task; for example someone might cite experience as a pet owner when applying for a job at a pet store*

2. *by being excited or moved in some way*

3. *no; new cars cost a great deal of money*

4. *if the friend missed the event*

5. *Students born in the United States cannot be repatriated, but it is possible for students who are immigrants.*

6. *by apologizing or promising not to repeat the behavior*

7. *Call for help from a doctor or other medical professional.*

8. *offer help or sympathy*

Vocabulary Strategy: Using Latin Prefixes

1. *recap: summarize or tell again*

2. *repatriated: go back to a country of birth*

3. *relocate: move or transfer*

4. *review: look again*

5. *reform: change ideas or form again; rethink: consider in a different way*

Strategies for Annotation ✐ 🖥 *Annotate it!*

Using Latin Prefixes

Have students locate the sentence containing the vocabulary word *recap* in line 263 of the selection. Encourage them to use their eBook annotation tools to apply the steps suggested in the activity:
- Highlight the prefix and think about its meaning.
- Use the prefix meaning and the meaning of the base word to define the prefixed word.

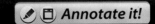

I wanted to recap this journey with Grandma. I waited enthusiastically for her summer visit.

Language Conventions: Active and Passive Voice

COMMON CORE L 1b, L 3a

Tell students that while active voice is generally preferred, there are situations in which passive voice is effective. Invite students to identify those situations as they read the text.

Answers:

1. *were affected; passive voice; subject receives the action; The Vietnam War affected the people of Laos.*

2. *changed; active voice; subject performs the action; Their country and their lives were changed forever by the war.*

3. *took; active voice; subject performs the action; Harsh actions were taken against the Hmong people.*

4. *were uprooted; passive voice; subject receives the action; The war and its aftermath uprooted the Hmong from their homes.*

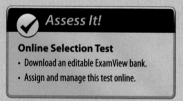

Assess It!

Online Selection Test
- Download an editable ExamView bank.
- Assign and manage this test online.

Language Conventions: Active and Passive Voice

COMMON CORE L 1b, L 3a

The **voice of a verb** shows whether its subject performs or receives the action expressed by the verb. When the subject performs the action, the verb is in the **active voice.** When the subject is the receiver of the action, the verb is in the **passive voice.**

	Definition	Examples	Use to...
Active Voice	• shows that a subject performs an action	• I walk. • She walked.	• emphasize the subject or actor • keep writing lively
Passive Voice	• shows that a subject is acted upon • uses helping verbs	• The dog is walked.	• emphasize the action • show that the doer is unknown or unimportant

A writer uses **active voice** to show that a subject performs the verb's action. In this example from *The Latehomecomer*, Kalia Kao Yang uses active voice to emphasize the role she and her sister had in the process of searching for a house:

> Dawb and I posed creative arguments for why owning such behemoths would never work for our family.

Writers use **passive voice** to show that a subject is being acted upon. Passive voice uses forms of *be* such as *am, is, are, was, were,* or *will be* to emphasize the receiver of the action, as in this example from *The Latehomecomer.*

> These houses were supposed to inspire us to work extra hard in school.

Practice and Apply Identify the voice of the verb in each sentence and tell if the subject performs or receives the action. Then rewrite the sentence in a different voice.

1. The people of Laos were affected by the Vietnam War.

2. The war changed their country and their lives forever.

3. New leaders took harsh actions against the Hmong people.

4. The Hmong were uprooted from their homes by the war and its aftermath.

Evaluating Sources

COMMON CORE
RI 8,
W 8

TEACH

Before students begin their research for the Performance Task, review the use of **credible,** or trustworthy, sources. Remind students that

- credible Internet sources often have the extensions *.org, .gov,* or *.edu*
- reference sources, such as dictionaries, encyclopedias, atlases, and almanacs are credible sources
- many newspapers and magazines are credible sources, but it is important to distinguish news articles from commentary or editorials that present opinions
- credible sources are those that are written by people who have expertise and knowledge with the topic

Guide students to identify sources that are not considered credible, such as blogs or other forms of social media.

PRACTICE AND APPLY

Work with students to develop a form or a short checklist that they can use to evaluate their sources as they conduct their research. The checklist should include:

Source:

Category: – Website – Print – Other

Author:

Author's background:

Why the source is credible:

 INTERACTIVE LESSON Have students complete the lessons within **Evaluating Sources.**

Figurative Language

COMMON CORE
RL 4,
RI 4

RETEACH

Review the terms *imagery, figurative language, simile,* and *metaphor.* Give simple examples of each, prompting students with relevant questions. For example:

The puppy's velvety ears brushed my arm while the puppy's cold, wet nose startled my hands.

- To which senses does this language appeal?
- What type of figurative language is this?

The puppy's fur was soft as velvet.

- What kind of comparison is this?
- Does it include the word *like* or *as*?
- What type of figurative language is this?

Follow a similar procedure for each type of figurative language.

 LEVEL UP TUTORIALS Assign the following *Level Up* tutorial: **Figurative Language and Imagery.**

CLOSE READING APPLICATION

Student partners can work together to apply the skill to another selection in Collection 1, or to a current magazine article.

Museum Indians

Memoir by Susan Power

Why This Text

Students may have difficulty understanding the difference between memoir and autobiography. Although there are similarities (both are written by the author about his or her life, with details drawn from memory as well as history), a memoir describes events in a very personal way. Sometimes, as in "Museum Indians," events will be described from a child's perspective. With the help of the close-reading questions, students will examine the author's use of language to convey details that, while true, are carefully chosen to create an emotional effect.

Background Have students read the background and information about the author. Point out that Power strongly identifies herself as a Dakota Sioux, but unlike her Great Plains ancestors, Power was raised in Chicago. Point out that this "contradiction" is a central theme of Power's writing. What fascinates her is the struggle to maintain her Sioux identity in light of the need to "fit in" and survive in today's world.

SETTING A PURPOSE Ask students to pay attention to the author's use of figurative language to describe the world she grew up in. Does her version of the events seem authentic? Is she able to tell her story from a child's perspective?

 Common Core Support

- cite textual evidence
- determine the meaning of words and phrases as they are used in a text, including figurative meanings
- analyze the impact of specific word choices on meaning, including allusions
- analyze a particular point of view in a memoir

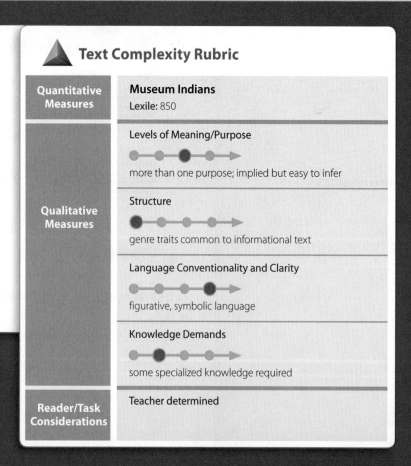

Text Complexity Rubric

Quantitative Measures	**Museum Indians** Lexile: 850
Qualitative Measures	**Levels of Meaning/Purpose** — more than one purpose; implied but easy to infer
	Structure — genre traits common to informational text
	Language Conventionality and Clarity — figurative, symbolic language
	Knowledge Demands — some specialized knowledge required
Reader/Task Considerations	Teacher determined

Strategies for CLOSE READING

Analyze the Meanings of Words and Phrases

Students should read this story carefully all the way through. Close-reading questions at the bottom of the page will help them to analyze how the author's word choices help set the tone and create meaning. As they read, students should jot down comments or questions about the text in the margins.

WHEN STUDENTS STRUGGLE . . .

To help students understand more about the world Susan Power wrote about in "Museum Indians," have them work in small groups to fill out a chart like the one shown below.

CITE TEXT EVIDENCE For practice in analyzing the figurative language the author uses in her observations and memories, ask students to cite text evidence for each point in the chart.

Figurative Language	Example	Effect
"A snake coils in my mother's dresser drawer; it is thick and black, glossy as sequins." (lines 1–2)	imagery	This description makes the reader "see" with a child's eyes.
"I am only half of her . . . in maturity [my braids] will look like tiny garden snakes." (lines 15–16)	metaphor	This shows how the narrator sees herself as less mature and not as strong as her mother.
"[W]hen I draw her picture in my notebook, she takes up the entire page." (lines 31–32)	personification/ symbolism	Here the narrator uses a drawing to represent the dominant role her mother had in her life.

Background *A member of the Standing Rock Sioux,* **Susan Power** *was born in 1961 and grew up in Chicago. She spent her childhood listening to her mother tell stories about their American Indian heritage. These stories later served as inspiration for Power's writing. As a young girl, Power made frequent visits with her mother to local museums—trips that inspired her memoir "Museum Indians."*

Museum Indians

Memoir by Susan Power

1. **READD** As you read lines 1–16, begin to cite text evidence.

- Underline a metaphor in the first paragraph that describes the mother's braid.
- Underline a metaphor in the second paragraph that describes the mother's braid differently.
- In the margin, note the adjectives the narrator uses to describe the braid.

CLOSE READ
Notes

(A) A snake coils in my mother's dresser drawer; it is thick and black, glossy as sequins. My mother cut her hair several years ago, before I was born, but she kept one heavy braid. It is the three-foot snake I lift from its nest and handle as if it were alive.

(B) "Mom, why did you cut your hair?" I ask. I am a little girl lifting a sleek black river into the light that streams through the kitchen window. Mom turns to me.

"It gave me headaches. Now put that away and wash your hands for lunch."

10 "You won't cut *my* hair, will you?" I'm sure this is a whine.

"No, just a little trim now and then to even the ends."

I return the dark snake to its nest among my mother's slips, arranging it so that its thin tail hides beneath the wide mouth sheared

thick
black
glossy

13

1. **READ AND CITE TEXT EVIDENCE** Point out that in this section the image of a snake is used to represent the mother's braid (lines 1–4). Explain that the narrator uses the snake metaphor again to refer to herself.

(A) **ASK STUDENTS** how the snake image in line 16 is used to underscore the idea that the narrator is "only half" of her mother. *Compared to her mother's braid (which she describes as a "3-foot snake" (lines 3–4), her own braids will be "tiny garden snakes" (line 16).*

by scissors. My mother keeps her promise and lets my hair grow long, but I am only half of her; my thin brown braids will reach the middle of my back, and in maturity will look like tiny garden snakes.

My mother tells me stories every day: while she cleans, while she cooks, on our way to the library, standing in the checkout line at the supermarket. I like to share her stories with other people, and chatter
20 like a monkey when I am able to command adult attention.

She likes to share her mother's stories to impress adults.

C "She left the reservation when she was sixteen years old," I tell my audience. Sixteen sounds very old to me, but I always state the number because it seems integral to my recitation. "She had never been on a train before, or used a telephone. She left Standing Rock to take a job in Chicago so she could help out the family during the war. She was petrified of all the strange people and new surroundings; she stayed in her seat all the way from McLaughlin, South Dakota, to Chicago, Illinois, and didn't move once."

I usually laugh after saying this, because I cannot imagine my
D 30 mother being afraid of anything. She is so tall, a true Dakota woman; she rises against the sun like a skyscraper, and when I draw her picture in my notebook, she takes up the entire page. She talks politics and attends sit-ins,[1] wrestles with the Chicago police and says what's on her mind.

The narrator sees her mother as being larger than life.

[1] **sit-ins:** organized protest demonstrations in which participants seat themselves in appropriate places and refuse to move; the act of occupying the seats or an area of a segregated establishment to protest racial discimination.

2. **REREAD** Reread lines 12–16. Explain what the narrator means when she says "I am only half of her." Support your answer with explicit textual evidence.

The narrator means that even as an adult, she will be only half the strong, proud woman her mother is. This idea is reinforced when she says her mother's hair is a "three-foot snake" while her own hair will look like "tiny garden snakes" when she matures.

3. **READ** As you read lines 17–34, continue to cite textual evidence.
- Underline a simile about the narrator, and in the margin, explain how it helps reveal the narrator's personality.
- Underline a simile about the mother, and in the margin, describe what it reveals about the narrator's view of her mother.

14

▲▲▲▲▲▲▲▲▲▲▲▲▲▲▲▲▲▲▲▲
" She is so tall, a true Dakota woman; she rises against the sun like a skyscraper. . . . "
▼▼▼▼▼▼▼▼▼▼▼▼▼▼

I am her small shadow and witness. I am the timid daughter who can rage only on paper.

We don't have much money, but Mom takes me from one end of the city to the other on foot, on buses. I will grow up believing that Chicago belongs to me, because it was given to me by my mother.
40 Nearly every week we tour the Historical Society, and Mom makes a point of complaining about the statue that depicts an Indian man about to kill a white woman and her children: "This is the only monument to the history of Indians in this area that you have on exhibit. It's a shame because it is completely one-sided. Children who see this will think this is what Indians are all about."

My mother lectures the guides and their bosses, until eventually that statue disappears.

Some days we haunt the Art Institute, and my mother pauses before a Picasso.[2]
50 "He did this during his blue period," she tells me.
I squint at the blue man holding a blue guitar. "Was he very sad?" I ask.
"Yes, I think he was." My mother takes my hand and looks away
E from the painting. I can see a story developing behind her eyes, and I tug on her arm to release the words. She will tell me why Picasso was blue, what his thoughts were as he painted this canvas. She relates anecdotes I will never find in books, never see footnoted in a

The narrator is outspoken only when writing, while her mother is strong, proud, and not afraid of speaking her mind.

[2] **Picasso:** Pablo Picasso (1881–1973), Spanish artist whose work is some of the most influential in modern art.

4. **READ** As you read lines 35–59, continue to cite textual evidence.
- Underline the text that reveals the mother's personality.
- Circle the text that reveals how the narrator sees herself.
- Make a note in the margin to explain the difference between the narrator and her mother.

15

2. **REREAD AND CITE TEXT EVIDENCE** Susan Power often reveals her characters through the use of symbol, metaphor, and analogy.

B **ASK STUDENTS** to review the mother's response to her daughter's question about her hair (line 5). How would you describe this response? What does it tell you about the mother? *Her braid personifies her heritage. She feels bad about cutting it off, and is defensive and irritated by her daughter's innocent question.*

3. **READ AND CITE TEXT EVIDENCE**

C **ASK STUDENTS** to review lines 21–28, in which the author describes the stories she told about her mother. Why would she have told these stories? *Students may suggest that the author is mythologizing her mother, emphasizing her uniqueness to make her seem larger than life.*

4. **REREAD AND CITE TEXT EVIDENCE** In lines 30–36, the narrator describes her mother as a skyscraper and herself as a shadow. Have students think about the relationship between a skyscraper and its shadow.

D **ASK STUDENTS** what this analogy suggests about the narrator's self-image. *She feels she is timid and dependent.*

FOR ELL STUDENTS Some Spanish-speaking students may be confused by the use of *lectures*, which is a false cognate for the Spanish word *lecturas* (readings). Clarify the meaning of *lectures* for them (in this context, a reprimand).

biography of the master artist. I don't even bother to check these references because I like my mother's version best.

(F) 60 When Mom is down, we go to see the mummies at the Field Museum of Natural History. The Egyptian dead sleep in the basement, most of them still shrouded in their wrappings.

"These were people like us," my mother whispers. She pulls me into her waist. "They had dreams and **intrigues** and problems with their teeth. They thought their one particular life was of the utmost significance. And now, just *look* at them." <u>My mother never fails to brighten. "So what's the use of worrying too hard or too long? Might as well be cheerful."</u>

intrigue:
a plot or scheme

Before we leave this place, we always visit my great-grandmother's
70 buckskin[3] dress. We mount the stairs and walk through the museum's main hall—past the dinosaur bones all strung together, and the stuffed elephants lifting their trunks in a mute trumpet.

The clothed figures are **disconcerting** because they have no heads. I think of them as dead Indians. We reach the traditional outfits of the Sioux in the Plains Indian section, and there is the dress, as magnificent as I remembered. The yoke[4] is completely beaded—I know the garment must be heavy to wear. My great-grandmother

disconcerting:
startling or upsetting

---

[3] **buckskin:** leather made from deerskin.
[4] **yoke:** a piece that supports the gathered parts of a garment.

---

5. **◄ REREAD** Reread lines 51–59. What does the narrator mean when she says "I can see a story developing behind her eyes" (line 54)? Support your answer with explicit textual evidence.

The narrator's mother is thinking of how to explain Picasso's painting. The narrator never sees these details about Picasso "in books" or "footnoted in a biography" so she knows her mother makes up the stories herself. However, they are more interesting than true stories about the artist would be.

6. **READ ▶** Read lines 60–79, and underline text that reveals the mother's outlook on life.

16

---

used blue beads as a background for the geometrical design, and I point to the azure expanse.

80 "Was this her blue period?" I ask my mother. She hushes me
(H) unexpectedly, she will not play the game. I come to understand that this is a solemn call, and we stand before the glass case as we would before a grave.

"I don't know how this got out of the family," Mom murmurs. I feel helpless beside her, wishing I could reach through the glass to disrobe the headless mannequin. My mother belongs in a grand buckskin dress such as this, even though her hair is now too short to braid and has been trained to curl at the edges in a saucy flip.

We leave our fingerprints on the glass, two sets of hands at
90 different heights pressing against the barrier. Mom is sad to leave.

"I hope she knows we visit her dress," my mother says.

There is a little buffalo across the hall, stuffed and staring. Mom doesn't always have the heart to greet him. Some days we slip out of the museum without finding his stall.

<u>"You don't belong here,"</u> Mom tells him on those rare occasions when she feels she must pay her respects. <u>"We honor you,"</u> she continues, <u>"because you are a creature of great endurance and great generosity. You provided us with so many things that helped us to</u>
(G) <u>survive. It makes me angry to see you like this."</u>
100 Few things can make my mother cry; the buffalo is one of them.

"I am just like you," she whispers. <u>"I don't belong here either. We should be in the Dakotas, somewhere a little bit east of the Missouri River. This crazy city is not a fit home for buffalo or Dakotas."</u>

She means that both of them belong on their ancestral land.

---

7. **READ ▶** As you read lines 80–110, continue to cite textual evidence.
• Underline what the mother says to the buffalo, and explain what she means in the margin.
• Circle text that reveals the narrator's feelings about the city.

17

---

5. **REREAD AND CITE TEXT EVIDENCE**

(E) ASK STUDENTS to find examples of the narrator's desire to accept an "alternate" version of the truth. *She says her mom "gave her" the city of Chicago; she prefers invented stories about Picasso.*

6. **READ AND CITE TEXT EVIDENCE**

(F) ASK STUDENTS to describe the mother's outlook on life. What text evidence supports or refutes this? *The mother tries to stay positive. Exhibits in the museum—the mummies, stuffed elephants, headless Indians—seem to undercut her positive outlook.*

Critical Vocabulary: intrigue (line 64) What examples of "intrigue" can students think of? *Students might mention news stories featuring schemes, secret deals, or cover-ups.*

Critical Vocabulary: disconcerting (line 73) Why were the mother and daughter "disconcerted" by the figures at the museum? *They had no heads.*

---

7. **READ AND CITE TEXT EVIDENCE** In line 99 the mother says to the buffalo, "It makes me angry to see you like this."

(G) ASK STUDENTS to find evidence that might explain her reaction. Why is she so angry when she sees the buffalo? *In line 101 she says, "I am just like you." She identifies with the buffalo: she feels dead, stuffed, and out of place in "this crazy city" (line 103).*

FOR ELL STUDENTS On this page there are several verbs that mean uttering soft sounds from your mouth, but that have different nuances. Demonstrate the differences between *hushing*, *murmuring*, and *whispering*.

I take my mother's hand to hold her in place. (I am a city child,) (nervous around livestock) and (lonely on the plains.) (I am afraid of a sky) (without light pollution)—I never knew there could be so many stars. I lead my mother from the museum so she will forget the sense of loss. From the marble steps we can see Lake Shore Drive spill ahead of us, and I sweep my arm to the side as if I were responsible for this view. I

110 introduce my mother to the city she gave me. I call her home.

8. ◀ **REREAD AND DISCUSS** Why does seeing the little buffalo make the mother cry? Discuss your thoughts with a partner.

SHORT RESPONSE

Cite Text Evidence Compare and contrast the personalities of the narrator and her mother. Review your reading notes, and be sure to **cite text evidence** in your response.

Both the narrator and her mother are American Indians, but the mother is tall, strong, and proud. Her daughter, the narrator, feels very small and timid beside her ("I am only half of her"). Although the mother keenly feels the loss of her traditional way of life, rooted in her ancestral lands in the Dakotas, the daughter feels at home in Chicago.

18

---

8. **REREAD AND DISCUSS USING TEXT EVIDENCE** In lines 81–83, the narrator likens standing before the glass case to standing before a grave. In what way is the glass case like a grave?

   Ⓗ ASK STUDENTS to discuss the comparison. What does the grave represent? Who died? *The headless Indians, empty buckskin dress, and stuffed buffalo represent a kind of spiritual death, the "death" of a culture.*

SHORT RESPONSE

Cite Text Evidence Students' responses will vary but should use text evidence to support their positions. Students should:

- explain how the personalities of the narrator and her mother are similar.
- explain how the personalities of the narrator and her mother are different.
- cite evidence to show how the mother's personality affected the way the narrator felt about herself.

TO CHALLENGE STUDENTS . . .

For more context and to deepen their understanding of the characteristics of memoir, students can look at some of the biographical information about Susan Power that is available online.

Have students note events in the author's life that seem most pivotal both professionally and personally, including background information about her parents, her upbringing, her education, and the writers that influenced her the most.

ASK STUDENTS to examine how Power used the real events of her life in her memoir. Which biographical details show up? Does reading about the author's life help students to better understand "Museum Indians"? Does it detract from their appreciation of its content?

DIG DEEPER

1. With the class, return to Question 3, Read. Have students share their responses to the question.

ASK STUDENTS to examine the way the author describes her mother.

• Throughout the story the narrator depicts her mother as larger than life. Have students review lines 29–34 and identify two images that show how big her mother seemed to her.

• Ask students to consider the stories the narrator told about her mother. Why did she tell these stories? Why did she need to "impress" people? Did she feel she had to "explain" her mother? What were the stories meant to illustrate?

2. With the class, return to Question 5, Reread. Have students share the results of their discussion.

ASK STUDENTS to consider the words and images the narrator uses to convey the mother's sense of loss.

• Have groups analyze the imagery used in the scene with the buffalo to depict the mother's grief. Groups should cite references to the "stuffed and staring buffalo," "headless mannequin," "grave," and "blue period."

• Have groups examine how hair is used as a symbol of cultural belonging in this story. Why do they think the mother cut off her braid? How does the narrator feel about her mother's short hair? Why did the narrator make her mother promise not to cut off her braids? How does the narrator use the image of a snake to compare her mother's braid to her own?

• Have groups find other instances in which the author conveys meaning through language and word choice, such as the narrator's characterization of herself as "nervous around livestock" and "lonely on the plains." How do these details underscore the difference between mother and daughter?

• Have groups explain the significance of the narrator's connection to the city of Chicago. How do her feelings for the city contrast with her mother's? Does this change the way the narrator perceives her mother?

ASK STUDENTS to return to their Short Response answer and revise it based on the class discussion.

CLOSE READING NOTES

New Immigrants Share Their Stories

Documentary

Why This Text?

Because documentaries share information along with the views and opinions of filmmakers, it is important for students to learn to analyze and evaluate the ideas that are presented. This lesson will guide students to evaluate a documentary about young immigrants in New York City.

Key Learning Objective: The student will be able to recognize the elements used in a documentary and understand and evaluate the purpose of each one.

 Common Core Standards

RI 1 Cite textual evidence.
RI 2 Determine main idea and details.
RI 3 Make connections.
RI 6 Determine an author's point of view and purpose.
RI 7 Determine the advantages and disadvantages of media.
SL 2 Analyze the purpose of information presented in diverse media.
SL 4 Present claims and findings in a focused manner.
SL 5 Integrate multimedia and visual displays into a presentation.
W 7 Conduct short research projects to answer a question.

▲ Text Complexity Rubric

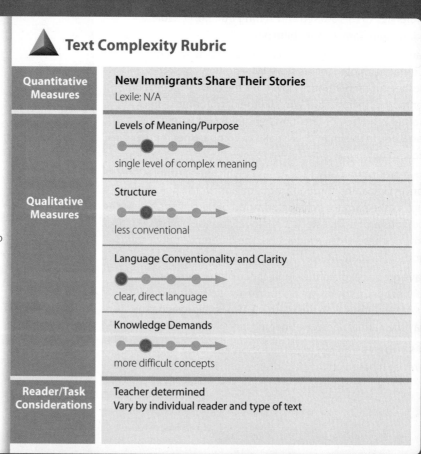

Quantitative Measures	**New Immigrants Share Their Stories** Lexile: N/A
Qualitative Measures	Levels of Meaning/Purpose — single level of complex meaning
	Structure — less conventional
	Language Conventionality and Clarity — clear, direct language
	Knowledge Demands — more difficult concepts
Reader/Task Considerations	Teacher determined Vary by individual reader and type of text

TEACH

CLOSE READ

Background Have students read the background about the Building Bridges project. Tell students that the documentary was made by Not in Our Town, an organization based in Oakland, California. For almost twenty years, its mission has been to guide, support, and inspire people and communities to work together to build safe, inclusive environments for all. Not in Our Town has completed many projects in an effort to achieve this goal. The documentary about the Building Bridges project was filmed in 2010.

SETTING A PURPOSE Direct students to use the Setting a Purpose information and prompts to focus their viewing. Remind them to generate questions as they view.

Background *A collaboration between two very different New York schools is at the heart of the Building Bridges project. Newcomers High School in Queens, New York, is dedicated to teaching recent immigrants, while St. Luke's is a private middle school in Manhattan where students have many advantages.*

MEDIA ANALYSIS

New Immigrants Share Their Stories

Documentary directed by Lisa Gossels

SETTING A PURPOSE Through letter writing, video diaries, and interviews, the English learners from Newcomers tell their personal immigration stories with support and encouragement from their St. Luke's "buddies." Together the students hope to change stereotyped ideas about immigrants, highlight their reasons for coming to America, and share their goals and dreams for the future. The documentary *New Immigrants Share Their Stories* chronicles the students' project.

As you view the film, pay attention to the interviews between the immigrant students and their "buddies." Listen to the questions asked and the answers given. Also watch the facial expressions and gestures of the individuals. Think about what you learn about the two groups from these conversations. Write down any questions you have as you view.

©The Working Group

SCAFFOLDING FOR ELL STUDENTS

Compound Words Guide students to recognize that *newcomer* is a **compound word,** a word that is formed from two smaller words. Explain that it is often possible to use the meanings of the smaller words to help define a compound word.

ASK STUDENTS to divide *newcomer* into its two smaller words. Discuss the meaning of each smaller word and guide students to define the compound word. Encourage students to follow a similar process when they encounter other compound words, such as *voice-over, filmmaker*, and *underlying*.

TEACH

CLOSE READ

As You View Tell students that they will be watching a documentary. Explain that a **documentary** is a nonfiction film that presents information about people or events. Point out that filmmakers combine visual and sound elements to convey information in documentaries. Have students read As You View to help them focus their viewing on the kinds of elements the director incorporated into the documentary, including interviews and video diaries.

Analyze Media
COMMON CORE **SL 2**

Explain to students that in this documentary, the director includes **interviews,** or conversations in which one speaker asks specific questions of another. The director also includes **video diaries**, which are video recordings that share a person's personal views and on-the-spot reactions over a period of time.

 ASK STUDENTS to watch the documentary to identify how the interviews and the video diaries are alike and different. *(They both tell about the lives of the students; interviews have the students answer questions about their lives; the students make video diaries to tell about their own lives; video diaries may include maps and photographs.)* Prompt students to discuss the filmmaker's purpose for including both types of footage. How do the two formats together present a more complete story? *(Possible answer: By their nature, video diaries present personal ideas and information that an individual finds important. The interviews reflect what someone else wants to know about the subject. Together, the formats provide a more complete view of the students.)*

COLLABORATIVE DISCUSSION Have students pair up and discuss the content of several interviews and video diaries. Then have them choose one that particularly affected them and share the concepts or ideas it conveys to viewers. Accept all reasonable responses.

ASK STUDENTS to share any questions they generated in the course of viewing and discussing the documentary.

Format: Documentary
Running Time: 7:47

AS YOU VIEW The documentary you are about to view includes interviews and video diaries. An interview is a conversation or dialogue in which one person, the interviewer, asks specific questions of another person, the interviewee. A video diary is a video recording that shares a subject's personal views and on-the-spot reactions over a period of time. In these video diaries, the individual featured narrates his or her own diary.

As you view the documentary, consider the director's choice of scenes, words, and images in the video diaries and interviews and how they work together to tell about the thoughts and lives of the students who have recently arrived in their new country.

COLLABORATIVE DISCUSSION Which of the student interviews and video diaries had the greatest impact on you? With a partner, discuss concepts or ideas people might learn from the students' conversations.

©The Working Group

APPLYING ACADEMIC VOCABULARY

immigrate	reaction

As you discuss the documentary, incorporate the following Collection 1 academic vocabulary words: *immigrate* and *reaction*. To probe responses to the personal stories, ask students how it might feel to **immigrate** to a new country. Ask them what kind of **reaction** they have to the Building Bridges project.

Analyze Media

COMMON CORE RI 7, SL 2

New Immigrants Share Their Stories is a **documentary,** a nonfiction film that presents, or documents, information about people or events. A documentary's **purpose** is the intent for which it is made: to inform, entertain, persuade, or express the feelings or opinions of the documentarian.

Documentary filmmakers use visual and sound techniques to present information in a way that meets their purpose and appeals to viewers. These techniques can include:

- **Voice-over**—the voice of an unseen commentator or narrator. The narrator explains or clarifies images or scenes shown on film and provides important new information. *New Immigrants Share Their Stories* uses several narrators, including an unidentified commentator and the teachers. In the video diaries, the students themselves are the narrators.
- **Stills**—images that are motionless, such as illustrations or photographs. Documentaries are composed mainly of moving images but often include stills. The students' video diaries include photographs from their years growing up in other countries.
- **Animation**—the process of creating images that appear to move and seem alive. *New Immigrants Share Their Stories* includes an animated graphic of travel across the globe.

Documentary filmmakers usually have a **motive,** or underlying reason for telling their story. The motive is why they feel the story is worth telling, and in telling it, they want to convey certain insights or angles on the subject. Here are some examples of motives and how they are revealed in a documentary.

Motive	How Motive Is Revealed
Social	Focus is on the interaction of people or on changing behaviors or attitudes
Commercial	Focus is on a product and encouraging viewers to buy it
Political	Focus is on support or opposition to government or laws

To **evaluate** a documentary, you examine the film's techniques and content to judge its value or worth. In evaluating, ask questions like these:

- What is the filmmaker's motive for making the film? How is the motive revealed?
- What techniques caught my interest? What made them effective?
- What is the main message of the film?

CLOSE READ

Analyze Media

COMMON CORE RI 7, SL 2

Guide students to relate elements and techniques used in "New Immigrants Share Their Stories" to the definitions and descriptions provided. Have students compare the different information that voice-over narration and interviews convey. *(The voice-over provides more general information about the project and what happened; the interviews provide more specific information about the students.)*

Draw attention to the list of questions for evaluating a documentary. Have students answer each question as it relates to "New Immigrants Share Their Stories." *(The filmmakers' motive is social: it is an effort to change attitudes toward immigrants. Students' ideas about effective techniques will vary. The film's main message is that immigrants have come to the United States for a variety of reasons and are willing to work hard to have a better life.)*

Ask students to point out reasons why a documentary is a good medium to use to present the information in "New Immigrants Share their Stories."

WHEN STUDENTS STRUGGLE...

To guide students' understanding of the information presented by the voice-over narration and the interviews, have pairs of students work together during another viewing of the film to list the different kinds of information provided in each format. Students can then use their lists to evaluate the purpose and effectiveness of the film.

Analyzing the Media

 RI 1, RI 2,
RI 3, RI 6,
RI 7

Answers:

1. *Possible answer: Sangjukta describes the discrimination she experienced because she is a girl. For example, she was not allowed outside alone and was required to stay inside and do housework. She shows photographs of herself as a young girl, of girls in an all-girl classroom, of boys in all-boy classroom and of her with a woman, probably her mother.*

2. *A social motive: their purpose is to lessen or eliminate bias and discrimination against immigrants; the central message is that getting to know immigrants personally will help Americans understand that they are thoughtful, responsible, intelligent people who contribute to society.*

3. *The filmmakers used narration, interviews, and video diaries. The interviews are effective because they help to make each immigrant's story personal.*

4. *The scenes students choose will vary; accept reasonable choices. The voice-over narration provides background and general information throughout. The stills capture a moment-in-time of the students' lives. The animation of the globe shows the route one immigrant traveled to get to New York.*

5. *The interviews reveal the students' personal reasons for immigrating: families immigrated to the United States because of economics, to have more opportunity, because of civil war.*

6. *Possible answer: The documentary clearly shows the experiences of immigrants from a variety of cultures in a short period of time. A disadvantage is that filmmakers could edit in a way that takes what people say out of context, or could choose to omit scenes that do not suit their purpose or motive.*

Analyzing the Media

 RI 1, RI 2, RI 3,
RI 6, RI 7, SL 2,
SL 5, W 7

Cite Text Evidence Support your responses with evidence from the media.

1. **Summarize** The documentary includes students' video diaries. Choose one of the video diaries and summarize the events shown and described.

2. **Analyze** What do you think is the purpose of this documentary and the filmmakers' motive in making it? What is the film's central message?

3. **Evaluate** What elements of the documentary reveal the filmmakers' motive and the film's message? How effectively are they revealed?

4. **Analyze** Complete a chart like the one shown to identify three of the techniques the filmmakers use. Explain what each technique emphasizes.

Technique	Scene from the Documentary
1. Voice-over	
2. Stills	
3. Animation	

5. **Critique** What information do you gain from the interviews included in the documentary? Is this information effective in helping to convey the documentary's overall message? Why or why not?

6. **Compare and Evaluate** Consider what you have read and viewed about immigration. What are the advantages of using a documentary format to present the topic of immigration? What are the disadvantages?

PERFORMANCE TASK

Media Activity: Video Work in small groups to create videos of your own personal stories.

- Prepare for your video by choosing a brief personal story to tell. It might be an immigration story, or it could be a story about another important event in your life. Write down a few notes or an outline of your story. Use it as a guide in your interview.

- Choose a "buddy" in the group to interview. Prepare a list of questions to ask your buddy. Use the types of interview questions from *New Immigrants Share Their Stories* to guide you in writing your questions. Remember to keep them general and open-ended.

- Record the interviews, modeling techniques you saw in the film.

PERFORMANCE TASK

 SL 5, W 7

Assign this performance task.

Media Activity: Video Have students work in pairs or small groups to conduct needed research and to plan interviews. Tell them that good interviews ask and answer these basic questions about a person's experience or story.

- Who is it about?
- What happened?
- Where did it take place?
- When did it happen?
- Why did it happen?

Have students write thoughtful questions they can use in their interviews to guide their subject to tell his or her story. Give students time to practice their interviews before they record them. See page 85 for additional support for creating a video.

Creating a Video

COMMON CORE
SL 4,
SL 5

TEACH

Before students begin the Performance Task, present the procedure for creating a video.

Prepare: The **preproduction,** or planning, stage is key to producing a good video.

- Explain that students should identify the roles needed to tell their personal stories and develop a script or outline.
- If they plan to conduct interviews, they will need to prepare questions. An **interview** is a formal conversation in which one person asks another person questions.
- Tell students that developing a simple storyboard will help them to plan the scenes they will film and to brainstorm ideas for camera angles, lighting, and narration.

Shoot the Footage: Tell students that they put their plans into action when they begin filming.

- Point out that varying camera angles adds interest to a film. Students may wish to include close-ups of interview subjects, while showing a long shot or wider view of the location where the filming takes place.
- Remind students to refer often to their storyboards and to add ideas or notes as needed during filming.

Edit the Film: Explain that when filming is complete, students will still have work to do. As needed, arrange a demonstration of editing software that will allow students to put scenes in an appropriate sequence and to create pacing that matches the feel of the story. Explain that quick cuts can create a sense of action or excitement, while longer cuts can create drama and time for reflection.

PRACTICE AND APPLY

Have students work with a partner to plan and shoot footage for a brief video before beginning the Performance Task.

 INTERACTIVE LESSON Have students complete the lessons within **Using Media in a Presentation**.

Evaluate a Documentary

COMMON CORE
RI 7,
SL 2

RETEACH

Review the term *motive* with students. Discuss different kinds of motives that filmmakers might have when they make a documentary, including social, commercial, or political. Then give students the following example of a motive that a filmmaker might have for making a documentary: *to support a law that prevents people from hurting certain endangered animals.*

Have students discuss the techniques that a filmmaker might use in this documentary, such as voice-over narration, stills, and animation. Prompt students to suggest how each technique might be used by asking questions such as:

- What kinds of information might a voice-over narrator give?
- What sorts of still photographs might be used?
- What could an animation show that a video could not?

Then explain that you can evaluate, or judge, whether the documentary is a good way to present information about this topic. Refer back to each of the techniques you discussed and analyze whether it is a good technique to use to provide the information in this kind of a documentary.

CLOSE VIEWING APPLICATION

Students can apply the skill to a current documentary. Have them work independently to name the filmmaker's motive and to outline the different techniques the filmmaker uses. Ask: *Were these good techniques to use to reveal the filmmaker's motive? Is a documentary a good choice to reveal this motive?*

The Powwow at the End of the World

Poem by Sherman Alexie

Why This Text?

The language of poetry is full of opportunities for students to interpret and gain insights about the speaker's message. This lesson focuses on making inferences about the poet's use of imagery and allusions.

Key Learning Objective: The student will learn how to use imagery and allusion to make inferences about the deeper meaning of a poem.

 COMMON CORE

Common Core Standards

RL 1 Cite textual evidence.

RL 4 Determine meanings of words and phrases.

RL 9 Analyze how a modern work draws on themes from traditional stories.

W 7 Conduct short research projects to answer a question.

W 9 Draw evidence from literary texts to support analysis, reflection, and research.

▲ Text Complexity Rubric

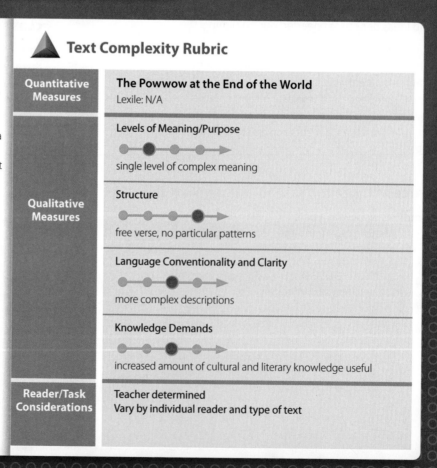

Quantitative Measures	**The Powwow at the End of the World** Lexile: N/A
Qualitative Measures	**Levels of Meaning/Purpose** — single level of complex meaning
	Structure — free verse, no particular patterns
	Language Conventionality and Clarity — more complex descriptions
	Knowledge Demands — increased amount of cultural and literary knowledge useful
Reader/Task Considerations	Teacher determined Vary by individual reader and type of text

TEACH

CLOSE READ

Background Have students read the background and information about the poet. Tell them that the building of the Grand Coulee Dam was one of the projects of President's Roosevelt's New Deal. While its intent was to help hard-working farmers by irrigating farmland, little consideration was given to the changes it would bring to the Columbia River and the Native Americans whose lives revolved around that river.

SETTING A PURPOSE Direct students to use the Setting a Purpose question to focus their reading. Tell students to write any additional questions they generate during reading.

Determine Meaning of Words and Phrases (LINES 1–5)

COMMON CORE · RL 4

Inform students that Alexie uses imagery to communicate ideas throughout the poem. Explain that **imagery** is vivid, descriptive language that appeals to one or more of the senses (sight, hearing, touch, smell, and taste).

(A) ASK STUDENTS to reread lines 1–5 to identify words and phrases that help them see, hear, taste, smell or feel. *(Possible answer: puts her shoulder to the Grand Coulee Dam, topples it, floodwaters burst)* What is the impact of these word choices? *(Word choices, such as "topples" and "floodwaters burst," suggest a destructive force that cannot be controlled, something the speaker would find appealing.)*

Make Inferences (LINES 1–8)

COMMON CORE · RL 1

Remind students that writers do not always tell readers everything they want the readers to know. Readers need to make educated guesses, or **inferences,** about what the poet is trying to say. Tell students that they make inferences by paying close attention to the details in the poem, and then using those details and their own prior knowledge and experiences to figure out what the poet does not directly say.

(B) ASK STUDENTS to reread lines 1–8. What feelings does the poet convey? *(anger, sarcasm)* What details in the poem help you understand this? *(The poet says that he will forgive but only when the dams are destroyed, which is unlikely to happen.)*

Background *Award-winning author and poet* **Sherman Alexie** *(b. 1966) was born on the Spokane Indian Reservation in the state of Washington. Salmon have long played an important role in the economic and spiritual life of Native Americans in the Washington area. The building of dams in the 20th century destroyed the population of the once plentiful salmon and the way of life of the people who depended upon them. Many of Alexie's poems and stories deal with how the Native American community has been affected by this destruction.*

The Powwow at the End of the World

Poem by Sherman Alexie

SETTING A PURPOSE As you read, pay attention to the details Alexie presents about the river and salmon. How do these details show his feelings about the dams and their effects on the lives of Native Americans?

I am told by many of you that I must forgive and so I shall
after an Indian woman puts her shoulder to the Grand Coulee
    Dam[1]
and topples it. I am told by many of you that I must forgive
and so I shall after the floodwaters burst each successive dam
5   downriver from the Grand Coulee. I am told by many of you
that I must forgive and so I shall after the floodwaters find
their way to the mouth of the Columbia River as it enters the
    Pacific
and causes all of it to rise. I am told by many of you that I
    must forgive

_____
[1] **Grand Coulee Dam:** a dam built across the Columbia River in the 1930s to provide hydroelectric power and irrigation.

(tl) ©Christopher Felver/Corbis; (cr) ©Andrey Burmakin/Shutterstock

---

SCAFFOLDING FOR ELL STUDENTS

Analyze Language Using a whiteboard, project lines 1–8. Highlight and discuss the repeated phrase "I must forgive and so I shall." Guide students to understand this unusual construction.

ASK STUDENTS to explain what the speaker means, and to identify the word the speaker leaves unsaid *(and so I shall forgive)*. Explain that since poetry is most effective when read aloud, students should practice the phrase, emphasizing the word *forgive.*

I am told by many of you that I must forgive and so I shall after an Indian woman puts her shoulder to the Grand Coulee Dam and topples it.

TEACH

CLOSE READ

Determine Meaning of Words and Phrases

  COMMON CORE RL 1, RL 4

(LINES 11–13)

Point out the reference to the Hanford reactors. Explain that these reactors were built as the core of America's atomic defense during World War II and the Cold War.

C **CITE TEXT EVIDENCE** What evidence in the text helps you infer the speaker's feelings about the Hanford reactors? *(The speaker says the reactors are "abandoned." His use of this word shows that he is unable to forgive the damage done to the land and the spirit of Native Americans by these technological advances: something that caused so much change is now considered useless.)*

Make Inferences

  COMMON CORE RL 1

(LINES 10–16)

Point out to students that the poem describes the journey of a salmon swimming upstream back from the Pacific to a secret bay. Reread lines 10–16 aloud.

D **ASK STUDENTS** what the salmon represents to the speaker. *(Possible answer: The salmon swimming upstream represents the struggles of the Native American peoples against the changes in their land and culture.)*

COLLABORATIVE DISCUSSION Have partners discuss their ideas and evidence about the feelings of the poem's speaker. Then have them share their ideas with the larger group.

ASK STUDENTS to share any questions they generated in the course of reading and discussing this selection.

---

and so I shall after the first drop of floodwater is swallowed by
    that salmon
10 waiting in the Pacific. I am told by many of you that I must
    forgive and so I shall

D after that salmon swims upstream, through the mouth of the   **C**
    Columbia
and then past the flooded cities, broken dams and abandoned
    reactors
of Hanford.[2] I am told by many of you that I must forgive and
    so I shall
after that salmon swims through the mouth of the Spokane
    River
15 as it meets the Columbia, then upstream, until it arrives
in the shallows of a secret bay on the reservation where I wait
    alone.
I am told by many of you that I must forgive and so I shall
    after
that salmon leaps into the night air above the water, throws
a lightning bolt at the brush near my feet, and starts the fire
20 which will lead all of the lost Indians home. I am told
by many of you that I must forgive and so I shall
after we Indians have gathered around the fire with that
    salmon
who has three stories it must tell before sunrise: one story will
    teach us
how to pray; another story will make us laugh for hours;
25 the third story will give us reason to dance. I am told by many
of you that I must forgive and so I shall when I am dancing
with my tribe during the powwow at the end of the world.

COLLABORATIVE DISCUSSION With a partner, discuss Alexie's feelings about the effects of the dam. Do his feelings seem justified? Cite specific evidence from the text to support your ideas.

---

[2] **reactors of Hanford:** a series of abandoned nuclear reactors along the Columbia River.

APPLYING ACADEMIC VOCABULARY

contribute	reaction

As you discuss the poem, incorporate the following Collection 1 academic vocabulary words: *contribute* and *reaction*. Have students explain the speaker's **reaction** to being told to forgive. Have them tell how the building of the dam and reactors and his sense of isolation **contribute** to his feelings.

Determine Meaning of Words and Phrases RL 4, RL 9

Each word in a poem contributes to its overall meaning and effect. One way poets create meaning is through the use of **imagery,** descriptions that appeal to the senses of sight, sound, smell, taste, and touch. Notice the way Sherman Alexie appeals to the senses of sight and touch with this image, which communicates feelings of power and importance:

> . . . after / that salmon leaps into the night air above the water, throws / a lightning bolt at the brush near my feet and starts the fire . . .

Another way poets can communicate meaning is through the use of **allusions,** or references to a famous person, place, event, or work of literature. Alexie creates a connection to the culture of Northwest Native Americans by alluding to characters and places that are important in their history. For example, "The Powwow at the End of the World" contains several references to salmon. Salmon have special significance to Northwest Coast peoples and are part of many traditional myths and ceremonies.

Identify at least one additional image and one allusion in "The Powwow at the End of the World" and explain how each creates an effect or contributes to the poem's meaning.

Make Inferences RL 1

When you **make inferences** about a poem, you combine clues from the text with your own knowledge and experience of the world to make educated guesses about meaning. Making inferences is sometimes called "reading between the lines," and it can be especially important in poetry, where much can be said in relatively few words. The diagram below shows one inference that can be made about "The Powwow at the End of the World."

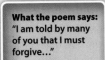

What the poem says: "I am told by many of you that I must forgive…" → **What I know:** People may choose to forgive someone who has hurt them in some way. → **What I infer:** The speaker believes he has been hurt by the actions of another.

The **speaker** of a poem is the voice that talks to the reader. Who is the speaker being asked to forgive? Tell what the poem says and what you already know that helps you make this inference.

The Powwow at the End of the World   77

CLOSE READ

Determine Meaning of Words and Phrases RL 4, RL 9

Guide students to identify examples of imagery, noting the sense or senses to which each one appeals. As needed, highlight the allusions Alexie uses to convey his message. *(Possible answers: Imagery: first drop of floodwater is swallowed by that salmon; The imagery suggests the contrast between a single drop of water and more overwhelming idea of floodwater. Allusion: The reference to the Grand Coulee Dam helps to explain what prevents the salmon from swimming upstream.)*

Prompt students to reread the poem, focusing on how Alexie draws on Northwest Native Americans' traditional ideas about salmon to support the speaker's views in this modern poem. *(Alexie wants the salmon to "start the fire which will lead all of the lost Indians home." He uses the salmon's power from the traditional stories to create the modern image of "the powwow at the end of the world.")*

Make Inferences RL 1

Reread the poem aloud to students. Have them think about the subject the speaker is addressing and who might be asking him to forgive and why. Have them record their ideas on a flowchart to help them answer the question. *(The speaker is asked to forgive the non-Indian leaders who made the decisions to building the dam and the reactor.)*

Strategies for Annotation   📝 📖 *Annotate it!*

Determine Meaning of Words and Phrases RL 4, RL 9

Have students use their eBook annotation tools to analyze the text. Ask them to do the following:

- Highlight in yellow sensory details.
- Underline allusions to people, places, or events.
- On a note, record the impact of the allusions.

I am told by many of you that I must forgive and so I shall after an <u>Indian woman</u> puts her shoulder to the <u>Grand Coulee Dam</u>

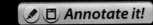

The allusions relate the imagery to his culture and environment, things that he knows.

and topples it. I am told by many of you tha and so I shall after the floodwaters burst each successive dam downriver from the Grand Coulee.

The Powwow at the End of the World   **77**

PRACTICE & APPLY

Analyzing the Text COMMON CORE RL 1, RL 4

Possible answers:

1. *To the speaker, the dam has caused great harm and must be destroyed. The image of an Indian woman putting her shoulder to the Grand Coulee Dam and making it topple suggests the speaker's anger toward the dam.*

2. *The image appeals to the sense of touch, sound, and sight. The power of the floodwaters breaking through each dam is similar to the powerful feelings the poet has for it to be destroyed.*

3. *The repeated phrase is "I am told by many of you that I must forgive and so I shall." By the phrase "many of you," the speaker means non-Native Americans, who want the speaker to forgive those responsible for altering the land and disrupting lives. The repetition ties the poem together by introducing each set of events that must happen before the speaker will forgive.*

4. *The speaker will never show forgiveness—not until impossible things happen, such as the Grand Coulee being toppled by a Native American woman and a salmon throwing a lightning bolt to start a signal fire. The speaker will forgive after all wrongs have been righted in a fictional future world.*

5. *As the world ends, Native American peoples will hold a powwow to celebrate their return to their ancestral lands and ways of life. All the "lost Indians" will find their way home and listen to the salmon tell stories that will teach them "how to pray," make them "laugh for hours," and give them a "reason to dance."*

6. *Students' word choices and oral readings should reflect their understanding of the speaker's feelings of both cultural pride and regret for what has been lost.*

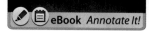

Analyzing the Text COMMON CORE RL 1, RL 4, RL 9, W 7, W 9

Cite Text Evidence   Support your responses with evidence from the poem.

1. **Infer** The poem begins with an allusion to the Grand Coulee Dam, built on the Columbia River in the mid-20th century and widely considered to be an engineering marvel. Reread lines 1–3. What is the speaker's view of the mighty dam? Tell what image helps you understand the speaker's feelings about the dam.

2. **Interpret** Identify the imagery in lines 4–5. To what senses does it appeal? Explain what this image suggests about the power of the speaker's feelings.

3. **Analyze** The technique in which a sound, word, or phrase is repeated for emphasis as well as to create rhythm is called **repetition.** Identify the phrase that is repeated in this poem. What is the effect of this repetition?

4. **Infer** When will the speaker show forgiveness? Identify the lines in the poem that help you answer.

5. **Draw Conclusions** Powwows are gatherings where Native Americans of North America share dancing, music, and other cultural traditions. What phrases from the poem suggest what will happen at "The Powwow at the End of the World"?

6. **Evaluate** The **tone** of a poem expresses the speaker's attitude toward the subject being addressed. Here are some words that can describe tone: *lighthearted, humorous, sharp, gloomy, angry, grateful, defiant, reflective, energetic, ironic.* What word describes the tone of this poem? Explain your choice. Then read part of the poem aloud to express the tone.

PERFORMANCE TASK

Speaking Activity: Discussion The speaker in the poem makes allusions to stories about salmon. Do research to locate a retelling of a salmon myth originating among the Native Americans of the Northwest Coast.

- Find a retelling of a myth such as "Salmon Boy," "The Legend of the Lost Salmon," or "How Salmon Came to the Squamish."

- After reading the myth, compare and contrast its ideas about the significance of salmon with those mentioned in the poem. How does the poem reflect traditional ideas in a new way?

- Discuss your conclusions with your classmates.

PERFORMANCE TASK COMMON CORE RL 9, W 7, W 9

 Assign this performance task.

Speaking Activity: Discussion Have students use print and digital sources to locate a retelling of a salmon myth or story. Have students compare and contrast the ideas in the myth and poem in a Venn diagram before and during their discussion. Students should note that the salmon is a powerful symbol in cultures that depend on it to sustain them. The mythical salmon in the poem can swim upstream, leap out of the water, throw a lightning bolt, and start a fire to show the way home to those who are lost. It tells three stories to show the Native Americans how to celebrate life. In their discussion students should analyze how Alexie's poem both draws on the traditional characterizations of salmon and uses them in a new way. See the lesson on page 91 for additional support.

Analyze Modern Fiction

COMMON CORE

RL 9

TEACH

Remind students that Sherman Alexie makes **allusions,** or references, to the importance of the salmon throughout "The Powwow at the End of the World." Explain that many modern works of fiction draw on themes, events, or character types from myths and traditional stories. Tell students that such stories often reflect characteristics and symbols that are important to a culture. Point out that recognizing elements of traditional stories in modern works of fiction can give readers deeper understanding and insight into the literature and the culture it reflects.

Before having students compare ideas about the significance of salmon for the Performance Task, use the Interactive Whiteboard Lesson "Comparing Texts" to help them learn how to compare and synthesize ideas across texts.

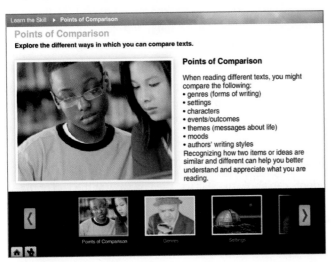

Discuss the steps for comparing exts:

- **Identify similarities.** Look for elements to compare, such as theme, imagery, mood, or symbolism.
- **Identify differences.** Tell how these elements are different in each text.
- **Synthesize ideas.** Combine details to develop new understanding or insights.

PRACTICE AND APPLY

Have students work in groups to apply the steps to the example texts in the Whiteboard Lesson. Have groups compare their results.

Analyze Lyric Poems

COMMON CORE

RL 4

TEACH

Explain to students that a **lyric** poem is a poem that expresses the personal thoughts and feelings of a speaker. The **speaker** of a lyric poem may be the poet or someone else who is responding to an experience.

Tell students that to understand a lyric poem, the reader must pay attention to details that reveal the speaker. Provide an example, such as the following lines from "The Powwow at the End of the World:"

"I am told by many of you that I must forgive and so I shall after an Indian woman puts her shoulder to the Grand Coulee Dam and topples it."

Guide students to understand that the words "I am told by many of you that I must forgive" suggest that the speaker is someone who feels mistreated. The remaining words suggest that the speaker is angry and will never forgive.

PRACTICE AND APPLY

Display the remaining lines of "The Powwow at the End of the World." Have students identify details that help them understand who the speaker is and how he feels about the subject.

 LEVEL UP TUTORIALS Assign the following *Level Up* tutorial: **Narrator and Speaker**

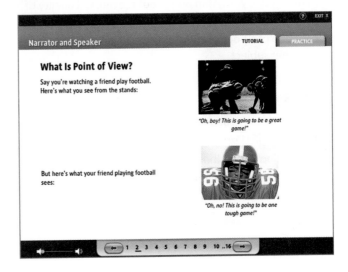

Analyze Poetry: Line Length

TEACH

Explain to students that the form of a poem is the way the poem is laid out on the page. Remind them that most poems are made up of lines and stanzas. A **line** is the core unit of a poem. A **stanza** is a group of two or more lines. The place where a line ends is called a **line break.** Point out that not all poems contain these sorts of regular patterns. Cite free verse as one example, explaining that **free verse** is poetry that does not follow regular patterns of rhyme or rhythm. The lines in free verse flow more naturally to achieve a rhythm that is more like that of everyday language.

Explain that line length is an essential element of a poem's meaning and rhythm, using these points:

- Line breaks do not always signal the end of a sentence or thought.
- A line break can occur in the middle of a sentence or phrase to create a meaningful pause or emphasis.
- Poets use a variety of line breaks to convey a wide range of effects, such as pace, mood, rhythm, and tone.

Discuss the following effects of line lengths:

- **Pace** is how fast or slow a poem is read. Short sentences speed up the pace of a poem. Longer sentences slow it down.
- **Mood** is the feeling or atmosphere that the poet creates for the reader.
- **Rhythm** is a pattern of stressed and unstressed syllables in a line of poetry. Rhythm brings out the musical quality of language, emphasizes ideas, and creates mood.
- The **tone** of a poem expresses the speaker's attitude toward his or her subject.

PRACTICE AND APPLY

Work with students to analyze the form of "The Powwow at the End of the World." Have them:

- describe how each thought begins and ends
- explain the effects that are created by the poem's line breaks

Determine Meaning of Words and Phrases: Allusion

RETEACH

Review that an **allusion** is a reference to a famous person, place, event, or other work of literature. Then discuss the following points:

- Poets use allusions to help them convey meaning in a single word or two.
- In order to understand an allusion, a reader must understand the reference.
- No reader can recognize every allusion. It is sometimes necessary to do research in order to understand the reference.

Guide students to interpret examples, such as the following:

My mom is no Scrooge, but she almost never buys things she doesn't need. *(Scrooge is a stingy and mean character from "A Christmas Carol" by Charles Dickens. A Scrooge refers to a person who is miserly.)*

That girl has a Mona Lisa smile. *(Leonardo DaVinci's Mona Lisa is a painting of a woman that is known for her mysterious smile. A Mona Lisa smile is one that is very hard to understand.)*

CLOSE READING APPLICATION

Students can apply the skill to "The Powwow at the End of the World." Have them complete a three-column chart like the one shown.

Allusion	What It References	Meaning in Poem
salmon		
Grand Coulee Dam		
Hanford reactors		

As needed, guide students to research to learn more about each allusion.

Interactive Lessons
If you need help . . .
• **Writing Informative Texts**
• **Writing as a Process**

Write an Expository Essay

This collection focuses on immigration and its impact. In the short story "My Favorite Chaperone," you read a fictional account of someone trying to establish a sense of belonging in a new culture. In other selections in this collection, you read first-hand, real-life accounts and informational texts about various aspects of adjusting to a new culture. In this activity, you will conduct research and write a short expository essay on the best ways for people from other countries to adjust to living in the United States.

COMMON CORE

W 2a–e Write informative/explanatory texts.
W 4 Produce clear and coherent writing.
W 5 Strengthen writing as needed.
W 8 Gather relevant and credible information from multiple print/digital sources while avoiding plagiarism and providing basic bibliographic information.

A successful expository essay

- provides an introduction that catches the reader's attention and clearly states the topic
- develops the topic using facts, definitions, examples, and quotations
- logically organizes main ideas and supporting evidence
- uses appropriate transitions to connect ideas
- provides a conclusion that summarizes and supports the topic

PLAN

Determine Your Topic Review the selections in the collection, and make a list of the issues that seem common to the characters and people in them. Choose one or more immigration-related issues to focus on, such as the cost of living or the maintaining of ties to the country of origin.

Formulate Ideas Prepare for research by jotting down questions that you will answer in your essay, such as:

- Where can people go to find tips for adjusting to life in the United States?
- What are some of the biggest obstacles to adjusting to life in a new country?
- What sources are available to immigrants when they first arrive?

my Notebook

Use the annotation tools in your eBook to find evidence to support your ideas. Save each piece of evidence to your notebook.

ACADEMIC VOCABULARY

As you write your essay, be sure to use the academic vocabulary words.

contribute
immigrate
reaction
relocate
shifting

Collection Performance Task A **79**

WRITE AN EXPOSITORY ESSAY

COMMON CORE W 2a-e, W 4, W 5, W 9

Introduce students to the Performance Task by reading the introductory paragraph with them and reviewing the criteria for what makes a good expository essay. Remind students that a good expository essay includes evidence that supports the main points the writer makes.

PLAN

DETERMINE YOUR TOPIC

View It!

Professional Development Podcast:
Performance Tasks

Share with students that, when they take notes during research, they can write information on individual file cards or color code information in their notebooks. Information about the same ideas can then easily be organized to include in their outlines.

Conduct Research Use print and digital sources to find additional definitions, information, and quotations from experts.

- Use relevant, credible sources. Use a search engine or Internet directories to find online sources. Find books using keywords or subject searches in the library.

- Search government immigration websites for helpful tips and resources.

- Cite real-life examples of people who have faced this issue.

- Explore and provide links to websites that can be used as resources.

- Copy information about the sources you use so you can give them credit in your essay.

Organize Your Ideas Think about how you will organize your essay. Create an outline showing the information you will present in each paragraph. Organize your ideas in a logical sequence, making sure they flow smoothly and are clearly connected.

> **I.** Use Roman numerals for main topics.
>   A. Indent and use capital letters for subtopics.
>   1. Indent and use numbers for supporting facts and details.
>   2. Indent and use numbers for supporting facts and details.
> **II.** Use Roman numerals for main topics.
>   B. Indent and use capital letters for subtopics.
>   1. Indent and use numbers for supporting facts and details.

Consider Your Purpose and Audience Think about who will read or listen to your essay and what you want them to understand. Keep your audience in mind as you prepare to write.

PRODUCE

Write Your Essay Review your notes and your outline as you begin your draft.

- Begin your essay with an unusual comment, fact, quote, or personal anecdote in order to grab your reader's interest.

- State or make clear the main idea or focus of your essay.

- Support your main idea with details, including facts, statistics, examples, and quotations from experts. Construct paragraphs around related information.

my **WriteSmart**

Write your rough draft in *my*WriteSmart. Focus on getting your ideas down, rather than on perfecting your choice of language.

PRODUCE

WRITE YOUR ESSAY

Remind students that they should keep their audience in mind when they draft their essays. Point out that the evidence students use to support their points may vary according to who that audience might be. Some audiences might be swayed more by evidence such as statistics, whereas others may respond more to personal stories.

- Include website links that offer helpful resources to your readers.
- Prepare a conclusion that summarizes your main idea and provides your reader with a memorable insight.

Prepare Visuals Add charts, graphs, photos, or statistical data to your essay. These visuals can be included in a sidebar to help clarify and further explain your ideas.

REVISE

Review Your Draft Use the chart on the next page to evaluate your draft. Work with a partner to determine whether you have explained your topic clearly and provided information that supports your main ideas. Consider the following:

- Does the introduction grab the reader's attention?
- Are the main idea and supporting evidence clearly defined?
- Does each paragraph have a main point with relevant supporting details?
- Are facts, details, examples, and quotations accurate?
- Are ideas organized in a logical sequence? Do transitions help the reader follow along?
- Does the conclusion support the information presented?

my **WriteSmart**

Have your partner or a group of peers review your draft in *my*WriteSmart. Ask your reviewers to note any details that do not support your ideas.

PRESENT

Create a Finished Copy Finalize your essay and choose a way to share it with your audience. Consider these options:

- Present your essay as a speech to the class.
- Post your essay as a blog on a classroom or school website.

REVISE

REVIEW YOUR DRAFT

Remind students that the purpose of an expository essay is to inform others. As they write, students should think about what it would be like to be the audience for their essay. Answering questions such as the following will help them make their finished essays better:

- Is there enough information?
- Is the information clear?
- Does the evidence support the main ideas in the essay?

PRESENT

CREATE A FINISHED COPY

Groups of students can present their essays as speeches to the class. Remind students that, when they give a speech, the delivery is just as important as the information they present. Students can videotape their speeches beforehand and then review them to make sure they are speaking effectively.

PERFORMANCE TASK A

ORGANIZATION

Have students use the chart to identify how they did on the performance task in each of the three main categories. Tell students to pay particular attention to the organization of their essays and to be sure they have used appropriate transitions throughout. You may want to provide examples of essays from previous years that successfully execute these aspects of expository writing. Have students compare their writing to the examples and note areas in which they can make improvements.

COLLECTION 1 TASK A
EXPOSITORY ESSAY

	Ideas and Evidence	Organization	Language
ADVANCED	• The introduction is appealing, is informative, and catches the reader's attention; the topic is clearly identified. • The topic is well developed with clear main ideas supported by facts, details, definitions, and examples from reliable sources. • The conclusion effectively summarizes the information presented.	• The organization is effective and logical throughout the essay. • Transitions logically connect related ideas.	• The writer maintains a formal style throughout the essay. • Language is strong and precise. • Sentences vary in pattern and structure. • Spelling, capitalization, punctuation, and other mechanics are correct. • Grammar and usage are correct.
COMPETENT	• The introduction could be more appealing and engaging; the topic is clearly identified. • One or two important points could use more support, but most main ideas are well supported by facts, details, definitions, and examples from reliable sources. • The conclusion summarizes the information presented.	• The organization of main ideas and details is confusing in a few places. • A few more transitions are needed to connect related ideas.	• The writing style is inconsistent in a few places. • Language is too vague or general in some places. • Sentences vary somewhat in pattern and structure. • Some spelling, capitalization, and punctuation mistakes occur. • Some grammar and usage errors are repeated.
LIMITED	• The introduction is only partly informative; the topic is unclear. • Most important points could use more support from relevant facts, details, definitions, and examples from reliable sources. • The conclusion is unclear or only partially summarizes the information presented.	• The organization of main ideas and details is logical in some places, but it often doesn't follow a pattern. • More transitions are needed throughout to connect related ideas.	• The writing style becomes informal in many places. • Language is too general or vague in many places. • Sentence pattern and structure hardly vary; some fragments or run-on sentences occur. • Spelling, capitalization, and punctuation are often incorrect but do not make reading difficult. • Grammar and usage are often incorrect, but the writer's ideas are still clear.
EMERGING	• The introduction is missing or confusing. • Supporting facts, details, definitions, or examples are unreliable or missing. • The conclusion is missing.	• The organization is not logical; main ideas and details are presented randomly. • No transitions are used, making the essay difficult to understand.	• The style is inappropriate for the essay. • Language is too general to convey the information. • Sentence structure is repetitive and monotonous; fragments and run-on sentences make the essay hard to follow. • Spelling, capitalization, and punctuation are incorrect and distracting throughout. • Many grammatical and usage errors obscure the meaning of the writer's ideas.

Write a Personal Narrative

COMMON CORE

W 3a–e Write narratives.
W 4 Produce writing appropriate to task, purpose, and audience.
W 5 Develop and strengthen writing.
W 10 Write routinely over extended time frames and shorter time frames.

Like the characters in "My Favorite Chaperone" and *The Latehomecomer,* many people struggle to adjust to new situations or to fit in with different groups. Think about a time when you faced that type of challenge. Using the excerpt from *The Latehomecomer* as a model, write a personal narrative about your own experience.

A successful personal narrative

- establishes a situation and introduces a narrator and characters
- organizes a well-structured event sequence that unfolds naturally and logically
- uses narrative techniques such as dialogue, pacing, relevant descriptive details, and reflection to develop experiences
- provides a conclusion that follows from and reflects on the narrated experiences and events

PLAN

*my*Notebook

Have your partner or a group of peers review your draft in *my*WriteSmart. Ask your reviewers to note any details that do not support your ideas.

Establish the Situation A personal narrative is a story that describes a memorable event from your past. Think about the following to help you choose an event.

- Have you faced a situation in which you needed to fit in or adjust to something new? How did you deal with it?
- How were the strategies you used similar to or different from the strategies that the characters in the selections used?
- What contributed to making the event significant for you?

ACADEMIC VOCABULARY

As you prepare your narrative, be sure to use the academic vocabulary words.

contribute
immigrate
reaction
relocate
shifting

List the Events In a personal narrative, you are the narrator, or the person telling the story. Develop a strong voice and avoid shifting points of view. Tell your story in an order that will make sense to readers. A graphic organizer, such as a flow chart, can help you describe the event in a logical way.

WRITE A PERSONAL NARRATIVE

COMMON CORE W 3a-e, W 4, W 5, W 10

Introduce students to the Performance Task by reading the introductory paragraph with them and reviewing the criteria for what makes a good personal narrative. Remind students that a good personal narrative is a story about real people and events that usually reflects the writer's experiences, feelings, and personality.

PLAN

ESTABLISH THE SITUATION

Share with students that, while brainstorming ideas for their personal narratives, they should think back over their lives. Have them list times that were particularly challenging and think about which of these ideas would be interesting to others. Then have students choose the single event that they want to write about.

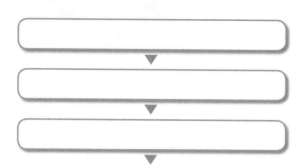

Brainstorm Images Think about your mental images of the event. Which aspects of those images seem most striking to you? Describe the images using words and phrases that convey

- vivid colors
- specific sounds
- scents, tastes, or feelings

Consider Your Purpose and Audience Think about those who will read or listen to your personal narrative, and decide how you want them to react to your experience. Consider that audience as you prepare to write. Keep in mind that your wording and tone may be different for a group of classmates or friends than it would be for a group of adults.

PRODUCE

WRITE YOUR PERSONAL NARRATIVE

Remind students that most personal narratives allow readers to see inside the mind of the writer. Before students begin to write, remind them to let readers know what their feelings and thoughts were when facing the challenges they tell about.

PRODUCE

*my***WriteSmart**

Write Your Personal Narrative Review your notes and your graphic organizer as you begin your draft.

Write your rough draft in *my*WriteSmart. Focus on getting your ideas down, rather than on perfecting your choice of language.

- Introduce your audience to the people, places, and events you are writing about. Begin with an attention-grabbing comment or some dialogue that will catch readers' interest. Provide any background on your experience that readers may need.

- Use your graphic organizer to describe the sequence of events and to ensure you establish the correct order of events. Include descriptive details to capture your experience for readers.

- Bring your personal narrative to a conclusion by telling how the events ended. Reflect on what made the experience significant for you by explaining what you learned from it or how the experience had an impact on your life.

REVISE

Review Your Draft Use the chart on the next page to evaluate your draft. Work with a partner to determine whether you both have described your experience clearly and used details that will interest readers. Be sure to consider these points.

my **WriteSmart**

Have your partner or a group of peers review your draft in *my*WriteSmart. Ask your reviewers to note any parts of the story that are confusing or that could benefit from more descriptive details.

- Examine your narrative's sequence of events. Delete any event that is not important to describing your experience. If necessary, add events that will help readers understand what happened. Check that you have made the order of events clear with transition words such as *next*, *finally*, or *a day later*.

- Look back to see if you have described your experience in a way that creates a vivid image for readers. Check that your descriptions include details that appeal to a variety of senses.

- Decide whether dialogue would add interest or reveal the problem you faced in a more interesting way. If it would, look for opportunities to include it in your story.

- Make sure it is clear why the experience you have described is significant to you. If necessary, add a sentence or two to show your thoughts and feelings about the experience.

PRESENT

Create a Finished Copy Finalize your written personal narrative and then choose a way to share it with your audience. Consider these additional options:

- Present your personal narrative as a speech to the class.
- Post your personal narrative as a blog on a school website.
- Dramatize your personal narrative in a one-person show.

REVISE

REVIEW YOUR DRAFT

Remind students that good personal narratives usually build to a climax. Have students reread their drafts and determine whether the action builds toward the climax and resolution of the problem. Help them understand that this in an important part of making their narratives engaging to readers.

PRESENT

CREATE A FINISHED COPY

Students can post their personal narratives as a blog on a school website. Encourage readers to post comments and questions after reading the narrative. The author can also respond to those comments and questions.

PERFORMANCE TASK B

LANGUAGE

Have students use the chart to identify how they did on the performance task in each of the three main categories. Prompt students to check the impact of their word choices and vivid details. Ask them to think about one way they could improve their writing in each of the categories.

	Ideas and Evidence	Organization	Language
ADVANCED	• The narrative establishes the situation using well-chosen details. • Dialogue and description are used effectively. • The conclusion unfolds naturally and reflects on the significance of the experience.	• The narrative has a coherent sequence that builds to a logical conclusion. • Well-chosen events result in effective pacing. • Transitions logically connect the sequence of events.	• The narrative successfully weaves in sensory language and vivid details. • The writer's word choice develops or enhances his or her voice. • Grammar, usage, and mechanics are correct.
COMPETENT	• The narrative conveys a real experience. • Some well-chosen details are included. • More dialogue or description could be used. • The conclusion could be strengthened.	• The narrative includes some extraneous events, resulting in ineffective pacing. • More transitions would make the sequence of events clearer.	• The narrative includes sensory language and descriptive details. • The writer's word choice is effective. • Some errors in grammar, usage, or mechanics create distractions.
LIMITED	• The narrative conveys a real experience but needs more development. • Details are lacking or irrelevant. • Dialogue and description are limited or lacking. • The conclusion is ineffective.	• The narrative has a confusing sequence caused by extraneous events or the lack of transitions. • Missing events or information creates ambiguity.	• The narrative needs more sensory language and descriptive details. • The writer's word choice needs improvement. • Multiple errors in grammar, usage, or mechanics create distractions.
EMERGING	• The narrative has no identifiable experience. • Details are vague or omitted. • Dialogue and description are not included. • A conclusion is not included.	• The narrative has no apparent organization.	• The narrative lacks sensory language and descriptive details. • The writer's word choice is vague or confusing. • Significant errors in grammar, usage, or mechanics create confusion and misunderstanding.

©Andreas Gradin/Shutterstock

The Thrill of Horror

❝There is a . . . horror story that is only two sentences long:
The last man on Earth sat alone in a room.
There was a knock at the door.❞

—Frederick Brown

CONNECTING WORD AND IMAGE

ASK STUDENTS to discuss how the Collection Opener image and the collection quotation work together to create a connection.

PERFORMANCE TASK PREVIEW

Point out to students that they will complete two Performance Tasks at the end of the collection. The Performance Tasks will require them to further analyze the selections in the collection and to synthesize ideas about these analyses. They will present their findings in a variety of products.

ACADEMIC VOCABULARY

View It!

Professional Development Podcast:

Academic Vocabulary

Students can acquire facility with the academic vocabulary words through frequent, repeated exposure as they analyze and discuss the selections in the collection. Academic vocabulary can be used in the instructional contexts shown below. This will enable students to incorporate the academic vocabulary words into their working vocabulary.

- Collaborative Discussion at the end of each selection
- Analyzing the Text questions for each selection
- Selection-level Performance Task
- Vocabulary instruction (for Critical Vocabulary and/or for Vocabulary Strategy)
- Language Conventions
- End-of-collection Performance Task for all selections in the collection

ASK STUDENTS to review the Academic Vocabulary word list for this collection. You may wish to pronounce each word aloud so students hear the correct pronunciation. Then, discuss the definitions and the related forms for each word. Remind students that they will encounter these five academic vocabulary words throughout the collection.

The Thrill of Horror

In this collection, you will examine why the horror genre both terrifies and fascinates.

hmhfyi.com

COLLECTION

PERFORMANCE TASK Preview

At the end of this collection, you will have the opportunity to complete two performance tasks:

- In one, you will give a speech arguing whether a classic horror story is appropriate for your age group to read.

- In the second, you will write a literary analysis that examines how the fiction in the collection meets the criteria for the horror genre.

ACADEMIC VOCABULARY

Study the words and their definitions in the chart below. You will use these words as you discuss and write about the texts in this collection.

Word	Definition	Related Forms
convention (kən-vĕn´shən) *n.*	a practice or procedure widely used by a group; a custom	conventional, conventionally
predict (prĭ-dĭkt´) *v.*	to tell about in advance, especially on the basis of special knowledge	prediction, predictable, predictive
psychology (sī-kŏl´ə-jē) *n.*	the study of mental processes and behaviors	psychological, psychologist
summary (sŭm´ə-rē) *n.*	a condensed, or shorter, report that includes the main points of a text or event	summarize, summation
technique (tĕk-nēk´) *n.*	the systematic or orderly procedure by which a task is accomplished	technical

88

USING COLLECTIONS YOUR WAY

Use the following information, along with the charts on the following pages, to help you decide how you want to introduce the collection. Based on your teaching style, your students' interests, or your instructional goals, you may want to structure this collection in various ways. You may choose different entry points each time you teach the collection.

"I rely heavily on novels and longer works."

Suspense builds as a seemingly innocent wish brings a devastating result in this short story.

William Wymark Jacobs (1863–1943) *grew up in London near the waterfront wharfs. As a boy, Jacobs absorbed the tales of strange, distant lands told by passing sailors. As a young man, Jacobs worked at a bank—a job that he hated—and wrote stories in his spare time. He eventually became a popular writer of humor. Ironically, his best-known work, "The Monkey's Paw," became a classic of the horror genre.*

The Monkey's Paw

Short Story by W. W. Jacobs

SETTING A PURPOSE As you read, pay attention to the relationships among the members of the White family. How does the appearance of the monkey's paw affect those relationships?

Part I

Without, the night was cold and wet, but in the small parlor of Laburnum Villa the blinds were drawn and the fire burned brightly. Father and son were at chess; the former, who possessed ideas about the game involving radical changes, putting his king into such sharp and unnecessary perils that it even provoked comment from the white-haired old lady knitting placidly by the fire.

"Hark at the wind," said Mr. White, who, having seen a fatal mistake after it was too late, was amiably desirous of preventing his son from seeing it.

"I'm listening," said the latter, grimly surveying the board as he stretched out his hand. "Check."

peril
(pĕr′əl) *n. A peril is something that is dangerous.*

The Monkey's Paw **105**

"I love teaching traditional literature."

A classic of the horror genre, this short story has fascinated—and frightened—generations of readers.

Edgar Allan Poe (1809–1849) *was born in Boston to parents who were traveling actors. Orphaned by the time he was three, he moved to Virginia where friends of his family raised him. As a young man, Poe worked as a journalist while writing the stories and poems that would earn him the title "father of the modern mystery." After his young wife died, Poe fell into despair. He passed away two years later. His dark and sometimes horrifying works perhaps mirror the darkness and sadness of his own short life.*

The Tell-Tale Heart

Short Story by Edgar Allan Poe

SETTING A PURPOSE As you read, pay attention to the way the narrator describes himself. What makes him unusual?

True!—nervous—very, very dreadfully nervous I had been and am! but why *will* you say that I am mad? The disease had sharpened my senses—not destroyed—not dulled them. Above all was the sense of hearing acute. I heard all things in the heaven and in the earth. I heard many things in hell. How, then, am I mad? Hearken! and observe how healthily—how calmly I can tell you the whole story.

It is impossible to say how first the idea entered my brain; but once **conceived**, it haunted me day and night. Object there was none. Passion there was none. I loved the old man. He had never wronged me. He had never given me insult. For his gold I had no desire. I think it was his eye! yes, it was this! He had the eye of a vulture—a pale blue eye, with a film over it. Whenever it fell upon me, my blood ran cold; and so by degrees—very gradually—I made up my mind to take the life of the old man, and thus rid myself of the eye forever.

Now this is the point. You fancy me mad. Madmen know nothing. But you should have seen *me*. You should have seen

conceive
(kən-sēv′) *v.* When you conceive an idea, you think of it.

The Tell-Tale Heart **89**

"I want to concentrate on standards coverage."

This literary criticism guides readers to define, analyze, and evaluate elements of the genre.

Sharon A. Russell (b. 1941) *is a retired professor of Communication and Women's Studies at Indiana State University, where she taught courses on film and television. Russell has published extensively on horror film and literature and detective fiction. She is the author of Stephen King: A Critical Companion, a book that analyzes several of King's famous horror novels and in which this essay appears.*

What Is the Horror Genre?

Literary Criticism by Sharon A. Russell

SETTING A PURPOSE As you read, pay attention to the points the author makes about horror stories. Do her ideas make you think about horror stories in new ways?

Many people define horror by its subjects. We all think of creatures like Frankenstein's monster, Dracula, and the wolfman[1] as monsters in the horror genre. Each one of these creatures has a history and developed over a period of time. But we also know that horror covers more than just these monsters. We could all make long lists of the kind of creatures we identify with horror, especially when we think of films as well as literature. The minute we would start to make such a list we would also realize that not all monsters are alike and that not all horror deals with monsters. The subject approach is not the clearest way to define this genre.

[1] **Frankenstein's monster, Dracula, and the wolfman:** legendary monsters. "Frankenstein's monster" is the creature created by Dr. Victor Frankenstein in Mary Shelley's novel; "Dracula" is the vampire in Bram Stoker's novel; in folklore, the wolfman is a man who can become a wolf.

What Is the Horror Genre? **125**

COLLECTION 2 DIGITAL OVERVIEW

mySmartPlanner | **eBook** | **myNotebook** | **myWriteSmart** | fyi hmhfyi.com

Collection 2 Lessons	Media	Teach and Practice
Student Edition | eBook	Video Links HISTORY A&E	**Close Reading and Evidence Tracking**
ANCHOR TEXT — **Short Story by Edgar Allan Poe** "The Tell-Tale Heart"	◉ **Audio** "The Tell-Tale Heart"	**Close Read Screencasts** • Modeled Discussion (lines 1–7) • Close Read Application (lines 164–175) **Strategies for Annotation** • Analyze Suspense • Use a Thesaurus
CLOSE READER — **Short Story by H.P. Lovecraft** "The Outsider"	◉ **Audio** "The Outsider"	
Essay by Jackie Torrence "Scary Tales"	◉ **Audio** "Scary Tales"	**Strategies for Annotation** • Determine Author's Viewpoint
Short Story by W.W. Jacobs "The Monkey's Paw"	⯈ **Video HISTORY** *British Imperialism* ◉ **Audio** "The Monkey's Paw"	**Strategies for Annotation** • Determine Theme • Analyze Stories: Dialogue • Analyze Stories: Foreshadowing • Using Latin Roots
CLOSE READER — **Poem by Edward Field** "Frankenstein"	◉ **Audio** "Frankenstein"	
Film by Ricky Lewis Jr. *The Monkey's Paw*		
ANCHOR TEXT — **Literary Criticism by Sharon A. Russell** "What Is the Horror Genre?"	◉ **Audio** "What Is the Horror Genre?"	**Close Read Screencasts** • Modeled Discussion (lines 1–11) • Close Read Application (lines 72–82) **Strategies for Annotation** • Analyze Text: Literary Criticism • Using Suffixes
CLOSE READER — **Essay by Daniel Cohen** "Man-Made Monsters"	◉ **Audio** "Man-Made Monsters"	
Collection 2 Performance Tasks: **A** Deliver a Persuasive Speech **B** Write a Literary Analysis	fyi hmhfyi.com **hmhfyi.com**	**Interactive Lessons** **A** Writing Arguments **A** Using Textual Evidence **A** Analyzing and Evaluating Presentations **B** Writing as a Process **B** Using Textual Evidence

For Systematic Coverage of Writing and Speaking & Listening Standards	**Interactive Lessons** Writing an Argument Analyzing and Evaluating Presentations

Assess		Extend	Reteach
Performance Task	**Online Assessment**	**Teacher eBook**	**Teacher eBook**
Writing Activity: Profile	Selection Test	**Analyze Stories: Plot > Interactive Whiteboard Lesson >** Plot and Conflict	**Analyze Point of View > Level Up Tutorial >** Point of View
Speaking Activity: Debate	Selection Test	**Conducting a Debate > Interactive Lesson >** Writing Arguments	**Determine Author's Viewpoint > Level Up Tutorial >** Author's Perspective
Writing Activity: Report	Selection Test	**Compare and Contrast Texts > Interactive Whiteboard Lesson >** Comparing Texts	**Determine Theme > Level Up Tutorial >** Theme
Media Activity: Storyboard	Selection Test	**Compare and Contrast a Film and a Story > Interactive Graphic Organizers >** Venn diagram	**Film Techniques**
Speaking Activity: Discussion	Selection Test	**Identifying Central Idea and Details in Literary Criticism > Interactive Whiteboard Lesson >** Main/Central Idea and Details **Monitor Comprehension Participating in Classroom Discussions > Interactive Lessons >** Participating in Collaborative Discussions	**Analyze Text: Literary Criticism**
A Deliver a Persuasive Speech **B** Write a Literary Analysis	Collection Test		

Lesson Assessments
Writing an Argument
Analyzing and Evaluating Presentations

Collection 2 Lessons	COMMON CORE Key Learning Objective	Performance Task
ANCHOR TEXT **Short Story by Edgar Allan Poe** **"The Tell-Tale Heart," p. 89A** **Lexile 850L**	**The student will be able to . . .** determine the point of view from which a story is told, evaluate the credibility of a narrator, and identify techniques used to create suspense in a fictional account.	Writing Activity: Profile
Essay by Jackie Torrence **"Scary Tales," p. 99A** **Lexile 710L**	**The student will be able to . . .** analyze an essay to determine the author's viewpoint, counterarguments, and elements of language that contribute to the author's style.	Speaking Activity: Debate
Short Story by W.W. Jacobs **"The Monkey's Paw," p. 105A** **Lexile 920L**	**The student will be able to . . .** determine and analyze a universal theme and to analyze foreshadowing in a short story.	Writing Activity: Report
Film by Ricky Lewis Jr. *The Monkey's Paw,* **p. 121A**	**The student will be able to . . .** analyze the choices a filmmaker makes when he or she decides to adapt a written story to movie form.	Media Activity: Storyboard
ANCHOR TEXT **Literary Criticism by Sharon A. Russell** **Lexile 1030L** **"What Is the Horror Genre?," p. 125A**	**The student will be able to . . .** analyze literary criticism to gain insight into literature.	Speaking Activity: Discussion

Collection 2 Performance Tasks:
A Deliver a Persuasive Speech
B Write a Literary Analysis

Vocabulary Strategy	Language and Style	Student Instructional Support	CLOSE READER Selection
Use a Thesaurus	Using Dashes	**Scaffolding for ELL Students:** Analyze Language: Repetition **When Students Struggle:** Track Sequence of Events **To Challenge Students:** Analyze Voice	Short Story by H.P. Lovecraft "The Outsider," p.98b **Lexile 1270L**
	Subject-Verb Agreement	**Scaffolding for ELL Students:** Analyze Language: Contractions	
Using Latin Roots	Subjunctive Mood	**Scaffolding for ELL Students:** Analyze Language: Archaic Terms **When Students Struggle:** Track Characters' Actions **To Challenge Students:** Analyze Stories	Poem by Edward Field "Frankenstein," p.120b
		Scaffolding for ELL Students: Multiple-Meaning Words **When Students Struggle:** Viewing with a Partner	
Using Suffixes	Commas	**Scaffolding for ELL Students:** Pronoun Referents **When Students Struggle:** Track Criteri	Essay by Daniel Cohen "Man-Made Monsters," p. 132b **Lexile 1210L**

ANCHOR TEXT

The Tell-Tale Heart

Short Story by Edgar Allan Poe

Why This Text?

Many students are fascinated by stories of terror and suspense. Using Edgar Allan Poe's classic tale, this lesson will introduce students to the horror genre and the techniques used by one of its most beloved writers.

 View It!

Professional Development Podcast:

Text-Dependent Analysis

Key Learning Objective: The student will be able to determine the point of view from which a story is told, evaluate the credibility of a narrator, and identify techniques used to create suspense in a fictional account.

For practice and application:

The Outsider

Close Reader selection
"The Outsider,"
Short Story by H.P. Lovecraft

COMMON CORE — Common Core Standards

RL 1 Cite textual evidence to support analysis and inferences.

RL 3 Analyze incidents in a story.

RL 4 Determine the meaning of words and phrases.

RL 6 Analyze how differences in points of view create suspense.

SL 1a Come to discussions prepared.

SL 4 Present claims and findings.

SL 6 Adapt speech to a variety of contexts and tasks.

W 2b Develop topic with relevant, well-chosen information and examples.

W 4 Produce clear and coherent writing.

W 9a Apply grade 8 Reading standards to literature.

W 10 Write routinely over extended and shorter time frames.

L 2a Use punctuation to indicate a pause or break.

L 4c Consult reference materials, both print and digital.

▲ Text Complexity Rubric

Quantitative Measures	**The Tell-Tale Heart** Lexile: 850L
Qualitative Measures	**Levels of Meaning/Purpose** single level of complex meaning **Structure** somewhat complex story concepts **Language Conventionality and Clarity** figurative, less accessible language **Knowledge Demands** distinctly unfamiliar experience
Reader/Task Considerations	**Teacher determined** Vary by individual reader and type of text

CLOSE READ

Edgar Allan Poe dreamed of being a writer at a very early age. By the time he was 13, he had already written many poems. In fact, Poe's first book was a collection of poetry that he published in 1827 when he was only 18 years old. However, it was the publication of his poem "The Raven" in 1845 that made Poe famous.

SETTING A PURPOSE Direct students to use the Setting a Purpose question to focus their reading. Tell students to generate additional questions as they read.

Analyze Point of View

COMMON CORE **RL 6**

(LINES 8–16)

Tell students that, in a story told from a **first-person point of view,** the narrator—the voice telling the story—is a character in the story.

A **ASK STUDENTS** to reread lines 8–16 and explain how they can tell that this story is being told from a first-person point of view. *(The narrator uses the first-person pronouns* my, me, *and* I.*)* How does the use of a first-person narrator contribute to the development of suspense? *(The first-person narrator makes the tone conversational, as if the narrator is calmly telling the reader why the idea of the murder is appropriate. This leads to immediate tension for the reader.)*

CRITICAL VOCABULARY

conceive: The narrator describes his thoughts about his relationship with the old man.

ASK STUDENTS to explain what led the narrator to conceive of the plan to kill the old man. *(The old man's "vulture" eye made the narrator's blood run cold, and he wanted to be rid of the eye forever.)*

Edgar Allan Poe (1809–1849) *was born in Boston to parents who were traveling actors. Orphaned by the time he was three, he moved to Virginia where friends of his family raised him. As a young man, Poe worked as a journalist while writing the stories and poems that would earn him the title "father of the modern mystery." After his young wife died, Poe fell into despair. He passed away two years later. His dark and sometimes horrifying works perhaps mirror the darkness and sadness of his own short life.*

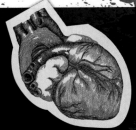

The Tell-Tale Heart

Short Story by Edgar Allan Poe

SETTING A PURPOSE As you read, pay attention to the way the narrator describes himself. What makes him unusual?

True!—nervous—very, very dreadfully nervous I had been and am! but why *will* you say that I am mad? The disease had sharpened my senses—not destroyed—not dulled them. Above all was the sense of hearing acute. I heard all things in the heaven and in the earth. I heard many things in hell. How, then, am I mad? Hearken! and observe how healthily—how calmly I can tell you the whole story.

It is impossible to say how first the idea entered my brain; but once **conceived**, it haunted me day and night. Object there
10 was none. Passion there was none. I loved the old man. He had never wronged me. He had never given me insult. For his gold I had no desire. I think it was his eye! yes, it was this! He had the eye of a vulture—a pale blue eye, with a film over it. Whenever it fell upon me, my blood ran cold; and so by degrees—very gradually—I made up my mind to take the life of the old man, and thus rid myself of the eye forever.

Now this is the point. You fancy me mad. Madmen know nothing. But you should have seen *me*. You should have seen

conceive
(kən-sēv´) *v.* When you *conceive* an idea, you think of it.

(tr) ©Bettmann/Corbis; 89 (cl) ©Alvor/Shutterstock; (cr) ©vadim nardin/Shutterstock; (c) ©vadim nardin/Shutterstock

The Tell-Tale Heart **89**

Close Read Screencasts ▶ View It!

Modeled Discussions

Have students click the *Close Read* icon in their eBooks to access a screencast in which readers discuss and annotate lines 1–7, a key passage that introduces the story.

As a class, view and discuss this video. Then have students work in pairs to do an independent close read of an additional passage—the narrator's description of what he experiences as he speaks with the police officers (lines 164–175).

CLOSE READ

Analyze Point of View

COMMON CORE RL 1, RL 6

(LINES 45–52)

Explain to students that an **unreliable narrator** is a narrator whose assessment of events cannot be trusted for some reason.

B **CITE TEXT EVIDENCE** Ask students to reread lines 45–52 and identify details in the text that suggest that the narrator of this story is not reliable. *(Possible answer: "I felt the extent of my own powers— of my sagacity"; "I could scarcely contain my feelings of triumph"; "I fairly chuckled at the idea")* What is it about this narrator that makes him seem unreliable? *(He appears to be mentally unstable.)*

CRITICAL VOCABULARY

vex: The narrator explains how he quietly entered the old man's room each night for seven nights but wasn't able to accomplish the task he had in mind.

ASK STUDENTS to tell what it was that vexed the narrator. *(the old man's Evil Eye)* Why wasn't the narrator able to kill the old man as he had planned to do? *(The old man's Evil Eye was closed as he slept.)*

---

how wisely I proceeded—with what caution—with what

20 foresight—with what dissimulation[1] I went to work!

I was never kinder to the old man than during the whole week before I killed him. And every night, about midnight, I turned the latch of his door and opened it—oh, so gently! And then, when I had made an opening sufficient for my head, I put in a dark lantern, all closed, closed, so that no light shone out, and then I thrust in my head. Oh, you would have laughed to see how cunningly I thrust it in! I moved it slowly—very, very slowly, so that I might not disturb the old man's sleep. It took me an hour to place my whole head within

30 the opening so far that I could see him as he lay upon his bed. Ha!—would a madman have been so wise as this? And then, when my head was well in the room, I undid the lantern cautiously—oh, so cautiously—cautiously (for the hinges creaked)—I undid it just so much that a single thin ray fell upon the vulture eye. And this I did for seven long nights— every night just at midnight—but I found the eye always closed; and so it was impossible to do the work; for it was not the old man who **vexed** me, but his Evil Eye. And every morning, when the day broke, I went boldly into the chamber,

40 and spoke courageously to him, calling him by name in a hearty tone, and inquiring how he had passed the night. So you see he would have been a very profound old man, indeed, to suspect that every night, just at twelve, I looked in upon him while he slept.

Upon the eighth night I was more than usually cautious in opening the door. A watch's minute hand moves more quickly than did mine. Never before that night had I *felt* the extent of my own powers—of my sagacity.[2] I could scarcely contain my feelings of triumph. To think that there I was, opening

50 the door, little by little, and he not even to dream of my secret deeds or thoughts. I fairly chuckled at the idea; and perhaps he heard me; for he moved on the bed suddenly, as if startled. Now you may think that I drew back—but no. His room was as black as pitch with the thick darkness (for the shutters were close fastened, through fear of robbers), and so I knew that he could not see the opening of the door, and I kept pushing it on steadily, steadily.

vex
(vĕks) *v.* If you *vex* someone, you annoy that person.

---

[1] **dissimulation** (dĭ-sĭm´yə-lā´shən): a hiding of one's true feelings.
[2] **sagacity** (sə-găs´ĭ-tē): sound judgment.

SCAFFOLDING FOR ELL STUDENTS

Analyze Language Students who are not yet fluent in English may be confused by Poe's frequent use of repetition since it deviates from standard sentence structure. Use a whiteboard to project lines 24–26 of the story.

- Highlight in yellow the repeated words "closed, closed."
- Read the sentence aloud both with and without the repetition.

Tell students that Poe repeats *closed* for emphasis only. Explain that the repeated word does not change the meaning of the sentence.

ASK STUDENTS to identify other sentences that include repeated words or phrases as they continue reading. Discuss the meaning of each of these sentences.

And then, when I had made an opening sufficient for my head, I put in a dark lantern, all closed, closed, so that no light shone out, and then I thrust in my head. Oh you would have laughed to see how cunningly I thurst it in! I moved it slowly—very, very slowly,

I had my head in, and was about to open the lantern, when my thumb slipped upon the tin fastening, and the old man sprang up in the bed, crying out—"Who's there?"

I kept quite still and said nothing. For a whole hour I did not move a muscle, and in the meantime I did not hear him lie down. He was still sitting up in the bed listening,—just as I have done, night after night, hearkening to the death watches[3] in the wall.

Presently I heard a slight groan, and I knew it was the groan of mortal terror. It was not a groan of pain or grief—oh, no!—it was the low, **stifled** sound that arises from the bottom of the soul when overcharged with awe. I knew the sound well. Many a night, just at midnight, when all the world slept, it has welled up from my own bosom, deepening, with its dreadful echo, the terrors that distracted me. I say I knew it well. I knew what the old man felt, and pitied him, although I chuckled at heart. I knew that he had been lying awake ever since the first slight noise, when he had turned in the bed. His fears had been ever since growing upon him. He had been trying to fancy them causeless, but could not. He had been saying to himself—"It is nothing but the wind in the chimney—it is only a mouse crossing the floor," or "it is merely a cricket which has made a single chirp." Yes, he has been trying to comfort himself with these suppositions; but he had found all in vain. *All in vain;* because Death, in approaching him, had stalked with his black shadow before him, and enveloped the victim. And it was the mournful influence of the unperceived shadow that caused him to feel—although he neither saw nor heard—to *feel* the presence of my head within the room.

When I had waited a long time, very patiently, without hearing him lie down, I resolved to open a little—a very, very little **crevice** in the lantern. So I opened it—you cannot imagine how stealthily, stealthily—until, at length, a single dim ray, like the thread of the spider, shot from out the crevice and fell full upon the vulture eye.

It was open—wide, wide open—and I grew furious as I gazed upon it. I saw it with perfect distinctness—all a dull blue, with a hideous veil over it that chilled the very marrow in my bones; but I could see nothing else of the old man's face

---

[3] **death watches:** deathwatch beetles—insects that make a tapping sound with their heads.

stifle
(stī´fəl) *v.* If you *stifle* something, you smother it.

crevice
(krĕv´ ĭs) *n.* A *crevice* is a narrow crack.

The Tell-Tale Heart **91**

CLOSE READ

Analyze Language

COMMON CORE RL 4

(LINES 80–93)

Tell students that **repetition,** the use of the same word or words more than once, can be used to emphasize a particular idea and to help create suspense. Point out that Poe uses repetition often throughout this story.

C **ASK STUDENTS** to reread lines 80–93 to identify four places where Poe repeats a word or phrase. *(all in vain; to feel; little; stealthily)* What idea does the repetition of "to feel" emphasize? *(Although the old man could not see or hear the narrator in the dark room, he could still sense that he was there.)* What impact does the repetition of the word "stealthily" have? *(It creates tension by slowing the story's pace at a very suspenseful moment and emphasizing that the narrator is acting in a cautious, secretive way.)*

CRITICAL VOCABULARY

stifle: On the eighth night, the old man sits up in bed listening for an hour after the narrator accidentally makes a noise that wakes him.

ASK STUDENTS what sound the old man makes after the hour has passed. *(a slight groan)* Why might he have stifled his groan? *(Possible answer: He was very fearful, believing that someone was in the room with him.)*

crevice: Standing in the dark room, the narrator decides to let some light shine from his lantern.

ASK STUDENTS to explain the effect of opening the covering of the lantern by only a crevice. *(The lantern emits a very thin ray of light that the narrator focuses on the old man's vulture eye.)*

APPLYING ACADEMIC VOCABULARY

predict	psychology

As you discuss the story, incorporate the following Collection 2 academic vocabulary words: *predict* and *psychology*. Ask students to pause occasionally as they read to **predict** what they think will happen next. Have them compare their predictions with actual story events. As students make predictions, ask them to consider the **psychology** of the narrator, analyzing his thought process and the ways his mental state may affect his telling of future events.

Analyze Suspense

COMMON CORE   RL 1, RL 6

(LINES 103–115)

Explain that **suspense** is a sense of growing tension, fear, and excitement felt by readers. Point out that authors often create suspense in a story by describing a character's anxiety or by using vivid language to tell about dramatic events.

D   **CITE TEXT EVIDENCE**   Have students reread lines 103–115 of the story. Ask students to find examples of the ways Poe creates suspense. *(Possible answers: "It increased my fury"; "I scarcely breathed"; "It grew louder, I say, louder every moment"; "this excited me to uncontrollable terror")* Why do these phrases create suspense? *(The description of the narrator's anxiety heightens the reader's fear that he will go through with his plan to kill the old man.)*

or person: for I had directed the ray as if by instinct, precisely upon the damned spot.

100   And now have I not told you that what you mistake for madness is but over-acuteness of the senses?—now, I say, there came to my ears a low, dull, quick sound, such as a watch makes when enveloped in cotton. I knew *that* sound well too. It was the beating of the old man's heart. It increased my fury, as the beating of a drum stimulates the soldier into courage.

But even yet I refrained and kept still. I scarcely breathed. I held the lantern motionless. I tried how steadily I could maintain the ray upon the eye. Meantime the hellish tattoo[4] of the heart increased. It grew quicker and quicker, and louder 110 and louder every instant. The old man's terror *must* have been extreme! It grew louder, I say, louder every moment!—do you mark me well? I have told you that I am nervous: so I am. And now at the dead hour of the night, amid the dreadful silence of that old house, so strange a noise as this excited me to uncontrollable terror. Yet, for some minutes longer I refrained and stood still. But the beating grew louder, louder! I thought the heart must burst. And now a new anxiety seized me—the sound would be heard by a neighbor! The old man's hour had come! With a loud yell, I threw open the lantern and leaped 120 into the room. He shrieked once—once only. In an instant

_____

[4] **hellish tattoo:** awful drumming.

92   Collection 2

WHEN STUDENTS STRUGGLE...

Direct students to lines 116–122. Ask students to reread this passage and to explain what has happened in this part of the story. *(The narrator becomes increasingly agitated by the beating of the old man's heart, and the narrator is afraid a neighbor will hear it. The narrator kills the old man by pulling him out of bed, dragging him to the floor, and then putting his heavy bed on top of him.)*

To help students gain a clearer understanding of the sequence of events in the story, have them fill out a chain of events graphic organizer like the one shown.

Chain of Events

First:

Then:

Then:

Finally:

(tl) ©Jinx Photography RF/Alamy Images; (tl) ©Richard Laschon/Shutterstock

I dragged him to the floor, and pulled the heavy bed over him. I then smiled gaily, to find the deed so far done. But, for many minutes, the heart beat on with a muffled sound. This, however, did not vex me; it would not be heard through the wall. At length it ceased. The old man was dead. I removed the bed and examined the corpse. Yes, he was stone, stone dead. I placed my hand upon the heart and held it there many minutes. There was no pulsation. He was stone dead. His eye would trouble me no more.

130   If still you think me mad, you will think so no longer when I describe the wise precautions I took for the concealment of the body. The night waned, and I worked hastily, but in silence. First of all I dismembered the corpse. I cut off the head and the arms and the legs.

I then took up three planks from the flooring of the chamber, and deposited all between the scantlings.[5] I then replaced the boards so cleverly, so cunningly, that no human eye—not even *his*—could have detected anything wrong. There was nothing to wash out—no stain of any kind—no
140   blood-spot whatever. I had been too wary for that. A tub had caught all—ha! ha!

When I made an end of these labors, it was four o'clock—still dark as midnight. As the bell sounded the hour, there came a knocking at the street door. I went down to open it with a light heart,—for what had I *now* to fear? There entered three men, who introduced themselves, with perfect suavity,[6] as officers of the police. A shriek had been heard by a neighbor during the night: suspicion of foul play had been aroused; information had been lodged at the police office, and they
150   (the officers) had been deputed to search the premises.

I smiled,—for *what* had I to fear? I bade the gentlemen welcome. The shriek, I said, was my own in a dream. The old man, I mentioned, was absent in the country. I took my visitors all over the house. I bade them search—search *well*. I led them, at length, to *his* chamber. I showed them his treasures, secure, undisturbed. In the enthusiasm of my confidence, I brought chairs into the room, and desired them *here* to rest from their fatigues, while I myself, in the wild **audacity** of my perfect triumph, placed my own seat upon the
160   very spot beneath which reposed the corpse of the victim.

audacity
(ô-dăs´ ĭ-tē) *n.*
Audacity is shameless daring or boldness.

---

[5] **scantlings:** small wooden beams supporting the floor.

[6] **suavity** (swä´vĭ-tē): graceful politeness.

The Tell-Tale Heart   **93**

CLOSE READ

Analyze Point of View

COMMON CORE RL 1, RL 6

(LINES 130–141)

Remind students that an unreliable narrator cannot be trusted to give an accurate assessment of events. Guide students to identify evidence that the narrator in the story is unreliable.

E   CITE TEXT EVIDENCE Have students reread lines 130–141. In this passage, how does the narrator try to convince readers that he is sane and reliable? *(He points to his "wise precautions" in his "concealment of the body" as evidence of his sanity.)* What effect do the narrator's explanations have on the reader? *(Far from convincing readers he is sane, the narrator's comments suggest that he is unstable or mentally ill.)*

CRITICAL VOCABULARY

audacity: The narrator leads the police to the old man's bedroom and shows them his belongings.

ASK STUDENTS which of the narrator's actions in his dealings with the police most clearly demonstrates his audacity. *(Possible answer: He brings chairs into the bedroom and invites the police to sit and rest. He places his own chair over the spot where he has hidden the corpse below the floorboards.)*

TEACH

CLOSE READ

Analyze Language

COMMON CORE RL 4

(LINES 170–178)

Point out that authors sometimes use italic type and repetition to emphasize a thought or an idea.

F **ASK STUDENTS** to examine lines 170–178. Why is the description in lines 172–174 in italic type? *(Poe wants to emphasize this idea that is repeated from lines 101–103.)* What does the narrator think the sound is? *(the beating of the old man's heart)* What is the likely source of the sound? *(Possible answer: the narrator's own heart)*

CRITICAL VOCABULARY

vehemently: As the narrator talks with the police, he begins to hear a disturbing sound.

ASK STUDENTS to explain why the narrator starts speaking more vehemently. *(As the sound gets louder, the narrator becomes more nervous. He tries to use his voice to mask the sound so the police won't hear it.)*

derision: Though the noise the narrator hears sounds louder and louder to him, the police go on chatting and smiling as if they do not notice it.

ASK STUDENTS why the narrator interprets the behavior of the police as derision. *(He thinks they know what he has done and are ridiculing him through their calm, composed attitude and actions.)*

hypocritical: The narrator can no longer tolerate his interaction with the police.

ASK STUDENTS to explain why the narrator calls the police officers' smiles "hypocritical." *(He believes they are mocking him, smiling kindly when really they know what he has done and are planning to arrest him.)*

COLLABORATIVE DISCUSSION Have student partners discuss specific ways that the story and its narrator are thought provoking. Prompt students with questions like: *What is unusual about the narrator's motive for murder?*

ASK STUDENTS to share any questions they generated in the course of reading and discussing the selection.

The officers were satisfied. My *manner* had convinced them. I was singularly at ease. They sat, and while I answered cheerily, they chatted of familiar things. But, ere long, I felt myself getting pale and wished them gone. My head ached, and I fancied a ringing in my ears: but still they sat and still chatted. The ringing became more distinct:—it continued and became more distinct: I talked more freely to get rid of the feeling: but it continued and gained definitiveness—until at length, I found that the noise was *not* within my ears.

170   No doubt I now grew *very* pale;—but I talked more fluently, and with a heightened voice. Yet the sound increased—and what could I do? It was *a low, dull, quick sound—much such a sound as a watch makes when enveloped in cotton.* I gasped for breath—and yet the officers heard it not. I talked more quickly—more **vehemently**; but the noise steadily increased. I arose and argued about trifles, in a high key and with violent gesticulations,[7] but the noise steadily increased. Why *would* they not be gone? I paced the floor to and fro with heavy strides, as if excited to fury by the

180 observation of the men—but the noise steadily increased. What *could* I do? I foamed—I raved—I swore. I swung the chair upon which I had been sitting, and grated it upon the boards, but the noise arose over all and continually increased. It grew louder—louder—*louder!* And still the men chatted pleasantly, and smiled. Was it possible they heard not?—no, no! They heard!—they suspected!—they *knew!*—they were making a *mockery* of my horror!—this I thought, and this I think. But anything was better than this agony! Anything was more tolerable than this **derision**! I could bear those

190 **hypocritical** smiles no longer! I felt that I must scream or die!—and now—again!—hark! louder! louder! *louder!*—

"Villains!" I shrieked, "dissemble[8] no more! I admit the deed!—tear up the planks!—here, here!—it is the beating of his hideous heart!"

vehemently
(vē′ə-mənt-lē) *adv.*
If you do something *vehemently*, you do it with intense emotion.

derision
(dĭ-rĭzh′ən) *n.*
Derision is jeering laughter or ridicule.

hypocritical
(hĭp′ə-krĭt′-kəl) *adj.*
If someone is *hypocritical*, the person is false or deceptive.

COLLABORATIVE DISCUSSION "The Tell-Tale Heart" is a well-known classic. With a partner, discuss what makes the story—and its narrator—so thought provoking. Cite specific evidence from the text to support your ideas.

---

[7] **gesticulations** (jĕ-stĭk′yə-lā′shəns): energetic gestures of the hands or arms.
[8] **dissemble**: pretend.

TO CHALLENGE STUDENTS . . .

Analyze Voice Tell students that the term **voice** refers to the unique use of language that allows readers to *hear* a human personality in a text. Invite students to analyze how Poe deviates from traditional rules of grammar to emphasize the deterioration of the narrator's mind.

ASK STUDENTS to identify sentence fragments, unusual placement of punctuation, and unconventional word order in "The Tell-Tale Heart." Have students discuss the effect of Poe's choices on the narrator's voice.

Analyze Point of View

COMMON CORE RL 6

Point of view is the method of narration used in a short story, novel, narrative poem, or work of nonfiction. In a story told from the **third-person point of view**, the **narrator**, or the voice that tells the story, is an outside observer. In a story told from **first-person point of view**, the narrator is a character in the story and uses the pronouns *I* and *me*.

Just as you can't believe everything everyone tells you, you can't always believe everything you learn from a first-person narrator. An **unreliable narrator** is a narrator whose assessment of events cannot be trusted for some reason—he or she might be purposefully lying, mentally unstable, or too young or unsophisticated to fully understand events. In order to determine whether or not a narrator is reliable, consider his or her actions, attitudes, and statements, and then decide whether he or she is generally trustworthy.

Do you think the narrator of "The Tell-Tale Heart" is reliable? Review the story and identify the lines that help you decide.

Analyze Suspense

COMMON CORE RL 6

Suspense is the sense of growing tension, fear, and excitement felt by the reader. When a story is suspenseful, the reader becomes increasingly curious about what will happen next. Writers use different techniques to create suspense in fiction. Notice these examples from "The Tell-Tale Heart."

Technique	Example
Describing a character's anxiety or fear	"... groan of mortal terror ... it was the low, stifled sound that arises from the bottom of the soul when overcharged with awe."
Using vivid words to describe dramatic sights, sounds, or feelings	"He had the eye of a vulture—a pale blue eye with a film over it. Whenever it fell upon me, my blood ran cold."
Repeating words, phrases, or characters' actions	the actions the narrator repeated as he entered the old man's room each night

As you analyze "The Tell-Tale Heart," look for additional examples of each technique.

TEACH

CLOSE READ

Analyze Point of View

COMMON CORE RL 1, RL 6

Discuss point of view with students, focusing on the distinctions between third-person point of view and first-person point of view.

Lead a conversation in which students suggest what circumstances might make a narrator an unreliable source of information. Then help them identify actions, attitudes, and statements in "The Tell-Tale Heart" that suggest whether or not the narrator in this story is a reliable witness. *(Possible answers: he has an abnormal motivation for murder, lines 8–16; he tries to make his irrational behavior sound normal, lines 100–101; he calls the police "Villains," line 192)*

Analyze Suspense

COMMON CORE RL 6

Review with students the three techniques authors may use to create suspense. Discuss each example shown in the chart. Then ask volunteers to find additional examples of each technique. *(Possible answers: (1) "And now a new anxiety seized me—the sound would be heard by a neighbor!", lines 117–118; (2) Poe describes the sound of the old man's heart; lines 108–110; 3. "It grew louder—louder—louder!", line 184)*

Strategies for Annotation

Annotate it!

Analyze Suspense

COMMON CORE RL 6

Share these strategies for guided or independent analysis:

- Highlight in yellow text that creates suspense by describing a character's anxiety or fear.
- Highlight in blue vivid words that create suspense by describing dramatic sights, sounds, or feelings.
- Highlight in pink words, phrases, or characters' actions that create suspense through repetition.

I arose and argued about trifles, in a high key and with violent gesticulations, but the noise steadily increased. Why *would* they not be gone? I paced the floor to and fro with heavy strides, as if excited to fury by the observation of the men—but the noise steadily increased. What *could* I do? I foamed—I raved—I swore.

Analyzing the Text

COMMON CORE · RL 1, RL 3, RL 4, RL 6

Possible answers:

1. The narrator's statements are immediately suspicious because he begins by mentioning "the disease" and its effects on his senses. This suggests a psychological or physical illness has affected his brain. His further comments in lines 19–20 about "how wisely I proceeded" and "with what foresight" suggests a distorted view of his intelligence.

2. The narrator waits to kill the old man because he believes he needs to wait for the "vulture eye" to be open. This creates suspense because readers can sense the narrator's mounting anxiety and can feel tension about what will happen if the old man's eye is ever open.

3. The narrator describes the "eye of the vulture" in detail ("a pale, blue eye, with a film over it"; "dull blue with a hideous veil") and as something that makes the narrator's "blood run cold." Every time the eye is mentioned, readers feel the narrator's dread growing. The sense that something very bad is going to happen creates suspense.

4. The first-person narrator claims to hear the old man's heart beating, a sound that drives him to finally kill the old man. The narrator describes his own anger of the sound, giving readers an awareness of his thinking and emotions that they would not otherwise have.

5. The narrator thinks he has convinced police of his innocence until he "fancied a ringing in his ears." The narrator's obsession with the sound grows until he confesses that, "it is the beating of his hideous heart!"

6. Yes. The narrator is obviously mentally ill and the reader cannot trust his view of reality, so the reader is left wondering what really happened and what this unbalanced person is going to do next, which adds to the tension.

Speaking and Listening

COMMON CORE · SL 1a, SL 4, SL 6

Before students begin rehearsing the scene they have chosen, ask them to consider the following:

- How will the emotional state of the character affect the way the character looks, moves, and sounds?
- Where should I change the volume, rate, and tone to bring out the meaning of the words and to best express the character's feelings?
- How can I be sure the audience will understand what I am saying? Am I speaking clearly and distinctly?

Analyzing the Text

COMMON CORE · RL 1, RL 3, RL 4, RL 6, W 2b, W 9a, SL 1a, SL 4, SL 6

Cite Text Evidence Support your responses with evidence from the text.

1. **Infer** Does the narrator's opinion of himself in lines 1–16 make him seem more or less reliable? Explain your choice.

2. **Analyze** What prevents the narrator from killing the old man during the first seven nights? Explain how his inaction contributes to the suspense.

3. **Interpret** In what way does the author's repeated image of the "eye of a vulture" help to create suspense?

4. **Draw Conclusions** Reread lines 88–105. What do readers learn from this first-person narration about the narrator's subjective, or personal, experience?

5. **Analyze** In lines 151–160, the narrator makes his case to the police and thinks he has convinced them of his innocence. What happens next that leads the narrator to finally confess? Tell what this suggests about his mental state.

6. **Evaluate** Do you think the reader's ability to trust the narrator increases the suspense in this story? Explain your answer.

Speaking and Listening

Working alone or with one or more partners, act out a scene from "The Tell-Tale Heart" that you consider especially suspenseful. Be prepared to identify the techniques or conventions that create suspense in the scene.

PERFORMANCE TASK

Writing Activity: Profile Criminals sometimes undergo a psychiatric evaluation during which their mental health is reviewed by a psychologist. If the narrator of this story underwent such an evaluation, what might the mental health experts say about his state of mind? Based on details from the story, write a profile of the narrator by answering the following questions:

- What crime did he commit?
- What was his motive? Was he insane, enraged, seeking revenge, or something else?
- Do you predict that the narrator will take responsibility for his crimes? Why or why not?
- What evidence, based on the narrator's account of events, supports your theory?

Assign this performance task.

PERFORMANCE TASK

COMMON CORE · W 2b, W 4, W 9a, W 10

Writing Activity: Profile Tell students that a profile is a type of explanatory writing in which a writer draws conclusions that are supported with facts, examples, and other kinds of details. Suggest that students begin their profiles by writing an introduction that gives a general assessment of the narrator. Each additional paragraph should address one specific aspect of their analysis.

Critical Vocabulary

conceive	vex	stifle	crevice
audacity	vehemently	derision	hypocritical

Practice and Apply Use what you know about the Vocabulary words to answer these questions.

1. Would it **vex** you if someone were **hypocritical**? Why?

2. Why does it take **audacity** to **vehemently** deny that you told a lie?

3. What method can you **conceive** to get something out of a **crevice**?

4. What can you do to **stifle derision** of another student?

Vocabulary Strategy: Use a Thesaurus

A **thesaurus** is a reference source that provides synonyms for many words. Writers use **synonyms,** or words that have a similar meaning as another word, to make writing precise and to avoid repeating the same word.

A good writer does not simply choose the first synonym provided in the thesaurus. He or she chooses the synonym that conveys the precise, or exact, meaning intended for a sentence. Look at the synonyms a thesaurus provides for the word *terror*:

fear, horror, fright, dread, shock, panic, alarm

Think about how each synonym might fit in this sentence from "The Tell-Tale Heart."

I knew it was a groan of mortal <u>terror</u>.

Does *a groan of terror* mean exactly the same as *a groan of alarm*? Which word conveys the idea of concern? Which conveys the idea of complete and total fear?

Practice and Apply Read these sentences. Use a print or digital thesaurus to replace the underlined words. Check that the synonym you chose fits the precise meaning of the sentence.

1. The narrator at first appears calm. By the end of the story, he is no longer <u>calm</u>.

2. As the story continues the narrator becomes increasingly nervous. His inability to stop talking shows how <u>nervous</u> he is.

3. "The Tell-Tale Heart" is a suspense-filled story. The narrator builds <u>suspense</u> as he reveals his carefully constructed plan to kill an old man.

PRACTICE & APPLY

Critical Vocabulary

COMMON CORE L 4c

Possible answers:

1. *Yes, it is annoying if someone is false or deceptive.*

2. *It is bold to show intense emotion while denying something you actually did.*

3. *I might be able to use tongs or tweezers to retrieve something that had fallen into a small crevice.*

4. *Students can speak up to demand the ridiculing stop or can ask adults for help in stopping it.*

Vocabulary Strategy: Use a Thesaurus

Possible answers:

(Accept all answers that work within the context of the sentence.)

1. *unruffled*

2. *anxious*

3. *tension*

Strategies for Annotation 🖊 📖 *Annotate it!*

Use a Thesaurus

COMMON CORE L 4c

Using a whiteboard, project a sample thesaurus entry such as the one shown to the right. Invite volunteers to mark the entry:

- Highlight in green words that fit the context of each sentence shown in the Practice and Apply activity.

- Highlight in blue words that do not fit the context of the sentence.

suspense: anticipation, expectation, apprehension, tension, anxiety, nervousness

Language Conventions: Using Dashes

COMMON CORE L 2a

Point out to students that the pause indicated by a dash is longer and more emphasized than the one indicated by a comma. To help students hear and understand the way that dashes affect the rhythm and meaning of a text, have student volunteers select and read aloud sentences from the story that include a dash or dashes.

Answers:

Students' paragraphs should show effective examples of dashes used to

- *signal a sudden break in thought*
- *signal the reader to pause and pay attention*
- *let the reader better hear the narrator's thoughts*

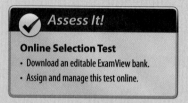

Assess It!

Online Selection Test
- Download an editable ExamView bank.
- Assign and manage this test online.

Language Conventions: Using Dashes

COMMON CORE L 2a

A writer's use of punctuation not only helps readers understand the writer's message, it can also signal how the writer wants the text to be read. A **dash** (—) is a horizontal line that is longer than a hyphen. Writers may use a dash for different purposes, as noted in the following chart.

Purpose	Example
to signal a sudden break in thought	"I did so for seven long nights—every night just after midnight—but found the eye always closed . . ."
to signal the reader to pause and pay attention	"I resolved to open a little—a very, very little crevice in the lantern."
to let the reader better hear a narrator's thoughts	"I went down to open it with a light heart—for what had I *now* to fear?"

Notice that when the interrupting thought appears in the middle of the sentence, one dash appears at the beginning of the thought and one dash appears at the end. Look at this example from "The Tell-Tale Heart":

> He had the eye of a vulture—a pale blue eye, with a film over it. Whenever it fell upon me, my blood ran cold; and so by degrees—very gradually—I made up my mind to take the life of the old man, and thus rid myself of the eye forever.

The dash after "vulture," signals the reader to pause and pay attention. The two dashes surrounding "very gradually" emphasize the slow, gradual process the narrator went through before deciding to kill the old man. Poe uses dashes not only to indicate pauses, but also to let the reader hear the excited, irrational voice of the narrator.

Practice and Apply Working with a partner, write a paragraph in which your narrator tells readers about him- or herself. Use dashes to

- set off a sudden break in thought.
- signal the reader to pause and pay attention.
- let the reader better hear your narrator's voice.

INTERACTIVE WHITEBOARD LESSON
Analyze Stories: Plot

COMMON CORE

RL 3

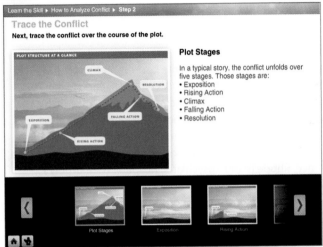

Learn the Skill ▶ How to Analyze Conflict ▶ Step 2

Trace the Conflict

Next, trace the conflict over the course of the plot.

PLOT STRUCTURE AT A GLANCE

CLIMAX

RESOLUTION

EXPOSITION

RISING ACTION

FALLING ACTION

Plot Stages

In a typical story, the conflict unfolds over five stages. Those stages are:
• Exposition
• Rising Action
• Climax
• Falling Action
• Resolution

Plot Stages   Exposition   Rising Action

TEACH

Explain that the **plot** is a series of events that takes place in a story.

Review with students these stages in a plot:

- Exposition
- Rising Action
- Climax
- Falling Action
- Resolution

Explain that during the exposition, readers learn about the conflict characters are facing. The **conflict** is the struggle between different forces. A conflict is **external** when the struggle is between a character and some outside force. It is **internal** when the conflict is within a character's mind.

PRACTICE AND APPLY

Work with students to identify and trace conflicts in the passages found in the Practice & Apply section of the whiteboard lesson. Then ask partners to apply the skill further by identifying and tracing the conflict in "The Tell-Tale Heart." Ask them to decide whether the narrator's conflict is external or internal.

Analyze Point of View

COMMON CORE

RL 6

RETEACH

Review the terms *point of view, first-person point of view, third-person point of view, narrator,* and *unreliable narrator.* Remind students that they can tell that the story "The Tell-Tale Heart" is told from a first-person point of view because the **narrator,** the person telling the story, is a character in the story.

Have students think of a familiar story, such as a fairy tale or folktale, that is typically told from a third-person point of view. Ask them to explain how that story might be different if it were told from a first-person point of view. For example, how might "The Three Little Pigs" change if it were told from a first-person point of view by

- the pig who built the straw house?
- the pig who built the brick house?
- the wolf?

LEVEL UP TUTORIALS Assign one or more of the following *Level Up* tutorials: **Point of View; First-Person Point of View; Third-Person Point of View; Narrator and Speaker.**

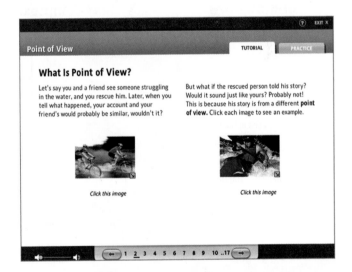

EXIT X

Point of View

TUTORIAL   PRACTICE

What Is Point of View?

Let's say you and a friend see someone struggling in the water, and you rescue him. Later, when you tell what happened, your account and your friend's would probably be similar, wouldn't it?

But what if the rescued person told his story? Would it sound just like yours? Probably not! This is because his story is from a different **point of view.** Click each image to see an example.

Click this image   Click this image

1 2 3 4 5 6 7 8 9 10 ..17

CLOSE READING APPLICATION

Student partners can work together to apply the skill to another fictional text they have read recently. Have students identify the point of view from which the story is told. Ask: *Is the narrator reliable or unreliable?* Have students cite evidence from the text to support their answers.

The Outsider

Short Story by H. P. Lovecraft

Why This Text

Students may not take the time to analyze how effects such as suspense are created. In "The Outsider," the contrast between the points of view of the narrator and the reader creates suspense. With the help of the close-reading questions, students will analyze the techniques Lovecraft uses to build suspense. They will draw conclusions about the narrator's reliability, and assess the effect of the narrator's reliability. This close reading will lead students to articulate a clear explanation of how the narrator contributed to the story's suspense.

Background Have students read the background and the information about the author. Introduce the selection by telling students that Howard Phillips Lovecraft had experiences in his childhood that would have predisposed anyone to have an interest in the emotion of fear. He and his family were vulnerable to mental illness, and his parents both died in Butler Hospital, Providence, Rhode Island's psychiatric hospital. *The Outsider and Others* was published in 1939—two years after Lovecraft's death in 1937—by two of his friends, who were determined to preserve Lovecraft's stories and share them with a wider audience than Lovecraft had reached during his lifetime.

SETTING A PURPOSE Ask students to pay attention to clues to the point of view of the narrator. How soon into the story can they begin to infer the narrator's identity?

 COMMON CORE

Common Core Support

- cite strong textual evidence
- determine the meaning of words and phrases as they are used in the text
- analyze how differences in points of view of the characters and the reader create suspense
- read and comprehend stories

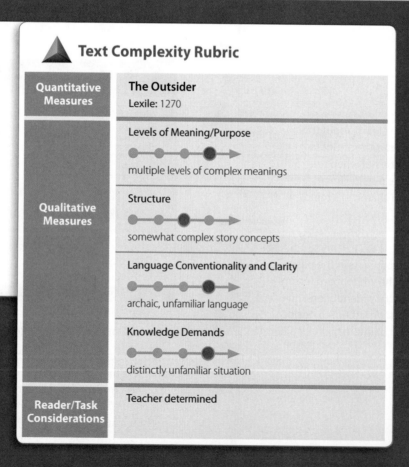

Text Complexity Rubric

Quantitative Measures

The Outsider
Lexile: 1270

Qualitative Measures

Levels of Meaning/Purpose

multiple levels of complex meanings

Structure

somewhat complex story concepts

Language Conventionality and Clarity

archaic, unfamiliar language

Knowledge Demands

distinctly unfamiliar situation

Reader/Task Considerations

Teacher determined

Strategies for CLOSE READING

Analyze Point of View

Students should read this story carefully all the way through. Close-reading questions at the bottom of the page will help them focus on a thorough analysis of the story. As they read, students should jot down comments or questions about the text in the side margins.

WHEN STUDENTS STRUGGLE . . .

To help students analyze how differences in the points of view of the narrator and the reader create suspense, have them work in a small group to fill out a chart like the one shown below as they analyze the story.

CITE TEXT EVIDENCE For practice in analyzing the narrator of "The Outsider," ask students to cite details that offer clues to the narrator's identity. After citing evidence they should circle "reliable" or "not reliable" in the center box.

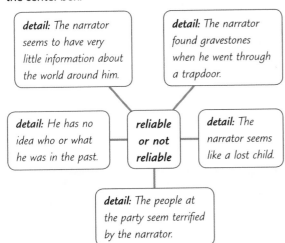

detail: The narrator seems to have very little information about the world around him.

detail: The narrator found gravestones when he went through a trapdoor.

detail: He has no idea who or what he was in the past.

reliable or not reliable

detail: The narrator seems like a lost child.

detail: The people at the party seem terrified by the narrator.

Background *"The oldest and strongest emotion of mankind is fear, and the oldest and strongest kind of fear is fear of the unknown." So says* **H. P. Lovecraft** *in the opening sentence of "Supernatural Horror in Literature," one of the best essays about horror fiction ever written. Plagued by nightmares and a fear of the unknown as a child, Lovecraft sought to exorcise his own fears by expressing them to his readers, believing that if his fears frightened him, they would terrify his audience.*

The Outsider

Short Story by H. P. Lovecraft

CLOSE READ
Notes

1. **READ ▶** As you read lines 1–21, begin to collect and cite text evidence.

- Circle the words that describe the narrator in lines 1–9.
- Underline the words that describe the narrator's surroundings.
- In the margin, write your impression of the narrator based on his description of himself and his surroundings.

A Unhappy is he to whom the memories of childhood bring only fear and sadness. Wretched is he who looks back upon lone hours in vast and dismal chambers with brown hangings and maddening rows of antique books, or upon awed watches in twilight groves of grotesque, gigantic, and vine-encumbered trees that silently wave twisted branches far aloft. Such a lot the gods gave to me—to me, the dazed, the disappointed; the barren, the broken. And yet I am strangely content, and cling desperately to those sere memories, when my mind momentarily threatens to reach beyond to *the other*.

B 10   I know not where I was born, save that the castle was infinitely old and infinitely horrible; full of dark passages and having high ceilings where the eye could find only cobwebs and shadows. The stones in the crumbling corridors seemed always hideously damp, and there

The narrator seems lonely and isolated.

21

---

1. **READ AND CITE TEXT EVIDENCE** Point out to students that the descriptions of the narrator and his surroundings tell the reader something about his identity and point of view.

A **ASK STUDENTS** to cite evidence to support their initial impressions of the narrator. *Answers will vary. Possible answer: students may describe the narrator as lonely, and cite evidence such as in line 2, "upon lone hours." They may describe the surroundings as isolated, and cite evidence such as in line 11, "infinitely horrible; full of dark passages."*

was an accursed smell everywhere, as of the piled-up corpses of dead
generations. It was never light, so that I used sometimes to light
candles and gaze steadily at them for relief; nor was there any sun
outdoors, since the terrible trees grew high above the topmost
20 accessible tower. There was one black tower which reached above the
trees into the unknown outer sky, but that was partly ruined and
could not be ascended save by a well-nigh impossible climb up the
sheer wall, stone by stone.

I must have lived years in this place, but I cannot measure the
time. Beings must have cared for my needs, yet I cannot recall any
person except myself; or anything alive but the noiseless rats and bats
and spiders. I think that whoever nursed me must have been
shockingly aged, since my first conception of a living person was that
of somebody mockingly like myself, yet distorted, shrivelled, and
decaying like the castle. To me there was nothing grotesque in the
bones and skeletons that strowed some of the stone crypts deep down
30 among the foundations. I fantastically associated these things with
every-day events, and thought them more natural than the coloured
pictures of living beings which I found in many of the mouldy books.
From such books I learned all that I know. No teacher urged or
guided me, and I do not recall hearing any human voice in all those
years—not even my own; for although I had read of speech, I had
never thought to try to speak aloud. My aspect[1] was a matter equally
unthought of, for there were no mirrors in the castle, and I merely
regarded myself by instinct as akin to the youthful figures I saw

[1] **aspect:** facial expression or appearance.

accessible:
easily
approached or
entered

C
D

---

2. **◀ REREAD** Reread lines 10–21. In this paragraph, how do the
narrator's statements about his background and his description of
his surroundings create suspense? Support your answer with explicit
textual evidence.

His mysterious background adds suspense to the story by reinforcing
a sense of the unknown. His description of the castle, with its dark
passages and lack of light, creates a sense of horror.

3. **READ ▶** Read lines 22–40. Underline details about the narrator's
upbringing that seem strange or unusual.

---

drawn and painted in the books. I felt conscious of youth because I
40 remembered so little.

Outside, across the **putrid** moat and under the dark mute trees, I
would often lie and dream for hours about what I read in the books;
and would longingly picture myself amidst gay crowds in the sunny
world beyond the endless forest. Once I tried to escape from the
forest, but as I went farther from the castle the shade grew denser and
the air more filled with brooding fear; so that I ran frantically back
lest I lose my way in a labyrinth of nighted silence.

So through endless twilights I dreamed and waited, though I
knew not what I waited for. Then in the shadowy solitude my longing
50 for light grew so frantic that I could rest no more, and I lifted
entreating hands to the single black ruined tower that reached above
the forest into the unknown outer sky. And at last I resolved to scale
that tower, fall though I might; since it were better to glimpse the sky
and perish, than to live without ever beholding day.

In the dank twilight I climbed the worn and aged stone stairs till I
reached the level where they ceased, and thereafter clung perilously to
small footholds leading upward. Ghastly and terrible was that dead,
stairless cylinder of rock; black, ruined, and deserted, and sinister
with startled bats whose wings made no noise. But more ghastly and
60 terrible still was the slowness of my progress; for climb as I might, the
darkness overhead grew no thinner, and a new chill as of haunted and
venerable mould **assailed** me. I shivered as I wondered why I did not
reach the light, and would have looked down had I dared. I fancied
that night had come suddenly upon me, and vainly groped with one
free hand for a window embrasure, that I might peer out and above,
and try to judge the height I had attained.

putrid:
foul-smelling
or rotten

He explains
that he is
desperate to
behold the sky
and daylight.

E

assailed:
attacked

---

4. **◀ REREAD AND DISCUSS** Reread lines 22–40. Discuss with a small
group whether the information the narrator shares about himself
makes him seem more or less reliable. Cite details in your discussion.

5. **READ ▶** As you read lines 41–100, continue to cite text evidence.

• Underline the reason the narrator gives for attempting to escape from
the castle, and restate it in the margin.

• Circle every use of the word *slab* in lines 67–83. In the margin, explain
what image it calls to mind.

• Underline the text in lines 84–100 that describes where the narrator
finds himself after scaling the tower.

---

2. **REREAD AND CITE TEXT EVIDENCE**

B **ASK STUDENTS** to read their answer aloud to a partner, and
then directly quote the text that supports their answer. Have
partners discuss and then rewrite their responses, including
explicit textual evidence. *Students should cite text in lines 10–12: "I*
know not where I was born . . ."

3. **READ AND CITE TEXT EVIDENCE** Remind students to
evaluate the reliability of the narrator.

C **ASK STUDENTS** to underline text that suggests that the
narrator had a strange childhood. *Students should cite lines 23–25,*
and lines 28–35, for their eerie details and sense of isolation.

Critical Vocabulary: accessible (line 18) Have students
compare their definitions of *accessible*.

4. **REREAD AND DISCUSS USING TEXT EVIDENCE**

D **ASK STUDENTS** to be prepared to share the results of their
discussions, including citing specific text evidence with line
numbers, such as 22–25, to support their analysis of whether the
narrator seems reliable or not.

5. **READ AND CITE TEXT EVIDENCE**

E **ASK STUDENTS** to cite evidence of the narrator's
motivations and surroundings. *Students should cite lines 53–55 as*
evidence of his motivations and lines 74, 77, 80, and 88–89 as
evidence that he is in a tomb.

Critical Vocabulary: putrid (line 41) Have students share
definitions for *putrid*, and explain how this word choice
contributes to tone in this story.

Critical Vocabulary: assailed (line 62) Have students compare
definitions for *assailed*.

> *Nothing I had before undergone could compare in terror with what I now saw . . .*

F All at once, after an infinity of awesome, sightless crawling up that concave and desperate precipice, I felt my head touch a solid thing, and I knew I must have gained the roof, or at least some kind of
70 floor. In the darkness I raised my free hand and tested the barrier, finding it stone and immovable. Then came a deadly circuit of the tower, clinging to whatever holds the slimy wall could give; till finally my testing hand found the barrier yielding, and I turned upward again, pushing the (slab) or door with my head as I used both hands in my fearful ascent. There was no light revealed above, and as my hands went higher I knew that my climb was for the nonce ended; since the (slab) was the trap-door of an aperture leading to a level surface of greater circumference than the lower tower, no doubt the floor of some lofty and capacious observation chamber. I crawled through
80 carefully, and tried to prevent the heavy (slab) from falling back into place, but failed in the latter attempt. As I lay exhausted on the stone floor I heard the eerie echoes of its fall, but hoped when necessary to pry it up again.

Believing I was now at a **prodigious** height, far above the accursed branches of the wood, I dragged myself up from the floor and fumbled about for windows, that I might look for the first time upon the sky, and the moon and stars of which I had read. But on every hand I was disappointed; since all that I found were vast shelves of marble, bearing odious oblong boxes of disturbing size. More and
90 more I reflected, and wondered what hoary secrets might abide in this high apartment so many aeons cut off from the castle below. Then unexpectedly my hands came upon a doorway, where hung a portal of stone, rough with strange chiselling. Trying it, I found it locked; but with a supreme burst of strength I overcame all obstacles and dragged it open inward. As I did so there came to me the purest ecstasy I have ever known; for shining tranquilly through an ornate grating of iron, and down a short stone passageway of steps that ascended from the newly found doorway, was the radiant full moon, which I had never before seen save in dreams and in vague visions I dared not call
100 memories.

The word slab *suggests a tomb.*

prodigious:
great in size

G Fancying now that I had attained the very **pinnacle** of the castle, I commenced to rush up the few steps beyond the door; but the sudden veiling of the moon by a cloud caused me to stumble, and I felt my way more slowly in the dark. It was still very dark when I reached the grating—which I tried carefully and found unlocked, but which I did not open for fear of falling from the amazing height to which I had climbed. Then the moon came out.

Most daemoniacal of all shocks is that of the abysmally unexpected and grotesquely unbelievable. Nothing I had before
110 undergone could compare in terror with what I now saw; with the bizarre marvels that sight implied. The sight itself was as simple as it was stupefying, for it was merely this: instead of a dizzying prospect of treetops seen from a lofty eminence, there stretched around me on the level through the grating nothing less than *the solid ground,* decked and diversified by marble slabs and columns, and overshadowed by an ancient stone church, whose ruined spire gleamed spectrally in the moonlight.

H Half unconscious, I opened the grating and staggered out upon the white gravel path that stretched away in two directions. (My mind,)
120 (stunned and chaotic as it was,) still held the frantic craving for light; and not even the fantastic wonder which had happened could stay my course. (I neither knew nor cared whether my experience was insanity,) (dreaming, or magic;) but was determined to gaze on brilliance and gaiety at any cost. (I knew not who I was or what I was, or what my) (surroundings might be;) though as I continued to stumble along I

pinnacle:
tower or spire

The narrator describes the setting of ruins, and he doesn't know where he is or where he is going.

6. **◄ REREAD** Reread lines 67–100. What vivid words in the narrator's description of the tower climb create suspense?

The narrator uses words such as "sightless crawling," "slimy," "eerie echoes," and "odious oblong boxes," to create a mood of terror and suspense.

7. **READ ▶** As you read lines 101–133, continue to cite textual evidence.

- Underline text that creates suspense by building anticipation of events.
- Circle text that describes the narrator's confused mental state.
- In the margin, state how the narrator continues to build suspense.

Critical Vocabulary: prodigious (line 84) Have students explain the meaning of *prodigious* as it is used here. Have students use a thesaurus to find synonyms for *prodigious.* Ask how Lovecraft's choice of the word *prodigious* impacts the meaning of this sentence. Have volunteers read the sentence with a synonym such as *extraordinary,* and discuss how the meaning changes.

FOR ELL STUDENTS If you have Spanish speakers in your class, ask a volunteer to explain what the word *ascent* means. They may recognize it as a cognate of the Spanish *ascenso.*

6. **REREAD AND CITE TEXT EVIDENCE**

F **ASK STUDENTS** to cite text evidence to support their analysis of how Lovecraft creates suspense in lines 67–100. *Students may cite line 67, "sightless crawling"; line 72, "slimy"; line 82, "eerie echoes"; and line 89, "odious oblong boxes."*

7. **READ AND CITE TEXT EVIDENCE**

G **ASK STUDENTS** to cite text that shows how Lovecraft creates suspense. *Students should cite specific evidence that shows how Lovecraft builds anticipation of events (lines 101–102, 103–104, 109–110, 125–127) and how Lovecraft reveals the narrator's confused mental state (lines 119–120, 122–125).*

Critical Vocabulary: pinnacle (line 101) Have students share definitions for *pinnacle,* and explain the meaning of the word as it is used in this context.

FOR ELL STUDENTS Clarify that the word *undergone* means "endured" or "experienced."

The Outsider **98e**

became conscious of a kind of fearsome latent memory that made my progress not wholly fortuitous. I passed under an arch out of that region of slabs and columns, and wandered through the open country; sometimes following the visible road, but sometimes leaving

130 it curiously to tread across meadows where only occasional ruins bespoke the ancient presence of a forgotten road. Once I swam across a swift river where crumbling, mossy masonry told of a bridge long vanished.

Over two hours must have passed before I reached what seemed to be my goal, a venerable ivied castle in a thickly wooded park; maddeningly familiar, yet full of perplexing strangeness to me. I saw that the moat was filled in, and that some of the well-known towers were demolished; whilst new wings existed to confuse the beholder. But what I observed with chief interest and delight were the open

140 windows—gorgeously ablaze with light and sending forth sound of the gayest **revelry**. Advancing to one of these I looked in and saw an oddly dressed company indeed; making merry, and speaking brightly to one another. I had never, seemingly, heard human speech before;

The castle feels familiar but it also feels odd or unusual to him.

revelry:
merrymaking

---

8. ◀ **REREAD** Reread lines 118–133. What impression do you form of the narrator's mental state? In what ways does his unreliability increase suspense? Cite explicit textual evidence in your answer.

His confused mental state calls into question his ability to tell the story accurately. Since the story is told solely from his point of view, the reader does not know what to believe or expect. His unreliability as a narrator builds suspense as the audience is prompted to wonder what will happen next.

9. **READ** ▶ As you read lines 134–160, continue to cite textual evidence.

- Circle each use of *I* in the text.
- Underline the narrator's contradictory statement in lines 134–138, and in the margin, paraphrase what he says.
- In lines 147–160, circle phrases that describe the actions of the partygoers.

26

---

and could guess only vaguely what was said. Some of the faces seemed to hold expressions that brought up incredibly remote recollections; others were utterly alien.

I now stepped through the low window into the brilliantly lighted room, stepping as I did so from my single bright moment of hope to my blackest convulsion of despair and realisation. The nightmare was

150 quick to come; for as I entered, there occurred immediately one of the most terrifying demonstrations I had ever conceived. Scarcely had I crossed the sill when there descended upon the whole company a sudden and unheralded fear of hideous intensity, distorting every face and evoking the most horrible screams from nearly every throat. Flight was universal, and in the clamour and panic several fell in a swoon and were dragged away by their madly fleeing companions. Many covered their eyes with their hands, and plunged blindly and awkwardly in their race to escape, overturning furniture and stumbling against the walls before they managed to reach one of

160 the many doors.

The cries were shocking; and as I stood in the brilliant apartment alone and dazed, listening to their vanishing echoes, I trembled at the thought of what might be lurking near me unseen. At a casual inspection the room seemed deserted, but when I moved toward one

---

10. ◀ **REREAD** Reread lines 147–160. Why does seeing the events in these lines from the narrator's point of view limit your understanding of what is actually happening? Support your answer with explicit textual evidence.

The partygoers are terrified of something but we don't know what it is because the narrator can only describe their reaction to what they see. He doesn't tell what people say. He only reports their panic.

11. **READ** ▶ As you read lines 161–182, continue to cite textual evidence.

- Underline the text that describes the sound the narrator makes.
- In the margin, explain what causes him to make that sound.
- Circle vivid words and phrases that describe what the narrator sees.

27

---

8. **REREAD AND CITE TEXT EVIDENCE**

H ASK STUDENTS to read their response to a partner, discuss how the narrator's unreliability increases suspense, and revise their response, citing text evidence. *Students should cite text evidence that shows that the narrator is unreliable from lines 118–127.*

9. **READ AND CITE TEXT EVIDENCE**

I ASK STUDENTS to cite clues to the narrator's identity. *Students should cite evidence that he once knew the castle, but that a lot of time has passed (lines 136–138), and that "oddly dressed" (line 142) is evidence of the passage of time. The responses of the revelers in lines 153–160 may be clues, but that will need to be confirmed later.*

Critical Vocabulary: revelry (line 141) Have students compare their definitions, and discuss the meaning of *revelry* as it is used here.

10. **REREAD AND CITE TEXT EVIDENCE**

J ASK STUDENTS to cite explicit textual evidence to explain why seeing events from the narrator's point of view limits the reader's understanding of of what is happening. *Students should cite evidence showing that the partygoers are terrified (lines 153–159). They should explain that the narrator cannot tell the reader what the partygoers are afraid of, because he does not know.*

11. **READ AND CITE TEXT EVIDENCE**

K ASK STUDENTS to cite clues that provide insights into the identity of the narrator. *Students should cite the sound the narrator makes (line 169), and the vivid description of what the narrator sees (lines 175–181), as possible clues to the narrator's identity. Reading further will be necessary to confirm the narrator's identity.*

FOR ELL STUDENTS Explain that *heralded* means "announced." Then ask a volunteer to deduce the meaning of the word *unheralded* ("unannounced, without warning").

The narrator has seen a "monstrosity" that is unbelievably hideous.

of the alcoves I thought I detected a presence there—a hint of motion beyond the golden-arched doorway leading to another and somewhat similar room. As I approached the arch I began to perceive the presence more clearly; and then, with the first and last sound I ever uttered—a ghastly ululation[2] that revolted me almost as poignantly as its noxious cause—I beheld in full, frightful vividness the inconceivable, indescribable, and unmentionable monstrosity which had by its simple appearance changed a merry company to a herd of delirious fugitives.

I cannot even hint what it was like, for it was a compound of all that is unclean, uncanny, unwelcome, abnormal, and detestable. It was the ghoulish shade of decay, antiquity, and desolation; the putrid, dripping eidolon[3] of unwholesome revelation; the awful baring of that which the merciful earth should always hide. God knows it was not of this world—or no longer of this world—yet to my horror I saw in its eaten-away and bone-revealing outlines and leering, abhorrent **travesty** on the human shape; and in its mouldy, disintegrating apparel an unspeakable quality that chilled me even more.

I was almost paralysed, but not too much so to make a feeble effort towards flight; a backward stumble which failed to break the spell in which the nameless, voiceless monster held me. My eyes bewitched by the glassy orbs which stared loathsomely into them, refused to close; though they were mercifully blurred, and shewed the terrible object but indistinctly after the first shock. I tried to raise my hand to shut out the sight, yet so stunned were my nerves that my

travesty:
a bizarre imitation

[2] **ululation:** howling or wailing.
[3] **eidolon:** phantom; image.

---

12. ◀ **REREAD** Reread lines 174–182. In what way do the descriptions in these lines create suspense?

The description in these lines is one of an other-worldly monster. We are curious about why such a creature has appeared.

13. **READ** ▶ Read lines 183–225. What has the narrator discovered about himself? What supernatural elements become clear in the story? Record your ideas in the margin. Continue to cite textual evidence.

28

> *I recognized, most terrible of all, the unholy abomination that stood leering before me . . .*

arm could not fully obey my will. The attempt, however, was enough to disturb my balance; so that I had to stagger forward several steps to avoid falling. As I did so I became suddenly and agonizingly aware of the *nearness* of the carrion[4] thing, whose hideous hollow breathing I half fancied I could hear. Nearly mad, I found myself yet able to throw out a hand to ward off the foetid apparition which pressed so close; when in one cataclysmic second of nightmarishness and hellish accident *my fingers touched the rotting outstretched paw of the monster beneath the golden arch.*

I did not shriek, but all the fiendish ghouls that ride the night-wind shrieked for me as in that same second there crashed down upon my mind a single fleeting avalanche of soul-annihilating memory. I knew in that second all that had been; I remembered beyond the frightful castle and the trees, and recognized the altered edifice in which I now stood; I recognized, most terrible of all, the unholy **abomination** that stood leering before me as I withdrew my sullied fingers from its own.

But in the cosmos there is balm as well as bitterness, and that balm is nepenthe.[5] In the supreme horror of that second I forgot what had horrified me, and the burst of black memory vanished in a chaos of echoing images. In a dream I fled from that haunted and accursed pile, and ran swiftly and silently in the moonlight. When I returned to the churchyard place of marble and went down the steps I found the stone trap-door immovable; but I was not sorry, for I had hated the antique castle and the trees. Now I ride with the mocking and friendly ghouls on the night-wind, and play by day amongst the catacombs of Nephren-Ka[6] in the sealed and unknown valley of Hadoth[7] by the Nile. I know that light is not for me, save that of the

abomination:
a disgusting thing

The narrator is not a human being; he is a ghost or one of the "undead."

[4] **carrion:** decaying flesh.
[5] **nepenthe:** a drug mentioned in the *Odyssey* as a remedy for grief.
[6] **Nephren-Ka:** one of Lovecraft's mythical creations.
[7] **Hadoth:** one of Lovecraft's creations; a sealed valley by the Nile amid the hills of Neb that holds the catacombs of Nephren-Ka.

29

---

12. REREAD AND CITE TEXT EVIDENCE

L **ASK STUDENTS** to add specific text evidence to their responses to support their analysis of how the descriptions create suspense. *Students may cite any text from lines 174–182, such as "its mouldy, disintegrating apparel," as examples of details that create growing tension in the reader.*

13. READ AND CITE TEXT EVIDENCE

M **ASK STUDENTS** to cite text evidence to support their explanations of the narrator's discovery. *Students should realize that the hideous monster the narrator described is in fact the narrator himself. They should cite line 225 as evidence and explain that what he saw was a reflection.*

Critical Vocabulary: travesty (line 181) Ask volunteers to read their definitions. Have students discuss the meaning of *travesty* as it is used here.

Critical Vocabulary: abomination (line 205) Have students compare definitions of *abomination*, and explain the meaning of *abomination* as it is used here. Have students also look up the adjective *abominable*.

The narrator discovers that he is the monster.

moon over the rock tombs of Neb, nor any gaiety save the unnamed feasts of Nitokris[8] beneath the Great Pyramid; yet in my new wildness and freedom I almost welcome the bitterness of alienage.

220 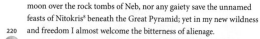 For although nepenthe has calmed me, I know always that I am an outsider; a stranger in this century and among those who are still men. This I have known ever since I stretched out my fingers to the abomination within that great gilded frame; stretched out my fingers and touched *a cold and unyielding surface of polished glass.*

---

[8] **Nitokris:** perhaps the last pharaoh of the Sixth Dynasty; she is used mythically in two of Lovecraft's stories.

---

14. ◄ REREAD AND DISCUSS   Reread lines 221–225. With a small group, discuss whether you were surprised by the revelation at the end of the story. Cite explicit text evidence in your discussion.

SHORT RESPONSE

Cite Text Evidence   Evaluate the narrator of "The Outsider." How credible is his presentation of events? Explain whether your understanding of the narrator added to the story's suspense. **Cite text evidence** in your response.

The narrator seems to have very little information about the world outside of his own, limited environment. Therefore, his presentation of events is not very credible. He had no idea of who or what he was, so he could provide no context for what he saw and experienced. The author provided clues to the reader, such as the gravestones the narrator found when he went through the trapdoor, hinting that things are not quite what they seem. Not understanding who or what the narrator was made the story more suspenseful. The narrator at first seemed like an unfortunate child, locked in a castle and cared for by invisible hands. There is no hint that the narrator is something sinister.

30

TO CHALLENGE STUDENTS . . .

Tell students that H. P. Lovecraft wrote in a subgenre of speculative fiction called "weird fiction". Weird tales are not simply about murder, bones, and ghosts. They must catch at the heart and leave the reader in a cold sweat. The following are the characteristics of weird fiction.

- A weird tale must evoke dread and suggest that mysterious forces are in effect.
- A weird tale treats the possibility of inexplicable ghastliness seriously.
- A weird tale implies that the natural laws we take for granted may dissolve against attacks from the unknown.

ASK STUDENTS to write a paragraph or more of their own weird fiction that creates tension, using techniques exemplified in *The Outsider*. Volunteers can read their writing aloud to the class.

---

14. REREAD AND DISCUSS USING TEXT EVIDENCE

(N) ASK STUDENTS to volunteer to record text evidence for their group. They should record quotations with line numbers for the most compelling evidence they can find. *Most students will probably not be surprised by the revelation at the end of the story. They may cite text as early in the story as lines 1–2, "memories of childhood bring only fear and sadness," as evidence pointing in the direction of a grim or ghoulish narrator.*

SHORT RESPONSE

Cite Text Evidence   Student responses will vary, but they should cite evidence from the text to support their evaluations. Students should:

- provide a text-based assessment of the credibility of the narrator.
- evaluate whether the credibility of the narrator contributed to the creation of suspense.
- cite strong textual evidence to support their response.

DIG DEEPER

1. With the class, return to Question 4, Reread and Discuss. Have students share the results of their discussion.

ASK STUDENTS whether they were satisfied with the outcome of their small-group discussions. Have each group share whether the majority opinion was that the narrator was reliable or unreliable. What compelling evidence did the groups cite from the story to support this opinion?

- Encourage students to tell whether there was any compelling evidence cited by group members holding the minority opinion. If so, why didn't it sway the group's position?

- Have students cite text that shows that the narrator is unreliable: *His memory is impaired (lines10, 39–40). His experience is limited: "lone hours in vast and dismal chambers." His experience is bizarre: "I cannot measure time."*

- After students have shared the results of their group's discussion, ask whether other groups presented evidence they wished they had identified.

2. With the class, return to Question 14, Reread and Discuss. Have students share the results of their discussion.

ASK STUDENTS whether they were satisfied with the outcome of their small-group discussions. Have each group share whether the majority opinion was that the ending was a surprise or not. What compelling evidence did the groups cite from the story to support this position?

- Point out that Lovecraft used foreshadowing to reveal the narrator, little by little.

- Have students cite text that reveals the narrator's identity. *He has been living underground (line114). He has been living in a graveyard: "vast shelves of marble, bearing odious oblong boxes of disturbing size," the partygoers are terrified of him.*

- After students have shared the results of their group's discussion, ask whether other groups presented evidence they wished they had identified.

ASK STUDENTS to return to their Short Response answer and revise it based on the class discussion.

CLOSE READING NOTES

Scary Tales

Essay by Jackie Torrence

Why This Text?

People often debate the kinds of ideas and activities that are appropriate for young people. This essay offers what some may think is an unusual position on sharing scary stories with young people. Students will explore how the author supports her viewpoint and will understand factors that influence her point of view.

Key Learning Objective: The student will be able to analyze an essay to determine the author's viewpoint, counterarguments, and elements of language that contribute to the author's style.

 ## Common Core Standards

RI 1 Cite textual evidence.

RI 2 Provide an objective summary.

RI 3 Analyze how a text makes connections among individuals, ideas, or events.

RI 4 Determine the meaning of words and phrases, including figurative meanings.

RI 6 Determine an author's point of view and analyze how the author responds to conflicting viewpoints.

SL 1 Engage effectively in a range of collaborative discussions.

SL 1a Come to discussions prepared.

SL 1c Pose and respond to questions.

SL 3 Delineate a speaker's argument and specific claims, evaluating the soundness of the reasoning.

SL 4 Present claims and findings in a focused, coherent manner.

L 1 Demonstrate command of the conventions of standard English grammar and usage.

 ## Text Complexity Rubric

Quantitative Measures	**Scary Tales** Lexile: 710L

Levels of Meaning/Purpose

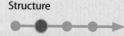

more than one purpose; implied but easy to infer

Structure

implicit problem-solution text structure

Qualitative Measures

Language Conventionality and Clarity

figurative, less accessible language

Knowledge Demands

some specialized knowledge required

Reader/Task Considerations
Teacher determined
Vary by individual reader and type of text

CLOSE READ

Background Have students read the background information about the author. Tell students that in many cultures the ability to tell a story well is a prized skill. Stories help to preserve traditions and forge connections between old and new generations. Explain that Jackie Torrence's grandfather first heard many of his stories from his own father who had been a slave. Stories, like "Br'er Rabbit" and other African American folktales that Torrence's audiences enjoyed hearing her tell, have historical importance because they preserve the dialect of the slaves and also include code words that once helped slaves in the American South escape to freedom on the Underground Railroad. Tell students they will learn more about slavery and the Civil War in Collection 3.

SETTING A PURPOSE Direct students to use the Setting a Purpose question to focus their reading. Tell students to generate their own questions as they read.

Analyze the Meanings of Words and Phrases

COMMON CORE **RI 4**

(LINES 13–18)

Tell students that **style** is the manner in which a work is written. Style involves *how* something is said rather than *what* is said. The style of a piece of writing can be described with words such as *formal, informal, serious,* or *conversational.* Explain that an author's **word choice,** or use of specific words, is one element that helps determine style.

A **ASK STUDENTS** to reread lines 13–18. What words describe the style of this essay? *(informal; conversational)* Which words or phrases in these lines help establish the style? *(Possible answer: "wears a rug," "That ain't nice.")* How does the author's use of the word *rug* contribute to her style? *(It is an informal term that means "a small wig"; it would not be used in formal writing.)*

Jackie Torrence (1944–2004) *spent much of her childhood on a North Carolina farm, where she grew up listening to traditional stories told by her grandfather. Years later, while working as a librarian, she was asked to read stories to some young children. She agreed, and the children were instantly captivated. Before long, Torrence was invited to tell stories in local and neighboring communities. Torrence, who was later dubbed "The Story Lady," went on to gain national prominence as a storyteller.*

SCARY TALES

Essay by Jackie Torrence

SETTING A PURPOSE As you read, pay attention to the points the author makes about scary tales. Would most people agree with her ideas?

I guess I like scary tales so much because my granddaddy liked scary tales. He'd have to tell one if it killed him. He was sick a lot, but if visitors came, he'd prop himself up in an armchair and put a quilt on his lap. So nobody could see his nightshirt. Then he'd put his derby hat on, he loved that derby, and somebody would say, "Mr. Jim, tell us about that time when the fire dog followed you down though the wheat field." And my grandma would say, "Hold it, let me leave the room, lightning's going to strike." She always said Granddaddy was
10 the biggest liar God ever blew breath into. So she'd leave, but not me. I'd get closer to Pa 'cause I wanted to watch the people listening to him.

There used to be an old man who came to our house named Hall. I would hear people say, "Mr. Hall wears a rug." I didn't know what a rug was. I'd lay down on the floor and Grandma would say, "What are you doing?" "I'm trying to

99 ©Danomyte/Shutterstock

SCAFFOLDING FOR ELL STUDENTS

Analyze Language Help students identify and understand the meanings of the many contractions that appear in this essay.

- Explain that a **contraction** is a short way of writing a word or words. An apostrophe takes the place of one or more letters that are omitted.

- Demonstrate by writing the contraction *isn't.* Tell students that *isn't* means "is not" and that the apostrophe takes the place of the missing letter *o.*

ASK STUDENTS to identify contractions and the words they stand for as they read. For example: *He'd* (line 2); *lightning's* (line 9); *didn't* (line 15).

Analyze the Meanings of Words and Phrases

COMMON CORE RI 1, RI 4

(LINES 25–33)

Explain that **syntax** refers to the way words are put together to form phrases and sentences. Sentence length and the use of formal or informal grammar are both part of syntax and contribute to a writer's style of writing.

B **CITE TEXT EVIDENCE** Have students reread lines 25–33 and identify examples of sentence structure and wording that help create the style of this essay. Are the sentences long and filled with details, or are they short and crisp? *(short and crisp)* Is the grammar formal or informal? *(informal)* Give an example. *(Possible answer: "Granddaddy scared the hair right off Mr. Hall's head!")*

Tell students that **figurative language** is language used imaginatively in ways that go beyond literal definitions. A **simile** is one type of figurative language that compares two unlike things using the words *like* or *as*. The use of figurative language also contributes to a writer's style.

C **ASK STUDENTS** to reread lines 25–33 to identify the simile Torrence uses. *("as naked as the palm of my hand")* What is the effect of the comparison? *(It paints a strong visual picture that is also humorous.)*

find Mr. Hall's rug." And Grandma would say, "Get up, *get up!* That ain't nice." Well, one day Mr. Hall was there and Grandpa started into one of his scary stories. There was a
20 piece of wood burning in the fireplace, sort of sticking out, and Pa spotted it. I watched him put his tobacco way back in his mouth so he could get a good long shot. At just the right moment in the story, he threw his head forward and that tobacco came out and hit that wood just right; it fell off on the floor and the fire sparked up. Somebody threw a baby on the floor, men ran out, and Mr. Hall ran out too. When he passed us, Mr. Hall's scalp was as naked as the palm of my hand. *Jesus have mercy!* Granddaddy scared the hair right off Mr. Hall's head! Well, I went over to his chair, and there in Mr.
30 Hall's hat was his scalp! I picked it up. "Grandma! Is this Mr. Hall's rug?" Grandma said, "Put that thing down and go wash your hands." Oh, I loved those days when Grandpa told his scary stories.

So when I started telling stories in school, that's what I chose, scary tales. I've got storytelling friends who'd rather be killed than go to junior high. But not me, I love junior high.

APPLYING ACADEMIC VOCABULARY

| summary | psychology |

As you discuss the essay, incorporate the following Collection 2 academic vocabulary words: *summary* and *psychology*. As students read the essay, ask them to pause occasionally to **summarize** the events that the author describes. Discuss with them the ways the author's grandpa used **psychology** to frighten her and how she uses it to tell stories in junior high schools.

That's sixth, seventh, and eighth grade, and those kids can't
believe they're going to have to sit there and listen to me tell
a story. So I do just what Grandpa said, "If you want to get the
40 attention of a mule who's too stubborn to listen, you take the
branch off a tree and come right down across the top of his
head." What is my branch? A good scary story. When I tell
those kids, "I'm going to scare you," when I start to give them
a little bit of fear, well, they're ready to listen.

A lot of people have told me I really shouldn't tell children
scary things. Well, children can frighten themselves without
your help. When they're alone in bed they hear things and
they see things. So I just help them along. "It's *daaaaaaark,*"
I say. And there's a strange voice, "Where's Myy Haaairy
50 Toe…" That's all they need. They remember the dark and
they're scared again and that's good.

Children need to be frightened. We all do. It's an emotion
that was given to all of us and it should be exercised. When
you don't exercise it, you lose your sense of fear. That's why my
granddaddy told me scary stories. He wanted me to know that
only fools rush in where angels fear to tread. You should be a
little hesitant sometimes, his stories were saying, you should
think twice before you go into the woods, there just might be a
hairy man and you need to be cautious.

60 My grandfather scared me to death. Grandma would say,
"Get up on your granddaddy's lap and kiss him good night."
I'd throw my arms around him and say, "I'm going to bed."
And he'd say, "It's dark up there." And I'd say, "I know." "You
know what's in the dark?" "Nooooo." "Monsters," he'd say.
"What do monsters do?" "They'll drag you off the bed and
put you in the keyhole," he'd say. Well, I yelled and screamed
going up the stairs. My grandmother would say to me on the
way up, "*Would you stop crying?* There's not a keyhole big
enough to put you in." So I remained fat for the rest of my life.
70 That's why no monsters have ever bothered me.

COLLABORATIVE DISCUSSION With a partner, discuss whether
you agree with Torrence's ideas about scary tales. Cite specific
evidence from the text to support your ideas.

TEACH

CLOSE READ

Determine Author's Viewpoint (LINES 45–59)   COMMON CORE RI 6

Tell students that an **author's viewpoint,** or
perspective, is the unique combination of ideas,
values, feelings, and beliefs that influence the way
the writer views a topic. Point out that good writers
anticipate that some readers may not agree with their
views and respond to the people who might disagree
by addressing **counterarguments,** arguments made
to oppose a view that is different from the author's.

D **ASK STUDENTS** to reread lines 45–59. What is
Torrence's view about telling children scary stories?
*(She thinks it's a good idea; "Children need to be
frightened," she says.)* What is one counterargument
that she provides? *(Possible answer: It's good to exercise
the emotion of fear because being fearful can keep
children safe in some situations.)*

COLLABORATIVE DISCUSSION Have partners
identify the author's views about telling children scary
tales and then decide whether they agree or disagree
with her ideas. Ask them to consider

- how hearing scary stories might be helpful
- how hearing scary stories might be harmful

Ask pairs to share their conclusions with the class.

ASK STUDENTS to share any questions they generated
in the course of reading and discussing the selection.

Strategies for Annotation   ✐ ▣ *Annotate it!*

Determine Author's Viewpoint   COMMON CORE RI 6

Have students use their eBook annotation tools to analyze the text.
Ask them to do the following:

- Highlight in yellow sentences that express the author's viewpoint.
- Highlight in blue sentences that provide counterarguments.

A lot of people have told me I really shouldn't tell children scary
things. Well, children can frighten themselves without your help.
When they're alone in bed they hear things and they see things. So I
just help them along. "It's *daaaaaaaark,*" I say. And there's a strange

TEACH

CLOSE READ

Determine Author's Viewpoint

Discuss with students how to determine an author's viewpoint.

- Using the four items in the bulleted list as a guide, help students identify evidence in the text that reveals Jackie Torrence's viewpoint.
- Have students explain how they think the author's background affected her outlook. *(Possible answer: She loved her grandfather's stories and thought they had a positive effect on her.)*

Next, discuss how providing counterarguments can strengthen an author's position or view. Work with students to identify two or more counterarguments in the essay. *(Possible answer: "Well, children can frighten themselves without your help"; "You should be a little hesitant sometimes, his stories were saying, you should think twice . . .")*

Analyze the Meanings of Words and Phrases

Guide students in a discussion of writing style, focusing on how different elements of language contribute to the style of a text.

- Have students suggest words they would use to describe the style of "Scary Tales." *(Possible answers: conversational; informal; humorous)*

Determine Author's Viewpoint

Why does Jackie Torrence feel the way she does about scary tales? In order to answer, you have to determine her viewpoint. An **author's viewpoint** is the unique combination of ideas, values, feelings, and beliefs that influence the way the writer looks at a topic. To determine an author's viewpoint, consider

- the opinions an author holds about a topic
- the details that suggest why he or she thinks a certain way
- the reasons offered in support of a certain view
- the way the author's background might affect his or her outlook

A good writer anticipates and acknowledges opposing views and responds to them. A **counterargument** is an argument made to oppose an alternative view. In "Scary Tales," Jackie Torrence includes this counterargument when discussing whether or not it's a good idea for children to experience fear:

> It's an emotion that was given to all of us and it should be exercised.

Review "Scary Tales" and identify at least two more counterarguments.

Analyze the Meanings of Words and Phrases

Style is a manner of writing. It involves *how* something is said rather than *what* is said. Writers show style through the choices they make about the following elements:

Elements of Style	Examples
Word choice and imagery are the use of specific words. Writers might choose elegant, specialized words or vivid, blunt language.	". . . there in Mr. Hall's hat was his scalp!"
Syntax refers to the way words are put together to form phrases and sentences. The length of a writer's sentences and the use of formal or informal grammar all contribute to style.	"And Grandma would say, 'Get up, get up! That ain't nice.'"
Figurative language is language used imaginatively in ways that go beyond literal definitions. The kinds and amount of images writers use can help define his or her style.	"My grandfather scared me to death."

Style can be described with words such as *formal, conversational, sophisticated,* and *humorous.* How would you describe the style in which "Scary Tales" is written? Review the selections and find examples to support your answer.

Strategies for Annotation Annotate it!

Determine Author's Viewpoint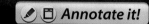

Have students use their eBook annotation tools to analyze the text. Ask them to do the following:

- Highlight in yellow sentences that express the author's viewpoint.
- Highlight in blue sentences that provide counterarguments.

> So when I started telling stories in school, that's what I chose, scary tales. I've got storytelling friends who'd rather be killed than go to junior high. But not me, I love junior high.

 **eBook** *Annotate It!*

Analyzing the Text

COMMON CORE RI 1, RI 2, RI 3, RI 4, RI 6, SL 1a, SL 1c, SL 3, SL 4

 Cite Text Evidence Support your responses with evidence from the text.

1. **Interpret** What does the author's grandma mean in lines 8–9 when she says, "Hold it, let me leave the room, lightning's going to strike"?

2. **Summarize** Tell what happens when Mr. Hall comes to visit.

3. **Analyze** An **analogy** is an extended comparison of two things that are alike in some way. Examine lines 39–42. What two things is the author comparing? Explain what this comparison reveals about the author's **tone,** or attitude, toward storytelling.

4. **Interpret** What does Grandpa Jim mean when he tells his granddaughter that "only fools rush in where angels fear to tread"? Explain what lesson scary stories can help teach.

5. **Analyze** Use a chart like the one shown to record examples of the word choice, syntax, and figurative language that contribute to Torrence's style.

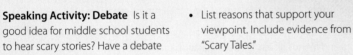

Elements of Style	Examples
Word choice	
Syntax	
Figurative language	

6. **Draw Conclusions** How would you describe Torrence's viewpoint on scary tales? Explain how her values, beliefs, and background contribute to the way she thinks about this topic.

7. **Evaluate** Are the author's counterarguments effective in proving her own view? Explain why or why not.

PERFORMANCE TASK

 my WriteSmart

Speaking Activity: Debate Is it a good idea for middle school students to hear scary stories? Have a debate about this topic.

- Working with a partner, decide which viewpoint you will argue: Is it a good idea for young people to hear scary stories, or is it a bad idea?

- List reasons that support your viewpoint. Include evidence from "Scary Tales."
- Prepare for counterarguments.
- Practice your arguments orally. Then debate another pair of students who have chosen the opposite position.

PRACTICE & APPLY

Analyzing the Text

COMMON CORE RI 1, RI 2, RI 3, RI 4, RI 6

Possible answers:

1. *She thinks the story about the fire dog is a lie and that God will hear it and strike them with lightning.*

2. *Mr. Hall and others listen to Mr. Jim as he tells a scary story. At an appropriate moment in the story, Mr. Jim spits tobacco at the fire. A piece of wood falls out and starts a fire. In the commotion, Mr. Hall's hairpiece falls off.*

3. *The writer's grandfather believed that a stubborn mule would be more willing to listen if hit with a branch. Stubborn students are willing to listen if you "hit" them with the idea that you are going to scare them. Both approaches involve getting full attention to make a task easier. The analogy contributes to a humorous tone that suggests storytelling should be fun.*

4. *Uninformed or inexperienced people will do something that those who are wise will approach with caution or avoid altogether. Scary stories can instill caution, which is a good thing.*

5. *Word Choice: 'cause, rug, ain't, sort of. Syntax: "Well, children can frighten themselves without your help." "So I remained fat for the rest of my life." Figurative Language: "God ever blew breath into"; "who'd rather be killed than go to junior high"*

6. *She thinks it's a good idea for children to hear scary things. She not only enjoyed hearing scary stories as a child, but she also believes the stories were helpful.*

7. *Responses should include the following counterarguments: Children frighten themselves anyway; fear is an emotion that needs to be exercised, or you lose it; it's good to be a little frightened because learning to be cautious can help you avoid dangerous situations. Her counterarguments are effective because she uses her own experiences to show that scary stories did her no harm as a child.*

PERFORMANCE TASK

COMMON CORE SL 1a, SL 1c, SL 3, SL 4

Assign this performance task.  **my WriteSmart**

Speaking Activity: Debate Have debating partners decide which position they will debate. See page 104a for instruction on conducting a debate.

- Help the class establish debating rules, including how long each speaker will be allowed to talk. Select a moderator for the debate.
- Remind students of the importance of speaking clearly and loudly enough so that everyone can hear.

- After each debate, ask students to evaluate the effectiveness of the speakers' arguments.

PRACTICE & APPLY

Language Conventions: L1
Subject-Verb Agreement

Tell students that to make a subject and verb agree, first they need to find the subject and verb in a sentence or clause. Explain that

- the **subject** tells whom or what the sentence or clause is about. The subject is usually a noun or a pronoun.
- the **verb** tells what the subject is, does, has, or feels.

Answers:

1. *listen*

2. *see*

3. *run*

4. *watches*

5. *love*

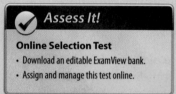

Language Conventions: L1
Subject-Verb Agreement

The subject and verb in a sentence or clause must agree in number. **Agreement** means that if the subject is singular, the verb must also be singular; if the subject is plural, the verb must also be plural. In this sentence from "Scary Tales," both the subject and the verb are plural.

Children need to be frightened.

Notice how the verb changes when the subject is singular:

A child needs to be frightened.

Add -s or -es to most verbs in the present tense to agree with a singular subject. Do not add -s if the subject is *I* or *you*.

Singular Subjects and Verbs	Plural Subjects and Verbs
I scream.	We scream.
You scream.	You scream.
He/She/It screams.	They scream.
Jacob screams.	My cousins scream.

Sometimes, other words in a sentence come between the subject and the verb. When this happens, first identify the subject, and then make sure the verb agrees with it.

My <u>friends</u> in the neighborhood <u>like</u> scary stories.

Use a plural verb with most compound subjects joined by the coordinating conjunction *and*.

The <u>students and their teacher</u> <u>watch</u> a horror movie.

When the parts of a compound subject are joined by *or*, *nor*, or the correlative conjunctions *either . . . or* or *neither . . . nor*, the verb should agree with the noun or pronoun nearest the verb.

<u>Neither the pupils nor Ms. Chen</u> <u>believes</u> that the house is really haunted.

Practice and Apply Choose the correct verb in parentheses to agree with its subject.

1. Grandma and friends (listen, listens) to Grandpa Jim's stories.

2. Visitors, who come to the house to visit, (see, sees) the image.

3. People not far from the author (run, runs) out of the room.

4. She (watch, watches) the commotion with interest.

5. Neither the grandmother nor the guests (love, loves) the scary tales.

Conducting a Debate

COMMON CORE

SL 1,
SL 3,
SL 4

TEACH

Before having students conduct the debate suggested in the Performance Task, discuss the process with them.

Tell students that a **debate** is a discussion in which people present and argue opposing ideas about a topic. Explain that the purpose of a debate is to allow speakers and audience members to consider and evaluate the merits of different viewpoints.

Planning a Debate Explain that a debate requires careful preparation. Discuss these steps:

- First, the class should choose an issue to debate.
- Next, students form debate teams. One team will argue the affirmative side, that is, *for* the issue. A second team will argue the negative side, *against* the issue.
- All team members must conduct research to find strong, reliable evidence that supports their claim or argument.
- Finally, team members should plan what they will say and practice their oral arguments.

Holding a Debate Tell students that a debate is conducted according to rules such as these:

- A moderator guides the debate, introducing the topic and each speaker. The moderator also keeps track of the time.
- Affirmative and negative speakers take turns making their presentations, using appropriate eye contact, adequate volume, and clear pronunciation.
- After all debaters have made their presentations, they may ask questions to members of the opposing team as well as point out any errors they see in the opposing team's claims or supporting evidence.

PRACTICE AND APPLY

INTERACTIVE WRITING LESSON To help students prepare for the debate, have them complete the Interactive Writing Lesson "Writing Arguments." Then have students debate the topic presented in the Performance Task or another topic that the class chooses.

Determine Author's Viewpoint

COMMON CORE

RI 6

RETEACH

Review the terms *author's viewpoint* and *counterargument*. Explain that sometimes *author's viewpoint* is also called "author's perspective." Remind students that an **author's viewpoint** is the unique combination of ideas, values, feelings, and beliefs that influences the way the writer looks at a topic.

Suggest a topic about which students may have strong opinions, such as whether they should be able to use mobile phones in school.

- Ask volunteers to share their views on the topic.
- Have speakers suggest events and ideas that have influenced their thoughts.
- Have students present **counterarguments,** statements that address possible opposing viewpoints.
- Ask what factors might contribute to people having different views. For example, how might a teacher's viewpoint be different from a student's? Why?

LEVEL UP TUTORIALS Assign one or more of the following *Level Up* tutorials: **Author's Perspective**; **Elements of an Argument**

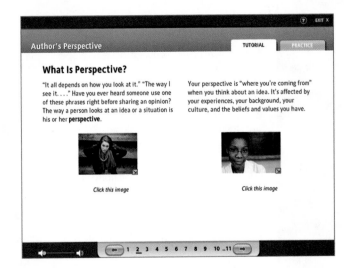

CLOSE READING APPLICATION

Student partners can work together to apply the skill to a recent editorial in a magazine or newspaper. Ask the pairs to identify the author's viewpoint as well as counterarguments presented in the text.

The Monkey's Paw

*my*SmartPlanner Create lesson plans and access resources online.

Short Story by W. W. Jacobs

Why This Text?

Students are often challenged to determine the theme of a story, play, or poem. This selection presents a strong, universal theme within a suspenseful and entertaining story.

Key Learning Objective: The student will be able to determine and analyze a universal theme and to analyze foreshadowing in a short story.

For practice and application:

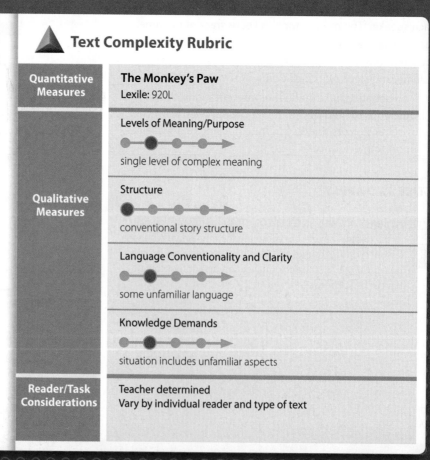

Frankenstein
Poem by Edward Field

Close Reader selection
"Frankenstein,"
Poem by Edward Field

COMMON CORE Common Core Standards

RL 1 Cite textual evidence.
RL 2 Determine a theme of a text.
RL 3 Analyze how dialogue or incidents propel action.
RL 4 Determine meaning of words and phrases.
RL 6 Analyze differences in points of view.
RL 9 Analyze how a modern work draws on themes from traditional stories.
W 2b Develop the topic.
W 7 Conduct short research projects.
W 8 Gather relevant information from multiple sources.
W 9a Apply grade 8 Reading standards to literature.
L 1c Use verbs in the subjunctive mood.
L 3a Use verbs in the subjunctive mood to achieve particular effects.
L 4a Use context as a clue to meaning.
L 4b Use Latin roots.
L 4c Consult reference materials.
L 4d Verify preliminary determination of the meaning of a word or phrase.

▲ Text Complexity Rubric

Quantitative Measures	**The Monkey's Paw** Lexile: 920L
Qualitative Measures	**Levels of Meaning/Purpose** single level of complex meaning
	Structure conventional story structure
	Language Conventionality and Clarity some unfamiliar language
	Knowledge Demands situation includes unfamiliar aspects
Reader/Task Considerations	Teacher determined Vary by individual reader and type of text

William Wymark Jacobs Have students read the information about the author. Tell students that William Wymark Jacobs was the son of a man who worked on the wharf, but he managed to get a good education. In addition to working in a bank, Jacobs began submitting stories to small magazines. Eventually, he was able to focus strictly on writing stories related to his childhood, the sea, and occasionally the supernatural.

SETTING A PURPOSE Direct students to use the Setting a Purpose question to focus their reading. Tell students to generate their own questions as they read.

Analyze Language (LINES 1–10) · COMMON CORE · RL 1, RL 4

Explain that the author contrasts the cold, stormy weather outside with the warm, cozy interior to establish the setting of the story.

A CITE TEXT EVIDENCE Ask students to reread lines 1–10 and cite the descriptive details that help establish the setting. *("Without, the night was cold and wet, but in the small parlor . . . the blinds were drawn and the fire burned brightly."; "white-haired old lady knitting placidly by the fire"; "'Hark at the wind'")*

Analyze Stories: Foreshadowing (LINES 3–7) · COMMON CORE · RL 3

Tell students that **foreshadowing** refers to clues an author gives that hint at what will happen later in the story. Explain that one way authors foreshadow events is through description.

B ASK STUDENTS to reread lines 3–7 and identify the details that tell something about the father's personality. Ask how this aspect of his personality could affect the plot. *("radical changes"; "sharp and unnecessary perils." The father seems like the type of person who might take risks or do dangerous things.)*

CRITICAL VOCABULARY

peril: The author is describing Mr. White's risky method of playing the game of chess.

ASK STUDENTS what can happen in chess or checkers if you put your game piece in peril. *(Your piece may be captured by your opponent.)*

William Wymark Jacobs (1863–1943) *grew up in London near the waterfront wharfs. As a boy, Jacobs absorbed the tales of strange, distant lands told by passing sailors. As a young man, Jacobs worked at a bank—a job that he hated—and wrote stories in his spare time. He eventually became a popular writer of humor. Ironically, his best-known work, "The Monkey's Paw," became a classic of the horror genre.*

The Monkey's Paw

Short Story by W. W. Jacobs

SETTING A PURPOSE As you read, pay attention to the relationships among the members of the White family. How does the appearance of the monkey's paw affect those relationships?

Part I

Without, the night was cold and wet, but in the small parlor of Laburnum Villa the blinds were drawn and the fire burned brightly. Father and son were at chess; the former, who possessed ideas about the game involving radical changes, putting his king into such sharp and unnecessary **perils** that it even provoked comment from the white-haired old lady knitting placidly by the fire.

"Hark at the wind," said Mr. White, who, having seen a fatal mistake after it was too late, was amiably desirous of preventing his son from seeing it.

10   "I'm listening," said the latter, grimly surveying the board as he stretched out his hand. "Check."

peril
(pĕr´əl) *n.* A *peril* is something that is dangerous.

(tr) ©Bettmann/Corbis; 105 (c) ©andreiuc88/Shutterstock

SCAFFOLDING FOR ELL STUDENTS

Analyze Language Explain that the author of this story uses some words that are **archaic**, or old-fashioned. Using a whiteboard, project the first two paragraphs.

- Highlight the word *Without* in the first sentence.
- Model how to use context and word parts to understand its meaning. *(the word part* out; *the fact that the word refers to the weather outside)*
- Replace the word *Without* with the word *Outside*, and have a volunteer read the sentence.

ASK STUDENTS to point out other archaic language in the first two paragraphs. (Hark) Guide them to use context to clarify meaning. Tell students to continue using this strategy as they read and to refer to a dictionary, as needed.

CLOSE READ

 For more context and historical background, students can view the video "British Imperialism" in their eBooks.

Analyze Stories: Foreshadowing (LINES 39–42)

 COMMON CORE **RL 1, RL 3**

Explain to students that the author of a horror story may use foreshadowing to prepare the reader for strange and unexpected events. Point out that this technique creates suspense by building the reader's expectations.

C **CITE TEXT EVIDENCE** Ask students to closely reread lines 39–42. Have them cite evidence to explain how this description of Sergeant-Major Morris helps build suspense. (*Sergeant-Major Morris is presented as a person who knows "wild scenes" and "strange peoples." The reader begins to expect him to cause something strange.*)

CRITICAL VOCABULARY

condole: When Mr. White greets the visitor at the door, he is heard condoling with the guest.

ASK STUDENTS what conditions might cause a host to condole with a guest who has just arrived at his door. (*The weather might be very bad, or the guest might have had a long or difficult journey.*)

"I should hardly think that he'd come tonight," said his father, with his hand poised over the board.

"Mate," replied the son.

"That's the worst of living so far out," bawled Mr. White, with sudden and unlooked-for violence; "of all the beastly, slushy, out-of-the-way places to live in, this is the worst. Pathway's a bog,[1] and the road's a torrent.[2] I don't know what 20 people are thinking about. I suppose because only two houses in the road are let,[3] they think it doesn't matter."

"Never mind, dear," said his wife soothingly; "perhaps you'll win the next one."

Mr. White looked up sharply, just in time to intercept a knowing glance between mother and son. The words died away on his lips, and he hid a guilty grin in his thin gray beard.

"There he is," said Herbert White, as the gate banged loudly and heavy footsteps came toward the door.

The old man rose with hospitable haste, and opening the 30 door, was heard **condoling** with the new arrival. The new arrival also condoled with himself, so that Mrs. White said, "Tut, tut!" and coughed gently as her husband entered the room, followed by a tall, burly man, beady of eye and rubicund of visage.[4]

"Sergeant-Major Morris," he said, introducing him.

The sergeant-major shook hands, and taking the proffered seat by the fire, watched contentedly while his host brought out drinks and stood a small copper kettle on the fire.

He began to talk, the little family circle regarding with 40 eager interest this visitor from distant parts, as he squared his broad shoulders in the chair and spoke of wild scenes and doughty[5] deeds; of wars and plagues and strange peoples.

"Twenty-one years of it," said Mr. White, nodding at his wife and son. "When he went away, he was a slip of a youth in the warehouse. Now look at him."

"He don't look to have taken much harm," said Mrs. White politely.

"I'd like to go to India myself," said the old man, "just to look round a bit, you know."

condole
(kən-dōl´) *v.* If you *condole* with someone, you express sympathy or sorrow.

---

[1] **bog:** a swamp.
[2] **torrent** (tôr´ənt): a swift-flowing stream.
[3] **let:** rented.
[4] **rubicund** (roo´bĭ-kənd) **of visage** (vĭz´ĭj): with a ruddy complexion.
[5] **doughty** (dou´tē): brave.

APPLYING ACADEMIC VOCABULARY

predict	convention	technique

As you discuss "The Monkey's Paw," incorporate the following Collection 2 academic vocabulary words: *predict, convention,* and *technique.* To help students understand foreshadowing, discuss how Jacobs helps the reader **predict** what will happen in the story. Ask students to discuss how the author uses the traditional **convention** of three wishes in a modern story. Explain that Jacobs uses the **technique** of communicating major plot developments through dialogue.

50 "Better where you are," said the sergeant-major, shaking his head. He put down the empty glass, and sighing softly, shook it again.

"I should like to see those old temples and fakirs and jugglers," said the old man. "What was that you started telling me the other day about a monkey's paw or something, Morris?"

"Nothing," said the soldier hastily. "Leastways nothing worth hearing."

"Monkey's paw?" said Mrs. White curiously.

60 "Well, it's just a bit of what you might call magic, perhaps," said the sergeant-major off-handedly.

His three listeners leaned forward eagerly. The visitor absent-mindedly put his empty glass to his lips and then set it down again. His host filled it for him.

"To look at," said the sergeant-major, fumbling in his pocket, "it's just an ordinary little paw, dried to a mummy."

He took something out of his pocket and proffered it. Mrs. White drew back with a **grimace**, but her son, taking it, examined it curiously.

grimace
(grĭm´ĭs) *n.* A *grimace* is a facial expression of pain or disgust.

70 "And what is there special about it?" inquired Mr. White as he took it from his son, and having examined it, placed it upon the table.

"It had a spell put on it by an old fakir," said the sergeant-major, "a very holy man. He wanted to show that **fate** ruled people's lives, and that those who interfered with it did so to their sorrow. He put a spell on it so that three separate men could each have three wishes from it."

His manner was so impressive that his hearers were conscious that their light laughter jarred somewhat.

fate
(fāt) *n. Fate* is a power that is thought to determine the course of events.

80 "Well, why don't you have three, sir?" said Herbert White cleverly.

The soldier regarded him in the way that middle age is wont to regard presumptuous youth. "I have," he said quietly, and his blotchy face whitened.

"And did you really have the three wishes granted?" asked Mrs. White.

"I did," said the sergeant-major, and his glass tapped against his strong teeth.

"And has anybody else wished?" persisted the old lady.

CLOSE READ

Determine Theme
COMMON CORE **RL 2**

(LINES 73–77)

Explain to students that a **theme** is a message about life or human nature that a writer wants to share with readers. Sometimes, a writer actually states the theme of a story. In other cases, readers must **infer,** or figure out, the theme from details the writer provides.

D **ASK STUDENTS** to reread lines 73–77 to identify ideas that suggest what the theme of this story might be. Ask what those ideas might foreshadow in the story. ("*He wanted to show that fate ruled people's lives, and that those who interfered with it did so to their sorrow.*" It might foreshadow that the family will try to change their lives and that sorrow will result.)

CRITICAL VOCABULARY

grimace: Mrs. White drew back with a grimace when she saw the monkey's paw.

ASK STUDENTS what Mrs. White looked like and what caused her to look that way. *(Her face showed a look of horror and disgust. She was repelled by the appearance of the paw.)*

fate: The Indian fakir wanted to warn people not to interfere with fate.

ASK STUDENTS how having a wish granted would be a way of trying to change fate. *(Having a wish granted would be trying to get something you hadn't worked for or earned or been predetermined to have. It could alter your life's course and change your fate for the worse.)*

Analyze Stories:
Foreshadowing (LINES 90–92)

COMMON CORE RL 1, RL 3

Tell students that foreshadowing in a horror story is often based on a reference to something bad that happened in the past and might happen again.

E **ASK STUDENTS** to reread lines 90–92 and explain what makes this foreshadowing effective. *(Sergeant-Major Morris suggests that the result of using the first two wishes was so bad that the man wanted to die. Since we already suspect that the Whites are going to use the monkey's paw, this foreshadows something bad for them.)*

Determine Theme

COMMON CORE RL 1, RL 2, RL 9

(LINES 110–116)

Explain to students that a **universal theme** is a theme found in the literature of different cultures and time periods. Point out that the granting of wishes is a convention used in the literature of many different cultures, such as the *Arabian Nights* and the fairy tales of the Brothers Grimm. The use of granting of wishes suggests a universal theme about interfering with fate.

F **CITE TEXT EVIDENCE** Have students reread lines 110–116 to identify evidence of a universal theme related to interfering with fate. Ask students to cite the words that warn of interfering with fate. *("If you keep it, don't blame me for what happens," and "I warn you of the consequences.")*

---

90   "The first man had his three wishes. Yes," was the reply; "I don't know what the first two were, but the third was for death. That's how I got the paw."

His tones were so grave that a hush fell upon the group.

"If you've had your three wishes, it's no good to you now, then, Morris," said the old man at last. "What do you keep it for?"

> ## ❝ His tones were so grave that a hush fell upon the room. ❞

The soldier shook his head. "Fancy, I suppose," he said slowly. "I did have some idea of selling it, but I don't think I will. It has caused enough mischief already. Besides, people won't buy. They think it's a fairy tale, some of them; and those

100   who do think anything of it want to try it first and pay me afterward."

"If you could have another three wishes," said the old man, eyeing him keenly, "would you have them?"

"I don't know," said the other. "I don't know."

He took the paw, and dangling it between his forefinger and thumb, suddenly threw it upon the fire. White, with a slight cry, stooped down and snatched it off.

"Better let it burn," said the soldier solemnly.

"If you don't want it, Morris," said the other, "give it to me."

110   "I won't," said his friend doggedly. "I threw it on the fire. If you keep it, don't blame me for what happens. Pitch it on the fire again like a sensible man."

The other shook his head and examined his new possession closely. "How do you do it?" he inquired.

"Hold it up in your right hand and wish aloud," said the sergeant-major, "but I warn you of the consequences."

"Sounds like the *Arabian Nights*,"[6] said Mrs. White, as she rose and began to set the supper. "Don't you think you might wish for four pairs of hands for me?"

---

[6] ***Arabian Nights:*** a famous collection of Asian stories.

Strategies for Annotation   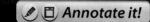 ✎ 🖥 Annotate it!

Determine Theme

COMMON CORE RL 2

To support students in determining the theme of the story, share these strategies for guided and independent analysis:

- As you read, highlight in yellow the evidence that helps you predict what lesson the characters might learn.
- In notes, jot down what that lesson might be.

> "I won't," said his friend doggedly. "I threw it on the fire. If you
>
> keep it, don't blame me for what happens. Pitch it on the fire again
>
> like a sensible man."

> If you interfere with fate, there may be negative consequences.

120 Her husband drew the talisman[7] from his pocket, and then all three burst into laughter as the sergeant-major, with a look of alarm on his face, caught him by the arm.

"If you must wish," he said gruffly, "wish for something sensible."

Mr. White dropped it back in his pocket, and placing chairs, motioned his friend to the table. In the business of supper the talisman was partly forgotten, and afterward the three sat listening in an enthralled fashion to a second installment of the soldier's adventures in India.

130 "If the tale about the monkey's paw is not more truthful than those he has been telling us," said Herbert, as the door closed behind their guest, just in time for him to catch the last train, "we shan't make much out of it."

"Did you give him anything for it, Father?" inquired Mrs. White, regarding her husband closely.

"A trifle," said he, coloring slightly. "He didn't want it, but I made him take it. And he pressed me again to throw it away."

"Likely," said Herbert, with pretended horror. "Why, we're going to be rich, and famous, and happy. Wish to be an 140 emperor, Father, to begin with; then you can't be henpecked."

He darted round the table, pursued by the maligned Mrs. White armed with an antimacassar.[8]

Mr. White took the paw from his pocket and eyed it dubiously. "I don't know what to wish for, and that's a fact," he said slowly. "It seems to me I've got all I want."

"If you only cleared the house, you'd be quite happy, wouldn't you?" said Herbert, with his hand on his shoulder. "Well, wish for two hundred pounds, then; that'll just do it."

His father, smiling shamefacedly at his own **credulity**,
150 held up the talisman, as his son, with a solemn face, somewhat marred by a wink at his mother, sat down at the piano and struck a few impressive chords.

"I wish for two hundred pounds," said the old man distinctly.

A fine crash from the piano greeted the words, interrupted by a shuddering cry from the old man. His wife and son ran toward him.

credulity
(krĭ-dōō′ lĭ-tē) *n.*
Credulity is a tendency to believe too readily.

---

[7] **talisman** (tăl′ĭs-mən): an object thought to have magical powers.
[8] **antimacassar** (ăn′tĭ-mə-kăs′ər): a cloth placed over an arm or the back of a chair.

The Monkey's Paw **109**

TEACH

CLOSE READ

Determine Theme
(LINES 138–152)

COMMON CORE — RL 1, RL 2, RL 9

Point out that the convention of granting wishes in a story is particularly effective when the person given the wishes is already happy and therefore has a lot to lose. The White family's comfort and happiness help establish the theme of how dangerous it is to play with fate.

G **CITE TEXT EVIDENCE** Have students reread lines 138–152, citing evidence of how this text contributes to the theme. *(Herbert's teasing of his mother, her playful response, and Mr. White's words about having all they want show that the White family is happy and doesn't need anything more than what they have.)* How does the author provide a new twist to the universal theme through the White family? *(The monkey's paw serves as a temptation for the family to challenge fate despite all of Morris's warnings.)*

CRITICAL VOCABULARY

credulity: The author explains that Mr. White is ashamed at his own credulity in believing the story about the paw.

ASK STUDENTS why credulity might be some thing to be ashamed of. *(It suggests that a person is gullible or too easily convinced.)*

Analyze Stories: Foreshadowing (LINES 176–182)

COMMON CORE RL 1, RL 3, RL 4

Explain that authors sometimes use vivid **imagery**, or descriptive language that appeals to the senses, to create foreshadowing. In a horror story, this imagery can create a mood of fear and impending danger, making readers feel eager to have more of the story's plot or action revealed.

(H) CITE TEXT EVIDENCE Have students reread lines 176–182 and cite the words and phrases that foreshadow something frightening. Ask what effect this word choice creates. *("The last face was so horrible and so simian that he gazed at it in amazement." A horrible face in the fire suggests that something frightening may happen. It adds to the suspenseful tone of the story and sets up the next event in the plot.)*

> ### CRITICAL VOCABULARY
>
> **prosaic:** The author is contrasting the exciting atmosphere of the night before with that of the new day.
>
> **ASK STUDENTS** what makes the house seem prosaic in the morning. *(In the daylight, the room looks as it always does, with its "ordinary breakfast table" and other furnishings.)*

---

160 "It moved," he cried, with a glance of disgust at the object as it lay on the floor. "As I wished, it twisted in my hand like a snake."

"Well, I don't see the money," said his son, as he picked it up and placed it on the table, "and I bet I never shall."

"It must have been your fancy, father," said his wife, regarding him anxiously.

He shook his head. "Never mind, though; there's no harm done, but it gave me a shock all the same."

They sat down by the fire again. Outside, the wind was higher than ever, and the old man started nervously at the sound of a door banging upstairs. A silence unusual and 170 depressing settled upon all three, which lasted until the old couple rose to retire for the night.

"I expect you'll find the cash tied up in a big bag in the middle of your bed," said Herbert, as he bade them good-night, "and something horrible squatting up on top of the wardrobe watching you as you pocket your ill-gotten gains."

(H) He sat alone in the darkness, gazing at the dying fire, and seeing faces in it. The last face was so horrible and so simian[9] that he gazed at it in amazement. It got so vivid that, with a little uneasy laugh, he felt on the table for a glass containing 180 a little water to throw over it. His hand grasped the monkey's paw, and with a little shiver he wiped his hand on his coat and went up to bed.

Part II

In the brightness of the wintry sun next morning as it streamed over the breakfast table he laughed at his fears. There was an air of **prosaic** wholesomeness about the room which it had lacked on the previous night, and the dirty, shriveled little paw was pitched on the sideboard[10] with a carelessness which betokened no great belief in its virtues.[11]

"I suppose all old soldiers are the same," said Mrs. White. 190 "The idea of our listening to such nonsense! How could wishes be granted in these days? And if they could, how could two hundred pounds hurt you, father?"

prosaic
(prō-zā´ĭk) *adj.* If something is *prosaic*, it is dull or ordinary.

---

9 **simian** (sĭm´ə-ən): monkey- or ape-like.
10 **sideboard:** a piece of furniture used to store linens and dishes.
11 **virtues:** powers.

"Might drop on his head from the sky," said the frivolous[12] Herbert.

"Morris said the things happened so naturally," said his father, "that you might if you so wished attribute it to coincidence."

"Well, don't break into the money before I come back," said Herbert as he rose from the table. "I'm afraid it'll turn you into a
200 mean, avaricious[13] man, and we shall have to disown you."

His mother laughed, and following him to the door, watched him down the road; and returning to the breakfast table, was very happy at the expense of her husband's credulity. All of which did not prevent her from scurrying to the door at the postman's knock, when she found that the post brought a tailor's bill.

"Herbert will have some more of his funny remarks, I expect, when he comes home," she said, as they sat at dinner.

"I dare say," said Mr. White, "but for all that, the thing
210 moved in my hand; that I'll swear to."

"You thought it did," said the old lady soothingly.

"I say it did," replied the other. "There was no thought about it; I had just—What's the matter?"

His wife made no reply. She was watching the mysterious movements of a man outside, who, peering in an undecided fashion at the house, appeared to be trying to make up his mind to enter. In mental connection with the two hundred pounds, she noticed that the stranger was well dressed, and wore a silk hat of glossy newness. Three times he paused at the
220 gate, and then walked on again. The fourth time he stood with his hand upon it, and then with sudden resolution flung it open and walked up the path. Mrs. White at the same moment placed her hands behind her, and hurriedly unfastening the strings of her apron, put that useful article of apparel beneath the cushion of her chair.

She brought the stranger, who seemed ill at ease, into the room. He gazed at her furtively, and listened in a preoccupied fashion as the old lady apologized for the appearance of the room, and her husband's coat, a garment which he usually
230 reserved for the garden. She then waited patiently for him to broach his business, but he was at first strangely silent.

---

[12]**frivolous** (frĭv´ə-ləs): inappropriately silly.
[13]**avaricious** (ăv´ə-rĭsh´es): greedy.

CLOSE READ

Analyze Stories: Foreshadowing (LINES 214–225)

COMMON CORE **RL 1, RL 3**

Explain to students that another way writers can foreshadow is through description of a character's behavior.

CITE TEXT EVIDENCE Ask students to reread lines 214–225 and to describe the behavior of the man outside. *(The man pauses several times at the gate and walks away. He seems to be putting off the moment when he will enter the house.)* Ask what might cause him to act that way. *(Something makes him reluctant to enter. He may have bad news.)* How does this foreshadowing propel the story's action? *(The man's actions provide a hint of foreboding and serve to introduce Herbert's death.)*

Analyze Stories: Dialogue (LINES 242–250)

COMMON CORE RL 3

Explain to students that **dialogue,** the words spoken by the characters, can be a very effective technique for communicating plot events. Explain that while narration makes readers feel that they are being told a story, dialogue makes them feel part of the action, as though they are seeing a story unfold.

J **ASK STUDENTS** to closely reread the dialogue in lines 242–250. Ask how these lines move the plot along. *(Through the dialogue between the visitor and Mrs. White, readers realize what has happened to Herbert at the same moment she does.)*

"I—was asked to call," he said at last, and stooped and picked a piece of cotton from his trousers. "I come from Maw and Meggins."

The old lady started. "Is anything the matter?" she asked breathlessly. "Has anything happened to Herbert? What is it? What is it?"

Her husband interposed. "There, there, mother," he said hastily. "Sit down, and don't jump to conclusions. You've not brought bad news, I'm sure, sir;" and he eyed the other wistfully.

"I'm sorry—" began the visitor.

"Is he hurt?" demanded the mother wildly.

The visitor bowed in assent. "Badly hurt," he said quietly, "but he is not in any pain."

"Oh!" said the old woman, clasping her hands. "Thank goodness for that! Thank—"

She broke off suddenly as the sinister meaning of the assurance dawned upon her and she saw the awful confirmation of her fears in the other's averted face. She caught her breath, and turning to her slower-witted husband, laid her trembling old hand upon his. There was a long silence.

"He was caught in the machinery," said the visitor at length in a low voice.

"Caught in the machinery," repeated Mr. White, in a dazed fashion, "yes."

He sat staring blankly out at the window, and taking his wife's hand between his own, pressed it as he had been wont to do in their old courting days nearly forty years before.

"He was the only one left to us," he said, turning gently to the visitor. "It is hard."

The other coughed, and rising, walked slowly to the window. "The firm wished me to convey their sincere sympathy with you in your great loss," he said, without looking round. "I beg that you will understand I am only their servant and merely obeying orders."

There was no reply; the old woman's face was white, her eyes staring, and her breath inaudible; on the husband's face was a look such as his friend the sergeant might have carried into his first action.

"I was to say that Maw and Meggins disclaim all responsibility," continued the other. "They admit no liability

---

Strategies for Annotation ✎ ▣ *Annotate it!*

Analyze Stories: Dialogue

COMMON CORE RL 3

Have students locate lines 242–250. Encourage them to use their eBook annotation tools to do the following:

- Highlight in blue the dialogue that Jacobs uses to let the reader know that Herbert is dead.
- Highlight in green the narration that Jacobs uses to confirm what the dialogue has told the reader.
- Continue to use this strategy as you read the story.

"Is he hurt?" demanded the mother wildly.

The visitor bowed in assent. "Badly hurt," he said quietly, "but he is not in any pain."

at all, but in consideration of your son's services, they wish to present you with a certain sum as **compensation**."

Mr. White dropped his wife's hand, and rising to his feet, gazed with a look of horror at his visitor. His dry lips shaped the words, "How much?"

"Two hundred pounds," was the answer.

280 Unconscious of his wife's shriek, the old man smiled faintly, put out his hands like a sightless man, and dropped, a senseless heap, to the floor.

Part III

In the huge new cemetery, some two miles distant, the old people buried their dead, and came back to a house steeped in shadow and silence. It was all over so quickly that at first they could hardly realize it, and remained in a state of expectation as though of something else to happen— something else which was to lighten this load, too heavy for old hearts to bear.

But the days passed, and expectation gave place to 290 **resignation**—the hopeless resignation of the old, sometimes miscalled apathy. Sometimes they hardly exchanged a word, for now they had nothing to talk about, and their days were long to weariness.

It was about a week after that the old man, waking suddenly in the night, stretched out his hand and found himself alone. The room was in darkness, and the sound of subdued weeping came from the window. He raised himself in bed and listened.

compensation
(kŏm´ pən-sā´ shən) *n.*
Compensation is something, such as money, that is received as payment.

resignation
(rĕz´ĭg-nā´shən) *n.*
Resignation is the acceptance of something that is inescapable.

©Corbis RF

The Monkey's Paw **113**

CLOSE READ

Determine Theme

COMMON CORE **RL 2, RL 9**

(LINES 271–281)

Remind students that W. W. Jacobs has already given many indications of what the theme of this story might be.

K **ASK STUDENTS** to reread lines 271–281 and then discuss how the information from the man from Maw and Meggins supports the theme of the story. *(When the man announces that the Whites will get two hundred pounds, it seems clear to them that the wish has caused their son's death. This supports the idea that the theme is to be careful of interfering with fate.) In what way have the Whites interfered with fate? (They had a comfortable and happy life, yet they chose to ask for more.)*

CRITICAL VOCABULARY

compensation: The man from Maw and Meggins offers the Whites two hundred pounds.

ASK STUDENTS why the Whites are offered compensation and how they probably feel about it. *(The company offers the money because Herbert died while working at their facility. The Whites probably feel that the money can never compensate for their loss.)*

resignation: The author says that resignation is "sometimes miscalled apathy."

ASK STUDENTS how resignation differs from apathy and why it might be mistaken for apathy. (Apathy *means "a lack of caring." When people have become resigned to something, it may appear that they don't care anymore, but this is not true.)*

Make Inferences

(COMMON CORE) RL 1

(LINES 330–340)

Remind students that they can use evidence in a text to figure out, or make **inferences**, about what the author does not state directly.

L CITE TEXT EVIDENCE Ask students to reread lines 330–340. Point out that in line 332, Mr. White calls the granting of the first wish "a coincidence." Ask students whether he really believes this and why he says it. Have them cite evidence to support their inference. (*Mr. White does not think it's a coincidence; he believes in the power of the paw. He does not want to make the wish his wife asks for, because he is afraid something even more horrible will be the result. Evidence: "a horrible fear that the unspoken wish might bring his mutilated son before him."*)

WHEN STUDENTS STRUGGLE . . .

Following the events of the story's conclusion may be difficult because the author presents what Mrs. White is doing at the door only by telling us what Mr. White is hearing.

Suggest that students use a graphic organizer, like the one shown to the right, to help them keep track of the actions of both characters. You might suggest that they use the interactive graphic organizer sequence chart instead.

"Come back," he said tenderly. "You will be cold."

300   "It is colder for my son," said the old woman, and wept afresh.

The sound of her sobs died away on his ears. The bed was warm, and his eyes heavy with sleep. He dozed fitfully, and then slept until a sudden wild cry from his wife awoke him with a start.

"*The paw!*" she cried wildly. "The monkey's paw!"

He started up in alarm. "Where? Where is it? What's the matter?"

She came stumbling across the room toward him. "I want

310   it," she said quietly. "You've not destroyed it?"

"It's in the parlor, on the bracket," he replied, marveling. "Why?"

She cried and laughed together, and bending over, kissed his cheek.

"I only just thought of it," she said hysterically. "Why didn't I think of it before? Why didn't *you* think of it?"

"Think of what?" he questioned.

"The other two wishes," she replied rapidly. "We've only had one."

320   "Was not that enough?" he demanded fiercely.

"No," she cried triumphantly; "we'll have one more. Go down and get it quickly, and wish our boy alive again."

The man sat up in bed and flung the bedclothes from his quaking limbs. "You are mad!" he cried, aghast.

"Get it," she panted; "get it quickly, and wish—Oh, my boy, my boy!"

Her husband struck a match and lit the candle. "Get back to bed," he said unsteadily. "You don't know what you are saying."

330   "We had the first wish granted," said the old woman feverishly; "why not the second?"

"A coincidence," stammered the old man.

"Go and get it and wish," cried his wife, quivering with excitement.

He went down in the darkness, and felt his way to the parlor, and then to the mantelpiece. The talisman was in its place, and a horrible fear that the unspoken wish might bring his mutilated son before him ere he could escape from the room seized upon him, and he caught his breath as he found

340   that he had lost the direction of the door. His brow cold with

Action	Character

sweat, he felt his way round the table, and groped along the wall until he found himself in the small passage with the unwholesome thing in his hand.

Even his wife's face seemed changed as he entered the room. It was white and expectant, and to his fears seemed to have an unnatural look upon it. He was afraid of her.

"*Wish!*" she cried, in a strong voice.

"It is foolish and wicked," he faltered.

"*Wish!*" repeated his wife.

350 He raised his hand. "I wish my son alive again."

The talisman fell to the floor, and he regarded it fearfully. Then he sank trembling into a chair as the old woman, with burning eyes, walked to the window and raised the blind.

He sat until he was chilled with the cold, glancing occasionally at the figure of the old woman peering through the window. The candle-end, which had burned below the rim of the china candlestick, was throwing pulsating shadows on the ceiling and walls, until, with a flicker larger than the rest, it expired. The old man, with an unspeakable sense of

360 relief at the failure of the talisman, crept back to his bed, and a minute or two afterward the old woman came silently and apathetically beside him.

Neither spoke, but lay silently listening to the ticking of the clock. A stair creaked, and a squeaky mouse scurried noisily through the wall. The darkness was oppressive, and after lying for some time gathering up his courage, he took the box of matches, and striking one, went downstairs for a candle.

At the foot of the stairs the match went out, and he paused

370 to strike another; and at the same moment a knock, so quiet and stealthy as to be scarcely audible, sounded on the front door.

The matches fell from his hand. He stood motionless, his breath suspended until the knock was repeated. Then he turned and fled swiftly back to his room, and closed the door behind him. A third knock sounded through the house.

"*What's that?*" cried the old woman, starting up.

"A rat," said the old man in shaking tones—"a rat. It passed me on the stairs."

380 His wife sat up in bed listening. A loud knock resounded through the house.

"It's Herbert!" she screamed. "It's Herbert!"

CLOSE READ

Analyze Stories: Foreshadowing (LINES 344–353)

COMMON CORE RL 1, RL 3, RL 4

Remind students that authors may use imagery as a technique to foreshadow future events and create suspense.

M **CITE TEXT EVIDENCE** Ask students to reread lines 344–353 and to identify the imagery. Ask what it might foreshadow and what effect it creates. *(Imagery: "It was white and expectant"; "an unnatural look"; "regarded it fearfully"; "sank trembling into a chair; "old woman, with burning eyes." The imagery foreshadows that something terrible may happen; it creates a feeling of fear and tension.)*

CLOSE READ

Determine Theme

COMMON CORE **RL 2**

(LINES 385–391)

Remind students that they can determine the theme of a story by asking what lesson the characters learn.

 ASK STUDENTS to reread the dialogue between Mr. and Mrs. White (lines 385–391). Ask what lesson, if any, each character has learned. *(Mr. White has learned not to try to change fate by making wishes. He is afraid that something terrible will result from his wish. Mrs. White has not learned a lesson. She is still convinced that wishing on the paw has brought her son back to life.)*

COLLABORATIVE DISCUSSION Have students independently reread the part of the story in which Mr. White decides to make a wish. Suggest that they take notes about the reasons for his choice and refer to them when they discuss the question with a partner. Remind students to cite evidence during the discussion.

ASK STUDENTS to share any questions they generated in the course of reading and discussing the selection.

She ran to the door, but her husband was before her, and catching her by the arm, held her tightly.

"What are you going to do?" he whispered hoarsely.

"It's my boy; it's Herbert!" she cried, struggling mechanically. "I forgot it was two miles away. What are you holding me for? Let go. I must open the door."

"Don't let it in," cried the old man, trembling.

390 "You're afraid of your own son," she cried, struggling. "Let me go. I'm coming, Herbert; I'm coming."

There was another knock, and another. The old woman with a sudden wrench broke free and ran from the room. Her husband followed to the landing, and called after her appealingly as she hurried downstairs. He heard the chain rattle back and the bottom bolt drawn slowly and stiffly from the socket. Then the old woman's voice, strained and panting.

"The bolt," she cried loudly. "Come down. I can't reach it."

But her husband was on his hands and knees groping

400 wildly on the floor in search of the paw. If he could only find it before the thing outside got in. A perfect fusillade[14] of knocks reverberated through the house, and he heard the scraping of a chair as his wife put it down in the passage against the door. He heard the creaking of the bolt as it came slowly back, and at the same moment he found the monkey's paw, and frantically breathed his third and last wish.

The knocking ceased suddenly, although the echoes of it were still in the house. He heard the chair drawn back, and the door opened. A cold wind rushed up the staircase, and a

410 long loud wail of disappointment and misery from his wife gave him courage to run down to her side, and then to the gate beyond. The streetlamp flickering opposite shone on a quiet and deserted road.

COLLABORATIVE DISCUSSION Mr. White decides to make a wish, even though he says he already has everything he wants. Discuss with a partner whether his wish is more for himself or for his family. Use evidence from the text to support your ideas.

---

[14]**fusillade** (fyoo′sə-läd′): discharge from many guns; a rapid outburst.

TO CHALLENGE STUDENTS . . .

Analyze Stories "The Monkey's Paw" might have ended very differently if Mrs. White had opened the door before her husband made the final wish.

ASK STUDENTS to consider what might have happened had she done that. Ask: *What do you think was on the other side of the door? Is it better for you as a reader not to know? Why?* Have students discuss these questions and the ending of the story in small groups.

Determine Theme

One reason people read literature is to learn how to avoid or understand common problems. Literature conveys these lessons through **themes,** the messages about life or human nature that writers share with readers.

- In some stories, the theme is stated directly in the text.
- In most cases, readers must **infer,** or make an educated guess about, the theme based on clues in the text.
- One way to determine a story's theme is to ask, "What lesson does the main character learn that applies to real people's lives?"

Contemporary literature often draws on the themes and patterns of events that have been expressed in myths and traditional stories passed down through the centuries. For example, you've probably been told many stories in which a theme about greed is revealed through the granting of three wishes. When the same message can be found in the literature of different cultures and in different time periods like this, it's called a **universal theme.**

Review "The Monkey's Paw" and identify the traditional pattern of events that reveals a universal theme.

Analyze Stories: Foreshadowing

Foreshadowing occurs when a writer provides hints that suggest future events in a story. Writers use this technique to create suspense and propel the action by making readers eager to find out what happens next.

Clues about future events may appear in dialogue, descriptions of events, or imagery. Think about how these examples from "The Monkey's Paw" foreshadow what will occur later in the story.

Dialogue (*lines 97–98*)	"I did have some idea of selling it, but I don't think I will. It has caused enough mischief already."
Event (*lines 106–107*)	"He took the paw, and dangling it between his forefinger and thumb, suddenly threw it upon the fire."
Imagery (*lines 176–182*)	"He sat . . . at the dying fire . . . seeing faces in it. The last face was so horrible . . . that he gazed at it in amazement. It got so vivid that, with a little uneasy laugh, he felt on the table for a glass containing a little water to throw over it. His hand grasped the monkey's paw and with a little shiver he wiped his hand on his coat and went to up to bed."

As you analyze "The Monkey's Paw," look for an additional example of each kind of foreshadowing.

CLOSE READ

Determine Theme

Review the definition of theme and the points about how to determine the theme. Recall the lesson that Mr. White learned in "The Monkey's Paw" and ask students how that lesson can apply to real people's lives. (*It suggests that you should be happy with what you have and not be greedy for more.*) Explain that this lesson from "The Monkey's Paw" is an example of a universal theme. Discuss examples of myths, fairy tales, and other stories that share this theme.

After students review the story to identify the pattern of events, ask: *How does W. W. Jacobs alter this pattern from the way it appears in traditional stories? (In "The Monkey's Paw," the characters are warned not to wish, but they do so anyway. The terrible result of the wish cannot be undone, and there is no happy ending.)*

Analyze Stories: Foreshadowing

Review the definition of foreshadowing and the three different ways in which writers foreshadow events. Discuss the additional examples that students identify. Have students analyze and explain how the incidents of foreshadowing propel the story forward, or provoke the characters to make a decision.

Possible answers:

Dialogue: (*lines 110–111*)
Event: (*lines 155–156*)
Imagery: (*lines 167–170*)

Strategies for Annotation   ✎ 🗐 *Annotate it!*

Analyze Stories: Foreshadowing

Share these strategies for guided or independent analysis:

- Highlight in yellow foreshadowing in dialogue.
- Highlight in blue foreshadowing through an event.
- Highlight in green foreshadowing in imagery.
- Use a note to explain the effect of each example.

The soldier shook his head. "Fancy, I suppose," he said slowly. "I did have some idea of selling it, but I don't think I will. It has caused enough mischief already. Besides, people won't buy."

Analyzing the Text

COMMON CORE RL 1, RL 2, RL 3, RL 6, RL 9

Possible answers:

1. *The description of the setting ("of all the beastly, slushy, out-of-the-way places to live in, this is the worst. Pathway's a bog, and the road's a torrent.") suggests potential danger or impending doom.*

2. *She refers to Arabian Nights, a collection of fantastical tales, which suggests that she doesn't take the paw seriously or believe its powers are real.*

3. *Morris throws the paw in the fire; he takes its powers seriously and seems afraid. White grabs the paw because he is more skeptical and curious. Morris looks alarmed and urges White to "wish for something sensible." This conflict between the two characters adds to the story's suspense. Readers have to finish the story to see which character's attitude toward the paw will prove right.*

4. *When the Whites hear that the amount being offered is two hundred pounds, Mrs. White screams and Mr. White faints. They clearly believe that the money is the fulfillment of the wish, and that means that they are responsible for their son's death.*

5. *Mr. White's fear of the evil that results from the monkey's paw prevents him from taking a risk. Mrs. White's overpowering love for her son still allows her to hope for a good outcome.*

6. *The main message or theme is to be careful what you wish for. Examples of how the theme is developed throughout the story may include that the first man who had the monkey's paw had three wishes granted, but "the third wish was for death"; Morris's desperation to be rid of the paw; and the death of the Whites' son.*

7. *In many stories, the result of making three wishes is positive in some way. Here the outcome is frightening and tragic.*

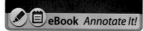 eBook *Annotate It!*

Analyzing the Text

COMMON CORE RL 1, RL 2, RL3, RL 6, RL 9, W 2b, W 7, W 8, W 9a

Cite Text Evidence Support your responses with evidence from the text.

1. **Infer** In what way does the setting described in lines 1–21 suggest or foreshadow later events?

2. **Analyze** Reread lines 110–119 and identify the **allusion,** or reference to a well-known work that Mrs. White makes. What does the allusion suggest about Mrs. White's view of the paw?

3. **Compare and Analyze** Complete the chart to identify how Morris's and Mr. White's views about the monkey's paw are different. Then explain how these differing points of view add to the suspense in the story.

Sergeant-Major Morris's View	Mr. White's View

4. **Draw Conclusions** Examine lines 271–281 to review the Whites' reaction as they realize what has happened to their son. What do they assume about the two hundred pounds they will receive "as compensation"?

5. **Compare** What do the actions of Mr. and Mrs. White at the end of the story reveal about their different expectations for wishes made on the monkey's paw? Identify what hopes or fears these expectations reveal.

6. **Analyze** What is the theme of "The Monkey's Paw"? Give examples of how the author develops the theme through the characters and plot.

7. **Connect** There are many traditional stories in which characters are granted three wishes. What theme do many of them share? Tell what makes "The Monkey's Paw" different from the others.

PERFORMANCE TASK

Writing Activity: Report Review lines 39–56. What ideas and attitudes about India are expressed here? Do research to learn more about the historical relationship between Britain and India. Write a short report in which you

- explain how Britain came to rule India, including the role of the British East India Company

- describe the attitudes the two peoples had toward one another during British rule

Then share your findings with the class. Be prepared to discuss the ways the attitudes in the story reflect the historical context.

Assign this performance task.

PERFORMANCE TASK

COMMON CORE W 2b, W 7, W 8, W 9a

Writing Activity: Report Have students work in pairs to discuss the attitudes about India expressed in the selection and to conduct their research.

- You might suggest that they consult the following website: http://www.bbc.co.uk/history/british/empire_seapower/east_india_01.shtml

- As needed, suggest that students refer to the Interactive Lesson "Conducting Research."

Critical Vocabulary

COMMON CORE L 4a, L 4b, L 4c, L 4d

peril	condole	grimace	fate
credulity	prosaic	compensation	resignation

Practice and Apply Explain what is alike and different about the meanings of the words in each pair.

1. peril/risk
2. grimace/frown
3. compensation/wages
4. fate/outcome
5. credulity/trust
6. resignation/acceptance
7. condole/encourage
8. prosaic/dull

Vocabulary Strategy: Latin Roots

A word **root** is a word part that contains the core meaning of a word. A root is combined with other word parts, such as a prefix or a suffix, to form a word. The root of many English words comes from Latin. Read this sentence from "The Monkey's Paw."

> His mother laughed, and following him to the door, watched him down the road; and returning to the breakfast table, was very happy at the expense of her husband's credulity.

The word *credulity* includes the Latin root *cred*, which means "believe" or "trust." You can use the meaning of the root *cred* as a clue to figure out that *credulity* means "a disposition to believe too readily."

Practice and Apply Find the word in each sentence that includes the Latin root *cred*. Use context and the meaning of the root to help you write a definition of the word. Then verify each of your definitions by finding the word's precise meaning in a print or digital dictionary.

1. Herbert was incredulous when he heard the sergeant-major's tale.
2. A person must have the proper credentials to enter a foreign country.
3. Mrs. White didn't give any credence to the notion that the monkey's paw moved.
4. Were the sergeant-major's stories about India credible?
5. One witness may discredit the story that another person tells.

The Monkey's Paw **119**

PRACTICE & APPLY

Critical Vocabulary

COMMON CORE L 4a, L 4b, L 4c, L 4d

Possible answers:

1. Peril *and* risk *both refer to a danger, but a peril is something more serious.*

2. *Both a grimace and a frown are facial expressions. A grimace may show pain or disgust. A frown shows disapproval or displeasure.*

3. *Compensation and wages are types of payment. However, compensation is often money given for some type of loss or suffering.*

4. *Both* fate *and* outcome *refer to a future event, but fate suggests an event is determined by an outside power.*

5. *Both* credulity *and* trust *have to do with a willingness to believe something, but credulity refers to believing something too readily or easily.*

6. Resignation *and* acceptance *both refer to deciding to put up with a situation. Resignation suggests that the situation is undesirable and inescapable.*

7. *Both* condole *and* encourage *suggest supporting another person, but condole suggests a particular type of support through the expression of sympathy.*

8. Prosaic *and* dull *both mean "ordinary" or "commonplace," but dull has a more negative connotation.*

Vocabulary Strategy: Latin Roots

Answers:

1. *incredulous: disbelieving or doubtful; skeptical*
2. *credentials: written evidence that promotes belief or trust*
3. *credence: belief, trust; acceptance as true*
4. *credible: believable*
5. *discredit: to cast doubt on; cause to be distrusted*

Strategies for Annotation ✎ 🗐 *Annotate it!*

Vocabulary Strategy: Latin Roots

COMMON CORE L 4a, L 4b, L 4c, L4d

Have students locate lines 149–152 and find the vocabulary word *credulity*. Encourage them to use their eBook annotation tools to do the following:

- Highlight the root and think about its meaning.
- Use the root to define the word.
- Check that the definition makes sense in the context. Use a dictionary to confirm, if necessary.

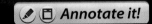

His father, smiling shamefacedly at his own **credulity,** held up the talisman, as his son, with a solemn face, somewhat marred by a wink at his mother, sat down at the piano and struck a few impressive chords.

PRACTICE & APPLY

Language Conventions: Subjunctive Mood

COMMON CORE L 1c, L 3a

Review the definition of subjunctive mood and that it is used to express a recommendation, a requirement, a wish or hypothetical situation, or a condition that is contrary to fact. Read the three bulleted examples with students, and ask them to give other examples of each use of the subjunctive.

Answers:

1. *The Whites recommend that Morris be seated by the fire.*

2. *My teacher suggests that the class predict what will happen next in the story.*

3. *Mrs. White acted as though she were mad.*

4. *Mr. White insists that his wife keep the door closed.*

5. *If Mrs. White were taller, she could reach the bolt on the door.*

6. *I move that each student be required to write a story summary after reading.*

 Assess It!

Online Selection Test
- Download an editable ExamView bank.
- Assign and manage this test online.

Language Conventions: Subjunctive Mood

COMMON CORE L 1c, L 3a

The **mood** of a verb shows a writer's judgment or attitude about a statement he or she makes. The **subjunctive mood** is used to express a recommendation, a requirement, a wish or hypothetical situation, or a condition that is contrary to fact. The subjunctive mood is generally used only in very formal English.

- Use the subjunctive, present-tense singular form of a verb in clauses beginning with *that* to express a recommendation or a requirement.

  Morris suggests <u>that</u> Mr. White let the monkey's paw burn.
  (*let* not *lets*)

  It is important <u>that</u> he think carefully before making a wish.
  (*think* not *thinks*)

- Use the subjunctive *be* in clauses beginning with *that* to express a recommendation or a requirement.

  Mrs. White insists <u>that</u> another wish be made.
  (*be* not *is*)

  I recommend <u>that</u> all students be required to read this story.
  (*be* not *are*)

- Use the subjunctive *were* to express a wish or hypothetical situation, or to state a condition that is contrary to fact.

  I wish Herbert were here with us.
  (*were* not *was*)

  The monkey's paw moved, as though it were alive.
  (*were* not *was*)

Practice and Apply One verb in each sentence is not correct. Rewrite each sentence correctly, using the subjunctive mood.

1. The Whites recommend that Morris is seated by the fire.

2. My teacher suggests that the class predicts what will happen next in the story.

3. Mrs. White acted as though she was mad.

4. Mr. White insists that his wife keeps the door closed.

5. If Mrs. White was taller, she could reach the bolt on the door.

6. I move that each student is required to write a story summary after reading.

Compare and Contrast Texts

COMMON CORE
RL 9

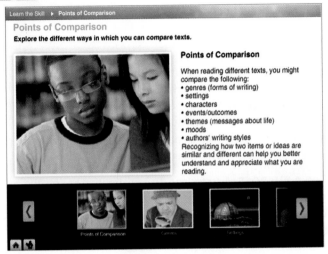

Learn the Skill ▶ Points of Comparison

Points of Comparison

Explore the different ways in which you can compare texts.

Points of Comparison

When reading different texts, you might compare the following:
- genres (forms of writing)
- settings
- characters
- events/outcomes
- themes (messages about life)
- moods
- authors' writing styles

Recognizing how two items or ideas are similar and different can help you better understand and appreciate what you are reading.

TEACH

Tell students that comparing texts with similar themes can deepen their understanding of both the texts and the theme. Briefly review the story of King Midas, who, when granted a wish, wished that everything he touched would turn to gold. Use these steps to model how to compare this story with "The Monkey's Paw."

- **Step 1: Look for Similarities** (*In both stories the characters make wishes, with disastrous results: Midas's daughter is turned to gold; the Whites' son is killed in an accident.*)
- **Step 2: Look for Differences** (*Midas is able to reverse his wish and get his daughter back. The Whites are not.*)
- **Step 3: Synthesize Your Ideas** (*The stories share a similar theme: be careful what you wish for. The lesson is much harsher in "The Monkey's Paw," because the wish cannot be undone.*)

 INTERACTIVE GRAPHIC ORGANIZER Demonstrate how to use an Interactive Graphic Organizer, such as a **Venn Diagram** or **Comparison-Contrast Chart,** to record similarities and differences.

PRACTICE AND APPLY

Have small groups follow the steps above to compare "The Monkey's Paw" with another horror story in Collection 2.

Determine Theme

COMMON CORE
RL 2,
RL 9

RETEACH

Review that a **theme** is a message about life or human nature that a writer shares with readers. It is not the same as the topic, or what the story is about. A theme is usually stated as a complete sentence. For example:

- Money can't buy happiness.
- Hard work pays off.

To determine the theme of a story, readers should ask, "What lesson does the character learn? How does this apply to real people's lives?"

Ask a volunteer to give a summary of a familiar fairy tale, such as "Beauty and the Beast." Then ask questions such as:

- How did Beauty change during the story?
- What lesson about life did she learn?

Stress that there may be many ideas in a story, a book, or a film. The theme, however, will be the most important message a story communicates. Prompt students to suggest modern stories whose themes draw on myths or other traditional stories.

 LEVEL UP TUTORIALS Assign the following *Level Up* tutorial: **Theme**

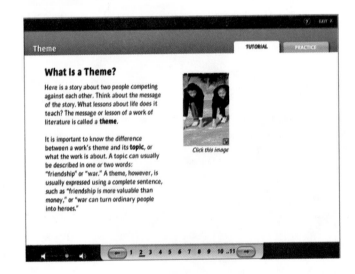

Theme   TUTORIAL   PRACTICE

What Is a Theme?

Here is a story about two people competing against each other. Think about the message of the story. What lessons about life does it teach? The message or lesson of a work of literature is called a **theme**.

It is important to know the difference between a work's theme and its **topic**, or what the work is about. A topic can usually be described in one or two words: "friendship" or "war." A theme, however, is usually expressed using a complete sentence, such as "friendship is more valuable than money," or "war can turn ordinary people into heroes."

Click this image

CLOSE READING APPLICATION

Student partners can work together to determine the theme of another story or of a current film. Encourage the student partners to discuss how the theme applies to everyday life.

Frankenstein

Poem by Edward Field

Why This Text

Few tales have withstood the test of time like *Frankenstein*. Originally published in 1818 as a Gothic novel, its universal themes have inspired adaptations in every medium you can think of, from animated cartoons to works of theater and film. Here, the poet Edward Field throws his hat into the ring with a version that is as lyrical as it is straightforward. With the help of the close-reading questions, students will examine a dark tale that has gripped the collective imagination for centuries.

Background Have students read the background information about Edward Field and the story that inspired his poem. The poem has more in common with the 1931 movie *Frankenstein* than it does with the novel. For instance, in the poem as well as the movie, it's "the Baron" who creates the monster; in the novel, this character is referred to as "Dr. Frankenstein."

SETTING A PURPOSE Ask students to pay attention to how the author uses foreshadowing to create suspense and advance the plot. What clues in the dialogue, events, and descriptions signal future events?

Common Core Support

- cite textual evidence
- determine the theme in a work of literature and analyze its development over the course of a text

Text Complexity Rubric

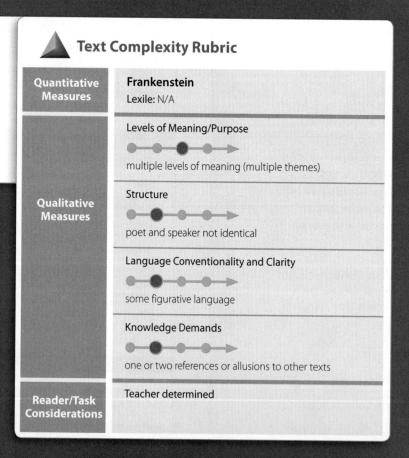

Quantitative Measures

Frankenstein
Lexile: N/A

Qualitative Measures

Levels of Meaning/Purpose
multiple levels of meaning (multiple themes)

Structure
poet and speaker not identical

Language Conventionality and Clarity
some figurative language

Knowledge Demands
one or two references or allusions to other texts

Reader/Task Considerations
Teacher determined

Strategies for CLOSE READING

Determine Theme

Students should read this poem carefully all the way through. Close-reading questions at the bottom of the page will help to clarify the poem's theme. As they read, students should jot down comments or questions about the text in the margins.

WHEN STUDENTS STRUGGLE . . .

To help students analyze the poem "Frankenstein," have them work in small groups to fill out a chart like the one shown below.

CITE TEXT EVIDENCE For practice in determining the story's theme, ask students to make inferences about each clue in the chart.

Clue	Inference
"He is pursued by the ignorant villagers . . . They wave firebrands at him and cudgels and rakes"	The monster has human affectations.
"tears come into our dear monster's eyes"	The monster is capable of strong emotion.
"the magic new words he has learned and above all of the friend he has found"	The monster has the power of speech.
"sits back like a banker, grunting and puffing"	Fear and ignorance drives the villagers to violence.
". . . his short unnatural life"	The monster's kindness is "unnatural."

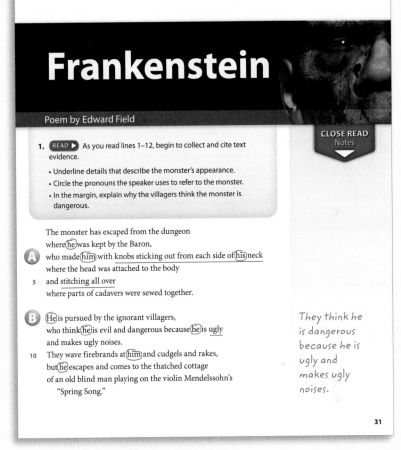

Background *This poem by Edward Field (born 1924) presents a new version of a famous character in literature, the monster brought to life by the scientist Dr. Frankenstein. In the original story by the English writer Mary Wollstonecraft Shelley, Dr. Frankenstein used portions of dead bodies to create a figure shaped like a man and then gave the creature the power to move and think by activating him with electricity.*

Frankenstein

Poem by Edward Field

CLOSE READ Notes

1. **READ ▶** As you read lines 1–12, begin to collect and cite text evidence.
    - Underline details that describe the monster's appearance.
    - Circle the pronouns the speaker uses to refer to the monster.
    - In the margin, explain why the villagers think the monster is dangerous.

The monster has escaped from the dungeon
where (he) was kept by the Baron,
A who made (him) with knobs sticking out from each side of (his) neck
where the head was attached to the body
5 and stitching all over
where parts of cadavers were sewed together.

B (He) is pursued by the ignorant villagers,
who think (he) is evil and dangerous because (he) is ugly
and makes ugly noises.
10 They wave firebrands at (him) and cudgels and rakes,
but (he) escapes and comes to the thatched cottage
of an old blind man playing on the violin Mendelssohn's
    "Spring Song."

They think he is dangerous because he is ugly and makes ugly noises.

31

1. **READ AND CITE TEXT EVIDENCE** Explain that although there are many versions of "Frankenstein," the monster's appearance stays remarkably the same: knobs sticking out of his neck and the giant stitches crisscrossing his body.

A **ASK STUDENTS** to explain the monster's physical features. *The knobs were used to attach the head to the body (line 3); the stitches were used to sew the cadaver parts together (line 6).*

Hearing him approach, the blind man welcomes him:
"Come in, my friend," and takes him by the arm.
15 "You must be weary," and sits him down inside the house.
For the blind man has long dreamed of having a friend
to share his lonely life.

The monster has never known kindness—the Baron was cruel—
but somehow he is able to accept it now,
20 and he really has no instincts to harm the old man,
D for in spite of his awful looks he has a tender heart:
Who knows what cadaver that part of him came from?

The monster rears back in terror because he cannot recognize honest kindness.

C The old man seats him at table, offers him bread,
and says, "Eat, my friend." The monster
25 rears back roaring in terror.
"No my friend, it is good. Eat—gooood"
and the old man shows him how to eat,
and reassured, the monster eats
and says, "Eat—gooood,"
30 trying out the words and finding them good too.

E The old man offers him a glass of wine,
"Drink, my friend. Drink—goood."
The monster drinks, slurping horribly, and says,
"Drink—goood," in his deep nutty voice
35 and smiles maybe for the first time in his life.

Then the blind man puts a cigar in the monster's mouth
and lights a large wooden match that flares up in his face.
The monster, remembering the torches of the villagers,
recoils, grunting in terror.
40 "No, my friend, smoke—goood,"
and the old man demonstrates with his own cigar.
The monster takes a tentative puff
and smiles hugely, saying, "Smoke—goood,"
and sits back like a banker, grunting and puffing.

45 Now the old man plays Mendelssohn's "Spring Song" on the violin
while tears come into our dear monster's eyes
as he thinks of the stones of the mob, the pleasures of mealtime,
the magic new words he has learned
and above all of the friend he has found.

---

2. ◀ REREAD   Reread lines 7–12. Does the speaker share the villagers' view that the monster is evil and dangerous? Support your answer with explicit textual evidence.

The speaker doesn't agree with the villagers—he says they are "ignorant." The speaker refers to the monster as "he" instead of "it," which suggests the speaker recognizes the monster's humanity.

3. READ ▶   As you read lines 13–30, continue to cite textual evidence.
• Circle details that suggest the blind man's kindness to the monster.
• Underline phrases that describe the monster's personality.
• In the margin, write the reason the monster "rears back roaring in terror" (line 25).

4. ◀ REREAD   Reread lines 13–30. Explain why the old man is quick to welcome the monster into his house. Support your answer with explicit textual evidence.

The man "has long dreamed of having a friend" to experience life with him. He welcomes the monster as a friend because he cannot see what he looks like and therefore is not afraid of him.

5. READ ▶   As you read lines 31–55, cite additional textual evidence.
• Circle actions by the old man that are similar to those he has made before.
• Underline details that reveal how happy the monster is.
• In the margin, restate what will happen to the monster when the mob finds him.

32

33

---

2. **REREAD AND CITE TEXT EVIDENCE**   Point out that the villagers think the monster is dangerous and pursue him with weapons.

B **ASK STUDENTS** to use this information to make inferences about the poem's theme. What universal truth is being addressed? *People in their ignorance will often make judgments based on appearance alone.*

3. **READ AND CITE TEXT EVIDENCE**   Point out that the monster has a strong reaction to the blind man's offer of bread.

C **ASK STUDENTS** to describe the reaction. *The monster is terrified.* Why does the monster react this way? *His only experience of humanity is the Baron, who is cruel.*

FOR ELL STUDENTS Explain that the phrase *in spite of* means "without being prevented by." The word *despite* can be used in place of *in spite of*.

4. **REREAD AND CITE TEXT EVIDENCE**   Explain that the blind man "sees" the monster as he really is.

D **ASK STUDENTS** what the blind man sees in the monster. *The monster has a "tender heart."* Why is he able to see the monster this way? *Since he is blind, he is unaware of the "awful looks" of him.*

5. **READ AND CITE TEXT EVIDENCE**

E **ASK STUDENTS** to explain how these lines foreshadow the monster's fate. How might the monster's new behavior push the villagers over the edge? *The monster is happy; he has human characteristics; he drinks, smiles, eats, uses language, listens to music, and smokes a cigar "like a banker."*

FOR ELL STUDENTS Some students may be familiar with the term *match* referring to a game of sport. Clarify that in this context *match* is a small strip of wood or cardboard that you strike to produce a flame.

The mob will drive the monster to his death.

F 50 It is just as well that he is unaware—
being simple enough to believe only in the present—
that the mob will find him and pursue him
for the rest of his short unnatural life,
until trapped at the whirlpool's edge
55 he plunges to his death.

6. ◀ REREAD AND DISCUSS Reread lines 31–55. With a small group, discuss whether the time spent with the blind musician ultimately brought the monster more joy or more pain.

SHORT RESPONSE

Cite Text Evidence "We should not judge people by their appearance" is one of the themes of "Frankenstein." How do the events in the story and the characters' behavior convey this? Cite text evidence from the text to support your claims.

The villagers believe that the monster is threatening because he is "ugly and makes ugly noises." The villagers wave firebrands, cudgels, and rakes at him, judging him solely on his appearance. However, he really has no "instincts to harm." This proves to be true when the monster meets the blind man. The blind man is happy to "have a friend to share his lonely life." The monster, who "has never known kindness," responds gently and positively to the blind man, showing that he is like other humans inside. Because the monster and the blind man do not judge each other, they are able to bring each other joy. On the other hand, the crowd's willingness to judge the monster brings about sadness and, eventually, death.

34

6. REREAD AND DISCUSS USING TEXT EVIDENCE

F ASK STUDENTS to consider the speaker's opinion when discussing this question. What does the speaker have to say about whether the monster's brief brush with life was worth it? Have groups share their responses. *Students may point out that according to the speaker, "It is just as well that he is unaware. . . " (line 50) suggesting that although the monster's life will be short, he will at least have known happiness and friendship—the best parts of being human.*

SHORT RESPONSE

Cite Text Evidence Students' responses should include text evidence that supports their positions. They should:

- analyze the poem's theme.
- cite events from the text that convey this theme.
- explain how the characters' behavior reinforces this theme.

TO CHALLENGE STUDENTS . . .

To deepen students' understanding, they can conduct research in a library or online to learn about other versions of the Frankenstein story. Challenge students to see how many treatments of the original story they can come up with.

ASK STUDENTS to compare two different treatments of the story. How do they differ? What do they have in common? How successfully does each one convey the theme of judging people by their physical appearance? Why do you think this theme is so prevalent in our culture?

DIG DEEPER

With the class, return to Question 3, Read. Have groups share their responses to the question.

ASK STUDENTS about the blind man's kindness to the monster.

- Have students discuss why the poem features a blind character. What does his blindness represent? *Since he cannot see the physical world, he must rely on his intuitive sense of a person's intrinsic worth. His blindness enables him to focus on what lies below the surface—on what is meaningful and enduring rather than what is surface and fleeting. Unlike his sighted counterparts, the blind man finds ways to connect with people.*

- Have students contrast the blind man with the villagers. *The villagers, who can see, have their sights trained on the surface layer of things—their appearance rather than their inner truth. Because they are shallow they see only what separates people, not what brings them together.*

- Ask students to describe how the blind man teaches the monster what it means to be human. What does the monster learn? What does he know now that he didn't know before? *Through the blind man's generosity the monster is able to experience some of life's simple pleasures: food, music, companionship, language. He learns he has the ability to feel emotion. He becomes, in essence, human—more human than those who base their lives around hate and fear.*

ASK STUDENTS to return to their Short Response answer and revise it based on the class discussion.

from The Monkey's Paw

Film by Ricky Lewis Jr.

Why This Text?

This film clip is from a movie based on the short story "The Monkey's Paw." By learning about the techniques the filmmaker uses to tell this familiar story, students will be better able to understand a movie's impact on viewers.

Key Learning Objective: The student will be able to analyze the choices a filmmaker makes when he or she decides to adapt a written story to movie form.

COMMON CORE Common Core Standards

RL 2 Provide a summary.

RL 7 Analyze the extent to which a filmed production of a story stays faithful to the text.

RI 7 Evaluate the advantages and disadvantages of using different mediums.

SL 2 Analyze the purpose of information presented in diverse media.

SL 4 Present findings with relevant evidence.

SL 5 Integrate multimedia and visual displays into presentations.

▲ Text Complexity Rubric

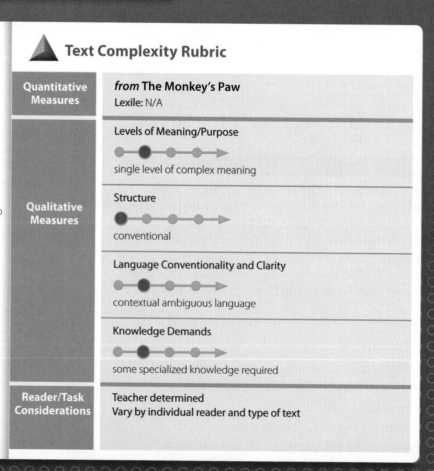

Quantitative Measures	*from* The Monkey's Paw Lexile: N/A
Qualitative Measures	**Levels of Meaning/Purpose** single level of complex meaning
	Structure conventional
	Language Conventionality and Clarity contextual ambiguous language
	Knowledge Demands some specialized knowledge required
Reader/Task Considerations	Teacher determined Vary by individual reader and type of text

Background Have students read the background about the film *The Monkey's Paw*. Point out that the film clip they are about to watch is only one part of a longer movie. Explain that the film clip deals with the very end of the story, following Herbert's death. Tell students that although the film was shot in only a handful of days, the production work took several years to complete. Point out that it is during this production time that a director incorporates many of the techniques that students will learn about in the lesson.

SETTING A PURPOSE Direct students to use the Setting a Purpose suggestions to focus their viewing. Remind students to write their own questions as they watch the clip.

Background *The film* The Monkey's Paw *is an adaptation of the short story of the same name. The film's writer and director, Ricky Lewis, Jr., had read the story as a child. He decided to make it into a movie because his "morbid curiosity wanted to see it." While other film adaptations of the story had modernized it, Lewis thought it was important that the film be set in the past, "when odd things were sure to happen." He chose to "let a little darkness" into his film to create its gloomy, sometimes spooky mood.*

MEDIA ANALYSIS

from THE MONKEY'S PAW

Film by Ricky Lewis Jr.

©Lewisworks Studio

SETTING A PURPOSE The film clip you will view deals with the ending of the short story "The Monkey's Paw." Keep your reading of the short story in mind as you view the film, and pay attention to any differences you notice between the content of the text version of the story and the content of the film. Think about how any differences affect the story being told. Also consider your own reaction to each version and how the choices made by the author of the short story and the director of the film helped bring about your reaction. Write down any questions you have during viewing.

The Monkey's Paw **121**

SCAFFOLDING FOR ELL STUDENTS

Multiple-Meaning Words Draw attention to the term *film clip* in Setting a Purpose. Elicit that the word *clip* can mean "to cut or trim something," but it can also refer to an excerpt or passage from a longer work. Explain that since many words in English have more than one meaning, it is important to consider the context in which the words are used.

ASK STUDENTS to use context to discuss and define other multiple-meaning words in this lesson, such as *running* (in "running time") and *shot* (as in "camera shot").

TEACH

CLOSE READ

As You View Explain that film directors rely on lighting and camera angles to get certain reactions from viewers and to help bring their stories to life. Have students read As You View to help them focus their viewing on the kinds of techniques the director used in this film.

Evaluate Media

COMMON CORE · RL 7, RI 7, SL 2

Explain to students that when a director makes a movie of a written story, he or she has to make choices about how closely to follow the written work.

Ⓐ ASK STUDENTS to think about the story "The Monkey's Paw." Prompt them to give reasons why a director might cut or add a scene. *(The director might cut a scene that is not important or one that slows the action; while a writer can state what a character thinks or feels, a director might need to add a scene to show what the character is experiencing.)*

COLLABORATIVE DISCUSSION Have pairs work together to outline the endings of both the story and the film. Then have them compare the outlines and ask them to tell how the endings are alike and different. Remind them to consider why the director might have chosen to tell the story differently.

ASK STUDENTS to share any questions they generated in the course of viewing and discussing the film.

Format: Film
Running Time: 6:02

AS YOU VIEW Directors use many different techniques to make stories come alive on the screen. As you view *The Monkey's Paw*, notice the lighting and camera angles the director uses. Notice how they vary or change as the scenes change. Think about the techniques being used and why Ricky Lewis, Jr. chose those particular techniques to tell the story.

Ⓐ

COLLABORATIVE DISCUSSION Review the ending of the print version of the short story. Then consider the ending of the film clip. With a partner, compare and contrast the two endings and decide how the film ending differs from the ending of the short story. Discuss why the director might have chosen to tell parts of the story in a different way. Cite specific evidence from the text and the film to support your ideas.

APPLYING ACADEMIC VOCABULARY

technique	summary

As you discuss the film clip, incorporate the following Collection 2 academic vocabulary words: *technique* and *summary*. As you discuss the film, ask students which of the director's **techniques** they found most effective. Ask students to give a **summary** of the film clip they viewed.

Evaluate Media

COMMON CORE RL 7, RI 7, SL 2

Like many movies, the film clip of *The Monkey's Paw* is based on a written story. When a film director decides to make a movie, he or she must make choices about how closely to follow the written work. Will the film

- include all of the same characters?
- have the same setting?
- show all of the same events?

Think about how the director's choices affect the content of the film clip of *The Monkey's Paw*.

Writers and directors use different techniques to create suspense and to tell the story.

- Writers use words to describe the rising action or the characters' struggles.
- Directors use a combination of visual and sound techniques.

For example, directors may use different camera shots to convey ideas, to track characters' emotions, or to show a situation from a character's viewpoint. Directors also use other techniques to build suspense.

Camera Shot	What It Is	Why It Is Used
Close-up shot	a shot that focuses on a character's face	to convey a character's emotions or thoughts
Low-angle shot	a shot in which the camera looks up at a subject	to create the impression of height or distance; to make a subject look more menacing
High-angle shot	a shot in which the camera looks down on a subject	to show a character in relation to his or her surroundings; to make a subject look unprotected or exposed
Point-of-view shot	a shot that shows what a character sees	to let viewers see what is happening from a character's point of view

- **Lighting** can create moods that are gloomy, mysterious, or scary. Suspenseful movies often use minimal lighting with frequent use of shadows.
- **Camera filters** are glass or plastic disks that are inserted in front of a camera lens. These filters can change the way that images appear, making them clearer, brighter, darker, or fuzzier.
- **Music** can signal dramatic events or tense moments. Music sometimes foreshadows, or hints at, what is going to happen.

As you analyze the film clip, **evaluate,** or make judgments about the different film techniques the director uses in *The Monkey's Paw*.

The Monkey's Paw **123**

WHEN STUDENTS STRUGGLE . . .

To guide students' understanding of the different techniques, have them work in teams. Name one technique and have students watch the film clip to find examples of its use and the effects it has on viewers. Encourage them to pause the film as needed while they take notes. Have them repeat the process to look for other techniques.

CLOSE READ

Evaluate Media

COMMON CORE RL 7, RI 7, SL 2

Help students compare the film clip of *The Monkey's Paw* with the original story by W. W. Jacobs, making notes of where and how the film stays faithful to or departs from the text. Then have them summarize their findings. *(The characters and the setting are the same, but some events are different. In the film clip, viewers see some of what happens when Mr. White uses the monkey's paw to wish that Herbert were still with them. Viewers also find out what happens after Mr. White wishes Herbert back to the grave.)*

Discuss the visual and sound techniques used in films, citing examples to evaluate and discuss the impact of each one.

- Explain that directors use different camera shots to achieve certain purposes. Prompt students to give examples of each type from *The Monkey's Paw*. Discuss how each shot helps to tell the story. Have students evaluate the director's choice for each camera shot, prompting them to describe what makes the shot effective or ineffective.
- Have students tell what kind of lighting the director uses in *The Monkey's Paw* and how it helps to build suspense.
- Discuss how music can affect the mood of a film. Have students identify the different kinds of music in the film clip and describe how it affects the viewer.

PRACTICE & APPLY

Analyzing the Media

COMMON CORE RL 2, RL 7, RI 7, SL 2

Possible answers:

1. *The film clip begins just after Herbert's funeral, when Mrs. White realizes that there are two remaining wishes for the monkey's paw. She begs her husband to wish that their son were alive, and after much pleading he agrees. Though Herbert returns to the house, he is not human, and Mr. White uses his third wish to return him to his grave. A year later Mrs. White has died and Mr. White is at her grave, near death.*

2. *The film clip is mainly faithful to the story. While it uses much of the dialogue from the print version, it adds some, such as Mr. White's explanation about how badly disfigured Herbert was when he died. Also, the clip continues beyond the end of the story to show that within a year Mrs. White has died, and Mr. White is at her grave, near death.*

3. *The film clip uses dark shadows and low lighting throughout, close-up shots of Mrs. White that reveal her extreme grief, and music that adds an eerie feeling. The low lighting is effective in creating a spooky, ominous feeling.*

4. *The dark lighting creates an ominous feeling while Herbert is trying to enter the house, while the flood of brighter blue lighting when Mr. White makes his third wish is somewhat mystical.*

5. *The close-up shots of Mrs. White reveal her torment and create a haunting, desperate mood; these shots are often in a brighter light that makes her a focal point. The point-of-view shots of Mrs. White from her husband's perspective show her grief, which helps viewers accept his second wish to try to help her. At the cemetery, the angles and filters highlight the cold reality of death.*

6. *One advantage of the story is that the narrator tells readers what characters are thinking ("If only he could find it before the thing outside got in.") An advantage of the film clip is the use of music and lighting to create a gloomy, frightening mood that enhances story events.*

Analyzing the Media

COMMON CORE RL 2, RL 7, RI 7, SL 2, SL 4, SL 5

Cite Text Evidence   Support your responses with evidence from the media.

1. **Summarize** The film clip shows several scenes from the short story "The Monkey's Paw." Summarize the events shown and described in the film.

2. **Compare** Has the director remained faithful to the written story? Name some of the ways that the story you read and the film clip are the same. Then name some of the ways that they are different.

3. **Evaluate** Complete a chart like the one shown to identify three of the techniques the director used. Then explain which one you found most effective and why.

Technique	Part in the Film
1.	
2.	
3.	

4. **Analyze** Consider the ways the director uses lighting in the film. What is the effect of the lighting in the scene where Herbert returns to the house?

5. **Analyze** How do the camera angles and camera filters that the director uses affect the mood of the film? How do they affect the impact of the final scenes at the cemetery?

6. **Compare and Evaluate** You have read a story and viewed a film clip of that story. What are some of the advantages of the written version of the story? What are some of the advantages of the film version?

PERFORMANCE TASK

Media Activity: Storyboard Work with a partner to create a storyboard for your own film retelling of a scene from "The Monkey's Paw." A storyboard is a device filmmakers use to plan the shooting of a movie. It serves as a map that includes images and descriptions.

- Decide whether you will stay faithful to the short story or depart from the text.

- Draw a series of at least 12 separate frames. Sketch the characters and scene for each frame.

- Underneath each frame, write descriptions of shots—such as close-up, medium, or distance shots—and write a line of dialogue or describe what characters will say.

- Consider what kind of music you will add and write where you'll include it.

Assign this performance task.

PERFORMANCE TASK

COMMON CORE SL 4, SL 5

Media Activity: Storyboard Have students work with a partner using these tips:

- Make the storyboard simple rather than too detailed. The images should be easy to understand.
- Include a variety of different camera shots.
- Include shots that show how characters react.

Compare and Contrast a Film and Story

RL 7

TEACH

Remind students that when directors decide to make a movie based on a written story or novel, they make choices about what to include and what to omit. Provide the following guidelines for comparing a story and a film adaptation of that story:

- **Compare the events.** Does the film include all of the events from the story or novel? Or does it focus on only one part of it? Does the film give more information about the plot than the written work? Or does it stay faithful to the story?
- **Compare the characters.** Are all of the characters from the written work included in the film? If not, why might the director have omitted those characters? How does that affect the plot?
- **Compare settings.** Is the setting in the film the same as the written work? If not, why does the director change the time or place in which the written work takes place? How does that affect the story?

 INTERACTIVE GRAPHIC ORGANIZER Have students use a Venn diagram to compare the events, characters, and settings.

PRACTICE AND APPLY

Have students choose a film they have seen that was based upon a written story they know. Ask them to complete a chart, like the one below, to compare the two versions. Then have students analyze the extent to which the film stays faithful to or changes the original text. Ask students to evaluate the choices made by the director and/or actors in bringing the story to life.

	Story	Film
Events		
Characters		
Setting		

Film Techniques

RL 7, SL 2

RETEACH

Review the following visual and sound techniques that directors use in films:

- close-up shots
- low-angle shots
- high-angle shots
- point-of-view shots
- lighting
- camera filters
- music

Ask questions such as: *What do you see on the screen when you see a close-up shot? Why would a director use a close-up shot in a film?*

Then run the film clip of *The Monkey's Paw*, stopping as needed to point out examples for each technique. Discuss the effects each of these techniques has on the viewer of the film.

CLOSE VIEWING APPLICATION

Students can apply the skill to another short film or an advertisement. Have them work independently to identify different techniques the director uses. Ask: *What effects do these techniques have? Why do you think the director chose these techniques?*

What Is the Horror Genre?

Literary Criticism by Sharon A. Russell

Why This Text?

It is often a challenge for students to analyze text beyond recognizing whether or not they liked it. Russell's essay provides a good model to break down that analysis into the parts that make up the whole. It is an especially good example of analyzing literature without making subjective judgments.

View It!

Professional Development Podcast:

Text Complexity

Key Learning Objective: The student will be able to analyze literary criticism to gain insight into the literature.

For practice and application:

Close Reader selection
"Man-Made Monsters,"
Essay by Daniel Cohe

COMMON CORE Common Core Standards

RI 1 Cite textual evidence.

RI 2 Provide an objective summary of the text.

RI 3 Analyze how a text makes connections.

RI 4 Determine the meaning of words and phrases.

RI 6 Determine author's purpose.

SL 1a Come to discussions prepared.

SL 1b Follow rules for collegial discussions and decision-making.

SL 1c Pose and respond to questions.

SL 1d Acknowledge new information expressed by others.

SL 4 Present claims and findings.

L 2a Use commas to indicate a pause or break.

L 4b Use affixes as clues to meaning.

▲ Text Complexity Rubric

Quantitative Measures	**What Is the Horror Genre?** Lexile: 1030L
Qualitative Measures	**Levels of Meaning/Purpose** ●━━●━━●━━●━━▶ single purpose, explicitly stated
	Structure ●━━●━━●━━●━━▶ organization of main ideas and details are complex, but clearly stated and generally sequential
	Language Conventionality and Clarity ●━━●━━●━━●━━▶ contemporary, familiar language
	Knowledge Demands ●━━●━━●━━●━━▶ some references to other texts
Reader/Task Considerations	Teacher determined Vary by individual reader and type of text

Sharon A. Russel Have students read the background and information about the author. Tell students that Stephen King is one of the most popular horror story writers in history, and Sharon A. Russell was the first person to write a book for the general public analyzing his work. Russell uses her expertise in the field to analyze how the horror genre works and what makes a good horror story.

SETTING A PURPOSE Direct students to use the Setting a Purpose question to focus their reading. Tell students to generate questions as they read.

Analyze Text: Literary Criticism (LINES 1–11)

COMMON CORE **RI 1, RI 2, RI 3, RI 6**

Explain that an **author's purpose** is his or her reason for writing. Discuss Russell's likely purpose for writing, based on the title of the essay (*to define the horror genre*). Point out that one way to define something is by discussing what it *isn't*.

Ⓐ CITE TEXT EVIDENCE Have students reread lines 1–11 to identify the phrase in which Russell states what horror stories do *not* have to include. (*"not all horror deals with monsters"*) What reason does she give for beginning in this way? (*"We all think of creatures like Frankenstein's monster, Dracula, and the wolfman . . . horror covers more than just these monsters."*) How might the author's statements relate to the central, or most important, idea in the literary criticism? (*She brings up a common misunderstanding about the genre to avoid later confusion when she offers her own ideas about how to define it.*)

Sharon A. Russell (b. 1941) *is a retired professor of Communication and Women's Studies at Indiana State University, where she taught courses on film and television. Russell has published extensively on horror film and literature and detective fiction. She is the author of* Stephen King: A Critical Companion, *a book that analyzes several of King's famous horror novels and in which this essay appears.*

What Is the Horror Genre?

Literary Criticism by Sharon A. Russell

SETTING A PURPOSE As you read, pay attention to the points the author makes about horror stories. Do her ideas make you think about horror stories in new ways?

Ⓐ   Many people define horror by its subjects. We all think of creatures like Frankenstein's monster, Dracula, and the wolfman[1] as monsters in the horror genre. Each one of these creatures has a history and developed over a period of time. But we also know that horror covers more than just these monsters. We could all make long lists of the kind of creatures we identify with horror, especially when we think of films as well as literature. The minute we would start to make such a list we would also realize that not all monsters are alike and that not all horror deals with monsters. The subject approach is not the clearest way to define this genre.

10

[1] **Frankenstein's monster, Dracula, and the wolfman:** legendary monsters. "Frankenstein's monster" is the creature created by Dr. Victor Frankenstein in Mary Shelley's novel; "Dracula" is the vampire in Bram Stoker's novel; in folklore, the wolfman is a man who can become a wolf.

Close Read Screencasts   View It!

Modeled Discussions

Have students click the *Close Read* icons in their eBooks to access a screencast in which readers discuss and annotate the following key passage:

- Note the rationale for not defining the horror genre by subjects, such as monsters (lines 1–11)

As a class, view and discuss the video. Then have students work in pairs to do an independent close read of an additional passage—the author's suggestion to categorize works of horror based on the source of the horror (lines 72–82).

Summarize Text

COMMON CORE RI 2

(LINES 12–32)

Tell students that when you **summarize,** you briefly retell the central ideas and most important details in a piece of writing. Explain that one of the most important steps in summarizing is determining a text's main, or most important, ideas. Point out that in lines 12–32, Russell explains one feature that can be used to define the horror genre.

B **ASK STUDENTS** to reread lines 12–32 to summarize the main idea. *(Readers expect something bad to happen just because the story is a horror story.)*

CRITICAL VOCABULARY

intensify: Russell is explaining the built-in element of suspense that readers find in horror stories.

ASK STUDENTS why knowing what to expect from a horror story might intensify suspense. *(Anticipating something bad increases tension.)*

justify: Russell is describing a character who fears that something bad is going to happen to her if she goes down into the basement.

ASK STUDENTS to explain whether having her fears justified is a good thing for the character. *(No. The character dies.)*

B Some students of this genre find that the best way to examine it is to deal with the way horror fiction is organized or structured. Examining the organization of a horror story shows that it shares certain traits with other types of fiction. Horror stories share the use of suspense as a tactic with many other kinds of literature. The tension we feel when a character goes into the attic, down into the basement, or just into the abandoned house is partially a result of suspense. We don't
20 know what is going to happen. But that suspense is **intensified** by our knowledge of the genre. We know that characters involved in the world of horror always meet something awful when they go where they shouldn't. Part of the tension is created because they are doing something we know is going to get them in trouble. Stephen King refers directly to our anticipation of horror. In *Salem's Lot*[2] Susan approaches the house which is the source of evil. "She found herself thinking of those drive-in horror movie epics where the heroine goes venturing up the narrow attic stairs…or down into some dark,
30 cobwebby cellar…and she…thinking: …*I'd never do that!*" Of course Susan's fears are **justified**. She does end up dead in the basement, a victim of the vampire.

If the horror genre uses the character's search for information to create suspense, it controls when and where we get our knowledge. Because we are outside of the situation we usually know more than the characters. Our advance knowledge creates suspense because we can anticipate what is going to happen. The author can play with those expectations by either confirming them or surprising us with a different
40 outcome. When suspense is an important element in fiction we may often find that the plot is the most critical part of the story. We care more about what happens next than about who the characters are or where the story is set. But setting is often considered a part of the horror genre. If the genre has traditional monsters, it also has traditional settings. Only authors who want to challenge the tradition place events in bright, beautiful parks. We expect a connection between the setting and the events in this genre. We are not surprised to find old houses, abandoned castles, damp cellars, or dark
50 forests as important elements in the horror story.

---

[2] **Salem's Lot:** a horror fiction novel written by Stephen A. King.

intensify
(ĭn-tĕn′sə-fī′) *v.* If you *intensify* something, you make it grow in strength.

justify
(jŭs′tə-fī′) *v.* If you *justify* something, you prove it is right or valid.

SCAFFOLDING FOR ELL STUDENTS

Pronoun Referents Using a whiteboard, project lines 21–23. Review with students that a **pronoun** is a word that takes the place of a noun. Guide students to do the following to clarify the connection between each pronoun and its referent:

- Highlight in green the phrase *characters involved in the world of horror* in the lines 21–22.
- Highlight in yellow all of the pronouns that refer to the phrase.

ASK STUDENTS to whom the pronoun *we* in the text refers. Encourage students to follow a similar process as they continue reading. As needed, point out the agreement between pronouns and their antecedents.

We know that characters involved in the world of horror always meet something awful when they go where they shouldn't. Part of the tension

The actor Boris Karloff as the monster in the 1931 film *Frankenstein,* based on the novel

The actor Lon Chaney as a werewolf in the 1941 film *The Wolf Man*

The actor Bela Lugosi as Dracula in the 1931 film by the same name

Some people make further distinctions based on how the stories are organized. We can divide stories into different categories based on how we come to believe in the events related and how they are explained to us. Stories that deal with **parallel** worlds expect us to accept those worlds without question. We just believe Dorothy is in Oz; we accept Oz as a parallel world separate from ours. Other times events seem to be supernatural but turn out to have natural explanations: the ghosts turn out to be squirrels in the attic, or things that
60 move mysteriously are part of a plot to drive someone crazy. Sometimes the supernatural is the result of the way the central character sees the world, as in stories told from the point of view of a crazy person. But at times we are not sure, and hesitate about believing in the possibility of the supernatural. When I first read Dracula I seriously considered hanging garlic on my windows because I believed that vampires could exist. This type of hesitation, when we almost believe, falls into the general category of the "fantastic" (Todorov 25).³ Often horror has its greatest effect on us because we almost

parallel
(păr´ə-lĕl´) *adj.*
If things are *parallel*, they have comparable or similar parts.

---
³ **Todorov 25:** the author is following MLA style to cite her source for the information just stated: page 25 of a work by an author named Todorov.

WHEN STUDENTS STRUGGLE...

Students may find it helpful to keep track of the criteria Russell discusses in a graphic organizer. Have them note the criteria along with an example or related idea.

CRITERIA	EXAMPLE
parallel world	The Wizard of Oz
supernatural, with natural explanations	ghosts turn out to be squirrels in the attic
supernatural	Dracula

CLOSE READ

Analyze Text: Literary Criticism (LINES 51–63)

 COMMON CORE RI 1, RI 2, RI 3, RI 6

Tell students that authors of literary criticism define and classify literature according to certain **criteria,** or standards. Explain that in lines 51–63, Russell is identifying criteria that helps to answer the question she posed in the title: what is the horror genre?

C **CITE TEXT EVIDENCE** Ask students to reread lines 51–63 and to identify two types of horror stories. *("Stories that deal with parallel worlds," "events that seem to be supernatural, but turn out to have natural explanations")* What is Russell's purpose for describing the two types of stories? *(They support her central idea by helping to define what the horror genre is.)*

Analyze Language

 COMMON CORE RI 4

(LINES 65–67)

Draw attention to the author's use of the personal pronoun *I* in lines 65–67. Point out that it is the first instance of its use in the literary criticism.

D **ASK STUDENTS** to reread the example the author provides in lines 65–67. Ask: *What is the impact of this personal detail? (Possible answer: The description of the author's experience with a classic horror story brings a more personal element into the literary criticism. It reveals that she is a fan of the genre as well as an academic person who studies and analyzes it.)*

CRITICAL VOCABULARY

parallel: Russell is using *The Wizard of Oz* as an example of what she means by "a parallel world."

ASK STUDENTS how a horror story could use a parallel world to scare its readers. *(The parallel world's similarity to reality can make scary events seem as if they could really happen.)*

Analyze Text:
Literary Criticism (LINES 72–83)

COMMON CORE RI 1, RI 2, RI 3, RI 6

Draw attention to the new criteria for horror stories that the author examines: the source of the horror.

 CITE TEXT EVIDENCE Have students reread lines 72–83 to identify the two ways a person in a horror story may become a source of horror. *(Lines 74–75: "Something goes wrong inside, and a person turns into a monster." Lines 79–80: "An outside force may invade the character and then force the evil out again.")* What is Russell's purpose for describing the source of horror in stories? *(The source of horror connects to her central idea by helping to define characteristics of the horror genre.)*

CRITICAL VOCABULARY

quest: Russell talks about a kind of search that is often the theme of horror fiction.

ASK STUDENTS what phrase names the quest that may be the theme of a horror story. *(forbidden knowledge)*

COLLABORATIVE DISCUSSION Have student partners use the text to review Russell's ideas about horror stories. Then tell partners to share their own ideas and experiences with the genre. Students may wish to use a Venn diagram or a chart to compare and contrast their ideas with Russell's.

ASK STUDENTS to share any questions they generated in the course of reading and discussing the selection.

---

70 believe, or believe while we are reading the book or watching the film, that the events are possible.

Yet another way of categorizing works of horror is by the source of the horror. Some horror comes from inside the characters. Something goes wrong inside, and a person turns into a monster. Dr. Frankenstein's need for knowledge turns him into the kind of person who creates a monster. Dr. Jekyll also values his desire for information above all else, and creates Mr. Hyde.[4] In another kind of horror story the threat to the central character or characters comes from outside. An 80 outside force may invade the character and then force the evil out again. The vampire attacks the victim, but then the victim becomes a vampire and attacks others. Stories of ghosts or demonic possession also fall into this category.

We can also look at the kinds of themes common to horror. Many works concentrate on the conflict between good and evil. Works about the fantastic may deal with the search for forbidden knowledge that appears in much horror literature. Such **quests** are used as a way of examining our attitude toward knowledge. While society may believe that 90 new knowledge is always good, the horror genre may question this assumption, examining how such advances affect the individual and society.

quest
(kwĕst) *n.* A *quest* is a search.

COLLABORATIVE DISCUSSION With a partner, discuss how Russell's ideas about horror stories compare with your own knowledge of this genre.

---

[4] **Dr. Jekyll . . . and . . . Mr. Hyde:** the good and evil sides of the same character in a novella by Robert Louis Stevenson.

APPLYING ACADEMIC VOCABULARY

psychology	technique

As you discuss "What Is the Horror Genre?" incorporate the following Collection 2 academic vocabulary words: *psychology* and *technique*. To help students understand tension and suspense, ask how authors take advantage of the **psychology** of the reader to create suspense. Invite students to explain or describe **techniques** used in horror stories that they find especially effective.

Analyze Text: Literary Criticism

COMMON CORE RI 2, RI 3, RI 6

One of the pleasures of reading literature is thinking about it afterward. **Literary criticism** is writing that examines, analyzes, and interprets a piece of literature or a general aspect of literature.

In literary criticism, the **author's purpose**—or the reason he or she is writing—is often to inform or to persuade other readers to view a text in a certain way. The chart shows some specific purposes an author might have when writing literary criticism.

Purpose	What the Author Does
To define a genre	explains the characteristics of a type of writing using specific examples as evidence
To categorize works of literature	defines and classifies works of literature based on certain **criteria,** or standards
To examine the structure of a work of literature	analyzes the organization of a piece of literature
To analyze an author's technique	explains and evaluates the effectiveness of literary techniques, such as using an unreliable narrator, recurring imagery, or flashbacks

What is the purpose of the work of literary criticism you have just read?

Summarize Text

COMMON CORE RI 2

A good way to check your comprehension and remember what you read is to summarize the text. When you **summarize,** you briefly retell the central ideas and most important details of a piece of writing in your own words. You can summarize a section of a text or an entire work.

- Begin with a clear, brief statement of the central idea of the section or work.
- Present the most important details that support the idea in the order in which they appear in the text.
- Write in your own words, but be careful not to change the author's meaning.

Summarize the first paragraph of "What Is the Horror Genre?"

TEACH

CLOSE READ

Analyze Text: Literary Criticism

COMMON CORE RI 3, RI 6

Use the chart to focus students' attention on the specific purposes an author may have when writing literary criticism. Prompt students to discuss each purpose, asking them to provide examples from the text as well as from other selections in the collection and their own experiences. Ask students to explain how each example connects to the ideas presented in the text. *(Students should note that the purpose of the literary criticism is to define the horror genre.)*

Summarize Text

COMMON CORE RI 2

Review each of the items in the bulleted list. Remind students that a summary does not include details that are not related to the central idea, and that a good summary is much shorter than the work it summarizes. *(Though monsters are a significant feature of many horror stories, there are more effective ways to explain what the horror genre is.)*

Strategies for Annotation 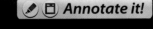 Annotate it!

Analyze Text: Literary Criticism

COMMON CORE RI 2, RI 3, RI 6

Share these strategies for guided or independent analysis:

- Highlight in yellow phrases or sentences that define the horror genre.
- Highlight in blue phrases or sentences that identify criteria that help to categorize elements of the horror genre.
- Highlight in green phrases or sentences that refer to an author's techniques.

Some students of this genre find that the best way to examine it is to deal with the way horror fiction is organized or structured. Examining the organization of a horror story shows that it shares certain traits with other types of fiction. Horror stories share the use of suspense as a tactic with many other kinds of literature.

Analyzing the Text

COMMON CORE RI 1, RI 2, RI 3, RI 4, RI 6

Possible answers:

1. The author argues that there are too many different kinds of monsters in horror stories to make the subject approach useful. She also points out that not all horror stories include monsters.

2. The author's purpose is to define a genre. Each paragraph is about characteristics of the genre: subjects and organization. At the end of the first paragraph, the author talks about "the clearest way to define this genre."

3. Readers know that awful things happen to characters in horror stories, most often when characters go to isolated or forbidding places, so when that happens, the readers' tension starts to mount.

4. Readers may have to suspend disbelief and accept the parallel reality presented in the world of the story, supernatural events may turn out to have natural explanations, and supernatural events may be presented in a way that leads readers to almost believe they are possible in the world in which we live.

5. "Forbidden knowledge" is knowledge that humans are not expected to have, such as how to control life and death. The author suggests that "forbidden knowledge" involves evil, as with Dr Jekyll, or an unnatural interest in life and death, such as that displayed by Dr. Frankenstein.

6. The horror genre refers to scary stories that use certain conventions to increase readers' suspense. The source of the horror may come from either within or outside of the character, and supernatural elements often, but not always, play a role.

7. Students might say her focus on how we come to believe in story events is a useful way of thinking about stories. In "The Monkey's Paw," the reader—along with the characters—might wonder whether the paw is actually magical or whether the events are a coincidence. Students might find their confidence in reality weakening by the end of the story.

 eBook *Annotate It!*

Analyzing the Text

COMMON CORE RI 1, RI 2, RI 3, RI 4, RI 6, SL 1a, SL 4

Cite Text Evidence   Support your responses with evidence from the text.

1. **Identify** Reread the first paragraph, lines 1–11. Why does the author reject characters or subjects as a way to categorize the horror genre?

2. **Infer** Reread the first two paragraphs of the essay, lines 1–32. What does the opening suggest about the author's purpose in writing this essay?

3. **Cause/Effect** In lines 20–21, the author says that in horror stories "suspense is intensified by our knowledge of the genre." What knowledge is the author referring to? Explain why it increases suspense.

4. **Analyze** Events described in the horror genre often defy everyday reality. According to Russell, what are three different reactions the reader might have to supernatural events depicted in horror stories?

5. **Interpret** In line 87, what does the author mean by "the search for forbidden knowledge"?

6. **Summarize** After reading this essay, what is your response to its title: "What Is the Horror Genre?" To answer, summarize the text.

7. **Synthesize** Consider your own knowledge of the horror genre. Which of Russell's proposed categories do you consider the most useful for gaining new understanding about these stories? Explain your answer by referring to horror stories with which you're familiar.

PERFORMANCE TASK

Speaking Activity: Discussion Use the characteristics of the horror genre described in the essay to categorize the horror stories you have read and the horror films you have seen.

- Work with a small group to create a list of stories and films.
- Review the characters, setting, events, structure, and organization of the stories and films.
- Decide how to categorize the stories and films. What creates the suspense in each one? Do they have similar themes or settings? Are the sources of horror alike in some way?
- Be prepared to explain your categories as you share your final list with the class or a small group.

Assign this performance task.

PERFORMANCE TASK

COMMON CORE SL 1a, SL 4

Speaking Activity: Discussion Some brainstorming may be useful to help student groups make their lists of horror stories and films. To prepare for the class discussion, suggest that students create a chart with a column for each category and place their story or film titles within those columns.

Critical Vocabulary

COMMON CORE L 4b

intensify	justify	parallel	quest

1. Which Vocabulary word goes with *similar*? Why?

2. Which Vocabulary word goes with *strengthen*? Why?

3. Which Vocabulary word goes with *search*? Why?

4. Which Vocabulary word goes with *defend*? Why?

Vocabulary Strategy: Using Suffixes

A **suffix** is a word part that is added to the end of a word. The suffix *-ied* is added to verbs that end in the letter *-y* and are preceded by a consonant. Adding *-ied* to such verbs changes the verb from the present to the past tense.

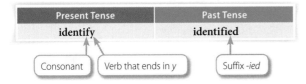

Present Tense	Past Tense
identify	identified

Consonant · Verb that ends in y · Suffix *-ied*

For example, to change a verb like *identify* to the past tense, you drop the *-y* and add *-ied*. Look at the sentences from "What Is the Horror Genre?" that show how the author uses the verbs *intensify* and *justify* in the past tense.

But that suspense is <u>intensified</u> by our knowledge of the genre.

Of course, Susan's fears are <u>justified</u>.

In the case of both *justify* and *intensify*, the author dropped the *-y* and added *-ied* to show the past tense.

Practice and Apply Read the sentences. Change the verbs in parentheses to the past tense by adding the suffix *-ied*.

1. In the horror story, the main character (rely) on her brother for help.

2. She was (mystify) when her calls to him were not answered.

3. She (hurry) to check that all her house doors were securely locked.

4. She was (petrify) when she thought she saw someone looking in the window.

5. Now she was (worry) that her brother would not show up to help her.

PRACTICE & APPLY

Critical Vocabulary

COMMON CORE L 4b

Possible answers:

1. *parallel; A parallel world is similar or comparable to the real world.*

2. *intensify; When something intensifies, it grows stronger.*

3. *quest; A quest is a search for something.*

4. *justify; To justify something is to explain or defend it.*

Vocabulary Strategy: Using Suffixes

1. *In the horror story, the main character relied on her brother for help.*

2. *She was mystified when her calls to him were not answered.*

3. *She hurried to check that all her house doors were securely locked.*

4. *She was petrified when she thought she saw someone looking in the window.*

5. *Now, she was worried that her brother would not show up to help her.*

Strategies for Annotation ✐ 🗐 **Annotate it!**

Using Suffixes

COMMON CORE L 4b

Have students locate the sentence containing the word *identify* in line 7 of the selection. Encourage them to use their eBook annotation tools to apply the steps suggested in the activity:

- Underline the word.
- Highlight the consonant before the *y* in blue.
- Highlight the *y* in yellow.
- Use a note to show the correct spelling when writing the word's past tense.

We could all make long lists of the kind of creatures we <u>identify</u> with horror, especially when we think of films as well as literature. The minute we would start to make such

identified

Language Conventions: Using Commas

COMMON CORE L 2a

Tell students that commas are often used to indicate pauses or breaks in a sentence.

Answers:

1. *Yes, I absolutely love horror stories.*

2. *You know, of course, that the main purpose of horror stories is to inspire fear and dread.*

3. *If Frankenstein is frightening, he is also sympathetic.*

4. *The long movie was terrifying, so much so that several times I closed my eyes and blocked my ears.*

5. *Writing a horror story, a big dream of mine, will take a lot of thought and hard work.*

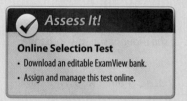

Assess It!

Online Selection Test
- Download an editable ExamView bank.
- Assign and manage this test online.

Language Conventions: Using Commas

COMMON CORE L 2a

A writer's use of punctuation not only helps readers understand the writer's message, but also signals how the writer wants the text to be read. In your writing, you can use commas to signal a break or a pause to the reader. When you write, read your sentences out loud, noticing where you pause. The parts where you pause probably need to be punctuated by a comma. Look at these examples from "What Is the Horror Genre?"

> So, she does end up dead in the basement, a victim of the vampire.

> This type of hesitation, when we almost believe, falls into the general category of the "fantastic."

Read the two sentences out loud, noticing where you pause. The commas after "So" and "basement" in the first sentence signal the reader to pause. The commas before and after "when we almost believe" do the same thing. They also signal a break in thought and make the sentence easier to understand. Additional examples are shown in the following chart.

Purpose of Comma	Example
to signal a break in thought	"Often horror has its greatest effect on us because we almost believe, or believe while we are reading the book or watching the film, that the events are possible."
to signal the reader to pause	"If a genre has traditional monsters, it also has traditional settings."

Practice and Apply These sentences include words, phrases, and clauses that need to be punctuated with commas. Rewrite the sentences, inserting the needed punctuation. If you get stuck, try reading the sentence out loud.

1. Yes I absolutely love horror stories.

2. You know of course that the main purpose of horror stories is to inspire fear and dread.

3. If Frankenstein is frightening he is also sympathetic.

4. The long movie was terrifying so much so that several times I just closed my eyes and blocked my ears.

5. Writing a horror story a big dream of mine will take a lot of thought and hard work.

Identifying Central Idea and Details in Literary Criticism

RI 2

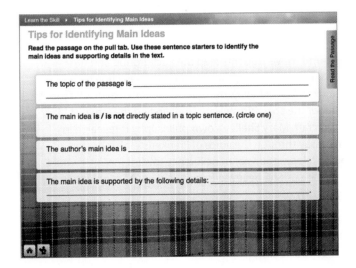

Learn the Skill ▸ Tips for Identifying Main Ideas

Tips for Identifying Main Ideas

Read the passage on the pull tab. Use these sentence starters to identify the main ideas and supporting details in the text.

The topic of the passage is _____

The main idea **is / is not** directly stated in a topic sentence. (circle one)

The author's main idea is _____

The main idea is supported by the following details: _____

TEACH

Tell students that the **central idea** of a text is its most important, or main, idea. Point out that details, such as examples, reasons, facts, or statistics, may be used to support or explain more about the central idea.

Explain to students that to identify the central idea in literary criticism they should follow these steps:

- Identify the topic and title. What do they suggest about the central idea of the text?
- Look for topic sentences that reveal the author's main points about the topic.
- Find the details the author uses to support the central idea.

Use the Interactive Whiteboard lesson on Identifying Main Idea and Details for additional instruction and support.

CLOSE READING APPLICATION

Student partners can work together to apply the skill to another article about a work of literature.

Analyze Text: Literary Criticism

RI 3,
RI 6

RETEACH

Remind students that **literary criticism** is writing that examines, analyzes, and interprets a piece of literature or a general aspect of literature. Review that the author of a piece of literary criticism may write for the following purposes:

- to define a genre
- to categorize works of literature
- to examine the structure of a work of literature
- to analyze an author's technique

Point out that book reviews are a type of literary criticism. Use children's book reviews from an online source, newspaper, or magazine to examine the author's purpose. Point out examples such as the following:

If the author . . .	The purpose may be . . .
discusses examples of certain type of book, such as picture books	to define a genre
explains the ways in which several books are similar	to categorize works of literature
discusses the way books are organized, such as chapter books	to examine the structure of a work of literature
focuses on an author's style and use of literary devices	to analyze the author's technique

Discuss the ways in which the purposes might overlap or connect to each other. For example, an analysis of an author's technique might connect to an effort to categorize literature. Point out that students themselves are often asked to write their own literary criticism after reading and enjoying a work of literature. Ask students which purpose or purposes they most often have when they write about a story or article.

CLOSE READING APPLICATION

Provide additional adolescent or adult book reviews, and have student partners work together to determine the specific purposes of the review.

Man-Made Monsters

Essay by Daniel Cohen

Why This Text

Students may finish reading the text of an essay without summarizing what they have read. Summarizing confirms comprehension of a text and helps students remember what they have read. Essays like this one by Daniel Cohen have more than one central idea, each with relationships to supporting ideas. With the help of the close-reading questions, students will identify the central ideas about Mary Shelley's Frankenstein monster. They will identify details that support the central ideas. This close reading will prepare students to summarize the central ideas.

Background Have students read the background and the information about the author. Introduce the selection by telling students that Mary Shelley, the author of *Frankenstein*, was the daughter of the anarchist William Godwin and the feminist Mary Wollstonecraft. Mary Shelley's own philosophy is revealed in Cohen's essay through the voice of Frankenstein's monster: "If any being felt emotions of benevolence toward me, . . . I would make peace . . . " She believed feminine ideals of cooperation and sympathy could transform society.

SETTING A PURPOSE Ask students to pay attention to details in Cohen's essay. How soon into the text can they identify one of Cohen's central ideas?

Common Core Support

- cite strong textual evidence

- determine a central idea and analyze its development

- provide an objective summary

- analyze how a text makes connections among ideas

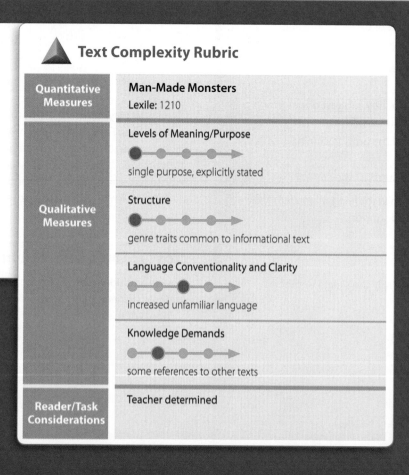

Text Complexity Rubric

	Man-Made Monsters
Quantitative Measures	Lexile: 1210

Qualitative Measures

Levels of Meaning/Purpose

single purpose, explicitly stated

Structure

genre traits common to informational text

Language Conventionality and Clarity

increased unfamiliar language

Knowledge Demands

some references to other texts

Reader/Task Considerations Teacher determined

Strategies for CLOSE READING

Summarize Text

Students should read this essay carefully all the way through. Close-reading questions at the bottom of the page will help them focus on a thorough analysis of the essay. As they read, students should jot down comments or questions about the text in the side margins.

WHEN STUDENTS STRUGGLE . . .

To help students analyze the development of one of Cohen's central ideas, have them work in a small group to fill out a chart, such as the one shown below, as they analyze the text.

CITE TEXT EVIDENCE For practice in summarizing an essay, ask students to identify details that support one of Cohen's central ideas.

detail: In Shelley's time science was becoming more important.

detail: Shelley's monster was very intelligent.

detail: The golem of Jewish legend had some aspects of humanity.

central idea: The monster is "a man of his time."

detail: Greek mythology had a man-made brass man called Talus.

detail: "Body snatchers" stole corpses and sold them to doctors who used them to explore the workings of the human body.

Background *Daniel Cohen has created over one hundred books for young readers on topics like sports, nature, history, and science fiction. In this essay, Cohen examines the Frankenstein monster. Mary Wollstonecraft Shelley, the monster's creator, began writing* Frankenstein: Or, The Modern Prometheus *in 1818 when she was only 18 years old. Frankenstein's monster has gone on to become an icon of popular culture. His image can be seen in movies, cartoons, and even cereal boxes.*

Man-Made Monsters

Essay by Daniel Cohen

CLOSE READ
Notes

1. **READ ▷** As you read lines 1–19, begin to collect and cite text evidence.

   • Underline adjectives used to describe the scientist and the sorcerer.
   • Circle what the scientist and the sorcerer are seeking to acquire.
   • In the margin, restate what you learn about Prometheus.

With the publication of Mary W. Shelley's novel, *Frankenstein: Or, The Modern Prometheus*, in 1818, the mad scientist replaced the evil sorcerer as the master of monsters. In many respects the mad scientist and the evil **sorcerer** were very similar. They were not necessarily either mad or evil, at least not at first. Often they were brilliant, selfless, and dedicated to the task of acquiring knowledge—for the sorcerer magical knowledge, for the scientist scientific knowledge—that might benefit the human race.

A

   But the knowledge they sought was forbidden to mankind. Often
10 for the best of motives, both sorcerer and scientist released great evil upon the world, and their knowledge ultimately destroyed them. That is why Mrs. Shelley chose the subtitle, *Or, the Modern Prometheus*, for her book. Prometheus was one of the Titans of Greek mythology. He was supposed to have given the human race the knowledge of fire, but this gift angered the gods and they punished him savagely.

B

*sorcerer:
magician,
wizard*

Prometheus was punished for trying to give humans the knowledge of fire.

35

---

1. **READ AND CITE TEXT EVIDENCE**

   A **ASK STUDENTS** to cite textual evidence that supports the restatement of what they learned about Prometheus. *Students should recognize that like mad scientists and sorcerers, Prometheus wanted to deliver something "that might benefit the human race," (line 8) and was punished for it (line 15).*

   Critical Vocabulary: sorcerer (line 4) Have students compare their definitions of *sorcerer*. Ask them to draw conclusions about why Cohen chose to use the word *sorcerer* rather than a synonym such as *magician* or *wizard*.

Mary Shelley's scientist, Baron Victor von Frankenstein, attempted something no medieval sorcerer, no matter how powerful, could even aspire to—he sought to create life. Thus, Dr. Frankenstein's creation is the first truly modern monster in fiction.

20   According to tradition, the idea of the Frankenstein monster was first put into words in Switzerland on a stormy evening in 1816. A group of friends decided to pass the evening by telling stories based on supernatural events. Among those attending this storytelling session were two English poets, Lord Byron and Percy Bysshe Shelley. Also in attendance were Shelley's wife, Mary, and Byron's personal physician and friend, Dr. John Polidori. Dr. Polidori was reported to have told the tale of Lord Ruthven, who was to become the first famous vampire in English fiction. But surely the high point of the evening must have been Mary Shelley's story of Dr. Frankenstein and

30 his creation.

    There had never been anything quite like the Frankenstein monster in legend or fiction, but there were a few creatures the monster might have counted among its ancestors. One was Talus, a sort of ancient robot of Greek mythology. Talus was said to have been made of brass by Hephaestus, a god of fire and craftsmen. The job of the brass man was to protect the island of Crete. He drove off strangers by throwing rocks at them, or by heating himself red-hot and clasping the intruders in a lethal bear hug. Talus was animated by a single vein of blood running from his head to his foot, where it was

40 closed with a nail. The powerful sorceress Medea put Talus to sleep and then cut the vein, allowing the vital fluid to pour out—thus killing the brass man.

The Talus was supposed to protect the island of Crete.

2. ◀ **REREAD** Reread lines 9–19. In what way is Dr. Frankenstein similar to Prometheus?

Both Dr. Frankenstein and Prometheus suffered because of the knowledge they had.

3. **READ** ▶ As you read lines 20–49, continue to cite textual evidence.

- Circle the names of the mythical creatures mentioned in lines 31–49.
- Underline a description of each creature.
- In the margin, describe the duty each mythical creature was supposed to perform.

36

Somewhat closer to the Frankenstein monster was the golem, a creature of medieval Jewish legend. It was a clay figure said to be given life by some sort of magical charm. According to the legends, golems had been created by several famous medieval European rabbis. The golem was supposed to be a servant and protector of the Jews but it was untrustworthy. Rabbi Low, of sixteenth-century Prague,[1] had to destroy the golem he created when it went berserk.

50   Frankenstein's castle was located in the hills above the picturesque Bavarian city of Ingolstadt. Some have **speculated** that the inspiration for the Frankenstein story may have come from a German legend. There is a ruined castle outside of Frankfurt am Main, Germany, that contains the tomb of a medieval knight. This knight was supposed to have been killed by a ferocious man-eating, man-made monster that resembled a wild boar. But the legend itself is not at all clear and there is no way of knowing if this story or anything like it was ever encountered by Mary Shelley, although she was known to have traveled extensively in Europe.

60   More likely Mrs. Shelley drew her inspiration for the story of Frankenstein from events of her own time. Science was becoming ever more important and it increasingly clashed with established beliefs and values. Frankenstein put life back into a creature that had been assembled from the limbs and organs of cadavers.[2]

The golem was supposed to serve and protect the Jews.

speculate: *guess*

---

[1] **Prague:** the capital and largest city of the Czech Republic.
[2] **cadaver:** a dead human body.

4. ◀ **REREAD** Reread lines 31–49. What is the writer's purpose for including the information on the Talus and the golem?

The writer wants to provide background information on two creatures who may have inspired the creation of the Frankenstein monster.

5. **READ** ▶ As you read lines 50–84, continue to cite textual evidence.

- Circle what the author believes inspired Mary Shelley to write her story.
- Underline reasons why body snatching was a flourishing trade in the eighteenth and nineteenth centuries.

37

---

2. **REREAD AND CITE TEXT EVIDENCE**

B **ASK STUDENTS** to read their response aloud to a partner. Then, have them cite strong textual evidence that supports their response. After discussing their response, ask students to rewrite it. *Students should make a connection between Prometheus's "knowledge of fire" (line 14) and Dr. Frankenstein's knowledge of the creation of life (line 18). Prometheus suffered for his knowledge, and we can anticipate that Dr. Frankenstein will as well.*

3. **READ AND CITE TEXT EVIDENCE**

C **ASK STUDENTS** to cite textual evidence to support their description of the duties Talus and the golem were supposed to perform. *Students should find evidence that the Talus was supposed to protect the island of Crete, in lines 35–36, and that the golem was supposed to serve and protect the Jews, in line 47.*

FOR ELL STUDENTS Explain that a *bear hug* is an embrace so tight and strong that it might hurt the person receiving it.

4. **REREAD AND CITE TEXT EVIDENCE**

D **ASK STUDENTS** to cite text evidence to support their analysis of the writer's purpose for including the Talus and the golem. *Students should cite lines 32–33: "creatures the monster might have counted among its ancestors."*

5. **READ AND CITE TEXT EVIDENCE**

E **ASK STUDENTS** to explain to a partner why body snatching was a flourishing trade. Have them cite text evidence with line numbers. *Students should explain the new importance of science (lines 61–62), science's clash with existing beliefs and values (lines 62–63, 75–76), the shortage of bodies for scientific study (line 66), and that doctors ignored the laws (lines 83–84).*

Critical Vocabulary: speculate (line 51) Have students explain Cohen's use of *speculate*.

During the eighteenth and much of the nineteenth centuries human bodies were not readily available for scientific study. Dissection of a corpse was considered both irreligious and illegal. The result was that doctors who wished to study the human anatomy had to employ the services of body snatchers who would exhume[3] newly
70 buried corpses or cut down the hanging corpses of executed criminals and deliver them in secret to the laboratories. (While doctors couldn't dissect a body legally, it was considered perfectly proper to leave the corpse of a hanged man swinging until it rotted, as an example to other potential wrongdoers.)

Interest in medical science had grown enormously while the laws concerning dissection had not kept pace, so the body snatchers (the Resurrectionists or Sack-em-up Men as they were called in England) had a flourishing trade. If an adequate supply of corpses was unavailable, some of the more enterprising body snatchers would
80 murder some unfortunates in order to sell their bodies. The most **notorious** of these murderers were Burke and Hare, who operated in Edinburgh, Scotland, at about the time that *Frankenstein* was written. The practice was fairly common throughout Europe, and many respectable doctors simply closed their eyes to what was happening.

notorious:
infamous;
known widely

[3] **exhume:** to dig out from the ground.

6. **◀ REREAD** Reread lines 60–84. How did the act of body snatching influence the writing of *Frankenstein*? Support your answer with explicit textual evidence.

Frankenstein's monster was assembled from the limbs and organs of dead human bodies. During the 18th and 19th centuries, secretly obtaining dead human bodies for dissection and study by doctors was a flourishing trade and rather common.

7. **READ ▶** As you read lines 85–102, continue to cite textual evidence.
   • Circle phrases used to describe Frankenstein's monster in Mary Shelley's book.
   • Underline phrases used to describe Frankenstein's monster in the 1931 film *Frankenstein*.
   • In the margin, write one similarity between the monster in Shelley's book and the monster in the film *Frankenstein*.

38

> **"He had not intended to create a monster, rather he had hoped to create a perfect human being."**

Dr. Frankenstein himself was forced to steal bodies for his experiments, and this was the first step in his crime. He had not intended to create a monster, rather he had hoped to create a perfect human being. But from the moment the creature opened its "dull yellow eye," the young scientist was overcome with disgust and
90 horror. He realized that he had made an abomination, not a superman.

The monster in Mary Shelley's book is described as being exceptionally tall, yellow-eyed, and having skin like parchment. But few picture the Frankenstein monster as looking like that. Our image was fixed in 1931 with the appearance of the movie *Frankenstein*, starring a then unknown actor named Boris Karloff as the monster. Karloff's monster was a masterpiece of horrific makeup. It had a flat head and the overhanging brows of a Neanderthal man. Its face was crisscrossed with crude stitching, and two electrodes[4] stuck out of its
100 neck. Like Mary Shelley's monster, the movie monster was unnaturally tall, but it also wore enormous leaden shoes and walked in a stiff, almost mechanical way.

The monster was unnaturally tall in both the movie and the book.

[4] **electrode:** a conductor used to establish electrical contact with a non-metallic surface.

8. **◀ REREAD AND DISCUSS** Reread lines 91–102. In a small group, discuss the differences between the monster's appearance in the book *Frankenstein* and its appearance in the movie *Frankenstein*.

9. **READ ▶** As you read lines 103–120, continue to cite evidence.
   • Underline phrases that describe the temperament of the monster in Mary Shelley's book.
   • Circle phrases that describe the temperament of Frankenstein's monster in movies.
   • In the margin, explain what would need to happen for the monster in Mary Shelley's book to stop being miserable.

39

---

6. **REREAD AND CITE TEXT EVIDENCE**

(F) ASK STUDENTS to cite textual evidence that supports their answer. *Students should connect the "flourishing" trade in corpses (lines 76–78) with the monster that was "assembled from the limbs and organs of cadavers" (line 64).*

7. **READ AND CITE TEXT EVIDENCE**

(G) ASK STUDENTS to cite text evidence that compares and contrasts Shelley's monster with the monster in the 1931 film *Frankenstein*. *Students should note differences in the monsters' appearances (line 93, lines 97–100, and lines 101–102) and the similarity that both monsters were unnaturally tall (lines 93 and 101).*

Critical Vocabulary: notorious (line 81) Have students compare their definitions. Ask students why Cohen describes Burke and Hare as *notorious*.

FOR ELL STUDENTS Point out that the phrase *to keep pace* is an expression that means "to keep up with."

8. **REREAD AND DISCUSS USING TEXT EVIDENCE**

(H) ASK STUDENTS to be prepared to cite text evidence in a class discussion. *Students should notice that there are more differences in the monster's appearance than similarities and cite evidence from line 93 and lines 97–102.*

9. **READ AND CITE TEXT EVIDENCE** Students have already cited evidence of differences in the appearance of the book and movie versions of Frankenstein's monster.

(I) ASK STUDENTS to continue to cite evidence comparing and contrasting the book and movie versions of the monster. *Students should cite similarities such as both monsters being described as "evil" (lines 103 and 119), and differences such as the monster of Shelley's book being "intelligent and highly articulate" (line 107), whereas the movie monster was only able to "mumble and grunt" (lines 115–118).*

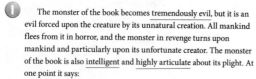

CLOSE READ
Notes

I   The monster of the book becomes tremendously evil, but it is an evil forced upon the creature by its unnatural creation. All mankind flees from it in horror, and the monster in revenge turns upon mankind and particularly upon its unfortunate creator. The monster of the book is also intelligent and highly articulate about its plight. At one point it says:

malicious:

intentionally harmful

110   "I am **malicious** because I am miserable.... If any being felt emotions of benevolence toward me, I should return them an hundred and an hundred fold. For that one creature's sake, I would make peace with the whole kind!"

The monster would stop being miserable if one person was charitable to him.

J   The first of the long series of Frankenstein films simplified Mrs. Shelley's plot but retained much of the sympathy toward the monster. However, the creature's intelligence is largely lost in the films. Instead of making long, soul-searching speeches, the monster can only mumble and grunt. In later films the monster loses even this rudimentary speaking ability. It is reduced to a stiff, stumbling, and thoroughly evil automaton, more of a mechanical man than anything 120   else.

10. ◀ **REREAD AND DISCUSS** Reread lines 113–120. With a small group, discuss why filmmakers do not emphasize the monster's intelligence. What effect might this have on viewers' perception of the monster?

SHORT RESPONSE

Cite Text Evidence Summarize what you learn about Mary Shelley's creation of Frankenstein's monster and the way the monster has been perceived since its creation. Review your reading notes, and **cite text evidence** of Mary Shelley's inspiration in the selection.

The monster is "a man of his time." The idea of a man-made monster wasn't new. The ancient robot of Greek mythology, Talus, and the golem of medieval Jewish legend both had some aspects of humanity. In Shelley's time, science was becoming more important. Corpses were being used to explore the workings of the human body, but some "body snatchers" were creating their own corpses. The monster in Shelley's book was very intelligent. The movies have made the monster almost unable to speak.

40

---

10. **REREAD AND DISCUSS USING TEXT EVIDENCE**

J **ASK STUDENTS** to be prepared to present textual evidence to support their group's conclusions in a class discussion. *Students will make inferences about how viewers might perceive a more intelligent monster and why filmmakers do not choose to emphasize the monster's intelligence.*

Critical Vocabulary: malicious (line 109) Have students share their definitions. Ask students why Shelley might have had her monster describe himself as malicious.

SHORT RESPONSE

Cite Text Evidence Students should:

- identify a central idea.
- identify related supporting ideas.
- cite text evidence that supports their summary.

TO CHALLENGE STUDENTS . . .

For an additional expert opinion about body snatchers in Victorian London, students can view the video *Body Snatching in London* in their eBooks.

ASK STUDENTS to cite evidence from the video that supports Cohen's points about body snatching, as well as evidence that adds to their understanding of body snatching. *Answers will vary. Students should cite each minute and second of their video evidence. For example, at 00:15, the narrator explains that graves were as shallow as six inches, making it easy for grave robbers to get corpses.*

DIG DEEPER

With the class, return to questions 8, 9, and 10, the comparison of the book and movie versions of Frankenstein's monster. Have students share the results of their discussions, and share the further evidence of similarities and differences identified independently.

ASK STUDENTS whether they were satisfied with the outcome of their small-group discussions. Have students share their findings about similarities and differences in the book and movie versions of the monster. What textual evidence did students find to support their conclusions?

- Encourage students to supply line numbers as they cite evidence. Ask them whether they found more evidence of the book and movie monsters being different or the same. In what ways are the monsters different? In what ways are they the same? *Students should cite evidence about the monster's appearance (lines 93, 97–102) and the monster's temperament (lines 103, 107, 109, 118, and 119).*

- Remind students of Cohen's statement, "Dr. Frankenstein's creation is the first truly modern monster in fiction" (lines 18–19). Tell students that the book was published in 1818, and remind them that the movie was made in 1931. In what ways could the movie version be considered a modernization? *Students might consider the "two electrodes" that "stuck out of its neck" a modernization (lines 99–100).* In what ways was Dr. Frankenstein's monster more modern than the Talus or the golem?

- Ask students to share the outcome of their discussion about movie viewers' perceptions of the monster. Why did filmmakers choose not to emphasize the monster's intelligence? *Answers will vary. Students should cite text evidence to support their responses.*

ASK STUDENTS to return to their Short Response answer and revise it based on the class discussion.

CLOSE READING NOTES

COLLECTION **2**
PERFORMANCE TASK A

Interactive Lessons

If you need help . . .
- **Writing Arguments**
- **Using Textual Evidence**
- **Analyzing and Evaluating Presentations**

Persuasive Speech

The horror genre is intended to inspire terror in its audience. While many people enjoy the sense of excitement the genre provides, some experience unwanted effects, such as the inability to sleep or overreactions to real-life situations that are similar to a scary film or story. In the following activity, you will give a speech arguing whether a classic of the horror genre, "The Tell-Tale Heart," is appropriate for your age group to read. You may use other selections in the collection to provide information or support for your argument.

A successful persuasive speech

- contains an engaging introduction that clearly establishes the claim being made
- supports the claim with reasons and relevant evidence from a variety of credible sources
- emphasizes key points in a focused, coherent manner
- uses language that effectively conveys ideas and adds interest
- concludes by leaving the audience with a lasting impression

COMMON CORE

W 1 a–e Write arguments.
W 4 Produce clear and coherent writing.
W 5 Develop and strengthen writing.
W 8 Gather relevant information.
W 10 Write routinely over extended time frames and shorter time frames.
SL 4 Present claims and findings.
SL 5 Include multimedia components and visual displays.
SL 6 Adapt speech to a variety of contexts and tasks.

PLAN

Choose Your Position Reread "The Tell-Tale Heart," and think about its effects on you as a reader. What emotions and images does it evoke? What kind of lasting impression does it create? Decide whether the story is appropriate reading for students your age. Choose a position and write out your claim in a statement.

Gather Information Focus on "The Tell-Tale Heart." Jot down details that provide reasons and evidence that support your claim.

- Identify quotations from the story that you can use as examples to support your claim.
- What might others say to oppose your claim? Look for story details that will help you convince people to agree with you.
- Search for conventions of the horror genre within the story that will help your audience understand your position.

myNotebook

Use the annotation tools in your eBook to find text evidence that supports your claim.

ACADEMIC VOCABULARY

As you share what you learned about creating suspense, be sure to use the academic vocabulary words.

conventions
predict
psychology
summary
technique

Collection Performance Task A   **133**

PERFORMANCE TASK A

PERSUASIVE SPEECH

COMMON CORE W 1a-e, W 4, W 5, W 8, SL 4, SL 5, SL 6

Introduce students to the Performance Task by reading the introductory paragraph with students and reviewing the criteria for what makes a good persuasive speech. Remind students that a good persuasive speech needs to be written well, but that the delivery of the speech is also important.

PLAN

GATHER INFORMATION

View It!

Professional Development Podcast:
Performance Tasks

Remind students to think about their audience as they identify reasons and gather evidence for their speeches. For example, if students were presenting their speeches to parents, they might present different reasons and evidence than if they were speaking to their classmates.

Collection Performance Task A   **133**

Do Further Research Use additional print and digital sources to find solid, credible evidence for your argument.

- Search for facts, quotations, and statistics about the story, the author, and the genre that support your claim.
- Anticipate arguments against your claim and develop counterclaims to refute them and persuade your audience more thoroughly.
- Identify any visuals, such as pictures or charts, that illustrate your ideas.

Organize Your Ideas Think about how you will organize your speech. A graphic organizer, such as a hierarchy chart, can help you present your ideas logically.

Consider Your Purpose and Audience Who will listen to your speech? Decide which specific ideas will be most convincing to your audience. Think about the psychology of that audience as you prepare to write. Your tone and word choices should be appealing and targeted toward your listeners.

> **PRODUCE**

PRODUCE

DRAFT YOUR SPEECH

Remind students to use their hierarchy charts to help them organize their speeches. Point out that students' claims should be supported by reasons, and that each reason should have logical evidence to support it.

Draft Your Speech As you draft your speech, keep the following in mind:

- Introduce your claim in an attention-grabbing way.
- Use your notes and graphic organizer to organize your reasons and evidence logically.
- Include quotes and other data from your sources. Remember to paraphrase this data, or put it into your own words.
- Use transitional words and phrases to clarify relationships among your claim, reasons, and evidence. Doing so will make your argument stronger and more cohesive.

my WriteSmart

Write your rough draft in myWriteSmart. Focus on getting your ideas down, rather than on perfecting your choice of language.

- Vary the length and type of sentences in your speech to create a lively flow of ideas.

- Bring your speech to a conclusion. Summarize your main points in a concluding statement and tell your audience what you want them to believe or be inspired to do.

Prepare Visuals Think about using multimedia resources to create pictures or charts that clarify and strengthen your claims. Plan how you will integrate these visuals into your speech.

REVISE ....

my **WriteSmart**

Have your partner or a group of peers review your draft in *my*WriteSmart. Ask your reviewers to note whether your claim, reasons, and evidence are clear and easy to understand.

Practice Your Speech Present your speech aloud. Try speaking in front of a mirror or making a recording of your speech and listening to it. Then practice your speech with a partner.

- Use your voice effectively, varying your pitch and tone.
- Maintain eye contact with the members of your audience.
- Use gestures and facial expressions that allow your audience to see how you feel.

Evaluate Your Speech Use the chart on the next page to evaluate the substance and style of your speech.

- Check that your claim is clear and logically supported with reasons and evidence.
- Examine your evidence to make sure it is relevant and based on accurate, credible sources.
- Determine whether your speech will keep your audience's attention.
- Ensure that your conclusion is strong and memorable.

PRESENT ....

Deliver your Speech Finalize your persuasive speech and present it to the class. Consider these additional options:

- Present your ideas in a debate with someone who makes an opposing argument.
- Publish your speech as a podcast and share it with classmates.

REVISE

PRACTICE YOUR SPEECH

Have students practice delivering their speeches. If students make recordings of themselves, have them use the recording to analyze the content and delivery of the speech. Point out that a poorly delivered speech will not be effective, even if the reasoning in it is sound. Remind students to speak clearly and at a rate that is easy for others to understand.

PRESENT

DELIVER YOUR SPEECH

If desired, pairs of students can present opposing views in a debate. After students listen to each other's speeches, allow time for them to question each other regarding their points of view. Remind students to be respectful when questioning the points of view of others.

PERFORMANCE TASK A

IDEAS AND EVIDENCE

Have students use the chart to evaluate how they did on the Performance Task in each of the three main categories. Suggest that students focus on the effectiveness of the reasons and evidence they presented. Then, have students discuss different ways in which they could have improved the delivery of their speeches.

COLLECTION 2 TASK A
PERSUASIVE SPEECH

	Ideas and Evidence	Organization	Language
ADVANCED	• The introduction immediately grabs the audience's attention; the claim clearly states the speaker's position on an issue. • Logical reasons and relevant evidence convincingly support the speaker's claim. • Opposing claims are anticipated and effectively addressed. • The concluding section effectively summarizes the claim.	• The reasons and evidence are organized logically and consistently throughout the speech. • Transitions logically connect reasons and evidence to the speaker's claim.	• The speech is written and delivered in a consistent formal style. • Sentence beginnings, lengths, and structures vary and have a rhythmic flow. • Grammar, usage, and mechanics are correct.
COMPETENT	• The introduction could do more to grab the audience's attention; the speaker's claim states a position on an issue. • Most reasons and evidence support the speaker's claim, but they could be more convincing. • Opposing claims are anticipated but need to be addressed more thoroughly. • The concluding section restates the claim.	• The organization of key points and supporting details is confusing in a few places. • A few more transitions are needed to clarify the relationships between ideas.	• The style is inconsistent in a few places. • Sentence beginnings, lengths, and structures vary somewhat. • Some grammatical and usage errors are repeated in the speech.
LIMITED	• The introduction is ordinary; the speaker's claim identifies an issue, but the position is not clearly stated. • The reasons and evidence are not always logical or relevant. • Opposing claims are anticipated but not addressed logically. • The concluding section includes an incomplete summary of the claim.	• The organization of reasons and evidence is logical in some places, but it often doesn't follow a pattern. • Many more transitions are needed to connect reasons and evidence to the speaker's claim.	• The style is inconsistent in many places. • Sentence structures barely vary, and some fragments or run-on sentences are present. • Grammar and usage are incorrect in many places, but the speaker's ideas are still clear.
EMERGING	• The introduction is confusing. • Supporting reasons and evidence are missing. • Opposing claims are neither anticipated nor addressed. • The concluding section is missing.	• A logical organization is not used; reasons and evidence are presented randomly. • Transitions are not used, making the speech difficult to understand.	• The style is completely inconsistent or inappropriate for the speech. • Repetitive sentence structure, fragments, and run-on sentences make the speech hard to follow. • Many grammatical and usage errors obscure the meanings of ideas.

COLLECTION 2
PERFORMANCE TASK B

Interactive Lessons
If you need help . . .
• Writing as a Process
• Using Textual Evidence

Write a Literary Analysis

This collection has given you both experience with and background about the horror genre. In this activity, you will write a literary analysis of one or both of the fictional horror stories in this collection. Use the criteria for horror explained in "What Is the Horror Genre?" by Sharon A. Russell to support your analysis. Think about the structure of horror fiction and the tools its authors use, such as suspense and plot. As you analyze your chosen story or stories, pay attention to setting, events, and details that make the work both believable and entertaining.

A successful literary analysis

- provides an introduction that captures the reader's attention and clearly states the topic
- cites textual evidence that strongly supports the writer's ideas
- clearly organizes ideas and concepts
- conveys key points through the selection, organization, and analysis of relevant content
- provides a strong conclusion that summarizes the analysis

COMMON CORE

RI 1 Cite textual evidence.
W 2a–f Write informative/ explanatory texts.
W 5 Develop and strengthen writing.
W 9a Apply grade 8 Reading standards to literature.
W 10 Write routinely over extended time frames and shorter time frames.

PLAN

Choose a Story for Analysis
Refresh your memory of "What Is the Horror Genre?" as well as "The Tell-Tale Heart" and "The Monkey's Paw."

- Take notes about the criteria for horror that are explained in "What Is the Horror Genre?"
- Reread "The Tell-Tale Heart" and "The Monkey's Paw" as if you were reading them for the first time. Identify aspects of the stories that impress—and horrify—you.
- Decide whether you will analyze one or both stories.

*my*Notebook

Use the annotation tools in your eBook to note the criteria in Sharon A. Russell's piece and to apply it to the story or stories you will analyze.

ACADEMIC VOCABULARY

As you share what you have learned about the horror genre, be sure to use the academic vocabulary words.

conventions
predict
psychology
summary
technique

WRITE A LITERARY ANALYSIS

COMMON CORE
RI 1, W 2a-f, W 5, W 9a, W10

Introduce students to the Performance Task by reading the introductory paragraph with them and reviewing the criteria for what makes a good literary analysis. Remind students that a literary analysis will use story details to support the main points a writer wants to make.

PLAN

CHOOSE A STORY FOR ANALYSIS

Point out to students that when taking notes for their analysis it will be helpful to create a separate file or sheet of paper for each of their criteria. By listing appropriate story details for each criterion, students will be better able to organize their points when getting ready to write.

Consider Audience and Purpose Think about your readers and what they need to know to understand your literary analysis.

- Classmates who have read this collection, and other fans of the horror genre, will already understand a lot about the techniques or conventions related to horror storytelling, such as suspense. Other readers may need support to understand "the language of horror."

- Decide what you want your audience to know about the horror genre in general, and about the specific story or stories you are analyzing.

Identify Your Criteria Use your notes about "What Is the Horror Genre?" to plan your analysis.

- Decide what your central idea will be. This idea is the main point you want to make in your analysis, so the criteria and textual evidence you discuss should relate to it.

- Create a graphic organizer for each of the criteria you identify.

- List story details that are relevant for each of your criteria.

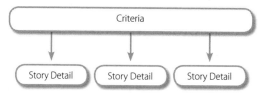

PRODUCE

WRITE YOUR LITERARY ANALYSIS

Point out to students that they should introduce each of the stories that they discuss in their analyses. Remind students to name the story and its author and to briefly describe what the story is about. Then, they can tell about the key points they want to make.

PRODUCE

Write Your Literary Analysis Use your notes and your graphic organizers to draft your literary analysis.

- Decide on a logical way to organize your ideas. You may wish to discuss each of your chosen criteria with examples from the story or stories. Another option would be to organize around the sequence of events in the story.

- Include a brief summary of the story or stories you will discuss.

- Be sure to include concrete details, quotations, or other examples from the story or stories to support your ideas. Use precise language to explain key concepts.

*my*WriteSmart

Write your rough draft in *my*WriteSmart. Concentrate on getting your ideas down rather than on crafting perfect sentences.

- Use transitions to show relationships between your ideas and the textual evidence that supports them.
- Consider adding headings or other formatting to help readers understand how you have organized your ideas.
- Conclude your analysis with a summary of your main points and your own insights about the appeal of the horror genre.

REVISE

Review Your Draft Use the chart on the next page to evaluate your draft. Work with a partner to determine whether you have achieved your purpose. Consider the following:

my **WriteSmart**

Have your partner or a group of peers review your draft in *my*WriteSmart and note any points that need clarification or better support from the texts.

- Examine your central idea to determine whether it is clearly stated.
- Check each of your main points and consider whether you have included enough supporting evidence from the text.
- Be sure your main points and evidence are organized in a logical manner.
- Evaluate whether your conclusion restates your main points and offers your insight about the horror genre.

PRESENT

Create a Finished Copy Finalize your literary analysis. Then choose a way to share it with your audience. Consider these options:

- Combine your analysis with those of your classmates to create a "Literary Review: Horror Edition" for your school's library.
- Present your literary analysis as a television advertisement for the horror genre.
- Organize a panel discussion in which you and other classmates share your insights into the horror genre.

REVISE

REVIEW YOUR DRAFT

Remind students that the purpose of a literary analysis is to inform others about a work of literature. Before they revise their lessons, students should ask themselves questions such as:

- Does my introduction clearly state the topic?
- Have I provided story details to support my main points?
- Does my conclusion summarize my ideas?

PRESENT

CREATE A FINISHED COPY

If desired, students can present their analyses in a panel discussion. Encourage students to compare and contrast the main points they present about each story. Students may also want to compare each of the stories to see which one is a better example of a horror story.

PERFORMANCE TASK B

LANGUAGE

Have students use the chart to evaluate how they did on the Performance Task in each of the three main categories. Prompt students to check their use of precise language to reflect the originality of their ideas. They may also want to exchange their literary analysis with a partner to get another perspective on how well they met the criteria and where they might be able to make improvements.

COLLECTION 2 TASK B
LITERARY ANALYSIS

	Ideas and Evidence	Organization	Language
ADVANCED	• The central idea presents a specific idea about the work(s). • Concrete, relevant details support the key points. • The concluding section summarizes the analysis and offers an insight.	• Key points and supporting details are organized effectively and logically throughout the literary analysis. • Transitions successfully show the relationships between ideas.	• Language is precise and captures the writer's thoughts with originality. • Grammar, usage, and mechanics are correct.
COMPETENT	• The central idea sets up criteria for the analysis. • Some key points need more support. • The concluding section summarizes most of the analysis but doesn't offer an insight.	• The organization of key points and supporting details is mostly clear. • A few more transitions are needed to clarify the relationships between ideas.	• Most language is precise. • Some errors in grammar, usage, and mechanics occur.
LIMITED	• The central idea only hints at a main point. • Details support some key points but often are too general. • The concluding section gives an incomplete summary without insight.	• Most key points are organized logically, but many supporting details are out of place. • More transitions are needed throughout the literary analysis to connect ideas.	• Language is repetitive or too general at times. • Many errors in grammar, usage, and mechanics occur, but the writer's ideas are still clear.
EMERGING	• The central idea is missing. • Details and evidence are irrelevant or missing. • The literary analysis lacks a concluding section.	• A logical organization is not apparent. • Transitions are not used.	• Language is inaccurate, repetitive, and too general. • Errors in grammar, usage, and mechanics obscure the meaning of the writer's ideas.

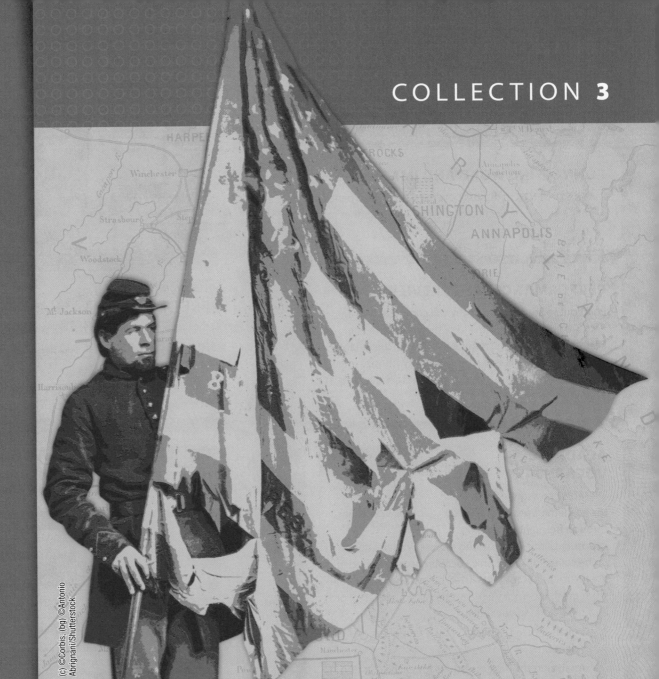

(c) ©Corbis; (bg) ©Antonio Abrignani/Shutterstock

The Move Toward Freedom

" I should fight for liberty as long as my strength lasted. **"**

—Harriet Tubman

CONNECTING WORD AND IMAGE

ASK STUDENTS to discuss how the Collection Opener image and the collection quotation work together to create a connection.

PERFORMANCE TASK PREVIEW

Point out to students that they will complete two Performance Tasks at the end of the collection. The Performance Tasks will require them to further analyze the selections in the collection and to synthesize ideas about these analyses. They will present their findings in a variety of products.

ACADEMIC VOCABULARY

View It!

Professional Development Podcast:

Academic Vocabulary

Students can acquire facility with the academic vocabulary words through frequent, repeated exposure as they analyze and discuss the selections in the collection. academic vocabulary can be used in the instructional contexts listed below. This will enable students to incorporate the academic vocabulary words into their working vocabulary.

- Collaborative Discussion at the end of each selection
- Analyzing the Text questions for each selection
- Selection-level Performance Tasks
- Vocabulary instruction (for Critical Vocabulary and/or for Vocabulary Strategy)
- Language Conventions
- End-of-collection Performance Task for all selections in the collection

ASK STUDENTS to review the academic vocabulary word list for this collection. You may wish to pronounce each word aloud, so students hear the correct pronunciation. Then, discuss the definitions and the related forms for each word. Remind students that they will encounter these five academic vocabulary words throughout the collection.

COLLECTION 3

The Move Toward Freedom

In this collection, you will focus on the quest for freedom that led to the American Civil War.

hmhfyi.com

COLLECTION

PERFORMANCE TASK Preview

At the end of this collection, you will complete two performance tasks:

- In the first, you will create a visual presentation to highlight the work of those who fought to end slavery.

- In the second, you will write a literary analysis in which you consider the symbolism in a story in light of its historical context.

ACADEMIC VOCABULARY

Study the words and their definitions in the chart below. You will use these words as you discuss and write about the texts in this collection.

Word	Definition	Related Forms
access (ăk´sĕs) *n.*	a way of approaching or making use of	accessible, accessed
civil (sĭv´əl) *adj.*	of, or related to, citizens and their relations with each other and the state	civilization, civilian, civil rights
demonstrate (dĕm´ən-stāt´) *v.*	to show clearly and deliberately	demonstration, demonstrable
document (dŏk´yə-mənt) *n.*	written or printed paper that provides evidence or information	documentary, documentation
symbolize (sĭm´bə-līz´) *v.*	to serve as a symbol of, or represent something else	symbol, symbolic, symbolism

142

USING COLLECTIONS YOUR WAY

Use the following information, along with the charts on the following pages, to help you decide how you want to introduce the collection. Based on your teaching style, your students' interests, or your instructional goals, you may want to structure this collection in various ways. You may choose different entry points each time you teach the collection.

"I like to connect literature to history."

Rife with symbolism, this historical fiction transports readers to the eve of a Civil War battle.

Background *Though Ray Bradbury (1920–2012) is best known as a science fiction writer, he's also written plays, mysteries, fantasies, realistic stories, and novels. In this story, Bradbury tells about a drummer boy on the night before the Battle of Shiloh in the Civil War. This two-day battle began on April 6, 1862, near the southwestern Tennessee church from which the bloody clash takes its name. More than 23,000 soldiers died during those two days. At that time, it was the bloodiest battle in American history.*

The Drummer Boy of Shiloh

Historical Fiction by Ray Bradbury

SETTING A PURPOSE As you read, pay attention to the details the author provides about the scene of the battle and about the men who were preparing to fight. What do the details suggest about the realities of war?

In the April night, more than once, blossoms fell from the orchard trees and lit with rustling taps on the drumskin. At midnight a peach stone left miraculously on a branch through winter, flicked by a bird, fell swift and unseen, struck once, like panic, which jerked the boy upright. In silence he listened to his own heart ruffle away, away, at last gone from his ears and back in his chest again.

After that, he turned the drum on its side, where its great lunar[1] face peered at him whenever he opened his eyes.

His face, alert or at rest, was **solemn**. It was indeed a solemn time and a solemn night for a boy just turned fourteen in the peach field near the Owl Creek not far from the church at Shiloh.

solemn
(sŏl´əm) *adj.* If an event is solemn, it is deeply serious.

[1] **lunar** (lōō´nər): of or relating to the moon.

The Drummer Boy of Shiloh **167**

"I stress the importance of language and style."

Douglass's vivid language and insight personified the call for the abolition of slavery.

Frederick Douglass *(1818–1895) was born into enslavement in Maryland at a time when slavery was still legal in many states in the Union. As Douglass grew up, he tried to escape several times. Finally, in 1838, he succeeded. Douglass went on to become a famous speaker and writer, fighting to abolish, or end, slavery. His autobiography,* Narrative of the Life of Frederick Douglass, an American Slave, *became a best seller in the United States and Europe.*

from Narrative of the Life of Frederick Douglass, an American Slave

Autobiography by Frederick Douglass

SETTING A PURPOSE As you read, consider why Frederick Douglass chose these particular events to write about. Think about what his focus on these events reveals about his character and his struggle for freedom.

I lived in Master Hugh's family about seven years. During this time, I succeeded in learning to read and write. In accomplishing this, I was compelled to resort to various stratagems. I had no regular teacher. My mistress, who had kindly commenced to instruct me, had, in compliance with the advice and direction of her husband, not only ceased to instruct, but had set her face against my being instructed by any one else. It is due, however, to my mistress to say of her, that she did not adopt this course of treatment immediately. She at first lacked the depravity[1] indispensable to shutting me up in mental darkness. It was at least necessary for her to have

[1] **depravity** (dǐ-prăv´ǐ-tē): moral corruption.

Narrative of the Life of Frederick Douglass, an American Slave **143**

"I emphasize informational texts."

This text focuses on the actions of two leaders during the final days of the Civil War.

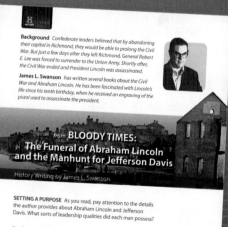

Background *Confederate leaders believed that by abandoning their capitol in Richmond, they would be able to prolong the Civil War. But just a few days after they left Richmond, General Robert E. Lee was forced to surrender to the Union Army. Shortly after, the Civil War ended and President Lincoln was assassinated.*

James L. Swanson *has written several books about the Civil War and Abraham Lincoln. He has been fascinated with Lincoln's life since his tenth birthday, when he received an engraving of the pistol used to assassinate the president.*

from BLOODY TIMES: The Funeral of Abraham Lincoln and the Manhunt for Jefferson Davis

History Writing by James L. Swanson

SETTING A PURPOSE As you read, pay attention to the details the author provides about Abraham Lincoln and Jefferson Davis. What sorts of leadership qualities did each man possess?

Prologue

In the spring of 1865, the country was divided in two: the Union in the North, led by Abraham Lincoln, fighting to keep the Southern states from **seceding** from the United States. The South, led by its president, Jefferson Davis, believed it had the absolute right to quit the Union in order to preserve its way of life, including the right to own slaves. The bloody Civil War had lasted four years and cost 620,000 lives. In April 1865, the war was about to end.

secede
(sǐ-sēd´) *v.* When you secede, you formally withdraw from an organization or association.

Introduction

In April of 1865, as the Civil War drew to a close, two men set out on very different journeys. One, Jefferson Davis, president

Bloody Times **177**

Collection 3 Lessons	**Media**	**Teach and Practice**	
**Student Edition	eBook**	▶ Video Links H HISTORY A&E	**Close Reading and Evidence Tracking**	
ANCHOR TEXT **Autobiography by Frederick Douglass** from *Narrative of the Life of Frederick Douglass, an American Slave*	▶ **Video HISTORY** *America: The Story of Us: Frederick Douglass* ◀ **Audio** from *Narrative of the Life of Frederick Douglass, an American Slave*	**Close Read Screencasts** • Modeled Discussion 1 (lines 8–13) • Modeled Discussion 2 (lines 93–102) • Close Read Application (lines 115–123)	**Strategies for Annotation** • Analyze Text: Autobiography • Use Context Clues
CLOSE READER **Historical Writing by Russell Freedman** "My Friend Douglass"	◀ **Audio** "My Friend Douglass"		
Biography by Ann Petry from *Harriet Tubman: Conductor on the Underground Railroad*	▶ **Video HISTORY** *America: The Story of Us: Harriet Tubman and the Underground Railroad* ◀ **Audio** from *Harriet Tubman: Conductor on the Underground Railroad*		**Strategies for Annotation** • Analyze Structure • Analyze Text: Biography • Use Word Relationships
ANCHOR TEXT **Historical Fiction by Ray Bradbury** "The Drummer Boy of Shiloh"	▶ **Video HISTORY** *Battle of Shiloh* ◀ **Audio** "The Drummer Boy of Shiloh"	**Close Read Screencasts** • Modeled Discussion (lines 42–52) • Close Read Application (lines 158–164)	**Strategies for Annotation** • Analyze Stories: Historical Fiction • Interpret Figures of Speech
CLOSE READER **Short Story by Stephen Crane** "A Mystery of Heroism"	◀ **Audio** "A Mystery of Heroism"		
History Writing by James L. Swanson from *Bloody Times: The Funeral of Abraham Lincoln and the Manhunt for Jefferson Davis*	◀ **Audio** from *Bloody Times: The Funeral of Abraham Lincoln and the Manhunt for Jefferson Davis*		**Strategies for Annotation** • Analyze Structure: Comparison-Contrast • Use Context Clues
CLOSE READER **Journal Entries by Louisa May Alcott** "Civil War Journal"	◀ **Audio** "Civil War Journal"		
Poem by Walt Whitman "O Captain! My Captain!"	◀ **Audio** "O Captain! My Captain!"		**Strategies for Annotation** • Determine Meaning of Words and Phrases
Collection 3 Performance Tasks: **A** Create a Visual Presentation **B** Write a Literary Analysis	fyi hmhfyi.com **hmhfyi.com**	**Interactive Lessons** **A** Conducting Research **A** Producing and Publishing with Technology	**B** Writing Informative Texts **B** Using Textual Evidence

For Systematic Coverage of Writing and Speaking & Listening Standards	**Interactive Lessons** Conducting Research Evaluating Sources

Assess		Extend	Reteach
Performance Task	**Online Assessment**	**Teacher eBook**	**Teacher eBook**
Writing Activity: Literary Analysis	Selection Test	**Collaborative Discussion > Interactive Lesson > ** Participating in Collaborative Discussions	**Analyze Text: Autobiography and Author's Purpose > Level Up Tutorial > ** Biographies and Autobiographies
Speaking Activity: Speech	Selection Test	**Cite Evidence > Interactive Whiteboard Lesson > ** Citing Textual Evidence	**Analyze Text: Biography > Level Up Tutorial > ** Biographies and Autobiographies
Speaking Activity: Research	Selection Test	**Draw Conclusions**	**Analyze Stories: Historical Fiction > Level Up Tutorial > ** Prose Forms > Historical Fiction
Writing Activity: Character Sketch	Selection Test	**Generating Questions for Research > Interactive Whiteboard Lesson > ** Doing Research on the Web	**Analyze Structure: Comparison and Contrast > Level Up Tutorial > ** Comparison-Contrast Organization
Speaking Activity: Respond by Speaking	Selection Test	**Analyze Style** **Analyze Structure: Stanza and Rhyme Scheme > Interactive Whiteboard Lesson > ** Form in Poetry **Meter and Scansion**	**Determine Meaning of Words and Phrases > Level Up Tutorial > ** Figurative Language
A Create a Visual Presentation **B** Write a Literary Analysis	Collection Test		

Lesson Assessments
Conducting Research
Evaluating Sources

Collection 3 Lessons	COMMON CORE **Key Learning Objective**	Performance Task
ANCHOR TEXT **Autobiography by Frederick Douglass** **Lexile 970L** from *Narrative of the Life of Frederick Douglass, an American Slave*, p. 143A	**The student will be able to . . .** analyze an autobiography and explain the author's purpose.	Writing Activity: Literary Analysis
Biography by Ann Petry **Lexile 1010L** from *Harriet Tubman: Conductor on the Underground Railroad*, p. 151A	**The student will be able to . . .** analyze methods of characterization in a biography and analyze the author's craft.	Speaking Activity: Speech
ANCHOR TEXT **Historical Fiction by Ray Bradbury** **Lexile 990L** **"The Drummer Boy of Shiloh," p. 167A**	**The student will be able to . . .** identify and analyze the key elements of historical fiction and examine how authors create mood in a story.	Speaking Activity: Research
History Writing by James L. Swanson **Lexile 1030L** from *Bloody Times: The Funeral of Abraham Lincoln and the Manhunt for Jefferson Davis*, p. 177A	**The student will be able to . . .** identify and analyze a compare and contrast organizational pattern in a text and understand the impact of a word's connotation on meaning.	Writing Activity: Character Sketch
Poem by Walt Whitman **"O Captain! My Captain!," p. 199A**	**The student will be able to . . .** recognize elegy as a poetic form and understand how extended metaphors can be used to express feelings and ideas.	Speaking Activity: Respond by Speaking

Collection 3 Performance Tasks:
A Create a Visual Presentation
B Write a Literary Analysis

Vocabulary Strategy	Language and Style	Student Instructional Support	CLOSE READER Selection
Use Context Clues		**Scaffolding for ELL Students:** Analyze Punctuation **When Students Struggle:** Read with Fluency	Historical Writing by Russell Freedman "My Friend Douglass," p. 150b **Lexile 1180L**
Use Word Relationships	Conditional Mood	**Scaffolding for ELL Students:** Analyze Structure: Phrases and Clauses **When Students Struggle:** Track Shifts in Time **To Challenge Students:** Analyze Allusions	
Interpret Figures of Speech	Indicative Mood	**Scaffolding for ELL Students:** Spanish Cognates **When Students Struggle:** Analyze Archaic Language **To Challenge Students:** Analyze Motivation	Short Story by Stephen Crane "A Mystery of Heroism," p. 176b **Lexile 1010L**
Use Context Clues	Gerunds	**Scaffolding for ELL Students:** • Analyze Language: Plurals • Analyze Language: Idiomatic Expressions **When Students Struggle:** • Analyze Compare-Contrast Structure • Create a Time Line **To Challenge Students:** Analyze Author's Perspective	Journal Entries by Louisa May Alcott "Civil War Journal," p.198b **Lexile 1480L**
		Scaffolding for ELL Students: Analyze Language: Structure Structure	

from Narrative of the Life of Frederick Douglass, an American Slave

Autobiography by Frederick Douglass

Why This Text?

Students will encounter autobiographies, first-person historical accounts, and other primary sources as they continue to study history and literature. This lesson helps students learn to understand the unique perspective such first-person accounts provide.

▶ **View It!**

Professional Development Podcast:

Text Complexity

Key Learning Objective: The student will be able to analyze an autobiography and explain the author's purpose.

For practice and application:

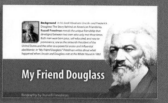

My Friend Douglass

Close Reader selection
"My Friend Douglass,"
Historical Writing by Russell Freedman

COMMON CORE Common Core Standards

RI 1 Cite textual evidence.

RI 3 Analyze how a text makes connections.

RI 4 Determine the meanings of words; analyze the impact of word choices.

RI 5 Analyze structure.

RI 6 Determine author's point of view or purpose.

W 2b Develop the topic with relevant details.

W 9b Apply grade 8 Reading standards to literary nonfiction.

SL 1a Come to discussions prepared.

SL 1b Follow rules for collegial discussions.

SL 1c Pose questions and respond to others' questions and comments.

SL 1d Acknowledge new information; qualify or justify views in light of evidence.

SL 4 Present claims and findings in a focused, coherent manner.

L 4a Use context as a clue to meaning.

L 4d Verify the preliminary determination of meaning.

▲ Text Complexity Rubric

Quantitative Measures

from **Narrative of the Life of Frederick Douglass, an American Slave**

Lexile: 970L

Qualitative Measures

Levels of Meaning/Purpose

more than one purpose; implied, but easily identified from context

Structure

more than one text structure

Language Conventionality and Clarity

some unfamiliar language; more complex sentence structure

Knowledge Demands

more difficult historical concepts

Reader/Task Considerations

Teacher determined
Vary by individual reader and type of text

CLOSE READ

Frederick Douglass Have students read the information about the author. Tell students that Frederick Douglass worked not only to end the injustice of slavery in the United States, but also to extend the rights of women, who at that time were not allowed to vote. Douglass also served as a speaker for the Massachusetts Anti-Slavery Society and published his own newspaper, *The North Star.* He was known internationally as a tireless worker not only for the abolition of slavery, but for justice and equal opportunity for all.

SETTING A PURPOSE Direct students to use the Setting a Purpose prompt to focus their reading. Remind students to write down questions that arise as they read.

Analyze Text: Autobiography (LINES 1–11)

COMMON CORE **RI 6**

Explain that an **autobiography** is an account of the writer's own life. Frederick Douglass is writing about himself and about real people and actual events. Note the use of the pronouns *I, me,* and *my.* Remind students that the pronouns used in a text can be clues to help them determine the author's point of view.

 ASK STUDENTS to locate the pronouns *I, me,* and *my* in the text. From what point of view is Douglass writing? How does this point of view help Douglass achieve his purpose? *(The text is written in first person. This point of view makes the text more personal, emphasizing the horror of slavery through his personal experience.)*

Analyze Language

COMMON CORE **RI 4**

(LINES 1–11)

Note that Douglass uses the words *master* and *mistress* to refer to the people to whom he was enslaved. Explain that these were the customary terms of address used by enslaved persons.

 ASK STUDENTS to tell what impact the use of *master* and *mistress* has on the text, given that Douglass had been a free man for seven years when he wrote this. What do these word choices reveal about Douglass? *(The use of* master *and* mistress *helps put readers into Douglass's shoes at the time of the events he is recounting. Douglass's word choices imply that his comments and feelings are directed to all who owned slaves.)*

 HISTORY VIDEO

Frederick Douglass (1818–1895) *was born into enslavement in Maryland at a time when slavery was still legal in many states in the Union. As Douglass grew up, he tried to escape several times. Finally, in 1838, he succeeded. Douglass went on to become a famous speaker and writer, fighting to abolish, or end, slavery. His autobiography,* Narrative of the Life of Frederick Douglass, an American Slave, *became a best seller in the United States and Europe.*

from
Narrative of the Life of Frederick Douglass, an American Slave

Autobiography by Frederick Douglass

SETTING A PURPOSE As you read, consider why Frederick Douglass chose these particular events to write about. Think about what his focus on these events reveals about his character and his struggle for freedom.

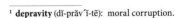

I lived in Master Hugh's family about seven years. During this time, I succeeded in learning to read and write. In accomplishing this, I was compelled to resort to various stratagems. I had no regular teacher. My mistress, who had kindly commenced to instruct me, had, in compliance with the advice and direction of her husband, not only ceased to instruct, but had set her face against my being instructed by any one else. It is due, however, to my mistress to say of her, that she did not adopt this course of treatment immediately.
10 She at first lacked the depravity[1] indispensable to shutting me up in mental darkness. It was at least necessary for her to have

(tr) ©Corbis; (c) ©aceshot1/Shutterstock

---

[1] **depravity** (dĭ-prăv´ĭ-tē): moral corruption.

Narrative of the Life of Frederick Douglass, an American Slave **143**

Close Read Screencasts ▶ **View It!**

Modeled Discussions

Have students click the *Close Read* icons in their eBooks to access two screencasts in which readers discuss and annotate the following key passages:

- Douglass's comments about his mistress (lines 8–13)
- Douglass's description of Sheridan's speeches (lines 93–102)

As a class, view and discuss at least one of these videos. Then, have students work in pairs to do an independent close read of an additional passage—Douglass's description of his discontentment (lines 115–123).

CLOSE READ

Analyze Text: Autobiography (LINES 14–41)

COMMON CORE RI 3, RI 6

Point out that Douglass writes a long paragraph about his mistress. He begins by praising her, but then he describes how her behavior changed because of her husband's influence and because of slavery itself.

C ASK STUDENTS to reread lines 14–41 and to explain Douglass's purpose in devoting so much space in his autobiography to describing his connection to this woman. *(Douglass's mistress had a big influence on him; she was one of the two people who were completely in control of his life. Describing the change in her behavior helps readers understand the effects that slavery had on slave owners, as well as on the enslaved people themselves.)*

Analyze Structure

COMMON CORE RI 1, RI 3

(LINES 26–29)

Explain that writers of autobiographies often tell events in order, but they may also show how events caused other events. Recognizing such causes and effects helps readers understand why and how events occur, and how those events are connected.

D CITE TEXT EVIDENCE Have students identify changes slavery brought about in Douglass's mistress. *(The mistress's "tender heart became stone," and her gentle nature "gave way to one of tigerlike fierceness.")*

CRITICAL VOCABULARY

commence: Douglass describes the nature of his mistress's early behavior.

ASK STUDENTS why it is significant that the mistress commenced to treat Douglass kindly. *(Her behavior in the beginning is in stark contrast to the way she treated him later. Douglass blames slavery for the terrible change in her.)*

apprehension: The mistress seems to fear the sight of Douglass with a newspaper.

ASK STUDENTS what Douglass implies by saying that the mistress showed apprehension about his reading. *(He implies that she feared what might happen if slaves were to become literate and educated.)*

---

some training in the exercise of irresponsible power, to make her equal to the task of treating me as though I were a brute.

My mistress was, as I have said, a kind and tender-hearted woman; and in the simplicity of her soul she **commenced**, when I first went to live with her, to treat me as she supposed one human being ought to treat another. In entering upon the duties of a slaveholder, she did not seem to perceive that I sustained to her the relation of a mere chattel,[2] and that for

20 her to treat me as a human being was not only wrong, but dangerously so. Slavery proved as injurious to her as it did to me. When I went there, she was a pious warm, and tender-hearted woman. There was no sorrow or suffering for which she had not a tear. She had bread for the hungry, clothes for the naked, and comfort for every mourner that came within her reach. Slavery soon proved its ability to divest her of these heavenly qualities. Under its influence, the tender heart became stone, and the lamblike disposition gave way to one of tigerlike fierceness. The first step in her downward course was

30 in her ceasing to instruct me. She now commenced to practise her husband's precepts.[3] She finally became even more violent in her opposition than her husband himself. She was not satisfied with simply doing as well as he had commanded; she seemed anxious to do better. Nothing seemed to make her more angry than to see me with a newspaper. She seemed to think that here lay the danger. I have had her rush at me with a face made all up of fury, and snatch from me a newspaper, in a manner that fully revealed her **apprehension**. She was an apt woman; and a little experience soon demonstrated, to

40 her satisfaction, that education and slavery were incompatible with each other.

From this time I was most narrowly watched. If I was in a separate room any considerable length of time, I was sure to be suspected of having a book, and was at once called to give an account of myself. All this, however, was too late. The first step had been taken. Mistress, in teaching me the alphabet, had given me the *inch*, and no precaution could prevent me from taking the *ell*.

commence
(kə-měns´) *v.* When things *commence*, they begin or start.

apprehension
(ăp´rĭ-hěn´shən) *n.* *Apprehension* is the fear or dread of the future.

---

[2] **chattle** (chăt´l): a property or slave.
[3] **precepts** (prē´sĕpts´): a rule or principal regarding action or conduct.

SCAFFOLDING FOR ELL STUDENTS

Analyze Punctuation Prompt students to use punctuation to break the sentences into more easily understood segments. Using a whiteboard, project lines 14–17.

- Highlight in yellow any commas.
- Highlight in blue the semi-colon.

ASK STUDENTS to describe the way Douglass was first treated by the mistress.

My mistress was, as I have said, a kind and tender-hearted woman;

and in the simplicity of her soul she **commenced**, when I first went to

live with

> ## "Slavery proved as injurious to her as it did to me."

The plan which I adopted, and the one by which I was most successful, was that of making friends of all the little white boys whom I met in the street. As many of these as I could, I converted into teachers. With their kindly aid, obtained at different times and in different places, I finally succeeded in learning to read. When I was sent of errands, I always took my book with me, and by going one part of my errand quickly, I found time to get a lesson before my return. I used also to carry bread with me, enough of which was always in the house, and to which I was always welcome; for I was much better off in this regard than many of the poor white children in our neighborhood. This bread I used to bestow upon the hungry little urchins, who, in return, would give me that more valuable bread of knowledge. I am strongly tempted to give the names of two or three of those little boys, as a testimonial of the gratitude and affection I bear them; but **prudence** forbids;—not that it would injure me, but it might embarrass them; for it is almost an unpardonable offence to teach slaves to read in this Christian country. It is enough to say of the dear little fellows, that they lived on Philpot Street, very near Durgin and Bailey's ship-yard. I used to talk this matter of slavery over with them. I would sometimes say to them, I wished I could be as free as they would be when they got to be men. "You will be free as soon as you are twenty-one, *but I am a slave for life!* Have not I as good a right to be free as you have?" These words used to trouble them; they would express for me the liveliest sympathy, and console me with the hope that something would occur by which I might be free.

I was now about twelve years old, and the thought of being *a slave for life* began to bear heavily upon my heart. Just about this time, I got hold of a book entitled "The Columbian Orator."[4] Every opportunity I got, I used to read this book. Among much of other interesting matter, I found in it a dialogue between a master and his slave. The slave was

prudence
(prŏŏd´ns) *n.*
Prudence is the wise handling of practical matters.

---

[4] **"The Columbian Orator":** a collection of political essays, poems, and dialogues that were used to teach reading and speaking at the beginning of the 19th century.

APPLYING ACADEMIC VOCABULARY

access	demonstrate

As you discuss the selection, incorporate the following Collection 3 academic vocabulary words: *access* and *demonstrate*. Explore the changes that Douglass describes in his mistress. What behaviors does she **demonstrate** that show how slavery affected her? Discuss the process of Douglass's self-education. How did having **access** to certain types of reading materials affect his ideas and his development?

TEACH

CLOSE READ

For more context and historical background, students can view the video "America The Story of Us: Federick Douglas" in their eBooks.

Analyze Text: Autobiography (LINES 49–76)

COMMON CORE RI 1, RI 3

Point out that, in this part of his autobiography, Douglass describes how he furthered his education after the mistress ceased to teach him.

E CITE TEXT EVIDENCE Have students reread lines 49–76 and cite evidence that shows the attitudes of the white boys. Ask: How are these attitudes similar to or different from the attitudes of the master and mistress? *(The boys provided "kindly aid," and they expressed "the liveliest sympathy" when Douglass talked about slavery. Their attitude toward Douglass is very different from the harsh treatment he is used to receiving from his master and mistress. The boys are willing to help him read because, as children, they don't share the fear that many slave owners had about the education of slaves.)*

CRITICAL VOCABULARY

prudence: Out of prudence, Douglass declines to name the boys who helped him.

ASK STUDENTS why it was prudent for Douglass not to name the boys. *(Since it was an "unpardonable offence" to teach slaves to read, Douglass doesn't want the boys—probably adults by the time he wrote his autobiography—to suffer any shame or consequences for helping him. He is grateful to them and has no desire to cause them trouble.)*

Analyze Structure
COMMON CORE · RI 5

(LINES 84–92)

Point out that Douglass describes a book he read at age twelve that had great influence on him. It included a dialogue between a master and a slave.

 ASK STUDENTS to reread lines 84–92 and explain what happens as a result of the dialogue. Ask why the dialogue was so interesting to Douglass and what effect it may have had on him. *(As a result of the dialogue, in which the slave argues successfully against slavery, the master frees the slave. This text awakened Douglass to the idea that there was a way out of slavery and that freedom was possible.)*

Analyze Text: Autobiography (LINES 112–120)
COMMON CORE · RI 1, RI 3

Beginning in line 112, Douglass describes the result of his having learned to read.

G **CITE TEXT EVIDENCE** Have students reread lines 112–120 and explain what Douglass believed his ability to read had caused. Ask them to cite evidence showing why he felt that way. *(Douglass says that reading exposed him to ideas that made his life unbearable because they confirmed what he knew to be the truth but offered no solution.)*

CRITICAL VOCABULARY

unabated: Douglass reads Sheridan's speeches over and over without tiring of them.

ASK STUDENTS to explain why Douglass's interest in these speeches was unabated. *(The more he read them, the more they helped him understand and express thoughts of his own about slavery—that it was wrong to "own" a person, and that it was right to treat all human beings with respect. He says, "It had given me a view of my wretched condition, without the remedy. It opened my eyes to the horrible pit, but no ladder upon which to get out." Douglass seemed to feel that learning to read had, in some ways, caused him more misery.)*

---

represented as having run away from his master three times. The dialogue represented the conversation which took place between them, when the slave was retaken the third time. In this dialogue, the whole argument in behalf of slavery was brought forward by the master, all of which was disposed of by the slave. The slave was made to say some very smart as well as impressive things in reply to his master—things which had the desired though unexpected effect; for the conversation resulted in the voluntary emancipation of the slave on the part of the master.

In the same book, I met with one of Sheridan's mighty speeches on and in behalf of Catholic emancipation.[5] These were choice documents to me. I read them over and over again with **unabated** interest. They gave tongue to interesting thoughts of my own soul, which had frequently flashed through my mind, and died away for want of utterance. The moral which I gained from the dialogue was the power of truth over the conscience of even a slaveholder. What I got from Sheridan was a bold **denunciation** of slavery, and a powerful **vindication** of human rights. The reading of these documents enabled me to utter my thoughts, and to meet the arguments brought forward to sustain slavery; but while they relieved me of one difficulty, they brought on another even more painful than the one of which I was relieved. The more I read, the more I was led to abhor and detest my enslavers. I could regard them in no other light than a band of successful robbers, who had left their homes, and gone to Africa, and stolen us from our homes, and in a strange land reduced us to slavery. I loathed them as being the meanest as well as the most wicked of men. As I read and contemplated the subject, behold! that very discontentment which Master Hugh had predicted would follow my learning to read had already come, to torment and sting my soul to unutterable anguish. As I writhed under it, I would at times feel that learning to read had been a curse rather than a blessing. It had given me a view of my wretched condition, without the remedy. It opened

unabated
(ŭn´ə-bā´tĭd) *adj.*
If something is *unabated*, it keeps its full force without decreasing.

denunciation
(dĭ-nŭn´sē-ā´shən) *n.*
A *denunciation* is the public condemnation of something as wrong or evil.

vindication
(vĭn´dĭ-kā´shən) *n.*
Vindication is the evidence or proof that someone's claim is correct.

---

[5] **one of Sheridan's mighty speeches on and behalf of Catholic emancipation:** Richard Brinsley Sheridan (1751–1816) was an Irish playwright and politician who made speeches about the rights of people who practiced the Roman Catholic religion in Britain and Ireland.

WHEN STUDENTS STRUGGLE...

Listening to fluently read text and being able to read fluently themselves will help students comprehend the long and fairly complex sentences in Douglass's text. Project on a whiteboard lines 93–100, in which Douglass explains the impact Sheridan's book had on him.

- Model reading the lines aloud with appropriate pacing, intonation, and expression. Demonstrate how to use punctuation as a guide to phrasing.
- Then have students turn to a partner and reread the same lines aloud as you listen, and monitor.
- Have students take turns partner-reading lines 100–107. Monitor their pacing, intonation, and expression.

my eyes to the horrible pit, but to no ladder upon which to
get out. In moments of agony, I envied my fellow-slaves for
their stupidity. I have often wished myself a beast. I preferred
the condition of the meanest reptile to my own. Any thing,
no matter what, to get rid of thinking! It was this everlasting
thinking of my condition that tormented me. There was no
getting rid of it. It was pressed upon me by every object within
sight or hearing, animate or inanimate. The silver trump of
freedom had roused my soul to eternal wakefulness. Freedom
now appeared, to disappear no more forever. It was heard
in every sound, and seen in every thing. It was ever present
to torment me with a sense of my wretched condition. I saw
nothing without seeing it, I heard nothing without hearing it,
and felt nothing without feeling it. It looked from every star, it
smiled in every calm, breathed in every wind, and moved in
every storm.

COLLABORATIVE DISCUSSION Frederick Douglass describes his
ability to read as a curse. With a partner, discuss why he comes to
think this way after working so hard to learn to read. Cite specific
evidence from the text to support your ideas.

CLOSE READ

Analyze Text: Autobiography (LINES 120–134)

COMMON CORE **RI 3, RI 6**

Remind students that Douglass escaped to freedom at age 20 and wrote this autobiography about seven years later.

 ASK STUDENTS to reread lines 120–134. Ask why Douglass, as a free man writing his autobiography, included these anguished thoughts that he had as a teenager. *(These thoughts help readers understand his despair and also his determination to gain freedom.)*

CRITICAL VOCABULARY

denunciation: In his reading, Douglass is glad to find a denunciation of slavery.

ASK STUDENTS where in the text Douglass made a denunciation of his own against slavery. *(When Douglass talked with the white boys, he denounced slavery by saying "Have not I as good a right to be free as you have?")*

vindication: Douglass finds powerful vindication for human rights in Sheridan's speeches.

ASK STUDENTS what the speeches might have said as a vindication of human rights. *(Most likely, the speeches expressed ideas similar to Douglass's—that it was wrong to "own" a person, and that it was right to treat all human beings with respect.)*

COLLABORATIVE DISCUSSION Have students work in pairs to discuss why Douglass views being able to read as a curse. You might suggest that students argue different sides of the issue, with one taking the stance that education is always a good thing and the other taking the stance, as Douglass does, that education can lead to torment or "trouble."

ASK STUDENTS to share any questions they generated in the course of reading and discussing the selection.

Analyze Text: Autobiography

Review with students the characteristics of an autobiography:

- Text is written from the first-person point of view.
- The focus is on significant events and/or people who influenced or had an impact on the writer.

Have students ask themselves, "Why did he include this?" about events and details in the autobiography. Asking and answering that question will help readers understand Douglass's purpose for writing.

Help students understand the connection Douglass makes between education and freedom.

Analyze Structure

Review the definitions of cause and effect. Explain that a cause is not always an event. In Douglass's autobiography, some of the causes he addresses are ideas or institutions, like slavery. For example, slavery makes it possible for Douglass's mistress to mistreat him. Later in the selection, Douglass calls his ability to read the cause of his discontentment with life.

Help students review the example and graphic showing the effects of slavery on the mistress. Then, have students analyze another paragraph. *(Possible answer: Lines 102–115 show the effect that reading Sheridan's speeches had on Douglass; it helped him express his own thoughts, but it also caused him to hate his enslavers.)*

Analyze Text: Autobiography

Narrative of the Life of Frederick Douglass is an **autobiography,** an account of the writer's own life. Almost all autobiographies

- are told from the first-person point of view using the pronouns *I* and *me*
- focus on the most significant events and people over a period of time in the author's life

Authors of autobiography often have a **purpose,** or reason for writing, beyond informing readers about what happened to one individual. For example, writers might also want to shed light on the time period in which they lived, or on an issue that has shaped their lives as well as the lives of others. Sometimes writers state their purpose directly, but often you must infer it by paying attention to what topics they come back to repeatedly and the thoughts, attitudes, and beliefs about these topics that they reveal.

What topic does Frederick Douglass focus on in this excerpt of his autobiography?

Analyze Structure

In an autobiography, authors often choose to focus on events that are related by **cause and effect,** which means that one event brings about another event or creates a change in attitude. The first event is the cause, and what follows is the effect. Paragraphs may be structured to show these cause-and-effect relationships.

For example, review the second paragraph of this selection. Douglass begins by saying his mistress was "a kind and tender-hearted woman," and he gives examples to support his statement. Then he explains how slavery caused her to change. "Under its influence, the tender heart became stone, and the lamblike disposition gave way to one of tigerlike fierceness." He supports this description of slavery's effects by giving examples. "Nothing seemed to make her more angry than to see me with a newspaper . . . I have had her rush at me with a face made all up of fury, and snatch from me a newspaper."

| **Cause:** Slavery ▶ | **Effect:** A kind woman turns angry and cruel. |

Review the autobiography and find another paragraph that explains a cause-and-effect relationship.

Strategies for Annotation

Analyze Text: Autobiography
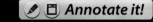

Share these strategies for guided or independent analysis:

- Highlight in blue references to the effects of being able to read.
- Add a note to explain Douglass's attitudes or feelings about being able to read.

powerful vindication of human rights. The reading of these documents enabled me to utter my thoughts, and to meet the arguments brought forward to sustain slavery; but

> Reading inspired him to express his thoughts on slavery.

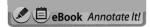

Analyzing the Text

COMMON CORE RI 1, RI 3, RI 4, RI 5, RI 6, SL 1a, SL 4, W 2b, W 9b

Cite Text Evidence Support your responses with evidence from the text.

1. **Cause/Effect** Read lines 14–48. Did the mistress's initial kindness or her eventual cruelty have a greater effect on Frederick Douglass? Explain.

2. **Interpret** When describing how he paid his child tutors, Douglass says, "This bread I used to bestow upon the hungry little urchins, who, in return, would give me that more valuable bread of knowledge." In what way is knowledge "bread"?

3. **Cause/Effect** Douglass reads a dialogue between a master and his slave as well as a speech by Sheridan. In a chart like the one shown, list several effects that resulted from reading these documents.

Cause: Douglass reads dialogue and speech. ▶ **Effect:** ▶ **Effect:** ▶ **Effect:**

4. **Analyze** Why does Douglass say in line 121, "I have often wished myself a beast"?

5. **Evaluate** Reread lines 105–112. What words reveal Douglass's perspective on, or view of, slaveholders?

6. **Analyze** What is Douglass's purpose for writing? Identify three events in this selection that help him achieve his goal.

Speaking and Listening

In lines 116–117, Douglass says "... I would at times feel that learning to read had been a curse rather than a blessing." With a partner or small group, discuss Douglass's statement and examine whether people today might share his attitude. Be sure to support your views with evidence from the text.

PERFORMANCE TASK

Writing Activity: Literary Analysis
How does the tone of Douglass's autobiography help him achieve his purpose? Write a short literary analysis.

- With a partner, discuss the author's purpose for writing. Identify the **tone** of the piece, or the writer's

attitude toward his subject.

- Next, find examples where Douglass's choice of words helps establish the tone.

- When you write, begin by stating your view. Then support that view with evidence from the text.

Narrative of the Life of Frederick Douglass **149**

Analyzing the Text

COMMON CORE RI 1, RI 3, RI 4, RI 5, RI 6

Possible answers:

1. *The mistress's initial kindness had a greater effect because it was during that time that she taught Douglass to read, an event which had enormous impact on his life. He acknowledges this when he says, "Mistress, in teaching me the alphabet, had given me the inch, and no precaution could prevent me from taking the ell."*

2. *People are fed and sustained not only by food, but also by ideas and understanding.*

3. *Effect: Douglass finds vindication for his belief that slavery is wrong. Effect: Douglass "was led to abhor and detest" his enslavers. Effect: Douglass comes to feel that learning to read had been a curse rather than a blessing.*

4. *He thinks that if he were an animal, he wouldn't have the ability to think and worry about his circumstances. Now that he can read, Douglass is tormented by his constant thoughts about his life as a slave and the impossibility of freedom.*

5. *He regards slaveholders as "a band of successful robbers" and as "the meanest as well as the most wicked of men."*

6. *Douglass's purpose is to express his thoughts and feelings about being enslaved and about the effects of literacy. He relates three events that help him achieve his goal: his mistress teaching him to read, his further pursuit of instruction from "all of the little white boys," and the acquisition of certain reading materials that encouraged his own thoughts and feelings about slavery.*

Speaking and Listening

COMMON CORE SL 1a, SL 4

Have students prepare by reviewing and citing the reasons Douglass gives for feeling that being able to read was a curse. For current examples, students may cite the case of girls and women in certain countries who are either not allowed to go to school or who may be punished for going to school and being able to read. Remind students to present their ideas in a clear and coherent manner. See page 150a for further instruction on participating in a collaborative discussion.

 Assign this performance task.

PERFORMANCE TASK

COMMON CORE W 2b, W 9b

Writing Activity: Literary Analysis Have pairs of students review the text together. Provide this additional guidance by

- reminding students that an author's tone is apparent in the attitudes the author expresses

- noting that the strong statements Douglass makes about slavery, slaveholders, and his own torment are key to the author's tone

PRACTICE & APPLY

Critical Vocabulary

Answers:

1. *relieved*

2. *saving an allowance*

3. *study the recipe*

4. *criticism*

5. *taking a test*

6. *many books*

Vocabulary Strategy: Use Context Clues

Word	Context Clues	Guessed Definition	Dictionary Definition
divest	"Slavery proved as injurious to her . . ."; "Under its influence, the tender heart became stone . . ."	to take away	to deprive of a particular quality
apt	"a little experience soon demonstrated, to her satisfaction . . ."	smart	quick to learn
bestow	"I used also to carry bread . . ."; "to bestow upon the hungry little urchins, who in return, . . ."	give	give, present
conconsole	"they would express for me the liveliest sympathy"	make to feel better	to comfort in time of disappointment or sorrow

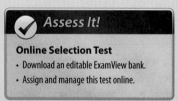

Assess It!

Online Selection Test
- Download an editable ExamView bank.
- Assign and manage this test online.

Critical Vocabulary

commence	apprehension	prudence
unabated	denunciation	vindication

Practice and Apply   Use what you know about the Vocabulary words to answer the following questions.

1. If a criminal receives **vindication,** will he feel relieved or upset?

2. Which demonstrates **prudence,** saving an allowance or spending it all?

3. To **commence** baking a cake, would you stir the batter or study the recipe?

4. Which is a type of **denunciation,** praise or criticism?

5. Would you feel **apprehension** about taking a test or about getting an A?

6. If your interest in Frederick Douglass is **unabated,** will you read many books about him or just one?

Vocabulary Strategy: Use Context Clues

Context clues are the words, phrases, and sentences surrounding a word that provide hints about a word's definition. These clues can be found either before or after the unfamiliar word. Look at this example:

> She seemed to think that here lay the danger. I have had her rush at me with a face made all up of fury . . . in a manner that fully revealed her <u>apprehension</u>.

The first sentence says that the subject perceives some danger. This provides a clue to the meaning of the word *apprehension*, which you can infer is a feeling of fear or dread that often arises in the face of danger. The dictionary definition confirms this guess.

Practice and Apply   Find the following words in Douglass's autobiography. Look at the surrounding words, phrases, and sentences for clues to each word's meaning. On a separate piece of paper, fill out a chart like the one shown.

Word	Context Clues	Guessed Definition	Dictionary Definition
divest (line 26)			
apt (line 39)			
bestow (line 61)			
console (line 75)			

Strategies for Annotation   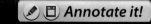 Annotate it!

Use Context Clues

Have students locate the sentences in Douglass's autobiography that contain *perceive, disposition, precaution,* and *testimonial.* Encourage them to use their eBook annotation tools to do the following:

- Highlight each word.
- Reread the surrounding sentences, looking for clues to the word's meaning. Underline any clues you find.
- Review the text and infer the word's meaning. If you are still uncertain, check the meaning in a dictionary.

these heavenly qualities. Under its influence, the tender heart became stone, and the <u>lamblike disposition</u> gave way to one of <u>tigerlike fierceness.</u> The first step in her downward course was

Collaborative Discussion

COMMON CORE

SL 1a,
SL 1b,
SL 1c,
SL 1d

TEACH

Point out to students that it is important to be able to discuss topics effectively and make decisions in a group. Provide these reminders:

- Prepare for the discussion by reading required material or by jotting down your thoughts.
- Effective discussion involves stating and supporting one's own opinions, listening to others' opinions, and respecting everyone's contributions.
- Ask questions that help group members connect the ideas of the speakers. Answer others' questions with relevant observations and ideas.
- Acknowledge new ideas or information and incorporate it into the discussion.

Explain to students that taking on specific roles in a group discussion helps make the discussion more productive. Suggest these roles:

- leader: introduces topic and goal; keeps the discussion on track; helps resolve conflicts and reach goal
- recorder: takes notes; reports on suggestions and decisions; participates in discussion
- participants: contribute relevant facts or ideas; respond constructively to one another's ideas; reach agreement or decision

PRACTICE AND APPLY

Have students assume roles and apply the tips above to their discussion in the Speaking and Listening assignment. Remind students that they should apply these tips any time they work in collaborative groups.

 INTERACTIVE WRITING/LISTENING AND SPEAKING Have students complete the tutorials in this lesson: **Participating in Collaborative Discussions**

Analyze Text: Autobiography and Author's Purpose

COMMON CORE

RI 3,
RI 5,
RI 6

RETEACH

Remind students that an **autobiography** is an account of the writer's own life. Review these characteristics:

- The writer uses the pronouns *I, me, my,* and *mine,* indicating that events are told from a first-person point of view.
- The text focuses on significant events and people in the life of the author.
- Events may be told in chronological order. The writer may use a cause-and-effect structure to connect ideas.

Explain that autobiographers have a purpose for writing. A politician might write to explain why he or she made certain decisions or to give an "insider's" perspective of political events. An actor with a reputation for being difficult might write to justify certain behaviors or events.

Explain that the thoughts, attitudes, and beliefs, as expressed in the autobiography, reveal the person's purpose for writing.

 LEVEL UP TUTORIALS Assign the following *Level Up* tutorial: **Biographies and Autobiographies**

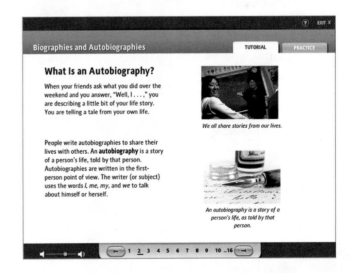

CLOSE READING APPLICATION

Students can apply their knowledge of autobiography and determining an author's purpose when they read other autobiographies. Use questions such as these to guide their reading and analysis: On what events does the author focus? What does the author's attitude toward events reveal about the author's purpose?

My Friend Douglass

Biography by Russell Freedman

Why This Text

Readers of biographies may get caught up in the life events of the subject and thus miss some of the underlying lessons revealed in the text: how the person related to, learned from, and thought about others. With the help of the close-reading questions, students will analyze the structure of the biography, examining the cause–and-effect relationships that the author uses to organize his writing. This close reading will lead students to understand Douglass and his friendship with Lincoln.

Background Have students read the background information about the biography. By early 1865, the Civil War was winding down—the Confederate army was largely defeated, and the Union army occupied most of the South. Two years before, Lincoln had issued his Emancipation Proclamation, freeing slaves in those parts of the Confederacy controlled by the Union army. However, slavery would not be abolished until the Thirteenth Amendment was passed at the end of 1865.

SETTING A PURPOSE Ask students to notice the cause-and-effect relationships in the text. Why is this an effective way to organize the text?

 ## Common Core Support

- cite strong textual evidence

- determine a central idea of a text

- analyze how a text makes connections between individuals

- determine the meaning of words

- analyze the structure of paragraphs in a text

- determine an author's point of view

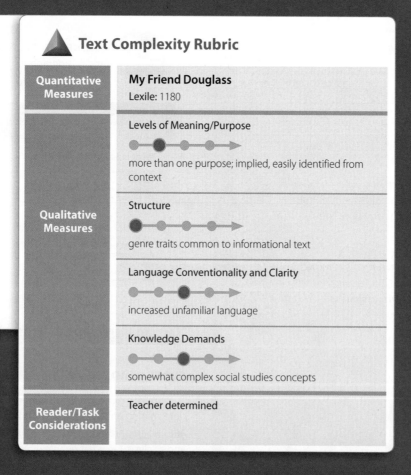

Text Complexity Rubric

Quantitative Measures	**My Friend Douglass** Lexile: 1180
Qualitative Measures	**Levels of Meaning/Purpose** more than one purpose; implied, easily identified from context
	Structure genre traits common to informational text
	Language Conventionality and Clarity increased unfamiliar language
	Knowledge Demands somewhat complex social studies concepts
Reader/Task Considerations	Teacher determined

Analyze the Structure of a Biography

Students should read this biography carefully all the way through. Close-reading questions at the bottom of the page will help them focus on a thorough analysis of the structure of specific paragraphs. As they read, students should jot down comments or questions about the text in the margins.

WHEN STUDENTS STRUGGLE . . .

To help students analyze "My Friend Douglass," have them work in small groups to fill out a chart like the one shown below.

CITE TEXT EVIDENCE For practice in analyzing the structure of a biography, ask students to cite text evidence for some of the cause-and-effect relationships.

Lines 1–9 "On the morning of . . ."	Lines 24–34 "Following the . . ."
Cause: Union troops were marching victoriously through the South. Everyone knew the war was almost over.	Cause: Freedom had become the law of the republic, and colored men were on the battlefield, mingling their blood with that of white men.
Effect: The crowd was in a mood to celebrate.	Effect: Douglass felt entitled to join the crowd heading to the gala inaugural reception.
Lines 35–39 "At the White House . . ."	Lines 105–117 "As he traveled . . ."
Cause: Their orders . . . were "to admit no person of my color."	Cause: Douglass realized that Lincoln needed the support and sympathy of his countrymen to save the nation and end slavery.
Effect: Douglass was stopped by two policemen at the door of the White House.	Effect: Douglass came to admire the political skills employed by Lincoln.

Background *In his book* Abraham Lincoln and Frederick Douglass: The Story Behind an American Friendship, **Russell Freedman** *reveals the unique friendship that developed between two men who only met three times. Both men were born poor, self-educated, and rose to prominence, one as the sixteenth President of the United States and the other as a powerful orator and influential abolitionist. In "My Friend Douglass," Freedman writes about what happened when Lincoln and Douglass met at the White House in 1865.*

My Friend Douglass

Biography by Russell Freedman

CLOSE READ
Notes

1. **READ ▶** As you read lines 1–23, begin to cite text evidence.
   - Underline the date, the place, the name of the person involved in the action, and the historical event in lines 1–9.
   - In the margin, restate what Lincoln says that slavery has caused.
   - In lines 14–23, underline what Lincoln says will be an effect of the end of slavery.

On the morning of March 4, 1865, Frederick Douglass joined a festive crowd of 30,000 spectators at the U.S. Capitol to witness Abraham Lincoln's second **inauguration**. Weeks of rain had turned Washington's unpaved streets into a sea of mud, but despite the wet and windy weather, the crowd was in a mood to celebrate. Union troops were marching victoriously through the South. Everyone knew that the war was almost over. When Lincoln's tall figure appeared, "cheer upon cheer arose, bands blatted upon the air, and flags waved all over the scene."

10   Douglass found a place for himself directly in front of the speaker's stand. He could see every crease in Lincoln's careworn face as the president stepped forward to deliver his second inaugural address.

B   The Civil War had cost more than 600,000 American lives. The fighting had been more bitter and lasted far longer than anyone could

inauguration:
a ceremony to place a leader into office

43

---

1. **READ AND CITE TEXT EVIDENCE**   Explain to students that Lincoln, like Douglass, saw the Civil War both in political and moral terms.

A ASK STUDENTS to discuss the cause-and-effect relationship that Lincoln presents. *Students should recognize that Lincoln believed slavery was "a sin in the sight of God" (line 18). Thus, the Civil War was a result of, or "terrible retribution" for, this sin (line 19).*

Critical Vocabulary: inauguration (line 3) Have students share their definitions of *inauguration*, and ask volunteers to use the noun in sentences with a political context. What happens at a presidential inauguration? *The new President is sworn in to his position, and he makes an address setting out his intentions.*

Lincoln says that slavery has divided the nation and caused the Civil War to begin.

have imagined. The "cause of the war" was slavery, Lincoln declared.

(A) Slavery was the one institution that divided the nation. And slavery was a hateful and evil practice—a sin in the sight of God. "This mighty scourge of war" was a terrible retribution, a punishment for

20 allowing human bondage to flourish on the nation's soil. Now that slavery was abolished, the time had come "to bind up the nation's wounds" and "cherish a just and lasting peace among ourselves and with all nations."

Following the "wonderfully quiet, earnest, and solemn" ceremony, Douglass wanted to congratulate Lincoln personally. That evening he joined the crowd heading to attend the gala inaugural reception at the White House—a building completed with slave labor just a half

(C) century earlier. "Though no colored persons had ever ventured to present themselves on such occasions," Douglass wrote, "it seemed,

30 now that freedom had become the law of the republic, and colored men were on the battlefield, mingling their blood with that of white men in one common effort to save the country, that it was not too great an assumption for a colored man to offer his congratulations to the President with those of other citizens."

At the White House door, Douglass was stopped by two policemen who "took me rudely by the arm and ordered me to stand

---

2. ◀ **REREAD** Reread lines 14–23. If slavery was the "cause of the war," what were the effects of slavery? Be sure to cite explicit textual evidence in your response.

The long bitter fight that divided the nation and the great loss of life were brought about by slavery. The awful war was "punishment" for allowing "human bondage" to exist in America.

3. **READ** ▶ As you read lines 24–62, continue to collect and cite textual evidence.

- Circle the reason Douglass feels justified in attending the inaugural gala.
- Explain in the margin what happens when Douglass tries to enter the White House.
- Underline what Lincoln says to Douglass in lines 47–62.

44

---

back." Their orders, they told him, were "to admit no persons of my color." Douglass didn't believe them. He was positive that no such order could have come from the president.

40 The police tried to steer Douglass away from the doorway and out a side exit. He refused to leave. "I shall not go out of this building till I see President Lincoln," he insisted. Just then he spotted an acquaintance who was entering the building and asked him to send word "to Mr. Lincoln that Frederick Douglass is detained by officers at the door." Within moments, Douglass was being escorted into the elegant East Room of the White House.

Lincoln stood among his guests "like a mountain pine high above all others." As Douglass approached through the crowd, Lincoln

(D) called out, "Here comes my friend Douglass." The president took

50 Douglass by the hand. "I am glad to see you," he said. "I saw you in the crowd today, listening to my inaugural address. How did you like it?"

Douglass hesitated. "Mr. Lincoln, I must not detain you with my poor opinion when there are thousands waiting to shake hands with you."

"No, no" said the president. "You must stop a little Douglass; there is no man whose opinion I value more than yours. I want to know what you think of it."

"Mr. Lincoln, that was a sacred effort," Douglass replied.

60 "I'm glad you liked it!"

And with that, Douglass moved on, making way for other guests who were waiting to shake the hand of Abraham Lincoln.

Police stop Douglass because of the color of his skin, but he refuses to leave. Someone tells Lincoln, who allows Douglass to enter.

---

4. ◀ **REREAD** Reread lines 47–62. Explain how Lincoln makes Douglass feel welcome. Cite specific textual evidence in your response.

Lincoln calls Douglass a "friend" and says he is glad to see him. Lincoln reveals his great respect for Douglass when he says "there is no man whose opinion I value more than yours."

45

---

2. **REREAD AND CITE TEXT EVIDENCE**

(B) ASK STUDENTS to outline two cause-and-effect chains that Lincoln traces back to slavery. One chain is empirical, the other is moral, or spiritual. *Students should note: 1) slavery ➔ divided nation ➔ Civil War ➔ 600,000 Americans dead ➔ time to bind the nation's wounds; 2) slavery ➔ a sin in God's eye ➔ punishment is Civil War ➔ slavery abolished ➔ lasting peace.*

3. **READ AND CITE TEXT EVIDENCE**

(C) ASK STUDENTS to summarize Douglass's reasons for believing that he could congratulate the President. *Freedom was the "law of the republic." Also, "colored men" were dying with white men on the battlefield trying to save the country.* How does Douglass view himself? *He sees himself as a "colored man" who is a citizen. He ought to be able to congratulate Lincoln.*

4. **REREAD AND CITE TEXT EVIDENCE**

(D) ASK STUDENTS to discuss the significance of this scene and why Douglass did not feel comfortable. *Students should recognize the painful irony: Lincoln had just finished a speech blaming the Civil War on slavery and arguing that the end of slavery gave the nation a chance to "bind up its wounds." Yet, Douglass, a black man, had just met resistance trying to enter the White House.* How does Lincoln set an example? *He begins the process of "binding up" the nation's wounds by welcoming Douglass as a friend and seeking his opinion. He shows others in the room that black men must be treated with the same respect as white men.*

FOR ELL STUDENTS In this context, *practice* (line 18) means the usual way of doing something.

1. The war ends.

jubilant:
overjoyed

(A month later, on April 9, 1865,) generals Grant and Lee met at Appomattox Courthouse in Virginia, where Grant accepted the surrender of Lee's Confederate army. After almost four years of savage fighting, the Civil War had ended. "Guns are firing, bells ringing, flags flying, men laughing, children cheering, all, all **jubilant**," Gideon Welles, Lincoln's secretary of the navy, recorded in his diary.

E

70   Throngs of people collected around the White House, calling for the president. When Lincoln appeared, he asked the band to play "Dixie," a popular minstrel tune that had become associated with the Confederate cause. "It is one of the best tunes I have ever heard," Lincoln told the crowd. He joked that the tune was now "a lawful prize," since "we fairly captured it." So the band played "Dixie," then struck up "Yankee Doodle."

2. Lincoln is shot.
3. Lincoln dies.

(Five days later,) as Lincoln sat watching a play with his wife at Ford's Theater in Washington, the president was shot in the head by actor John Wilkes Booth. Lincoln died (early the next morning, April 15, 1865.)

F   80   "A dreadful disaster has befallen the nation," Frederick Douglass told a memorial service in Rochester that afternoon. "It is a day for silence and meditation; for grief and tears."

calamity:
disaster

For Douglass, Lincoln's death was "a personal as well as a national **calamity**." He felt that he had lost a friend, and how deeply he mourned that day for Abraham Lincoln, "I dare not attempt to tell. It was only a few days ago that I shook his brave, honest hand, and looked into his gentle eye and heard his kindly voice."

---

5. **READ** ▶ As you read lines 63–87, continue to cite textual evidence.
- Circle words that indicate the sequence of events. List the events in the margin.
- Underline Douglass's response to the news of Lincoln's death.

6. **◀ REREAD** Reread lines 80–87. In what way is Lincoln's death a "calamity" for Douglass? In what way is it a calamity for the nation?

On a personal level, Lincoln's death has caused Douglass to lose a
friend, which has had a profound effect on him. It is a terrible loss
for the nation as well because Lincoln maintained the union of the
United States and abolished slavery.

46

A few months later Douglass received in the mail a long, slender package from Washington, D.C., along with a note from Mary Todd
90   Lincoln. Her husband had considered Douglass a special friend, she wrote, and before he died, he had wanted to do something to express his warm personal regard. Since he hadn't had the chance, Mary had decided to send Douglass her husband's favorite walking stick as a memento of their friendship.

When Abraham Lincoln was assassinated, Frederick Douglass, in his mid-forties, was America's most influential black citizen. For the rest of his long life, he continued in his speeches and writings to be a powerful voice for social justice, denouncing racism and demanding equal rights for blacks and whites alike. During the Reconstruction
100   era[1] of the 1870s and 1880s, when many of the rights gained after **emancipation** were snatched away in the South, Douglass spoke out against lynchings, the terrorism of the Ku Klux Klan, and the Jim Crow laws[2] that were devised to keep blacks in their place and away from the ballot box.

emancipation:
freedom from
slavery

G

As he traveled widely, lecturing on social issues and national politics, Douglass spoke often about Abraham Lincoln. During the war, he had criticized the president for being slow to move against slavery, for resisting the enlistment of black soldiers, for inviting blacks "to leave the land in which we were born." But with
110   emancipation, and in the aftermath of the war, Douglass had come to appreciate Lincoln's sensitivity to popular opinion and to admire the political skills Lincoln employed to win public support. "His greatest mission was to accomplish two things: first, to save the country from dismemberment and ruin; and, second, to free his country from the great crime of slavery. To do one or the other, or both," Douglass said, Lincoln needed "the earnest sympathy and the powerful cooperation of his fellow countrymen."

Lincoln
successfully
gathered
support to
preserve the
country and
end slavery.

In the 1870s, Douglass moved with his family to Washington, D.C., where he edited a newspaper, held a succession of federal

---

[1] **Reconstruction era:** the period after the American Civil War when the Southern states were under the federal government's control.
[2] **Jim Crow laws:** the practice of separating African Americans from whites in the South during and after Reconstruction.

---

7. **READ** ▶ Read lines 88–139. In the margin, paraphrase what Douglass says about Lincoln in lines 112–117. Continue to cite evidence.

47

---

5. **READ AND CITE TEXT EVIDENCE**

E **ASK STUDENTS** what the immediate results of Lee's surrender at Appomattox were. *People in the North were jubilant and celebrated the end of the war. Many people gathered at the White House and called for the President.*

6. **REREAD AND CITE TEXT EVIDENCE**

F **ASK STUDENTS** to cite some of the evocative language used by Douglass to indicate the scope of the national calamity. *Students should cite, "dreadful disaster" (line 80), and "a day for silence and meditation; for grief and tears" (lines 81–82).*

Critical Vocabulary: jubilant (line 67) Have students suggest synonyms for *jubilant. elated, joyous, exultant, rejoicing*

Critical Vocabulary: calamity (line 84) Have students share their definitions of *calamity*, and ask volunteers to use the noun in sentences.

---

7. **READ AND CITE TEXT EVIDENCE**

G **ASK STUDENTS** why Douglass criticized Lincoln during the war. *He thought Lincoln was slow to end slavery, resisted letting blacks enlist in the army, and wanted blacks to leave the United States.* What did Douglass come to understand after the war? *He realized that Lincoln first needed to win public support—the sympathy and cooperation of "his fellow countrymen" (line 117).*

Critical Vocabulary: emancipation (line 101) Have students compare how blacks and whites in the South might have thought of the word *emancipation. Blacks probably viewed the word with pride, as a symbol of their entry into citizenship. Southern whites may have viewed the word with anger, as a symbol of their defeat.*

FOR ELL STUDENTS Encourage Spanish-speaking students to describe what the verb *denounce* means (*denouncing*, line 98). They may recognize it from its Spanish cognate *denunciar*.

120 appointments, and clearly enjoyed his exalted position as an elder
statesman of America's black citizens. And he continued to denounce
injustice and inequality with the undiminished fervor of an old
warrior.

His last home was a large, comfortable house called Cedar Hill,
perched high on a hilltop looking down at the Anacostia River and
the U.S. capital beyond. Cedar Hill had a spacious library, large
enough to hold Douglass's collection of some two thousand books.
From time to time, as he picked a book from his shelves and settled
down to read, he must have recalled those distant days in Baltimore
130 when he was a young slave named Frederick Bailey, a determined boy
who owned just one book, a single volume that he kept hidden from
view and read in secret.

Lincoln had read and studied the same book as a young man in
New Salem. That was something they had in common, a shared
experience that helped each of them rise from obscurity to greatness.
"He was the architect of his own fortune, a self-made man," Douglass
wrote of Lincoln. He had "ascended high, but with hard hands and
honest work built the ladder on which he climbed"—words that
Douglass, as he was aware, could easily have applied to himself.

8. ◀ REREAD AND DISCUSS Reread lines 128–135. With a small group,
discuss the author's purpose for including the information about the
shared book. What point is Freedman making about a childhood
experience common to both men?

SHORT RESPONSE

Cite Text Evidence What effect did Lincoln have on Douglass's life? In what
respect did Douglass carry on Lincoln's work? **Cite text evidence** in your
response.

Lincoln's assassination caused Douglass to lose a friend and feel a
great loss; but it also put Douglass in the spotlight, as he carried on
Lincoln's work of speaking out against social injustice and racism,
and in demanding equal rights for African Americans. Later,
Douglass became an elder statesman, and he held federal
appointments, enjoying his influential positions.

48

---

8. REREAD AND DISCUSS USING TEXT EVIDENCE

ASK STUDENTS in each group to review the life experiences
of Douglass and Lincoln. Have students pay close attention to
those parts of the men's lives that parallel, intersect, or overlap.
*Students should understand that although Douglass and Lincoln
were born into remarkably different circumstances—one a slave, the
other a free man—they shared some experiences, had similar
personalities, fought against the same injustices, rose to national
prominence, and in some ways came to resemble one another
politically.*

SHORT RESPONSE

Cite Text Evidence Students' responses should include text
evidence that supports their positions. They should:

- describe the connections between Lincoln and Douglass.
- give examples of how Lincoln affected Douglass's life.
- explain how Douglass carried on Lincoln's work.

TO CHALLENGE STUDENTS . . .

For more context and expert opinion on Douglass, students can
view the video "Frederick Douglass" in their eBooks.

ASK STUDENTS what some of the personality traits that led to
Douglass to rise as a great abolitionist were. *First, he had to have
the vision to imagine himself as a free man. For a slave, trapped in a
world where slave owners controlled everything from one's personal
life to the highest government bodies, imagining freedom required
fortitude and tenacity. Then, to escape slavery, Douglass needed
courage, of course, plus "drive." Later, as a free man, Douglass had to
have the "audacity" to think that he, a black man, could speak about
the issues of slavery as well or better than white abolitionists.*

Have students discuss how Douglass's circumstances allowed
him to act as a "bridge," advancing the abolitionist cause. *The
abolitionist movement was led by men and women who for religious
and political reasons felt that slavery was wrong. As an ex-slave,
Douglass brought a new perspective to the movement. He could
speak about slavery from personal experience, something that white
abolitionists could not do. So he bridged the divide between slavery
and freedom, and between blacks and whites. He also traveled and
spoke in Europe, thus helping bridge another divide.*

DIG DEEPER

1. With the class, return to Question 1, Read. Have students summarize what Lincoln says will be an effect of slavery's abolishment.

   ASK STUDENTS to discuss how the process of "binding up" the nation's wounds influenced the rest of Douglass's life.

   • Was the end of the war the beginning of a "just and lasting peace" for Douglass? *In some ways, the end of the war was just the beginning, a new chapter in the struggle for racial equality. Slaves were emancipated, but all of the old prejudices and discriminatory institutions still existed. Right away, Douglass is blocked at the White House door because of the color of his skin. This is a forewarning—Douglass would spend the rest of his life working to "bind up" the nation's wounds from slavery.*

2. With the class, return to Question 3, Read. Have students share their responses.

   ASK STUDENTS to imagine themselves in Douglass's shoes as he attends the inaugural celebration.

   • What was an initial lesson learned by Douglass at the inaugural reception? *Policemen rudely held him back and said he couldn't enter the White House because of his "color." So Douglass must have realized that not much had changed—society still didn't view or treat him as an equal citizen.*

   • What was a subsequent lesson learned by Douglass that evening? *Lincoln greeted Douglass as a respected friend and insisted that Douglass stop and tell him what he thought of Lincoln's address. So here Douglass must have taken heart, realizing the process of "binding up" the nation's wounds had indeed begun. The president of the United States was treating him as a citizen, a peer whose opinion he valued.*

   ASK STUDENTS to return to their Short Response answer and revise it based on the class discussion.

CLOSE READING NOTES

EXEMPLAR

from *Harriet Tubman: Conductor on the Underground Railroad*

Biography by Ann Petry

*my*SmartPlanner — Create lesson plans and access resources online.

Why This Text?

Students expand their understanding of a historical period by reading biographies of the people who played significant roles in events. This lesson focuses attention on the biographer's techniques for revealing character and creating interest.

Key Learning Objective: The student will be able to identify methods of characterization in a biography and analyze the author's craft.

COMMON CORE — Common Core Standards

RI 1 Cite text evidence to support analysis.
RI 3 Analyze text connections among individuals, ideas, or events.
RI 4 Determine meanings of words and phrases.
RI 5 Analyze paragraph structure.
W 7 Conduct short research projects.
W 9b Apply Grade 8 Reading standards to literary nonfiction.
SL 1a Come to discussions prepared with research.
SL 4 Present claims and findings in a focused, coherent manner.
L 1c Form and use verbs in the conditional mood.
L 3a Use verbs in the conditional mood to achieve particular effects.
L 5b Use word relationships to understand meanings.
L 6 Acquire and use grade-appropriate academic vocabulary.

Text Complexity Rubric

Quantitative Measures	**from *Harriet Tubman: Conductor on the Underground Railroad*** Lexile: 1010L

Levels of Meaning/Purpose

multiple levels of meaning

Qualitative Measures

Structure

no major shifts in chronology; occasional use of flashback

Language Conventionality and Clarity

some figurative language

Knowledge Demands

distinctly unfamiliar experience

Reader/Task Considerations	Teacher determined Vary by individual reader and type of text

TEACH

CLOSE READ

Background Have students read the background and information about the author. Clarify that the word *underground* means "secret or hidden," in this context, and not literally underground. Also clarify the Biblical allusion: The subject of this biography had the nickname Moses because, like the Biblical Moses, she led enslaved people to freedom.

SETTING A PURPOSE Direct students to use the Setting a Purpose question to focus their reading.

Analyze Text: Biography (LINES 1–6)

COMMON CORE RI 3, RI 5

Tell students that a **biography** is a true account of a person's life that is told by someone other than the subject. Tell students that this excerpt from a biography begins with information about how the subject—Harriet Tubman—is viewed by others.

Ⓐ ASK STUDENTS to reread lines 1–6 and tell what is revealed about the subject. *(Tubman is known as "Moses" and is a figure of mystery to the masters of slaves in Maryland.)* How does the structure of the paragraph show the masters' illogical reaction to Moses? *(The first sentences say that the masters did not believe Moses existed, but later sentences indicate that they watched for him and offered rewards for his capture.)*

Background *Before the Civil War, many enslaved people fled north to freedom along the Underground Railroad, a secret network of safe houses. One of the Underground Railroad's most famous "conductors" was Harriet Tubman.*

Ann Lane Petry (1908–1997) *grew up in a small town in Connecticut, where she and her family were the only African American residents. Much of her writing focused on the important contributions of African Americans.*

from HARRIET TUBMAN: Conductor on the Underground Railroad

Biography by Ann Petry

SETTING A PURPOSE As you read, look for clues about the kind of person Harriet Tubman was. What qualities led others to trust her as a leader? Write down any questions you have.

The Railroad Runs to Canada

Along the Eastern Shore of Maryland, in Dorchester County, in Caroline County, the masters kept hearing whispers about the man named Moses, who was running off slaves. At first they did not believe in his existence. The stories about him were fantastic, unbelievable. Yet they watched for him. They offered rewards for his capture.

They never saw him. Now and then they heard whispered rumors to the effect that he was in the neighborhood. The woods were searched. The roads were watched. There was
10 never anything to indicate his whereabouts. But a few days afterward, a goodly number of slaves would be gone from the plantation. Neither the master nor the overseer had heard or

©Jacob Harris/AP/Wide World Photos

SCAFFOLDING FOR ELL STUDENTS

Analyze Structure Using a whiteboard, offer support for long sentences with multiple phrases and clauses by prompting students to find units of ideas.

• Highlight in yellow phrases describing places, and in green for details about action.

ASK STUDENTS what the multiple locations suggest about Moses' work. *(He helps runaway slaves in a large area.)*

> Along the Eastern Shore of Maryland, in Dorchester County, in Caroline County, the masters kept hearing whispers about the man named Moses, who was running off slaves. At first they did not believe

Analyze Text: Biography (LINES 33–46)

COMMON CORE RI 3, RI 5

Explain that authors use a technique called **characterization** to reveal what a person is like. Characterization can be shown through the traits and actions of the person or through how the person is seen by others. Point out that the author's characterization of Harriet Tubman shifts from the viewpoint of the masters to the viewpoint of Tubman herself: her actions reveal her qualities.

 ASK STUDENTS to reread lines 33–46 to summarize Tubman's actions in "running off slaves." Have students tell what those actions show about her character. *(She announces her arrival by singing the spiritual "Go down, Moses" near the slaves' quarter. She spends days planning the trip and selecting the slaves. She waits for a clear Saturday night and then calls like a whippoorwill or a hoot owl to signal time for departure. These actions show that Tubman is careful, organized, and brave.)*

Analyze Structure

COMMON CORE RI 4, RI 5

(LINES 42–46)

Tell students that **author's craft** refers to the methods authors use to make their writing lively and vivid.

 ASK STUDENTS to reread the paragraph beginning on line 42, which describes Tubman's voice. What is the effect of the author's choice to describe her voice in this vivid way? *(By comparing Tubman's voice to a "murmur borne on the wind," the author is suggesting secrecy and also helping readers hear a gentle, soft, low song.)*

---

seen anything unusual in the quarter.[1] Sometimes one or the other would vaguely remember having heard a whippoorwill call somewhere in the woods, close by, late at night. Though it was the wrong season for whippoorwills.

Sometimes the masters thought they had heard the cry of a hoot owl, repeated, and would remember having thought that the intervals between the low moaning cry were wrong, that it had been repeated four times in succession instead of three. There was never anything more than that to suggest that all was not well in the quarter. Yet when morning came, they invariably discovered that a group of the finest slaves had taken to their heels.

Unfortunately, the discovery was almost always made on a Sunday. Thus a whole day was lost before the machinery of pursuit could be set in motion. The posters offering rewards for the fugitives could not be printed until Monday. The men who made a living hunting for runaway slaves were out of reach, off in the woods with their dogs and their guns, in pursuit of four-footed game, or they were in camp meetings saying their prayers with their wives and families beside them.

Harriet Tubman could have told them that there was far more involved in this matter of running off slaves than signaling the would-be runaways by imitating the call of a whippoorwill, or a hoot owl, far more involved than a matter of waiting for a clear night when the North Star was visible.

In December, 1851, when she started out with the band of fugitives that she planned to take to Canada, she had been in the vicinity of the plantation for days, planning the trip, carefully selecting the slaves that she would take with her.

She had announced her arrival in the quarter by singing the forbidden spiritual—"Go down, Moses, 'way down to Egypt Land"[2]—singing it softly outside the door of a slave cabin, late at night. The husky voice was beautiful even when it was barely more than a murmur borne[3] on the wind.

Once she had made her presence known, word of her coming spread from cabin to cabin. The slaves whispered to each other, ear to mouth, mouth to ear, "Moses is here." "Moses has come." "Get ready. Moses is back again." The ones

---

[1] **quarter:** the area in which enslaved people lived.

[2] **"Go down, Moses, 'way down to Egypt Land":** a line from an African American folk song.

[3] **borne:** carried.

APPLYING ACADEMIC VOCABULARY

demonstrate	symbolize

As you discuss the author's characterization of Harriet Tubman, incorporate the following Collection 3 academic vocabulary words: *demonstrate* and *symbolize*. Talk about what a song, Biblical allusion, Canada, and other things **symbolize** for the people described. Talk about the qualities that Tubman **demonstrates** through her actions.

who had agreed to go North with her put ashcake and salt herring in an old bandanna, hastily tied it into a bundle, and then waited patiently for the signal that meant it was time to start.

There were eleven in this party, including one of her brothers and his wife. It was the largest group that she had ever conducted, but she was determined that more and more slaves should know what freedom was like.

She had to take them all the way to Canada. The Fugitive
60 Slave Law[4] was no longer a great many incomprehensible words written down on the country's lawbooks. The new law had become a reality. It was Thomas Sims, a boy, picked up on the streets of Boston at night and shipped back to Georgia. It was Jerry and Shadrach, arrested and jailed with no warning.

She had never been in Canada. The route beyond Philadelphia was strange to her. But she could not let the runaways who accompanied her know this. As they walked along she told them stories of her own first flight, she kept painting vivid word pictures of what it would be like to be
70 free.

But there were so many of them this time. She knew moments of doubt when she was half-afraid, and kept looking back over her shoulder, imagining that she heard the sound of pursuit. They would certainly be pursued. Eleven of them. Eleven thousand dollars' worth of flesh and bone and muscle that belonged to Maryland planters. If they were caught, the eleven runaways would be whipped and sold South, but she— she would probably be hanged.

They tried to sleep during the day but they never could
80 wholly relax into sleep. She could tell by the positions they assumed, by their restless movements. And they walked at night. Their progress was slow. It took them three nights of walking to reach the first stop. She had told them about the place where they would stay, promising warmth and good food, holding these things out to them as an incentive to keep going.

When she knocked on the door of a farmhouse, a place where she and her parties of runaways had always been welcome, always been given shelter and plenty to eat, there

---

[4] **Fugitive Slave Law:** a law by which enslaved people who escaped could be recovered by their owners.

CLOSE READ

Analyze Text: Biography (LINES 71–78)

Tell students that characterization in a biography includes information about the subject's thoughts and feelings.

D ASK STUDENTS to reread lines 71–78 to tell how Tubman seems to deal with feelings of fear. *(She knows that the group is being pursued and is "half-afraid" of being caught, knowing that she will be hanged. But she doesn't let these fears control her and keeps going.)* How does the author compare Tubman's possible fate to that of the runaways? *(While the runaways will be whipped and sold South, Tubman will be hanged.)*

Analyze Structure

COMMON CORE RI 1, RI 4, RI 5

(LINES 74–76)

Point out that an author may use sentence fragments, or incomplete sentences, for their effects. A fragment may suggest a powerful idea or a short burst of thought.

E CITE TEXT EVIDENCE Have students reread the text that begins on line 74 to identify the sentence fragments. Ask students what effect these fragments have on the reader. *("Eleven of them. Eleven thousand dollars' worth of flesh and bone and muscle that belonged to Maryland planters." The fragments have emotional impact because they emphasize that eleven human beings are not individuals, just "flesh and bone and muscle," property worth one thousand dollars each.)*

Analyze Structure

COMMON CORE **RI 4, RI 5**

(LINES 104–108)

Tell students that repeated grammatical constructions are called **parallelism.** Point out that an author may use parallelism to create rhythm and to emphasize similar ideas.

F **CITE TEXT EVIDENCE** Have students identify the parallelism in lines 104–108. Suggest that students read the sentence aloud to listen for the effects of repetition. (*"Somehow she* would have to *instill courage into these eleven people, most of them strangers,* would have to *feed them on hope and bright dreams of freedom . . ." Students should note that the parallelism emphasizes the challenge Tubman is facing.*)

CRITICAL VOCABULARY

disheveled: The author is explaining how the fugitives look after three nights of walking.

ASK STUDENTS to describe how the disheveled people might look. (*Their clothes are wrinkled and spotted with dirt.*)

instill: Harriet Tubman wants to instill courage into the people she is leading.

ASK STUDENTS to explain why Tubman needs to instill courage. (*They are facing a frightening and unfamiliar situation.*)

dispel: Harriet Tubman is trying to keep the runaways calm in the situation they face.

ASK STUDENTS why it is important for Tubman to dispel their fears. (*If they are too frightened, they might panic and run or make noise.*)

---

90 was no answer. She knocked again, softly. A voice from within said, "Who is it?" There was fear in the voice.

She knew instantly from the sound of the voice that there was something wrong. She said, "A friend with friends," the password on the Underground Railroad.

The door opened, slowly. The man who stood in the doorway looked at her coldly, looked with unconcealed astonishment and fear at the eleven **disheveled** runaways who were standing near her. Then he shouted, "Too many, too many. It's not safe. My place was searched last week. It's not 100 safe!" and slammed the door in her face.

She turned away from the house, frowning. She had promised her passengers food and rest and warmth, and instead of that, there would be hunger and cold and more **F** walking over the frozen ground. Somehow she would have to **instill** courage into these eleven people, most of them strangers, would have to feed them on hope and bright dreams of freedom instead of the fried pork and corn bread and milk she had promised them.

They stumbled along behind her, half-dead for sleep, 110 and she urged them on, though she was as tired and as discouraged as they were. She had never been in Canada but she kept painting wondrous word pictures of what it would be like. She managed to **dispel** their fear of pursuit, so that they would not become hysterical, panic-stricken. Then she had to bring some of the fear back, so that they would stay awake and keep walking though they drooped with sleep.

Yet during the day, when they lay down deep in a thicket, they never really slept, because if a twig snapped or the wind sighed in the branches of a pine tree, they jumped to their 120 feet, afraid of their own shadows, shivering and shaking. It was very cold, but they dared not make fires because someone would see the smoke and wonder about it.

She kept thinking, eleven of them. Eleven thousand dollars' worth of slaves. And she had to take them all the way to Canada. Sometimes she told them about Thomas Garrett, in Wilmington. She said he was their friend even though he did not know them. He was the friend of all fugitives. He called them God's poor. He was a Quaker[5] and his speech was a little different from that of other people. His clothing was

disheveled
(dĭ-shəv´əld) *adj.*
When something is *disheveled*, it is messy or untidy.

instill
(ĭn-stĭl´) *v.* When you *instill* something, you supply it gradually.

dispel
(dĭ-spĕl´) *v.* to drive away.

---

[5] **Quaker:** a member of a religious group called the Society of Friends.

WHEN STUDENTS STRUGGLE . . .

Help students follow the narrative by focusing their attention on shifts in time. The author refers to earlier events and provides background information, and also refers to events that will take place after the main action of the narrative.

Have partners identify each sentence that signals time shifting away from Tubman's trip north with eleven fugitives and each sentence that signals a return to that main action. Ask students to sum up the information given between those points.

Harriet Tubman

130 different, too. He wore the wide-brimmed hat that the
Quakers wear.

 She said that he had thick white hair, soft, almost like a
baby's, and the kindest eyes she had ever seen. He was a big
man and strong, but he had never used his strength to harm
anyone, always to help people. He would give all of them
a new pair of shoes. Everybody. He always did. Once they
reached his house in Wilmington, they would be safe. He
would see to it that they were.

She described the house where he lived, told them about
140 the store where he sold shoes. She said he kept a pail of milk
and a loaf of bread in the drawer of his desk so that he would
have food ready at hand for any of God's poor who should

Harriet Tubman: Conductor on the Underground Railroad   **155**

Time shifts back:	Sometimes she told them about Thomas Garrett in Wilmington. (lines 125–126)
Return to main action:	While she talked, she kept watching them. (line 150)
Summary:	Tubman describes the Quaker Thomas Garrett who has a shoe store and hiding place for fugitives.

CLOSE READ

Analyze Text: Biography (LINES 132–148)

 COMMON CORE RI 3

Point out that the author is providing historical information about a person and place on the Underground Railroad.

G **ASK STUDENTS** to reread lines 132–148 and explain the connection between Thomas Garrett and Tubman. Prompt students to identify details that suggest Tubman's view of Garrett. *(His shoe store was a stop on the Underground Railroad where Tubman brought fugitives for rest and safety. She viewed him as a kind, generous person doing God's work: "kept a pail of milk and a loaf of bread . . . for any of God's poor." She thought he was clever: "boxes of shoes—so that you would never guess that the wall actually opened.")*

Analyze Structure

COMMON CORE RI 1, RI 4, RI 5

(LINES 133–135)

Tell students that syntax is the arrangement of words, phrases, and clauses within sentences. Explain that because there are many correct ways to shape a sentence, an author's choices reflect his or her craft and style.

H **CITE TEXT EVIDENCE** Have students reread the sentence that begins on line 133, "He was a big man . . . ," and pay special attention to word order. Ask for ideas about why the author chose that syntax. *(Instead of writing, "He was a big, strong man," the author writes, "He was a big man and strong." Instead of writing, "He used his strength only to help people and never to harm them," the author uses a less straightforward syntax. The effect is to emphasize the contrast between harm and help. The effect is also a storytelling voice, as if Tubman is telling a story to her followers.)*

TEACH

CLOSE READ

Analyze Structure

COMMON CORE · RI 1, RI 4, RI 5

(LINES 158–161)

Tell students that the author is using a variety of techniques to make sound-meaning connections, including syntax, repetition, and punctuation.

① **CITE TEXT EVIDENCE** Tell students to reread aloud softly to themselves the sentence that begins on line 158 ("She hesitated before . . .") and listen for word order, repetition, and pauses. Have students describe the impact of these techniques. (*The author interrupts the sentence, "She hesitated before she approached the door and knocked softly" with words between* door *and and* knocked. *The commas, repeated word* suppose, *and bigger thought between dashes all emphasize the hesitation she feels.*)

CRITICAL VOCABULARY

linger: The author is describing how the people feel after they spent the night in a safe kitchen.

ASK STUDENTS to describe the feelings that lingered on. (*The warm, peaceful feelings they had inside the kitchen stayed with them.*)

---

suddenly appear before him, fainting with hunger. There was a hidden room in the store. A whole wall swung open, and behind it was a room where he could hide fugitives. On the wall there were shelves filled with small boxes— boxes of shoes—so that you would never guess that the wall actually opened.

150 While she talked, she kept watching them. They did not believe her. She could tell by their expressions. They were thinking, New shoes, Thomas Garrett, Quaker, Wilmington— what foolishness was this? Who knew if she told the truth? Where was she taking them anyway?

That night they reached the next stop—a farm that belonged to a German. She made the runaways take shelter behind trees at the edge of the fields before she knocked at the door. She hesitated before she approached the door, thinking, suppose that he, too, should refuse shelter, suppose—Then she thought, Lord, I'm going to hold steady on to You and You've

160 got to see me through—and knocked softly.

She heard the familiar guttural voice say, "Who's there?"
She answered quickly, "A friend with friends."
He opened the door and greeted her warmly. "How many this time?" he asked."Eleven," she said and waited, doubting, wondering.
He said, "Good. Bring them in."
He and his wife fed them in the lamplit kitchen, their faces glowing, as they offered food and more food, urging them to eat, saying there was plenty for everybody, have more milk,

170 have more bread, have more meat.

They spent the night in the warm kitchen. They really slept, all that night and until dusk the next day. When they left, it was with reluctance. They had all been warm and safe and well-fed. It was hard to exchange the security offered by that clean warm kitchen for the darkness and the cold of a December night.

"Go On or Die"

Harriet had found it hard to leave the warmth and friendliness, too. But she urged them on. For a while, as they walked, they seemed to carry in them a measure of

180 contentment; some of the serenity and the cleanliness of that big warm kitchen **lingered** on inside them. But as they walked farther and farther away from the warmth and the light, the

linger
(lĭng′gər) *v.* When you *linger*, you remain or stay longer.

Strategies for Annotation 🖉 📋 Annotate it!

Analyze Structure

COMMON CORE · RI 4, RI 5

Share these strategies for guided or independent analysis:

- Underline repeated grammatical constructions.
- Highlight in yellow repeated words.
- Highlight in green punctuation that signals pauses.
- Write a note about the general effect of the sentence(s).

He and his wife fed them in the lamplit kitchen, their faces

glowing, as they offered food and more food, urging them to eat,

saying there was plenty for everybody, have more milk,

have more bread, have more meat.

abundance, coming in a rush

cold and the darkness entered into them. They fell silent, **sullen**, suspicious. She waited for the moment when some one of them would turn mutinous. It did not happen that night.

Two nights later she was aware that the feet behind her were moving slower and slower. She heard the irritability in their voices, knew that soon someone would refuse to go on.

190 She started talking about William Still and the Philadelphia Vigilance Committee.[6] No one commented. No one asked any questions. She told them the story of William and Ellen Craft and how they escaped from Georgia. Ellen was so fair that she looked as though she were white, and so she dressed up in a man's clothing and she looked like a wealthy young planter. Her husband, William, who was dark, played the role of her slave. Thus they traveled from Macon, Georgia, to Philadelphia, riding on the trains, staying at the finest hotels. Ellen pretended to be very ill—her right arm was in a sling, and her right hand was bandaged, because she was 200 supposed to have rheumatism. Thus she avoided having to sign the register at the hotels for she could not read or write. They finally arrived safely in Philadelphia, and then went on to Boston.

No one said anything. Not one of them seemed to have heard her.

She told them about Frederick Douglass, the most famous of the escaped slaves, of his **eloquence**, of his magnificent appearance. Then she told them of her own first vain effort at running away, **evoking** the memory of that miserable life she 210 had led as a child, reliving it for a moment in the telling.

But they had been tired too long, hungry too long, afraid too long, footsore too long. One of them suddenly cried out in despair, "Let me go back. It is better to be a slave than to suffer like this in order to be free."

She carried a gun with her on these trips. She had never used it—except as a threat. Now as she aimed it, she experienced a feeling of guilt, remembering that time, years ago, when she had prayed for the death of Edward Brodas, the Master, and then not too long afterward had heard that great 220 wailing cry that came from the throats of the field hands, and knew from the sound that the Master was dead.

---

[6] **Philadelphia Vigilance Committee:** fundraising organization that helped people who escaped enslavement.

---

sullen
(sŭl´ən) *adj.* Sullen people give the silent resentment.

eloquence
(ĕl´ə-kwəns) *n.* Eloquence is the ability to speak powerfully and persuasively.

evoke
(ĭ-vōk´) *v.* When you *evoke* something, you summon it.

CLOSE READ

Analyze Text: Biography (LINES 216–222)

COMMON CORE RI 1, RI 3

Tell students that, in an earlier chapter of the biography, readers learn that Tubman had prayed for the death of her master because she feared that he was going to sell her South on a chain gang. Explain that, when her master died, she felt responsible.

Ⓙ CITE TEXT EVIDENCE Ask students to find the information in lines 216–222 that connects to earlier events. *(As Tubman aims a gun to threaten a follower, she experiences "a feeling of guilt, remembering that time, years ago, when she had prayed for the death of Edward Brodas, the Master.")* What does this comparison to an earlier event suggest about Tubman? *(Possible answer: She has a respect for life, even for the lives of those who enslaved her.)*

CRITICAL VOCABULARY

sullen: Harriet Tubman sees sullen looks on the people's faces.

ASK STUDENTS to explain why sullen feelings are a problem for Harriet Tubman. *(She fears the people might give up or even turn against her.)*

eloquence: The author is describing Tubman's stories about the abolitionist Frederick Douglass.

ASK STUDENTS why eloquence might make a person famous. *(When someone speaks with eloquence, he or she can persuade and inspire others.)*

evoke: Harriet Tubman shares a painful memory of her miserable childhood.

ASK STUDENTS why telling a story might evoke a memory. *(Talking about her past brings the pain back to mind.)*

Analyze Text: Biography (LINES 225–239)

COMMON CORE · RI 1, RI 3

Point out that the author describes Tubman's action toward a despairing fugitive to reveal another aspect of her character.

 CITE TEXT EVIDENCE Have students cite Tubman's words and other details in lines 225–239 to tell whether they think she would have killed the "despairing slave." *(Tubman repeats, "Go on with us or die" and "We got to go free or die." She would have killed him in order to protect the larger group and all the helpers on the Underground Railroad, who would be "ruined, fined, imprisoned.")* How does this situation connect, or fit in with, what readers have already learned about Tubman? *(Possible answer: It supports the determination she has shown; it adds a new dimension by showing that she will do whatever it takes to get the runaways to freedom.)*

Analyze Structure (LINES 240–243)

COMMON CORE · RI 1, RI 4, RI 5

Tell students that the author's careful word choice has an emotional impact.

L **CITE TEXT EVIDENCE** Direct students to reread lines 240–243 to note words that describe the Middle Passage. *(The phrases "long agony" and "black horror")* What is the impact of the word choices in this paragraph? *(They suggest the terrible misery experienced by the people's forebears.)* How does the first sentence develop the text's key idea: that the escape from slavery was terrifying? *(The comparison to the Middle Passage brings the idea full circle; their people's slavery began in terror and agony, and their escape from it will be difficult as well.)*

A stop on the Underground Railroad

One of the runaways said, again, "Let me go back. Let me go back," and stood still, and then turned around and said, over his shoulder, "I am going back."

She lifted the gun, aimed it at the despairing slave. She said, "Go on with us or die." The husky low-pitched voice was grim.

He hesitated for a moment and then he joined the others. They started walking again. She tried to explain to them why 230 none of them could go back to the plantation. If a runaway returned, he would turn traitor, the master and the overseer would force him to turn traitor. The returned slave would disclose the stopping places, the hiding places, the cornstacks they had used with the full knowledge of the owner of the farm, the name of the German farmer who had fed them and sheltered them. These people who had risked their own security to help runaways would be ruined, fined, imprisoned.

She said, "We got to go free or die. And freedom's not bought with dust."

240 This time she told them about the long agony of the Middle Passage[7] on the old slave ships, about the black horror of the holds, about the chains and the whips. They too knew these stories. But she wanted to remind them of the long hard

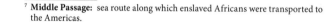

[7] **Middle Passage:** sea route along which enslaved Africans were transported to the Americas.

way they had come, about the long hard way they had yet to go. She told them about Thomas Sims, the boy picked up on the streets of Boston and sent back to Georgia. She said when they got him back to Savannah, got him in prison there, they whipped him until a doctor who was standing by watching said, "You will kill him if you strike him again!" His master
250 said, "Let him die!"

Thus she forced them to go on. Sometimes she thought she had become nothing but a voice speaking in the darkness, **cajoling**, urging, threatening. Sometimes she told them things to make them laugh, sometimes she sang to them, and heard the eleven voices behind her blending softly with hers, and then she knew that for the moment all was well with them.

She gave the impression of being a short, muscular, indomitable woman who could never be defeated. Yet at any moment she was liable to be seized by one of those curious fits
260 of sleep, which might last for a few minutes or for hours.

Even on this trip, she suddenly fell asleep in the woods. The runaways, ragged, dirty, hungry, cold, did not steal the gun as they might have, and set off by themselves, or turn back. They sat on the ground near her and waited patiently until she awakened. They had come to trust her implicitly, totally. They, too, had come to believe her repeated statement, "We got to go free or die." She was leading them into freedom, and so they waited until she was ready to go on.

Finally, they reached Thomas Garrett's house in
270 Wilmington, Delaware. Just as Harriet had promised, Garrett gave them all new shoes, and provided carriages to take them on to the next stop.

By slow stages they reached Philadelphia, where William Still hastily recorded their names, and the plantations whence they had come, and something of the life they had led in slavery. Then he carefully hid what he had written, for fear it might be discovered. In 1872 he published this record in book form and called it *The Underground Railroad*. In the foreword to his book he said: "While I knew the danger of keeping
280 strict records, and while I did not then dream that in my day slavery would be blotted out, or that the time would come when I could publish these records, it used to afford me great satisfaction to take them down, fresh from the lips of fugitives on the way to freedom, and to preserve them as they had given them."

cajole
(kə-jōl´) *v.* When you *cajole*, you coax or urge gently.

CLOSE READ

Analyze Structure
(LINES 261–268)

Point out that, after the incident in which Tubman threatens to shoot the runaway, the group seems to have changed its view of her.

(M) **CITE TEXT EVIDENCE** Have students reread lines 261–268 to identify a sentence that expresses the fugitives' changed attitude. *("They had come to trust her implicitly, totally.")* Ask students to suggest the impact of the author's use of the synonyms *implicitly* and *totally*. *(to emphasize complete trust)*

Analyze Text: Biography (LINES 273–285)

Tell students that a biographer's research includes **primary sources,** which are documents and other materials produced by people who witnessed or took part in historical events.

(N) **ASK STUDENTS** to reread lines 273–285 to explain what is suggested about the author's research. *(The author read William Still's record of fugitive slaves, which he published in 1872 with the title* The Underground Railroad. *The author has identified Still as a member of the Philadelphia Vigilance Committee in lines 189–190.)*

CRITICAL VOCABULARY

cajole: The author uses three verbs—*cajoles, urges, threatens*—to show what Harriet Tubman does to keep her followers from giving up.

ASK STUDENTS for ideas about why the author puts *cajole* first in the list. *(Cajoling is the mildest form of urging.* Cajoles *is followed by the stronger verb,* urges, *and then the strongest,* threatens.*)*

Analyze Text: Biography (LINES 300–316)

COMMON CORE RI 1, RI 3

Tell students that biographers draw conclusions based on their research.

 CITE TEXT EVIDENCE Have students reread lines 300–316 and note the words that show the author's reasoning. *("Here they almost certainly stayed with Frederick Douglass" shows that she is using details in Douglass's autobiography to reason that the eleven fugitives who stayed with Douglass were in fact the people Tubman was leading north.)*

William Still, who was familiar with all the station stops on the Underground Railroad, supplied Harriet with money and sent her and her eleven fugitives on to Burlington, New Jersey.

290   Harriet felt safer now, though there were danger spots ahead. But the biggest part of her job was over. As they went farther and farther north, it grew colder; she was aware of the wind on the Jersey ferry and aware of the cold damp in New York. From New York they went on to Syracuse, where the temperature was even lower.

   In Syracuse she met the Reverend J. W. Loguen, known as "Jarm" Loguen. This was the beginning of a lifelong friendship. Both Harriet and Jarm Loguen were to become friends and supporters of Old John Brown.[8]

300   From Syracuse they went north again, into a colder, snowier city—Rochester. Here they almost certainly stayed with Frederick Douglass, for he wrote in his autobiography:

> On one occasion I had eleven
> fugitives at the same time under my
> roof, and it was necessary for them to
> remain with me until I could collect
> sufficient money to get them to Canada.
> It was the largest number I ever had at
> any one time, and I had some difficulty
310 > in providing so many with food and
> shelter, but, as may well be imagined,
> they were not very fastidious in either
> direction, and were well content with
> very plain food, and a strip of carpet
> on the floor for a bed, or a place on the
> straw in the barnloft.

   Late in December, 1851, Harriet arrived in St. Catharines, Canada West (now Ontario), with the eleven fugitives. It had taken almost a month to complete this journey; most of the
320 time had been spent getting out of Maryland.

---

[8] **Old John Brown:** anti-slavery leader who was executed.

St. Catharine's, Prince Edward Island, Canada

That first winter in St. Catharines was a terrible one. Canada was a strange frozen land, snow everywhere, ice everywhere, and a bone-biting cold the like of which none of them had ever experienced before. Harriet rented a small frame house in the town and set to work to make a home. The fugitives boarded with her. They worked in the forests, felling trees, and so did she. Sometimes she took other jobs, cooking or cleaning house for people in the town. She cheered on these newly arrived fugitives, working herself, finding work for them, finding food for them, praying for them, sometimes begging for them.

330

Often she found herself thinking of the beauty of Maryland, the mellowness of the soil, the richness of the plant life there. The climate itself made for an ease of living that could never be duplicated in this bleak, barren countryside.

In spite of the severe cold, the hard work, she came to love St. Catharines, and the other towns and cities in Canada where black men lived. She discovered that freedom meant more than the right to change jobs at will, more than the right to keep the money that one earned. It was the right to vote and to sit on juries. It was the right to be elected to office. In Canada there were black men who were county officials and members of school boards. St. Catharines had a

340

Harriet Tubman: Conductor on the Underground Railroad **161**

CLOSE READ

Analyze Text: Biography (LINES 321–331)

COMMON CORE **RI 3**

Explain that readers use what the biographer tells and shows, along with what they can figure out, to answer the question, "What is this person like?"

P ASK STUDENTS what they can tell about Tubman from the information provided in lines 321–331. *(Possible answers: She was hardworking, generous, strong, encouraging, and independent.)*

Analyze Structure

COMMON CORE **RI 1, RI 4, RI 5**

(LINES 332–335)

Point out that the author is contrasting Tubman's destination with her starting point. As needed, refer them to the description of Canada in lines 322–324.

Q CITE TEXT EVIDENCE Have students identify details that develop the contrasts between Canada and Maryland. Discuss the impact of the author's word choices, parallelism, and repetition. *("Canada was a strange frozen land, snow everywhere, ice everywhere, and a bone-biting cold the like of which none of them had ever experienced before." "Often she found herself thinking of the beauty of Maryland, the mellowness of the soil, the richness of the plant life there. The climate itself made for an ease of living that could never be duplicated in this bleak, barren countryside." The overall impact is to create a series of stark contrasts, which reinforces the idea that Tubman is able to adapt to her environment.)*

Strategies for Annotation ✐ ▱ *Annotate it!*

Analyze Text: Biography

COMMON CORE **RI 3**

Share these strategies for guided or independent analysis:

- Highlight direct statements of the subject's thoughts, feelings, and qualities.
- Underline actions that provide clues about the subject's qualities.
- Note your own thoughts about the subject.

She cheered on these newly arrived fugitives, working herself, finding work for them, finding food for them, praying for them, sometimes begging for them.

hardworking, inspirational, heroic, religious, free

For more context and historical background, students can view the video "America The Story of Us: Harriet Rubman and the Underground Railroad" in their eBooks.

Analyze Structure

COMMON CORE **RI 4, RI 5**

(LINES 352–357)

Tell students that an author's word choices impact both the meaning and tone, or feeling, in a text. Elicit that in lines 352–357, the author is highlighting a comparison.

R **ASK STUDENTS** to reread lines 352–357. Prompt students to identify the comparison the author is making and explain how it develops the concept of freedom. *(The author is contrasting the warmth of summer—and Maryland—with the severe cold of Canada to emphasize the price the escaping slaves paid for their freedom.)* How do word choices such as "bone-biting cold" impact the tone of the paragraph? *(Word choices that describe the extreme cold create a harsh feeling that suggests what life will be like for the newly freed slaves.)*

COLLABORATIVE DISCUSSION Have students work in pairs to share ideas from the text and their own thinking about the character of Harriet Tubman. Suggest that they start with a list of adjectives that seem to describe her.

ASK STUDENTS to share any questions they generated in the course of reading and discussing the selection.

---

large colony of ex-slaves, and they owned their own homes, kept them neat and clean and in good repair. They lived in whatever part of town they chose and sent their children to the schools.

When spring came she decided that she would make this small Canadian city her home—as much as any place could be
350 said to be home to a woman who traveled from Canada to the Eastern Shore of Maryland as often as she did.

R In the spring of 1852, she went back to Cape May, New Jersey. She spent the summer there, cooking in a hotel. That fall she returned, as usual, to Dorchester County, and brought out nine more slaves, conducting them all the way to St. Catharines, in Canada West, to the bone-biting cold, the snow-covered forests—and freedom.

She continued to live in this fashion, spending the winter in Canada, and the spring and summer working in Cape May,
360 New Jersey, or in Philadelphia. She made two trips a year into slave territory, one in the fall and another in the spring. She now had a definite crystallized purpose, and in carrying it out, her life fell into a pattern which remained unchanged for the next six years.

COLLABORATIVE DISCUSSION What did you find most interesting about Harriet Tubman? With a partner, discuss the characteristics that surprised or impressed you. Cite specific evidence from the text to support your ideas.

TO CHALLENGE STUDENTS . . .

Analyze Allusions Remind students that an **allusion** is a reference to a famous person, place, event, or work of literature. Point out that Harriet Tubman was known as "Moses" and that she used a spiritual to let would-be runaways know that she was in their area.

ASK STUDENTS to determine what these allusions suggest about Tubman and about the runaways. Invite them to discuss the impact of these allusions on their view of Tubman.

Analyze Text: Biography

 COMMON CORE RI 3, RI 5

A good way to gain an understanding of a historical figure is to read his or her **biography,** a true account of a person's life told by someone other than the subject, usually in the third-person point of view. Biographers thoroughly research the people they write about. They then use the research to give readers access to their subjects through one or more methods of **characterization,** techniques that reveal a person's qualities and personality.

To analyze the biography you have just read, examine how the author characterizes the subject.

- Look at what the author says about Harriet Tubman's hopes, thoughts, and worries.
- Consider what Harriet Tubman says and does. What is her motivation, or reason, for her words and actions?
- Think about how others behave toward Harriet Tubman.

Analyze Structure

 COMMON CORE RI 4, RI 5

Author's craft refers to the methods authors use to make their writing come alive. Notice how Ann Petry combines the techniques below to develop and refine ideas about Harriet Tubman in the paragraphs cited in these examples. Review the text to find an additional example of each technique.

Technique	Definition	Examples
word choice	the author's use of specific words to impact the reader	"The man who stood in the doorway looked at her coldly, looked with an <u>unconcealed astonishment and fear</u> . . ."
sentence variety and punctuation	variations in sentence length and use of dashes for dramatic effect	"She had never used it—except as a threat."
parallelism	similar grammatical constructions used to express ideas that are related or equal in importance	"When she knocked on the door of a farmhouse, a place where she and her parties of runaways had <u>always been welcome, always been given shelter</u>. . ."
syntax	the arrangement of words and phrases in sentences used to convey accurate meaning and tone	"Sometimes the masters thought they heard the cry of a hoot owl, repeated, and would remember having thought the intervals between the low moaning cry were wrong."

TEACH

CLOSE READ

Analyze Text: Biography COMMON CORE RI 3

Discuss what makes a biography different from other nonfiction works and from fiction.

Point out that, just as fiction writers use characterization techniques, biographers also try to show their subject's qualities and motivations. For each bulleted characterization technique, ask students to find an example in the text, explaining what they learn about Tubman from each one.

Analyze Structure COMMON CORE RI 4, RI 5

Discuss what it means to make "writing come alive." Guide students to understand that this biography is an example of literary nonfiction, in which the author has carefully chosen words, constructed sentences, and structured paragraphs and details so that meaning, sound, and feeling are conveyed.

After reviewing the four examples in the chart, have students identify additional examples. Discuss the effects on the reader.

Strategies for Annotation 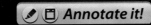 Annotate it!

Analyze Structure COMMON CORE RI 4, RI 5

Share these strategies for guided or independent analysis:

- Select a segment to analyze.
- Highlight in yellow striking word choices.
- Highlight in green repetition or parallelism.
- Underline a sentence with interesting or unusual syntax.
- On a note, comment on the effect of the segment on you, the reader.

Sometimes she thought she had become nothing but a voice speaking in the darkness, cajoling, urging, threatening. Sometimes she told them things to make them laugh, sometimes she sang to them, and heard the eleven voices behind her blending softly with hers, and then she knew that for the moment all was well with them.

Analyzing the Text RI 1, RI 3, RI 4, RI 5

Possible answers:

1. The description gives the impression that Moses is more clever and powerful than any of the plantation owners. No one can figure out who or where he is: "the stories about him were fantastic, unbelievable . . . Yet they watched for him."

2. The phrase suggests that the hunters also pursued two-footed game, hunting runaway slaves as if they were animals. The phrase suggests that slaves were not considered human beings.

3. The parallelism in "ear to mouth, mouth to ear" lets readers hear and visualize how the messages are passed from slave to slave.

4. Although Tubman is worried and afraid herself, she keeps up a brave front, indicating that she is a strong, selfless, and determined person.

5. Parallelism: The list of adjectives after runaways—ragged, dirty, hungry, cold—emphasizes their desperate condition.
Word Choice: "short, muscular, indomitable" helps readers picture Tubman's physical appearance and inner strength.
Syntax: The word order in the sentence that begins with "The runaways" points out the contrast between the actions they did not take and their decision to remain with Tubman.

6. What Harriet Tubman thinks: She must instill courage in her followers; "more and more slaves should know what freedom is like"; she will be hanged if caught.
What Harriet Tubman does: Plans an escape route and leads fugitives from Maryland to Canada.
What Harriet Tubman says: tells stories about successful escapes; describes help on the Underground Railroad; gives warnings about the Fugitive Slave Law; says, "We got to go free or die."
What others think and say about her: Masters think the existence of "Moses" is too fantastic to believe. Her followers come to trust her implicitly.
Description: Harriet Tubman was a determined, selfless, capable person whose work with the Underground Railroad was inspiring and heroic.

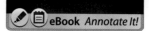

Analyzing the Text  RI 1, RI 3, RI 4, RI 5, SL 1a, SL 4, W 7, W 9b

Cite Text Evidence Support your responses with evidence from the text.

1. **Infer** Reread lines 1–16. What does the description suggest about the qualities of the person called Moses?

2. **Interpret** Reread lines 28–32. What is the effect of the author's use of the phrase "in pursuit of four-footed game"?

3. **Interpret** Identify the parallelism in lines 47–49. How does this technique contribute to the effectiveness of these lines?

4. **Infer** In lines 59–70, the author describes the difficulty of the task facing Harriet Tubman. What is Tubman's response? Explain what her words and actions reveal about her.

5. **Analyze** Reread lines 258–265. Find and explain three examples of the techniques the author uses to make the events come alive in this paragraph.

6. **Draw Conclusions** Based on the characterization of Harriet Tubman in this biography, how would you describe her? Fill out a chart like the one shown with examples from the selection, and then write a one-sentence description of this famous woman.

What Harriet Tubman thinks	
What Harriet Tubman does	
What Harriet Tubman says	
What others think and say about her	

PERFORMANCE TASK

Speaking Activity: Speech Imagine that Harriet Tubman will be honored at a "Hall of Fame" for those who fought slavery. Prepare and give a speech explaining why she is a heroic figure. Consult sources in addition to the selection. Consider the following:

- What kind of person was Harriet Tubman?

- What was Tubman's motivation for bringing enslaved people to freedom?

- What examples demonstrate Tubman's heroism?

- How do historians judge Tubman's impact on the quest for freedom prior to the Civil War?

Assign this performance task.

PERFORMANCE TASK SL 1a, SL 4, W 7, W 9b

Speaking Activity: Speech Students' speeches should include

- a summary of Harriet Tubman's character

- an analysis of her motivation for helping enslaved people

- examples from the selection that illustrate Tubman's heroism

- additional examples of her heroism gleaned from research

- an assessment of Tubman's impact on American history

Critical Vocabulary

COMMON CORE L 5b

disheveled	instill	dispel	linger
sullen	eloquence	evoke	cajole

Practice and Apply Use what you know about the Vocabulary words to answer the following questions.

1. Would you **linger** at a party if you were **disheveled**? Why or why not?

2. Could someone **instill eloquence** in you? Why or why not?

3. What might someone do to **evoke** a **sullen** response?

4. Would you **cajole** a friend to **dispel** a bad mood? Why or why not?

Vocabulary Strategy: Use Word Relationships

You can use relationships among words to help you figure out the meaning of an unfamiliar word. Look at this sentence from *Harriet Tubman*:

> "Sometimes she thought she had become nothing but a voice speaking in the darkness, <u>cajoling, urging, threatening</u>."

The words "cajoling, urging, threatening" are synonyms, or words that have similar meanings.

> Look at this sentence from *Harriet Tubman*:
>
> "She had promised her passengers food and . . . <u>warmth</u>, and instead of that, there would be hunger and <u>cold</u> . . ."

The phrase "instead of" provides a clue that the words *warmth* and *cold* are **antonyms,** or words that have opposite meanings. If you know the meaning of one word in a synonym or antonym pair, you can often guess the meaning of the other.

Practice and Apply For each sentence, write an S if the underlined word is a synonym and an A if it is an antonym. Identify the other word or words in the synonym or antonym pair. Then write a definition of the underlined word.

1. Instead of becoming discouraged, she grew more <u>determined</u>.

2. The effect of the Fugitive Slave Law was <u>appalling</u>, horrifying, and dismaying.

3. Her <u>incentive</u> for leading her first group north was the same as her reason for leading the tenth group: she wanted others to know freedom.

Critical Vocabulary

COMMON CORE L 5b

Possible answers:

1. *You might not want to stay at a party if you were the only guest not dressed nicely.*

2. *It might be possible to teach someone to speak in an eloquent way, but it would likely take a long time.*

3. *Someone might say or do something to hurt a person's feelings to evoke a sullen response.*

4. *Yes; you could try to coax a friend out of a bad mood with gentle suggestions or humor.*

Vocabulary Strategy: Use Word Relationships

1. *A,* discouraged; *meaning for* determined: *"set on a goal"*

2. *S,* horrifying, dismaying; *meaning for* appalling: *"causing disgust"*

3. *S,* reason; *meaning for* incentive: *"something that motivates"*

Vocabulary Strategy: Use Word Relationships

COMMON CORE L 5b

Tell students that few synonyms have identical meanings; synonyms have meaning variations related to usage and connotation. Have students use their eBook annotation tools to identify synonyms in the sentences shown.

- Highlight the synonyms.
- Use a print or digital dictionary to check meanings.
- On a note, tell how the synonym meanings are similar, and how they differ.

She managed to dispel their fear of pursuit, so that they would not become hysterical, panic-stricken. Then sh[...] both mean "unable to think clearly," "hysterical" sounds more desperate than "panic-stricken"

PRACTICE & APPLY

Language Conventions: Conditional Mood

COMMON CORE L 1c, L 3a

Use the example sentences to point out that the effect named in the independent clause has not actually occurred—it *would* occur, *might* have occurred, or *could* have occurred.

Possible answers:

1. *If Max had done more research, he would have written a good report.*

2. *If Kim had studied harder, she would have done better on the test.*

3. *Maria could have succeeded if she had decided to study rather than play computer games.*

4. *If you had done thorough research on the topic, you would have earned a good grade.*

5. *If the weather had been good, gym class would have been held outside.*

 Assess It!

Online Selection Test
- Download an editable ExamView bank.
- Assign and manage this test online.

Language Conventions: Conditional Mood

COMMON CORE L 1c, L 3c

The **mood** of a verb indicates the tone or attitude with which a statement is made. Writers use the **conditional mood** when they want to make a statement about what might happen if something else happens. The conditional mood often includes the words *might, could, would,* or *if.* Look at this example from *Harriet Tubman*. Notice that the sentence describes what might happen ("he would turn traitor") if something else happens ("If a runaway slave returned").

If a runaway slave returned, he **would** turn traitor, the master and the overseer **would** force him to turn traitor.

If this happens it might cause . . .   . . . this to happen

Study these examples.

If he did not forge ahead, he **would** not reach his goal.

He **might** have succeeded **if** he had tried harder.

She **could** have won the game **if** she had practiced.

Practice and Apply Read the sentences. Rewrite them so that they are in the conditional mood.

1. Max did not write a good report because he had not done enough research.

2. Kim did not study hard and did not do well on the test.

3. Maria wanted to succeed but decided to play computer games rather than to study.

4. To earn a good grade you have to do thorough research on the topic.

5. The weather has to be good in order for gym class to be held outside.

INTERACTIVE WHITEBOARD LESSON
Cite Evidence

COMMON CORE

RI 1

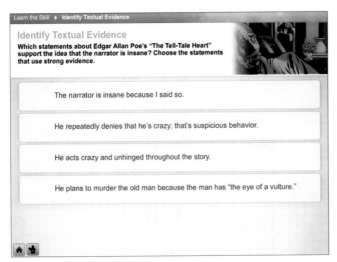

Learn the Skill ▶ Identify Textual Evidence

Identify Textual Evidence

Which statements about Edgar Allan Poe's "The Tell-Tale Heart" support the idea that the narrator is insane? Choose the statements that use strong evidence.

> The narrator is insane because I said so.

> He repeatedly denies that he's crazy; that's suspicious behavior.

> He acts crazy and unhinged throughout the story.

> He plans to murder the old man because the man has "the eye of a vulture."

TEACH

Explain that a biography, or any other informational text, may be read and reread for different purposes. For example, readers may give ideas and opinions about the text, use it for research, draw conclusions based on it, and summarize the most important ideas. Point out that these activities all require finding and using evidence from the text. Review that evidence is information in the text, such as facts and figures, details, quotations, and examples.

PRACTICE AND APPLY

As a group, review the selection about Harriet Tubman to cite evidence that supports statements such as these:

- Being a conductor on the Underground Railroad required special qualities.
- Religious faith was important to Harriet Tubman.
- Harriet Tubman relied on others to help her do her work.
- Leading a group of eleven fugitives posed special challenges.

Then, have students reread lines 336–351. Ask partners to cite evidence that supports Harriet Tubman's reasons for making St. Catharine's her home.

Analyze Text: Biography

COMMON CORE

RI 3, RI 5

RETEACH

Review that a **biography** is a true story about a person's life written by someone other than the subject. With students, list a few names of famous people. Discuss what a reader would expect to learn in a biography about each one. Prompt students to identify chronological order and cause/effect as common text structures in a biography.

Guide students to understand how a biographer uses **characterization** to help readers learn about the subject by

- telling about the subject's thoughts and feelings
- quoting statements the subject has made
- connecting to what others have said about the subject

Discuss what can be learned from each of these examples:

- Harriet Beecher Stowe, author of *Uncle Tom's Cabin,* wanted to show the evils of slavery.
- Abraham Lincoln said, "As I would not be a slave, so I would not be a master."
- Some said that John Brown was a fanatical murderer; others said he was the noblest, bravest abolitionist of them all.

LEVEL UP TUTORIALS Assign the following *Level Up* tutorial: **Biographies and Autobiographies**

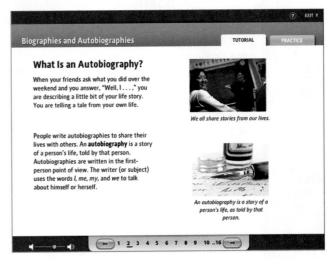

Biographies and Autobiographies

TUTORIAL   PRACTICE

What Is an Autobiography?

When your friends ask what you did over the weekend and you answer, "Well, I . . . ," you are describing a little bit of your life story. You are telling a tale from your own life.

We all share stories from our lives.

People write autobiographies to share their lives with others. **An autobiography** is a story of a person's life, told by that person. Autobiographies are written in the first-person point of view. The writer (or subject) uses the words *I, me, my,* and *we* to talk about himself or herself.

An autobiography is a story of a person's life, as told by that person.

1 2 3 4 5 6 7 8 9 10 ..16

CLOSE READING APPLICATION

Help students find a biography of a historical figure. Have them show examples of quotations from the subject, the biographer's descriptions of the subject's thoughts and feelings, and information about the viewpoints of others.

ANCHOR TEXT The Drummer Boy of Shiloh

Historical Fiction by Ray Bradbury

Why This Text?

Historical fiction adds a human perspective to the facts, dates, and statistics that often come with the study of the past. Reading stories such as "The Drummer Boy of Shiloh" allows students to gain insight into key events in their country's history in a way that textbooks cannot provide.

▶ **View It!**

Professional Development Podcast:
Text-Dependent Analysis

For practice and application:

A Mystery of Heroism

Close Reader selection
"A Mystery of Heroism,"
Short Story by Stephen Crane

Key Learning Objective: Student will identify and analyze the key elements of historical fiction and examine how authors create mood in a story.

COMMON CORE Common Core Standards

RL 1 Cite textual evidence.
RL 2 Determine a theme; summarize.
RL 3 Analyze dialogue or incidents.
RL 4 Determine the meaning of words and phrases.
SL 1 Engage in collaborative discussions on grade 8 topics.
SL 2 Analyze the purpose of information in diverse media.
SL 4 Present claims and findings with relevant evidence.
L 1c Form and use verbs in the indicative mood.
L 4a Use context as a clue to the meaning of a word or phrase.
L 5a Interpret figures of speech.
L 6 Acquire and use grade-appropriate general academic vocabulary.
W 7 Conduct short research projects.
W 8 Gather information from print and digital sources.

▲ Text Complexity Rubric

Quantitative Measures	**The Drummer Boy of Shiloh** Lexile: 990L
Qualitative Measures	Levels of Meaning/Purpose  multiple levels of meaning (multiple themes)
	Structure somewhat complex story concepts
	Language Conventionality and Clarity some figurative language
	Knowledge Demands some cultural and literary knowledge useful
Reader/Task Considerations	Teacher determined Vary by individual reader and type of text

CLOSE READ

Background Have students read the background and information about the author. As needed, remind them that the Civil War lasted from 1861 to 1865 and led to the abolition of slavery in the United States. Tell students that at the time, drummers, young boys from about 7 to 12 years old, marched with the armed soldiers into battle. Point out the irony of the fact that the Hebrew word *shiloh* means "place of peace."

SETTING A PURPOSE Direct students to use the Setting a Purpose question to focus their reading. Tell students to generate their own questions as they read.

Analyze Stories:
Historical Fiction (LINES 1–13)

COMMON CORE **RL 1, RL 2**

Tell students that the **setting,** or the time and place, is especially important to understanding this story. Review the setting information provided in the Background section of the student book.

Ⓐ CITE TEXT EVIDENCE Tell students to reread lines 1–13 and identify details that describe the setting. *(The time is "in the April night." The place is "in the peach field near the Owl Creek not far from the church at Shiloh.")* How might the details of the setting contribute to the theme? *(They provide a stark contrast to what will become a battlefield.)*

 HISTORY VIDEO

Background *Though **Ray Bradbury** (1920–2012) is best known as a science fiction writer, he's also written plays, mysteries, fantasies, realistic stories, and novels. In this story, Bradbury tells about a drummer boy on the night before the Battle of Shiloh in the Civil War. This two-day battle began on April 6, 1862, near the southwestern Tennessee church from which the bloody clash takes its name. More than 23,000 soldiers died during those two days. At that time, it was the bloodiest battle in American history.*

The
Drummer Boy
of Shiloh

Historical Fiction by Ray Bradbury

SETTING A PURPOSE As you read, pay attention to the details the author provides about the scene of the battle and about the men who were preparing to fight. What do the details suggest about the realities of war?

In the April night, more than once, blossoms fell from the orchard trees and lit with rustling taps on the drumskin. At midnight a peach stone left miraculously on a branch through winter, flicked by a bird, fell swift and unseen, struck once, like panic, which jerked the boy upright. In silence he listened to his own heart ruffle away, away, at last gone from his ears and back in his chest again.

After that, he turned the drum on its side, where its great lunar[1] face peered at him whenever he opened his eyes.

10 His face, alert or at rest, was **solemn.** It was indeed a solemn time and a solemn night for a boy just turned fourteen in the peach field near the Owl Creek not far from the church at Shiloh.

solemn
(sŏl´əm) *adj.* If an event is *solemn,* it is deeply serious.

---
[1] **lunar** (lōō´nər): of or relating to the moon.

(tr) ©Jean-Claude Amiel/Kipa/CORBIS; (cr) ©Stockbyte/Getty Images

---

Close Read Screencasts ▶ **View It!**

Modeled Discussions

Have students click the *Close Read* icons in their eBooks to access a screencast in which readers discuss and annotate the key passage describing the difference between the armed soldiers and the unarmed drummer boy (lines 42–52).

As a class, view and discuss this video. Then have students work in pairs to do an independent close read of an additional passage—the General's description of the effects on the soldiers of Joby's beating a faster rhythm (lines 158–164).

Determine Meanings of Words and Phrases

(LINES 24–39)

Explain to students that authors use descriptions and language that appeals to the senses to create a **mood,** the feeling or atmosphere in a story. Explain that the mood, whether it is one of humor, sadness, or tension, is intended to evoke an emotional response from readers.

B CITE TEXT EVIDENCE Have students reread lines 24–39 and identify language that describes the mood in the camp during the night before the battle. *(Possible answer: Word choices such as "whispering to itself in the dark," "I'll live through it," "careless bones harvested by night," and "strewn steel bones" help create the mood of muffled tension or foreboding.)*

Draw Conclusion

(LINES 40–42)

Explain that when readers **draw conclusions,** they use story details and their own knowledge and experiences to figure out things that an author has not explicitly stated about characters and events in a story.

C ASK STUDENTS to use what they have read so far and lines 40–42 to draw a conclusion about how the drummer boy feels at this point. *(Possible answer: Because he is awake and very alert to the sounds around him and is thinking about not having a rifle for protection, students should conclude that he is scared.)*

CRITICAL VOCABULARY

askew: The author is describing the sleeping soldiers in the camp.

ASK STUDENTS to explain why the resting soldiers might lie askew. *(They might be curled up in strange positions to try to get comfortable on the ground.)*

strew: The author is explaining the appearance of the other army.

ASK STUDENTS what the phrase "strewn helter-skelter" suggests about the other army. *(They are sleeping anywhere they can, in an unorganized way.)*

"... thirty-one, thirty-two, thirty-three ..."
Unable to see, he stopped counting.

Beyond the thirty-three familiar shadows, forty thousand men, exhausted by nervous expectation, unable to sleep for romantic dreams of battles yet unfought, lay crazily **askew** in their uniforms. A mile yet farther on, another army was 20 **strewn** helter-skelter, turning slow, basting themselves with the thought of what they would do when the time came: a leap, a yell, a blind plunge their strategy, raw youth their protection and benediction.[2]

B Now and again the boy heard a vast wind come up, that gently stirred the air. But he knew what it was, the army here, the army there, whispering to itself in the dark. Some men talking to others, others murmuring to themselves, and all so quiet it was like a natural element arisen from south or north with the motion of the earth toward dawn.

30 What the men whispered the boy could only guess, and he guessed that it was: Me, I'm the one, I'm the one of all the rest won't die. I'll live through it. I'll go home. The band will play. And I'll be there to hear it.

Yes, thought the boy, that's all very well for them, they can give as good as they get!

For with the careless bones of the young men harvested by night and bindled[3] around campfires were the similarly strewn steel bones of their rifles, with bayonets fixed like eternal lightning lost in the orchard grass.

C 40 Me, thought the boy, I got only a drum, two sticks to beat it, and no shield.

There wasn't a man-boy on this ground tonight did not have a shield he cast, riveted or carved himself on his way to his first attack, compounded of remote but nonetheless firm and fiery family devotion, flag-blown patriotism and cocksure immortality strengthened by the touchstone of very real gunpowder, ramrod, minnieball and flint.[4] But without these last the boy felt his family move yet farther off away in the dark, as if one of those great prairie-burning trains had 50 chanted them away never to return, leaving him with this drum which was worse than a toy in the game to be played tomorrow or some day much too soon.

---

[2] **benediction** (bĕn´ĭ-dĭk´shən): a blessing.
[3] **bindled:** fastened or wrapped by encircling, as with a belt.
[4] **ramrod, minnieball, and flint:** items used to fire a rifle.

askew (ə-skyōō´) *adj.* When something is *askew*, it is off center.

strew (strōō) *v.* If you *strew* something, you spread it here and there, or scatter it.

SCAFFOLDING FOR ELL STUDENTS

Spanish Cognates Using a whiteboard, project lines 19–23. Point out that some English words are similar to Spanish words with the same meaning. Ask volunteers from Spanish-speaking backgrounds to mark up lines 19–23.

- Highlight in green English words that are similar to Spanish words.
- Use a note to show the Spanish word with the same meaning.

a leap, a yell, a blind plunge their strategy, raw youth their protection and benediction.

The boy turned on his side. A moth brushed his face, but it was peach blossom. A peach blossom flicked him, but it was a moth. Noting stayed put. Nothing had a name. Nothing was as it once was.

If he lay very still, when the dawn came up and the soldiers put on their bravery with their caps, perhaps they might go away, the war with them, and not notice him lying
60 small here, no more than a toy himself.

"Well, by God, now," said a voice.

The boy shut up his eyes, to hide inside himself, but it was too late. Someone, walking by in the night, stood over him.

"Well," said the voice quietly, "here's a soldier crying *before* the fight. Good. Get it over. Won't be time once it all starts."

And the voice was about to move on when the boy, startled, touched the drum at his elbow. The man above, hearing this, stopped. The boy could feel his eyes, sense him slowly bending near. A hand must have come down out of the
70 night, for there was a little rat-tat as the fingernails brushed and the man's breath fanned his face.

"Why, it's the drummer boy, isn't it?"

The boy nodded, not knowing if his nod was seen. "Sir, is that *you?*" he said.

"I assume it is." The man's knees cracked as he bent still closer.

He smelled as all fathers should smell, of salt sweat, ginger tobacco, horse and boot leather, and the earth he walked upon. He had many eyes. No, not eyes, brass buttons that watched
80 the boy.

He could only be, and was, the General.

"What's your name, boy?" he asked.

"Joby," whispered the boy, starting to sit up.

"All right, Joby, don't stir." A hand pressed his chest gently, and the boy relaxed. "How long you been with us, Joby?"

"Three weeks, sir."

"Run off from home or joined **legitimately**, boy?"
Silence.

"Damn-fool question," said the General. "Do you shave
90 yet, boy? Even more of a damn-fool. There's your cheek, fell right off the tree overhead. And the others here not much older. Raw, raw, damn raw, the lot of you. You ready for tomorrow or the next day, Joby?"

"I think so, sir.

legitimately
(lə-jĭt′ə-mĭt-lē) *adv.*
When you do
something
legitimately, you do it
lawfully.

The Drummer Boy of Shiloh   **169**

APPLYING ACADEMIC VOCABULARY

civil	symbolize

As you discuss the story, incorporate the following Collection 3 academic vocabulary words: *civil* and *symbolize*. Have students explain how a war between different parts of the same country can be considered a "**civil** war." Have students discuss what the figure of the General **symbolizes** to the drummer boy.

CLOSE READ

Analyze Stories: Historical Fiction (LINES 72–81)

 COMMON CORE RL 1, RL 3

Explain that, while some events in historical fiction really happened, the author may also make up some events. Point out that authors rely on research to make made-up events realistic and true to the time period in which they happened.

D CITE TEXT EVIDENCE Have students reread lines 72–81. Which details make Joby think that the man talking to him is the General? (*The man says, "I assume it is" when Joby asks him if he is the General. Also, the way the man smelled and the brass buttons of his uniform help Joby identify him.*) How does their dialogue propel the story's action? (*Their encounter suggests that the General is also anxious about the upcoming battle.*)

Determine Meanings of Words and Phrases

COMMON CORE RL 4

(LINES 82–94)

Explain that the person's words and actions can also impact a story's mood.

E ASK STUDENTS to reread lines 82–94. Draw attention to the General's statement, "There's your cheek, fell right off the tree overhead." Discuss what his words suggest (*Joby is too young to shave; his cheek is like peach fuzz*) and the mood that his words help to create. (*The General takes time to be kind to Joby, but his words suggest a feeling of frustration with his army's inexperience and youth.*)

CRITICAL VOCABULARY

legitimately: The general asks the drummer boy how he came to join the army.

ASK STUDENTS to explain what the boy might have had to do to join the army legitimately. (*The boy would have had his parents' consent to serve as a drummer boy. He would have had to prove how old he was.*)

Draw Conclusions RL 1

(LINES 106–115)

Direct students' attention to the General's description of the young soldiers on both sides in lines 106–115.

F **CITE TEXT EVIDENCE** Ask students to reread lines 106–115 to draw a conclusion about how the General feels about the upcoming battle. *(Possible answer: He is dismayed that the soldiers on both sides are so young and thinks that they should "train for four months" before going into battle. He is probably saddened by his knowledge that many of the young soldiers will die in the battle.)*

Determine Meanings of Words and Phrases   COMMON CORE RL 4

(LINES 125–129)

Explain that authors sometimes use a **symbol,** a thing that stands for something beyond itself, to create mood in a story.

G **ASK STUDENTS** to discuss what the pile of leaves and twigs described in lines 125–129 might symbolize. *(Possible answer: They may symbolize the guidance the General is seeking. Set afire, the pile of leaves could help him see how best to conduct the battle and save as many soldiers as possible.)* Prompt students to suggest how this image impacts the mood of the story. *(It emphasizes the darkness and thus the uncertainty the General feels about the coming battle.)*

WHEN STUDENTS STRUGGLE . . .

To aid understanding of archaic, or old-fashioned, phrases in the text, have students work in pairs to fill out a chart like the one shown. Model using context to explain "turn tail" (line 111). Point out that the General is talking about having the armies leave the battlefield to train for four months. Tell students that this context can help them understand that "turn tail" means "to turn in the opposite direction." Follow a similar process with other expressions in the text.

"You want to cry some more, go on ahead. I did the same last night."

"*You, sir?*"

"God's truth. Thinking of everything ahead. Both sides figuring the other side will just give up, and soon, and the war done in weeks, and us all home. Well, that's not how it's going to be. And maybe that's why I cried."

"Yes, sir," said Joby.

The General must have taken out a cigar now, for the dark was suddenly filled with the Indian smell of tobacco unlit as yet, but chewed as the man thought what next to say.

"It's going to be a crazy time," said the General. "Counting both sides, there's a hundred thousand men, give or take a few thousand out there tonight, not one as can spit a sparrow off a tree, or knows a horse clod from a minnieball. Stand up, bare the breast, ask to be a target, thank them and sit down, that's us, that's them. We should turn tail and train four months, they should do the same. But here we are, taken with spring fever and thinking it blood lust, taking our sulphur with cannons instead of with molasses[5] as it should be, going to be a hero, going to live forever. And I can see all of them over there nodding agreement, save the other way around. It's wrong, boy, it's wrong as a head put on hind side front and a man marching backward through life. It will be a double massacre if one of their itchy generals decides to picnic his lads on our grass. More innocents will get shot out of pure Cherokee enthusiasm than ever got shot before. Owl Creek was full of boys splashing around in the noonday sun just a few hours ago. I fear it will be full of boys again, just floating, at sundown tomorrow, not caring where the tide takes them."

The General stopped and made a little pile of winter leaves and twigs in the darkness, as if he might at any moment strike fire to them to see his way through the coming days when the sun might not show its face because of what was happening here and just beyond. **G**

The boy watched the hand stirring the leaves and opened his lips to say something, but did not say it. The General heard the boy's breath and spoke himself.

---

[5] **taking our sulphur with cannons instead of with molasses:** sulphur was an ingredient in gunpowder that was used to fire cannons; at that time sulphur was also used as a tonic or medical treatment. Molasses is a thick, brown syrup, used to mask the unpleasant taste of medicines.

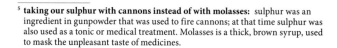

EXPRESSION	POSSIBLE MEANING
"spit a sparrow off a tree" (lines 108–109)	old enough to chew tobacco and spit it accurately enough to scare a bird away
"not caring where the tide takes them" (line 124)	The soldiers are dead and floating in the creek.

"Why am I telling you this? That's what you wanted to ask, eh? Well, when you got a bunch of wild horses on a loose rein somewhere, somehow you got to bring order, rein them in. These lads, fresh out of the milkshed, don't know what I know, and I can't tell them: men actually die, in war. So each is his own army. I got to make *one* army of them. And for that, boy, I need you."

140 "Me!" The boy's lips barely twitched.

 "Now, boy," said the General quietly, "you are the heart of the army. Think of that. You're the heart of the army. Listen, now."

And, lying there, Joby listened.

And the General spoke on.

If he, Joby, beat slow tomorrow, the heart would beat slow in the men. They would lag by the wayside.[6] They would drowse in the fields on their muskets. They would sleep

"You're the heart of the army."

forever, after that, in those same fields, their hearts slowed by 150 a drummer boy and stopped by enemy lead.

But if he beat a sure, steady, ever faster rhythm, then, then their knees would come up in a long line down over that hill, one knee after the other, like a wave on the ocean shore! Had he seen the ocean ever? Seen the waves rolling in like a well-ordered cavalry charge to the sand? Well, that was it, that's what he wanted, that's what was needed! Joby was his right hand and his left. He gave the orders, but Joby set the pace!

So bring the right knee up and the right foot out and the left knee up and the left foot out. One following the other in good 160 time, in brisk time. Move the blood up the body and make the head proud and the spine stiff and the jaw **resolute**. Focus the eye and set the teeth, flare the nostrils and tighten the hands, put steel armor all over the men, for blood moving fast in them does indeed make men feel as if they'd put on steel. He must keep at it, at it! Long and steady, steady and long! Then, even though shot or torn, those wounds got in hot blood—in blood he'd helped

resolute
(rĕz´ə-lo͞ot´) *adj.*
If you are *resolute*, you are firm or determined.

---

[6] **lag by the wayside:** fall behind.

The Drummer Boy of Shiloh **171**

CLOSE READ

Determine Meanings of Words and Phrases
COMMON CORE RL 4

(LINES 141–157)

Point out to students that what a character says and how it is said can affect the mood in a story.

H ASK STUDENTS to reread lines 141–157. Ask students how they think Joby feels when the General tells him that he is "the heart of the army." *(He probably feels excited, suddenly important, and maybe less scared.)* Direct students' attention to the descriptive words "a sure, steady, ever faster rhythm" that the General uses to describe Joby's drumming. What mood does the General's speech to Joby create? *(Possible answer: The mood is one of increasing excitement and inspiration.)*

CRITICAL VOCABULARY

resolute: The General is describing what he wants the soldiers to look like going into battle.

ASK STUDENTS to think about how they look when they are determined to do something. Have volunteers model how a "resolute jaw" might look. *(Students should demonstrate appropriate actions, such as giving a determined look as they jut out their jaws.)*

For more context and historical background, students can view the video "Battle of Shiloh" in their eBooks.

Determine Meanings of Words and Phrases

 COMMON CORE **RL 4**

(LINES 170–176)

Explain to students that the emotions that a symbol evokes in the reader affect the reader's sense of the story's mood.

ⓘ ASK STUDENTS to reread lines 170–176. Draw attention to the General's statement to Joby that "you're the general of the army when the General's left behind." What will Joby and his drum symbolize during battle? *(Possible answer: the General's strength and inspiration)* How do the General's words impact the mood at the end of the story? *(The mood is hopeful and heroic.)*

> **CRITICAL VOCABULARY**
>
> **muted**: The author is describing Joby's reaction to his conversation with the General.
>
> **ASK STUDENTS** why Joby might hear muted sounds. *(He is imagining how the drum will sound as the army marches into battle.)*

COLLABORATIVE DISCUSSION Have students work in pairs to discuss the question and cite text evidence to support their ideas about how the drummer boy feels about being in the army. Have them share their results with the class. Accept all reasonable responses.

ASK STUDENTS to share any questions they generated in the course of reading and discussing the story.

---

stir—would feel less pain. If their blood was cold, it would be more than slaughter, it would be murderous nightmare and pain best not told and no one to guess.

170   The General spoke and stopped, letting his breath slack off. Then, after a moment, he said, "So there you are, that's it. Will you do that, boy? Do you know now you're general of the army when the General's left behind?"

The boy nodded mutely.

"You'll run them through for me then, boy?"

"Yes, sir."

"Good. And, God willing, many nights from tonight, many years from now, when you're as old or far much older than me, when they ask you what you did in this awful time,

180   you will tell them—one part humble and one part proud— 'I was the drummer boy at the battle of Owl Creek,' or the Tennessee River, or maybe they'll just name it after the church there. 'I was the drummer boy at Shiloh.' Good grief, that has a beat and sound to it fitting for Mr. Longfellow. 'I was the drummer boy at Shiloh.' Who will ever hear those words and not know you, boy, or what you thought this night, or what you'll think tomorrow or the next day when we must get up on our legs and *move!*"

The general stood up. "Well, then. God bless you, boy.

190   Good night."

"Good night, sir."

And, tobacco, brass, boot polish, salt sweat and leather, the man moved away through the grass.

Joby lay for a moment, staring but unable to see where the man had gone.

He swallowed. He wiped his eyes. He cleared his throat. He settled himself. Then, at last, very slowly and firmly, he turned the drum so that it faced up toward the sky.

He lay next to it, his arm around it, feeling the tremor, the

200   touch, the **muted** thunder as, all the rest of the April night in the year 1862, near the Tennessee River, not far from the Owl Creek, very close to the church named Shiloh, the peach blossoms fell on the drum.

> **muted**
> (myōō′tĭd) *adj.* When something is *muted*, it is softened or muffled.

COLLABORATIVE DISCUSSION Do you think the drummer boy regretted his decision to become part of the Army once he begins to realize what war is like? With a partner, discuss your impressions of him and the choice that he made. Cite specific evidence from the text to support your ideas.

172 Collection 3

TO CHALLENGE STUDENTS . . .

Analyze Motivation Remind students that characters have **motivations,** or reasons, for their actions in a story. Point out that, at the time the Battle of Shiloh took place, the Civil War had been going on for close to two years.

ASK STUDENTS to analyze the text to determine Joby's possible motivation for joining the army. What role might the ongoing war have played in his decision and that of the other young soldiers who were about to go into battle? As needed, prompt students to do some research to determine why so few experienced soldiers were available for the battle. *(Students should note that there were extremely high casualty rates throughout the war.)*

Analyze Stories: Historical Fiction

COMMON CORE RL2, RL3

Every story has a **setting,** the time and place in which the action occurs. In historical fiction such as "The Drummer Boy of Shiloh," the setting is usually a key aspect of the work.

Historical fiction refers to stories that are set in the past and include real places and events from the time period. Like other works of historical fiction, Ray Bradbury's story involves characters that may be based on real people, plot developments that reflect real events, and details that are historically accurate. Sometimes, you may not know whether elements of a work of historical fiction are based on something real unless you do some research.

Review "The Drummer Boy of Shiloh" for additional examples of historical details and references to actual events.

Determine Meanings of Words and Phrases

COMMON CORE RL 4

When you get a general sense of anxiety, sadness, giddiness, or some other emotion as you read a story, you are responding to the work's **mood,** the feeling or atmosphere that the writer creates for readers. Various elements work together to contribute to a story's mood.

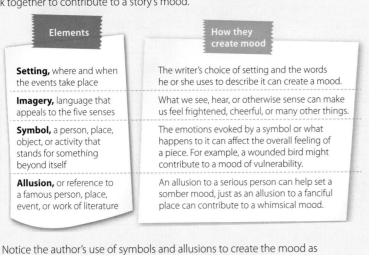

Elements	How they create mood
Setting, where and when the events take place	The writer's choice of setting and the words he or she uses to describe it can create a mood.
Imagery, language that appeals to the five senses	What we see, hear, or otherwise sense can make us feel frightened, cheerful, or many other things.
Symbol, a person, place, object, or activity that stands for something beyond itself	The emotions evoked by a symbol or what happens to it can affect the overall feeling of a piece. For example, a wounded bird might contribute to a mood of vulnerability.
Allusion, or reference to a famous person, place, event, or work of literature	An allusion to a serious person can help set a somber mood, just as an allusion to a fanciful place can contribute to a whimsical mood.

Notice the author's use of symbols and allusions to create the mood as you analyze "The Drummer Boy of Shiloh."

CLOSE READ

Analyze Stories: Historical Fiction

COMMON CORE RL 2, RL 3

Guide students to understand the terms *historical fiction* and *setting.* Discuss how the accuracy of details used to describe the setting of "The Drummer Boy of Shiloh" helps readers get a better sense of the reality of the situation. *(Students may note, for example, that the description in lines 24–29 helps readers understand just how close the two armies were to each other. They should also note that the story takes place the night before the Battle of Shiloh during the Civil War. Both the battle and the war are real events in American history.)*

Determine Meanings of Words and Phrases

COMMON CORE RL 4

Discuss each of the elements that may contribute to creating a story's mood, prompting students to cite examples from the selection or from other familiar stories. For example:

- the imagery describing the boy surrounded by thousands of young soldiers who are trying to relax and sleep helps create the tense mood in the beginning of the story
- the presence of the General, an important and symbolic character, creates a dramatic and serious mood

Have students reread to identify other details that help create the changing moods of the story.

Strategies for Annotation   Annotate it!

Analyze Stories: Historical Fiction

COMMON CORE RL 2, RL 3

Direct students' attention to lines 10–13 and share these strategies for annotating details that tell about the story's setting:

- Highlight in green any words that tell when the story is taking place.
- Highlight in yellow any words or phrases that describe where the action is occurring.

Students can use this strategy throughout the story:

- Use a note to explain how details of the setting connect to the story's theme.

> His face, alert or at rest, was solemn. It was indeed a solemn time and a solemn night for a boy just turned fourteen in the peach field near the Owl Creek not far from the church at Shiloh.

PRACTICE & APPLY

Analyzing the Text RL 1, RL 2, RL 3, RL 4

Possible answers:

1. The sound, which the boy at first interprets as the wind, is the sound of both armies. The fact that he can hear the soldiers on both sides implies that the armies are camped very near one another. This detail helps create the mood of anxiety and tension in the beginning of the story.

2. The author mentions the smells of sweat, tobacco, horse, and boot leather. These are all odors that an older army officer of the time might have. He would probably smoke cigars, and he would be wearing leather boots. The smell of horse is especially associated with a general, as generals usually were mounted, whereas the soldiers were usually on foot.

3. The sound of the boy's drumming, like the beating of a heart, will give life to, or inspire, the soldiers.

4. "...that has a beat and sound to it fitting for Mr. Longfellow"; the idea that a prominent author would immortalize the battle helps create the mood of seriousness and heroism.

5. The General's description of what he wants the drummer boy to do not only tells the reader how the boy will play the next day but also has the effect on Joby that the beating of the drum will have on the soldiers: it excites him and gives him courage.

6. The falling of the peach blossoms occurs toward the end of spring and symbolizes the loss of youth and innocence associated with the ensuing battle. They contribute to the overall mood of sadness in the story.

Speaking and Listening SL 1, SL 2

Student pairs should use the text (lines 62–192) to prepare their scripts. Before they begin, students should discuss the General's motives for speaking to the boy *(to calm him and give him courage)* and how these motivations would affect the rate and tone with which the General speaks.

 eBook *Annotate It!*

Analyzing the Text RL 1, RL 2, RL 3, RL 4, SL1, SL2, SL4

Cite Text Evidence   Support your responses with evidence from the text.

1. **Analyze** In the description of the setting in lines 24–26, what does the special wind suggest about the locations of the two armies? Identify what mood this description helps create.

2. **Cite Evidence** What are the descriptive details that the author provides about the General in lines 76–79 that help make this historical fiction accurate for its time? What is the effect of providing these details?

3. **Interpret** Why does the General refer to the pace of the boy's drumming as "the heart of the army" in lines 142–157?

4. **Analyze** Henry Wadsworth Longfellow was a popular American author who wrote "Paul Revere's Ride" and other works immortalizing early American history. Identify the allusion to him in lines 178–186. What mood does this allusion help create in the last paragraph?

5. **Compare** What is the similarity between the General's talk with the drummer boy and the drummer boy's role in the next day's battle?

6. **Analyze** What do the peach blossoms symbolize in this story? Explain how this symbol contributes to the overall mood.

Speaking and Listening

Working with a partner, act out the scene in which the General discusses the boy's fears and his role in the coming battle. Prepare by discussing the General's motivation for the conversation and how that might affect the way the General speaks.

PERFORMANCE TASK

Respond by Speaking Research the Battle of Shiloh, including the legend of the drummer boy. Find out how many people died and how the significance of the battle is viewed today. Discuss whether your reaction to the following parts of the story has changed as a result of your research:

- lines 99–102
- lines 107–125
- lines 152–159
- lines 180–191

 Assign this performance task.

PERFORMANCE TASK W 7, W 8, SL 4

Speaking Activity: Research Have students work in pairs or small groups to conduct their research. Suggest that they

- focus their research on the specific sections of the selection listed
- plan to present their ideas in a way that clearly shows the connections between story events and their research findings
- use appropriate eye contact and clear pronunciation to share research

Critical Vocabulary

COMMON CORE L 4a, L 5a, L 6

solemn	askew	strew
legitimately	resolute	muted

Practice and Apply Use what you know about the Vocabulary words to answer the following questions.

1. When did you have to act in a **resolute** way to face a challenge?
2. When did you **legitimately** claim that someone owed you something?
3. When did you **strew** things across a room? Why did you do it?
4. When would you need to be **solemn** in a group of people?
5. When has your response to news been **muted**?
6. When has your hat been **askew** on your head?

Vocabulary Strategy: Interpret Figures of Speech

A **figure of speech** is a word or phrase that communicates meanings beyond the literal definition of the words. **Idioms,** or expressions in which the entire phrase means something different from the words in it, are one kind of figure of speech. Consider this idiom from the story.

> "These lads, <u>fresh out of the milkshed</u>, don't know what I know, and I can't tell them . . ."

You can use nearby words and phrases, or **context,** to help you understand that "fresh out of the milkshed" implies that not long ago these lads were farmer hands milking cows. The phrase "don't know what I know" helps you understand that the General is using a figure of speech to express concern that his soldiers lack battle experience.

Practice and Apply Use context to explain the meaning of each underlined figure of speech below.

1. ". . . Yes, thought the boy, that's all very well for them, <u>they can give as good as they get</u>! . . . Me, thought the boy, I only got a drum, two sticks to beat it, and no shield"
2. ". . . there's a hundred thousand men, . . . <u>not one as can spit a sparrow off a tree, or knows a horse clod from a minnieball</u> . . . should turn tail and train . . ."
3. ". . . he might at any moment strike fire to them to see his way through the coming days when the <u>sun might not show its face</u> . . ."

PRACTICE & APPLY

Critical Vocabulary

COMMON CORE L 4a, L 5a, L 6

Possible answers:

1. *when I had to write a report on a weekend*
2. *when I returned some unopened batteries to a store and asked for a refund*
3. *when I tossed my books on my bedroom floor because I was glad it was Friday*
4. *when I was attending a sad event, such as a funeral*
5. *when I didn't care about the news, such as who won an election in another state*
6. *when my older brother tipped it in fun*

Vocabulary Strategy: Interpret Figures of Speech

1. *they can give as good as they get!*
   Explanation: *The soldiers on both sides have weapons that enable them to fight each other fairly.*
   Context Clues: *I only got a drum, two sticks to beat it, and no shield.*

2. *not one as can spit a sparrow off a tree, or knows a horse clod from a minnieball*
   Explanation: *The soldiers are all untrained and inexperienced.*
   Context Clues: *We should . . . train four months. They should do the same.*

3. *sun might not show its face*
   Explanation: *gloomy or depressing stretches of time*
   Context Clues: *the coming days; because of what was happening here*

Strategies for Annotation 🖊 📖 *Annotate it!*

Interpret Figures of Speech

Have students locate other examples of figures of speech and idioms in the story. Encourage them to use their eBook annotation tools to apply the steps suggested in the activity:

- Highlight in green the words or phrase that make up the figure of speech.
- Highlight in yellow surrounding context clues that help you understand the figure of speech.
- Use a note to explain the meaning of the figure of speech.

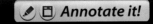

It's wrong, boy, it's wrong as a head put on hind side front and a man marching backward through life.

> doing something backward or incorrectly

Language Conventions: Indicative Mood

COMMON CORE L 1c

Explain to students that they will probably have to add words and details to rewrite the sentences.

Possible answers:

1. *We did not lose the document that proves we own this land.*

2. *The children decided to stop crying and to do something useful.*

3. *Did you get some sleep before the sun came up?*

4. *Now that the troops are guarding the camp, everyone will be safer.*

5. *The troops charged when they heard the order.*

6. *The cause was lost because we did not succeed.*

7. *The war will end soon, and many lives will be saved.*

8. *We prepared for battle so that we would have a greater chance of surviving it.*

Assess It!

Online Selection Test
- Download an editable ExamView bank.
- Assign and manage this test online.

Language Conventions: Indicative Mood   COMMON CORE L 1c

The **mood of a verb** shows the speaker's attitude toward what is being said. There are several moods for verbs.

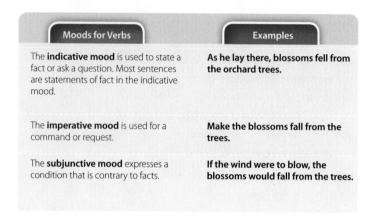

Moods for Verbs	Examples
The **indicative mood** is used to state a fact or ask a question. Most sentences are statements of fact in the indicative mood.	As he lay there, blossoms fell from the orchard trees.
The **imperative mood** is used for a command or request.	Make the blossoms fall from the trees.
The **subjunctive mood** expresses a condition that is contrary to facts.	If the wind were to blow, the blossoms would fall from the trees.

Notice how Ray Bradbury uses the indicative mood for effect. Read these sentences from the story aloud and hear how they use statements of fact to express difficult truths about the uncertainty of battle:

> "The boy turned on his side. A moth brushed his face, but it was peach blossom. A peach blossom flicked him, but it was a moth. Nothing stayed put. Nothing had a name. Nothing was as it once was . . . the peach blossoms fell on the drum."

Practice and Apply Rewrite each sentence using the indicative mood.

1. I hope we have not lost the document that proves we own this land.

2. Stop crying and do something useful!

3. Try to get some sleep before the sun comes up.

4. If the troops guard the camp, everyone will be safer.

5. Don't charge until I give the order.

6. The cause may be lost if we do not succeed.

7. If the war ended sooner, many lives would have been saved.

8. Prepare for battle so you have a greater chance to survive it.

Draw Conclusions

TEACH

Tell students that they **draw conclusions** when they make a judgment or arrive at a belief based on evidence, experience, and reasoning. Explain that readers often draw conclusions about things a writer does not say directly. These conclusions may be about

- characters
- settings
- events in the story

Use events from "The Drummer Boy of Shiloh" to discuss these steps for drawing conclusions. For example:

Step 1: Notice Evidence in the Text Have students reread lines 133–139. Guide students to identify details that suggest the General's purpose in making the statements. *("Why am I telling you this?" "I can't tell them: men actually die, in war." "I got to make one army of them." "I need you.")*

Step 2: Consider Prior Knowledge and Experience Tell students to think about "pep talks" they have had from adults, and ask them to suggest the reasons why those talks take place. *(Possible answer: to encourage, to ask for help, to change behavior)*

Step 3: Draw a Conclusion Based on the details in the text and what they know from experience, ask students to draw conclusions about what the General says. *(Possible answer: the General wants to encourage an inexperienced boy, to help him understand his importance in the coming battle.)*

PRACTICE AND APPLY

Direct partners to work together to draw conclusions about other sections of the story, such as the following:

- lines 16–23 *(Most of the soldiers have not been in battle before.)*
- lines 61–71 *(The General mistakes the boy for a soldier.)*

Have groups compare and discuss their conclusions.

Analyze Stories: Historical Fiction

RETEACH

Review the terms *historical fiction* and *setting*. Point out that students have probably seen movies or television programs that are examples of historical fiction. Ask volunteers to name movies or TV programs that are set in the past. Recent examples include the movies *Lincoln* and *The King's Speech*. Have students

- identify the setting and discuss its impact on the story's central idea or theme
- recall real events depicted in the movie and explain how they propel the story's action
- name any real characters in the movie or program

 LEVEL UP TUTORIALS Assign the following *Level Up* tutorial: **Prose Forms**

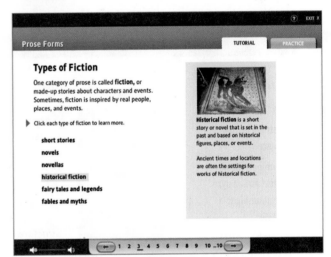

CLOSE READING APPLICATION

Student partners can work together to apply the skill to other historical fiction, identifying the time and place of the story and other details characteristic of historical fiction, such as the presence of famous people and events that really happened. Ask:

- When and where does the story take place?
- What historical events does the story describe?
- What real characters from history appear in the story?
- How does the story's historical setting, events, and content develop its theme?

A Mystery of Heroism

Short Story by Stephen Crane

Why This Text

Students do not always take the time to determine the theme of a story and its relationship to characters. In "A Mystery of Heroism" a third-person narrator reveals the actions of the main character, Collins. The reader must infer Collins's motivations from his actions. With the help of the close-reading questions, students will analyze Collins's character and how it relates to the theme of heroism. This close reading will help students analyze this piece of historical fiction.

Background Have students read the background and the information about the author. "A Mystery of Heroism" asks questions about what makes a person a hero. Introduce the selection by telling students that Stephen Crane was born in Newark, New Jersey, six years after the Civil War ended. His famous novel *The Red Badge of Courage* is a realistic depiction of the battlefields of the Civil War. He is known for writing about characters with complex psychology.

SETTING A PURPOSE Ask students to pay attention to the development of the characters. How soon into the story can students identify the main character?

Common Core Support

- cite strong textual evidence
- determine a theme of a text and analyze its relationship to a character
- analyze how incidents in a story reveal aspects of a character
- determine the meaning of words and phrases as they are used in a text

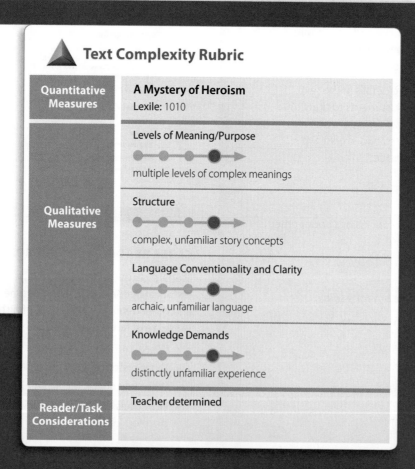

Text Complexity Rubric

	A Mystery of Heroism
Quantitative Measures	Lexile: 1010
Qualitative Measures	**Levels of Meaning/Purpose** — multiple levels of complex meanings
	Structure — complex, unfamiliar story concepts
	Language Conventionality and Clarity — archaic, unfamiliar language
	Knowledge Demands — distinctly unfamiliar experience
Reader/Task Considerations	Teacher determined

Strategies for CLOSE READING

Analyze Historical Fiction

Students should read this story carefully all the way through. Close-reading questions at the bottom of the page will help them focus on a thorough analysis of the story. As they read, students should jot down comments or questions about the text in the side margins.

WHEN STUDENTS STRUGGLE . . .

To help students analyze the main character, have them work in small groups to fill out a chart, such as the one shown below, as they analyze the story.

CITE TEXT EVIDENCE For practice in analyzing a character and story theme, ask students to cite evidence from the text to describe Collins's' actions and motivations.

detail: Collins says, "Thunder, I wisht I had a drink. Ain't there any water round here?"

detail: Collins seems like he wants to impress his fellow soldiers.

detail: Collins thinks he is a hero because he is not afraid to get the water.

Fred Collins

detail: The reader thinks he is a hero when he gives the dying man water.

detail: He seems uncertain when he talks to the captain and the colonel about why or whether he wants to go to the well.

Background *Born in November of 1871,* **Stephen Crane** *began writing at the age of four. The Red Badge of Courage, his famous novel on the Civil War, was published when he was only twenty-four years old. The book made Crane a celebrity and national expert on the war. Crane interviewed Civil War veterans for his fictional writing, but they seemed unable to articulate their feelings about the war. As a result, Crane drew on his own imagination to fill in their thoughts and feelings to give his words larger meaning.*

A Mystery of Heroism

Short Story by Stephen Crane

CLOSE READ
Notes

1. **READ ▶** As you read lines 1–23, begin to cite text evidence.
   - Underline details that reveal the setting, time, and place the action occurs. Write the setting in the margin.
   - Circle images that appeal to your sense of sight, smell, or hearing.
   - In the margin, restate what Fred Collins says in lines 13–15.

The <u>dark uniforms</u> of the men were so coated with dust from the incessant wrestling of the <u>two armies</u> that the regiment almost seemed a part of the clay bank which shielded them from the shells. On the top of the hill a battery[1] was (arguing in tremendous roars) with some other guns, and to the eye of the <u>infantry</u>, the <u>artillerymen, the guns, the caissons</u>,[2] <u>the horses</u>, were distinctly outlined (upon the blue sky.) When a piece was fired, (a red streak as round as a log flashed low in the heavens, like a monstrous bolt of lightning.) The men of the battery wore (white duck trousers,) which somehow emphasized their
10 legs, and when they ran and crowded in little groups at the bidding of the shouting officers, it was more impressive than usual to the infantry.

   Fred Collins of <u>A Company</u> was saying: "Thunder, I wisht I had a drink. Ain't there any water round here?" Then somebody yelled: "There goes th' bugler!"

---
[1] **battery:** set of heavy guns.
[2] **caissons:** ammunition wagons.

49

This story is set during a war.

Fred Collins says he wants a drink of water.

---

1. **READ AND CITE TEXT EVIDENCE** Remind students that authors appeal to readers' senses to evoke feelings and establish a mood.

   A ASK STUDENTS to describe the mood at the beginning of the story, using the sensory images they circled as text evidence. *Answers will vary. Students might cite evidence in line 4, "arguing in tremendous roars," line 8, "a monstrous bolt of lightning," and line 20, "crimson terror," to describe a mood of fear and danger in the opening of the story.*

CLOSE READ Notes

B As the eyes of half of the regiment swept in one machine-like movement, there was an instant's picture of a horse in a great convulsive leap of a death wound and a rider leaning back with a crooked arm and spread fingers before his face. On the ground was
20 the crimson terror of an exploding shell, with fibers of flame that seemed like lances. A glittering bugle swung clear of the rider's back as fell headlong the horse and the man. In the air was an odor as from a conflagration.[3]

The house and barn have been destroyed by shells and by soldiers salvaging wood to burn.

Sometimes they of the infantry looked down at a fair little meadow which spread at their feet. Its long, green grass was rippling
C gently in a breeze. Beyond it was the gray form of a house half torn to pieces by shells and by the busy axes of soldiers who had pursued firewood. The line of an old fence was now dimly marked by long weeds and by an occasional post. A shell had blown the well house to
30 fragments. Little lines of gray smoke ribboning upward from some embers indicated the place where had stood the barn.

From beyond a curtain of green woods there came the sound of some stupendous scuffle as if two animals of the size of islands were fighting. At a distance there were occasional appearances of swift-moving men, horses, batteries, flags, and, with the crashing of infantry, volleys were heard, often, wild and frenzied cheers. In the midst of it all, Smith and Ferguson, two privates of A Company, were engaged in a heated discussion, which involved the greatest questions of the national existence.

[3] **conflagration:** huge fire.

---

2. ◀ **REREAD** Reread lines 1–23. What is unexpected about Fred Collins's statement in lines 13–15? Support your answer with explicit textual evidence.

Crane vividly describes a wartime scene of chaos and destruction. It is surprising that a soldier would be concerned about getting a drink of water under such circumstances.

3. **READ ▶** As you read lines 24–71, continue to cite textual evidence.
- Circle phrases that describe the meadow.
- In the margin, explain what happens to the house and barn in lines 24–31.
- Underline images in lines 40–50 that suggest fear and terror.

50

---

40 The battery on the hill presently engaged in a frightful duel. The white legs of the gunners scampered this way and that way and the officers redoubled their shouts. The guns, with their demeanors of **stolidity** and courage, were typical of something infinitely self-possessed in this clamor of death that swirled around the hill.

One of a "swing" team was suddenly smitten quivering to the ground and his maddened brethren dragged his torn body in their struggle to escape from this turmoil and danger. A young soldier astride one of the leaders swore and fumed in his saddle and furiously jerked at the bridle. An officer screamed out an order so violently that
50 his voice broke and ended the sentence in a falsetto shriek.

The leading company of the infantry regiment was somewhat exposed and the colonel ordered it moved more fully under the shelter of the hill. There was the clank of steel against steel.

A lieutenant of the battery rode down and passed them, holding his right arm carefully in his left hand. And it was as if this arm was not at all a part of him, but belonged to another man. His sober and reflective charger went slowly. The officer's face was grimy and perspiring and his uniform was tousled as if he had been in direct grapple with an enemy. He smiled grimly when the men stared at
60 him. He turned his horse toward the meadow.

Collins of A Company said: "I wisht I had a drink. I bet there's water in that there ol' well yonder!"

"Yes; but how you gain' to git it?"

D For the little meadow which intervened was now suffering a terrible onslaught of shells. Its green and beautiful calm had vanished utterly. Brown earth was being flung in monstrous handfuls. And there was a massacre of the young blades of grass. They were being torn, burned, obliterated. Some curious fortune of the battle had made this gentle little meadow the object of the red hate of the shells
70 and each one as it exploded seemed like an imprecation[4] in the face of a maiden.

[4] **imprecation:** curse.

stolidity: *showing no emotion*

---

4. ◀ **REREAD** Reread lines 64–71. How might the destruction of the meadow reflect the impact of war? Cite text evidence in your answer.

Often in war, "beautiful" things like the "gentle little" meadow are destroyed because they lie in the path of an "onslaught of shells."

51

---

2. **REREAD AND CITE TEXT EVIDENCE**

B **ASK STUDENTS** to work with a partner. Have them read aloud their conclusion, and cite text evidence to support it. *Students should cite text that describes the chaos of war: lines 4–5, "a battery was arguing in tremendous roars with some other guns," and lines 7–8, "a red streak as round as a log flashed low in the heavens, like a monstrous bolt of lightning," to support a conclusion that it is unexpected that Fred Collins's attention would turn to his thirst.*

3. **READ AND CITE TEXT EVIDENCE**

C **ASK STUDENTS** to cite text evidence to support their explanation of what happens to the house and barn. *Students will find evidence in lines 26–28 that the house and barn have been destroyed by shells and by soldiers "who had pursued firewood."*

4. **REREAD AND CITE TEXT EVIDENCE**

D **ASK STUDENTS** to cite textual evidence to support their analysis of how the destruction of the meadow reflects the impact of war. *Students should cite evidence of what the meadow represents, such as line 65 which describes the meadow as "green and beautiful calm" and line 69, "gentle little meadow," and point out its destruction in lines 64–65, "a terrible onslaught of shells," or line 67, "a massacre of the young blades of grass."*

Critical Vocabulary: stolidity (line 43) Have students compare definitions for *stolidity* and then explain why Crane uses this word here. *Students should recognize that the word* stolidity *contrasts with the scene which would typically evoke strong emotions in a person.*

FOR ELL STUDENTS Clarify that the multiple-meaning word *battery,* in this context, refers to a group of two or more big guns. Your Spanish-speakers may recognize it from its cognate *batería.*

176d Collection 3

The wounded officer who was riding across this expanse said to himself: "Why, they couldn't shoot any harder if the whole army was massed here!"

A shell struck the gray ruins of the house and as, after the roar the shattered wall fell in fragments, there was a noise which resembled the flapping of shutters during a wild gale of winter. Indeed the infantry paused in the shelter of the bank, appeared as men standing upon a shore contemplating a madness of the sea. The angel of the calamity had under its glance the battery upon the hill. Fewer white-legged men labored about the guns. A shell had smitten one of the pieces and after the flare, the smoke, the dust, the wrath of this blow was gone, it was possible to see white legs stretched horizontally upon the ground. And at that interval to the rear, where it is the business of battery horses to stand with their noses to the fight awaiting the command to drag their guns out of the destruction or into it or wheresoever these incomprehensible humans demanded with whip and spur—in this line of passive and dumb spectators, whose fluttering hearts yet would not let them forget the iron laws of man's control of them—in this rank of brute soldiers there had been relentless and hideous carnage. From the ruck⁵ of bleeding and **prostrate** horses, the men of the infantry could see one animal raising its stricken body with its forelegs and turning its nose with mystic and profound eloquence toward the sky.

Some comrades joked Collins about his thirst. "Well, if yeh want a drink so bad, why don't yeh go git it?"

"Well, I will in a minnet if yeh don't shut up."

A lieutenant of the artillery floundered his horse straight down the hill with as great concern as of it were level ground. As he

---
⁵ **ruck:** mass, crowd.

The white legs
might
symbolize
innocence.
Crane may be
drawing a
contrast with
the bloodshed
in this scene.

prostrate:
lying flat on
the ground

80

E

90

G F

galloped past the colonel of the infantry, he threw up his hand in a swift salute. "We've got to get out of that," he roared angrily. He was a black-bearded officer, and his eyes, which resembled beads, sparkled like those of an insane man. His jumping horse sped along the column of infantry.

The fat major standing carelessly with his sword held horizontally behind him and with his legs far apart, looked after the receding horseman and laughed. "He wants to get back with orders pretty quick or there'll be no batt'ry left," he observed.

The wise young captain of the second company hazarded to the lieutenant colonel that the enemy's infantry would probably soon attack the hill, and the lieutenant colonel snubbed him.

A private in one of the rear companies looked out over the meadow and then turned to a companion and said: "Look there, Jim." It was the wounded officer from the battery, who some time before had started to ride across the meadow, supporting his right arm carefully with his left hand. This man had encountered a shell apparently at a time when no one perceived him and he could now be seen lying face downward with a stirruped foot stretched across the body of his dead horse. A leg of the charger extended slantingly upward precisely as stiff as a stake. Around this motionless pair the shells still howled.

There was a quarrel in A Company. Collins was shaking his fist in the faces of some laughing comrades. "Dern yeh! I ain't afraid t' go. If yeh say much, I will go!"

"Of course, yeh will! Yeh'll run through that there medder, won't yeh?"

Collins said, in a terrible voice: "You see, now!" At this **ominous** threat his comrades broke into renewed jeers.

100

110

120

---

5. **READ ▶** As you read lines 72–94, circle the repeated image. In the margin, explain why Crane may have chosen to emphasize this image. Consider what the image may symbolize in your response.

6. **READ ▶** As you read lines 95–154, continue to cite textual evidence.
   - Underline what Collins says in response to his fellow officers.
   - Circle the words the colonel uses to refer to Collins. In the margin, explain what this dialogue reveals about the colonel.

---

5. **READ AND CITE TEXT EVIDENCE** Students have already noted the chaos and carnage of the war.

E **ASK STUDENTS** to circle the repeated image and to infer what it may symbolize. *Students should circle "white-legged men" in lines 80–81 and "white legs" in line 83. Students may infer that the white legs represent the men's innocence in contrast to the bloodshed in the scene.*

Critical Vocabulary: prostrate (line 92) Have students explain Crane's use of *prostrate*. What does Crane describe as *prostrate*? *Students should note the contrast between the horses lying prostrate and the one horse "raising its stricken body."*

6. **READ AND CITE TEXT EVIDENCE** Bring students' attention to lines 145–146 and Collins's feelings of "resentment toward his companions."

F **ASK STUDENTS** to underline what Collins says in response to his fellow officers in lines 122–128. What do his responses suggest about his relationship with them? *Students should underline quotations in lines 123–124 and line 127. Students should note that Collins has a contentious relationship with his fellow officers.*

Critical Vocabulary: ominous (line 127) Have students explain Crane's use of *ominous*. Ask them to define the related word *omen*, and then consider the connotations of the synonyms *ominous, threatening,* and *menacing*. Why did Crane choose *ominous*?

Collins gave them a dark scowl and went to find his captain. The
130 latter was conversing with the colonel of the regiment.

"Captain," said Collins, saluting and standing at attention. In
those days all trousers bagged at the knees. "Captain, I want t' git
permission to go git some water from that there well over yonder!"

The colonel and the captain swung about simultaneously and
stared across the meadow. The captain laughed. "You must be pretty
thirsty, Collins?"

"Yes, sir; I am."

"Well—ah," said the captain. After a moment he asked: "Can't you
wait?"

140 "No, sir."

The colonel was watching Collins's face. "Look here, my lad," he
said, in a pious sort of a voice. "Look here, my lad." Collins was not a
lad. "Don't you think that's taking pretty big risks for a little drink of
water?"

"I dunno," said Collins, uncomfortably. Some of the resentment
toward his companions, which perhaps had forced him into this
affair, was beginning to fade. "I dunno wether 'tis."

The colonel and the captain contemplated him for a time.

"Well," said the captain finally.

150 "Well," said the colonel, "if you want to go, why go."

Collins saluted. "Much obliged t' yeh."

As he moved away the colonel called after him. "Take some of the
other boys' canteens with you an' hurry back now."

"Yes, sir. I will."

*The colonel
might feel
protective of
Collins.*

---

7. **◀ REREAD** Reread lines 95–154. What does Collins's dialogue reveal
about his character? Support your answer with explicit text evidence.

*In saying "I ain't afraid t' go," Collins seems sensitive to what his
fellow officers think. However, when he says "I dunno whether 'tis,"
he seems a little unsure if he wants to go through with getting the
water after all.*

8. **READ ▶** As you read lines 155–183, continue to cite text evidence.

• Underline details that describe Collins's appearance.
• In the margin, explain what is "curious" about Collins's manner.

54

> " *I never thought Fred
> Collins had the blood
> in him for that kind
> of business.* "

The colonel and the captain looked at each other then, for it had
suddenly occurred that they could not for the life of them tell whether
Collins wanted to go or whether he did not.

They turned to regard Collins and as they perceived him
surrounded by **gesticulating** comrades the colonel said: "Well, by
160 thunder! I guess he's going."

Collins appeared as a man dreaming. In the midst of the
questions, the advice, the warnings, all the excited talk of his
company mates, he maintained a curious silence.

They were very busy in preparing him for his ordeal. When they
inspected him carefully it was somewhat like the examination that
grooms give a horse before a race; and they were amazed, staggered by
the whole affair. Their astonishment found vent in strange repetitions.

"Are yeh sure a-goin'?" they demanded again and again.

"Certainly I am," cried Collins, at last furiously.

170 He strode sullenly away from them. He was swinging five or six
canteens by their cords. It seemed that his cap would not remain
firmly on his head, and often he reached and pulled it down over his
brow.

There was a general movement in the compact column. The long
animal-like thing moved slightly. Its four hundred eyes were turned
upon the figure of Collins.

"Well, sir, if that ain't th' derndest thing. I never thought Fred
Collins had the blood in him for that kind of business."

"What's he goin' to do, anyhow?"

180 "He's goin' to that well there after water."

"We ain't dyin' of thirst, are we? That's foolishness."

*gesticulating:
gesturing
while speaking*

*He appears
oblivious to
the danger he
is about to
face.*

55

---

7. **REREAD AND CITE TEXT EVIDENCE** Remind students to make
inferences about Collins's character based on what he says.

G **ASK STUDENTS** to cite text evidence to support their
inferences about Collins's character. *Students should cite specific
evidence about Collins's sensitivity to what his fellow officers think
(lines 123–124) and his uncertainty about whether he really wants to
go through with getting the water (line 147).*

8. **READ AND CITE TEXT EVIDENCE**

H **ASK STUDENTS** to cite text evidence to support their
explanation of what is "curious" about Collins's manner. *Collins
appears oblivious to the danger he is about to face, and "appeared
as a man dreaming" (line 161). Students should cite the reactions of
his concerned fellow soldiers in lines 166–167.*

WHEN STUDENTS STRUGGLE . . .

To help students analyze the main character, Collins, ask them to
reread lines 168–183. Invite them to work with a small group to
discuss Collins's actions and motivations. Remind students that we
learn about characters through what the author tells us directly, and
through what other characters tell us.

CITE TEXT EVIDENCE For practice in analyzing a character, ask
students to make an inference about what motivates Collins. *Students
may conclude that Collins is taking an unnecessary risk, because he is
reacting emotionally to the taunts of his fellow soldiers, citing evidence
from lines 169, 170, 181, and 183.*

Critical Vocabulary: gesticulating (line 159) Have students
determine the meaning of *gesticulating* as it is used here. Why does
Crane describe Collins's comrades as *gesticulating*?

FOR ELL STUDENTS Explain that the idiom *had the blood in him*
means "dared."

"Well, somebody put him up to it an' he's doin' it."

"Say, he must be a desperate cuss."

When Collins faced the meadow and walked away from the regiment, he was vaguely conscious that a chasm, the deep valley of all prides, was suddenly between him and his comrades. It was provisional, but the provision was that he return as a victor. He had blindly been led by quaint emotions and laid himself under an obligation to walk squarely up to the face of death.

190 But he was not sure that he wished to make a retraction even if he could do so without shame. As a matter of truth he was sure of very little. He was mainly surprised.

It seemed to him supernaturally strange that he had allowed his mind to maneuver his body into such a situation. He understood that it might be called dramatically great.

However, he had no full appreciation of anything excepting that he was actually conscious of being dazed. He could feel his dulled mind groping after the form and color of this incident.

200 Too, he wondered why he did not feel some keen agony of fear cutting his sense like a knife. He wondered at this because human expression had said loudly for centuries that men should feel afraid of certain things and that all men who did not feel this fear were phenomena, heroes.

Collins thinks he is a hero because he is not afraid of going to get the water.

He was then a hero. He suffered that disappointment which we would all have if we discovered that we were ourselves capable of those deeds which we most admire in history and legend. This, then, was a hero. After all, heroes were not much.

No, it could not be true. He was not a hero. Heroes had no shames in their lives and, as for him, he remembered borrowing fifteen 210 dollars from a friend and promising to pay it back the next day, and then avoiding that friend for ten months. When at home his mother had aroused him for the early labor of his life on the farm, it had often been his fashion to be irritable, childish, diabolical, and his mother had died since he had come to the war.

He saw that in this matter of the well, the canteens, the shells, he was an intruder in the land of fine deeds.

He was now about thirty paces from his comrades. The regiment had just turned its many faces toward him.

From the forest of terrific noises there suddenly emerged a little 220 uneven line of men. They fired fiercely and rapidly at distant foliage on which appeared little puffs of white smoke. The spatter of skirmish firing was added to the thunder of the guns on the hill. The little line of men ran forward. A color sergeant fell flat with his flag as if he had slipped on ice. There was hoarse cheering from a distant field.

Collins's thoughts are interrupted by the sounds of battle. A sergeant is killed.

---

9. ◀ REREAD Reread lines 164–183. What do you think finally provokes Collins's decision to leave the regiment and go to the well?

Collins does not want to be embarrassed in front of his fellow soldiers so he realizes it would be better for him to go get the water.

10. READ ▶ As you read lines 184–218, continue to cite textual evidence.

- Circle the phrases in 184–203 that describe Collins's thoughts and feelings about his situation.
- In the margin, explain why Collins thinks he is a hero.
- In lines 208–218, underline reasons why Collins says he is not a hero.

56

---

11. ◀ REREAD Reread lines 184–218. What attributes does Collins possess that make him an unlikely hero? Cite explicit textual evidence in your response.

Even though he is about to commit a brave act, Collins's thoughts and feelings do not seem particularly heroic. Although he doesn't feel afraid of getting the water, he is "conscious of being dazed" and "mainly surprised" by the absence of fear, which creates a feeling of "disappointment" to the activity. The shame he feels about his past is also unusual for a hero to express.

12. READ ▶ As you read lines 219–240, continue to cite text evidence.

- Underline images that appeal to your sense of hearing.
- In the margin, summarize what happens in lines 219–224.
- Circle details in lines 233–240 that describe the setting.

57

---

9. REREAD AND CITE TEXT EVIDENCE

🄸 **ASK STUDENTS** to read aloud their analysis of Collins's decision to a partner. Have partners work together to identify text evidence to support their analysis. *Students should find that Collins is reacting emotionally to his fellow soldiers, citing evidence from lines 169, "furiously," and line 170, "sullenly."*

10. READ AND CITE TEXT EVIDENCE

🄹 **ASK STUDENTS** to cite evidence of Collins's reflections on whether or not he is a hero. *Students should cite evidence showing that Collins thinks he is a hero because he is not afraid of going to get the water (lines 199–203). They should cite evidence that Collins also thinks he is not a hero, because he feels shame over incidents in his past (lines 208–216). Collins concluded, "he was an intruder in the land of fine deeds."*

11. REREAD AND CITE TEXT EVIDENCE

🄺 **ASK STUDENTS** to compare their responses about Collins as an unlikely hero. *Students should see that Collins's thoughts and feelings do not seem particularly heroic. Students may cite evidence from line 192, "He was mainly surprised," and line 197, he was "conscious of being dazed." He suffers a sense of "disappointment" at what a hero might be (lines 204–207). Collins's shame also makes him an unlikely hero (lines 208–214).*

12. READ AND CITE TEXT EVIDENCE

🄻 **ASK STUDENTS** to cite text evidence to support their summary of lines 219–224. *Students should cite lines 223–224, "A color sergeant fell flat with his flag as if he had slipped on ice," as evidence that a sergeant has been killed. Ask students to describe the setting based on evidence they circled in lines 233–240. Students should describe the home as in ruins, and the danger of flying bullets.*

Collins suddenly felt that two demon fingers were pressed into his ears. He could see nothing but flying arrows, flaming red. He lurched from the shock of this explosion, but he made a mad rush for the house, which he viewed as a man submerged to the neck in a boiling surf might view the shore. In the air, little pieces of shell howled and

230 the earthquake explosions drove him insane with the menace of their roar. As he ran the canteens knocked together with a rhythmical tinkling.

As he neared the house, each detail of the scene became vivid to him. He was aware of some bricks of the vanished chimney lying on the sod. There was a door which hung by one hinge. Rifle bullets called forth by the insistent skirmishers came from the far-off bank of foliage. They mingled with the shells and the pieces of shells until the air was torn in all directions by hootings, yells, howls. The sky was full of fiends who directed all their wild rage

240 at his head.

13. ◀ **REREAD** Reread lines 219–240. How does Crane's word choice create a frightening mood? Support your answer with specific text evidence.

Crane uses vivid imagery such as "the sky was full of fiends" to describe the scene with words and phrases that evoke fear. He also chooses harsh words to describe sounds: "thunder of the guns"; "the air was torn in all directions by hootings, yells, howls."

14. **READ** ▶ As you read lines 241–278, continue to cite text evidence.
- Underline phrases that provide detail about the setting.
- In the margin, summarize what happens at the well.
- In the margin, write what the "long blue line of the regiment" may refer to.

58

> *And now as he lay with his face turned away he was suddenly smitten with the terror.*

 When he came to the well he flung himself face downward and peered into its darkness. There were furtive silver glintings some feet from the surface. He grabbed one of the canteens and, unfastening its cap, swung it down by the cord. The water flowed slowly in with an **indolent** gurgle.

And now as he lay with his face turned away he was suddenly smitten with the terror. It came upon his heart like the grasp of claws. All the power faded from his muscles. For an instant he was no more than a dead man.

250 The canteen filled with a maddening slowness in the manner of all bottles. Presently he recovered his strength and addressed a screaming oath to it. He leaned over until it seemed as if he intended to try to push water into it with his hands. His eyes as he gazed down into the well shone like two pieces of metal and in their expression was a great appeal and a great curse. The stupid water derided him.

There was the blaring thunder of a shell. Crimson light shone through the swift-boiling smoke and made a pink reflection on part of the wall of the well. Collins jerked out his arm and canteen with the same motion that a man would use in withdrawing his head from

260 a furnace.

He scrambled erect and glared and hesitated. On the ground near him lay the old well bucket, with a length of rusty chain. He lowered it swiftly into the well. The bucket struck the water and then turning lazily over, sank. When, with hand reaching tremblingly over hand, he hauled it out, it knocked often against the walls of the well and spilled some of its contents.

indolent:
lazy

Collins struggles to get the water quickly amidst all the chaos surrounding him.

59

---

13. **REREAD AND CITE TEXT EVIDENCE**

Ⓜ ASK STUDENTS to compare the imagery they identified that creates a frightening mood. *Students will cite harsh sounds such as the "thunder of guns" in line 222, and imagery such as "air was torn in all directions by hootings, yells, howls," in lines 238–239, and "the sky was full of fiends" in line 239.*

14. **READ AND CITE TEXT EVIDENCE**

Ⓝ ASK STUDENTS to cite text evidence that describes what happens at the well. *Students will find evidence in lines 241–245 that Collins looked into the well and saw water, in lines 246–249 that Collins became terrified, in lines 250–251 that the canteen filled with a "maddening slowness," and in lines 261–266 that he abandoned the slow-filling canteens and instead filled "the old well bucket." They should conclude that at the well, Collins struggles to get the water quickly amidst all the chaos surrounding him.*

Critical Vocabulary: indolent (line 245) Ask students to determine the meaning of *indolent* as Crane uses it here. Have students discuss whether Crane's use of the word *indolent* is an example of personification.

FOR ELL STUDENTS For ELL students, the meaning of the verb *derided* can be difficult to grasp since it is used in a figure of speech. Explain that it means "ridiculed" or "laughed at."

In running with a filled bucket, a man can adopt but one kind of gait. So through this terrible field over which screamed practical angels of death Collins ran in the manner of a farmer chased out of a dairy by a bull.

His face went staring white with anticipation—anticipation of a blow that would whirl him around and down. He would fall as he had seen other men fall, the life knocked out of them so suddenly that their knees were no more quick to touch the ground than their heads. He saw the long blue line of the regiment, but his comrades were standing looking at him from the edge of an impossible star. He was aware of some deep wheel ruts and hoof prints in the sod beneath his feet.

The artillery officer who had fallen in this meadow had been making groans in the teeth of the tempest of sound. These futile cries, wrenched from him by his agony, were heard only by shells, bullets. When wild-eyed Collins came running, this officer raised himself. His face contorted and blanched from pain, he was about to utter some great beseeching cry. But suddenly his face straightened and he called: "Say, young man, give me a drink of water, will you?"

Collins had no room amid his emotions for surprise. He was mad from the threats of destruction.

"I can't," he screamed, and in this reply was a full description of his quaking apprehension. His cap was gone and his hair was riotous.

The "long blue line of the regiment" refers to the color of the actual uniforms worn by soldiers during the Civil War.

His clothes made it appear that he had been dragged over the ground by the heels. He ran on.

The officer's head sank down and one elbow crooked. His foot in its brass-bound stirrup still stretched over the body of his horse and the other leg was under the steed.

But Collins turned. He came dashing back. His face had now turned gray and in his eye was all terror. "Here it is! Here it is!"

The officer was as a man gone in drink. His arm bended like a twig. His head drooped as if his neck was of willow. He was sinking to the ground to lie face downward.

Collins grabbed him by the shoulder. "Here it is. Here's your drink. Turn over! Turn over, man, for God's sake!"

With Collins hauling at his shoulder, the officer twisted his body and fell with his face turned toward that region where lived the unspeakable noises of the swirling missiles. There was the faintest shadow of a smile on his lips as he looked at Collins. He gave a sigh, a little primitive breath like that from a child.

Collins tried to hold the bucket steadily, but his shaking hands caused the water to splash all over the face of the dying man. Then he jerked it away and ran on.

The regiment gave him a welcoming roar. The grimed faces were wrinkled in laughter.

His captain waved the bucket away. "Give it to the men!"

Collins runs past an officer who asks him for a drink of water. Then he turns around to give him a drink.

---

15. ◀ REREAD Reread lines 241–278. How does the author create a scary and chaotic mood in these lines? Support your answer with explicit textual evidence.

The author uses frightening imagery to describe the battlefield, such as when he says "practical angels of death" screamed over the field. He also conveys the urgency Collins feels as he tries to fill the canteens while his life is at serious risk.

16. READ ▶ As you read lines 279–301, continue to cite textual evidence.

- Underline details that tell you the artillery officer is in pain.
- Circle details that describe Collins's physical appearance.
- In the margin, summarize Collins's actions in these lines.

17. ◀ REREAD Reread lines 279–301. Which details in these lines suggest that Collins acted heroically? Cite text evidence in your response.

Even though Collins looks haggard and would be safer if he ran on, he still chooses to put himself at risk to ease someone else's considerable pain. The look on his face is "all terror," but he decides to do something kind for someone else.

18. READ ▶ As you read lines 302–320, continue to cite textual evidence.

- Underline the officer's reaction to Collins's kindness.
- In the margin, restate what happens to the bucket of water.
- Circle the words used to describe the regiment.

---

15. REREAD AND CITE TEXT EVIDENCE

O ASK STUDENTS to compare the imagery they identified that creates a scary and chaotic mood. *Students should cite evidence of Collins's concern as he tries to fill the canteens, such as lines 246–249, and imagery such as "practical angels of death," in lines 268–269.*

16. READ AND CITE TEXT EVIDENCE

P ASK STUDENTS to cite text evidence to support their summaries of the action in lines 279–301. *Students should cite evidence that Collins ran past a wounded officer who asked him for a drink of water (lines 284–288). They should cite evidence that he turns around to give the officer a drink (lines 295–309).*

17. REREAD AND CITE TEXT EVIDENCE

Q ASK STUDENTS to cite text evidence that suggests that Collins acted heroically. *Students should cite evidence of the risk Collins is taking, such as his appearance in lines 289–291, and his expression in lines 295–296.*

18. READ AND CITE TEXT EVIDENCE

R ASK STUDENTS to cite text evidence to support their restatement of what happens to the bucket of water. *Students should cite evidence that the bucket of water gets dropped and the water spills on the ground: "Suddenly there was an oath, the thud of wood on the ground," (line 318), and "The bucket lay on the ground empty," (line 320).*

The two (genial, skylarking young) lieutenants were the first to gain possession of it. They played over it in their fashion.

When one tried to drink, the other teasingly knocked his elbow. "Don't, Billie! You'll make me spill it," said the one. The other laughed.

 Suddenly there was an oath, the thud of wood on the ground, and a swift murmur of astonishment from the ranks. The two lieutenants 320 glared at each other. The bucket lay on the ground empty.

The bucket of water gets dropped and the water spills on the ground.

19. ◀ **REREAD AND DISCUSS** Reread lines 302–320. With a small group, discuss the story's ironic, or unexpected, ending. How does this ending affect your impression of the events in the story?

SHORT ANSWER

Cite Text Evidence Explain whether you think Collins acted heroically during his mission to get the water. **Cite evidence** from the text and your reading notes to support your opinion.

At first, Collins seems to want the bucket of water out of necessity to quench his thirst. After conversing with his fellow soldiers, it seems he wants to get the water to impress them. These do not seem like heroic reasons for action. However, as the story progresses and Collins is racing across the battlefield, the retrieval of the bucket becomes a heroic endeavor. He acts bravely in a scary situation and selflessly gives some of his water to a soldier on the ground. Even though his motivation is questionable and the water is eventually spilled, Collins's actions are those of a hero.

19. **REREAD AND DISCUSS USING TEXT EVIDENCE**

S **ASK STUDENTS** to share the results of their small group discussion. *Students should cite evidence of the irony of the story's ending: after all that Collins went through to get the water, two "genial skylarking young lieutenants" (line 313) spill the water on the ground.*

SHORT RESPONSE

Cite Text Evidence Student responses will vary, but they should cite evidence from the text to support their opinions. Students should:

- explain whether or not they believe Collins is a hero.
- provide text-based insights into Collins's motivation.
- focus on details of Collins's behavior that develop the theme of heroism.

TO CHALLENGE STUDENTS . . .

Remind students that "A Mystery of Heroism" is historical fiction. For more context on the history of the Civil War, students can view the following videos about famous Civil War battles in their eBooks: *Battle of Shiloh, Battle of Fredericksburg, First Battle of Bull Run,* and *Chamberlain Defends Little Round Top.*

ASK STUDENTS to work in small groups to compare and contrast a video about an actual Civil War battle with "A Mystery of Heroism." Each group should learn about one battle.

Stephen Crane is famous for his realism. The Poetry Foundation writes: *Stephen Crane was one of America's foremost realistic writers.* Have groups discuss the realism of "A Mystery of Heroism." What realistic details did Crane include in his story? *Crane describes the sounds and sights of the battleground without softening them. The dialogue he uses is convincing and faithful to the kinds of men who would speak it. Crane does not shy away from describing the violence suffered by the men, the animals, and the earth.*

As a class, discuss whether there is value in reading both history and historical fiction to understand an event such as the Civil War. If so, how does reading historical fiction contribute to a full understanding?

DIG DEEPER

With the class, return to Question 4, Reread. Have students share their responses.

ASK STUDENTS to cite the text evidence that led to their inferences about what the meadow might symbolize.

- Point out that lines 19–26 introduce a contrast between the battle and the meadow. Ask students to cite evidence of the contrast. *Students should cite evidence such as "the crimson terror of an exploding shell" (lines 19–20), and "an odor as from a conflagration" (lines 22–23) to show the horror of battle, and contrast it to "a fair little meadow" (lines 24–25) and "long, green, grass was rippling gently in a breeze (lines 25–26).*

- Ask students what the meadow might represent symbolically. *Students should understand that the meadow may represent life, peace, and innocence.*

- Ask a volunteer to reread lines 64–71 aloud.

- Have volunteers identity how Crane contrasts the innocence of the meadow with the horror of war. *Students should identify these contrasting phrases in lines 64–65: "little meadow" and "suffering a terrible onslaught of shells." And in lines 65–66: "Its green and beautiful calm had vanished utterly. Brown earth was bring flung in monstrous handfuls." And in lines 67–68, "young blades of grass" is contrasted with "massacre" and "torn, burned, obliterated." Finally, in lines 69–71, the "gentle little meadow" is contrasted with "the red hate of the shells" and "an imprecation in the face of a maiden."*

- Ask students how this description of the meadow's destruction contributes to an analysis of Collins's heroism. *Students should understand the risk Collins took running toward the well.*

ASK STUDENTS to return to their Short Response answer and revise it based on the class discussion.

CLOSE READING NOTES

*my*SmartPlanner — Create lesson plans and access resources online.

from *Bloody Times: The Funeral of Abraham Lincoln and the Manhunt for Jefferson Davis*

History Writing by James L. Swanson

Why This Text?

The Civil War forever changed the United States. This selection provides important insight into the lives of the two leaders who guided that conflict. Detailed descriptions of events surrounding the fall of Richmond allow students to hear the voices of those who were there.

▶ **View It!**

Professional Development Podcast:

Informational Text

Key Learning Objective: The student will be able to identify and analyze a compare-and-contrast organizational pattern in a text and understand the impact of a word's connotation on meaning.

For practice and application:

Civil War Journal
Journal Entries by Louisa May Alcott

Close Reader selection
"Civil War Journal,"
Journal Entries by Louisa May Alcott

COMMON CORE — Common Core Standards

RI 1 Cite textual evidence.

RI 3 Analyze how a text makes connections among and distinctions between individuals, ideas, or events.

RI 4 Determine the meaning of words and phrases; analyze the impact of specific word choices.

RI 5 Analyze the structure of a text.

RI 6 Determine an author's point of view and purpose.

W 2 Write informative/explanatory texts.

W 7 Conduct short research projects.

W 8 Gather relevant information from print and digital sources.

W 9b Apply grade 8 Reading standards to literary nonfiction.

L 1a Explain the function of verbals.

L 4a Use context as a clue to meaning.

L 4d Verify the preliminary determination of the meaning of a word by checking in a dictionary.

L 5c Distinguish among the connotations of words with similar denotations.

▲ Text Complexity Rubric

Quantitative Measures	*from* **Bloody Times: The Funeral of Abraham Lincoln and the Manhunt for Jefferson Davis** Lexile: 1030L
Qualitative Measures	**Levels of Meaning/Purpose** more than one purpose; implied but easy to infer **Structure** implicit compare-contrast text structure **Language Conventionality and Clarity** some unfamiliar, academic, or domain-specific words **Knowledge Demands** some specialized knowledge required
Reader/Task Considerations	Teacher determined Vary by individual reader and type of text

TEACH

CLOSE READ

Background Have students read the background information about the end of the Civil War and author James Swanson. Explain that the capital of the Confederacy, originally located in Montgomery, Alabama, was moved to Richmond, Virginia, in June 1861. The residents of Richmond were used to threats of possible invasion by Union forces, but they had such confidence in General Lee that they believed it wouldn't happen. Lee had warned President Davis weeks before that Richmond might soon be lost. And although Davis evacuated his own family, the general public suspected nothing. It was the sight of fires in front of government offices that led many to wonder what was happening as officials burned government records.

SETTING A PURPOSE Direct students to use the Setting a Purpose question to focus their reading. Tell students to generate questions as they read.

CRITICAL VOCABULARY

secede: Swanson introduces his topic by giving a general account of historical events as the American Civil War is about to end.

ASK STUDENTS to explain why the Southern states decided to secede from the United States. *(The citizens of these states wanted to preserve their way of life, which included owning slaves.)*

Background *Confederate leaders believed that by abandoning their capitol in Richmond, they would be able to prolong the Civil War. But just a few days after they left Richmond, General Robert E. Lee was forced to surrender to the Union Army. Shortly after, the Civil War ended and President Lincoln was assassinated.*

James L. Swanson *has written several books about the Civil War and Abraham Lincoln. He has been fascinated with Lincoln's life since his tenth birthday, when he received an engraving of the pistol used to assassinate the president.*

from BLOODY TIMES: The Funeral of Abraham Lincoln and the Manhunt for Jefferson Davis

History Writing by James L. Swanson

SETTING A PURPOSE As you read, pay attention to the details the author provides about Abraham Lincoln and Jefferson Davis. What sorts of leadership qualities did each man possess?

Prologue

In the spring of 1865, the country was divided in two: the Union in the North, led by Abraham Lincoln, fighting to keep the Southern states from **seceding** from the United States. The South, led by its president, Jefferson Davis, believed it had the absolute right to quit the Union in order to preserve its way of life, including the right to own slaves. The bloody Civil War had lasted four years and cost 620,000 lives. In April 1865, the war was about to end.

secede
(sĭ-sēd´) *v.* When you *secede*, you formally withdraw from an organization or association.

Introduction

In April of 1865, as the Civil War drew to a close, two men set
10 out on very different journeys. One, Jefferson Davis, president

(tr) ©Getty Images; (c) ©Library of Congress Prints & Photographs Division

Bloody Times **177**

SCAFFOLDING FOR ELL STUDENTS

Analyze Language Because several languages either have no plural form for nouns or form plurals in a different way than in English, these nouns may be confusing to some students.

- Explain that plural nouns name more than one person, place, or thing and that most plural nouns end in *-s*.
- Use a whiteboard to project the Prologue (lines 1–8). Lead a discussion of the plural nouns in the text.

ASK STUDENTS to identify the plural nouns. Highlight these nouns as students name them: *states, States, slaves, years, lives.* Discuss the meaning of each plural. Point out the number markers *four* and *620,000* before the plural nouns *years* and *lives.*

Analyze Structure: Comparison and Contrast

COMMON CORE   RI 1, RI 3, RI 5

(LINES 15–21)

Tell students that, when authors **contrast** individuals, ideas, or events, they explain how they are different. Point out that sometimes two subjects can be contrasted within a single paragraph.

 CITE TEXT EVIDENCE Have students reread lines 15–21 and describe the contrast that Swanson draws between Abraham Lincoln and Jefferson Davis. *(While "few people had heard of " Lincoln in 1858, many "recognized the name of Jefferson Davis" and were aware of his leadership potential.)*

CRITICAL VOCABULARY

succumb: Jefferson Davis and his young wife, Sarah Knox Taylor, both became ill shortly after they were married.

ASK STUDENTS to what disease did Sarah Knox Taylor succumb? *(malaria)* What happened as a result? *(She died.)* What kept Jefferson Davis from succumbing to the disease? *(He was strong and had a strong will to live.)*

WHEN STUDENTS STRUGGLE . . .

If students have difficulty comparing and contrasting ideas presented in the text, have them work in pairs to fill out a Venn diagram graphic organizer like the one shown. Explain that students can use this type of graphic organizer to help identify similarities or differences between two subjects, or topics.

Demonstrate by writing similarities between Lincoln and Davis in the overlapping portions of the circles and differences in the outside portions. Students might create several Venn diagrams about Lincoln and Davis that they can add to as they read *Bloody Times*.

---

of the Confederate States of America,[1] was on the run, desperate to save his family, his country, and his cause. The other, Abraham Lincoln, murdered on April 14, was bound for a different destination: home, the grave, and everlasting glory.

Today everybody knows the name of Abraham Lincoln. But before 1858, when Lincoln ran for the United States Senate (and lost the election), very few people had heard of him. Most people of those days would have recognized the name of Jefferson Davis. Many would have predicted Davis,
20 not Lincoln, would become president of the United States someday.

Born in 1808, Jefferson Davis went to private schools and studied at a university, then moved on to the United States Military Academy at West Point. A fine horseback rider, he looked elegant in the saddle. He served as an officer in the United States army on the western frontier, and then became a planter, or a farmer, in Mississippi and was later elected a United States Congressman and later a senator. As a colonel in the Mexican-American War, he was wounded in battle and
30 came home a hero.

Davis knew many of the powerful leaders of his time, including presidents Zachary Taylor and Franklin Pierce. He was a polished speech maker with a beautiful speaking voice. Put simply, he was well-known, respected, and admired in both the North and the South of the country.

What Davis had accomplished was even more remarkable because he was often ill. He was slowly going blind in one eye, and he periodically suffered from malaria, which gave him fevers, as well as a painful condition called neuralgia. He and
40 his young wife, Sarah Knox Taylor, contracted malaria shortly after they were married. She **succumbed** to the disease. More than once he almost died. But his strength and his will to live kept him going.

Abraham Lincoln's life started out much different from Jefferson Davis's. Born in 1809, he had no wealthy relatives to help give him a start in life. His father was a farmer who could not read or write and who gave Abe an ax at the age of nine and sent him to split logs into rails for fences. His mother died while Lincoln was still a young boy. When his father

succumb
(sə-kŭm´) *v.* To *succumb* is to give in to an overwhelming force.

---

[1] **Confederate States of America:** the government formed by the 11 southern states that seceded from the United States.

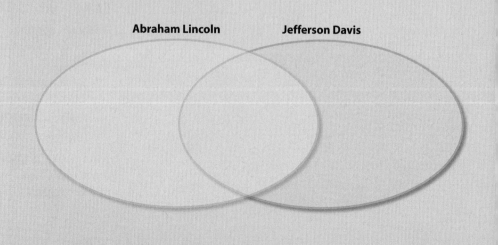
Abraham Lincoln   **Jefferson Davis**

50 remarried, Abe's stepmother, Sarah, took a special interest
in Abe.

By the time Abe Lincoln grew up, he'd had less than a year
of school. But he'd managed to learn to read and write, and
he wanted a better life for himself than that of a poor farmer.
He tried many different kinds of jobs: piloting a riverboat,
surveying (taking careful measurement of land to set up
boundaries), keeping a store, and working as a postmaster.

He read books to teach himself law so that he could
practice as an attorney. Finally in 1846 he was elected to
60 the U.S. Congress. He served an unremarkable term, and
at the end of two years, he left Washington and returned to
Illinois and his law office. He was hardworking, well-off, and
respected by the people who knew him—but not nearly as
well-known or as widely admired as Jefferson Davis.

It may seem that two men could not be more different
than Abraham Lincoln and Jefferson Davis. But in fact, they
had many things in common. Both Davis and Lincoln loved
books and reading. Both had children who died young. One
of Davis's sons, Samuel, died when he was still a baby, and
70 another, Joseph, died after an accident while Davis was the
president of the Confederacy. Lincoln, too, lost one son, Eddie,
at a very young age and another, Willie, his favorite, while he
was president of the United States.

Both men fell in love young, and both lost the women they
loved to illness. When he was twenty-four years old, Davis
fell for Sarah Knox Taylor. Called Knox, she was just eighteen
and was the daughter of army general and future president
Zachary Taylor. It took Davis two years to convince her family
to allow her to marry him—but at last he did. Married in June

80 of 1835, just three months later both he and Knox fell ill with
malaria, and she died. Davis was devastated. His grief changed
him—afterward he was quieter, sterner, a different man.

Eight years later, he found someone else to love. He
married Varina Howell, the daughter of a wealthy family.
For the rest of his life, Davis would depend on Varina's love,
advice, and loyalty. They would eventually have six children;
only two would outlive Jefferson Davis.

Lincoln was still a young man when he met and fell in love
with Ann Rutledge. Everyone expected them to get married,
90 but before that could happen, Ann became ill and died.
Lincoln himself never talked or wrote about Ann after her

CLOSE READ

Analyze Structure: Comparison and Contrast (LINES 65–75)

 COMMON CORE RI 1, RI 3, RI 5

Tell students that when authors **compare** individuals, ideas, or events, they explain how they are similar, or alike. Point out that two subjects can be compared within one paragraph or in separate paragraphs.

B ASK STUDENTS to reread lines 65–75 and identify details in the paragraph that show how Lincoln and Davis were similar. *(They both "loved books and reading." They both "had children who died young." They both "fell in love young" with women who became ill and died.)*

Analyze Connotative Meanings (LINES 78–79)

COMMON CORE RI 4, L 5c

Explain that although some words may have a similar **denotation,** or dictionary definition, they can have very different **connotations,** the feelings or ideas associated with a word. Point out that words can have a positive, neutral, or negative connotation.

C ASK STUDENTS to reread lines 78–79. Draw attention to the word *convince* and have students name other words that have a similar denotation. *(Possible answers: coax, coerce, persuade, pressure)* How does the author's use of *convince* impact the sentence differently than words such as *coerce* or *pressure*? *(Words such as* coerce *or* pressure *have a negative connotation and would give a poor impression of Davis's behavior.)*

Analyze Structure: Comparison and Contrast

COMMON CORE — RI 1, RI 3, RI 5

(LINES 100–116)

Remind students that when authors contrast subjects, they describe the ways in which they are different. Explain that sometimes a contrast is made in two separate paragraphs, with one paragraph covering various aspects of the first subject and the next paragraph covering similar aspects of the second subject.

D **CITE TEXT EVIDENCE** Have students reread lines 100–116 to contrast Davis's and Lincoln's views on slavery. What were Davis's beliefs about slavery? *(He "believed that white people were superior to blacks," that slavery was good for blacks, and that the founding fathers "had intended slavery to be part of America forever.")* How were Lincoln's views different? *(Lincoln "thought slavery was simply wrong" and that the founding fathers "hadn't intended it always to exist." He was willing to allow slavery in states where it was already legal but didn't want it to spread to new states.)*

Abraham Lincoln, president of the United States of America

death. But those who knew him at the time remembered how crushed and miserable he was to lose her. Some even worried that he might kill himself.

Abraham Lincoln recovered and eventually married Mary Todd. But their marriage was not as happy as that of Jefferson and Varina. Mary was a woman of shifting moods. Jealous, insulting, rude, selfish, careless with money, she was difficult to live with.

100 By far the greatest difference between Davis and Lincoln was their view on slavery. Davis, a slave owner, firmly believed that white people were superior to blacks, and that slavery was good for black people, who needed and benefited from having masters to rule over them. He also believed that the founding fathers of the United States, the men who had written the Constitution and the Declaration of Independence, a number of whom had owned slaves, had intended slavery to be part of America forever.

Lincoln thought slavery was simply wrong, and he 110 believed that the founders hadn't intended it always to exist in the United States. Lincoln was willing to let slavery remain legal in the states where it was already permitted. But he

©Corbis

thought that slavery should not be allowed to spread into the new states entering the Union in the American south and southwest. Every new state to join the country, Lincoln firmly believed, should prohibit slavery.

Lincoln explained his views in several famous debates during his campaign for Senate in 1858. The campaign debates between Lincoln and Stephen Douglas brought
120 Lincoln to national attention for the first time. Though he lost that Senate race, his new visibility enabled Lincoln to win the presidential nomination and election in 1860. To the surprise of many, it was Abraham Lincoln who became the president of the United States by winning less than 40 percent of the popular vote. More people voted for the other three candidates running for president than for Lincoln.

Chapter One

On the morning of Sunday, April 2, 1865, Richmond, Virginia, capital city of the Confederate States of America, did not look like a city at war. The White House of the Confederacy was
130 surprisingly close to—one hundred miles from—the White House in Washington, D.C. But the armies of the North had never been able to capture Richmond. After four years of war, Richmond had not been invaded by Yankees. The people there had thus far been spared many of the horrors of fighting. This morning everything appeared beautiful and serene. The air smelled of spring, and fresh green growth promised a season of new life.

As he usually did on Sundays, President Jefferson Davis walked from his mansion to St. Paul's Episcopal Church. One
140 of the worshippers, a young woman named Constance Cary, recalled the day: "On the Sunday morning of April 2, a perfect Sunday of the Southern spring, a large congregation assembled as usual at St. Paul's." As the service went on, a messenger entered the church. He brought Jefferson Davis a telegram from Robert E. Lee.

The telegram was not addressed to Davis, but to his secretary of war, John C. Breckinridge. Breckinridge had sent it on to Davis. It told devastating news: The Union army was approaching the city gates, and the Army of Northern
150 Virginia, with Lee in command, was powerless to stop them.

CLOSE READ

Analyze Language

COMMON CORE RI 4

(LINES 134–145)

Tell students that **imagery** is descriptive language that appeals to one or more of the five senses—sight, hearing, smell, taste, and touch. Imagery helps readers imagine, or form an image of, what is being described.

E **ASK STUDENTS** to reread lines 134–145. What descriptive details help you imagine the scene in Richmond the morning of April 2, 1865? *(Possible answers: "beautiful and serene"; "air smelled of spring"; "fresh green growth"; "a perfect Sunday of the Southern spring"; "a large congregation")* What impact does the description have on the tone of the selection? *(The imagery provides a stark contrast to the references to war, such as "the horrors of fighting" in lines 133–134.)*

WHEN STUDENTS STRUGGLE...

To help students follow the sequence of events that the author describes, ask them to make a timeline showing the dates listed below. Beside each date, have students write what happened on that day. Tell students that they will find information about each day's events in the text.

- Thursday, March 23
- Wednesday, March 29
- Thursday, March 30
- Sunday, April 2
- Monday, April 3
- Tuesday, April 4
- Friday, April 14

SPRING 1865

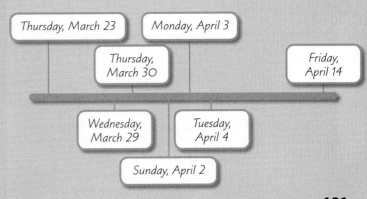

Thursday, March 23 | Monday, April 3 | Thursday, March 30 | Friday, April 14 | Wednesday, March 29 | Tuesday, April 4 | Sunday, April 2

Determine Author's Purpose (LINES 151–157)

COMMON CORE RI 1, RI 6

Explain that an **author's purpose** is his or her reason for writing. Draw attention to General Lee's telegram to General Breckinridge.

F **CITE TEXT EVIDENCE** Ask students to reread lines 151–157. Which words and phrases show the dire circumstances facing Richmond? *("no prospect of doing more than holding our position," "not certain that I can do that")* How does the telegram better support the author's purpose of informing readers about the fall of Richmond than a description of the event? *(The note provides the exact words of a key historical figure. It is a powerful statement of the danger the city faces.)*

F

Headquarters, April 2, 1865

General J. C. Breckinridge:

I see no prospect of doing more than holding our position here till night. I am not certain that I can do that. . . . I advise that all preparation be made for leaving Richmond tonight. I will advise you later, according to circumstances.

R. E. Lee

On reading the telegram, Davis did not panic, but he turned pale and quietly rose to leave the church. The news
160 quickly spread through Richmond. "As if by a flash of electricity, Richmond knew that on the morrow her streets would be crowded by her captors, her rulers fled... her high hopes crushed to earth," Constance Cary wrote later. "I saw many pale faces, some trembling lips, but in all that day I heard no expression of a weakling fear."

Many people did not believe that Richmond would be captured. General Lee would not allow it to happen, they told themselves. He would protect the city, just as the army had before. In the spring of 1865, Robert E. Lee was the
170 greatest hero in the Confederacy, more popular than Jefferson Davis, who many people blamed for their country's present misfortunes. With Lee to defend them, many people of Richmond refused to believe that before the sun rose the next morning, life as they knew it would come to an end.

Jefferson Davis walked from St. Paul's to his office. He summoned the leaders of his government to meet with him there at once. Davis explained to his cabinet[2] that the fall of Richmond would not mean the death of the Confederate States of America. He would not stay behind to surrender the
180 capital. If Richmond was doomed to fall, then the president and the government would leave the city, travel south, and set up a new capital in Danville, Virginia, 140 miles to the southwest. The war would go on.

Davis told the cabinet to pack their most important records and send them to the railroad station. What they could not take, they must burn. The train would leave tonight, and he expected all of them to be on it. Secretary of War John C. Breckinridge would stay behind in Richmond to make sure

---

[2] **cabinet:** a government leader's advisers.

APPLYING ACADEMIC VOCABULARY

access	document

As you discuss the selection, incorporate the following Collection 3 academic vocabulary words: *access* and *document*. Have students discuss the impact of primary source **documents** quoted by Swanson, such as the telegram on this page and first-hand accounts of those who had direct **access** to Lincoln and Davis. Ask students to share their thoughts about the historical significance of these records and what readers today can learn from them.

the evacuation of the government went smoothly, and then
190 follow the train to Danville. Davis ordered the train to take on other cargo, too: the Confederate treasury, consisting of half a million dollars in gold and silver coins.

After spending most of the afternoon working at his office, Davis walked home to pack his few remaining possessions. The house was eerily still. His wife, Varina, and their four children had already evacuated to Charlotte, North Carolina. His private secretary, Burton Harrison, had gone with them to make sure they reached safety.

Varina had begged to stay with her husband in Richmond
200 until the end. Jefferson said no, that for their safety, she and the children must go. He understood that she wanted to help and comfort him, he told her, "but you can do this in but one way, and that is by going yourself and taking our children to a place of safety." What he said next was frightening: "If I live," he promised, "you can come to me when the struggle is ended."

On March 29, the day before Varina and the children left Richmond, Davis gave his wife a revolver and taught her how to use it. He also gave her all the money he had, saving just
210 one five-dollar gold piece for himself. Varina and the children left the White House on Thursday, March 30. "Leaving the house as it was," Varina wrote later, "and taking only our clothing, I made ready with my young sister and my four little children, the eldest only nine years old, to go forth into the unknown." The children did not want to leave their father. "Our little Jeff begged to remain with him," Varina wrote, "and Maggie clung to him . . . for it was evident he thought he was looking his last upon us." The president took his family to the station and put them aboard a train.

220 While Jefferson Davis spent his last night in the Confederate White House, alone, without his family, he did not know that Abraham Lincoln had left his own White House several days ago and was now traveling in Virginia. Lincoln was visiting the Union Army.[3] The Union president did not want to go home until he had won the war. And he dreamed of seeing Richmond.

---

[3] **Union Army:** the land force of the military that fought for the northern states during the Civil War.

Analyze Language

(LINES 199–219)

Help students understand that Jefferson Davis was now aware that both he and the Confederacy were in danger.

G CITE TEXT EVIDENCE Have students reread lines 199–219 to identify details in the text that signal how serious Jefferson Davis thought the situation was. *(He insisted his family evacuate Richmond and told his wife, "If I live, you can come to me when the struggle is ended." He gave his wife a gun and virtually all their money. He looked and acted as though he was seeing his family for the last time.)* What is the impact of these word choices? *(The personal details about Davis and his family suggest the impact that the defeat of the South will have on individuals, rather than the larger political implications for the South.)*

Analyze Language

COMMON CORE **RI 4**

(LINES 232–253)

Explain to students that President Lincoln was known for telling stories. Point out that he could use a story to make an **analogy,** a comparison between two things that are alike in some respect.

H **ASK STUDENTS** to reread lines 232–253. Why does Lincoln tell the story about the lemonade? *(He tells the story to address indirectly the question of how to treat Jefferson Davis.)* What analogy does General Sherman think Lincoln is making? *(He believes Lincoln is comparing himself to the man in the story who wouldn't mind having brandy in his lemonade so long as he didn't have to add it himself. Sherman understands that Lincoln feels it is fine to let Davis escape and disappear but is unable to issue the order himself or be directly involved.)*

Chapter Two

On March 23 at 1:00 P.M., Lincoln left Washington, bound south on the ship *River Queen*. His wife, Mary, came with him, along with their son Tad. A day later the vessel anchored
230 off City Point, Virginia, headquarters of General Grant and the Armies of the United States.

Lincoln met with his commanders to discuss the war. General William Tecumseh Sherman asked Lincoln about his plans for Jefferson Davis. Many in the North wanted Davis hanged if he was captured. Did Lincoln think so, too? Lincoln answered Sherman by saying that all he wanted was for the Southern armies to be defeated. He wanted the Confederate soldiers sent back to their homes, their farms, and their shops. Lincoln didn't answer Sherman's question about Jefferson
240 Davis directly. But he told a story.

There was a man, Lincoln said, who had sworn never to touch alcohol. He visited a friend who offered him a drink of lemonade. Then the friend suggested that the lemonade would taste better with a little brandy in it. The man replied that if some of the brandy were to get into the lemonade "unbeknown to him," that would be fine.

Sherman believed that Lincoln meant it would be the best thing for the country if Jefferson Davis were simply to leave and never return. As the Union president, Lincoln could
250 hardly say in public that he wanted a man who had rebelled against his government to get away without punishment. But if Davis were to escape "unbeknown to him," as Lincoln seemed to be suggesting, that would be fine.

At City Point Lincoln received reports and sent messages. He haunted the army telegraph office for news of the battles raging in Virginia. He knew that soon Robert E. Lee must make a major decision: Would he sacrifice his army in a final, hopeless battle to defend Richmond, or would he abandon the Confederate capital and save his men to fight another day?
260 In the afternoon of April 2, Lee telegraphed another warning to Jefferson Davis in Richmond. "I think it absolutely necessary that we should abandon our position tonight," he wrote. Lee had made his choice. His army would retreat. Richmond would be captured.

Davis packed some clothes, retrieved important papers and letters from his private office, and waited at the mansion.

Jefferson Davis, president of the Confederate States of America

Then a messenger brought him word: The officials of his government had assembled at the station. The train that would carry the president and the cabinet of the Confederacy was
270 loaded and ready to depart.

Davis and a few friends left the White House, mounted their horses, and rode to the railroad station. Crowds did not line the streets to cheer their president or to shout best wishes for his journey. The citizens of Richmond were locking up their homes, hiding their valuables, or fleeing the city before the Yankees arrived. Throughout the day and into the night, countless people left however they could—on foot, on horseback, in carriages, in carts, or in wagons. Some rushed to the railroad station, hoping to catch the last train south. Few
280 would escape.

But not all of Richmond's inhabitants dreaded the capital's fall. Among the blacks of Richmond, the mood was happy. At the African church, it was a day of **jubilation**. Worshippers poured into the streets, congratulated one another, and prayed for the coming of the Union army.

When Jefferson Davis got to the station, he hesitated. Perhaps the fortunes of war had turned in the Confederacy's

jubilation
(jōō´bə-lā´shən) *n.*
Jubilation is the act of celebrating.

CLOSE READ

Analyze Structure: Comparison and Contrast (LINES 271–285)

COMMON CORE · RI 1, RI 3, RI 5

Review that an author contrasts people, ideas, or events by explaining how they are different. Have students recall that a contrast can be made in two separate paragraphs, the first paragraph describing aspects of one subject and the second paragraph describing similar aspects of another subject.

CITE TEXT EVIDENCE Have students reread lines 271–285 to contrast the moods and actions of Richmond's residents. How are most people feeling and behaving? *(They are despondent as they try to protect their belongings and flee the city: "did not line the streets to cheer," "hiding valuables, or fleeing.")* How is the black population feeling and behaving? *(They are happy, congratulating one another, and praying for the arrival of the Union soldiers: "the mood was happy," "a day of jubilation.")*

CRITICAL VOCABULARY

jubilation: Many residents of Richmond, the capital of the Confederacy, prepare to leave the city before the Union army arrives.

ASK STUDENTS why the anticipated arrival of the Union army is a cause for jubilation, instead of dread, for the African American community in Richmond. *(The African Americans in Richmond celebrate because the Union soldiers are fighting to defeat the South and its practice of slavery.)*

Analyze Connotative Meanings (LINES 295–296)

COMMON CORE RI 4, L 5c

Remind students that a word's denotation is its dictionary definition, while its connotations are the ideas and feelings associated with the word.

 ASK STUDENTS to reread lines 295–296. Point out the word *common*. Have students name other words with a similar denotation. *(Possible answers: ordinary, regular, standard, inferior, low-class)* What is the impact of the author's choice to use *common* rather than words such as *inferior* or *low-class*? *(Those words have a negative connotation and would give a worse impression of Davis's travel accommodations.)*

CRITICAL VOCABULARY

oppress: As Richmond is about to fall, President Jefferson Davis and his cabinet evacuate, traveling by train to Danville, Virginia, where they will set up their new capital.

ASK STUDENTS why these government officials are oppressed with sorrow. *(They are overwhelmed with sadness, fearing that people who remained in Richmond, as well as General Lee and his soldiers, will be injured, captured, or killed by the Union army.)*

ruffian: After Jefferson Davis leaves Richmond, there is chaos in the city.

ASK STUDENTS who the ruffians in the city may have been. *(thieves; deserters from the army)* What is it about their behavior that disturbs Captain Parker? *(They are drinking and traveling in mobs.)*

looter: Captain Parker and his men are charged with guarding the special cargo on their train.

ASK STUDENTS why Captain Parker is concerned about looters. *(Parker is afraid that if the crowd finds out that the train is carrying the treasury of the Confederacy, they will attack and steal the money.)*

---

favor that night. Perhaps Lee had defeated the enemy after all, as he had done so many times before. For an hour Davis held the loaded and waiting train in hopes of receiving good news from Lee. That telegram never came. The Army of Northern Virginia would not save Richmond from its fate.

Dejected, the president boarded the train. He did not have a private luxurious sleeping car built for the leader of a country. Davis took his seat in a common coach packed with the officials of his government. The train gathered steam and crept out of the station at slow speed, no more than ten miles per hour. It was a humble, sobering departure of the president of the Confederate States of America from his capital city.

As the train rolled out of Richmond, most of the passengers were somber. There was nothing left to say. "It was near midnight," Postmaster General John Reagan, on board the train, remembered, "when the President and his cabinet left the heroic city. As our train, frightfully overcrowded, rolled along toward Danville we were **oppressed** with sorrow for those we left behind us and fears for the safety of General Lee and his army."

The presidential train was not the last one to leave Richmond that night. A second one carried another cargo from the city—the treasure of the Confederacy, half a million dollars in gold and silver coins, plus deposits from the Richmond banks. Captain William Parker, an officer in the Confederate States Navy, was put in charge of the treasure and ordered to guard it during the trip to Danville. Men desperate to escape Richmond and who had failed to make it on to Davis's train climbed aboard their last hope, the treasure train. The wild mood at the station alarmed Parker, and he ordered his men—some were only boys—to guard the doors and not allow "another soul to enter."

Once Jefferson Davis was gone, and as the night wore on, Parker witnessed the breakdown of order: "The whiskey…was running in the gutters, and men were getting drunk upon it…. Large numbers of **ruffians** suddenly sprung into existence—I suppose thieves, deserters…who had been hiding." If the mob learned what cargo Parker and his men guarded, then the **looters**, driven mad by greed, would have attacked the train. Parker was prepared to order his men to fire on the crowd.

oppress
(ə-prĕs′) *v.* When you *oppress* someone, you overwhelm or crush them.

ruffian
(rŭf′ē-ən) *n.* A *ruffian* is a thug or a gangster.

looter
(lōōt′ər) *n.* A *looter* is someone who steals during a war or riot.

Before that became necessary, the treasure train got up steam and followed Jefferson Davis into the night.

330   To add to the chaos caused by the mobs, soon there would be fire. And it would not be the Union troops who would burn the city. The Confederates accidentally set their own city afire when they burned supplies to keep them from Union hands. The flames spread out of control and reduced much of the capital to ruins.

Union troops outside Richmond would see the fire and hear the explosions. "About 2 o'clock on the morning of April 3d bright fires were seen in the direction of Richmond. Shortly after, while we were looking at these fires, we heard

340   explosions," one witness reported.

On the way to Danville, the president's train stopped at Clover Station. It was three o'clock in the morning. There a young army lieutenant, eighteen years old, saw the train pull in. He spotted Davis through a window, waving to the people gathered at the station. Later he witnessed the treasure train pass, and others, too. "I saw a government on wheels," he said. From one car in the rear a man cried out, to no one in particular, "Richmond's burning. Gone. All gone."

As Jefferson Davis continued his journey to Danville,

350   Richmond burned and Union troops approached. Around dawn a black man who had escaped the city reached Union lines and reported what Lincoln and U. S. Grant, the commanding general of the Armies of the United States, suspected. The Confederate government had abandoned the capital during the night and the road to the city was open. There would be no battle for Richmond. The Union army could march in and occupy the rebel capital without firing a shot.

The first Union troops entered Richmond shortly

360   after sunrise on Monday, April 3. They marched through the streets, arrived downtown, and took control of the government buildings. They tried to put out the fires, which still burned in some sections of the city. Just a few hours since Davis had left it, the White House of the Confederacy was seized by the Union and made into their new headquarters.

SCAFFOLDING FOR ELL STUDENTS

Analyze Language Use a whiteboard to draw attention to specific words and phrases, like the ones below, that may be unfamiliar to students who are not yet fluent in English. Guide students to use context and prior knowledge to define each phrase.

- "spotted Davis"
- "treasure train"
- "a government on wheels"
- "Gone. All gone."

ASK STUDENTS to explain the events described in lines 330–349. Tell students to ask questions about any parts of the text that they do not understand.

He spotted Davis through a window, waving to the people gathered at the station. Later he witnessed the treasure train pass, and others, too. "I saw a government on wheels," he said. From one car in the rear a man cried out, to no one in particular, "Richmond's burning. Gone. All gone."

Analyze Structure: Comparison and Contrast

COMMON CORE RI 1, RI 3, RI 5

(LINES 366–388)

Tell students that the author is, once again, showing a stark contrast in the way groups of people experience the ongoing events.

 CITE TEXT EVIDENCE Have students reread lines 366–388 to contrast the mood and actions of the government officials with that of Richmond's residents. How are the government officials reacting? *("trying to brighten the mood," "hope and good humor [were] inexhaustible," "a playful air")* How are the people of Richmond feeling and behaving? *("endured a night of terror," "ruins and smoke presented a terrible sight," "a mob . . . gathered . . . half-starved")* What do these contrasting reactions suggest about each group's situation? *(Government officials are headed toward relative safety, while the people of Richmond continue to fear for their lives, either from starvation or from the impending invasion of enemy troops.)*

CRITICAL VOCABULARY

provisions: Richmond burns as Union troops enter the city on the morning of April 3.

ASK STUDENTS to explain why the people of Richmond have such a great need for provisions. *(There were already food shortages in the South during the war, and now the fire has burned what little many people had.)* What kinds of provisions do the people fight over at the warehouse? *(They struggle with one another to get ham, bacon, whisky, flour, sugar, and coffee.)*

Chapter Three

K The gloom that filled President Davis's train eased with the morning sun. Some of the officials of the Confederate government began to talk and tell jokes, trying to brighten the mood. Judah Benjamin, the secretary of state, talked

370 about food and told stories. "[H]is hope and good humor [were] inexhaustible," one official recalled. With a playful air, he discussed the fine points of a sandwich, analyzed his daily diet given the food shortages that plagued the South, and as an example of doing much with little, showed off his coat and pants, both made from an old shawl, which had kept him warm through three winters. Colonel Frank Lubbock, a former governor of Texas, entertained his fellow travelers with wild western tales.

But back in Richmond, the people had endured a night of
380 terror. The ruins and the smoke presented a terrible sight. A Confederate army officer wrote about what he saw at a depot, or warehouse, where food supplies were stored. "By daylight, on the 3d," he noted, "a mob of men, women, and children, to the number of several thousands, had gathered at the corner of 14th and Cary streets…for it must be remembered that in 1865 Richmond was a half-starved city, and the Confederate Government had that morning removed its guards and abandoned the removal of the **provisions**. . . . The depot doors

provisions
(prə-vĭzh′ənz) *n.*
Provisions are a stock of necessary supplies, such as food.

Richmond, Virginia shortly after Union forces entered the city on April 3, 1865.

©Bettmann/Corbis

were forced open and a demoniacal struggle for the countless
barrels of hams, bacon, whisky, flour, sugar, coffee . . . raged
about the buildings among the hungry mob. The gutters ran
with whisky, and it was lapped up as it flowed down the
streets, while all fought for a share of the plunder."

A Union officer wrote about what he saw as he entered the
city in early morning, when it was still burning. "As we neared
the city the fires seemed to increase in number and size,
and at intervals loud explosions were heard. On entering the
square we found Capitol Square covered with people who had
fled there to escape the fire and were utterly worn out with
fatigue and fright. Details were at once made to scour the city
and press into service every able-bodied man, white or black,
and make them assist in extinguishing the flames."

Constance Cary ventured outside to see her ruined
and fallen city. Horrified, she discovered that Yankees had
occupied the Confederate White House. "I looked over at the
President's house, and saw the porch crowded with Union
soldiers and politicians, the street in front filled with curious
gaping negroes." The sight of ex-slaves roving freely about
disgusted her. "It is no longer our Richmond," she complained,
and added that the Confederate anthem still had the power to
raise some people's spirits: "One of the girls tells me she finds
great comfort in singing 'Dixie' with her head buried in a
feather pillow."

All day on April 3, Washington, D.C., celebrated the fall
of Richmond. The *Washington Star* newspaper captured the
joyous mood: "As we write Washington city is in such a blaze
of excitement and enthusiasm as we never before witnessed
here. . . . The thunder of cannon; the ringing of bells; the
eruption of flags from every window and housetop, the shouts
of enthusiastic gatherings in the streets; all echo the glorious
report. RICHMOND IS OURS!!!"

The Union capital celebrated without President Lincoln,
who was still with the army. While Washington rejoiced,
the secretary of war, Edwin Stanton, worried about Lincoln's
safety. He believed that the president was traveling in enemy
territory without sufficient protection. Stanton urged Lincoln
to return to Washington. But Lincoln didn't take the warning.
He telegraphed back:

CLOSE READ

Analyze Language

COMMON CORE **RI 4**

(LINES 414–421)

Review that imagery is descriptive language that
appeals to the sense of sight, hearing, smell, taste, or
touch. Remind students that imagery helps readers
form a mental picture of what is being described.

L **ASK STUDENTS** to reread lines 414–421. What
descriptive details help you imagine events in
Washington, D.C., on April 3, 1865? *(Possible answers:
"joyous mood"; "blaze of excitement and enthusiasm";
"thunder of cannon"; "ringing of bells"; "eruption of
flags from every window and housetop"; "shouts of
enthusiastic gatherings")* Have students compare
this description with the description of Richmond
in lines 394–402. *("worn out with fatigue and fright,"
"extinguishing the flames")* How do the contrasting
images affect the meaning of the text? *(The images
reinforce the idea that victory for one side means
destruction and desolation for the other.)*

Analyze Structure: Comparison and Contrast

COMMON CORE RI 1, RI 3

(LINES 458–463)

Guide students in contrasting the people's reaction to President Davis as he leaves Richmond with the reception he receives the next day in Danville.

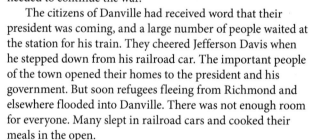 **CITE TEXT EVIDENCE** Have students reread lines 458–463. How do the citizens of Danville respond to Davis when he arrives? *(A large crowd cheers him. Families open their homes to him and other government officials.)* How is this different from the response he received as he left Richmond (lines 272–276)? *(Crowds did not line up to cheer him or offer words of encouragement—many were in the process of fleeing the city themselves.)*

430

> *Head Quarters Armies of the United States*
> *City-Point,*
> *April 3. 5 P.M. 1865*
>
> Hon. Sec. of War
> Washington, D.C.
>
> *Yours received. Thanks for your caution; but I have already been to Petersburg, stayed with Gen. Grant an hour & a half and returned here. It is certain now that Richmond is in our hands, and I think I will go there to-morrow. I will take care of myself.*
>
> A. Lincoln

440   President Davis did not arrive in Danville until 4:00 P.M. on the afternoon of April 3. It had taken eighteen hours to travel just 140 miles. The plodding journey from Richmond to Danville made clear an uncomfortable truth. If Jefferson Davis hoped to avoid capture, continue the war, and save the Confederacy, he would have to move a lot faster than this. Still, the trip had served its purpose. It had saved, for at least another day, the Confederate States of America.

On the afternoon and evening of Monday, April 3, the government on wheels unpacked and set up shop in 450 Danville, Virginia. Jefferson Davis hoped to remain there as long as possible. In Danville he could send and receive communications so that he could issue orders and control the movements of his armies. It would be hard for his commanders to telegraph the president or send riders with the latest news if he stayed on the move and they had to chase him from town to town. In Danville he had the bare minimum he needed to continue the war.

The citizens of Danville had received word that their president was coming, and a large number of people waited at 460 the station for his train. They cheered Jefferson Davis when he stepped down from his railroad car. The important people of the town opened their homes to the president and his government. But soon refugees fleeing from Richmond and elsewhere flooded into Danville. There was not enough room for everyone. Many slept in railroad cars and cooked their meals in the open.

But in Danville Davis and his government had little to do except wait for news. The future course of the war in Virginia

depended upon Robert E. Lee and what was left of his army.
470 Davis expected news from Lee on April 4, but none came. The president longed for action: He wanted to rally armies, send them to strategic places, and continue fighting. Instead, he had to sit still and wait for word from the Army of Northern Virginia.

"April 4 and the succeeding four days passed," noted Stephen R. Mallory, the secretary of the navy, "without bringing word from Lee or Breckinridge, or of the operations of the army; and the anxiety of the President and his followers was intense." Refugees from Richmond carried wild stories.
480 Some said Lee had won "a glorious victory." Others said Lee was too busy fighting to send messengers. Jefferson Davis ignored the rumors.

On April 4, as Davis waited impatiently for news, Lincoln experienced one of the most thrilling days of his life. "Thank God that I have lived to see this!" he wrote. "It seems to me that I have been dreaming a horrid dream for four years, and now the nightmare is gone. I want to go to Richmond."

Admiral Porter, a Union navy admiral, agreed to take him there, "[i]f there is any of it left. There is black smoke over the
490 city." On the *River Queen* they traveled up the river toward Richmond. When the water became too shallow for big boats, Porter transferred the president and Tad to his personal craft, the "admiral's barge." Despite the fancy name, it was no more than a big rowboat. But it allowed them to continue.

The city looked eerie. Lincoln and Porter peered at the rebel capital but saw no one. They saw smoke from the fires. The only sound was the creaking of the oars. "The street along the river-front was as deserted," Porter observed, "as if this had been a city of the dead." Although the Union army
500 had controlled the city for several hours, "not a soldier was to be seen."

The oarsmen rowed for a wharf, and Lincoln stepped out of the boat. Admiral Porter described what happened next: "There was a small house on this landing, and behind it were some twelve negroes digging with spades. The leader of them was an old man sixty years of age. He raised himself to an upright position as we landed, and put his hands up to his eyes. Then he dropped his spade and sprang forward." The man knelt at Lincoln's feet, praising him, calling him

CLOSE READ

Analyze Language

COMMON CORE **RI 1, RI 4**

(LINES 495–501)

Help students identify sensory details used to describe Lincoln's approach to Richmond.

N CITE TEXT EVIDENCE Have students reread the paragraph that begins on line 495. What sensory details does the author use to describe what President Lincoln saw and heard as he arrived in Richmond on a boat? *(sight: "looked eerie," "saw no one," "smoke from the fires," "street along the river-front was . . . deserted"; sound: "creaking of the oars")* How do the descriptive details support the meaning of this section of the text? *(Possible answer: The silence and lack of human presence support the idea that the battle for the city has ended and Richmond is basically deserted.)*

APPLYING ACADEMIC VOCABULARY

demonstrate	symbolize

As you discuss the remainder of the selection, incorporate the following Collection 3 academic vocabulary words: *demonstrate* and *symbolize*. Ask students to suggest what they think the actions and decisions of Lincoln and Davis **demonstrate** about each man's character. What do students think the fall of Richmond **symbolized** to the people of the North? of the South? What did Lincoln **symbolize** to the slaves?

Analyze Connotative Meanings (LINES 524–528)

 COMMON CORE · RI 4, L 5c

Review that some words with a similar denotation, or dictionary definition, can have quite different connotations, or the ideas and feelings associated with a word.

ASK STUDENTS to reread lines 524–528. Point out the word *foolish*. Have students name other words with a similar denotation. *(Possible answers: silly, thoughtless, unwise, imprudent, stupid, dumb, idiotic)* What is the impact of the author's choice to use *foolish* rather than words such as *dumb* or *idiotic*? *(Those words have more negative connotations and would give a worse impression of Admiral Porter's decision. They also are a bit more informal and do not suit the tone and voice of the text.)*

CRITICAL VOCABULARY

throng: Lincoln enters the captured city of Richmond by boat. As he steps onto a wharf, he is greeted by a group of newly freed slaves.

ASK STUDENTS how the throng of grateful slaves reacts to Lincoln's arrival. *(They kneel in front of him and kiss his feet. They joyfully sing a hymn.)* What increases the size of the throng? *(Hundreds of other African Americans hear the singing and come to the wharf.)*

boon: President Lincoln speaks to the large crowd that surrounds him.

ASK STUDENTS to explain what boon these former slaves have received. *(their freedom)* What advice does Lincoln offer regarding this boon? *(He tells the freed slaves that they must act in a way that shows they deserve liberty. They should do good works and learn and obey the laws.)*

---

510 the messiah[4] come to free his children from slavery. "Glory, Hallelujah!" he cried, and kissed the president's feet. The others did the same.

Lincoln was embarrassed. He did not want to enter Richmond like a king. He spoke to the **throng** of former slaves. "Don't kneel to me. That is not right. You must kneel to God only, and thank him for the liberty you will hereafter enjoy."

Before allowing Lincoln to leave them and proceed on foot into Richmond, the freed slaves burst into joyous song:

520   *Oh, all ye people clap your hands,*
        And with triumphant voices sing;
        No force the mighty power withstands
        Of God, the universal King.

The hymn drew hundreds of blacks to the landing. They surrounded Lincoln, making it impossible for him to move. Admiral Porter recognized how foolish he had been to bring the president of the United States ashore without enough soldiers to protect him.

The crowd went wild. Some rushed forward, laid their
530 hands upon the president, and collapsed in joy. Some, too awed to approach Father Abraham, kept their distance and, speechless, just stared at him. Others yelled for joy and performed somersaults. Lincoln spoke to them: "My poor friends, you are free—free as air. You can cast off the name of slave and trample upon it. . . . Liberty is your birthright. . . . But you must try to deserve this priceless **boon**. Let the world see that you merit it, and are able to maintain it by your good works. Don't let your joy carry you into excesses. Learn the laws and obey them. . . . There, now, let me pass on; I have but
540 little time to spare. I want to see the capital."

Porter ordered six marines to march ahead of the president and six behind him, and the landing party walked toward downtown Richmond. The streets were dusty, and smoke from the fires still hung in the air. Lincoln could smell Richmond burning. By now thousands of people, blacks and whites, crowded the streets.

throng
(thrông) *n.* A *throng* is a large group of people.

boon
(bo̅o̅n) *n.* A *boon* is a gift or benefit.

---

[4] **messiah:** the savior or liberator.

> ## "The crowd went wild. Some rushed forward, laid their hands upon the president, and collapsed in joy."

A beautiful girl, about seventeen years old, carrying a bouquet of roses, stepped into the street and advanced toward the president. Admiral Porter watched her struggle
550 through the crowd. "She had a hard time in reaching him," he remembered. "I reached out and helped her within the circle of the sailors' bayonets, where, although nearly stifled with dust, she gracefully presented her bouquet to the President and made a neat little speech, while he held her hand. . . . There was a card on the bouquet with these simple words: 'From Eva to the Liberator of the slaves.'"

Porter spotted a sole soldier on horseback and called out to him: "Go to the general, and tell him to send a military escort here to guard the President and get him through this crowd!"
560 "Is that old Abe?" the trooper asked before galloping off.

Lincoln went on to the Confederate White House and entered Jefferson Davis's study. One of the men with him remembered watching Lincoln sit down and say, "This must have been President Davis's chair." Lincoln crossed his legs and "looked far off with a serious, dreamy expression." Lincoln knew the Confederate president had been here, in this room, no more than thirty-six hours ago. This was the closest Abraham Lincoln had ever come to Jefferson Davis.

One observer remembered that Lincoln "lay back in the
570 chair like a tired man whose nerves had carried him beyond his strength." Sitting in the quiet study of the Confederate president, perhaps Lincoln weighed the cost—more than 620,000 American lives[5]—paid to get there. He did not speak. Then he requested a glass of water.

After Lincoln left the Confederate White House, he toured Richmond in a buggy. Blacks flocked to him and rejoiced, just

---

[5] **more than 620,000 American lives:** the number of deaths caused by the Civil War.

CLOSE READ

Draw Conclusions

COMMON CORE · RI 1, RI 4

(LINES 561–574)

Point out that as President Lincoln entered the Confederate White House, he was accompanied by others who later recorded their observations.

P ASK STUDENTS to reread lines 561–574 to draw conclusions about Lincoln. Based on details in these paragraphs, what conclusions can you draw about the president's thoughts and feelings at this time? What does the author's use of the word "dreamy" suggest about Lincoln's state of mind as he sits in Jefferson Davis's study? *(Possible answer: He was feeling a combination of relief, sadness, and exhaustion. The word* dreamy *suggests that he may have found it hard to believe that this day of victory had finally come.)*

CRITICAL VOCABULARY

vengeance: Although the North is victorious in the Civil War, Lincoln's attitude toward the South is one of compassion.

ASK STUDENTS why they think President Lincoln wanted no vengeance taken on the rebel leaders or their followers. *(Possible answer: He wanted the wounds of war to heal as quickly as possible.)* Why does the author think the period following the fall of Richmond showed "Abraham Lincoln at his best"? *(Possible answer: Lincoln's decision not to inflict vengeance on his opponents showed wisdom, humility, and a great strength of character.)*

COLLABORATIVE DISCUSSION Before partners begin their discussion, have the class suggest qualities or traits they think someone should have to be an effective leader. List students' suggestions, such as

- intelligence
- fairness
- integrity
- persistence
- a vision of the future
- humility
- dedication
- care for others

After pairs have identified ways that Lincoln and Davis demonstrated leadership qualities, ask them to share their conclusions with the class.

ASK STUDENTS to share any questions they generated in the course of reading and discussing the selection.

---

as they had done at the river landing. But not all of Richmond welcomed him to the ruined capital. Most whites stayed in their homes behind locked doors and closed shutters, with
580 some glaring at the unwelcome conqueror through their windows.

It was a miracle that no one poked a rifle or a pistol through an open window and opened fire on the despised Yankee president. Lincoln knew the risk. "I walked alone on the street, and anyone could have shot me from a second-story window," he said. His Richmond tour was one of Lincoln's triumphs. It was the most important day of his presidency. It was also one of the most dangerous days of his life. No American president before or since has ever placed himself
590 at that much risk.

Before Lincoln left Richmond, the Union general left in charge of the city asked Lincoln to tell him how he should deal with the conquered rebels. Lincoln's answer became an American legend. He replied that he didn't want to give any orders, but, "If I were in your place I'd let 'em up easy, let 'em up easy."

During his time in Richmond, Lincoln did not order arrests of any rebel leaders who stayed in the city, did not order their property seized, and said nothing of **vengeance**
600 or punishment. Nor did he order a manhunt for Davis and the officials who had left the city less than two days ago. It was a moment of remarkable greatness and generosity. It was Abraham Lincoln at his best.

vengeance
(věn´jəns) *n.*
Vengeance is a punishment given in return for a wrong.

COLLABORATIVE DISCUSSION With a partner, discuss how Abraham Lincoln and Jefferson Davis demonstrated leadership qualities in the last days of the war. Cite specific evidence from the text to support your ideas.

TO CHALLENGE STUDENTS...

Analyze Author's Perspective Have students reread the background information about James L. Swanson at the beginning of the selection, pointing out his near lifelong fascination with Lincoln.

ASK STUDENTS to work in small groups to review the text with a focus on Swanson's perspective on Lincoln and his actions as opposed to his views of Davis and his actions. Ask groups to discuss whether the text reflects a bias toward Lincoln or whether Swanson offers a balanced perspective. Remind students to support their views with evidence from the text.

Analyze Structure: Comparison and Contrast

COMMON CORE RI 3, RI 5

The Civil War is a topic that lends itself to the examination of two sides. One way to do that in writing is through the use of **compare and contrast organization,** a pattern of organization in which an author compares two or more subjects by explaining how they are similar and contrasts them by explaining how they are different.

- Two subjects can be compared and contrasted within a single paragraph. In this example from *Bloody Times*, Swanson identifies ways that Abraham Lincoln and Jefferson Davis were alike:

  It may seem that two men could not be more different . . . But in fact, they had many things in common. Both . . . loved books and reading. Both had children who died young.

- A comparison and contrast can be made in two separate paragraphs, with one paragraph covering various aspects of the first subject and the next paragraph covering similar aspects of the second subject.
- A comparison and contrast can be made within larger sections of a piece, such as chapter by chapter.

Look for examples of each type of compare and contrast organization as you analyze *Bloody Times*.

Analyze Connotative Meanings

COMMON CORE RI 4, L 5c

Word choice, an author's selection of words, can affect a reader's attitude toward a subject. For example, every word has a dictionary definition, or **denotation.** Words also have **connotations**—the feelings or ideas that people associate with that word. Words with a similar denotation can have a positive, neutral, or negative connotation.

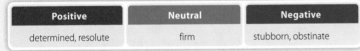

Positive	Neutral	Negative
determined, resolute	firm	stubborn, obstinate

Study this sentence. How would your feelings about Lincoln be different if the author had used the word *stubbornly* instead of *firmly*?

Every new state to join the country, Lincoln firmly believed, should prohibit slavery.

Review *Bloody Times* to find another sentence whose meaning would change if a word with a similar denotation but different connotation was used.

CLOSE READ

Analyze Structure: Comparison and Contrast

COMMON CORE RI 3, RI 5

Explain to students that writers can organize their ideas in various ways. Point out that a compare and contrast organization is one of several organizational patterns a writer might use.

Help students find examples of different forms of compare and contrast organization in *Bloody Times*:

- comparing or contrasting subjects in one paragraph *(Example: The paragraph that begins on line 65 and the paragraph that begins on line 575.)*
- contrasting subjects in larger selections *(Example: A group of paragraphs beginning on line 22.)*

Analyze Connotative Meanings

COMMON CORE RI 4, L 5c

To demonstrate how connotation influences meaning, have students make up original sentences using a word, such as *determined,* from the chart.

- Ask students to replace that word with another from the chart to see how the meaning is affected.
- Then, ask volunteers to identify sentences whose meaning would change by using a word with a similar denotation but different connotation. *(Example: "Lincoln was embarrassed"; replace embarrassed with humiliated)*

Strategies for Annotation   *Annotate it!*

Analyze Structure: Comparison and Contrast

COMMON CORE RI 3, RI 5

Have students use their eBook annotation tools to analyze the text. Ask students to do the following:

- Highlight in yellow details that compare subjects.
- Highlight in blue details that contrast subjects.

But before 1858, when Lincoln ran for the United States Senate (and lost the election), very few people had heard of him. Most people of those days would have recognized the name of Jefferson Davis.

Analyzing the Text COMMON CORE RI 1, RI 3, RI 4, RI 5

Possible answers:

1. *The selection has a compare and contrast organization. The Introduction makes direct comparisons between the two men in single paragraphs and in groups of paragraphs. Chapter 1 is entirely about Davis. Chapters 2 and 3 tell information about both men in chronological order.*

2. Stern *evokes the image of someone who is very serious.* Harsh *and* authoritarian *both have more negative connotations.*

3. *The greatest difference was their view on slavery. Davis believed in slavery (lines 101–108). Lincoln held the opposite view (lines 109–116). Their differences led them to become enemies at war.*

4. *He is calm, thoughtful, and resolute. He is a man fully committed to his cause.*

5. *"The man knelt at Lincoln's feet, praising him"; "messiah come to free his children from slavery"; "'Glory, Hallelujah!'"; "kissed the president's feet"; "Father Abraham." Lincoln was viewed by many as a savior.*

Writing and Research COMMON CORE W 2, W 7, W 8

Have students form small groups to conduct research.

- Use the lesson on page 198a to help each group formulate research questions.
- Assist groups that need help locating appropriate print and digital resources to answer their questions.
- Have each group present their findings to the class by summarizing the key points in their completed report.

 eBook *Annotate It!*

Analyzing the Text  COMMON CORE RI 1, RI 3, RI 4, RI 5, W 2, W 7, W 8, W 9b

Cite Text Evidence   Support your responses with evidence from the text.

1. **Identify Patterns** Review the overall pattern of organization that author James Swanson used in this piece. How is the organizational pattern in the introduction different from each of the chapters?

2. **Interpret** Reread lines 74–82. Swanson writes that Davis was "sterner." How is the connotation of *stern* different from words such as *harsh* and *authoritarian* that have similar denotations?

3. **Compare** What does the author identify as the greatest difference between Davis and Lincoln? How did this difference affect the life course of these two men?

4. **Draw Conclusions** Reread lines 175–183. Describe Jefferson Davis's behavior. What does his conduct reveal about his character?

5. **Evaluate** When an author refers to another literary work without naming it, it is called an **allusion.** Identify several allusions to the Bible in lines 502–545. What do these suggest about the way Lincoln was viewed by the end of the Civil War?

Writing and Research

With a small group, conduct research and write a short report about how Lincoln's views on slavery and emancipation changed over time. Explain his thoughts about emancipation before, during, and after the Civil War, and describe what led to his changing attitudes. Share your findings with the class.

PERFORMANCE TASK  my WriteSmart

Respond in Writing Create a poster that compares and contrasts Abraham Lincoln and Jefferson Davis.

- First, draw a Venn diagram on your poster. Label each side of the diagram with one man's name and include an image to represent him.

- Next, revisit the text of *Bloody Times* to identify character traits of these two leaders. Write the traits in the appropriate sections of your Venn diagram.
- Finally, use the traits you identified to write a brief character sketch of each man below the corresponding parts of the diagram.

PERFORMANCE TASK   COMMON CORE W9b

Assign this performance task. my WriteSmart

Respond in Writing As needed, model how to complete a Venn diagram. Then, tell students that a **character sketch** is a brief description of a character or person that gives readers a general picture of what the person is like. It does not tell a person's entire life story.

- Explain that a character sketch may include information related to a person's background, beliefs or values, strengths, weaknesses, goals, talents, appearance, and behavior.

- Have students work in pairs to review *Bloody Times* and identify important character traits of Lincoln and Davis.

Critical Vocabulary

secede	succumb	jubilation	oppress
ruffian	looter	provisions	throng
boon	vengeance		

Practice and Apply Use your understanding of the Vocabulary words to complete each sentence.

1. A store owner might **succumb** to a **looter** because . . .

2. Some wanted **vengeance** against those who tried to **secede** because . . .

3. It would be scary to see a **throng** of **ruffians** because . . .

4. **Provisions** would be a **boon** to people following a hurricane because . . .

5. There is no **jubilation** when someone tries to **oppress** people because . . .

Vocabulary Strategy: Use Context Clues

Context clues are the words and phrases surrounding a word that provide hints about its meaning. Sometimes, you may find a context clue in the same sentence as the unfamiliar word you are trying to understand. The overall meaning of a sentence can also be a good context clue. Look at this example:

> If the mob learned what cargo Parker and his men guarded, then the looters, driven mad by greed, would have attacked the train.

If you didn't know what *looters* means, the words *greed* and *attacked* are clues. The overall meaning of the sentence is another context clue. Together, these hints can help you guess that looters are "robbers who use violent means during times of chaos." You can confirm your guess by checking a print or a digital dictionary.

Practice and Apply Find each of the following words in the selection and look for clues to the word's meaning. Then, complete a chart like the one shown.

Word	Context Clues	Guessed Definition	Dictionary Definition
fatigue (line 400)			
anthem (line 410)			
despised (line 583)			

Critical Vocabulary

Possible answers:

1. *he or she wants to avoid being injured.*

2. *they believed seceding had damaged the country.*

3. *they often cause damage and injuries.*

4. *a hurricane may destroy provisions such as food, water, and medical supplies.*

5. *people do not celebrate being oppressed.*

Vocabulary Strategy: Use Context Clues

Word	Context Clues	Guessed Definition	Dictionary Definition
fatigue	"people who had fled there to escape the fire"; "utterly worn out"	tiredness	weariness or exhaustion resulting from great effort
anthem	"still had the power to raise some people's spirits"; "finds great comfort in singing 'Dixie'"	song	a song of praise or loyalty
despised	"a miracle that no one poked a rifle or a pistol through an open window and opened fire on"; "Yankee"	hated	to regard with contempt or scorn

---

Strategies for Annotation   **Annotate it!**

Use Context Clues

Have students locate the sentences containing *fatigue*, *anthem*, and *despised*. Encourage them to use their eBook annotation tools to do the following:

- Highlight each of the three words.
- Reread the sentence in which each word appears as well as the surrounding sentences. Underline any context clues.
- Using the underlined text as well as the overall meaning of the sentence, try to infer each word's meaning.

> "It is no longer our Richmond," she complained, and added that the Confederate anthem still had the power to raise some people's spirits: "One of the girls tells me she finds great comfort in singing 'Dixie' with her head buried in a feather pillow."

PRACTICE & APPLY

Language Conventions: Gerunds

Tell students that, like a noun, a gerund is a word that names something. Using the chart on page 198, help students understand the function of the gerund *fighting* in each sentence. Explain that

- the **subject** of a sentence tells who or what the sentence is about (here, *fighting* tells what the sentence is about)

- a **direct object** receives the action of a verb; it answers the question *whom?* or *what?* (*fighting* answers the question "Stopped *what?*")

- the **object of a preposition** is the last word in a prepositional phrase (*fighting* is the object of the preposition *from*)

- a **predicate noun** comes after a linking verb and is linked to or renames another noun in the sentence (the linking verb *was* links *fighting* and *solution*)

Answers:

1. *Reading: subject*

2. *singing: object of preposition*

3. *fleeing: direct object*

4. *Studying: subject*

5. *losing: predicate noun*

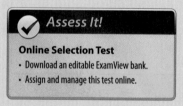

✓ Assess It!

Online Selection Test
- Download an editable ExamView bank.
- Assign and manage this test online.

Language Conventions: Gerunds

Recall that a **verbal** is a word that is formed from a verb but is used as a noun, an adjective, or an adverb.

A **gerund** is one type of verbal. It is a verb form ending in *-ing* that functions as a noun. In this sentence, the word *fighting* is a gerund:

> He wanted to rally armies, send them to strategic places, and continue *fighting.*

Gerunds can perform the same functions as nouns in a sentence.

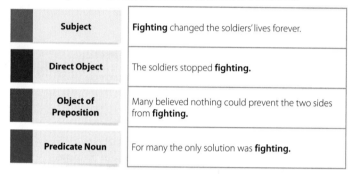

Subject	**Fighting** changed the soldiers' lives forever.
Direct Object	The soldiers stopped **fighting.**
Object of Preposition	Many believed nothing could prevent the two sides from **fighting.**
Predicate Noun	For many the only solution was **fighting.**

Don't confuse gerunds with other kinds of words that end in *-ing*. A verb can end in *-ing*. A participle that modifies a noun or a pronoun can also end in *-ing*.

Gerund	Verb	Participle
Thinking became a torment for Davis.	The slaves were **thinking** about freedom.	Lincoln was a **thinking** person.

Practice and Apply Write each gerund. Label it *subject, direct object, object of preposition,* or *predicate noun* to explain its function in the sentence.

1. Reading gave Lincoln and Davis access to inspiring ideas.

2. The former slaves were demonstrating their joy by singing.

3. Davis and other promising leaders eventually stopped fleeing.

4. Studying was what allowed Lincoln to become a lawyer.

5. Vengeance meant losing because Lincoln believed it would destroy the healing nation.

INTERACTIVE WHITEBOARD LESSON
Generating Questions for Research

COMMON CORE
W 7

TEACH

Tell students that before they write a report or informative essay, they will need to conduct research to find information on their topic. Explain that good writers begin this process by making a list of research questions. Review these steps:

1. Choose your topic.
2. Think about what you want to explain in your paper.
3. List questions you have about your topic. These questions will help guide your research.
4. Be sure your questions aren't too broad or too narrow.

Use the Interactive Whiteboard lesson "Doing Research on the Web" to help students consider the types of questions that will best focus their search for information. As needed, point out that writers often look for answers to the questions *who? what? where? when? why?* and *how?*

PRACTICE AND APPLY

Have small groups apply this skill by generating research questions for this lesson's Writing and Research activity, found in the student book. Review and evaluate each group's questions before they begin their research to be sure the questions are focused and are neither too broad nor too narrow.

Analyze Structure:
Comparison and Contrast

COMMON CORE
RI 3,
RI 5

RETEACH

Review the terms *compare, contrast,* and *organization.* Remind students that when writers use a compare and contrast organizational pattern, they examine the similarities and differences between two or more subjects.

Give a familiar example of two people an author might describe. For example: two historical figures, two popular figures in today's culture, or two fictional characters. Ask students to

- compare the two individuals by naming ways they are similar
- contrast the two individuals by naming ways they are different

As volunteers suggest similarities and differences, point out how this leads them to a better understanding of both people. Remind students that authors often use a compare-and-contrast structure to make connections among individuals and to deepen readers' understanding of people, ideas, and events.

 LEVEL UP TUTORIALS Assign the following *Level Up* tutorial: **Comparison-Contrast Organization**

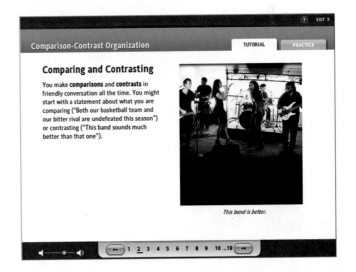

CLOSE READING APPLICATION

Student partners can work together to analyze structure and causes and effects in another selection they have read recently or in a recent newspaper or magazine article.

Civil War Journal

Journal Entries by Louisa May Alcott

Why This Text

Students do not always analyze comparisons authors make. Journal excerpts like these by Louisa May Alcott contain comparisons that might be overlooked without close reading. With the help of the close-reading questions, students will compare Alcott's first experience of becoming a Civil War nurse with her later experience of facing difficulties as a nurse. Close reading will help students understand this historical text.

Background Have students read the background and the information about the author. Introduce the selection by telling students that these journal entries are excerpted from *Hospital Sketches*, which was published in 1863. The complete work is a memoir of the six weeks Alcott spent volunteering as a nurse for the Union Army. To save her family the embarrassment of her service, she published the sketches under the pseudonym Tribulation Periwinkle.

SETTING A PURPOSE Ask students to pay attention to shifts in tone and content as they read. How soon into the text can they identify Alcott's mood?

 Common Core Support

- cite strong textual evidence
- analyze how a text makes distinctions between ideas and events
- determine the meaning of words and phrases as they are used in a text
- analyze the structure of a specific paragraph in a text

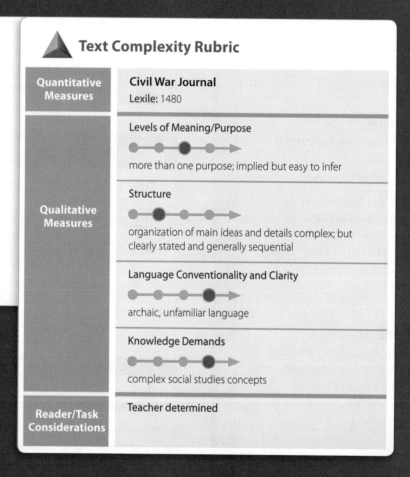

Text Complexity Rubric

Quantitative Measures	**Civil War Journal** Lexile: 1480
Qualitative Measures	**Levels of Meaning/Purpose** more than one purpose; implied but easy to infer
	Structure organization of main ideas and details complex; but clearly stated and generally sequential
	Language Conventionality and Clarity archaic, unfamiliar language
	Knowledge Demands complex social studies concepts
Reader/Task Considerations	Teacher determined

Strategies for CLOSE READING

Analyze Structure: Comparison and Contrast

Students should read these journal excerpts carefully all the way through. Close-reading questions at the bottom of the page will help them focus on a thorough analysis of the text. As they read, students should jot down comments or questions about the journal entries in the side margins.

WHEN STUDENTS STRUGGLE . . .

To help students compare and contrast sections of the selection, have them work in small groups to fill out a chart, such as the one shown below, as they analyze the text.

CITE TEXT EVIDENCE For practice in comparing sections of text, ask students to identify key concepts from the 1861 and 1862 entries and compare them to Alcott's writing in 1863.

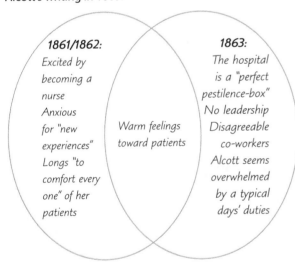

1861/1862:

Excited by becoming a nurse
Anxious for "new experiences"
Longs "to comfort every one" of her patients

Warm feelings toward patients

1863:

The hospital is a "perfect pestilence-box"
No leadership
Disagreeable co-workers
Alcott seems overwhelmed by a typical days' duties

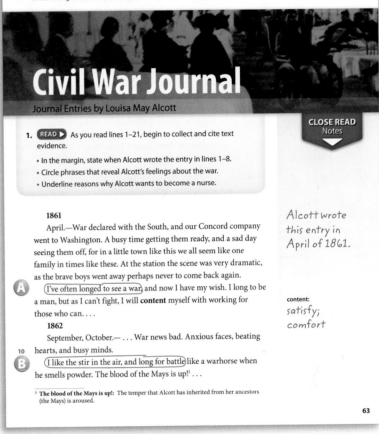

Background Louisa May Alcott *(1832–1888) published her first work when she was 22, and she published over 30 books and story collections during her lifetime. In addition to writing literary masterworks such as* Little Women, *she is also known for the journal she kept during the Civil War. During the war she nursed wounded soldiers in Washington, D.C., hospitals. The army thought that female nurses would improve the morale of the wounded men, even though critics said the work was "indecent" for women and fretted that women would flirt with the soldiers. Alcott's journal proved critics wrong about female nurses.*

Civil War Journal

Journal Entries by Louisa May Alcott

CLOSE READ
Notes

1. **READ ▶** As you read lines 1–21, begin to collect and cite text evidence.

   • In the margin, state when Alcott wrote the entry in lines 1–8.
   • Circle phrases that reveal Alcott's feelings about the war.
   • Underline reasons why Alcott wants to become a nurse.

1861

April.—War declared with the South, and our Concord company went to Washington. A busy time getting them ready, and a sad day seeing them off, for in a little town like this we all seem like one family in times like these. At the station the scene was very dramatic, as the brave boys went away perhaps never to come back again.

(A) I've often longed to see a war, and now I have my wish. I long to be a man, but as I can't fight, I will **content** myself with working for those who can. . . .

1862

September, October.— . . . War news bad. Anxious faces, beating hearts, and busy minds.

10 **(B)** I like the stir in the air, and long for battle like a warhorse when he smells powder. The blood of the Mays is up![1] . . .

[1] **The blood of the Mays is up!:** The temper that Alcott has inherited from her ancestors (the Mays) is aroused.

Alcott wrote this entry in April of 1861.

content:
satisfy; comfort

63

---

1. **READ AND CITE TEXT EVIDENCE**

   (A) ASK STUDENTS to cite textual evidence that explains Alcott's motivations for becoming a nurse for the Union Army. *Students will find evidence of Alcott's feelings about the war in lines 6 and 11. They will find reasons Alcott wants to become a nurse in lines 14–18.*

   Critical Vocabulary: content (line 7) Have students compare their definitions of *content*. Ask them what part of speech Alcott uses here, and what homographs they came across spelled *c-o-n-t-e-n-t* that Alcott did not use here.

November.—Thirty years old. Decided to go to Washington as a nurse if I could find a place. Help needed, and I love nursing, and *must* let out my pent-up energy in some new way. Winter is always a hard and a dull time, and if I am away there is one less to feed and warm and worry over.

I want new experiences, and am sure to get 'em if I go. So I've sent in my name, and bide my time[2] writing tales, to leave all snug behind
20 me, and mending up my old clothes,—for nurses don't need nice things, thank goodness!

December.—On the 11th I received a note from Miss H. M. Stevenson telling me to start for Georgetown next day to fill a place in the Union Hotel Hospital. Mrs. Ropes of Boston was matron, and Miss Kendall of Plymouth was a nurse there, and though a hard place, help was needed. I was ready, and when my commander said "March!" I marched. Packed my trunk, and reported in B.[oston] that same evening.

We had all been full of courage till the last moment came, then we
30 all broke down. I realized that I had taken my life in my hand, and might never see them all again. I said, "Shall I stay, Mother?" as I hugged her close. "No, go!" answered the Spartan[3] woman, and till I turned the corner she bravely smiled and waved her wet handkerchief on the doorstep. Shall I ever see that dear old face again?

---

[2] **bide my time:** wait around.
[3] **Spartan:** strong and self-disciplined.

---

2. **REREAD** Reread lines 1–21. How does Alcott use words with positive connotations to explain her desire to become a Civil War nurse? Support your answer with explicit textual evidence.

Alcott says that there is a "stir in the air" which creates a feeling of excitement. Alcott's "pent-up energy" and desire for "new experiences" also make the prospect of becoming a Civil War nurse a worthwhile endeavor.

3. **READ** As you read lines 22–64, continue to cite textual evidence.

• Underline details in lines 22–37 that suggest a similarity between Alcott and a soldier.
• In the margin, paraphrase Alcott's thoughts in lines 48–49.
• Circle the little boy's description of Alcott in lines 52–64.

64

> I want new experiences, and am sure to get 'em if I go.

So I set forth in the December twilight, with May and Julian Hawthorne as escort, feeling as if I was the son of the house going to war.

Friday, the 12th, was a very memorable day, spent in running all over Boston to get my pass, etc., calling for parcels, getting a tooth
40 filled, and buying a veil,—my only purchase. A. C. gave me some old clothes, the dear Sewalls money for myself and boys, lots of love and help, and at 5 P.M., saying "good-by" to a group of tearful faces at the station, I started on my long journey, full of hope and sorrow, courage and plans.

A most interesting journey into a new world full of stirring sights and sounds, new adventures, and an evergrowing sense of the great task I had undertaken.

I said my prayers as I went rushing through the country white with tents, all alive with patriotism, and already red with blood.
50 A solemn time, but I'm glad to live in it, and am sure it will do me good whether I come out alive or dead.

All went well, and I got to Georgetown one evening very tired. Was kindly welcomed, slept in my narrow bed with two other room-mates, and on the morrow began my new life by seeing a poor man die at dawn, and sitting all day between a boy with pneumonia and a man shot through the lungs. A strange day, but I did my best, and when I put mother's little black shawl round the boy while he sat up panting for breath, he smiled and said, "You are real motherly,

There is enthusiasm for the war but there is also a significant number of injured soldiers for Alcott to tend to.

65

---

2. **REREAD AND CITE TEXT EVIDENCE**

B **ASK STUDENTS** to read aloud their response, including explicit textual evidence, to a partner. After discussing their response, allow time for revisions of their connotations. *Answers will vary. Students should cite words and phrases with positive connotations such as "the stir in the air" from line 11, and "pent up energy," from line 15.*

3. **READ AND CITE TEXT EVIDENCE**

C **ASK STUDENTS** to cite textual evidence that contrasts Alcott's view of herself before she begins nursing with one patient's view of her after she becomes a nurse. *Students should underline evidence that Alcott sees herself as similar to a soldier in lines 26–28, line 30, and lines 36–37. They should circle the contrasting view that comes from one of her patients in lines 58–59, "You are real motherly, ma'am."*

WHEN STUDENTS STRUGGLE . . .

To help students identify key concepts in Alcott's journal entries from 1861 and 1862, have them review their reading notes and their responses to questions 1–3. Have them discuss and draft entries for the left circle of the Venn diagram. What are the key concepts in lines 1–64? They will revise their answers as they read further.

CITE TEXT EVIDENCE Ask students to cite textual evidence of the key concepts in lines 1–64. *Students should cite evidence of Alcott's excitement about becoming a nurse, such as lines 14–15: "I love nursing and must let out my pent-up energy . . ." They should cite evidence of her enthusiasm, and her desire to help others, such as line 18, "I want new experiences," and lines 63–64 "the suffering round me made me long to comfort every one. . . ."*

"ma'am." I felt as if I was getting on. The man only lay and stared with his big black eyes, and made me very nervous. But all were well behaved, and I sat looking at the twenty strong faces as they looked back at me,—hoping that I looked "motherly" to them, for my thirty years made me feel old, and the suffering round me made me long to comfort every one. . . .

1863

January.—I never began the year in a stranger place than this, five hundred miles from home, alone among strangers, doing painful duties all day long, & leading a life of constant excitement in this greathouse surrounded by 3 or 4 hundred men in all stages of suffering, disease & death. Though often home sick, heart sick & worn out, I like it—find real pleasure in comforting tending & cheering these poor souls who seem to love me, to feel my sympathy though unspoken, & acknowledge my hearty good will in spite of the ignorance, awkwardness, & bashfulness which I cannot help showing in so new & trying a situation. The men are docile, respectful, & affectionate, with but few exceptions, truly lovable & manly many of them. John Suhre a Virginia blacksmith is the prince of patients & though what we call a common man, in education & condition, to me is all that I could expect or ask from the first gentleman in the land. Under his plain speech & unpolished manner I seem to see a noble character, a heart as warm & tender as a woman's, a nature fresh &

Alcott is tired and homesick, but she is pleased that she can ease the pain of the wounded and has warm feelings toward her patients.

---

4. ◀ **REREAD** Reread lines 52–64. Alcott says she hopes to appear "motherly" to all her patients. How would your perception of Alcott change if she had used a word such as *watchful* or *protective*, which has a similar denotation but different connotation?

The word "motherly" implies a strong bond between two people. A word such as "watchful" or "protective" conveys that Alcott is focused on her duties, but does not suggest the close relationship she wants to develop with her patients.

5. **READ** ▶ As you read lines 65–86, continue to cite text evidence.
- Underline details that describe Alcott's duties.
- Circle details that describe Alcott's patients, including John Suhre.
- In the margin, summarize Alcott's feelings about her experiences.

66

---

frank as any child's. He is about thirty, I think, tall & handsome, mortally wounded & dying royally, without **reproach**, repining,[4] or remorse. Mrs. Ropes & myself love him & feel indignant that such a man should be so early lost, for though he might never distinguish himself before the world, his influence & example cannot be without effect, for real goodness is never wasted.

Mon 4th—I shall record the events of a day as a sample of the days I spend—

Up at six, dress by gas light, run through my ward & fling up the windows though the men grumble & shiver; but the air is bad enough to breed a pestilence & as no notice is taken of our frequent appeals for better ventilation I must do what I can. Poke up the fire, add blankets, joke, coax & command, but continue to open doors & windows as if life depended on it; mine does, & doubtless many another, for a more perfect pestilence-box than this house I never saw—cold, damp, dirty, full of vile odors from wounds, kitchens, wash rooms, & stables. No competent head, male or female, to right matters, & a jumble of good, bad, & indifferent nurses, surgeons & attendants to complicate the Chaos still more.

After this unwelcome progress through my **stifling** ward I go to breakfast with what appetite I may; find the inevitable fried beef, salt butter, husky bread & washy coffee; listen to the clack of eight women & a dozen men; the first silly, stupid or possessed of but one idea, the last absorbed in their breakfast & themselves to a degree that is both **ludicrous** and provoking, for all the dishes are ordered down the table *full* & returned *empty*, the conversation is entirely among themselves

[4] **repining:** fretting, being discontented.

reproach:
shame

Alcott uses this entry to provide an example of a typical day.

stifling:
hot and stuffy; suffocating

ludicrous:
ridiculous

---

6. ◀ **REREAD AND DISCUSS** Reread lines 65–86. In a small group, compare and contrast Alcott's feelings about the war in this entry with the way she felt in previous journal entries. Cite explicit textual evidence in your discussion.

7. **READ** ▶ As you read lines 87–117, continue to cite textual evidence.
- In the margin, restate what Alcott says about the journal entry for Monday the 4th in lines 87–88.
- Circle the phrases that describe the conditions in the hospital.
- Underline the desctiption of Alcott's duties as a nurse on a typical day.

67

---

4. **REREAD AND CITE TEXT EVIDENCE**

D **ASK STUDENTS** to discuss their analysis of Alcott's choice of the word *motherly* in line 62. Ask students to find evidence in the text that Alcott would like to develop a "motherly" relationship with her patients. *Students may cite that she offered her "mother's little black shawl" (line 57) to a suffering patient, or that she wanted to "comfort every one" (line 64).*

5. **READ AND CITE TEXT EVIDENCE**

E **ASK STUDENTS** to cite textual evidence that describes Alcott's nursing experience. *Students should underline details that describe Alcott's duties (lines 66–69, lines 70–72, and line 74) and circle details that describe Alcott's patients (lines 74–77 and 79–83).*

FOR ELL STUDENTS *Sympathy* is a term that is usually confusing for Spanish-speakers, since it has a false cognate, *simpatía* (friendliness, charm). Clarify that in English it means the "feeling of support or concern for someone else's trouble."

6. **REREAD AND DISCUSS USING TEXT EVIDENCE**

F **ASK STUDENTS** to appoint a reporter for each group to cite specific text evidence and line number references to support their conclusions.

7. **READ AND CITE TEXT EVIDENCE**

G **ASK STUDENTS** to cite text evidence that describes the experience of nursing in a Union hospital. *Students should cite lines 95–99 and lines 110–116.*

Critical Vocabulary: reproach (line 82) Have students explain Alcott's use of *reproach* in this context.

Critical Vocabulary: stifling (line 100) Ask why Alcott used *stifling* rather than a synonym such as *hot* or *stuffy*.

Critical Vocabulary: ludicrous (line 105) Have students explain what Alcott finds ludicrous.

& each announces his opinion with an air of importance that frequently causes me to choke in my cup or bolt my meals with undignified speed lest a laugh betray to these pompous beings that a "child's among them takin' notes." Till noon I trot, trot, giving out rations, cutting up food for helpless "boys," washing faces, teaching my attendants how beds are made or floors swept, dressing wounds, taking Dr. FitzPatrick's orders, (privately wishing all the time that he would be more gentle with my big babies), dusting tables, sewing bandages, keeping my tray tidy, rushing up & down after pillows, bed linen, sponges, book & directions, till it seems as if I would joyfully pay down all I possess for a fifteen minutes rest.

110

8. **◀ REREAD** Reread lines 87–117. Which details in these lines develop Alcott's concept of the poor working conditions in the hospital? Explain, citing explicit textual evidence in your answer.

Alcott calls the hospital a "perfect-pestilence box" filled with "vile odors." She describes her colleagues as "stupid" and "absorbed . . . in themselves." Her many duties exhaust her. These details suggest that the hospital is a chaotic and unpleasant place.

SHORT RESPONSE

Cite Text Evidence Compare and contrast Alcott's journal entry in lines 1–64 with her entry in lines 87–117. Which concepts do each of these entries develop? Be sure to **cite text evidence** in your response.

At first, Alcott is excited by becoming a nurse. She is anxious for "new experiences" and longs "to comfort every one" of her patients. These entries develop her enthusiasm and desire to help others. On the other hand, Alcott's later journal entries emphasize the difficulties she faces. The hospital is a "perfect pestilence-box" with no leadership and disagreeable coworkers. She is also seems overwhelmed by the duties she completes in a typical day.

68

8. **REREAD AND CITE TEXT EVIDENCE**

(H) ASK STUDENTS to cite text evidence to support their explanation of how Alcott develops the concept of poor working conditions in the hospital. *Students should cite evidence of the shortcomings of the hospital itself (lines 95–96), evidence of the mismanagement (lines 97–99), and evidence that Alcott does not like her co-workers (lines 102–110).*

FOR ELL STUDENTS Clarify the meaning of *lest*. Explain to students that it is equivalent to the expression "for fear that."

SHORT RESPONSE

Cite Text Evidence Students should:

- summarize and explain key concepts in lines 1–64 and 87–117.
- compare and contrast key concepts in lines 1–64 with key concepts in lines 87–117.
- cite text evidence to support their comparison.

TO CHALLENGE STUDENTS . . .

For additional expert opinions about the meaning of the American Civil War, students can view the video *Civil War in One Word* in their eBooks.

ASK STUDENTS to create a chart like the one below to organize the information presented in the video. The first row is filled in as an example. After filling in the chart, ask students to make an inference about how Alcott might have described the war. What word might Alcott have chosen to describe the war as she anticipated her nursing experience? What word might she have chosen after spending some time as a nurse in a Union Army hospital?

Time	Expert	Credentials	Word	Reasons
0:03	Ira Berlin	Professor of History, University of Maryland	Freedom	This is what the war comes to mean to people

DIG DEEPER

1. With the class, return to Question 6, Reread and Discuss. Have students share the results of their discussion.

   ASK STUDENTS whether they were satisfied with the outcome of their small-group discussions. Have each group share the textual evidence they cited as they compared and contrasted Alcott's feelings about the war in lines 65–86 with previous journal entries.

   - Encourage students to supply line number references as they cite evidence of Alcott's feelings about the war in lines 65–86. *Students should cite evidence of Alcott's loneliness (lines 65–66), the extent of the suffering around her (lines 68–69 and lines 79–83), and her desire to help alleviate the suffering of the wounded and dying (lines 70–71).*

   - Encourage students to supply line number references as they cite evidence of Alcott's feelings about the war in previous journal entries. *Students should cite evidence of Alcott's excitement (lines 6, 11–12, and 18). They should cite evidence of her fear (lines 29–34). They should also cite evidence of her desire to "comfort every one . . ." (lines 63–64).*

   - After students have shared the results of their group's discussion, ask whether another group found evidence they would like to include in their comparison.

2. With the class, return to Question 8, Reread. Have students share their responses.

   ASK STUDENTS to discuss how Alcott portrayed the poor working conditions at the hospital. Remind them to cite textual evidence in their discussion.

   - What clues let you know that the hospital is an unpleasant place to work? *Alcott describes the hospital as a "perfect pestilence-box" (line 95); she writes that it is "cold, damp, dirty, full of vile odors" (line 96).*

   - How does Alcott describe the administration of the hospital? *There is "no competent head" (line 97) and the "nurses, surgeons and attendants" are a "jumble of good, bad, & indifferent" (line 98), She uses the word "Chaos" (line 99) and capitalizes it, giving it even more importance.*

   - What clues tell you that Alcott does not enjoy her co-workers? *Students should cite descriptions of women who are "silly, stupid, or possessed of but one idea" (line 103) and men who are "absorbed in their breakfast & themselves to a degree that is both ludicrous and provoking" (lines 104–105).*

   ASK STUDENTS to return to their Short Response answer and revise it based on the class discussion.

CLOSE READING NOTES

O Captain! My Captain!

Poem by Walt Whitman

Why This Text?

Poetry can express the powerful emotions of those affected by significant events. This classic elegy—a poetic form that expresses mourning and reflection—was written at the time of Abraham Lincoln's death.

Key Learning Objective: The student will learn about elegy as a poetic form and understand how extended metaphors can be used to express feelings and ideas.

 COMMON CORE

Common Core Standards

RL 1 Cite textual evidence.
RL 4 Determine the meaning of words and phrases.
RL 5 Compare and contrast the structure of two or more texts.
SL 1 Engage effectively in a range of collaborative discussions.
SL 6 Adapt speech to context or task.

 ## Text Complexity Rubric

Quantitative Measures	**O Captain! My Captain!** Lexile: N/A
Qualitative Measures	**Levels of Meaning/Purpose** single level of complex meaning
	Structure regular stanzas, predictable rhyme scheme
	Language Conventionality and Clarity figurative, symbolic language
	Knowledge Demands cultural and literary knowledge essential to understanding
Reader/Task Considerations	Teacher determined Vary by individual reader and type of text

CLOSE READ

Background Have students read the background and information about the author. Tell them that Walt Whitman worked as a printer, teacher, and journalist before publishing *Leaves of Grass,* the first collection of poems to be written in free verse with no regular patterns of rhythm or rhyme. He self-published the first edition, which contained only twelve poems, almost ten years before the Civil War. Over the course of his career, Whitman added to, revised, and rearranged the poems, publishing several more editions until his death in 1892.

Walt Whitman Whitman's poems focus on American life during the 19th century, idealizing both its leaders and working citizens, giving narrative accounts of Civil War battles, and celebrating industry and innovation. Whitman was greatly influenced by the time he spent visiting and caring for wounded soldiers during the Civil War.

SETTING A PURPOSE Direct students to use the Setting a Purpose prompt and question to focus their reading. Remind students to generate additional questions as they read the text.

Background *On April 14, 1865, only five days after the Civil War ended, President Abraham Lincoln was assassinated at the Ford Theater in Washington, D.C., where he was watching a performance. Lincoln was shot by John Wilkes Booth, a famous actor and a Confederate sympathizer. Although Booth initially escaped, he was discovered days later by Union soldiers. Booth was killed while trying to avoid capture.*

O Captain! My Captain!

Poem by Walt Whitman

Walt Whitman (1819–1892) *was a great admirer of President Lincoln. After the president was assassinated, Whitman wrote "O Captain! My Captain!" to capture the sense of tragedy that descended upon the country. Largely unknown to the public when he wrote this poem, Whitman eventually gained a reputation as one of the greatest American writers. "O Captain! My Captain!" is among his most famous works, and his book of poems,* Leaves of Grass, *is considered one of the masterpieces of American literature.*

SETTING A PURPOSE As you read, look for evidence of Whitman's feelings about Lincoln. Do others seem to share his feelings? Write down any questions you have as you read.

(cr) ©Jupiterimages/Getty Images; (r) ©inxti/Shutterstock; (br) ©CORBIS

O Captain! My Captain! **199**

SCAFFOLDING FOR ELL STUDENTS

Analyze Language Help students understand the sentence structure in the poem. Use a whiteboard to display lines 5–9.

- Highlight in yellow: "While follow eyes the steady keel." Explain the meaning of the phrase "steady keel."
- Discuss how the sentence structure is grammatically irregular.
- Rewrite the phrase using conventional word order, and read it aloud.
- Discuss the differences between the two versions.

ASK STUDENTS to identify other lines with an irregular word order, and discuss how the word order affects rhythm, mood, and meaning.

> While follow eyes the steady keel, the vessel grim and daring:
>
> But O heart! heart! heart!
>
> O the bleeding drops of red,
>
> Where on the deck my Captain lies,
>
> Fallen cold and dead.

Analyze Structure

COMMON CORE — RL 1, RL 4, RL 5

(LINES 1–18)

Tell students that "O Captain! My Captain!" is an **elegy,** a poem that offers tribute to someone who has died. Guide students to recognize that Whitman contrasts sorrow with the joy surrounding a great achievement.

(A) CITE TEXT EVIDENCE Have students reread lines 1–18 to identify words and phrases that evoke sorrow or joy. Describe the effect on the reader. *("Prize we sought is won" and "people all exulting" give a feeling of excitement, which is quickly overshadowed by the sadness in "fallen cold and dead." The contrast makes the poem more emotionally powerful.)*

Determine Meanings of Words and Phrases

COMMON CORE — RL 4

(LINES 1–3)

Explain that Whitman uses both metaphor and extended metaphor in this poem. Discuss these definitions:

- A **metaphor** is a comparison of two things that are basically unlike but have some qualities in common. A metaphor does not contain the words *like* or *as*.

- An **extended metaphor** compares two essentially unlike things at some length and in several ways.

Tell students that lines 1–3 introduce an extended metaphor that unifies the entire poem.

(B) ASK STUDENTS to reread lines 1–3. Have them use their knowledge of the selections in Collection 3 to infer who the "Captain" is and what the "fearful trip" refers to. *(Abraham Lincoln; the Civil War)*

COLLABORATIVE DISCUSSION Before their discussion, have partners make a list of words and phrases from the poem that represent conflicting thoughts and feelings.

ASK STUDENTS to share any questions they generated in the course of reading and discussing this selection.

O Captain! My Captain!

O Captain! my Captain! our fearful trip is done,
The ship has weather'd every rack,[1] the prize we sought[2]
is won,

The port is near, the bells I hear, the people all exulting,
5 While follow eyes the steady keel,[3] the vessel grim and daring:
But O heart! heart! heart!
O the bleeding drops of red,
Where on the deck my Captain lies,
Fallen cold and dead.

10 O Captain! my Captain! rise up and hear the bells;
Rise up—for you the flag is flung[4]—for you the bugle trills,
For you bouquets and ribbon'd wreaths—for you the shores
a-crowding,
For you they call, the swaying mass, their eager faces turning;
15 Here Captain! dear father!
This arm beneath your head!
It is some dream that on the deck,
You've fallen cold and dead.

My Captain does not answer, his lips are pale and still,
20 My father does not feel my arm, he has no pulse nor will,
The ship is anchor'd safe and sound, its voyage closed
and done,
From fearful trip the victor ship comes in with object won;
Exult O shores, and ring O bells!
But I with mournful tread,[5]
Walk the deck my Captain lies,
Fallen cold and dead.

COLLABORATIVE DISCUSSION What conflicting thoughts and feelings does this poem express about the end of the Civil War? With a partner, discuss whether you think many Americans shared Walt Whitman's feelings. Cite specific evidence from the text to support your ideas.

---

[1] **rack:** a mass of wind-driven clouds.
[2] **sought (sôt):** searched for; tried to gain.
[3] **keel:** the main part of a ship's structure.
[4] **flung:** suddenly put out.
[5] **tread (trĕd):** footsteps.

APPLYING ACADEMIC VOCABULARY

demonstrate	symbolize

As you discuss the poem, incorporate the following Collection 3 academic vocabulary words: *demonstrate* and *symbolize*. Have students give examples of how Whitman **demonstrates** his feelings toward Lincoln in the poem. Ask students to suggest what the flag, bells, and bugle **symbolize.**

Determine Meaning of Words and Phrases

COMMON CORE RL 4, RL 5

One way poets can help readers understand things in new ways is by using **figurative language,** or imaginative descriptions that are not literally true. A **metaphor** is a type of figurative language in which an author compares two things that are generally different but have some quality or qualities in common. In an **extended metaphor,** this comparison between two things is developed at some length and in different ways.

An extended metaphor in a poem may continue, or extend, through several lines or stanzas or throughout the entire poem. In "O Captain! My Captain!" Whitman uses an extended metaphor to express his feelings about Lincoln and the Civil War. Reread the poem and determine what is being compared.

Analyze Structure

COMMON CORE RL 5

Certain forms of poetry are associated with particular topics. For example, sonnets are often associated with love, and limericks are often associated with humor. "O Captain! My Captain!" is an elegy. An **elegy** is a poem in which the speaker reflects on death. In contrast to other forms of poetry, elegies often pay tribute to someone who has recently died.

Most elegies use formal, dignified language and are serious in **tone,** which is the writer's attitude toward the subject. Elegies may also express

- sorrow and grief
- praise for the person who has died
- comforting thoughts or ideas

In these lines from "O Captain! My Captain!," Whitman expresses his own sorrow.

> But I with mournful tread,
> Walk the deck my Captain lies,

Review "O Captain! My Captain!" and identify words and phrases that pay tribute to Lincoln's greatness.

CLOSE READ

Determine Meanings of Words and Phrases

COMMON CORE RL 4, RL 5

Review the information about figurative language. Work with students to identify how the metaphors for Lincoln and the Civil War are extended throughout the poem. Remind students that Whitman compares Lincoln to a ship's captain, using the ship to represent the country. Then, have students reread the poem and find additional examples of metaphor in the poem. *(ship; father)* Discuss the impact each one has on meaning and emotion.

Analyze Structure

COMMON CORE RL 4, RL 5

Prompt students to analyze the ways in which an elegy is different from other forms of poetry. Guide students to understand how the arrangement of the stanzas contributes to the powerful tone of the poem and pays tribute to Lincoln's greatness.

- Point out that, in the first two stanzas, Whitman introduces the extended metaphor and sets the context of the poem, expressing his dismay at the death of his Captain.
- In the third stanza, he continues to mourn—this time that the Captain will not receive the recognition that is due.
- In the last stanza, Whitman celebrates him as not just a leader but as a father of a nation.

Have students reread the poem and identify words and phrases that convey these ideas.

Strategies for Annotation   📝 📖 *Annotate it!*

Determine Meanings of Words and Phrases

COMMON CORE RL 4

Share these strategies for guided or independent analysis:

- Highlight in yellow examples of the Captain as an extended metaphor.
- Highlight in blue examples of other extended metaphors.
- Use a note to explain the meaning and effect of each example.

My Captain does not answer, his lips are pale and s

My father does not feel my arm, he has no pulse no

The ship is anchor'd safe and sound, its voyage clo

From fearful trip the victor ship comes in with object won;

> It shows the close relationship and respect the narrator has for Lincoln.

Analyzing the Text COMMON CORE RL 1, RL 4, RL 5

Possible answers:

1. The "fearful trip" is the Civil War. The "ship" is the United States, and the "prize" is the preservation of the Union. The "port" is the peace that will follow the war.

2. People are "exulting." They are ringing bells, waving flags, and playing bugles. The crowds have brought flowers and wreaths for Lincoln. They are celebrating the end of the Civil War.

3. Readers would expect the people to be sad as they mourn the death of President Lincoln, but the people are also celebrating the end of the Civil War.

4. He cries "But O heart! heart! heart!" upon learning of his death. He calls to Lincoln to "rise up" from death and speaks of his passing as "some dream." In the last stanza, he cannot join in celebrating the end of the war because Lincoln has died.

5. Though the United States has survived the Civil War and is now "safe and sound," its leader, Lincoln, is dead. The mission of preserving the Union has been accomplished.

 **eBook** *Annotate It!*

Analyzing the Text COMMON CORE RL 1, RL 4, RL 5, SL 1, SL 6

Cite Text Evidence Support your responses with evidence from the text.

1. **Interpret** Reread lines 1–3. In Whitman's metaphor, what is the "fearful trip," the "ship," and the "prize" that was won? What is the "port"? Express your answer in a chart like the one shown.

Element	What It Represents
fearful	
trip	
ship	
prize	
port	

2. **Interpret** Examine lines 3–13. Describe the grand celebration that Whitman tells about in these lines. Why are the crowds rejoicing?

3. **Evaluate** When there is a contrast between appearance and reality, **irony** results. Why is it ironic that the crowds are celebrating in this poem?

4. **Cite Evidence** How does Whitman express his own grief about Lincoln's death? Cite three specific examples.

5. **Evaluate** Reread lines 20–21. What is the meaning of these lines in terms of Whitman's extended metaphor?

PERFORMANCE TASK

Respond by Speaking Work with a small group to present a choral reading of "O Captain! My Captain!"

- Begin by rereading the poem carefully. As a group, decide how each line should be read based on its message. Are the words expressing sorrow? praise? comfort?

- Next, decide who will read each line or part of a line. Should some words be read by one speaker? by two speakers? by your entire group?

- The choices you make about how the lines will be spoken should reflect your analysis of the poem. Be prepared to explain your choices.

Assign this performance task.

PERFORMANCE TASK COMMON CORE SL 1, SL 6

Respond by Speaking As students practice their reading, have them speak in front of a mirror or record their reading, and listen to it. Direct students to

- keep the emotions they want to convey in mind as they speak
- use their voices effectively, speaking with adequate volume and clear pronunciation
- use gestures and facial expressions to emphasize rhythm and feeling

Analyze Style

COMMON CORE
RL 4, RL 5

TEACH

Explain that **style** refers to a manner of writing, focusing on *how* something is said rather than *what* is said. Tell students that Walt Whitman is considered one of the most influential American poets, known for his unconventional use of language and for his focus on political and current events. Point out that Whitman also is often referred to as "the father of free verse." As needed, explain that **free verse** is poetry that does not contain regular patterns of rhythm or rhyme.

Explain that Whitman uses other poetic devices, such as metaphor, alliteration, and repetition of words and phrases, in his poems to emphasize emotion and meaning. His poems often include long lines, and the **meter,** or repeated pattern of rhythm, often imitates natural speech.

Guide students to identify examples of these elements in "O Captain! My Captain!"

> The port is near, the bells I hear, the people all exulting,
> While follow eyes the steady keel, the vessel grim and daring:
> But O heart! heart! heart!
> O the bleeding drops of red,
> Where on the deck my Captain lies,
> Fallen cold and dead.

PRACTICE AND APPLY

Have partners work together to analyze the style of another poem by Walt Whitman, such as "Turn O Libertad" or "A Paumanok Picture." Have students tell how the devices used in the poem affect its meaning.

INTERACTIVE WHITEBOARD LESSON
COMMON CORE
RL 5

Analyze Structure: Stanza and Rhyme Scheme

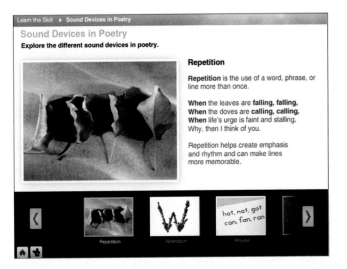

TEACH

Explain to students that the form of a poem is the way the poem is laid out on the page. A poem is made up of lines and stanzas. A **line** is the core unit of a poem. A **stanza** is a group of two or more lines.

Explain that each stanza in a poem may have the same number of lines, or the number of lines may vary. Point out that a break between stanzas often indicates a pause in thoughts, ideas, or actions.

Tell students that poets often use rhyme to emphasize meaning, create rhythm, or express emotion. Explain that **rhyme** is the repetition of sounds at the ends of words, as in *pig* and *dig*.

Explain that a pattern of end rhymes in a poem is called a **rhyme scheme.** Poets often use a rhyme scheme to give a poem a regular beat, or rhythm. Model how to identify a rhyme scheme by assigning a letter to each line in a poem and assigning the same letter to any lines that rhyme.

PRACTICE AND APPLY

Have students work with a partner to analyze the rhyme scheme in "O Captain! My Captain!" stanza by stanza. As they work, ask them to note the effect of the rhyme scheme and how it contributes to the poem's structure, meaning, and style.

Meter and Scansion

TEACH

Tell students that, like the beat in music, **rhythm** in a poem is a regular pattern of sound that is created by stressed and unstressed words or syllables. Point out that poets intentionally arrange words to create a rhythm that emphasizes words or ideas and conveys feelings and meaning.

Explain that **scansion** is the process of marking the stressed and unstressed words or syllables in a poem to find its rhythm, and that a repeated pattern of rhythm is called **meter.** Display and read aloud the following sentence:

The **time** to **act** is **now**!

Point out that the boldfaced words are stressed, and the meter is that every other word is stressed.

Then, explain that a common way to show the rhythm of a line of poetry is by marking an acute accent (´) over the stressed words or syllables and a breve (˘) over the unstressed words or syllables. Display the sentence again, marking it as shown:

˘ ´ ˘ ´ ˘ ´
The time to act is now!

PRACTICE AND APPLY

Have partners work together to mark the stressed and unstressed syllables in the first two stanzas of "O Captain! My Captain!" Have students discuss how its rhythm and meter affect the poem's meaning.

Determine Meanings of Words and Phrases

RETEACH

Review that **figurative language** is a way of using language to communicate meanings beyond the literal meanings of words. Guide students to recall the following:

- A **metaphor** is a comparison of two things that are basically unlike but have some qualities in common. A metaphor does not contain the words *like* or *as*.
- An **extended metaphor** compares in a detailed way two unlike things through several lines of a text.

Provide a simple example, prompting students with relevant questions. For instance:

Our classroom is a train, passengers arriving or leaving at each stop. With the conductor's help, each passenger reaches the right destination.

- What two things are being compared?
- How is the metaphor extended?

 LEVEL UP TUTORIALS Assign the following *Level Up* tutorial: **Figurative Language**

CLOSE READING APPLICATION

Invite students to explore the use of extended metaphors in other poems they have read. Have students identify examples and explain the effect and meaning of each one.

COLLECTION 3
PERFORMANCE TASK A

Interactive Lessons

If you need help . . .
• **Conducting Research**
• **Producing and Publishing with Technology**

Create a Visual Presentation

This collection focuses on slavery and the Civil War. The people who led the fight during this period in American history to end slavery were called **abolitionists.** In the excerpt from *Narrative of the Life of Frederick Douglass*, you read about some of the experiences of one of the key figures in the abolitionist movement. In this activity, you will highlight the work of four or more abolitionists by creating an American Abolitionists Hall of Fame. Combining text with a poster or multimedia, you will create a visual presentation that gives viewers access to the words and deeds that made these heroes worth celebrating.

A successful visual presentation

- integrates text, multimedia, and visuals to clarify information and add interest
- is organized in a way that is appropriate to purpose and audience
- provides accurate information based on research
- includes information from texts and additional sources

COMMON CORE

W 4 Produce clear and coherent writing.
W 6 Use technology to produce and publish writing.
W 7 Conduct short research projects to answer a question.
SL 5 Integrate multimedia and visual displays into presentations.

PLAN

Gather Information Identify the abolitionists you will honor.

- Consider the variety of roles abolitionists played in their efforts to end slavery. While some worked through the government to change laws related to slavery, others demonstrated their skills for public speaking or writing to rally support. Still others risked imprisonment or death as part of the Underground Railroad. Determine which role or roles you will represent in your Hall of Fame.
- Review the selections in this collection to choose at least two individuals to include.
- Then use additional sources to identify other abolitionists whose work led to the end of slavery.

my **Notebook**

Use the annotation tools in your eBook to review the abolitionists you have studied in this collection and to note information about them that can be used in your presentation.

ACADEMIC VOCABULARY

As you share what you learned about abolitionists and their work, be sure to use the academic vocabulary words.

access
civil
demonstrate
document
symbolize

Collection Performance Task A   **203**

PERFORMANCE TASK A

VISUAL PRESENTATION

COMMON CORE W 4, W 6, W 7, SL 5

Introduce students to the Performance Task by reading the introductory paragraph with them and reviewing the criteria for what makes a good visual presentation. Remind students that an effective visual presentation combines information and multimedia or visuals in a cohesive and well-organized way.

PLAN

GATHER INFORMATION

▶ *View It!*

Professional Development Podcast:
Performance Tasks

Guide students to begin their planning with research into a variety of abolitionists and their roles. As needed, suggest keyword searches, such as "abolitionist movement leaders" or "Quaker abolitionists," that will help students identify lawmakers, speakers, writers, and others.

Conduct Research Use both print and digital resources such as encyclopedia entries and biographies, web pages, and historical documents to gather information about the abolitionists.

- Research each abolitionist's life. Focus on the skill or action for which the abolitionist was best known.
- Take notes on how the person's work helped to end slavery.
- Identify the qualities or traits that make the abolitionist a worthy choice for your Hall of Fame.

Evaluate Your Materials As you learn about your chosen abolitionists, evaluate each source you use.

- Is the source relevant? Does it focus on your topic?
- Is the source accurate? Is the information supported by what you read in the collection?
- Does the author of the source have the necessary background and experience to write about this topic?

Gather Images Identify multimedia and visuals that help show the person's accomplishments. You might include

- photographs and illustrations
- film clips from movies or documentaries
- maps, sketches, graphs, or charts

Consider Your Purpose and Audience Think about those who will view your visual presentation, and decide how you want them to react to the experience. The tone you use may be one of serious respect, or one of awe and admiration.

PRODUCE

Write Biographical Sketches Review your notes and draft a brief profile of each abolitionist.

- Introduce the abolitionist to your audience with background and an attention-grabbing accomplishment or anecdote.
- Highlight the events in the person's life that relate to his or her work as an abolitionist. Explain how that work shaped the person's life and impacted American history.

*my*WriteSmart

Write your rough draft in *my*WriteSmart. Focus on getting your ideas down, rather than on perfecting your choice of language.

PRODUCE

WRITE BIOGRAPHICAL SKETCHES

Explain to students that the text and visuals in their presentations need to work together to provide insight into the lives and accomplishments of the abolitionists. Point out that visuals should be chosen to support or enhance the information students collected during their research. Although some visuals might be interesting on their own, remind students that they should include only those visuals that relate to the events and accomplishments in their profiles.

Design Your Visual Presentation Think about the impression you want your visual presentation to create. A poster can be an excellent way to display images, while multimedia might be more effective for combining visuals and sound.

- Organize your visuals and multimedia to highlight the accomplishments of the abolitionists you have chosen.
- Draft captions that describe each visual or piece of multimedia, and decide how to incorporate each visual.
- Sketch out how you will display or present your materials.
- Cite your research sources appropriately.

REVISE

Review Your Production Use the chart on the next page to evaluate your draft. Work with a partner to critique your visual presentation. Consider the following:

- Is the layout clear and easy to understand? Do all the visuals and other pieces of media clearly represent the abolitionists' work and accomplishments?
- Do the captions and biographical sketches include specific and accurate details?
- Are the captions and biographical sketches easy to read and free of grammatical errors?
- Does the presentation feel cohesive and respectful?

my **WriteSmart**

Have your partner or a group of peers review your biographical sketch drafts in *my*WriteSmart and note any statements about the abolitionists that need additional support, such as facts or details.

PRESENT

Create a Finished Visual Presentation Finalize your project and put it together. Then choose a way to share it with your audience. Consider these options:

- Lead "visitors" through your Hall of Fame as if you were a museum guide.
- Become an expert on one of the abolitionists for a panel discussion with classmates who have created similar visual displays.
- Post your visual presentation on a bulletin board.

REVISE

REVIEW YOUR PRODUCTION

Remind students that the text, visuals, and multimedia need to be evaluated on their own, but that good visual presentations are dependent upon all of these elements working together. Suggest that students edit text to make sure it aligns with their visuals and multimedia. Point out that some visuals and multimedia can also be edited or removed if they are not essential to the presentation.

PRESENT

CREATE A FINISHED VISUAL PRESENTATION

Students can

- act as museum guides as they lead others through their Halls of Fame. Beforehand, discuss what kinds of information a museum guide might give to visitors.
- participate in a panel discussion about abolitionists. Have students choose one of the abolitionists to research further for the discussion.
- post their visual presentations to a bulletin board. Encourage viewers to leave comments about the displays.

PERFORMANCE TASK A

ORGANIZATION

Have students use the chart to evaluate how they did on the performance task in each of the three main categories. Tell students to pay particular attention to the organization of their presentations and to think about ways to improve the links between text and visuals in future assignments. Small groups of students can evaluate different presentations and point out elements that are good examples for each of the criteria.

COLLECTION 3 TASK A
VISUAL PRESENTATION

	Ideas and Evidence	Organization	Language
ADVANCED	• The presentation combines text, multimedia, and visuals in a coherent manner. • Information about each abolitionist is detailed and factual. • Relevant, reliable research sources are cited appropriately.	• Visuals and multimedia are organized to connect related ideas logically. • Text and visuals are clearly linked. • Sound elements used support or enhance the overall message.	• Text provides specific and accurate details. • Grammar, usage, and mechanics are correct.
COMPETENT	• The presentation combines text and visuals in a clear way. • Information about each abolitionist is factual. • Research sources are cited appropriately.	• Visuals and multimedia are mostly organized in a way that connects related ideas. • Text and visuals are connected. • If used, sound elements are appropriate.	• Text provides details that are mostly specific and accurate. • Grammar, usage, and mechanics are generally correct.
LIMITED	• The presentation includes both text and visuals. • Most information is factual. • Sources used for research are cited incorrectly or are not relevant.	• The organization of visuals and multimedia is confusing or haphazard. • The connection between text and visuals is not clear. • If used, sound elements are distracting.	• Many text details are vague or inaccurate. • Multiple errors in grammar, usage, or mechanics are present.
EMERGING	• The presentation shows irrelevant or unconnected visuals. • Some or all of the information is inaccurate. • Sources used for research are not cited.	• The visuals and multimedia have no apparent organization. • Text is irrelevant or unconnected to visuals. • If used, sound elements are inappropriate.	• Most text details are vague or irrelevant. • Significant errors in grammar, usage, or mechanics create misunderstanding.

COLLECTION 3
PERFORMANCE TASK B

Interactive Lessons
If you need help . . .
• **Writing Informative Texts**
• **Using Textual Evidence**

Write a Literary Analysis

Ray Bradbury's "The Drummer Boy of Shiloh" invites readers to experience the night before a Civil War battle through the eyes of a young boy. In this activity, you will conduct research (or review your earlier research) to learn how the historical details of the Battle of Shiloh are relevant to the story. Following a small-group discussion about your fresh insights into the story, you will write a literary analysis essay in which you offer an interpretation of the story's symbolism.

A successful literary analysis

- cites evidence from the text that strongly supports ideas and analysis
- is organized in a way that is appropriate to purpose and audience
- conveys ideas through the selection, organization, and analysis of relevant content

> **COMMON CORE**
>
> **RL 1** Cite textual evidence that supports analysis and inferences.
> **W 2a–f** Write informative/explanatory texts.
> **W 5** Develop and strengthen writing.
> **W 7** Conduct short research projects to answer a question.
> **W 9a** Apply grade 8 Reading standards to literature.
> **SL 1a** Come to discussions prepared.

PLAN

Conduct Research Use both print and digital sources to research the Battle of Shiloh.

- Find out why the battle was fought, and learn about the geography of the area, including the Peach Orchard.
- Identify the significance of the battle and its aftermath for each side.
- Use relevant sources. Find books by using keyword or subject searches in the library. Use a search engine or Internet directories to find credible online sources.

Reread the Story Develop fresh insights during a second reading of "The Drummer Boy of Shiloh." Look for

- events or descriptions that gain significance as a result of your research
- new or sharper understanding of symbols Ray Bradbury uses in the story

> **my Notebook**
>
> Use the annotation tools in your eBook to find details, descriptions, and events that support your impressions of the story.
>
> **ACADEMIC VOCABULARY**
>
> As you share your insights into the symbolism in the story, be sure to use the academic vocabulary words.
>
> *access*
> *civil*
> *demonstrate*
> *document*
> *symbolize*

PERFORMANCE TASK B

LITERARY ANALYSIS RL 1, W 2a-f, W 6, W 7, W 9a, SL 1a

Introduce students to the Performance Task by reading the introductory paragraph with them and reviewing the criteria for what makes a good literary analysis. Remind students that a literary analysis will use evidence from the text to support the main points a writer wants to make.

PLAN

CONDUCT RESEARCH

Tell students that it is important to assess the credibility of the research sources they find on the Internet. Remind students that most reliable websites will contain extensions such as .gov, .org, and .edu. Tell students that when they come across a source that seems questionable, they should ask themselves the following:

- Who created the site?
- Why was the site created?
- Are there credits?
- Are there more reliable sources with information about the topic?

PERFORMANCE TASK B

PRODUCE

WRITE A LITERARY ANALYSIS

Tell students to experiment with different ways of beginning their analyses. For example, a quotation from or about the text is one way to garner attention. Students might also consider beginning with a blunt statement of opinion. Suggest that students meet with a partner to discuss which beginning is the most effective in engaging readers.

Participate in a Group Discussion Join two or three classmates to discuss the story and its symbols. Focus on

- repeated events or images that may be symbols, such as peach blossoms, the drum, or even Joby himself
- how research affected your understanding and awareness of symbolism in the story
- symbolism that you understood during your second reading that was not apparent during your first reading

Plan Your Analysis Compile ideas for your literary analysis based on your research, reading, and discussion.

- Decide what your central idea will be. This idea is the main point you want to make in your analysis, so all of the ideas you discuss should relate or connect to it.
- Use a graphic organizer like the one shown to jot down ideas for your literary analysis.

Symbol	Connection to the Battle	Effect in the Story

> **PRODUCE**

Write Your Literary Analysis Use your research, ideas from your group discussion, and your graphic organizer to draft a literary analysis of the symbolism in "The Drummer Boy of Shiloh."

- Decide on a logical way to organize your ideas. You may wish to discuss each symbol in the order in which it appears in the story. Another option would be to organize around story events, discussing the appearance or reappearance of symbols as appropriate.
- Include a brief summary of the story and of the Battle of Shiloh.
- Be sure to include concrete details, quotations, or other examples from the story and from your research to support your interpretation of the symbols. Use precise language to explain key concepts.

my WriteSmart

Write your rough draft in *my*WriteSmart. Concentrate on supporting your main points and connecting ideas rather than on creating perfect sentences.

- Consider using headings or other formatting to help readers understand how you have organized your ideas.
- Conclude your analysis with a summary of your main points and your own insights into the symbolism in the story.

REVISE

Review Your Draft Use the chart on the next page to evaluate your draft. Work with a partner to determine whether you have achieved your purpose. Consider the following:

*my*WriteSmart

Have your partner or a group of peers review your draft in *my*WriteSmart and note any parts of your analysis that are unclear or that could be moved to improve your organization.

- Examine your central idea to decide whether it clearly represents your thoughts about the symbolism in the story.
- Look at the flow of ideas in your analysis to be sure the organization is clear and logical.
- Check each symbol you have discussed and consider whether you have explained it clearly based on supporting evidence from the story and from your research.
- Evaluate whether your conclusion restates your main points and shares your insight about symbolism in the story.

PRESENT

Create a Finished Copy Finalize your literary analysis. Then choose a way to share it with your audience. Consider these additional options:

- Share your literary analysis in an oral report to members of your discussion group.
- Post your literary analysis on a classroom or school website and invite comments from others who have read "The Drummer Boy of Shiloh."

REVISE

REVIEW THE DRAFT

Remind students that when they revise, they will evaluate the content, organization, and style of their analyses. Have students work with a partner to find ways to improve their drafts. Students may want to direct their partners to particular sections of their drafts that might need clarification. Suggest that students discuss ways to make the ideas clearer.

PRESENT

CREATE A FINISHED COPY

Students can
- share their literary analyses as oral reports. Remind students that the delivery of an oral report is as important as the content. Suggest that students practice by giving their report in front of a mirror or by recording themselves.
- post their literary analyses on a class or school website. Encourage students to respond to readers' comments.

PERFORMANCE TASK B

LANGUAGE

Have students use the chart to evaluate how they did on the performance task in each of the three main categories. Prompt students to check their use of precise language to reflect the originality of their ideas. Partners can help each other evaluate their writing and determine areas in which they can make improvements for future writing assignments.

COLLECTION 3 TASK B
LITERARY ANALYSIS

	Ideas and Evidence	Organization	Language
ADVANCED	• The central idea is clearly presented and makes a strong statement about symbolism in the text. • Specific, relevant details support the key points. • The concluding section summarizes the analysis and offers an insight.	• Key points and supporting details are organized effectively and logically throughout the literary analysis. • Transitions successfully show the relationships between ideas.	• Language is precise and captures the writer's thoughts with originality. • Grammar, usage, and mechanics are correct.
COMPETENT	• The central idea makes a point about symbols in the text. • Some key points need more support. • The concluding section summarizes most of the analysis but does not offer an insight.	• The organization of key points and supporting details is mostly clear. • A few more transitions are needed to clarify the relationships between ideas.	• Most language is precise. • Some errors in grammar, usage, and mechanics occur.
LIMITED	• The central idea only hints at a main point. • Details support some key points but often are too general. • The concluding section gives an incomplete summary without insight.	• Most key points are organized logically, but many supporting details are out of place. • More transitions are needed throughout the literary analysis to connect ideas.	• Language is repetitive or too general at times. • Several errors in grammar, usage, and mechanics occur, but the writer's ideas are still clear.
EMERGING	• The central idea is missing. • Details and evidence are irrelevant or missing. • The literary analysis lacks a concluding section.	• A logical organization is not apparent. • Transitions are not used.	• Language is inaccurate, repetitive, and too general. • Errors in grammar, usage, and mechanics obscure the meaning of the writer's ideas.

©jumpingsack/Shutterstock

Approaching Adulthood

❝ When you become a teenager, you step onto a bridge. . . . The opposite shore is adulthood. ❞

—Gail Carson Levin

CONNECTING WORD AND IMAGE

ASK STUDENTS to discuss how the collection opener image and the collection quotation work together to create a connection.

PERFORMANCE TASK PREVIEW

Point out to students that they will complete two performance tasks at the end of the collection. The performance tasks will require them to further analyze the selections in the collection and to synthesize ideas about these analyses. They will present their findings in a variety of products.

ACADEMIC VOCABULARY

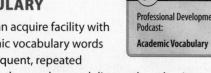

View It!

Professional Development Podcast:

Academic Vocabulary

Students can acquire facility with the academic vocabulary words through frequent, repeated exposure as they analyze and discuss the selections in the collection. Academic vocabulary can be used in the following instructional contexts. This will enable students to incorporate the academic vocabulary words into their working vocabulary.

- Collaborative Discussion at the end of each selection
- Analyzing the Text questions for each selection
- Selection-level Performance Tasks
- Vocabulary instruction (for Critical Vocabulary and/or for Vocabulary Strategy)
- Language Conventions
- End-of-collection Performance Task for all selections in the collection

ASK STUDENTS to review the Academic Vocabulary word list for this collection. You may wish to pronounce each word aloud, so students hear the correct pronunciation. Then, discuss the definitions and the related forms for each word. Remind students that they will encounter these five academic vocabulary words throughout the collection.

COLLECTION 4

Approaching Adulthood

hmhfyi.com

In this collection, you will explore the passage from childhood to adulthood.

COLLECTION

PERFORMANCE TASK Preview

At the end of this collection, you will complete two performance tasks:

- You will write an essay to analyze how the theme of a story set in the past is relevant to the life of modern-day adolescents.

- You will create a campaign to recognize a certain life event—such as voting, getting a driver's license, or living independently—as the start of adulthood.

ACADEMIC VOCABULARY

Study the words and their definitions in the chart below. You will use these words as you discuss and write about the texts in this collection.

Word	Definition	Related Forms
debate (dĭ-bāt´) v.	to engage in arguments by discussing opposing points	debatable
deduce (dĭ-do͞os´) v.	to reach a conclusion or decision through reasoning	deduction, deductive, deducible
license (lī´səns) n.	a document that is issued as proof of legal permission to do something	licensed
sufficient (sə-fĭsh´ənt) adj.	being enough, or as much as needed	sufficiently
trend (trĕnd) n.	the general direction of something; a current style	trendy

USING COLLECTIONS YOUR WAY

Use the following information, along with the charts on the following pages, to help you decide how you want to introduce the collection. Based on your teaching style, your students' interests, or your instructional goals, you may want to structure this collection in various ways. You may choose different entry points each time you teach the collection.

"I want to challenge my students to the utmost."

Readers analyze the scientific, political, legal, and emotional answers to the question posed in the title.

Background *"Room for Debate" is a weekly feature of the New York Times newspaper. Each week, the Times poses a question to a group of knowledgeable outside contributors about a news event or other timely issue. The contributors each bring different perspectives to the question and often offer conflicting opinions. Readers are invited to comment on the topic as well.*

When Do Kids Become Adults?

Arguments from "Room for Debate" in the *New York Times*

What the Brain Says about Maturity by Laurence Steinberg

Leave the Voting Age Alone by Jenny Diamond Cheng

Better Training for New Drivers by Jamie Lincoln Kitman

A Parent's Role in the Path to Adulthood by Barbara Hofer

Mandatory Service to Become an Adult by Michael Thompson

SETTING A PURPOSE As you read, pay attention to the points each writer makes about when and how children mature into adults. Why do you think it is so hard to define when this happens?

Is it time to rethink the age of adulthood? Do the age requirements for certain rights need to be lowered or raised? Shouldn't they at least be consistent?

When Do Kids Become Adults? 235

Background *During the Great Depression of the 1930s, millions of Americans experienced poverty due to widespread unemployment. African Americans were particularly affected by the weak economy. In an age of racial segregation and prejudice, they generally had fewer job opportunities.*

Eugenia Collier *(b. 1928) was raised in Baltimore, Maryland. After working for the Department of Public Welfare, she became a college professor and began writing. "Marigolds" won the Gwendolyn Brooks Award for Fiction in 1969.*

Marigolds

Short Story by Eugenia Collier

SETTING A PURPOSE As you read, notice the story details that suggest how the Great Depression influenced the life of the narrator and her family. Write down any questions you have when reading.

When I think of the home town of my youth, all that I seem to remember is dust—the brown, crumbly dust of late summer—arid, sterile dust that gets into the eyes and makes them water, gets into the throat and between the toes of bare brown feet. I don't know why I should remember only the dust. Surely there must have been lush green lawns and paved streets under leafy shade trees somewhere in town; but memory is an abstract painting—it does not present things as they are, but rather as they *feel*. And so, when I think of that time and that place, I remember only the dry September of the dirt roads and grassless yards of the shanty-town where I lived. And one other thing I remember, another incongruency of memory—a brilliant splash of sunny yellow against the dust—Miss Lottie's marigolds.

Marigolds 213

"I emphasize building vocabulary."

Rich descriptions take readers to a defining moment in a Depression-era girl's transition to adulthood.

"I like to teach by comparing texts."

Related articles offer readers the opportunity for in-depth comparison and contrast on a topic that is relevant for many young people.

COMPARE TEXTS

Background *Although driver's licenses were required by some states by the early 1900s, age restrictions on drivers did not begin until later. These restrictions were motivated by the need to protect the public from young drivers, who were increasingly viewed as a problem on the highways. Some states selected 16 as the age at which people could drive, while others chose 18. Eventually, 16 became the recommended legal age for drivers. Although there are a few exceptions today, most states now allow teenagers to get a driver's license at the age of 16.*

Is 16 Too Young to Drive a Car?

Article by Robert Davis

Fatal Car Crashes Drop for 16-Year-Olds, Rise for Older Teens

Article by Allison Aubrey

SETTING A PURPOSE As you read, think about the points each writer makes regarding the age requirements for drivers. Look for evidence that supports each point.

Raise the driving age. That radical idea is gaining momentum in the fight to save the lives of teenage drivers—the most dangerous on the USA's roads—and their passengers.

Brain and auto safety experts fear that 16-year-olds, the youngest drivers licensed in most states, are too immature to handle today's cars and roadway risks.

New findings from brain researchers at the National Institutes of Health explain for the first time why efforts to protect the youngest drivers usually fail. The weak link: what's called "the executive branch" of the teen brain—the part that weighs risks, makes judgments and controls impulsive behavior.

Scientists at the NIH campus in Bethesda, Md., have found that this vital area develops through the teenage years

Compare Texts 247

mySmartPlanner | **eBook** | **myNotebook** | **myWriteSmart** | **fyi** hmhfyi.com

Collection 4 Lessons	Media	Teach and Practice
Student Edition | eBook	▶ **Video Links** H HISTORY A&E	**Close Reading and Evidence Tracking**
ANCHOR TEXT Short Story by Eugenia Collier "Marigolds"	🔊 **Audio** "Marigolds"	**Close Read Screencasts** • Modeled Discussion 1 (lines 27–42) • Modeled Discussion 2 (lines 287–293) • Close Read Application (lines 316–323)	**Strategies for Annotation** • Analyze Language • Analyze Stories: Characters' Motivation • Determine Theme • Use Latin Suffixes
CLOSE READER Short Story by Anne Estevis "The Whistle"	🔊 **Audio** "The Whistle"		
Poem by Audre Lord "Hanging Fire" **Poem by Pat Mora "Teenagers"**	🔊 **Audio** "Hanging Fire" "Teenagers"		**Strategies for Annotation** • Determine Meaning of Words and Phrases • Make Inferences
CLOSE READER Poem by Julio Noboa Polanco "Identity" Poem by Janet S. Wong "Hard on Gas"	🔊 **Audio** "Identity" "Hard on Gas"		
ANCHOR TEXT Arguments from "Room for Debate" in the New York Times "When Do Kids Become Adults?"	🔊 **Audio** "When Do Kids Become Adults?"	**Close Read Screencasts** • Modeled Discussion (lines 12–20) • Close Read Application (lines 198–205)	**Strategies for Annotation** • Trace and Evaluate an Argument • Greek Roots
CLOSE READER History Article by Naoki Tanaka "Much Too Young to Work So Hard"	🔊 **Audio** "Much Too Young to Work So Hard"		
Article by Robert Davis "Is 16 Too Young to Drive a Car?" **Article by Allison Aubrey "Fatal Car Crashes Drop for 16-Year-Olds, Rise for Older Teens"**	🔊 **Audio** "Is 16 Too Young to Drive a Car?" "Fatal Car Crashes Drop for 16-Year-Olds, Rise for Older Teens"		**Strategies for Annotation** • Determine Central Idea and Details • Analyze Text • Analyze Information in Texts • Domain-Specific Words
Public Service Announcement "Your Phone Can Wait" **Poster "Driving Distracted"**			
Collection 4 Performance Tasks: **A** Write a Literary Analysis **B** Produce a Multimedia Campaign	**fyi** hmhfyi.com	**Interactive Lessons** **A** Writing Informative Texts **A** Writing as a Process **A** Using Textual Evidence	**B** Producing and Publishing with Technology **B** Conducting Research

For Systematic Coverage of Writing and Speaking & Listening Standards	**Interactive Lessons** Using Textual Evidence Using Media in a Presentation

Assess		Extend	Reteach
Performance Task	**Online Assessment**	**Teacher eBook**	**Teacher eBook**
Writing Activity: Essay	Selection Test	**Make Inferences > Interactive Whiteboard Lesson >** Make Inferences	**Analyze Stories: Characters' Motivation > Level Up Tutorial >** Character Motivation
Writing Activity: Comparison	Selection Test	**Determine Meaning of Words and Phrases > Interactive Whiteboard Lesson >** Figurative Language and Imagery	**Determine Theme > Level Up Tutorial >** Theme
Speaking Activity: Debate	Selection Test	**Fact and Opinion**	**Trace and Evaluate an Argument > Level Up Tutorial >** Analyzing Arguments
Writing Activity: Opinion	Selection Test	**Write an Objective Summary > Interactive Whiteboard Lesson >** Summarizing Text	**Analyze Information in Texts**
Media Activity: Public Service Announcement	Selection Test	**Camera Shots and Shot Selections Persuasive Techniques: Visual and Print/ Narration > Level Up Tutorial >** Persuasive Techniques **How to Create a Public Service Announcement**	**Evaluating Advantages and Disadvantages of Media**
A Write a Literary Analysis **B** Produce a Multimedia Campaign	Collection Test		

Lesson Assessments
Using Textual Evidence
Using Media in a Presentation

Collection 4 Lessons	COMMON CORE Key Learning Objective	Performance Task
ANCHOR TEXT **Short Story by Eugenia Collier** **"Marigolds," p. 213A** — Lexile 1140L	**The student will be able to . . .** identify the motivations of characters in a story and determine the factors that help them understand the theme of the story.	Writing Activity: Essay
Poem by Audre Lord **"Hanging Fire," p. 229A** **Poem by Pat Mora** **"Teenagers," p. 229A**	**The student will be able to . . .** make inferences and determine the theme of a poem.	Writing Activity: Comparison
ANCHOR TEXT **Arguments from "Room for Debate"** **in the *New York Times*** **"When Do Kids Become Adults?," p. 235A** — Lexile 1440L	**The student will be able to . . .** trace and evaluate arguments and evaluate supporting evidence to determine whether it is relevant or irrelevant.	Speaking Activity: Debate
Article by Robert Davis — Lexile 1150L **"Is 16 Too Young to Drive a Car?," p. 247A** **Article by Allison Aubrey** — Lexile 1070L **"Fatal Car Crashes Drop for 16-Year-Olds, Rise for Older Teens," p. 247A**	**The student will be able to . . .** determine central ideas and details while analyzing relationships between ideas.	Writing Activity: Opinion
Public Service Announcement **"Your Phone Can Wait," p. 263A** **Poster** **"Driving Distracted," p. 263A**	**The student will be able to . . .** analyze the purpose of a public service announcement and understand the elements used in it.	Media Activity: Public Service Announcement

Collection 4 Performance Tasks:
A Write a Literary Analysis
B Produce a Multimedia Campaign

Vocabulary Strategy	Language and Style	Student Instructional Support	CLOSE READER Selection
Use Latin Suffixes	Infinitives	**Scaffolding for ELL Students:** Analyze Language: Complex and Compound Sentences **When Students Struggle:** Visualize Descriptions **To Challenge Students:** Create Dialogue	Short Story by Anne Estevis "The Whistle" p. 228b **Lexile 800L**
	Words Ending in y	**Scaffolding for ELL Students:** Model Fluency	Poem by Julio Noboa Polanco "Identity" p. 234b Poem by Janet S. Wong "Hard on Gas," p. 234b
Greek Roots	Shifts in Voice and Mood	**Scaffolding for ELL Students:** Analyze Language: Base Words and Word Families **When Students Struggle:** Analyze Graphics	History Article by Naoki Tanaka "Much Too Young to Work So Hard" p. 246b **Lexile 1050L**
Domain-Specific Words	Fragments	**Scaffolding for ELL Students:** Analyze Punctuation **When Students Struggle:** Use a Chart to Track Details **To Challenge Students:** Analyze Argument	
		Scaffolding for ELL Students: Analyze Shortened Words and Acronyms **When Students Struggle:** • Track Visual and Sound Elements • Analyze Percentages	

ANCHOR TEXT
Marigolds

my SmartPlanner — Create lesson plans and access resources online.

Short Story by Eugenia Collier

Why This Text?

Though "Marigolds" takes place in the 1930s, the thoughts and emotions of the characters will strike a chord with today's youth. The narrator's acknowledgement of these emotions is one of the important contributions of "Marigolds."

▶ View It!
Professional Development Podcast:
Text-Dependent Analysis

Key Learning Objective: The student will be able to identify the motivations of characters in a story and determine the factors that help him or her understand the theme of the story.

For Practice and Application:

The Whistle
Short Story by Anne Estevis

Close Reader selection
"The Whistle,"
Short Story by Anne Estevis

COMMON CORE
Common Core Standards

RL 1 Cite text evidence.
RL 2 Determine a theme.
RL 3 Analyze how incidents in a story reveal a character.
RL 4 Determine the meaning of words and phrases in a text.
W 2 Write explanatory texts to examine a topic.
W 4 Produce clear and coherent writing.
W 9a Apply grade 8 Reading standards to literature.
W 10 Write routinely over extended time frames and shorter time frames.
L 1a Explain the function of infinitives.
L 4b Use Latin affixes as clues to meaning.
L 4d Verify preliminary determination of meaning.
L 6 Acquire and use grade-appropriate academic and domain-specific words and phrases.

▲ Text Complexity Rubric

Quantitative Measures	**Marigolds** Lexile: 1140L
	Levels of Meaning/Purpose
Qualitative Measures	multiple levels of meaning (multiple themes)
	Structure
	somewhat complex story concepts
	Language Conventionality and Clarity
	some figurative language
	Knowledge Demands
	fairly complex theme
Reader/Task Considerations	Teacher determined Vary by individual reader and type of text

CLOSE READ

Background Have students read the background and information about the author. Explain that the Great Depression began in 1929 and lasted well into the 1930s. Point out that high unemployment rates led to greater competition for jobs among white males, leaving black males with lower-paying jobs or no jobs at all. As a result, it became more common for black women to work outside the home as domestic servants or clerks.

SETTING A PURPOSE Direct students to use the Setting a Purpose directive about the Great Depression to focus their reading.

Determine Theme (LINES 1–12) COMMON CORE RL 1, RL 2

Tell students that details in a story can help them understand its **theme,** the writer's message about life or human nature. Point out that because the authors usually do not directly state a story's theme, and develop it gradually over the course of the text, students will need to look for clues such as setting, plot events, and the main character's responses to challenges. Explain that a story's theme sometimes does not become truly clear to readers until the main character's conflict has been resolved.

 CITE TEXT EVIDENCE Tell students to reread lines 1–12 and identify details that help them understand the time and place of the story. *("the home town of my youth"; "dust of late summer"; "lush green lawns and paved streets under leafy shade trees somewhere in town"; "dry September of dirt roads and grassless yards of the shanty-town where I lived")* What do these details suggest about what might be important to the theme? *(Possible answer: The theme may relate to poverty.)*

Background *During the Great Depression of the 1930s, millions of Americans experienced poverty due to widespread unemployment. African Americans were particularly affected by the weak economy. In an age of racial segregation and prejudice, they generally had fewer job opportunities.*

Eugenia Collier (b. 1928) *was raised in Baltimore, Maryland. After working for the Department of Public Welfare, she became a college professor and began writing. "Marigolds" won the Gwendolyn Brooks Award for Fiction in 1969.*

Marigolds

Short Story by Eugenia Collier

SETTING A PURPOSE As you read, notice the story details that suggest how the Great Depression influenced the life of the narrator and her family. Write down any questions you have when reading.

When I think of the home town of my youth, all that I seem to remember is dust—the brown, crumbly dust of late summer—arid, sterile dust that gets into the eyes and makes them water, gets into the throat and between the toes of bare brown feet. I don't know why I should remember only the dust. Surely there must have been lush green lawns and paved streets under leafy shade trees somewhere in town; but memory is an abstract painting—it does not present things as they are, but rather as they *feel*. And so, when

10 I think of that time and that place, I remember only the dry September of the dirt roads and grassless yards of the shanty-town where I lived. And one other thing I remember, another incongruency of memory—a brilliant splash of sunny yellow against the dust—Miss Lottie's marigolds.

Close Read Screencasts ▶ View It!

Modeled Discussions

Have students click the *Close Read* icons in their eBooks to access two screencasts in which readers discuss and annotate the following key passages:

- the narrator's description of her community (lines 27–42)
- the narrator's description of her parents' problems and her reaction to them (lines 287–293)

As a class, view and discuss at least one of these videos. Then, have students work in pairs to do an independent close read of an additional passage—the narrator's description of her frenzied arrival at Miss Lottie's yard (lines 316–323).

Determine Theme

COMMON CORE RL 1, RL 2

(LINES 15–26)

Remind students that writers rarely state a story's theme. Tell students that details about plot events and characters, as well as what the narrator says throughout a story, provide clues about its theme.

B CITE TEXT EVIDENCE Have students reread lines 15–26 to identify details that may relate to the author's lesson or message. *("the memory of those marigolds . . . remains long after the picture has faded"; "devastating moment when I was suddenly more woman than child, years ago in Miss Lottie's yard"; "think of those marigolds at the strangest times.")* **What do the details suggest about the theme?** *(Possible answer: The theme has to do with growing up. It is related to an event connected to the marigolds in Miss Lottie's yard.)*

Analyze Language

COMMON CORE RL 4

(LINES 27–29)

Remind students that a **metaphor** is a comparison of two things that are basically unlike but have some qualities in common. Review that a metaphor does not contain the words *like* or *as*.

C ASK STUDENTS to reread lines 27–29 to identify the comparison. *("Futile waiting" is compared to "sorrowful background music.")* **How does this comparison affect the tone or feeling in the story?** *(Possible answer: It suggests a feeling of desperation and ongoing sadness.)*

SCAFFOLDING FOR ELL STUDENTS

Analyze Language The author's use of complex and compound sentences may challenge English learners. Using a whiteboard, project lines 31–34 to model using punctuation to identify and separate key ideas within a longer sentence. Have volunteers mark up the text.

- Highlight in yellow the semicolon.
- Highlight in green the commas.

ASK STUDENTS how the author feels that her family is different from "white folks." *(They do not expect prosperity.)*

Whenever the memory of those marigolds flashes across my mind, a strange nostalgia[1] comes with it and remains long after the picture has faded. I feel again the chaotic emotions of adolescence, illusive as smoke, yet as real as the potted geranium before me now. Joy and rage and wild
20 animal gladness and shame become tangled together in the multicolored skein of 14-going-on-15 as I recall that devastating moment when I was suddenly more woman than child, years ago in Miss Lottie's yard. I think of those marigolds at the strangest times; I remember them vividly now as I desperately pass away the time waiting for you, who will not come.

   I suppose that futile[2] waiting was the sorrowful background music of our impoverished little community when I was young. The Depression that gripped the nation
30 was no new thing to us, for the black workers of rural Maryland had always been depressed. I don't know what it was that we were waiting for; certainly not for the prosperity that was "just around the corner," for those were white folks' words, which we never believed. Nor did we wait for hard work and thrift to pay off in shining success as the American Dream[3] promised, for we knew better than that, too. Perhaps we waited for a miracle, amorphous in concept but necessary if one were to have the grit to rise before dawn each day and labor in the white man's vineyard until after dark, or to
40 wander about in the September dust, offering one's sweat in return for some meager share of bread. But God was chary[4] with miracles in those days, and so we waited—and waited.

   We children, of course, were only vaguely aware of the extent of our poverty. Having no radios, few newspapers, and no magazines, we were somewhat unaware of the world outside our community. Nowadays we would be called "culturally deprived" and people would write books and hold conferences about us. In those days everybody we knew was just as hungry and ill-clad as we were. Poverty was the cage
50 in which we all were trapped, and our hatred of it was still the

---

[1] **nostalgia** (nŏ-stăl′jə): bittersweet longing for things from the past.

[2] **futile** (fyo͞ot′l): having no useful result.

[3] **American dream:** the belief that through hard work one will achieve a comfortable and prosperous life.

[4] **chary** (châr′ē): sparing or stingy.

214 Collection 4

I don't know what it was that we were waiting for; certainly not for the

prosperity that was "just around the corner," for those were white folks'

words, which we never believed. Nor did we wait for hard work and vague, undirected restlessness of the zoo-bred flamingo who knows that nature created him to fly free.

As I think of those days I feel most **poignantly** the tag-end of summer, the bright dry times when we began to have a sense of shortening days and the imminence of the cold.

By the time I was 14 my brother Joey and I were the only children left at our house, the older ones having left home for early marriage or the lure of the city, and the two babies having been sent to relatives who might care for them better
60 than we. Joey was three years younger than I, and a boy, and therefore vastly inferior. Each morning our mother and father trudged wearily down the dirt road and around the bend, she to her domestic job, he to his daily unsuccessful quest for work. After our few chores around the tumbledown shanty, Joey and I were free to run wild in the sun with other children similarly situated.

For the most part, those days are ill-defined in my memory, running together and combining like a fresh water-color painting left out in the rain. I remember squatting in the
70 road drawing a picture in the dust, a picture that Joey gleefully erased with one sweep of his dirty foot. I remember fishing for minnows in a muddy creek and watching sadly as they eluded my cupped hands, while Joey laughed uproariously. And I remember, that year, a strange restlessness of body and of spirit, a feeling that something old and familiar was ending, and something unknown and therefore terrifying was beginning.

One day returns to me with special clarity for some reason, perhaps because it was the beginning of the experience
80 that in some inexplicable way marked the end of innocence. I was loafing under the great oak tree in our yard, deep in some reverie which I have now forgotten except that it involved some secret, secret thoughts of one of the Harris boys across the yard. Joey and a bunch of kids were bored now with the old tire suspended from an oak limb which had kept them entertained for a while.

"Hey, Lizabeth," Joey yelled. He never talked when he could yell. "Hey, Lizabeth, let's us go somewhere."

I came reluctantly from my private world. "Where you
90 want to go? What you want to do?"

The truth was that we were becoming tired of the formlessness of our summer days. The idleness whose

poignant
(poin′yənt) *adj.*
If something is *poignant*, it is profoundly moving or touching.

CLOSE READ

Analyze Stories: Characters' Motivation
COMMON CORE RL 1, RL 3
(LINES 78–88)

Explain that a character's **motivations** are the reasons for his or her actions. Point out that an author may state a character's motivation directly, or readers may need to use details to figure it out.

D CITE TEXT EVIDENCE Have students reread lines 78–88 to identify how Joey and his friends feel at this point. *("Joey and a bunch of kids were bored now")* How might their feelings move the story forward? *(They want to "go somewhere" to find a new activity or some adventure.)*

CRITICAL VOCABULARY

poignant: The narrator is describing her feelings about the events at the end of the summer.

ASK STUDENTS why the narrator might describe her feelings about the time period as poignant. What does her use of that word suggest about the events she is describing? *(The events of the time were important to her or impacted her greatly.)*

APPLYING ACADEMIC VOCABULARY

deduce	sufficient

As you discuss the story, incorporate the following Collection 4 academic vocabulary words: *deduce* and *sufficient*. As you discuss the story, periodically ask students what they can **deduce** about its theme. Prompt students to provide **sufficient** evidence when they make inferences about characters' motivations.

Make Inferences

COMMON CORE **RL 1**

(LINES 104–105)

Tell students that an **inference** is a logical guess that is made based on facts and one's own knowledge. Explain that in a story readers can use details from the text as the facts on which they base their inferences.

E **ASK STUDENTS** to reread the sentence in lines 104–105. What can you guess about the children and Miss Lottie? Explain the evidence you use to make your inference. *(Possible answer: The narrator says that "annoying Miss Lottie was always fun," which suggests that it is something the children do often.)*

CRITICAL VOCABULARY

ostensible: The narrator is explaining why the group stops when they are close to Miss Lottie's house.

ASK STUDENTS why the children need an ostensible reason to stop before continuing to Miss Lottie's house. *(Possible answer: They do not want to admit to themselves or each other that they are afraid.)*

WHEN STUDENTS STRUGGLE ...

Explain to students that visualizing, or seeing in their mind, details of the setting and action can help them understand what is happening in a story. Using a whiteboard, project the paragraph that begins on line 114. Have volunteers mark up the text.

- Highlight in yellow descriptive details that help readers visualize Miss Lottie's house.

- Highlight in green the phrase that tells what Miss Lottie's house represented to the narrator.

---

prospect had seemed so beautiful during the busy days of spring now had degenerated to an almost desperate effort to fill up the empty midday hours.

"Let's go see can we find some locusts on the hill," someone suggested.

Joey was scornful. "Ain't no more locusts there. Y'all got 'em all while they was still green."

100 The argument that followed was brief and not really worth the effort. Hunting locust trees wasn't fun any more by now.

"Tell you what," said Joey finally, his eyes sparkling. "Let's go over to Miss Lottie's."

The idea caught on at once, for annoying Miss Lottie was always fun. I was still child enough to scamper along with the group over rickety fences and through bushes that tore our already raggedy clothes, back to where Miss Lottie lived. I think now that we must have made a tragicomic spectacle, five or six kids of different ages, each of us clad in only one 110 garment—the girls in faded dresses that were too long or too short, the boys in patchy pants, their sweaty brown chests gleaming in the hot sun. A little cloud of dust followed our thin legs and bare feet as we tramped over the barren land.

When Miss Lottie's house came into view we stopped, **ostensibly** to plan our strategy, but actually to reinforce our courage. Miss Lottie's house was the most ramshackle of all our ramshackle homes. The sun and rain had long since faded its rickety frame siding from white to a sullen gray. The boards themselves seemed to remain upright not from 120 being nailed together but rather from leaning together like a house that a child might have constructed from cards. A brisk wind might have blown it down, and the fact that it was still standing implied a kind of enchantment that was stronger than the elements. There it stood, and as far as I know is standing yet—a gray rotting thing with no porch, no shutters, no steps, set on a cramped lot with no grass, not even any weeds—a monument to decay.

In front of the house in a squeaky rocking chair sat Miss Lottie's son, John Burke, completing the impression of decay. 130 John Burke was what was known as "queer-headed." Black and ageless, he sat, rocking day in and day out in a mindless stupor, lulled by the monotonous squeak-squawk of the chair. A battered hat atop his shaggy head shaded him from the sun. Usually John Burke was totally unaware of everything

ostensible
(ŏ-stĕn′sə-blē) *adj.*
If something is *ostensible*, it is apparent or supposed.

216 Collection 4

ASK STUDENTS how their image of Miss Lottie's house contributes to the general tone or feeling of the story. *(Possible answer: It adds to the overall feeling of poverty and desperation.)*

—a gray rotting thing with no porch, no shutters, no steps, set on a cramped lot with no grass, not even any weeds—a monument to decay.

outside his quiet dream world. But if you disturbed him, if you intruded upon his fantasies, he would become enraged, strike out at you, and curse at you in some strange enchanted language which only he could understand. We children made a game of thinking of ways to disturb John Burke and then to elude his violent **retribution**.

140

F But our real fun and our real fear lay in Miss Lottie herself. Miss Lottie seemed to be at least a hundred years old. Her big

retribution
(rĕt´rə-byōō´shən) *n.* *Retribution* is something given in repayment, usually as a punishment.

CLOSE READ

Analyze Stories: Characters' Motivation

COMMON CORE RL 3

(LINE 141)

Remind students that details in a text can help them understand what is motivating characters to do what they do.

F **ASK STUDENTS** to reread the sentence on line 141. Ask students what is motivating the children to annoy Miss Lottie. *(Possible answer: They find Miss Lottie to be some sort of challenge. She is a poor, elderly woman, yet they are a little afraid of her, which is probably exciting to them.)*

CRITICAL VOCABULARY

retribution: The narrator is describing the children's practice of goading Miss Lottie's son into a violent reaction.

ASK STUDENTS whether the children deserve retribution for their actions. *(The children are being deliberately cruel to a mentally challenged man, so they deserve punishment. That punishment, however, should not be violent.)*

Determine Theme

COMMON CORE · RL 1, RL 2

(LINES 158–174)

Point out that the narrator is once again focusing on Miss Lottie's marigolds. Prompt students to recall that in addition to being the title of the story, the marigolds were described as a key memory for the narrator.

Ⓖ CITE TEXT EVIDENCE Have students reread lines 158–174 to identify the narrator's description of, and reaction to, seeing the marigolds. *("them crazy flowers"; "strangest part of the picture"; "did not fit with the crumbling decay"; "dazzling strip of bright blossoms, clumped together in enormous mounds, warm and passionate and sun-golden"; "interfered with the perfect ugliness of the place; they were too beautiful"; "they did not make sense")* How might this aspect of the setting contribute to the story's theme? *(Possible answer: The narrator may learn something from the beauty of the flowers.)*

CRITICAL VOCABULARY

stoicism: The narrator is describing Miss Lottie's face.

ASK STUDENTS why Miss Lottie's face might show "stern stoicism." *(Possible answer: Based on her home and her son, it seems that she has had a difficult life in which she has had to move forward regardless of how she was feeling. She also knows that the children enjoy taunting her, and may not want them to know how much it bothers her.)*

perverse: The narrator describes the children's hatred of Miss Lottie's flowers as perverse.

ASK STUDENTS to explain why the narrator's use of *perverse* is appropriate. *(Miss Lottie's flowers are probably one of the few pretty things in the neighborhood. A natural response would be to admire and like the flowers, but the children have the opposite reaction.)*

---

frame still held traces of the tall, powerful woman she must have been in youth, although it was now bent and drawn. Her smooth skin was a dark reddish-brown, and her face had Indian-like features and the stern **stoicism** that one associates with Indian faces. Miss Lottie didn't like intruders either, especially children. She never left her yard, and nobody ever visited her. We never knew how she managed those necessities
150 that depend on human interaction—how she ate, for example, or even whether she ate. When we were tiny children, we thought Miss Lottie was a witch and we made up tales, that we half believed ourselves, about her exploits. We were far too sophisticated now, of course, to believe the witchnonsense. But old fears have a way of clinging like cobwebs, and so when we sighted the tumble-down shack, we had to stop to reinforce our nerves.

Ⓖ "Look, there she is," I whispered, forgetting that Miss Lottie could not possibly have heard me from that distance.
160 "She's fooling with them crazy flowers."

"Yeh, look at 'er."

Miss Lottie's marigolds were perhaps the strangest part of the picture. Certainly they did not fit in with the crumbling decay of the rest of her yard. Beyond the dusty brown yard, in front of the sorry gray house, rose suddenly and shockingly a dazzling strip of bright blossoms, clumped together in enormous mounds, warm and passionate and sun-golden. The old black witch-woman worked on them all summer, every summer, down on her creaky knees, weeding and cultivating
170 and arranging, while the house crumbled and John Burke rocked. For some **perverse** reason, we children hated those marigolds. They interfered with the perfect ugliness of the place; they were too beautiful; they said too much that we could not understand; they did not make sense. There was something in the vigor with which the old woman destroyed the weeds that intimidated us. It should have been a comical sight—the old woman with the man's hat on her cropped white head, leaning over the bright mounds, her big backside in the air—but it wasn't comical, it was something we could
180 not name. We had to annoy her by whizzing a pebble into her flowers or by yelling a dirty word, then dancing away from her rage, reveling in our youth and mocking her age. Actually, I think it was the flowers we wanted to destroy, but nobody had

stoicism
(stō´ĭ-sĭz´əm) *n.* Stoicism is indifference to pleasure or pain, or a lack of visible emotion.

perverse
(pər-vûrs´) *adj.* If something is *perverse*, it is stubbornly contrary, wrong, or harmful.

the nerve to try it, not even Joey, who was usually fool enough to try anything.

"Y'all git some stones," commanded Joey now, and was met with instant giggling obedience as everyone except me began to gather pebbles from the dusty ground. "Come on, Lizabeth."

190 I just stood there peering through the bushes, torn between wanting to join the fun and feeling that it was all a bit silly.

"You scared, Lizabeth?"

I cursed and spat on the ground—my favorite gesture of phony **bravado**. "Y'all children get the stones; I'll show you how to use 'em."

I said before that we children were not consciously aware of how thick were the bars of our cage. I wonder now, though, whether we were not more aware of it than I thought. Perhaps 200 we had some dim notion of what we were, and how little chance we had of being anything else. Otherwise, why would we have been so preoccupied with destruction? Anyway, the pebbles were collected quickly, and everybody looked at me to begin the fun.

"Come on, y'all."

We crept to the edge of the bushes that bordered the narrow road in front of Miss Lottie's place. She was working placidly, kneeling over the flowers, her dark hand plunged into the golden mound. Suddenly "zing"—an expertlyaimed stone 210 cut the head off one of the blossoms.

"Who out there?" Miss Lottie's backside came down and her head came up as her sharp eyes searched the bushes. "You better git!"

We had crouched down out of sight in the bushes, where we stifled the giggles that insisted on coming. Miss Lottie gazed warily across the road for a moment, then cautiously returned to her weeding. "Zing"—Joey sent a pebble into the blooms, and another marigold was beheaded.

Miss Lottie was enraged now. She began struggling to her 220 feet, leaning on a rickety cane and shouting, "Y'all git! Go on home!" Then the rest of the kids let loose with their pebbles, storming the flowers and laughing wildly and senselessly at Miss Lottie's **impotent** rage. She shook her stick at us and started shakily toward the road crying, "Git 'long! John Burke! John Burke, come help!"

bravado
(brə-vä´dō) *n.*
Bravado is a false show of bravery.

impotent
(ĭm´pə-tənt) *adj.* If someone is *impotent*, he or she is lacking strength or vigor.

Marigolds **219**

CLOSE READ

Analyze Language

COMMON CORE RL 4

(LINES 197–201)

Remind students that authors often use comparisons, such as metaphors, to create an image or explain an idea.

H ASK STUDENTS to reread lines 197–201 and explain what the phrase "the bars of our cage" refers to. *(The poverty of children's lives is like a cage from which they cannot escape.)* How does the comparison add to readers' understanding of the characters? *(Possible answer: It emphasizes how little control they have over their lives; they have little chance of escaping the poverty in which they live.)*

CRITICAL VOCABULARY

bravado: The narrator is taking the lead to show the younger children what they should do.

ASK STUDENTS why Lizabeth might make a "gesture of phony bravado." *(Possible answer: She wants the younger children to think she is tough and brave.)*

impotent: The children laugh at Miss Lottie as they storm her marigold garden.

ASK STUDENTS to explain why Miss Lottie's rage might be considered impotent. *(She is very old and no longer physically powerful.)*

Strategies for Annotation

🖊 📋 **Annotate it!**

Analyze Language (LINES 197–201)

COMMON CORE RL 4

Share these strategies for guided or independent analysis:

- Highlight in yellow the comparison the author makes.
- Underline any clues in the text that help explain the comparison.
- Use a note to explain the comparison.

I said before that we children were not consciously aware of how thick were the bars of our cage. I wonder now, though, whether we were not more aware of it than I thought. Perhaps we had some dim notion of what we were, and how little chance we had of being anything else. Oth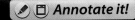ould we have been so preoccupied

no control of their lives

Make Inferences

COMMON CORE **RL 1**

(LINES 237–248)

Remind students that readers can use details in the text and their own knowledge to make inferences about a character. Direct students' attention to the description of Lizabeth's feelings about the incident in Miss Lottie's yard in lines 237–248.

ASK STUDENTS to reread lines 237–248 to identify the conflicting feelings Lizabeth is experiencing. *("The child in me sulked and said it was all in fun, but the woman in me flinched at the thought of the malicious attack")* Why does she have "a particularly bitter argument" with Joey? *(Possible answer: She is taking her anger at herself out on him.)*

CRITICAL VOCABULARY

exuberance: The narrator is describing Joey's behavior during dinner.

ASK STUDENTS to explain why they think Joey is exuberant so long after the incident at Miss Lottie's. *(Possible answer: Joey is young and probably still excited and pleased about the attack the children made on Miss Lottie and her marigolds.)*

Then I lost my head entirely, mad with the power of inciting such rage, and ran out of the bushes in the storm of pebbles, straight toward Miss Lottie chanting madly, "Old witch, fell in a ditch, picked up a penny and thought she was
230 rich!" The children screamed with delight, dropped their pebbles and joined the crazy dance, swarming around Miss Lottie like bees and chanting, "Old lady witch!" while she screamed curses at us. The madness lasted only a moment, for John Burke, startled at last, lurched out of his chair, and we dashed for the bushes just as Miss Lottie's cane went whizzing at my head.

I did not join the merriment when the kids gathered again under the oak in our bare yard. Suddenly I was ashamed, and I did not like being ashamed. The child in me sulked and said
240 it was all in fun, but the woman in me flinched at the thought of the malicious attack that I had led. The mood lasted all afternoon. When we ate the beans and rice that was supper that night, I did not notice my father's silence, for he was always silent these days, nor did I notice my mother's absence, for she always worked until well into evening. Joey and I had a particularly bitter argument after supper; his **exuberance** got on my nerves. Finally I stretched out upon the palette in the room we shared and fell into a fitful doze.

exuberance
(ĭg-zōō′bər-əns) *n.*
Exuberance is
a condition of
unrestrained joy.

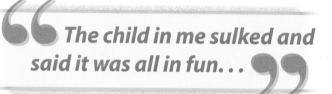

> ## *The child in me sulked and said it was all in fun. . .*

When I awoke, somewhere in the middle of the night,
250 my mother had returned, and I vaguely listened to the conversation that was audible through the thin walls that separated our rooms. At first I heard no words, only voices. My mother's voice was like a cool, dark room in summer— peaceful, soothing, quiet. I loved to listen to it; it made things seem all right somehow. But my father's voice cut through hers, shattering the peace.

"Twenty-two years, Maybelle, twenty-two years," he was saying, "and I got nothing for you, nothing, nothing."

"It's all right, honey, you'll get something. Everybody's out of work now, you know that."

"It ain't right. Ain't no man ought to eat his woman's food year in and year out, and see his children running wild. Ain't nothing right about that."

"Honey, you took good care of us when you had it. Ain't nobody got nothing nowadays."

"I ain't talking about nobody else, I'm talking about me. God knows I try." My mother said something I could not hear, and my father cried out louder, "What must a man do, tell me that?"

"Look, we ain't starving. I git paid every week, and Mrs. Ellis is real nice about giving me things. She gonna let me have Mr. Ellis' old coat for you this winter—"

"Damn Mr. Ellis' coat! And damn his money! You think I want white folks' leavings? Damn, Maybelle"—and suddenly he sobbed, loudly and painfully, and cried helplessly and hopelessly in the dark night. I had never heard a man cry before. I did not know men ever cried. I covered my ears with my hands but could not cut off the sound of my father's harsh, painful, despairing sobs. My father was a strong man who would whisk a child upon his shoulders and go singing through the house. My father whittled toys for us and laughed so loud that the great oak seemed to laugh with him, and taught us how to fish and hunt rabbits. How could it be that my father was crying? But the sobs went on, unstifled, finally quieting until I could hear my mother's voice, deep and rich, humming softly as she used to hum to a frightened child.

The world had lost its boundary lines. My mother, who was small and soft, was now the strength of the family; my father, who was the rock on which the family had been built, was sobbing like the tiniest child. Everything was suddenly out of tune, like a broken accordion. Where did I fit into this crazy picture? I do not now remember my thoughts, only a feeling of great bewilderment and fear.

Long after the sobbing and the humming had stopped, I lay on the palette, still as stone with my hands over my ears, wishing that I too could cry and be comforted. The night was silent now except for the sound of the crickets and of Joey's soft breathing. But the room was too crowded with fear to allow me to sleep, and finally, feeling the terrible aloneness of 4 A.M., I decided to awaken Joey.

CLOSE READ

Analyze Language
COMMON CORE **RL 4**

(LINES 287–293)

Point out that the author uses vivid language, including similes and metaphors, to describe Lizabeth's reaction to her parents' conversation. Explain that a **simile** is a comparison that includes the words *like* or *as.*

J ASK STUDENTS to reread lines 287–293 to identify the comparisons the author makes. *("my father, who was the rock on which the family had been built"; "sobbing like the tiniest child"; "out of tune, like a broken accordion")* What is the impact of these comparisons? *(They emphasize the narrator's fragile and confused state.)*

Analyze Stories: Characters' Motivation
COMMON CORE **RL 1, RL 3**

(LINES 287–300)

Point out that a character's reaction to story events or a situation is often a motivation for his or her actions.

K CITE TEXT EVIDENCE Have students reread lines 287–300 to identify details that help explain what motivates Lizabeth to wake Joey. *("The world had lost its boundary lines"; "Everything was suddenly out of tune"; "a feeling of great bewilderment and fear"; "wishing that I too could cry and be comforted"; "the room was too crowded with fear"; "the terrible aloneness of 4 A.M.")* How might Lizabeth's actions move the story forward? *(Between the incident with Miss Lottie and overhearing her parents, she seems to be at an emotional turning point. Whatever she does next will help bring about the story's resolution.)*

TEACH

CLOSE READ

Analyze Stories: Characters' Motivation

COMMON CORE RL 1, RL 3

(LINES 324–338)

Remind students that a character's motivation is his or her reason for acting in a particular way.

Ⓛ CITE TEXT EVIDENCE Have students reread lines 324–338 to identify the different feelings that are causing Lizabeth to return to Miss Lottie's. *(the "need for my mother who was never there"; "hopelessness of poverty and degradation"; "bewilderment of being neither child nor woman"; "fear unleashed by my father's tears")* Why do these feelings provoke her actions at Miss Lottie's? *(Her feelings "combined in one great impulse toward destruction," leading her to ruin the marigold garden.)*

CRITICAL VOCABULARY

degradation: The author is describing Lizabeth's feelings about her family's poverty.

ASK STUDENTS why Lizabeth might have a sense of degradation about living in poverty. *(Possible answer: She feels hopeless, that the family's poverty will always keep her down.)*

"Ouch! What's the matter with you? What you want?" he demanded disagreeably when I had pinched and slapped him awake.

"Come on, wake up."

"What for? Go 'way."

I was lost for a reasonable reply. I could not say, "I'm scared, and I don't want to be alone," so I merely said, "I'm going out. If you want to come, come on."

The promise of adventure awoke him. "Going out now? 310 Where to, Lizabeth? What you going to do?"

I was pulling my dress over my head. Until now I had not thought of going out. "Just come on," I replied tersely.

I was out the window and halfway down the road before Joey caught up with me.

"Wait, Lizabeth, where you going?"

I was running as if the Furies[5] were after me, as perhaps they were—running silently and furiously until I came to where I had half-known I was headed: to Miss Lottie's yard.

The half-dawn light was more eerie than complete 320 darkness, and in it the old house was like the ruin that my world had become—foul and crumbling, a grotesque caricature.[6] It looked haunted, but I was not afraid because I was haunted too.

"Lizabeth, you lost your mind?" panted Joey.

I had indeed lost my mind, for all the smoldering emotions of that summer swelled in me and burst—the great need for my mother who was never there, the hopelessness of our poverty and **degradation**, the bewilderment of being neither 330 child nor woman and yet both at once, the fear unleashed by my father's tears. And these feelings combined in one great impulse toward destruction.

"Lizabeth!"

I leaped furiously into the mounds of marigolds and pulled madly, trampling and pulling and destroying the perfect yellow blooms. The fresh smell of early morning and of dew-soaked marigolds spurred me on as I went tearing and mangling and sobbing while Joey tugged my dress or my waist crying, "Lizabeth stop, please stop!"

degradation
(dĕg´rə-dā´shən) *n.*
Degradation is the condition of being brought to a lower level or humiliated.

---

[5] **Furies:** In Greek and Roman mythology, the Furies were three goddesses of vengeance, or revenge.

[6] **a grotesque caricature** (grō-tĕsk´ kăr´ĭ-kə-chŏor): a bizarre and absurdly exaggerated representation of something.

Strategies for Annotation ✏️ 🅱 *Annotate it!*

Analyze Stories: Characters' Motivation (LINES 324–338)

COMMON CORE RL 1, RL 3

Share these strategies for guided or independent analysis:

- Underline the reasons Lizabeth gives for her actions.
- Highlight in yellow the action she takes.

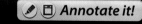

I had indeed lost my mind, for all the smoldering emotions of that summer swelled in me and burst—the great need for my mother who was never there, the hopelessness of our poverty and degradation, the bewilderment of being neither a child nor woman and yet both at once, the fear unleashed by my father's tears. And these feelings combined in one great impulse toward destruction.

And then I was sitting in the ruined little garden among
340 the uprooted and ruined flowers, crying and crying, and it
was too late to undo what I had done. Joey was sitting beside
me, silent and frightened, not knowing what to say. Then,
"Lizabeth, look."

I opened my swollen eyes and saw in front of me a pair of
large calloused feet; my gaze lifted to the swollen legs, the
age-distorted body clad in a tight cotton night dress, and then
the shadowed Indian face surrounded by stubby white hair.
And there was no rage in the face now, now that the garden
was destroyed and there was nothing any longer to be
350 protected.

"M-miss Lottie!" I scrambled to my feet and just stood
there and stared at her, and that was the moment when
childhood faded and womanhood began. That violent,
crazy act was the last act of childhood. For as I gazed at the
immobile face with the sad, weary eyes, I gazed upon a kind
of reality that is hidden to childhood. The witch was no longer
a witch but only a broken old woman who had dared to create
beauty in the midst of ugliness and sterility. She had been
born in **squalor** and lived in it all her life. Now at the end of
360 that life she had nothing except a falling-down hut, a wrecked
body, and John Burke, the mindless son of her passion.
Whatever verve there was left in her, whatever was of love and

squalor
(skwŏl´ər) *n. Squalor*
is a filthy, shabby, and
wretched condition,
as from poverty.

Marigolds **223**

CLOSE READ

Determine Theme

COMMON CORE RL 1, RL 2

(LINES 351–361)

Explain that a **symbol** is a person, place, or thing
that stands for something beyond itself. Point out
that thinking about what symbols stand for can help
readers understand the theme of the story.

 ASK STUDENTS to reread lines 351–361. What
do Miss Lottie and her marigolds symbolize to the
narrator? (*Possible answer: Miss Lottie symbolizes the
ugliness and failure of the narrator's life. The marigolds
symbolize the beauty that Miss Lottie had tried to create,
which was ultimately destroyed. Miss Lottie's effort to
create beauty in the midst of her ugly surroundings was
seemingly futile.*) What does Lizabeth's reaction to
seeing Miss Lottie reveal about her? (*She feels she is no
longer a child. Through Miss Lottie, she has begun to see
the world through an adult's eyes.*)

CRITICAL VOCABULARY

squalor: The author is describing the way
Miss Lottie lived.

ASK STUDENTS why the marigolds might have
been so important to a woman who lived in
squalor. (*Possible answer: They served as an antidote
to the wretched conditions in which she lived.*)

CLOSE READ

Determine Theme

COMMON CORE RL 1, RL 2

(LINES 365–386)

Remind students that a theme is the message or lesson about life that an author wants to share.

N **ASK STUDENTS** to reread lines 365–386. What is a theme of this story? *(Possible answer: There is beauty in life for those who are willing to see it.)* What details in the text support the theme? *("... one does not have to be ignorant and poor to find that one's life is barren as the dusty yards of one's town. And I too have planted marigolds.")*

Make Inferences

COMMON CORE RL 1

(LINES 385–386)

Guide students to make inferences about the final sentence of the story.

O **ASK STUDENTS** to reread the last sentence of the story. What does the narrator mean when she says she has "planted marigolds"? *(Possible answer: She has looked for elements of beauty at times when things were otherwise ugly.)*

COLLABORATIVE DISCUSSION Have students work in pairs to identify the circumstances of Lizabeth's life that led her to destroy Miss Lottie's flowers. Tell partners to share ideas about which of the circumstances had the greatest influence on Lizabeth's actions. Accept all reasonable responses.

ASK STUDENTS to share any questions they generated in the course of reading and discussing the selection.

beauty and joy that had not been squeezed out by life, had been there in the marigolds she had so tenderly cared for.

N Of course I could not express the things that I knew about Miss Lottie as I stood there awkward and ashamed. The years have put words to the things I knew in that moment, and as I look back upon it, I know that that moment marked the end of innocence. People think of the loss of innocence as meaning

370 the loss of virginity, but this is far from true. Innocence involves an unseeing acceptance of things at face value, an ignorance of the area below the surface. In that humiliating moment I looked beyond myself and into the depths of another person. This was the beginning of compassion, and one cannot have both compassion and innocence.

The years have taken me worlds away from that time and that place, from the dust and squalor of our lives and from the bright thing that I destroyed in a blind childish striking out at God-knows-what. Miss Lottie died long ago and many years

380 have passed since I last saw her hut, completely barren at last, for despite my wild contrition she never planted marigolds again. Yet, there are times when the image of those passionate yellow mounds returns with a painful poignancy. For one does not have to be ignorant and poor to find that one's life is barren as the dusty yards of one's town. And I too have **O** planted marigolds.

COLLABORATIVE DISCUSSION With a partner, discuss which aspects of Lizabeth's life contributed to her reaction to Miss Lottie's flowers.

TO CHALLENGE STUDENTS . . .

Create Dialogue Have students reread lines 379–382, drawing attention to the narrator's statement that "despite my wild contrition, she never planted marigolds again."

ASK STUDENTS to imagine the dialogue that might have taken place between Lizabeth and Miss Lottie. Have partners work together to write and role-play the conversation.

Analyze Stories: Characters' Motivation

COMMON CORE RL 3

To fully understand a story, you need to think about the characters' **motivations,** or the reasons for their actions. Sometimes a narrator will state a character's motivations directly. For example, notice what the narrator of "Marigolds" says about why the children go to Miss Lottie's.

> . . . we were becoming tired of the formlessness of our days. The idleness . . . had degenerated to an almost desperate effort to fill the time.

> "Tell you what," said Joey finally, his eyes sparkling. "Let's go over to Miss Lottie's."

> The idea caught on at once, for annoying Miss Lottie was always fun.

Other times, you will need to **infer,** or guess, a character's motivations. To do this, think about the character's personality, notice his or her reactions, and consider the situation. Then ask yourself what you might want to achieve if you were in his or her place.

Determine Theme

COMMON CORE RL 2, RL 4

A **theme** is a message about life or human nature that a writer shares with the reader. Writers rarely state a story's theme directly. More often, readers deduce, or figure out, the writer's message by looking at clues, such as the symbols in a story. A **symbol** is a person, place, or thing that stands for something beyond itself. Other clues to a story's theme can be found in the following chart.

Clues to Theme	Questions to Ask
Plot and conflict	How are the conflicts resolved?
Characters	What lesson does the main character learn?
Setting	How does the setting affect the characters? What might the setting represent to readers?
Symbols	What might the symbol mean to the main character? What might it represent to the readers? What happens to the symbol?
Title	What idea or symbol does the title highlight?

Review "Marigolds" to identify clues to the story's theme.

TEACH

CLOSE READ

Analyze Stories: Characters' Motivation

COMMON CORE RL 3

Tell students that identifying characters' motives for doing things in a story usually involves these steps:

- Read the story closely to identify details that explain or partially explain why a character does what he or she does.
- Consider comparable situations in real life and the reasons a real person might have for taking similar actions.
- Form ideas about why characters are doing what they do.

Determine Theme

COMMON CORE RL 2, RL 4

Discuss the definition of *theme* and the clues presented in the chart, focusing on the possible answers to each of the questions:

Plot and conflict: After destroying the marigolds, Lizabeth begins to see herself as an adult rather than a child.

Characters: Lizabeth learns that it is possible to see beauty in ugly circumstances.

Setting: The squalor of the shanty-town surrounds all of the characters.

Symbols: The marigolds represent the beauty and opportunity Lizabeth may find in life if she is willing.

Title: "Marigolds"

Strategies for Annotation 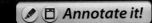 Annotate it!

Determine Theme

COMMON CORE RL 2, RL 4

Share these strategies for guided or independent analysis:

- Highlight in green details related to plot or conflict.
- Highlight in yellow details about characters.
- Highlight in blue details about setting.
- Highlight in pink details about symbols in the story.

Now at the end of that life she had nothing except a falling-down hut, a wrecked body, and John Burke, the mindless son of her passion. Whatever verve there was left in her, whatever was of love and beauty and joy that had not been squeezed out by life, had been there in the marigolds she had so tenderly cared for.

Analyzing the Text COMMON CORE RL 1, RL 2, RL 3, RL 4

Possible answers:

1. The shanty-town is full of dusty dirt roads and grassless yards. It is a community of poor people living in ramshackle homes. The crushing poverty of the setting permeates Lizabeth's adolescence, filling her with half-understood rage.

2. The conflicts and emotions associated with Lizabeth's age play a significant role in motivating her actions. She is old enough to feel the pain and rage of her circumstances, but not old enough to know how to control her reactions to these emotions.

3. The colorful beauty of the flowers does not make sense to the children, who are too young to articulate their feelings of anger and humiliation about their impoverished lives. They feel that they must destroy the intrusion of beauty on their otherwise ugly world.

4. The role reversal represented by her father's crying and her mother's strength fills Lizabeth with fear and bewilderment. This incident unleashes Lizabeth's smoldering fear and rage and compels her to commit the story's climactic, destructive act.

5. In the beginning, the narrator sees Miss Lottie as a crazy old woman obsessed with her flowers. At the end, Lizabeth feels compassion for Miss Lottie and understands that she was a poor old woman who tried to create beauty in the midst of ugliness.

6. With the loss of youth's innocence comes compassion for others and a deeper understanding of life. The description of Miss Lottie in lines 354–356, details in lines 370–375, and the direct statement in the last sentence of this passage all support the theme.

7. In the beginning of the story, the marigolds represent to the children something that does not make sense in their dusty, colorless world. At the end, the marigolds symbolize the possibility of beauty in a bleak existence.

8. The narrator describes her present life as barren. I, too, have tried to create something of beauty to combat the emptiness of my life.

Analyzing the Text COMMON CORE RL 1, RL 2, RL 3, RL 4, W 2, W 4, W 9a, W 10

Cite Text Evidence Support your responses with evidence from the text.

1. **Infer** In lines 8–9, Collier writes that an abstract painting "does not present things as they are, but rather as they *feel*." What can you infer about the narrator's childhood experiences based on her description of her home town?

2. **Synthesize** What part do the "chaotic emotions of adolescence" (lines 17–18) play in motivating Lizabeth to taunt Miss Lottie?

3. **Infer** Reread lines 162–185. What might explain the children's reactions to the marigolds?

4. **Analyze** Review lines 257–293. How does the conversation between Lizabeth's parents motivate Lizabeth's later actions?

5. **Compare** How does the narrator's understanding of Miss Lottie at the end of the story compare to her feelings about the woman at the beginning of the story?

6. **Draw Conclusions** What is the story's theme? Note at least three clues that help you recognize the message the author is sharing.

7. **Analyze** What do the marigolds symbolize in this story? Explain how they contribute to the development of the story's theme.

8. **Draw Conclusions** What conclusions can you draw about the narrator's present life from the last paragraph in the story? Drawing on your understanding of the story's symbolism, paraphrase the last line.

PERFORMANCE TASK

Writing Activity: Essay Write a short essay in which you analyze how Lizabeth changes over the course of "Marigolds." Be sure to support your ideas with sufficient evidence from the text. Consider the following questions before you write.

- How aware is Lizabeth of her own surroundings and the wider world?
- What does Lizabeth's reflection at the end of the story suggest about her feelings toward the move into adulthood?

Assign this performance task.

PERFORMANCE TASK COMMON CORE W 2, W 4, W 9a, W 10

Writing Activity: Essay Have students work in pairs to discuss the questions and take notes. Then, have students write independently. Essays should be organized in a clear and coherent manner and provide details that differentiate Lizabeth as a child and as an adult.

Critical Vocabulary

COMMON CORE L 4b, L 4d, L 6

poignant	ostensible	retribution	stoicism
perverse	bravado	impotent	exuberance
degradation	squalor		

Practice and Apply Use your understanding of the Vocabulary words to answer each question.

1. Is it **perverse** to seek **retribution** for stolen property? Why?

2. Why might homeowners who feel **impotent** show **bravado** at an approaching wildfire?

3. Is suppressing a cry of pain showing **exuberance** or **stoicism**? Why?

4. Why might someone tell a **poignant** story about living in **squalor**?

5. What might be the **ostensible** reason for telling about **degradation**?

Vocabulary Strategy: Use Latin Suffixes

Suffixes—word parts added to the end of a root or base word—often provide clues about the meaning of a word. For example, knowing that the Latin suffix -ation usually means "state, condition, or quality of" helps you to understand the word *degradation* in the phrase below from "Marigolds":

> ". . . the hopelessness of our poverty and degradation . . ."

When you break the longer word *degradation* into its parts (*degrad* + *ation*), it is easier to read and understand the word. The base word *degrade*, which means "to lower in dignity" combines with the suffix -ation to mean "the state of being lowered in dignity."

Practice and Apply Identify the -ation word or words in each of the following sentences. Use the base or root word and the suffix meaning to define the word. Check a dictionary to confirm your definition.

1. Lizabeth overheard her parents' heated conversation.

2. The combination of poverty and discrimination hurt Lizabeth's family.

3. The feeling of exhilaration from the release of rage and tension didn't last.

4. The desire to succeed filled Lizabeth with the determination to work hard.

5. Receiving the writing medal was affirmation of her hard work.

PRACTICE & APPLY

Critical Vocabulary

COMMON CORE L 4b, L 4d, L 6

Possible answers:

1. *No; seeking punishment of someone who has stolen something seems natural and appropriate.*

2. *Helpless before a raging wildfire, homeowners might act with bravado to make themselves feel better.*

3. *It shows stoicism. Trying not to cry, or show that you are in pain, is a way of not showing emotion.*

4. *They might be trying to get readers or listeners to be sympathetic to people living in poverty.*

5. *There might be no way to conceal the circumstances of degradation.*

Vocabulary Strategy: Use Latin Suffixes

1. *converse + ation; the state of conversing*

2. *combine + ation; the condition of being combined; discriminate + ation; the state of discriminating*

3. *exhilerate + ation; the state of being exhilarated*

4. *determine + ation; the state of being determined*

5. *affirm + ation; the state of being affirmed*

Strategies for Annotation 🖉 📖 *Annotate it!*

Vocabulary Strategy: Use Latin Suffixes

COMMON CORE L 4b

Share these strategies for guided or independent analysis:

- Highlight in blue the vocabulary word.
- Use a note to break the word into its parts and to tell what it means.

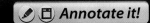

the hopelessness of our poverty and **degradation,** the

bewilderment

> degrade + ation: the state of being lowered in dignity

Language Conventions: Infinitives

Prompt students to describe how the infinitive functions in each sentence. For example, if the infinitive is used as a noun, is it the subject or a direct object of the sentence?

Possible answers:

1. *To hurl stone at flowers; noun (subject)*

2. *to run wild with the other children; adverb (modifies free)*

3. *to be avoided; adjective (modifies one)*

4. *to listen to her mother's soothing voice; noun (direct object)*

5. *to do mischief; adjective (modifies time)*

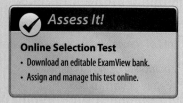

Assess It!

Online Selection Test
- Download an editable ExamView bank.
- Assign and manage this test online.

Language Conventions: Infinitives

Along with participles and gerunds, another kind of **verbal**—or verb form that is used as another part of speech—is the infinitive. An **infinitive** is a verb form that usually begins with *to* and functions as a noun, an adjective, or an adverb. An infinitive phrase consists of an infinitive plus its modifiers and complements.

In this example from "Marigolds," the author uses an infinitive phrase as an adverb modifying the adjective *sophisticated*:

> We were far too <u>sophisticated</u> now, of course, <u>to believe the witch-nonsense.</u>

Because *to*, the sign of the infinitive, precedes infinitives, it is usually easy to recognize them. However, sometimes *to* may be omitted, as in this example:

> Let no one dare [to] come into my garden.

Look at these examples of the uses of infinitives and infinitive phrases:

Uses of Infinitives	Examples
As a noun	<u>To taunt</u> is cruel. (subject)
	She wanted **to destroy the flowers**. (direct object)
	She wanted nothing except **to escape her room**. (object of preposition)
As an adjective	Now is the time **to grow up**. (modifies a noun)
	She was someone **to ridicule**. (modifies a pronoun)
As an adverb	<u>To escape</u>, jump out the window. (modifies a verb)
	The children were armed and ready **to do mischief**. (modifies an adjective)
	It was enough mischief **to do for one night**. (modifies an adverb)

Practice and Apply Identify the infinitive phrase in each sentence and tell whether it is being used as a noun, an adjective, or an adverb. Be careful not to confuse an infinitive with a prepositional phrase beginning with *to*.

1. To hurl stones at flowers is silly.

2. Lizabeth and Joey were free to run wild with the other children.

3. The road to Miss Lottie's was one to be avoided.

4. She loved to listen to her mother's soothing voice.

5. The children had too much time to do mischief.

INTERACTIVE WHITEBOARD LESSON
Make Inferences

COMMON CORE

RL 1

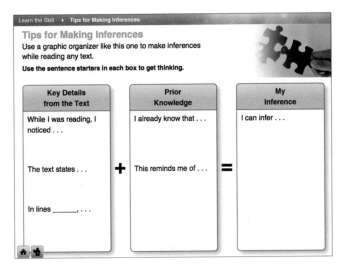

Learn the Skill ▸ Tips for Making Inferences

Tips for Making Inferences
Use a graphic organizer like this one to make inferences while reading any text.

Use the sentence starters in each box to get thinking.

Key Details from the Text		Prior Knowledge		My Inference
While I was reading, I noticed . . .		I already know that . . .		I can infer . . .
The text states . . .	**+**	This reminds me of . . .	**=**	
In lines _____, . . .				

TEACH

Tell students that an **inference** is a logical guess that is made based on facts and one's own knowledge and experience. Remind students that authors do not always state directly what a character is thinking or feeling. Explain that when this is so readers can make inferences about the character's thoughts and feelings.

Present the following steps:

- First, notice key details in the text.
- Then, think about any prior knowledge that relates to the passage. Prior knowledge may be something readers know about characters in another story or something they know from experience.
- Use the details from the text and prior knowledge to make an inference about the characters.

PRACTICE AND APPLY

Work with students to make inferences based on the passages in the Practice & Apply section of the Interactive Whiteboard Lesson. Then, have small groups of students choose a passage from "Marigolds" that describes how Lizabeth feels at that point in the story. Have students follow the steps to make an inference about Lizabeth.

Analyze Stories:
Characters' Motivation

COMMON CORE

RL 3

RETEACH

Review the terms **character, motivation,** and **infer.** Then, retell, or have a volunteer retell, a simple, familiar folk tale or fairy tale, such as "Goldilocks and the Three Bears." Prompt students to analyze the characters' motivation using questions such as the following:

- What is the reason that Goldilocks goes into the three bears' home? How do you know?
- Why does Goldilocks try different chairs? How do you know?
- What is Goldilocks' motivation to run away when the bears return home? How do you know?

LEVEL UP TUTORIALS Assign the following *Level Up* tutorial: **Character Motivation**

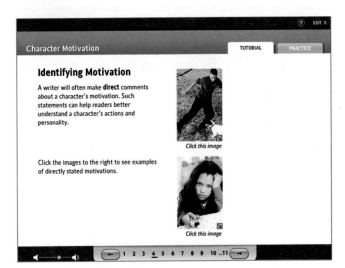

CLOSE READING APPLICATION

Student partners can work together to apply the skill to another selection or to a story they are reading as an independent assignment. After determining character motivations, students should discuss how incidents in the story move the plot forward, reveal aspects of a character, or provoke a character to make a decision.

The Whistle

Short Story by Anne Estevis

Why This Text

Students may read a short story without understanding the characters' motivations for their actions. Sometimes a narrator states a character's motivations directly. Other times, the reader must infer why a character acts in a certain way. Stories such as this one by Anne Estevis become clear by studying the characters and the situations that occur. With the help of the close-reading questions, students can infer a character's motivations by combining textual evidence with their own knowledge and experience.

Background Have students read the background and the biographical information about the author. Introduce the selection by telling students that Anne Estevis is a contemporary author who writes books rich with the traditions of rural Mexican-American life, as seen in her popular novels for young people, *Down Garrapata Road* and *Chicken Foot Farm*.

SETTING A PURPOSE Ask students to pay close attention to the characters' personalities and reactions to situations or problems. How soon into the story can they begin to identify a conflict that needs to be resolved?

 COMMON CORE

Common Core Support

- cite textual evidence to support inferences drawn from the text
- determine a theme or central idea and summarize events
- analyze how dialogue or incidents in a story propel the action and reveal character

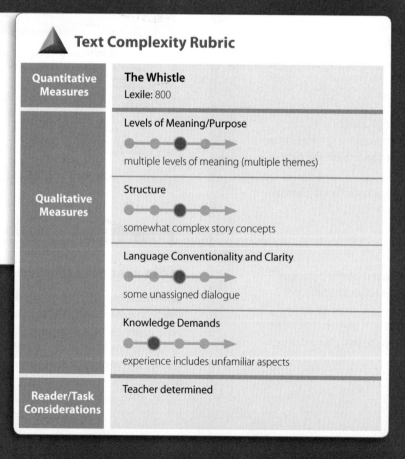

Text Complexity Rubric

Quantitative Measures	**The Whistle** Lexile: 800
Qualitative Measures	**Levels of Meaning/Purpose** multiple levels of meaning (multiple themes)
	Structure somewhat complex story concepts
	Language Conventionality and Clarity some unassigned dialogue
	Knowledge Demands experience includes unfamiliar aspects
Reader/Task Considerations	Teacher determined

Strategies for CLOSE READING

Analyze Stories: Characters' Motivation

Students should read this short story carefully all the way through. Close-reading questions at the bottom of the page will help them focus on a thorough analysis of the characters' motivations. As they read, students should record comments or questions about the text in the side margins.

WHEN STUDENTS STRUGGLE . . .

To help students understand the structural elements in a fictional narrative, have them work in a small group to fill out a story map, such as the one shown below, as they analyze the text.

CITE TEXT EVIDENCE For practice in tracing a character's motivations and reactions to the events of the plot, have students cite specific textual evidence to complete the story map.

> **Setting:** *The Southwest, a few decades ago*

⬇

> **Major Characters:** *Chatita, Abuelita*
>
> **Minor Characters:** *Chatita's mother and father and her two brothers, Keno and Chuy*

⬇

> **Plot/Problem:** *The grandmother gets locked in the shed and calls for help. Chatita should be keeping an eye on her, but mistakes her cries for the bleating of a goat.*

⬇

> **Event 1:** *Mother tells Abuelita and the children to care for each other while she is away.*

> **Event 2:** *The narrator mistakes the trapped Abuelita's cries for the bleating of a goat.*

> **Event 3:** *The narrator rescues Abuelita, who is angry at her, shaming the narrator.*

⬇

> **Outcome:** *The narrator buys Abuelita a whistle. When Abuelita locks herself in the shed—this time, probably on purpose—she blows the whistle to "test" that her granddaughter can hear her call.*

Background *An award-winning author, **Anne Estevis** (born 1936) grew up in Corpus Christi, Texas. Shortly after high school, she and her mother moved to a ranch in New Mexico. Her mother, a native New Mexican, was the family historian and storyteller. Through her stories, she imbued in her daughter an appreciation for the history and diverse cultures of Mexico and the American Southwest, which Estevis later used in her novels.*

The Whistle

Short Story by Anne Estevis

CLOSE READ
Notes

1. **READ ▶** As you read lines 1–12, begin to cite text evidence.

- Circle the reason the grandmother comes to live with the family.
- Underline what the mother tells the abuela.
- Underline what the mother tells her children.

My **paternal** grandmother Carmen was a tiny woman, not even five feet tall. She came to live with us because she said she needed to help my mother with the heavy load of raising a family. Having my grandmother around was usually pleasant; however, I remember a time when I wished she would find another family to care for. It was during the late autumn when I was fourteen years old. My parents had gone to San Antonio because my mother's father was very ill.

A **B** Before leaving, Mamá said to my abuela,[1] "Please take care of
10 Chatita and the boys while I am gone."

Then Mamá turned around and quietly said to my brothers and me, "Children, please take care of your grandmother."

_____
[1] **abuela** (ä bwe′ lə): Spanish for "Grandmother."

paternal:
related through the father

71

---

1. **READ AND CITE TEXT EVIDENCE**

A **ASK STUDENTS** to determine how Estevis uses dialogue at the opening of the story to introduce the main characters and a potential conflict of the plot. *Students should recognize that the mother's admonition to the children and their grandmother to take care of one another while she is gone reveals a caring aspect of her personality, while establishing a potential conflict in the plot—that the grandmother will be taking care of the children, while unbeknownst to her, the children will be taking care of her. Students should cite specific textual evidence from lines 9–12.*

Critical Vocabulary: paternal (line 1) Have students explain the meaning of *paternal* as Estevis uses it here. Ask students how *paternal* fits in with the narrator's discussion of her grandmother. *It explains how her grandmother, who has come to live with the family, is her father's mother.*

For several days we all took good care of one another. Then, on Saturday, the third day of my parents' absence, a cool front blew in a short while after we had eaten our noon meal. It wasn't terribly cold, just a little nippy.

My grandmother took note of the pleasant weather and remarked, ("What a nice day it is! I think I will clean the storage shed.") She retied her sagging apron, put on her sweater, and marched directly out to the
20 shed.

D

While my grandmother toiled in the shed, I went about my Saturday chores as usual: washing the bedding, cleaning out the ice box, feeding the chickens, cleaning the lantern chimneys, and polishing my only pair of shoes. My brothers Keno and Chuy had been instructed by our father to prepare the fields for winter vegetable planting, so I was alone in the house. I liked it this way because I could do my work without interruption and get finished sooner.

C

In the late afternoon I took some vegetable peelings out to the
30 chickens and noticed that the sky was cloudy and the wind was blowing harder than it had earlier. The day was turning cold. I glanced toward the storage shed and wondered how much longer my abuela would be working. I faintly heard what sounded like a goat bleating, so I looked around. Seeing nothing, I hurried back into the house to finish my chores. I especially wanted to get the lanterns put back together before dark.

The wind starts to blow and the day gets colder. The narrator thinks she hears a goat bleating.

Later I went out to get some firewood and while picking up small pieces of kindling from near the woodpile I heard again what I thought was a bleating goat. Still, I couldn't see the animal. Perhaps Keno or Chuy had brought home a kid to slaughter. They did that
40 occasionally. We all enjoyed the **savory** meat of *cabrito*;[2] I was beginning to feel hungry just thinking about it. I thought I should look for the animal, but decided to get the fire in the stove going first because I could see Chuy coming toward the house on the tractor. Keno was already at the tractor shed, and the boys usually wanted coffee as soon as they got to the house.

The house quickly warmed from the fire in the cookstove. I was just putting on the pot for coffee when my brothers stomped into the kitchen.

"It's really getting cold out there!" said Chuy as he hovered over
50 the big stove.

E

"Is the coffee ready, Chatita?" Keno asked.

I shook my head. "What about the goat? Are you going to butcher it?"

savory:

appetizing; tasty

[2] **cabrito** (kä brē' tô): Spanish for the "meat of a young goat, or kid."

---

2. **◀ REREAD** Reread lines 9–12. Write what you can infer about the mother's motivation for telling the children and the grandmother to take care of one another.

The mother knows the children's grandmother also needs looking after. She wants her mother-in-law to think that she is in charge while she and her husband are away, but she knows the children will need to keep an eye on her, too.

3. **READ ▶** As you read lines 13–48, continue to cite text evidence.

- Circle what the grandmother decides to do when the cool front arrives.
- Underline each of the narrator's chores.
- Explain in the margin how the weather changes and what the narrator hears as she finishes her chores.

4. **◀ REREAD** Reread lines 21–48. Briefly summarize what the characters are doing that day.

The grandmother cleans the shed, the narrator washes clothes, feeds chickens, and gets firewood, and her brothers prepare the fields for planting. Several times the narrator thinks she hears a goat, but doesn't take the time to look for the animal.

5. **READ ▶** As you read lines 49–71, continue to cite text evidence.

- Underline what Chuy says about the weather and the goats.
- Explain in the margin what the narrator suddenly realizes when she hears Chuy's comment about the goats.

---

2. **REREAD AND CITE TEXT EVIDENCE**

B **ASK STUDENTS** to draw an inference from the text to explain the reasons for the mother's words and actions concerning who should look after whom while she is away. *Students should infer that the mother knows that both the children and their abuela need looking after. Students should cite specific textual evidence from lines 9–12.*

3. **READ AND CITE TEXT EVIDENCE**

C **ASK STUDENTS** to read their margin notes and write one response that describes how the weather is changing and what the narrator thinks she hears as she completes her chores, citing specific textual evidence. *Students should note that the sky is getting cloudy, the wind is blowing harder, and the day is getting colder; she thinks she hears a bleating goat. Students should cite evidence from lines 28–30, 32–34, and 36–40.*

4. **REREAD AND CITE TEXT EVIDENCE**

D **ASK STUDENTS** to find the central ideas in lines 21–48 and use them to write a summary of the section. *Students should cite evidence from lines 21–26, 28–34, and 36–40 to restate the central ideas in their summary, recognizing that their summary will include the characters' actions, the change in the weather, and the narrator's mistake about the sound she hears.*

5. **READ AND CITE TEXT EVIDENCE**

E **ASK STUDENTS** to read their margin notes and write one response that explains the narrator's sudden realization about the sound she has heard. Remind students to use the dialogue between Keno and the narrator to see how it propels the action and provokes the narrator's decision to act quickly. *Students should cite specific textual evidence from lines 51–53, 57–60, 62–66.*

Critical Vocabulary: savory (line 40) Have students share their definitions of *savory* and use the word in several sentences.

Neither answered. Chuy stopped warming his hands and turned away from the stove to look at me. Keno continued washing up in the enamel wash pan.

"I said, are you going to butcher the goat?"

"What goat are you talking about?" responded Keno.

"We don't have any goats," said Chuy.

60 I gasped and said, "Oh, my goodness! Come with me! Hurry!" I bounded out the kitchen door with my brothers behind me.

As we approached the storage shed I could see that the outside latch hook on the door was in place. I flipped the hook up and flung open the door. There, sitting on the floor, wrapped up in burlap bags like a mummy, was a cold and shivering grandmother. She tried to talk, but her voice was almost gone.

My brother helped the tiny woman to her feet and Keno carried her into the house as quickly as he could. All the way she was croaking like a frog, but I'm sure I discerned the words *"¡Huercos*
70 *desgraciados!"* repeated over and over. This meant that we were wretched brats, or maybe worse.

(F)

The narrator realizes that the bleating she heard was not a goat. It was her grandmother calling for help.

6. **◄ REREAD** Reread lines 62–66 and continue to cite text evidence. What can you infer from knowing that the shed's latch hook was in place when the children found their grandmother? What can you infer about the bleating goat?

The grandmother got locked in the shed, most likely when the door shut behind her as she started to clean the shed earlier that day. The sound of the goat the narrator thought she had heard during the day was really the grandmother crying for help.

7. **READ ►** As you read lines 72–93, continue to collect text evidence.
- Underline what the narrator learns in lines 88–93.
- In the margin, explain what the narrator could have done to keep her grandmother from being trapped.

74

> **" I knew she was very angry with me because she used my real name. "**

My brothers placed her in the chair nearest the kitchen stove while I fetched a soft woolen blanket to wrap her in. Chuy poured a cup of coffee and set it before her. Then we all sat down around the table staring at our obviously **infuriated** grandmother.

(H)

"What unfortunate children you are. You have no brains!" she said in a raspy voice. Her entire body was shivering. "You left me to die out there!" She shook her fist at each one of us and then looked squarely at me. "You, Telésfora. You must be deaf!" She shook a
80 crooked index finger at me.

I knew she was very angry with me because she used my real name.

"I called and called for you. The wind blew the door shut and it locked. All afternoon I yelled, but you didn't come. I nearly froze to death!" She scowled and slowly turned her head away from me.

"But I didn't hear you," I answered. "I'm sorry. Please, Abuelita. I'm truly sorry!"

(G) How could I have confused my grandmother's voice with that of a bleating goat? I felt terribly guilty and ashamed. I knew that the shed
90 door was prone to latch by itself if it was slammed. That's why a wooden stake for propping the door open was usually kept nearby. But this time the stake had not been used, and now my grandmother was shaking and shivering and glaring at me.

infuriated:

angry; enraged

Chatita should have remembered to tell her grandmother to prop the shed door open.

8. **◄ REREAD AND DISCUSS** With a small group, discuss whether the evidence in the text justifies the grandmother's feelings toward the narrator once she is rescued, and the narrator's feelings once she realizes the mistake she has made (lines 76–93).

75

---

6. **REREAD AND CITE TEXT EVIDENCE**

(F) ASK STUDENTS to cite specific evidence from the text and use their own knowledge and experience to support their inferences about how the grandmother got locked in the shed and how the narrator mistook the sound she heard. *Students should cite textual evidence from lines 62–66 to infer that the grandmother got locked in the shed, most likely when the wind blew the door shut, and that the sound the narrator heard was probably that of her grandmother's raspy voice crying for help.*

7. **READ AND CITE TEXT EVIDENCE**

(G) ASK STUDENTS to read their margin notes to a partner or a small group and then write one response that states what the narrator forgot to tell her grandmother about the latch on the shed door and what she could do about it. *Students should cite specific textual evidence from lines 88–93.*

8. **REREAD AND DISCUSS USING TEXT EVIDENCE**

(H) ASK STUDENTS to appoint a reporter for each group to cite textual evidence and line numbers to support their position about whether the evidence in the text justifies the grandmother's furious reaction toward the narrator and the narrator's self-reproach and guilt once she realizes her mistake. *Students should cite textual evidence from lines 76–93.*

Critical Vocabulary: infuriated (line 75) Have students define *infuriated* and list familiar words that also come from the Latin *furia* or *furere*. Students might list *fury, furious,* and *furor.*

FOR ELL STUDENTS ELL students will better understand Abuelita's furious reaction in lines 76–93 if they engage in total physical response (TPR) to role-play the anger displayed toward the narrator. Have students act out these angry commands as you give them, with you playing the narrator: *Shake your fist at me (line 78); Call my name loudly (line 83); Scowl at me (line 85); Turn your head away from me (line 85); Glare at me (line 93).*

The Whistle **228e**

Ⓘ "Just you wait, Telésfora. Just you wait until your father gets home. I'll have him punish you," she said and her bottom lip quivered and her nostrils flared.

My parents came home in a few days and of course the first thing that occurred was that Abuelita told her story to my father.

100 "Son, Telésfora left me locked in the storage shed all afternoon on Saturday. I called and called for her, but she declares she didn't hear me. She says she heard a goat bleating. Can you imagine that I could possibly sound like a goat?" my grandmother said.

Ⓙ My father was very concerned, of course. I admitted to him that, indeed, I had mistakenly thought I heard a goat and that I was terribly sorry that I hadn't checked on Abuelita as I should have. He scolded me severely. But this wasn't enough punishment, according to my grandmother, so she decided to penalize me herself by refusing to speak to me. This made me very sad, and it seemed to affect all of us. A sense of sorrow and discomfort permeated our family.

She is furious at the narrator for having confused her cries with the bleating of a goat.

9. **READ** ▶ As you read lines 94–109, continue to cite text evidence.
   - Underline text evidence that confirms that the relationship between the narrator and her grandmother has taken a turn for the worse.
   - In the margin, make an inference about Abuelita's motivation for "telling on" the narrator. What does this tell you about her?

10. ◀ **REREAD** Reread lines 103–109, noting what the narrator tells her father in her own defense. What does this tell you about her personality?

It shows that she is willing to admit her mistakes and to take responsibility for her actions.

76

> **... this wasn't enough punishment, according to my grandmother ...**

Ⓚ 110 Two weeks later I asked to go with my father to the big yellow store in town. While Papa made his purchases, I bought a silver (whistle) and a long piece of blue satin ribbon. I threaded the ribbon through the ring on the (whistle) and tied the ends of the ribbon together.

That evening, I placed the (whistle) in a little box and wrapped it in some colored paper. After supper, I approached my grandmother.

"This is for you, Abuelita. I'm terribly sorry about what happened to you in the shed. I hope you can forgive me."

My grandmother looked at me and said nothing. Then she took 120 the box and opened it. She pulled the (whistle) out by its ribbon.

"Well, Telésfora, whatever is this for?" she asked, keeping her eyes on the whistle.

"It's to wear around your neck when you are outside. If you need me, just blow the (whistle) and I'll come to you," I said.

"And how can I be sure you'll hear this little (whistle)? You couldn't even hear me yelling at you!" But Abuela put it around her neck anyway.

Ⓛ "The next evening, while I was feeding the chickens, I heard a faint (whistle.) I stopped what I was doing and stood very still. Then I 130 heard the (whistle) more distinctly. Yes! It was definitely coming from inside the storage shed. I rushed to the shed and found the door latched. That surprised me because the wind wasn't blowing at all.

The repetition calls attention to the whistle's— and the grandmother's— unique importance.

11. **READ** ▶ As you read lines 110–141, continue to cite textual evidence.
   - Circle each use of the word *whistle.*
   - In the margin, explain what idea the narrator might be emphasizing by repeating this word.
   - Underline details of Abuelita's behavior in lines 128–141.

77

---

9. **READ AND CITE TEXT EVIDENCE**

Ⓘ **ASK STUDENTS** to consider what they know about Abuelita's personality in order to draw an inference from the text about her reason for telling her son about the narrator's mistake and the terrible situation that occurred as a result. *Students should support their assessment of Abuelita's personality and her motivation for "telling on" the narrator by citing evidence from lines 94–96 and 97–102, pointing out personality traits that include Abuelita's ability to become violently angry and to seek retribution.*

10. **REREAD AND CITE TEXT EVIDENCE**

Ⓙ **ASK STUDENTS** to combine textual evidence with their own prior knowledge and experience to make an inference about the narrator's personality based on her truthful admission to her father. *Students should cite textual evidence from lines 103–109 to support the inference that the narrator is mature enough to admit her mistakes and shortcomings and to take responsibility for her behavior.*

11. **READ AND CITE TEXT EVIDENCE**

Ⓚ **ASK STUDENTS** to read their margin notes and write one response that explains why *whistle* is repeated several times in lines 110–141. *Students should note that its repetition emphasizes its importance to the story and its figurative or symbolic significance as a peace offering from the narrator to her grandmother. The whistle may also represent the future of this family, including Abuelita's renewed trust in her granddaughter and the important role Abuelita will play in the family. Students should cite textual evidence from lines 110–114, 117–118, 123–127, 128–133, 135–141.*

FOR ELL STUDENTS Act out the common meaning of *faint* by pretending to swoon. Ask students if this is the meaning of the word as used here (line 129). *No.* Point out that *faint* is a multiple-meaning word, and ask students to define it in context. *Here, it means "not clearly heard."* Ask students to find and cite other multiple-meaning words in lines 110–141 and cite them in the margin.

There was no way that the door could have slammed shut by itself. Something seemed really strange about this, and I was suspicious. I unlatched the door and opened it. There stood my grandmother with the (whistle) in her mouth. She quickly removed it and said, "I think your papá needs to do something about that crazy door latch. Don't you think so, Chatita?"

140 She hurried out of the shed and we started toward the house. I could see that she was smiling, and I think I even heard her chuckling.

12. ◀ **REREAD** Reread lines 128–141. How did Abuelita get locked in the shed this time? Cite text evidence in your response.

Abuelita locked herself in the shed on purpose. She wanted to be sure Chatita was listening for the whistle. Her "smiling" and "chuckling" at the end of the story suggests this is the case.

SHORT RESPONSE

Cite Text Evidence   Explain what the whistle symbolizes for both Chatita and Abuelita. **Cite text evidence** to support your ideas.

After being locked in the shed all day, Abuelita felt ignored and abandoned by her granddaughter. Once Chatita realized her mistake and recognized how angry her grandmother was, she knew that she needed to find a way to make a heartfelt apology. For Chatita, the whistle symbolizes the remorse she feels for not noticing Abuelita's predicament, as well as her pledge never to ignore her grandmother again. For Abuelita, the whistle symbolizes the renewed trust she has in her granddaughter.

78

TO CHALLENGE STUDENTS . . .

For more context about extended families, in which parents, dependent children, and other relatives live together, students can do print or online research to write a persuasive essay to argue in favor of the extended family system over the nuclear family, in which just parents and dependent children live together, or vice versa.

ASK STUDENTS to take a position and argue it in their essay, discussing the advantages and disadvantages of one family group over the other. Point out that students will need to present a strong argument to persuade their audience to agree with their point of view.

DIG DEEPER

With the class, return to Question 8, Reread and Discuss. Have students share the results of their discussion.

ASK STUDENTS whether they were satisfied with the outcome of their group discussions. Have each group share what the majority opinion was concerning whether or not the textual evidence justified the reactions of the grandmother and the narrator after the rescue.

- Encourage each group to share the compelling evidence from the text that the group cited to support the majority opinion. Ask if there was any other convincing evidence cited by group members holding a different opinion.

- Have groups explain how they decided whether or not they had found sufficient textual evidence to justify the reactions of Abuelita and the narrator. Did everyone in the group agree as to what made the evidence sufficient? How did the groups resolve any differences of opinion?

- After groups have shared the results of their discussion, ask what compelling ideas were shared by other groups.

ASK STUDENTS to return to their Short Response answer and to revise it based on the class discussion.

---

12. **REREAD AND CITE TEXT EVIDENCE** Explain to students that they will need to "read between the lines" to infer how Abuelita got locked in the shed the second time.

ⓛ **ASK STUDENTS** to combine textual evidence with what they already know to make an inference about Abuelita and the situation of being locked in the shed the second time. *Students should cite textual evidence from lines 128–141 to support the inference that Abuelita locked herself in the shed to see if the narrator was listening for the whistle. Abuelita's "smiling" (line 140) and "chuckling" (line 141) suggest that her motivation is to "test" Chatita.*

SHORT RESPONSE

Cite Text Evidence   Students should:

- explain the symbolic significance of the whistle for both the narrator and her grandmother.
- give reasons for their point of view.
- cite specific evidence from the text to support their reasons.

Hanging Fire

Teenagers

Poem by Audre Lorde

Poem by Pat Mora

Why These Texts?

Students sometimes have difficulty connecting to or feeling comfortable with the poetry genre. These two poems express feelings that today's teenagers can readily grasp and relate to. At the same time, the poems are complex texts that present opportunities to analyze theme and figurative language as well as to compare points of view.

Key Learning Objective: The student will be able to make inferences and determine the theme of a poem.

For practice and application:

Close Reader selection
Poems About Growing Up
"Identity," *Poem by Julio Noboa Polanco*
"Hard On the Gas" *Poem by Janet S. Wong*

COMMON CORE Common Core Standards

RL 1 Cite textual evidence.

RL 2 Determine a theme.

RL 4 Determine figurative meanings.

RL 5 Compare and contrast the structure of two texts.

W 4 Produce clear and coherent writing.

W 9a Apply grade 8 Reading standards to literature.

W 10 Write routinely for a range of purposes.

SL 1a Come to discussions prepared.

SL 6 Adapt speech to context and tasks.

L 2c Spell correctly.

Text Complexity Rubric

	Hanging Fire	Teenagers
Quantitative Measures	Lexile: N/A	Lexile: N/A
Qualitative Measures	**Levels of Meaning/Purpose** single level of complex meaning	**Levels of Meaning/Purpose** single level of complex meaning
	Structure free verse, no particular patterns	**Structure** free verse, no particular patterns
	Language Conventionality and Clarity less straightforward sentence structure	**Language Conventionality and Clarity** some figurative language
	Knowledge Demands single, familiar perspective	**Knowledge Demands** somewhat unfamiliar perspective
Reader/Task Considerations	Teacher determined Vary by individual reader and type of text	Teacher determined Vary by individual reader and type of text

CLOSE READ

Audre Lorde and Pat Mora Have students read the information about the two poets. Point out that each of the poets demonstrates pride in her cultural heritage. Discuss why Audre Lorde's African name, Gamba Adisa, is a particularly appropriate one for a poet.

SETTING A PURPOSE Direct students to use the Setting a Purpose question to focus their reading. Remind students to generate their own questions as they read.

SCAFFOLDING FOR ELL STUDENTS

Model Fluency Project the first stanza of "Hanging Fire" on a whiteboard. Explain to students that poets sometimes write without punctuation to produce the effect of natural speech or to draw attention to a speaker's uninterrupted thoughts. Read the lines aloud with expression, modeling how to pause at logical points to convey meaning.

ASK STUDENTS to read the stanza aloud with you and to think about the meaning of the lines. Tell them to use this strategy as they read the rest of the poetry in this lesson.

HANGING FIRE   TEENAGERS

Poem by Audre Lorde   Poem by Pat Mora

Audre Lorde (1934–1992) *was born in New York City and found early success in writing poetry. Lorde used poetry as a means of expression and a way to communicate. She became a published author when a popular magazine published one of her poems while she was still in high school. In addition to poetry, Lorde also wrote acclaimed essays and novels. She won many important awards for her writing and worked to support several social causes close to her heart. Toward the end of her life, Lorde took the African name Gamba Adisa, which is believed to mean "she who makes her meaning clear."*

Pat Mora (b. 1942) *was born in El Paso, Texas. She comes from a Mexican American family and considers herself fortunate to be bilingual and have the ability to write in both Spanish and English. She has written several books of poetry, as well as children's books and essays. Mora takes pride in being a Hispanic writer. She says that she will continue to write and to struggle to say what no other writer can say in quite the same way she can. Family, Mexican American culture, and the desert are all important themes in Mora's work.*

SETTING A PURPOSE Both of these poems focus on communication during adolescence. As you read, think about the subject and how it is presented from two different points of view. How is the message in each poem communicated to readers?

©nuttakit/Shutterstock

I am fourteen
and my skin has betrayed me
the boy I cannot live without
still sucks his thumb
in secret
how come my knees are

always so ashy
what if I die
before morning
and momma's in the bedroom
with the door closed.

TEACH

CLOSE READ

Determine Theme

COMMON CORE **RL 1, RL 2**

(LINES 12–21)

Tell students that the **theme** of a poem is a message about life or human nature that the writer wants to convey. Readers can make **inferences,** or logical guesses, about the theme from the title as well as from statements and images in the poem.

Ⓐ CITE TEXT EVIDENCE Explain that the phrase *hang fire* means "to delay or be delayed in taking action or progressing." Ask students what the title "Hanging Fire" suggests about the theme of the poem. *(Teenagers often feel stuck in place while also feeling that there is so much to be done.)* Have students reread lines 12–21 and cite evidence that supports this inference about the theme. *("I have to learn how to dance / in time for the next party"; "suppose I die before graduation"; "There is nothing I want to do /and too much / that has to be done")*

Make Inferences

COMMON CORE **RL 1**

(LINES 24–35)

Review that the **speaker** in a poem is the voice that talks to readers. From evidence in the poem, readers can make inferences about the speaker.

Ⓑ CITE TEXT EVIDENCE Have students reread lines 24–35. Ask what they can infer about the speaker and what evidence supports the inference. *(The speaker is overly dramatic and sees herself as persecuted and misunderstood. Evidence: "Nobody ever stops to think about my side of it"; "why do I have to be the one wearing braces"; "I have nothing to wear tomorrow")*

Determine Theme (LINES 1–5)

COMMON CORE **RL 1, RL 2**

Point out to students that both poems use the image of a closed door.

Ⓒ ASK STUDENTS to reread the first stanza of "Teenagers" and identify where this image is used. *(line 3: "Doors and lips shut.")* Ask what the image suggests about a similar theme in both poems. *(It suggests a theme that parents and teenagers should "open the door" to communication with each other.)*

Hanging Fire
Poem by Audre Lorde

I am fourteen
and my skin has betrayed me
the boy I cannot live without
still sucks his thumb
5   in secret
how come my knees are
always so ashy
what if I die
before morning
10 and momma's in the bedroom
with the door closed.

Ⓐ   I have to learn how to dance
in time for the next party
my room is too small for me
15 suppose I die before graduation
they will sing sad melodies
but finally
tell the truth about me
There is nothing I want to do
20 and too much
that has to be done
and momma's in the bedroom
with the door closed.

Ⓑ   Nobody even stops to think
25 about my side of it
I should have been on Math Team
my marks were better than his
why do I have to be
the one
30 wearing braces
I have nothing to wear tomorrow
will I live long enough
to grow up
and momma's in the bedroom
35 with the door closed.

©nuttakit/Shutterstock

APPLYING ACADEMIC VOCABULARY

deduce	sufficient

As you discuss the two poems, incorporate the following Collection 4 academic vocabulary words: *deduce* and *sufficient*. Ask students what they can **deduce** about adolescence from reading these poems. Remind students to be sure that they have **sufficient** evidence to support the inferences they make while reading.

Teenagers
Poem by Pat Mora

C

One day they disappear
into their rooms.
Doors and lips shut,
and we become strangers
5 in our own home.

I pace the hall, hear whispers,
a code I knew but can't remember,
mouthed by mouths I taught to speak.

D

Years later the door opens.
10 I see faces I once held,
open as sunflowers in my hands. I see
familiar skin now stretched on long bodies
that move past me
glowing
15 almost like pearls.

COLLABORATIVE DISCUSSION Both speakers address the
idea of a lack of communication between parents and children.
With a partner, discuss what might be the cause of this lack of
communication. Cite specific evidence from the texts to support
your ideas.

©nuttakit/Shutterstock

CLOSE READ

Determine Meaning of Words and Phrases

COMMON CORE RL 4

(LINES 9–15)

Explain that one type of figurative language poets
often use is a **simile**, a comparison between two
unlike things using the words *like* or *as*.

D **ASK STUDENTS** to reread lines 9–11 and identify
the simile. (*"I see faces I once held, / open as sunflowers
in my hands."*) Ask what two things are being
compared. *(faces and sunflowers)* Then, have students
identify another simile in lines 11–15. (*"long bodies /
that move past me / glowing / almost like pearls."*)
Discuss what effect the similes have on the last stanza
of the poem. *(The images of sunflowers and glowing
pearls create a joyful tone, in contrast to the darker tone
of the earlier stanzas. They also help convey the image
of teenagers blooming or cultivating into something
beautiful as they pass through those difficult years of
development.)*

COLLABORATIVE DISCUSSION Have students work
in pairs to discuss the specific lines in each poem that
show ideas about lack of communication. Encourage
pairs to take notes as they discuss the causes of this
problem. Then, have each pair share its ideas with
the class.

ASK STUDENTS to share any additional questions they
generated in the course of reading and discussing the
selection.

Strategies for Annotation

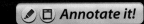 Annotate it!

Determine Meanings of Words and Phrases

COMMON CORE RL 4

To help students identify and understand figurative language in
the poems, have them use their eBook annotation tools to do
the following:

- Highlight similes in blue.
- In notes, write your analysis of what the figurative
  language adds to the poem.

Years later the door opens.

I see faces I once held,

open as sunflowers in my hands. I see

familiar skin now stretched on long bodies

that move past me

glowing

almost like pearls.

similes add
brightness

CLOSE READ

Make Inferences

COMMON CORE RL 1, RL 2

Review the definition of *speaker*. Emphasize that the speaker in a poem is not necessarily the poet, just as the narrator in a story may not be the story's author.

Point out that the chart illustrates the process of making an inference: use text clues, plus your own knowledge and experience, to make an educated guess about what the author does not say directly.

Have students make other inferences about the speaker of each poem. (*The speaker in "Hanging Fire" is a teenager who feels misunderstood: "I am fourteen," "think about my side of it."*)

Determine Theme

COMMON CORE RL 1, RL 2

Discuss the definition of *theme*. Guide students to understand that a theme is different from a topic, or what the text is about. Point out that the topic of both "Hanging Fire" and "Teenagers" is adolescence. However, the themes of the poems are ideas about this topic that the poets want to share with readers. Emphasize that a poem can have multiple themes.

Direct students to work in pairs to "dig deeper" into the poems, using the bulleted list to help them analyze themes. Ask students to identify a theme that is common to both poems. (*Possible answer: Both poems share the theme that teenagers and parents can benefit from more open communication with each other.*)

Make Inferences

COMMON CORE RL 1, RL 2

Both "Hanging Fire" and "Teenagers" are poems about adolescence, but they offer starkly different points of view—in part because the speakers in the poems are quite different. In poetry, the **speaker** is the voice that "talks" to the reader and shares his or her point of view, similar to the narrator in a story. A poem's speaker may or may not be the poet.

Often readers must make an **inference,** or logical guess based on text clues and their own knowledge and experience, in order to identify a poem's speaker. For example, in "Teenagers," text clues help readers figure out that the speaker is an adult, probably a parent or guardian, commenting on the behavior of a child becoming a teen.

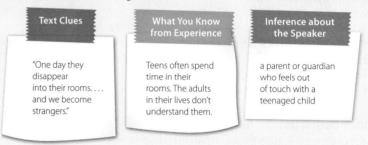

Text Clues	What You Know from Experience	Inference about the Speaker
"One day they disappear into their rooms. . . . and we become strangers."	Teens often spend time in their rooms. The adults in their lives don't understand them.	a parent or guardian who feels out of touch with a teenaged child

As you continue to analyze the two poems, think about what text-based inferences you can make about each speaker and his or her point of view.

Determine Theme

COMMON CORE RL 1, RL 2

Readers also may need to make inferences about themes in a poem. A **theme** is a message about life or human nature that a writer shares with readers. A theme usually is developed over the course of a poem, rather than stated directly at the beginning or end. Sometimes the lesson a speaker or character learns is a sufficient clue to help readers determine theme. Other elements within the text should be considered as well.

- the poem's title
- important statements the speaker makes
- images and details that stand out
- repeated words and phrases

Pay attention to text details as you dig deeper into the poems. Use text clues to determine the themes in each poem and to analyze how those themes are developed through word choice, imagery, and the speaker.

Strategies for Annotation  Annotate it!

Make Inferences

COMMON CORE RL 1, RL 2

Share these strategies for guided and independent analysis:

- Highlight in yellow evidence that helps make inferences about the speaker of the poem.
- Highlight in blue evidence that suggests a theme.
- In notes, write inferences about the speaker and theme.

how come my knees are
always so ashy
what if I die

before morning
and momma's in the bedroom
with the door closed.

The speaker does not like her appearance.

 eBook *Annotate It!*

Analyzing the Text

COMMON CORE RL 1, RL 2, RL 4, RL 5, W 4, W 9a, W 10, SL 1a, SL 6

Cite Text Evidence   Support your responses with evidence from the texts.

1. **Infer** Figurative language in which human qualities are given to an object, idea, or animal is called **personification.** What does the example of personification in the first stanza of "Hanging Fire" reveal about the speaker?

2. **Infer** Reread lines 1–7 of "Hanging Fire." Based on these lines, what inferences can you make about the speaker of the poem?

3. **Analyze** Reread lines 19–21 of "Hanging Fire." What does the contradiction or inconsistency expressed in these lines suggest about the speaker?

4. **Analyze** Several themes are touched on in "Hanging Fire." Identify and explain one or two of these themes, using text evidence as support.

5. **Interpret** A **simile** is a figure of speech that compares two unlike things using the word *like* or *as*. Identify a simile Mora uses in "Teenagers" that suggests what the speaker's grown children are like.

6. **Compare** The speaker in each poem has a specific point of view, or position about the subject matter of the poem. Tell one way the points of view are similar and one way they are different.

Speaking and Listening

Work with a partner to prepare a dramatic reading of one of the poems. Begin by discussing the impact of the poet's word choices. Practice reading each line of your chosen poem in a way that conveys what you think it means. Then share your dramatic reading with the class.

PERFORMANCE TASK

Writing Activity: Comparison
Compare and contrast the two poems.

- In a small group, work together to create Venn diagrams that show the similarities and differences between the poems' speakers, themes, and points of view.
- Then each group member should

write a paragraph in which she or he reflects on the advice the speaker in each poem might give to the other. Include text evidence from the poems to support your thoughts.

Assign this performance task.

PERFORMANCE TASK

COMMON CORE W 4, W 9a, W 10

Writing Activity: Comparison Students can use the Interactive Graphic Organizer Venn Diagram to create their comparisons.

- After students have written their paragraphs, switch them into different groups to share and discuss their comparisons.
- Challenge students to rewrite their paragraphs as a dialogue between the speakers of the two poems.

PRACTICE & APPLY

Analyzing the Text

COMMON CORE RL 1, RL 2, RL 4, RL 5

Possible answers:

1. *"My skin has betrayed me" is personification. The phrase suggests that the speaker is a teenager whose skin is breaking out. She sees this as a personal attack.*

2. *The speaker is a typical teenager who worries about her appearance and her boyfriend. She has many questions but feels like no one will stop to listen to her.*

3. *The contradiction of having nothing one wants to do but knowing there is much to be done suggests that the speaker is thoughtful and self-aware. She feels the pressures of school and the future weighing on her. Sometimes the reaction to pressure is a desire to do nothing at all.*

4. *One theme of "Hanging Fire" is that even though teens may resent adults for not giving them credit for their ideas and accomplishments ("Nobody even stops to think / about my side of it"; "I should have been on Math Team"), they still need the love and support of adults they can trust ("momma's in the bedroom / with the door closed.")*

5. *"long bodies / that move past me / glowing / almost like pearls." In this simile, the speaker's adult children are compared to pearls. The speaker is overjoyed when they finally emerge from behind the shut door of their teenage years like pearls from closed oysters.*

6. *One way the speakers' points of view are similar is that both feel isolated. They are different because the teenaged speaker in "Hanging Fire" feels her mother has abandoned her, whereas the adult speaker in "Teenagers" feels shut out by the teenaged children.*

Speaking and Listening

COMMON CORE SL 1a, SL 6

As partners prepare their dramatic readings, suggest that they alternate the roles of speaker and listener, with the listener giving the speaker feedback on the clarity and expression of the presentation.

Language Conventions: Words Ending in *y*

 COMMON CORE **L 2c**

Review the rules and examples shown in the chart. Before assigning Practice and Apply, have students give additional examples for each rule.

Answers:

1. *Teenagers' emotions can swing from lofty peaks to deep valleys in a single day.*

2. *Children that once played board games with parents now disappeared into their rooms after dinner.*

3. *My sister is a drama queen. She flies into a panic if she isn't able to call her friends.*

4. *During my older brother's teen years, his moods varied quite a bit.*

5. *Work hard at your studies in high school if you want to be successful.*

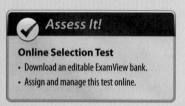

Assess It!

Online Selection Test
• Download an editable ExamView bank.
• Assign and manage this test online.

Language Conventions: Words Ending in *y*

 COMMON CORE **L 2c**

The plurals of most nouns are formed by adding -*s* to the singular, as in *teenager/teenagers*. However, different rules may apply to nouns ending in *y*. Regular verbs follow similar spelling rules in order to agree with their subjects in number and to form verb parts.

Note these examples from the poems of correctly spelled words ending in *y*:

> "I am fourteen / and my skin has <u>betrayed</u> me"
> (past participle of the verb *betray*)

> "I see / familiar skin now stretched on long <u>bodies</u>"
> (plural form of the noun *body*)

Keep the following rules in mind for words ending in *y*:

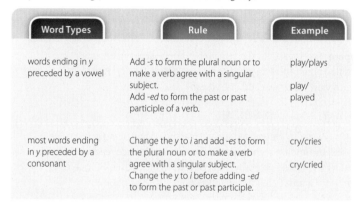

Word Types	Rule	Example
words ending in *y* preceded by a vowel	Add -*s* to form the plural noun or to make a verb agree with a singular subject. Add -*ed* to form the past or past participle of a verb.	play/plays play/ played
most words ending in *y* preceded by a consonant	Change the *y* to *i* and add -*es* to form the plural noun or to make a verb agree with a singular subject. Change the *y* to *i* before adding -*ed* to form the past or past participle.	cry/cries cry/cried

Practice and Apply   Rewrite these sentences, correcting any incorrectly spelled words.

1. Teenagers' emotions can swing from lofty peaks to deep vallies in a single day.

2. Children that once plaied board games with parents now disappeared into their rooms after dinner.

3. My sister is a drama queen. She flys into a panic if she isn't able to call her friends.

4. During my older brother's teen years, his moods varyed quite a bit.

5. Work hard at your studys in high school if you want to be successful.

INTERACTIVE WHITEBOARD LESSON
Determine Meaning of Words and Phrases

COMMON CORE

RL 4

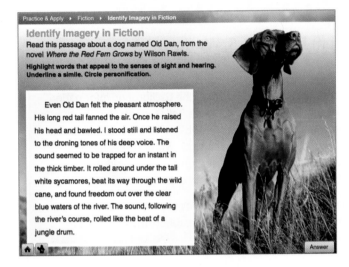

Practice & Apply ▸ Fiction ▸ Identify Imagery in Fiction

Identify Imagery in Fiction

Read this passage about a dog named Old Dan, from the novel *Where the Red Fern Grows* by Wilson Rawls.

Highlight words that appeal to the senses of sight and hearing. Underline a simile. Circle personification.

Even Old Dan felt the pleasant atmosphere. His long red tail fanned the air. Once he raised his head and bawled. I stood still and listened to the droning tones of his deep voice. The sound seemed to be trapped for an instant in the thick timber. It rolled around under the tall white sycamores, beat its way through the wild cane, and found freedom out over the clear blue waters of the river. The sound, following the river's course, rolled like the beat of a jungle drum.

Answer

TEACH

Explain that writers—especially poets—use figurative language to help readers see things in new ways. Discuss the following types of figurative language:

- **Simile:** A comparison between two things that uses the words *like* or *as*. (*"faces I once held, / open **as** sunflowers in my hands."*)

- **Metaphor:** A comparison that does not use the words *like* or *as*. (*"faces I once held **are** sunflowers in my hands."*)

- **Personification:** Giving human qualities to something that is not human. (*"my skin has betrayed me"*)

Share and discuss these steps for understanding figurative language:

- **Step 1:** Identify the figurative language.
- **Step 2:** Analyze the meaning. Ask what things are being compared and what the figure of speech contributes to the poem.

COLLABORATIVE DISCUSSION

Direct small groups of students to reread previously read poems and work together to analyze the poets' use of figurative language. Have students create a three-column chart to categorize examples of simile, metaphor, and personification.

Determine Theme

COMMON CORE

RL 2

RETEACH

Review that a **theme** is a message about life or human nature that a writer wants to share with readers. To determine th theme of a poem, The theme of a poem is usually not stated directly. Instead, the reader must make inferences based on elements such as statements made by the speaker, images and details, and repeated words and phrases. Work with students to determine the theme of a simple poem such as the following:

> Please take care of me.
> And I did.
> Puppy feeding, walking, playing.
> Puppy teething, howling, woofing.
>
> Please take care of me.
> And she did.
> Puppy defending, understanding, accepting.
> Puppy sharing, greeting, watching.

(speaker's statement: "Please take care of me. / And I did."; images and details: "teething, howling, woofing"; repeated words and phrases: "Please take care of me.")

Ask what inference students can make about the theme based on this evidence. *(Possible answer: Dogs are man's best friend.)*

LEVEL UP TUTORIALS Assign the following *Level Up* tutorial: **Theme**

CLOSE READING APPLICATION

Students can apply the skill to other poems that they choose. You might want to provide anthologies of appropriate poems and have partners work together to select and analyze a poem.

Poems About Growing Up

Identity

Poem by Julio Noboa Polanco

Hard on the Gas

Poem by Janet S. Wong

Why These Texts

Both poems examine the process of growing up. Because they are poems, students may have difficulty understanding the form and the figurative language the authors use to convey their meaning. With the help of the close-reading questions, students will examine what the speaker of each poem is saying about growing up. The results of their close reading will help students make inferences to determine the larger meaning of the poems.

Background Have students read the background information describing what poetry is and does. Tell students that the theme of reaching adulthood is a common one with poets and that, depending on the poet you read, you will find very different takes on the subject. Remind students that it is important to note how they relate or do not relate to a poem as they read it.

SETTING A PURPOSE Tell students to pay close attention to the images (word pictures) and metaphors the poets use to convey meaning.

 Common Core Support

- cite strong textual evidence
- make inferences
- determine the theme of a text
- compare and contrast the structure of two or more texts

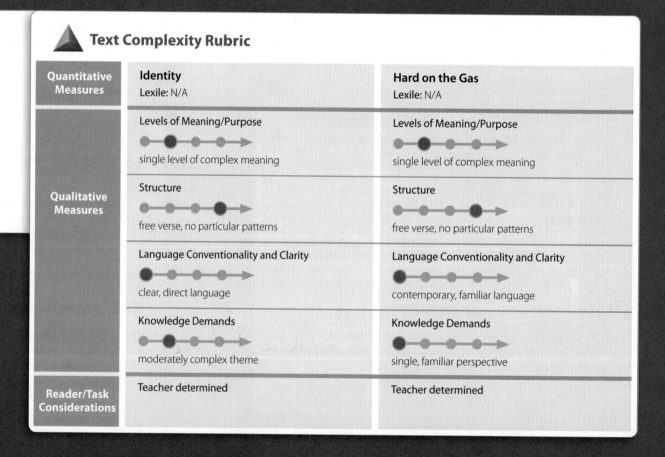

Text Complexity Rubric

	Identity Lexile: N/A	Hard on the Gas Lexile: N/A
Quantitative Measures		
Qualitative Measures	Levels of Meaning/Purpose single level of complex meaning	Levels of Meaning/Purpose single level of complex meaning
	Structure free verse, no particular patterns	Structure free verse, no particular patterns
	Language Conventionality and Clarity clear, direct language	Language Conventionality and Clarity contemporary, familiar language
	Knowledge Demands moderately complex theme	Knowledge Demands single, familiar perspective
Reader/Task Considerations	Teacher determined	Teacher determined

Strategies for CLOSE READING

Make Inferences

Students should read both poems carefully and slowly, thinking about what each speaker is saying about the process of growing up. Close-reading questions will help students cite text evidence that will help them make inferences about the poems and better understand the poems. Students should jot down in the margin details that will help them better understand the poems.

WHEN STUDENTS STRUGGLE . . .

To help students make inferences, have them work in small groups to fill out a chart like the one shown below.

CITE TEXT EVIDENCE For practice making inferences, ask students to make inferences based on lines from the poems.

Lines from the Poem	Inferences
"I'd rather be a tall, ugly weed, clinging on cliffs, like an eagle wind-wavering above high, jagged rocks." ("Identity," lines 4–6)	The speaker compares weeds to an eagle—a strong and free bird—and that's what he wants to be like.
"My grandfather taught himself to drive rough, the way he learned to live," ("Hard on the Gas," lines 1–2)	The speaker compares the way her grandfather taught himself to drive to the way he learned to live: rough. I think her grandfather is a tough person.

Background *The Italian poet Salvatore Quasimodo once wrote that "Poetry is the revelation of a feeling that the poet believes to be interior and personal which the reader recognizes as his own." While you read the following poems, think about how each speaker feels about growing up. Perhaps you will relate to the feelings the poems express about approaching adulthood.*

Poems About Growing Up

Identity . . . . Julio Noboa Polanco

Hard on the Gas . . . . Janet S. Wong

Julio Noboa Polanco *(born 1949) grew up in the Bronx, a part of New York City. He now lives in Texas. Polanco wrote "Identity," his best-known poem, when he was in the eighth grade. He had just broken up with his girlfriend, an event that marked a turning point in the young poet's life. He continued to write poetry for many years until he decided to focus on writing essays and articles on educational and cultural issues.*

Janet S. Wong *(born 1962) decided to become a poet after working as a lawyer for several years. Many of Wong's poems are about her experiences as an Asian American. Wong has said that a poem is a bit like shouting—since it's impossible to yell for very long, "you have to decide what you really need to say, and say it quickly."*

79

1. **READ ▶** As you read, collect and cite textual evidence.

- Circle where flowers and weeds grow.
- Underline what the speaker wants each time he says "I'd rather."
- In the margin next to stanzas 2, 5, and 6, write one or two words that describe the speaker.

Identity
Julio Noboa Polanco

B Let them be as flowers,
always watered, fed, guarded, admired,
but harnessed to a pot of dirt.

independent, adventurous

A I'd rather be a tall, ugly weed,
5   clinging on cliffs, like an eagle
wind-wavering above high, jagged rocks.

To have broken through the surface of stone
to live, to feel exposed to madness
of the vast, eternal sky.

10   To be swayed by the breezes of an ancient sea,
carrying my soul, my seed, beyond the mountains of time
or into the abyss of the bizarre.

loner, outsider

I'd rather be unseen, and if
then shunned by everyone
15   than to be a pleasant-smelling flower,
growing in clusters in the fertile valley
where they're praised, handled, and plucked
by greedy, human hands.

self-reliant, competent, powerful

I'd rather smell of musty, green stench
20   than of sweet, fragrant lilac.
If I could stand alone, strong and free,
I'd rather be a tall, ugly weed.

80

2. **◀ REREAD** Reread the poem. What can you infer about what the flowers and the weed represent?

The flowers and the weed represent two different types of people. The flowers are people who don't think for themselves and follow the trends and fashions of the moment. They follow the crowd. The weed is the person who thinks for himself and who is satisfied with who he is, because he is independent.

SHORT RESPONSE

Cite Text Evidence Why does the speaker want to be a weed? Review your reading notes and be sure to **cite evidence from the text** in your response.

The writer wants to be a weed because weeds are "alone, strong, and free." While flowers are contained in one location—"harnessed to a pot of dirt"—weeds live in wild and exciting places. Weeds are not pampered and owe nothing to caretakers and their "greedy, human hands." The speaker wants to stand out from the crowd as a unique individual.

81

---

1. **READ AND CITE TEXT EVIDENCE** Explain to students that they should try to understand what the speaker of the poem is like.

A **ASK STUDENTS** to find details and phrases in lines 4–12 that help them infer what the speaker of the poem wants to be like. *Possible responses: "tall ugly weed," "like an eagle," "to feel exposed to the madness," "swayed by the breezes of the ancient seas"*

FOR ELL STUDENTS Clarify the meaning of *harnessed*. Just as a horse may be harnessed to a plough or a cart, the poet is saying that flowers are confined or bound to a pot.

2. **REREAD AND CITE TEXT EVIDENCE**

B **ASK STUDENTS** to explain why the speaker spends so much time talking about weeds and flowers. *Possible response: Flowers and weeds represent two kinds of people. The speaker talks about flowers because he wants to show why being like a weed is what he prefers.*

SHORT RESPONSE

Cite Text Evidence Students' responses will vary, but they should cite evidence from the text to support their answers. Students should:

- explain what flowers and weeds represent to the speaker.
- explain what the speaker thinks flowers are like.
- explain what the speaker thinks weeds are like, and why he would prefer to be a weed.
- cite specific evidence from the text to support their ideas.

CLOSE READ
Notes

1. **READ ▶** As you read, collect and cite text evidence.
   - Underline the two things the speaker compares in the first stanza.
   - In the margin, explain what line 6 means.

Hard on the Gas
Janet S. Wong

"Rush, rest" refers to the ups and downs and starts and stops in the grandfather's life.

C My grandfather <u>taught himself to drive</u>
<u>rough, the way he learned to live,</u>

push the pedal, hard on the gas,
rush up to 50,
5 coast a bit,

rush, rest, rush, rest—

D When you clutch the bar above your right shoulder
he shoots you a look that asks,
Who said the ride would be smooth?

2. **◀ REREAD AND DISCUSS** Reread the poem. With a small group, discuss why the grandfather "shoots a look" at the speaker. Why does the speaker clutch the bar? Cite evidence from the poem in your discussion.

SHORT RESPONSE

Cite Text Evidence This poem is about more than the grandfather's driving ability. Explain the message, or larger meaning, of the question *"Who said the ride would be smooth?"* **Cite text evidence** in your response.

This poem is about the way people live their lives as they grow up. Perhaps the grandfather's driving applies to life: "rush up to 50, coast a bit." He wants his granddaughter to be tougher than she is. When she holds on, his look implies that she should be stronger and able to deal with the wild drive. Her interpretation of his glance—"Who said the ride would be smooth?"—lets the reader know that she understands his warning that life will not always be easy.

82

---

1. **READ AND CITE TEXT EVIDENCE**

C **ASK STUDENTS** to explain what two things the speaker compares in the first stanza. *The speaker compares the way her grandfather drove his car to the way he lived his life.*

2. **REREAD AND DISCUSS USING TEXT EVIDENCE**

D **ASK STUDENTS** to assign a reporter for each group. Have students infer why the speaker clutches the bar in line 7. *Possible response: If riding with the grandfather was probably a series of really fast starts, a passenger might get alarmed and grab the bar.*

SHORT RESPONSE

Cite Text Evidence Students should:
- explain the larger meaning of the grandfather's driving.
- explain why the speaker clutches the bar and why the grandfather, in response, shoots her a look.
- explain the larger meaning of *"Who said the ride would be smooth?"*

TO CHALLENGE STUDENTS . . .

To extend students' understanding of the these poems and of poetry in general, have them think about what kind of person they would like to become or what they have learned from others about growing up. Have students use either images or metaphors, as Julio Noboa Polanco did in "Identity," or use a personal anecdote as a metaphor, as Janet S. Wong did in "Hard on the Gas," to express their thoughts and feelings about growing up.

ASK STUDENTS to choose their images or anecdotes carefully. Then have them create their own poem based on their images or anecdotes. Their poems should:

- focus on the theme of growing up.
- use images or anecdotes as metaphors.
- express a larger meaning that other people can relate to about the topic of growing up.

When their poems are complete, ask volunteers to share them with the class.

DIG DEEPER

With the class, return to Question 2, Reread and Discuss on page 82. Have students share and discuss their responses.

ASK STUDENTS to comment on how their responses are alike and how they are different.

- Have students discuss a time when someone shot them a "look." What were the circumstances and what did they infer the "look" meant?
- Then, have students think about a time when they or someone else grabbed the bar over their shoulder in a car. What was happening?

Building on their responses, have students reread the last line of the poem and reassess its meaning.

ASK STUDENTS to return to their answers to the Short Response question and revise them.

ANCHOR TEXT

When Do Kids Become Adults?

Arguments from "Room for Debate" in the *New York Times*

Why This Text?

Students regularly encounter arguments that present a variety of viewpoints on a single topic. This lesson outlines tracing and evaluating an argument of particular interest to young people: When are they considered adults?

▶ View It!

Professional Development Podcast:

Teaching Argument

Key Learning Objective: The student will be able to trace and evaluate arguments and evaluate supporting evidence to determine whether the evidence is relevant or irrelevant.

For practice and application:

Close Reader selection

"Much Too Young to Work So Hard," *History Article by Naoki Tanaka*

COMMON CORE Common Core Standards

RI 1 Cite text evidence.

RI 2 Determine central idea; summarize.

RI 3 Analyze how an idea is introduced and elaborated.

RI 4 Determine the meaning of words and phrases.

RI 5 Analyze structure.

RI 6 Determine an author's point of view and how it is conveyed.

RI 8 Trace and evaluate an argument.

RI 9 Compare and contrast texts.

W 7 Conduct short research projects.

L 1d Recognize and correct inappropriate shifts in verb voice and mood..

L 4b Use common Greek affixes as clues to meaning.

L 4d Verify preliminary determination of meaning.

SL 3 Delineate a speaker's argument and specific claims.

SL 4 Present claims and findings.

SL 5 Integrate visual displays into presentations.

SL 6 Adapt speech to a variety of contexts and tasks.

▲ Text Complexity Rubric

Quantitative Measures	**When Do Kids Become Adults?** Lexile: 1440L
Qualitative Measures	Levels of Meaning/Purpose more than one purpose; implied but easy to infer
	Structure more than one text structure
	Language Conventionality and Clarity some unfamiliar, academic, or domain-specific words
	Knowledge Demands more difficult science or civics concepts
Reader/Task Considerations	Teacher determined Vary by individual reader and type of text

Background Have students read the background information about "Room for Debate." Explain to students that the *New York Times*, which began publication in 1851, is one of the most widely read newspapers in the world.

SETTING A PURPOSE Direct students to use the Setting a Purpose question to focus their reading. Remind students to generate questions as they read.

Trace and Evaluate an Argument (TITLES, LINES 1–3)

 COMMON CORE RI 6

Explain that an **argument** is speaking or writing that expresses a **claim,** or a position on a problem or issue. Point out that an argument's title often gives readers a good idea of what an author's claim will be, or his or her position on a particular issue.

A ASK STUDENTS to review the titles of the five arguments and identify those that seem to indicate claims the authors might make and those that do not give readers a clear sense of what the author's position on a topic or issue might be. *(Possible answers: "Leave the Voting Age Alone," "Better Training for New Drivers," and "Mandatory Service to Become an Adult" all indicate clear claims that show a position on an issue. "What the Brain Says about Maturity" and "A Parent's Role in the Path to Adulthood" do not give readers a clear idea of what the author's position on those issues might be.)*

Then, have students reread lines 1–3. Point out that that these questions posed by the *New York Times* are general ideas that authors of the pieces that follow may examine or address, but that the primary question the newspaper asks is the selection's title *When Do Kids Become Adults?*

Background *"Room for Debate" is a weekly feature of the New York Times newspaper. Each week, the Times poses a question to a group of knowledgeable outside contributors about a news event or other timely issue. The contributors each bring different perspectives to the question and often offer conflicting opinions. Readers are invited to comment on the topic as well.*

When Do Kids Become Adults?

Arguments from "Room for Debate" in the *New York Times*

A **What the Brain Says about Maturity** by Laurence Steinberg

Leave the Voting Age Alone by Jenny Diamond Cheng

Better Training for New Drivers by Jamie Lincoln Kitman

A Parent's Role in the Path to Adulthood by Barbara Hofer

Mandatory Service to Become an Adult by Michael Thompson

SETTING A PURPOSE As you read, pay attention to the points each writer makes about when and how children mature into adults. Why do you think it is so hard to define when this happens?

Is it time to rethink the age of adulthood? Do the age requirements for certain rights need to be lowered or raised? Shouldn't they at least be consistent?

When Do Kids Become Adults? **235**

Close Read Screencasts ▶ View It!

Modeled Discussions

Have students click the *Close Read* icon in their eBooks to access a screencast in which readers discuss and annotate lines 12–20, a key passage that introduces an author's claim and presents reasons to support it.

As a class, view and discuss the video. Then, have students work in pairs to do an independent close read of a different claim and the reasons to support it in lines 198–205.

Trace and Evaluate an Argument

COMMON CORE · RI 5, RI 6, RI 8

(LINES 12–14; 27–31)

Remind students that a claim is an author's position on a topic or issue. Explain that a claim may be stated directly or indirectly, so that sometimes readers need to figure it out on their own.

B **ASK STUDENTS** to reread lines 12–14 to identify the writer's claim. *(lines 12–13: "Should this new knowledge prompt us to rethink where we draw the legal boundaries between minors and adults?")* Why might the writer have presented his claim in question-and-answer form? *(Possible answer: It connects his claim to the first of his supporting reasons.)*

Explain that, in an argument, an author provides **support,** or information, to back up his or her claim. Support includes reasons and **evidence,** such as facts, examples, and statistics.

C **CITE TEXT EVIDENCE** Have students reread lines 27–31 and tell how the author uses examples to support his claim that scientific information about brain maturity is not the primary way our society decides when maturity occurs. *(The author states that "teenagers can drive before they can see R-rated movies" on their own, and that they can fight in wars "before they can buy beer.")*

What the Brain Says about Maturity
By Laurence Steinberg

Neuroscientists[1] now know that brain maturation continues far later into development than had been believed previously. Significant changes in brain anatomy and activity are still taking place during young adulthood, especially in prefrontal regions that are important for planning ahead, anticipating the future consequences of one's decisions, controlling

10 impulses, and comparing risk and reward. Indeed, some brain regions and systems do not reach full maturity until the early or mid 20s. Should this new knowledge prompt us to rethink where we draw legal boundaries between minors and adults?

Maybe, but it's not as straightforward as it seems, for at least two reasons. First, different brain regions and systems mature along different timetables. There is no single age at which the adolescent brain becomes an adult brain. Systems responsible for logical reasoning mature by the time people are 16, but those involved in self-regulation are still developing

20 in young adulthood. This is why 16-year-olds are just as competent as adults when it comes to granting informed medical consent, but still immature in ways that diminish their criminal responsibility, as the Supreme Court has noted in several recent cases. Using different ages for different legal boundaries seems odd, but it would make neuroscientific sense if we did it rationally.

Second, science has never had much of an influence on these sorts of decisions. If it did, we wouldn't have ended up with a society that permits teenagers to drive before they can

30 see R-rated movies on their own, or go to war before they can buy beer. Surely the maturity required to operate a car or face combat exceeds that required to handle sexy movies or drinking. Age boundaries are drawn for mainly political reasons, not scientific ones. It's unlikely that brain science will have much of an impact on these thresholds, no matter what the science says.

[1] **neuroscientists:** people who study the brain and nervous system.

©Hadi Djunaedi/Shutterstock

SCAFFOLDING FOR ELL STUDENTS

Analyze Language Guide students to use base words and word families to explore related terms and ideas. Using a whiteboard, project lines 4–24. Point out *mature* in line 16 and explain its meaning. Then, tell students to highlight in yellow words that share the base word *mature*. *(maturation, maturity, immature)* Have students use word analysis and a dictionary to check or confirm their meanings.

ASK STUDENTS to follow a similar process to analyze other selection words, such as *neuroscientists, neuroscientific,* and *science.*

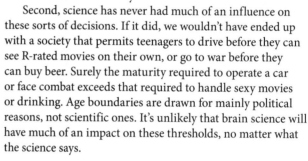

Neuroscientists now know that brain maturation continues far later into development than had been believed previously. Significant

Leave the Voting Age Alone
By Jenny Diamond Cheng

The 26th Amendment, ratified in 1971, establishes 18 as the minimum voting age for both state and federal elections. Like all lines that divide legal childhood from adulthood, the
40 voting age is essentially **arbitrary**. Indeed, in modern America 18-year-old voting has become **unmoored** from one of its more important original justifications, which was matching the minimum age for draft eligibility (itself also an arbitrary line). Despite this, raising or lowering the voting age, as some groups have suggested, seems a waste of time at best.

The American colonies mostly set their voting ages at 21, reflecting British common law.[2] This requirement went largely unchallenged until World War II, when several members of Congress proposed amending the Constitution to lower
50 the age to 18. Between 1942 and 1970 federal legislators introduced hundreds of such proposals, but the issue lacked momentum until the late 1960s, when a **confluence** of factors—including the escalating war in Vietnam[3]—pushed 18-year-old voting closer to the surface of the national political agenda. The 26th Amendment itself was the culmination of some creative political maneuvering by Congressional advocates, with a crucial assist from the Supreme Court in Oregon v. Mitchell.[4]

As a historical matter, the significance of the soldier-voter
60 link has been somewhat overstated. The amendment's passage was propelled by a small group of federal legislators whose motivations and rationales were considerably more complex than commonly thought. Still, the Vietnam-era slogan, "Old enough to fight, old enough to vote," was unquestionably a powerful claim, encompassing deeply embedded ideas about civic virtue, adulthood and fairness.

Tying voting to soldiering was always problematic, though, and it is even more so today. The contemporary U.S. military is an all-volunteer force and only a small fraction of
70 Americans ever serve. Selective Service registration applies only to males and the possibility of an actual draft is remote.

---

[2] **British common law:** the laws of England.

[3] **Vietnam:** a country in Southeast Asia where the United States fought a war in the 1960s and 1970s.

[4] **Supreme Court in Oregon v. Mitchell:** In this case, the Supreme Court decided that the U.S. Congress could set qualification rules for national elections.

arbitrary
(är´bĭ-trĕr´ē) *adj.*
If something is *arbitrary*, it is determined by chance or whim.

unmoor
(ŭn-mo͞or´) *v.* If you *unmoor* something, you release it from a place.

confluence
(kŏn´flo͞o-əns) *n.*
A *confluence* is a gathering or joining together in one place.

APPLYING ACADEMIC VOCABULARY

debate	sufficient

As you discuss the texts, incorporate the following Collection 4 academic vocabulary words: *debate* and *sufficient*. Ask students to discuss why adults seem so interested in **debating** issues such as the voting age or when teenagers can get a driver's license. Ask students to tell whether authors provide **sufficient** evidence to back up their claims.

CLOSE READ

Trace and Evaluate an Argument (LINES 44–58)

COMMON CORE RI 6, RI 8

Remind students that in an argument, a claim (the author's position on an issue) is backed up with reasons and evidence.

D **ASK STUDENTS** to reread lines 44–45 and use their own words to summarize the author's claim. *(Possible answer: It doesn't make sense to change the voting age.)*

E **CITE TEXT EVIDENCE** Ask students to review lines 44–58 and identify examples the author uses to support her claim. *(Possible answers: She points out that the "American colonies... reflecting British common laws," and that it took many tries, from World War II to the Vietnam era, to get the voting age changed from 21 to 18.)*

CRITICAL VOCABULARY

arbitrary: The author is explaining how the 26th Amendment made 18 the legal voting age in our country.

ASK STUDENTS to tell why choosing one single age that determines adulthood is arbitrary. *(People do not automatically mature in all ways when they turn 18, 19, or 21, so there is no good reason to explain why one should be able to vote at age 18 rather than at 17.)*

unmoor: The author is suggesting that the voting age is no longer related to when one can be drafted into the military.

ASK STUDENTS to tell what the author thinks that the unmooring of the voting age from draft eligibility proves. *(that trying to set one age as a dividing line between childhood and adulthood doesn't make sense)*

confluence: The author is discussing the long path to the passage of the 26th Amendment.

ASK STUDENTS to explain why it might have taken a confluence of events and factors to get the amendment passed. *(Possible answer: It didn't have great support for many years until a number of events related to the Vietnam War pushed legislators to take action.)*

Trace and Evaluate an Argument (LINES 75–81)

COMMON CORE RI 6, RI 8

Explain to students that usually an author will focus on one main claim in a text, but sometimes an author will include multiple claims.

 ASK STUDENTS to reread lines 75–81 to identify a second claim the author presents. Ask students to tell how the author supports this claim. *(The author makes the claim that it would be more useful to help young people get more involved in politics by getting rid of barriers that prevent them from voting. She gives an example of an unfair voting regulation in Tennessee that makes it difficult for college students to vote.)*

Analyze Language

COMMON CORE RI 4

(LINES 81–84)

Point out that an author's word choices often have an impact on the meaning of a text. Explain that while words may have a similar **denotation,** or dictionary definition, they can have very different connotations. Tell students that **connotations** are the feelings or ideas associated with a word.

G **ASK STUDENTS** to reread lines 81–84, drawing attention to the word *suffer*. Have students name words that have a similar denotation. *(Possible answers: experience, bear, undergo)* How does the author's use of *suffer* impact the sentence differently than a word such as *experience*? *(Suffer suggests a more painful or difficult situation. It makes the problems facing young people sound more dire.)*

> **CRITICAL VOCABULARY**
>
> **egregious:** The author is explaining that laws regarding voting do not always help voters.
>
> **ASK STUDENTS** to discuss why a new voting law in Tennessee seems egregious. *(It lets people who work at a university use their ID cards to vote, but students at the same university are not given that privilege, and this seems unfair, even suspicious.)*

Yet there is no life moment to which the voting age might be more obviously tethered, and any bright-line rule will inevitably seem unfair to some.

F Interest in improving young adults' political participation would be better focused on attacking barriers like residency requirements that exclude college students and voter ID laws that disfavor young and mobile voters, sometimes **egregiously**. Tennessee's new law, for example, specifically

80 disallows students, but not university employees, from using state university ID cards at the polls. More broadly, young **G** Americans suffer from the same challenges to meaningful representation and governance that plague our democracy at all levels. The voting age is the least of their problems.

egregious
(ĭ-grē´jəs) *adj.*
If something is *egregious*, it is very bad or offensive.

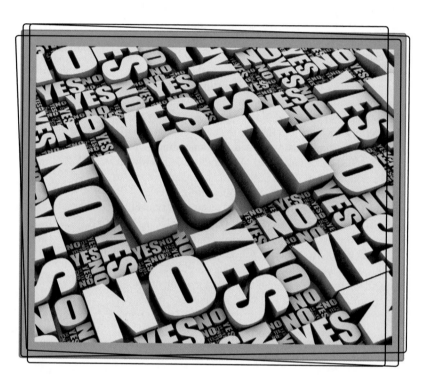

©Victor Correia/Shutterstock

Better Training for New Drivers
By Jamie Lincoln Kitman

Bright and early on the day I turned 17 you would have found me at the front of the line at the local New Jersey D.M.V. office, applying for a permit to drive. In due course, I got my full license and it wasn't long before I got my first ticket for speeding. And soon after that I got another for failing to
90 observe a stop sign. After which failure, I'd turned without signaling and then traveled 40 mph in a 25 mph zone, a points cluster-bomb that resulted in the suspension of my license until I enrolled in a driver-training course. Which, I might add, like the driving instruction I'd received in school, was virtually useless.

Americans (with an assist from the automobile and oil industries) tend to treat driving like a right, rather than the privilege it most assuredly is. And now that I'm grown and I like to think a more responsible driver, two factors leave me
100 convinced that the driving age shouldn't be lowered, indeed the right to drive should be doled out gradually to teens as it has been in New York since 2010.

The first problem is the utter **inadequacy** of our driver training. American states would do well to follow the example of European countries where licensing procedures require considerably more training and proven skill before new drivers are let loose on public roads. The second decider for me is the discovery by scientists that poor decision-making, the hallmark of many teenagers' existence, has its
110 roots in biology.

So graduated licenses like we have in New York—where young drivers cannot drive past nightfall or with more than one unrelated person under the age of 21 in their car—make good sense.

Is it the case that many teenagers can and will drive responsibly, regardless of the hour, number of young passengers or brain chemistry? Yes. Is there any inconsistency in the fact that a teen may work but not drive at night? Sure.

But, as every parent worth his or her salt[5] has reminded
120 their child at least a hundred times, Sometimes, life isn't fair.

inadequate
(ĭn-ăd´ĭ-kwĭt) *adj.*
If something is *inadequate*, it is insufficient or not enough.

---
[5] **worth his or her salt:** good at his or her job.

When Do Kids Become Adults? **239**

TEACH

CLOSE READ

Trace and Evaluate an Argument (LINES 98–110, LINES 115–120)

COMMON CORE — RI 5, RI 6, RI 8

Tell students that to **trace** an argument, they follow its reasoning. Explain that they first identify the claim and then locate evidence that supports it.

H **CITE TEXT EVIDENCE** Have students reread lines 98–110 to identify the sentence in which the author develops the key ideas in his claim. *("And now that I'm grown . . . as it has been in New York since 2010.")*

Explain that readers can also trace an argument by identifying **counterarguments,** statements that address opposing viewpoints. Point out that a good argument anticipates opposing views and disproves them.

I **ASK STUDENTS** to review lines 115–120 and to explain how the author uses a counterargument. *(Possible answer: He notes that some teenagers will drive responsibly, and that it doesn't make sense that teens can work but won't be allowed to drive there.)*

CRITICAL VOCABULARY

inadequate: The author believes that our driver's education requirements should "follow the example of European countries."

ASK STUDENTS why the author thinks our requirements are inadequate compared to those in Europe. *(The training and testing young drivers in Europe need to have are more appropriate.)*

Strategies for Annotation

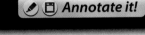 **Annotate it!**

Trace and Evaluate an Argument (LINES 103–110)

COMMON CORE — RI 5, RI 6, RI 8

Have students locate lines 103–110. Have them use their eBook annotation tools to do the following:

- Highlight in yellow reasons the author gives as evidence for his claim.
- Underline signal phrases that help identify the evidence.
- Write a note to tell whether the evidence is clearly connected to the claim.

The first problem is the utter inadequacy of our driver training. American states would do well to follow the example of European countries where licensing procedures require considerably more training and proven skill before new drivers are let loose on public roads. The second decider for me is the discovery by scientists that poor decision-making, the hallmark of many teenagers' existence, has its roots in biology.

Trace and Evaluate an Argument (LINES 133–145)

COMMON CORE RI 6, RI 8

Explain that when readers **evaluate** an argument, they examine it carefully and judge its value or worth. One way to evaluate an argument is to weigh the evidence an author presents. Explain that evidence is **relevant** if it supports the claim in a logical way. It is **irrelevant** if the connection to the claim is not clear.

 ASK STUDENTS to note the author's claim in lines 135–136 that "individuals are taking longer to recognize themselves as adults." Have students examine the evidence the author presents in lines 136–145, and evaluate whether each piece is relevant or irrelevant. (*Possible answers: The evidence about how first marriages and the birth of the first child seems relevant because it shows a clear connection to the claim. That more young people delay marriage or parenthood seems irrelevant because it is not clearly connected to the claim. The evidence about how young adults are financially dependent on their parents could be seen as an interpretation, but it is connected to the claim.*)

CRITICAL VOCABULARY

diffuse: The author is discussing how the age of adulthood varies from culture to culture.

ASK STUDENTS to explain how the author's examples prove her point that reaching adulthood can be diffuse. (*They show that in some cultures, like in the United States, the acquisition of rights is gradual, or spread out over time.*)

autonomous: The author is discussing how young people feel as they become adults.

ASK STUDENTS why it might be difficult for a young adult to become autonomous if his or her parents help too much in the making of choices. (*The young person will not learn to depend on him- or herself or feel comfortable making choices alone.*)

A Parent's Role in the Path to Adulthood

By Barbara Hofer

The transition to adulthood can be either clear or **diffuse**, depending on whether a culture chooses to offer all the privileges and responsibilities at one distinct age or spread them across time. In some countries, the ability to vote, drink, enter into legal contracts and serve in the military all occur at once. In the United States, these rights are not only spread out, but often without clear rationale. Serving in the military before one is considered responsible enough to purchase alcohol is one of the glaring inconsistencies. Some cultures

130 also mark the transition formally, as in Japan, where "Coming of Age Day" (Seijin Shiki) is a national holiday to celebrate all who reached adulthood in the current year.

Becoming an adult is also a subjective experience, of course, and there is little doubt from recent research that individuals are taking longer to recognize themselves as adults. The age of first marriage and birth of a first child, often perceived by individuals as adult markers, are now occurring later than at any time in history in the U.S. (and greater numbers of individuals are also choosing to forge

140 lives without either of these traditional markers). With increased numbers of individuals attending college and with the tremendous rise in the cost of education and the loans necessary for many, young people are also remaining dependent on parents financially far longer, often leaving them less likely to perceive themselves as adults.

Another psychological aspect of being an adult is feeling **autonomous**, and individuals whose autonomy is supported—at any age—are more personally motivated. As a college professor who studies adolescents and emerging adults, I am

150 particularly concerned that college students are not getting the opportunities they need to grow into autonomous, healthily connected adults when parents are still hyper-involved in their lives. "Emerging adults"—whom Jeffrey Arnett[6] defines as individuals between 18 and 25—need opportunities to make their own choices, whether that's about their major, what courses to take, their social lives or summer plans, and

diffuse
(dĭ-fyo͞os´) *adj.* If something is *diffuse*, it is very spread out or scattered.

autonomous
(ô-tŏn´ə-məs) *adj.* If someone is *autonomous*, the person is independent and not controlled by outside forces.

---

[6] **Jeffrey Arnett:** a doctor who studies emerging adulthood.

they need practice in making mistakes and recovering, and in owning the outcomes of their choices. They don't arrive in college fully formed as adults, but we hope they will use these
160 years to make significant progress toward adult behavior, with all the support and safety nets that college can offer.

Yet my research with Abigail Sullivan Moore, reported in our book, shows that many college students are in frequent contact with their parents—nearly twice daily, on average—and that frequency of contact is related to lower autonomy. Parents who are using technology (calls, Skype, texting, e-mail, Facebook, etc.) to micromanage lives from afar may be **thwarting** the timely passage to adulthood. Not surprisingly, these college students are also not likely to see themselves as
170 adults, nor fully prepared to take the responsibilities of their actions, nor even getting the benefits of college that they and their parents are paying for. One in five students in our study report parents are editing and proofing their papers, for example. College parents can help with the transition by serving as a sounding board rather than being directive, by steering their college-age kids to campus resources for help, by considering long-range goals rather than short-term ones and by giving their "kids" space to grow up.

thwart
(thwôrt) *v.* If you *thwart* something, you stop it from happening.

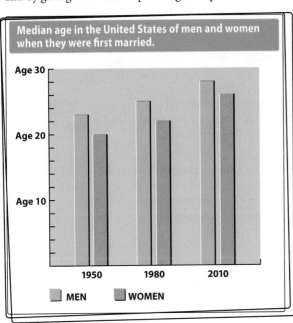

Median age in the United States of men and women when they were first married.

MEN   WOMEN

WHEN STUDENTS STRUGGLE...

Prompt students to read and examine the caption, the key, and the labels on each axis of the bar graph. Have students use information from the graph to draw conclusions about how patterns of the age at first marriages have changed in the United States over time. Then, have students review the author's claim in lines 134–136 and explain whether the information in the bar graph supports it.

CLOSE READ

Trace and Evaluate an Argument (BAR GRAPH)

 COMMON CORE RI 6, RI 8

Remind students that to evaluate an argument they need to determine whether the evidence is relevant or irrelevant. Explain that authors sometimes include graphic features such as charts and bar graphs like the one shown to support their claims.

K CITE TEXT EVIDENCE Have students examine the bar graph that follows line 178. Ask whether they think the bar graph is relevant and helps readers understand the author's claim. *(It is relevant because it supports her earlier point that the age of first marriages are seen as a marker for adulthood; the graph clearly backs up the claim that "individuals are taking longer to recognize themselves as adults" because it shows that men and women have been marrying later and later over the last 60 years.)*

CRITICAL VOCABULARY

thwart: The author is explaining that her research shows that parents are in frequent contact with their college-age children.

ASK STUDENTS how having a parent help their college student write and edit papers might end up thwarting their child's education. *(If college students never write papers on their own, they are not thinking independently or getting the full benefit of a college education.)*

Trace and Evaluate an Argument (LINES 198–205)

 COMMON CORE RI 6, RI 8

Explain that other ways readers can evaluate an argument include determining whether the evidence an author presents is accurate and sufficient and whether opposing viewpoints have been addressed. Draw attention to the author's new claim in lines 198–205.

(K) ASK STUDENTS to reread lines 198–205 to identify the claim. *(All 18-year-olds should be required to spend a year in service to others.)* Have students evaluate whether the author presents evidence that is accurate and sufficient and whether he has addressed opposing viewpoints. *(Possible answer: There is very little evidence presented to support this claim, other than a reason that it would result in "better workers and better citizens." The author has not addressed any opposing viewpoints.)*

CRITICAL VOCABULARY

cohort: The author is discussing what might happen as a result of requiring a mandatory year of service for all 18-year-olds.

ASK STUDENTS to discuss what a cohort of teenagers who have shared an experience of mandatory service might have in common. *(Possible answers: They might be more caring people; they might be more politically aware and active; they might want to work together to solve or improve some societal problems.)*

COLLABORATIVE DISCUSSION Before groups meet, have students work individually to review the texts to find support for their opinions. As students discuss their opinions in a group, remind them to cite evidence from the text to support their ideas.

ASK STUDENTS to share any questions they generated in the course of reading and discussing the selection.

Mandatory Service to Become an Adult

By Michael Thompson

180 Children are so variable in their growth and the ways in which cultures understand child development are so different, it is futile to attempt to pin down the "right" age of majority. The Dutch, for example, allow children to drink at the age of 16 but not to drive until they are 19. Even if I thought it was a good idea to lower the drinking age and raise the driving age—and I do—I recognize that the U.S. would never embrace it.

I am more concerned with the issue of maturity than I am with the technical age of majority. Researchers and observers have noted that while our children are getting brighter (I.Q.
190 scores have been going up for the last two decades), they are relatively immature for their ages in comparison to earlier generations. Over-protected by their parents and spending vast amounts of time in front of TV, computers and cellphones (over 50 hours a week by middle adolescence, according to the Kaiser Family Foundation), they are less skilled in the world, less able to build friendships and function in groups, and more reliant on their parents.

 Instead of fiddling with the age of majority, we should encourage our children to grow up, and mandatory service
200 would do just that. We should require all 18-year-olds in America to leave home and give a year to society, either in the military or in community-based projects like tutoring younger children or working in retirement homes or the inner city. The result would be a **cohort** of more mature 19-year-olds who would make better workers and better citizens.

cohort
(kō´hôrt´) *n.* A *cohort* is a group or band of people.

COLLABORATIVE DISCUSSION With a small group, discuss two of the questions posed at the beginning of the selection: Should the age requirements for certain rights be lowered or raised? Should these age requirements be consistent? Cite specific evidence from the texts to support your ideas.

Trace and Evaluate an Argument

COMMON CORE · RI 5, RI 6, RI 8

Each writer who responded to the question "When Do Kids Become Adults?" presents an **argument**, or a claim supported with reasons and evidence. A **claim** is the writer's position on an issue or problem. There is usually one main claim in a text, but sometimes a writer may make multiple claims in a single piece of writing. **Evidence** is any information that helps prove a claim. Facts, quotations, examples, anecdotes, and statistics can all be used as evidence.

Look at this example of a claim made by Jamie Lincoln Kitman in "Better Training for New Drivers." The claim states the author's opinion:

> . . . the driving age shouldn't be lowered, indeed the right to drive should be doled out gradually to teens as it has been in New York since 2010.

- To **trace**, or follow, the reasoning in an argument, you should
  - Identify the claims that the author states directly or indirectly.
  - Locate evidence that supports the claims.
  - Identify **counterarguments**, statements that address opposing viewpoints. A good argument anticipates opposing views and provides counterarguments to disprove them.

- Once you trace an author's argument, it's important to **evaluate** it by examining the support and deciding if it is valid and convincing.
  - Consider whether the evidence is accurate and sufficient.
  - Evaluate the evidence to determine if it is relevant. Evidence is **relevant** if it supports the claim in a logical way. It is **irrelevant** if it isn't based on sound reasoning or isn't clearly connected to the claim.
  - Consider whether opposing viewpoints have been addressed.
  - Identify persuasive techniques, such as exaggeration or appeals to a reader's emotions, that might distort a reader's views.

Here, Kitman presents personal experiences as relevant evidence to support his claim:

> . . . I got my full license and it wasn't long before I got my first ticket for speeding. And soon after that I got another for failing to observe a stop sign.

As you review each writer's argument in "When Do Kids Become Adults?" identify the main claim and prepare to evaluate it.

CLOSE READ

Trace and Evaluate an Argument

COMMON CORE · RI 5, RI 6, RI 8

Discuss the terms **argument, claim,** and **evidence.** Emphasize the following points:

- An argument refers to speaking or writing that expresses a position, or makes a claim, and supports it with reasons and evidence.
- A claim helps readers determine an author's point of view. An argument may include one or multiple claims.
- A claim may be stated directly in the text, but if it is stated indirectly, readers must figure it out on their own.

Have volunteers identify the sentence that states Barbara Hofer's claim in lines 133–145 of "A Parent's Role in the Path to Adulthood." *(Lines 133–136: "Becoming an adult . . . taking longer to recognize themselves as adults.")*

Prompt students to discuss how to trace and evaluate an argument, including that readers should:

- examine whether evidence is sound, sufficient, relevant, and clearly connects to the claim
- look for counterarguments that address opposing viewpoints
- identify language choices an author includes to persuade or sway readers

Point out that evaluating an argument helps students become critical readers and independent thinkers.

Strategies for Annotation 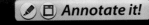 Annotate it!

Trace and Evaluate an Argument

COMMON CORE · RI 4, RI 8

Share these strategies for guided or independent analysis:

- Highlight in yellow language that appeals to readers' logic.
- Highlight in green language with strong negative associations or that appeals to readers' emotions.
- Use a note to tell whether you think the language choices are effective in persuading readers.

> Interest in improving young adults' political participation would be better focused on attacking barriers like residency requirements that exclude college students and voter ID laws that disfavor young and mobile voters, sometimes egregiously.
>
> Yes, they are effective.

PRACTICE & APPLY

Analyzing the Text RI 1, RI 3, RI 4, RI 6, RI 8, RI 9

Possible answers:

1. Steinberg's position is that there is not one particular age at which a minor becomes an adult; the main reason he gives is that brain science shows that different parts of the brain mature at different times.

2. Chang suggests that a better strategy for increasing participation is eliminating barriers like residency requirements and voter ID laws that disfavor young and mobile voters. Also, young Americans suffer from the same challenges to meaningful representation and governance that older Americans do.

3. Answers will vary; students should cite evidence from the text.

4. People are getting married later; they're having children later. Because more young people have large student loans for college, they are financially dependent on parents longer.

5.

Ways Parents Promote Autonomy	Ways Parents Thwart Autonomy
allow opportunities to make own choices	too much daily contact
allow opportunities to make mistakes and recover	using technology to micromanage
steer young people to campus resources	editing and proofing papers

6. There is no specific age when someone becomes an adult. People mature at different times based on age, experience, and family circumstances.

---

 eBook *Annotate It!*

Analyzing the Text RI 1, RI 3, RI 4, RI 6, RI 8, RI 9, W 7, SL 3, SL 4, SL 5, SL 6

Cite Text Evidence Support your responses with evidence from the text.

1. **Evaluate** In "What the Brain Says about Maturity," what is the main reason the author gives to support his claim?

2. **Analyze** In "Leave the Voting Age Alone," what counterargument does the author make to respond to people who want to lower the voting age in order to increase teenagers' participation in the political process?

3. **Evaluate** Evaluate the argument made in "Better Training for New Drivers." Does the author provide sufficient relevant evidence to support his claim? Explain why or why not.

4. **Cite Evidence** The author of "A Parent's Role in the Path to Adulthood" says people are "taking longer to recognize themselves as adults." What trends does she note to support this claim?

5. **Analyze** According to "A Parent's Role in the Path to Adulthood," how could parents promote autonomy in college-age students, and how do they limit autonomy? Record your answer in a chart.

Ways Parents Promote Autonomy	Ways Parents Thwart Autonomy

6. **Synthesize** The title of this selection asks, "When Do Kids Become Adults?" Based on what you have read, how would you answer this question?

PERFORMANCE TASK

Speaking Activity: Debate When are kids ready to assume adult responsibilities? Working with a group, choose one issue presented in the selection and have a debate.

- Assign one position on the issue to one half of your group, and assign the other position to the other half.
- Research the issue. Find answers to any questions you have.
- Decide on a claim. Prepare to support your claim with evidence

from the selections as well as from your own research. Consider displaying your evidence in visuals, such as charts or graphs.

- When you debate, be sure to address counterarguments.
- As you listen to other groups, carefully evaluate each speaker's reasoning and evidence.

PERFORMANCE TASK W 7, SL 3, SL 4, SL 5, SL 6

Assign this performance task.

Speaking Activity: Debate Have groups assign specific roles and issues to research. Have students prepare for the debate by

- anticipating arguments that the opposing side will present and preparing counterarguments
- making sure that evidence clearly supports and connects to claims
- having sides rehearse how they will present their arguments and prepare any visuals they need

- setting rules for the debate, such as taking turns, considering time limits for speakers, and listening attentively and respectfully

Critical Vocabulary

arbitrary	confluence	inadequate	autonomous	cohort
unmoor	egregious	diffuse	thwart	

Practice and Apply Use your understanding of the Vocabulary words to answer each question.

1. What have you done that made you feel **autonomous**?

2. Have you ever disagreed with a decision that seemed **arbitrary**? Explain.

3. When did a **confluence** of events cause a change in your life?

4. When has something happened to **thwart** your progress? Explain.

5. When have you seen someone treated in an **egregious** way?

6. What trends in your school appear to be **diffuse**?

7. When have you felt **inadequate** to complete an assignment?

8. What is something you accomplished as part of a **cohort**?

9. When is a good time to **unmoor** from your family or classmates? Explain.

Vocabulary Strategy: Greek Roots

A word **root** is a word part that forms the basis of a word's meaning. A root is combined with other word parts, such as a prefix or a suffix, to make a word. Many English words have a root that comes from Greek. Look at this sentence from "When Do Kids Become Adults?":

> . . . Young Americans suffer from the same challenges . . . that plague our <u>democracy</u> at all levels.

The word *democracy* includes the Greek root *dem*, which means "people." The meaning of the root *dem* is a clue that can help you figure out that *democracy* means "a government by the people."

Practice and Apply Find the word in each sentence that includes the Greek root *dem*. Use the meaning of the root to help you write a definition of the word. Then check each definition you write against the dictionary definition.

1. In some areas, dropping out of school has reached epidemic levels.

2. Researchers feared the pandemic would spread rapidly among teenagers.

3. Certain cars are most popular with a younger demographic.

4. The demagogue convinced many that the voting age should be raised.

5. Is spending vast amounts of time texting endemic among adolescents?

PRACTICE & APPLY

Critical Vocabulary

Possible answers:

1. *Saving money from babysitting to buy my own cell phone made me feel autonomous.*

2. *I suggested that we take a family vote on places we might like to visit because my father's plans seemed arbitrary.*

3. *Last year, the confluence of a winter storm, the flu, and a power outage all resulted in my missing a lot of school.*

4. *I was hoping to be captain of the soccer team last spring, but breaking my ankle thwarted that dream.*

5. *I once treated my younger sister egregiously and pretended that she simply didn't exist.*

6. *Fashion trends like hip-hop gear are diffuse at school.*

7. *My poor navigational skills made me an inadequate leader on a hike that should have taken less time.*

8. *As part of a cohort of kids, I helped clean up the park.*

9. *When you have a new interest, it's time to unmoor from friends and follow your own desires.*

Vocabulary Strategy: Greek Roots

1. *epidemic: a rapid spread or development of something undesirable among people*

2. *pandemic: a disease that spreads among people over a wide geographic area*

3. *demographic: a certain segment of the population*

4. *demagogue: a leader who wins people's favor by appealing to their emotions or prejudices*

5. *endemic: common in or restricted to a particular area, country, or group of people*

 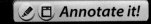

Greek Roots

Have students locate the sentence with the vocabulary word *democracy* in the selection. Share these strategies for guided and independent analysis:

- Highlight the word in yellow. Underline the Greek root and think about its meaning.
- Highlight in green context clues in the surrounding text.
- Use the root's meaning and context clues to determine the word's meaning.

> state university ID cards at the polls. More broadly, young Americans suffer from the same challenges to meaningful representation and governance that plague our <u>democracy</u> at all levels. The voting age is the least of their problems.

PRACTICE & APPLY

Language Conventions: Shifts in Voice and Mood

COMMON CORE L 1d

Point out to students that keeping mood and voice consistent is not simply a matter of grammar. Remind students that the point of writing is to communicate ideas effectively. Shifts in voice and mood can confuse readers or distract them in a way that lessens the impact of what a writer is trying to get across.

Answers:

1. *When Liam turned 18, he filled out a voter registration form.*

2. *Lil chose classes after her mom made some suggestions.*

3. *Watch less TV and tutor young children instead.*

4. *Niki volunteers at a retirement home and learns many valuable skills.*

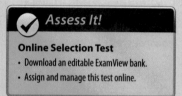

Assess It!

Online Selection Test
- Download an editable ExamView bank.
- Assign and manage this test online.

Language Conventions: Shifts in Voice and Mood

COMMON CORE L 1d

Verbs have different voices and moods. The **voice of a verb** tells whether its subject performs or receives the action. A verb is in the **active voice** when the subject performs the action of the verb. A verb is in the **passive voice** when the subject receives the action of the verb.

Active Voice   Neuroscientists **study** the brain.

Passive Voice   The brain **is studied** by neuroscientists.

To change a verb from active to passive voice, use a form of the verb *be* with the past participle of the verb.

Active Voice   Politicians **write** laws about age.

Passive Voice   Laws **are written** about age.

The **mood of a verb** expresses a writer's judgment or attitude about a statement. The **indicative mood** is used when making a statement. The **imperative mood** is used in a request or a command.

Indicative Mood   Her teenage daughter **drives** responsibly.

Imperative Mood   Always **drive** responsibly!

A shift, or change, in verb voice or mood can make meaning unclear. It is usually correct to make the voice and mood in a sentence consistent.

Shift	Correct
From active to passive: They took driver training but very little was learned.	They took driver training but learned very little.
From imperative to indicative: Enroll in a good class, and it is helpful to learn traffic safety rules.	Enroll in a good class, and learn traffic safety rules.

Practice and Apply Write each item correctly by fixing the inappropriate shift in verb voice or mood.

1. When Liam turned 18, a voter registration form was filled out by him.

2. Classes were chosen by Lil after her mom made some suggestions.

3. Watch less TV and you should be tutoring young children instead.

4. Niki volunteers at a retirement home. Learn many valuable skills.

Fact and Opinion

COMMON CORE

RI 2,
RI 8

TEACH

Explain to students that when they read persuasive texts they need to be critical readers and recognize the difference between facts and opinions. Discuss the following points:

- A **fact** is a statement that can be proved, or verified.
- An **opinion** is a statement that cannot be proved because it expresses a person's beliefs, feelings, or thoughts.
- Most often, a writer's claim in a persuasive text is an opinion. The writer uses facts, such as examples and statistics, to support his or her opinion.

Display the following example on the board or on a device:

Today's teenagers are lazy and uninterested in community service. A recent study of our local schools shows that less than ten percent of students are involved in volunteer activities.

Ask volunteers to summarize the central idea in the passage. Then, elicit that the first sentence, the claim, is the author's opinion. The second sentence presents a fact that can be proved. Point out that while the fact supports the author's claim, the claim is still an opinion.

PRACTICE AND APPLY

Display lines 187–197 from "When Do Kids Become Adults?" Tell students to summarize the central idea of the passage. Then, have students indicate the statements that are facts and those that are opinions. Guide students to explain how the author uses facts such as statistics and studies to support his opinions, and thus his central idea.

Next, have partners work together to locate other examples from the selection that show how an author uses facts to support an opinion. Have students discuss their examples with the class.

Trace and Evaluate an Argument

COMMON CORE

RI 6,
RI 8

RETEACH

Review the terms *argument, claim, evidence,* and *counterargument.* Remind students that when they **evaluate** an argument they examine it carefully and judge its value or worth.

Use a recent editorial or other opinion writing on a topic of interest to students. Guide students to identify its argument, claim, evidence, and counterargument. Work together to evaluate the argument and determine if the evidence provided is relevant.

 LEVEL UP TUTORIALS Assign the following *Level Up* tutorials: **Analyzing Arguments; Evidence; Persuasive Techniques**

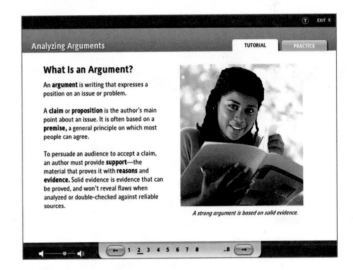

CLOSE READING APPLICATION

Students can apply the skill to a current magazine or newspaper editorial. Have students work independently to identify the claim and support and then note whether counterarguments address opposing views. Have students tell whether the support the author provides is accurate, sufficient, and connects logically to the claim.

Much Too Young to Work So Hard

History Article by Naoki Tanaka

Why This Text

This nonfiction article presents arguments for and against child labor. Students may have difficulty understanding these arguments and the evidence cited in support of them. With the help of the close-reading questions, students will trace and cite evidence for both points of view and summarize parts of the article. The results of their close reading will help students develop a solid understanding of the issue and of how the problem of child labor in the U.S. was finally resolved.

Background Have students read the background information about child labor and the photographer Lewis Hine. Tell students that Hine is an example of a documentary photographer, that is, a photographer who uses images to document important social issues or historical events. Other well-known American documentary photographers are Jacob Riis, Walker Evans, and Dorothea Lange.

SETTING A PURPOSE Tell students to pay close attention to the arguments cited for and against child labor and the text evidence given to support each argument.

 Common Core Support

- cite strong textual evidence
- determine the author's purpose
- evaluate the use of different mediums to present a topic
- trace and evaluate an argument

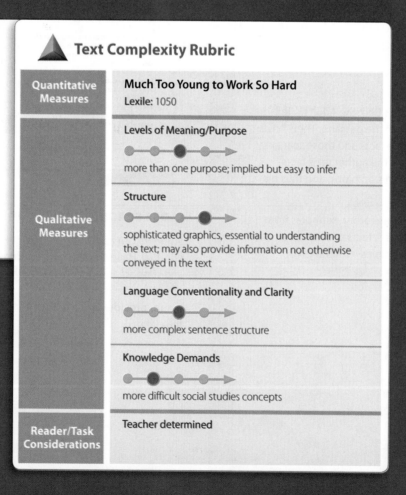 **Text Complexity Rubric**

Quantitative Measures	**Much Too Young to Work So Hard** Lexile: 1050
Qualitative Measures	**Levels of Meaning/Purpose** more than one purpose; implied but easy to infer
	Structure sophisticated graphics, essential to understanding the text; may also provide information not otherwise conveyed in the text
	Language Conventionality and Clarity more complex sentence structure
	Knowledge Demands more difficult social studies concepts
Reader/Task Considerations	Teacher determined

Strategies for CLOSE READING

Trace and Evaluate an Argument

Students should read the article, keeping track of the arguments for and against child labor. Close-reading questions at the bottom of the page will help students collect and cite text evidence to better understand both sides of the argument. As they read, students should jot down in the margin paraphrases, comments, and responses to the article.

WHEN STUDENTS STRUGGLE . . .

To help students trace and evaluate an argument, have them work in small groups to fill out a chart like the one shown below.

CITE TEXT EVIDENCE For practice tracing and evaluating an argument, ask students to cite text evidence that explains the effects of child labor listed below.

Effects of Child Labor	Text Evidence
Conditions for boys working in mines were both brutal and dangerous. (lines 1–10)	The foreman hits the boys; they bend over until their backs ache; their faces are covered with soot; they have chronic coughs. (lines 6–10)
Children working on farms also often did backbreaking work. (lines 17–23)	Children picked cotton in the sweltering Texas heat from dawn until the sun set. (lines 20–23)

Background *By the end of the nineteenth century, more than 1.5 million children under the age of fifteen were hard at work in the United States. By 1900, the number had increased to 2 million, and many people started to refer to child labor as "child slavery." Lewis Hine was a great crusader against child labor. A former schoolteacher, Hine's photographs for the National Child Labor Committee documented the dreadful working conditions inflicted on children as young as three years old. Two of Hine's photographs of children at work illustrate the article you are about to read.*

Much Too Young to Work So Hard

History Article by Naoki Tanaka

CLOSE READ
Notes

1. **READ ▶** As you read lines 1–10, begin to collect text evidence.
   - Circle the time and place cited at the beginning of the article.
   - Underline the description of the boys' job.
   - In the margin, explain what the author says about the working conditions in the first paragraph.

A Picture of Child Labor

Ⓐ Ⓑ The year is 1911. Boys, aged nine and ten, are working as coal breakers at a coal mine in Pennsylvania. They are sitting in rows on boards placed over conveyor belts that are carrying coal from the mine to large bins and dump trucks. The boys' job is to pick out any pieces of slate and stone embedded in the coal. The boys must watch very carefully because coal and slate look very much alike. A foreman, armed with a broom handle, raps the heads of boys who are not working hard or fast enough. The boys bend over the conveyor belts until their backs ache. Their faces are covered with soot. Often they
10 have chronic coughs from breathing in air thick with coal dust.

Conditions are brutal, and the boys are sick from the coal dust. A foreman hits them for not working hard or fast enough.

83

---

1. **READ AND CITE TEXT EVIDENCE** Remind students that they are looking for evidence of what child labor was like in the early 1900s.

Ⓐ **ASK STUDENTS** to find details and phrases in lines 1–10 that help them identify the time period and what the boys had to do and endure for work. *The time period is 1911. The boys had to sort coal and slate. The foreman hits the boys, the boys' backs ache, and they breathe in unhealthy coal dust.*

Breaker boys sorting coal, South Pittston, Pennsylvania, 1911;
photograph by Lewis Hine. While Hine was taking photographs at a
coal mine, two breaker boys fell into a coal chute and were
smothered to death.

Small Hired Hands

     Young girls were not exempt from such hard labor. During the
early 1900s, when many crops were still planted and harvested by
hand, children—both boys and girls—worked on farms in large
numbers. People who were opposed to children working in factories
often saw nothing wrong with them working on farms. After all, they
were working with their families and breathing in fresh air. Some

---

2. **◀ REREAD** Reread lines 1–10, and study the photograph on this
page. What does the image add to your understanding of the boys'
situation?

*The way the boys are sitting suggests that this is backbreaking work.
One boy has even propped himself up with two pieces of wood. These
boys had to sit like this for hours at a time in a dark, dirty place.*

3. **READ ▶** As you read lines 11–23, continue to cite text evidence.

• Circle each use of the words *girls*, *boys*, and *children*.

• Underline the positive opinion some people had about children
working on farms. Then study the photograph of the children picking
cotton. In the margin next to the image explain your reaction to that
opinion.

84

This photograph, taken by Lewis Hine in 1913 at a farm in Bells, Texas,
shows four children picking cotton.

*Children as
young as five
probably do
not benefit
from "fresh
air" when they
are carrying
heavy bags of
cotton.*

children did help out on old-fashioned family farms. But many others
traveled from farm to farm as hired hands doing the same
backbreaking work as the adults. A 1913 photograph shows three girls
20 and a boy, ranging in age from five to nine years, picking cotton in
the sweltering Texas heat. Some of these cotton pickers were orphans.
Others were the children of migrant workers. All of them picked
cotton from dawn until the sun set.

Documenting Child Labor

In 1908, Lewis Hine wrote: "There is work that profits children,
and there is work that brings profit only to employers. The object of

---

4. **◀ REREAD AND DISCUSS** According to the Background information
on page 83, many people in the 1900s thought that child labor was
really "child slavery." With a small group, discuss whether the
information presented in lines 11–23 and in the photograph on this
page support this claim.

5. **READ ▶** As you read lines 24–42, continue to cite text evidence.

• Paraphrase Hine's statement about the object of employing children
in the margin.

• Underline Hine's purpose for exposing the hardships endured by
working children.

85

---

2. **REREAD AND CITE TEXT EVIDENCE** Remind students to look
at the photograph carefully and to study the caption.

B **ASK STUDENTS** to identify details in the photograph and
its caption and in lines 1–10 that help them better understand
what the boys went through. *Possible response: The boys' work was
hard and dangerous; two boys who fell into the coal chute were
smothered.*

3. **READ AND CITE TEXT EVIDENCE** Explain to students that the
author is trying to give both sides of the argument concerning
child labor.

C **ASK STUDENTS** to find text evidence in lines 11–23 that
explains why some people thought working on farms might be
good for children. *Children would be working with their families
and breathing fresh air.*

4. **REREAD AND DISCUSS USING TEXT EVIDENCE**

D **ASK STUDENTS** to appoint a reporter for each group to cite
specific text evidence from lines 11–23 and from the photograph
to support the claim that child labor was really "child slavery."

5. **READ AND CITE TEXT EVIDENCE** Tell students that *to
paraphrase* means "to restate information in your own words."

E **ASK STUDENTS** to write in their own words what Hine
means when he says, "The object of employing children is not to
train them, but to get high profits from their work." *Possible
response: The reason children were employed was so that their
employers could make money.*

Hine says that the reason for employing children is that employers make more money by not having to pay them adult wages.

E employing children is not to train them, but to get high profits from their work." From 1908 until 1918, Hine documented in groundbreaking photographs children as young as three years old
30 working long hours in often dangerous conditions. The children worked in factories, on farms, and in mines in the United States. As early as the 1830s, various states had passed laws restricting or prohibiting the employment of young children in industrial settings. Unfortunately, many of these laws were not enforced. Hine's goal was to publicize the fate of child laborers and the damage done to their young lives. His hope was that public outrage would stop the practice of employing children to do the work of adults.

F America's army of child laborers had been growing steadily over the nineteenth century, fueled largely by an expanding economy. Factories, mines, and mills needed cheap labor, which children could
40 and did supply. By 1911, more than 2 million American children under the age of sixteen were a regular part of the country's workforce.

Exploiting Children

Hine and others devoted to the rights of working children had no argument with children helping out with family tasks. Their focus was on the exploitation of children. Children were **exploited** because

exploited:
taken advantage of

6. **REREAD** Reread lines 24–42. Summarize the information about "America's army of child laborers" (line 37).

A growing economy demanded cheap labor. By 1911, over 2 million children under the age of 16 went to work in mills, factories, and mines every day.

7. **READ** As you read lines 43–81, continue to cite text evidence.

- Underline the reasons children were often exploited (lines 43–52).
- Underline the reasons cited by advocates for child labor (lines 53–60).
- In the margin, explain what finally stopped the practice of employing children.

86

" What finally slowed the widespread use of children as laborers, however, was the Great Depression of the 1930s. "

as workers their labor was cheap and because their age made them easy to order around. In addition, these working children were systematically robbed of education. Many were **illiterate,** and most had never attended school or, if they had, attended only sporadically.
50 They were forced to be adults, shouldering adult responsibilities, long before they were ready. Finally, the work they did was dangerous and hazardous to their health.

illiterate:
unable to read or write

Child-Labor Advocates

G Those who argued for the continued use of children in industry and on farms argued that the work helped children develop a solid work ethic and that their work was necessary to support their impoverished families. Others claimed that after having worked hard labor, children would be more motivated to go back to school and become educated. Still others claimed that the cheap labor provided by children was needed to keep certain industries up and running,
60 which in turn kept the nation's economy healthy.

The photographs of Louis Hine succeeded in publicizing and proving what many Americans had refused to believe: that numerous American children were being cruelly exploited. What finally slowed the widespread use of children as laborers, however, was the Great Depression of the 1930s. Sentiment against the use of child laborers had grown in the years preceding the Great Depression. With the economic catastrophe of the 1930s, however, many adults found themselves unemployed and struggling to find work. These adults wanted for themselves the jobs that traditionally had been held by
70 children. Sadly, this more than any other reason may have turned the tide on using children as cheap labor in the United States.

Unemployed adults wanted the jobs that children usually did.

87

---

6. **REREAD AND CITE TEXT EVIDENCE**

F **ASK STUDENTS** to identify the lines that summarize the information in lines 24–42. *The expanding economy needed cheap labor. By 1911, more than two million children under the age of 16 worked throughout the United States (lines 37–42).*

7. **READ AND CITE TEXT EVIDENCE**

G **ASK STUDENTS** what reasons advocates, or people who thought that child labor was a good thing, gave to support their point of view. *Work helped children develop a solid work ethic; their families needed them to work; work would motivate children to get an education.*

Critical Vocabulary: exploited (line 45) Ask students to think of other groups of people who could be exploited by powerful people. *Answers will vary. Possible responses: people with mental or physical disabilities; people who desperately need money.*

Critical Vocabulary: illiterate (line 48) Discuss with students how lines 48–49 give clues about the meaning of *illiterate*. *They suggest that being illiterate has something to do with not going to school.* Then, have students share their definitions of *illiterate*.

FOR ELL STUDENTS Challenge students to explain the meaning of the adverb *sporadically*. Spanish-speaking students may recognize the word from its Spanish cognate, *esporádicamente*.

A Long-Overdue Victory

It took until 1938 for federal legislation banning the use of child labor to finally pass Congress. In 1941, the Supreme Court declared the Fair Labor Standards Act constitutional and made it the law of the land. With the exception of agricultural work, the law prohibited child labor for children under the age of 16. It set 18 as the minimum age for working hazardous jobs. It allowed children aged 14 and 15 to work in non-manufacturing, non-mining, and non-hazardous jobs outside of school hours. They could also work for limited times
80 during school vacations. In the fight to protect the rights of children, this law was a great and long-overdue victory.

8. ◀ REREAD Reread lines 72–81. Explain the way the passing of the Fair Labor Standards Act had an impact on the lives of children.

The Fair Labor Standards Act was a wide-reaching ban on child labor. As a result of its passing, children were protected from working long hours and exposure to hazardous conditions.

SHORT RESPONSE

Cite Text Evidence Using the text, the photographs, and your reading notes, explain why many people felt that child labor exploited children. **Cite text evidence** in your response.

Many people believed that the practice of child labor exploited children and put them at risk. Children were exploited as workers because their labor was cheap and their age made them easy to order around. Working children were systematically robbed of education. Many were illiterate, and most had never attended school. In particular, the photographs of Lewis Hine plainly showed that the work the children did was dangerous and hazardous to their health.

88

TO CHALLENGE STUDENTS . . .

To extend students' understanding of the power and effectiveness of documentary photography, such as that created by Lewis Hine, have them research the work of three American documentary photographers: Mathew Brady, Jacob Riis, and Dorothea Lange.

ASK STUDENTS to compare and contrast the work of these photographers by addressing the following questions:

- When did the photographer live?
- What was the photographer's subject matter?
- Why did the photographer choose this subject matter?
- What was the photographer's larger purpose? Did the photographer want to educate people, record history, change society, or something else?
- None of these photographers had the benefits of modern camera equipment or large camera crews. Describe how each photographer did his or her work. Explain how the work was easy or difficult for these photographers.
- Describe the effect of each photographer's work on people who lived during the time period in which the photographer worked, on subsequent generations, and on you as you viewed the photographs.

---

8. **REREAD AND CITE TEXT EVIDENCE**

🅗 **ASK STUDENTS** to find specific examples of the ways in which the new law would improve the lives of children. *Possible responses: with the exception of agricultural work, children under 16 would no longer be allowed to have full-time jobs; children could work, but only when school was not in session; children could now attend school because they did not have to work.*

SHORT RESPONSE

Cite Text Evidence Students should:

- explain why employers wanted child laborers.
- cite the dangers and health hazards child laborers regularly encountered.
- explain what children missed out on as a result of working full-time.
- cite specific evidence from the text to support their ideas.

DIG DEEPER

With the class, return to Question 4, Reread and Discuss. Have students share and discuss their responses.

ASK STUDENTS what their responses generally have in common. Most students probably will have mentioned that the children picking cotton looked worn down and very young.

- Building on their responses, have students find other examples from the text that support the idea that child labor was really "child slavery." *Answers will vary. Possible responses: the boys' work was hard and very dangerous, the children worked in intolerable conditions, children aren't big enough to fight back, working was not a choice for these children, it was impossible for working children to get an education and better themselves, some of the children were defenseless orphans.*

- Then, direct students' attention to the two photographs in the article (pages 84 and 85). Ask them to use text evidence and to imagine what kinds of things Lewis Hine wanted to show and teach Americans about the real lives of America's working children. *Answers will vary. Possible responses: that these children were very young, that they had no one looking out for or protecting them, that they were doing work that should have been done by adults, that what was happening to them was neither fair or just, that work was ruining their lives and condemning them to a life of poverty.*

- Ask students to use text evidence and to imagine how a parent or an employer might justify the use of child labor. *Answers will vary. Possible responses: A parent might say that it is the child's responsibility to help support the family, that the child is exaggerating how bad work conditions are, or that the child will only have to work for a short time until the family gets back on its feet. Employers might say that children are better off working than causing trouble, that work helps build character, that children make better employees because they're easier to manage, or that society needs the work of children to keep industry humming.*

ASK STUDENTS to return to their response to the Short Response and revise it based on the class discussion.

CLOSE READING NOTES

Is 16 Too Young to Drive a Car?

Article by Robert Davis

Fatal Car Crashes Drop for 16-Year-Olds, Rise in Older Teens

Article by Allison Aubrey

Why These Texts?

Articles about similar or related topics allow students to compare and contrast information and ideas. These texts explore a topic of great interest to young people—driving— while providing an opportunity to analyze and interpret the facts they encounter in their reading.

Key Learning Objective: The student will be able to determine central ideas and details while analyzing relationships between ideas.

COMMON CORE Common Core Standards

RI 1 Cite textual evidence; make inferences.
RI 2 Determine a central idea; provide a summary.
RI 3 Analyze text connections.
RI 4 Determine the meaning of words and phrases.
RI 5 Analyze structure.
RI 8 Evaluate argument and specific claims.
RI 9 Analyze conflicting information on the same topic.
W 1a Introduce claims and organize reasons and evidence logically.
W1b Support claims with logical reasoning and relevant evidence.
W 2 Write informative/explanatory texts.
W 4 Produce clear and coherent writing.
W 9b Apply grade 8 Reading standards to literary nonfiction.
W 10 Write routinely over extended time frames and shorter time frames.
L 1 Demonstrate command of grammar and usage.
L 4a Use context as a clue to meaning.

Text Complexity Rubric

	Is 16 Too Young to Drive a Car? Lexile: 1150L	Fatal Car Crashes Drop for 16-Year-Olds, Rise in Older Teens Lexile: 1070L
Quantitative Measures		
Qualitative Measures	**Levels of Meaning/Purpose** more than one purpose; implied, easily identified from context	**Levels of Meaning/Purpose** more than one purpose; implied, easily identified from context
	Structure implicit problem-solution text structure	**Structure** organization of main ideas and details is complex, but clearly stated and sequential
	Language Conventionality and Clarity increased unfamiliar academic or domain-specific words	**Language Conventionality and Clarity** increased unfamiliar academic or domain-specific words
	Knowledge Demands somewhat complex science, civics concepts	**Knowledge Demands** some specialized knowledge required
Reader/Task Considerations	**Teacher determined** Vary by individual reader and type of text	**Teacher determined** Vary by individual reader and type of text

TEACH

CLOSE READ

Background Have students read the information about the age restrictions imposed on drivers. Point out that when automobiles were first being sold, there were no requirements for training and testing of driving skills. A friend, a relative, or perhaps a car salesman taught people how to drive. As more and more people began to drive, especially in congested cities, the need for more rules and regulations became clear, as did the need for better-trained drivers.

SETTING A PURPOSE Direct students to use the Setting a Purpose prompt to focus their reading. Remind students to write down questions as they read.

Determine Central Ideas and Details (LINES 1–7)

COMMON CORE RI 1, RI 2, RI 5

Explain that the central idea of a piece of writing is the main concept a writer wants to convey.

A CITE TEXT EVIDENCE Have students reread lines 1–7 to identify the statement that describes the central idea of the article. *("Raise the driving age.")* How does the placement of the statement impact the text? *(Placing the statement at the beginning of the article's first paragraph gives it prominence.)*

SCAFFOLDING FOR ELL STUDENTS

Analyze Punctuation Point out that commas and dashes signal readers to pause and are also used to separate or draw attention to ideas. Using a whiteboard, project lines 1–4 of the text. Have volunteers mark up the text.

- Highlight in yellow the dashes.
- Highlight in green the phrase between the dashes.
- Read the text with and without the phrase set off by the dashes.

ASK STUDENTS to explain in a note the writer's purpose in using dashes in lines 1–4.

Background *Although driver's licenses were required by some states by the early 1900s, age restrictions on drivers did not begin until later. These restrictions were motivated by the need to protect the public from young drivers, who were increasingly viewed as a problem on the highways. Some states selected 16 as the age at which people could drive, while others chose 18. Eventually, 16 became the recommended legal age for drivers. Although there are a few exceptions today, most states now allow teenagers to get a driver's license at the age of 16.*

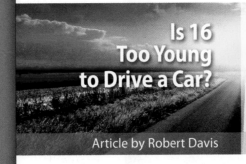

Is 16 Too Young to Drive a Car?
Article by Robert Davis

Fatal Car Crashes Drop for 16-Year-Olds, Rise for Older Teens
Article by Allison Aubrey

SETTING A PURPOSE As you read, think about the points each writer makes regarding the age requirements for drivers. Look for evidence that supports each point.

A Raise the driving age. That radical idea is gaining momentum in the fight to save the lives of teenage drivers—the most dangerous on the USA's roads—and their passengers.

Brain and auto safety experts fear that 16-year-olds, the youngest drivers licensed in most states, are too immature to handle today's cars and roadway risks.

New findings from brain researchers at the National Institutes of Health explain for the first time why efforts to
10 protect the youngest drivers usually fail. The weak link: what's called "the executive branch" of the teen brain—the part that weighs risks, makes judgments and controls impulsive behavior.

Scientists at the NIH campus in Bethesda, Md., have found that this vital area develops through the teenage years

©Photodisc/Getty Images

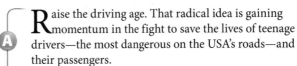

Raise the driving age. That radical idea is gaining momentum in the fight to save the lives of teenage drivers—the most dangerous on the USA's roads— and their passengers.

> draws attention to dangerous drivers

Determine Central Ideas and Details (LINES 39–49)

 COMMON CORE RI 1, RI 2, RI 3

Explain to students that authors use details to support a central, or main, idea. Point out that **details** are specific facts, statistics, or quotations that tell more about the central idea.

B **CITE TEXT EVIDENCE** Ask students to reread lines 39–49 to find details that support the author's statement that states have begun to restrict 16-year-old drivers. *("limiting the number of passengers they can carry," "barring late-night driving," and parental supervision)* Have students explain how the details in these two paragraphs connect to the overall central idea in the article. *(Possible answer: The details show some of the ways states are beginning to restrict what 16-year-old drivers can do.)*

and isn't fully mature until age 25. One 16-year-old's brain might be more developed than another 18-year-old's, just as a younger teen might be taller than an older one. But evidence is mounting that a 16-year-old's brain is generally far less
20 developed than those of teens just a little older.

The research seems to help explain why 16-year-old drivers crash at far higher rates than older teens. The studies have convinced a growing number of safety experts that 16-year-olds are too young to drive safely without supervision.

"Privately, a lot of people in safety think it's a good idea to raise the driving age," says Barbara Harsha, executive director of the Governors Highway Safety Association. "It's a topic that is emerging."

Americans increasingly favor raising the driving age,
30 a USA TODAY/CNN/Gallup Poll[1] has found. Nearly two-thirds—61%—say they think a 16-year-old is too young to have a driver's license. Only 37% of those polled thought it was OK to license 16-year-olds, compared with 50% who thought so in 1995.

A slight majority, 53%, think teens should be at least 18 to get a license.

The poll of 1,002 adults, conducted Dec. 17–19, 2004, has an error margin of +/-3 percentage points.

Many states have begun to raise the age by imposing
B 40 restrictions on 16-year-old drivers. Examples: limiting the number of passengers they can carry or barring late-night driving. But the idea of flatly forbidding 16-year-olds to drive without parental supervision—as New Jersey does—has run into resistance from many lawmakers and parents around the country.

Irving Slosberg, a Florida state representative who lost his 14-year-old daughter in a 1995 crash, says that when he proposed a law to raise the driving age, other lawmakers "laughed at me."
50 Bill Van Tassel, AAA's[2] national manager of driving training programs, hears both sides of the argument. "We have parents who are pretty much tired of chauffeuring their

---

[1] **Gallup Poll:** a survey done by the Gallup company to measure people's opinions.
[2] **AAA:** the American Automobile Association, an organization that provides benefits and information to drivers.

WHEN STUDENTS STRUGGLE . . .

To help students keep track of the details the author provides to support his idea of raising the driving age, have students list the facts, statistics, or quotations in a chart like the one shown.

Author Idea	Fact	Statistic	Quotation
States impose restrictions	NJ requires parental supervision		

kids around, and they want their children to be able to drive," he says. "Driving is a very emotional issue."

But safety experts fear inaction could lead to more young lives lost. Some sound a note of urgency about changing course. The reason: A record number of American teenagers will soon be behind the wheel as the peak of the "baby boomlet" hits driving age.

60 Already, on average, two people die every day across the USA in vehicles driven by 16-year-old drivers. One in five 16-year-olds will have a reportable car crash within the first year.

In 2003, there were 937 drivers age 16 who were involved in fatal crashes. In those wrecks, 411 of the 16-year-old drivers died and 352 of their passengers were killed. Sixteen-year-old drivers are involved in fatal crashes at a rate nearly five times the rate of drivers 20 or older.

Gayle Bell, whose 16-year-old daughter, Jessie, rolled her 70 small car into a Missouri ditch and died in July 2003, says she used to happily be Jessie's "ride." She would give anything for the chance to drive Jessie again.

"We were always together, but not as much after she got her license," Bell says. "If I could bring her back, I'd lasso the moon."

Most states have focused their fixes on giving teens more driving experience before granting them unrestricted licenses. But the new brain research suggests that a separate factor is just as crucial: maturity. A new 17- or 18-year-old driver is 80 considered safer than a new 16-year-old driver.

Even some teens are acknowledging that 16-year-olds are generally not ready to face the life-threatening risks that drivers can encounter behind the wheel.

"Raising the driving age from 16 to 17 would benefit society as a whole," says Liza Darwin, 17, of Nashville. Though many parents would be inconvenienced and teens would be frustrated, she says, "It makes sense to raise the driving age to save more lives."

Focus on lawmakers

But those in a position to raise the driving age—legislators in 90 states throughout the USA—have mostly refused to do so.

Adrienne Mandel, a Maryland state legislator, has tried since 1997 to pass tougher teen driving laws. Even lawmakers

CLOSE READ

Draw Conclusions
COMMON CORE RI 1

(LINES 55–68)

Explain to students that readers **draw conclusions** when they make a judgment based on evidence, experience, and reasoning.

C **ASK STUDENTS** to reread lines 55–68. What conclusion can you draw about what a "baby boomlet" is? Why does it create urgency about laws related to teenage drivers? *(A "baby boomlet" is a period when a higher-than-average number of babies are born; when those babies reach their teenage years, there will be a higher-than-average number of teenage drivers. Statistics cited in lines 60–68 indicate that teen drivers are already involved in a high percentage of serious accidents; more teen drivers will likely lead to more serious accidents unless laws are changed.)*

Determine Central Ideas and Details (LINES 84–88)
COMMON CORE RI 1, RI 2, RI 3, RI 5

Remind students that quotations can be used to support a central idea. Point out that writers often use quotations from **experts,** people with skills or knowledge about a particular topic.

D **ASK STUDENTS** to reread the quotations in lines 84–85 and 87–88. In what way might the speaker be considered an expert about teenage driving? *(Possible answer: As a teenager, she has had a good deal of experience with young people who drive.)* Why does the author end this section of the article with her quotation? *(Her quotation connects to the author's central point about raising the driving age due to safety concerns.)*

TEACH

CLOSE READ

who recognize that a higher driving age could save lives, Mandel notes, resist the **notion** of having to drive their 16-year-olds to after-school activities that the teens could drive to themselves.

"Other delegates said, 'What are you doing? You're going to make me drive my kid to the movies on Friday night for another six months?' " Mandel says. "Parents are talking about 100 inconvenience, and I'm talking about saving lives."

Yet the USA TODAY poll found that among the general public, majorities in both suburbs (65%) and urban areas (60%) favor licensing ages above 16.

While a smaller percentage in rural areas (54%) favor raising the driving age, experts say it's striking that majority support exists even there, considering that teens on farms often start driving very young to help with workloads.

For those who oppose raising the minimum age, their argument is often this: Responsible teen drivers shouldn't be 110 punished for the mistakes of the small fraction who cause deadly crashes.

The debate stirs images of reckless teens drag-racing or driving drunk. But such flagrant misdeeds account for only a small portion of the fatal actions of 16-year-old drivers. Only about 10% of the 16-year-old drivers killed in 2003 had blood-alcohol concentrations of 0.10 or higher, compared with 43% of 20- to 49-year-old drivers killed, according to the Insurance Institute for Highway Safety.

Instead, most fatal crashes with 16-year-old drivers (77%) 120 involved driver errors, especially the kind most common among **novices**. Examples: speeding, overcorrecting after veering off the road, and losing control when facing a roadway obstacle that a more mature driver would be more likely to handle safely. That's the highest percentage of error for any age group.

For years, researchers suspected that inexperience—the **bane** of any new driver—was mostly to blame for deadly crashes involving teens. When trouble arose, the theory went, the young driver simply made the wrong move. But 130 in recent years, safety researchers have noticed a pattern emerge—one that seems to stem more from immaturity than from inexperience.

notion
(nō′shən) *n.* A notion is a belief or opinion.

novice
(nŏv′ĭs) *n.* A novice is a beginner.

bane
(bān) *n.* A bane is a cause of death, destruction, or ruin.

APPLYING ACADEMIC VOCABULARY

debate	deduce

As you discuss the articles, incorporate the following Collection 4 academic vocabulary words: *debate* and *deduce*. Ask students to **debate** whether the author's suggestion to raise the driving age is a valid one. Have students **deduce** why the author might feel so strongly about raising the driving age.

"Skills are a minor factor in most cases," says Allan Williams, former chief scientist at the insurance institute. "It's really attitudes and emotions."

A peek inside the brain

The NIH brain research suggests that the problem is human biology. A crucial part of the teen's brain—the area that peers ahead and considers consequences—remains undeveloped. That means careless attitudes and rash emotions often drive teen decisions, says Jay Giedd, chief of brain imaging in the child psychiatric unit at the National Institute of Mental Health, who's leading the study.

"It all comes down to impulse control," Giedd says. "The brain is changing a lot longer than we used to think. And that part of the brain involved in decision-making and controlling impulses is among the latest to come on board."

The teen brain is a **paradox**. Some areas—those that control senses, reactions and physical abilities—are fully developed in teenagers. "Physically, they should be ruling the world," Giedd says. "But (adolescence) is not that great of a time emotionally."

Giedd and an international research team have analyzed 4,000 brain scans from 2,000 volunteers to document how brains evolve as children mature.

paradox
(păr´ə-dŏks´) *n.* A *paradox* is a true statement that seems like it would not be true.

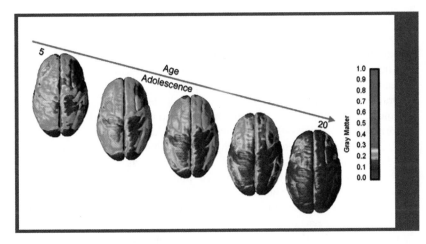

The human brain continues to develop throughout adolescence. As the brain prunes cells, there is an increase in reasoning skills.

CLOSE READ

Determine Central Ideas and Details (LINES 136–151)

COMMON CORE RI 1, RI 2, RI 3

Remind students that authors provide details to support a central idea. Elicit that a variety of effective supporting details make it more likely that readers will accept and agree with the author's central idea.

E **CITE TEXT EVIDENCE** Have students reread lines 136–151 to identify details in the text that support the author's central idea. *(Details that support the central idea of raising the driving age include "the part of the brain involved in decision-making and controlling impulses" is underdeveloped in teenagers.)* How does this detail connect to the supporting details the author has already presented? *(The author has presented research about driving ability, statistics about accidents, and legal efforts. He is providing scientific evidence to further support his idea.)*

CRITICAL VOCABULARY

paradox: Point out that the author is explaining the truth of an idea that may not seem true at first.

ASK STUDENTS what sort of problem the paradox of a teen brain might present for a driver. *(Possible answer: Teenagers may have the physical ability to be excellent drivers, but their emotional issues lead them to make poor choices and be careless.)*

Analyze Language

COMMON CORE RI 4

(LINES 181–188)

Point out that authors use descriptive language and idioms to make their points more clearly. Tell students that an **idiom** is an expression that has a meaning that is different from the meaning of its individual words.

F **CITE TEXT EVIDENCE** Have students reread lines 181–188 to identify the idiom the author uses and explain its meaning. *(The idiom "leave the nest" refers to leaving parents' care to live on one's own.)* How does the use of the idiom affect the meaning of the text? *(Possible answer: It emphasizes that making decisions and becoming independent are part of a natural growing process.)*

CRITICAL VOCABULARY

impetuous: The author is explaining the impact of brain functions on teenagers' decision-making processes.

ASK STUDENTS why someone who is impetuous is less likely to be a careful driver. *(Someone who is impetuous is not restrained by thoughts of long-term consequences or concerned about the result of poor decision making. He or she might, for example, drive too fast without worrying about getting in an accident or being unable to stop quickly if necessary.)*

In his office at the NIH, Giedd points to an image of a brain on his computer screen that illustrates brain development from childhood to adulthood. As he sets the time lapse in motion, the brain turns blue rapidly in some areas and more slowly in others. One area that's slow to turn blue—

160 which represents development over time—is the right side just over the temple. It's the spot on the head where a parent might tap a frustrated finger while asking his teen, "What were you thinking?"

This underdeveloped area is called the dorsal lateral prefrontal cortex. The underdeveloped blue on Giedd's screen is where thoughts of long-term consequences spring to consciousness. And in teen after teen, the research team found, it's not fully mature.

"This is the top rung," Giedd says. "This is the part of

170 the brain that, in a sense, associates everything. All of our hopes and dreams for the future. All of our memories of the past. Our values. Everything going on in our environment. Everything to make a decision."

When a smart, talented and very mature teen does something a parent might call "stupid," Giedd says, it's this underdeveloped part of the brain that has most likely failed.

"That's the part of the brain that helps look farther ahead," he says. "In a sense, increasing the time between impulse and decisions. It seems not to get as good as it's going to get until

180 age 25."

F

This slow process plays a kind of dirty trick on teens, whose hormones are churning. As their bodies turn more adultlike, the hormones encourage more risk-taking and thrill-seeking. That might be nature's way of helping them leave the nest. But as the hormones fire up the part of the brain that responds to pleasure, known as the limbic system, emotions run high. Those emotions make it hard to quickly form wise judgments—the kind drivers must make every day.

That's also why teens often seem more **impetuous** than

190 adults. In making decisions, they rely more on the parts of their brain that control emotion. They're "hotter" when angry and "colder" when sad, Giedd says.

When a teen is traveling 15 to 20 miles per hour over the speed limit, the part of his or her brain that processes a thrill is working brilliantly. But the part that warns of negative consequences? It's all but useless.

impetuous
(ĭm-pĕch′ōō-əs) *adj.*
If someone is *impetuous*, he or she acts without thinking things through.

"It may not seem that fast to them," Giedd says, because they're not weighing the same factors an adult might. They're not asking themselves, he says, " 'Should I go fast or not?' And dying is not really part of the equation."

Precisely how brain development plays out on the roads has yet to be studied. Giedd says brain scans of teens in driving simulations might tell researchers exactly what's going on in their heads. That could lead to better training and a clearer understanding of which teens are ready to make critical driving decisions.

In theory, a teen's brain could eventually be scanned to determine whether he or she was neurologically fit to drive. But Giedd says that ethical crossroad is too radical to seriously consider today. "We are just at the threshold of this," he says.

Finding explanations

The new insights into the teen brain might help explain why efforts to protect young drivers, ranging from driver education to laws that restrict teen driving, have had only modest success. With the judgment center of the teen brain not fully developed, parents and states must struggle to instill decision-making skills in still-immature drivers.

In nearly every state, 16-year-old drivers face limits known as "graduated licensing" rules. These restrictions vary. But typically, they bar 16-year-olds from carrying other teen passengers, driving at night or driving alone until they have driven a certain number of hours under parental supervision.

These states have, in effect, already raised their driving age. Safety experts say lives have been saved as a result. But it's mostly left to parents to enforce the restrictions, and the evidence suggests enforcement has been weak.

Teens probably appear to their parents at the dinner table to be more in control than they are behind the wheel. They might recite perfectly the risks of speeding, drinking and driving or distractions, such as carrying passengers or talking on a cell phone, Giedd says. But their brains are built to learn more from example.

For teenagers, years of watching parents drive after downing a few glasses of wine or while chatting on a cell phone might make a deeper imprint than a lecture from a driver education teacher.

CLOSE READ

Determine Central Ideas and Details (LINES 211–225)

COMMON CORE RI 1, RI 2, RI 5

Tell students that when reading an informational article they must pay close attention to facts, details, and other support for the writer's central idea. Explain that sometimes readers must weigh the relevance of that support and decide whether it is sufficient or helpful. Point out that while facts and staticistics may seem especially convincing, they might not provide the whole picture.

G CITE TEXT EVIDENCE Have students reread lines 211–225 to identify details that explain "graduated licensing." *(These rules may "bar 16-year-olds from carrying other teen passengers, driving at night, or driving alone until they have driven a certain number of hours under parental supervision.")* Why should readers be careful about interpreting the effectiveness of these rules? *(Safety experts say the rules save lives, but parents must enforce the rules, and "evidence suggests enforcement has been weak.")*

Strategies for Annotation 🖉 📋 *Annotate it!*

Determine Central Ideas and Details

COMMON CORE RI 1, RI 2, RI 5

Share these strategies for guided or independent analysis:
- Highlight in yellow details that explain graduated licensing.
- Highlight in blue the author's interpretation of the details.
- Use a note to state why the rules may not be effective.

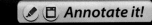

These restrictions vary. But typically, they bar 16-year-olds from carrying other teen passengers, driving at night or driving alone until they have driven a certain number of hours under parental supervision.

These states have, in effect, already raised their driving age.

> Parents must enforce rules.

Determine Central Ideas and Details (LINES 242–255)

 COMMON CORE RI 1, RI 2, RI 3

Point out that authors may support a central idea by making a comparison to a similar situation. Guide students to recognize the comparison the writer uses to end the article.

H **ASK STUDENTS** to reread lines 242–255 to identify the comparison the author makes. *(The author is comparing efforts to raise the legal drinking age to efforts to raise the driving age.)* How do the ideas presented in these last paragraphs of the article connect to the author's central idea? *(The efforts to raise the legal drinking age met resistance, but "public support for stricter laws grew" and Congress was pressured to pass a law. Efforts to raise the driving age have also met resistance.)*

Remind students that quotations are one type of support for a central idea.

I **ASK STUDENTS** to reread lines 251–255. What makes this quotation an effective way to end the article? *(The author has presented facts and statistics. This quotation is more emotional, suggesting that having more young people injured or killed in driving accidents will spur change. Such an ending is likely to make a strong impression on readers.)*

The brain research raises this question: How well can teen brains respond to the stresses of driving?

More research on teen driving decisions is needed, safety advocates say, before definitive conclusions can be drawn. 240 And more public support is probably needed before politicians would seriously consider raising the driving age.

H In the 1980s, Congress pressured states to raise their legal age to buy alcohol to 21. The goal was to stop teens from crossing borders to buy alcohol, after reports of drunken teens dying in auto crashes. Fueled by groups such as Mothers Against Drunk Driving, public support for stricter laws grew until Congress forced a rise in the drinking age.

Those laws have saved an estimated 20,000 lives in the past 20 years. Yet safety advocates say politicians remain generally 250 unwilling to raise the driving age.

"If this were forced on the states, it would not be accepted very well," Harsha says. "What it usually takes for politicians **I** to change their minds is a series of crashes involving young people. When enough of those kind of things happen, then politicians are more likely to be open to other suggestions."

TO CHALLENGE STUDENTS . . .

Analyze Argument Explain that writers use a variety of persuasive techniques to create an effective argument. Elicit that often some supporting details appeal to a reader's sense of logic, while others are aimed at a reader's emotions.

ASK STUDENTS to work with a partner to analyze the details Robert Davis presents in his article. Tell partners to categorize the details according to whether they appeal to logic or emotion and decide which are more effective.

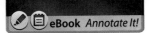

Determine Central Idea and Details

COMMON CORE RI 1, RI 2, RI 3, RI 5

The **central idea** of a piece of writing is the main concept about a topic that a writer conveys. Entire pieces of writing can be based around a central idea, and so can individual paragraphs.

A central idea is supported by **details**—facts, statistics, or quotations—that tell more about it. Note these details from "Is 16 Too Young to Drive a Car?"

Detail	What It Is	Example
fact	a statement that can be proved	Many states have begun to raise the age by imposing restrictions on 16-year-old drivers.
statistic	information that deals with numbers	Already, on average, <u>two people die every day across the USA in vehicles driven by 16-year-old drivers.</u>
quotation by experts	an expert's exact written or spoken words	"Skills are a minor factor in most cases," says Allan Williams, former chief scientist at the insurance institute. "<u>It's really attitudes and emotions.</u>"

It's important to remember that although facts, quotations by experts, and especially statistics can seem undeniable, there are often multiple ways to interpret them, depending on the information or attitudes a reader already has. For example, the statistic in the chart can be interpreted to mean

- Every day, 16-year-old drivers are to blame for deaths.
- 16-year-olds are driving in only a small percentage of fatal accidents that occur each day.

Readers have to decide how—or if—a statistic helps to support a central idea. Study the supporting details carefully as you analyze "Is 16 Too Young to Drive a Car?"

Analyzing the Text

COMMON CORE RI 1, RI 2, RI 3, RI 5

Cite Text Evidence   Support your responses with evidence from the text.

1. **Draw Conclusions** What is the central idea of "Is 16 Too Young to Drive a Car?"

2. **Evaluate** Reread lines 101–125. Explain how the statistics the author provides support his central idea. Is there another way to interpret the statistics? Support your answer.

3. **Cause/Effect** Reread lines 155–173. Which details explain why teen drivers make poor decisions?

PRACTICE & APPLY

Determine Central Ideas and Details

COMMON CORE RI 1, RI 2, RI 3, RI 5

Discuss the definitions of *central idea* and *details*. Help students differentiate between the types of details by going over the definitions and examples offered in the chart. Prompt students to focus on the parts of each example that are underlined, as they are specific to the definition. Ask students to explain how the statistics in the example help the author develop the central idea. Refer students to the paragraphs in lines 60–68 to identify additional statements that develop the author's key concept. Have students offer additional examples of each type of detail from the text.

Then discuss the idea that facts, quotations, and statistics must be interpreted. Elicit that experience or attitudes may lead readers to different conclusions. Review the example offered, focusing on how statistics can be misleading.

Analyzing the Text

COMMON CORE RI 1, RI 2, RI 3, RI 5

Possible answers:

1. *Raising the legal age for driving is an idea that could save lives.*

2. *The statistics show that driver errors cause most accidents for 16-year-old drivers, which supports the effort to raise the legal age for driving. Students may note that the statistics could be used to suggest that drunk driving is not a significant issue among teen drivers.*

3. *Giedd demonstrates how the dorsal lateral prefrontal cortex is underdeveloped in teen drivers and explains that this results in bad decision making.*

 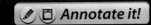

Determine Central Ideas and Details

COMMON CORE RI 1, RI 2, RI 3, RI 5

Share these strategies for guided or independent analysis:

- Highlight in yellow evidence that supports the central idea.
- Highlight in blue quotations that support the central idea.
- Highlight in pink statistics that support the central idea.

The teen brain is a paradox. Some areas—those that control senses, reactions, and physical abilities—are fully developed in teenagers. "Physically, they should be ruling the world," Giedd says. "But (adolescence) is not that great of a time emotionally." Giedd and an international research team have analyzed 4,000 brain scans from 2,000 volunteers to document how brains evolve as children mature.

Analyze Text (LINES 5–15)

COMMON CORE · RI 1, RI 3, RI 8

Explain that readers use **reasoning**, or logic, to evaluate an author's conclusions. Point out that **deductive reasoning** begins with a general statement and then presents a specific situation and provides facts and evidence toward a logical conclusion. Tell students that another type of reasoning is called inductive reasoning. **Inductive reasoning** starts with observations, examples, and facts and moves toward a conclusion.

 ASK STUDENTS to reread lines 5–15 to identify the type of reasoning the author uses. Have students provide text details that support their answer. *(The author uses inductive reasoning. He presents observations, "they don't have to jump through hoops"; examples, "they can opt out of driver's ed"; and facts, "they are not subject to nighttime driving restrictions," to reach the conclusion that teens are waiting until they are old enough to get a license without restrictions.)*

Determine Central Ideas and Details (LINES 21–25)

COMMON CORE · RI 1, RI 2, RI 3

Point out that the author doesn't express the central idea of the article until lines 21–25.

K **CITE TEXT EVIDENCE** Have students reread lines 21–25 to identify the central idea of the article. *(Although tougher licensing laws have led to fewer deaths for 16-year-old drivers, "fatal crashes involving 18-year-old drivers have increased.")* What details in the text support the central idea? *(Possible answers: Students should cite lines 2–4 for decreasing fatalities in 16-year-olds and note the article's title.)*

Fatal Car Crashes Drop for 16-Year-Olds, Rise for Older Teens
Article by Allison Aubrey

Terrified to see your teenager behind the wheel? You're not alone. But a new study finds tougher state licensing laws have led to a decrease in fatal accidents, at least among 16-year-olds. That's the good news.

But here's the rub. Some kids are waiting until they're 18-years-old to get their driver's licenses. At this point, they're considered adults, and they don't have to jump through the hoops required of younger teens. They can opt out of driver's ed. And they are not subject to nighttime driving restrictions 10 or passenger restrictions.

"[Older teens] are saying, 'The heck with your more complicated process,'" says Justin McNaull, director of state relations for the American Automobile Association. At 18, teenagers can, in many cases, get their license in a matter of weeks.

It's one explanation for the latest findings published in the *Journal of the American Medical Association*. Researchers at the University of North Carolina and the California Department of Motor Vehicles analyzed more than 130,000 20 fatal teen crashes over 22 years.

They found that tougher licensing laws have led to 1,348 fewer fatal car crashes involving 16-year-old drivers. But during the same period, fatal crashes involving 18-year-old drivers increased. They were behind the wheel in 1,086 more fatal accidents.

States have made the licensing process more rigorous in many ways: longer permitting times, driver's ed requirements, and restrictions on nighttime driving and carrying fellow teenage passengers. Experts say all of these requirements help 30 give teenagers the experience they need on the road. "In the last 15 years, we've made great strides in getting the licensing process to do a better job in helping teens get through it safely," says McNaull.

California has seen a big drop in 16-year-olds getting their driver's license. Back in 1986, 27 percent got licensed. By 2007, the figure dropped to 14 percent.

"We have more novices on the road at 18," says Scott
Masten of the California DMV and an author of the study.
And some of them may not have enough experience under
40 their belts to face risky conditions. Masten says this may help
explain the increase in fatal crashes.

It's not clear whether there are significantly fewer 16-year-
olds behind the wheel in other states because there's no
national database. But **anecdotally**, experts see this as a trend.

"There's a belief that graduated licensing has led to a
delay," says Anne McCart, a senior vice president at the
Insurance Institute for Highway Safety.

A survey of teens conducted by the Allstate Foundation
found that there are many reasons teens are delaying the
50 process of getting a license. Some say they don't have a car
or can't afford it. Others report that their parents are not
available to help them, or that they're too busy with other
activities.

But parents who do want to be more proactive can refer to
the tips the AAA has compiled on how to keep teens behind
the wheel safe. And they might also consider another recent
study, which showed that starting the school day a little bit
later seems to reduce the accident rate for teen drivers.

anecdote
(ănˊĭk-dōtˊ) *n.* An
anecdote is a short
account of an
incident.

COLLABORATIVE DISCUSSION In your opinion, at what age
should people begin driving? With a partner, discuss the reasons
for your view. Cite specific evidence from the text to support your
ideas.

CLOSE READ

Analyze Text (LINES 37–41)

COMMON CORE RI 1, RI 3, RI 8

Remind students that authors may use inductive or
deductive reasoning when presenting conclusions.
Review each type of reasoning.

🅛 **ASK STUDENTS** to reread lines 37–41. What
type of reasoning is the author using? How do you
know? *(The author is using deductive reasoning: the
first statement is a fact, and the next is a situation being
considered. The last sentence is a conclusion.)* In what
way does the reasoning in the paragraph support
the author's claim? *(It includes a quotation from an
expert to explain why more 18-year-olds are involved in
fatal crashes.)*

CRITICAL VOCABULARY

anecdote: The author is explaining the conclusion
that experts have reached regarding teen drivers.

ASK STUDENTS why the author mentions
anecdotal evidence to support the conclusion.
*(Students should note that the author has "no
national database," so she is relying on what experts
have concluded is "a trend.")*

COLLABORATIVE DISCUSSION Have students
form partnerships to locate details from the text that
would support their argument for the best age to begin
driving.

ASK STUDENTS to share any questions they generated
in the course of reading and discussing the selection.

TEACH

CLOSE READ

Analyze Text
COMMON CORE RI 3, RI 8

Discuss the definitions of deductive and inductive reasoning, explaining that both are valid and logical. Note that the major difference between these two types of thinking is that deductive reasoning begins with a generally accepted principle and applies it to a situation, while inductive reasoning takes two seemingly unrelated facts and uses them to form a conclusion.

Review the examples of each type of reasoning with students and discuss why each is effective.

Analyzing the Text
COMMON CORE RI 1, RI 3, RI 4, RI 8

1. *Lawmakers most likely believe that 18-year-olds don't need the laws designed to restrict 16-year-old drivers because 18-year-olds are presumed to be more mature and ready to drive.*

2. *The author uses inductive reasoning by presenting observations of what the states have done to make the licensing process more rigorous, as well as their effects, and then provides a conclusion about the licensing process in the quotation by McNaull.*

3. *The use of the word* belief *implies that the impact of graduated licensing has not been proven.*

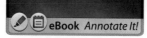 eBook *Annotate It!*

Analyze Text
COMMON CORE RI 1, RI 3, RI 4, RI 7, RI 8

When you evaluate an author's conclusions, it's important to consider the **reasoning,** or logic, that links his or her ideas together. Two of the most commonly used methods of reasoning are deductive reasoning and inductive reasoning.

Deductive reasoning occurs when a person uses a general principle to form a conclusion about a particular situation or problem.

General principle	The situation being considered	Conclusion
To drive safely, new drivers must receive training.	High schools train students in many areas.	New drivers should get their license while in high school.

Inductive reasoning occurs when a person uses specific observations or examples to arrive at a general conclusion or statement.

Fact	Fact	Conclusion
Automobile accidents are more severe when cars drive at high speeds.	Severe automobile accidents are more likely to occur on highways than on roads.	Lower speed limits on highways will save lives.

As you analyze "Fatal Car Crashes Drop for 16-Year-Olds, Rise for Older Teens," identify what kind of reasoning the author is using.

Analyzing the Text
COMMON CORE RI 1, RI 3, RI 4, RI 7, RI 8

Cite Text Evidence   Support your responses with evidence from the text.

1. **Draw Conclusions** What conclusions can you draw about why there are fewer laws designed to restrict 18-year-old drivers or force them to take driver's education?

2. **Interpret** Reread lines 26–33. What kind of reasoning does the author use? Explain your answer.

3. **Analyze** What is the effect of the use of the word *belief* in this statement from the selection: "There's a belief that graduated licensing has led to a delay"?

Strategies for Annotation   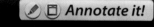 *Annotate it!*

Analyze Text
COMMON CORE RI 1

Share these strategies for guided or independent analysis:

- Highlight in yellow a fact that the author presents.
- Highlight in green information related to the first fact.
- Highlight in blue the author's conclusion.

States have made the licensing process more rigorous in many ways: longer permitting times, driver's ed requirements, and restrictions on nighttime driving and carrying fellow teenage passengers. Experts say all of these requirements help give teenagers the experience they need on the road. "In the last 15 years, we've made great strides in getting the licensing process to do a better job in helping teens get through it safely," says McNaull.

Analyze Information in Texts

A **fact** is a statement that can be proved. Most writers are careful to choose facts that support their central idea, while omitting facts that do not. However, similar facts can be used to support opposing ideas. That's because a fact can be **interpreted**—or understood—differently by different people.

It's important to identify when writers are supporting their ideas with facts and when they are supporting their ideas with interpretations of the facts, which you may or may not agree with. For example, look at this passage from "Is 16 Too Young to Drive a Car?"

> Scientists at the NIH campus in Bethesda, Md, have found that this vital area [the executive branch] develops through the teenage years and isn't fully mature until after age 25. — **fact**
>
> One 16-year-old's brain might be more developed than another 18-year-old's, just as a younger teen might be taller than an older one. But evidence is mounting that a 16-year-old's brain is generally far less developed than those of teens just a little older. — **fact**
>
> The research seems to help explain why 16-year-old drivers crash at far higher rates than older teens. — **interpretation**

Even if the executive branch of the brain is not fully developed, there may be other explanations of why 16-year-old drivers have more-frequent crashes than older teens, as "Fatal Car Crashes Drop for 16-Year-Olds, Rise for Older Teens" points out.

As you compare and contrast the two articles, read carefully to identify each writer's central idea and the facts and interpretations used to support it. Identify where the texts disagree on matters of fact and interpretation.

PRACTICE & APPLY

Analyze Information in Texts

Help students to understand the distinction between facts and interpretations. Point out that interpretations of facts may be different without disproving the facts themselves. Note that people form different opinions based on the same facts because they interpret or react to the ideas in a fact in their own particular way.

Discuss the example of facts and interpretation presented. Elicit that the words "seems to help explain" suggest that these facts could be interpreted in another way. Ask volunteers to offer other reasons why 16-year-olds have more frequent crashes than older teens, based on information in the second article. *(Possible answer: The crashes may be more the result of inexperience rather than brain development.)*

Strategies for Annotation 📝 📋 *Annotate it!*

Analyze Information in Texts

Share these strategies for guided or independent analysis:

- Highlight in yellow the first set of facts.
- Highlight in green the next fact.
- Highlight in pink an interpretation of the facts.

> California has seen a big drop in 16-year-olds getting their driver's license. Back in 1986, 27 percent got licensed. By 2007, the figure dropped to 14 percent.
>
> "We have more novices on the road at 18," says Scott Masten of the California DMV and an author of the study. And some of them may not have enough experience under their belts to face risky conditions.

Analyzing the Text

COMMON CORE RI 1, RI 2, RI 3, RI 5, RI 8, RI 9

Possible answers:

1. The central idea of "Is 16 Too Young to Drive a Car?" is that delays in brain development may make 16-year-olds too immature to drive. The central idea of "Fatal Car Crashes Drop for 16-Year-Olds" is that raising the legal age for driving may have the unintended consequence of giving 18-year-olds less training than they need to be good drivers.

2. Both selections offer facts about why the driving age should be raised, and both provide quotations that support the idea that good driving is the result of training and legal restrictions. Their facts differ in that the first selection provides proof that underdeveloped areas of a 16-year-old's brain keep 16-year-olds from making appropriate decisions, and the second selection cites a lack of training and regulation on why 18-year-olds make bad drivers.

3. The study says an 18-year-old's brain is also less developed and won't be fully developed until age 25, which would help to explain why 18-year-olds have trouble driving as well.

4. Allison Aubrey makes a case that young drivers are waiting until they are 18 to get their licenses so they can avoid driver's ed and skip the driving restrictions younger drivers face, which causes them to lack proper training behind the wheel. In lines 133–135 of "Is 16 Too Young to Drive a Car?" Aubrey's argument is undercut by Alan Williams, who says attitudes and emotions are more important than skills learned in training.

5. The facts in Allison Aubrey's article do not seem to support the idea that 18-year-olds, who are just a little older than 16-year-olds, have better-developed brains that will keep them out of accidents. Aubrey's article shows that 18-year-olds are also having problems with driving, although perhaps for different reasons than 16-year-olds.

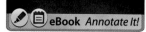

 eBook *Annotate It!*

Analyzing the Text

COMMON CORE RI 1, RI 2, RI 3, RI 5, RI 8, RI 9, W 1a, W 1b, W 4, W 9b, W 10

Cite Text Evidence   Support your responses with evidence from the texts.

1. **Summarize** In your own words, explain the central idea of each selection.

2. **Compare** Identify similar facts that both selections use to support their central idea. What key facts on this topic are included in one selection but omitted in the other?

3. **Draw Conclusions** How does the study on brain development in the first article support the conclusions about the performance of 18-year-old drivers in the second selection?

4. **Compare** Reread lines 16–20 in "Fatal Car Crashes Drop for 16-Year-Olds, Rise for Older Teens." According to Allison Aubrey, what is one interpretation for the fact that there's been an increase in fatal car crashes among 18-year-olds? How does this interpretation conflict with the quotation in lines 133–135 of "Is 16 Too Young to Drive a Car?"

5. **Evaluate** Reread lines 19–20 in "Is 16 Too Young to Drive a Car?" Do the facts found in the other article support or conflict with this interpretation? Explain.

PERFORMANCE TASK

Writing Activity: Opinion Which selection is most convincing to you?

- Review the two selections, and jot down notes to support your opinion.
- Meet with a small group to discuss which selection makes a stronger case by using sufficient details to prove its central idea. Use your notes to support your opinion.
- Next, write a paragraph or two to explain and give reasons for your opinion.
- Share your paragraph with the class. Discuss any opinions that you might not have considered during your group discussion.

Assign this performance task.

PERFORMANCE TASK

COMMON CORE W 1a, W1b, W 4, W 9, W 10

Writing Activity: Opinion Have students work in small groups and help each other to make notes about facts and evidence from the two selections that support their opinions. Remind students to locate specific reasons in the text to support their opinions and to clearly state their claims when they begin their paragraphs.

Critical Vocabulary

COMMON CORE L 4a, L 6

notion	bane	paradox	impetuous
novice	anecdote		

Practice and Apply Explain your response to answer each question.

1. Which Vocabulary word goes with *contradiction*?

2. Which Vocabulary word goes with *impulsive*?

3. Which Vocabulary word goes with *story*?

4. Which Vocabulary word goes with *idea*?

5. Which Vocabulary word goes with *nuisance*?

6. Which Vocabulary word goes with *beginner*?

Vocabulary Strategy: Domain-Specific Words

In some nonfiction texts, you may come across an unfamiliar word whose meaning is specific to its subject matter. As with any unfamiliar word, your first clue to the word's meaning should come from the surrounding text, or context. If context is not sufficient to help you define the word, you need to consult a dictionary. Read the following example:

> . . . Giedd points to an image of a brain on his computer screen... the right side just over the temple . . . is called the dorsal lateral prefrontal cortex.

The term *dorsal lateral prefrontal cortex* is not one you would know unless you were a doctor or a scientist. However, the nearby word *brain* is a clue to its meaning. Another clue is the phrase "the right side just over the temple." These clues allow you to guess that the term describes a section of the brain.

Practice and Apply Find the following terms in "Is 16 Too Young to Drive a Car?" On a separate piece of paper, fill out a chart like this one.

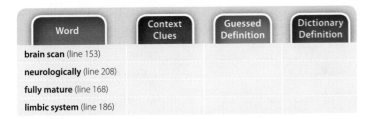

Word	Context Clues	Guessed Definition	Dictionary Definition
brain scan (line 153)			
neurologically (line 208)			
fully mature (line 168)			
limbic system (line 186)			

PRACTICE & APPLY

Critical Vocabulary

COMMON CORE L 4a, L 6

Possible answers:

1. *paradox*

2. *impetuous*

3. *anecdote*

4. *notion*

5. *bane*

6. *novice*

Vocabulary Strategy: Domain-Specific Words

Possible answers:

Word	Context Clue	Guessed Definition	Dictionary Definition
brain scan	"image of a brain"	a device that can map the brain	a CAT scan of brain activity
neurologically	"brain development"	related to the brain	of or related to the nervous system
fully mature	underdeveloped	completely grown or experienced	completely grown
limbic system	"part of the brain that responds to pleasure"	areas of the body that control behavior	parts of the brain that control emotions and behavior

---

Strategies for Annotation   *Annotate it!*

Domain-Specific Words

COMMON CORE L 4a, L 6

Have students locate domain specific words in "Is 16 Too Young to Drive a Car?" Tell students to use their eBook annotation tools to do the following:

- Highlight in green any scientific words used in the text.
- Highlight in yellow any words or phrases that help to define the scientific word.

> Giedd points to an image of a brain on his computer screen . . . one area that's slow to turn blue—which represents development over time—is the right side just over the temple . . . is called the dorsal lateral prefrontal cortex.

Language Conventions: Fragments

COMMON CORE L1

Discuss the accepted reasons for using sentence fragments in writing.

Fragment	Missing Part	Why Use Fragment
"In a sense, increasing the time between impulse and decisions."	subject and predicate	emphasize ideas
'The heck with your more complicated process,"	predicate	reproduce what was said and craft a style of writing

Assess It!

Online Selection Test
- Download an editable ExamView bank.
- Assign and manage this test online.

Language Conventions: Fragments

COMMON CORE L1

Usually, writers use grammatically correct sentences to make their meaning clear. However, they may occasionally include **fragments,** or incomplete sentences that lack a subject or predicate. Reasons for using fragments include

- to reproduce exactly what someone said in a quote
- to capture someone's voice or manner of speaking
- to emphasize particular ideas
- to avoid repeating sentence parts
- to craft a style of writing

Study this example from "Is 16 Too Young to Drive a Car?" The sentence fragments have been underlined.

> **"This is the top rung," Giedd says. "This is the part of the brain that, in a sense, associates everything. <u>All of our hopes and dreams for the future.</u> <u>All of our memories of the past.</u> <u>Our values.</u> <u>Everything going on in our environment.</u> <u>Everything to make a decision."</u>**

These fragments define *everything*. They capture the speaker's exact words and emphasize the idea that the brain can associate the parts of our lives with each other.

Practice and Apply Read these fragments from the selections. In a chart like the one shown, tell what sentence part is missing and why the author used a fragment in each case.

1. "In a sense, increasing the time between impulse and decisions." (lines 178–179) [Selection 1]

2. 'The heck with your more complicated process,'" (lines 11–12) [Selection 2]

Missing Part	Why Use the Fragment
1.	
2.	

Write an Objective Summary

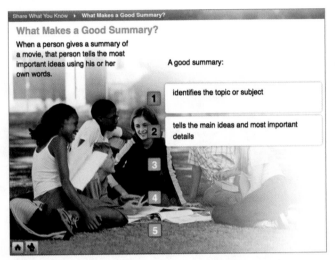

Share What You Know ▸ What Makes a Good Summary?

What Makes a Good Summary?

When a person gives a summary of a movie, that person tells the most important ideas using his or her own words.

A good summary:

1 identifies the topic or subject

2 tells the main ideas and most important details

3

4

5

TEACH

Tell students that a **summary** is a brief retelling of the main ideas of a piece of writing in one's own words. Explain that an **objective summary** is a summary that is free of the opinions of the person summarizing; writers restate the main ideas and significant details of the text in their own words but avoid personal interpretation of the facts. Share these steps for summarizing with students:

- **Use the Title** Many titles state the author's purpose or topic. Begin by checking whether the title is an expression of the main idea.
- **Combine Main Ideas** An informational article may have one main idea, but often there are many contributing ideas. They may be paragraphs or sections describing these ideas. Break the article down into major ideas and restate them in a sentence or two.
- **Reread for Opinion** When writers summarize, they tend to combine ideas in the way they understood the topics. An objective summary should include only the author's interpretation of facts.

Tell students that a summary should be shorter than the original article but should include every important detail and fully state the main ideas.

PRACTICE AND APPLY

Have students complete the Practice and Apply screens of the whiteboard lesson. Then have partners work together to create objective summaries of both articles.

Analyze Information in Texts

RETEACH

Review that a **fact** is a statement that can be proved. Explain that readers interpret, or understand, facts whenever they read.

Provide a familiar fact such as "School begins at 8:00. Ninety-five percent of students are on time for school." Ask students which interpretations they could make from the facts.

- Most students like having school start at 8:00.
- 5% of students do not care if they are on time for school.
- Most students try to be on time for school.

Discuss students' interpretations, asking them to explain their reasoning.

Then select related facts from the two articles and have students practice interpreting them. For example, in "Is 16 Too Young To Drive a Car?" the author says 61% of Americans "say they think a 16-year-old is too young to drive." Prompt students to interpret the fact by asking questions such as the following:

- Does the fact prove people want to raise the driving age?
- Are people willing to find another way of transporting 16-year-olds?

Then present this statement from "Fatal Car Crashes Drop": "We have more novices on the road at 18." Ask students to interpret the statement, focusing on whether it conflicts with the belief that 16 is too young to drive.

CLOSE READING APPLICATION

Have partners analyze the two articles, focusing on related statistics, facts, and/or quotations. Tell students to evaluate the author's interpretations as well as make some of their own. Remind them to differentiate between facts and interpretations when the texts provide conflicting information.

Persuading Viewers through Ads

Public Service Announcements

Why This Text?

Students regularly encounter public service announcements in media. This lesson will explore two public service announcements—a film and a poster. By learning about the elements these media use to convey their points, students will be better able to understand their messages and purposes.

Key Learning Objective: The student will be able to analyze the purpose of a public service announcement and understand the elements used in it.

COMMON CORE Common Core Standards

RI 7 Evaluate the advantages and disadvantages of media.

W 1a Introduce claims and organize the reasons and evidence logically.

W 1b Support claims with logical reasoning and relevant evidence.

W 7 Conduct short research projects to answer a question.

SL 2 Analyze the purpose of information presented in diverse media.

SL 5 Integrate multimedia and visual displays into a presentation.

▲ Text Complexity Rubric

	Your Phone Can Wait Lexile: N/A	Driving Distracted Lexile: N/A
Quantitative Measures		
Qualitative Measures	**Levels of Meaning/Purpose** single level of complex meaning	**Levels of Meaning/Purpose** multiple levels of complex meanings
	Structure organization of main ideas and details is complex but clearly stated and generally sequential	**Structure** some sophisticated graphics, occasionally essential to understanding the text
	Language Conventionality and Clarity contemporary, familiar language	**Language Conventionality and Clarity** some unfamiliar, academic, or domain-specific words
	Knowledge Demands some specialized knowledge required	**Knowledge Demands** some specialized knowledge required
Reader/Task Considerations	Teacher determined Vary by individual reader and type of text	Teacher determined Vary by individual reader and type of text

TEACH

CLOSE READ

Background Have students read the background information about public service announcements. Explain that **public service announcements,** or PSAs, are messages in the public interest distributed by the media without charge. Their objective is to raise awareness or change public attitudes and behavior in relation to a social issue. The first PSAs in the United States were produced during the Civil War. At that time, the government sold bonds via free newspaper advertisements throughout the North to raise money to support the war. Today, PSAs try to create awareness regarding a wide variety of topics, including littering, forest fires, and personal health.

SETTING A PURPOSE Direct students to use the Setting a Purpose prompt to focus their viewing. Remind students to generate questions as they view.

SCAFFOLDING FOR ELL STUDENTS

Shortened Words and Acronyms Explain that many common English words are shortened forms of longer words. Guide students to recall shortened words such as *phone/telephone* and familiar acronyms such as *LOL*. Using a whiteboard, project the Background information. Have volunteers mark up shortened words and acronyms in the text.

- Highlight in yellow shortened words and any phrases that help explain the words.
- Highlight in green any word formed from the first letters of several words and the phrase that explains the letters.

Background *Ads are everywhere around us—on websites, in football and baseball stadiums, and even on clothing. Ads draw our attention to products or services and try to convince us to buy what we see advertised. Companies make billions of dollars from purchases made because ads were successful in persuading us.*

One type of ad is not trying to sell something that costs money. Public service announcements, or PSAs, deliver a completely different kind of message—ideas that are for the public good.

MEDIA ANALYSIS

Persuading Viewers through Ads

Your Phone Can Wait
Public Service Announcement Film
by Stephanie Ramirez

Driving Distracted
Public Service Announcement Poster

SETTING A PURPOSE In this lesson, you will view and analyze two types of public service announcements—a film and a poster. Both try to convince people to change their attitudes and behaviors regarding aspects of driving in order to help them drive safely. Examine each public service announcement carefully to determine what particular points about safe driving it promotes and whom it is trying to persuade.

(t) ©Stephanie Ramirez; (m) (t) ©Stephanie Ramirez; (b) ©Jacqui Lindo/Pacific Gas and Electric Company

---

Ads draw our attention to products or services and try to convince us to buy what we see advertised. Companies make billions of dollars from purchases made because ads were successful in persuading us.

One type of ad is not trying to sell something that costs money. Public service announcements, or PSAs, deliver a completely different kind of message…

TEACH

CLOSE READ

As You View Tell students that they will be watching a public service announcement film. Explain that PSA filmmakers use different elements and techniques to target their audience and to convey information. Have students read As You View to help them focus their viewing on the elements the filmmaker uses in "Your Phone Can Wait."

Analyze Ideas in Media COMMON CORE SL 2

Explain to students that filmmakers make creative choices to ensure that their messages are clear and appealing to their intended audience.

A **ASK STUDENTS** to watch the film and explain why the filmmaker chooses a teenager to act in it. *(Possible answer: The filmmaker wants other teenagers to identify with the girl in the film.)*

Your Phone Can Wait

Format: Public service announcement film
Running Time: 2:0 minutes

AS YOU VIEW The film you are about to view was created for the National Safety Council for a specific purpose and audience. Think about whom the filmmaker might have wanted to appeal to as you watch the film. How do the various parts of the film appeal to that audience? Also think about the specific message that the film delivers and the variety of techniques—verbal and visual—that the filmmaker uses.

Pause the video and write notes about techniques and ideas that impress you as you view. Also write down any questions you have during viewing. Replay or rewind the video as needed.

©Stephanie Ramirez

264 Collection 4

APPLYING ACADEMIC VOCABULARY

deduce	license

As you discuss the film, incorporate the following Collection 4 academic vocabulary words: *deduce* and *license*. Ask students what message they might **deduce** from the film. Ask students what other kinds of information they think people should learn when they apply for a driver's **license.**

Analyze Ideas in Media

The creators of public service announcements like "Your Phone Can Wait" design them with a specific audience and purpose in mind. A **target audience** is the group that the creators want to appeal to. The individuals in the target audience may share certain attributes, such as age, gender, ethnic background, values, or lifestyle. The **purpose** of a film may be to share information or to persuade the audience to change behaviors or attitudes.

The creators of filmed public service announcements combine different techniques and elements to deliver their **message**—the idea that the film promotes.

- **Persuasive techniques** are methods used to convince viewers to agree with a message. Some language may appeal to viewers' sense of reason, while other words appeal to viewers' emotions. Repeated words help viewers remember the message.
- **Visual elements,** such as graphics or **animation**—the process of displaying images so they appear to move—can engage the audience. Fast-paced scene changes can convey excitement.
- **Sound elements** such as music or sound effects can emphasize a point or grab viewers' attention. A **narrator,** or the person who speaks and explains the message, also has an impact. An older voice may sound responsible and mature, while a younger voice may seem friendlier to a younger audience.

Consider how these elements are used in "Your Phone Can Wait."

Analyzing the Media

Cite Text Evidence   Support your responses with evidence from the media.

1. **Identify and Infer** Review the public service announcement film and fill out a chart like this one.

Who is the target audience?
What is the message of the announcement?
What is the purpose of the announcement?

2. **Evaluate** Which persuasive techniques, visual elements, and sound elements are used to deliver the film's message? How do these techniques and elements help make the message more appealing?

Analyze Ideas in Media   COMMON CORE SL 2

Help students to understand the terms *target audience* and *purpose.* Then explain that filmmakers use different techniques and elements to deliver the messages they promote in public service announcements. Define and discuss the different techniques and elements with students. Discuss how these elements are used in the public service announcement students have just viewed. (*The film uses a young girl as a narrator. The narrator uses persuasive language when she speaks to the audience. The words "on the road, off the phone" are repeated. Animation and contemporary music are used in the film. Statistics about accidents are also used.*)

Analyzing the Media   COMMON CORE SL 2

Possible Answers:

1. *The target audience is teenagers. The message is that the use of a phone for talking or texting distracts drivers and leads to accidents. The purpose of the announcement is to convince teenagers not to use their phones while driving.*

2. *The film uses a friendly young narrator, persuasive language, statistics, repetition, and music to deliver its point. The narrator generally delivers information in front of a plain white background, which makes her stand out. She seems likeable so that young viewers will want to identify with her. The animation has a lighthearted tone, but suggests serious information about what drivers may miss when distracted by a phone conversation. Text headlines, such as "What you aren't seeing" and "On the road, off the phone," reinforce spoken messages.*

WHEN STUDENTS STRUGGLE . . .

To guide students' understanding of the information about different elements, have pairs of students work together to make a two-column chart that lists different visual and sound elements in the film. Students can then look at their list and use it to compare and contrast the effects each element has on a viewer.

Visual Elements	Sound Elements
animation	music

As You View Tell students that the poster they are looking at is a public service announcement. Explain that the poster contains specific elements to convey its message. Have students read As You View to help them focus their viewing on the kinds of elements found in the "Driving Distracted" poster.

COLLABORATIVE DISCUSSION Have students work in pairs and discuss the messages in the film and poster. Have students compare the two messages by telling how they are alike and different. Then have partners each choose one of the public service announcements. Have them tell whether they think the message in the announcement is powerful and why. Accept all reasonable responses.

ASK STUDENTS to share any questions they generated in the course of viewing and discussing the film and poster.

MEDIA

Driving Distracted

Format: Public service announcement poster

AS YOU VIEW In this poster, the writer and designer create a particular scene for a particular purpose. They include facts and figures as well as images. Think about how these visual and textual elements work together to convey the message.

Consider specific elements, such as
- the objects that are included
- the use of light and dark colors
- the content and placement of text and figures

What points do each of these elements make or emphasize?

©Jacqui Lindo/Pacific Gas and Electric Company

COLLABORATIVE DISCUSSION Evaluate how well the film and the poster work as public service announcements. Is the message in each announcement a powerful one? Why or why not?

Analyze Diverse Media

Public service announcements are communicated through various media, including magazines, billboards, or posters such as the "Driving Distracted" poster. These media use different elements to help make their messages more exciting.

Public service announcements quite often include **statistics,** mathematical information that is collected and analyzed to help people understand a situation or a trend. Statistics help make a message more convincing.

A public service poster, or any similar type of media, also includes visual elements, such as the following:

- **Graphics** are visual designs or elements that call attention to certain information. For example, the starbursts in the "Driving Distracted" poster call attention to the objects contained within.
- **Color** can be used to create certain feelings or to convey emphasis. For example, red can suggest danger, while blue can create a calm, peaceful feeling. Text in vivid colors will stand out more than text in darker colors. Viewers are more likely to read something bold or vivid because it catches their attention immediately.

Consider the impact of these elements as you analyze the "Driving Distracted" poster.

Analyzing the Media

 COMMON CORE SL 2

Cite Text Evidence Support your responses with evidence from the media.

1. **Infer** To what does the heading "Distraction/Rate" refer?

2. **Interpret** Each of the five yellow starbursts within the car contains an image with a percentage shown next to it. What does this use of visuals and statistics convey? What impact do these elements have on the message?

3. **Analyze** Why is the starburst containing the image of the deer placed within the windshield area? What message does this symbol and its placement convey?

WHEN STUDENTS STRUGGLE . . .

Guide students to understand the statistics shown on the poster. Provide a simple example such as the following to help them understand what percentages represent.

- Explain that all percentages are based on 100%.
- If a statistic shows that something happens 10% of the time, it means that out of every 100 events, this thing happens 10 times.
- Prompt students to explain the meaning of other percentages shown on the poster.

Analyze Diverse Media

 COMMON CORE SL 2

Discuss each of the different elements that public service announcements may use to deliver their messages. Prompt students to identify how each of those elements is used in "Driving Distracted." Then have students consider the impact of graphics and color upon viewers. *(The orange type and starburst call attention to the information they convey. The chart of statistics shows how often different kinds of distractions cause accidents.)* Ask students to consider the possible motives for creating the poster, and discuss how the use of graphics and color support that motive. *(Possible answer: The motive is social, to change driving behavior; the color and graphics call attention to the consequences of distracted driving that should prompt drivers to become more focused.)*

Analyzing the Media

 COMMON CORE SL 2

Possible Answers:

1. *"2010 Rate" most likely refers to the percentage of accidents caused by each driving distraction during the year 2010.*

2. *Each starburst in the car highlights a driving distraction; the nearby percentage shows the volume of accidents related to that distraction. Together, these graphics highlight the connection between each distraction and accidents.*

3. *The bright yellow starbursts call attention to each distraction in the car, while the dark blue starburst is more subtle and easy to miss—just as the deer would be in comparison to the distractions in the car.*

PRACTICE & APPLY

Evaluate Media

COMMON CORE RI 7, SL 2

Help students understand how the techniques used in a public service announcement film and poster differ. Discuss examples of oral and quantitative information from each one with students. Then have students tell which kinds of information are provided in each form of media. *(Oral information is only presented in the film; quantitative information is provided in both the film and the poster.)*

Analyzing the Media

COMMON CORE RI 7, SL 2, SL 5

Possible Answers:

1. *Both give statistics about the numbers of accidents caused by distractions. "Your Phone Can Wait" focuses on phone calls and texting; "Driving Distracted" also addresses other types of distractions. The poster conveys the information more effectively because the numbers are visible and easy to scan. In the film, the numbers can easily be forgotten.*

2. *The combination of the narrator and the animation is more effective because they show a variety of driving situations and potential problems. The poster shows a single situation.*

Evaluate Media

COMMON CORE RI 7, SL 2

"Your Phone Can Wait" and "Driving Distracted" both deliver similar messages. However, because they are presented in different forms of media, they can emphasize different types of information to make their message clear.

- **Oral information** uses spoken language to make its point. While words can be logical and factual, some words can appeal to feelings and emotions. A speaker's tone or emphasis can also have an impact.
- **Quantitative information** conveys facts and details through numbers. It tells about information that is measurable.

Think about the techniques—or combination of techniques—each media form uses as you evaluate "Your Phone Can Wait" and "Driving Distracted."

Analyzing the Media

COMMON CORE RI 7, W 1a, W 1b, W 7, SL 2, SL 5

Cite Text Evidence Support your responses with evidence from the media.

1. **Analyze** "Your Phone Can Wait" and "Driving Distracted" both provide quantitative information about the dangers of distracted driving. Complete a chart like this to gather details about the specific information each public service announcement provides. Which announcement more effectively conveys quantitative information?

Public Service Announcement	Quantitative Information	How Information Is Shared
Your Phone Can Wait		
Driving Distracted		

2. **Compare** "Your Phone Can Wait" includes a narrator who provides spoken information. It also includes an animated re-creation of a driving experience. Are these methods of conveying information more or less effective than the use of text and graphics in "Driving Distracted"? Explain.

PERFORMANCE TASK

Media Activity: Public Service Announcement Work with your group to create your own print media public service announcement about safe driving for teenagers.

- Brainstorm with your group for ideas to include.

- Discuss the different techniques that would help you effectively deliver your message.
- Research the topic and gather statistics that will help make your message more persuasive.
- Create and lay out visuals that reflect your ideas.

PERFORMANCE TASK

COMMON CORE W 1a, W 1b, W 7, SL 2, SL 5

Media Activity: Public Service Announcement Have students work in small groups to plan their public service announcements. The groups should answer these questions as they plan:

- What message do we want to convey?
- What information will make our message persuasive?
- What techniques will make our message more effective?

Assign this performance task.

Have students try out several ways of presenting their information. Then have students choose the most effective one and produce their final announcements. See page 318 for further instruction on creating a public service announcement.

Camera Shots and Shot Selections

RI 7,
SL 2

TEACH

Explain to students that filmmakers use different kinds of camera shots to convey ideas, to track characters' emotions, or to show a situation from a character's point of view. Point out that the makers of public service announcements also use different camera shots to convey information and ideas to viewers.

Review the following kinds of shots that the filmmaker uses is "Your Phone Can Wait":

- A **close-up shot** focuses on a person's face. The filmmaker uses the close-up shot to focus on the face of the narrator. This makes the narrator seem attractive to the viewer and makes the viewer want to identify with her.
- A **point-of-view shot** shows what a character sees. The filmmaker uses a point-of-view shot to show what the narrator sees when she is driving. The filmmaker uses this shot to help viewers realize the potential dangers of driving while talking on a phone.

Explain to students that filmmakers may use some of these shots as well.

- **Establishing shots** present a wide view of an area. They are used to introduce viewers to a location.
- **Long shots** give a wide view of a scene. They allow viewers to see the "big picture" and show the relationship between characters and their environment.
- **Low-angle shots** are shots where the camera looks up at a subject. They might make a subject look larger or more menacing.
- **High-angle shots** are shots where a camera looks down upon a subject. They might make a subject look vulnerable or exposed.

PRACTICE AND APPLY

Have students view another public service announcement film. Have them list the different camera shots the filmmaker uses. Then have them tell the effect each kind of shot has on a viewer.

Persuasive Techniques: Visual and Print/Narration

RI 7,
SL 2

TEACH

Explain to students that advertisers use the following persuasive techniques when trying to convince readers and viewers to agree with an idea or to buy a product:

- **Emotional appeals** use strong feelings, such as fear or pity, to persuade viewers.
- **Bandwagon appeals** suggest that "everyone else" does or believes a certain thing.
- **Slogans** use memorable phrases that viewers will remember.
- **Logical appeals** rely on facts and the use of reason.

 LEVEL UP TUTORIALS Assign the following *Level Up* tutorial: **Persuasive Techniques**

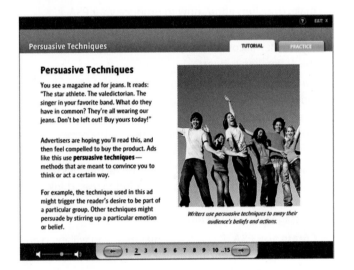

PRACTICE AND APPLY

Have students view "Your Phone Call Can Wait." Ask them to name the different persuasive techniques the filmmaker uses to convince viewers not to talk on the telephone and drive at the same time. Then have students look at the "Driving Distracted" poster. Ask them to name the persuasive techniques the poster maker uses to convince drivers not to drive while distracted. Discuss what makes the techniques effective in each medium.

How to Create a Public Service Announcement

TEACH

Before students begin the performance task, provide the following information. Remind them that a **public service announcement**, or PSA, is a message in the public interest that is distributed by the media without charge. Review that the objective of a PSA is to raise awareness or change public attitudes and behavior over a social issue.

The following guidelines can help students create their own public service announcement.

- **Choose a topic.** A public service announcement is supposed to raise awareness to help people. When choosing a topic, think about which kinds of issues are really for the public good. Keep in mind that many PSAs are about health, safety, and the environment.
- **Target your audience.** Think about who you want to reach with your message. Knowing your audience will help you make decisions about how to produce your PSA.
- **Research your topic.** Gather information and statistics that you think will convince your audience that they should take the action you suggest.
- **Choose a medium.** Ask yourself what kind of medium would work best for your message. Would a poster work best? Or would an audio or video recording work best? Decide which medium would work best to convey the information you researched.
- **Choose techniques.** Think about the techniques that work best for the medium you have decided to use. Think about how color, graphics, or sound might help to convey the message you want to deliver.
- **Create you PSA.** Produce the materials you will need and then assemble them into your PSA. If you are making an audio or video PSA, you will have to make a recording. Review your recording and then make a final version.

PRACTICE AND APPLY

Have students choose topics for their own public service announcements and produce them. Students can present their PSAs to the class.

Evaluating Advantages and Disadvantages of Media

RI 7, SL 2

RETEACH

Remind students that public service announcements use different kinds of media to convey their messages, including posters, billboards, newspaper ads, radio broadcasts, and videos. Point out that different kinds of information may be better suited for one type of media.

- **Oral information** uses spoken language to make its point. Video or audio can be effective in transmitting oral information. Some words can be logical and factual, but others can appeal to feelings and emotions. A speaker's voice can make this kind of oral information more persuasive.
- **Quantitative information** conveys facts and details through numbers. It tells about information that is measurable. Although a speaker could convey this kind of information, seeing this information on a poster or billboard might make the information easier to understand and remember. Those types of media convey this quantitative information better than spoken language.

CLOSE VIEWING APPLICATION

Students can view a variety of different kinds of public service announcements. Have them discuss the kinds of information each one conveys. Then have them discuss whether the medium of each public service announcement is best suited for that kind of information.

COLLECTION 4
PERFORMANCE TASK A

Interactive Lessons
If you need help . . .
• **Writing Informative Texts**
• **Writing as a Process**
• **Using Textual Evidence**

Write a Literary Analysis

The transition from childhood to adulthood can be complicated, as you have learned in this collection. In this activity, you will write a literary analysis about what the theme of "Marigolds" reveals about that transition and explore how the story's theme is relevant to modern life.

A successful literary analysis

- cites evidence from the text that strongly supports the writer's ideas and analysis

- is organized in a way that is appropriate to purpose and audience

- conveys ideas through the selection, organization, and analysis of relevant content

COMMON CORE

RL 1 Cite textual evidence to support analysis.
RL 2 Determine theme.
W 2a–f Write informative/ explanatory texts.
W 5 Develop and strengthen writing.
W 9a Apply grade 8 Reading standards to literature.
W 10 Write routinely over extended time frames and shorter time frames.

> **PLAN**

> *my* **Notebook**

Use the annotation tools in your eBook to find evidence in the text that supports your ideas about the story's theme.

Analyze the Story Refresh your memory of "Marigolds."

- Reread "Marigolds" to review the lesson or theme that stands out for you. Consider Lizabeth's experiences as a teenager, as well as her view of those experiences as an adult.

- Take notes about evidence from the text that reveals the story's theme. Remember to look for clues in the story's setting and in symbols that represent ideas or feelings.

- Though "Marigolds" is set in the 1930s, many adolescents today can recognize something of themselves in Lizabeth's feelings or actions. List some ways that the story's theme connects to modern trends or to the experiences of modern teens.

Consider Audience and Purpose Think about your readers and what they need to know to understand and appreciate your literary analysis.

- Keep in mind that peers, and especially classmates who have read this collection, may be more in tune with issues and experiences related to adolescence than older readers.

- Decide how you will appeal to readers who may have different views about the theme of the story.

ACADEMIC VOCABULARY

As you share what you learned about the transition to adulthood, be sure to use the academic vocabulary words.

debate
deduce
license
sufficient
trend

WRITE A LITERARY ANALYSIS

 COMMON CORE RL 1, RL 2, W 2a-f, W 6, W 9a, W 10

Introduce students to the performance pask by reading the introductory paragraph with them and reviewing the criteria for what makes a good literary analysis. Remind students that a literary analysis will use evidence from the text to support the main points a writer wants to make.

PLAN

CONSIDER AUDIENCE AND PURPOSE

> ▶ *View It!*
>
> **Professional Development Podcast:**
>
> **Performance Tasks**

Remind students that they should keep their audience in mind as they draw conclusions about how the story relates to modern teenagers. Point out that an audience of peers might be able to understand familiar references to modern teenage life, whereas an older audience may not. Suggest that students choose references based upon their audience.

Develop a Central Idea Use your notes about "Marigolds" to plan your analysis.

- Draft your central idea. This idea is the main point you want to make in your analysis, so everything you discuss should relate to it. Remember that you can modify or refine your central idea as needed when you write.

- Decide what theme you will discuss, and identify evidence from the story that reveals the theme and supports your thoughts.

- Create a graphic organizer like this one to help you plan your writing. Use it to note how different aspects of the story might resonate with modern teenagers.

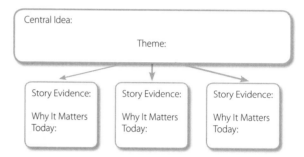

Central Idea:

Theme:

Story Evidence:	Story Evidence:	Story Evidence:
Why It Matters Today:	Why It Matters Today:	Why It Matters Today:

PRODUCE

WRITE YOUR LITERARY ANALYSIS

Tell students that writers often come up with new ideas about a topic when they begin writing. Point out that it may be helpful to incorporate any new ideas into their graphic organizer to help guide the writing of their drafts. Explain that doing so will help clarify how these new ideas fit with the organization students have created and make their drafts flow more logically.

PRODUCE

Write Your Literary Analysis Use your notes and your graphic organizer to draft your literary analysis.

- Start with an attention-grabbing question or comment, and state your central idea to introduce your analysis. Provide a brief summary of the story.

- Organize your ideas in a logical way. You may wish to discuss the theme along with related story evidence, and then explain how the theme is relevant for today's young people. Another option would be to organize around the major events in the story, explaining how each one helps to reveal the theme and connects to today's teenagers.

- Be sure to include concrete details, quotations, or other examples from the story to support your ideas.

- Conclude your analysis with a summary of your main points and your own insights about the theme.

my **WriteSmart**

Write your rough draft in *my*WriteSmart. Focus on getting your ideas down, rather than on perfecting your choice of language.

REVISE

Review Your Draft Use the chart on the next page to evaluate your draft. Work with a partner to determine whether you have achieved your purpose. Consider the following:

- Examine your central idea to decide whether it clearly represents the focus you have chosen.

- Review the flow of ideas in your analysis to be sure the organization is clear and logical.

- Check whether you have included sufficient supporting evidence from the story.

- Evaluate whether your conclusion restates your main points and offers insight about the theme's relevance.

my **WriteSmart**

Have your partner or a group of peers review your draft in *my*WriteSmart. Ask your reviewers to note any reasons that do not support the claim or that lack sufficient evidence.

PRESENT

Create a Finished Copy Finalize your literary analysis. Then choose a way to share it with your audience. Consider these options:

- Present your literary analysis in a speech to your classmates.

- Send your analysis to a magazine that publishes articles of interest to adolescents.

- Organize a debate in which you and other classmates argue your views about the relevance of "Marigolds" for today's teenagers.

REVISE

REVIEW YOUR DRAFT

Suggest to students that, when they revise, they should first focus on improving the content, organization, and style of their analyses. Point out that they can correct grammar, spelling, and punctuation when they prepare their final drafts.

PRESENT

CREATE A FINISHED COPY

Students can:

- present their analyses as speeches. Remind students that the delivery of a speech is as important as the content.

- send their analyses to a magazine. Have students research magazines that publish articles of interest to adolescents.

- form small groups with others who have differing views and debate their contrasting points of view. Remind students to use supporting story evidence when they argue why their points are relevant.

PERFORMANCE TASK A

IDEAS AND EVIDENCE

Have students use the chart to evaluate how they did on the performance task in each of the three main categories. Suggest that students focus on the relevance of the reasons and evidence they presented. Partners can critique each other's analyses. Encourage them to give reasons for their criticisms and to offer each other ideas about ways they can improve their writing.

COLLECTION 4 TASK A
LITERARY ANALYSIS

	Ideas and Evidence	Organization	Language
ADVANCED	• The central idea clearly identifies the story's theme and its relevance. • Specific, relevant details support key points in the analysis. • The concluding section summarizes the analysis and offers an insight.	• Key points and supporting details are organized effectively and logically throughout the literary analysis. • Transitions successfully show the relationships between ideas.	• Language is precise and captures the writer's thoughts with originality. • Grammar, usage, and mechanics are correct.
COMPETENT	• The central idea makes a point about the relevance of the theme. • Some key points need more support. • The concluding section summarizes most of the analysis but doesn't offer an insight.	• The organization of key points and supporting details is confusing in a few places. • A few more transitions are needed to clarify the relationships between ideas.	• Most language is precise and shows some originality. • Some errors in grammar, usage, and mechanics occur.
LIMITED	• The central idea only hints at a main point. • Details support some key points but often are too general. • The concluding section gives an incomplete summary without insight.	• Most key points are organized logically, but many supporting details are out of place. • More transitions are needed throughout the literary analysis to connect ideas.	• Language is repetitive or too general at times. • Many errors in grammar, usage, and mechanics occur, but the writer's ideas are still clear.
EMERGING	• The central idea is missing. • Details and evidence are irrelevant or missing. • The literary analysis lacks a concluding section.	• A logical organization is not apparent. • Transitions are not used.	• Language is inaccurate, repetitive, and too general. • Errors in grammar, usage, and mechanics obscure the meaning of the writer's ideas.

COLLECTION 4
PERFORMANCE TASK B

Interactive Lessons

If you need help . . .
• **Producing and Publishing with Technology**
• **Conducting Research**

Produce a Multimedia Campaign

One selection in Collection 4 asks, "When Do Kids Become Adults?" In this activity, you will create a multimedia campaign to present your response to that age-old question. Your campaign will include an editorial along with messages in one or two other mediums.

A successful campaign

- presents an argument that supports claims with clear reasons and relevant evidence
- draws evidence from informational texts and from print and digital research
- integrates multimedia and visual displays to strengthen claims and to add interest

COMMON CORE

RI 1 Cite textual evidence to support analysis.
W 1a–e Write arguments.
W 5 Develop and strengthen writing.
W 6 Use technology to produce and publish writing.
W 8 Gather relevant information from multiple print/digital sources.
W 9b Apply grade 8 Reading standards to literary nonfiction.
SL 4 Present claims, findings, and evidence.
SL 5 Integrate multimedia and visual displays into presentations.

PLAN

Gather Information Review the selections in Collection 4 to find events or trends that may mark the beginning of adulthood.

- Identify the event, action, or age that reflects your position.
- Gather at least two pieces of evidence to support your position from selections in the collection.

Conduct Research Use both print and digital resources to gather information about the start of adulthood.

- If you have chosen to focus on an event such as obtaining a driver's license or voting for the first time, research the legal age for those events in the United States as well as in other countries.
- If your focus is on living independently, research laws or traditions that signal legal adulthood.
- Take notes and gather sufficient statistics to support your claim.

Consider Audience and Purpose Keep your intended audience in mind as you develop your campaign.

my Notebook

Use the annotation tools in your eBook to identify textual evidence from the collection that will help shape and support your argument.

ACADEMIC VOCABULARY

As you share your ideas about the event or age that should mark the start of adulthood, be sure to use the academic vocabulary words.

debate
deduce
license
sufficient
trend

PRODUCE A MULTIMEDIA CAMPAIGN

COMMON CORE

RI 1, W 1a-e,
W 5, W 6,
W8, W 9b,
SL 4, SL 5

Introduce students to the performance task by reading the introductory paragraph with them and reviewing the criteria for what makes a good multimedia campaign. Remind students that an editorial is an opinion piece that tries to convince its audience to think in a particular way.

PLAN

GATHER INFORMATION

Remind students that, after they complete their research, they will need to decide which kinds of media are best for conveying their information and targeting their audience. Have them think of questions like these:

- Who is my target audience?
- Which medium would this audience respond to?
- Which medium would best deliver this message?

- Your language and tone will generally be different for classmates and other peers than for adults.

- Your campaign will include an editorial, but you will also use other formats to present your ideas effectively. You might consider using a poster, a television or radio commercial, or a direct mail advertisement to effectively reach your audience.

Develop Your Argument Use your notes from your review of the collection and your research to plan your argument.

- Whether advertising a product or promoting a political candidate, a good campaign has a central message or claim. Plan how to deliver your message in writing for your editorial and in the other formats you choose.

- Create a graphic organizer like the one shown to develop an argument that includes a claim, supporting evidence, and a counterargument.

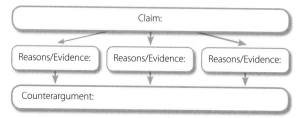

Claim:

Reasons/Evidence: | Reasons/Evidence: | Reasons/Evidence:

Counterargument:

PRODUCE

Write Your Editorial Use your notes and your graphic organizer to draft your editorial.

- Use quotations or unexpected statistics to get your audience's attention, and state your position with a strong claim.

- Organize your ideas in a logical way. You might begin with the strongest reason and progress to less strong reasons. Another option would be to start with the least important reason and build to the most important.

- Be sure to include concrete details, quotations, or examples from the selections and your research to support your claim.

- Conclude your editorial by restating your claim and by encouraging readers to show their support for your argument.

*my*WriteSmart

Write your rough draft in *my*WriteSmart. Focus on getting your ideas down, rather than on perfecting your choice of language.

PRODUCE

WRITE YOUR EDITORIAL

Explain to students that, as they write, they should anticipate readers' concerns and questions. Point out that by including counterarguments to these questions and concerns, students will make their opinions more convincing.

Design Other Formats The best campaigns use more than one medium to share their message. Using multimedia technology to mix visuals with sound is the latest trend, but something as "low-tech" as a poster, a T-shirt, or a bumper sticker may also reach a wide audience.

- Choose one or two other mediums to add to your campaign.
- Draft any necessary text and decide how to incorporate it with related visuals.
- Sketch out how you will display or present your visuals.
- Cite your research sources, following your teacher's choice of style.

REVISE

Review Your Draft Use the chart on the next page to evaluate your draft. Work with a partner to determine whether you have presented a strong argument in your campaign. Consider the following:

- Review your editorial to make sure you have clearly stated your claim and provided sufficient supporting reasons and evidence.
- Check that the other formats you have chosen clearly support your claim. Is each layout clear and easy to understand? Do all the visuals clearly represent your focus? Confirm that the text is easy to read and free of grammatical errors.
- Evaluate whether all the elements of your campaign send a unified message that will appeal to your audience.

my **WriteSmart**

Have your partner or a group of peers review the draft of your editorial in *my*WriteSmart. Ask your reviewers to note any reasons that do not support the claim or that lack sufficient evidence.

PRESENT

Create a Finished Product Finalize all the parts of your campaign. Then choose a way to share it with your audience. Consider these options:

- Plan a campaign rally or kick-off event to share your ideas with classmates.
- Create a blog or website to share your argument with a wider audience.
- Organize a debate with classmates who claim a different age or event as the mark of adulthood.

REVISE

REVIEW YOUR DRAFT

Have students work with a partner to revise their editorial and other formats. Encourage students to look for ways to improve the individual pieces, but also to think about how well the pieces work together.

- Do each of the pieces contribute to a cohesive message?
- Do the pieces together have a unified message?

PRESENT

CREATE A FINISHED PRODUCT

Students can:

- share their campaigns at a rally. After all students have presented their materials, have them discuss what made their campaigns effective.
- create a blog or website to share their campaigns with a wider audience. Students can ask a school technology expert for assistance.
- debate their contrasting points of views with others. Remind students to take turns asking and answering questions and to listen politely to others.

PERFORMANCE TASK B

ORGANIZATION

Have students use the chart to evaluate how they did on the performance task in each of the three main categories. Tell students to pay particular attention to their organization of ideas and how that organization affects the persuasiveness of the campaign. Partners can work together to first assess the individual pieces they created. Then

MULTIMEDIA CAMPAIGN

	Ideas and Evidence	Organization	Language
ADVANCED	• All parts of the campaign clearly state a position and a call for action. • Logical reasons and relevant evidence support the claim. • Counterarguments are addressed. • The campaign's message is strong and unified throughout.	• The reasons and evidence are organized logically and consistently to persuasive effect. • Transitions connect reasons and evidence to the writer's claim.	• The editorial is presented in a consistent, formal style. • Grammar, mechanics, and usage are correct.
COMPETENT	• A position is stated but could be more clear. • Reasons and evidence could be more convincing. • Responses to counterarguments need development. • The campaign's message is strong and mostly unified.	• The organization of reasons and evidence is confusing in places. • A few more transitions are needed to connect reasons and evidence to the claim.	• The style of the editorial becomes informal in a few places. • Some errors in grammar, usage, and mechanics occur.
LIMITED	• The writer's position is not clear. • Some reasons and evidence are not logical or relevant. • Opposing claims are not addressed logically. • The campaign's message is somewhat inconsistent.	• The organization of reasons and evidence is logical in some places, but it does not follow a clear pattern. • Many more transitions are needed to connect reasons and evidence to the claim.	• The style of the editorial becomes informal in many places. • Grammar, usage, and mechanics are incorrect in many places.
EMERGING	• No position is stated. • Reasons and evidence are missing. • Opposing claims are not anticipated or addressed. • The campaign lacks a unified message.	• A logical organization is not used; reasons and evidence are presented randomly. • Transitions are not used, making the argument difficult to understand.	• The style is inappropriate for the argument. • Errors in grammar, usage, and mechanics obscure the meaning of ideas.

©Tim De Waele/Corbis

Anne Frank's Legacy

❝ I don't want to have lived in vain like most people…
I want to go on living even after my death! ❞

—Anne Frank

277

PLAN

CONNECTING WORD AND IMAGE

ASK STUDENTS to discuss how the collection opener image and the collection quotation work together to create a connection.

PERFORMANCE TASK PREVIEW

Point out to students that they will complete a performance task at the end of the collection. The performance task will require them to further analyze the selections in the collection and to synthesize ideas about these analyses. They will present their findings in an expository essay.

ACADEMIC VOCABULARY

View It!

Professional Development Podcast:
Academic Vocabulary

Students can acquire facility with the academic vocabulary words through frequent, repeated exposure as they analyze and discuss the selections in the collection. Academic vocabulary can be used in the following instructional contexts . This will enable students to incorporate the academic vocabulary words into their working vocabulary.

- Collaborative Discussion at the end of each selection
- Analyzing the Text questions for each selection
- Selection-level Performance Tasks
- Vocabulary instruction (for Critical Vocabulary and/or for Vocabulary Strategy)
- Language Conventions
- End-of-collection Performance Task for all selections in the collection

ASK STUDENTS to review the Academic Vocabulary word list for this collection. You may wish to pronounce each word aloud, so students hear the correct pronunciation. Then, discuss the definitions and the related forms for each word. Remind students that they will encounter these five academic vocabulary words throughout the collection.

Anne Frank's Legacy

In this collection, you will learn about the lasting impact of a young girl and her diary.

hmhfyi.com

COLLECTION

PERFORMANCE TASK Preview

At the end of this collection, you will write an expository essay about the living conditions in the Annex, the secret section of a building where Anne Frank and others hid for more than two years during World War II.

ACADEMIC VOCABULARY

Study the words and their definitions in the chart below. You will use these words as you discuss and write about the texts in this collection.

Word	Definition	Related Forms
communicate (kə-myōō´nĭ-kāt´) v.	to convey information or exchange ideas	communicated, communicable
draft (drăft) n.; v.	early versions or stages of a written document or plan; to write such a version	drafting, drafted
liberation (lĭb´ə-rā´shən) n.	the act of freeing or the state of being free	liberate, liberal
philosophy (fĭ-lŏs´ə-fē) n.	the underlying theory or set of ideas related to life as a whole	philosopher, philosophic
publish (pŭb´lĭsh) v.	to prepare and issue a book or other material to the public	publishing, publication, public

USING COLLECTIONS YOUR WAY

Use the following information, along with the charts on the following pages, to help you decide how you want to introduce the collection. Based on your teaching style, your students' interests, or your instructional goals, you may want to structure this collection in various ways. You may choose different entry points each time you teach the collection.

"I stress the importance of language and style."

This literary criticism examines Anne Frank's legacy as a writer.

Background *Anne Frank's The Diary of a Young Girl has become one of the most well-known books in the world, but it is not always recognized as a skillfully crafted piece of literature. Author Francine Prose (b. 1947), a successful novelist and nonfiction writer, researched the diary to learn more about how it was written, how it came to be published, and how it has been received over time. She published her findings in a book, from which this selection is excerpted.*

from
ANNE FRANK:
The Book, The Life, The Afterlife

Literary Criticism by Francine Prose

SETTING A PURPOSE Has *The Diary of a Young Girl* become a classic because of its author's tragically short life, or because of the quality of the writing? As you read, focus on the differing opinions about this question.

THE FIRST TIME I READ THE DIARY OF ANNE FRANK, I was younger than its author was when, at the age of thirteen, she began to write it. I can still picture myself sitting cross-legged on the floor of the bedroom in the house in which I grew up and reading until the daylight faded around me and I had to turn on the lamp. I lost track of my surroundings and felt as if I were entering the Amsterdam attic in which a Jewish girl and her family hid from the Nazis, and where, with the aid of their Dutch "helpers," they survived for two
10 years and a month, until they were betrayed to the authorities, arrested, and deported. I was enthralled by Anne's vivid descriptions of her adored father, Otto; of her conflicts with her mother, Edith, and her sister, Margot; of her romance with Peter van Pels; and of her irritation with Hermann

---

Anne Frank *(1929–1945) was 13 years old when she and her family went into hiding to avoid being sent to concentration camps by the Nazis. During the two years she spent living in an attic, she kept a diary, which she called "Kitty." After the war, Anne's father, the only family member to survive the concentration camps the family was eventually sent to, chose to publish the diary. The selection you are about to read consists of entries taken from throughout the work.*

from
The Diary of a Young Girl

Diary by Anne Frank

SETTING A PURPOSE As you read, think about which of Anne's thoughts and feelings are similar to that of any teenager and which are unique to her family's particularly dire, or urgent, situation.

WEDNESDAY, JANUARY 13, 1943

Dearest Kitty,

This morning I was constantly interrupted, and as a result I haven't been able to finish a single thing I've begun.

We have a new pastime, namely, filling packages with powdered gravy. The gravy is one of Gies & Co.'s[1] products. Mr. Kugler hasn't been able to find anyone else to fill the packages, and besides, it's cheaper if we do the job. It's the kind of work they do in prisons. It's incredibly boring and
10 makes us dizzy and giggly.

Terrible things are happening outside. At any time of night and day, poor helpless people are being dragged out of their homes. They're allowed to take only a knapsack and a

---

[1] **Gies (gēs) & Co.:** the name of Mr. Frank's company in Amsterdam.

"I like to connect literature to history."

Anne Frank's words have brought the tragic realities of the Holocaust to millions.

Background *The first German concentration camps were built only for opponents of the Nazi Party. Later, these camps were also used to imprison Jews and other supposed enemies of the state. Auschwitz, the largest Nazi concentration camp, was opened in 1940 in southern Poland. Inside, prisoners were forced to do work for the Nazi government. Those who were unable to do useful work were killed. Over one million Jews were sent to Auschwitz. Most of them died inside its walls. The camp was finally abandoned by German soldiers as the Russian army advanced upon it in 1945.*

"I want to challenge my students to the utmost."

As a survivor of the camp, Elie Wiesel shares his unique understanding of the evil Auschwitz represented.

After Auschwitz

Speech by Elie Wiesel

Elie Wiesel *(b. 1928) was born in Romania. After the Germans invaded his town, Wiesel and his family were sent to Auschwitz. Only Wiesel and two of his sisters survived. After the war, Wiesel moved to France and became a journalist. It was there that he wrote Night, a book about his experiences at Auschwitz. The book has sold millions of copies in many different languages. Wiesel later moved to the United States. There he devoted himself to ensuring that the deaths of millions of Jews in concentration camps would never be forgotten, and that other human beings would never be subjected to such crimes. In 1986, Wiesel was awarded the Nobel Peace Prize for his life's work.*

SETTING A PURPOSE The horrible crimes committed in Nazi concentration camps occurred long ago. As you read, think about why the author continues to reflect on these events. Why does he believe people need to be reminded of them? Write down any questions you have.

COLLECTION 5 DIGITAL OVERVIEW

mySmartPlanner | eBook | myNotebook | WriteSmart | fyi hmhfyi.com

Collection 5 Lessons	Media	Teach and Practice
**Student Edition	eBook**	▶ Video Links HISTORY A&E	**Close Reading and Evidence Tracking**
ANCHOR TEXT Drama by Frances Goodrich and Albert Hackett *The Diary of Anne Frank*	▶ **Video** HISTORY *Holocaust* ◀ **Audio** *The Diary of Anne Frank*	**Close Read Screencasts** • Modeled Discussion 1 (Act One: lines 124–138) • Modeled Discussion 2 (Act One: lines 2737–2756) • Close Read Application (Act Two: lines 1915–1937) / **Strategies for Annotation** • Analyze Drama • Understand Idioms • Analyze Characters • Analyze Dialogue in Drama
CLOSE READER Drama by Frances Goodrich and Albert Hackett *The Diary of Anne Frank; Act I, Scenes 1 and 2*	◀ **Audio** *The Diary of Anne Frank; Act I, Scenes 1 and 2*	
Diary by Anne Frank *The Diary of a Young Girl*	◀ **Audio** *The Diary of a Young Girl*	**Strategies for Annotation** • Make Inferences • Analyze Text: Elements of a Diary • Connotation and Denotation
Literary Criticism by Francine Prose from *Anne Frank: The Book, The Life, The Afterlife*	◀ **Audio** from *Anne Frank: The Book, The Life, The Afterlife*	**Strategies for Annotation** • Determine Author's Point of View • Analyze the Meaning of Words and Phrases • Latin Suffixes
Speech by Elie Wiesel "After Auschwitz"	▶ **Video** HISTORY *Holocaust* ◀ **Audio** "After Auschwitz"	**Strategies for Annotation** • Analyze Word Choices
Poem by Wislawa Szymborska "There but for the Grace"	◀ **Audio** "There but for the Grace"	**Strategies for Annotation** • Analyze Sound Devices
Collection 5 Performance Tasks: **A** Write an Expository Essay	fyi hmhfyi.com **hmhfyi.com**	**Interactive Lessons** **A** Writing Informative Texts **A** Writing as a Process / **B** Conducting Research
	For Systematic Coverage of Writing and Speaking & Listening Standards	**Interactive Lessons** Writing a Narrative Producing and Publishing with Technology

Assess		Extend	Reteach
Performance Task	**Online Assessment**	**Teacher eBook**	**Teacher eBook**
Writing Activity: Character Sketch	Selection Test	**Analyze Characters > Interactive Whiteboard Lesson >** Character Development	**Analyze Elements of Drama > Level Up Tutorial >** Elements of Drama
Speaking Activity: Performance	Selection Test	**Compare and Contrast Structure > Interactive Graphic Organizer >** Comparison-Contrast Chart	**Analyze Text: Elements of a Diary**
Writing Activity: Analysis	Selection Test	**Evaluate Reasoning**	**Determine Author's Point of View > Level Up Tutorial >** Author's Perspective
Speaking Activity: Discussion	Selection Test	**Analyze Elements of a Speech**	**Analyze Persuasive Techniques > Level Up Tutorial >** Persuasive Techniques
Writing Activity: Analysis	Selection Test	**Theme > Interactive Whiteboard Lesson >** Theme/Central Idea **Paraphrase** **Analyze Imagery > Interactive Whiteboard Lesson >** Figurative Language and Imagery	**Analyze Sound Devices > Level Up Tutorial >** Elements of Poetry
A Write an Expository Essay	Collection Test		

Lesson Assessments
Writing a Narrative
Producing and Publishing with Technology

Collection 5 Lessons	Key Learning Objective	Performance Task
ANCHOR TEXT **Drama by Frances Goodrich and Albert Hackett** *The Diary of Anne Frank*, **p. 279A**	**The student will be able to . . .** analyze the key elements of a drama, including its structure, characters, dialogue, and events.	Writing Activity: Character Sketch
Diary by Anne Frank *The Diary of a Young Girl*, **p. 355A** **Lexile 1020L**	**The student will be able to . . .** analyze the elements of a diary entry, and make and support inferences about the text.	Speaking Activity: Performance
Literary Criticism by Francine Prose from *Anne Frank: The Book, The Life, The Afterlife*, **p. 369A** **Lexile 1410L**	**The student will be able to . . .** determine an author's point of view in a work of literary criticism and analyze how the author's word choices impact the tone of the text.	Writing Activity: Analysis
Speech by Elie Wiesel "After Auschwitz," **p. 379A**	**The student will be able to . . .** identify persuasive techniques and rhetorical devices in a speech.	Speaking Activity: Discussion
Poem by Wislawa Szymborska "There but for the Grace," **p. 385A**	**The student will be able to . . .** analyze the use of sound devices in a poem to understand how they impact meaning.	Writing Activity: Analysis

Collection 5 Performance Tasks:
A Write an Expository Essay

Vocabulary Strategy	Language and Style	Student Instructional Support	CLOSE READER Selection
		Scaffolding for ELL Students: • Analyze Language: Setting Details • Understand Idioms • Analyze Language: Adverbs **When Students Struggle:** • Analyze Ellipses and Sentence Fragments • Track Sequence of Events • Analyze Relationships **To Challenge Students:** • Analyze Motivation • Analyze the Impact of Perspective • Debate Issues • Analyze the Impact of Setting	Drama by Frances Goodrich and Albert Hackett *The Diary of Anne Frank* Act I, Scenes 1 and 2, p. 354b
Connotation and Denotation		**Scaffolding for ELL Students:** Analyze Language: Suffixes **When Students Struggle:** Analyze Figurative Language **To Challenge Students:** Analyze the Diary's Effect	
Latin Suffixes	Use Ellipses	**Scaffolding for ELL Students:** Analyze Language: Prepositional Phrases **When Students Struggle:** Track Differing Views **To Challenge Students:** Analyze Voice	
		Scaffolding for ELL Students: Analyze Context **When Students Struggle:** Analyze Imagery **To Challenge Students:** Analyze the Speaker	
		Scaffolding for ELL Students: Punctuation and Print Cues **When Students Struggle:** Track Opposites	

ANCHOR TEXT EXEMPLAR

The Diary of Anne Frank

Play by Frances Goodrich and Albert Hackett

Why This Text?

The Holocaust was a defining event of the 20th century, and to many, Anne Frank has become its face. Her story of courage and hope is brought to life through the dialogue in this play, helping students understand in some small degree the ways this tragedy touched the lives of ordinary families not unlike their own.

Key Learning Objective: The student will be able to analyze the key elements of a drama, including its structure, characters, dialogue, and events.

For practice and application:

Close Reader selection
The Diary of Anne Frank (Act One, Scenes 1 and 2),
Play by Frances Goodrich and Albert Hackett

COMMON CORE | Common Core Standards

RL 1 Cite textual evidence that supports inferences.

RL 3 Analyze how dialogue or incidents in a drama propel the action, reveal aspects of a character, or provoke a decision.

RL 4 Determine the meaning of words and phrases in a text.

RL 6 Analyze how differences in points of view create suspense.

W 4 Produce clear and coherent writing.

W 9a Apply grade 8 Reading standards to literature.

W 10 Write routinely over extended time frames and shorter time frames.

SL 1a Come to discussions prepared.

SL 6 Adapt speech to a variety of contexts and tasks.

L 5a Interpret figures of speech in context.

▲ Text Complexity Rubric

Quantitative Measures	The Diary of Anne Frank
	Lexile: N/A

Qualitative Measures	
	Levels of Meaning/Purpose multiple levels of meaning (multiple themes)
	Structure no major shifts in chronology; occasional use of flashback
	Language Conventionality and Clarity some unfamiliar language
	Knowledge Demands distinctly unfamiliar experience

Reader/Task Considerations	Teacher determined Vary by individual reader and type of text

TEACH

CLOSE READ

Background Have students read the background information about Anne Frank and her family. Explain that after the Nazis found the Franks' hiding place the family was sent to the Auschwitz concentration camp in Poland. At the camp, the men and women were separated, and Mr. Frank never saw his wife and daughters again. Anne and her sister were eventually transferred to another concentration camp, Bergen-Belsen.

After the war, Mr. Frank returned to Amsterdam and discovered Anne's diary, which had been found and saved by a friend. The diary, originally published in Dutch in 1947, has now been printed in many other languages. This has allowed millions of people around the world to read Anne's words.

SETTING A PURPOSE Direct students to use the Setting a Purpose question to focus their reading. Remind students to generate questions as they read.

Analyze Drama

COMMON CORE **RL 1**

Tell students that a **drama,** or play, is a form of literature meant to be performed by actors for an audience. The author of a play is called a **playwright,** and the text of a play is called a **script.**

A ASK STUDENTS to read the background information about the playwrights. What did the playwrights use as the source of information for their script? *(They based their script on Anne Frank's diary entries.)* Why is it important for readers to know how the playwrights used Anne's diary? *(It is important to remember that the play is based on Anne's diary, but it is not an exact account of what happened.)*

HISTORY VIDEO

The Diary of Anne Frank

Play by Frances Goodrich and Albert Hackett

Background *Anne Frank and her family were Jewish citizens of Germany. When the Nazi party, led by Adolf Hitler, came to power in 1933, the Nazis blamed the country's problems on the Jews. Jews were stripped of their rights. Many were eventually sent to concentration camps, where more than 6 million died in what became known as the Holocaust. The Franks moved to the Netherlands to escape persecution, but the Nazis invaded that country in 1940. In order to survive, Anne's family went into hiding when she was 13 years old. They hid in attic rooms behind Mr. Frank's office, and several other Jews joined them. In this "Secret Annex," Anne kept a diary about her life in hiding. More than two years later, the group's worst fears came true when the Nazis found them. Everyone who had been living there was sent to concentration camps. Anne's diary was discovered later.*

Frances Goodrich (1890–1984) *and* **Albert Hackett** (1900–1995) *were a married couple who worked together to write screenplays for movies. They wrote the play called* The Diary of Anne Frank *based on Anne's actual diary entries. Although the play differs from the diary in many ways, Anne's father, who survived the Holocaust, believed it captured the essence of his daughter's diary. The play won a Pulitzer Prize for Drama. It was later made into a movie.*

SETTING A PURPOSE As you read, think about what the play reveals about Anne Frank's philosophy of life. How are her thoughts communicated?

(tr) ©Alex Kalmbach/Shutterstock; (t) ©Rasmus Holmboe Dahl/Shutterstock; (br) © Bettmann/CORBIS

The Diary of Anne Frank: Act One **279**

Close Read Screencasts

 ▶ *View It!*

Modeled Discussions

Have students click the *Close Read* icons in their eBooks to access two screencasts in which readers discuss and annotate the following key passages:

- The audience hears Anne's voice join Mr. Frank's as he reads from her diary (Act One: lines 124–138).
- Residents of the Annex fear their hiding place has been discovered (Act One: lines 2737–2756).

As a class, view and discuss at least one of these videos. Then, have students work in pairs to do an independent close read of an additional passage—Mr. Frank's description of events after he was released from the camp (Act Two: lines 1915–1937).

CLOSE READ

Analyze Drama

COMMON CORE **RL 1**

Explain that the script of a play includes a **cast of characters,** a list of all the characters in the play. Sometimes this list may include additional information about some or all of the characters.

B **ASK STUDENTS** to review the cast of characters at the beginning of the play. How many families are living in the Secret Annex? Who are the members of each family? *(There are two families; Anne, Margot, Mr. Frank, and Mrs. Frank are members of the Frank family; the Van Daan family is made up of Peter, Mr. Van Daan, and Mrs. Van Daan.)*

Point out to students that in addition to a cast of characters a script also includes stage directions. **Stage directions** are instructions that give readers, actors, the director, and the stage crew important details that explain what is happening in the play. Explain that stage directions are often in italic type and include information about the **setting,** the time and place of the action.

C **ASK STUDENTS** to reread the stage directions that appear below the listing of characters. During what years does this play take place? *(1942–1945)* In what city does it take place? *(Amsterdam, Netherlands)* Why do you think the stage directions include a description of the sounds outside the Annex? *(Possible answer: Because the residents can't go outside, the sounds they hear are very important. They remind readers that these sounds are one of the few sources of information the residents have about the outside world. The church bells tell the time. The "marching feet" are a constant reminder that German soldiers are close by.)*

SCAFFOLDING FOR ELL STUDENTS

Analyze Language Because the layout of the Secret Annex is key to understanding the events in the play, be sure students are able to visualize the space. Guide them to identify prepositional phrases that help to describe the setting. Have volunteers mark up the text.

- Highlight in yellow phrases beginning with *on, in,* or *of.*

ASK STUDENTS what the setting details suggest about the space.

B

CHARACTERS

SECRET ANNEX RESIDENTS

Anne Frank	Peter Van Daan
Margot Frank	Mr. Van Daan
Mr. Frank	Mrs. Van Daan
Mrs. Frank	Mr. Dussel

WORKERS IN MR. FRANK'S BUSINESS

Miep Gies (mēp gēs)

Mr. Kraler (krä´lər)

The Time. *July 1942–August 1944, November 1945*

The Place. *Amsterdam, the Netherlands*

The scene remains the same throughout the play. It is the top floor of a warehouse and office building in Amsterdam, Holland. The sharply peaked roof of the building is outlined against a sea of other rooftops, stretching away into the distance. Nearby is the belfry of a church tower, the Westertoren, whose carillon rings out the hours. Occasionally faint sounds float up from below: the voices of children playing in the street, the tramp of marching feet, a boat whistle from the canal.

C

The three rooms of the top floor and a small attic space above are exposed to our view. The largest of the rooms is in the center, with two small rooms, slightly raised, on either side. On the right is a bathroom, out of sight. A narrow steep flight of stairs at the back leads up to the attic. The rooms are sparsely furnished with a few chairs, cots, a table or two. The windows are painted over, or covered with makeshift blackout curtains. In the main room there is a sink, a gas ring for cooking and a wood-burning stove for warmth.

The room on the left is hardly more than a closet. There is a skylight in the sloping ceiling. Directly under this room is a small steep stairwell, with steps leading down to a door. This is the only entrance from the building below. When the door is opened we see that it has been concealed on the outer side by a bookcase attached to it.

The three rooms of the top floor and a small attic space above are exposed to our view. The largest of the rooms is in the center, with two small rooms, slightly raised on either side. On the right is a bathroom, out of sight. A narrow steep flight of stairs at the back leads up to the

©Bettmann/Corbis

ACT ONE

Scene 1

The curtain rises on an empty stage. It is late afternoon November, 1945.

The rooms are dusty, the curtains in rags. Chairs and tables are overturned.

The door at the foot of the small stairwell swings open. Mr. Frank comes up the steps into view. He is 10 *a gentle, cultured European in his* middle years. There is still a trace of a German accent in his speech.

He stands looking slowly around, making a supreme effort at self-control. He is weak, ill. His clothes are threadbare.

After a second he drops his rucksack on the couch and moves slowly about. He opens the door to 20 *one of the smaller rooms, and then abruptly closes it again, turning away. He goes to the window at the back, looking off at the Westertoren as its carillon strikes the hour of six, then he moves restlessly on.*

The Diary of Anne Frank: Act One **281**

CLOSE READ

Analyze Drama

COMMON CORE RL 1

(HEADINGS, LINES 1–25)

Tell students that the **structure** of a literary work is the way in which it is arranged or organized. The script of a play is often divided into sections. An **act** is a major section in a play, similar to a chapter in a book. An act may be divided into smaller sections, called **scenes.**

D ASK STUDENTS to explain which act and scene begin the play. *(Act One, Scene 1)*

As needed, explain that stage directions include different kinds of information, such as details about scenery, lighting, sound effects, and ways for actors to move and speak.

E CITE TEXT EVIDENCE Have students reread lines 1–25 to identify the different types of information found in these stage directions. What does the audience see on the stage when the curtain rises? *(They see empty rooms that are dusty. The curtains are tattered. The chairs and tables are turned over.)* What kinds of information do the stage directions give about Mr. Frank? *(The directions tell Mr. Frank's age and manner; they explain how he looks, sounds, feels, and moves.)* What does the description suggest about Mr. Frank? *(Possible answer: He has been through a difficult ordeal.)*

Analyze Characters

COMMON CORE RL 1, RL 3

(LINES 26–37)

Tell students that one way authors reveal what characters are like is through their actions.

 CITE TEXT EVIDENCE Have students reread lines 26–37 to identify Mr. Frank's thoughts and feelings. How does the white glove affect Mr. Frank? *("all his self-control is gone. He breaks down crying.")* What does this detail reveal about him? *(Possible answer: The glove probably belonged to someone he loved. He is caring and sensitive.)*

Analyze Drama

COMMON CORE RL 1, RL 3

(LINES 91–103)

Remind students that stage directions in a script provide important information about how to perform a play. Point out that these directions are sometimes set off in parentheses to separate them from the words characters say.

 ASK STUDENTS to identify the various stage directions in lines 91–103. What do these directions say that Miep does? *(She gets a bundle of papers from a cupboard and gives it to Mr. Frank.)* What do the directions indicate that Mr. Frank does? *(He puts the white glove he found into his rucksack.)* Why is it important to know that Mr. Frank saves the glove but wants his papers to be burned? *(The glove represents a part of his former life that is still meaningful to him; he thinks the papers do not.)*

WHEN STUDENTS STRUGGLE...

Help students access the text by understanding the use of ellipses and sentence fragments in dialogue. Using a whiteboard, highlight examples of both:

- Explain that an ellipsis is a punctuation mark that consists of three dots. It is used to indicate a pause, an interruption, or speech that trails off.
- Tell students that dialogue is written the way people actually speak, so sometimes words are left out.

Have students read aloud passages that include ellipses so they can hear how each character's voice would sound. In addition, have them identify any omitted words.

From the street below we hear the sound of a barrel organ and children's voices at play. There is a many-colored scarf hanging from a
30 *nail. Mr. Frank takes it, putting it around his neck. As he starts back for his rucksack, his eye is caught by something lying on the floor. It is a woman's white glove. He holds it in his hand and suddenly all of his self-control is gone. He breaks down, crying.*

We hear footsteps on the stairs. Miep Gies comes up, looking for
40 *Mr. Frank. Miep is a Dutch girl of about twenty-two. She wears a coat and hat, ready to go home. She is pregnant. Her attitude toward Mr. Frank is protective, compassionate.*

Miep. Are you all right, Mr. Frank?

Mr. Frank (*quickly controlling himself*). Yes, Miep, yes.

Miep. Everyone in the office has
50 gone home . . . It's after six. (*then pleading*) Don't stay up here, Mr. Frank. What's the use of torturing yourself like this?

Mr. Frank. I've come to say good-bye . . . I'm leaving here, Miep.

Miep. What do you mean? Where are you going? Where?

Mr. Frank. I don't know yet. I haven't decided.

60 **Miep.** Mr. Frank, you can't leave here! This is your home! Amsterdam is your home. Your business is here, waiting for you . . . You're needed here . . . Now that

the war is over, there are things that . . .

Mr. Frank. I can't stay in Amsterdam, Miep. It has too many memories for me.
70 Everywhere there's something . . . the house we lived in . . . the school . . . that street organ playing out there . . . I'm not the person you used to know, Miep. I'm a bitter old man. (*breaking off*) Forgive me. I shouldn't speak to you like this . . . after all that you did for us . . . the suffering . . .

Miep. No. No. It wasn't suffering.
80 You can't say we suffered. (*As she speaks, she straightens a chair which is overturned.*)

Mr. Frank. I know what you went through, you and Mr. Kraler. I'll remember it as long as I live. (*He gives one last look around.*) Come, Miep.

(*He starts for the steps, then remembers his rucksack, going back*
90 *to get it.*)

Miep (*hurrying up to a cupboard*). Mr. Frank, did you see? There are some of your papers here. (*She brings a bundle of papers to him.*) We found them in a heap of rubbish on the floor after . . . after you left.

Mr. Frank. Burn them.

(*He opens his rucksack to put the*
100 *glove in it.*)

Miep. But, Mr. Frank, there are letters, notes . . .

Mr. Frank. Burn them. All of them.

Mr. Frank. I can't stay in Amsterdam, Miep. It has too many memories for me. Everywhere there's something . . . the house we lived in . . . the school . . . that street organ playing out there . . . I'm not the person you used to know, Miep. I'm a bitter old man. (*breaking off*) Forgive me. I

Miep. Burn *this?*

(*She hands him a paperbound notebook.*)

Mr. Frank (*quietly*). Anne's diary. (*He opens the diary and begins to read.*) "Monday, the sixth of July,
110 nineteen forty-two." (*to Miep*) Nineteen forty-two. Is it possible, Miep? . . . Only three years ago. (*As he continues his reading, he sits down on the couch.*) "Dear Diary, since you and I are going to be great friends, I will start by telling you about myself. My name is Anne Frank. I am thirteen years old. I was born in Germany the
120 twelfth of June, nineteen twenty-nine. As my family is Jewish, we emigrated to Holland when Hitler came to power."

(*As* Mr. Frank *reads on, another voice joins his, as if coming from the air. It is* Anne's Voice.)

Mr. Frank and Anne. "My father started a business, importing spice and herbs. Things went well for us
130 until nineteen forty. Then the war came, and the Dutch capitulation, followed by the arrival of the Germans. Then things got very bad for the Jews."

(Mr. Frank's Voice *dies out.* Anne's Voice *continues alone. The lights dim slowly to darkness. The curtain falls on the scene.*)

Anne's Voice. You could not do
140 this and you could not do that. They forced Father out of his business. We had to wear yellow

stars.¹ I had to turn in my bike. I couldn't go to a Dutch school any more. I couldn't go to the movies, or ride in an automobile, or even on a streetcar, and a million other things. But somehow we children still managed to have
150 fun. Yesterday Father told me we were going into hiding. Where, he wouldn't say. At five o'clock this morning Mother woke me and told me to hurry and get dressed. I was to put on as many clothes as I could. It would look too suspicious if we walked along carrying suitcases. It wasn't until we were on our way that I learned
160 where we were going. Our hiding place was to be upstairs in the building where Father used to have his business. Three other people were coming in with us . . . the Van Daans and their son Peter . . . Father knew the Van Daans but we had never met them . . .

(*During the last lines the curtain rises on the scene. The lights dim on.*
170 Anne's Voice *fades out.*)

Scene 2

It is early morning, July, 1942. The rooms are bare, as before, but they are now clean and orderly.

Mr. Van Daan, *a tall, portly man in his late forties, is in the main room, pacing up and down, nervously smoking a cigarette. His*

---

¹ **yellow stars:** the six-pointed Stars of David that the Nazis ordered all Jews to wear for identification.

The Diary of Anne Frank: Act One **283**

CLOSE READ

 For more content and historical background, students can view the video "Holocaust" in their eBooks.

Analyze Language
COMMON CORE RL 1, RL 4

(LINES 124–138)

Point out to students that the script of a play always indicates which character or characters are speaking.

H **ASK STUDENTS** to reread lines 124–138. What shift takes place in who is saying the words from Anne's diary? (*First Mr. Frank is reading, then Anne's voice joins him, and then the audience hears only Anne's voice.*) What is the impact of this shift in speakers? How does it affect the tone, or feeling of the scene? (*The playwrights are emphasizing that there is a shift in time, moving from the present to the past. The tone changes from one of sadness, when Mr. Frank speaks, to a more hopeful one, as Anne speaks.*)

Analyze Drama
COMMON CORE RL 1, RL 3

(LINES 171–173)

Remind students that an act in a play is often divided into smaller sections called scenes. Explain that a playwright often creates a new scene when the time or place of the action has changed.

I **ASK STUDENTS** to explain why a new scene begins at line 171. (*The time has changed from the present to the past. Scene 1 took place in 1945; it is now 1942.*)

Analyze Characters

COMMON CORE RL 1, RL 3

(LINES 180–193)

Tell students that another way an audience gets to know and understand characters is through descriptions of their physical appearance.

 CITE TEXT EVIDENCE Have students reread lines 180–193 to note the physical appearance of Mrs. Van Daan and her son, Peter. What does Mrs. Van Daan look like? *("She is a pretty woman in her early forties," and wears a fur coat. She is "clutching her possessions.")* How does Peter Van Daan look? *(He is sixteen; he "is a shy, awkward boy"; he has a cat carrier.)* What do these details reveal about Mrs. Van Daan? about Peter? *(Possible answer: Because Mrs. Van Daan is "clutching" her belongings, they are probably very important to her. As a boy who is "shy, awkward," Peter may have difficulty living with the Frank family because he has never met them.)*

Analyze Drama

COMMON CORE RL 1, RL 3

(LINES 196–207)

Explain that **dialogue** is the written conversation between two or more characters. Point out the format for dialogue in a play: the name of a character is given, followed by the words that he or she speaks.

 ASK STUDENTS to reread lines 196–207. What two characters are having a dialogue here? *(Mrs. Van Daan and Mr. Van Daan)* What do the ellipses in the dialogue indicate? *(The ellipses show where there is a break or pause in the dialogue as the characters interrupt one another.)* What does the dialogue reveal about Mrs. Van Daan? *(She is nervous and excited; she is afraid that the Franks have been arrested by the Nazis.)*

---

clothes and overcoat are expensive and well cut.

180 Mrs. Van Daan *sits on the couch, clutching her possessions, a hatbox, bags, etc. She is a pretty woman in her early forties. She wears a fur coat over her other clothes.*

Peter Van Daan *is standing at the window of the room on the right, looking down at the street below. He is a shy, awkward boy of* 190 *sixteen. He wears a cap, a raincoat, and long Dutch trousers, like "plus fours." At his feet is a black case, a carrier for his cat.*

The yellow Star of David is conspicuous on all of their clothes.

Mrs. Van Daan (*rising, nervous, excited*). Something's happened to them! I know it!

Mr. Van Daan. Now, Kerli!

200 **Mrs. Van Daan.** Mr. Frank said they'd be here at seven o'clock. He said . . .

Mr. Van Daan. They have two miles to walk. You can't expect . . .

Mrs. Van Daan. They've been picked up. That's what's happened. They've been taken . . .

(Mr. Van Daan *indicates that he hears someone coming.*)

210 **Mr. Van Daan.** You see?

(Peter *takes up his carrier and his schoolbag, etc., and goes into the main room as* Mr. Frank *comes up the stairwell from below.* Mr. Frank *looks much younger now. His movements are brisk, his manner*

confident. He wears an overcoat and carries his hat and a small cardboard box. He crosses to the 220 Van Daans, *shaking hands with each of them.*)

Mr. Frank. Mrs. Van Daan, Mr. Van Daan, Peter. (*then, in explanation of their lateness*) There were too many of the Green Police[2] on the streets . . . we had to take the long way around.

(*Up the steps come* Margot Frank, Mrs. Frank, Miep [*not pregnant now*] *and* Mr. Kraler. *All of them* 230 *carry bags, packages, and so forth. The Star of David is conspicuous on all of the Franks' clothing.* Margot *is eighteen, beautiful, quiet, shy.* Mrs. Frank *is a young mother, gently bred, reserved. She, like* Mr. Frank, *has a slight German accent.* Mr. Kraler *is a Dutchman, dependable, kindly.*

240 As Mr. Kraler *and* Miep *go upstage to put down their parcels,* Mrs. Frank *turns back to call* Anne.)

Mrs. Frank. Anne?

(Anne *comes running up the stairs. She is thirteen, quick in her movements, interested in everything, mercurial in her emotions. She wears a cape, long* 250 *wool socks and carries a schoolbag.*)

Mr. Frank (*introducing them*). My wife, Edith. Mr. and Mrs. Van Daan (Mrs. Frank *hurries over, shaking hands with them.*) . . .

---

[2] **Green Police:** the Nazi police who wore green uniforms.

their son, Peter . . . my daughters, Margot and Anne.

(*Anne gives a polite little curtsy as she shakes* Mr. Van Daan's *hand. Then she immediately starts off on a tour of investigation of her new home, going upstairs to the attic room.* Miep *and* Mr. Kraler *are putting the various things they have brought on the shelves.*)

Mr. Kraler. I'm sorry there is still so much confusion.

Mr. Frank. Please. Don't think of it. After all, we'll have plenty of leisure to arrange everything ourselves.

Miep (*to* Mrs. Frank). We put the stores of food you sent in here. Your drugs are here . . . soap, linen here.

Mrs. Frank. Thank you, Miep.

Miep. I made up the beds . . . the way Mr. Frank and Mr. Kraler said. (*She starts out.*) Forgive me. I have to hurry. I've got to go to the other side of town to get some ration books[3] for you.

Mrs. Van Daan. Ration books? If they see our names on ration books, they'll know we're here.

Mr. Kraler. There isn't anything . . . ⎫
Miep. Don't worry. Your names won't be on them. (*as she hurries out*) I'll be up later. ⎭ *Together*

---
[3] **ration books:** books of stamps or coupons issued by the government in wartime. With these coupons, people could purchase scarce items, such as food, clothing, and gasoline.

Mr. Frank. Thank you, Miep.

Mrs. Frank (*to* Mr. Kraler). It's illegal, then, the ration books? We've never done anything illegal.

Mr. Frank. We won't be living here exactly according to regulations. (*As* Mr. Kraler *reassures* Mrs. Frank, *he takes various small things, such as matches, soap, etc., from his pockets, handing them to her.*)

Mr. Kraler. This isn't the black market,[4] Mrs. Frank. This is what we call the white market . . . helping all of the hundreds and hundreds who are hiding out in Amsterdam.

(*The carillon is heard playing the quarter-hour before eight.* Mr. Kraler *looks at his watch.* Anne *stops at the window as she comes down the stairs.*)

Anne. It's the Westertoren!

Mr. Kraler. I must go. I must be out of here and downstairs in the office before the workmen get here. (*He starts for the stairs leading out.*) Miep or I, or both of us, will be up each day to bring you food and news and find out what your needs are. Tomorrow I'll get you a better bolt for the door at the foot of the stairs. It needs a bolt that you can throw yourself and open only at our signal. (*to* Mr. Frank) Oh . . . You'll tell them about the noise?

Mr. Frank. I'll tell them.

---
[4] **black market:** a system for selling goods illegally, in violation of rationing and other restrictions.

The Diary of Anne Frank: Act One **285**

CLOSE READ

Analyze Language

COMMON CORE RL 4

(LINES 291–306)

Prompt students to consider some of the moral and legal dilemmas people faced during the Holocaust.

Ⓛ ASK STUDENTS to examine lines 291–306. Why is Mrs. Frank concerned about the legality of the ration books? (*She has always been law abiding; even though she is being treated so unfairly, she wants to remain honest.*) What is the impact of Mr. Kraler's distinction between the "black market" and the "white market"? (*His contrast suggests that the "black market" is a bad thing, while implying that what he is doing, although technically illegal, is good and moral.*)

Analyze Characters   COMMON CORE RL 1, RL 3

(LINES 334–337)

Tell students that another way an audience gets to know and understand a character is through the reactions of other characters in the play.

Ⓜ ASK STUDENTS to reread lines 334–337. What does this comment by Mr. Kraler reveal about Mr. Frank? *(Mr. Frank is highly respected by others.)*

Mr. Kraler. Good-bye then for the moment. I'll come up again, after the workmen leave.

330 **Mr. Frank.** Good-bye, Mr. Kraler.

Mrs. Frank (*shaking his hand*). How can we thank you? (*The others murmur their good-byes.*)

Mr. Kraler. I never thought I'd live to see the day when a man like Mr. Frank would have to go into hiding. When you think—(*He breaks off, going out. Mr. Frank follows him down the steps, bolting the door after* 340 *him. In the interval before he returns,* Peter *goes over to* Margot, *shaking hands with her. As* Mr. Frank *comes back up the steps,* Mrs. Frank *questions him anxiously.*)

Mrs. Frank. What did he mean, about the noise?

Mr. Frank. First let us take off some of these clothes. (*They all start to take off garment after garment. On* 350 *each of their coats, sweaters, blouses, suits, dresses, is another yellow Star of David. Mr. and* Mrs. Frank *are underdressed quite simply. The others wear several things, sweaters, extra dresses, bathrobes, aprons, nightgowns, etc.*)

Mr. Van Daan. It's a wonder we weren't arrested, walking along the streets . . . Petronella with a 360 fur coat in July . . . and that cat of Peter's crying all the way.

Anne (*as she is removing a pair of panties*). A cat?

Mrs. Frank (*shocked*). Anne, please!

Anne. It's all right. I've got on three more. (*She pulls off two more. Finally, as they have all removed their surplus clothes, they look to Mr. Frank, waiting for him* 370 *to speak.*)

Mr. Frank. Now. About the noise. While the men are in the building below, we must have complete quiet. Every sound can be heard down there, not only in the workrooms, but in the offices too. The men come at about eight-thirty, and leave at about five-thirty. So, to be perfectly safe, 380 from eight in the morning until six in the evening we must move only when it is necessary, and then in stockinged feet. We must not speak above a whisper. We must not run any water. We cannot use the sink, or even, forgive me, the w.c.[5] The pipes go down through the workrooms. It would be heard. No trash . . . (*Mr. Frank stops* 390 *abruptly as he hears the sound of marching feet from the street below. Everyone is motionless, paralyzed with fear. Mr. Frank goes quietly into the room on the right to look down out of the window. Anne runs after him, peering out with him. The tramping feet pass without stopping. The tension is relieved. Mr. Frank, followed by Anne, returns to* 400 *the main room and resumes his instructions to the group.*) . . . No trash must ever be thrown out which might reveal that someone is living up here . . . not even a potato

---

[5] **w.c.:** water closet; toilet.

paring. We must burn everything in the stove at night. This is the way we must live until it is over, if we are to survive.

(*There is silence for a second.*)

410 **Mrs. Frank.** Until it is over.

Mr. Frank (*reassuringly*). After six we can move about . . . we can talk and laugh and have our supper and read and play games . . . just as we would at home. (*He looks at his watch.*) And now I think it would be wise if we all went to our rooms, and were settled before eight o'clock. Mrs. Van Daan, you

420 and your husband will be upstairs. I regret that there's no place up there for Peter. But he will be here, near us. This will be our common room, where we'll meet to talk and eat and read, like one family.

Mr. Van Daan. And where do you and Mrs. Frank sleep?

Mr. Frank. This room is also our bedroom.

430 **Mrs. Van Daan.** That isn't right. We'll sleep here and you take the room upstairs. } *Together*

Mr. Van Daan. It's your place. }

Mr. Frank. Please. I've thought this out for weeks. It's the best arrangement. The only arrangement.

Mrs. Van Daan (*to* Mr. Frank).
440 Never, never can we thank you. (*then to* Mrs. Frank) I don't know what would have happened to us, if it hadn't been for Mr. Frank.

Mr. Frank. You don't know how your husband helped me when I came to this country . . . knowing no one . . . not able to speak the language. I can never repay him for that. (*going to* Van Daan) May
450 I help you with your things?

Mr. Van Daan. No. No. (*to* Mrs. Van Daan) Come along, *liefje.*[6]

Mrs. Van Daan. You'll be all right, Peter? You're not afraid?

Peter (*embarrassed*). Please, Mother.

(*They start up the stairs to the attic room above.* Mr. Frank *turns to* Mrs. Frank.)

460 **Mr. Frank.** You too must have some rest, Edith. You didn't close your eyes last night. Nor you, Margot.

Anne. I slept, Father. Wasn't that funny? I knew it was the last night in my own bed, and yet I slept soundly.

Mr. Frank. I'm glad, Anne. Now you'll be able to help me straighten things in here. (*to* Mrs. Frank *and*
470 Margot) Come with me . . . You and Margot rest in this room for the time being. (*He picks up their clothes, starting for the room on the right.*)

Mrs. Frank. You're sure . . . ? I could help . . . And Anne hasn't had her milk . . .

Mr. Frank. I'll give it to her. (*to* Anne *and* Peter) Anne, Peter . . .
480 it's best that you take off your

---
[6] *liefje* (lēf´yə) *Dutch*: little darling.

The Diary of Anne Frank: Act One **287**

CLOSE READ

Analyze Language

COMMON CORE RL 1, RL 4

(LINES 453–456)

Direct students' attention to the language Mrs. Van Daan and Peter use as they speak to one another.

Ⓝ ASK STUDENTS to reread the dialogue in lines 453–456. Why does Mrs. Van Daan think Peter might be afraid? (*His parents will be sleeping in an upstairs room away from him. Peter will be sleeping in a room below with the Franks, a family he doesn't know.*) What does Peter mean when he says "Please, Mother"? (*Possible answer: "Please don't embarrass me, Mother. I'm not a little boy, and I'll be fine."*)

APPLYING ACADEMIC VOCABULARY

communicate	philosophy

As you discuss the selection, incorporate the following Collection 5 academic vocabulary words: *communicate* and *philosophy*. Have students describe the ways various characters **communicate** with one another. Are they patient? thoughtful? rude? For example, in line 452, Mr. Van Daan communicates with his wife in a tender way when he calls her *liefje*. Ask students to comment on what the characters' words and actions reveal about their **philosophy** of life.

Analyze Drama

COMMON CORE · RL 1, RL 3

(LINES 498–516)

Remind students that stage directions provide important information about how a scene in a play should be performed.

Ⓞ CITE TEXT EVIDENCE Have students reread lines 498–516, paying particular attention to the stage directions. What do the stage directions indicate about how the performers should interact with Peter's cat? *(Peter takes his cat out of its carrier. Anne picks up the cat and walks away with it. Then, Peter takes the cat from her and puts it back in the carrier.)* What do these directions reveal about Peter? *(Possible answer: He is very possessive about his cat.)*

Analyze Language

COMMON CORE · RL 3, RL 4

(LINES 530–540)

Explain that when authors draw a **contrast** they identify the differences in two or more subjects.

Ⓟ ASK STUDENTS to reread lines 530–540. What does Peter mean when he says he is "a lone wolf"? *(He is someone who prefers to act or be alone.)* What contrast do the playwrights reveal between Anne and Peter in this passage? *(While Anne is very social and enjoys being with others, Peter prefers being alone.)*

---

shoes now, before you forget. (*He leads the way to the room, followed by* Margot.)

Mrs. Frank. You're sure you're not tired, Anne?

Anne. I feel fine. I'm going to help Father.

Mrs. Frank. Peter, I'm glad you are to be with us.

490 **Peter.** Yes, Mrs. Frank.

(Mrs. Frank *goes to join* Mr. Frank *and* Margot.)(*During the following scene* Mr. Frank *helps* Margot *and* Mrs. Frank *to hang up their clothes. Then he persuades them both to lie down and rest. The* Van Daans *in their room above settle themselves. In the main room* Anne *and* Peter *remove their shoes.* Peter *takes his*

500 *cat out of the carrier.*)

Anne. What's your cat's name?

Peter. Mouschi.[7]

Anne. Mouschi! Mouschi! Mouschi! (*She picks up the cat, walking away with it. To* Peter.) I love cats. I have one . . . a darling little cat. But they made me leave her behind. I left some food and a note for the neighbors to take care

510 of her . . . I'm going to miss her terribly. What is yours? A him or a her?

Peter. He's a tom. He doesn't like strangers.

(*He takes the cat from her, putting it back in its carrier.*)

---

[7] **Mouschi** (mōō´shē)

Anne (*unabashed*). Then I'll have to stop being a stranger, won't I? Is he fixed?

520 **Peter** (*startled*). Huh?

Anne. Did you have him fixed?

Peter. No.

Anne. Oh, you ought to have him fixed—to keep him from—you know, fighting. Where did you go to school?

Peter. Jewish Secondary.

Anne. But that's where Margot and I go! I never saw you around.

530 **Peter.** I used to see you . . . sometimes . . .

Anne. You did?

Peter. . . . in the school yard. You were always in the middle of a bunch of kids. (*He takes a penknife from his pocket.*)

Anne. Why didn't you ever come over?

Peter. I'm sort of a lone wolf. (*He*

540 *starts to rip off his Star of David.*)

Anne. What are you doing?

Peter. Taking it off.

Anne. But you can't do that. They'll arrest you if you go out without your star.

(*He tosses his knife on the table.*)

Peter. Who's going out?

Anne. Why, of course! You're right! Of course we don't need them any

550 more. (*She picks up his knife and starts to take her star off.*) I wonder

what our friends will think when we don't show up today?

Peter. I didn't have any dates with anyone.

Anne. Oh, I did. I had a date with Jopie to go and play ping-pong at her house. Do you know Jopie de Waal?[8]

560 **Peter.** No.

Anne. Jopie's my best friend. I wonder what she'll think when she telephones and there's no answer? . . . Probably she'll go over to the house . . . I wonder what she'll think . . . we left everything as if we'd suddenly been called away . . . breakfast dishes in the sink . . . beds not made . . .

570 (*As she pulls off her star, the cloth underneath shows clearly the color and form of the star.*) Look! It's still there! (*Peter goes over to the stove with his star.*) What're you going to do with yours?

Peter. Burn it.

Anne (*She starts to throw hers in, and cannot.*) It's funny, I can't throw mine away. I don't

580 know why.

Peter. You can't throw . . . ? Something they branded you with . . . ? That they made you wear so they could spit on you?

Anne. I know. I know. But after all, it *is* the Star of David, isn't it?

---

[8] **Jopie de Waal** (yō′pē də väl′)

(*In the bedroom, right, Margot and Mrs. Frank are lying down. Mr. Frank starts quietly out.*)

590 **Peter.** Maybe it's different for a girl.

(*Mr. Frank comes into the main room.*)

Mr. Frank. Forgive me, Peter. Now let me see. We must find a bed for your cat. (*He goes to a cupboard.*) I'm glad you brought your cat. Anne was feeling so badly about hers. (*getting a used small washtub*)

600 Here we are. Will it be comfortable in that?

Peter (*gathering up his things*). Thanks.

Mr. Frank (*opening the door of the room on the left*). And here is your room. But I warn you, Peter, you can't grow any more. Not an inch, or you'll have to sleep with your feet out of the skylight. Are you

610 hungry?

Peter. No.

Mr. Frank. We have some bread and butter.

Peter. No, thank you.

Mr. Frank. You can have it for luncheon then. And tonight we will have a real supper . . . our first supper together.

Peter. Thanks. Thanks.

620 (*He goes into his room. During the following scene he arranges his possessions in his new room.*)

Mr. Frank. That's a nice boy, Peter.

Anne. He's awfully shy, isn't he?

The Diary of Anne Frank: Act One **289**

CLOSE READ

Analyze Language

(LINES 570–586)

Tell students that a **symbol** is a person, a place, or an object that stands for something beyond itself.

Q **ASK STUDENTS** to reread lines 570–586. What does the Star of David symbolize? (*The Star of David is a symbol of the Jewish people and Judaism.*) What do Peter's and Ann's views about the star reveal about them? (*Peter views it as a symbol of Nazi persecution and wants to burn it. Anne still sees it as a sacred symbol and an important part of her Jewish identity.*)

TEACH

CLOSE READ

Analyze Characters

COMMON CORE RL 1, RL 3

(LINES 631–656)

Remind students that a character's actions can reveal something about what the character is like.

(R) CITE TEXT EVIDENCE Have students examine lines 631–656 to discover more about Mr. Frank's nature. What surprises does Mr. Frank have for Anne? *(He gives her a box that contains Anne's treasured pictures of movie stars as well as a photo of the queen of the Netherlands. He also gives her a diary.)* What can you infer about Mr. Frank from this part of the script? *(Possible answer: He is an understanding father who wants his daughter to thrive in a difficult situation. Mr. Frank may already be aware that Anne is a talented writer, but he also wants his energetic daughter to have something meaningful to do while in hiding.)*

Mr. Frank. You'll like him, I know.

Anne. I certainly hope so, since he's the only boy I'm likely to see for months and months.

(Mr. Frank *sits down, taking off his* 630 *shoes.*)

Mr. Frank. Annele,[9] there's a box there. Will you open it? (*He indicates a carton on the couch.* Anne *brings it to the center table. In the street below there is the sound of children playing.*)

Anne (*as she opens the carton*). You know the way I'm going to think of it here? I'm going to think of it as 640 a boarding house. A very peculiar summer boarding house, like the one that we—(*She breaks off as she pulls out some photographs.*) Father! My movie stars! I was wondering where they were! I was looking for them this morning . . . and Queen Wilhelmina! How wonderful!

Mr. Frank. There's something more. Go on. Look further. (*He* 650 *goes over to the sink, pouring a glass of milk from a thermos bottle.*)

Anne (*pulling out a pasteboard-bound book*). A diary! (*She throws her arms around her father.*) I've never had a diary. And I've always longed for one. (*She looks around the room.*) Pencil, pencil, pencil, pencil. (*She starts down the stairs.*) I'm going down to the office to get 660 a pencil.

---

[9] **Annele/Anneke:** a nickname for Anne.

Mr. Frank. Anne! No! (*He goes after her, catching her by the arm and pulling her back.*)

Anne (*startled*). But there's no one in the building now.

Mr. Frank. It doesn't matter. I don't want you ever to go beyond that door.

Anne (*sobered*). Never . . . ? Not 670 even at nighttime, when everyone is gone? Or on Sundays? Can't I go down to listen to the radio?

Mr. Frank. Never. I am sorry, Anneke. It isn't safe. No, you must never go beyond that door.

(*For the first time* Anne *realizes what "going into hiding" means.*)

Anne. I see.

Mr. Frank. It'll be hard, I know. 680 But always remember this, Anneke. There are no walls, there are no bolts, no locks that anyone can put on your mind. Miep will bring us books. We will read history, poetry, mythology. (*He gives her the glass of milk.*) Here's your milk. (*With his arm about her, they go over to the couch, sitting down side by side.*) As a matter of fact, between 690 us, Anne, being here has certain advantages for you. For instance, you remember the battle you had with your mother the other day on the subject of overshoes? You said you'd rather die than wear overshoes. But in the end you had to wear them? Well now, you see, for as long as we are here you will never have to wear overshoes! 700 Isn't that good? And the coat that

---

WHEN STUDENTS STRUGGLE...

To help students understand and recall the sequence of events in the play, have them complete a Flow Chart graphic organizer.

Ask students to use one frame for each scene in the play. Have students write the scene number, the time when the scene takes place, and notes about key events in the scene.

SCENE 1:

▼

SCENE 2:

▼

SCENE 3:

▼

you inherited from Margot, you won't have to wear that any more. And the piano! You won't have to practice on the piano. I tell you, this is going to be a fine life for you!

(Anne's *panic is gone.* Peter *appears in the doorway of his room, with a saucer in his hand. He is carrying his cat.*)

710

Peter. I . . . I . . . I thought I'd better get some water for Mouschi before . . .

Mr. Frank. Of course.

(*As he starts toward the sink the carillon begins to chime the hour of eight. He tiptoes to the window at the back and looks down at the street below. He turns to Peter,*

720 *indicating in pantomime that it is too late.* Peter *starts back for his room. He steps on a creaking board. The three of them are frozen for a minute in fear. As* Peter *starts away again,* Anne *tiptoes over to him and pours some of the milk from her glass into the saucer for the cat.* Peter *squats on the floor, putting the milk before the cat.* Mr. Frank *gives*

730 Anne *his fountain pen, and then goes into the room at the right. For a second* Anne *watches the cat, then she goes over to the center table, and opens her diary.*

In the room at the right, Mrs. Frank *has sat up quickly at the sound of the carillon.* Mr. Frank *comes in and sits down beside her on the settee, his arm comfortingly*

740 *around her.*

Upstairs, in the attic room, Mr. *and* Mrs. Van Daan *have hung their clothes in the closet and are now seated on the iron bed.* Mrs. Van Daan *leans back exhausted.* Mr. Van Daan *fans her with a newspaper.*

Anne *starts to write in her diary. The lights dim out, the curtain falls.*

750 *In the darkness* Anne's Voice *comes to us again, faintly at first, and then with growing strength.*)

Anne's Voice. I expect I should be describing what it feels like to go into hiding. But I really don't know yet myself. I only know it's funny never to be able to go outdoors . . . never to breathe fresh air . . . never to run and shout and jump. It's the

760 silence in the nights that frightens me most. Every time I hear a creak in the house, or a step on the street outside, I'm sure they're coming for us. The days aren't so bad. At least we know that Miep and Mr. Kraler are down there below us in the office. Our protectors, we call them. I asked Father what would happen to them if the Nazis found

770 out they were hiding us. Pim said that they would suffer the same fate that we would . . . Imagine! They know this, and yet when they come up here, they're always cheerful and gay as if there were nothing in the world to bother them . . . Friday, the twenty-first of August, nineteen forty-two. Today I'm going to tell you our general

780 news. Mother is unbearable. She insists on treating me like a baby,

CLOSE READ

Analyze Drama

COMMON CORE **RL 1**

(LINES 748–759)

Prompt students to note the various kinds of cues in the script and what they signal to actors, the director, and the stage crew.

Ⓢ **ASK STUDENTS** to reread lines 748–759. What instructions do the stage directions give about lighting? (*The lights gradually dim to complete darkness.*) What happens to the stage curtain? What does this signal? (*The curtain "falls" [comes down]. This signals that a scene is ending.*) Why does the beginning of line 753 say "Anne's Voice" instead of just "Anne"? (*Anne is no longer on the stage. The audience hears only her voice speaking the words she is writing in her diary.*)

which I loathe. Otherwise things are going better. The weather is . . .

(*As Anne's Voice is fading out, the curtain rises on the scene.*)

Scene 3

It is a little after six o'clock in the evening, two months later.

Margot *is in the bedroom at the right, studying.* Mr. Van Daan *is* 790 *lying down in the attic room above.*

The rest of the "family" is in the main room. Anne *and* Peter *sit opposite each other at the center table, where they have been doing their lessons.* Mrs. Frank *is on the couch.* Mrs. Van Daan *is seated with her fur coat, on which she has been sewing, in her lap. None of them are wearing their shoes.*

800 *Their eyes are on* Mr. Frank, *waiting for him to give them the signal which will release them from their day-long quiet.* Mr. Frank, *his shoes in his hand, stands looking down out of the window at the back, watching to be sure that all of the workmen have left the building below.*

After a few seconds of motionless 810 *silence,* Mr. Frank *turns from the window.*

Mr. Frank (*quietly, to the group*). It's safe now. The last workman has left. (*There is an immediate stir of relief.*)

Anne (*Her pent-up energy explodes*). WHEE!

Mrs. Frank (*startled, amused*). Anne!

820 **Mrs. Van Daan.** I'm first for the w.c. (*She hurries off to the bathroom.* Mrs. Frank *puts on her shoes and starts up to the sink to prepare supper.* Anne *sneaks* Peter's *shoes from under the table and hides them behind her back.* Mr. Frank *goes in to* Margot's *room.*)

Mr. Frank (*to* Margot). Six o'clock. School's over.

830 (Margot *gets up, stretching.* Mr. Frank *sits down to put on his shoes. In the main room* Peter *tries to find his.*)

Peter (*to* Anne). Have you seen my shoes?

Anne (*innocently*). Your shoes?

Peter. You've taken them, haven't you?

Anne. I don't know what you're 840 talking about.

Peter. You're going to be sorry!

Anne. Am I? (Peter *goes after her.* Anne, *with his shoes in her hand, runs from him, dodging behind her mother.*)

Mrs. Frank (*protesting*). Anne, dear!

Peter. Wait till I get you!

Anne. I'm waiting! (Peter *makes a* 850 *lunge for her. They both fall to the floor.* Peter *pins her down, wrestling with her to get the shoes.*) Don't! Don't! Peter, stop it. Ouch!

Mrs. Frank. Anne! . . . Peter! (*Suddenly* Peter *becomes*

APPLYING ACADEMIC VOCABULARY

communicate	liberation

As you discuss the selection, incorporate the following Collection 5 academic vocabulary words: *communicate* and *liberation*. Ask students to describe the different ways the residents of the Annex feel about their **liberation** each evening after the workers in the rooms below go home. How does this change the way the "family" members are able to **communicate** with one another?

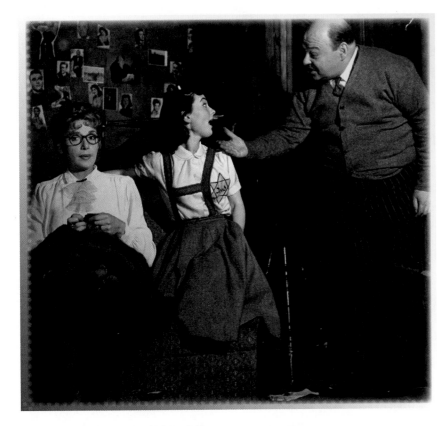

self-conscious. He grabs his shoes roughly and starts for his room.)

Anne (*following him*). Peter, where are you going? Come dance
860 with me.

Peter. I tell you I don't know how.

Anne. I'll teach you.

Peter. I'm going to give Mouschi his dinner.

Anne. Can I watch?

Peter. He doesn't like people around while he eats.

Anne. Peter, please.

Peter. No! (*He goes into his room.*
870 Anne *slams his door after him.*)

Mrs. Frank. Anne, dear, I think you shouldn't play like that with Peter. It's not dignified.

Anne. Who cares if it's dignified? I don't want to be dignified.

(Mr. Frank *and* Margot *come from the room on the right. Margot goes to help her mother. Mr. Frank starts for the center table to correct*
880 Margot's *school papers.*)

The Diary of Anne Frank: Act One   **293**

©Daily Mail/Rex/Alamy Images

Analyze Language

COMMON CORE · RL 3, RL 4

(LINES 907–917)

Discuss the meanings of expressions used in the dialogue. Explain that **hyperbole** is a figure of speech in which the truth is exaggerated for emphasis or humorous effect.

🅣 **ASK STUDENTS** to reread lines 907–917. What does Anne mean when she responds to Mrs. Van Daan by saying, "Where would he be!" *(She is implying that Peter is always in the same place, in his room with his cat.)* Which expression used by Mrs. Van Daan is hyperbole? *("His father'll kill him")* What does this expression reveal about Mr. Van Daan? *(Although Mr. Van Daan won't really kill his son, Mrs. Van Daan is emphasizing how upset her husband will be.)*

Mrs. Frank (*to* Anne). You complain that I don't treat you like a grownup. But when I do, you resent it.

Anne. I only want some fun . . . someone to laugh and clown with . . . After you've sat still all day and hardly moved, you've got to have some fun. I don't know 890 what's the matter with that boy.

Mr. Frank. He isn't used to girls. Give him a little time.

Anne. Time? Isn't two months time? I could cry. (*catching hold of* Margot) Come on, Margot . . . dance with me. Come on, please.

Margot. I have to help with supper.

Anne. You know we're going to forget how to dance . . . When we 900 get out we won't remember a thing.

(*She starts to sing and dance by herself.* Mr. Frank *takes her in his arms, waltzing with her.* Mrs. Van Daan *comes in from the bathroom.*)

Mrs. Van Daan. Next? (*She looks around as she starts putting on her shoes.*) Where's Peter?

Anne (*as they are dancing*). Where would he be!

910 **Mrs. Van Daan.** He hasn't finished his lessons, has he? His father'll kill him if he catches him in there with that cat and his work not done.

(Mr. Frank *and* Anne *finish their dance. They bow to each other with extravagant formality.*) Anne, get him out of there, will you?

Anne (*at* Peter's *door*). Peter? Peter?

Peter (*opening the door a crack*). 920 What is it?

Anne. Your mother says to come out.

Peter. I'm giving Mouschi his dinner.

Mrs. Van Daan. You know what your father says. (*She sits on the couch, sewing on the lining of her fur coat.*)

Peter. For heaven's sake, I haven't 930 even looked at him since lunch.

Mrs. Van Daan. I'm just telling you, that's all.

Anne. I'll feed him.

Peter. I don't want you in there.

Mrs. Van Daan. Peter!

Peter (*to* Anne). Then give him his dinner and come right out, you hear? (*He comes back to the table.* Anne *shuts the door of* Peter's *room* 940 *after her and disappears behind the curtain covering his closet.*)

Mrs. Van Daan (*to* Peter). Now is that any way to talk to your little girl friend?

Peter. Mother . . . for heaven's sake . . . will you please stop saying that?

Mrs. Van Daan. Look at him blush! Look at him!

950 **Peter.** Please! I'm not . . . anyway . . . let me alone, will you?

Mrs. Van Daan. He acts like it was something to be ashamed of. It's nothing to be ashamed of, to have a little girl friend.

Peter. You're crazy. She's only thirteen.

Mrs. Van Daan. So what? And you're sixteen. Just perfect. Your
960 father's ten years older than I am. (*to* Mr. Frank) I warn you, Mr. Frank, if this war lasts much longer, we're going to be related and then . . .

Mr. Frank. *Mazeltov!*[10]

Mrs. Frank (*deliberately changing the conversation*). I wonder where Miep is. She's usually so prompt.
970 (*Suddenly everything else is forgotten as they hear the sound of an automobile coming to a screeching stop in the street below. They are tense, motionless in their terror. The car starts away. A wave of relief sweeps over them. They pick up their occupations again.* Anne *flings open the door of* Peter's *room, making a dramatic entrance. She is dressed in* Peter's *clothes.* Peter *looks at her in*
980 *fury. The others are amused.*)

Anne. Good evening, everyone. Forgive me if I don't stay. (*She jumps up on a chair.*) I have a friend waiting for me in there. My friend Tom. Tom Cat. Some people say that we look alike. But Tom has the most beautiful whiskers, and I have only a little fuzz. I am hoping . . . in time . . .

990 **Peter.** All right, Mrs. Quack Quack!

Anne (*outraged—jumping down*). Peter!

---

[10] **Mazeltov!** (mä´zəl tôf´)
   Hebrew: Congratulations!

Peter. I heard about you . . . How you talked so much in class they called you Mrs. Quack Quack. How Mr. Smitter made you write a composition . . . "'Quack, quack,' said Mrs. Quack Quack."

1000 **Anne.** Well, go on. Tell them the rest. How it was so good he read it out loud to the class and then read it to all his other classes!

Peter. Quack! Quack! Quack . . . Quack . . . Quack . . .

(Anne *pulls off the coat and trousers.*)

Anne. You are the most intolerable, insufferable boy I've ever met!

1010 (*She throws the clothes down the stairwell.* Peter *goes down after them.*)

Peter. Quack, quack, quack!

Mrs. Van Daan (*to* Anne). That's right, Anneke! Give it to him!

Anne. With all the boys in the world . . . Why I had to get locked up with one like you! . . .

Peter. Quack, quack, quack, and
1020 from now on stay out of my room!

(*As* Peter *passes her,* Anne *puts out her foot, tripping him. He picks himself up, and goes on into his room.*)

Mrs. Frank (*quietly*). Anne, dear . . . your hair. (*She feels* Anne's *forehead.*) You're warm. Are you feeling all right?

Anne. Please, Mother. (*She goes
1030 over to the center table, slipping into her shoes.*)

CLOSE READ

Analyze Characters

COMMON CORE **RL 1, RL 3**

(LINES 976–993)

Remind students that one way to learn about characters is through their actions. Explain that students can also determine what characters are like by what the characters say as well as by direct comments playwrights make in the stage directions.

U **CITE TEXT EVIDENCE** Have students reread lines 976–993 to draw conclusions about Anne and Peter. What direct comments by the playwrights show Peter's and Anne's thoughts and feelings? (*Peter responds "in fury" when Anne appears wearing his clothes. Anne is "outraged" when Peter calls her Mrs. Quack Quack.*) What conclusions can you draw about Anne and Peter based on their actions, speech, and comments by the playwrights? (*Possible answer: Anne is high spirited and willing to tease someone for the sake of amusement. Peter is more withdrawn. They both show a lack of sensitivity to the other's feelings.*)

Mrs. Frank (*following her*). You haven't a fever, have you?

Anne (*pulling away*). No. No.

Mrs. Frank. You know we can't call a doctor here, ever. There's only one thing to do . . . watch carefully. Prevent an illness before it comes. Let me see your tongue.

1040 **Anne.** Mother, this is perfectly absurd.

Mrs. Frank. Anne, dear, don't be such a baby. Let me see your tongue. (*As Anne refuses, Mrs. Frank appeals to Mr. Frank.*) Otto . . . ?

Mr. Frank. You hear your mother, Anne. (*Anne flicks out her tongue for a second, then turns away.*)

1050 **Mrs. Frank.** Come on—open up! (*as Anne opens her mouth very wide*) You seem all right . . . but perhaps an aspirin . . .

Mrs. Van Daan. For heaven's sake, don't give that child any pills. I waited for fifteen minutes this morning for her to come out of the w.c.

Anne. I was washing my hair!

1060 **Mr. Frank.** I think there's nothing the matter with our Anne that a ride on her bike, or a visit with her friend Jopie de Waal wouldn't cure. Isn't that so, Anne?

(*Mr. Van Daan comes down into the room. From outside we hear faint sounds of bombers going over and a burst of ack-ack.*)

Mr. Van Daan. Miep not come yet?

1070 **Mrs. Van Daan.** The workmen just left, a little while ago.

Mr. Van Daan. What's for dinner tonight?

Mrs. Van Daan. Beans.

Mr. Van Daan. Not again!

Mrs. Van Daan. Poor Putti! I know. But what can we do? That's all that Miep brought us.

(*Mr. Van Daan starts to pace, his hands behind his back. Anne follows behind him, imitating him.*)

1080 **Anne.** We are now in what is known as the "bean cycle." Beans boiled, beans en casserole, beans with strings, beans without strings . . .

(*Peter has come out of his room. He slides into his place at the table, becoming immediately absorbed in his studies.*)

1090 **Mr. Van Daan** (*to* Peter). I saw you . . . in there, playing with your cat.

Mrs. Van Daan. He just went in for a second, putting his coat away. He's been out here all the time, doing his lessons.

Mr. Frank (*looking up from the papers*). Anne, you got an excellent in your history paper today . . . and very good in Latin.

1100 **Anne** (*sitting beside him*). How about algebra?

Mr. Frank. I'll have to make a confession. Up until now I've managed to stay ahead of you in algebra. Today you caught up with

---

Strategies for Annotation

 Annotate it!

Analyze Drama

COMMON CORE RL 3

Point out that when playwrights develop the script for a play they may carry one idea or topic in the script through several scenes or through the entire play. Share these strategies for guided or independent analysis:

- Highlight in yellow all parts of the dialogue related to an element in the plot, such as Peter and his cat.
- Record on notes how the highlighted text propels the action and what it reveals about the characters.

(Peter *has come out of his room. He slides into his place* becoming *immediately absorbed in his studies.*)

> Mr. Van Daan does not like Peter's interest in the cat.

Mr. Van Daan (*to* Peter). I saw you . . . in there, playing with your cat.

Mrs. Van Daan. He just went in for a second, putting his coat away. He's been out here all the time, doing his lessons.

me. We'll leave it to Margot to correct.

V 1110 **Anne.** Isn't algebra *vile*, Pim!

Mr. Frank. Vile!

Margot (*to* Mr. Frank). How did I do?

Anne (*getting up*). Excellent, excellent, excellent, excellent!

Mr. Frank (*to* Margot). You should have used the subjunctive here . . .

Margot. Should I? . . . I thought . . . look here . . . I didn't use it here . . . 1120 (*The two become absorbed in the papers.*)

Anne. Mrs. Van Daan, may I try on your coat?

Mrs. Frank. No, Anne.

Mrs. Van Daan (*giving it to* Anne). It's all right . . . but careful with it. (Anne *puts it on and struts with it.*) My father gave me that the year before he died. He always bought 1130 the best that money could buy.

Anne. Mrs. Van Daan, did you have a lot of boy friends before you were married?

Mrs. Frank. Anne, that's a personal question. It's not courteous to ask personal questions.

Mrs. Van Daan. Oh I don't mind. (*to* Anne) Our house was always swarming with boys. When I was a 1140 girl we had . . .

Mr. Van Daan. Oh, God. Not again!

Mrs. Van Daan (*good-humored*). Shut up! (*Without a pause, to* Anne.

 Mr. Van Daan *mimics* Mrs. Van Daan, *speaking the first few words in unison with her.*) One summer we had a big house in Hilversum. The boys came buzzing round 1150 like bees around a jam pot. And when I was sixteen! . . . We were wearing our skirts very short those days and I had good-looking legs. (*She pulls up her skirt, going to* Mr. Frank.) I still have 'em. I may not be as pretty as I used to be, but I still have my legs. How about it, Mr. Frank?

Mr. Van Daan. All right. All right. 1160 We see them.

Mrs. Van Daan. I'm not asking you. I'm asking Mr. Frank.

Peter. Mother, for heaven's sake.

Mrs. Van Daan. Oh, I embarrass you, do I? Well, I just hope the girl you marry has as good. (*then to* Anne) My father used to worry about me, with so many boys hanging round. He told 1170 me, if any of them gets fresh, you say to him . . . "Remember, Mr. So-and-So, remember I'm a lady."

Anne. "Remember, Mr. So-and-So, remember I'm a lady." (*She gives* Mrs. Van Daan *her coat.*)

Mr. Van Daan. Look at you, talking that way in front of her! Don't you know she puts it all down in that 1180 diary?

Mrs. Van Daan. So, if she does? I'm only telling the truth!

CLOSE READ

Analyze Language
COMMON CORE **RL 4**

(LINES 1110–1111)

Tell students that even brief exchanges between characters can reveal or reinforce a reader's ideas about them.

V **ASK STUDENTS** to reread lines 1110–1111 to identify "Pim." (*"Pim" is a nickname Anne uses for her father.*) How does their use of the word *vile* impact their exchange? (*Anne's use of* vile *emphasizes her tendency to overdramatize; Mr. Frank's use of* vile *suggests that he wants to humor her, or help her realize how silly she sounds.*)

Analyze Drama
COMMON CORE **RL 1**

(LINES 1145–1147)

Guide students in drawing a conclusion based on the stage directions.

W **ASK STUDENTS** what the stage directions in lines 1145–1147 imply about the story that Mrs. Van Daan is about to tell. (*Mr. Van Daan has heard the story so many times that he can repeat it word for word.*)

Analyze Drama

COMMON CORE **RL 1, RL 3**

(LINES 1203–1237)

Tell students that playwrights use both dialogue and stage directions to help actors and audiences understand the relationships between characters.

X **CITE TEXT EVIDENCE** Have students reread lines 1203–1237 to identify Mrs. Van Daan's attitudes toward her husband and Mr. Frank. What are her thoughts about Mr. Van Daan? about Mr. Frank? *(Mrs. Van Daan is critical of her husband but has great respect and admiration for Mr. Frank.)* Give evidence from the text. *(Possible answers: Mrs. Van Daan says Peter doesn't have anyone to help him as the girls do. She kisses Mr. Frank on the lips and calls him "an angel." She implies that she would have preferred to marry Mr. Frank and calls her husband "that one there" instead of using his name. She refers to Mr. Frank as a "highly educated man.")*

(Anne *stretches out, putting her ear to the floor, listening to what is going on below. The sound of the bombers fades away.*)

Mrs. Frank (*setting the table*). Would you mind, Peter, if I moved you over to the couch?

1190 **Anne** (*listening*). Miep must have the radio on.

(Peter *picks up his papers, going over to the couch beside Mrs. Van Daan.*)

Mr. Van Daan (*accusingly, to* Peter). Haven't you finished yet?

Peter. No.

Mr. Van Daan. You ought to be ashamed of yourself.

1200 **Peter.** All right. All right. I'm a dunce. I'm a hopeless case. Why do I go on?

 Mrs. Van Daan. You're not hopeless. Don't talk that way. It's just that you haven't anyone to help you, like the girls have. (*to* Mr. Frank) Maybe you could help him, Mr. Frank?

Mr. Frank. I'm sure that his 1210 father . . . ?

Mr. Van Daan. Not me. I can't do anything with him. He won't listen to me. You go ahead . . . if you want.

Mr. Frank (*going to* Peter). What about it, Peter? Shall we make our school coeducational?

Mrs. Van Daan (*kissing* Mr. Frank). You're an angel, Mr. Frank. An 1220 angel. I don't know why I didn't

meet you before I met that one there.

Here, sit down, Mr. Frank . . . (*She forces him down on the couch beside* Peter.) Now, Peter, you listen to Mr. Frank.

Mr. Frank. It might be better for us to go into Peter's room. (Peter *jumps up eagerly, leading the way.*)

1230 **Mrs. Van Daan.** That's right. You go in there, Peter. You listen to Mr. Frank. Mr. Frank is a highly educated man. (*As* Mr. Frank *is about to follow* Peter *into his room,* Mrs. Frank *stops him and wipes the lipstick from his lips. Then she closes the door after them.*)

Anne (*on the floor, listening*). Shh! I can hear a man's voice talking.

1240 **Mr. Van Daan** (*to* Anne). Isn't it bad enough here without your sprawling all over the place? (Anne *sits up.*)

Mrs. Van Daan (*to* Mr. Van Daan). If you didn't smoke so much, you wouldn't be so bad-tempered.

Mr. Van Daan. Am I smoking? Do you see me smoking?

Mrs. Van Daan. Don't tell me 1250 you've used up all those cigarettes.

Mr. Van Daan. One package. Miep only brought me one package.

Mrs. Van Daan. It's a filthy habit anyway. It's a good time to break yourself.

Mr. Van Daan. Oh, stop it, please.

Mrs. Van Daan. You're smoking up all our money. You know that, don't you?

1260 **Mr. Van Daan.** Will you shut up? (*During this,* Mrs. Frank *and* Margot *have studiously kept their eyes down. But* Anne, *seated on the floor, has been following the discussion interestedly.* Mr. Van Daan *turns to see her staring up at him.*) And what are you staring at?

Anne. I never heard grownups quarrel before. I thought only
1270 children quarreled.

Mr. Van Daan. This isn't a quarrel! It's a discussion. And I never heard children so rude before.

Anne (*rising, indignantly*). I, rude!

Mr. Van Daan. Yes!

Mrs. Frank (*quickly*). Anne, will you get me my knitting? (Anne *goes to get it.*) I must remember, when Miep comes, to ask her to
1280 bring me some more wool.

Margot (*going to her room*). I need some hairpins and some soap. I made a list. (*She goes into her bedroom to get the list.*)

Mrs. Frank (*to* Anne). Have you some library books for Miep when she comes?

Anne. It's a wonder that Miep has a life of her own, the way we make
1290 her run errands for us. Please, Miep, get me some starch. Please take my hair out and have it cut. Tell me all the latest news, Miep.

(*She goes over, kneeling on the couch beside* Mrs. Van Daan.) Did you

know she was engaged? His name is Dirk, and Miep's afraid the Nazis will ship him off to Germany to work in one of their war plants.
1300 That's what they're doing with some of the young Dutchmen . . . they pick them up off the streets—

Mr. Van Daan (*interrupting*). Don't you ever get tired of talking? Suppose you try keeping still for five minutes. Just five minutes. (*He starts to pace again. Again* Anne *follows him, mimicking him.* Mrs. Frank *jumps up and takes her*
1310 *by the arm up to the sink, and gives her a glass of milk.*)

Mrs. Frank. Come here, Anne. It's time for your glass of milk.

Mr. Van Daan. Talk, talk, talk. I never heard such a child. Where is my . . . ? Every evening it's the same, talk, talk, talk. (*He looks around.*) Where is my . . . ?

Mrs. Van Daan. What're you
1320 looking for?

Mr. Van Daan. My pipe. Have you seen my pipe?

Mrs. Van Daan. What good's a pipe? You haven't got any tobacco.

Mr. Van Daan. At least I'll have something to hold in my mouth! (*opening* Margot's *bedroom door*) Margot, have you seen my pipe?

Margot. It was on the table last
1330 night. (Anne *puts her glass of milk on the table and picks up his pipe, hiding it behind her back.*)

CLOSE READ

Analyze Language

COMMON CORE **RL 4**

(LINES 1268–1273)

Explain to students that words with a similar **denotation,** or dictionary definition, can have different **connotations,** the feelings or ideas associated with a word. Words can have a positive, neutral, or negative connotation.

Y **ASK STUDENTS** to reread lines 1268–1273. How are the connotations of the words *discussion* and *quarrel* different? (*Although both words are about people talking together,* quarrel *has a negative connotation because it includes the idea of anger.* Discussion *has a neutral connotation.*) Why is the distinction between the words important to Mr. Van Daan? (*Possible answer: He does not want to be viewed as a child.*)

Analyze Characters

COMMON CORE RL 1, RL 3

(LINES 1349–1370)

Review with students that they can learn something about what characters in a play are like by examining the words they say.

Ⓩ CITE TEXT EVIDENCE Have students reread lines 1349–1370 to draw conclusions about Mr. Van Daan and Anne. How does Mr. Van Daan think women and girls should behave? (*He thinks they should be quiet, focusing their attention on keeping their "house shining" for their husbands and "to cook and sew."*) What do Mr. Van Daan's words reveal about him? (*Possible answer: He is old fashioned, narrow minded, and condescending.*) What does Anne's response reveal about her? (*Possible answer: She is idealistic, independent, and wants to have her own career. She is ambitious and expects to do something "remarkable" and "wonderful" with her life.*)

Mr. Van Daan. I know. I know. Anne, did you see my pipe? . . . Anne!

Mrs. Frank. Anne, Mr. Van Daan is speaking to you.

Anne. Am I allowed to talk now?

1340 **Mr. Van Daan.** You're the most aggravating . . . The trouble with you is, you've been spoiled. What you need is a good old-fashioned spanking.

Anne (*mimicking* Mrs. Van Daan). "Remember, Mr. So-and-So, remember I'm a lady." (*She thrusts the pipe into his mouth, then picks up her glass of milk.*)

1350 **Mr. Van Daan** (*restraining himself with difficulty*). Why aren't you nice and quiet like your sister Margot? Why do you have to show off all the time? Let me give you a little advice, young lady. Men don't like that kind of thing in a girl. You know that? A man likes a girl who'll listen to him once in a while . . . a domestic girl, who'll keep her house shining for her 1360 husband . . . who loves to cook and sew and . . .

Anne. I'd cut my throat first! I'd open my veins! I'm going to be remarkable! I'm going to Paris . . .

Mr. Van Daan (*scoffingly*). Paris!

Anne. . . . to study music and art.

Mr. Van Daan. Yeah! Yeah!

Anne. I'm going to be a famous dancer or singer . . . or something 1370 wonderful. (*She makes a wide gesture, spilling the glass of milk on*

the fur coat in Mrs. Van Daan's *lap.* Margot *rushes quickly over with a towel.* Anne *tries to brush the milk off with her skirt.*)

Mrs. Van Daan. Now look what you've done . . . you clumsy little fool! My beautiful fur coat my father gave me . . .

1380 **Anne.** I'm so sorry.

Mrs. Van Daan. What do you care? It isn't yours . . . So go on, ruin it! Do you know what that coat cost? Do you? And now look at it! Look at it!

Anne. I'm very, very sorry.

Mrs. Van Daan. I could kill you for this. I could just kill you! (Mrs. Van Daan *goes up the stairs,* 1390 *clutching the coat.* Mr. Van Daan *starts after her.*)

Mr. Van Daan. Petronella . . . *liefje! Liefje!* . . . Come back . . . the supper . . . come back!

Mrs. Frank. Anne, you must not behave in that way.

Anne. It was an accident. Anyone can have an accident.

Mrs. Frank. I don't mean that. I 1400 mean the answering back. You must not answer back. They are our guests. We must always show the greatest courtesy to them. We're all living under terrible tension. (*She stops as* Margot *indicates that* Van Daan *can hear. When he is gone, she continues.*) That's why we must control ourselves . . . You don't hear Margot 1410 getting into arguments with them, do you? Watch Margot. She's always courteous with them. Never familiar. She keeps her distance. And they respect her for it. Try to be like Margot.

Anne. And have them walk all over me, the way they do her? No, thanks!

Mrs. Frank. I'm not afraid that anyone is going to walk all over you, Anne. I'm afraid for other people, that you'll walk on them. I don't know what happens to you, Anne. You are wild, self-willed. If I had ever talked to my mother as you talk to me . . .

Anne. Things have changed. People aren't like that any more. "Yes, Mother." "No, Mother." "Anything you say, Mother." I've got to fight things out for myself! Make something of myself!

Mrs. Frank. It isn't necessary to fight to do it. Margot doesn't fight, and isn't she . . . ?

Anne (*violently rebellious*). Margot! Margot! Margot! That's all I hear from everyone . . . how wonderful Margot is . . . "Why aren't you like Margot?"

Margot (*protesting*). Oh, come on, Anne, don't be so . . .

Anne (*paying no attention*). Everything she does is right, and everything I do is wrong! I'm the goat around here! . . . You're all against me! . . . And you worst of all!

(*She rushes off into her room and throws herself down on the settee, stifling her sobs. Mrs. Frank sighs and starts toward the stove.*)

Mrs. Frank (*to* Margot). Let's put the soup on the stove . . . if there's anyone who cares to eat. Margot, will you take the bread out? (*Margot gets the bread from the cupboard.*) I don't know how we can go on living this way . . . I can't say a word to Anne . . . she flies at me . . .

Margot. You know Anne. In half an hour she'll be out here, laughing and joking.

Mrs. Frank. And . . . (*She makes a motion upwards, indicating the Van Daans.*) . . . I told your father it wouldn't work . . . but no . . . no . . . he had to ask them, he said . . . he owed it to him, he said. Well, he knows now that I was right! These quarrels! . . . This bickering!

Margot (*with a warning look*). Shush. Shush.

(*The buzzer for the door sounds. Mrs. Frank gasps, startled.*)

Mrs. Frank. Every time I hear that sound, my heart stops!

Margot (*starting for* Peter's *door*). It's Miep. (*She knocks at the door.*) Father?

(*Mr. Frank comes quickly from* Peter's *room.*)

Mr. Frank. Thank you, Margot. (*as he goes down the steps to open the outer door*) Has everyone his list?

Margot. I'll get my books. (*giving her mother a list*) Here's your list.

CLOSE READ

Analyze Language

(LINES 1414–1432)

Tell students that an **idiom** is an expression that has a meaning different from the meaning of its individual words.

A2 ASK STUDENTS to reread lines 1414–1432. Anne doesn't want the Van Daans to "walk all over" her. What variation of the idiom does Mrs. Frank use in her response to Anne? (*She doesn't want Anne to "walk on" others.*) What does the idiom "walk all over" or "walk on" mean? (*to treat someone badly or in a disrespectful way; to be overbearing*) What is the impact of the use of the idiom on readers' understanding of the characters? (*Anne is confident enough to stand up for herself; Mrs. Frank understands this quality in her daughter but wishes she would temper it.*)

Analyze Drama

COMMON CORE · RL 1, RL 4

(LINES 1509–1514)

Point out that stage directions often explain what characters' facial expressions should be during particular scenes in a drama.

B2 ASK STUDENTS to read the stage directions in lines 1509–1514. What word do the playwrights use to explain how Mr. Frank and Mr. Kraler should look? *(grave)* What does the description signal to the audience? *(that something distressing has happened)*

(Margot *goes into her and Anne's bedroom on the right.* Anne *sits up,*
1490 *hiding her tears, as* Margot *comes in.*) Miep's here.

(Margot *picks up her books and goes back.* Anne *hurries over to the mirror, smoothing her hair.*)

Mr. Van Daan (*coming down the stairs*). Is it Miep?

Margot. Yes. Father's gone down to let her in.

Mr. Van Daan. At last I'll have
1500 some cigarettes!

Mrs. Frank (*to* Mr. Van Daan). I can't tell you how unhappy I am about Mrs. Van Daan's coat. Anne should never have touched it.

Mr. Van Daan. She'll be all right.

Mrs. Frank. Is there anything I can do?

Mr. Van Daan. Don't worry.

(*He turns to meet* Miep. *But it is not*
1510 Miep *who comes up the steps. It is* Mr. Kraler, *followed by* Mr. Frank. *Their faces are grave.* Anne *comes from the bedroom.* Peter *comes from his room.*)

Mrs. Frank. Mr. Kraler!

Mr. Van Daan. How are you, Mr. Kraler?

Margot. This is a surprise.

Mrs. Frank. When Mr. Kraler
1520 comes, the sun begins to shine.

Mr. Van Daan. Miep is coming?

Mr. Kraler. Not tonight.

(Kraler *goes to* Margot *and* Mrs. Frank *and* Anne, *shaking hands with them.*)

Mrs. Frank. Wouldn't you like a cup of coffee? . . . Or, better still, will you have supper with us?

Mr. Frank. Mr. Kraler has
1530 something to talk over with us. Something has happened, he says, which demands an immediate decision.

Mrs. Frank (*fearful*). What is it?

(Mr. Kraler *sits down on the couch. As he talks he takes bread, cabbages, milk, etc., from his briefcase, giving them to* Margot *and* Anne *to put away.*)

1540 **Mr. Kraler.** Usually, when I come up here, I try to bring you some bit of good news. What's the use of telling you the bad news when there's nothing that you can do about it? But today something has happened . . . Dirk . . . Miep's Dirk, you know, came to me just now. He tells me that he has a Jewish friend living near him. A dentist.
1550 He says he's in trouble. He begged me, could I do anything for this man? Could I find him a hiding place? . . . So I've come to you . . . I know it's a terrible thing to ask of you, living as you are, but would you take him in with you?

Mr. Frank. Of course we will.

Mr. Kraler (*rising*). It'll be just for a night or two . . . until I find some
1560 other place. This happened so suddenly that I didn't know where to turn.

Mr. Frank. Where is he?

Mr. Kraler. Downstairs in the office.

Mr. Frank. Good. Bring him up.

Mr. Kraler. His name is Dussel . . . Jan Dussel.

Mr. Frank. Dussel . . . I think I know him.

1570 **Mr. Kraler.** I'll get him. (*He goes quickly down the steps and out. Mr. Frank suddenly becomes conscious of the others.*)

Mr. Frank. Forgive me. I spoke without consulting you. But I knew you'd feel as I do.

Mr. Van Daan. There's no reason for you to consult anyone. This is your place. You have a right to
1580 do exactly as you please. The only thing I feel . . . there's so little food as it is . . . and to take in another person . . .

(*Peter turns away, ashamed of his father.*)

Mr. Frank. We can stretch the food a little. It's only for a few days.

Mr. Van Daan. You want to make a bet?

1590 **Mrs. Frank.** I think it's fine to have him. But, Otto, where are you going to put him? Where?

Peter. He can have my bed. I can sleep on the floor. I wouldn't mind.

Mr. Frank. That's good of you, Peter. But your room's too small . . . even for *you*.

Anne. I have a much better idea. I'll come in here with you and

1600 Mother, and Margot can take Peter's room and Peter can go in our room with Mr. Dussel.

Margot. That's right. We could do that.

Mr. Frank. No, Margot. You mustn't sleep in that room . . . neither you nor Anne. Mouschi has caught some rats in there. Peter's brave. He doesn't mind.

1610 **Anne.** Then how about *this*? I'll come in here with you and Mother, and Mr. Dussel can have my bed.

Mrs. Frank. No. No. *No!* Margot will come in here with us and he can have her bed. It's the only way. Margot, bring your things in here. Help her, Anne.

(Margot *hurries into her room to get her things.*)

1620 **Anne** (*to her mother*). Why Margot? Why can't I come in here?

Mrs. Frank. Because it wouldn't be proper for Margot to sleep with a . . . Please, Anne. Don't argue. Please. (Anne *starts slowly away.*)

Mr. Frank. (*to* Anne). You don't mind sharing your room with Mr. Dussel, do you, Anne?

Anne. No. No, of course not.

1630 **Mr. Frank.** Good. (Anne *goes off into her bedroom, helping* Margot. Mr. Frank *starts to search in the cupboards.*) Where's the cognac?

Mrs. Frank. It's there. But, Otto, I was saving it in case of illness.

TO CHALLENGE STUDENTS . . .

Analyze Motivation Remind students that characters have **motivations,** or reasons, for their actions. Draw attention to Mr. Frank's words and actions in lines 1572–1576, and tell students to consider Mr. Frank's motivations.

ASK STUDENTS to consider whether

- Mr. Frank acted on instinct, and thus it did not occur to him to discuss his decision with the others, or
- Mr. Frank feared the others would not agree to have Dussel join them, and so he made the choice without consulting anyone

Prompt them to cite evidence from the text to support their opinions.

©Time Life Pictures/Getty Images

Mr. Frank. I think we couldn't find a better time to use it. Peter, will you get five glasses for me?

1640 (Peter *goes for the glasses. Margot comes out of her bedroom, carrying her possessions, which she hangs behind a curtain in the main room. Mr. Frank finds the cognac and pours it into the five glasses that* Peter *brings him. Mr. Van Daan stands looking on sourly. Mrs. Van Daan comes downstairs and looks around at all the bustle.*)

Mrs. Van Daan. What's happening?
1650 What's going on?

Mr. Van Daan. Someone's moving in with us.

Mrs. Van Daan. In here? You're joking.

Margot. It's only for a night or two . . . until Mr. Kraler finds him another place.

Mr. Van Daan. Yeah! Yeah!

1660 (*Mr. Frank hurries over as Mr. Kraler and Dussel come up. Dussel is a man in his late fifties, meticulous, finicky . . . bewildered now. He wears a raincoat. He carries a briefcase, stuffed full, and a small medicine case.*)

Mr. Frank. Come in, Mr. Dussel.

Mr. Kraler. This is Mr. Frank.

Dussel. Mr. Otto Frank?

Mr. Frank. Yes. Let me take your
1670 things.

(*He takes the hat and briefcase, but Dussel clings to his medicine case.*) This is my wife Edith . . . Mr. and Mrs. Van Daan . . . their son, Peter . . . and my daughters, Margot and Anne.

(*Dussel shakes hands with everyone.*)

Mr. Kraler. Thank you, Mr. Frank.
1680 Thank you all. Mr. Dussel, I leave you in good hands. Oh . . . Dirk's coat.

(*Dussel hurriedly takes off the raincoat, giving it to Mr. Kraler. Underneath is his white dentist's jacket, with a yellow Star of David on it.*)

Dussel (*to Mr. Kraler*). What can I say to thank you . . .?

1690 **Mrs. Frank** (*to Dussel*). Mr. Kraler and Miep . . . They're our life line. Without them we couldn't live.

Mr. Kraler. Please. Please. You make us seem very heroic. It isn't that at all. We simply don't like the Nazis. (*to Mr. Frank, who offers him a drink*) No, thanks. (*then going on*) We don't like their methods. We don't like . . .

1700 **Mr. Frank** (*smiling*). I know. I know. "No one's going to tell us Dutchmen what to do with our damn Jews!"

Mr. Kraler (*to Dussel*). Pay no attention to Mr. Frank. I'll be up tomorrow to see that they're treating you right. (*to Mr. Frank*) Don't trouble to come down again. Peter will bolt the door after me,
1710 won't you, Peter?

Peter. Yes, sir.

Mr. Frank. Thank you, Peter. I'll do it.

Mr. Kraler. Good night. Good night.

Group. Good night, Mr. Kraler. We'll see you tomorrow, (*etc., etc.*)

(*Mr. Kraler goes out with Mr. Frank. Mrs. Frank gives each
1720 one of the "grownups" a glass of cognac.*)

Mrs. Frank. Please, Mr. Dussel, sit down.

(*Mr. Dussel sinks into a chair. Mrs. Frank gives him a glass of cognac.*)

The Diary of Anne Frank: Act One **305**

SCAFFOLDING FOR ELL STUDENTS

Understand Idioms Draw attention to the idiom in lines 1680–1681: *leave you in good hands*. Tell students that an **idiom** is an expression that has a meaning different from the meanings of its individual words. Model these steps for determining an idiom's meaning:

- Use context to understand the meaning.
- Analyze the image suggested by the idiom.

ASK STUDENTS to identify the general action in lines 1653–1681. (*Someone new is arriving to stay at the Annex.*) Ask what kind of help someone new might want. (*to feel welcomed; to have an ally*) Based on these responses, discuss what Mr. Kraler is suggesting to Dussel. (*that Mr. Frank is his ally*) Tell students to follow a similar process with other idioms in the text.

CLOSE READ

Analyze Language

COMMON CORE **RL 4**

(LINES 1752–1773)

Discuss with students the playwrights' choice of words and the impact particular words have on meaning.

C2 **ASK STUDENTS** to reread the description of Mr. Dussel's welcome to the Annex in lines 1752–1773. What does *bolt* mean in this context? *(to gulp down)* What does this word suggest about Mr. Dussel? *(Possible answer: He is very nervous.)* Mr. and Mrs. Van Daan "murmur" their welcome. What are the playwrights indicating by using the word *murmur*? *(The Van Daans are not sincere in their welcome.)* Peter is "humiliated" by his father's comment to Mr. Dussel. What is the impact of the playwright's use of the word *humiliated* instead of a word such as *upset* or *embarrassed*? *(Humiliated has a stronger sense of shame and disapproval.)*

Dussel. I'm dreaming. I know it. I can't believe my eyes. Mr. Otto Frank here! (*to* Mrs. Frank) You're 1730 not in Switzerland then? A woman told me . . . She said she'd gone to your house . . . the door was open, everything was in disorder, dishes in the sink. She said she found a piece of paper in the wastebasket with an address scribbled on it . . . an address in Zurich. She said you must have escaped to Zurich.

Anne. Father put that there 1740 purposely . . . just so people would think that very thing!

Dussel. And you've been here all the time?

Mrs. Frank. All the time . . . ever since July.

(Anne *speaks to her father as he comes back.*)

Anne. It worked, Pim . . . the address you left! Mr. Dussel says 1750 that people believe we escaped to Switzerland.

Mr. Frank. I'm glad . . . And now let's have a little drink to welcome Mr. Dussel. (*Before they can drink,* Mr. Dussel *bolts his drink.* Mr. Frank *smiles and raises his glass.*) To Mr. Dussel. Welcome. We're very honored to have you with us.

1760 **Mrs. Frank.** To Mr. Dussel, welcome.

(*The* Van Daans *murmur a welcome. The "grown-ups" drink.*)

Mrs. Van Daan. Um. That was good.

Mr. Van Daan. Did Mr. Kraler warn you that you won't get much to eat here? You can imagine . . . three ration books among the 1770 seven of us . . . and now you make eight.

(Peter *walks away, humiliated. Outside a street organ is heard dimly.*)

Dussel (*rising*). Mr. Van Daan, you don't realize what is happening outside that you should warn me of a thing like that. You don't realize what's going on . . . (As Mr. Van Daan *starts his characteristic pacing,* 1780 Dussel *turns to speak to the others.*) Right here in Amsterdam every day hundreds of Jews disappear . . . They surround a block and search house by house. Children come home from school to find their parents gone. Hundreds are being deported . . . people that you and I know . . . the Hallensteins . . . the Wessels . . .

1790 **Mrs. Frank** (*in tears*). Oh, no. No!

Dussel. They get their call-up notice . . . come to the Jewish theatre on such and such a day and hour . . . bring only what you can carry in a rucksack. And if you refuse the call-up notice, then they come and drag you from your home and ship you off to Mauthausen.[11] The death camp!

1800 **Mrs. Frank.** We didn't know that things had got so much worse.

Dussel. Forgive me for speaking so.

---

[11] **Mauthausen** (mout´hou´zən): a Nazi concentration camp in Austria.

Anne (*coming to* Dussel). Do you know the de Waals? . . . What's become of them? Their daughter Jopie and I are in the same class. Jopie's my best friend.

Dussel. They are gone.

Anne. Gone?

1810 **Dussel.** With all the others.

Anne. Oh, no. Not Jopie!

(*She turns away, in tears. Mrs. Frank motions to Margot to comfort her. Margot goes to Anne, putting her arms comfortingly around her.*)

Mrs. Van Daan. There were some people called Wagner. They lived near us . . . ?

1820 **Mr. Frank** (*interrupting, with a glance at* Anne). I think we should put this off until later. We all have many questions we want to ask . . . But I'm sure that Mr. Dussel would like to get settled before supper.

Dussel. Thank you. I would. I brought very little with me.

Mr. Frank (*giving him his hat and briefcase*). I'm sorry we can't give
1830 you a room alone. But I hope you won't be too uncomfortable. We've had to make strict rules here . . . a schedule of hours . . . We'll tell you after supper. Anne, would you like to take Mr. Dussel to his room?

Anne (*controlling her tears*). If you'll come with me, Mr. Dussel? (*She starts for her room.*)

Dussel (*shaking hands with each in
1840 turn*). Forgive me if I haven't really

expressed my gratitude to all of you. This has been such a shock to me. I'd always thought of myself as Dutch. I was born in Holland. My father was born in Holland, and my grandfather. And now . . . after all these years . . . (*He breaks off.*) If you'll excuse me.

(Dussel *gives a little bow and
1850 hurries off after* Anne. Mr. Frank *and the others are subdued.*)

Anne (*turning on the light*). Well, here we are.

(Dussel *looks around the room. In the main room* Margot *speaks to her mother.*)

Margot. The news sounds pretty bad, doesn't it? It's so different from what Mr. Kraler tells
1860 us. Mr. Kraler says things are improving.

Mr. Van Daan. I like it better the way Kraler tells it.

(*They resume their occupations, quietly.* Peter *goes off into his room. In* Anne's *room,* Anne *turns to* Dussel.)

Anne. You're going to share the room with me.

1870 **Dussel.** I'm a man who's always lived alone. I haven't had to adjust myself to others. I hope you'll bear with me until I learn.

Anne. Let me help you. (*She takes his briefcase.*) Do you always live all alone? Have you no family at all?

Dussel. No one. (*He opens his medicine case and spreads his bottles on the dressing table.*)

The Diary of Anne Frank: Act One **307**

CLOSE READ

Analyze Characters

COMMON CORE RL 1, RL 3

(LINES 1875–1954)

Remind students that playwrights often reveal what characters are like through their actions and speech as well as through direct comments in the stage directions.

 CITE TEXT EVIDENCE Have students reread lines 1875–1954 to identify clues in the text that reveal what Mr. Dussel is like. What do Mr. Dussel's words and behavior, along with notes in the stage directions, reveal about him? *(Possible answer: Dussel is "used to" being alone. He is allergic to animals with fur. He "takes some pills to fortify himself." Dussel is focused mainly on himself, is not flexible, and seems worried about having to deal "with all the people" on a regular basis.)*

1880 **Anne.** How dreadful. You must be terribly lonely.

Dussel. I'm used to it.

Anne. I don't think I could ever get used to it. Didn't you even have a pet? A cat, or a dog?

Dussel. I have an allergy for fur-bearing animals. They give me asthma.

Anne. Oh, dear. Peter has a cat.

1890 **Dussel.** Here? He has it here?

Anne. Yes. But we hardly ever see it. He keeps it in his room all the time. I'm sure it will be all right.

Dussel. Let us hope so.

(*He takes some pills to fortify himself.*)

Anne. That's Margot's bed, where you're going to sleep. I sleep on the sofa there. (*indicating the clothes*
1900 *hooks on the wall*) We cleared these off for your things. (*She goes over to the window.*) The best part about this room . . . you can look down and see a bit of the street and the canal. There's a houseboat . . . you can see the end of it . . . a bargeman lives there with his family . . . They have a baby and he's just beginning to walk and I'm so afraid he's going
1910 to fall into the canal some day. I watch him . . .

Dussel (*interrupting*). Your father spoke of a schedule.

Anne (*coming away from the window*). Oh, yes. It's mostly about the times we have to be quiet. And times for the w.c. You can use it now if you like.

Dussel (*stiffly*). No, thank you.

1920 **Anne.** I suppose you think it's awful, my talking about a thing like that. But you don't know how important it can get to be, especially when you're frightened . . . About this room, the way Margot and I did . . . she had it to herself in the afternoons for studying, reading . . . lessons, you know . . . and I took the mornings.
1930 Would that be all right with you?

Dussel. I'm not at my best in the morning.

Anne. You stay here in the mornings then. I'll take the room in the afternoons.

Dussel. Tell me, when you're in here, what happens to me? Where am I spending my time? In there, with all the people?

1940 **Anne.** Yes.

Dussel. I see. I see.

Anne. We have supper at half past six.

Dussel (*going over to the sofa*). Then, if you don't mind . . . I like to lie down quietly for ten minutes before eating. I find it helps the digestion.

Anne. Of course. I hope I'm not
1950 going to be too much of a bother to you. I seem to be able to get everyone's back up.

(Dussel *lies down on the sofa, curled up, his back to her.*)

Dussel. I always get along very well with children. My patients all bring their children to me, because they know I get on well with them. So don't you worry about that.

1960 (Anne *leans over him, taking his hand and shaking it gratefully.*)

Anne. Thank you. Thank you, Mr. Dussel.

(*The lights dim to darkness. The curtain falls on the scene. Anne's Voice* comes to us faintly at first, and then with increasing power.*)

Anne's Voice. . . . And yesterday I finished Cissy Van Marxvelt's
1970 latest book. I think she is a first-class writer. I shall definitely let my children read her. Monday the twenty-first of September, nineteen forty-two. Mr. Dussel and I had another battle yesterday. Yes, Mr. Dussel! According to him, nothing, I repeat . . . nothing, is right about me . . . my appearance, my character, my manners. While he
1980 was going on at me I thought . . . sometime I'll give you such a smack that you'll fly right up to the ceiling! Why is it that every grownup thinks he knows the way to bring up children? Particularly the grownups that never had any. I keep wishing that Peter was a girl instead of a boy. Then I would have someone to talk to. Margot's
1990 a darling, but she takes everything too seriously. To pause for a moment on the subject of Mrs. Van Daan. I must tell you that her attempts to flirt with Father are

getting her nowhere. Pim, thank goodness, won't play.

(*As she is saying the last lines, the curtain rises on the darkened scene. Anne's Voice* fades out.*)

Scene 4

2000 *It is the middle of the night, several months later. The stage is dark except for a little light which comes through the skylight in Peter's room.*

Everyone is in bed. Mr. and Mrs. Frank lie on the couch in the main room, which has been pulled out to serve as a makeshift double bed.

2010 *Margot is sleeping on a mattress on the floor in the main room, behind a curtain stretched across for privacy. The others are all in their accustomed rooms.*

*From outside we hear two drunken soldiers singing "Lili Marlene." A girl's high giggle is heard. The sound of running feet is heard coming closer and then fading
2020 in the distance. Throughout the scene there is the distant sound of airplanes passing overhead.*

*A match suddenly flares up in the attic. We dimly see Mr. Van Daan. He is getting his bearings. He comes quickly down the stairs, and goes to the cupboard where the food is stored. Again the match flares up, and is as quickly
2030 blown out. The dim figure is seen to steal back up the stairs.*

The Diary of Anne Frank: Act One **309**

CLOSE READ

Analyze Drama

COMMON CORE RL 1

(LINES 2000–2004)

Review that acts in a play are divided into smaller sections called scenes.

E2 **ASK STUDENTS** to explain why the playwrights begin a new scene here. (*The time of the action has changed.*) When does this scene take place? (*It is the middle of the night a few months after Scene 3.*)

Analyze Drama

COMMON CORE RL 1, RL 3

(LINES 2040–2066)

Tell students that playwrights can use **dialogue,** the written conversation between two or more characters, to make a contrast.

F2 **CITE TEXT EVIDENCE** Have students reread lines 2040–2066 to contrast the ways Mr. Dussel and Mrs. Frank communicate with Anne. *(Mr. Dussel is "furious" and speaks to her using harsh language. Mrs. Frank is loving and gentle. She uses comforting language such as "my darling.")* What does this dialogue reveal about the characters? *(It suggests that Dussel is not any more comfortable with the other residents than he was when he arrived; Anne's nightmare suggests that the tension of being in hiding is having an impact on her.)*

There is quiet for a second or two, broken only by the sound of airplanes, and running feet on the street below.

Suddenly, out of the silence and the dark, we hear Anne scream.

Anne (*screaming*). No! No! Don't . . . don't take me!

2040 (*She moans, tossing and crying in her sleep. The other people wake, terrified. Dussel sits up in bed, furious.*)

Dussel. Shush! Anne! Anne, for God's sake, shush!

Anne (*still in her nightmare*). Save me! Save me!

(*She screams and screams. Dussel gets out of bed, going over to her,* 2050 *trying to wake her.*)

Dussel. For God's sake! Quiet! Quiet! You want someone to hear?

(*In the main room Mrs. Frank grabs a shawl and pulls it around her. She rushes in to Anne, taking her in her arms. Mr. Frank hurriedly gets up, putting on his overcoat. Margot sits up, terrified. Peter's light goes on in his room.*)

2060 **Mrs. Frank** (*to Anne, in her room*). Hush, darling, hush. It's all right. It's all right. (*over her shoulder to Dussel*) Will you be kind enough to turn on the light, Mr. Dussel? (*back to Anne*) It's nothing, my darling. It was just a dream.

(*Dussel turns on the light in the bedroom. Mrs. Frank holds Anne in her arms. Gradually Anne comes* 2070 *out of her nightmare, still trembling*

with horror. Mr. Frank comes into the room, and goes quickly to the window, looking out to be sure that no one outside had heard Anne's screams. Mrs. Frank holds Anne, talking softly to her. In the main room Margot stands on a chair, turning on the center hanging lamp. A light goes on in the Van Daan's 2080 *room overhead. Peter puts his robe on, coming out of his room.*)

Dussel (*to Mrs. Frank, blowing his nose*). Something must be done about that child, Mrs. Frank. Yelling like that! Who knows but there's somebody on the streets? She's endangering all our lives.

Mrs. Frank. Anne, darling.

Dussel. Every night she twists and 2090 turns. I don't sleep. I spend half my night shushing her. And now it's nightmares!

(*Margot comes to the door of Anne's room, followed by Peter. Mr. Frank goes to them, indicating that everything is all right. Peter takes Margot back.*)

Mrs. Frank (*to Anne*). You're here, safe, you see? Nothing has 2100 happened. (*to Dussel*) Please, Mr. Dussel, go back to bed. She'll be herself in a minute or two. Won't you, Anne?

Dussel (*picking up a book and a pillow*). Thank you, but I'm going to the w.c. The one place where there's peace! (*He stalks out. Mr. Van Daan, in underwear and trousers, comes down the stairs.*)

©Rex/Daily Mail/Alamy Images

2110 **Mr. Van Daan** (*to* Dussel). What is it? What happened?

Dussel. A nightmare. She was having a nightmare!

Mr. Van Daan. I thought someone was murdering her.

Dussel. Unfortunately, no.

(*He goes into the bathroom. Mr. Van Daan goes back up the stairs. Mr. Frank, in the main room, sends*
2120 Peter *back to his own bedroom.*)

Mr. Frank. Thank you, Peter. Go back to bed.

(Peter *goes back to his room. Mr. Frank follows him, turning*

The Diary of Anne Frank: Act One **311**

Analyze Drama

COMMON CORE RL 1, RL 4

(LINES 2151–2168)

Point out that although most of the play is written in English here the playwrights present parts of the dialogue in German.

G2 **ASK STUDENTS** to reread lines 2151–2168. Why do you think the playwrights have Mr. and Mrs. Frank speak German in this part of the script? *(Possible answer: People who speak more than one language may revert to the one they feel most comfortable with in times of stress. Because the play is written in English, the playwrights may be emphasizing that Mr. and Mrs. Frank are under extreme stress.)*

---

out the light and looking out the window. Then he goes back to the main room, and gets up on a chair, turning out the center hanging lamp.)

2130 **Mrs. Frank** (*to* Anne). Would you like some water? (Anne *shakes her head.*) Was it a very bad dream? Perhaps if you told me . . . ?

Anne. I'd rather not talk about it.

Mrs. Frank. Poor darling. Try to sleep then. I'll sit right here beside you until you fall asleep.

(*She brings a stool over, sitting there.*)

2140 **Anne.** You don't have to.

Mrs. Frank. But I'd like to stay with you . . . very much. Really.

Anne. I'd rather you didn't.

Mrs. Frank. Good night, then. (*She leans down to kiss* Anne. Anne *throws her arm up over her face, turning away.* Mrs. Frank, *hiding her hurt, kisses* Anne's *arm.*) You'll be all right? There's nothing that you want?

2150 **Anne.** Will you please ask Father to come.

Mrs. Frank (*after a second*). Of course, Anne dear. (*She hurries out into the other room.* Mr. Frank *comes to her as she comes in.*) Sie verlangt nach Dir!¹²

Mr. Frank (*sensing her hurt*). Edith, Liebe, schau . . .¹³

2160 **Mrs. Frank.** *Es macht nichts! Ich danke dem lieben Herrgott, dass sie sich wenigstens an Dich wendet, wenn sie Trost braucht! Geh hinein, Otto, sie ist ganz hysterisch vor Angst.*¹⁴ (*as* Mr. Frank *hesitates*) *Geh zu ihr.*¹⁵ (*He looks at her for a second and then goes to get a cup of water for* Anne. Mrs. Frank *sinks down on the bed, her face in her hands, trying to keep from sobbing aloud.* Margot *comes over to her, putting her arms around her.*) She wants nothing of me. She pulled away when I leaned down to kiss her.

Margot. It's a phase . . . You heard Father . . . Most girls go through it . . . they turn to their fathers at this age . . . they give all their love to their fathers.

Mrs. Frank. You weren't like this. You didn't shut me out.

Margot. She'll get over it . . . (*She smooths the bed for* Mrs. Frank *and sits beside her a moment as* Mrs. Frank *lies down. In* Anne's *room* Mr. Frank *comes in, sitting down by* Anne. Anne *flings her arms around him, clinging to him.*

---

¹³ *Liebe, schau* (lē´bə shou´) German: Dear, look.

¹⁴ *Es macht . . .* (ĕs mäкнt´ nĭкнts´! ĭкн dängk´ə dām lē´bən hĕr´gôt´, däs zē zĭкн´ vān´ĭкн-shtənz än dĭкн´ vĕn´dət, vĕn zē trôst´ brouкнt´! gä hĭn-īn´, ôt´tô; zē ĭst gänts hü-stĕr´ĭsh fŏr ängst´) *German:* It's all right. I thank dear God that at least she turns to you when she needs comfort. Go in, Otto; she is hysterical with fear.

¹⁵ *Geh zu ihr* (gä´ tsoō îr´) German: Go to her.

---

¹² *Sie verlangt nach Dir* (zē fer-längt´näкн dîr) *German:* She is asking for you.

2190 *In the distance we hear the sound of ack-ack.*)

Anne. Oh, Pim. I dreamed that they came to get us! The Green Police! They broke down the door and grabbed me and started to drag me out the way they did Jopie.

Mr. Frank. I want you to take this pill. H2

Anne. What is it?

2200 **Mr. Frank.** Something to quiet you.

(*She takes it and drinks the water. In the main room* Margot *turns out the light and goes back to her bed.*)

Mr. Frank (*to* Anne). Do you want me to read to you for a while?

Anne. No. Just sit with me for a minute. Was I awful? Did I yell terribly loud? Do you think anyone outside could have heard?

2210 **Mr. Frank.** No. No. Lie quietly now. Try to sleep.

Anne. I'm a terrible coward. I'm so disappointed in myself. I think I've conquered my fear . . . I think I'm really grown-up . . . and then something happens . . . and I run to you like a baby . . . I love you, Father. I don't love anyone but you.

Mr. Frank (*reproachfully*). Annele!

2220 **Anne.** It's true. I've been thinking about it for a long time. You're the only one I love.

Mr. Frank. It's fine to hear you tell me that you love me. But I'd be happier if you said you loved your mother as well . . . She needs your help so much . . . your love . . .

Anne. We have nothing in common. She doesn't understand me. Whenever I try to explain my
2230 views on life to her she asks me if I'm constipated.

Mr. Frank. You hurt her very much just now. She's crying. She's in there crying.

Anne. I can't help it. I only told the truth. I didn't want her here . . . (*then, with sudden change*) Oh, Pim, I was horrible, wasn't I? And
2240 the worst of it is, I can stand off and look at myself doing it and know it's cruel and yet I can't stop doing it. What's the matter with me? Tell me. Don't say it's just a phase! Help me.

Mr. Frank. There is so little that we parents can do to help our children. We can only try to set a good example . . . point the way.
2250 The rest you must do yourself. You must build your own character.

Anne. I'm trying. Really I am. Every night I think back over all of the things I did that day that were wrong . . . like putting the wet mop in Mr. Dussel's bed . . . and this thing now with Mother. I say to myself, that was wrong. I make up my mind, I'm never going to do
2260 that again. Never! Of course I may do something worse . . . but at least I'll never do *that* again! . . . I have a nicer side, Father . . . a sweeter, nicer side. But I'm scared to show it. I'm afraid that people are going to laugh at me if I'm serious. So the mean Anne comes to the outside and the good Anne stays on the

The Diary of Anne Frank: Act One **313**

Analyze Characters

COMMON CORE RL 1, RL 3

(LINES 2233–2274)

Explain to students that another way authors reveal what characters are like is through a character's own thoughts.

H2 **CITE TEXT EVIDENCE** Have students reread lines 2233–2274 to examine Anne's thoughts about herself. What do Anne's thoughts tell the audience about her nature? (*Possible answer: Anne is self-aware and knows that sometimes her behavior hurts others: "I was horrible, wasn't I?" She sincerely wishes to be kinder: "I'm never going to do that again. Never! Of course I may do something worse." Her sometimes-brash behavior is a way of hiding an inner fear of ridicule: "I'm afraid that people are going to laugh at me if I'm serious."*)

Analyze Drama

COMMON CORE **RL 1**

(LINES 2320–2328)

Call attention to the stage directions at the beginning of Scene 5.

⑫ ASK STUDENTS to reread lines 2320–2328. Based on these stage directions, what will the focus of Scene 5 be? *(the celebration of Hanukkah)* Who is leading the Hanukkah celebration? *(Mr. Frank)* Why might the playwrights have chosen to focus on this celebration? *(Hanukkah is a sacred holiday for the Jewish people. The celebration reinforces that being Jewish is the reason the families are in hiding.)*

inside, and I keep on trying to switch them around and have the good Anne outside and the bad Anne inside and be what I'd like to be . . . and might be . . . if only . . . only . . . (*She is asleep. Mr. Frank watches her for a moment and then turns off the light, and starts out. The lights dim out. The curtain falls on the scene. Anne's Voice is heard dimly at first, and then with growing strength.*)

Anne's Voice. . . . The air raids are getting worse. They come over day and night. The noise is terrifying. Pim says it should be music to our ears. The more planes, the sooner will come the end of the war. Mrs. Van Daan pretends to be a fatalist. What will be, will be. But when the planes come over, who is the most frightened? No one else but Petronella! . . . Monday, the ninth of November, nineteen forty-two. Wonderful news! The Allies have landed in Africa. Pim says that we can look for an early finish to the war. Just for fun he asked each of us what was the first thing we wanted to do when we got out of here. Mrs. Van Daan longs to be home with her own things, her needle-point chairs, the Beckstein piano her father gave her . . . the best that money could buy. Peter would like to go to a movie. Mr. Dussel wants to get back to his dentist's drill. He's afraid he is losing his touch. For myself, there are so many things . . . to ride a bike again . . . to laugh till my belly aches . . . to

have new clothes from the skin out . . . to have a hot tub filled to overflowing and wallow in it for hours . . . to be back in school with my friends . . .

(*As the last lines are being said, the curtain rises on the scene. The lights dim on as Anne's Voice fades away.*)

Scene 5

It is the first night of the Hanukkah[16] *celebration. Mr. Frank is standing at the head of the table on which is the Menorah.*[17] *He lights the Shamos, or servant candle, and holds it as he says the blessing. Seated listening is all of the "family," dressed in their best. The men wear hats,* Peter *wears his cap.*

Mr. Frank (*reading from a prayer book*). "Praised be Thou, oh Lord our God, Ruler of the universe, who has sanctified us with Thy commandments and bidden us kindle the Hanukkah lights. Praised be Thou, oh Lord our God, Ruler of the universe, who has wrought wondrous deliverances for our fathers in days of old. Praised be Thou, oh Lord our God, Ruler of the universe, that Thou has given us life and sustenance and brought us to this happy season." (Mr. Frank *lights the one candle*

---

[16] **Hanukkah** (hä´nə-kə): a Jewish holiday, celebrated in December and lasting eight days.

[17] **Menorah** (mə-nôr´ə): a candleholder with nine branches, used in the celebration of Hanukkah.

of the Menorah *as he continues.*) "We kindle this Hanukkah light to celebrate the great and wonderful deeds wrought through the zeal with which God filled the hearts of the heroic Maccabees, two thousand years ago. They fought against indifference, against tyranny and oppression, and they restored our Temple to us. May these lights remind us that we should ever look to God, whence cometh our help." Amen. [Pronounced O-mayn.]

All. Amen.

(Mr. Frank *hands* Mrs. Frank *the prayer book.*)

Mrs. Frank (*reading*). "I lift up mine eyes unto the mountains, from whence cometh my help. My help cometh from the Lord who made heaven and earth. He will not suffer thy foot to be moved. He that keepeth thee will not slumber. He that keepeth Israel doth neither slumber nor sleep. The Lord is thy keeper. The Lord is thy shade upon thy right hand. The sun shall not smite thee by day, nor the moon by night. The Lord shall keep thee from all evil. He shall keep thy soul. The Lord shall guard thy going out and thy coming in, from this time forth and forevermore." Amen.

All. Amen.

(Mrs. Frank *puts down the prayer book and goes to get the food and wine.* Margot *helps her.* Mr. Frank takes the men's hats and puts them aside.)

Dussel (*rising*). That was very moving.

Anne (*pulling him back*). It isn't over yet!

Mrs. Van Daan. Sit down! Sit down!

Anne. There's a lot more, songs and presents.

Dussel. Presents?

Mrs. Frank. Not this year, unfortunately.

Mrs. Van Daan. But always on Hanukkah everyone gives presents . . . everyone!

Dussel. Like our St. Nicholas' Day.[18] (*There is a chorus of "no's" from the group.*)

Mrs. Van Daan. No! Not like St. Nicholas! What kind of a Jew are you that you don't know Hanukkah?

Mrs. Frank (*as she brings the food*). I remember particularly the candles . . . First one, as we have tonight. Then the second night you light two candles, the next night three . . . and so on until you have eight candles burning. When there are eight candles it is truly beautiful.

Mrs. Van Daan. And the potato pancakes.

---

[18] **St. Nicholas's Day:** December 6, the day that Christian children in the Netherlands receive gifts.

CLOSE READ

Analyze Language

COMMON CORE **RL 4**

(LINES 2359–2378)

Tell students that sometimes authors may include passages from other texts in their own work. As needed, explain that playwrights are quoting Psalm 121 from the Bible.

J2 ASK STUDENTS to reread lines 2359–2378. Why is most of this text shown within quotation marks? (*The quotation marks indicate that the words are from another source, a prayer book.*) What is the impact of the ancient prayer that Mrs. Frank reads? (*Although the prayer is ancient, its solemn language offers hope for the families' current situation: "The Lord shall keep thee from all evil. . . . from this time forth and forevermore."*)

CLOSE READ

Analyze Language

COMMON CORE RL 4, L 5a

(LINES 2451–2459)

Explain that a **pun** is a humorous play on words and that some puns involve using different meanings of the same word.

K2 **ASK STUDENTS** to reread lines 2451–2459. Who is the author of this poem? *(Anne)* What pun does Anne include to make the poem humorous? *("Cross words" and "crossword" sound alike but have different meanings. "Cross words" are angry words; "crosswords" are a type of word puzzle.)* What is the impact of Anne's pun? *(It recalls both the tension with which everyone is living and their need for activities that will keep their minds active.)*

Mr. Van Daan. Don't talk about them!

2420 **Mrs. Van Daan.** I make the best *latkes*[19] you ever tasted!

Mrs. Frank. Invite us all next year . . . in your own home.

Mr. Frank. God willing!

Mrs. Van Daan. God willing.

Margot. What I remember best is the presents we used to get when we were little . . . eight days of presents . . . and each day they got better and better.

2430 **Mrs. Frank** (*sitting down*). We are all here, alive. That is present enough.

Anne. No, it isn't. I've got something . . .

(*She rushes into her room, hurriedly puts on a little hat improvised from the lamp shade, grabs a satchel bulging with parcels and comes running back.*)

2440 **Mrs. Frank.** What is it?

Anne. Presents!

Mrs. Van Daan. Presents!

Dussel. Look!

Mr. Van Daan. What's she got on her head?

Peter. A lamp shade!

Anne (*She picks out one at random*). This is for Margot. (*She hands it to Margot, pulling her to her feet.*)
2450 Read it out loud.

 Margot (*reading*).

---

[19] **latkes** (lät´kəz): potato pancakes.

"You have never lost your temper. You never will, I fear,

You are so good.

But if you should,

Put all your cross words here."

(*She tears open the package.*)

A new crossword puzzle book! Where did you get it?

2460 **Anne.** It isn't new. It's one that you've done. But I rubbed it all out, and if you wait a little and forget, you can do it all over again.

Margot (*sitting*). It's wonderful, Anne. Thank you. You'd never know it wasn't new.

(*From outside we hear the sound of a streetcar passing.*)

Anne (*with another gift*). Mrs. Van
2470 Daan.

Mrs. Van Daan (*taking it*). This is awful . . . I haven't anything for anyone . . . I never thought . . .

Mr. Frank. This is all Anne's idea.

Mrs. Van Daan (*holding up a bottle*). What is it?

Anne. It's hair shampoo. I took all the odds and ends of soap and mixed them with the last of my
2480 toilet water.

Mrs. Van Daan. Oh, Anneke!

Anne. I wanted to write a poem for all of them, but I didn't have time. (*offering a large box to* Mr. Van Daan) Yours, Mr. Van Daan, is really something . . . something you want more than anything. (*as she* *waits for him to open it)* Look! Cigarettes!

2490 **Mr. Van Daan.** Cigarettes!

Anne. Two of them! Pim found some old pipe tobacco in the pocket lining of his coat . . . and we made them . . . or rather, Pim did.

Mrs. Van Daan. Let me see . . . Well, look at that! Light it, Putti! Light it.

(Mr. Van Daan hesitates.)

2500 **Anne.** It's tobacco, really it is! There's a little fluff in it, but not much.

(Everyone watches intently as Mr. Van Daan cautiously lights it. The cigarette flares up. Everyone laughs.)

Peter. It works!

Mrs. Van Daan. Look at him.

Mr. Van Daan *(spluttering).* Thank
2510 you, Anne. Thank you.

(Anne rushes back to her satchel for another present.)

Anne *(handing her mother a piece of paper).* For Mother, Hanukkah greeting. *(She pulls her mother to her feet.)*

Mrs. Frank *(She reads.)* "Here's an I.O.U. that I promise to pay. Ten hours of doing whatever you say.
2520 Signed, Anne Frank." *(Mrs. Frank, touched, takes Anne in her arms, holding her close.)*

Dussel *(to Anne).* Ten hours of doing what you're told? *Anything* you're told?

Anne. That's right.

Dussel. You wouldn't want to sell that, Mrs. Frank?

Mrs. Frank. Never! This is the
2530 most precious gift I've ever had!

(She sits, showing her present to the others. Anne hurries back to the satchel and pulls out a scarf, the scarf that Mr. Frank found in the first scene.)

Anne *(offering it to her father).* For Pim.

Mr. Frank. Anneke . . . I wasn't supposed to have a present! *(He
2540 takes it, unfolding it and showing it to the others.)*

Anne. It's a muffler . . . to put round your neck . . . like an ascot, you know. I made it myself out of odds and ends . . . I knitted it in the dark each night, after I'd gone to bed. I'm afraid it looks better in the dark!

Mr. Frank *(putting it on).* It's fine.
2550 It fits me perfectly. Thank you, Annele.

(Anne hands Peter a ball of paper, with a string attached to it.)

Anne. That's for Mouschi.

Peter *(rising to bow).* On behalf of Mouschi, I thank you.

Anne *(hesitant, handing him a gift).* And . . . this is yours . . . from Mrs. Quack Quack. *(as he holds it
2560 gingerly in his hands)* Well . . . open it . . . Aren't you going to open it?

CLOSE READ

Analyze Drama

COMMON CORE **RL 1**

(LINES 2532–2551)

Point out that stage directions can provide important information that links scenes in a play.

L2 **CITE TEXT EVIDENCE** Ask students to reread lines 2532–2551 to determine how the action in this scene is connected to Scene 1. *(The scarf that Anne makes for her father as a Hanukkah gift is the same scarf that Mr. Frank puts around his neck in Scene 1.)* Why is this detail in the stage directions important to know? *(It explains why the scarf is still important to Mr. Frank after the war and why he saves it when he comes back to the Annex.)*

Peter. I'm scared to. I know something's going to jump out and hit me.

Anne. No. It's nothing like that, really.

Mrs. Van Daan (*as he is opening it*). What is it, Peter? Go on. Show it.

Anne (*excitedly*). It's a safety razor!

2570 **Dussel.** A what?

Anne. A razor!

Mrs. Van Daan (*looking at it*). You didn't make that out of odds and ends.

Anne (*to* Peter). Miep got it for me. It's not new. It's second-hand. But you really do need a razor now.

Dussel. For what?

Anne. Look on his upper lip . . .
2580 you can see the beginning of a mustache.

Dussel. He wants to get rid of that? Put a little milk on it and let the cat lick it off.

Peter (*starting for his room*). Think you're funny, don't you.

Dussel. Look! He can't wait! He's going in to try it!

Peter. I'm going to give Mouschi
2590 his present! (*He goes into his room, slamming the door behind him.*)

Mr. Van Daan (*disgustedly*). Mouschi, Mouschi, Mouschi.

(*In the distance we hear a dog persistently barking. Anne brings a gift to* Dussel.)

Anne. And last but never least, my roommate, Mr. Dussel.

Dussel. For me? You have
2600 something for me? (*He opens the small box she gives him.*)

Anne. I made them myself.

Dussel (*puzzled*). Capsules! Two capsules!

Anne. They're ear-plugs!

Dussel. Ear-plugs?

Anne. To put in your ears so you won't hear me when I thrash around at night. I saw them
2610 advertised in a magazine. They're not real ones . . . I made them out of cotton and candle wax. Try them . . . See if they don't work . . . see if you can hear me talk . . .

Dussel (*putting them in his ears*). Wait now until I get them in . . . so.

Anne. Are you ready?

Dussel. Huh?

Anne. Are you ready?

2620 **Dussel.** Good God! They've gone inside! I can't get them out! (*They laugh as* Mr. Dussel *jumps about, trying to shake the plugs out of his ears. Finally he gets them out. Putting them away.*) Thank you, Anne! Thank you!

Mr. Van Daan. A real Hanukkah!

Mrs. Van Daan. Wasn't it
2630 cute of her?   *Together*

Mrs. Frank. I don't know when she did it.

Margot. I love my present.

Anne (*sitting at the table*). And now let's have the song, Father . . .

TO CHALLENGE STUDENTS . . .

Analyze the Impact of Perspective Remind students the Frances Goodrich and Albert Hackett wrote their play based on Anne's diary. Have students form small groups to create diary entries that one of the other characters might have written about the Hanukkah celebration. You may wish to assign a specific character to each group.

ASK STUDENTS to review the main events of the celebration and to consider what they have learned about each character. How would that character describe the celebration differently? In what ways would the character's description be similar to what the play presents? Have groups share their diary entries with the class.

©Time Life Pictures/Getty Images

please . . . (*to* Dussel) Have you heard the Hanukkah song, Mr. Dussel? The song is the whole thing! (*She sings.*) "Oh, Hanukkah! Oh Hanukkah! The sweet celebration . . . "

Mr. Frank (*quieting her*). I'm afraid, Anne, we shouldn't sing that song tonight. (*to* Dussel) It's a song of jubilation, of rejoicing. One is apt to become too enthusiastic.

Anne. Oh, please, please. Let's sing the song. I promise not to shout!

Mr. Frank. Very well. But quietly now . . . I'll keep an eye on you and when . . .

(*As* Anne *starts to sing, she is interrupted by* Dussel, *who is snorting and wheezing.*)

Dussel (*pointing to* Peter). You . . . You! (Peter *is coming from his bedroom, ostentatiously holding a bulge in his coat as if he were holding his cat, and dangling* Anne's *present before it.*) How many times . . . I told you . . . Out! Out!

The Diary of Anne Frank: Act One **319**

CLOSE READ

Analyze Characters

COMMON CORE **RL 1, RL 3**

(LINES 2668–2699)

Help students understand more about what Mr. Van Daan is like by examining his words.

M2 **CITE TEXT EVIDENCE** Have students reread lines 2668–2699 to draw conclusions about Mr. Van Daan. What can you infer about Mr. Van Daan from the words he speaks to Peter and to Mr. Dussel? *(Possible answer: Mr. Van Daan is very direct and isn't afraid to say just what he thinks. His thoughts can be based more on emotion than on facts and logic: "Don't tell me! He gets fatter every day! Damn cat looks better than any of us." His threat to get rid of Peter's cat and to allow Peter himself to leave show that he is not an understanding or supportive parent.)*

Analyze Drama

COMMON CORE **RL 1**

(LINES 2720–2736)

Tell students that the series of events in a story or play is called the plot. Explain that stage directions in a play may describe a key event in the plot.

N2 **CITE TEXT EVIDENCE** Ask students to reread lines 2720–2736 to identify the most significant event that occurs at this point in the play. *(Although no one should be downstairs, the residents of the Annex hear "a crash of something falling below." After Peter and a lamp shade fall, making a loud noise upstairs, the residents hear the sound of running feet below.)* Why is this event such an important part of the plot? *(The residents of the Annex fear that their hiding place has been discovered.)*

Mr. Van Daan (*going to* Peter). What's the matter with you? Haven't you any sense? Get that cat out of here.

Peter (*innocently*). Cat?

Mr. Van Daan. You heard me. Get it out of here!

Peter. I have no cat. (*Delighted with his joke, he opens his coat and pulls* 2670 *out a bath towel. The group at the table laugh, enjoying the joke.*)

Dussel (*still wheezing*). It doesn't need to be the cat . . . his clothes are enough . . . when he comes out of that room . . .

Mr. Van Daan. Don't worry. You won't be bothered any more. We're getting rid of it.

Dussel. At last you listen to me. 2680 (*He goes off into his bedroom.*)

Mr. Van Daan (*calling after him*). I'm not doing it for you. That's all in your mind . . . all of it! (*He starts back to his place at the table.*) I'm doing it because I'm sick of seeing that cat eat all our food.

Peter. That's not true! I only give him bones . . . scraps . . .

Mr. Van Daan. Don't tell me! He 2690 gets fatter every day! Damn cat looks better than any of us. Out he goes tonight!

Peter. No! No!

Anne. Mr. Van Daan, you can't do that! That's Peter's cat.

Mrs. Frank (*quietly*). Anne.

Peter (*to* Mr. Van Daan). If he goes, I go.

Mr. Van Daan. Go! Go!

2700 **Mrs. Van Daan.** You're not going and the cat's not going! Now please . . . this is Hanukkah . . . Hanukkah . . . this is the time to celebrate . . . What's the matter with all of you? Come on, Anne. Let's have the song.

Anne (*singing*). "Oh, Hanukkah! Oh, Hanukkah! The sweet celebration."

Mr. Frank (*rising*). I think we should first blow out the candle . . . 2710 then we'll have something for tomorrow night.

Margot. But, Father, you're supposed to let it burn itself out.

Mr. Frank. I'm sure that God understands shortages. (*before blowing it out*) "Praised be Thou, oh Lord our God, who hast sustained us and permitted us to celebrate this joyous festival."

2720 (*He is about to blow out the candle when suddenly there is a crash of something falling below. They all freeze in horror, motionless. For a few seconds there is complete silence. Mr. Frank slips off his shoes. The others noiselessly follow his example. Mr. Frank turns out a light near him. He motions to Peter to turn off the center lamp. Peter tries to reach* 2730 *it, realizes he cannot and gets up on a chair. Just as he is touching the lamp he loses his balance. The chair goes out from under him. He falls. The iron lamp shade crashes to the floor. There is a sound of feet below, running down the stairs.*)

Mr. Van Daan (*under his breath*). God Almighty! (*The only light left comes from the Hanukkah*

2740 candle. Dussel *comes from his room. Mr. Frank creeps over to the stairwell and stands listening. The dog is heard barking excitedly.*) Do you hear anything?

Mr. Frank (*in a whisper*). No. I think they've gone.

Mrs. Van Daan. It's the Green Police. They've found us.

Mr. Frank. If they had, they
2750 wouldn't have left. They'd be up here by now.

Mrs. Van Daan. I know it's the Green Police. They've gone to get help. That's all. They'll be back!

Mr. Van Daan. Or it may have been the Gestapo,[20] looking for papers . . .

Mr. Frank (*interrupting*). Or a thief, looking for money.

Mrs. Van Daan. We've got to do
2760 something . . . Quick! Quick! Before they come back.

Mr. Van Daan. There isn't anything to do. Just wait.

(*Mr. Frank holds up his hand for them to be quiet. He is listening intently. There is complete silence as they all strain to hear any sound from below. Suddenly Anne begins to sway. With a low cry she falls to*
2770 *the floor in a faint. Mrs. Frank goes to her quickly, sitting beside her on the floor and taking her in her arms.*)

Mrs. Frank. Get some water, please! Get some water!

(*Margot starts for the sink.*)

[20] **Gestapo** (gə-stä′pō): the Nazi secret police force, known for its terrorism and brutality.

Mr. Van Daan (*grabbing* Margot). No! No! No one's going to run water!

Mr. Frank. If they've found us, they've found us. Get the water.
2780 (Margot *starts again for the sink.* Mr. Frank, *getting a flashlight*) I'm going down.

(Margot *rushes to him, clinging to him.* Anne *struggles to consciousness.*)

Margot. No, Father, no! There may be someone there, waiting . . . It may be a trap!

Mr. Frank. This is Saturday. There
2790 is no way for us to know what has happened until Miep or Mr. Kraler comes on Monday morning. We cannot live with this uncertainty.

Margot. Don't go, Father!

Mrs. Frank. Hush, darling, hush. (Mr. Frank *slips quietly out, down the steps and out through the door below.*) Margot! Stay close to me.

(Margot *goes to her mother.*)

2800 **Mr. Van Daan.** Shush! Shush!

(Mrs. Frank *whispers to* Margot *to get the water.* Margot *goes for it.*)

Mrs. Van Daan. Putti, where's our money? Get our money. I hear you can buy the Green Police off, so much a head. Go upstairs quick! Get the money!

Mr. Van Daan. Keep still!

Mrs. Van Daan (*kneeling before*
2810 *him, pleading*). Do you want to be dragged off to a concentration camp? Are you going to stand there

and wait for them to come up and get you? Do something, I tell you!

Mr. Van Daan (*pushing her aside*). Will you keep still! (*He goes over to the stairwell to listen. Peter goes to his mother, helping her up onto the sofa. There is a second of silence,*
2820 *then Anne can stand it no longer.*)

Anne. Someone go after Father! Make Father come back!

Peter (*starting for the door*). I'll go.

Mr. Van Daan. Haven't you done enough?

(*He pushes Peter roughly away. In his anger against his father Peter grabs a chair as if to hit him with it, then puts it down, burying his face*
2830 *in his hands. Mrs. Frank begins to pray softly.*)

Anne. Please, please, Mr. Van Daan. Get Father.

Mr. Van Daan. Quiet! Quiet!

(*Anne is shocked into silence. Mrs. Frank pulls her closer, holding her protectively in her arms.*)

Mrs. Frank (*softly, praying*). "I lift up mine eyes unto the mountains,
2840 from whence cometh my help. My help cometh from the Lord who made heaven and earth. He will not suffer thy foot to be moved . . . He that keepeth thee will not slumber . . . " (*She stops as she hears someone coming. They all watch the door tensely. Mr. Frank comes quietly in. Anne rushes to him, holding him tight.*)

2850 **Mr. Frank.** It was a thief. That noise must have scared him away.

Mrs. Van Daan. Thank God.

Mr. Frank. He took the cash box. And the radio. He ran away in such a hurry that he didn't stop to shut the street door. It was swinging wide open. (*A breath of relief sweeps over them.*) I think it would be good to have some light.

2860 **Margot.** Are you sure it's all right?

Mr. Frank. The danger has passed. (*Margot goes to light the small lamp.*) Don't be so terrified, Anne. We're safe.

Dussel. Who says the danger has passed? Don't you realize we are in greater danger than ever?

Mr. Frank. Mr. Dussel, will you be still!

2870 (*Mr. Frank takes Anne back to the table, making her sit down with him, trying to calm her.*)

Dussel (*pointing to Peter*). Thanks to this clumsy fool, there's someone now who knows we're up here! Someone now knows we're up here, hiding!

Mrs. Van Daan (*going to Dussel*). Someone knows we're here, yes.
2880 But who is the someone? A thief! A thief! You think a thief is going to go to the Green Police and say . . . I was robbing a place the other night and I heard a noise up over my head? You think a thief is going to do that?

Dussel. Yes. I think he will.

Mrs. Van Daan (*hysterically*). You're crazy! (*She stumbles back to*

2890 *her seat at the table.* Peter *follows protectively, pushing* Dussel *aside.*)

Dussel. I think some day he'll be caught and then he'll make a bargain with the Green Police . . . if they'll let him off, he'll tell them where some Jews are hiding!

(*He goes off into the bedroom. There is a second of appalled silence.*)

Mr. Van Daan. He's right.

2900 **Anne.** Father, let's get out of here! We can't stay here now . . . Let's go . . .

Mr. Van Daan. Go! Where?

Mrs. Frank (*sinking into her chair at the table*). Yes. Where?

Mr. Frank (*rising, to them all*). Have we lost all faith? All courage? A moment ago we thought that they'd come for us. We were sure it

2910 was the end. But it wasn't the end. We're alive, safe. (Mr. Van Daan *goes to the table and sits.* Mr. Frank *prays.*) "We thank Thee, oh Lord our God, that in Thy infinite mercy Thou hast again seen fit to spare us." (*He blows out the candle, then turns to* Anne.) Come on, Anne. The song! Let's have the song! (*He starts to sing.* Anne

2920 *finally starts falteringly to sing, as* Mr. Frank *urges her on. Her voice is hardly audible at first.*)

Anne (*singing*). "Oh, Hanukkah! Oh, Hanukkah! The sweet . . .

celebration . . . " (*As she goes on singing, the others gradually join in, their voices still shaking with fear.* Mrs. Van Daan *sobs as she sings.*)

Group. "Around the feast . . .
2930 we . . . gather

In complete . . . jubilation . . .

Happiest of sea . . . sons

Now is here. Many are the reasons for good cheer."

(Dussel *comes from the bedroom. He comes over to the table, standing beside* Margot, *listening to them as they sing.*)

"Together

2940 We'll weather

Whatever tomorrow may bring."

(*As they sing on with growing courage, the lights start to dim.*)

"So hear us rejoicing

And merrily voicing

The Hanukkah song that we sing.

Hoy!"

(*The lights are out. The curtain starts slowly to fall.*)

2950 "Hear us rejoicing

And merrily voicing

The Hanukkah song that we sing."

(*They are still singing, as the curtain falls.*)

The Curtain Falls.

CLOSE READ

Analyze Characters

 COMMON CORE RL 1, RL 3

(LINES 2906–2922)

Remind students that one way playwrights reveal what a character is like is through the words a character speaks.

02 CITE TEXT EVIDENCE Have students reread lines 2906–2922 to discover more about Mr. Frank's character. What can you infer about Mr. Frank from the words he says to all the residents of the Annex? (*Possible answer: Mr. Frank is a strong person who instills hope and courage: "We're alive, safe." He is a calming influence who tries to ease others' fears. He has faith in God: "We thank Thee, oh Lord our God, that in Thy infinite mercy Thou hast again seen fit to spare us."*) Why does Mr. Frank want the "family" to sing the Hanukkah song? (*Possible answer: to build their courage*)

Analyze Language

COMMON CORE RL 1, RL 4

(LINES 2923–2952)

Discuss with students the general history behind the celebration of Hanukkah, including the victory of the Jewish people over foreign invaders and the rededication of the Temple in Jerusalem in 165 BCE. Explain that an **analogy** is a comparison between two things that are alike in some way.

P2 ASK STUDENTS to reread lines 2923–2952. What analogy are the playwrights making between the ancient Jews and the residents in the Annex? What is the impact of their analogy? (*Possible answer: Like the ancient Jews, the Jews in the Annex are oppressed by another group of people. These Jews hope to be successful in their struggle as the ancient Jews were.*) Which words in the Hanukkah song bring out the idea of victory through unity? (*"Together / We'll weather / Whatever tomorrow may bring."*)

Analyze Drama

COMMON CORE RL 1, RL 3

Review with students the terms defined on the page. Have students cite examples of each from Act One.

Discuss the important differences between the first two scenes in Act One and how these differences help explain events in the play. *(Possible answer: Scene 1 occurs in the Annex after the war, and we see the effect of the war on Mr. Frank and his family. Scene 2 takes place three years earlier. It explains conditions in the Annex. The differences in the scenes highlight the impact of the Holocaust, especially on Mr. Frank.)*

Analyzing the Text

COMMON CORE RL 1, RL 3

Possible answers:

1. *Mr. Frank is caring and compassionate. He shows wisdom and strength in his ability to allay his young daughter's fears.*

2. *There are five scenes in Act One. They began a new scene because the time has changed, and they are going to tell about a new episode in the plot.*

3. *Possible answer: Mr. Van Daan is narrow minded and traditional in his views. Anne is idealistic, hopeful, and forward thinking. Mrs. Van Daan is materialistic.*

4. *He explains that Jews in Amsterdam are disappearing. There are additional strains on food and space. He is a loner who has difficulty adjusting to living with children and other adults. He is allergic to Peter's cat.*

Analyze Drama

A **drama,** or play, is a form of literature meant to be performed by actors for an audience. In a drama, the characters' words and actions tell the story. The author of a drama is called a **playwright,** and the text of the play is the **script.** The script for a drama includes several different elements:

- The **cast of characters** is a list of all the characters in the play. This list may also include a brief description of each character.
- **Stage directions** are instructions about how to perform the drama. They are often italicized, and they may also be set off with parentheses. They give readers, actors, and directors important details that explain what is happening. For example, these stage directions help readers imagine how Mr. Frank looks and feels when the play begins.

He stands looking slowly around, making a supreme effort at self-control. He is weak, ill. His clothes are threadbare.

- **Dialogue** is the written conversation between two or more characters. The name of a character is followed by the words that he or she speaks.

The **structure** of a text is the way in which it is arranged or organized. In a drama, the script is often divided into acts and scenes.

- An **act** is a major division within a play, similar to a chapter in a book.
- Each act may be divided into smaller sections, called **scenes.**
- A new act or scene often shows that the time or place of the action has changed.

As you review Act One, notice the important differences between Scene 1 and Scene 2. What does this difference help you to understand?

Analyzing the Text

Cite Text Evidence   Support your responses with evidence from the text.

1. **Draw Conclusions** Reread lines 679–706. What do the stage directions and dialogue reveal about Mr. Frank?

2. **Identify Patterns** How many scenes are there in Act One of this play? Why do the playwrights begin a new scene after line 785?

3. **Draw Conclusions** Examine lines 1341–1391. What do the stage directions and dialogue reveal about the characters?

4. **Analyze** How does the arrival of Mr. Dussel heighten tensions in the Annex?

Strategies for Annotation   ✎ 🗐 Annotate it!

Analyze Drama

COMMON CORE RL 1, RL 3

Have students use their eBook annotation tools to mark up a section of the text for oral reading:

- Highlight in yellow any stage directions.
- Highlight in blue, pink, or green the words spoken by different characters. Use one color for each character.

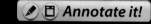

Peter (*to* Anne). Have you seen my shoes?

Anne (*innocently*). Your shoes?

Peter. You've taken them, haven't you?

Anne. I don't know what you're talking about.

Peter. You're going to be sorry!

ACT TWO

Scene 1

In the darkness we hear Anne's Voice, again reading from the diary.

Anne's Voice. Saturday, the first of January, nineteen forty-four. Another new year has begun and we find ourselves still in our hiding place. We have been here now for one year, five months and twenty-five days. It seems that our life is at
10 a standstill.

*The curtain rises on the scene. It is late afternoon. Everyone is bundled up against the cold. In the main room Mrs. Frank is taking down the laundry which is hung across the back. Mr. Frank sits in the chair down left, reading. Margot is lying on the couch with a blanket over her and the many-colored
20 knitted scarf around her throat. Anne is seated at the center table, writing in her diary. Peter, Mr. and Mrs. Van Daan, and Dussel are all in their own rooms, reading or lying down.*

As the lights dim on, Anne's Voice *continues, without a break.*

Anne's Voice. We are all a little thinner. The Van Daans'
30 "discussions" are as violent as ever. Mother still does not understand me. But then I don't understand her either. There is one great change, however. A change in myself. I read somewhere that girls of my age don't feel quite

certain of themselves. That they become quiet within and begin to think of the miracle that is taking
40 place in their bodies. I think that what is happening to me is so wonderful . . . not only what can be seen, but what is taking place inside. Each time it has happened I have a feeling that I have a sweet secret. (*We hear the chimes and then a hymn being played on the carillon outside.*) And in spite of any pain, I long for the time when
50 I shall feel that secret within me again.

(*The buzzer of the door below suddenly sounds. Everyone is startled, Mr. Frank tiptoes cautiously to the top of the steps and listens. Again the buzzer sounds, in Miep's V-for-Victory signal.*)

Mr. Frank. It's Miep! (*He goes quickly down the steps to unbolt the
60 door. Mrs. Frank calls upstairs to the Van Daans and then to Peter.*)

Mrs. Frank. Wake up, everyone! Miep is here! (Anne *quickly puts her diary away. Margot sits up, pulling the blanket around her shoulders. Mr. Dussel sits on the edge of his bed, listening, disgruntled. Miep comes up the steps, followed by Mr. Kraler. They
70 bring flowers, books, newspapers, etc. Anne rushes to Miep, throwing her arms affectionately around her.*) Miep . . . and Mr. Kraler . . . What a delightful surprise!

Mr. Kraler. We came to bring you New Year's greetings.

The Diary of Anne Frank: Act Two **325**

CLOSE READ

Analyze Drama

COMMON CORE **RL 1**

(LINES 1–10)

Point out that a new act and scene begin at this point, signaling a change in the time of the action.

A **ASK STUDENTS** to reread lines 1–10. How much time has passed since the end of Act 1? *(a little over a year)* What does this suggest about the suspected thief who may have heard noise from the Annex? *(Possible answer: If there was a thief, he or she has not revealed to police that there was noise.)*

SCAFFOLDING FOR ELL STUDENTS

Analyze Language Help students understand the meaning and use of adverbs in the text. Explain that adverbs modify, or describe, verbs. Point out that adverbs ending in -*ly* tell how something is done and that this kind of adverb is often found in stage directions. Using a whiteboard, project lines 52–61.

- Highlight in yellow adverbs that tell *how*.
- Underline the verb the adverb describes.

ASK STUDENTS to explain or demonstrate the meaning of each highlighted adverb.

(*The buzzer of the door below suddenly sounds. Everyone is startled, Mr. Frank tiptoes cautiously to the top of the steps and listens. Again the buzzer sounds, in Miep's V-for-Victory signal.*)

Mr. Frank. It's Miep! (*He goes quickly down the steps to unbolt the door. Mrs. Frank calls upstairs to the Van Daans and then to Peter.*)

Analyze Incidents in Drama (LINES 123–141)

COMMON CORE RL 3

Tell students that playwrights usually describe events in **chronological order,** the order in which they occurred.

B **ASK STUDENTS** to reread lines 123–141. How does this passage help the audience and readers understand the order of events? *(The dates on the cakes are one indication that events are being described in chronological order.)* How do these events propel the story? *(Because sugar is still being rationed and Miep is still hoping for peace, readers know that the war continues.)*

Mrs. Frank. You shouldn't . . . you should have at least one day to yourselves. (*She goes quickly to the*
80 *stove and brings down teacups and tea for all of them.*)

Anne. Don't say that, it's so wonderful to see them! (*sniffing at* Miep's *coat*) I can smell the wind and the cold on your clothes.

Miep (*giving her the flowers*). There you are. (*then to* Margot, *feeling her forehead*) How are you, Margot? . . . Feeling any better?

90 **Margot.** I'm all right.

Anne. We filled her full of every kind of pill so she won't cough and make a noise. (*She runs into her room to put the flowers in water.* Mr. *and* Mrs. Van Daan *come from upstairs. Outside there is the sound of a band playing.*)

Mrs. Van Daan. Well, hello, Miep. Mr. Kraler.

100 **Mr. Kraler** (*giving a bouquet of flowers to* Mrs. Van Daan). With my hope for peace in the New Year.

Peter (*anxiously*). Miep, have you seen Mouschi? Have you seen him anywhere around?

Miep. I'm sorry, Peter. I asked everyone in the neighborhood had they seen a gray cat. But they said no.

110 (Mrs. Frank *gives* Miep *a cup of tea.* Mr. Frank *comes up the steps, carrying a small cake on a plate.*)

Mr. Frank. Look what Miep's brought for us!

Mrs. Frank (*taking it*). A cake!

Mr. Van Daan. A cake! (*He pinches* Miep's *cheeks gaily and hurries up to the cupboard.*) I'll get some plates.

120 (Dussel, *in his room, hastily puts a coat on and starts out to join the others.*)

Mrs. Frank. Thank you, Miepia. You shouldn't have done it. You must have used all of your sugar ration for weeks. (*giving it to* Mrs. Van Daan) It's beautiful, isn't it?

Mrs. Van Daan. It's been ages since
130 I even saw a cake. Not since you brought us one last year. (*without looking at the cake, to* Miep) Remember? Don't you remember, you gave us one on New Year's Day? Just this time last year? I'll never forget it because you had "Peace in nineteen forty-three" on it. (*She looks at the cake and reads.*) "Peace in nineteen forty-four!"

140 **Miep.** Well, it has to come sometime, you know. (*as* Dussel *comes from his room*) Hello, Mr. Dussel.

Mr. Kraler. How are you?

Mr. Van Daan (*bringing plates and a knife*). Here's the knife, *liefje.* Now, how many of us are there?

Miep. None for me, thank you.

Mr. Frank. Oh, please. You must.

150 **Miep.** I couldn't.

Mr. Van Daan. Good! That leaves one . . . two . . . three . . . seven of us.

Dussel. Eight! Eight! It's the same number as it always is!

Mr. Van Daan. I left Margot out. I take it for granted Margot won't eat any.

Anne. Why wouldn't she!

160 **Mrs. Frank.** I think it won't harm her.

Mr. Van Daan. All right! All right! I just didn't want her to start coughing again, that's all.

Dussel. And please, Mrs. Frank should cut the cake.

Mr. Van Daan. What's the difference?

Mrs. Van Daan. It's not 170 Mrs. Frank's cake, is it, Miep? It's for all of us. } *Together*

Dussel. Mrs. Frank divides things better.

Mrs. Van Daan (*going to* Dussel). What are you trying to say? } *Together*

Mr. Van Daan. Oh, come on! Stop wasting time!

Mrs. Van Daan (*to* Dussel). Don't I 180 always give everybody exactly the same? Don't I?

Mr. Van Daan. Forget it, Kerli.

Mrs. Van Daan. No. I want an answer! Don't I?

Dussel. Yes. Yes. Everybody gets exactly the same . . . except

Mr. Van Daan always gets a little bit more.

(Mr. Van Daan *advances on* 190 Dussel, *the knife still in his hand*.)

Mr. Van Daan. That's a lie!

(Dussel *retreats before the onslaught of the* Van Daans.)

Mr. Frank. Please, please! (*then to* Miep) You see what a little sugar cake does to us? It goes right to our heads!

Mr. Van Daan (*handing* Mrs. Frank *the knife*). Here you are, 200 Mrs. Frank.

Mrs. Frank. Thank you. (*then to* Miep *as she goes to the table to cut the cake*) Are you sure you won't have some?

Miep (*drinking her tea*). No, really, I have to go in a minute.

(*The sound of the band fades out in the distance.*)

Peter (*to* Miep). Maybe Mouschi 210 went back to our house . . . they say that cats . . . Do you ever get over there . . . ? I mean . . . do you suppose you could . . . ?

Miep. I'll try, Peter. The first minute I get I'll try. But I'm afraid, with him gone a week . . .

Dussel. Make up your mind, already someone has had a nice big dinner from that cat!

220 (Peter *is furious, inarticulate. He starts toward* Dussel *as if to hit him.* Mr. Frank *stops him.* Mrs. Frank *speaks quickly to ease the situation.*)

CLOSE READ

Analyze Dialogue in Drama (LINES 145–200)

COMMON CORE **RL 3**

Remind students that the story in a play is told mainly through dialogue and that the words characters say and the way they say them reveal personal qualities, or **character traits,** such as kindness, humility, or fear.

C **ASK STUDENTS** to reread lines 145–200 to determine character traits. What does the dialogue about cutting the cake reveal about Mrs. Frank? Mr. Frank? the Van Daans? (*Possible answers: Mrs. Frank is fair minded: "Mrs. Frank divides things better.";* Mr. Frank *is a peacemaker: "You see what a little sugar does to us?";* Mr. Van Daan *is self-centered and has a temper: "That's a lie!";* Mrs. Van Daan *is petty and defensive: "Don't I always give everybody exactly the same? Don't I?"*)

CLOSE READ

Analyze Dialogue in Drama (LINES 241–278)

 COMMON CORE RL 3

Point out that dialogue in a play sometimes establishes a conflict that provokes characters to make a decision.

D CITE TEXT EVIDENCE Have students reread lines 241–278 to analyze the conflict described in this scene. How does Peter explain the conflict? *(In lines 251–254, Peter explains that his father wants to sell the fur coat that his mother is "crazy about.")* According to Mrs. Van Daan, why is the coat so important to her? *(It was a gift from her father.)* What decision does Mr. Van Daan make? *(He gives the coat to Miep to sell.)*

Analyze Language (LINES 279–291)

COMMON CORE RL 4, RL 6

Remind students that although words may have a similar dictionary definition, they can have different connotations, the feelings or ideas associated with a word. Also explain that **irony** is a special kind of contrast between appearance and reality.

E ASK STUDENTS to reread lines 279–291. Have them compare Mr. Van Daan's words here with his comment to Anne in lines 1271–1273 of Act One. What is the impact of Van Daan again using the word *discussion* rather than *quarrel*? *(He wants to make the situation seem better than it is by avoiding using a word with a negative connotation.)* What is ironic about Mr. Van Daan's use of the word *selfish*? *(It is really Mr. Van Daan who is being selfish, not his wife.)*

Mrs. Frank (*to* Miep). This is delicious, Miep!

Mrs. Van Daan (*eating hers*). Delicious!

Mr. Van Daan (*finishing it in one gulp*). Dirk's in luck to get a girl who can bake like this!

Miep (*putting down her empty teacup*). I have to run. Dirk's taking me to a party tonight.

Anne. How heavenly! Remember now what everyone is wearing, and what you have to eat and everything, so you can tell us tomorrow.

Miep. I'll give you a full report! Good-bye, everyone!

Mr. Van Daan (*to* Miep). Just a minute. There's something I'd like you to do for me. (*He hurries off up the stairs to his room.*)

Mrs. Van Daan (*sharply*). Putti, where are you going? (*She rushes up the stairs after him, calling hysterically.*) What do you want? Putti, what are you going to do?

Miep (*to* Peter). What's wrong?

Peter (*his sympathy is with his mother*). Father says he's going to sell her fur coat. She's crazy about that old fur coat.

Dussel. Is it possible? Is it possible that anyone is so silly as to worry about a fur coat in times like this?

Peter. It's none of your darn business . . . and if you say one more thing . . . I'll, I'll take you and I'll . . . I mean it . . . I'll . . .

(*There is a piercing scream from Mrs. Van Daan above. She grabs at the fur coat as Mr. Van Daan is starting downstairs with it.*)

Mrs. Van Daan. No! No! No! Don't you dare take that! You hear? It's mine! (*Downstairs* Peter *turns away, embarrassed, miserable.*) My father gave me that! You didn't give it to me. You have no right. Let go of it . . . you hear?

(*Mr. Van Daan pulls the coat from her hands and hurries downstairs. Mrs. Van Daan sinks to the floor, sobbing. As Mr. Van Daan comes into the main room the others look away, embarrassed for him.*)

Mr. Van Daan (*to* Mr. Kraler). Just a little—discussion over the advisability of selling this coat. As I have often reminded Mrs. Van Daan, it's very selfish of her to keep it when people outside are in such desperate need of clothing . . . (*He gives the coat to* Miep.) So if you will please to sell it for us? It should fetch a good price. And by the way, will you get me cigarettes. I don't care what kind they are . . . get all you can.

Miep. It's terribly difficult to get them, Mr. Van Daan. But I'll try. Good-bye.

(*She goes.* Mr. Frank *follows her down the steps to bolt the door after her.* Mrs. Frank *gives* Mr. Kraler *a cup of tea.*)

Mrs. Frank. Are you sure you won't have some cake, Mr. Kraler?

Mr. Kraler. I'd better not.

Mr. Van Daan. You're still feeling badly? What does your doctor say?

Mr. Kraler. I haven't been to him.

Mrs. Frank. Now, Mr. Kraler! . . .

Mr. Kraler (*sitting at the table*). Oh, I tried. But you can't get near a doctor these days . . . they're so busy. After weeks I 310 finally managed to get one on the telephone. I told him I'd like an appointment . . . I wasn't feeling very well. You know what he answers . . . over the telephone . . . Stick out your tongue! (*They laugh. He turns to Mr. Frank as Mr. Frank comes back.*) I have some contracts here . . . I wonder if you'd look over them with me . . .

320 **Mr. Frank** (*putting out his hand*). Of course.

Mr. Kraler (*He rises*). If we could go downstairs . . . (*Mr. Frank starts ahead, Mr. Kraler speaks to the others.*) Will you forgive us? I won't keep him but a minute. (*He starts to follow* Mr. Frank *down the steps.*)

Margot (*with sudden foreboding*). What's happened? Something's 330 happened! Hasn't it, Mr. Kraler?

(*Mr. Kraler stops and comes back, trying to reassure* Margot *with a pretense of casualness.*)

Mr. Kraler. No, really. I want your father's advice . . .

Margot. Something's gone wrong! I know it!

Mr. Frank (*coming back, to* Mr. Kraler). If it's something that 340 concerns us here, it's better that we all hear it.

Mr. Kraler (*turning to him, quietly*). But . . . the children . . . ?

Mr. Frank. What they'd imagine would be worse than any reality.

(*As Mr. Kraler speaks, they all listen with intense apprehension. Mrs. Van Daan comes down the stairs and sits on the bottom step.*)

350 **Mr. Kraler.** It's a man in the storeroom . . . I don't know whether or not you remember him . . . Carl, about fifty, heavy-set, near-sighted . . . He came with us just before you left.

Mr. Frank. He was from Utrecht?

Mr. Kraler. That's the man. A couple of weeks ago, when I was in the storeroom, he closed 360 the door and asked me . . . how's Mr. Frank? What do you hear from Mr. Frank? I told him I only knew there was a rumor that you were in Switzerland. He said he'd heard that rumor too, but he thought I might know something more. I didn't pay any attention to it . . . but then a thing happened yesterday . . . He'd brought some 370 invoices to the office for me to sign. As I was going through them, I looked up. He was standing staring at the bookcase . . . your bookcase. He said he thought he remembered a door there . . . Wasn't there a door there that used to go up to the loft? Then he told

CLOSE READ

Analyze Dialogue in Drama (LINES 350–380)

COMMON CORE **RL 3**

Guide students to understand that dialogue can propel the action in a play, moving the plot forward. Point out that sometimes dialogue increases tension and forces characters to make a decision.

(F) CITE TEXT EVIDENCE Have students reread lines 350–380 to identify important details in the plot. What problem does Mr. Kraler describe to the group? (*An employee, Carl, wonders where Mr. Frank has gone, asks about the bookcase, and wants a raise.*) Why is the bookcase important? (*It is hiding the door and stairs to the upstairs rooms.*) How does this dialogue move the plot forward and provoke a decision? (*The tension is heightened as the residents wonder if their hiding place has been discovered. Mr. Frank will have to decide whether or not to pay Carl more and if this is blackmail.*)

me he wanted more money. Twenty guilders[1] more a week.

380 **Mr. Van Daan.** Blackmail!

Mr. Frank. Twenty guilders? Very modest blackmail.

Mr. Van Daan. That's just the beginning.

Dussel (*coming to Mr. Frank*). You know what I think? He was the thief who was down there that night. That's how he knows we're here.

390 **Mr. Frank** (*to Mr. Kraler*). How was it left? What did you tell him?

Mr. Kraler. I said I had to think about it. What shall I do? Pay him the money? . . Take a chance on firing him . . . or what? I don't know.

Dussel (*frantic*). For God's sake don't fire him! Pay him what he asks . . . keep him here where you 400 can have your eye on him.

Mr. Frank. Is it so much that he's asking? What are they paying nowadays?

Mr. Kraler. He could get it in a war plant. But this isn't a war plant. Mind you, I don't know if he really knows . . . or if he doesn't know.

Mr. Frank. Offer him half. Then we'll soon find out if it's blackmail 410 or not.

Dussel. And if it is? We've got to pay it, haven't we? Anything he asks we've got to pay!

---

[1] **guilders** (gĭl´dərz): the basic monetary unit of the Netherlands at the time.

Mr. Frank. Let's decide that when the time comes.

Mr. Kraler. This may be all my imagination. You get to a point, these days, where you suspect everyone and everything. Again 420 and again . . . on some simple look or word, I've found myself . . . (*The telephone rings in the office below.*)

Mrs. Van Daan (*hurrying to Mr. Kraler*). There's the telephone! What does that mean, the telephone ringing on a holiday?

Mr. Kraler. That's my wife. I told her I had to go over some papers in my office . . . to call me there when 430 she got out of church. (*He starts out.*) I'll offer him half then. Good-bye . . . we'll hope for the best!

(*The group call their good-byes half-heartedly. Mr. Frank follows Mr. Kraler, to bolt the door below. During the following scene, Mr. Frank comes back up and stands listening, disturbed.*)

Dussel (*to Mr. Van Daan*). You 440 can thank your son for this . . . smashing the light! I tell you, it's just a question of time now. (*He goes to the window at the back and stands looking out.*)

Margot. Sometimes I wish the end would come . . . whatever it is.

Mrs. Frank (*shocked*). Margot!

(*Anne goes to Margot, sitting beside her on the couch with her arms 450 around her.*)

Margot. Then at least we'd know where we were.

TO CHALLENGE STUDENTS . . .

Debate Issues Draw attention to the characters' discussion of the potential blackmail situation described in lines 380–416. Tell students to reread the section to note the questions, concerns, and suggestions that each character describes.

ASK STUDENTS to form two groups to conduct an informal debate about an appropriate response to the blackmail situation. Remind students to use text evidence as well as logic and reasoning to present their arguments.

Mrs. Frank. You should be ashamed of yourself! Talking that way! Think how lucky we are! Think of the thousands dying in the war, every day. Think of the people in concentration camps.

Anne (*interrupting*). What's the
460 good of that? What's the good of thinking of misery when you're already miserable? That's stupid!

Mrs. Frank. Anne!

(*As Anne goes on raging at her mother, Mrs. Frank tries to break in, in an effort to quiet her.*)

Anne. We're young, Margot and Peter and I! You grownups have had your chance! But look
470 at us . . . If we begin thinking of all the horror in the world, we're lost! We're trying to hold onto some kind of ideals . . . when everything . . . ideals, hopes . . . everything, are being destroyed! It isn't our fault that the world is in such a mess! We weren't around when all this started! So don't try to take it out on us!

480 (*She rushes off to her room, slamming the door after her. She picks up a brush from the chest and hurls it to the floor. Then she sits on the settee, trying to control her anger.*)

Mr. Van Daan. She talks as if we started the war! Did we start the war? (*He spots Anne's cake. As he starts to take it, Peter anticipates*
490 *him.*)

Peter. She left her cake. (*He starts for Anne's room with the cake. There is silence in the main room. Mrs. Van Daan goes up to her room, followed by Van Daan. Dussel stays looking out the window. Mr. Frank brings Mrs. Frank her cake. She eats it slowly, without relish. Mr. Frank takes his cake to Margot and sits*
500 *quietly on the sofa beside her. Peter stands in the doorway of Anne's darkened room, looking at her, then makes a little movement to let her know he is there. Anne sits up, quickly, trying to hide the signs of her tears. Peter holds out the cake to her.*) You left this.

Anne (*dully*). Thanks.

(*Peter starts to go out, then comes*
510 *back.*)

Peter. I thought you were fine just now. You know just how to talk to them. You know just how to say it. I'm no good . . . I never can think . . . especially when I'm mad . . . That Dussel . . . when he said that about Mouschi . . . someone eating him . . . all I could think is . . . I wanted to hit him.
520 I wanted to give him such a . . . a . . . that he'd . . . That's what I used to do when there was an argument at school . . . That's the way I . . . but here . . . And an old man like that . . . it wouldn't be so good.

Anne. You're making a big mistake about me. I do it all wrong. I say too much. I go too far. I hurt
530 people's feelings . . .

Analyze Characters

COMMON CORE RL 1, RL 3

(LINES 500–546)

Review that playwrights can reveal what characters are like through their speech, thoughts, and actions.

G **CITE TEXT EVIDENCE** Have students reread lines 500–546 to draw conclusions about the relationship between Peter and Anne. What does Peter do to show his concern for Anne? (*He brings Anne cake when he knows she is upset.*) What does he say to encourage her? (*He praises the way she is able to speak to the adults, clearly expressing her feelings.*) What does Peter think about Anne's presence in the Annex? (*He deeply appreciates her being there.*) What is the impact of the incident on their relationship? (*It shows that the relationship between the two is changing. They are becoming friends and allies.*)

(Dussel *leaves the window, going to his room.*)

Peter. I think you're just fine . . . What I want to say . . . if it wasn't for you around here, I don't know. What I mean . . .

(Peter *is interrupted by* Dussel's *turning on the light.* Dussel *stands in the doorway, startled to see* 540 Peter. Peter *advances toward him forbiddingly.* Dussel *backs out of the room.* Peter *closes the door on him.*)

Anne. Do you mean it, Peter? Do you really mean it?

Peter. I said it, didn't I?

Anne. Thank you, Peter!

(*In the main room* Mr. *and* Mrs. Frank *collect the dishes and take them to the sink, washing* 550 *them.* Margot *lies down again on the couch.* Dussel, *lost, wanders into* Peter's *room and takes up a book, starting to read.*)

Peter (*looking at the photographs on the wall*). You've got quite a collection.

Anne. Wouldn't you like some in your room? I could give you some. Heaven knows you spend enough 560 time in there . . . doing heaven knows what . . .

Peter. It's easier. A fight starts, or an argument . . . I duck in there.

Anne. You're lucky, having a room to go to. His lordship is always here . . . I hardly ever get a minute alone. When they start in on me, I can't duck away. I have to stand there and take it.

570 **Peter.** You gave some of it back just now.

Anne. I get so mad. They've formed their opinions . . . about everything . . . but we . . . we're still trying to find out . . . We have problems here that no other people our age have ever had. And just as you think you've solved them, something comes along and bang! 580 You have to start all over again.

Peter. At least you've got someone you can talk to.

Anne. Not really. Mother . . . I never discuss anything serious with her. She doesn't understand. Father's all right. We can talk about everything . . . everything but one thing. Mother. He simply won't talk about her. I don't think 590 you can be really intimate with anyone if he holds something back, do you?

Peter. I think your father's fine.

Anne. Oh, he is, Peter! He is! He's the only one who's ever given me the feeling that I have any sense. But anyway, nothing can take the place of school and play and friends of your own age . . . or near your 600 age . . . can it?

Peter. I suppose you miss your friends and all.

Anne. It isn't just . . . (*She breaks off, staring up at him for a second.*) Isn't it funny, you and I? Here we've been seeing each other every minute for almost a year and a half, and this is the first time we've ever really talked. It helps a lot to

---

Strategies for Annotation *Annotate it!*

Analyze Characters

COMMON CORE RL 1, RL 3

Share these strategies for guided or independent analysis:

- Highlight in yellow dialogue in the play that explains Anne's relationship with her mother.
- Highlight in blue dialogue that explains Anne's relationship with her father.
- On notes, compare and contrast the relationships Anne has with her parents.

Peter. At least you've got someone you can talk to.

Anne. Not really. Mother . . . I never discuss anything serious with her. She doesn't understand. Father's all right. We can talk about everything . . . everything but one thing. Mother. He simply won't talk about her. I don't think you can be really intimate with anyone if he holds something back, do you?

©John Springer Collection/Corbis

The Diary of Anne Frank: Act Two **333**

Analyze Language

COMMON CORE RL 4, L 5a

(LINES 638–657)

Tell students that a **simile** is a figure of speech that compares two unlike things and uses the words *like* or *as*. A **metaphor** is also a comparison between things that are basically unlike. However, unlike a simile, a metaphor does not contain *like* or *as*.

 ASK STUDENTS to reread lines 638–657 to identify three similes and a metaphor. What comparisons does Anne make using a simile? *(She compares the sound of Mr. Van Daan's hungry stomach to a bass fiddle, her stomach to a whistling flute, and the group's stomachs to an orchestra tuning up.)* What is the impact of these similes? *(They help the readers/audience imagine the sounds.)* What does Anne compare in a metaphor? *(She compares Mr. Kraler's ulcers with the "family.")* What does the metaphor mean? *(Caring for the group in hiding is the cause of Mr. Kraler's pain.)*

---

610 have someone to talk to, don't you think? It helps you to let off steam.

Peter (*going to the door*). Well, any time you want to let off steam, you can come into my room.

Anne (*following him*). I can get up an awful lot of steam. You'll have to be careful how you say that.

Peter. It's all right with me.

Anne. Do you mean it?

620 **Peter.** I said it, didn't I?

(*He goes out. Anne stands in her doorway looking after him. As Peter gets to his door he stands for a minute looking back at her. Then he goes into his room. Dussel rises as he comes in, and quickly passes him, going out. He starts across for his room. Anne sees him coming, and pulls her door shut. Dussel turns*
630 *back toward Peter's room. Peter pulls his door shut. Dussel stands there, bewildered, forlorn.*

The scene slowly dims out. The curtain falls on the scene. Anne's Voice comes over in the darkness . . . faintly at first, and then with growing strength.)

Anne's Voice. We've had bad news. The people from whom Miep
640 got our ration books have been arrested. So we have had to cut down on our food. Our stomachs are so empty that they rumble and make strange noises, all in different keys. Mr. Van Daan's is deep and low, like a bass fiddle. Mine is high, whistling like a flute. As we all sit around waiting for supper,

it's like an orchestra tuning up.
650 It only needs Toscanini[2] to raise his baton and we'd be off in the Ride of the Valkyries.[3] Monday, the sixth of March, nineteen forty-four. Mr. Kraler is in the hospital. It seems he has ulcers. Pim says we are his ulcers. Miep has to run the business and us too. The Americans have landed on the southern tip of Italy. Father
660 looks for a quick finish to the war. Mr. Dussel is waiting every day for the warehouse man to demand more money. Have I been skipping too much from one subject to another? I can't help it. I feel that spring is coming. I feel it in my whole body and soul. I feel utterly confused. I am longing . . . so longing . . . for everything . . .
670 for friends . . . for someone to talk to . . . someone who understands . . . someone young, who feels as I do . . .

(*As these last lines are being said, the curtain rises on the scene. The lights dim on. Anne's Voice fades out.*)

Scene 2

It is evening, after supper. From outside we hear the sound of
680 *children playing. The "grownups," with the exception of Mr. Van Daan, are all in the main room.*

---

[2] **Toscanini** (tŏs´-kə-nē´nē): Arturo Toscanini, a famous Italian orchestral conductor.

[3] **Ride of the Valkyries** (văl-kîr´əz): a moving passage from an opera by Richard Wagner, a German composer.

334 Collection 5

Mrs. Frank *is doing some mending,* Mrs. Van Daan *is reading a fashion magazine.* Mr. Frank *is going over business accounts.* Dussel, *in his dentist's jacket, is pacing up and down, impatient to get into his bedroom.* Mr. Van Daan *is upstairs* 690 *working on a piece of embroidery in an embroidery frame.*

In his room Peter *is sitting before the mirror, smoothing his hair. As the scene goes on, he puts on his tie, brushes his coat and puts it on, preparing himself meticulously for a visit from* Anne. *On his wall are now hung some of* Anne's *motion picture stars.*

700 *In her room* Anne *too is getting dressed. She stands before the mirror in her slip, trying various ways of dressing her hair.* Margot *is seated on the sofa, hemming a skirt for* Anne *to wear.*

In the main room Dussel *can stand it no longer. He comes over, rapping sharply on the door of his and* Anne's *bedroom.*

710 **Anne** (*calling to him*). No, no, Mr. Dussel! I am not dressed yet. (Dussel *walks away, furious, sitting down and burying his head in his hands.* Anne *turns to* Margot.) How is that? How does that look?

Margot (*glancing at her briefly*). Fine.

Anne. You didn't even look.

Margot. Of course I did. It's fine.

720 **Anne.** Margot, tell me, am I terribly ugly?

Margot. Oh, stop fishing.

Anne. No. No. Tell me.

Margot. Of course you're not. You've got nice eyes . . . and a lot of animation, and . . .

Anne. A little vague, aren't you?

(*She reaches over and takes a brassière out of* Margot's *sewing* 730 *basket. She holds it up to herself, studying the effect in the mirror. Outside,* Mrs. Frank, *feeling sorry for* Dussel, *comes over, knocking at the girls' door.*)

Mrs. Frank (*outside*). May I come in?

Margot. Come in, Mother.

Mrs. Frank (*shutting the door behind her*). Mr. Dussel's impatient 740 to get in here.

Anne (*still with the brassière*). Heavens, he takes the room for himself the entire day.

Mrs. Frank (*gently*). Anne, dear, you're not going in again tonight to see Peter?

Anne (*dignified*). That is my intention.

Mrs. Frank. But you've already 750 spent a great deal of time in there today.

Anne. I was in there exactly twice. Once to get the dictionary, and then three-quarters of an hour before supper.

Mrs. Frank. Aren't you afraid you're disturbing him?

CLOSE READ

Analyze Incidents in Drama (LINES 692–705)

COMMON CORE RL 1, RL 3

Remind students that playwrights often tell what happens in a play in **chronological order,** the order in which events occur. Explain that an event in a drama sometimes signals what will happen next.

ⓘ **CITE TEXT EVIDENCE** Have students reread lines 692–705 to analyze events in the plot. What is Peter doing? *(He is dressing himself very carefully: "brushes his coat and puts it on, preparing himself meticulously.")* What is Anne doing? *(She is also dressing carefully.)* Which detail shows that Anne wants her appearance to be just right? *(She tries "various ways of dressing her hair.")* What do the events in these stage directions suggest will happen next? *(Peter and Anne will visit together.)*

Analyze Dialogue in Drama (LINES 792–832)

 COMMON CORE RL 3

Prompt students to recognize character traits revealed through this section of dialogue between Anne and Margot.

Ⓙ CITE TEXT EVIDENCE Have students reread lines 792–832. What parts of the dialogue show that Margot is an understanding daughter? *(Possible answer: She realizes that Mrs. Frank is bothered by Mrs. Van Daan's comments and that her gentle nature makes it difficult for her to speak up.)* What statements by Anne show that she is a caring sister? *(Possible answer: She is concerned that Margot may be jealous of her relationship with Peter. She invites Margot to join them.)*

Anne. Mother, I have some intuition.

760 **Mrs. Frank.** Then may I ask you this much, Anne. Please don't shut the door when you go in.

Anne. You sound like Mrs. Van Daan! (*She throws the brassière back in* Margot's *sewing basket and picks up her blouse, putting it on.*)

Mrs. Frank. No. No. I don't mean to suggest anything wrong. I only wish that you wouldn't expose 770 yourself to criticism . . . that you wouldn't give Mrs. Van Daan the opportunity to be unpleasant.

Anne. Mrs. Van Daan doesn't need an opportunity to be unpleasant!

Mrs. Frank. Everyone's on edge, worried about Mr. Kraler. This is one more thing . . .

Anne. I'm sorry, Mother. I'm going to Peter's room. I'm not going to 780 let Petronella Van Daan spoil our friendship.

(Mrs. Frank *hesitates for a second, then goes out, closing the door after her. She gets a pack of playing cards and sits at the center table, playing solitaire. In* Anne's *room* Margot *hands the finished skirt to* Anne. *As* Anne *is putting it on,* Margot *takes off her high-heeled shoes and stuffs* 790 *paper in the toes so that* Anne *can wear them.*)

 Margot (*to* Anne). Why don't you two talk in the main room? It'd save a lot of trouble. It's hard on Mother, having to listen to those remarks from Mrs. Van Daan and not say a word.

Anne. Why doesn't she say a word? I think it's ridiculous to take it and 800 take it.

Margot. You don't understand Mother at all, do you? She can't talk back. She's not like you. It's just not in her nature to fight back.

Anne. Anyway . . . the only one I worry about is you. I feel awfully guilty about you.

(*She sits on the stool near* Margot, *putting on* Margot's *high-heeled* 810 *shoes.*)

Margot. What about?

Anne. I mean, every time I go into Peter's room, I have a feeling I may be hurting you. (Margot *shakes her head.*) I know if it were me, I'd be wild. I'd be desperately jealous, if it were me.

Margot. Well, I'm not.

Anne. You don't feel badly? Really? 820 Truly? You're not jealous?

Margot. Of course I'm jealous . . . jealous that you've got something to get up in the morning for . . . But jealous of you and Peter? No.

(Anne *goes back to the mirror.*)

Anne. Maybe there's nothing to be jealous of. Maybe he doesn't really like me. Maybe I'm just taking the place of his cat . . . (*She picks up a* 830 *pair of short white gloves, putting them on.*) Wouldn't you like to come in with us?

Margot. I have a book.

(*The sound of the children playing outside fades out. In the main room*

Dussel *can stand it no longer. He jumps up, going to the bedroom door and knocking sharply.*)

Dussel. Will you please let me in
840 my room!

Anne. Just a minute, dear, dear Mr. Dussel. (*She picks up her Mother's pink stole and adjusts it elegantly over her shoulders, then gives a last look in the mirror.*) Well, here I go . . . to run the gauntlet.[4] (*She starts out, followed by* Margot.)

Dussel (*as she appears—sarcastic*). Thank you so much.

850 (Dussel *goes into his room. Anne goes toward* Peter's *room, passing* Mrs. Van Daan *and her parents at the center table.*)

Mrs. Van Daan. My God, look at her! (Anne *pays no attention. She knocks at* Peter's *door.*) I don't know what good it is to have a son. I never see him. He wouldn't care if I killed myself. (Peter *opens the*
860 *door and stands aside for* Anne *to come in.*) Just a minute, Anne. (*She goes to them at the door.*) I'd like to say a few words to my son. Do you mind? (Peter *and* Anne *stand waiting.*) Peter, I don't want you staying up till all hours tonight. You've got to have your sleep. You're a growing boy. You hear?

Mrs. Frank. Anne won't stay late.
870 She's going to bed promptly at nine. Aren't you, Anne?

---

4 **to run the gauntlet:** to endure a series of troubles or difficulties.

Anne. Yes, Mother . . . (*to* Mrs. Van Daan) May we go now?

Mrs. Van Daan. Are you asking me? I didn't know I had anything to say about it.

Mrs. Frank. Listen for the chimes, Anne dear.

(*The two young people go off into*
880 Peter's *room, shutting the door after them.*)

Mrs. Van Daan (*to* Mrs. Frank). In my day it was the boys who called on the girls. Not the girls on the boys.

Mrs. Frank. You know how young people like to feel that they have secrets. Peter's room is the only place where they can talk.

890 **Mrs. Van Daan.** Talk! That's not what they called it when I was young.

(Mrs. Van Daan *goes off to the bathroom.* Margot *settles down to read her book.* Mr. Frank *puts his papers away and brings a chess game to the center table. He and* Mrs. Frank *start to play. In* Peter's *room,* Anne *speaks to* Peter,
900 *indignant, humiliated.*)

Anne. Aren't they awful? Aren't they impossible? Treating us as if we were still in the nursery.

(*She sits on the cot.* Peter *gets a bottle of pop and two glasses.*)

Peter. Don't let it bother you. It doesn't bother me.

Anne. I suppose you can't really blame them . . . they think back

CLOSE READ

Analyze Language

COMMON CORE **RL 4**

(LINES 854–868)

Explain that in a play a character's **tone** is the attitude he or she expresses toward a subject or another character. Point out that the speaker's choice of words influences the tone.

Ⓚ **CITE TEXT EVIDENCE** Have students reread lines 854–868 to determine Mrs. Van Daan's tone. (*Possible answer: critical, sarcastic, arrogant*) What words does Mrs. Van Daan use to suggest the tone? (*Possible answer: "My God, look at her!"; "I don't know what good it is to have a son"; "Do you mind?"*) What is the impact of her tone? (*She makes herself sound selfish; she injects herself into what should be a tender moment between Peter and Anne.*)

910 to what *they* were like at our age. They don't realize how much more advanced we are . . . When you think what wonderful discussions we've had! . . . Oh, I forgot. I was going to bring you some more pictures.

Peter. Oh, these are fine, thanks.

Anne. Don't you want some more? Miep just brought me some new 920 ones.

Peter. Maybe later. (*He gives her a glass of pop and, taking some for himself, sits down facing her.*)

Anne (*looking up at one of the photographs*). I remember when I got that . . . I won it. I bet Jopie that I could eat five ice-cream cones. We'd all been playing ping-pong . . . We used to have heavenly 930 times . . . we'd finish up with ice cream at the Delphi, or the Oasis, where Jews were allowed . . . there'd always be a lot of boys . . . we'd laugh and joke . . . I'd like to go back to it for a few days or a week. But after that I know I'd be bored to death. I think more seriously about life now. I want to be a journalist . . . or something. I love 940 to write. What do you want to do?

Peter. I thought I might go off some place . . . work on a farm or something . . . some job that doesn't take much brains.

Anne. You shouldn't talk that way. You've got the most awful inferiority complex.

Peter. I know I'm not smart.

Anne. That isn't true. You're much 950 better than I am in dozens of things . . . arithmetic and algebra and . . . well, you're a million times better than I am in algebra. (*with sudden directness*) You like Margot, don't you? Right from the start you liked her, liked her much better than me.

Peter (*uncomfortably*). Oh, I don't know.

960 (*In the main room* Mrs. Van Daan *comes from the bathroom and goes over to the sink, polishing a coffee pot.*)

Anne. It's all right. Everyone feels that way. Margot's so good. She's sweet and bright and beautiful and I'm not.

Peter. I wouldn't say that.

Anne. Oh, no, I'm not. I know that. 970 I know quite well that I'm not a beauty. I never have been and never shall be.

Peter. I don't agree at all. I think you're pretty.

Anne. That's not true!

Peter. And another thing. You've changed . . . from at first, I mean.

Anne. I have?

Peter. I used to think you were 980 awful noisy.

Anne. And what do you think now, Peter? How have I changed?

Peter. Well . . . er . . . you're . . . quieter.

(*In his room* Dussel *takes his pajamas and toilet articles and goes into the bathroom to change.*)

Anne. I'm glad you don't just hate me.

990 **Peter.** I never said that.

Anne. I bet when you get out of here you'll never think of me again.

Peter. That's crazy.

Anne. When you get back with all of your friends, you're going to say . . . now what did I ever see in that Mrs. Quack Quack.

Peter. I haven't got any friends.

Anne. Oh, Peter, of course you
1000 have. Everyone has friends.

Peter. Not me. I don't want any. I get along all right without them.

Anne. Does that mean you can get along without me? I think of myself as your friend.

Peter. No. If they were all like you, it'd be different.

(*He takes the glasses and the bottle and puts them away. There is a*
1010 *second's silence and then* Anne *speaks, hesitantly, shyly.*)

Anne. Peter, did you ever kiss a girl?

Peter. Yes. Once.

Anne (*to cover her feelings*). That picture's crooked. (Peter *goes over, straightening the photograph.*) Was she pretty?

Peter. Huh?

1020 **Anne.** The girl that you kissed.

Peter. I don't know. I was blindfolded. (*He comes back and sits down again.*) It was at a party. One of those kissing games.

Anne (*relieved*). Oh. I don't suppose that really counts, does it?

Peter. It didn't with me.

Anne. I've been kissed twice. Once a man I'd never seen before kissed
1030 me on the cheek when he picked me up off the ice and I was crying. And the other was Mr. Koophuis, a friend of Father's who kissed my hand. You wouldn't say those counted, would you?

Peter. I wouldn't say so.

Anne. I know almost for certain that Margot would never kiss anyone unless she was engaged
1040 to them. And I'm sure too that Mother never touched a man before Pim. But I don't know . . . things are so different now . . . What do you think? Do you think a girl shouldn't kiss anyone except if she's engaged or something? It's so hard to try to think what to do, when here we are with the whole world falling around our
1050 ears and you think . . . well . . . you don't know what's going to happen tomorrow and . . . What do you think?

Peter. I suppose it'd depend on the girl. Some girls, anything they do's wrong. But others . . . well . . . it wouldn't necessarily be wrong with them. (*The carillon starts to strike nine o'clock.*) I've always thought
1060 that when two people . . .

The Diary of Anne Frank: Act Two **339**

WHEN STUDENTS STRUGGLE . . .

Provide support for students to analyze the changes in the relationship between Anne and Peter in Act One and in Act Two. Prompt students to compare and contrast the relationship using a chart like the one shown.

	Act One	Act Two
What Anne Thinks of Peter		
What Peter Thinks of Anne		

Anne. Nine o'clock. I have to go.

Peter. That's right.

Anne (*without moving*). Good night.

(*There is a second's pause, then Peter gets up and moves toward the door.*)

Peter. You won't let them stop you coming?

1070 **Anne.** No. (*She rises and starts for the door.*) Sometime I might bring my diary. There are so many things in it that I want to talk over with you. There's a lot about you.

Peter. What kind of things?

Anne. I wouldn't want you to see some of it. I thought you were a nothing, just the way you thought about me.

1080 **Peter.** Did you change your mind, the way I changed my mind about you?

Anne. Well . . . You'll see . . .

(*For a second Anne stands looking up at Peter, longing for him to kiss her. As he makes no move she turns away. Then suddenly Peter grabs her awkwardly in his arms, kissing her on the cheek. Anne walks out*
1090 *dazed. She stands for a minute, her back to the people in the main room. As she regains her poise she goes to her mother and father and Margot, silently kissing them. They murmur their good nights to her. As she is about to open her bedroom door, she catches sight of Mrs. Van Daan. She goes quickly to her, taking her face in her hands and kissing her first*
1100 *on one cheek and then on the other. Then she hurries off into her room. Mrs. Van Daan looks after her, and then looks over at Peter's room. Her suspicions are confirmed.*)

Mrs. Van Daan (*She knows*). Ah hah!

(*The lights dim out. The curtain falls on the scene. In the darkness Anne's Voice comes faintly at first and then*
1110 *with growing strength.*)

Anne's Voice. By this time we all know each other so well that if anyone starts to tell a story, the rest can finish it for him. We're having to cut down still further on our meals. What makes it worse, the rats have been at work again. They've carried off some of our precious food. Even Mr. Dussel
1120 wishes now that Mouschi was here. Thursday, the twentieth of April, nineteen forty-four. Invasion fever is mounting every day. Miep tells us that people outside talk of nothing else. For myself, life has become much more pleasant. I often go to Peter's room after supper. Oh, don't think I'm in love, because I'm not. But it does make
1130 life more bearable to have someone with whom you can exchange views. No more tonight. P.S. . . . I must be honest. I must confess that I actually live for the next meeting. Is there anything lovelier than to sit under the skylight and feel the sun on your cheeks and have a darling boy in your arms? I admit now that I'm glad the
1140 Van Daans had a son and not a

daughter. I've outgrown another dress. That's the third. I'm having to wear Margot's clothes after all. I'm working hard on my French and am now reading *La Belle Nivernaise.*

(*As she is saying the last lines—the curtain rises on the scene. The lights dim on, as Anne's Voice fades out.*)

Scene 3

1150   *It is night, a few weeks later. Everyone is in bed. There is complete quiet. In the* Van Daans' *room a match flares up for a moment and then is quickly put out. Mr. Van Daan, in bare feet, dressed in underwear and trousers, is dimly seen coming stealthily down the stairs and into the main room, where Mr. and Mrs. Frank and*
1160   Margot *are sleeping. He goes to the food safe and again lights a match. Then he cautiously opens the safe, taking out a half-loaf of bread. As he closes the safe, it creaks. He stands rigid.* Mrs. Frank *sits up in bed. She sees him.*

Mrs. Frank (*screaming*). Otto! Otto! Komme schnell!⁵

(*The rest of the people wake,*
1170   *hurriedly getting up.*)

Mr. Frank. *Was ist los? Was ist passiert?*⁶

---

⁵ *Komme schnell!* (kôm´e shněl´) *German:* Come quickly!

⁶ *Was ist los? Was ist passiert?* (väs ĭst lôs´? väs ĭst päsērt´?) *German:* What's the matter? What has happened?

(Dussel, *followed by* Anne, *comes from his room.*)

Mrs. Frank (*as she rushes over to* Mr. Van Daan). *Er stiehlt das Essen!*⁷

Dussel (*grabbing* Mr. Van Daan). You! You! Give me that.

1180   **Mrs. Van Daan** (*coming down the stairs*). Putti . . . Putti . . . what is it?

Dussel (*his hands on* Van Daan's *neck*). You dirty thief . . . stealing food . . . you good-for-nothing . . .

Mr. Frank. Mr. Dussel! For God's sake! Help me, Peter!

(Peter *comes over, trying, with* Mr. Frank, *to separate the two struggling men.*)

1190   **Peter.** Let him go! Let go!

(Dussel *drops* Mr. Van Daan, *pushing him away. He shows them the end of a loaf of bread that he has taken from* Van Daan.)

Dussel. You greedy, selfish . . . !

(Margot *turns on the lights.*)

Mrs. Van Daan. Putti . . . what is it?

(*All of* Mrs. Frank's *gentleness, her self-control, is gone. She is outraged,*
1200   *in a frenzy of indignation.*)

Mrs. Frank. The bread! He was stealing the bread!

Dussel. It was you, and all the time we thought it was the rats!

Mr. Frank. Mr. Van Daan, how could you!

---

⁷ *Er stiehlt das Essen!* (ĕr shtēlt´ däs ĕs´ən) *German:* He is stealing food!

CLOSE READ

Analyze Dialogue in Drama (LINES 1150–1186)

COMMON CORE RL 3

Review that dialogue in a play, along with the stage directions, may establish a conflict that the characters must then resolve.

Ⓛ ASK STUDENTS to reread lines 1150–1186. What conflict arises in this scene? (*Mr. Van Daan steals bread from the food safe.*) Who reacts most strongly to the theft? (*Mrs. Frank; Mr. Dussel*) How does this event propel the action of the plot forward? (*Now the characters must decide what to do about Mr. Van Daan's betrayal of their trust.*)

TEACH

CLOSE READ

Analyze Language

COMMON CORE RL 4

(LINES 1222–1264)

Discuss the meaning and impact of language in this section of dialogue. Point out that, in **situational irony,** a playwright contrasts what readers or characters expect with what actually exists or happens. In **dramatic irony,** the reader or audience knows something that a character does not.

Ⓜ ASK STUDENTS to reread lines 1222–1264. What does Mrs. Frank mean when she says "you sacrifice your child to this man"? *(She is accusing Mrs. Van Daan of failing to protect Peter from his father's abuse.)* What is ironic about Mrs. Frank's language in this section? *(The characters and audience expect that she will be calm and speak kindly as she always does; instead she surprises them by expressing great anger.)* Why is Mrs. Frank's statement "He steals once! He'll steal again!" an example of irony? *(Mrs. Frank and the other characters do not know that Mr. Van Daan stole food another time [see Act One, line 2023].)* What is the impact of Mrs. Frank's anger? *(She is forcing a decision about a possible change in their living arrangement.)*

Mr. Van Daan. I'm hungry.

Mrs. Frank. We're all of us hungry! I see the children getting thinner
1210 and thinner. Your own son Peter . . . I've heard him moan in his sleep, he's so hungry. And you come in the night and steal food that should go to them . . . to the children!

Mrs. Van Daan (*going to* Mr. Van Daan *protectively*). He needs more food than the rest of us. He's used to more. He's a big man.

1220 (Mr. Van Daan *breaks away, going over and sitting on the couch.*)

Ⓜ **Mrs. Frank** (*turning on* Mrs. Van Daan). And you . . . you're worse than he is! You're a mother, and yet you sacrifice your child to this man . . . this . . . this . . .

Mr. Frank. Edith! Edith!

(Margot *picks up the pink woolen stole, putting it over her mother's*
1230 *shoulders.*)

Mrs. Frank (*paying no attention, going on to* Mrs. Van Daan). Don't think I haven't seen you! Always saving the choicest bits for him! I've watched you day after day and I've held my tongue. But not any longer! Not after this! Now I want him to go! I want him to get out of here!

1240 **Mr. Frank.** Edith!

Mr. Van Daan. Get out of here? ⎫
                                    ⎬ *Together*
Mrs. Van Daan. What do you mean? ⎭

Mrs. Frank. Just that! Take your things and get out!

Mr. Frank (*to* Mrs. Frank). You're speaking in anger. You cannot mean what you are saying.

1250 **Mrs. Frank.** I mean exactly that!

(Mrs. Van Daan *takes a cover from the* Franks' *bed, pulling it about her.*)

Mr. Frank. For two long years we have lived here, side by side. We have respected each other's rights . . . we have managed to live in peace. Are we now going to throw it all away? I know this will
1260 never happen again, will it, Mr. Van Daan?

Mr. Van Daan. No. No.

Mrs. Frank. He steals once! He'll steal again!

(Mr. Van Daan, *holding his stomach, starts for the bathroom.* Anne *puts her arms around him, helping him up the step.*)

Mr. Frank. Edith, please. Let us be
1270 calm. We'll all go to our rooms . . . and afterwards we'll sit down quietly and talk this out . . . we'll find some way . . .

Mrs. Frank. No! No! No more talk! I want them to leave!

Mrs. Van Daan. You'd put us out, on the streets?

Mrs. Frank. There are other hiding places.

1280 **Mrs. Van Daan.** A cellar . . . a closet. I know. And we have no money left even to pay for that.

Mrs. Frank. I'll give you money. Out of my own pocket I'll give it gladly. (*She gets her purse from a shelf and comes back with it.*)

Mrs. Van Daan. Mr. Frank, you told Putti you'd never forget what he'd done for you when you came 1290 to Amsterdam. You said you could never repay him, that you . . .

Mrs. Frank (*counting out money*). If my husband had any obligation to you, he's paid it, over and over.

Mr. Frank. Edith, I've never seen you like this before. I don't know you.

Mrs. Frank. I should have spoken out long ago.

1300 **Dussel.** You can't be nice to some people.

The Diary of Anne Frank: Act Two **343**

Analyze Characters

COMMON CORE RL 1, RL 3

(LINES 1306–1310)

Remind students that a character's traits, or qualities, can be revealed through his or her speech and actions.

 CITE TEXT EVIDENCE Have students reread lines 1306–1310 to draw conclusions about Mr. Frank. What do Mr. Frank's words reveal about him? *(Possible answer: Even in the midst of intense conflict, he still tries to be a peacemaker.)* What do his actions reveal? *(Possible answer: The way he is holding his head shows that even the usually steady and hopeful Mr. Frank is feeling discouraged.)*

Mrs. Van Daan (*turning on* Dussel). There would have been plenty for all of us, if you hadn't come in here!

Mr. Frank. We don't need the Nazis to destroy us. We're destroying ourselves.

1310 (*He sits down, with his head in his hands.* Mrs. Frank *goes to* Mrs. Van Daan.)

Mrs. Frank (*giving* Mrs. Van Daan *some money*). Give this to Miep. She'll find you a place.

Anne. Mother, you're not putting *Peter* out. Peter hasn't done anything.

Mrs. Frank. He'll stay, of course. When I say I must protect the 1320 children, I mean Peter too.

(Peter *rises from the steps where he has been sitting.*)

Peter. I'd have to go if Father goes.

(Mr. Van Daan *comes from the bathroom.* Mrs. Van Daan *hurries to him and takes him to the couch. Then she gets water from the sink to bathe his face.*)

Mrs. Frank (*while this is going on*). 1330 He's no father to you . . . that man! He doesn't know what it is to be a father!

Peter (*starting for his room*). I wouldn't feel right. I couldn't stay.

Mrs. Frank. Very well, then. I'm sorry.

Anne (*rushing over to* Peter). No, Peter! No! (Peter *goes into his room,*

closing the door after him. Anne 1340 *turns back to her mother, crying.*) I don't care about the food. They can have mine! I don't want it! Only don't send them away. It'll be daylight soon. They'll be caught . . .

Margot (*putting her arms comfortingly around* Anne). Please, Mother!

Mrs. Frank. They're not going now. They'll stay here until Miep finds 1350 them a place. (*to* Mrs. Van Daan) But one thing I insist on! He must never come down here again! He must never come to this room where the food is stored! We'll divide what we have . . . an equal share for each! (Dussel *hurries over to get a sack of potatoes from the food safe.* Mrs. Frank *goes on, to* Mrs. Van Daan.) You can cook it 1360 here and take it up to him.

(Dussel *brings the sack of potatoes back to the center table.*)

Margot. Oh, no. No. We haven't sunk so far that we're going to fight over a handful of rotten potatoes.

Dussel (*dividing the potatoes into piles*). Mrs. Frank, Mr. Frank, Margot, Anne, Peter, Mrs. Van Daan, Mr. Van Daan, myself . . . 1370 Mrs. Frank . . .

(The buzzer sounds in Miep's signal.)

Mr. Frank. It's Miep! (*He hurries over, getting his overcoat and putting it on.*)

Margot. At this hour?

Mrs. Frank. It is trouble.

Mr. Frank (*as he starts down to unbolt the door*). I beg you, don't let her see a thing like this!

1380 **Mr. Dussel** (*counting without stopping*). . . . Anne, Peter, Mrs. Van Daan, Mr. Van Daan, myself . . .

Margot (*to* Dussel). Stop it! Stop it!

Dussel.. . . . Mr. Frank, Margot, Anne, Peter, Mrs. Van Daan, Mr. Van Daan, myself, Mrs. Frank . . .

Mrs. Van Daan. You're keeping the big ones for yourself! All the big
1390 ones . . . Look at the size of that! . . . And that! . . .

(Dussel *continues on with his dividing.* Peter, *with his shirt and trousers on, comes from his room.*)

Margot. Stop it! Stop it!

(*We hear* Miep's *excited voice speaking to* Mr. Frank *below.*)

Miep. Mr. Frank . . . the most wonderful news! . . . The invasion
1400 has begun!

Mr. Frank. Go on, tell them! Tell them!

(Miep *comes running up the steps, ahead of* Mr. Frank. *She has a man's raincoat on over her nightclothes and a bunch of orange-colored flowers in her hand.*)

Miep. Did you hear that, everybody? Did you hear what
1410 I said? The invasion has begun! The invasion!

(*They all stare at* Miep, *unable to grasp what she is telling them.* Peter *is the first to recover his wits.*)

Peter. Where?

Mrs. Van Daan. When? When, Miep?

Miep. It began early this morning . . .

1420 (*As she talks on, the realization of what she has said begins to dawn on them. Everyone goes crazy. A wild demonstration takes place.* Mrs. Frank *hugs* Mr. Van Daan.)

Mrs. Frank. Oh, Mr. Van Daan, did you hear that? (Dussel *embraces* Mrs. Van Daan. Peter *grabs a frying pan and parades around the room, beating on it, singing the*
1430 *Dutch National Anthem.* Anne *and* Margot *follow him, singing, weaving in and out among the excited grownups.* Margot *breaks away to take the flowers from* Miep *and distribute them to everyone. While this pandemonium is going on* Mrs. Frank *tries to make herself heard above the excitement.*)

Mrs. Frank (*to* Miep). How do you
1440 know?

Miep. The radio . . . The B.B.C.! They said they landed on the coast of Normandy!

Peter. The British?

Miep. British, Americans, French, Dutch, Poles, Norwegians . . . all of them! More than four thousand ships! Churchill spoke, and General Eisenhower! D-Day they
1450 call it!

Mr. Frank. Thank God, it's come!

Mrs. Van Daan. At last!

CLOSE READ

Analyze Incidents in Drama (LINES 1408–1450)   COMMON CORE RL 1, RL 3

Guide students to understand the significance of D-Day and its impact on the plot.

ASK STUDENTS to reread lines 1408–1450. Why do the residents of the Annex go "crazy" and have a "wild demonstration"? (*The news that the Allies have landed in Normandy, France, leads them to believe that the Nazis will soon be defeated, and they will finally be free.*) How does the mention of D-Day help establish the chronology of events and propel the action of the story? (*D-Day, June 6, 1944, was a turning point in World War II, and it should be a turning point in the lives of the characters.*)

Miep (*starting out*). I'm going to tell Mr. Kraler. This'll be better than any blood transfusion.

Mr. Frank (*stopping her*). What part of Normandy did they land, did they say?

1460 **Miep.** Normandy . . . that's all I know now . . . I'll be up the minute I hear some more! (*She goes hurriedly out.*)

Mr. Frank (*to* Mrs. Frank). What did I tell you? What did I tell you?

(Mrs. Frank *indicates that he has forgotten to bolt the door after* Miep. *He hurries down the steps.* Mr. Van Daan, *sitting on the couch, suddenly breaks into a convulsive* 1470 *sob. Everybody looks at him, bewildered.*)

Mrs. Van Daan (*hurrying to him*). Putti! Putti! What is it? What happened?

Mr. Van Daan. Please. I'm so ashamed.

(Mr. Frank *comes back up the steps.*)

Dussel. Oh, for God's sake!

1480 **Mrs. Van Daan.** Don't, Putti.

Margot. It doesn't matter now!

Mr. Frank (*going to* Mr. Van Daan). Didn't you hear what Miep said? The invasion has come! We're going to be liberated! This is a time to celebrate!

(*He embraces* Mrs. Frank *and then hurries to the cupboard and gets the cognac and a glass.*)

1490 **Mr. Van Daan.** To steal bread from children!

Mrs. Frank. We've all done things that we're ashamed of.

Anne. Look at me, the way I've treated Mother . . . so mean and horrid to her.

Mrs. Frank. No, Anneke, no.

(Anne *runs to her mother, putting her arms around her.*)

1500 **Anne.** Oh, Mother, I was. I was awful.

Mr. Van Daan. Not like me. No one is as bad as me!

Dussel (*to* Mr. Van Daan). Stop it now! Let's be happy!

Mr. Frank (*giving* Mr. Van Daan *a glass of cognac*). Here! Here! *Schnapps! L'chaim!*[8] (Van Daan *takes the cognac. They all watch* 1510 *him. He gives them a feeble smile.* Anne *puts up her fingers in a V-for-Victory sign. As* Van Daan *gives an answering V-sign, they are startled to hear a loud sob from behind them. It is* Mrs. Frank, *stricken with remorse. She is sitting on the other side of the room.*)

Mrs. Frank (*through her sobs*). When I think of the terrible things 1520 I said . . .

(Mr. Frank, Anne, *and* Margot *hurry to her, trying to comfort her.* Mr. Van Daan *brings her his glass of cognac.*)

---

[8] *Schnapps!* (shnäps) *German:* Brandy! *L'chaim!* (lə khä´yǐm) *Hebrew:* To life!

TO CHALLENGE STUDENTS . . .

Impact of Setting Point out that the residents of the Secret Annex had to rely on Miep and Mr. Kraler for most of their information about the outside world. Prompt students to recall that the residents spend the majority of their time in silence, unable to speak more than a whisper.

ASK STUDENTS to meet in a small group to consider how the characters' sense of isolation might have impacted the tensions in the Annex. Remind students to use text evidence as well as logic and reasoning to present their arguments.

Mr. Van Daan. No! No! You were right!

Mrs. Frank. That I should speak that way to you! . . . Our friends! . . . Our guests! (*She starts to cry again.*)

Dussel. Stop it, you're spoiling the whole invasion!

(*As they are comforting her, the lights dim out. The curtain falls.*)

Anne's Voice (*faintly at first and then with growing strength*). We're all in much better spirits these days. There's still excellent news of the invasion. The best part about it is that I have a feeling that friends are coming. Who knows? Maybe I'll be back in school by fall. Ha, ha! The joke is on us! The warehouse man doesn't know a thing and we are paying him all that money! . . . Wednesday, the second of July, nineteen forty-four. The invasion seems temporarily to be bogged down. Mr. Kraler has to have an operation, which looks bad. The Gestapo have found the radio that was stolen. Mr. Dussel says they'll trace it back and back to the thief, and then, it's just a matter of time till they get to us. Everyone is low. Even poor Pim can't raise their spirits. I have often been downcast myself . . . but never in despair. I can shake off everything if I write. But . . . and that is the great question . . . will I ever be able to write well? I want to so much. I want to go on living even after my death. Another birthday has gone by, so now I am fifteen. Already I know what I want. I have a goal, an opinion.

(*As this is being said—the curtain rises on the scene, the lights dim on, and Anne's Voice fades out.*)

Scene 4

It is an afternoon a few weeks later . . . Everyone but Margot *is in the main room. There is a sense of great tension.*

Both Mrs. Frank *and* Mr. Van Daan *are nervously pacing back and forth,* Dussel *is standing at the window, looking down fixedly at the street below.* Peter *is at the center table, trying to do his lessons.* Anne *sits opposite him, writing in her diary.* Mrs. Van Daan *is seated on the couch, her eyes on* Mr. Frank *as he sits reading.*

The sound of a telephone ringing comes from the office below. They all are rigid, listening tensely. Mr. Dussel *rushes down to* Mr. Frank.

Dussel. There it goes again, the telephone! Mr. Frank, do you hear?

Mr. Frank (*quietly*). Yes. I hear.

Dussel (*pleading, insistent*). But this is the third time, Mr. Frank! The third time in quick succession! It's a signal! I tell you it's Miep, trying to get us! For some reason she can't come to us and she's trying to warn us of something!

Mr. Frank. Please. Please.

Mr. Van Daan (*to* Dussel). You're wasting your breath.

CLOSE READ

Analyze Drama

COMMON CORE **RL 1**

(LINES 1535–1566)

Review that the structure of a text is the way it is arranged or organized and that playwrights often arrange events for acts and scenes in chronological order, the order in which they occurred.

P **CITE TEXT EVIDENCE** Ask students to reread lines 1535–1566. How have the playwrights used Anne's diary to structure their play? (*Diary entries are written in chronological order by date. The playwrights used Anne's diary to present events in the order she wrote about them.*) What phrases and sentences in this diary entry are time clues? (*Possible answers: "Maybe I'll be back in school by fall"; "Wednesday, the second of July, nineteen forty-four"; "Another birthday has gone by, so now I am fifteen"*)

Analyze Language COMMON CORE RL 4

(LINES 1611–1612)

Draw attention to Mr. Van Daan's choice of words and their impact on the tone or feeling he portrays.

Q **ASK STUDENTS** to reread lines 1611–1612. How does Mr. Van Daan refer to Anne? *(He says "You with the diary" instead of using her name.)* What tone do these words create, and what is the impact of that tone? *(His tone is arrogant, disrespectful. His tone adds to increasing tension in the scene.)* How has Mr. Van Daan's attitude changed from the previous scene? *(He has lost his brief sense of humility and remorse.)*

Dussel. Something has happened, Mr. Frank. For three days now Miep hasn't been to see us! And today not a man has come to work. There hasn't been a sound in the building!

Mrs. Frank. Perhaps it's Sunday.
1610 We may have lost track of the days.

Q Mr. Van Daan (*to* Anne). You with the diary there. What day is it?

Dussel (*going to* Mrs. Frank). I don't lose track of the days! I know exactly what day it is! It's Friday, the fourth of August. Friday, and not a man at work. (*He rushes back to* Mr. Frank, *pleading with him, almost in tears.*) I tell you
1620 Mr. Kraler's dead. That's the only explanation. He's dead and they've closed down the building, and Miep's trying to tell us!

Mr. Frank. She'd never telephone us.

Dussel (*frantic*). Mr. Frank, answer that! I beg you, answer it!

Mr. Frank. No.

Mr. Van Daan. Just pick it up and
1630 listen. You don't have to speak. Just listen and see if it's Miep.

Dussel (*speaking at the same time*). For God's sake . . . I ask you.

Mr. Frank. No. I've told you, no. I'll do nothing that might let anyone know we're in the building.

Peter. Mr. Frank's right.

Mr. Van Daan. There's no need to tell us what side you're on.

1640 **Mr. Frank.** If we wait patiently, quietly, I believe that help will come.

(*There is silence for a minute as they all listen to the telephone ringing.*)

Dussel. I'm going down. (*He rushes down the steps.* Mr. Frank *tries ineffectually to hold him.* Dussel *runs to the lower door, unbolting it. The telephone stops ringing.* Dussel
1650 *bolts the door and comes slowly back up the steps.*) Too late. (Mr. Frank *goes to* Margot *in* Anne's *bedroom.*)

Mr. Van Daan. So we just wait here until we die.

Mrs. Van Daan (*hysterically*). I can't stand it! I'll kill myself ! I'll kill myself !

Mr. Van Daan. For God's sake, stop it!

(*In the distance, a German military
1660 band is heard playing a Viennese waltz.*)

Mrs. Van Daan. I think you'd be glad if I did! I think you want me to die!

Mr. Van Daan. Whose fault is it we're here? (Mrs. Van Daan *starts for her room. He follows, talking at her.*) We could've been safe somewhere . . . in America
1670 or Switzerland. But no! No! You wouldn't leave when I wanted to. You couldn't leave your things. You couldn't leave your precious furniture.

Mrs. Van Daan. Don't touch me!

(*She hurries up the stairs, followed by* Mr. Van Daan. Peter, *unable to bear it, goes to his room.* Anne *looks*

after him, deeply concerned. Dussel returns to his post at the window. Mr. Frank *comes back into the main room and takes a book, trying to read.* Mrs. Frank *sits near the sink, starting to peel some potatoes.* Anne *quietly goes to* Peter's *room, closing the door after her.* Peter *is lying face down on the cot.* Anne *leans over him, holding him in her arms, trying to bring him out of his despair.*)

1690 **Anne.** Look, Peter, the sky. (*She looks up through the skylight.*) What a lovely, lovely day! Aren't the clouds beautiful? You know what I do when it seems as if I couldn't stand being cooped up for one more minute? I *think* myself out. I think myself on a walk in the park where I used to go with Pim. Where the jonquils and the

1700 crocus and the violets grow down the slopes. You know the most wonderful part about *thinking* yourself out? You can have it any way you like. You can have roses and violets and chrysanthemums all blooming at the same time . . . It's funny . . . I used to take it all for granted . . . and now I've gone crazy about everything to do with

1710 nature. Haven't you?

Peter. I've just gone crazy. I think if something doesn't happen soon . . . if we don't get out of here . . . I can't stand much more of it!

Anne (*softly*). I wish you had a religion, Peter.

Peter. No, thanks! Not me!

Anne. Oh, I don't mean you have to be Orthodox[9] . . . or believe in
1720 heaven and hell and purgatory and things . . . I just mean some religion . . . it doesn't matter what. Just to believe in something! When I think of all that's out there . . . the trees . . . and flowers . . . and seagulls . . . when I think of the dearness of you, Peter . . . and the goodness of the people we know . . . Mr. Kraler, Miep, Dirk,
1730 the vegetable man, all risking their lives for us every day . . . When I think of these good things, I'm not afraid any more . . . I find myself, and God, and I . . . (Peter *interrupts, getting up and walking away.*)

Peter. That's fine! But when I begin to think, I get mad! Look at us, hiding out for two years. Not
1740 able to move! Caught here like . . . waiting for them to come and get us . . . and all for what?

Anne. We're not the only people that've had to suffer. There've always been people that've had to . . . sometimes one race . . . sometimes another . . . and yet . . .

Peter. That doesn't make me feel any better!

1750 **Anne** (*going to him*). I know it's terrible, trying to have any faith . . . when people are doing such horrible . . . But you know what I sometimes think? I think the world may be going through a

---

9 **Orthodox:** Orthodox Jews who strictly observe Jewish laws and traditions.

The Diary of Anne Frank: Act Two **349**

Analyze Dialogue in Drama (LINES 1718–1734)

COMMON CORE RL 3

Prompt students to evaluate Anne's comments to Peter to determine what they reveal about her.

R CITE TEXT EVIDENCE Have students reread lines 1718–1734. What evidence of good does Anne see in the world? (*She points out the beauty and variety of nature, Peter's "dearness," and the people who have risked their own lives to protect the residents of the Annex.*) What does this part of the dialogue reveal about Anne? (*Possible answer: She hasn't let the horrors around her destroy her hope, her loving nature, or her faith in God.*)

The Diary of Anne Frank Act Two **349**

phase, the way I was with Mother. It'll pass, maybe not for hundreds of years, but some day . . . I still believe, in spite of everything, that 1760 people are really good at heart.

Peter. I want to see something now . . . Not a thousand years from now! (*He goes over, sitting down again on the cot.*)

Anne. But, Peter, if you'd only look at it as part of a great pattern . . . that we're just a little minute in the life . . . (*She breaks off.*) Listen to us, going at each other like a 1770 couple of stupid grownups! Look at the sky now. Isn't it lovely? (*She holds out her hand to him. Peter takes it and rises, standing with her at the window looking out, his arms around her.*) Some day, when we're outside again, I'm going to . . .

(*She breaks off as she hears the sound of a car, its brakes squealing as it comes to a sudden stop. The 1780 people in the other rooms also become aware of the sound. They listen tensely. Another car roars up to a screeching stop. Anne and Peter come from Peter's room. Mr. and Mrs. Van Daan creep down the stairs. Dussel comes out from his room. Everyone is listening, hardly breathing. A doorbell clangs again and again in the building below.* 1790 Mr. Frank *starts quietly down the steps to the door.* Dussel *and* Peter *follow him. The others stand rigid, waiting, terrified.*

In a few seconds Dussel *comes stumbling back up the steps. He shakes off* Peter's *help and goes to*

his room. Mr. Frank *bolts the door below, and comes slowly back up the steps. Their eyes are all on him* 1800 *as he stands there for a minute. They realize that what they feared has happened.* Mrs. Van Daan *starts to whimper.* Mr. Van Daan *puts her gently in a chair, and then hurries off up the stairs to their room to collect their things.* Peter *goes to comfort his mother. There is a sound of violent pounding on a door below.*)

1810 **Mr. Frank** (*quietly*). For the past two years we have lived in fear. Now we can live in hope.

(*The pounding below becomes more insistent. There are muffled sounds of voices, shouting commands.*)

Men's Voices. *Auf machen! Da drinnen! Auf machen! Schnell! Schnell! Schnell! etc., etc.*[10]

(*The street door below is forced open.* 1820 *We hear the heavy tread of footsteps coming up.* Mr. Frank *gets two school bags from the shelves, and gives one to* Anne *and the other to* Margot. *He goes to get a bag for* Mrs. Frank. *The sound of feet coming up grows louder.* Peter *comes to* Anne, *kissing her good-bye, then he goes to his room to collect his things. The buzzer of their door starts to ring.* Mr. Frank 1830 *brings* Mrs. Frank *a bag. They stand together, waiting. We hear the thud of gun butts on the door, trying to break it down.*

---

[10] **Auf machen! . . . Schnell!** (ouf´ mäzкн´ən! dä drĭn´ən! ouf´ mäкн´ən! shnĕl! shnĕl! shnĕl!) *German:* Open up! Inside there! Open up! Quick! Quick! Quick!

Anne *stands, holding her school satchel, looking over at her father and mother with a soft, reassuring smile. She is no longer a child, but a woman with courage to meet whatever lies ahead.*

1840   *The lights dim out. The curtain falls on the scene. We hear a mighty crash as the door is shattered. After a second* Anne's Voice *is heard.*)

Anne's Voice. And so it seems our stay here is over. They are waiting for us now. They've allowed us five minutes to get our things. We can each take a bag and whatever it will hold of clothing. Nothing else.
1850   So, dear Diary, that means I must leave you behind. Good-bye for a while. P.S. Please, please, Miep, or Mr. Kraler, or anyone else. If you should find this diary, will you please keep it safe for me, because some day I hope . . .

(*Her voice stops abruptly. There is silence. After a second the curtain rises.*)

Scene 5

1860   *It is again the afternoon in November, 1945. The rooms are as we saw them in the first scene.* Mr. Kraler *has joined* Miep *and* Mr. Frank. *There are coffee cups on the table. We see a great change in* Mr. Frank. *He is calm now. His bitterness is gone. He slowly turns a few pages of the diary. They are blank.*

1870   **Mr. Frank.** No more. (*He closes the diary and puts it down on the couch beside him.*)

Miep. I'd gone to the country to find food. When I got back the block was surrounded by police . . .

Mr. Kraler. We made it our business to learn how they knew. It was the thief . . . the thief who told them.

1880   (Miep *goes up to the gas burner, bringing back a pot of coffee.*)

Mr. Frank (*after a pause*). It seems strange to say this, that anyone could be happy in a concentration camp. But Anne was happy in the camp in Holland where they first took us. After two years of being shut up in these rooms, she could be out . . . out in the sunshine and
1890   the fresh air that she loved.

Miep (*offering the coffee to* Mr. Frank). A little more?

Mr. Frank (*holding out his cup to her*). The news of the war was good. The British and Americans were sweeping through France. We felt sure that they would get to us in time. In September we were told that we were to be shipped to
1900   Poland . . . The men to one camp. The women to another. I was sent to Auschwitz. They went to Belsen. In January we were freed, the few of us who were left. The war wasn't yet over, so it took us a long time to get home. We'd be sent here and there behind the lines where

Analyze Drama   COMMON CORE **RL 1**
(LINES 1863–1872)

Remind students that stage directions provide information about the time and place of the action in a play.

S CITE TEXT EVIDENCE Ask students to reread lines 1863–1872. How does the setting of Scene 5 complete the structure of the play? (*"It is again the afternoon in November, 1945." The play has returned to its starting point as it reaches its conclusion.*) What sentences show that some time has passed since that first scene? (*"We see a great change in Mr. Frank. He is calm now. His bitterness is gone."*)

APPLYING ACADEMIC VOCABULARY

draft	publish

As you discuss the end of the selection, incorporate the following Collection 5 academic vocabulary words: *draft* and *publish*. Have students suggest how they think Anne would have finished her last sentence in Scene 4: "*If you should find this diary, will you please keep it safe for me, because some day I hope . . .*" Do they think Anne would have wanted to **publish** her diary? Would she have wanted to make any changes to her original **draft**? Ask students to support their opinions with evidence from the play.

TEACH

CLOSE READ

COLLABORATIVE DISCUSSION Before partners begin their discussion, remind them to examine Anne's speech, thoughts, and actions to find examples that support her statement. Point out that they can do this by looking again at the dialogue, the stage directions, and the excerpts from Anne's diary that appear in the play. Once pairs have identified several examples, ask them to share their findings with the class.

ASK STUDENTS to share any questions they generated in the course of reading and discussing the selection.

we'd be safe. Each time our train would stop . . . at a siding, or a
1910 crossing . . . we'd all get out and go from group to group . . . Where were you? Were you at Belsen? At Buchenwald? At Mauthausen? Is it possible that you knew my wife? Did you ever see my husband? My son? My daughter? That's how I found out about my wife's death . . . of Margot, the Van Daans . . . Dussel. But Anne . . . I
1920 still hoped . . . Yesterday I went to Rotterdam. I'd heard of a woman there . . . She'd been in Belsen with Anne . . . I know now.

(*He picks up the diary again, and turns the pages back to find a certain passage. As he finds it we hear* Anne's Voice.)

Anne's Voice. In spite of everything, I still believe that
1930 people are really good at heart.

(Mr. Frank *slowly closes the diary.*)

Mr. Frank. She puts me to shame. (*They are silent.*)

The Curtain Falls.

COLLABORATIVE DISCUSSION Mr. Frank read this from Anne's diary: "In spite of everything, I still believe that people are really good at heart." With a partner, discuss examples from the play that demonstrate that Anne really believed this to be true.

Analyze Dialogue in Drama

The story in a play is told mainly through dialogue, not only by the words characters speak but also by the way in which they say them. Through the dialogue, a playwright accomplishes different purposes:

- Dialogue propels the action in the story, moving the plot forward.
- Sometimes dialogue establishes a conflict that prompts characters to make a decision.
- Dialogue reveals different qualities, or **character traits,** of characters, because what people say and how they say it can reveal things such as fear, arrogance, doubt, or bravery.

Notice how the following dialogue increases tension in the play and reveals that Mr. Frank is forced to make a decision about a worker who may be blackmailing them:

> **Mr. Frank** (*to* Mr. Kraler). How was it left? What did you tell him?
>
> **Mr. Kraler.** I said I had to think about it. What shall I do? Pay him the money? . . . Take a chance on firing him . . . or what? I don't know.

As you analyze the dialogue, ask yourself, "What are these words explaining about the plot? What are they revealing about this character?"

Analyze Incidents in Drama

Playwrights usually tell events in **chronological order,** the order in which they occurred. They may, however, tell some events in a different order.

When an author interrupts the chronological order by describing something that took place at an earlier time, it is called a **flashback.** A flashback provides information that helps readers better understand a current situation. For example, in *The Diary of Anne Frank,* the first scene begins in November of 1945. Mr. Frank is speaking with Miep after World War II is over. The scene ends with a flashback as the audience hears words that Anne wrote in her diary during the war:

> Our hiding place was to be upstairs in the building where Father used to have his business. Three other people were coming in with us . . . the Van Daans and their son Peter . . . Father knew the Van Daans but we had never met them . . .

As you analyze *The Diary of Anne Frank,* identify where the flashback ends.

TEACH

CLOSE READ

Analyze Dialogue in Drama

As you discuss the different ways playwrights use dialogue to develop a play, ask students to provide examples from this play:

	Possible examples:
Dialogue can propel the action in a play.	*As Peter and Anne talk and get to know one another, their relationship changes.*
Dialogue can establish a conflict, forcing a decision.	*When Mr. Van Daan steals food, the characters must decide what to do.*
Dialogue can reveal character traits.	*Mr. Dussel's words to the others reveal that he is fearful and self-centered.*

Analyze Incidents in Drama

Be sure students understand that Anne's diary served as the basic outline for the story in this play, and that, like her diary, the story is told mainly in **chronological order,** the order in which events occurred.

- Ask students to identify where the flashback begins and ends. (*It begins in Act One, Scene 2 and ends in Act Two, Scene 4.*)
- Have students explain when the flashback takes place and when the opening and closing scenes take place. (*during World War II; in November 1945, after World War II*)

Strategies for Annotation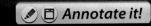

Analyze Dialogue in Drama

Have students use their eBook annotation tools to analyze the text. Ask students to do the following:

- Choose two characters, such as Mr. and Mrs. Van Daan or Anne and Mr. Dussel. Find examples of dialogue between the two.
- Highlight in green the words of one character.
- Highlight in blue the words of the other character.
- Record on notes what the dialogue reveals about both the relationship and the individual characters.

> **Mrs. Van Daan** (*hysterically*). I can't stand it! I'll kill myself! I'll kill myself!
>
> **Mr. Van Daan.** For God's sake, stop it!

Analyzing the Text COMMON CORE RL 1, RL 3

Possible answers:

1. *Mrs. Van Daan is overly concerned with material things. Mr. Van Daan is really no better because, although he is critical of his wife's attachment to the coat, he thinks it's fine to sell it to buy cigarettes for himself. Although Peter doesn't feel a closeness to his parents, he is still protective of them.*

2. *In Act One, Peter and Anne tease one another and quarrel. In Act Two, they develop an appreciation and admiration for one another and begin what may be the beginnings of a romantic relationship.*

3. *This is the event that finally causes Mrs. Frank to lose her temper, and she expresses feelings that she has so far kept to herself. She insists that Mr. Van Daan leave. This event precipitates a long discussion about whether or not the Van Daans should be allowed to stay.*

4. *Mr. Frank is speaking of the Allied invasion of Normandy on the coast of France. He anticipates that the Allies will defeat Germany and end the oppression of the Jewish people throughout Europe.*

5. *As they argue about whether or not to answer the phone that is ringing downstairs, Mr. Dussel is panicked. Mr. Frank is calm and remains a clear thinker despite outside pressures.*

6. *Students should note that the first and last scenes take place in the present, and that the rest of the play is a flashback. They may point out that seeing Mr. Frank in the first scene adds to the play's impact by showing him as an essentially broken man; it is a stark contrast to his portrayal in the flashback.*

Speaking and Listening COMMON CORE SL 1a, SL 6

Before small groups work together, have the class suggest scenes from the play in which the dialogue provokes a decision. Possible scenes include:

- Mr. Van Daan wants Miep to sell his wife's coat.
- Mr. Kraler thinks Carl may suspect something.
- Anne visits Peter despite her mother's objections.
- Mr. Van Daan steals food from the food safe.

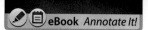

 eBook *Annotate It!*

Analyzing the Text COMMON CORE RL 1, RL 3, SL 1a, SL 6, W 4, W 9a, W 10

Cite Text Evidence Support your responses with evidence from the text.

1. **Interpret** Reread lines 241–291 in Act Two. What does this part of the dialogue reveal about each of the Van Daans?

2. **Compare** Explain the differences between Peter and Anne's relationship in Act One and in Act Two.

3. **Cause/Effect** Examine the dialogue in lines 1167–1239 that describes the aftermath of Mr. Van Daan's theft. Explain the effect of this event and how it propels the action of the story.

4. **Infer** Mr. Frank says, "The invasion has come! We're going to be liberated!" What invasion is Mr. Frank speaking about?

5. **Analyze** Reread lines 1625–1651. What does this section of dialogue demonstrate about Mr. Frank and Mr. Dussel?

6. **Evaluate** Does the use of an extended flashback add or detract from the impact of this play? Explain your opinion.

Speaking and Listening

With a small group, choose a section from the play in which the dialogue provokes a character to make a decision. Consider how each character would sound. Rehearse the lines. Then stage a dramatic reading of the section that communicates clearly the characters' thoughts and feelings.

PERFORMANCE TASK

Writing Activity: Character Sketch Choose three characters from the play, and write a character analysis of each one. Use the character's words, actions, and interactions with others to support your analysis.

- Identify each character and explain his or her role in the play.
- Describe the character's physical appearance and age.

- Discuss positive character traits as well as any weaknesses.
- Explain the character's motivations, actions, and reactions in relation to others and to historical events.
- Analyze the character's attitudes and feelings and how these change or remain the same over time.

Assign this performance task.

PERFORMANCE TASK COMMON CORE W 4, W 9a, W 10

Writing Activity: Character Sketch Tell students that a **character sketch** is a brief description of a character that gives a general picture of the character.

- Use the lesson on page 354a to teach students about character development and identifying character traits.
- After choosing three characters to write about, have students work in pairs to review the play and identify key details about each person.

INTERACTIVE WHITEBOARD LESSON
Analyze Characters

COMMON CORE

RL 1,
RL 3

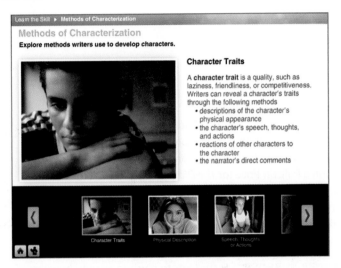

Learn the Skill ▶ Methods of Characterization

Methods of Characterization
Explore methods writers use to develop characters.

Character Traits

A **character trait** is a quality, such as laziness, friendliness, or competitiveness. Writers can reveal a character's traits through the following methods
• descriptions of the character's physical appearance
• the character's speech, thoughts, and actions
• reactions of other characters to the character
• the narrator's direct comments

Character Traits   Physical Description   Speech, Thoughts or Actions

TEACH

Before students begin the Performance Task, provide instruction on how to understand and analyze characters. Explain that like real people characters display certain qualities, or **character traits,** that develop and change over time and that authors may reveal these traits through

• descriptions of a character's physical appearance
• a character's speech, thoughts, and actions
• the reactions of other characters
• the narrator's or playwright's direct comments

Tells students that to analyze a character in a text they can

• find key details about the character
• create a character map
• use the key details to infer character traits

Point out that another important part of understanding characters is figuring out their **motivations,** or reasons, for their behaviors.

PRACTICE AND APPLY

Work with students to analyze characters in the Practice & Apply section of the Interactive Whiteboard Lesson. Then, ask partners to apply the skill further by choosing and analyzing one character from the play *The Diary of Anne Frank.* Remind students to choose a character they did not previously analyze when completing the Performance Task.

Analyze Elements of Drama

COMMON CORE

RL 1,
RL 3

RETEACH

Review the terms *drama, playwright, script, cast of characters, stage directions, structure, act, scene, dialogue, character traits, chronological order,* and *flashback.* Explain that a drama is a story that is told primarily through the dialogue and actions of actors. Point out that a play is one kind of drama, but that students regularly see other types of drama, including screenplays such as movies and television programs.

Ask students to suggest several dramas that most class members have seen. Have students choose one to discuss as a class. Guide the class discussion, focusing on these elements of the drama:

• the cast of characters
• the structure of the drama (acts and scenes)
• character traits of the main characters
• one or more compelling sections of dialogue
• stage directions the writer or writers may have included for one important scene

LEVEL UP TUTORIALS Assign the following *Level Up* tutorial: **Elements of Drama**

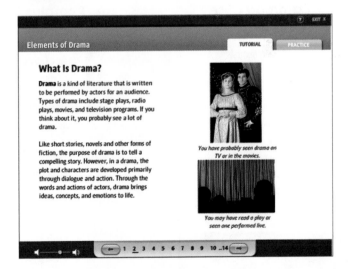

Elements of Drama   TUTORIAL   PRACTICE

What Is Drama?

Drama is a kind of literature that is written to be performed by actors for an audience. Types of drama include stage plays, radio plays, movies, and television programs. If you think about it, you probably see a lot of drama.

Like short stories, novels and other forms of fiction, the purpose of drama is to tell a compelling story. However, in a drama, the plot and characters are developed primarily through dialogue and action. Through the words and actions of actors, drama brings ideas, concepts, and emotions to life.

You have probably seen drama on TV or in the movies.

You may have read a play or seen one performed live.

CLOSE READING APPLICATION

Student partners can apply the skill by working together to identify elements of drama in another play.

The Diary of Anne Frank
Act I, Scenes 1 and 2

Drama by Frances Goodrich and Albert Hackett

Why This Text

Students may have limited experience analyzing drama. This excerpt from *The Diary of Anne Frank* provides an opportunity to analyze how dialogue reveals character and propels a plot. With the help of the close-reading questions, students will analyze how Goodrich and Hackett dramatize a series of events in the life of the Frank family. This close reading will lead students to analyze Anne Frank's character as well as some events that took place in the secret annex.

Background Have students read the background and the information about the authors. Goodrich and Hackett were a husband and wife writing team, nominated for Academy Awards for *The Thin Man* and *Father of the Bride* among others, before they won a Pulitzer Prize for *The Diary of Anne Frank*. Introduce the selection by telling students that Anne's father, Otto Frank, returned to his former home in Amsterdam after the end of World War II. Very little remained of the life he had known, but a friend of his had saved Anne's diary.

SETTING A PURPOSE Ask students to pay attention to how the playwrights reveal the characters and events. What is the setting of the opening scene?

 Common Core Support

- cite strong textual evidence
- analyze how particular lines of dialogue in a drama propel the action and reveal aspects of a character
- determine the meaning of words and phrases as they are used in the text

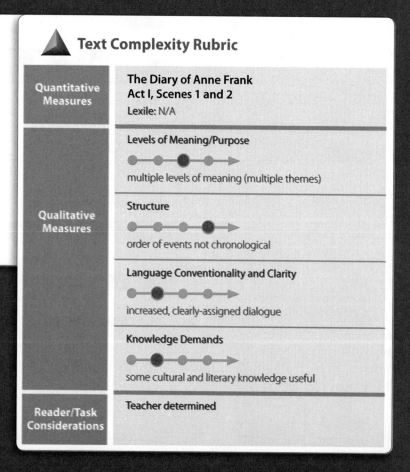

Text Complexity Rubric

Quantitative Measures	**The Diary of Anne Frank Act I, Scenes 1 and 2** Lexile: N/A
Qualitative Measures	**Levels of Meaning/Purpose** multiple levels of meaning (multiple themes)
	Structure order of events not chronological
	Language Conventionality and Clarity increased, clearly-assigned dialogue
	Knowledge Demands some cultural and literary knowledge useful
Reader/Task Considerations	Teacher determined

Strategies for CLOSE READING

Analyze Dialogue in Drama

Students should read this drama carefully all the way through. Close-reading questions at the bottom of the page will help them focus on a thorough analysis of the text. As they read, students should jot down comments or questions about the script in the side margins.

WHEN STUDENTS STRUGGLE . . .

To help students analyze the dialogue in *The Diary of Anne Frank*, have them work in small groups to fill out a chart, such as the one shown below, as they read the script.

CITE TEXT EVIDENCE For practice analyzing dialogue to understand Anne Frank's character, ask students to cite evidence from the text.

detail: *She is self-confident when she is taking off her layered clothes.*

detail: *had to wear a yellow star to identify herself as Jewish*

detail: *emigrated to Holland when Hitler came to power*

Anne Frank

detail: *13 years old, born June 19, 1929*

detail: *She is "sobered" by her realization of what "going into hiding" means.*

Background Anne Frank *was born in Germany in 1929. Her family relocated to the Netherlands in 1933 after the Nazi party came to power. In 1940, Germany invaded the Netherlands; in July 1942, the Frank and Van Daan families went into hiding. Anne's father survived the Holocaust. He was given Anne's diary at the end of World War II, and published it in 1947. It has since been translated into 67 languages and is considered one of the most affecting memoirs of the Holocaust.* **Frances Goodrich** *(1890–1984) and* **Albert Hackett** *(1900–1995) wrote the play called* The Diary of Anne Frank *based upon Anne's diary entries.*

The Diary of Anne Frank
Act I, Scenes 1 and 2

Drama by Frances Goodrich and Albert Hackett

CLOSE READ
Notes

CHARACTERS

SECRET ANNEX RESIDENTS
Anne Frank
Margot Frank
Mr. Frank
Mrs. Frank
Peter Van Daan
Mr. Van Daan
Mrs. Van Daan

WORKERS IN MR. FRANK'S BUSINESS
Miep Gies (mēp gēs)
Mr. Kraler (krä´lər)

A moveable bookcase hid the stairs to the hiding place, the Secret Annex.

91

1. **READ** ▶ As you read the stage directions and lines 1–42, begin to collect and cite text evidence.

- Underline details of the setting that show this is not an ordinary room.
- Circle the text that lets you know Mr. Frank has been through a very hard time.
- In the margin, make an inference about how Mr. Frank feels about being in the warehouse.

The Time. July 1942–August 1944, November 1945

The Place. Amsterdam, the Netherlands

The scene remains the same throughout the play. It is the top floor of a warehouse and office building in Amsterdam, Holland. The sharply peaked roof of the building is outlined against a sea of other rooftops, stretching away into the distance. Nearby is the belfry of a church tower, the Westertoren, whose carillon[1] *rings out the hours. Occasionally faint sounds float up from below: the voices of children playing in the street, the tramp of marching feet, a boat whistle from the canal.*

The three rooms of the top floor and a small attic space above are exposed to our view. The largest of the rooms is in the center, with two small rooms, slightly raised, on either side. On the right is a bathroom, out of sight. A narrow steep flight of stairs at the back leads up to the attic. The rooms are sparsely furnished with a few chairs, cots, a table or two. The windows are painted over, or covered with makeshift blackout curtains. In the main room there is a sink, a gas ring for cooking and a wood-burning stove for warmth.

The room on the left is hardly more than a closet. There is a skylight in the sloping ceiling. Directly under this room is a small steep stairwell, with steps leading down to a door. This is the only entrance from the building below. When the door is opened we see that it has been concealed on the outer side by a bookcase attached to it.

---

[1] **carillon:** a set of bells, commonly found in church bell towers.

ACT ONE
Scene 1

The curtain rises on an empty stage. It is late afternoon November, 1945.

The rooms are dusty, the curtains in rags. Chairs and tables are overturned.

The door at the foot of the small stairwell swings open. Mr. Frank comes up the steps into view. He is a gentle, cultured European in his middle years. There is still a trace of a German accent in his speech.

(A) *He stands looking slowly around, making a supreme effort at self-control. He is weak, ill.*

10   *His clothes are threadbare.*

After a second he drops his rucksack on the couch and moves slowly about. He opens the door to one of the smaller rooms, and then abruptly closes it again, turning away. He goes to the window at the back, looking off at the Westertoren as its carillon strikes the hour of six, then he moves restlessly on.

From the street below we hear the sound of a barrel organ and children's voices at play. There is a many-colored scarf hanging from a nail. Mr. Frank takes it, putting it around his neck. As he starts back for his rucksack, his eye is caught by something lying on the floor. It is a

20   *woman's white glove. He holds it in his hand and suddenly all of his self-control is gone. He breaks down, crying.*

We hear footsteps on the stairs. Miep Gies comes up, looking for Mr. Frank. Miep is a Dutch girl of about twenty-two. She wears a coat and hat, ready to go home. She is pregnant. Her attitude toward Mr. Frank is protective, compassionate.

Miep. Are you all right, Mr. Frank?

Mr. Frank (*quickly controlling himself*). Yes, Miep, yes.

Miep. Everyone in the office has gone home . . . It's after six. (*then pleading*) Don't stay up here, Mr. Frank. What's the use of torturing

30   yourself like this?

Mr. Frank. I've come to say good-bye . . . I'm leaving here, Miep.

Miep. What do you mean? Where are you going? Where?

Mr. Frank. I don't know yet. I haven't decided.

Miep. Mr. Frank, you can't leave here! This is your home! Amsterdam

(B) is your home. Your business is here, waiting for you . . . You're needed here . . . Now that the war is over, there are things that . . .

This is a place that holds painful memories for Mr. Frank. It is very difficult for him to be there.

1. **READ AND CITE TEXT EVIDENCE**

(A) **ASK STUDENTS** to cite text evidence that shows how Mr. Frank feels about being in the warehouse. *Students should cite evidence from lines 8–9, "making a supreme effort at self-control," line 15, "he moves restlessly," and lines 20–21, "suddenly all of his self-control is gone. He breaks down, crying."*

FOR ELL STUDENTS Explain to students that a rucksack (line 11) is the same as a backpack.

Mr. Frank. I can't stay in Amsterdam, Miep. It has too many memories for me. Everywhere there's something . . . the house we lived in . . . the school . . . that street organ playing out there . . . I'm
40 not the person you used to know, Miep. I'm a bitter old man. (*breaking off*) Forgive me. I shouldn't speak to you like this . . . after all that you did for us . . . the suffering . . .

Miep. No. No. It wasn't suffering. You can't say we suffered. (*As she speaks, she straightens a chair which is overturned.*)

Mr. Frank. I know what you went through, you and Mr. Kraler. I'll remember it as long as I live. (*He gives one last look around.*) Come, Miep.

(*He starts for the steps, then remembers his rucksack, going back to get it.*)

50 **Miep** (*hurrying up to a cupboard*). Mr. Frank, did you see? There are some of your papers here. (*She brings a bundle of papers to him.*) We found them in a heap of rubbish on the floor after . . . after you left.

Mr. Frank. Burn them.

(*He opens his rucksack to put the glove in it.*)

Miep. But, Mr. Frank, there are letters, notes . . .

Mr. Frank. Burn them. All of them.

Miep. Burn *this*?

(*She hands him a paperbound notebook.*)

Mr. Frank (*quietly*). Anne's diary. (*He opens the diary and begins to*
60 *read.*) "Monday, the sixth of July, nineteen forty-two." (*to Miep*) Nineteen forty-two. Is it possible, Miep? . . . Only three years ago. (*As he continues his reading, he sits down on the couch.*) "Dear Diary, since you and I are going to be great friends, I will start by telling you about myself. My name is Anne Frank. I am thirteen years old. I was born in Germany the twelfth of June, nineteen twenty-nine. As my family is Jewish, we emigrated to Holland when Hitler came to power."

Mr. Frank wants to destroy all memories of his time in the annex because they are so painful to him.

(*As Mr. Frank reads on, another voice joins his, as if coming from the air. It is Anne's Voice.*)

Mr. Frank and Anne. "My father started a business, importing spice
70 and herbs. Things went well for us until nineteen forty. Then the war came, and the Dutch **capitulation**, followed by the arrival of the Germans. Then things got very bad for the Jews."

(*Mr. Frank's Voice dies out. Anne's Voice continues alone. The lights dim slowly to darkness. The curtain falls on the scene.*)

Anne's Voice. You could not do this and you could not do that. They forced Father out of his business. We had to wear yellow stars.[2] I had to turn in my bike. I couldn't go to a Dutch school any more. I couldn't go to the movies, or ride in an automobile, or even on a streetcar, and a million other things. But somehow we children still
80 managed to have fun. Yesterday Father told me we were going into hiding. Where, he wouldn't say. At five o'clock this morning Mother woke me and told me to hurry and get dressed. I was to put on as many clothes as I could. It would look too suspicious if we walked along carrying suitcases. It wasn't until we were on our way that I learned where we were going. Our hiding place was to be upstairs in the building where Father used to have his business. Three other people were coming in with us . . . the Van Daans and their son Peter . . . Father knew the Van Daans but we had never met them . . . (*During the last lines the curtain rises on the scene. The lights dim on.*
90 Anne's Voice *fades out.*)

capitulation:
surrender;
defeat

[2] **yellow stars:** the six-pointed Stars of David that the Nazis ordered all Jews to wear for identification.

---

2. **REREAD AND DISCUSS** Reread lines 26–42. In a small group, discuss the clues that hint at what happened to Miep and Mr. Frank.

3. **READ** As you read lines 43–90, continue to cite textual evidence.
   - Circle what Mr. Frank instructs Miep to do with the papers, and in the margin explain what this reveals about him.
   - Underline what you learn about Anne from her diary.

94

---

4. **REREAD** Reread lines 58–90. How does the structure of the drama change? What is the effect of this change?

The drama starts in the present (1945), with Mr. Frank. When he reads Anne's diary, the play shifts to the past. This brings us closer to Anne; we see things as they happen to her, instead of experiencing the action through her diary entries, read by her father.

95

---

2. **REREAD AND DISCUSS USING TEXT EVIDENCE**

   B **ASK STUDENTS** to cite evidence as they discuss what happened to Miep and Mr. Frank. *Students should cite text in lines 35–36 to show that war has affected these characters. They should cite lines 1–2 and infer that it was the Second World War.*

3. **READ AND CITE TEXT EVIDENCE**

   C **ASK STUDENTS** to use their underlined text as evidence to describe Anne. *Students should describe Anne as young and German-Jewish based on evidence in lines 64–66. They should describe her hardships after the Germans arrived in Holland citing evidence from lines 76–77, 79, and 80–81.*

4. **REREAD AND CITE TEXT EVIDENCE**

   D **ASK STUDENTS** to read their response aloud to a partner. Have partners work together to locate text evidence that supports their answers. Then, have each student rewrite his or her response with text evidence. *Students may cite the date in the stage directions in lines 1–2. They may cite line 69 as the first time we hear Anne's voice. They might explain that we are being drawn into Anne's point of view.*

   Critical Vocabulary: capitulation (line 71) Have students explain the meaning of *capitulation* as it is used here. What connotation does the word *capitulation* have that its synonym *surrender* does not have? Why did the authors choose *capitulation*?

It didn't
matter how
well-off you
were; if you
were Jewish,
you were in
danger.

Scene 2

It is early morning, July, 1942. The rooms are bare, as before, but they are now clean and orderly.

Mr. Van Daan, *a tall, portly man in his late forties, is in the main room, pacing up and down, nervously smoking a cigarette. His clothes and overcoat are expensive and well cut.*

Mrs. Van Daan *sits on the couch, clutching her possessions, a hatbox, bags, etc. She is a pretty woman in her early forties. She wears a fur coat over her other clothes.*

100 Peter Van Daan *is standing at the window of the room on the right, looking down at the street below. He is a shy, awkward boy of sixteen. He wears a cap, a raincoat, and long Dutch trousers, like "plus fours."³ At his feet is a black case, a carrier for his cat.*

The yellow Star of David is conspicuous on all of their clothes.

Mrs. Van Daan (*rising, nervous, excited*). Something's happened to them! I know it!

Mr. Van Daan. Now, Kerli!

Mrs. Van Daan. Mr. Frank said they'd be here at seven o'clock. He said . . .

Mr. Van Daan. They have two miles to walk. You can't expect . . .

110 **Mrs. Van Daan.** They've been picked up. That's what's happened. They've been taken . . .

(Mr. Van Daan *indicates that he hears someone coming.*)

Mr. Van Daan. You see?

(Peter *takes up his carrier and his schoolbag, etc., and goes into the main room as* Mr. Frank *comes up the stairwell from below.* Mr. Frank *looks much younger now. His movements are brisk, his manner confident. He wears an overcoat and carries his hat and a small cardboard box. He crosses to the* Van Daans, *shaking hands with each of them.*)

³ **plus fours:** pants that end just below the knee.

120 **Mr. Frank.** Mrs. Van Daan, Mr. Van Daan, Peter. (*then, in explanation of their lateness*) There were too many of the Green Police⁴ on the streets . . . we had to take the long way around.

(*Up the steps come* Margot Frank, Mrs. Frank, Miep [*not pregnant now*] *and* Mr. Kraler. *All of them carry bags, packages, and so forth. The Star of David is* **conspicuous** *on all of the* Franks' *clothing.* Margot *is eighteen, beautiful, quiet, shy.* Mrs. Frank *is a young mother, gently bred, reserved. She, like* Mr. Frank, *has a slight German accent.* Mr. Kraler *is a Dutchman, dependable, kindly.*

As Mr. Kraler *and* Miep *go upstage to put down their parcels,* Mrs. 130 Frank *turns back to call* Anne.)

Mrs. Frank. Anne?

(Anne *comes running up the stairs. She is thirteen, quick in her movements, interested in everything,* **mercurial** *in her emotions. She wears a cape, long wool socks and carries a schoolbag.*)

Mr. Frank (*introducing them*). My wife, Edith. Mr. and Mrs. Van Daan (Mrs. Frank *hurries over, shaking hands with them.*) . . . their son, Peter . . . my daughters, Margot and Anne.

(Anne *gives a polite little curtsy as she shakes* Mr. Van Daan's *hand. Then she immediately starts off on a tour of investigation of her new* 140 *home, going upstairs to the attic room.* Miep *and* Mr. Kraler *are putting the various things they have brought on the shelves.*)

Mr. Kraler. I'm sorry there is still so much confusion.

Mr. Frank. Please. Don't think of it. After all, we'll have plenty of leisure to arrange everything ourselves.

Miep (*to* Mrs. Frank). We put the stores of food you sent in here. Your drugs are here . . . soap, linen here.

Mrs. Frank. Thank you, Miep.

⁴ **Green Police:** the Nazi police who wore green uniforms.

conspicuous:
visible; obvious

mercurial:
unpredictable; impulsive

5. **READ** As you read lines 91–147, continue to cite text evidence.
- Circle the stage directions that explain the setting.
- Underline what the Van Daans are wearing, and write in the margin what this tells you about people who went into hiding.

6. **REREAD AND DISCUSS** Reread lines 142–147. In a small group, discuss why Miep and Mr. Kraler are helping the Franks and the Van Daans. How do you think Miep and Mr. Kraler feel about helping them?

96

97

5. READ AND CITE TEXT EVIDENCE

E ASK STUDENTS to analyze the Van Daans using their underlined text as evidence. *Students should notice that the Van Daans are well-to-do and should cite as evidence lines 95–96, describing Mr. Van Daan's coat, and lines 97–98, describing Mrs. Van Daan's coat. They should infer that Jewish people were in danger whether they were well-off or not.*

FOR ELL STUDENTS Explain to students that in this context, *picked up* (line 110) means "taken into custody by the police."

6. REREAD AND DISCUSS USING TEXT EVIDENCE

F ASK STUDENTS to be prepared to cite evidence to support their inferences in a class discussion. Their evidence should be specific and should include line numbers. *Students should cite line 142 as evidence that Mr. Kraler regrets the Franks' situation. They may cite lines 145–146 as evidence that Miep is being thorough in her attention to the needs of the Frank family.*

Critical Vocabulary: conspicuous (line 125) Have students explain the meaning of *conspicuous* as it is used here.

Critical Vocabulary: mercurial (line 133) Have students compare definitions of *mercurial* and come to an agreement about which definition is intended here.

Miep. I made up the beds . . . the way Mr. Frank and Mr. Kraler said. (*She starts out.*) Forgive me. I have to hurry. I've got to go to the other

150 side of town to get some ration books⁵ for you.

Mrs. Van Daan. Ration books? If they see our names on ration books, they'll know we're here.

Mr. Kraler. There isn't anything . . .

Miep. Don't worry. Your names won't be on them. *(as she hurries out)* I'll be up later. } *Together*

Mr. Frank. Thank you, Miep.

Mrs. Frank (*to Mr. Kraler*). It's illegal, then, the ration books? We've never done anything illegal.

Mr. Frank. We won't be living here exactly according to regulations.

160 (*As Mr. Kraler reassures Mrs. Frank, he takes various small things, such as matches, soap, etc., from his pockets, handing them to her.*)

Mr. Kraler. This isn't the black market,⁶ Mrs. Frank. This is what we call the white market . . . helping all of the hundreds and hundreds who are hiding out in Amsterdam.

(*The carillon is heard playing the quarter-hour before eight. Mr. Kraler looks at his watch. Anne stops at the window as she comes down the stairs.*)

Anne. It's the Westertoren!

Mr. Kraler. I must go. I must be out of here and downstairs in the

170 office before the workmen get here. (*He starts for the stairs leading*

Kraler shows he's kind through his actions.

---

⁵ **ration books:** books of stamps or coupons issued by the government in wartime. With these coupons, people could purchase scarce items, such as food, clothing, and gasoline.

⁶ **black market:** a system for selling goods illegally, in violation of rationing and other restrictions.

---

7. **READ** ▶ As you read lines 148–201, continue to cite evidence from the text.

- Underline examples of Mr. Kraler's words and actions toward the Franks and Van Daans. In the margin, explain what they reveal about his character.
- Circle the clothing that the Franks and Van Daans are wearing, and explain in the margin why they are wearing so many layers of clothing.

98

---

out.) Miep or I, or both of us, will be up each day to bring you food and news and find out what your needs are. Tomorrow I'll get you a better bolt for the door at the foot of the stairs. It needs a bolt that you can throw yourself and open only at our signal. (*to Mr. Frank*) Oh . . . You'll tell them about the noise?

Mr. Frank. I'll tell them.

Mr. Kraler. Good-bye then for the moment. I'll come up again, after the workmen leave.

Mr. Frank. Good-bye, Mr. Kraler.

180 **Mrs. Frank** (*shaking his hand*). How can we thank you? (*The others murmur their good-byes.*)

Mr. Kraler. I never thought I'd live to see the day when a man like Mr. Frank would have to go into hiding. When you think—(*He breaks off, going out. Mr. Frank follows him down the steps, bolting the door after him. In the interval before he returns, Peter goes over to Margot, shaking hands with her. As Mr. Frank comes back up the steps, Mrs. Frank questions him anxiously.*)

Mrs. Frank. What did he mean, about the noise?

Mr. Frank. First let us take off some of these clothes. (*They all start to*

190 *take off garment after garment. On each of their coats, sweaters, blouses, suits, dresses, is another yellow Star of David. Mr. and Mrs. Frank are underdressed quite simply. The others wear several things, sweaters, extra dresses, bathrobes, aprons, nightgowns, etc.*)

Mr. Van Daan. It's a wonder we weren't arrested, walking along the streets . . . Petronella with a fur coat in July . . . and that cat of Peter's crying all the way.

Anne (*as she is removing a pair of panties*) A cat?

Mrs. Frank (*shocked*). Anne, please!

Anne. It's all right. I've got on three more. (*She pulls off two more.*

200 *Finally, as they have all removed their surplus clothes, they look to Mr. Frank, waiting for him to speak.*)

Kraler's words reveal his protective nature.

Kraler's words show his empathy.

They had to wear all of the clothes they were bringing into hiding. Carrying suitcases would have looked suspicious.

---

8. **◀ REREAD** Reread lines 165–168. What do these lines reveal about Anne's character?

Despite terrible circumstances, she still appreciates the wonders of life, even something as simple as seeing a church through the window.

99

---

7. **READ AND CITE TEXT EVIDENCE**

G **ASK STUDENTS** to cite text evidence that explains Mr. Kraler's character. *Students should find evidence of Kraler's kindness (line 160), his protective nature (lines 171–173), and his empathy (lines 182–183).*

8. **REREAD AND CITE TEXT EVIDENCE** Make sure that students understand the terms *carillon* and *Westertoren*. The carillon is a set of bells sounded by hammers controlled from a keyboard. The Westertoren is the bell tower of the famous Westerkerk church in Amsterdam.

H **ASK STUDENTS** to make an inference about Anne's character and to support it with specific evidence from the text. *Students may conclude that Anne still appreciates the wonders of life, and they may cite as evidence lines 166–168.*

FOR ELL STUDENTS Challenge students to guess the meaning of the noun *bolt* (line 173) by looking at context clues around the word.

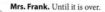

The view from a window in the Secret Annex.

Mr. Frank. Now. About the noise. While the men are in the building below, we must have complete quiet. Every sound can be heard down there, not only in the workrooms, but in the offices too. The men come at about eight-thirty, and leave at about five-thirty. So, to be perfectly safe, from eight in the morning until six in the evening we must move only when it is necessary, and then in stockinged feet. We must not speak above a whisper. We must not run any water. We cannot use the sink, or even, forgive me, the w.c.[7] The pipes go down

210 through the workrooms. It would be heard. No trash . . . (*Mr. Frank stops* **abruptly** *as he hears the sound of marching feet from the street below. Everyone is motionless, paralyzed with fear. Mr. Frank goes quietly into the room on the right to look down out of the window. Anne runs after him, peering out with him. The tramping feet pass without stopping. The tension is relieved. Mr. Frank, followed by Anne, returns to the main room and resumes his instructions to the group.*) . . . No trash must ever be thrown out which might reveal that someone is living up here . . . not even a potato paring. We must burn everything in the stove at night. This is the way we must live until it is over, if we

220 are to survive.

(*There is silence for a second.*)

abruptly:

quickly, without warning

---
[7] **w.c.:** water closet; toilet.

---

9. (READ ▶) As you read lines 202–266, continue to cite evidence from the text.
   • Underline the rules that the Franks and Van Daans must follow.
   • Circle ways in which Mr. Frank makes the situation more normal.

100

Mrs. Frank. Until it is over.
Mr. Frank (*reassuringly*). After six we can move about . . . we can talk and laugh and have our supper and read and play games . . . just as we would at home. (*He looks at his watch.*) And now I think it would be wise if we all went to our rooms, and were settled before eight o'clock. Mrs. Van Daan, you and your husband will be upstairs. I regret that there's no place up there for Peter. But he will be here, near us. This will be our common room, where we'll meet to talk and eat and read,

230 like one family.
Mr. Van Daan. And where do you and Mrs. Frank sleep?
Mr. Frank. This room is also our bedroom.
Mrs. Van Daan. That isn't right. We'll sleep here and you take the room upstairs.
Mr. Van Daan. It's your place.

} *Together*

Mr. Frank. Please. I've thought this out for weeks. It's the best arrangement. The only arrangement.
Mrs. Van Daan (*to* Mr. Frank). Never, never can we thank you. (*then to* Mrs. Frank) I don't know what would have happened to us, if it

240 hadn't been for Mr. Frank.
Mr. Frank. You don't know how your husband helped me when I came to this country . . . knowing no one . . . not able to speak the language. I can never repay him for that. (*going to* Van Daan) May I help you with your things?
Mr. Van Daan. No. No. (*to* Mrs. Van Daan) Come along, *liefje*.[8]
Mrs. Van Daan. You'll be all right, Peter? You're not afraid?
Peter (*embarrassed*). Please, Mother.
(*They start up the stairs to the attic room above.* Mr. Frank *turns to* Mrs. Frank.)

250 **Mr. Frank.** You too must have some rest, Edith. You didn't close your eyes last night. Nor you, Margot.
Anne. I slept, Father. Wasn't that funny? I knew it was the last night in my own bed, and yet I slept soundly.

---
[8] **liefje** (lēfʹyə): *Dutch:* little darling.

101

---

9. **READ AND CITE TEXT EVIDENCE**

(I) **ASK STUDENTS** to cite evidence of ways in which life is unusual in the secret annex, as well as efforts Mr. Frank makes to normalize their situation. *Students should cite evidence of rules those in the annex must follow during the workday from eight in the morning to six in the evening. Students should cite evidence that the residents of the secret annex must be silent from eight in the morning until six in the evening (lines 206–209), and that they must not throw out any trash (lines 216–219). Mr. Frank reassures them in lines 223–235: we can "talk and laugh and have our supper and read and play games" after six in the evening.*

Critical Vocabulary: abruptly (line 211) Ask students to explain the meaning of *abruptly* as it is used here. Why did Mr. Frank stop abruptly?

FOR ELL STUDENTS Some students may think that the adverb *soundly* (line 253) is related to sound. Clarify that *soundly* means "fully, deeply, completely."

Mr. Frank. I'm glad, Anne. Now you'll be able to help me straighten things in here. (*to* Mrs. Frank *and* Margot) Come with me . . . You and Margot rest in this room for the time being. (*He picks up their clothes, starting for the room on the right.*)

Mrs. Frank. You're sure . . .? I could help . . . And Anne hasn't had her milk . . .

260 **Mr. Frank.** I'll give it to her. (*to* Anne *and* Peter) Anne, Peter . . . it's best that you take off your shoes now, before you forget. (*He leads the way to the room, followed by* Margot.)

Mrs. Frank. You're sure you're not tired, Anne?

Anne. I feel fine. I'm going to help Father.

Mrs. Frank. Peter, I'm glad you are to be with us.

Peter. Yes, Mrs. Frank.

(Mrs. Frank *goes to join* Mr. Frank *and* Margot.)

(*During the following scene* Mr. Frank *helps* Margot *and* Mrs. Frank *to hang up their clothes. Then he persuades them both to lie down and*
270 *rest. The* Van Daans *in their room above settle themselves. In the main room* Anne *and* Peter *remove their shoes.* Peter *takes his cat out of the carrier.*)

(K) **Anne.** What's your cat's name?

Peter. Mouschi.[9]

---

[9] **Mouschi** (mōō´shē).

---

10. **◀ REREAD** Reread lines 222–262. Why is it important for Mr. Frank to normalize the situation? Support your answer with explicit textual evidence.

Making the space seem like a home is the only way he can make the people living there feel more comfortable and make hiding from the Nazis less frightening.

11. **READ ▶** As you read lines 267–325, continue to cite evidence from the text.

- Underline the questions Anne asks Peter, and explain in the margin what is significant about their exchange.
- Circle stage directions that explain what Anne and Peter do to their Star of David badges.

102

Anne. Mouschi! Mouschi! Mouschi! (*She picks up the cat, walking away with it. To* Peter.) I love cats. I have one . . . a darling little cat. But they made me leave her behind. I left some food and a note for the neighbors to take care of her . . . I'm going to miss her terribly. What is yours? A him or a her?

280 **Peter.** He's a tom. He doesn't like strangers.

(*He takes the cat from her, putting it back in its carrier.*)

Anne (*unabashed*). Then I'll have to stop being a stranger, won't I? Is he fixed?

Peter (*startled*). Huh?

Anne. Did you have him fixed?

Peter. No.

Anne. Oh, you ought to have him fixed—to keep him from—you know, fighting. Where did you go to school?

Peter. Jewish Secondary.

290 **Anne.** But that's where Margot and I go! I never saw you around.

Peter. I used to see you . . . sometimes . . .

Anne. You did?

Peter. . . . in the school yard. You were always in the middle of a bunch of kids. (*He takes a penknife from his pocket.*)

Anne. Why didn't you ever come over?

(L) **Peter.** I'm sort of a lone wolf. (*He starts to rip off his Star of David.*)

Anne. What are you doing?

Peter. Taking it off.

Anne. But you can't do that. They'll arrest you if you go out without
300 your star.

(*He tosses his knife on the table.*)

Peter. Who's going out?

Anne. Why, of course! You're right! Of course we don't need them any more. (*She picks up his knife and starts to take her star off.*) I wonder what our friends will think when we don't show up today?

Peter. I didn't have any dates with anyone.

This is an ordinary conversation. It is surprising that they can discuss everyday matters under such frightening circumstances.

103

---

10. **REREAD AND CITE TEXT EVIDENCE**

(J) **ASK STUDENTS** to make an inference about the reason Mr. Frank tries to normalize the situation. Ask students to read aloud specific evidence from the text that supports their response. *Students should cite evidence such as the stage direction in line 223 to show that Mr. Frank is motivated by a desire to make the people feel more comfortable.*

11. **READ AND CITE TEXT EVIDENCE**

(K) **ASK STUDENTS** to cite evidence of two ways that Anne and Peter rise above their frightening circumstances. *Students should cite evidence from Anne and Peter's conversation in lines 273–295 to show that they have a normal conversation despite their frightening circumstances. They also rise above their situation by defying the orders of the Nazis and removing the yellow stars (lines 296, 304, 314–316, and 318).*

FOR ELL STUDENTS Explain that to have an animal fixed (line 283) means to neuter it, making it unable to reproduce.

Anne. Oh, I did. I had a date with Jopie to go and play ping-pong at her house. <u>Do you know Jopie de Waal?</u>[10]

Peter. No.

310 **Anne.** Jopie's my best friend. <u>I wonder what she'll think when she</u> <u>telephones and there's no answer?</u> . . . Probably she'll go over to the house . . . I wonder what she'll think . . . we left everything as if we'd suddenly been called away . . . breakfast dishes in the sink . . . beds not made . . . (As she pulls off her star, the cloth underneath shows clearly the color and form of the star.) Look! It's still there! (Peter goes over to the stove with his star.) What're you going to do with yours?

Peter. Burn it.

Anne (She starts to throw hers in, and cannot.) It's funny, I can't throw mine away. I don't know why.

320 **Peter.** You can't throw . . .? Something they branded you with . . .? That they made you wear so they could spit on you?

Anne. I know. I know. But after all, it *is* the Star of David, isn't it? (In the bedroom, right, Margot and Mrs. Frank are lying down. Mr. Frank starts quietly out.)

Peter. Maybe it's different for a girl.

(Mr. Frank comes into the main room.)

Mr. Frank. Forgive me, Peter. Now let me see. We must find a bed for your cat. (He goes to a cupboard.) I'm glad you brought your cat. Anne was feeling so badly about hers. (getting a used small washtub) Here

330 we are. Will it be comfortable in that?

---

[10] **Jopie de Waal** (yō′pē də väl′).

---

12. ◀ REREAD Reread lines 291–325. What do Peter's words and actions reveal about his character?

Peter is angry that they are in hiding. He wants to have some control over the situation. He wants to remove the identifying mark that the Nazis assigned to the Jews.

13. READ ▶ As you read lines 326–388, continue to cite text evidence.

• Underline several examples of dialogue that reveal different aspects of Mr. Frank's personality, and describe his behavior in the margin.

• Explain in the margin how the diary helps you understand Scene 1.

• Circle the advice Mr. Frank tells Anne to remember and write in the margin why this advice is important.

104

> ❝ *I'm going to think of it as a boarding house. A very peculiar summer boarding house . . .* ❞

Peter (gathering up his things). Thanks.

Mr. Frank (opening the door of the room on the left)**.** And here is your room. But I warn you, Peter, you can't grow any more. <u>Not an inch, or you'll have to sleep with your feet out of the skylight.</u> Are you hungry?

Peter. No.

Mr. Frank. We have some bread and butter.

Peter. No, thank you.

Mr. Frank. You can have it for luncheon then. And tonight we will have a real supper . . . our first supper together.

340 **Peter.** Thanks. Thanks.

(He goes into his room. During the following scene he arranges his possessions in his new room.)

Mr. Frank. That's a nice boy, Peter.

Anne. He's awfully shy, isn't he?

Mr. Frank. <u>You'll like him, I know.</u>

Anne. I certainly hope so, since he's the only boy I'm likely to see for months and months.

(Mr. Frank sits down, taking off his shoes.)

Mr. Frank. Annele,[11] there's a box there. Will you open it?

350 (He indicates a carton on the couch. Anne brings it to the center table. In the street below there is the sound of children playing.)

Anne (as she opens the carton). You know the way I'm going to think of it here? I'm going to think of it as a boarding house. A very peculiar summer boarding house, like the one that we—(She breaks off as she pulls out some photographs.) Father! My movie stars! I was wondering

---

[11] **Annele/Anneke:** a nickname for Anne.

105

Mr. Frank is teasing Peter.

Mr. Frank is being fatherly and caring.

---

12. REREAD AND CITE TEXT EVIDENCE

Ⓛ ASK STUDENTS to work with a partner. Have them read aloud their response and cite specific text evidence with line numbers to support their inferences about Peter's character. *Students may think that Peter is angry and wants to defy the Nazi orders (lines 296, 315–316, and 320–321).*

13. READ AND CITE TEXT EVIDENCE

Ⓜ ASK STUDENTS to cite text evidence that reveals Mr. Frank's personality. *Students should cite evidence that Mr. Frank is keeping things light (lines 333–334 and lines 384–387), that he is fatherly and caring with Anne (line 345), and that he is protective and firm (lines 367–368).*

We learn that
Mr. Frank gave
Anne the
diary on their
first day of
hiding, so it
has a huge
emotional
impact on him.

Mr. Frank is
protective and
firm.

The Nazis
cannot take
away their
freedom to
think.

Mr. Frank is
joking again.

where they were! I was looking for them this morning . . . and Queen Wilhelmina! How wonderful!

Mr. Frank. There's something more. Go on. Look further.

(*He goes over to the sink, pouring a glass of milk from a thermos bottle.*)

360 **Anne** (*pulling out a pasteboard-bound book*). A diary! (*She throws her arms around her father.*) I've never had a diary. And I've always longed for one. (*She looks around the room.*) Pencil, pencil, pencil, pencil. (*She starts down the stairs.*) I'm going down to the office to get a pencil.

Mr. Frank. Anne! No! (*He goes after her, catching her by the arm and pulling her back.*)

Anne (*startled*). But there's no one in the building now.

Mr. Frank. It doesn't matter. I don't want you ever to go beyond that door.

Anne (*sobered*). Never . . .? Not even at nighttime, when everyone is

370 gone? Or on Sundays? Can't I go down to listen to the radio?

Mr. Frank. Never. I am sorry, Anneke. It isn't safe. No, you must never go beyond that door.

(*For the first time Anne realizes what "going into hiding" means.*)

Anne. I see.

Mr. Frank. It'll be hard, I know. But always remember this, Anneke.

Ⓝ There are no walls, there are no bolts, no locks that anyone can put on your mind. Miep will bring us books. We will read history, poetry, mythology. (*He gives her the glass of milk.*) Here's your milk. (*With his arm about her, they go over to the couch, sitting down side by side.*) As a

380 matter of fact, between us, Anne, being here has certain advantages for you. For instance, you remember the battle you had with your mother the other day on the subject of overshoes? You said you'd rather die than wear overshoes? But in the end you had to wear them? Well now, you see, for as long as we are here you will never have to wear overshoes! Isn't that good? And the coat that you inherited from Margot, you won't have to wear that any more. And the piano! You won't have to practice on the piano. I tell you, this is going to be a fine life for you!

(*Anne's panic is gone.* Peter *appears in the doorway of his room, with a*

390 *saucer in his hand. He is carrying his cat.*)

Peter. I . . . I . . . I thought I'd better get some water for Mouschi before . . .

Mr. Frank. Of course.

(*As he starts toward the sink the carillon begins to chime the hour of eight. He tiptoes to the window at the back and looks down at the street below. He turns to Peter, indicating in pantomime that it is too late. Peter starts back for his room. He steps on a creaking board. The three of them are frozen for a minute in fear. As Peter starts away again,*

Ⓞ Anne *tiptoes over to him and pours some of the milk from her glass into*

400 *the saucer for the cat.* Peter *squats on the floor, putting the milk before the cat.* Mr. Frank *gives Anne his fountain pen, and then goes into the room at the right. For a second Anne watches the cat, then she goes over to the center table, and opens her diary.*

In the room at the right, Mrs. Frank *has sat up quickly at the sound of the carillon.* Mr. Frank *comes in and sits down beside her on the settee, his arm comfortingly around her.*

Upstairs, in the attic room, Mr. *and* Mrs. Van Daan *have hung their clothes in the closet and are now seated on the iron bed.* Mrs. Van Daan *leans back exhausted.* Mr. Van Daan *fans her with a newspaper.*

410 Anne *starts to write in her diary. The lights dim out, the curtain falls.*

In the darkness Anne's Voice comes to us again, faintly at first, and then with growing strength.)

Ⓟ **Anne's Voice.** I expect I should be describing what it feels like to go into hiding. But I really don't know yet myself. I only know it's funny never to be able to go outdoors . . . never to breathe fresh air . . . never to run and shout and jump. It's the silence in the nights that frightens me most. Every time I hear a creak in the house, or a step on the street outside, I'm sure they're coming for us. The days aren't so bad.

420 At least we know that Miep and Mr. Kraler are down there below us

Anne is kind
and brave.

---

15. **READ ▶** As you read lines 389–430, continue to cite text evidence.

- Explain in the margin what Anne's actions as described in the stage directions reveal about her character, and underline examples to support your conclusion.
- Circle what Anne says it means to be in hiding.

---

14. **◀ REREAD AND DISCUSS** Reread lines 360–377. Think about Mr. Frank's advice. In a small group, discuss why he might have given the diary to Anne.

---

14. **REREAD AND DISCUSS USING TEXT EVIDENCE**

Ⓝ **ASK STUDENTS** to be prepared to share the results of their small-group discussions with the class. They should be ready to cite specific text evidence with line numbers to support their inferences about why Mr. Frank might have given the diary to Anne. *Students should cite lines 376–377 as evidence that Mr. Frank might have given Anne the diary so that she could exercise her freedom to think.*

FOR ELL STUDENTS Explain that a pasteboard-bound book (line 360) is similar to a hardcover book; it is a book with covers made of cardboard, with paper pasted on it.

15. **READ AND CITE TEXT EVIDENCE**

Ⓞ **ASK STUDENTS** to cite text evidence that reveals Anne's character. *Students should cite evidence that Anne is kind from lines 399–400. They should understand that it requires courage for her to tiptoe across the floor to feed the cat.*

in the office. Our protectors, we call them. I asked Father what would happen to them if the Nazis found out they were hiding us. Pim said that they would suffer the same fate that we would . . . Imagine! They know this, and yet when they come up here, they're always cheerful and gay as if there were nothing in the world to bother them . . . Friday, the twenty-first of August, nineteen forty-two. Today I'm going to tell you our general news. Mother is unbearable. She insists on treating me like a baby, which I loathe. Otherwise things are going better. The weather is . . .

430 (*As Anne's Voice is fading out, the curtain rises on the scene.*)

---

16. ◀ **REREAD** Reread lines 414–429. Anne's reading from her diary is a form of soliloquy, a speech in which a character speaks private thoughts aloud. What is the effect of Anne's reading from her diary?

The diary passage explains what Anne is thinking and feeling—things she might not tell other characters. The diary tells what really happened in the annex, so it becomes more moving to know exactly what she thought and felt.

SHORT RESPONSE

Cite Text Evidence When does Anne begin to understand what going into hiding will mean? Describe some of the ways life in the secret annex is different from life outside. Review your reading notes, and be sure to **cite text evidence** in your response.

Anne begins to understand what going into hiding will mean when Mr. Frank tells her she must "never go beyond that door." The stage directions describe Anne as "sobered" after Mr. Frank prevents her from leaving and then she "realizes what 'going into hiding' means." The people staying in the secret annex must live in tight quarters with little privacy. They cannot make noise ("never to run and shout and jump") and cannot make contact with the outside world.

108

TO CHALLENGE STUDENTS . . .

Remind students that this drama is based on nonfiction. The photograph of Anne Frank shows her at age 12, in May of 1942, a few months before she went into hiding. The other photos on pages 91 and 100 show the actual secret annex. Goodrich and Hackett use realistic details in their stage directions. Today, there is a wealth of information available in the library and online about Anne Frank, the other residents of the secret annex, and the people who helped them. Because of the popularity of Anne Frank's diary, it is possible to learn a great deal about the Franks, the people around them, the circumstances that drove them into hiding, and the place where they hid.

ASK STUDENTS to do research to fact check this drama. Which details are accurate, and which are fabricated? Each student should choose a unique area of research, such as Anne's father, Otto Frank, or Amsterdam in the early 1940s. Have students share the results of their research with the class, and discuss the value of remembering Anne Frank. How can we apply the lessons of her life to our lives today? What does the holocaust teach us about prejudice?

---

16. REREAD AND CITE TEXT EVIDENCE

Ⓟ **ASK STUDENTS** to exchange their response with a partner for a peer review. Partners should work together to identify text evidence that supports their response. *Students should cite lines such as 415–419 as evidence that Anne is sharing her internal world, thoughts that she might not tell other characters.*

SHORT RESPONSE

Cite Text Evidence Student responses will vary, but they should cite evidence from the text to support their conclusions and descriptions. Students should:

- analyze how Anne came to understand what it meant to be in hiding.
- describe some of the ways life in the secret annex is different from life outside.
- cite strong textual evidence to support their response.

DIG DEEPER

1. With the class, return to Question 8, Reread. Have students share their responses.

ASK STUDENTS to cite the text evidence that supports their analysis of Anne's character.

- Point out that lines 165–168 include stage directions and dialogue. Ask students what they learned about Anne from the stage directions. *Something grabs Anne's attention and she stops to look out the window.*
- Ask students how line 168 clarifies the significance of her action. *It clarifies that she stopped because she heard the carillon.*
- Have students explain how they arrived at a conclusion about how she was feeling. *Anne's exclamation makes it clear that she is not feeling sad or depressed. Students might say she is feeling happy, delighted, or excited.*
- Have students read aloud lines 148–176. Assign students to read the parts of Miep, Mrs. Van Daan, Mr. Kraler, Mr. Frank, Mrs. Frank, and Anne. Discuss contrasts in the characters. *Students should recognize that Mrs. Van Daan is frightened, Miep is worried, Mrs. Frank is concerned.*

2. With the class, return to Question 14, Reread and Discuss. Have students share the results of their discussion.

ASK STUDENTS whether they were satisfied with the outcome of their small-group discussions. Have each group share the evidence they found to support their conclusions about why Mr. Frank might have given the diary to Anne.

- Have students read aloud lines 349–388. Assign students to read the parts of Anne and Mr. Frank.
- Ask students to infer Mr. Frank's emotions and motivations in lines 375–388. *Students should infer Mr. Frank's concern for his daughter's safety, his love for her, and his motivation to make her time in hiding bearable.*
- Why does Mr. Frank talk about walls, bolts, and locks in lines 376–377? *Students should talk about his values and his desire to be reassuring to his daughter.*

ASK STUDENTS to return to their Short Response answer and revise it based on the class discussion.

CLOSE READING NOTES

from The Diary of a Young Girl

Diary by Anne Frank

Why This Text?

The Diary of a Young Girl gives students a rare look at history through a first-person account of someone their own age. It shows students that many of their experiences are common to people their age across time, culture, and circumstance. The diary is also an important cultural document that has had an enormous impact throughout the world.

Key Learning Objective: The student will be able to analyze the elements of a diary entry and make and support inferences about the text.

COMMON CORE Common Core Standards

RL 5 Compare and contrast the structure of two texts.
RI 1 Cite textual evidence.
RI 2 Determine a central idea.
RI 3 Analyze how a text makes connections.
RI 4 Determine the meaning of words and phrases.
RI 5 Analyze in detail the structure of a specific paragraph in a text.
RI 6 Determine an author's point of view or purpose.
SL 1a Come to discussions prepared.
SL 1b Follow rules for collegial discussions.
L 4a Use context as a clue to the meaning of a word or phrase.
L 4d Verify meaning by checking in context or in a dictionary.
L 5c Distinguish among the connotations of words with similar denotations.

▲ Text Complexity Rubric

Quantitative Measures	***From* Diary of a Young Girl** **Lexile:** 1020L
Qualitative Measures	**Levels of Meaning/Purpose**  more than one purpose, easily identified from context
	Structure genre traits less common to informational text (diary elements)
	Language Conventionality and Clarity some figurative language and less straightforward sentence structure; some longer descriptions
	Knowledge Demands  somewhat complex social studies concepts and historical references
Reader/Task Considerations	**Teacher determined** Vary by individual reader and type of text

Background Have students read the background and information about the author. Tell students that these diary entries are excerpted from a longer work, which has been published in several forms and translated into many languages. In the years since World War II, Anne Frank's diary has been recognized not only for how it shows the effects of war on a young person's spirit but also because it describes the emerging adulthood of a young girl.

SETTING A PURPOSE Direct students to use the Setting a Purpose prompt to focus their reading. Remind students to generate questions of their own as they read.

Analyze Text: Elements of a Diary (LINES 1–2)

COMMON CORE RI 3

Remind students that a **diary** is a daily record of a writer's thoughts, experiences, and feelings. Most diary entries include a **heading,** or the date on which the entry is made. When diaries are published, headings help readers monitor the passage of time.

Ⓐ ASK STUDENTS to reread the heading on this diary entry. How is this line important to the students' understanding of the diary entry? *(The heading, or date, allows readers to place the diary entry in historical time. The headings also show how much time has elapsed from one diary entry to the next.)*

SCAFFOLDING FOR ELL STUDENTS

Analyze Language Using a whiteboard, display lines 1-10. Draw attention to words ending with the suffix *-ly,* explaining that it can mean "like" or "in a way that is." Have volunteers mark up the text.

- Highlight in blue words ending with the suffix *-ly.*
- Underline the base word.
- Use the meanings of the base word and suffix to infer the word's meaning.

ASK STUDENTS what what these words ending in *-ly* suggest about the way Anne writes. *(She describes things carefully.)*

Anne Frank (1929–1945) *was 13 years old when she and her family went into hiding to avoid being sent to concentration camps by the Nazis. During the two years she spent living in an attic, she kept a diary, which she called "Kitty." After the war, Anne's father, the only family member to survive the concentration camps the family was eventually sent to, chose to publish the diary. The selection you are about to read consists of entries taken from throughout the work.*

from

The Diary of a Young Girl

Diary by Anne Frank

SETTING A PURPOSE As you read, think about which of Anne's thoughts and feelings are similar to that of any teenager and which are unique to her family's particularly dire, or urgent, situation.

WEDNESDAY, JANUARY 13, 1943

Ⓐ *Dearest Kitty,*

This morning I was constantly interrupted, and as a result I haven't been able to finish a single thing I've begun.

We have a new pastime, namely, filling packages with powdered gravy. The gravy is one of Gies & Co.'s[1] products. Mr. Kugler hasn't been able to find anyone else to fill the packages, and besides, it's cheaper if we do the job. It's the kind of work they do in prisons. It's incredibly boring and makes us dizzy and giggly.

Terrible things are happening outside. At any time of night and day, poor helpless people are being dragged out of their homes. They're allowed to take only a knapsack and a

[1] **Gies** (gēs) **& Co.:** the name of Mr. Frank's company in Amsterdam.

It's <u>incredibly</u> boring and makes us dizzy and <u>giggly</u>.

Make Inferences

COMMON CORE **RI 1**

(LINES 27–32)

Explain that an **inference** is a logical guess based on information from the text along with the reader's own knowledge and experiences. Remind students that Anne and her family are hiding in a fairly small space with another family. Yet, in lines 27–32, she says that she feels "quite fortunate."

B **CITE TEXT EVIDENCE** Ask students to reread lines 27–32. Have students use their own sense of how they would feel in such a situation, combined with clues in the text, to infer what else Anne may be feeling. *(Possible answer: Because other people are in even worse situations, Anne may indeed feel fortunate. However, because of their living situation, she likely feels trapped as well. She says she is feeling "so selfish" for looking forward to a return to normal life rather than helping others. This may cause her to feel guilty about her family's relative good fortune.)*

little cash with them, and even then, they're robbed of these possessions on the way. Families are torn apart; men, women and children are separated. Children come home from school to find that their parents have disappeared. Women return from shopping to find their houses sealed, their families gone. The Christians in Holland are also living in fear because

20 their sons are being sent to Germany. Everyone is scared. Every night hundreds of planes pass over Holland on their way to German cities, to sow their bombs on German soil. Every hour hundreds, or maybe even thousands, of people are being killed in Russia and Africa. No one can keep out of the conflict, the entire world is at war, and even though the Allies[2] are doing better, the end is nowhere in sight.

B   As for us, we're quite fortunate. Luckier than millions of people. It's quiet and safe here, and we're using our money to buy food. We're so selfish that we talk about "after the war"

30 and look forward to new clothes and shoes, when actually we should be saving every penny to help others when the war is over, to salvage whatever we can.

The children in this neighborhood run around in thin shirts and wooden shoes. They have no coats, no socks, no caps and no one to help them. Gnawing on a carrot to still their hunger pangs, they walk from their cold houses through cold streets to an even colder classroom. Things have gotten so bad in Holland that hordes of children stop passersby in the streets to beg for a piece of bread.

40   I could spend hours telling you about the suffering the war has brought, but I'd only make myself more miserable. All we can do is wait, as calmly as possible, for it to end. Jews and Christians alike are waiting, the whole world is waiting, and many are waiting for death.

Yours, Anne

---

[2] **Allies:** the group of countries that fought against Hitler and Germany.

SATURDAY, JANUARY 30, 1943

Dearest Kitty,

I'm seething with rage, yet I can't show it. I'd like to scream,
stamp my foot, give Mother a good shaking, cry and I don't
50 know what else because of the nasty words, mocking looks
and accusations that she hurls at me day after day, piercing
me like arrows from a tightly strung bow, which are nearly
impossible to pull from my body. I'd like to scream at Mother,
Margot, the van Daans, Dussel and Father too: "Leave me
alone, let me have at least one night when I don't cry myself
to sleep with my eyes burning and my head pounding. Let me
get away, away from everything, away from this world!" But
I can't do that. I can't let them see my doubts, or the wounds
they've inflicted on me. I couldn't bear their sympathy or
60 their good-humored **derision**.. It would only make me want to
scream even more.

Everyone thinks I'm showing off when I talk, ridiculous
when I'm silent, **insolent** when I answer, cunning when I have
a good idea, lazy when I'm tired, selfish when I eat one bit
more than I should, stupid, cowardly, calculating, etc., etc.
All day long I hear nothing but what an exasperating child I
am, and although I laugh it off and pretend not to mind, I do
mind. I wish I could ask God to give me another personality,
one that doesn't antagonize everyone.

70 But that's impossible. I'm stuck with the character I was
born with, and yet I'm sure I'm not a bad person. I do my best
to please everyone, more than they'd ever suspect in a million
years. When I'm upstairs, I try to laugh it off because I don't
want them to see my troubles.

More than once, after a series of absurd **reproaches**, I've
snapped at Mother: "I don't care what you say. Why don't you
just wash your hands of me—I'm a hopeless case." Of course,
she'd tell me not to talk back and virtually ignore me for two
days. Then suddenly all would be forgotten and she'd treat me
80 like everyone else.

insolent
(ĭn´ sə-lənt) *adj.* If
someone is *insolent,*
he or she is rude or
disrespectful.

reproach
(rĭ-prōch´) *n.* A
reproach is a scolding
or blaming.

The Diary of a Young Girl   **357**

CLOSE READ

Analyze Text: Elements of a Diary

COMMON CORE RI 1, RI 3, RI 6

(LINES 48–61)

Explain to students that a diary is usually written
using **first-person point of view**, as shown by
the use of pronouns such as *I* and *me*. As such, it
expresses the personal thoughts and feelings of
the writer.

G **CITE TEXT EVIDENCE** Have students reread
lines 48–61 and identify the pronouns that signal
first-person point of view. Ask what this text reveals
about Anne's feelings toward her mother—and about
Anne herself. *(Anne feels angry and frustrated with her
mother, but she knows she can't show her feelings. She
feels her mother doesn't understand her. These feelings
show that Anne is much like a typical teenager. The
comparison of her mother's "nasty words" to "arrows
from a tightly strung bow" show that Anne is dramatic
and has a flair for writing. Her words "I can't let them see
my doubts" and "I couldn't bear their sympathy" show
that she is proud.)*

CRITICAL VOCABULARY

insolent: Anne is perceived as insolent when she
responds to others' comments.

ASK STUDENTS to suggest which of Anne's
responses might be considered insolent. *(Possible
answer: "I don't care what you say.")*

reproach: Anne received reproaches from her
mother for her behavior.

ASK STUDENTS why Anne might have called the
reproaches "absurd." *(She felt that she was being
blamed for things that were not really wrong or not
her fault.)*

APPLYING ACADEMIC VOCABULARY

communicate	publish

As you discuss Anne Frank's diary, incorporate the following Collection 5
academic vocabulary words: *communicate* and *publish*. Discuss what Anne
Frank's diary **communicates** about life in hiding as well as about feelings
and experiences common to teenagers everywhere. Also discuss why Anne
Frank's father might have decided to **publish** her diary and what effect this
publication has had.

Make Inferences

COMMON CORE **RI 1**

(LINES 93–102)

Remind students that they can use what Anne writes in her diary, plus their own knowledge and experience, to infer her true feelings.

 CITE TEXT EVIDENCE Have students reread lines 93–102. Ask what they can infer about Anne's ideas about growing up, citing supporting evidence. *(Anne seems to have mixed feelings about growing up. She doesn't want to become "quiet and boring" like Margot and Peter. She hates being told to "follow your sister's example" and she has "no desire to be like Margot." She is afraid that she will lose something of herself by growing up.)*

CRITICAL VOCABULARY

mediate: Anne is explaining Mr. Dussel's role in the Annex.

ASK STUDENTS why Mr. Dussel might have given up on trying to mediate the squabbles between the Franks and the Van Daans. *(He realized that his efforts were useless because the squabbles continued.)*

It's impossible for me to be all smiles one day and venomous[3] the next. I'd rather choose the golden mean,[4] which isn't so golden, and keep my thoughts to myself. Perhaps sometime I'll treat the others with the same contempt as they treat me. Oh, if only I could.

Yours, Anne

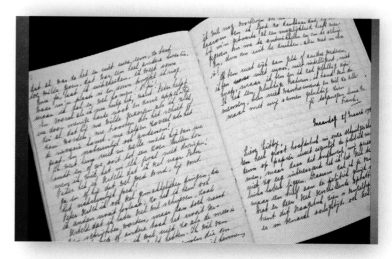

Anne Frank's diaries are on display at the Anne Frank House in Amsterdam, the Netherlands.

FRIDAY, FEBRUARY 5, 1943

Dearest Kitty,

Though it's been ages since I've written to you about the squabbles, there's still no change. In the beginning Mr. Dussel took our soon-forgotten clashes very seriously, but now he's grown used to them and no longer tries to **mediate**.

Margot and Peter aren't exactly what you'd call "young"; they're both so quiet and boring. Next to them, I stick out like a sore thumb, and I'm always being told, "Margot and Peter don't act that way. Why don't you follow your sister's example!" I hate that.

mediate
(mē´dē-āt´) *v.* If you *mediate* a conflict, you try to settle the differences.

---

[3] **venomous** (vĕn´ ə-məs): spiteful or bitter.
[4] **golden mean:** the middle between two extremes.

I confess that I have absolutely no desire to be like Margot.
She's too weak-willed and passive to suit me; she lets herself
be swayed by others and always backs down under pressure.
I want to have more spunk! But I keep ideas like these to
myself. They'd only laugh at me if I offered this in my defense.

During meals the air is filled with tension. Fortunately, the
outbursts are sometimes held in check by the "soup eaters,"
the people from the office who come up to have a cup of soup
for lunch.

This afternoon Mr. van Daan again brought up the fact
that Margot eats so little. "I suppose you do it to keep your
figure," he added in a mocking tone.

Mother, who always comes to Margot's defense, said
in a loud voice, "I can't stand that stupid chatter of yours a
minute longer."

Mrs. van D. turned red as a beet. Mr. van D. stared
straight ahead and said nothing.

Still, we often have a good laugh. Not long ago Mrs. van D.
was entertaining us with some bit of nonsense or another.
She was talking about the past, about how well she got along
with her father and what a flirt she was. "And you know," she
continued, "my father told me that if a gentleman ever got
fresh, I was to say, 'Remember, sir, that I'm a lady,' and he'd
know what I meant." We split our sides laughing, as if she'd
told us a good joke . . .

Yours, Anne

MONDAY EVENING, NOVEMBER 8, 1943

Dearest Kitty,

If you were to read all my letters in one sitting, you'd be
struck by the fact that they were written in a variety of moods.
It annoys me to be so dependent on the moods here in the
Annex, but I'm not the only one: we're all subject to them.
If I'm engrossed in a book, I have to rearrange my thoughts
before I can mingle with other people, because otherwise they
might think I was strange. As you can see, I'm currently in
the middle of a depression. I couldn't really tell you what set it
off, but I think it stems from my cowardice, which confronts

CLOSE READ

Make Inferences
COMMON CORE **RI 1**

(LINES 107–114)

Explain that because diaries are written from the first-person point of view, readers don't know what the other characters in the Annex are feeling or thinking. However, readers can make inferences based on clues in the diary. For example, a person's actions or reactions can provide an insight into his or her feelings.

E **CITE TEXT EVIDENCE** Ask students to reread lines 107–114 and to infer how Mr. and Mrs. van Daan felt after Mother's comment. Cite the text evidence that supports this inference. *(Mr. and Mrs. van Daan were likely angry or embarrassed. Evidence: "Mrs. van D. turned red as a beet. Mr. van D. stared straight ahead and said nothing.")*

Analyze Text: Elements of a Diary
COMMON CORE **RI 6**

(LINES 115–122)

Point out that, like all writers, writers of diaries make choices about what incidents and experiences to include.

F **ASK STUDENTS** to reread lines 115–122. Ask why Anne Frank might have chosen to record this scene in her diary. *(After describing so much anger and conflict, she might have wanted to show that there were also times of laughter and fun.)*

Analyze Language

COMMON CORE RI 4

(LINES 152–164)

Explain that writers often use figurative language in order to communicate ideas in an especially vivid way. One type of figurative language is a **simile**, or a comparison between two things that are basically unlike, using *like* or *as*.

G **ASK STUDENTS** to reread lines 152–164 and identify two similes. Have students explain what is being compared in each simile and what tone or feeling the similes create. *(The first simile compares the eight people in the Annex to "a patch of blue sky surrounded by menacing black clouds." The next one compares the figurative black clouds to "an impenetrable wall." Together, the similes convey a tone of dread and fear. They help the reader picture not only the current safety of the people's position but also the trap they are caught in.)*

me at every turn. This evening, when Bep was still here, the doorbell rang long and loud. I instantly turned white, my stomach churned, and my heart beat wildly—and all because I was afraid.

140　　At night in bed I see myself alone in a dungeon, without Father and Mother. Or I'm roaming the streets, or the Annex is on fire, or they come in the middle of the night to take us away and I crawl under my bed in desperation. I see everything as if it were actually taking place. And to think it might all happen soon!

Miep often says she envies us because we have such peace and quiet here. That may be true, but she's obviously not thinking about our fear.

I simply can't imagine the world will ever be normal again for us. I do talk about "after the war," but it's as if I were 150　talking about a castle in the air, something that can never come true.

I see the eight of us in the Annex as if we were a patch of blue sky surrounded by menacing black clouds. The perfectly round spot on which we're standing is still safe, but the clouds are moving in on us, and the ring between us and the approaching danger is being pulled tighter and tighter. We're surrounded by darkness and danger, and in our desperate search for a way out we keep bumping into each other. We look at the fighting down below and the peace and beauty up 160　above. In the meantime, we've been cut off by the dark mass of clouds, so that we can go neither up nor down. It looms before us like an impenetrable wall, trying to crush us, but not yet able to. I can only cry out and implore, "Oh, ring, ring, open wide and let us out!"

Yours, Anne

WHEN STUDENTS STRUGGLE...

To support students' understanding of the author's use of figurative language, have them work in pairs to complete a chart like the one shown. For each example students encounter, tell them to reread the comparison carefully and analyze what it reveals about Anne's feelings.

Figurative Language	What It Reveals
"patch of blue sky surrounded by menacing black clouds"	Anne is feeling temporarily safe, but also trapped, surrounded by trouble.

THURSDAY, NOVEMBER 11, 1943

Dearest Kitty,

I have a good title for this chapter:

Ode to My Fountain Pen

In Memoriam

170   My fountain pen was always one of my most prized possessions; I valued it highly, especially because it had a thick nib, and I can only write neatly with thick nibs. It has led a long and interesting fountain-pen life, which I will summarize below.

When I was nine, my fountain pen (packed in cotton) arrived as a "sample of no commercial value" all the way from Aachen,[5] where my grandmother (the kindly donor) used to live. I lay in bed with the flu, while the February winds howled
180   around the apartment house. This **splendid** fountain pen came in a red leather case, and I showed it to my girlfriends the first chance I got. Me, Anne Frank, the proud owner of a fountain pen.

When I was ten, I was allowed to take the pen to school, and to my surprise, the teacher even let me write with it. When I was eleven, however, my treasure had to be tucked away again, because my sixth-grade teacher allowed us to use only school pens and inkpots. When I was twelve, I started at the Jewish Lyceum and my fountain pen was given a new
190   case in honor of the occasion. Not only did it have room for a pencil, it also had a zipper, which was much more impressive. When I was thirteen, the fountain pen went with me to the Annex, and together we've raced through countless diaries and compositions. I'd turned fourteen and my fountain pen was enjoying the last year of its life with me when …

It was just after five on Friday afternoon. I came out of my room and was about to sit down at the table to write when I was roughly pushed to one side to make room for Margot and Father, who wanted to practice their Latin. The fountain pen
200   remained unused on the table, while its owner, sighing, was forced to make do with a very tiny corner of the table, where she began rubbing beans. That's how we remove mold from the beans and restore them to their original state. At a quarter to six I swept the floor, dumped the dirt into a newspaper, along with the rotten beans, and tossed it into the stove.

splendid
(splĕn´ dĭd) *adj.* If something is *splendid,* it is magnificent or very good.

---

[5] **Aachen** (ä´kən): a city in Germany.

The Diary of a Young Girl   **361**

Analyze Text: Elements of a Diary

COMMON CORE RI 3, RI 6

(LINES 168–195)

Remind students that writers of diaries choose to record events that are important and meaningful to them.

(H) ASK STUDENTS to reread lines 168–195, in which Anne tells a story about something that happened before she and her family went into hiding. Ask what Anne's purpose was for telling this story. *(Possible answer: The story recalls a happier time in Anne's life. It also demonstrates the importance of the pen, which she has had for so long.)*

Also point out that the three dots at the end of line 195 are called **ellipses**. Usually, ellipses are used to indicate that material has been omitted. Here, Anne uses them for a different purpose.

(I) ASK STUDENTS the purpose of the ellipses at the end of line 195. *(It creates suspense, making readers wonder what comes next.)*

Analyze Language

COMMON CORE RI 4

(LINES 194–195)

Point out that, in her story about the fountain pen, Anne uses another example of figurative language— personification. In **personification**, human characteristics are given to something nonhuman.

(J) ASK STUDENTS to identify the example of personification and explain why Anne uses it. *(She says that the fountain pen "was enjoying the last year of its life." She uses this expression to enliven her story and to convey her feelings about the pen.)*

> **CRITICAL VOCABULARY**
>
> **splendid**: Anne is describing her special fountain pen.
>
> **ASK STUDENTS** why Anne describes her fountain pen as "splendid." *(It came in a red leather case. It was something that none of her friends had, and Anne was very proud of it.)*

Analyze Text: Elements of a Diary (LINE 227)

COMMON CORE RI 3

Remind students that this selection consists of excerpts from Anne Frank's diary. Point out that students can use the headings, or dates, to determine how much time has elapsed between one excerpt and the next.

 ASK STUDENTS to reread the heading on line 227 and look back at the previous heading. Ask how much time has elapsed. *(over two months)* Point out that as students read the entry they will need to make inferences about what has occurred during those two months.

Make Inferences

COMMON CORE RI 1

(LINES 229–234)

Point out that Anne explicitly states that she is leaving out details of quarrels: "There's no reason for me to go on . . ." Her statement, "It's enough to tell you that . . ." is essentially an invitation to the reader to infer the extent of the quarrels that have taken place since the last diary entry.

 CITE TEXT EVIDENCE Have students reread lines 229–234. Ask what inference they can make, based on text evidence, about the quarrels that have occurred. *(The fact that the families are dividing up food and cooking separately is evidence that there was probably a lot of arguing about food and that people were worried there might not be enough.)*

CRITICAL VOCABULARY

conjecture: Anne presents her father's theory about what happened to her treasured pen.

ASK STUDENTS to explain why the author used the word *conjectured* rather than *claimed* or *stated*. *(Father believed that the nib had turned to stone, but he couldn't be certain because there was no trace left.)*

A giant flame shot up, and I thought it was wonderful that the stove, which had been gasping its last breath, had made such a miraculous recovery.

All was quiet again. The Latin students had left, and I sat down at the table to pick up where I'd left off. But no matter where I looked, my fountain pen was nowhere in sight. I took another look. Margot looked, Mother looked, Father looked, Dussel looked. But it had vanished.

"Maybe it fell into the stove, along with the beans!" Margot suggested.

"No, it couldn't have!" I replied.

But that evening, when my fountain pen still hadn't turned up, we all assumed it had been burned, especially because celluloid is highly inflammable. Our darkest fears were confirmed the next day when Father went to empty the stove and discovered the clip, used to fasten it to a pocket, among the ashes. Not a trace of the gold nib was left. "It must have melted into stone," Father **conjectured**.

I'm left with one consolation, small though it may be: my fountain pen was cremated,[6] just as I would like to be someday!

conjecture
(kən-jĕk´ chər) *v.* If you *conjecture*, you guess or suppose.

Saturday, January 15, 1944

My dearest Kitty,

There's no reason for me to go on describing all our quarrels and arguments down to the last detail. It's enough to tell you that we've divided many things like meat and fats and oils and are frying our own potatoes. Recently we've been eating a little extra rye bread because by four o'clock we're so hungry for dinner we can barely control our rumbling stomachs.

Mother's birthday is rapidly approaching. She received some extra sugar from Mr. Kugler, which sparked off jealousy on the part of the van Daans, because Mrs. van D. didn't receive any on her birthday. But what's the point of boring you with harsh words, spiteful conversations and tears when you know they bore us even more?

---

[6] **cremated** (krē´ māt´ əd): burned to ashes.

Mother has expressed a wish, which isn't likely to come true any time soon: not to have to see Mr. van Daan's face for two whole weeks. I wonder if everyone who shares a house sooner or later ends up at odds with their fellow residents. Or have we just had a stroke of bad luck? At mealtime, when Dussel helps himself to a quarter of the half-filled gravy boat and leaves the rest of us to do without, I lose my appetite and feel like jumping to my feet, knocking him off his chair and throwing him out the door.

250 Are most people so stingy and selfish? I've gained some insight into human nature since I came here, which is good, but I've had enough for the present. Peter says the same.

The war is going to go on despite our quarrels and our longing for freedom and fresh air, so we should try to make the best of our stay here.

I'm preaching, but I also believe that if I live here much longer, I'll turn into a dried-up old beanstalk. And all I really want is to be an honest-to-goodness teenager!

Yours, Anne

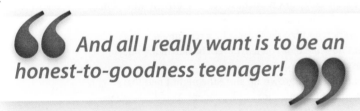

" And all I really want is to be an honest-to-goodness teenager! "

260 WEDNESDAY EVENING, JANUARY 19, 1944

Dearest Kitty,

 I (there I go again!) don't know what's happened, but since my dream I keep noticing how I've changed. By the way, I dreamed about Peter again last night and once again I felt his eyes penetrate mine, but this dream was less vivid and not quite as beautiful as the last.

You know that I always used to be jealous of Margot's relationship with Father. There's not a trace of my jealousy left now; I still feel hurt when Father's nerves cause him to be
270 unreasonable toward me, but then I think, "I can't blame you for being the way you are. You talk so much about the minds of children and adolescents, but you don't know the first thing about them!" I long for more than Father's affection, more than his hugs and kisses. Isn't it awful of me to be so

The Diary of a Young Girl **363**

Make Inferences

(LINES 281–284)

COMMON CORE **RI 1**

Point out that "PS." in line 282 stands for *postscript*, an additional remark that a letter-writer includes after the signature. It is usually information the writer forgot to include before signing the letter.

 **CITE TEXT EVIDENCE** Have students closely reread lines 281–284. Ask why Anne might have written this information as a postscript and what evidence supports their inference. *(She had probably forgotten about it until after she finished the entry because she says, "there's no room in my head for things like that.")* Ask what other inferences students can make based on the information in the postscript. *(Students may infer that Anne's father takes an interest in her writing because he asked if she had written about the cake. He may also have wanted to be sure she was writing about happy times instead of just dwelling on problems and difficulties.)*

---

preoccupied with myself? Shouldn't I, who want to be good and kind, forgive them first? I forgive Mother too, but every time she makes a sarcastic remark or laughs at me, it's all I can do to control myself.

I know I'm far from being what I should; will I ever be?

Anne Frank

280

PS. Father asked if I told you about the cake. For Mother's birthday, she received a real mocha cake, prewar quality,[7] from the office. It was a really nice day! But at the moment there's no room in my head for things like that.

SATURDAY, JANUARY 22, 1944

Dearest Kitty,

Can you tell me why people go to such lengths to hide their real selves? Or why I always behave very differently when I'm in the company of others? Why do people have so little trust

290 in one another? I know there must be a reason, but sometimes I think it's horrible that you can't ever confide in anyone, not even those closest to you.

It seems as if I've grown up since the night I had that dream, as if I've become more independent. You'll be amazed when I tell you that even my attitude toward the van Daans has changed. I've stopped looking at all the discussions and arguments from my family's biased point of view. What's brought on such a radical change? Well, you see, I suddenly realized that if Mother had been different, if she'd been a real

300 mom, our relationship would have been very, very different. Mrs. van Daan is by no means a wonderful person, yet half the arguments could have been avoided if Mother hadn't been so hard to deal with every time they got onto a tricky subject. Mrs. van Daan does have one good point, though: you can talk to her. She may be selfish, stingy and underhanded, but she'll readily back down as long as you don't provoke her and make her unreasonable. This tactic doesn't work every time,

---

[7] **prewar quality:** the better standard of goods before the war when there were no shortages of materials.

but if you're patient, you can keep trying and see how far you get.

All the conflicts about our upbringing, about not pampering children, about the food—about everything, absolutely everything—might have taken a different turn if we'd remained open and on friendly terms instead of always seeing the worst side.

I know exactly what you're going to say, Kitty. "But, Anne, are these words really coming from your lips? From you, who have had to put up with so many unkind words from upstairs? From you, who are aware of all the injustices?"

And yet they are coming from me. I want to take a fresh look at things and form my own opinion, not just ape my parents, as in the proverb "The apple never falls far from the tree." I want to reexamine the van Daans and decide for myself what's true and what's been blown out of proportion. If I wind up being disappointed in them, I can always side with Father and Mother. But if not, I can try to change their attitude. And if that doesn't work, I'll have to stick with my own opinions and judgment. I'll take every opportunity to speak openly to Mrs. van D. about our many differences and not be afraid—despite my reputation as a smart aleck—to offer my impartial opinion. I won't say anything negative about my own family, though that doesn't mean I won't defend them if somebody else does, and as of today, my gossiping is a thing of the past.

Up to now I was absolutely convinced that the van Daans were entirely to blame for the quarrels, but now I'm sure the fault was largely ours. We were right as far as the issues were concerned, but intelligent people (such as ourselves!) should have more insight into how to deal with others.

I hope I've got at least a touch of that insight, and that I'll find an occasion to put it to good use.

Yours, Anne

COLLABORATIVE DISCUSSION With a partner, discuss how Anne's ideas and reactions compare to those of you and your friends. Cite specific evidence from the text to support your ideas.

CLOSE READ

Analyze Text: Elements of a Diary

COMMON CORE RL 1, RL 3, RL 6

(LINES 319–338)

Point out that writers often chronicle personal growth in their diaries. In this last excerpt, Anne Frank explores the contrast between the way she has acted in the past and the way she would like to behave in the future.

ASK STUDENTS Have students reread lines 319–338 and cite evidence to explain the contrast between Anne's actions in the past and her new expectations for herself. (*Up to now, she has been "aping her parents," or adopting their attitudes. Now she wants to "form my own opinions" about the van Daans. She is going to speak openly to Mrs. van Daan, which she has been afraid to do in the past. She says she is not going to speak against her family or gossip, so she has probably been doing those things in the past.*)

COLLABORATIVE DISCUSSION Have students work in pairs and discuss how ideas expressed in Anne's diary compare to their own. Remind students to cite textual evidence in their discussion.

ASK STUDENTS to share any questions they generated in the course of reading and discussing the diary.

TO CHALLENGE STUDENTS . . .

Analyzing Effects Anne Frank's diary has been translated into numerous languages and has made an impact on people all over the world.

ASK STUDENTS in small groups to analyze Anne Frank's legacy. Have students share ideas about why people might identify with Anne Frank and draw inspiration from her life. Suggest that students do some brief additional research about Anne Frank and her diary before meeting with the group.

TEACH

Analyze Text: Elements of a Diary
 COMMON CORE RI 3, RI 6

Point out the elements of a diary, and clarify the terms *heading*, *salutation*, and *first-person point of view*. Discuss with students why a person might decide to keep a diary and how a diary differs from a journal.

Then have students review the selection and identify the elements in each diary entry.

Make Inferences
COMMON CORE RI 1

Review the definition of an inference, and discuss why it is particularly necessary to make inferences when reading a diary.

Point out that the chart shows the process of making an inference. Have students work in small groups to review the selection and use the chart to make additional inferences.

Analyze Text: Elements of a Diary
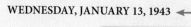 COMMON CORE RI 3, RI 6

A **diary** is a daily record of a writer's thoughts, experiences, and feelings. While the term *journal* has a similar definition, diary entries are often composed in the form of a letter addressed to the diary itself, as they are in *The Diary of a Young Girl*. The first lines of *The Diary of a Young Girl* reveal many of a diary's main elements:

WEDNESDAY, JANUARY 13, 1943 ← The **heading** contains the date on which the entry was made.

Dearest Kitty, ← The **salutation** reveals to whom the entry has been addressed.

This morning I was constantly interrupted, and as a result I haven't been able to finish a single thing I've begun. ← **First-person point of view** is used to share thoughts and experiences using pronouns such as *I* and *me*.

As you review *The Diary of a Young Girl*, notice whether Anne Frank uses the same elements with each diary entry.

Make Inferences
COMMON CORE RI 1

Though some writers intend to publish their diaries, most writers assume their diaries will remain private. As a result, certain explanations may be omitted. To make sense of the text, readers may need to make **inferences,** or logical guesses about meaning based on clues in the text and one's own knowledge. For example, look at this passage from *The Diary of a Young Girl:*

This evening, when Bep was still here, the doorbell rang long and loud. I instantly turned white, my stomach churned, and my heart beat wildly—and all because I was afraid.

Anne does not explain why the sound of the doorbell frightens her, but you can make an inference about it.

| **What the text says:**
The doorbell rang. | **+** | **What I know:**
The Franks are hiding from the Nazis. | **=** | **Inference:**
Anne is afraid they have been discovered. |

Use your knowledge of the Franks' situation to make other inferences as you analyze the diary.

Strategies for Annotation
 Annotate it!

Analyze Text: Elements of a Diary
COMMON CORE RI 3, RI 6

Share these strategies for guided or independent analysis of each diary entry:

- Highlight the heading in yellow. Make a note about how much time has passed since the last entry.
- Highlight the salutation in blue.
- Underline words that show first-person point of view.
- In a note, explain what the entry reveals and why Anne might have chosen to include it.

SATURDAY, JANUARY 30, 1943

Dearest Kitty,

I'm seething with rage, yet I can't show it. I'd like to scream, stamp my foot, give Mother a good shaking, cry and I don't know what else because of the nasty words, mocking loo and accusations that she hurls at me day after day, pierc

She's venting her frustration and anger.

 eBook *Annotate It!*

Analyzing the Text

 COMMON CORE RI 1, RI 2, RI 3, RI 4, RI 5, RI 6, SL 1a, SL 1b

Cite Text Evidence   Support your responses with evidence from the text.

1. **Infer**   Reread lines 5–26. What clues in the entry help readers make inferences about why "Mr. Kugler hasn't been able to find anyone else to fill the packages" of powdered gravy?

2. **Analyze**   What is the effect of the repetition in Anne's statement that "All we can do is wait . . . Jews and Christians alike are waiting, the whole world is waiting, and many are waiting for death"?

3. **Infer**   Read over lines 48–80. What is Anne's view of the tension between herself and her family? Consider how Anne's living conditions might contribute to her frustrations.

4. **Interpret**   A **simile** makes a comparison between two unlike things using the word *like* or *as*. Reread lines 152–164. What does Anne Frank reveal about her perspective with her use of the simile "I see the eight of us in the Annex as if we were a patch of blue sky surrounded by menacing black clouds."

5. **Draw Conclusions**   Reread lines 167–175. Notice that the elements of this entry differ from the others. Why might Anne Frank have used a slightly different form here?

6. **Compare**   How does Anne compare her situation in the Annex to what others are facing, particularly to the other two young people there?

7. **Draw Conclusions**   Over what span of time are the entries in this excerpt from the diary written? Explain how Anne's perspective has changed during this time.

PERFORMANCE TASK

Speaking Activity: Performance
What does the story that Anne tells about her fountain pen reveal about her as a writer and a person? Perform this story as a skit for the class.

- Working in groups, analyze Anne's purpose for including the story of her pen. What makes the pen so special to her? Why is the pen especially important during her time in the Annex?

- As you prepare your skit, be sure to maintain Anne's style and use of details to describe the pen. Show how the events of the day led her to destroy her beloved pen.

- After performing the skit, discuss how Anne's narrative, voice, and vivid description helped to bring this story to life.

The Diary of a Young Girl   **367**

PRACTICE & APPLY

Analyzing the Text

 COMMON CORE RI 1, RI 2, RI 3, RI 4, RI 5, RI 6,

Possible answers:

1. *Anne refers to people being taken away and families disappearing as well as the fact that "the war" is causing great upheaval in society. Readers can infer that the arrests and calls to military service leave fewer workers for Mr. Kugler to hire.*

2. *Anne's statement emphasizes the powerlessness people feel over events that are beyond their control. Their only options are to die or to wait for the situation to improve.*

3. *Anne feels isolated; she is confiding to her diary because she feels she has no one with whom she can share her feelings. The fact that the family is living in such close quarters probably adds to her frustration.*

4. *Anne sees the Annex as a safe place amid impending dangers. She says they are surrounded by danger looming "like an impenetrable wall" threatening to crush them. By using a simile, she is trying to describe her fear of what will happen if they are found.*

5. *Anne puts what she calls a chapter title, "Ode to My Fountain Pen—In Memoriam," on this entry as if she were writing a novel. She changes the form to enliven her writing and to focus on telling a story rather than describing her feelings. The form may suggest her desire to be a writer.*

6. *Anne tries to understand the van Daans even though the two families are quarrelling, and she realizes that they are as afraid and stressed as she is. She also notes that Margot and Peter aren't "young" like she is because they are quiet and boring. She does not want to be like Margot, and she appears to have a fascination with Peter.*

7. *The entries span about a year, from January 1943 to January 1944. Anne has become more mature during this time. In the beginning of the excerpt, she was simply rebellious—struggling against her family. Now her criticisms of her own family are less emotional, and she is developing a new perspective on life in the Annex.*

Assign this performance task.

PERFORMANCE TASK

COMMON CORE SL 1a, SL 1b

Speaking Activity: Performance   Have students work in groups to prepare their skits about the loss of Anne's fountain pen. Tell students to review her November 11, 1943, entry and

- determine why the pen was so important to Anne
- maintain Anne's writing style as they develop their dialogue
- discuss which details of the diary entry can help them bring the story to life

The Diary of a Young Girl   **367**

PRACTICE & APPLY

Critical Vocabulary

COMMON CORE L 4a, L 4d, L 5c

Possible answers:

1. choices to end a disagreement. Resolving the choices to end a disagreement might require someone to mediate. It is unlikely that such help would be needed for the choices on a menu.

2. someone guessing. Someone guessing is a conjecture because they are venturing a guess as to what happened without having a clear answer.

3. a disobedient child. Someone who is insolent says nasty things and talks back like a disobedient child, not a confused hiker.

4. a lovely view. A lovely view is satisfying and filled with splendor or magnificence. A challenging test is not a grand experience.

5. a thorough scolding. A reproach is a scolding or criticism, not a repeated attempt.

Vocabulary Strategy: Connotation and Denotation

Possible answers:

1. Stingy *has a connotation of meanness; using* sparing *instead would suggest a sharing of food that is judicious rather than unkind.*

2. Splendid *suggests something magnificent or very good, while* fine *suggests something that is okay but not great.*

3. Conflicts *suggests disagreements, while* battles *suggests more violent arguments.*

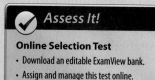

Assess It!

Online Selection Test
- Download an editable ExamView bank.
- Assign and manage this test online.

Critical Vocabulary

COMMON CORE L 4a, L 4d, L 5c

insolent	reproach	mediate
mediate	conjecture	

Practice and Apply Explain your response to each question.

1. Which of the following might require someone to **mediate**? Why?
   choices to end a disagreement   choices on a menu

2. Which of the following would you describe as **conjecture**? Why?
   someone explaining   someone guessing

3. Which of the following would you describe as **insolent**? Why?
   a disobedient child   a lost hiker

4. Which of the following would you describe as **splendid**? Why?
   a lovely view   a challenging test

5. Which of the following would you describe as a **reproach**? Why?
   a second draft of a story   a thorough scolding

Vocabulary Strategy: Connotation and Denotation

Many words have both a denotation and a connotation. A word's **denotation** is its dictionary definition. A word's **connotations** are the ideas and feelings associated with the word. Study this example from *The Diary of a Young Girl*:

> Things have gotten so bad in Holland that <u>hordes</u> of children . . . beg for a piece of bread.

While the denotation of *horde* is "a large group," the word's connotation suggests an out-of-control swarm that is desperate for food.

Practice and Apply Tell how the meaning of each sentence would change if the underlined word were replaced by the word in parentheses.

1. The families in the Annex had to be <u>stingy</u> with their food. (sparing)

2. The view from a certain window in the Annex was <u>splendid</u>. (fine)

3. Anne was bothered by the <u>conflicts</u> between the families. (battles)

Strategies for Annotation ✎ 🖥 Annotate it!

Vocabulary Strategy: Connotation and Denotation

COMMON CORE L 5c

Have students locate lines 62–65. Encourage students to use their eBook annotation tools to do the following:

- Highlight the word *insolent* in yellow.
- Use a thesaurus to locate synonyms for *insolent*.
- Read the sentence in which *insolent* occurs, replacing the word with a synonym that has a different connotation.

- In a note, explain how the different connotation changes the meaning of the sentence.
- Repeat with other Critical Vocabulary words.

> Everyone thinks that I'm showing off when I talk, ridiculous when I'm silent, **insolent** when I answer, cunning when I have a good idea, lazy when I'm tired, selfish when I eat one bit more than

Compare and Contrast Structure

COMMON CORE

RL 5

TEACH

Tell students that the **structure** of a work of literature is the way in which it is put together. Different genres have different structures. For example, a poem has a different structure from a story. A diary, like the one students have just read, has a different structure from a poem or a play.

Remind students that the play *The Diary of Anne Frank* and the excerpts from *The Diary of a Young Girl* recount some of the same experiences using different structures.

Discuss the following:

- Structural elements in a play include acts, scenes, dialogue, and stage directions. Ask students to find examples of each in *The Diary of Anne Frank*.
- Structural elements of a diary include headings and salutations. The use of pronouns such as *I* and *me* reveal that a diary uses first-person point of view. Ask students to find examples of each element in *Diary of a Young Girl*.
- Point out that in a diary we learn about characters and events only from what the writer tells us. In a play, we learn about characters from their own dialogue and actions. Discuss how in *The Diary of Anne Frank* the playwrights had to make inferences based on Anne Frank's writing in order to bring the characters to life.

PRACTICE AND APPLY

Have pairs of students work together to use a Comparison-Contrast Chart to record additional comparisons between the diary and the play. Suggest, for example, that they compare and contrast what readers learn about Anne from the two selections. Have students share their completed charts with another pair of students and discuss the similarities and differences. Did students prefer one presentation over the other, and, if so, why?

 INTERACTIVE GRAPHIC ORGANIZER Students can use a **Comparison-Contrast Chart** to organize and integrate information.

Analyze Text: Elements of a Diary

COMMON CORE

RI 3, RI 6

RETEACH

Explain that the elements of a diary entry are similar to those of a letter. Like a letter, a diary entry has a **heading** that tells the date the entry was written and a **salutation**, or greeting, that tells to whom the entry is addressed. Like a letter, a diary entry is written in the **first person**, using pronouns such as *I* and *me*.

Use lines 1–4 and lines 40–45 from *The Diary of a Young Girl* to point out the elements of a diary and explain the following:

- Readers can use headings to identify the historical context of an entry and to tell how much time has elapsed between one entry and another.
- Most diary writers simply use the salutation "Dear Diary." Anne addresses her diary to an imaginary friend named Kitty.
- Anne writes in the first person about her own feelings and experiences.
- Like all writers, diarists write with a particular purpose in mind. Readers can make inferences about the writer's purpose from the events that he or she has chosen to include and the way in which they are described. Have students reread lines 40–44 and discuss the writer's purpose. *(Anne's purpose in these lines is to express her feeling of helplessness about the war: "All we can do is wait.")*
- The closing, shown on line 45, is another element that diary entries share with letters.

CLOSE READING APPLICATION

Students can apply the skill to another published diary. You might want to make available copies of the complete work, *Diary of a Young Girl*. Have students work in small groups to read additional entries and discuss Anne Frank's purpose in writing them.

from Anne Frank: The Book, The Life, The Afterlife

Literary Criticism by Francine Prose

Why This Text?

To encounter a fresh, unusual perspective in a work of literary criticism is intellectually stimulating. Francine Prose's essay on Anne Frank should appeal to students as a fresh "take" on a familiar, age-appropriate topic and as a keen model of a well-crafted argument.

> ▶ **View It!**
> Professional Development Podcast:
> **Text Complexity**

Key Learning Objective: The student will be able to determine an author's point of view in a work of literary criticism and analyze how the author's word choices impact the tone of the text.

COMMON CORE Common Core Standards

RI 1 Cite textual evidence.

RI 2 Determine a central idea.

RI 3 Analyze connections between individuals, ideas, or events.

RI 4 Analyze the impact of word choices on tone.

RI 6 Determine an author's point of view and analyze how the author responds to conflicting viewpoints.

RI 8 Evaluate the argument.

W 4 Produce clear and coherent writing.

W 9b Apply grade 8 Reading standards to literary nonfiction.

W 10 Write over extended time frames and shorter time frames.

SL 1a Come to discussions prepared.

SL 1b Follow rules for discussions.

L 2a Use punctuation to indicate a pause or break.

L 2b Use an ellipsis to indicate an omission.

L 4b Use common Latin affixes as clues to meaning.

L 4d Verify the meaning of a word or phrase.

▲ Text Complexity Rubric

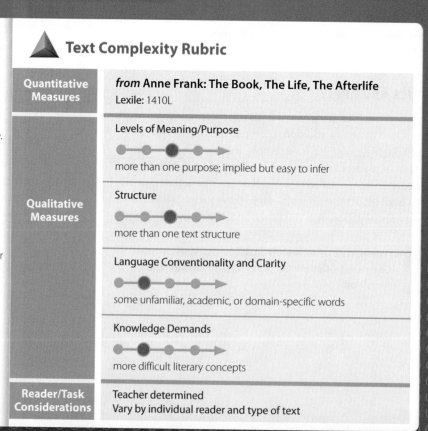

Quantitative Measures	*from* **Anne Frank: The Book, The Life, The Afterlife** Lexile: 1410L
Qualitative Measures	**Levels of Meaning/Purpose** more than one purpose; implied but easy to infer
	Structure more than one text structure
	Language Conventionality and Clarity some unfamiliar, academic, or domain-specific words
	Knowledge Demands more difficult literary concepts
Reader/Task Considerations	Teacher determined Vary by individual reader and type of text

Background Have students read the background and information about the author. Tell students that Otto Frank, the only surviving family member, published his daughter's diary in June of 1947, two years after the war ended. The 1,500 copies from that first printing quickly sold out, as did a second printing. In February 1948, there was a third printing of 10,000 copies. By the 1950s, the book had been translated into German, French, and English, paving the way for it to become a worldwide sensation.

SETTING A PURPOSE Direct students to use the Setting a Purpose question to focus their reading.

Determine Author's Point of View (LINES 3–12)

COMMON CORE RI 6

Explain that an **author's point of view** is his or her position or perspective on a subject. Tell students that the facts, reasons, and other details that an author includes reveal his or her point of view.

(A) CITE TEXT EVIDENCE Tell students to reread lines 3–12 and identify details that describe the author's feelings about reading Anne Frank's diary for the first time. (*"reading until the daylight faded"; "lost track of my surroundings"; "felt as if I were entering the Amsterdam attic"; "I was enthralled by Anne's vivid descriptions"*) Have students explain what these details suggest about the author's point of view. (*She read this diary when she was younger and is an admirer of Anne Frank's work.*)

SCAFFOLDING FOR ELL STUDENTS

Prepositional Phrases Explain that prepositions such as *in, on,* and *of* often signal phrases that explain more about an idea. Guide students to identify prepositions to help them segment the ideas in longer sentences. On a whiteboard, project lines 3–6. Have volunteers mark up the text.

- Highlight in yellow the words *in, on,* and *of*.
- Highlight in green the words that complete each phrase.

ASK STUDENTS how the details the author includes help them to imagine the scene. (*The phrases create a specific place and time.*)

Background *Anne Frank's The Diary of a Young Girl has become one of the most well-known books in the world, but it is not always recognized as a skillfully crafted piece of literature. Author **Francine Prose** (b. 1947), a successful novelist and nonfiction writer, researched the diary to learn more about how it was written, how it came to be published, and how it has been received over time. She published her findings in a book, from which this selection is excerpted.*

from
ANNE FRANK:
The Book, The Life, The Afterlife

Literary Criticism by Francine Prose

SETTING A PURPOSE Has *The Diary of a Young Girl* become a classic because of its author's tragically short life, or because of the quality of the writing? As you read, focus on the differing opinions about this question.

THE FIRST TIME I READ THE DIARY OF ANNE FRANK, I was younger than its author was when, at the age of thirteen, she began to write it. I can still picture myself sitting cross-legged on the floor of the bedroom in the house in which I grew up and reading until the daylight faded around me and I had to turn on the lamp. I lost track of my surroundings and felt as if I were entering the Amsterdam attic in which a Jewish girl and her family hid from the Nazis, and where, with the aid of their Dutch "helpers," they survived for two

10 years and a month, until they were betrayed to the authorities, arrested, and deported. I was enthralled by Anne's vivid descriptions of her adored father, Otto; of her conflicts with her mother, Edith, and her sister, Margot; of her romance with Peter van Pels; and of her irritation with Hermann

I can still picture myself sitting cross-legged on the floor of the bedroom in the house in which I grew up and reading until the daylight faded around me and I had to turn on the lamp. I lost track of my surroundings and felt as if I were entering the Amsterdam attic

(c) ©Oleksiy Mark/Shutterstock; (tr) ©Paul Hawthorne/AP Images; (bg) ©gregor/Shutterstock

Determine Author's Point of View

 COMMON CORE RI 6

(LINES 29–37)

Tell students that identifying an author's opinions and the reasons given to support those opinions can help them determine the author's point of view.

B **CITE TEXT EVIDENCE** Have students reread lines 29–37, first identifying the author's opinion of Anne Frank's book and then identifying several reasons used to support the opinion. *(opinion: "I was in the presence of a consciously crafted work of literature"; supporting reasons: "how much art is required to give the impression of artlessness, how much control is necessary in order to seem natural . . . nothing is more difficult for a writer than to find a narrative voice as fresh and unaffected as Anne Frank's")* **What does the author's opinion suggest about her point of view?** *(She views the diary as something carefully crafted and sees Anne as a skilled writer rather than as an adolescent sharing random thoughts.)*

CRITICAL VOCABULARY

intersperse: The author is describing Anne Frank's style as a writer.

ASK STUDENTS to recall what they read from Anne Frank's diary and to explain the impact of interspersing reflection with dramatized scenes. *(By interspersing the two, Anne gave the diary good pacing: enough action to keep readers' interest while presenting thought-provoking ideas.)*

---

and Auguste van Pels and the dentist, Fritz Pfeffer, with whom the Franks shared the secret annex. I remember that when I finished the book, I went back to the first page and started again, and that I read and reread the diary until I was older than Anne Frank was when she died, at fifteen, 20 in Bergen-Belsen.[1]

In the summer of 2005, I read the diary once more. I had just begun making notes for a novel that, I knew, would be narrated in the voice of a thirteen-year-old girl. Having written a book suggesting that writers seek guidance from a close and thoughtful reading of the classics, I thought I should follow my own advice, and it occurred to me that the greatest book ever written about a thirteen-year-old girl was Anne Frank's diary.

B Like most of Anne Frank's readers, I had viewed her book 30 as the innocent and spontaneous outpourings of a teenager. But now, rereading it as an adult, I quickly became convinced that I was in the presence of a consciously crafted work of literature. I understood, as I could not have as a child, how much art is required to give the impression of artlessness, how much control is necessary in order to seem natural, how almost nothing is more difficult for a writer than to find a narrative voice as fresh and unaffected as Anne Frank's. I appreciated, as I did not when I was a girl, her technical proficiency, the novelistic qualities of her diary, her ability to 40 turn living people into characters, her observational powers, her eye for detail, her ear for dialogue and monologue, and the sense of pacing that guides her as she **intersperses** sections of reflection with dramatized scenes.

I kept pausing to marvel at the fact that one of the greatest books about the Nazi genocide[2] should have been written by a girl between the ages of thirteen and fifteen—not a demographic[3] we commonly associate with literary genius. How astonishing that a teenager could have written so intelligently and so movingly about a subject that continues to 50 overwhelm the adult imagination. What makes it even more impressive is that this deceptively unassuming book focuses on a particular moment and on specific people, and at the same time speaks, in ways that seem timeless and universal,

intersperse
(ĭn´tər-spûrs´) *adj.*
If you *intersperse* something, you distribute it in different places.

---

[1] **Bergen-Belsen:** the Nazi concentration camp where Anne Frank was sent.
[2] **Nazi genocide:** the systematic killing of Jews by the Nazis.
[3] **demographic** (dĕm´ə-grăf´ĭk): part of a population.

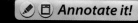
Strategies for Annotation   *Annotate it!*

Determine Author's Point of View (LINES 29–37)

 COMMON CORE RI 6

Direct students' attention to lines 31–34, and share these strategies for guided or independent analysis:

- Highlight in green the author's opinion.
- Highlight in yellow reasons that the author gives to support her opinion.
- Use a note to tell about the author's point of view.

But now, rereading it as an adult, I quickly became convinced that I was in the presence of a consciously crafted work of literature. I understood, as I could not have as a child, how much art is required to give the impression of artlessness, how much control is ne order to seem natural, how almost nothing is

The author sees Anne as a serious writer.

about adolescence and family life. It tells the truth about certain human beings' **ineradicable** desire to exterminate the largest possible number of other human beings, even as it celebrates the will to survive and the determination to maintain one's decency and dignity under the most dehumanizing circumstances.

60   Anne Frank thought of herself not merely as a girl who happened to be keeping a diary, but as a writer. According to Hanneli Goslar, a childhood friend, Anne's passion for writing began when she was still in school. "Anne would sit in class between lessons and she would shield her diary and she would write and write. Everybody would ask her, 'What are you writing?' And the answer always was, 'It's none of your business.'" In April 1944, four months before the attic in which the Franks found **refuge** was raided by the Nazis, Anne Frank recorded her wish to become a writer. "If I haven't any

70   talent for writing books or newspaper articles, well, then I can always write for myself.… I want to go on living even after my death! And therefore I am grateful to God for giving me this gift, this possibility of developing myself and of writing, of expressing all that is in me!"

    Much has been made of how differently we see Anne Frank after the so-called *Definitive Edition* of her diary, published in 1995, restored certain passages that Otto Frank had cut from the version that appeared in Holland in 1947 and in the United States in 1952. In fact, though

80   the *Definitive Edition* is almost a third longer than the first published version of *The Diary of a Young Girl*, the sections that were reinstated—barbed comments about Edith Frank and the Van Pelses, and other entries revealing the extent of Anne's curiosity about sexuality and about her body—don't substantially change our perception of her.

    On the other hand, there is a scene in Miep Gies's memoir, *Anne Frank Remembered*, that actually *does* alter our image of Anne. Along with the other helpers, the employees of Opekta, Otto Frank's spice and pectin business, Miep risked her life to

90   keep eight Jews alive for two years and a month, an experience she describes in a book that sharpens and enhances our sense of what the hidden Jews and their Dutch rescuers endured. The scene begins when Miep accidentally interrupts Anne while she is at work on her diary.

ineradicable
(ĭn´ĭ răd´ĭ-kə-bəl) *adj.* If something is *ineradicable*, it is impossible to remove.

refuge
(rĕf´yōōj) *n.* A *refuge* is shelter from danger.

CLOSE READ

Analyze the Meanings of Words and Phrases

COMMON CORE RI 4

(LINES 60–74)

Explain that **tone** expresses the author's attitude toward his or her subject. Point out that the author's selection of words, or **word choice**, contributes to the feeling associated with a text.

C **ASK STUDENTS** to reread lines 60–74 to identify the tone of the passage and word choices that reflect the tone. *(Possible answer: respectful; "not merely as a girl," "Anne's passion for writing")* What is the impact of the author's choice of the word *passion*? *(It emphasizes Anne's intensity as a writer.)*

CRITICAL VOCABULARY

ineradicable: The author is describing certain people's desire to exterminate large numbers of other people.

ASK STUDENTS how the Nazis' ineradicable desire to exterminate others affected the Frank family. *(Because the Nazis were relentless in their efforts, they eventually found the Frank family and arrested them.)*

refuge: The Franks were living in some hidden rooms in Mr. Frank's office building.

ASK STUDENTS to explain why the Franks needed to take refuge. *(The Nazis were arresting any Jews they could find and imprisoning them in concentration camps.)*

APPLYING ACADEMIC VOCABULARY

philosophy	publish

As you discuss the selection, incorporate the following Collection 5 academic vocabulary words: *philosophy* and *publish*. Ask students how the author's personal **philosophy** might help to determine her point of view. Ask students to explain why different editions of Anne Frank's diary were **published.**

CLOSE READ

Determine Author's Point of View (LINES 95–110)

 COMMON CORE RI 6

Point out that an **author's purpose** is his or her reason for writing. Explain or elicit that nonfiction writing is usually intended to inform or persuade readers.

Ⓓ ASK STUDENTS to reread lines 95–110. Prompt them to identify Prose's purpose in writing the literary criticism and in including this passage from Miep Gies's memoir. *(Prose's general purpose is to persuade readers to agree with her view that Anne Frank should be respected as a writer. Including the passage from Gies's memoir supports that purpose by describing a startling view of Anne's intensity as a writer.)*

CRITICAL VOCABULARY

incisive: The author is describing an essay about Anne Frank.

ASK STUDENTS to explain whether an incisive essay would be considered good writing or bad. *(It is likely to be considered good because it is clear and penetrating.)*

precocious: Many critics recognize Anne's literary talent.

ASK STUDENTS if a precocious talent is something that many people have. *(No. It is not common for a young person to have a talent that does not usually develop until adulthood, if at all.)*

tangential: The author is describing the many views of Anne Frank's diary.

ASK STUDENTS why the author says that Anne's diary is only tangentially about the war. *(Anne and her family were in hiding because of the war, but their lives were separate from it for the most part.)*

Ⓓ *I saw that Anne was writing intently, and hadn't heard me. I was quite close to her and was about to turn and go when she looked up, surprised, and saw me standing there. In our many encounters over the years, I'd seen Anne, like a chameleon, go from mood to mood, but always with friendliness. …But I saw a look on her face at this moment that I'd never seen before. It was a look of dark concentration, as if she had a throbbing headache. The look pierced me, and I was speechless. She was suddenly another person there writing at that table.*

100

The Anne whom Miep observed *was* another person: a writer, interrupted.

110

In his 1967 essay, "The Development of Anne Frank," John Berryman[4] asked "whether Anne Frank has *had* any serious readers, for I find no indication in anything written about her that anyone has taken her with real seriousness." That is no longer completely true. In an **incisive** 1989 *New Yorker* essay, "Not Even a Nice Girl," Judith Thurman remarked on the skill with which Anne Frank constructed her narrative. A small number of critics and historians have called attention to Anne's **precocious** literary talent. In her introduction

120

to the British edition of *The Tales from the House Behind*, a collection of Anne's fiction and her autobiographical compositions, the British author G. B. Stern wrote, "One thing is certain, that Anne was a writer in embryo." But is a "writer in embryo" the same as one who has emerged, at once newborn and mature?

The fact remains that Anne Frank has only rarely been given her due as a writer. With few exceptions, her diary has still never been taken seriously as literature, perhaps because it *is* a diary, or, more likely, because its author was a girl. Her

130

book has been discussed as eyewitness testimony, as a war document, as a Holocaust narrative or not, as a book written during the time of war that is only **tangentially** about the war, and as a springboard for conversations about racism

incisive
(ĭn-sī′sĭv) *adj.* If something is *incisive*, it is penetrating, clear, and sharp.

precocious
(prĭ-kō′shəs) *adj.* If someone is *precocious*, the person is mentally advanced for his or her age.

tangential
(tăn-jĕn′shəl) *adj.* If something is *tangential*, it is only slightly connected.

---

[4] **John Berryman:** an American poet and scholar.

WHEN STUDENTS STRUGGLE...

Have students begin a chart to identify and track the differing views presented in the literary criticism regarding Anne Frank as a writer.

Francine Prose's View	Other Views
Anne was a talented writer.	Judith Thurman: "the skill with which Anne Frank constructed her narrative"

and intolerance. But it has hardly ever been viewed as a work of art.

Harold Bloom tells us why: "A child's diary, even when she was so natural a writer, rarely could sustain literary criticism. Since *this* diary is **emblematic** of hundreds of thousands of murdered children, criticism is irrelevant. I myself have no qualifications except as a literary critic. One cannot write about Anne Frank's *Diary* as if Shakespeare, or Philip Roth,[5] is the subject."

140

emblematic
(ĕm´blə măt´ ĭk) *adj.*
If something is *emblematic*, it is a symbol for something else.

> " *A child's diary, even when she was so natural a writer, rarely could sustain literary criticism.* "

The Dutch novelist Harry Mulisch attributed the diary's popularity to the fact that its young author died soon after writing it: "The work by this child is not simply *not* a work of art, but in a certain sense it is a work of art made by life itself: it is a found object. It was after all literally found among the debris on the floor after the eight characters departed . . . ." Writing in the *New Republic*, Robert Alter, a critic and biblical scholar, agreed: "I do not mean to sound **impervious** to the **poignancy** of the *Diary*. Still, many diaries of Jews who perished have been published that reflect a complexity of adult perspective and, in some instances, of a direct grappling with the barbarity[6] of Nazism; and these are absent from Anne Frank's writing . . . . Anne may have been a bright and admirably introspective girl, but there is not much in her diary that is emotionally demanding, and her reflections on the world have the quality of **banality** that one would expect from a 14-year-old. What makes the *Diary* moving is the shadow cast back over it by the notice of the death at the end. Try to imagine (as Philip Roth did, for other reasons, in *The Ghost Writer*) an Anne Frank who survived Bergen-Belsen, and, let us say, settled in Cleveland, became a journalist, married and

150

160

impervious
(ĭm-pûr´vē-əs) *adj.*
If something is *impervious*, it is impossible to penetrate.

poignant
(poin´yənt) *adj.*
If something is *poignant*, it is profoundly moving or touching.

banal
(bə-năl´) *adj.* If something is *banal*, it is very commonplace, dull, and unoriginal.

---

[5] **Philip Roth:** an award-winning American novelist known for his depictions of American Jewish life.
[6] **barbarity** (bär-băr´ĭ-tē): savage cruelty or brutality.

CLOSE READ

Analyze the Meanings of Words and Phrases

COMMON CORE **RI 4**

(LINES 143–148)

Remind students that tone expresses the author's attitude toward his or her subject and that word choices reflect that attitude.

E **CITE TEXT EVIDENCE** Have students reread lines 143–148 to identify the tone of Harry Mulisch's quotation. How do his word choices reflect that tone? *(Possible answer: His tone is dismissive and somewhat arrogant; "The work by this child," "literally found among the debris")* What does Mulisch mean by the phrase found art? *(Possible answer: something that occurred naturally, without human creativity)*

CRITICAL VOCABULARY

emblematic: Harold Bloom says that Anne's diary represents hundreds of thousands of murdered children.

ASK STUDENTS why Anne's diary might be considered emblematic. *(It describes the experiences of many young Jewish children during the war.)*

impervious: A critic is explaining why he does not consider Anne's diary to be art.

ASK STUDENTS why a critic would not want to sound impervious to Anne's diary. *(Possible answer: He does not want to sound as if he is insensitive or not affected.)*

poignant: A critic is describing Anne's diary.

ASK STUDENTS why Anne's diary is thought of as poignant. *(Most people agree that the diary is moving and touching.)*

banal: One critic is arguing that Anne's diary is written in the way one would expect a 14-year-old girl to write.

ASK STUDENTS whether describing Anne's diary as banal is a compliment. *(No. Something banal is common and unoriginal.)*

Determine Author's Point of View (LINES 184–190)

 COMMON CORE RI 6

Remind students that an author's point of view is reflected in his or her descriptions, word choices, supporting evidence, and tone.

F **CITE TEXT EVIDENCE** Have students reread lines 184–190 to identify the words that reflect and reinforce the author's point of view about Anne Frank as a writer. *("she managed to create something that transcended what she herself called 'the unbosomings of a thirteen-year-old'"; "should be awarded its place among the great memoirs")*

COLLABORATIVE DISCUSSION Have students work in small groups to discuss the question and cite text evidence to support their ideas about what distinguishes ordinary writing from great literature. Have students share their results with the class. Accept all reasonable responses.

ASK STUDENTS to share any questions they generated in the course of reading and discussing the piece of literary criticism.

---

had two children. Would anyone care about her wartime diary except as an account of the material circumstances of hiding out from the Nazis in Amsterdam?"

At once admiring of Anne's gifts and troubled by a sense of how they have been underestimated, I began to think it might be interesting and perhaps useful for students newly
170 introduced to Anne's diary and for readers who have grown accustomed to seeing it in a certain light to consider her work from a more literary perspective. What aspects of the book have helped to ensure its long and influential afterlife? Why has Anne Frank become such an iconic figure for so many readers, in so many countries? What is it about her voice that continues to engage and move her audience? How have the various interpretations and versions of her diary—the Broadway play, the Hollywood film, the schoolroom lessons, the newspaper articles that keep her in the public eye—
180 influenced our idea of who she was and what she wrote?

The book I imagined would address those questions, mostly through a close reading of the diary. Such a book would explore the ways in which Anne's diary found an enduring place in the culture and consciousness of the world. I would argue for Anne Frank's *talent as a writer*. Regardless of her age and her gender, she managed to create something that transcended[7] what she herself called "the unbosomings[8] of a thirteen-year-old" and that should be awarded its place among the great memoirs and spiritual confessions, as well as among the most
190 significant records of the era in which she lived.

COLLABORATIVE DISCUSSION What do you think distinguishes an ordinary piece of writing from great literature? With a partner, discuss which of the author's reasons for considering Anne Frank's diary a work of art seem most convincing to you. Cite specific evidence from the text to support your ideas.

---

[7] **transcended** (trăn-sĕnd´əd): surpassed or went beyond the limits.
[8] **unbosoming** (ŭn-bŏŏz´əm-ing): revealing one's personal thoughts.

TO CHALLENGE STUDENTS . . .

Analyze Voice Have students reread lines 21–28, noting Francine Prose's goal of narrating a story in the voice of a thirteen-year-old girl. Tell students that the term *voice* refers to the unique use of language that allows readers to "hear" a human personality in a text.

ASK STUDENTS to work in small groups to discuss whether Anne Frank's diary would serve as a good model for Prose to achieve her goal. In what ways was Anne a typical teenage girl? In what ways was she not? Remind students to cite evidence from the text, including comments from the various critics, to support their ideas.

Determine Author's Point of View

An **author's viewpoint** is his or her position or attitude about a particular subject. This viewpoint is formed by the combination of ideas, values, feelings, and philosophy that influence and shape a writer's opinions. When determining an author's viewpoint, ask yourself,

- What opinions does the author express about this topic?
- What facts or other details suggest how the author feels?
- Are reasons provided to support a particular view?
- How has the author's background affected his or her attitudes?

Sometimes an author will mention the viewpoints of others. If these views are similar to the author's own, they may be used to support the author's opinions. If these viewpoints are different than the author's own, they may be presented so that the author can disprove them by offering a **counterargument.**

As you analyze the essay, look for clues to help you determine Francine Prose's viewpoint on the literary quality of Anne Frank's diary.

Analyze the Meanings of Words and Phrases

Every piece of writing has a particular tone. The **tone** expresses the author's attitude toward his or her subject. For example, a literary work might have a serious, humorous, sad, or respectful tone.

An author's selection of words, or **word choice,** contributes to the tone because words not only communicate ideas, they also convey specific feelings. Notice the word choice in this passage from *Anne Frank: The Book, the Life, the Afterlife.*

> I kept pausing to marvel at the fact that one of the greatest books about the Nazi genocide should have been written by a girl between the ages of thirteen and fifteen—not a demographic we commonly associate with literary genius. How astonishing that a teenager could have written so intelligently and so movingly about a subject that continues to overwhelm the adult imagination.

Words such as these help create a respectful, admiring tone.

Choose a passage from this selection and identify the words that contribute to the tone.

Anne Frank: The Book, The Life, the Afterlife **375**

TEACH

CLOSE READ

Determine Author's Point of View

Help students understand the term *author's viewpoint.* Discuss how an author's background or values might shape his or her viewpoint. Prompt students to examine how each of the questions in the bulleted list can help to determine an author's viewpoint.

Guide students to recognize that presenting a counterargument allows an author to refute an opposing idea, further strengthening his or her own ideas.

Analyze the Meanings of Words and Phrases

Discuss the meaning of *tone,* prompting students to suggest examples of word choices that impact tone. For example, that describing a school playground as "chaotic" suggests a more serious tone than describing that playground as "a three-ring circus."

Prompt students to examine the sample passage for words that help communicate its respectful, admiring tone. (*Possible answers: marvel, astonishing, intelligently, movingly*) Then have students work independently to identify another passage from the selection in which word choices impact the tone.

Strategies for Annotation

Analyze the Meanings of Words and Phrases (LINES 50–53)

Share these strategies for guided or independent analysis:

- Reread the passage closely, thinking about its overall tone or feeling.
- Highlight in yellow any words or phrases that help create the tone.

> What makes it even more impressive is that this deceptively unassuming book focuses on a particular moment and on specific people, and at the same time speaks, in ways that seem timeless and universal, about adolescence and family life. It tells the truth

Analyzing the Text

 COMMON CORE RI 1, RI 2, RI 3, RI 4, RI 6

Possible answers:

1. *Francine Prose was "enthralled by Anne's vivid descriptions." She read the book over and over.*

2. *The author originally viewed the book "as the innocent and spontaneous outpourings of a teenager." Later, she saw it as "a consciously crafted work of literature." She probably changed her mind as she discovered these things about Anne's writing: her technical proficiency, the novelistic qualities of her diary, her ability to turn living people into characters, her observational powers, her eye for detail, her ear for dialogue and monologue, and her sense of pacing.*

3. *The Definitive Edition is about a third longer than the first published version. Anne's father probably omitted parts of the diary ("barbed comments about Edith Frank and the Van Pelses"; "entries revealing Anne's curiosity about sexuality") in an effort to avoid hurting or embarrassing others.*

4. *She counters Berryman's view by citing the opposing opinions of other literary critics.*

5. *Alter's question is dismissive of Anne as a writer. He suggests that it is only her death that makes her diary popular. Prose's counterargument to the view represented by Alter is that on the contrary Anne's diary exhibits very sophisticated literary qualities.*

6. *Prose's main claim is that contrary to the opinions of many Anne Frank was a gifted, talented writer and that her diary is a work of literature that deserves recognition as such.*

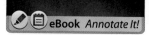

 COMMON CORE RI 1, RI 2, RI 3, RI 4, RI 6, RI 8, W 4, W 9b, W 10, SL 1a, SL 1b

Analyzing the Text

Cite Text Evidence   Support your responses with evidence from the text.

1. **Cite Evidence** What evidence in the essay demonstrates clearly that even as a young girl, Francine Prose loved the book *The Diary of Anne Frank*?

2. **Compare** Reread lines 29–43. Complete a chart like this one to show how the author's view of Anne Frank's diary changed over time. What might explain the change?

Prose's Viewpoint as a Child	Prose's Viewpoint as an Adult

3. **Draw Conclusions** How is the *Definitive Edition* of Anne Frank's diary different from the version that was originally published? Identify the evidence Prose provides to suggest why Anne's father made the decisions he did about the first edition.

4. **Evaluate** How does Francine Prose respond to John Berryman's view, expressed in lines 111–115, that Anne Frank never had any "serious readers"?

5. **Analyze** Why do you think Prose chose to include the quote from Robert Alter that appears in lines 150–166? Identify her counterargument to his view.

6. **Analyze** A **claim** is a writer's position on an issue. What is the main claim Prose makes about Anne Frank's writing?

PERFORMANCE TASK

Writing Activity: Analysis At the end of her essay, Francine Prose writes, "I would argue for Anne Frank's *talent as a writer*." Do you think Prose has made a convincing argument? Write an analysis that explains why or why not.

- Work with a partner to analyze the argument. Remember to listen politely and to share ideas in a respectful way as you complete a graphic organizer showing Prose's claims and supporting evidence.

- Discuss whether the evidence Prose presents is relevant and sufficient and if her reasoning is sound.

- Next, work together to evaluate the author's tone and word choice. Do they strengthen her claims? Why or why not?

- When you are ready to write, begin your analysis by stating your view. Then support that view with evidence from the text.

Assign this performance task.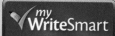

PERFORMANCE TASK

 COMMON CORE RI 8, W 4, W 9b, W 10, SL 1a, SL 1b

Writing Activity: Analysis Have students work in pairs to analyze and discuss Prose's argument. Instruct students to

- prepare for their discussions by beginning a graphic organizer that shows Prose's claims and supporting evidence,

- share ideas respectfully and follow the rules for collegial discussions, and

- state their views clearly when they begin writing their analyses.

Critical Vocabulary

COMMON CORE L 4b, L 4d

intersperse	ineradicable	refuge	incisive
precocious	tangential	emblematic	impervious
poignant	banal		

Practice and Apply Use your understanding of the Vocabulary words to answer each question.

1. Are birds likely to take **refuge** in a nest or in the sky?

2. Is an **incisive** news article insightful and clear or vague and confusing?

3. Would a **precocious** child write a note or a novel?

4. Which is **emblematic** of royalty, a star or a crown?

5. If you are **impervious** to bullies' taunts, will you remain calm or get upset?

6. Are bad habits eradicable or **ineradicable**?

7. Which has a **tangential** connection to astronomy, biology or astrology?

8. To **intersperse** a story with illustrations, would you place the drawings throughout the text or all at the end?

9. Would a **banal** TV commercial lead you to buy a product or not?

10. Would a **poignant** story be more likely to be forgotten or remembered?

Vocabulary Strategy: Latin Suffixes

You know that a **suffix** is a word part added to the end of a base word or a word root. The Latin suffixes -*able* and -*ible* form adjectives and mean "able to be," "capable of," or "worthy of." Look at this example from the text:

> It tells the truth about certain human beings' <u>ineradicable</u> desire to exterminate . . .

Knowing the meaning of the suffix -*able* can help you figure out that *ineradicable* means "not able to be eliminated."

Practice and Apply Find the word in each sentence that has the Latin suffix -*able* or -*ible*. Use the meaning of the suffix to help you write a definition of the word. Check each definition you write in a dictionary.

1. Anne Frank's vivid descriptions are enthralling and credible.

2. Critics find her writing commendable but do not consider it literature.

3. Is it conceivable that a teenager could write a great book about genocide?

4. Anne Frank made complex personal and historical events comprehensible.

Critical Vocabulary

COMMON CORE L 4b, L 4d

Possible answers:

1. *in a nest*

2. *insightful and clear*

3. *a novel*

4. *a crown*

5. *remain calm*

6. *eradicable*

7. *astrology*

8. *throughout the text*

9. *not*

10. *remembered*

Vocabulary Strategy: Latin Suffixes

1. *credible: worthy of confidence or belief; believable*

2. *commendable: able to be commended or praised*

3. *conceivable: able to be thought of; imaginable*

4. *comprehensible: able to be comprehended or understood*

Strategies for Annotation Annotate it!

Latin Suffixes

COMMON CORE L 4b, L 4d

Have students locate the sentence containing *ineradicable* in lines 54–59. Encourage students to use their eBook annotation tools to do the following:

- Underline the vocabulary word.
- Highlight in yellow the prefix *in-* and the Latin suffix -*able*.
- Use a note to tell the word's meaning.

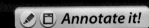

> It tells the truth about certain human beings' <u>ineradicable</u> desire to exterminate the largest possible number of other human beings,

not able to be eradicated

Language Conventions: Use Ellipses

 COMMON CORE L 2a, L 2b

Have students compare the first example in the chart with the actual text in the essay (lines 3–5) to see which words have been omitted. Also point out that the ellipsis at the end of the first example has also been placed after the period.

Read aloud the second example sentence so that students can hear the effect of the ellipsis.

Possible answers:

1. *She had an amazing gift as a writer . . . a fresh voice . . . technical proficiency.*

2. *"Anne Frank thought of herself not merely as a girl . . . keeping a diary, but as a writer. According to . . . a childhood friend, Anne's passion for writing began when she was still in school."*

3. *"At once admiring of Anne's gifts and troubled by a sense of how they have been underestimated, I began to think it might be interesting . . . to consider her work from a more literary perspective. . . . "*

4. *On the other hand, there is a scene in Miep Gies's memoir, . . . that actually does alter our image of Anne. . . . The scene begins when Miep accidentally interrupts Anne while she is at work on her diary.*

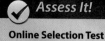

Assess It!

Online Selection Test

• Download an editable ExamView bank.
• Assign and manage this test online.

Language Conventions: Use Ellipses

 COMMON CORE L 2a, L 2b

An **ellipsis** is a punctuation mark that consists of three dots, or periods. Ellipses are used to indicate an omission in text or a long pause.

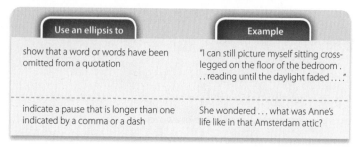

Use an ellipsis to	Example
show that a word or words have been omitted from a quotation	"I can still picture myself sitting cross-legged on the floor of the bedroom . . . reading until the daylight faded . . . ."
indicate a pause that is longer than one indicated by a comma or a dash	She wondered . . . what was Anne's life like in that Amsterdam attic?

Notice that when the omitted words are at the end of a sentence, the ellipsis are placed after the period or other end punctuation mark.

"**In our many encounters over the years, I'd seen Anne, like a chameleon, go from mood to mood, but always with friendliness. . . .** "

Practice and Apply Rewrite the sentences. Add one or more ellipses to indicate a long pause or to take the place of the underlined words in the quotation.

1. She had an amazing gift as a writer a fresh voice technical proficiency.

2. "Anne Frank thought of herself not merely as a girl <u>who happened to be</u> keeping a diary, but as a writer. According to <u>Hanneli Goslar</u>, a childhood friend, Anne's passion for writing began when she was still in school."

3. "At once admiring of Anne's gifts and troubled by a sense of how they have been underestimated, I began to think it might be interesting <u>and perhaps useful for students newly introduced to Anne's diary and for readers who have grown accustomed to seeing it in a certain light</u> to consider her work from a more literary perspective."

4. "On the other hand, there is a scene in Miep Gies's memoir, *Anne Frank Remembered*, that actually *does* alter our image of Anne. <u>Along with the other helpers, the employees of Opekta, Otto Frank's spice and pectin business, Miep risked her life to keep eight Jews alive for two years and a month, an experience she describes in a book that sharpens and enhances our sense of what the hidden Jews and their Dutch rescuers endured.</u> The scene begins when Miep accidentally interrupts Anne while she is at work on her diary."

Evaluate Reasoning

TEACH

Tell students that part of evaluating an author's claim or conclusions is to **evaluate**, or judge, the author's reasoning. Explain that **reasoning** is the logic that links ideas together.

Present these two commonly used methods of reasoning:

- When a writer uses **deductive reasoning**, he or she begins with a general principle and applies it to a particular situation in order to reach a conclusion.
General principle: Skilled writers must be adults.
Situation: Anne Frank was a teenager when she wrote her diary.
Conclusion: Anne Frank was not a skilled writer.

- When a writer uses **inductive reasoning**, he or she uses facts and observations to reach a conclusion.
Fact: Anne Frank was a teenager when she wrote her diary.
Fact: Millions of people all over the world have read and enjoyed Anne Frank's diary.
Conclusion: Anne Frank's diary is well written.

Tell students that while either type of reasoning can be used to reach a logical conclusion, it is important to evaluate conclusions to determine whether they are the result of sound reasoning. Ask students which of the conclusions presented above may not be sound reasoning. *(Anne Frank was not a skilled writer.)*

PRACTICE AND APPLY

Have partners work together to evaluate Francine Prose's reasoning in specific sections of *Anne Frank: The Book, The Life, The Afterlife*. As needed, provide specific passages such as lines 86–110 for students to evaluate. Prompt students to evaluate the logic and soundness of Prose's reasoning.

Determine Author's Point of View

RETEACH

Review that an **author's viewpoint** is his or her position or attitude about a particular subject. Explain to students that they can think of an author's viewpoint as his or her "stand" on an issue. Ask students how they "stand" on certain issues at school, such as healthy lunches, elimination of vending machines, or a longer school day.

Discuss the following clues that help reveal an author's viewpoint:

- opinions about a topic
- the author's choice of facts or details
- reasons provided to support an opinion
- the author's background

Point out that authors often include viewpoints other than their own and then challenge those views using a counterargument.

 LEVEL UP TUTORIALS Assign the following *Level Up* tutorial: **Author's Perspective**

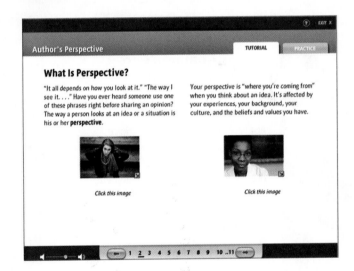

CLOSE READING APPLICATION

Student partners can work together to identify the author's viewpoint in a selection they have read, such as "When Do Kids Become Adults?" in Collection 4, or to a recent magazine article or newspaper opinion piece. Tell partners to cite opinions, facts, reasons, or other evidence in the text that reveals the author's viewpoint.

After Auschwitz

Speech by Elie Wiesel

Why This Text?

Students regularly encounter opinions and persuasive language in texts, speech, and media. Reading Elie Wiesel's heartfelt Holocaust memorial speech will give students the opportunity to analyze persuasive techniques and powerful word choices that convey emotion.

View It!

Professional Development Podcast:

Text-Dependent Analysis

Key Learning Objective: The student will be able to identify persuasive techniques and rhetorical devices in a speech.

COMMON CORE Common Core Standards

RI 1 Cite text evidence to support analysis.
RI 2 Determine central idea.
RI 4 Analyze impact of word choices.
RI 5 Analyze structure.
RI 6 Determine author's point of view or purpose.
RI 8 Delineate and evaluate argument.
W 7 Conduct short research projects.
W 8 Gather information from multiple sources.
SL 1a Come to discussions prepared.
SL 1b Follow rules for collegial discussions.

Text Complexity Rubric

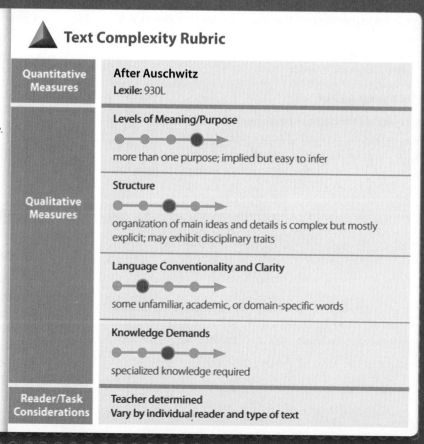

Quantitative Measures	**After Auschwitz** Lexile: 930L
	Levels of Meaning/Purpose more than one purpose; implied but easy to infer
Qualitative Measures	**Structure** organization of main ideas and details is complex but mostly explicit; may exhibit disciplinary traits
	Language Conventionality and Clarity some unfamiliar, academic, or domain-specific words
	Knowledge Demands specialized knowledge required
Reader/Task Considerations	**Teacher determined** Vary by individual reader and type of text

CLOSE READ

Background Have students read the background and information about the author, Elie Wiesel. Supplement the information by telling students about the place where the speech was made. The combined sites of Auschwitz and its mass-extermination center at Birkenau are considered the biggest cemetery in the world. The Auschwitz-Birkenau State Museum is an exhibition of Nazi prisons and death chambers. The museum, originally devised by Holocaust survivors during the 1950s, is the most visited tourist site in Poland.

Prepare students to recognize the line of prayer repeated throughout the speech. Explain that the text set off in boldface is an English transliteration of Aramaic, the language spoken by Jews in ancient times. The words are the beginning of a solemn prayer that is also known as the mourner's prayer.

SETTING A PURPOSE Direct students to use the Setting a Purpose question to focus their reading.

SCAFFOLDING FOR ELL STUDENTS

Analyze Context Using a whiteboard, model how to use context to determine the meanings of unfamiliar words. Have volunteers mark up lines 12–13.

- Underline unfamiliar words or phrases.
- Highlight in blue any words that provide clues to the meaning of the unfamiliar word.
- Write a synonym or brief definition on a note. Check a print or digital dictionary if necessary.

Background *The first German concentration camps were built only for opponents of the Nazi Party. Later, these camps were also used to imprison Jews and other supposed enemies of the state. Auschwitz, the largest Nazi concentration camp, was opened in 1940 in southern Poland. Inside, prisoners were forced to do work for the Nazi government. Those who were unable to do useful work were killed. Over one million Jews were sent to Auschwitz. Most of them died inside its walls. The camp was finally abandoned by German soldiers as the Russian army advanced upon it in 1945.*

After Auschwitz

Speech by Elie Wiesel

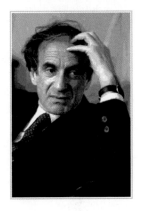

Elie Wiesel (b. 1928) *was born in Romania. After the Germans invaded his town, Wiesel and his family were sent to Auschwitz. Only Wiesel and two of his sisters survived. After the war, Wiesel moved to France and became a journalist. It was there that he wrote* Night, *a book about his experiences at Auschwitz. The book has sold millions of copies in many different languages. Wiesel later moved to the United States. There he devoted himself to ensuring that the deaths of millions of Jews in concentration camps would never be forgotten, and that other human beings would never be subjected to such crimes. In 1986, Wiesel was awarded the Nobel Peace Prize for his life's work.*

SETTING A PURPOSE The horrible crimes committed in Nazi concentration camps occurred long ago. As you read, think about why the author continues to reflect on these events. Why does he believe people need to be reminded of them? Write down any questions you have.

ASK STUDENTS to tell what image the phrase *nocturnal processions* suggests.

Close your eyes and look: endless <u>nocturnal</u> <u>processions</u> are <u>converging</u> here, and here it is always night. Here heaven and earth are on fire.

nocturnal = night

For more context and historical background, students can view the video "Holocaust" in their eBooks.

Analyze Structure: Speech

COMMON CORE · RI 5

(LINES 1–19)

Tell students that speakers try to capture their audience's attention by beginning speeches with a striking or memorable image.

A **ASK STUDENTS** to reread lines 1–19. What does Wiesel do to get listeners' attention at the beginning of his speech? *(He describes personal memories of Auschwitz. He repeats, "Here, heaven and earth are on fire.")* Why might Wiesel have chosen to begin this way? *(He feels terrible pain in this place because of what he experienced there fifty years earlier. He is arousing his listeners' compassion and making them interested in what he has learned: "Close your eyes and look"; "Close your eyes and listen.")*

Analyze Word Choices

COMMON CORE · RI 4

(LINES 3, 14)

Explain that **rhetorical devices** are the techniques writers use to enhance their arguments and communicate more effectively. Point out that **repetition**—repeating a word, phrase, or line—is one such device.

B **CITE TEXT EVIDENCE** Ask students to reread lines 4–6 to identify the repetition. *(Wiesel repeats the word* no: *"no name, no hope, no future.")* What is the impact of the repetition? *(The repetition emphasizes the desolation and lack of humanity in the camp.)*

A "*After Auschwitz, the human condition is not the same, nothing will be the same.*"

Here heaven and earth are on fire. **B**

I speak to you as a man, who 50 years and nine days ago had no name, no hope, no future and was known only by his number, A7713.[1]

I speak as a Jew who has seen what humanity has done to itself by trying to exterminate an entire people and inflict suffering and humiliation and death on so many others.

10   In this place of darkness and malediction[2] we can but stand in awe and remember its stateless, faceless and nameless victims. Close your eyes and look: endless nocturnal processions are converging here, and here it is always night.

 Here heaven and earth are on fire.

Close your eyes and listen. Listen to the silent screams of terrified mothers, the prayers of anguished old men and women. Listen to the tears of children, Jewish children, a beautiful little girl among them, with golden hair, whose vulnerable tenderness has never left me. Look and listen as

---

[1] **A7713:** the identification number tattooed on Wiesel at Auschwitz.
[2] **malediction** (măl´ĭ–dĭk´shən): curse.

WHEN STUDENTS STRUGGLE . . .

The powerful imagery of Wiesel's speech may be challenging for some readers to follow and understand. Suggest that students record the sights and sounds he describes in a chart like the one shown.

Sights	Sounds
"heaven and earth are on fire"	"silent screams of terrified mothers"
"here it always night"	"the tears of children"

20 they quietly walk towards dark flames so gigantic that the
planet itself seemed in danger.

All these men and women and children came from
everywhere, a gathering of exiles drawn by death.

Yitgadal veyitkadash, Shmay Rabba.[3]

In this kingdom of darkness there were many people.
People who came from all the occupied lands of Europe. And
then there were the Gypsies and the Poles and the Czechs . . .
It is true that not all the victims were Jews. But all the Jews
were victims.

30   Now, as then, we ask the question of all questions: what
was the meaning of what was so routinely going on in this
kingdom of eternal night. What kind of demented mind could
have invented this system?

And it worked. The killers killed, the victims died and
the world was the world and everything else was going on,
life as usual. In the towns nearby, what happened? In the
lands nearby, what happened? Life was going on where God's   **D**
creation was condemned to blasphemy[4] by their killers and
their accomplices.

40   **Yitgadal veyitkadash, Shmay Rabba.**

Turning point or watershed,[5] Birkenau[6] produced a
mutation[7] on a cosmic scale, affecting man's dreams and
endeavours. After Auschwitz, the human condition is no
longer the same. After Auschwitz, nothing will ever be
the same.

Yitgadal veyitkadash, Shmay Rabba.

As we remember the solitude and the pain of its
victims, let us declare this day marks our commitment to
commemorate their death, not to celebrate our own victory
50   over death.

---

[3] **Yitgadal veyitkadash, Shmay Rabba:** the Hebrew words that begin a Jewish
   prayer for the dead.
[4] **blasphemy** (blăs′fə-mē): a disrespect for religion.
[5] **watershed:** a place that marks a change of course or direction.
[6] **Birkenau:** the sub-camp at Auschwitz where prisoners were killed.
[7] **mutation** (myo͞o-tā′shən): change.

CLOSE READ

Analyze Word Choices   COMMON CORE RI 4
(LINES 25–39)

Tell students that **parallelism** is a rhetorical device in
which similar grammatical structures are repeated.
Explain that parallelism and word repetition in a
speech can have rhythmical effects, helping listeners
connect meaning, sound, and feeling.

C **CITE TEXT EVIDENCE** Have students reread
lines 25–33, noting the phrase *kingdom of darkness*
in line 25. Have students find a parallel phrase in
the next paragraph and describe the impact of both
phrases. *(The phrases "kingdom of darkness" and
"kingdom of eternal night" suggest an entire land of
hopelessness, fear, and pain, in which there is never any
light or happiness.)*

As needed, explain that traditional Judaism forbids
cremation; the bodies of the dead are required to be
buried in the earth.

D **ASK STUDENTS** to reread the sentence in
lines 37–39 and tell what meaning Wiesel's choice of
the word *blasphemy* conveys. *(When he says, "God's
creation was condemned to blasphemy," he may mean
that the Jewish people who were cremated here were
not properly buried. He suggests that the feeling of grief
is even greater because there are no bodies and no
individual graves.)*

Strategies for Annotation   🖉 🗐 *Annotate it!*

Analyze Word Choices   COMMON CORE RI 4

Have students use their eBook annotation tools to do the following:

- Highlight in yellow repeated words.
- Highlight in green parallel structures.
- Underline words that have emotional impact.
- Write a note with a short description of the emotion conveyed.

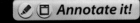

And it worked. The killers killed, the victims died and the
world was the world and everything else was going on, life as usual.
In the towns nearby, what happened? In the lands nearby, what
happened? Life was going on where God's creation was
to blasphemy by their killers and their accomplices.

helpless
anger at the
indifference
to a terrible
crime

Analyze Word Choices COMMON CORE RI 4

(LINES 51–60)

Tell students that an **ethical appeal** is a persuasive technique in which a speaker appeals to his listeners' sense of morality—in this case, the accepted belief that bloodshed and terror are wrong. Explain that Wiesel gave this speech in 1995 and makes references to ethnic strife and genocide in the world at that time.

 CITE TEXT EVIDENCE Have students reread lines 51–60 to identify words and phrases that convey an ethical appeal. *("In the name of all that is sacred in memory, let us stop the bloodshed . . . the vicious and ruthless terror attacks"; "Let us reject and oppose more effectively religious fanaticism and racial hate"; "Remember the morality of the human condition.")* What is the impact of this language on the tone of the speech? *(It offers a more hopeful tone, that it is possible to create a less violent world.)*

Analyze Structure: Speech COMMON CORE RI 5

(LINES 61–64)

Tell students that in the conclusion of a speech, a speaker leaves listeners with something to think about.

 ASK STUDENTS to reread lines 61–64. What elements of Wiesel's conclusion make it an effective ending for the speech? *(He repeats the first line of the prayer for the dead and addresses God. The ending has an emotional impact as he reminds listeners that the dead are around them, never buried or mourned as they should have been. He is reminding his listeners about why they have gathered in this place.)*

COLLABORATIVE DISCUSSION Have students work in pairs to discuss the appropriateness of the speech. Suggest that they reread segments of the speech aloud to one another to try to capture the sound-meaning-feeling connections.

ASK STUDENTS to share any questions they generated in the course of reading and discussing the selection.

 As we reflect upon the past, we must address ourselves to the present and the future. In the name of all that is sacred in memory, let us stop the bloodshed in Bosnia, Rwanda and Chechnia; the vicious and ruthless terror attacks against Jews in the Holy Land.[8] Let us reject and oppose more effectively religious fanaticism and racial hate.

Where else can we say to the world *"Remember the morality of the human condition,"* if not here?

For the sake of our children, we must remember Birkenau,
60 so that it does not become their future.

 Yitgadal veyitkadash, Shmay Rabba: Weep for Thy children whose death was not mourned then: weep for them, our Father in heaven, for they were deprived of their right to be buried, for heaven itself became their cemetery.

COLLABORATIVE DISCUSSION Elie Wiesel delivered the speech you just read at a ceremony marking the 50th anniversary of the liberation of Auschwitz. With a partner, discuss whether you think his message was the right one for the occasion. Cite evidence from the text to support your thoughts.

---

[8] **Holy Land:** the ancient kingdom of Israel.

TO CHALLENGE STUDENTS . . .

Analyze the Speaker Have students reread the speech with a focus on Elie Wiesel as a person. Prompt them to identify what they learn about Wiesel's life and experiences and to infer what his speech suggests about his personality.

ASK STUDENTS to work in small groups to use their findings to develop a brief description that might have been used to introduce Wiesel prior to his speech. Point out that while such introductions often focus on a person's successes and accomplishments, their emphasis should be on Wiesel's personal qualities.

Analyze Word Choices

 COMMON CORE RI 4

In "After Auschwitz," Elie Wiesel's goal is to persuade, or convince, his audience to adopt a particular viewpoint. To do so, he uses **persuasive techniques,** methods or devices designed to appeal to audiences' feelings and values and thus influence their opinions.

- An **emotional appeal** is a message that creates strong feelings in order to make a point. These appeals can tap into people's feelings such as fear, pity, or vanity. In this passage from his speech, Elie Wiesel appeals to feelings of sympathy and compassion for others.

  "**Close your eyes and listen. Listen to the silent screams of terrified mothers, the prayers of anguished old men and women. Listen to the tears of children, Jewish children . . .**"

- In an **ethical appeal,** a speaker or writer links a claim to a widely accepted value in order to gain moral support for the claim. In his speech, Wiesel appeals to the established belief that human beings should neither murder one another nor be indifferent to suffering.

  "**And it worked. The killers killed, the victims died and the world was the world and everything else was going on, life as usual.**"

Speakers can also attempt to persuade listeners by using different rhetorical devices. **Rhetorical devices** are techniques writers use to enhance their arguments and communicate more effectively.

- **Repetition** is a rhetorical device in which a sound, word, phrase, clause, or line is repeated for emphasis or to give a text or speech a sense of unity. Repetition also helps reinforce meaning and can create an appealing rhythm, as in this example.

  "**After Auschwitz, the human condition is no longer the same. After Auschwitz, nothing will ever be the same.**"

- **Parallelism** is the use of words, phrases, clauses, or lines that have a similar structure or grammatical form. Like repetition, parallelism can emphasize meaning and also produce a pleasing rhythm.

  "**In this place of darkness and malediction we can but stand in awe and remember its stateless, faceless and nameless victims.**"

Study the persuasive techniques Elie Wiesel uses as you analyze his speech.

 TEACH

CLOSE READ

Analyze Word Choices

COMMON CORE RI 4

After students read each of the two sections, discuss the boldfaced terms. Incorporate the terms *viewpoint* and *author's purpose* during discussion.

Have students use their own words to explain why each of the excerpts shown is an example of the listed persuasive technique or rhetorical device. Direct students to look back through the speech to find at least one more example of an emotional appeal, ethical appeal, repetition, and parallelism. In each case, have students explain the impact of the technique's use.

Strategies for Annotation 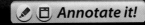 Annotate it!

Analyze Word Choices

COMMON CORE RI 4

Share these strategies for guided or independent analysis:

- Select a passage to analyze.
- Highlight in yellow repeated words or parallel structures.
- Underline words that have emotional impact.
- Note the impact of the word choices.

As we remember the solitude and the pain of its victims, let us declare this day marks our commitment to commemorate their death, not to celebrate our own victory over death.

> creates a sad tone

As we reflect upon the past, we must address ourselves to the present and the future. In the name of all that is sacred in memory,

PRACTICE & APPLY

Analyzing the Text RI 1, RI 2, RI 4, RI 5, RI 6, RI 8

Possible answers:

1. *The words are repeated in a slightly different form near the end of the speech. The repetition emphasizes this key idea in the speech and ties the whole text together, including by making a connection to the title.*

2. *"I speak to you as a man/I speak as a Jew": this parallel text emphasizes the universality of Wiesel's experience; "no name, no hope, no future": this parallel text emphasizes the utter despair in the situation.*

3. *He uses the imagery of fire to capture the idea that massive numbers of people were killed during the Holocaust. Fire was also literally a feature of the death camps, where bodies were burned in crematoria.*

4. *Wiesel is making an ethical appeal; he is calling on his audience to learn from the past and not turn a blind eye to genocide and other forms of discrimination that are occurring in the present.*

5. *Wiesel is making an emotional appeal; he is tapping into feelings of fear and pity.*

6. *Wiesel repeats this opening line of a prayer for the dead to emphasize the tragedy of what has happened; it is also perhaps a way of saying that now God's creation is comforted by God alone. It is effective because this is an ancient, sacred prayer for Jews. It honors God and the Jewish people who were killed.*

7. *Wiesel wants people to remember the horror of what happened during the Holocaust so that they step in and prevent similar events in the present and future. It is effective because of his emotional and ethical appeals.*

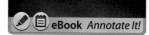

eBook *Annotate It!*

Analyzing the Text  RI 1, RI 2, RI 4, RI 5, RI 6, W 7, W 8, W 9b, SL 1a, SL 1b

Cite Text Evidence Support your responses with evidence from the text.

1. **Analyze** Wiesel's speech begins: "After Auschwitz, the human condition is not the same, nothing will be the same." Identify where similar language is repeated later in his speech. What is the effect of this repetition?

2. **Analyze** Reread lines 4–9. Identify two examples of parallelism in these lines and describe the effect of each.

3. **Interpret Imagery** Imagery consists of descriptive words and phrases that create sensory experiences for the reader. Wiesel writes: "Here heaven and earth are on fire." What image is he communicating? What effect does it have on the reader?

4. **Identify** Examine lines 51–60. What kind of appeal is Wiesel making in this part of his speech? What human values is he calling on his audience to consider?

5. **Identify** Reread lines 61–64. What kind of appeal is Wiesel making in this part of his speech? What human feelings is he tapping into to make his point?

6. **Evaluate** The sentence *Yitgadal veyitkadash, Shmay Rabba* is repeated three times in the speech. Is the use of this rhetorical device effective? Why or why not?

7. **Evaluate** Considering the author's purpose and audience, which persuasive techniques make the speech effective? Explain.

PERFORMANCE TASK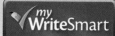

Speaking Activity: Discussion
Imagine that you have been put in charge of a museum exhibit about the Holocaust. Create a remembrance poster for the exhibit based on Elie Wiesel's speech.

- Choose two key quotes or ideas from the speech to highlight on your poster.
- Research the Holocaust, collecting information from print and digital sources.

- Select important facts, dates, quotes, and photographs to support the main points in Wiesel's speech.
- On the poster, include visuals such as a timeline or your own artwork or symbols.
- Describe your completed work to the class in an oral presentation. Discuss with classmates Wiesel's purpose and message and how your poster relates to them.

Assign this performance task.

PERFORMANCE TASK COMMON CORE W 7, W 8, SL 1a, SL 1b

Speaking Activity: Discussion Guide students to reliable sources of information about the Holocaust; offer suggestions for narrowing their search, along with these additional suggestions:

- decide on just one or two central ideas to convey
- reflect on ways to show visually the emotional content of the speech
- plan a presentation that conveys information effectively

Analyze Elements of a Speech

COMMON CORE

RI 5

TEACH

Explain that when Elie Wiesel wrote the speech students have just read, he thought about what he wanted to say and how he would organize those ideas. Tell students that most speeches have a basic organizational structure.

Display the terms *Introduction, Body,* and *Conclusion.* Present the following features of those three parts:

The **Introduction** grabs the audience's attention.

- A speaker might start with a personal story, a joke, a quotation, or an intriguing fact.
- The speaker tells what qualifies him or her to speak on this topic. The speaker also offers a preview—letting the audience know what main points will be covered in the speech.

In the **Body**, the speaker leads the audience from one main point to another.

- As the speaker shifts from one point to the next, he or she makes a connection, or **transition**, between the two. One way to make a clear transition is to sum up the main point just made and explain how it is related to the next point.

The **Conclusion** brings the speech to a satisfying close.

- The speaker reminds the audience of the main points that have been covered.
- The speech ends with a statement about what is most important to remember.
- The conclusion may refer to an idea from the Introduction.

PRACTICE AND APPLY

Have small groups work together to plan and write a speech on an issue that concerns them, from a classroom or school policy to a global problem.

- After choosing and discussing a topic, tell group members to share ideas about how the speaker might introduce the topic, present the main points, and bring the speech to a conclusion.
- Have the group divide the speech into parts and assign a writer to each.
- After the writers read their drafts aloud, other group members offer suggestions for revising to make the speech even more effective for an audience.

Analyze Persuasive Techniques

COMMON CORE

RI 4

RETEACH

Review that some forms of writing are intended mainly to **persuade**—to make readers agree with the author's viewpoint and possibly to take action. Explain that authors whose main purpose is to persuade choose words carefully and try to appeal to their readers' emotions and values.

Display the terms *emotional appeal* and *ethical appeal.* Explain that an **emotional appeal** has words that provoke strong feelings and memories. An **ethical appeal** makes readers think about values such as justice, fairness, patriotism, and opportunity.

Offer each of these examples so that students can identify the persuasive technique used—emotional or ethical appeal.

- Today is Election Day. Don't stay home! Voting is not just your right as a citizen—it's your responsibility. *(ethical appeal)*
- Here in the animal shelter, affectionate, adorable Buddy is a one-year-old mixed-breed dog in desperate need of a loving home. *(emotional appeal)*

Have students identify the impact of the word choices in each example.

 LEVEL UP TUTORIALS Assign the following *Level Up* tutorial: **Persuasive Techniques**

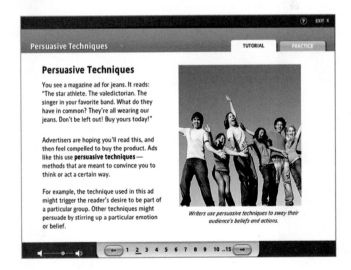

CLOSE READING APPLICATION

Direct students to common persuasive texts, such as advertisements, charity requests, political speeches, and blogs. Have students identify persuasive techniques and cite evidence to support their judgment.

There But for the Grace

Poem by Wislawa Szymborska

Why This Text?

Poetry often examines the questions and experiences of everyday life, prompting readers to think more deeply about their meaning. This poem discusses the role of chance in life, an especially provocative question for those—like Anne Frank—who experienced the Holocaust.

► View It!

Professional Development Podcast:
Teaching Argument

Key Learning Objective: The student will be able to analyze the use of sound devices in a poem to understand how they impact meaning.

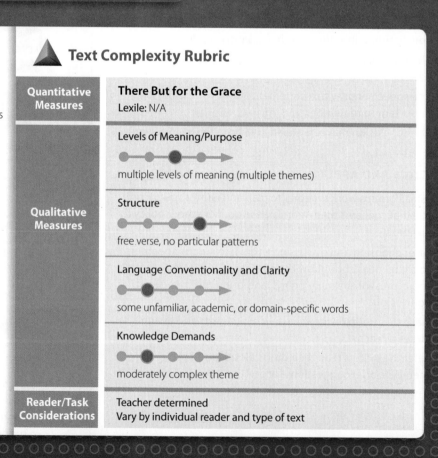

COMMON CORE Common Core Standards

RL 1 Cite textual evidence.
RL 2 Determine a theme or central idea.
RL 4 Analyze the impact of specific word choices on meaning and tone.
W 1a–e Write arguments to support claims.
W 4 Produce clear and coherent writing.
W 9a Apply Grade 8 Reading standards to literature.
W 10 Write routinely over extended time frames and shorter time frames.

▲ Text Complexity Rubric

Quantitative Measures	**There But for the Grace** Lexile: N/A
Qualitative Measures	**Levels of Meaning/Purpose** multiple levels of meaning (multiple themes)
	Structure free verse, no particular patterns
	Language Conventionality and Clarity some unfamiliar, academic, or domain-specific words
	Knowledge Demands moderately complex theme
Reader/Task Considerations	Teacher determined Vary by individual reader and type of text

Wislawa Szymborska wrote the poem "There But for the Grace" to express her feelings about why some people survived the Holocaust and some didn't. Have students read the background and information about the poet. Tell them that in "There But for the Grace," Wislawa Szymborska looks back at the German occupation of Poland and some people's seemingly arbitrary survival. While her early works were influenced by Polish history from World War II through Stalinism, her later works focus on people and everyday life. The Nobel award committee described Szymborska as the "Mozart of Poetry."

SETTING A PURPOSE Direct students to use the Setting a Purpose prompt to focus their reading. Remind them to write down their own questions as they read.

Background *On September 1, 1939, Germany invaded Poland, triggering the start of World War II. The defeat of Poland was swift, and the occupation of the country that followed became one of the cruelest chapters of the war. After their downfall, many Polish soldiers and citizens were slaughtered by the German army. Surviving Polish political leaders, Jews, and others were later collected and sent to concentration camps to be killed or to work as slaves for the Nazis. By the end of the war, more than five million Poles had died.*

There But for the Grace

Poem by Wisława Szymborska

Wisława Szymborska (1923–2012) *was born in a small town in western Poland. She was in high school when Germany invaded Poland. Despite the ban on high school education put in place by the Germans, Szymborska continued taking classes. Unlike many Poles, Szymborska was fortunate to avoid imprisonment and death at the hands of the Nazis. Szymborska has published more than a dozen collections of poetry. She has won numerous awards for her poetry, including the Nobel Prize for Literature in 1996.*

SETTING A PURPOSE As you read, think about the role that chance plays in a person's life. Write down any questions you have.

(cr) ©Mushakesa/Shutterstock; (bg) ©LiuDallas/Shutterstock; (tl) ©Czarek Sokolowski/AP/Corbis;

SCAFFOLDING FOR ELL STUDENTS

Punctuation and Print Cues Explain to students that poets sometimes use punctuation in unusual ways to establish pace or rhythm, to draw attention to an image or line, or to help convey the poet's state of mind. Tell students that a poem may contain many punctuation marks to indicate pauses or to create emphasis, or it may contain no puctuation at all. Explain that because poems are usually shorter than stories, poets use each word and punctuation mark to achieve the desired result.

ASK STUDENTS to reread lines 1–5. Have them tell how the punctuation affects the rhythm and meaning of the poem. *(Short, one word sentences followed by longer pauses give it a quick pace and emphasize the idea that things happen just by chance.)*

It could have happened.

It had to happen.

It happened sooner. Later.

Nearer. Farther.

It happened not to you.

CLOSE READ

Analyze Sound Devices COMMON CORE RL 4

(LINES 12–16)

Explain to students that poets manipulate sounds to emphasize meaning, affect mood, or unify a poem. Point out that in order to create the exact feeling and meaning a poet wants to achieve, he or she uses a variety of **sound devices**—the use of words for their connection to the sense of hearing.

A **ASK STUDENTS** to reread lines 12–16 to identify a sound or word that Szymborska emphasizes and to describe its impact. *(The word "Luckily" is repeated throughout, creating rhythm and emphasizing the idea that survival happened by chance.)*

Analyze Language COMMON CORE RL 4

(LINES 23–25)

Point out that **syntax** is the organization of words in a sentence. Explain that poets may use syntax to create an effect or to emphasize meaning.

B **CITE TEXT EVIDENCE** Ask students to reread lines 23–25. What phrase suggests that the speaker has survived a difficult situation? *("how fast your heart beats in me")* What is the impact of the choice to end the poem with the words *in me*? *(Possible answer: The words* in me *emphasize a personal aspect of the speaker's message: random events or situations can save, or doom, anyone—including the speaker.)*

COLLABORATIVE DISCUSSION During their discussions, prompt partners to share experiences they have had in which things happened that were beyond their control, as well as those in which determination affected the outcome. Remind students to also cite evidence from the text to support their ideas.

ASK STUDENTS to share any questions they generated in the course of reading and discussing this selection.

There But for the Grace

It could have happened.
It had to happen.
It happened sooner. Later.
Nearer. Farther.
5 It happened not to you.

You survived because you were the first.
You survived because you were the last.
Because you were alone. Because of people.
Because you turned left. Because you turned right.
10 Because rain fell. Because a shadow fell.
Because sunny weather prevailed.[1]

A
Luckily there was a wood.
Luckily there were no trees.
Luckily there was a rail, a hook, a beam, a brake,
15 a frame, a bend, a millimeter, a second.
Luckily a straw was floating on the surface.

Thanks to, because, and yet, in spite of.
What would have happened had not a hand, a foot,
by a step, a hairsbreadth[2]
20 by sheer coincidence.

So you're here? Straight from a moment still ajar?
The net had one eyehole, and you got through it?

B
There's no end to my wonder, my silence.
Listen
25 how fast your heart beats in me.

COLLABORATIVE DISCUSSION The speaker suggests that luck or chance plays a big part in survival. Do you agree? With a partner, discuss whether chance or determination is more likely to help a person in a difficult situation. Cite specific evidence from the text and your own knowledge or experiences to support your thoughts.

---

[1] **prevailed:** was common or frequent.
[2] **hairsbreadth:** a tiny space.

WHEN STUDENTS STRUGGLE . . .

To guide students in understanding the poem, have them create a chart to identify the series of opposites the speaker describes.

Idea	Its Opposite
happened sooner	happened later

ASK STUDENTS to tell how the opposite ideas impact the meaning of the poem. *(Possible answer: Some people survived, but others did not. Opposite ideas do not necessarily affect the outcome.)*

Analyze Sound Devices COMMON CORE RL 4

Like songs, poems are meant to be heard. **Sound devices** are the use of certain words for their connection to the sense of hearing. Poets use various sound devices to convey meaning and mood, to draw attention to certain lines or images, to engage readers, and, sometimes, to unify a work.

Poets use a sound device called **rhythm** to bring out the musical quality of language, to emphasize ideas, and to create moods. Rhythm is a pattern of stressed and unstressed syllables in a line of poetry. Notice how the speaker in "There But for the Grace" emphasizes ideas with the rhythm of one-syllable words:

> "Luckily there was a rail, a hook, a beam, a brake, . . ."

Poets also employ a variety of other sound devices to emphasize certain words or to unify a poem. The repetition of sounds, words, phrases, or lines often helps to reinforce meaning and create an appealing rhythm.

Sound Device	Definition	Example from the Poem
alliteration	repetition of consonant sounds at the beginnings of words	What would have happened had not a hand, a foot, . . .
assonance	repetition of vowel sounds within non-rhyming words	Because rain fell. Because a shadow fell. Because sunny weather prevailed.
consonance	repetition of consonant sounds within and at the ends of words	It happened sooner. Later. Nearer. Farther.
repetition	a technique in which a sound, word, phrase, or line is repeated for emphasis or unity	It could have happened. It had to happen. It happened sooner. Later.
parallelism	use of similar grammatical constructions to express ideas that are related or equal in importance	Luckily there was a wood. Luckily there were no trees.

Notice the impact of these sound devices as you continue to analyze "There But for the Grace." How does the poet's use of sound devices affect you as a reader?

TEACH

CLOSE READ

Analyze Sound Devices COMMON CORE RL 4

Review the definition of **sound devices.** Tell students that because sound devices relate to the sense of hearing, the reader can best understand their effects by reading a poem aloud.

Discuss each type of sound device, using the examples in the chart to help students understand each one. Guide students to find additional examples of sound devices in the poem.

Then have partners reread the poem. Have students discuss the impact of sound devices on the meaning and mood of the poem.

Strategies for Annotation   Annotate it!

Analyze Sound Devices COMMON CORE RL 4

Share these strategies for guided or independent analysis:

- Highlight in yellow examples of repetition.
- Highlight in green examples of alliteration.
- Continue highlighting examples of other sound devices in different colors.
- Use a note to explain the meaning and effect of each example.

Luckily there was a wood.

Luckily there were no trees.

Luckily there was a rail, a hook, a beam, a brake,

a frame, a bend, a millimeter, a second.

Luckily a straw was floating on the surface.

PRACTICE & APPLY

Analyzing the Text

COMMON CORE RL 1, RL 2, RL 4

Possible answers:

1. The theme is that there is no explanation for why some things happen in life, that they happen only by luck or chance. Sound devices—especially repetition and parallelism—help to emphasize the role that chance plays in survival.

2. The sound device used is repetition. Students should note the pattern: the words are exactly the same except for the final word. Beyond the meanings of those final words, the speaker suggests that everything could be the same in an accident or an event and that being first or last doesn't save or doom you.

3. The parallel structure of these lines emphasizes the ideas of alternating possibilities. The speaker is suggesting that all, each, or none of these causes and effects could have affected the outcome of events. Parallel structure is carried out both by the repetition of key words (because, you, of) as well as the paired phrases of each line ending with a period.

4. The sound device used is assonance. Students should note that the short a sound unifies most of the words (a, straw, was, surface) in the line and together produce a sense of finality in the stanza.

5. Students should note the alliteration in the first sounds of the words "step" and "sheer," and the consonance of the s sound in "hairsbreadth" and "coincidence." The two devices work together to unify the idea that the tiniest of things make all the difference in the way things work out.

6. The poet uses repetition to establish rhythm. The rhythm gives emphasis to the idea that many things could have happened to affect the person's survival.

7. The poem's overall tone is earnest and understated. In the last stanza, and especially in line 23, the tone changes to one that is more sarcastic or caustic.

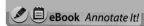

Analyzing the Text

COMMON CORE RL 1, RL 2, RL 4, W 1a–e, W 4, W 9a, W 10

Cite Text Evidence   Support your responses with evidence from the text.

1. **Interpret** What is the theme, or overall message, of this poem? Explain how the sound devices in the poem help to communicate that theme.

2. **Identify Patterns** Reread lines 6–7. What sound device is used in these lines, and what effect does it have?

3. **Analyze** Reread lines 8–11. How does the speaker use parallelism to emphasize chance?

4. **Cause/Effect** Examine line 16. Identify the sound device used, and explain how it affects the ending of the stanza.

5. **Infer** What two sound devices are used in the lines "by a step, a hairsbreadth / by sheer coincidence"? What impact does this combination of sound devices have?

6. **Evaluate** Reread stanzas 2 and 3. What does the poet do to establish rhythm in this part of the poem? How does that rhythm enhance the speaker's message?

7. **Draw Conclusions** The tone of a literary work expresses the writer's attitude toward his or her subject. Describe the overall tone of the poem, as well as the tone in line 23, "There's no end to my wonder, my silence."

PERFORMANCE TASK

Writing Activity: Analysis Respond to the poem by analyzing its connection to the topic of this collection.

- With a partner, discuss the poem's theme and how it relates to the themes present in other selections within the collection.
- Compare and contrast how similar ideas are presented across the texts.

- Identify the relationships you see between the poem's language and the events described in the other texts.
- Write one draft of your response, and then share it with your partner. Use your partner's feedback to improve and finalize your analysis.
- Publish your responses in a collection you can share with the whole class.

Assign this performance task.

PERFORMANCE TASK

COMMON CORE W 1a–e, W 4, W 9a, W 10

Writing Activity: Analysis Have students work independently. Direct them to

- create Venn diagrams to compare and contrast the theme of the poem with the themes in each selection
- use the diagrams to draft their analysis and organize their ideas
- include evidence from the texts that support their argument
- conclude by restating their main idea and insights

Theme

COMMON CORE
RL 2

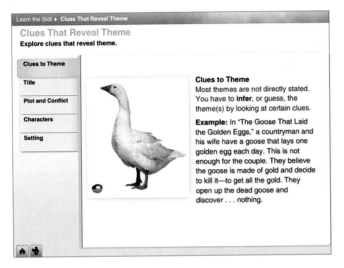

Learn the Skill ▶ Clues That Reveal Theme

Clues That Reveal Theme
Explore clues that reveal theme.

Clues to Theme
Title
Plot and Conflict
Characters
Setting

Clues to Theme
Most themes are not directly stated. You have to **infer**, or guess, the theme(s) by looking at certain clues.

Example: In "The Goose That Laid the Golden Eggs," a countryman and his wife have a goose that lays one golden egg each day. This is not enough for the couple. They believe the goose is made of gold and decide to kill it—to get all the gold. They open up the dead goose and discover . . . nothing.

TEACH

Explain that the **theme** of a poem is the message about life or human nature that a poet communicates to the reader. The theme is often implied, rather than directly stated. Readers can identify the theme by paying attention to the words and details in a poem and by asking themselves, "What big message about life is the poet trying to tell me?"

Review these steps for identifying theme:

Step 1. Examine clues in the text.

- What lesson does the title suggest?
- Which words and phrases convey a message? Is there repetition? parallelism?

Step 2. Use the clues to infer the theme.

PRACTICE AND APPLY

Have students work with a partner to apply the steps to a familiar poem they have read. After their analysis, have students share their ideas about theme with other pairs of students in the class.

Paraphrase

COMMON CORE
RL 1,
RL 2

TEACH

Tell students that one way to better understand a poem is to **paraphrase** it. Explain that to paraphrase means to restate or express a text's ideas in your own words without changing or adding to the original text's meaning.

Explain that readers often must infer ideas from the details in a poem. Point out that stopping occasionally to paraphrase can help readers be sure they understand the meaning of a poem.

Display the following lines from "There But for the Grace":

> So you're here? Straight from a moment still ajar?
>
> The net had one eyehole, and you got through it?
>
> There's no end to my wonder, my silence.
>
> Listen
>
> how fast your heart beats in me.

Work with students to paraphrase the lines. Have students

- identify the main idea, or what the poet is trying to say
- look up any unfamiliar words or phrases
- restate important ideas in their own words

Point out that the paraphrase says the same thing as the lines in the poem but uses different words.

PRACTICE AND APPLY

Have students work in small groups. Have them discuss the meaning of other stanzas in the poem. Then have students take turns paraphrasing each one.

INTERACTIVE WHITEBOARD LESSON
Analyze Imagery

Learn the Skill ▸ What Is Imagery?

What Is Imagery?

Find Out ⌄

Imagery refers to the vivid language and details writers use to create word pictures. Imagery draws on **sensory language**, words that appeal to the senses of sight, hearing, smell, taste, and touch.

TEACH

Review with students that **figurative language** is language that communicates meanings beyond the literal meanings of words. Remind them that poets use figurative language to make comparisons, create vivid images, emphasize ideas, or convey emotions.

Tell students that imagery is one type of figurative language. Explain that **imagery** is the use of words and phrases that appeal to the senses. Poets use imagery to help the reader imagine how things look, feel, smell, sound, and taste.

Guide students to identify sensory details and imagery, focusing on these steps:

Step 1. Identify sensory details. Look for words and phrases that appeal to your sense of sight, hearing, smell, taste, and touch.

Step 2. Analyze the meaning. Think about what you felt and imagined as you read the text. What mood was created? Which words and phrases helped create that mood?

PRACTICE AND APPLY

Have students work in groups to apply the steps to "There But for the Grace." Have groups compare their findings.

Analyze Sound Devices

RETEACH

Review that **sound devices** are the use of words for their connection to the sense of hearing. Prompt students to recall that poets use sound devices to emphasize meaning, affect mood, or unify a poem. Define and discuss the following sound devices:

- rhythm
- alliteration
- assonance
- consonance
- repetition
- parallelism

Provide simple examples of each, prompting students with relevant questions. For example:

> The sand sizzled in the summer sun. *(alliteration)*
> I try to light the fire alone. *(assonance)*
> I only woke by a stroke of luck. *(consonance)*

- How does this technique affect meaning?
- What mood is conveyed?

LEVEL UP TUTORIALS Assign the following *Level Up* tutorial: **Elements of Poetry**

? EXIT X

Elements of Poetry   TUTORIAL   PRACTICE

Sound Devices

Sound devices are techniques used to give poetry a musical quality. Both traditional and free verse poetry often contain sound devices.

▸ Click each sound device to learn more.

rhyme
rhythm
onomatopoeia
alliteration
assonance and consonance

← 11 12 13 14 15 16 17 18 19 20 ..21 →

CLOSE READING APPLICATION

Tell students to explore the use of sound devices in other poems they have read. Have students identify examples and explain the effect and meaning of each one.

Interactive Lessons

If you need help . . .
• **Writing Informative Texts**
• **Writing as a Process**
• **Conducting Research**

Write an Expository Essay

In Collection 5 you read about the experiences that Anne Frank and others had during the time they spent hiding from the Nazis in a small attic. What was it like to live in their secret Annex? In this activity, you will write an expository essay about the living conditions in the Annex, using details from *The Diary of Anne Frank*, other texts in the collection, and additional research.

COMMON CORE

W 2a–f Write informative/explanatory texts.

W 4 Produce clear and coherent writing.

W 5 Develop and strengthen writing.

W 7 Conduct short research projects.

W 9b Apply grade 8 Reading standards to literary nonfiction.

W 10 Write routinely over extended time frames and shorter time frames.

A successful expository essay

- provides an engaging introduction that clearly states the topic
- clearly organizes ideas and concepts to make important connections and distinctions
- includes relevant facts, definitions, and examples that support central ideas
- uses appropriate transitions to clarify relationships among ideas
- provides a conclusion that follows from and supports the information presented

PLAN

Gather Information Review *The Diary of Anne Frank* and other texts in the collection. Take notes about Anne's and her companions' experiences inside the Annex.

- Consider Anne's descriptions of the secret Annex. What do they suggest about what it was like to live in the Annex and why Anne's father may have chosen it as a hiding place?
- How did the people in hiding obtain food and other supplies? What did they eat and drink? What were they deprived of?
- Think about how the people coped with their loss of freedom. What did they do to pass the time during the day? During the evening? How were their lives different during the week and on the weekends?
- Consider the dangers the people faced. How did their helpers keep them safe? How did they communicate with them?

my Notebook

Use the annotation tools in your eBook to find evidence that supports your points about the living conditions in the Annex. Save each piece of evidence to your notebook.

ACADEMIC VOCABULARY

As you write about the living conditions of the Annex, be sure to use the academic vocabulary words.

communicate

draft

liberation

philosophy

publish

PERFORMANCE TASK

WRITE AN EXPOSITORY ESSAY

Introduce students to the Performance Task by reading the introductory paragraph with them and reviewing the criteria for what makes a good expository essay. Remind students that a good expository essay includes evidence that supports the main points the writer makes.

PLAN

CONDUCT RESEARCH

Remind students that even though the Internet can provide a lot of good information, not every website is a source that can be verified. Tell students that when conducting online research they should look for author and publication information for each website or sponsoring organization to help them determine whether the source is a credible one. Remind students that the most reliable websites usually have the extensions *.gov*, *.org*, and *.edu*. Point out that if students have concerns they should look for more reliable sources.

▶ View It!

Professional Development Podcast:

Performance Tasks

- Think about the extent to which the people in hiding were aware of events taking place in the outside world. How did they get information?

Conduct Research Use both print and digital sources to further investigate the living conditions of the Annex.

- Find facts, quotes, and examples that expand upon the information you learned in the collection.
- Search for other descriptions or photographs of the Annex. In what ways do they support the information you already gathered?
- Use credible sources. Find books using keyword or subject searches in the library. Use a search engine or Internet directories to find Internet sources.

Organize Your Ideas Think about how you will organize your essay. Group related ideas together and create an outline that identifies the central ideas and information you will include in each paragraph.

> **I.** Use Roman numerals for main topics.
>   *A.* Indent and use capital letters for subtopics.
>   1. Indent and use numbers for supporting facts and details.
>   2. Indent and use numbers for supporting facts and details.
> **II.** Use Roman numerals for main topics.
>   *B.* Indent and use capital letters for subtopics.
>   1. Indent and use numbers for supporting facts and details.

Consider Your Purpose and Audience Think about who will read or listen to your report, and what you want them to understand. What does the audience already know? What background information will they need? Keep these questions in mind as you prepare to write.

PRODUCE

Draft Your Essay Review your notes and your outline as you begin your draft.

- Introduce the topic clearly, previewing what is to follow. Include an unusual comment, fact, quote, or story to grab the reader's attention.
- Organize your information into paragraphs of similar information. Include relevant details, facts, and examples.

my **WriteSmart**

Write your rough draft in *my*WriteSmart. Focus on getting your ideas down, rather than on perfecting your choice of language.

PRODUCE

DRAFT YOUR ESSAY

As students begin their first drafts, point out that each main idea should be supported by relevant details and evidence. Suggest that students keep their outlines nearby, checking off details and facts as they write. Remind students to include only one main idea in each paragraph.

- Establish and maintain a formal style by using complete sentences with precise language. Avoid contractions and pronouns such as *I* and *you*.

- Include transition words and phrases such as *because, also, in addition, nearby,* and *finally* to clarify the relationships between ideas.

- Write a conclusion that follows from and supports your explanation.

REVISE

Evaluate Your Draft Use the chart on the next page to evaluate the content and style of your draft.

- Check that your topic is clearly defined.

- Examine your paragraphs. Does each one have a distinct central idea? Is that idea supported with relevant facts, details, and examples?

- Be sure that your ideas are organized in a logical sequence. Do transition words help readers follow along?

- Check that your conclusion summarizes the central ideas and supports the information presented.

my WriteSmart

Have a partner or a group of peers review your draft in *my*WriteSmart. Ask your reviewers to note any ideas presented in your draft that need clarification or further support.

PRESENT

Create a Finished Copy Finalize your essay and choose a way to share it with your audience. Consider these options:

- Give an oral report to classmates or community members.

- Produce a video or audio recording of you reading your essay aloud, and post the recording on an approved video- or audio-sharing website.

- Dramatize your essay, presenting the information from the perspective of a person living in the Annex.

PERFORMANCE TASK

REVISE

EVALUATE YOUR DRAFT

Have students work with a partner to revise their essays. Students can take turns reading or listening to each other's essays and offering suggestions to make them more effective. After students revise their essays, partners can reread them and discuss whether they need further revisions.

PRESENT

CREATE A FINISHED COPY

Students can
- present their essays orally to the class. Remind students to speak loudly and clearly, look directly at the audience, and use gestures and facial expressions to emphasize ideas.
- produce video or audio recordings of their essays. Students can practice with partners to help them refine their performances before recording.
- dramatize their essays from the perspective of one of the people living in the Annex. Students can work with partners to determine how to adapt their essays so that they can be performed.

PERFORMANCE TASK

LANGUAGE

Have students use the chart to evaluate how they did on the performance task in each of the three main categories. Ask them to choose one category and think about how they could improve that aspect of their writing when they write their next essay. Prompt students to check their use of precise language and formal style. You may want to provide some good models of expository writing and have students compare their essays to them.

	Ideas and Evidence	Organization	Language
ADVANCED	• The introduction is appealing and informative. • The topic is well developed with relevant facts, concrete details, interesting quotations, and examples from reliable sources. • The concluding section capably summarizes the information presented.	• The organization is effective and logical throughout the essay. • Transitions successfully connect related ideas.	• The writing maintains a formal style throughout. • Language is strong and precise. • Grammar, usage, and mechanics are correct.
COMPETENT	• The introduction could do more to grab readers' attention. • Some key points need more support from relevant facts, concrete details, quotations, and examples from reliable sources. • The concluding section summarizes the information presented.	• The organization is confusing in a few places. • A few more transitions are needed to connect related ideas.	• The style is inconsistent in a few places. • Language is too general in some places. • Some errors in grammar, usage, and mechanics are repeated in the essay.
LIMITED	• The introduction is only partly informative and could be more engaging. • Most key points need more support in the form of relevant facts, concrete details, quotations, and examples from reliable sources. • The concluding section partially summarizes the information presented.	• The organization is logical in some places but often doesn't follow a pattern. • More transitions are needed throughout to connect related ideas.	• The style becomes informal in many places. • Overly general language is used in many places. • Grammar, usage, and mechanics are incorrect in many places, but the writer's ideas are still clear.
EMERGING	• The introduction is missing. • Facts, details, quotations, and examples are from unreliable sources or are missing. • The essay lacks a concluding section.	• A logical organization is not used; information is presented randomly. • Transitions are not used, making the essay difficult to understand.	• The style is inappropriate for the essay. • Language is too general to convey the information. • Many errors in grammar, usage, and mechanics obscure the meaning of the writer's ideas.

©Debra Hughes/Shutterstock

The Value of Work

"Every job is a learning experience, and we can develop and grow in every one."

—Colin Powell

CONNECTING WORD AND IMAGE

ASK STUDENTS to discuss how the Collection Opener image and the collection quotation work together to create a connection.

PERFORMANCE TASK PREVIEW

Point out to students that they will complete two Performance Tasks at the end of the collection. The Performance Tasks will require them to further analyze the selections in the collection and to synthesize ideas about these analyses. Students will present their findings in a variety of products.

ACADEMIC VOCABULARY

View It!

Professional Development Podcast:
Academic Vocabulary

Students can acquire facility with the academic vocabulary words through frequent, repeated exposure as they analyze and discuss the selections in the collection. Academic vocabulary can be used in the instructional contexts shown below to enable students to incorporate the academic vocabulary words into their working vocabulary.

- Collaborative Discussion at the end of each selection
- Analyzing the Text questions for each selection
- Selection-level Performance Tasks
- Vocabulary instruction (for Critical Vocabulary and/or for Vocabulary Strategy)
- Language Conventions
- End-of-collection Performance Task for all selections in the collection

ASK STUDENTS to review the Academic Vocabulary word list for this collection. You may wish to pronounce each word aloud so students hear the correct pronunciation. Then, discuss the definitions and the related forms for each word. Remind students that they will encounter these five academic vocabulary words throughout the collection.

The Value of Work

In this collection, you will explore the benefits and challenges that are part of being a worker.

hmhfyi.com

COLLECTION

PERFORMANCE TASK Preview

At the end of this collection, you will complete two performance tasks:

- You will write a short story about a character who works or a character who finds a way to avoid work.

- You will write an argument to support your views about whether it is important for teenagers to get work experience during their school years.

ACADEMIC VOCABULARY

Study the words and their definitions in the chart below. You will use these words as you discuss and write about the texts in this collection.

Word	Definition	Related Forms
commentary (kŏm´ən-tĕr´ē) n.	explanation or interpretation in the form of comments or observations	comment, commentator, commentaries
minors (mī´nərz) n.	people who have not reached legal adulthood	minority, minorities
occupation (ŏk´yə-pā´shən) n.	an activity that serves as one's source of income	occupy, occupational
option (ŏp´shən) n.	something chosen or available as a choice	optional, opt
style (stīl) n.	the way in which something is said, done, expressed, or performed	stylistic, styled, stylized

©Debra Hughes/Shutterstock

394

USING COLLECTIONS YOUR WAY

Use the following information, along with the charts on the following pages, to help you decide how you want to introduce the collection. Based on your teaching style, your students' interests, or your instructional goals, you may want to structure this collection in various ways. You may choose different entry points each time you teach the collection.

"I want to challenge my students to the utmost."

Readers evaluate two arguments that focus on the reasons that teenagers need work experience.

Background *In 2008, the United States entered into what many called the Great Recession, generally considered to be America's worst economic crisis since the Great Depression of the late 1920s and 1930s. A recession is a slowdown of economic activity. During a recession, people and businesses tend to spend less money, which contributes to a cycle of job losses and decreases in profits. The effects of the Great Recession were felt for years. At the time these arguments were written, the unemployment rate was high for adult workers and even higher for young workers.*

Teens Need Jobs, Not Just Cash

Teens at Work

Argument by Anne Michaud   Argument from *The Record-Journal*

SETTING A PURPOSE As you read, consider the points each author makes about the importance of jobs for teenagers. Which reasons seem most valid to you?

I well remember how my first job made me feel: capable, creative, in charge. I was a summer counselor at a YMCA day camp, and still practically a kid myself, just out of 10th grade. I made a lot of mistakes.

As the arts and crafts counselor, I blew most of my $200 budget on Popsicle sticks and gimp.[1] We ran out of arts and crafts supplies halfway through the summer, and so taking long "nature walks" became our fallback. I wonder what the campers' parents thought.

10   Making mistakes like that is partly what early jobs are all about. We learn, and then make better decisions when the "real" job comes along.

[1] **gimp:** a narrow, flat braid used to make crafts such as a key chain.

Teens Need Jobs, Not Just Cash   **419**

"I rely heavily on novels and longer works."

This excerpt from a classic American novel shows that "work" can be a matter of perspective.

Mark Twain *(1835–1910) is the pen name of Samuel Clemens, who grew up in Missouri along the Mississippi River. Twain worked as a printer, riverboat captain, and a gold miner before finding his calling as a writer. In 1876, he published The Adventures of Tom Sawyer, which became one of his most famous works and contributed to his reputation as "the father of American literature." The excerpt included here takes place early in the book, when Tom has been commanded by his Aunt Sally to paint a fence.*

from
The Adventures of
Tom Sawyer

Novel by Mark Twain

SETTING A PURPOSE As you read, notice Tom's attitude toward his task. What lessons does he learn about work?

Tom's energy did not last. He began to think of the fun he had planned for this day, and his sorrows multiplied. Soon the free boys would come tripping along on all sorts of delicious expeditions, and they would make a world of fun of him for having to work—the very thought of it burnt him like fire. He got out his worldly wealth and examined it—bits of toys, marbles and trash; enough to buy an exchange of *work*, maybe, but not half enough to buy so much as half an hour of pure freedom. So he returned his straitened means to his pocket, and gave up the idea of trying to buy the boys. At this dark and hopeless moment an inspiration burst upon him! Nothing less than a great, magnificent inspiration.

The Adventures of Tom Sawyer   **395**

"I like to teach by comparing texts."

Related poems provide the opportunity to compare and contrast the role of work in people's lives.

ANCHOR TEXT: COMPARE POEMS

CHICAGO   FIND WORK   MY MOTHER ENTERS THE WORK FORCE

Poem by Carl Sandburg   Poem by Rhina P. Espaillat   Poem by Rita Dove

Carl Sandburg *(1878–1967) was born in Galesburg, Illinois to Swedish immigrant parents. After the eighth grade, Sandburg quit school so he could help support his family. He worked a variety of jobs, from shining shoes to delivering milk. Later, he began hopping on freight trains to explore the West. Eventually, Sandburg settled in Chicago. With the publication of his poetry collections Chicago Poems, Cornhuskers, and Smoke and Steel, Sandburg gained a reputation as a poet of the workers and common people.*

Rhina P. Espaillat *(b. 1932) was born in the Dominican Republic, but had to leave when her family was exiled for opposing the dictatorship in that country. Espaillat's family settled in New York City, where as a young girl she began writing poetry. She wrote in both English and Spanish, and has been published in both languages. Espaillat's collections of poetry have won her many prestigious literary awards.*

Rita Dove *(b. 1952) was the first African American to be named Poet Laureate of the United States, one of the highest official honors for American poets. Born in Akron, Ohio, Dove was encouraged to read by her parents and excelled at school. She was named a Presidential Scholar, one of the top one hundred high-school graduates in the country. Dove has published short stories and novels, as well as her award-winning collections of poetry. She has also written the lyrics for the songs of many renowned musical composers.*

SETTING A PURPOSE All of the poems you are about to read share a view about workers. As you read, think about what each of the poets suggests about the impact of workers on those around them.

Compare Poems   **427**

mySmartPlanner | **eBook** | **my**Notebook | **my**WriteSmart | **fyi** hmhfyi.com

Collection 6 Lessons	Media	Teach and Practice
**Student Edition	eBook**	▶ Video Links **H** HISTORY **A&E**	**Close Reading and Evidence Tracking**

ANCHOR TEXT Novel by Mark Twain from *The Adventures of Tom Sawyer*	🔊 **Audio** from *The Adventures of Tom Sawyer*	**Close Read Screencasts** • Modeled Discussion (lines 67–73) • Close Read Application (lines 120–127) **Strategies for Annotation** • Determine Meaning of Words and Phrases • Analyze Point of View • Verbal Irony and Puns
CLOSE READER Short Story by Ray Bradbury "The Flying Machine" Graphic Story by Bernard Krigstein "The Flying Machine"	🔊 **Audio** "The Flying Machine" "The Flying Machine"	
Memoir by Gary Soto "One Last Time"	🔊 **Audio** "One Last Time"	**Strategies for Annotation** • Analyze the Meanings of Words and Phrases • Using a Dictionary
CLOSE READER Biography by Jim Haskins "The Real McCoy"	🔊 **Audio** "The Real McCoy"	
Argument by Anne Michaud "Teens Need Jobs, Not Just Cash" Argument from The Record-Journal "Teens at Work"	🔊 **Audio** "Teens Need Jobs, Not Just Cash" "Teens at Work"	**Strategies for Annotation** • Delineate and Evaluate an Argument • Analyze Structure • Using Greek Suffixes
Poem by Carl Sandburg "Chicago" Poem by Rhina P. Espaillat "Find Work" Poem by Rita Dove "My Mother Enters the Work Force"	🔊 **Audio** "Chicago" "Find Work" "My Mother Enters the Work Force"	**Close Read Screencasts** • Modeled Discussion: "Chicago" (lines 11–17) "Find Work" (lines 1–5) "My Mother Enters the Work Force" (lines 8–15) • Close Read Application: "Chicago" (lines 21–26)" "Find Work" (lines 14–19) "My Mother Enters the Work Force" (lines 16–23) **Strategies for Annotation** • Determine Meaning of Words and Phrases • Analyze Structure
CLOSE READER Poem by Marge Piercy "To be of use" Poem by Simon J. Ortiz "The Story of How a Wall Stands"	🔊 **Audio** "To be of use" "The Story of How a Wall Stands"	
Collection 6 Performance Tasks: A Write a Short Story B Write an Argument	**fyi** hmhfyi.com	**Interactive Lessons** A Writing Narratives A Writing as a Process B Writing Arguments B Writing as a Process B Using Textual Evidence

For Systematic Coverage of Writing and Speaking & Listening Standards	**Interactive Lessons** Writing Informative Texts Giving a Presentation

Assess		Extend	Reteach
Performance Task	**Online Assessment**	**Teacher eBook**	**Teacher eBook**
Writing Activity: Analysis	Selection Test	**Determine Theme > Interactive Whiteboard Lesson >** Theme	**Analyze Point of View > Level Up Tutorial >** Point of View
Speaking Activity: Presentation	Selection Test	**Analyze Paragraph Structure > Interactive Whiteboard Lesson >** Patterns of Organization	**Draw Conclusions > Level Up Tutorial >** Drawing Conclusions
Speaking Activity: Oral Report	Selection Test	**Present Claims and Findings**	**Delineate and Evaluate an Argument > Level Up Tutorial >** Analyzing Arguments
Writing Activity: Compare and Contrast Essay	Selection Test	**Tone > Interactive Whiteboard Lesson >** Word Choice and Tone **Style** **Cite Evidence > Interactive Whiteboard Lesson >** Citing Textual Evidence	**Compare and Contrast Structure**
A Write a Short Story **B** Write an Argument	Collection Test		

Lesson Assessments
Writing Informative Texts
Giving a Presentation

Collection 6 Lessons	COMMON CORE Key Learning Objective	Performance Task
ANCHOR TEXT **Novel by Mark Twain** **Lexile 1040L** **from *The Adventures of Tom Sawyer,* p. 395A**	**The student will be able to . . .** recognize the characteristics of a story told by an omniscient, third-person narrator, how a third-person point of view creates dramatic irony, and how elements of a writer's style contribute to a humorous tone.	Writing Activity: Analysis
Memoir by Gary Soto **Lexile 1140L** **"One Last Time," p. 405A**	**The student will be able to . . .** cite evidence to draw conclusions about a text and analyze imagery and sensory details.	Speaking Activity: Presentation
Argument by Anne Michaud **"Teens Need Jobs, Not Just Cash," p. 419A** **Argument from *The Record-Journal* Lexile 1310L** **"Teens at Work," p. 419A**	**The student will be able to . . .** analyze an argument and determine whether its claims are sufficiently supported.	Speaking Activity: Oral Report
Poem by Carl Sandburg **"Chicago" p. 427A** **Poem by Rhina P. Espaillat** **"Find Work" p. 427A** **Poem by Rita Dove** **"My Mother Enters the Work Force," p. 427A**	**The student will be able to . . .** analyze a poem's form to understand how the use of figurative language emphasizes certain ideas.	Writing Activity: Compare and Contrast Ess

Collection 6 Performance Tasks:
A Write a Short Story
B Write an Argument

Vocabulary Strategy	Language and Style	Student Instructional Support	CLOSE READER Selection
Verbal Irony and Puns	Interrogative Mood	**Scaffolding for ELL Students:** Analyze Language: Dialect **When Students Struggle:** Model Fluency **To Challenge Students:** Create Dialogue	Short Story by Ray Bradbury "The Flying Machine," p. 404b **Lexile 790L** Graphic Story by Bernard Krigstein *"The Flying Machine,"* p. 404b
Using a Dictionary	Semicolons and Run-ons	**Scaffolding for ELL Students:** Analyze Language: Homophones **When Students Struggle:** Track Sequence of Events **To Challenge Students:** Brainstorm Titles	Biography by Jim Haskins "The Real McCoy," p. 418b **Lexile 1250L**
Using Greek Suffixes		**Scaffolding for ELL Students:** Analyze Informal Language **When Students Struggle:** Track Reasons and Evidence	
		Scaffolding for ELL Students: • Analyze Language: Suffixes • Use Cognates **When Students Struggle:** Analyze Rhythm	Poem by Marge Piercy "To be of use," p. 436b Poem by Simon J. Ortiz "The Story of How a Wall Stands," p. 436b

ANCHOR TEXT

from The Adventures of Tom Sawyer

*my*SmartPlanner Create lesson plans and access resources online.

Novel by Mark Twain

Why This Text?

This literary classic offers readers a fresh insight into what makes a task "work." In this portion of the novel, Tom Sawyer demonstrates a valuable lesson about work and the circumstances under which it can seem like play.

Key Learning Objective: The student will be able to recognize how an omniscient, third-person point of view creates dramatic irony and how elements of a writer's style contribute to a humorous tone.

For practice and application:

Close Reader selections
"The Flying Machine"
Short Story by Ray Bradbury

"The Flying Machine"
Graphic Story by Bernard Krigstein

COMMON CORE Common Core Standards

RL 1 Cite textual evidence that supports inferences.

RL 2 Determine a theme and analyze its development.

RL 3 Analyze how particular lines of dialogue in a story propel the action.

RL 4 Determine the meaning of words and phrases; analyze the impact of word choices on meaning and tone.

RL 6 Analyze how differences in points of view create dramatic irony or humor.

W 4 Produce clear and coherent writing.

W 9a Apply grade 8 Reading standards to literature.

W 10 Write routinely over extended time frames and shorter time frames.

L 1c Form and use verbs in the interrogative mood.

L 5a Interpret figures of speech (e.g., verbal irony, puns) in context.

Text Complexity Rubric

Quantitative Measures	*from* The Adventures of Tom Sawyer Lexile: 1040L
Qualitative Measures	**Levels of Meaning/Purpose** multiple levels of meaning (multiple themes)
	Structure simple, linear chronology
	Language Conventionality and Clarity some unfamiliar, academic, or domain-specific words
	Knowledge Demands experience includes unfamiliar aspects
Reader/Task Considerations	Teacher determined Vary by individual reader and type of text

Mark Twain Have students read the background information about Mark Twain and his famed novel *The Adventures of Tom Sawyer*. Explain that Twain (Samuel Clemens) was one of seven children and spent most of his childhood in Hannibal, Missouri. Twain entered the field of publishing when he was very young. To help the family after his father died, Twain got a job as a printer's apprentice at a local newspaper; he was only 12. At 15, he took a job at another newspaper, owned by his older brother.

Later in life, Twain drew on his experiences in Hannibal. In the Preface to *Tom Sawyer,* he explains: "Most of the adventures recorded in this book really occurred; one or two were experiences of my own, the rest those of boys who were schoolmates of mine. Huck Finn is drawn from life; Tom Sawyer also, but not from an individual—he is a combination of the characteristics of three boys whom I knew, and therefore belongs to the composite order of architecture."

SETTING A PURPOSE Direct students to use the Setting a Purpose question to focus their reading. Tell students to generate questions as they read.

Analyze Point of View   COMMON CORE   RL 6
(LINES 1–12)

Tell students that the **narrator** in a story or novel is the voice that is telling the story. The **point of view** is the view or perspective from which the narrator tells events. When the narrator is an outside voice, not a character in the story, the story is told from a **third-person point of view.**

A **ASK STUDENTS** to reread lines 1–12. How can you tell the point of view from which this story is told? *(The narrator refers to Tom as "he." The voice telling the story is an outside voice, not the voice of a character in the story. It is third-person point of view.)* What effect does this point of view create? *(Possible answer: The narrator is able to present a humorous view of Tom's situation.)*

Mark Twain (1835–1910) *is the pen name of Samuel Clemens, who grew up in Missouri along the Mississippi River. Twain worked as a printer, riverboat captain, and a gold miner before finding his calling as a writer. In 1876, he published* The Adventures of Tom Sawyer, *which became one of his most famous works and contributed to his reputation as "the father of American literature." The excerpt included here takes place early in the book, when Tom has been commanded by his Aunt Sally to paint a fence.*

from
The Adventures of Tom Sawyer

Novel by Mark Twain

(cr) ©PoodlesRock/Corbis; (c) ©Rikard Stadler/Shutterstock; (tl) ©A.F. Bradley, New York/New York World-Telegram & Sun Collection/Library of Congress Prints & Photographs Division; (c) ©RLN/Shutterstock

SETTING A PURPOSE As you read, notice Tom's attitude toward his task. What lessons does he learn about work?

Tom's energy did not last. He began to think of the fun he had planned for this day, and his sorrows multiplied. Soon the free boys would come tripping along on all sorts of delicious expeditions, and they would make a world of fun of him for having to work—the very thought of it burnt him like fire. He got out his worldly wealth and examined it—bits of toys, marbles and trash; enough to buy an exchange of *work*, maybe, but not half enough to buy so much as half an hour of pure freedom. So he returned his straitened means to his
10 pocket, and gave up the idea of trying to buy the boys. At this dark and hopeless moment an inspiration burst upon him! Nothing less than a great, magnificent inspiration.

A

Close Read Screencasts   View It!

Modeled Discussions

Have students click the *Close Read* icon in their eBooks to access a screencast in which readers discuss and annotate lines 67–73, a key passage describing Tom's encounter with his friend Ben Rogers.

As a class, view and discuss this video. Then, have students work in pairs to do an independent close read of an additional passage—the lesson Tom learns by convincing his friends to whitewash the fence (lines 120–127).

Analyze Language

COMMON CORE RL 4, RL 6

(LINES 15–17)

Draw attention to Twain's description of Ben Rogers's approach.

B **ASK STUDENTS** to reread lines 15–17. What does Twain mean when he says Ben's "heart was light and his anticipations high"? *(Possible answer: Ben is feeling happy and carefree.)* What is the impact of the phrase on the tone or feeling of the text? *(It creates some suspense about how Ben's encounter with Tom will go because his good mood is in stark contrast to the way Tom is feeling.)*

CRITICAL VOCABULARY

tranquil: Although Tom is unhappy about having to miss the fun he had planned for the day, he calmly begins his work.

ASK STUDENTS to explain why Tom is painting in a tranquil way. *(He wants to appear undisturbed and relaxed in order to give the impression that the work he is doing is enjoyable.)*

SCAFFOLDING FOR ELL STUDENTS

Analyze Language Using a whiteboard, project passages that include dialogue between the two boys. Explain that **dialect** is a form of a language spoken in a particular place or by a particular group of people. Guide students to use context to determine the meaning of dialect used by Tom and his friend Ben.

ASK STUDENTS to tell the meaning of the highlighted text by restating it in standard English.

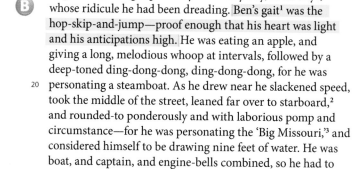

B   He took up his brush and went **tranquilly** to work. Ben Rogers hove in sight presently—the very boy, of all boys, whose ridicule he had been dreading. Ben's gait[1] was the hop-skip-and-jump—proof enough that his heart was light and his anticipations high. He was eating an apple, and giving a long, melodious whoop at intervals, followed by a deep-toned ding-dong-dong, ding-dong-dong, for he was

20   personating a steamboat. As he drew near he slackened speed, took the middle of the street, leaned far over to starboard,[2] and rounded-to ponderously and with laborious pomp and circumstance—for he was personating the 'Big Missouri,'[3] and considered himself to be drawing nine feet of water. He was boat, and captain, and engine-bells combined, so he had to imagine himself standing on his own hurricane deck giving the orders and executing them:

tranquil
(trăng′kwəl) *adj.* If something is *tranquil*, it is calm.

---

[1] **gait:** a rhythmical way of walking.
[2] **starboard:** the right side of a boat or ship.
[3] **Big Missouri:** the name of a riverboat.

396   Collection 6

©PoodlesRock/Corbis

'Why, it's you. Ben! I warn't noticing.'

'Say—*I'm* going in a-swimming, *I* am. Don't you wish

you could? But of course you'd druther *work*—wouldn't you?'

'Stop her, sir! Ting-a-ling-ling.' The headway ran almost out, and he drew up slowly toward the sidewalk.

30 'Ship up to back! Ting-a-ling-ling!' His arms straightened and stiffened down his sides.

'Set her back on the stabboard! Ting-a-ling-ling! Chow! ch-chow-wow! Chow!' His right hand meantime describing stately circles, for it was representing a forty-foot wheel.

'Let her go back on the labboard! Ting-a-ling-ling! Chow-ch-chow-chow!' The left hand began to describe circles.

'Stop the stabboard! Ting-a-ling-ling! Stop the labboard! Come ahead on the stabboard! Stop her! Let your outside turn over slow! Ting-a-ling-ling! Chow-ow-ow! Get out that

40 head-line! *Lively*, now! Come—out with your spring-line— what're you about there? Take a turn round that stump with the bight of it! Stand by that stage now—let her go! Done with the engines, sir! Ting-a-ling-ling! *Sh't! s'h't! s'h't!*' (trying the gauge-cocks).

Tom went on whitewashing—paid no attention to the steam-boat. Ben stared a moment, and then said:

'Hi-*yi! You're* up a stump,[4] ain't you?'

No answer. Tom **surveyed** his last touch with the eye of an artist; then he gave his brush another gentle sweep, and

50 surveyed the result, as before. Ben ranged up alongside of him. Tom's mouth watered for the apple, but he stuck to his work. Ben said:

'Hello, old chap; you got to work, hey?'

Tom wheeled suddenly and said:

'Why, it's you. Ben! I warn't noticing.'

'Say—*I'm* going in a-swimming, *I* am. Don't you wish you could? But of course you'd druther[5] *work*—wouldn't you? Course you would!'

Tom **contemplated** the boy a bit, and said:

60 'What do you call work?'

'Why, ain't *that* work?'

Tom resumed his whitewashing, and answered carelessly:

'Well, maybe it is, and maybe it ain't. All I know is, it suits Tom Sawyer.'

survey
(sər-vā´) *v.* If you *survey* something, you inspect it.

contemplate
(kŏn´təm-plāt´) *v.* When you *contemplate*, you look at something attentively and thoughtfully.

---

[4] **up a stump:** an expression that means someone has a big problem.
[5] **druther:** rather.

The Adventures of Tom Sawyer **397**

CLOSE READ

Analyze Point of View

COMMON CORE RL 1, RL 6

(LINES 53–64)

Tell students that a third-person narrator can sometimes be **omniscient,** or all knowing. Explain that an omniscient narrator knows everything about the characters and the story events.

C **CITE TEXT EVIDENCE** Have students reread lines 53–64. What are two things that the omniscient narrator knows and tells readers that Ben Rogers does not know? *(Tom actually* does *notice Ben's presence even though he says he "warn't noticing." Tom considers painting the fence work although he says otherwise and claims that it "suits" him.)* What effect does the narrator's point of view create? *(Possible answer: The narrator is leading readers to suspect what Tom might do to avoid his work.)*

> **CRITICAL VOCABULARY**
>
> **survey**: Tom continues whitewashing, ignoring his friend Ben as he pretends to be a steamboat.
>
> **ASK STUDENTS** to tell what impression Tom is trying to give as he surveys his work. *(Tom wants Ben to think that like an artist at work he is focused intently on his painting and is unaware of Ben's presence.)*
>
> **contemplate**: Ben invites Tom to go swimming with him and suggests that perhaps Tom would rather work.
>
> **ASK STUDENTS** why Tom contemplates Ben after Ben offers his invitation. *(Part of Tom's scheme is to seem thoughtful and serious in order to blur the line between appearance and reality.)*

APPLYING ACADEMIC VOCABULARY

commentary	style

As you discuss the novel excerpt, incorporate the following Collection 6 academic vocabulary words: *commentary* and *style*. Ask students to discuss what **commentary** they think Twain is making on human nature as well as on the meaning of work. Have students analyze Twain's **style** as they read. How do they think word choice, sentence structure, imagery, and tone contribute to his style?

Analyze Point of View

 RL 6

(LINES 80–92)

Explain that **irony** is a special kind of contrast in which reality is the opposite of what it seems. In one type of irony, **dramatic irony,** the reader knows something that a story character does not.

D **ASK STUDENTS** to reread lines 80–92. What do readers know that Ben does not? *(Ben doesn't know that Tom really wants him to paint the fence and that the story Tom is telling is untrue.)* How does Twain create dramatic irony here? *(The true situation is revealed to readers by the omniscient narrator who tells the story from the third-person point of view.)*

CRITICAL VOCABULARY

particular: Although Ben offers to help whitewash the fence, Tom says Aunt Polly probably wouldn't approve.

ASK STUDENTS why, according to Tom, Aunt Polly is particular about this fence. *(It's in the front of the house, right "on the street" where everyone will see it.)* Which fence would she be less particular about? *(the back fence)*

alacrity: Although Tom looks reluctant as he hands his paintbrush to Ben, his true feelings are quite different.

ASK STUDENTS to explain why Tom feels "alacrity in his heart" as Ben is about to begin working. *(Tom is cheerful and eager on the inside because he has gotten what he wants all along: Ben will do his work while he relaxes and enjoys eating the apple. However, Tom can't allow his true feelings to show because then Ben might realize he has been tricked.)*

'Oh, come now, you don't mean to let on that you *like* it?'

The brush continued to move.

'Like it? Well, I don't see why I oughtn't to like it. Does a boy get a chance to whitewash a fence every day?'

That put the thing in a new light. Ben stopped nibbling his
70 apple. Tom swept his brush daintily back and forth—stepped back to note the effect—added a touch here and there—criticized the effect again—Ben watching every move, and getting more and more interested, more and more absorbed.

Presently he said: 'Say, Tom, let *me* whitewash a little.'

Tom considered—was about to consent; but he altered his mind:

'No, no; I reckon it wouldn't hardly do, Ben. You see, Aunt Polly's awful **particular** about this fence—right here on the street, you know—but if it was the back fence I wouldn't mind,
80 and *she* wouldn't. Yes, she's awful particular about this fence; it's got to be done very careful; I reckon there ain't one boy in a thousand, maybe two thousand, that can do it the way it's got to be done.'

'No—is that so? Oh, come now; lemme just try, only just a little. I'd let *you*, if you was me, Tom.'

'Ben, I'd like to, honest Injun; but Aunt Polly—well, Jim wanted to do it, but she wouldn't let him. Sid wanted to do it, and she wouldn't let Sid. Now, don't you see how I'm fixed? If you was to tackle this fence, and anything was to happen
90 to it—'

'Oh, shucks; I'll be just as careful. Now lemme try. Say—I'll give you the core of my apple.'

'Well, here—No, Ben; now don't; I'm afeard—'

'I'll give you *all* of it!'

Tom gave up the brush with reluctance in his face but **alacrity** in his heart. And while the late steamer 'Big Missouri' worked and sweated in the sun, the retired artist sat on a barrel in the shade close by, dangled his legs, munched his apple, and planned the slaughter of more innocents. There
100 was no lack of material; boys happened along every little while; they came to jeer, but remained to whitewash. By the time Ben was fagged out,[6] Tom had traded the next chance

particular
(pər-tĭk′yə-lər) *adj.*
If you are *particular* about something, you are fussy about it and pay attention to its details.

alacrity
(ə-lăk′rĭ-tē) *n. Alacrity* is cheerful willingness or eagerness.

---

[6] **fagged out:** tired.

WHEN STUDENTS STRUGGLE . . .

Use the text on page 398 to help students develop automaticity and improve oral proficiency. Remind students that fluent readers read with expression and at a good pace.

- Explain how to use punctuation marks, such as commas, dashes, and question marks, to know where to pause and when to change intonation.
- Model for students an effective reading of the text.
- Finally, have students work in groups of three to practice reading the page. Ask one student to read the part of the narrator, another the words spoken by Tom, and the third the part of Ben.

> ❝ Tom gave up the brush with reluctance in his face but *alacrity* in his heart. ❞

to Billy Fisher for a kite, in good repair; and when *he* played out, Johnny Miller bought in for a dead rat and a string to swing it with; and so on, and so on, hour after hour. And when the middle of the afternoon came, from being a poor poverty-stricken boy in the morning, Tom was literally rolling in wealth. He had, beside the things before mentioned, twelve marbles, part of a jew's-harp,[7] a piece of blue bottle-glass to
110 look through, a spool-cannon,* a key that wouldn't unlock anything, a fragment of chalk, a glass stopper of a decanter,[8] a tin soldier, a couple of tadpoles, six fire-crackers, a kitten with only one eye, a brass door-knob, a dog-collar—but no dog—the handle of a knife, four pieces of orange-peel, and a **dilapidated** old window-sash. He had had a nice, good, idle time all the while—plenty of company—and the fence had three coats of whitewash on it! If he hadn't run out of whitewash, he would have bankrupted every boy in the village.
120   Tom said to himself that it was not such a hollow world, after all. He had discovered a great law of human action, without knowing it—namely, that in order to make a man

dilapidated
(dĭ-lăp´ĭ-dā´tĭd) *adj.*
If something is *dilapidated*, it is falling apart.

---
[7] **jew's-harp:** a musical instrument that is held between the teeth and plucked to produce a sound.
[8] **glass stopper of a decanter:** the glass top of a special kind of bottle.

The Adventures of Tom Sawyer **399**

©RLN/Shutterstock

CLOSE READ

Determine Meaning of Words and Phrases

COMMON CORE RL 1, RL 4, RL 6

(LINES 105–118)

Help students understand that the style of a literary work is the way in which it is written. **Style** refers to *how* something is said, not *what* is said. Explain that Twain's **tone,** or attitude toward his subject, is part of his writing style.

🅔 **CITE TEXT EVIDENCE** Have students reread lines 105–118 to identify parts of the text that contribute to Twain's style. How do Twain's word choices impact the tone? *(Possible answer: "from being a poor poverty-stricken boy in the morning, Tom was literally rolling in wealth"; "a key that wouldn't unlock anything"; "a dog-collar—but no dog"; "If he hadn't run out of whitewash, he would have bankrupted every boy in the village." Twain's word choices create a humorous tone.)*

> **CRITICAL VOCABULARY**
>
> **dilapidated**: Tom's friends give up many prized possessions for the privilege of painting the fence.
>
> **ASK STUDENTS** how one boy may have come to own a dilapidated window sash. *(Possible answer: Because the window sash was in poor condition, it was likely thrown out after being replaced with a new sash.)*

Strategies for Annotation   🖉 📋 *Annotate it!*

Determine Meaning of Words and Phrases (LINES 105–118)

COMMON CORE RL 1, RL 4, RL 6

Share these strategies for guided or independent analysis:

- Highlight in blue phrases that contribute to Twain's style.
- Add a note explaining how word choices impact tone.

a key that wouldn't unlock anything, a fragment of chalk, a glass stopper of a decanter, a tin soldier, a couple of tadpoles, six fire-crackers, a kitten with only one eye, a brass door-knob, a dog-collar— but no dog —the handle of a knife, four pieces of oran

Tom is glad to have useless things; creates a funny tone

Determine Meaning of Words and Phrases

 COMMON CORE RL 1, RL 4

(LINES 124–127)

Remind students that the tone is a writer's attitude toward his or her subject.

F CITE TEXT EVIDENCE Have students reread the sentence in lines 124–127. What is the impact of this sentence on the tone of the text? *(The sentence creates a humorous tone.)* Who is Twain making fun of? *(himself: "a great and wise philosopher, like the writer of this book")*

CRITICAL VOCABULARY

covet: Tom figured out a way to make his friends covet something.

ASK STUDENTS What was Tom able to make the other boys covet? *(They coveted the opportunity to help whitewash the fence.)*

attain: Tom thinks he has discovered a law of human nature.

ASK STUDENTS what Tom learns about things that are difficult to attain. *(People desire and will work to gain things that are hard to attain.)*

COLLABORATIVE DISCUSSION Before partners begin their discussion, remind them to study what the characters say and do as well as what the omniscient narrator explains about events. Once pairs have identified specific evidence from the text about the boys' work experiences, ask them to share their conclusions with the class.

ASK STUDENTS to share any questions they generated in the course of reading and discussing the selection.

---

or a boy **covet** a thing, it is only necessary to make the thing difficult to **attain**. If he had been a great and wise philosopher, like the writer of this book, he would now have comprehended that Work consists of whatever a body is *obliged*[9] to do, and that Play consists of whatever a body is not obliged to do. And this would help him to understand why constructing artificial flowers or performing on a treadmill is work, while
130 rolling ten-pins[10] or climbing Mont Blanc is only amusement. There are wealthy gentlemen in England who drive four-horse passenger-coaches twenty or thirty miles on a daily line in the summer, because the privilege costs them considerable money; but if they were offered wages for the service, that would turn it into work, and then they would resign.

The boy mused a while over the substantial change which had taken place in his worldly circumstances, and then wended[11] toward head-quarters to report.

covet
(kŭv´ĭt) *v.* If you *covet* something, you strongly wish for it.

attain
(ə-tān´) *v.* If you *attain* something, you gain it or achieve it.

COLLABORATIVE DISCUSSION With a partner, discuss what you think Tom learned from this work experience. What do you imagine the other boys learned? Cite specific evidence from the text to support your ideas.

---

[9] **obliged:** forced.
[10] **rolling ten-pins:** bowling.
[11] **wended:** proceeded or traveled.

TO CHALLENGE STUDENTS . . .

Create Dialogue Have students reread lines 120–124, focusing on what Tom Sawyer learned from his experience with the fence. Ask students to consider what Ben Rogers might have learned.

ASK STUDENTS to imagine the dialogue that might take place between Ben Rogers and his parents were he to describe how he came to whitewash the fence. Tell students to reread appropriate sections of the text to find details that will make the dialogue reflect Ben's personality. Have partners work together to write and role-play the conversation.

Analyze Point of View

COMMON CORE RL 4, RL 6

The **narrator** in a story or novel is the voice that is telling the story. The narrator may be a story character or an outside voice created by the author. The **point of view** in a story is the view or perspective from which the narrator tells events. When the narrator is an outside voice, the story is told from a **third-person point of view**. A third-person narrator may sometimes be **omniscient,** or all-knowing. An omniscient narrator

- knows everything about all the characters, including their thoughts and feelings
- knows everything about story events

An author's use of an omniscient narrator can create dramatic irony in a story. **Irony** is a special kind of contrast in which reality is the opposite of what it seems. In **dramatic irony,** the narrator reveals to readers something that a story character does not know. For example, in the following passage the reader knows something that Ben Rogers does not:

> Tom surveyed his last touch with the eye of an artist; then he gave his brush another gentle sweep, and surveyed the result, as before. Ben ranged up alongside of him. Tom's mouth watered for the apple, but he stuck to his work.

As you analyze the story, look for another example of how the third-person point of view creates dramatic irony.

Determine Meaning of Words and Phrases

COMMON CORE RL 4, RL 6

The **style** of a literary work is the way in which the work is written. Style refers to how something is said rather than to what is said. Word choice, sentence structure, imagery, and tone all contribute to the style of a piece of writing.

Mark Twain's **humorous tone,** or amused attitude toward his subject, is part of his famous writing style. Notice the way Twain's word choice and use of irony create humor in this passage:

> Tom gave us the brush with reluctance in his face but alacrity in his heart. And while the late steamer 'Big Missouri' worked and sweated in the sun, the retired artist say on a barrel . . . and planned the slaughter of more innocents.

Look for more examples of Twain's style as you analyze the text.

CLOSE READ

Analyze Point of View

COMMON CORE RL 4, RL 6

Discuss and define *narrator, point of view, third-person point of view,* and *omniscient.* Point out that a third-person narrator is called **omniscient** when the narrator knows everything about the characters and about story events. As needed, explain that the prefix *omni-* means "all."

Point out the explanations of *irony* and *dramatic irony.* Ask students to explain why the passage in bold type is an example of how an omniscient third-person point of view can create dramatic irony. *(Readers understand that Tom is not actually absorbed in his work, but Ben does not.)* Then, have students point out another example from the text. *(Possible answer: Readers know that Tom really wants to go swimming, but he convinces Ben otherwise.)* What is the effect of Twain's use of dramatic irony? *(Possible answer: The combination of Tom's cleverness and Ben's gullibillity creates humor.)*

Determine Meaning of Words and Phrases

COMMON CORE RL 4, RL 6

Discuss with students the meanings of the terms *word choice, sentence structure, imagery,* and *tone.* Ask students to point out and explain an example of each from the selection.

Have students find and share distinct phrases or individual word choices from the text and explain their appeal as well as how they contribute to Twain's style and to the tone of the text.

Strategies for Annotation   *Annotate it!*

Analyze Point of View

COMMON CORE RL 4, RL 6

Share these strategies for guided or independent analysis:

- Highlight in green text in which the omniscient narrator reveals to readers Tom's true thoughts or feelings.
- Add a note explaining how the text helps create dramatic irony.

So he returned his straitened means to his pocket, and gave up the idea of trying to buy the boys. At this dark and hopeless moment an inspiration burst upon him! Nothing less than a great, magnificent inspiration.

> Readers know Tom has an idea to solve his problem.

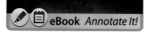

Analyzing the Text

COMMON CORE RL 1, RL 2, RL 3, RL 4

Possible answers:

1. The narrator is third-person omniscient: the narrator refers to Tom as "he" and knows what Tom is thinking: "began to think of the fun he had planned." The narrator also knows what Ben is thinking: "for he was personating a steamboat."

2. As Ben approaches Tom, he is eating an apple and impersonating a steamboat. He is at once the boat, the captain, and the engine-bells, making the sounds and movements of each. He is both giving orders (as captain) and then executing them.

3. Tom is successful in convincing Ben that whitewashing the fence is a highly skilled task that can be done only by certain people.

4. One example of Twain's use of dramatic irony to create humor is when Tom manipulates Ben by explaining to him how "particular" Aunt Polly is about the fence. Readers know that Tom is planning "the slaughter of more innocents," but the characters in the story are unaware of his intentions.

5. Tom's friends generally avoid work but will give up a lot for what they consider fun.

6. Twain's style incorporates informal language and humor, as in lines 60–61: 'What do you call work?' 'Why ain't that work?' Twain's use of an omniscient narrator lets readers in on the joke as Tom continues to manipulate Ben.

7. The message combines a serious and humorous tone. Though Twain pokes fun at himself ("a great and wise philosopher, like the writer of this book"), he also shares a serious message that play can be anything a person is not required to do.

Analyzing the Text

 eBook Annotate It!

COMMON CORE RL 1, RL 2, RL 3, RL 4, RL 6, W 4, W 9a, W 10

Cite Text Evidence Support your responses with evidence from the text.

1. **Identify** In lines 1–29, what words and phrases help you to determine the type of narrator telling this story? Identify the point of view being used.

2. **Summarize** Summarize Ben Rogers' sounds and movements in lines 20–44. Identify the phrases that best help you picture what he's doing.

3. **Analyze** The written conversation between two or more characters in a story is called **dialogue**. Analyze the dialogue between Tom and Ben that occurs in lines 53–94. What leads Ben to change his attitude about whitewashing the fence?

4. **Analyze** How does Mark Twain use dramatic irony to create humor? Give at least one specific example.

5. **Draw Conclusions** Reread lines 99–105. What conclusions can you draw about Tom's friends' attitudes toward work from this passage?

6. **Evaluate** Describe Mark Twain's writing style in this selection. In a chart like the one below, give examples of the word choices and use of irony that contribute to his style.

Word choice	Irony

7. **Evaluate** Reread lines 120–138. Do you think the message in this passage is serious or humorous, or some combination of both? Use examples from the text to explain your answer.

PERFORMANCE TASK

Writing Activity: Analysis Write an analysis that explains how the **theme**—the lesson or message— of this selection is developed through the character of Tom Sawyer.

- Work with a partner to create a character chart for Tom. In the left column, list his qualities. In the right column, list the passages from the text that demonstrate each quality.

- Next, determine the theme of the selection, drawing on the narrator's description of the lesson Tom learns.
- When you are ready, begin your analysis by stating the theme. Then, describe how the theme is developed in relation to Tom's thoughts, feelings, speech, and actions.

PERFORMANCE TASK

COMMON CORE RL 2, W 4, W 9a, W 10

Assign this performance task.

Writing Activity: Analysis See the lesson on page 404a for instruction on identifying theme.

- Before partners begin their work, review that a theme is a message or lesson about life that an author wants to share. As needed, discuss the themes of other familiar stories.

- Then, ask students to suggest character traits, or qualities, that Tom exhibits. Prompt students to consider how those qualities might reflect the theme.

Critical Vocabulary

 COMMON CORE L 5a

tranquil	survey	contemplate	particular
alacrity	dilapidated	covet	attain

Practice and Apply Use what you know about the Vocabulary words to answer the following questions.

1. When did you **contemplate** something very carefully? Why?

2. What have you worked hard to **attain**? Explain the steps you took.

3. When did someone **covet** something of yours? What happened?

4. What in your school or town has become **dilapidated**? Why?

5. What places do you think are **tranquil**?

6. When did you **survey** a situation before taking action? Why?

7. What is something that your teacher is **particular** about?

8. When did you begin a task with **alacrity**? Why?

Vocabulary Strategy: Verbal Irony and Puns

A **figure of speech** is a word or phrase that goes beyond the literal meanings of the words to create a special effect. Verbal irony and puns are two kinds of figures of speech. Verbal irony exists when someone knowingly exaggerates or says one thing while meaning another, such as in this example.

> "Say—I'm going in a swimming, I am. Don't you wish you could? But of course you'd druther *work*—wouldn't you?"

A **pun** is a humorous play on words. Some puns involve using different meanings of the same word, as in this passage where "played out" can mean "tired out; exhausted" or "finished play that was once considered work":

> "... Tom had traded the next chance to Billy Fisher for a kite, in good repair; and when he played out, Johnny Miller bought in for a dead rat and a string to swing it with ..."

Practice and Apply Identify the verbal irony or pun in each sentence and explain its meaning.

1. Ned said, "I just love working in the hot sun. When can we do this again?"

2. Billy Fisher was a minor character and remained one as an adult.

3. Kara read that Tom Sawyer tricked the boys. "What a good friend!" she remarked.

4. His friends none the wiser, Tom surveyed the results of his whitewashing.

PRACTICE & APPLY

Critical Vocabulary

 COMMON CORE L 5a

Possible answers:

1. *I contemplated something very carefully when I had to decide how to spend my allowance.*

2. *I had to practice every day to have a successful piano recital.*

3. *My sister coveted a new sweater I got as a gift.*

4. *A building near school is very rundown.*

5. *A beach at dawn is tranquil.*

6. *I surveyed a hill before starting to ski down.*

7. *My teacher is particular about using clear handwriting.*

8. *I began a task with alacrity when I was in charge of making ice-cream cones at the town fair.*

Vocabulary Strategy: Verbal Irony and Puns

Answers:

1. *This is verbal irony because Ned really doesn't want to work in the hot sun again.*

2. *In this pun,* minor *can mean "lesser in importance" or "not yet a legal adult."*

3. *This is verbal irony because Tom Sawyer wasn't acting like a good friend.*

4. *In this pun,* whitewashing *can mean "painting with a lime/water mixture to make something white" or "deception."*

Strategies for Annotation *Annotate it!*

Verbal Irony and Puns

COMMON CORE L 5a

Share these strategies for guided or independent analysis:

- Highlight in green words or phrases that can have more than one meaning.
- Add a note explaining how the word or phrase creates a pun.

> By the time Ben was fagged out, Tom had traded the next chance to Billy Fisher for a kite, in good repair; and when *he* played out, Johnny Miller bought in for a dead rat and a string to s
> and so on, and so on, hour after hour. And when the m

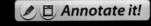

"Played" can mean "had fun" or "to be finished."

Language Conventions: Interrogative Mood

COMMON CORE L 1c

Use the chart to explain the function of the interrogative, indicative, and imperative moods. Discuss the examples, pointing out that each one comes from the selection.

Next, ask students to find another example of each mood in the text, for example:

- "What do you call work?" (interrogative)
- "I'll give you the core of my apple." (indicative)
- "Come ahead on the stabboard!" (imperative)

Possible answers:

1. indicative; Will Tom have a moment of great inspiration?

2. indicative; Did Ben scratch his nose as he stood by the fence?

3. imperative; Will you let me whitewash a little?

4. imperative; Will Tom give Ben the brush and then watch him work?

5. indicative; Was Tom rolling in wealth after a while?

6. imperative; Who traded tadpoles for a chance to whitewash the fence?

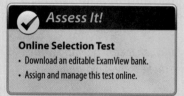

Language Conventions: Interrogative Mood

COMMON CORE L 1c

The **mood of a verb** shows the status of the action or condition it describes. The following chart shows several kinds of verb moods and their purposes.

Type of Mood	When It's Used	Example
interrogative mood	when asking a question	"Does a boy get a chance to whitewash a fence every day?"
indicative mood	when stating a fact or an opinion	"Tom's energy did not last."
imperative mood	when making a command or a request	"Stop her!"

Sentences that use the **interrogative mood,** or the mood that asks a question, often invert the subject-verb order so that the helping verb comes before the subject. In the examples below, notice how the subject-verb order changes between the sentence in the indicative mood and the one in the interrogative mood.

Indicative mood: **You can earn a paycheck.**

Interrogative mood: **Can you earn a paycheck?**

Practice and Apply Identify the mood of the boldfaced verbs in each sentence. Then, rewrite each sentence using the interrogative mood.

1. Tom **will have** a moment of great inspiration.

2. Ben **scratched** his nose as he **stood** by the fence.

3. **Let** me whitewash a little!

4. **Give** Ben the brush, and then **watch** him work.

5. After a while, Tom **was rolling** in wealth.

6. **Trade** the tadpoles for a chance to whitewash the fence.

Determine Theme

COMMON CORE

RL 2

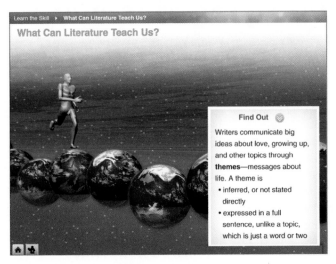

Learn the Skill ▶ What Can Literature Teach Us?

What Can Literature Teach Us?

Find Out

Writers communicate big ideas about love, growing up, and other topics through **themes**—messages about life. A theme is
• inferred, or not stated directly
• expressed in a full sentence, unlike a topic, which is just a word or two

TEACH

Provide instruction in theme before students begin the performance task. Explain that the **theme** of a literary work is a message about life or human nature that the writer shares with readers and that often readers must infer what the writer's message is. Point out that one way of determining a story's theme is to analyze how the main character responds to conflict and what he or she learns as a result.

Discuss the difference between a topic and a theme. Then, review these four types of clues that may help reveal a story's theme:

Title	The title may reflect a story's theme.
Plot and Conflict	A story's plot often revolves around a conflict that relates to a theme.
Characters	What characters do, say, and learn can reflect a theme.
Setting	A setting can suggest a theme through its effects on the characters and on story events.

PRACTICE AND APPLY

Work with students to determine the theme of a fable and a poem in the Practice & Apply section of the Interactive Whiteboard lesson. Then, ask partners to apply the skill further by identifying the theme of the excerpt they just read from *The Adventures of Tom Sawyer.*

Analyze Point of View

COMMON CORE

RL 6

RETEACH

Review the terms *narrator, point of view, third-person point of view,* and *omniscient.* Remind students that **point of view** is the vantage point, or position, from which a story is told. Explain that an author creates the point of view by choosing a **narrator,** the voice that tells the story.

Ask students to imagine that they attended a performance by a favorite music group. Have them consider how different people, or narrators, might describe what took place at the concert:

• What would the story be like if they were telling about the performance?
• How might the story be different if the performers themselves were describing what happened or if the students' parents were describing the event?

Point out that a narrator can either be a character in the story or an outside observer. A narrator from outside the story is sometimes **omniscient,** or all knowing.

LEVEL UP TUTORIALS Assign one or more of the following *Level Up* tutorials: **Point of View; Third-Person Point of View; Narrator and Speaker**

? EXIT X

Point of View

TUTORIAL   PRACTICE

What Is Point of View?

Let's say you and a friend see someone struggling in the water, and you rescue him. Later, when you tell what happened, your account and your friend's would probably be similar, wouldn't it?

But what if the rescued person told his story? Would it sound just like yours? Probably not! This is because his story is from a different **point of view.** Click each image to see an example.

Click this image   Click this image

1 **2** 3 4 5 6 7 8 9 10 ..17

CLOSE READING APPLICATION

Student partners can work together to apply the skill to other works of fiction. Have students find examples of literature in which the narrator is a character in the story, as well as examples in which the narrator is an omniscient, outside observer who tells the story from a third-person point of view.

Comparing Versions of The Flying Machine

The Flying Machine

Short Story by Ray Bradbury

The Flying Machine

Graphic Story by Ray Bradbury, *illustrated by* **Bernard Krigstein**

Why These Texts

Students need practice comparing two versions of the same story, written in two different forms. "The Flying Machine" provides an opportunity to analyze Ray Bradbury's short story and compare it to a graphic story version. With the help of close-reading questions, students will analyze both versions of the story, and grasp their meaning. This close reading will prepare students to compare the two forms of the story and to consider the advantages of one form over the other.

Background Have students read the background and the information about the author. Introduce the selection by emphasizing that Bradbury has said he tells tales to warn people about the dangers in the world around them. Tell students they are going to read two versions of the same story. After they read the short story, they will read a graphic version of the story that is illustrated by Bernard Krigstein.

SETTING A PURPOSE Ask students to pay attention to Bradbury's message. How soon do you begin to understand Bradbury's warning in "The Flying Machine"?

Common Core Support

- cite strong textual evidence
- determine the meaning of words and phrases as they are used in text
- analyze the impact of specific word choices on meaning and tone
- compare and contrast the structure of two or more texts
- analyze how differences in points of view create effects such as suspense

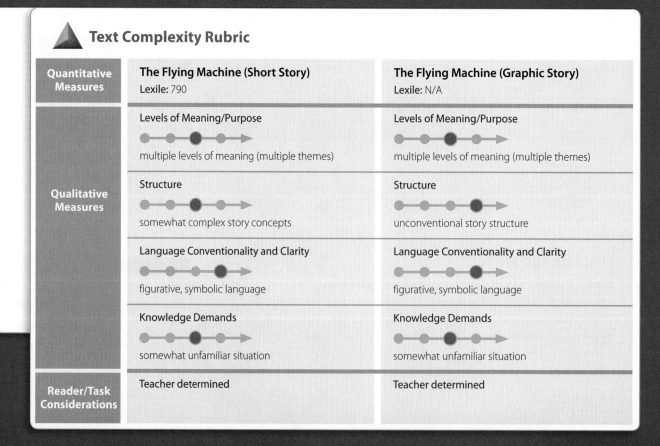

Text Complexity Rubric

	The Flying Machine (Short Story)	The Flying Machine (Graphic Story)
Quantitative Measures	Lexile: 790	Lexile: N/A
Qualitative Measures	Levels of Meaning/Purpose — multiple levels of meaning (multiple themes)	Levels of Meaning/Purpose — multiple levels of meaning (multiple themes)
	Structure — somewhat complex story concepts	Structure — unconventional story structure
	Language Conventionality and Clarity — figurative, symbolic language	Language Conventionality and Clarity — figurative, symbolic language
	Knowledge Demands — somewhat unfamiliar situation	Knowledge Demands — somewhat unfamiliar situation
Reader/Task Considerations	Teacher determined	Teacher determined

Strategies for CLOSE READING

Compare Versions of a Text

Students should read both versions of this story carefully all the way through. Close-reading questions at the bottom of the page will help them focus on a thorough analysis of the texts. As they read, students should jot down comments or questions about the texts in the side margins.

WHEN STUDENTS STRUGGLE . . .

To help students compare two versions of "The Flying Machine," have them work in small groups to fill out a chart, such as the one shown below, as they analyze the texts.

CITE TEXT EVIDENCE For practice comparing and contrasting two versions of a story, ask students to cite evidence of similarities and differences in the two versions of the story.

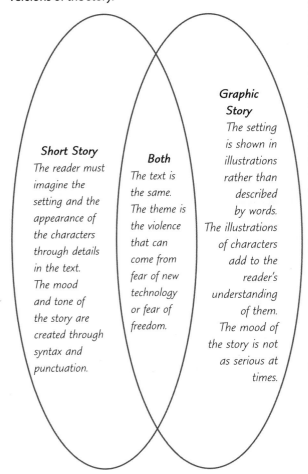

Short Story
The reader must imagine the setting and the appearance of the characters through details in the text. The mood and tone of the story are created through syntax and punctuation.

Both
The text is the same. The theme is the violence that can come from fear of new technology or fear of freedom.

Graphic Story
The setting is shown in illustrations rather than described by words. The illustrations of characters add to the reader's understanding of them. The mood of the story is not as serious at times.

Background Ray Bradbury *wrote hundreds of short stories in his 70-year career. He has said he tells tales to warn people about the dangers in the world around them. You are about to read a story that takes place in the distant past. As you read, think about the way this story connects to the world today. Then, read the graphic version of "The Flying Machine," illustrated by* Bernard Krigstein.

COMPARING VERSIONS OF
The Flying Machine

CLOSE READ
Notes

1. **READ** ▶ As you read lines 1–45, begin to collect and cite text evidence.

 • Circle repetitions of the word *miracle*. In the margin, state what the emperor says are miracles.
 • Circle what the servant says he sees.
 • Underline imagery that describes what they see.

The Flying Machine
Short Story by Ray Bradbury

In the year A.D. 400, the Emperor Yuan held his throne by the Great Wall of China, and the land was green with rain, readying itself toward the harvest, at peace, the people in his dominion[1] neither too happy nor too sad.

　Early on the morning of the first day of the first week of the second month of the new year, the Emperor Yuan was sipping tea and fanning himself against a warm breeze when a servant ran across the scarlet and blue garden tiles, calling, "Oh, Emperor, Emperor, a miracle!"

10　"Yes" said the Emperor, "the air *is* sweet this morning."
　"No, no, a miracle!" said the servant, bowing quickly.
　"And this tea is good in my mouth, surely that is a miracle."

The Emperor says the sweet air and delicious tea are miracles.

---
[1] **dominion:** country; territory.

111

---

1. **READ AND CITE TEXT EVIDENCE**

 A ASK STUDENTS to use their marked text as evidence of differences they notice between the Emperor and the servant. *Students should cite evidence that the Emperor sees the miraculous in the everyday, whereas the servant is using the word "miracle" to talk about a spectacular event (lines 8–16). They should see that the servant's response to the flying man is excited, whereas the Emperor's response is disbelief, "It is early...and you have just wakened from a dream" (lines 22–23).*

The Emperor says the sunrise and the sea are miracles.

"No, no, Your Excellency."

"Let me guess then—the sun has risen and a new day is upon us. Or the sea is blue. *That* now is the finest of all miracles."

"Excellency, a man is flying!"

"What?" The Emperor stopped his fan.

"I saw him in the air, a man flying with wings, I heard a voice call out of the sky, and when I looked up, there he was, a dragon in the
20   heavens with a man in its mouth, a dragon of paper and bamboo, colored like the sun and the grass."

"It is early," said the Emperor, "and you have just wakened from a dream."

"It is early, but I have seen what I have seen! Come, and you will see it too."

"Sit down with me here," said the Emperor. "Drink some tea. It must be a strange thing, if it is true, to see a man fly. You must have time to think of it, even as I must have time to prepare myself for the sight."
30   They drank tea.

"Please," said the servant at last, "or he will be gone."

The Emperor rose thoughtfully. "Now you may show me what you have seen."

They walked into a garden, across a meadow of grass, over a small bridge, through a grove of trees, and up a tiny hill.

"There!" said the servant.

The Emperor looked into the sky.

And in the sky, laughing so high that you could hardly hear him laugh, was a man; and the man was clothed in bright papers and reeds

---

40   to make wings and a beautiful yellow tail, and he was soaring all about like the largest bird in a universe of birds, like a new dragon in a land of ancient dragons.

The man called down to them from high in the cool winds of morning. "I fly, I fly!"

The servant waved to him. "Yes, *yes!*"

The Emperor Yuan did not move. Instead he looked at the Great Wall of China now taking shape out of the farthest mist in the green hills, that splendid snake of stones which **writhed** with majesty across the entire land. That wonderful wall which had protected them for a
50   timeless time from enemy **hordes** and preserved peace for years without number. He saw the town, nestled to itself by a river and a road and a hill, beginning to waken.

"Tell me," he said to his servant, "has anyone else seen this flying man?"

"I am the only one, Excellency," said the servant, smiling at the sky, waving.

The Emperor watched the heavens another minute and then said, "Call him down to me."

"Ho, come down, come down! The Emperor wishes to see you!"
60   called the servant, hands cupped to his shouting mouth.

The Emperor glanced in all directions while the flying man soared down the morning wind. He saw a farmer, early in his fields, watching the sky, and he noted where the farmer stood.

The flying man alit with a rustle of paper and a creak of bamboo reeds. He came proudly to the Emperor, clumsy in his rig, at last bowing before the old man.

"What have you done?" demanded the Emperor.

"I have flown in the sky, Your Excellency," replied the man.

"What *have* you done?" said the Emperor again.
70   "I have just told you!" cried the flier.

writhe:
turned

hordes:
masses, crowds

---

2. **◀ REREAD** Reread lines 5–37. Analyze the dialogue between the servant and the Emperor. What does the dialogue reveal about each character's feelings regarding the flying man?

The servant is thrilled with excitement. He speaks in quick, excited bursts: "Oh, Emperor, Emperor, a miracle!" His sentences are often punctuated with exclamation points. The Emperor seems more skeptical and speaks "thoughtfully" about the "miracle."

3. **READ ▶** As you read lines 46–103, continue to cite text evidence.
   • Underline descriptions of the Great Wall of China in lines 46–52.
   • In the margin, summarize what happens in lines 87–100.

---

2. **REREAD AND CITE TEXT EVIDENCE**

Ⓑ ASK STUDENTS to cite evidence to support their analysis of the dialogue between the servant and the Emperor. *Students may cite evidence that the servant speaks in quick, excited bursts punctuated with exclamation points (lines 8–9, 11, 13, and 16). They may cite evidence that the Emperor is skeptical (lines 22–23), and speaks "thoughtfully" (line 32).*

3. **READ AND CITE TEXT EVIDENCE**

Ⓒ ASK STUDENTS to cite text evidence to support their summary of what happens in lines 87–100. *Students should cite evidence that the Emperor has his guards seize the flying man (lines 90–93), and calls his executioner (line 94).*

Critical Vocabulary: writhe (line 48) Have students determine the meaning of *writhe* as it is used here. Ask students to discuss the symbolism of this word choice.

Critical Vocabulary: hordes (line 50) Have students determine the meaning of *hordes* as it is used here. How does the word *hordes* relate to the Emperor's concern? *The Emperor was reflecting on how the Great Wall has efficiently kept enemy hordes out of his kingdom all these years. The current way of life in the kingdom includes the safety of its borders.*

"You have told me nothing at all." The Emperor reached out a thin hand to touch the pretty paper and the birdlike keel of the apparatus. It smelled cool, of the wind.

"Is it not beautiful, Excellency?"

"Yes, too beautiful."

"It is the only one in the world!" smiled the man. "And I am the inventor."

"The *only* one in the world?"

"I swear it!"

80   "Who else knows of this?"

"No one. Not even my wife, who would think me mad with the sun. She thought I was making a kite. I rose in the night and walked to the cliffs far away. And when the morning breezes blew and the sun rose, I gathered my courage, Excellency, and leaped from the cliff. I flew! But my wife does not know of it."

"Well for her, then," said the Emperor. "Come along."

They walked back to the great house. The sun was full in the sky now, and the smell of the grass was refreshing. The Emperor, the servant, and the flier paused within the huge garden.

90   The Emperor clapped his hands. "Ho, guards!"

The guards came running.

"Hold this man."

The guards seized the flier.

"Call the executioner," said the Emperor.

"What's this!" cried the flier, bewildered. "What have I done?" He began to weep, so that the beautiful paper apparatus rustled.

"Here is the man who has made a certain machine," said the Emperor, "and yet asks us what he has created. He does not know himself. It is only necessary that he create, without knowing why he

100   has done so, or what this thing will do."

C

The Emperor has his guards seize the flier and calls for the executioner.

---

4. ◀ REREAD AND DISCUSS Reread lines 64–100. With a small group, discuss the reason why the Emperor captured the flier. Cite text evidence in your discussion.

5. READ ▶ As you read lines 104–150, continue to cite text evidence.

• Underline imagery that describes the Emperor's invention.
• Circle what the flier says he has done.
• In the margin, summarize the Emperor's concern.

The executioner came running with a sharp silver ax. He stood with his naked, large-muscled arms ready, his face covered with a **serene** white mask.

"One moment," said the Emperor. He turned to a nearby table upon which sat a machine that he himself had created. The Emperor took a tiny golden key from his own neck. He fitted his key to the tiny, delicate machine and wound it up. Then he set the machine going.

F
110   The machine was a garden of metal and jewels. Set in motion, the birds sang in tiny metal trees, wolves walked through miniature forests, and tiny people ran in and out of sun and shadow, fanning themselves with miniature fans, listening to tiny emerald birds, and standing by impossibly small but tinkling fountains.

"Is *it* not beautiful?" said the Emperor. "If you asked me what I have done here, I could answer you well. I have made birds sing, I have made forests murmur, I have set people to walking in this woodland, enjoying the leaves and shadows and songs. That is what I have done."

"But, oh, Emperor!" pleaded the flier, on his knees, the tears
120   pouring down his face. "I have done a similar thing! I have found beauty. I have flown on the morning wind. I have looked down on all the sleeping houses and gardens. I have smelled the sea and even *seen* it, beyond the hills, from my high place. And I have soared like a bird; oh, I cannot say how beautiful it is up there, in the sky, with the wind about me, the wind blowing me here like a feather, there like a fan, the way the sky smells in the morning! And how free one feels! *That* is beautiful, Emperor, that is beautiful too!"

"Yes," said the Emperor sadly, "I know it must be true. For I felt
E   my heart move with you in the air and I wondered: What is it like?
130   How does it feel? How do the distant pools look from so high? And how my houses and servants? Like ants? And how the distant towns not yet awake?"

"Then spare me!"

"But there are times," said the Emperor, more sadly still, "when one must lose a little beauty if one is to keep what little beauty one already has. I do not fear you, yourself, but I fear another man."

"What man?"

serene:
calm; undisturbed

114

115

---

4. **REREAD AND DISCUSS USING TEXT EVIDENCE**

D **ASK STUDENTS** to appoint a reporter for each group to cite specific evidence and line numbers to support their explanation of why the Emperor captured the flier. *Students should cite evidence from lines 97–100.*

5. **READ AND CITE TEXT EVIDENCE**

E **ASK STUDENTS** to cite text evidence to explain the Emperor's specific concern about the flying machine. *Students should cite evidence from lines 129–132 that the Emperor thinks about what his kingdom looks like from so far up. They should cite line 136, "I fear another man," and lines 139–140. Finally, they should cite lines 142–144 as evidence that the Emperor fears attack from above.*

Critical Vocabulary: serene (line 103) Have students determine the meaning of serene as it is used here. Ask them to explain why *serene* is a surprising word choice to use in a description of an executioner. Discuss why Bradbury might have made this choice. *Students might say the use of the word* serene *draws a contrast with the horror the flying man must feel.*

FOR ELL STUDENTS Spanish speakers will probably know the Spanish cognate for *murmur, murmurar*. Ask a volunteer to state the meaning ("to make a low indistinct sound"). Point out that the word is an example of *onomatopoeia*, the property of some words to imitate the sounds of what they describe.

"Some other man who, seeing you, will build a thing of bright papers and bamboo like this. But the other man will have an evil face and an evil heart, and the beauty will be gone. It is this man I fear."

"Why? Why?"

"Who is to say that someday just such a man, in just such an apparatus of paper and reed, might not fly in the sky and drop huge stones upon the Great Wall of China?" said the Emperor.

No one moved or said a word.

"Off with his head," said the Emperor.

The executioner whirled his silver ax.

"Burn the kite and the inventor's body and bury their ashes together," said the Emperor.

150 The servants retreated to obey.

(G) The Emperor turned to his hand-servant, who had seen the man flying. "Hold your tongue. It was all a dream, a most sorrowful and beautiful dream. And that farmer in the distant field who also saw, tell him it would pay him to consider it only a vision. If ever the word passes around, you and the farmer die within the hour."

"You are merciful, Emperor."

"No, not merciful," said the old man. Beyond the garden wall he saw the guards burning the beautiful machine of paper and reeds that

The Emperor fears that someone will use a flying machine to attack his kingdom.

The Emperor wants anyone who saw the flying machine to forget it immediately.

smelled of the morning wind. He saw he dark smoke climb into the sky. "No, only very much bewildered and afraid." He saw the guards digging a tiny pit wherein to bury the ashes. "What is the life of one man against those of a million others? I must take **solace** from that thought."

He took the key from its chain about his neck and once more wound up the beautiful miniature garden. He stood looking out across the land at the Great Wall, the peaceful town, the green fields, the rivers and streams. He sighed. The tiny garden whirred its hidden and delicate machinery and set itself in motion; tiny people walked in forests, tiny faces loped through sun-speckled glades in beautiful shining pelts, and among the tiny trees flew little bits of high song and bright blue and yellow colour, flying, flying, flying in that small sky.

(H) "Oh," said the Emperor, closing his eyes, "look at the birds, look at the birds!"

solace:
comfort

8. **◀ REREAD AND DISCUSS** Reread lines 173–174. With a small group, discuss your interpretation of the story's ending. What is the Emperor thinking about? Support your ideas with explicit textual evidence.

SHORT RESPONSE

Cite Text Evidence Recall that Bradbury says that he writes to warn people about dangers in the world around them. What warning is evident in "The Flying Machine"? **Cite text evidence** in your response.

Bradbury seems to warn that new technology can inspire fear and cause destruction. The Emperor's dialogue tells us he is immediately concerned about the flying machine. We soon find out the reason why: The flier does not realize it, but his advancement has the potential to endanger the Emperor's entire kingdom.

6. **◀ REREAD** Reread lines 110–145. Compare and contrast the two inventions in "The Flying Machine." Why does the Emperor only see beauty in his own creation? Cite textual evidence in your response.

The Emperor sees beauty in his own creation because it is a representation of nature that is self-contained. He can explain what it is and knows it will not cause harm. On the other hand, he sees potential for harm in the flying machine. The flier does not realize his invention surpasses nature and could cause destruction.

7. **READ ▶** As you read lines 151–174, continue to cite text evidence.

• In the margin, explain what the Emperor says in lines 151–155.
• Circle what the Emperor says in lines 160–163.
• Underline what the Emperor looks at in lines 164–172.

116

117

6. REREAD AND DISCUSS USING TEXT EVIDENCE

(F) **ASK STUDENTS** to cite evidence to support their comparison of the two inventions in the story, and their explanation of why the Emperor only sees beauty in his own creation. *Students should cite evidence of the nature of the Emperor's machine from lines 109–113. They should cite evidence of the Emperor's attitude toward his machine from lines 114–118. They should cite evidence of the Emperor's concerns from lines 142–144.*

7. READ AND CITE TEXT EVIDENCE

(G) **ASK STUDENTS** to use the text they marked as evidence to explain what they learned about the Emperor. *Students should explain that the Emperor wants anyone who saw the flying machine to forget it immediately (lines 151–155), that he feels "bewildered and afraid" (line 160), and that he feels responsible for the lives of people in his kingdom (lines 161–163).*

8. REREAD AND DISCUSS USING TEXT EVIDENCE

(H) **ASK STUDENTS** to work with a small group to cite specific text evidence that supports an interpretation of the story's ending, and an analysis of what the Emperor is thinking. *Students should cite textual evidence from lines 173–174.*

Critical Vocabulary: solace (line 162) Ask students what they learn about the Emperor from this use of the word *solace*.

SHORT RESPONSE

Cite Text Evidence Student responses will vary, but they should cite evidence to support their analysis of the text. Students should:

• provide a text-based analysis of Bradbury's warning.
• analyze the Emperor's words and actions.
• cite strong textual evidence to support their response.

1. **READ** ▶ As you read the following two pages, begin to collect and cite text evidence.

• Circle illustrations that show the characters' reactions to the "miracle."

• Circle illustrations and text that tell you about the flying machine.

• Circle the illustration of the Great Wall and explain its importance in the margin.

B

A

The Great Wall protects the kingdom.

2. **◀ REREAD** Contrast the drawings of the Emperor with the drawings of the servant. How do the illustrations convey each character's feelings about the flying machine?

The servant is leaping up and down and gesturing to explain what he saw. The flying machine makes him excited. The Emperor stops what he is doing when he hears about the flying machine. He is concerned.

118

119

1. **READ AND CITE TEXT EVIDENCE**

A **ASK STUDENTS** to use their marked text as evidence and show a partner how the man flew, and how the Great Wall protects the kingdom. *Students should cite evidence from panels 5 and 6 on the next page.*

2. **REREAD AND CITE TEXT EVIDENCE**

B **ASK STUDENTS** to cite evidence to support their comparison of the drawings of the Emperor and servant. *Students should cite evidence from panels 3 and 4 on the previous page.*

The Emperor is asking whether anyone else has a flying machine or knows about this one.

C

3. **READ ▶** As you read this page and the next, continue to cite text evidence.

- In the margin, explain the purpose of the Emperor's questions.
- On the next page, underline the question the flying man asks.
- Circle the close up of the Emperor's face.

120

4. **◀ REREAD AND DISCUSS** In a small group, discuss how the Emperor's expression in the close-up image might affect your perception of the story. Cite textual evidence in your discussion.

121

---

3. READ AND CITE TEXT EVIDENCE

C **ASK STUDENTS** why the Emperor wants to know if anyone else knows about the flying machine. *He is concerned that someone else might replicate the machine or get the idea to invent a similar machine. Flying machines could be used by enemies to invade the kingdom.*

FOR ELL STUDENTS Point out that the word *rustle* has two meanings. It can mean "to steal cattle" or "a faint crackling sound." In this context it means the latter. Tell students that this is another example of onomatopoeia, as is the word *creak* in the same sentence.

4. REREAD AND DISCUSS USING TEXT EVIDENCE

D **ASK STUDENTS** to appoint a reporter for each group to cite specific evidence to support their explanation of how the Emperor's expression in the close-up image affects their perception of the story. *The isolation of his face causes the reader to focus solely on the Emperor and his words—they gain importance and gravity from the seclusion and from the Emperor's solemn expression.*

The flier appeals to the Emperor's appreciation of beauty.

We do not see the death of the flying man. His death is described in text while birds flying in the air are depicted in an illustration.

5. **READ** ▶ As you read this page and the next, continue to cite text evidence.

- Circle repetitions of "beauty" and "beautiful," and in the margin, explain the flier's argument that his life should be spared.
- In the margin, explain the imagery that illustrates the flier's death.
- Circle birds in the last frame.

5. **READ AND CITE TEXT EVIDENCE**

E **ASK STUDENTS** to return to the text and pick the image that symbolizes the flying man's death. Have them read their explanation of the imagery that illustrates the flying man's death to a partner. *Students should cite the panel that is headed "THE EXECUTIONER WHIRLED HIS SILVER AX . . ."*

WHEN STUDENTS STRUGGLE . . .

To help students understand the differences in style between the short story and the graphic story, have them work in small groups to analyze the imagery on page 123. Ask them to describe the characters and the setting based on details they see in the pictures.

CITE TEXT EVIDENCE Ask students to point to specific images that support their descriptions. *Students might describe the servant as humble and point to his bowed posture. They might describe the setting as beautiful and point to the mountains, the birds, and the trees.*

6. ◀ REREAD AND DISCUSS With a small group, discuss why the death of the flier was depicted as it was. What feelings might the writers have been trying to evoke by depicting his death this way? Cite text evidence in your discussion.

SHORT RESPONSE

Cite Text Evidence What are the advantages of reading "The Flying Machine" as a graphic story instead of a short story? Review your reading notes, and remember to **cite text evidence** in your response.

The graphic story writer can emphasize words by making them bigger or darker. In the first frame, emphasizing the word "Emperor" makes it seem louder and more urgent. These choices affect the mood and tone of the story. The visual imagery—such as the setting—is shown rather than imagined. The isolation of the kingdom is shown in the first frame. Its natural beauty is seen throughout. Choices such as representing the execution with a startled flock of birds cause readers to make associations they might not make when reading Bradbury's short story.

124

TO CHALLENGE STUDENTS . . .

For more historical context and an expert opinion on the Great Wall of China, students can view the video *Building the Great Wall* in their eBooks.

ASK STUDENTS what similarities and differences they can identify between Bradbury's Emperor Yuan and history's Emperor Qin Shi Huang. *Students might recognize both Emperors' preoccupation with protecting the kingdom. They might point out that the Great Wall did not prove effective, and conclude that Emperor Yuan's efforts to protect his kingdom by destroying the knowledge of flight were only temporarily successful.*

For insight into ancient Chinese warfare, students can view the video *Ancient Chinese Weapons* in their eBooks.

ASK STUDENTS how a flying machine might have changed how wars were fought in ancient China. *Students should recognize that all the advantages China enjoyed due to the sophistication of their metallurgy and arrow design would have been meaningless if they confronted an army that had the means of flight.*

---

6. ⬬ **REREAD AND DISCUSS USING TEXT EVIDENCE**

F **ASK STUDENTS** to cite evidence to support their inferences about why the death of the flier was depicted as it was. *Students should understand that birds are a symbol of the flying man. They might conclude that the illustrator wanted to evoke feelings of sadness and beauty.*

SHORT RESPONSE

Cite Text Evidence Student responses will vary, but they should cite evidence from the text to support their explanation of the advantages of reading "The Flying Machine" as a graphic story. Students should:

- contrast the style of the text in the short story and graphic story.
- provide a text-based analysis of the impact of the graphic story's illustrations.
- cite strong textual evidence to support their response.

DIG DEEPER

1. With the class, return to short story Question 4, Reread and Discuss. Have students share the results of their discussion.

   ASK STUDENTS whether they were satisfied with the outcome of their small-group discussions. Have each group share their explanation of why the Emperor captured the flier. What compelling evidence did the groups cite from the text to support their explanation?

   - Ask students whether they all agreed on why the Emperor captured the flier. Ask groups to share their minority opinions.
   - Have groups explain how they decided which explanation made the most sense. Did everyone agree about which evidence was the most compelling? How were disagreements resolved?
   - After students have shared the results of their group's discussion, ask whether another group shared any ideas they wished they had brought to the table.

2. With the class, return to graphic story Question 6, Reread and Discuss. Have students share the results of their discussion.

   ASK STUDENTS whether they were satisfied with the outcome of their small-group discussions. Have each group share their inferences about why the death of the flier was depicted as it was. What evidence did the groups cite from the graphic story to support their inference?

   - Ask students whether they all agreed on the meaning of the imagery. Ask groups to share their minority opinions.
   - Have groups explain how they decided which inference made the most sense. Did everyone agree about which evidence was the most compelling? How were disagreements resolved?
   - After students have shared the results of their group's discussion, ask whether another group shared any ideas they wished they had brought to the table.

   ASK STUDENTS to return to their Short Response answer and revise it based on the class discussion.

CLOSE READING NOTES

One Last Time

Memoir by Gary Soto

Why This Text?

In this memoir, students will gain insight into the life and work of a popular author, Gary Soto. Long before he found success as a writer, Soto learned the value—and the hardship—involved in a day's work.

► **View It!**

Professional Development Podcast:

Text-Dependent Analysis

For practice and application:

Background *Jim Haskins (1941–2005) was born into a large family in Demopolis, Alabama. After graduating from college, Haskins moved to New York City, where he taught special education classes in Harlem. He drew from his experiences there to write his first book, Diary of a Harlem Schoolteacher. Haskins's books for young adults often highlight the lives of famous African Americans, as well as African language and culture. A few of the books have been turned into movies, including the award-winning The Cotton Club.*

The Real McCoy

Close Reader selection
"The Real McCoy,"
Biography by Jim Haskins

Key Learning Objective: The student will be able to cite evidence to draw conclusions about a text and analyze imagery and sensory details.

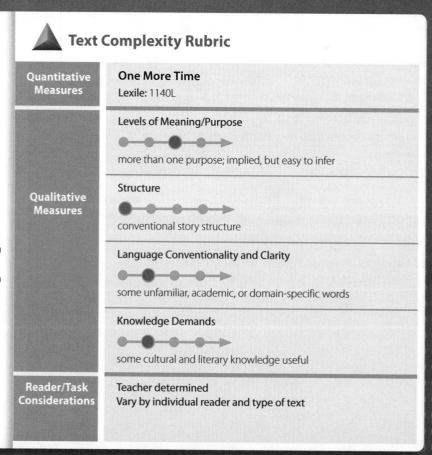

COMMON CORE

Common Core Standards

RI 1 Cite textual evidence that supports inferences.

RI 2 Determine a central idea; provide a summary.

RI 3 Analyze text connections.

RI 4 Determine the meaning of words and phrases.

RI 5 Analyze structure in a text.

RI 6 Determine an author's purpose.

SL 1a Come to discussions prepared.

SL 1b Follow rules for discussions and decision-making.

L 1 Demonstrate command of standard English grammar and usage.

L 2 Demonstrate command of standard English punctuation.

L 4c Consult dictionaries to find pronunciation, meaning, or part of speech.

L 4d Verify the meaning of a word or phrase by checking a dictionary.

Text Complexity Rubric

Quantitative Measures

One More Time
Lexile: 1140L

Qualitative Measures

Levels of Meaning/Purpose

more than one purpose; implied, but easy to infer

Structure

conventional story structure

Language Conventionality and Clarity

some unfamiliar, academic, or domain-specific words

Knowledge Demands

some cultural and literary knowledge useful

Reader/Task Considerations

Teacher determined
Vary by individual reader and type of text

Gary Soto Have students read the information about Gary Soto's life and use it to make a prediction about what his memoir might be about. As needed, explain that Soto is an award-winning writer of poetry, short stories, novels, and plays who bases much of his writing on his own life experiences. Although his stories often include Mexican American characters, Soto believes that young people from any background can recognize the experiences and feelings he writes about.

SETTING A PURPOSE Direct students to use the Setting a Purpose prompt to focus their reading. Remind students to generate questions as they read.

Analyze the Meanings of Words and Phrases (LINES 2–7)

COMMON CORE RI 1, RI 4

Tell students that authors use imagery to help readers imagine the things they are describing. Explain that **imagery** is the use of descriptive words and phrases that appeal to the sense of sight, hearing, smell, taste, or touch.

 CITE TEXT EVIDENCE Have students reread lines 2–7, focusing on the description of the workers. To what sense or senses does the description appeal? *(Sight: "dusty and thin as sparrows"; "squinting, eyes small and veined.")* What impact does the description have on the tone or feeling of the text? *(The description creates a sharp contrast between the comfortable movie audience and the exhausted workers; it suggests a feeling of hopelessness.)*

SCAFFOLDING FOR ELL STUDENTS

Homophones Using a whiteboard, project lines 4–7. Explain that some English words sound the same but have different spellings and meanings. Guide students to mark up the text.

- Highlight in yellow words that sound the same but have different spellings.
- Use a note to give the words' meanings.

ASK STUDENTS to explain what they learn about the workers.

Gary Soto (b.1952) *was born to parents of Mexican decent in Fresno, California. His father died when he was five years old, and Soto worked in the fields and factories when he was young. He struggled in school, but he managed to enroll in college, where a book of poetry inspired him to begin writing. Much of Soto's poetry, fiction, and nonfiction reflects his experience growing up as a Mexican American.*

ONE LAST TIME

Memoir by Gary Soto

SETTING A PURPOSE As you read, notice Soto's experiences and attitudes about work. Think about how his family history affects the way he thinks about working.

Yesterday I saw the movie *Gandhi*[1] and recognized a few of the people—not in the theater but in the film. I saw my relatives, dusty and thin as sparrows, returning from the fields with hoes balanced on their shoulders. The workers were squinting, eyes small and veined, and were using their hands to say what there was to say to those in the audience with popcorn. . . . I didn't have any, though. I sat thinking of my family and their years in the fields, beginning with Grandmother who came to the United States after the
10 Mexican revolution[2] to settle in Fresno where she met her

---

[1] *Gandhi* (gän´dē): a 1982 film biography of Mohandas Gandhi (1869–1948), an Indian spiritual and political leader who, through nonviolent struggle, forced England to grant India's independence.

[2] **Mexican revolution (1910–1920):** an armed conflict during which revolutionaries overthrew Mexico's longtime dictator and reformed the government.

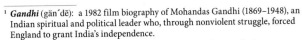

The workers were squinting, eyes small and veined, and were using their hands to say what there was to say to those in the audience with popcorn. . . . I didn't have any, though. I sat thinking of my family

Analyze Structure

COMMON CORE **RI 5**

(LINES 11–18)

Draw attention to the author's description of his grandmother as a worker. Prompt students to examine how each sentence in the description contributes to developing Soto's key concept.

B **ASK STUDENTS** to reread lines 11–18. What key concept does Soto develop? How do the sentences in lines 11–18 build on that idea? *(Soto's key concept is that his grandmother was a hard worker. Each sentence tells more about the intense physical work she did throughout her life.)*

CRITICAL VOCABULARY

ramble: The author is describing a conversation with his mother on his first day of work in the fields.

ASK STUDENTS what the contrast between Soto's rambling and his mother's silence suggests. *(Possible answer: Soto is enthusiastic and hopeful that his work will change the family's situation; his mother's silence implies that she knows his work will make little difference, or that she is exhausted even before the work begins.)*

foreman: Soto is describing what he is told to do to begin work.

ASK STUDENTS why the foreman tells Soto where to work. *(The foreman is in charge; he makes sure each worker has a specific area in which to work.)*

grope: Soto has begun to collect grapes.

ASK STUDENTS why Soto needs to grope for each bunch of grapes. *(Possible answer: Soto cannot see the bunches of grapes that are on the inner part of the vines, so he would have to search around and get a grip on the loose cluster.)*

B husband and bore children, many of them. She worked in the fields around Fresno, picking grapes, oranges, plums, peaches, and cotton, dragging a large white sack like a sled. She worked in the packing houses, Bonner and Sun-Maid Raisin, where she stood at a conveyor belt passing her hand over streams of raisins to pluck out leaves and pebbles. For over twenty years she worked at a machine that boxed raisins until she retired at sixty-five.

Grandfather worked in the fields, as did his children.
20 Mother also found herself out there when she separated from Father for three weeks. I remember her coming home, dusty and so tired that she had to rest on the porch before she trudged inside to wash and start dinner. I didn't understand the complaints about her ankles or the small of her back, even though I had been in the grape fields watching her work. With my brother and sister I ran in and out of the rows; we enjoyed ourselves and pretended not to hear Mother scolding us to sit down and behave ourselves. A few years later, however, I caught on when I went to pick grapes rather than play in
30 the rows.

Mother and I got up before dawn and ate quick bowls of cereal. She drove in silence while I **rambled** on how everything was now solved, how I was going to make enough money to end our misery and even buy her a beautiful copper tea pot, the one I had shown her in Long's Drugs. When we arrived I was frisky and ready to go, self-consciously aware of my grape knife dangling at my wrist. I almost ran to the row the **foreman** had pointed out, but I returned to help Mother with the grape pans and jug of water. She told me to settle
40 down and reminded me not to lose my knife. I walked at her side and listened to her explain how to cut grapes; bent down, hands on knees, I watched her demonstrate by cutting a few bunches into my pan. She stood over me as I tried it myself, tugging at a bunch of grapes that pulled loose like beads from a necklace. "Cut the stem all the way," she told me as last advice before she walked away, her shoes sinking in the loose dirt, to begin work on her own row.

I cut another bunch, then another, fighting the snap and whip of vines. After ten minutes of **groping** for grapes, my
50 first pan brimmed with bunches. I poured them on the paper tray, which was bordered by a wooden frame that kept the grapes from rolling off, and they spilled like jewels from a

ramble
(răm´bəl) *v.* When you *ramble*, you talk at length in an aimless way

foreman
(fôr´mən) *n.* A *foreman* is the leader of a work crew.

grope
(grōp) *v.* When you *grope*, you reach about in an uncertain way.

pirate's chest. The tray was only half filled, so I hurried to jump under the vines and begin groping, cutting, and tugging at the grapes again. I emptied the pan, raked the grapes with my hands to make them look like they filled the tray, and jumped back under the vine on my knees. I tried to cut faster because Mother, in the next row, was slowly moving ahead.

60   I peeked into her row and saw five trays gleaming in the early morning. I cut, pulled hard, and stopped to gather the grapes that missed the pan; already bored, I spat on a few to wash them before tossing them like popcorn into my mouth.

So it went. Two pans equaled one tray—or six cents. By lunchtime I had a trail of thirty-seven trays behind me while Mother had sixty or more. We met about halfway from our last trays, and I sat down with a grunt, knees wet from kneeling on dropped grapes. I washed my hands with the water from the jug, drying them on the inside of my shirt sleeve before I opened the paper bag for the first sandwich,

70   which I gave to Mother. I dipped my hand in again to unwrap a sandwich without looking at it. I took a first bite and chewed it slowly for the tang of mustard. Eating in silence I looked straight ahead at the vines, and only when we were finished with cookies did we talk.

"Are you tired?" she asked.

"No, but I got a sliver from the frame," I told her. I showed her the web of skin between my thumb and index finger. She wrinkled her forehead but said it was nothing.

"How many trays did you do?"

80   I looked straight ahead, not answering at first. I recounted in my mind the whole morning of bend, cut, pour again and again, before answering a **feeble** "thirty-seven." No elaboration, no detail. Without looking at me she told me how she had done field work in Texas and Michigan as a child. But I had a difficult time listening to her stories. I played with my grape knife, stabbing it into the ground, but stopped when Mother reminded me that I had better not lose it. I left the knife sticking up like a small, leafless plant. She then talked about school, the junior high I would be going to that fall,

90   and then about Rick and Debra, how sorry they would be that they hadn't come out to pick grapes because they'd have no new clothes for the school year. She stopped talking when she peeked at her watch, a bandless one she kept in her pocket. She

feeble
(fē´bəl) *adj.* If someone is *feeble*, the person is very weak.

CLOSE READ

Draw Conclusions

COMMON CORE RI 1

(LINES 63–79)

Remind students that authors expect readers to draw their own conclusions about ideas that are not stated in a text. Explain that a conclusion is a statement of belief or a logical judgment based on evidence, personal knowledge, and reasoning.

C **CITE TEXT EVIDENCE** Have students reread lines 63–79. What evidence in the text suggests how Soto and his mother are feeling? (*They are both exhausted: "sat down with a grunt"; "unwrap a sandwich without looking at it"; "chewed slowly"; "eating in silence I looked straight ahead."*) What conclusion can you draw about the work they are doing? (*The work is tedious and difficult; they are so tired and bored by the work that they can't even chat.*)

CRITICAL VOCABULARY

feeble: Soto is commenting on the amount of work he completed during his first morning.

ASK STUDENTS why Soto describes the number of trays he filled as *feeble*. (*Possible answer: He is embarrassed by the low number of trays he has filled, especially in comparison to his mother.*)

APPLYING ACADEMIC VOCABULARY

occupation	option

As you discuss "One Last Time," incorporate the following Collection 6 academic vocabulary words: *occupation* and *option*. Ask students what makes the **occupation** Soto describes such difficult work. Discuss whether or not Soto and his mother had the **option** of choosing to do other work.

Analyze the Meanings of Words and Phrases
COMMON CORE RI 4

(LINES 97–108)

Tell students that a **metaphor** is a comparison of two things without the use of the word *like* or *as*. Explain that authors often compare something unfamiliar to something familiar in order to help readers relate to what is being described.

 ASK STUDENTS to reread lines 97–108. What metaphor does Soto use to explain how he feels as he begins the second half of his workday? *("boredom was a terror almost as awful as the work itself.")* What is the impact of his metaphor on the tone or feeling of the text? *(The metaphor suggests a feeling of desperation; he is resigned to surviving the experience but no longer sees any hope in it.)*

Draw Conclusions
COMMON CORE RI 1

(LINES 120–132)

Remind students that when they draw conclusions they rely on evidence stated in the text.

 CITE TEXT EVIDENCE Have students reread lines 120–132 to find evidence of how Soto's first day of work has affected him. *("walked slowly to our car"; "little joy in trying to avoid their tags because I couldn't get the fields out of my mind"; "when I closed my eyes, I saw the fields")* What conclusion can you draw based on that evidence? *(Possible answer: Soto is haunted by the idea of a lifetime of working in the fields.)*

got up with an *"Ay, Dios,"*[3] and told me that we'd work until three, leaving me cutting figures in the sand with my knife and dreading the return to work.

Finally I rose and walked slowly back to where I had left off, again kneeling under the vine and fixing the pan under bunches of grapes. By that time, 11:30, the sun was over my 100 shoulder and made me squint and think of the pool at the Y.M.C.A. where I was a summer member. I saw myself diving face first into the water and loving it. I saw myself gleaming like something new, at the edge of the pool. I had to daydream and keep my mind busy because boredom was a terror almost as awful as the work itself. My mind went dumb with stupid things, and I had to keep it moving with dreams of baseball and would-be girlfriends. I even sang, however softly, to keep my mind moving, my hands moving.

I worked less hurriedly and with less vision. I no longer 110 saw that copper pot sitting squat on our stove or Mother waiting for it to whistle. The wardrobe that I imagined, crisp and bright in the closet, numbered only one pair of jeans and two shirts because, in half a day, six cents times thirty-seven trays was two dollars and twenty-two cents. It became clear to me. If I worked eight hours, I might make four dollars. I'd take this, even gladly, and walk downtown to look into store windows on the mall and long for the bright madras[4] shirts from Walter Smith or Coffee's, but settling for two imitation ones from Penney's.

120 That first day I laid down seventy-three trays while Mother had a hundred and twenty behind her. On the back of an old envelope, she wrote out our numbers and hours. We washed at the pump behind the farm house and walked slowly to our car for the drive back to town in the afternoon heat. That evening after dinner I sat in a lawn chair listening to music from a transistor radio while Rick and David King played catch. I joined them in a game of pickle, but there was little joy in trying to avoid their tags because I couldn't get the fields out of my mind: I saw myself dropping on my knees 130 under a vine to tug at a branch that wouldn't come off. In bed, when I closed my eyes, I saw the fields, yellow with kicked up dust, and a crooked trail of trays rotting behind me.

---

[3] *Ay, Dios* (ī dē-ōs´) *Spanish:* "Oh, God."
[4] **madras** (măd´rəs): cotton cloth, usually with a plaid pattern.

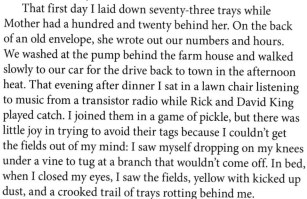

The next day I woke tired and started picking tired. The
grapes rained into the pan, slowly filling like a belly, until I
had my first tray and started my second. So it went all day, and
the next, and all through the following week, so that by the
end of thirteen days the foreman counted out, in tens mostly,
my pay of fifty-three dollars. Mother earned one hundred
and forty-eight dollars. She wrote this on her envelope, with a
140 message I didn't bother to ask her about.

The next day I walked with my friend Scott to the
downtown mall where we drooled over the clothes behind
fancy windows, bought popcorn, and sat at a tier of outdoor
fountains to talk about girls. Finally we went into Penney's for
more popcorn, which we ate walking around, before we
returned home without buying anything. It wasn't until a
few days before school that I let my fifty-three dollars slip
quietly from my hands, buying a pair of pants, two shirts, and
a maroon T-shirt, the kind that was in style. At home I tried
150 them on while Rick looked on enviously; later, the day before
school started, I tried them on again wondering not so much if
they were worth it as who would see me first in those clothes.

CLOSE READ

Analyze the Meanings of Words and Phrases

 COMMON CORE RI 4

(LINES 133–135)

Explain to students that authors use carefully chosen
words to help readers imagine what an experience is
like. Point out that in addition to imagery an author
may also use **similes,** comparisons of two things
using the word *like* or *as.*

F ASK STUDENTS to reread lines 133–135 to
identify Soto's use of imagery and simile. *(imagery:
"grapes rained into the pan"; simile: "slowly filling like
a belly")* What is the impact of these word choices?
*(The image of grapes "raining" into the pan shows how
hard he is working, but it also contrasts the dry, dusty
fields with the idea of soothing rain. "Filling like a belly"
implies that Soto is working to feed himself. The word
choices suggest that Soto has resigned himself to the
need to work.)*

Strategies for Annotation ✎ 🗐 *Annotate it!*

Analyze the Meanings of Words
and Phrases (LINES 133–135)

 COMMON CORE RI 4

Share these strategies for guided or independent analysis:

- Highlight in yellow the word *like* or *as.*
- Highlight in green the things being compared
- On a note, describe the impact of the simile.

The grapes rained into the pan, slowly filling like a belly, until I

had my first tray and started my second. So it went

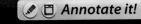

Connects to eating:
he is working so he
can eat.

Draw Conclusions

COMMON CORE RI 1

(LINES 153–162)

Guide students to use evidence in the text to draw conclusions about Soto's family.

G **CITE TEXT EVIDENCE** Have students reread lines 153–162 to find evidence of the expectations for the children in Soto's family. What conclusion can you draw about what Soto's mother provided for the children? *("Along with my brother and sister I picked grapes until I was fifteen, before giving up and saying I'd rather wear old clothes"; "there would be no new clothes for me in the fall"; "Mother bought me two pairs of socks, a packet of colored T-shirts, and underwear"; Soto's mother provided the necessities, but the children were expected to work for "extras.")*

CRITICAL VOCABULARY

stoop: Soto is describing the position in which a person stands to pick grapes.

ASK STUDENTS why Soto doesn't want to stoop any longer. *(Possible answer: He finds the work degrading; he thinks he should not have to do that type of work.)*

contractor: Explain that Soto is describing how he and his brother find different jobs.

ASK STUDENTS to explain why the contractors are shouting "Cotton" or "Beets." *(The contractors are identifying the crops that workers will be required to harvest if they are hired.)*

G Along with my brother and sister I picked grapes until I was fifteen, before giving up and saying that I'd rather wear old clothes than **stoop** like a Mexican. Mother thought I was being stuck-up, even stupid, because there would be no clothes for me in the fall. I told her I didn't care, but when Rick and Debra rose at five in the morning, I lay awake in bed feeling that perhaps I had made a mistake but unwilling to change
160 my mind. That fall Mother bought me two pairs of socks, a packet of colored T-shirts, and underwear. The T-shirts would help, I thought, but who would see that I had new underwear and socks? I wore a new T-shirt on the first day of school, then an old shirt on Tuesday, then another T-shirt on Wednesday, and on Thursday an old Nehru shirt[5] that was embarrassingly out of style. On Friday I changed into the corduroy pants my brother had handed down to me and slipped into my last new T-shirt. I worked like a magician, blinding my classmates, who were all clothes conscious and small-time social climbers, by
170 arranging my wardrobe to make it seem larger than it really was. But by spring I had to do something—my blue jeans were almost silver and my shoes had lost their form, puddling like black ice around my feet. That spring of my sixteenth year, Rick and I decided to take a labor bus to chop cotton. In his old Volkswagen, which was more noise than power, we drove on a Saturday morning to West Fresno—or Chinatown as some call it—parked, walked slowly toward a bus, and stood gawking at the . . . blacks, Okies,[6] *Tejanos*[7] with gold teeth, . . . Mexican families, and labor **contractors** shouting "Cotton" or
180 "Beets," the work of spring.

We boarded the "Cotton" bus without looking at the contractor who stood almost blocking the entrance. . . . We boarded scared. . . . We sat . . . looking straight ahead, and only glanced briefly at the others who boarded, almost all of them broken and poorly dressed in loudly mismatched clothes. Finally when the contractor banged his palm against the side of the bus, the young man at the wheel, smiling and talking in Spanish, started the engine, idled it for a moment while he adjusted the mirrors, and started off in slow chugs.
190 Except for the windshield there was no glass in the windows,

stoop
(stoop) *v.* If you *stoop*, you bend forward and down from the waist.

contractor
(kŏn´trăk´tər) *n.*
A *contractor* is a person who agrees to provide services for a specific price.

---

[5] **Nehru** (nā´roo) **shirt**: an Indian-style shirt with a stand-up collar.

[6] **Okies** (ō´kēz): people from Oklahoma and other midwestern states who moved to California to find work during the Great Depression of the 1930s.

[7] *Tejanos* (tā-hä´nōs): Texans of Mexican ancestry.

WHEN STUDENTS STRUGGLE . . .

Provide support for students to follow the sequence of events Soto is describing. Have students create a chart like the one shown to keep track of Soto's jobs.

Soto's job	Soto's age/Clues in text
picking grapes	about 12–13: "the junior high I would be going to that fall"
picking cotton	about 15: "until I was fifteen"; "By that spring"

so as soon as we were on the rural roads outside Fresno, the dust and sand began to be sucked into the bus, whipping about like **irate** wasps as the gravel ticked about us. We closed our eyes, clotted up our mouths that wanted to open with embarrassed laughter because we couldn't believe we were on that bus with those people and the dust attacking us for no reason.

When we arrived at a field we followed the others to a pickup where we each took a hoe and marched to stand 200 before a row. Rick and I, self-conscious and unsure, looked around at the others who leaned on their hoes or squatted in front of the rows, almost all talking in Spanish, joking . . . all waiting for the foreman's whistle to begin work. Mother had explained how to chop cotton by showing us with a broom in the backyard.

"Like this," she said, her broom swishing down weeds. "Leave one plant and cut four—and cut them! Don't leave them standing or the foreman will get mad."

The foreman whistled and we started up the row stealing 210 glances at other workers to see if we were doing it right. But after awhile we worked like we knew what we were doing, neither of us hurrying or falling behind. But slowly the clot of men, women, and kids began to spread and loosen. Even Rick pulled away. I didn't hurry, though. I cut smoothly and cleanly as I walked at a slow pace, in a sort of funeral march. My eyes measured each space of cotton plants before I cut. If I missed the plants, I swished again. I worked intently, seldom looking up, so when I did I was amazed to see the sun, like a broken orange coin, in the east. It looked blurry, unbelievable, like 220 something not of this world. I looked around in amazement, scanning the eastern horizon that was a taut line jutted with an occasional mountain. The horizon was beautiful, like a snapshot of the moon, in the early light of morning, in the quiet of no cars and few people.

The foreman trudged in boots in my direction, stepping awkwardly over the plants, to inspect the work. No one around me looked up. We all worked steadily while we waited for him to leave. When he did leave, with a feeble complaint addressed to no one in particular, we looked up smiling under 230 straw hats and bandanas.

irate
(ī-rāt´) *adj.* If you are *irate*, you are very angry.

One Last Time **411**

CLOSE READ

Analyze the Meanings of Words and Phrases

 COMMON CORE RI 1, RI 4

(LINES 217–224)

Draw attention to the imagery in the details that the author uses to convey the experience of working in the fields. Remind students that imagery appeals to one or more of the five senses.

H **CITE TEXT EVIDENCE** Have students reread lines 217–224 to identify descriptive words and phrases the author uses to describe what he can see from the field. To what sense do these descriptions appeal? *(Students should note that "sun, like a broken orange coin"; "something not of this world"; "taut line jutted with an occasional mountain"; and "snapshot of the moon" all appeal to the sense of sight.)* How does Soto's description impact the tone or feeling in the text? *(Possible answer: Soto is recognizing the beauty in an otherwise dismal place. This provides a more hopeful feeling and suggests that he may be becoming more positive about his life.)*

CRITICAL VOCABULARY

irate: The author is describing the bus ride from Fresno to the cotton fields.

ASK STUDENTS what made the dust and sand seem like irate wasps. *(An angry wasp will respond with a furious assault that is difficult to escape, much like the dust surrounding the passengers on the bus.)*

Draw Conclusions

  COMMON CORE **RI 1**

(LINES 256–266)

Remind students that they can use evidence from the text to draw conclusions about things that the author does not explicitly state.

 ASK STUDENTS to reread lines 256–266 with a focus on what Soto says about his home life. What conclusion can you draw from the evidence in the text about problems Soto had at home? *(Soto says that he had "a difficult stepfather" and was told that "I would never do anything, be anyone." He refers to "the way I was treated at home." Readers can conclude that he had a bad relationship with his stepfather and received little love or positive reinforcement from him.)*

CRITICAL VOCABULARY

predicament: Though they laugh about it, Soto is describing the unpleasant situation he and his brother are in.

ASK STUDENTS to describe Soto's predicament. *(He and his brother need to do better in school or they will likely have to work in the fields for the rest of their lives.)*

By 11:00, our lunch time, my ankles were hurting from walking on clods[8] the size of hardballs. My arms ached and my face was dusted by a wind that was perpetual, always busy whipping about. But the work was not bad, I thought. It was better, so much better, than picking grapes, especially with the hourly wage of a dollar twenty-five instead of piece work. Rick and I walked sorely toward the bus where we washed and drank water. Instead of eating in the bus or in the shade of the bus, we kept to ourselves by walking down to

240 the irrigation canal[9] that ran the length of the field, to open our lunch of sandwiches and crackers. We laughed at the crackers, which seemed like a cruel joke from our Mother, because we were working under the sun and the last thing we wanted was a salty dessert. We ate them anyway and drank more water before we returned to the field, both of us limping in exaggeration. Working side by side, we talked and laughed at our **predicament** because our Mother had warned us year after year that if we didn't get on track in school we'd have to work in the fields and then we would see. We mimicked

250 Mother's whining voice and smirked at her smoky view of the future in which we'd be trapped by marriage and screaming kids. We'd eat beans and then we'd see.

Rick pulled slowly away to the rhythm of his hoe falling faster and smoother. It was better that way, to work alone. I could hum made-up songs or songs from the radio and think to myself about school and friends. At the time I was doing badly in my classes, mainly because of a difficult stepfather, but also because I didn't care anymore. All through junior high and into my first year of high school there were those

260 who said I would never do anything, be anyone. They said I'd work like a donkey and marry the first Mexican girl that came along. I was reminded so often, verbally and in the way I was treated at home, that I began to believe that chopping cotton might be a lifetime job for me. If not chopping cotton, then I might get lucky and find myself in a car wash or restaurant or junkyard. But it was clear; I'd work, and work hard.

I cleared my mind by humming and looking about. The sun was directly above with a few soft blades of clouds against a sky that seemed bluer and more beautiful than our sky in

270 the city. Occasionally the breeze flurried and picked up dust

predicament
(prĭ-dĭk´ə-mənt) *n.*
A *predicament* is an unpleasant situation from which it is difficult to free oneself.

---

[8] **clods:** hardened clumps of soil.
[9] **irrigation canal:** a ditch that brings water to crops.

412 Collection 6

Cotton field

so that I had to cover my eyes and screw up my face. The workers were hunched, brown as the clods under our feet, and spread across the field that ran without end—fields that were owned by corporations, not families.

I hoed trying to keep my mind busy with scenes from school and pretend girlfriends until finally my brain turned off and my thinking went fuzzy with boredom. I looked about, no longer mesmerized by the beauty of the landscape, . . . no longer dreaming of the clothes I'd buy with my pay. My eyes

280 followed my chopping as the plants, thin as their shadows, fell with each strike. I worked slowly with ankles and arms hurting, neck stiff, and eyes stinging from the dust and the sun that glanced off the field like a mirror.

By quitting time, 3:00, there was such an excruciating pain in my ankles that I walked as if I were wearing snowshoes. Rick laughed at me and I laughed too, embarrassed that most of the men were walking normally and I was among the first timers who had to get used to this work. "And what about you . . ." I came back at Rick. His eyes were meshed red and

290 his long hippie hair was flecked with dust and gnats and bits of leaves. We placed our hoes in the back of a pickup and stood in line for our pay, which was twelve fifty. I was amazed at the pay, which was the most I had ever earned in one day, and thought that I'd come back the next day, Sunday. This was too good.

Instead of joining the others in the labor bus, we jumped in the back of a pickup when the driver said we'd get to town sooner and were welcome to join him. We scrambled

One Last Time **413**

(t) ©Cyrille Gibot/Alamy Images; (inset) ©Getty Images

CLOSE READ

Analyze the Meanings of Words and Phrases

COMMON CORE RI 1, RI 4

(LINES 279–291)

Remind students that authors often use comparisons, such as similes, along with other imagery to convey a visual impression.

J **CITE TEXT EVIDENCE** Have students reread lines 279–291 and identify similes and imagery Soto uses. *(Similes: "thin as their shadows," "glanced off the field like a mirror," and "walked as if I were wearing snowshoes." Imagery: "eyes were meshed red" and "long hippie hair was flecked with dust and gnats and bits of leaves.")* **How does Soto's description impact the tone?** *(Possible answer: The description creates a feeling of powerlessness, as if the brothers had gone up against a force of nature and lost.)*

Analyze the Meanings of Words and Phrases

COMMON CORE RI 4

(LINES 311–322)

Explain to students that authors use imagery and descriptive details to create a feeling or tone in a text.

 ASK STUDENTS to reread lines 311–322 to identify the imagery and descriptive details Soto uses to describe his return to Fresno after a day's work in the fields. How do these details impact the tone or feeling of the text? (*"like a soldier coming home from war"; "necks following us, owl-like"; "cadaverous faces"; "music blared"; "cue balls cracked like dull ice." The tone becomes almost celebratory and suggests a parade-like atmosphere in which the workers are honored for having survived.*)

COLLABORATIVE DISCUSSION Have student partners work together to identify evidence in the text of experiences that influenced Soto as a writer.

ASK STUDENTS to share any questions they generated in the course of reading and discussing the selection.

---

into the truck bed to be joined by a heavy-set and laughing
300 *Tejano* whose head was shaped like an egg, particularly so because the bandana he wore ended in a point on the top of his head. He laughed almost demonically as the pickup roared up the dirt path, a gray cape of dust rising behind us. On the highway, with the wind in our faces, we squinted at the fields as if we were looking for someone. The *Tejano* had quit laughing but was smiling broadly, occasionally chortling tunes he never finished. I was scared of him, though Rick, two years older and five inches taller, wasn't. If the *Tejano* looked at him, Rick stared back for a second or two before he looked away to
310 the fields.

    I felt like a soldier coming home from war when we rattled into Chinatown. People leaning against car hoods stared, their necks following us, owl-like; . . . Chinese grocers stopped brooming their storefronts to raise their cadaverous faces at us. We stopped in front of the Chi Chi Club where Mexican music blared from the juke box and cue balls cracked like dull ice. The *Tejano*, who was dirty as we were, stepped awkwardly over the side rail, dusted himself off with his bandana, and sauntered into the club.

320   Rick and I jumped from the back, thanked the driver who said *de nada*[10] and popped his clutch, so that the pickup jerked and coughed blue smoke. We returned smiling to our car, happy with the money we had made and pleased that we had, in a small way, proved ourselves to be tough; that we worked as well as other men and earned the same pay.

    We returned the next day and the next week until the season was over and there was nothing to do. I told myself that I wouldn't pick grapes that summer, saying all through June and July that it was for Mexicans, not me. When August
330 came around and I still had not found a summer job, I ate my words, sharpened my knife, and joined Mother, Rick, and Debra for one last time.

COLLABORATIVE DISCUSSION How do you think Gary Soto's experiences working in the fields influenced his attitudes toward work? With a partner, discuss how those early work experiences might affect him as a writer. Cite specific evidence from the text to support your ideas.

---

[10] *de nada* (də nä´də) *Spanish:* "You're welcome—it's nothing."

TO CHALLENGE STUDENTS . . .

Brainstorm Titles Have students reread the memoir's title and lines 329–332, reminding students that authors carefully choose titles that reflect key concepts and ideas in a text. Prompt students to consider how "One Last Time" reflects the message and ideas that Gary Soto wants to share in his memoir.

ASK STUDENTS to consider the ideas that Soto emphasizes in his memoir. Have students work in small groups to brainstorm other titles that might be equally appropriate for the memoir. Allow time for groups to share their ideas with the class.

Cite Evidence

COMMON CORE RI 1

Readers rely on more than an author's words to understand a text's complete meaning. Readers also draw conclusions about ideas that are not stated directly in a text. A **conclusion** is a statement of belief or a logical judgement made based on:

- evidence stated in the text
- inferences, or guesses, made about what the text does not say explicitly
- knowledge gained from personal experience
- reasoning that connects what you know and what you read

To help you draw a conclusion, you can fill in a statement like this:

"Based on _____ and _____, I believe _____."

Reread the first two paragraphs of "One Last Time" and draw a conclusion about Soto's attitude toward his family and the kind of work they did.

Analyze the Meanings of Words and Phrases

COMMON CORE RI 4

Authors choose words carefully to help readers imagine the things they are describing. **Imagery** is the use of descriptive words and phrases to create word pictures, or images. These images are formed through the use of **sensory details,** details that appeal to one or more of the five senses—sight, hearing, smell, taste, and touch.

Notice the many sensory details in these sentences from "One Last Time."

> I cut another bunch, then another, fighting the <u>snap</u> and <u>whip</u> of vines. After ten minutes of groping for grapes, my first pan brimmed with bunches. I poured them on the paper tray, which was <u>bordered by a wooden frame</u> that kept the grapes from rolling off, and they spilled like <u>jewels from a pirate's chest</u>.

 Appeal to hearing and touch

Appeal to sight

Identify other words in the passage that appeal to the five senses, and continue to notice Soto's use of imagery and senory details as you review the text.

TEACH

CLOSE READ

Cite Evidence

COMMON CORE RI 1

Discuss the definition of *conclusion* and each of the items in the bulleted list. Prompt students to complete the cloze statement to model using text evidence, inferences, personal experience, and reasoning to draw a conclusion about "One Last Time."

Analyze the Meanings of Words and Phrases

COMMON CORE RI 4

Review the definition of *imagery,* and ask students to suggest examples of sensory details that appeal to sight, hearing, smell, taste, and touch.

Guide students to consider how the sensory details in the example shown from "One Last Time" impact the tone or feeling of the passage. *(Possible answer: The details suggest an adventurous feeling.)* Have students identify sensory details in another passage from the selection and explain their impact.

Strategies for Annotation 🖊 🗐 *Annotate it!*

Analyze the Meanings of Words and Phrases

COMMON CORE RI 4

Share these strategies for guided or independent analysis:

- Highlight in yellow details that appeal to hearing.
- Highlight in green details that appeal to touch.
- Highlight in blue details that appeal to sight.
- On a note, record what the imagery makes you feel.

> We <u>scrambled</u> into the truck bed to be joined by a <u>heavy-set</u> and laughing *Tejano* whose head was <u>shaped like an egg</u>, particularly so because the bandana he wore ended <u>in a point on the top of his</u> head. He laughed almost demonically as the pickup roa— humorous feeling

PRACTICE & APPLY

Analyzing the Text RI 1, RI 3, RI 4, RI 6

Possible answers:

1. Soto "got a sliver" and thinks of "the whole morning of bend, cut, pour again and again." When he first arrived, Soto was energetic and eager to work. Now he dreads the idea of returning to work.

2. He feels that having nice/new clothing is an important part of fitting in at school. He compares himself to a magician because, like a magician, he creates an illusion to make it seem that he has a bigger wardrobe than he really does.

3. The imagery creates a vivid scene and adds some humor with the suggestion that they are under attack by dust.

Sight	Hearing	Taste	Touch
poorly dressed; loudly mismatched colors	banged palm against side of bus; idled; slow chugs	dusty	whipping about like irate wasps; gravel ticked about us

4. Sights: heavy-set; head shaped like an egg; bandana ended in a point on the top of his head; smiling broadly; Sounds: laughing; laughed demonically; chortled tunes

5. Soto prefers chopping cotton because he is paid by the hour rather than by the number of trays he fills; as a result, he makes a lot more money than he has ever made before. Even though his body aches and the conditions are difficult, he thinks it's "not bad."

6. Based on the physical and mental toll it takes on his body and mind and based on the poor pay it returns, I believe Gary Soto thinks of agricultural work as a difficult way to make a living.

 eBook *Annotate It!*

Analyzing the Text 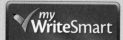 COMMON CORE RI 1, RI 2, RI 3, RI 4, RI 6, SL 1a, SL 1b

Cite Text Evidence   Support your responses with evidence from the text.

1. **Compare** Examine lines 75–85. Identify statements that show how Soto feels about the work he's doing. What change has occurred in his attitude since he first arrived at the farm?

2. **Make Inferences** Reread lines 141–172 to draw conclusions about the author's attitude toward clothing when he was a teenager. What does he mean when he says "I worked like a magician"?

3. **Analyze** Use a chart like the one shown to identify sensory details in the paragraph that begins on line 182. What do these details help you to understand about Soto?

Sight	Hearing	Taste	Touch

4. **Analyze** Reread lines 299–310. Which sensory details help you imagine how the *Tejano* looks and sounds?

5. **Draw Conclusions** What type of agricultural work does Soto prefer? Draw a conclusion about why he has this preference.

6. **Draw Conclusions** What is Soto's attitude toward agricultural work? Express your ideas by filling in a statement like the following, expanding it as necessary: Based on _____ and _____, I believe Gary Soto thinks of agricultural work as _____ .

PERFORMANCE TASK

Speaking Activity: Presentation
With a small group, make a poster that illustrates the central idea of "One Last Time."

• First, work with your group to determine the central idea of the memoir. What is the main message you think Gary Soto wants to communicate. Discuss the imagery and events that support this idea.

• Next, make a poster. In the center, write the central idea. Then, create a collage of words and images from the selection that helps illustrate this idea. The images can be illustrations you draw or photos from other sources.

• Present your work to the class, explaining how the images and quotations in the poster connect to the central idea of the memoir.

Assign this performance task.

PERFORMANCE TASK   COMMON CORE RI 2, SL 1a, SL 1b

Speaking Activity: Presentation After small groups determine the central idea of "One Last Time," have them brainstorm the images and words that will convey that idea on the poster. Tell students to practice explaining their central idea and poster before they present it to the class. Remind group members to follow the rules for classroom discussion as presentations are made.

Critical Vocabulary

COMMON CORE L 4c, L 4d

ramble	foreman	grope	feeble
stoop	contractor	irate	predicament

Practice and Apply Complete each sentence in a way that shows the meaning of the vocabulary word.

1. The principal became **irate** because . . .

2. Each day the **foreman** at the factory has to . . .

3. My friend found himself in a **predicament** when . . .

4. Our neighbors hired a **contractor** because . . .

5. You have to **stoop** if you want to . . .

6. Henry still felt **feeble** because . . .

7. Be sure you don't **ramble** when . . .

8. Alissa had to **grope** for some candles because . . .

Vocabulary Strategy: Using a Dictionary

A **dictionary** is a reference work—either print or digital—that gives information about words. Notice the parts of a dictionary entry:

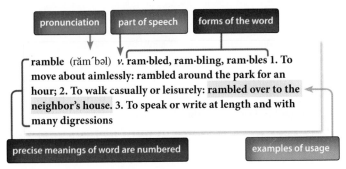

Practice and Apply Use a dictionary to look up the following words from "One Last Time." Then fill out a chart like the one shown.

Word	Pronunciation	Part of Speech	Guessed Definition	Dictionary Definition
elaboration (line 83)				
mesmerized (line 278)				
chortling (line 286)				

PRACTICE & APPLY

Critical Vocabulary

COMMON CORE L 4c, L 4d

Possible answers:

1. *some students broke school windows.*

2. *assign each worker a task.*

3. *he left his books and homework on the bus.*

4. *they need someone to repair their leaky roof.*

5. *be able to reach down and weed the garden.*

6. *he was recovering from the flu.*

7. *you are asked to give a short answer in class.*

8. *she couldn't see in the dark when the power went out.*

Vocabulary Strategy: Using a Dictionary

Word	Pronunciation	Part of Speech	Dictionary Definition
elaboration	î-lăb´ ə-rā´ shən	*noun*	*additional information*
mesmerized	mĕz´ mə rīzd´	*verb*	*fascinated; enthralled*
chortling	chôr´ tlĭng	*verb*	*laughing in a snorting, joyful manner*

Strategies for Annotation ✎ 📖 *Annotate it!*

Using a Dictionary

COMMON CORE L 4c, L 4d

Have students use their eBook annotation tools to do the following:

- Highlight in yellow the entry word.
- Highlight in blue the pronunciation.
- Highlight in pink the part of speech.
- Highlight in green the meaning of the sample word.

The *Tejano* had quit laughing but was smiling broadly, occasionally chortling tunes he never finished. I was scared of him, though Rick

chortle (chôr´ tl) *n.* chortled, chortling, chortles. **1.** a snorting joyful laugh or chuckle.

Language Conventions: Semicolons and Run-ons

Tell students that they should have a reason to use a semicolon in each of the practice sentences. If a sentence is correct, they should be able to identify the reason why it is correct.

1. *Soto and his friend went to the mall; they drooled over clothes in the fancy windows.*

2. *When Soto couldn't find another job, he ate his words; he joined his mother, brother, and sister picking grapes.*

3. *correct: the sentence begins with a dependent clause, so the comma is appropriate punctuation.*

4. *Rick, Soto's brother, didn't appear to be sore; his hair was flecked with dust, gnats, and bits of leaves.*

Assess It!

Online Selection Test
- Download an editable ExamView bank.
- Assign and manage this test online.

Language Conventions: Semicolons and Run-ons

 COMMON CORE L 1, L 2

A **run-on sentence** is made up of two or more independent clauses—or a group of words that contains a subject and predicate and can stand alone as a sentence—that are written as though they were one. Some run-ons have no punctuation within them, as in this example.

Incorrect: I didn't want to work I wanted to stay home.

Other run-ons may have independent clauses that are sepearted with a comma where a conjuncion or a semicolon is needed.

Incorrect: I thought I had enough clothes, I was wrong.

A **semicolon (;)** is a type of punctuation mark that can be used to separate the two independent clauses in a compound sentence.

Use a semicolon . . .	Example
. . . between two independent clauses when the relationship between the two clauses is very clear. The semicolon takes the place of a coordinating conjunction, such as *and, but, or,* or *nor*.	"At home I tried them on while Rick looked on enviously; later, the day before school started, I tried them on again wondering not so much if they were worth it as who would see me first in those clothes."
. . . before a conjunction to separate two independent clauses when one or both of the clauses contain commas.	He asked for new socks, T-shirts, and shoes; but what he really wanted was a phone.

One way to fix a run-on sentence is to break it into two separate sentences. Another way is to use a semicolon between the two independent clauses.

Correct: I didn't want to work. I wanted to stay home.

Correct: I thought I had enough clothes; I was wrong.

Practice and Apply Correct each sentence that has an error by rewriting it and adding a semicolon. If a sentence is already correct, write *correct*.

1. Soto and his friend went to the mall they drooled over clothes.

2. When Soto couldn't find another job, he ate his words, and he joined his mother, brother, and sister picking grapes.

3. Instead of joining the other workers in the labor bus, the boys jumped in the back of a pickup truck to get to town sooner.

4. Rick, Soto's brother, didn't appear to be sore, but his hair was flecked with dust, gnats, and bits of leaves.

INTERACTIVE WHITEBOARD LESSON
Analyze Paragraph Structure

COMMON CORE
RI 5

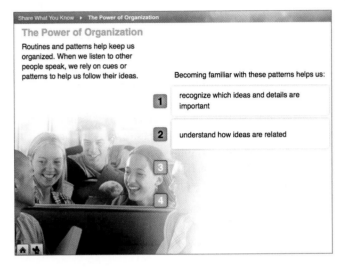

Share What You Know ▸ The Power of Organization

The Power of Organization

Routines and patterns help keep us organized. When we listen to other people speak, we rely on cues or patterns to help us follow their ideas.

Becoming familiar with these patterns helps us:

1 recognize which ideas and details are important

2 understand how ideas are related

3

4

TEACH

Explain to students that each paragraph within a text can have a structure that helps a writer to develop and refine key concepts. Point out that writers select a pattern of organization that helps them emphasize key ideas. Discuss the following paragraph structures:

- **Main Ideas and Details:** A paragraph presents a central concept and provides facts to support it.
- **Chronological Order:** A paragraph presents events in the order in which they occurred.
- **Cause and Effect:** A paragraph presents events and the reason(s) they happen.
- **Comparison-Contrast:** A paragraph presents the similarities and differences between two things.
- **Problem-Solution:** A paragraph presents an issue or problem and suggests a solution.

COLLABORATIVE DISCUSSION

Have small groups analyze the different paragraph structures Gary Soto uses to help define his key ideas in "One Last Time." Students should evaluate how each sentence in a given paragraph contributes to its structure and helps to develop or refine a key concept.

Draw Conclusions

COMMON CORE
RI 1

RETEACH

Review the terms *conclusions, text evidence, inferences, prior knowledge,* and *reasoning.* Then, provide examples such as the following, and ask students to draw conclusions:

"I can't believe the bus is late," Deena thought. "What will my new boss think of me?"

Have students use the cloze statement to explain their conclusions:

- "Based on _____ and _____, I believe _____."

(Possible answer: Based on "the bus is late" and "new boss," I believe it is Deena's first day on a new job.)

LEVEL UP TUTORIALS Assign the following *Level Up* tutorial: **Drawing Conclusions**

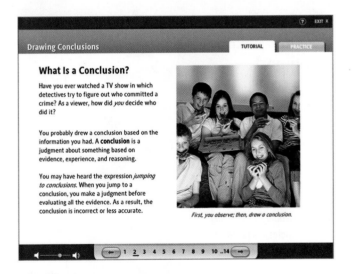

? EXIT X

Drawing Conclusions   TUTORIAL   PRACTICE

What Is a Conclusion?

Have you ever watched a TV show in which detectives try to figure out who committed a crime? As a viewer, how did *you* decide who did it?

You probably drew a conclusion based on the information you had. A **conclusion** is a judgment about something based on evidence, experience, and reasoning.

You may have heard the expression *jumping to conclusions.* When you jump to a conclusion, you make a judgment before evaluating all the evidence. As a result, the conclusion is incorrect or less accurate.

First, you observe; then, draw a conclusion.

1 2 3 4 5 6 7 8 9 10 ..14

CLOSE READING APPLICATION

Individual students can apply the skill to another selection in Collection 6 or to passages from the memoir. Ask students to use the cloze statement to explain how they reached each of their conclusions.

The Real McCoy

Biography by Jim Haskins

Why This Text

Students may be so captivated by the subject of a biography that they fail to pay attention to some of the author's more subtle ideas. If the subject of the biography lived in an era that is unfamiliar to students, they may have difficulty comprehending the text. With the help of the close-reading questions, students will draw conclusions from the biography, supporting them with text evidence. This close reading will lead students to understand the biography and the life of McCoy.

Background Have students read the background and information about the author. Introduce the selection by telling students that the United States became an industrial power in the second half of the nineteenth century. Steam engines allowed railroads to revolutionize transportation across the continent. Even more importantly, they made factory manufacturing possible. The era, however, was one of great turmoil—and promise—for black Americans.

SETTING A PURPOSE Ask students to pay attention to conclusions they draw about McCoy. What kind of evidence does the author provide to support these conclusions?

 COMMON CORE

Common Core Support

- cite strong textual evidence
- determine a central idea of a text
- analyze connections among individuals, ideas, and events
- determine the meaning of words and phrases as they are used in a text
- evaluate the argument and claims in a text

▲ Text Complexity Rubric

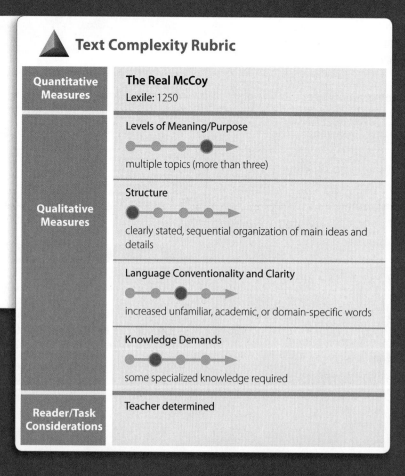

Quantitative Measures	**The Real McCoy** Lexile: 1250
Qualitative Measures	**Levels of Meaning/Purpose** multiple topics (more than three)
	Structure clearly stated, sequential organization of main ideas and details
	Language Conventionality and Clarity increased unfamiliar, academic, or domain-specific words
	Knowledge Demands some specialized knowledge required
Reader/Task Considerations	Teacher determined

Strategies for CLOSE READING

Cite Evidence for Conclusions

Students should read this biography carefully all the way through. Close-reading questions at the bottom of the page will help them focus on a thorough analysis of the text as they cite evidence and draw conclusions. As they read, students should jot down comments or questions about the text in the margins.

WHEN STUDENTS STRUGGLE . . .

To help students cite evidence that supports conclusions they draw from "The Real McCoy," have them work in small groups to fill out a chart like the one shown below.

CITE TEXT EVIDENCE For practice in drawing conclusions in a biography, ask students to cite text evidence for each cell in the chart.

Evidence	Evidence
McCoy got an apprenticeship in Scotland, where bias against his color was less than in America..	McCoy couldn't get a job as a mechanical engineer because of racial prejudice.

Conclusion
Blacks still had to confront discrimination after the Civil War.

Evidence	Evidence
He became interested in the problems of lubricating machinery.	He worked on the problem of automatic lubrication on his own time for two years.

Conclusion
McCoy was not demoralized by his repetitive, mindless job.

Background *Jim Haskins (1941–2005) was born into a large family in Demopolis, Alabama. After graduating from college, Haskins moved to New York City, where he taught special education classes in Harlem. He drew from his experiences there to write his first book, Diary of a Harlem Schoolteacher. Haskins's books for young adults often highlight the lives of famous African Americans, as well as African language and culture. A few of his books have been turned into movies, including the award-winning The Cotton Club.*

The Real McCoy

Biography by Jim Haskins

CLOSE READ
Notes

1. **READD** As you read lines 1–29, begin to collect and cite text evidence.
   - Underline details about the environment Elijah McCoy was born into and the different places where he lived.
   - Circle two sources of power during the age of the machine, and in the margin, explain why McCoy was fortunate to be born into that era.
   - In the margin, explain why McCoy could not get the kind of job he had been trained for.

Elijah McCoy's name is still remembered today and has become **synonymous** with the ideas of perfection and quality. When we say that something is "the real McCoy," we are remembering Elijah McCoy whether we are aware of it or not.

(A) Elijah McCoy (1843–1929) was born on May 2, 1843, in Colchester, Ontario, Canada, the son of two runaway slaves, fugitives who had escaped from Kentucky by way of the Underground Railroad. After the Civil War, Elijah and his parents returned to the (B) United States, settling down near Ypsilanti, Michigan. There Elijah
10 attended school and worked in a machine shop.

McCoy, even as a boy, was fascinated with machines and tools. He was fortunate to have been born into an era that suited him perfectly, a time when newer and better machines were being invented—the age

synonymous:
equivalent;
comparable

McCoy was
fascinated
with the
machinery of
the age.

125

---

1. **READ AND CITE TEXT EVIDENCE** Explain to students that Great Britain outlawed slavery before the United States did, so escaped slaves often tried to make their way to Canada, a British territory.

(A) ASK STUDENTS to find references to the various places that McCoy lived. *McCoy was born in Colchester, Ontario, Canada (lines 5–6). He and his family moved near Ypsilanti, Michigan, after the Civil War (lines 8–9). He later moved to Edinburgh, Scotland, to get an apprenticeship in mechanical engineering (line 18). After he finished the apprenticeship, he returned to the United States, most likely to Michigan, since he got a job with the Michigan Central Railroad (lines 21, 27–29).*

Critical Vocabulary: synonymous (line 2) Have students share their definitions of *synonymous*, and ask volunteers to use the adjective in sentences.

of the machine. Following the footsteps of ⟨steam⟩ was that new energy source ⟨electricity,⟩ which opened up even more opportunities for the inventive mind.

McCoy's interest only deepened with the emergence of each new device. He decided to go to Edinburgh, Scotland, where the bias against his color was not so evident, and serve an apprenticeship in
20 mechanical engineering. After finishing his apprenticeship, McCoy returned to the United States a mechanical engineer, eager to put his skills to work. But companies at that time were reluctant to hire a black man to fill such a highly skilled position. Prejudice was strong and the myth that blacks were intellectually inferior to whites persisted. Companies felt that McCoy could not possibly be as skilled as he claimed to be and, even if he were, the white workers he might have to supervise would never take orders from a black man. The only job he was able to find was as a fireman on the Michigan Central Railroad.
30   The job of fireman was hardly one that required the sophisticated
C skills McCoy had obtained. His duties consisted of fueling the firebox of the engine to "keep the steam up" and oiling the engine. The way
D train and other types of engines were built meant that it was necessary to stop the train periodically—or to shut down whatever

---

2. **◀ REREAD** Reread lines 1–29. What conclusions can you draw about each time McCoy changed his home? Support your answer with explicit textual evidence.

Elijah McCoy moved back from Canada with his parents after the Civil War, when they would no longer be considered "fugitives." McCoy traveled to Scotland to learn his trade because "the bias against his color was not so evident" there. He returned to Michigan "eager to put his skills to work."

3. **READ ▶** As you read lines 30–49, continue to cite textual evidence.

- Underline the words and images that describe a fireman's job.
- In the margin, explain what McCoy did to overcome "unthinking lethargy" (line 40).
- Circle what McCoy wanted to achieve.

" For two years he worked on the problem on his own time . . . "

engine was being used—so the moving parts could be lubricated. If the engines were not oiled, the parts would wear out quickly or friction would cause the parts to heat up, causing fires. Hand-lubricating engines was an inefficient but necessary procedure.

Many men or women, when faced with a repetitive, essentially
40 mindless task, might sink into an unthinking **lethargy,** doing only that which is required of them and no more, but this was not true of Elijah McCoy. He did his job—oiling the engines—but that job led him to become interested in the problems of lubricating any kind of machinery that was in motion. For two years he worked on the problem on his own time in his own homemade machine shop. His

McCoy's "mindless" job inspired him to work on his own for two years to solve a problem.

lethargy
boredom

---

4. **◀ REREAD** Reread lines 31–38. Is there enough evidence to support the conclusion the author makes in lines 37–38? Support your response with explicit textual evidence.

There is enough evidence. To keep engine parts in good shape ad prevent fires, "it was necessary to stop the train periodically—or to shut down whatever engine was being used."

---

2. **REREAD AND CITE TEXT EVIDENCE**

B **ASK STUDENTS** to state or infer the reason behind each of McCoy's moves. *The family moved back to the United States after the Civil War, so we can infer that the abolishment of slavery was the main reason. He went to Scotland for an apprenticeship because the there was less racial bias there. And he returned to the United States because he wanted to work as a mechanical engineer.*

3. **READ AND CITE TEXT EVIDENCE**

C **ASK STUDENTS** to find and cite text evidence about the job of fireman. What did the fireman do? *He fueled the firebox and oiled the engine (lines 31–32).* Why was lubricating the engine important? *Lubrication was necessary to keep the engine running; without oil, the parts would wear out and maybe cause fires (lines 35–38).* What inference can you make about the job of lubrication? *It must have been boring because the author calls it a "repetitive, essentially mindless task" (lines 39–40).*

4. **REREAD AND CITE TEXT EVIDENCE**

D **ASK STUDENTS** to discuss the author's conclusion about lubricating engines by hand. What are the two parts of his conclusion? *He concludes that lubricating engines by hand was a) inefficient, and b) necessary.* What inference can you make about the job's inefficiency? *Stopping the train to lubricate the engine is inefficient, since the train was no longer transporting goods or people (lines 32–35).* What evidence does the author give for the job's necessity? *Lubrication was a necessity because without oil the engine parts would wear out or heat up and cause fires (lines 35–37).*

Critical Vocabulary: lethargy (line 40) Have students share their definitions of *lethargy.* What might make an engine fireman fall into lethargy? *The repetitiveness of the job, combined with the noise and heat, may make someone fall into lethargy.*

FOR ELL STUDENTS Explain the idiom *on his own time* (line 45) to students. It means "during the time he was not at work."

initial idea was to manufacture the machines with canals cut into them with connecting devices between their various parts to distribute the oil throughout the machines while they were running. He wanted to make lubrication automatic.

50   Finally McCoy came up with what he called "the lubricating cup," or "drip cup." The lubricating cup was a small container filled with oil, with a stopcock to regulate the flow of oil into the parts of a moving machine. The lubricating or drip cup seemed an obvious invention, yet no one had thought of it before McCoy; it has since been described as the "key device in perfecting the overall lubrication system used in large industry today." With a drip cup installed, it was no longer necessary to shut down a machine in order to oil it, thus saving both time and money. McCoy received his patent for it on July 12, 1872.

5. **READ ▶** As you read lines 50–72, continue to cite textual evidence.

- Circle the benefits of the "drip cup."
- In the margin, write why people would ask if a machine contained "the real McCoy."

6. **◀ REREAD** Reread lines 50–59. What conclusions can you draw about why Elijah McCoy was the first to imagine the "drip cup," even though it seemed to be an "obvious invention"? Support your answer with explicit textual evidence.

Many people, "when faced with a repetitive, essentially mindless task, might sink into an unthinking lethargy." Elijah McCoy, however, was invested in his job due to his interest in machines, and became "interested in the problems of lubricating any kind of machinery that was in motion."

128

E 60 The drip cup could be used on machinery of all types and it was quickly adopted by machine manufacturers everywhere. Of course, there were imitators, but their devices were not as effective or efficient as McCoy's. It soon became standard practice for an equipment buyer to inquire if the machine contained "the real McCoy." So commonly was this expression used that it soon spread outside the machine industry and came to have the general meaning of the "real thing," or perfection. Nowadays if someone states that they want "the real McCoy," it is taken to mean that they want the genuine article, the best, not a shoddy imitation. In 1872, of course, Elijah McCoy could 70 not foresee that his name would soon become associated with the idea of perfection. All he knew was that the thing worked and worked well on machinery of all types.

The lubrication of machinery fascinated McCoy and he continued to work in that area. In 1892 he invented and patented a number of devices for lubricating locomotive engines. These inventions were used in all western railroads and on steamers plying the Great Lakes. Eventually McCoy would invent a total of twenty-three lubricators for different kinds of equipment and, in 1920, he applied his system to air brakes on vehicles.

80   During his lifetime, Elijah McCoy was awarded over fifty-seven patents and became known as one of the most prolific black inventors of the nineteenth century. In addition to his patents on various kinds of lubricating systems, he also received patents for such "homey" objects as an ironing table (a forerunner of today's ironing board), a lawn sprinkler, a steam dome and a dope cup (a cup for administering medicine). He eventually founded the Elijah McCoy Manufacturing Company in Detroit, Michigan, to develop and sell his inventions.

"The real McCoy" was superior to imitators' drip cups.

7. **READ ▶** As you read lines 73–92, continue to cite textual evidence.

- Underline McCoy's inventions.
- Circle a phrase that uses sensory details to appeal to the sense of hearing.
- In line 92, infer what "paean" means, and write your inference in the margin.

---

5. **READ AND CITE TEXT EVIDENCE**

E ASK STUDENTS to discuss the phrase "the real McCoy." What did "the real McCoy" refer to originally? *It referred to Elijah McCoy's invention, the drip cup (lines 60–67).* Why did equipment buyers want "the real McCoy?" *It worked better and more efficiently than drip cups made by other machine manufacturers (lines 62–63).*

6. **REREAD AND CITE TEXT EVIDENCE**

F ASK STUDENTS to state possible conclusions about McCoy's invention of the drip cup. *McCoy was well-positioned to invent the drip cup.* What evidence supports your conclusion? *McCoy was a mechanical engineer so he had the skills to solve mechanical problems. He worked as a fireman, which meant that he saw how inefficient it was to hand-lubricate engines. Instead of sinking into lethargy at his mindless job, he viewed the problems of lubrication as a challenge. He worked on a solution for two years on his own time.*

7. **READ AND CITE TEXT EVIDENCE**

G ASK STUDENTS to cite text evidence of McCoy's later inventions. *Students should mention his 1892 devices for lubricating locomotive engines (lines 74–75), his twenty-three other lubricators (lines 77–79), the total of fifty-seven patents (lines 80–81), and his patents for "homey" objects (lines 83–86).*

FOR ELL STUDENTS Ask students to guess the meaning of the informal adjective *homey* (line 83). Point out that the meaning is fairly apparent. The context clues should help students understand that *homey* means "having the feeling of home."

The Real McCoy **418e**

A paean is a testament or tribute.

Until his death in 1929, McCoy continued working and inventing, sometimes patenting two or three new devices a year. Today, although 90 many may not know who he was or what he did, his name remains to remind us of the idea of quality, and the steady, ceaseless roar of machinery is a paean to his inventiveness.

H

8. **◄ REREAD** Reread lines 72–92. What conclusion can you make about why the author feels "the steady, ceaseless roar of machinery is a paean to" McCoy's "inventiveness"? Support your answer with explicit textual evidence.

Without McCoy's invention of the "drip cup," "the steady, ceaseless roar of machinery" would not be "ceaseless." The "drip cup" allows machines to be lubricated without being stopped.

SHORT RESPONSE

Cite Text Evidence What conclusions can you make about the way Elijah McCoy was treated after he invented the "drip cup"? Support your answer with **explicit textual evidence.**

Before Elijah McCoy invented the "drip cup," companies "were reluctant to hire a black man" due to the myth that "blacks were intellectually inferior to whites." However, with the invention of the "drip cup," McCoy soon became a household name, as "it became standard practice for an equipment buyer to inquire if the machine contained 'the real McCoy.'" One can conclude that McCoy became extremely successful despite the color of his skin, since he "was awarded over fifty-seven patents and became known as one of the most prolific black inventors of the nineteenth century."

130

TO CHALLENGE STUDENTS . . .

For deeper understanding and more context, students can research the importance of steam engines in U.S. development in the nineteenth century.

ASK STUDENTS to discuss the way steam engines revolutionized transportation. *Railroads and shipping companies were the first industries to adopt steam engines as a new power source. In both cases, the effect was to "shorten" the great distances separating different towns and regions. Steamships could carry goods and people quickly and cheaply between coastal cities, across the Great Lakes, and the lengths of rivers such as the Mississippi, Ohio, and Hudson. Steam-powered trains could make the trip to western towns like Chicago, St. Louis, and, eventually, San Francisco in a matter of days, rather than months. The steam engine thus helped open the interior of the country to settlement, as emigrants could now be sure that they would be able to buy manufactured goods from—and sell agricultural products to—eastern markets.*

8. **REREAD AND DISCUSS USING TEXT EVIDENCE**

H **ASK STUDENTS** to analyze the image of today's machinery that the author creates. Why is today's machinery roaring "steadily" and "ceaselessly"? *Students should note that the author implies that today's machinery never needs to stop because it employs one of McCoy's automatic lubrication systems. Before McCoy's drip cup and other lubrication inventions, machinery had to be stopped periodically to be oiled by hand.*

SHORT RESPONSE

Cite Text Evidence Students' responses should include text evidence that supports their positions. They should:

- describe the racial prejudice experienced by McCoy.
- state conclusions about McCoy's life after the drip cup.
- support conclusions with evidence from the biography.

DIG DEEPER

1. With the class, return to Question 1, Read. Have students share their margin notes about McCoy's good fortune.

   ASK STUDENTS to discuss sources of power before and during McCoy's era.

   - What power sources did humans use before steam and electricity? *Students should mention animal power, such as mules, horses, and oxen, which were crucial for farming and transportation. Wind power was used to pump water from underground. Water-powered mills were used to grind grains and cut lumber.*

   - What kinds of tools or machinery were associated with these early power sources? *Most human endeavors were accompanied by tools, such as plows, saws, and looms. However, some mechanical devices and even simple machines were employed in mills and early manufactories.*

   - Why was the age of steam power also the age of machinery? *Steam power itself was produced by a remarkably complex machine, the steam engine. To make, maintain, and repair steam engines, a new class of skilled workers was needed. As more and more of these mechanics gained experience and proficiency, they were able to see— and tackle—other tasks that could be improved by new machinery.*

2. With the class, return to Question 3, Read.

   ASK STUDENTS to discuss how McCoy was well-positioned to invent the drip cup.

   - Why did McCoy become a fireman? *He couldn't get a job as a mechanical engineer because of racial prejudice. Companies didn't think black men were smart enough to be engineers and white men wouldn't take orders from them.*

   - How did McCoy respond to work for which he was overqualified? *Even though it was boring work, McCoy found something challenging in it. He recognized the inefficiency of hand-lubrication and applied his mechanical knowledge to inventing an automatic lubricator.*

   ASK STUDENTS to return to their Short Response answer and revise it based on the class discussion.

CLOSE READING NOTES

Teens Need Jobs, Not Just Cash

Teens at Work

Argument by Anne Michaud

Argument from *The Record-Journal*

Why These Texts?

Students regularly encounter differing positions on the economy in print, online, and other media. The ability to evaluate such arguments is a key skill for students who need to become responsible citizens and informed consumers. This lesson explores the features that come together to create sound arguments.

Key Learning Objective: The student will be able to analyze an argument and determine whether its claims are sufficiently supported.

 Common Core Standards

RI 1 Cite textual evidence to support analysis.
RI 2 Determine a central idea; provide an objective summary.
RI 4 Determine the meaning of words and phrases.
RI 5 Analyze the structure of a paragraph.
RI 6 Determine how the author acknowledges and responds to other viewpoints.
RI 8 Delineate and evaluate an argument's claims.
W 7 Conduct short research projects.
SL 4 Present claims and findings in a focused, coherent manner.
SL 5 Integrate multimedia and visual displays into presentations.
SL 6 Adapt speech to a variety of contexts.
L 4b Use Greek affixes as clues to meaning.
L 4d Verify preliminary meaning of a word or phrase.

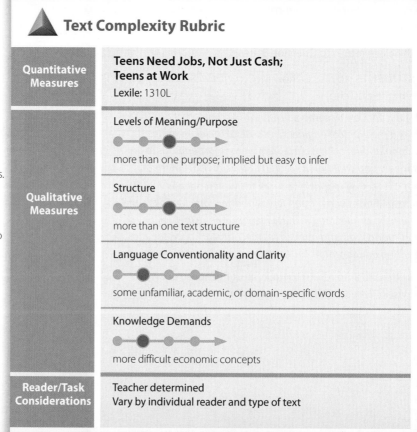

▲ **Text Complexity Rubric**

Quantitative Measures

Teens Need Jobs, Not Just Cash; Teens at Work
Lexile: 1310L

Qualitative Measures

Levels of Meaning/Purpose

more than one purpose; implied but easy to infer

Structure

more than one text structure

Language Conventionality and Clarity

some unfamiliar, academic, or domain-specific words

Knowledge Demands

more difficult economic concepts

Reader/Task Considerations

Teacher determined
Vary by individual reader and type of text

CLOSE READ

Background Have students read the background information. As needed, explain that during an economic recession jobs are difficult to find, and the problem is more extreme for teenagers than it is for adults. Point out the cyclical nature of unemployment: people who do not have jobs buy fewer products, so manufacturers make fewer products and may lay off employees, leaving even more people unemployed.

SETTING A PURPOSE Direct students to use the Setting a Purpose question to focus their reading. Remind students to generate questions as they read.

Delineate and Evaluate an Argument (LINES 1–12)

COMMON CORE RI 8

Tell students that an **argument** is writing that makes a claim and supports it with reasons and evidence. Point out that this author begins her argument with an **anecdote,** a brief account of an interesting incident or event that is usually intended to entertain or make a point.

 ASK STUDENTS to reread lines 1–12 to determine how the anecdote might be relevant, or related to the author's argument. *(Possible answer: The anecdote describes a mistake the author made in her first job; it is relevant to the point she makes in lines 10–12: "Making mistakes like that is partly what early jobs are all about. We learn, and then make better decisions . . . ")*

SCAFFOLDING FOR ELL STUDENTS

Analyze Informal Language Using a whiteboard, project lines 1–9. Explain that the author uses slang, idioms, and other informal language to tell a brief story. Guide students to use context to determine meaning, checking a dictionary as needed.

ASK STUDENTS what makes the author's use of informal language effective in the story.

Background *In 2008, the United States entered into what many called the Great Recession, generally considered to be America's worst economic crisis since the Great Depression of the late 1920s and 1930s. A recession is a slowdown of economic activity. During a recession, people and businesses tend to spend less money, which contributes to a cycle of job losses and decreases in profits. The effects of the Great Recession were felt for years. At the time these arguments were written, the unemployment rate was high for adult workers and even higher for young workers.*

Teens Need Jobs, Not Just Cash

Teens at Work

Argument by Anne Michaud   Argument from *The Record-Journal*

SETTING A PURPOSE As you read, consider the points each author makes about the importance of jobs for teenagers. Which reasons seem most valid to you?

I well remember how my first job made me feel: capable, creative, in charge. I was a summer counselor at a YMCA day camp, and still practically a kid myself, just out of 10th grade. I made a lot of mistakes.

As the arts and crafts counselor, I blew most of my $200 budget on Popsicle sticks and gimp.[1] We ran out of arts and crafts supplies halfway through the summer, and so taking long "nature walks" became our fallback. I wonder what the campers' parents thought.

10 Making mistakes like that is partly what early jobs are all about. We learn, and then make better decisions when the "real" job comes along.

---

[1] **gimp:** a narrow, flat braid used to make crafts such as a key chain.

Teens Need Jobs, Not Just Cash **419**

---

creative, in charge. I was a summer counselor at a YMCA

day camp, and still practically a kid myself, just out of 10th

grade. I made a lot of mistakes.

As the arts and crafts counselor, I blew most of my $200

budget on Popsicle sticks and gimp. We ran out of arts and

crafts supplies halfway through the summer, and so taking

long "nature walks" became our fallback. I wonder what the

Evaluate an Argument

COMMON CORE RI 1, RI 5, RI 6

(LINES 20–27)

Explain that authors of persuasive texts often anticipate ways in which others might disagree with their arguments, so authors include **counterarguments** to challenge those opposing views.

 CITE TEXT EVIDENCE Ask students to reread lines 20–27 to identify the opposing view presented by the author. How does the last sentence in the paragraph support the author's counterargument? *(The author presents the opposing view that some parents "debate the merits of teens taking jobs bagging groceries" rather than focusing on enrichment activities. The final sentence provides statistics to prove the author's counterargument that many teens need to work in order to help support their families.)*

CRITICAL VOCABULARY

sustain: The author is describing an unexpected impact of unemployment.

ASK STUDENTS why a sustained period of unemployment might have long-term effects. *(Possible answer: It may make someone seem like he or she did not want to work.)*

borne: The author is explaining the ups and downs of the business cycle.

ASK STUDENTS what example the author uses to show that problems in the business cycle should be borne by everyone. *(The author cites the availability of unemployment insurance.)*

renowned: The author is describing a training program in Germany.

ASK STUDENTS what might make a job-training program renowned. *(Possible answer: A program might become well known if its trainees were often successful.)*

So it's troubling that teens today are facing their third straight summer of bleak employment prospects—in fact, the worst since World War II, when the government began keeping track. In April, the jobless rate for 16-to 19-year-olds approached 25 percent. And the unemployment rate only counts those actively looking. Many are too discouraged by the dismal economy to try.

20 **B** Parents may debate the merits of teens taking jobs bagging groceries versus studying or pursuing music, sports or college-level courses. But the poorest Americans don't have that choice, and to double down[2] on their woes, they are hit hardest by teen unemployment. Last summer, just one in five teenagers with annual family income below $20,000 had a job, according to a report by Northeastern University's Center for Labor Market Studies.

Not only aren't these teens earning needed cash— or learning the life lessons I got at the YMCA—but the 30 joblessness they experience now may drag them down for years. One study in the United States and Britain said that 37-year-old men who had **sustained** a year of unemployment before age 23 made 23 percent less than their peers. The equivalent gap was 16 percent for women.

College graduates who took jobs beneath their education or outside of their fields often never got back to where they might have been, according to what the Japanese learned from their "lost decade" of economic doldrums[3] in the 1990s and early 2000s. When the Japanese economy recovered, 40 employers preferred graduates fresh out of school, creating a generation that suffers higher rates of depression, heart attack and suicide, and lower life expectancy.[4]

These structural problems with capitalism—the ups and downs of the business cycle—should not be **borne** by individuals, but collectively. That's why we have unemployment insurance, for example.

Other countries seem to have a better understanding of this. Germany's **renowned** apprenticeship program, a training period of two to four years, attracts roughly two-

sustain
(sə-stān´) v.
When you *sustain* something, you keep it in existence or continue it.

borne
(bôrn) v. If something is *borne*, it is carried or supported.

renowned
(rĭ-nound´) adj.
If something is *renowned*, it is famous.

---

[2] **double down:** to increase one's bet to two times.
[3] **doldrums:** stagnations or slumps.
[4] **life expectancy:** the number of years that an individual is expected to live.

420 Collection 6

APPLYING ACADEMIC VOCABULARY

minors	option

As you discuss "Teens Need Jobs, Not Just Cash" and "Teens at Work," incorporate the following Collection 6 academic vocabulary words: *minors* and *option*. Ask students whether they believe **minors** should be allowed to leave school in order to go to work. What **options** should be available to train young people for jobs as adults?

thirds of vocational school[5] students there. They're often
hired afterward, one reason Germany has a far lower youth
unemployment rate than us, at 9.5 percent. Firms and
government share the apprenticeship expenses.

The Netherlands, also keen on **averting** a lost generation
of workers, is dividing full-time private sector[6] jobs into
two or three part-time ones, with government providing
supplemental income for part-time workers. When the
economy improves, Dutch 20-somethings will be ready with
skills and experience.

The New York Youth Works program has the right idea.
On Long Island, at least 64 employers have signed up. The
program offers them tax credits for hiring low-income youth.
Given that unemployment among teens is more than twice the
7.4 percent rate for adults on Long Island, we should expand
this program.

When teens work, it teaches them independence,
responsibility, a good work ethic[7] and how to get along with
others. Our collective future depends on investing in their
success.

avert
(ə-vûrt´) *v.* If you
avert something,
you prevent it from
happening.

---

[5] **vocational school:** a school that teaches trades, such as plumbing or graphic
design.
[6] **private sector:** the privately owned part of the economy that is not funded by
the government.
[7] **work ethic:** the belief in the value of work.

Teens Need Jobs, Not Just Cash **421**

CLOSE READ

Delineate and Evaluate an Argument (LINES 60–65)

 COMMON CORE RI 5, RI 8

Point out that the author is building toward the
conclusion of her argument. Draw attention to the
way in which the paragraph in lines 60–65 develops
a key point.

C **ASK STUDENTS** to reread lines 60–65 to
determine the purpose of the paragraph in the
argument. Which sentences in the paragraph best
support the author's key point? *(The two previous
paragraphs provided examples of effective job programs
in other countries. In lines 60–65, the author cites a New
York program, bringing her argument "closer to home."
The second and third sentences in the paragraph give
facts that show that the program could be successful.)*

CRITICAL VOCABULARY

avert: A program in the Netherlands is aimed at
providing jobs for young people.

ASK STUDENTS why the Netherlands wants to
avert high unemployment among young people.
*(The government wants to avoid the mental and
physical problems that can be long-term effects of
high unemployment.)*

Strategies for Annotation ✏️ 📖 *Annotate it!*

Analyze Structure (LINES 60–65) COMMON CORE RI 5

Tell students to use their eBook annotation tools to do the following:

- Highlight in yellow the key point of the paragraph.
- Underline details in other sentences that support the key point.

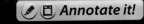

The New York Youth Works program has the right idea.
On Long Island, at least 64 employers have signed up. The
program offers them tax credits for hiring low-income youth.
Given that unemployment among teens is more than twice the
7.4 percent rate for adults on Long Island, we should expand
this program.

Teens Need Jobs, Not Just Cash **421**

Delineate and Evaluate an Argument

COMMON CORE — RI 1, RI 5, RI 8

(LINES 1–10)

Point out that whereas the writer of the first argument started with an anecdote this writer begins with a more specific statement of his or her **claim,** or position on the problem.

D CITE TEXT EVIDENCE Ask students to reread lines 1–10 to identify the author's claim. *(lines 1–3: "To combat high national unemployment for teens, . . . creation of summer and part-time work opportunities.")* How does the position of the sentence stating the claim help to develop the argument? *(The fact that it is the first sentence in the editorial gives the claim added prominence.)*

CRITICAL VOCABULARY

initiative: The author claims that legislators need to help create jobs for teens.

ASK STUDENTS what a jobs initiative would be intended to do. *(An initiative would be a first step in a plan to create many jobs.)*

detrimental: The author is explaining the impact of filling jobs with adults instead of teens.

ASK STUDENTS whether the practice of hiring adults rather than teens is detrimental to adults or to teens. *(It is detrimental to teens, who remain unemployed.)*

Teens at Work

Online Editorial from *The Record-Journal*

To combat high national unemployment rates for teens, legislators[8] must craft more **initiatives** which help induce creation of summer and part-time work opportunities.

According to the U.S. Bureau of Labor Statistics, America's unemployment rate in 2011 for job-aspirants 16 to 19 years old was 24.4 percent, which does not include those who do not apply for openings. Since the Bureau began compiling such data in the late 1940s, last year's number was the second highest ever recorded. Worst of all time was 25.9 percent, in 10 2010. More must be done to address this issue.

Entire families can suffer when wages are not available for older kids. Many teenagers, fortunate enough to have work, contribute portions of paychecks to households' overall budgets. With fewer chances for adolescents to secure employment, steady sources of domestic income disappear. Moreover, when jobs are scarce, even youths who simply want discretionary money[9] must instead request finances from mom, dad or guardians, which places added levels of stress upon the family.

initiative
(ĭ-nĭsh´ə-tĭv) *n.*
An *initiative* is a beginning step in a plan.

> **" Entire families can suffer when wages are not available for older kids. "**

20 One factor behind increased teen joblessness is that youths will often come up against experienced adults willing to work part-time for stable pay. While anyone's successful ascension[10] out of unemployment-status in this sluggish economy is positive, too much position-filling at newer generations' expense is **detrimental** long-term.

detrimental
(dĕt´rə-mĕn´tl) *adj.*
If something is *detrimental*, it causes damage or harm.

---

[8] **legislators:** lawmakers.
[9] **discretionary money:** money to be spent on things you want but do not need.
[10] **ascension:** rise.

©atribut/Shutterstock

WHEN STUDENTS STRUGGLE . . .

To help students delineate, or describe the argument, have them complete a chart like the one shown. Students can then use their charts to see at a glance whether the reasons and evidence provided are relevant.

Claim	Reasons and evidence
Lawmakers must create more jobs for teens.	Unemployment for 16- to 19-year-olds is 24.4 percent.

For at part-time jobs is where most members of tomorrow's labor force will first learn valuable workplace skills. Delaying or denying this experience, crucial to one's ongoing professional development, will engender[11] negative economic **implications** in future decades. People who miss out on employment early may not reach full potential. Already, businesses nationwide report **deficiencies** in quantities of candidates who can fill positions which require advanced capabilities.

Teenagers' employment statistics have worsened also because of automated machines' replacement of personnel at low-level tasks—for example, grocery stores' self-scan aisles—and continued closures of businesses which utilize large staffs … Commendably, the White House and U.S. Department of Labor have begun a campaign to generate 250,000 private-sector jobs, with at least 100,000 being paid spots. While this is a start, even more government-backed employment stimulus[12] is necessary. Otherwise, a generation whose future is already threatened by the Great Recession's aftermath could fall even further behind—an unacceptable, dangerous prospect.

implication
(ĭm′plĭ-kā′shən) *n.*
An *implication* is a connection or consequence.

deficiency
(dĭ-fĭsh′ən-sē) *n.*
A *deficiency* is a lack or shortage of something.

COLLABORATIVE DISCUSSION Both authors mention the value of work experience for teenagers. With a partner, discuss whether the authors have convinced you that getting a job is more important than other school or sports activities you might enjoy. Cite specific evidence from the text to support your ideas.

---

[11] **engender:** produce or create.
[12] **employment stimulus:** funds, special programs, or other incentives provided by the government to generate new jobs or to encourage employers to hire more workers.

CLOSE READ

Delineate and Evaluate an Argument (LINES 26–34)

COMMON CORE **RI 8**

Tell students that information that is **relevant** has a sensible connection to the idea being discussed.

E **ASK STUDENTS** to reread lines 26–34 to determine whether all of the support the author provides is relevant to the claim. *(The author's claim is that more job opportunities should be available for teens. The lack of "candidates who can fill positions which require advanced capabilities" is not clearly connected to jobs for teenagers.)*

> **CRITICAL VOCABULARY**
>
> **implication:** The author is describing possible consequences of high unemployment among teens.
>
> **ASK STUDENTS** what the author believes about the implications of a lack of teen jobs. *(The teens may not reach their full potential.)*
>
> **deficiency:** Businesses have difficulty filling some jobs.
>
> **ASK STUDENTS** what a business might do if there was a deficiency of workers who could do a certain job. *(A business could leave the job empty or take time to train someone to do the job.)*

COLLABORATIVE DISCUSSION Have students work with a partner to discuss the reasons each author presents to support the importance of jobs for teenagers. Remind students to cite evidence from the text as they share their views about whether the authors' claims are convincing.

ASK STUDENTS to share any questions they generated in the course of reading and discussing the selection.

CLOSE READ

Delineate and Evaluate an Argument COMMON CORE RI 5, RI 8

Define and discuss the terms *argument, claim, support,* and *counterargument,* citing examples of each from the two editorials. After reviewing the criteria for evaluating an argument, have volunteers share their thoughts regarding the effectiveness of the arguments in the two editorials. Remind students to cite relevant evidence from the text to support their opinions.

Select one paragraph from the first argument and one paragraph from the second. Then, have partners evaluate each paragraph. The pairs should analyze the role of each sentence within the paragraph in developing the author's claim.

Delineate and Evaluate an Argument COMMON CORE RI 5, RI 8

"Teens Need Jobs, Not Just Cash" and "Teens at Work" both cite the need for the creation of more jobs for adolescents. Writing such as this that makes a claim and supports it with reasons and evidence is called an **argument**.

- A **claim** is the writer's position on an issue or problem. It is often stated directly at the beginning or end of an argument.
- **Support** consists of the reasons and evidence presented to prove the claim. Support may include explanations, specific facts, statistics, or examples.

A good argument anticipates opposing viewpoints and provides counterarguments to disprove them. **Counterarguments** are arguments made to oppose another argument. Notice this example in "Teens at Work."

> . . . youths will often come up against experienced adults willing to work part-time for stable pay. While anyone's successful ascension out of unemployment-status in this sluggish economy is positive, too much position-filling at newer generations' expense is detrimental long-term.

The reasons and evidence given in support of a claim must be **relevant,** or have some sensible connection. Writers may include information that appeals to readers' emotions, but is not really relevant to the claim. It is up to the reader to **evaluate,** or examine carefully, the support for the argument and determine whether it makes sense and is convincing.

Although "Teens Need Jobs, Not Just Cash" and "Teens at Work" both deal with the same topic and make similar claims, there are differences in the strength and relevance of the evidence. As you evaluate each claim, ask yourself the following questions:

- What claim is being made?
- What reasons and evidence are presented in support of the claim?
- Is the support presented in a way that makes sense?
- Are all the reasons and evidence relevant?
- Is an opposing argument addressed with a counterargument?

Strategies for Annotation Annotate it!

Delineate and Evaluate an Argument 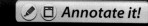 COMMON CORE RI 8

Share these strategies for guided or independent analysis:

- Highlight in yellow claims made by the author.
- Underline counterarguments that the author has included.
- On a note, state whether the author sufficiently rebutted the counterargument.

One factor behind increased teen joblessness is th[ ] will often come up against experienced adults willing [ ] part-time for stable pay. While <u>anyone's successful ascension out of unemployment-status in this sluggish economy is positive,</u> too much position-filling at newer generations' expense is **detrimental** long-term.

> Author explains more in lines 26–34.

 **eBook** *Annotate It!*

Analyzing the Text

Cite Text Evidence   Support your responses with evidence from the texts.

1. **Interpret** In lines 1–12 of "Teens Need Jobs, Not Just Cash," the author includes an **anecdote,** a brief account of an interesting incident or event that is usually intended to entertain or make a point. What impact does this anecdote have on the tone of the article? Explain how it supports the author's claim.

2. **Interpret** What opposing viewpoint is presented in "Teens Need Jobs, Not Just Cash"? What counterargument does the author make?

3. **Evaluate** Reread lines 43–46 of "Teens Need Jobs, Not Just Cash." Is this information relevant as support for the author's claim about the need for jobs for teens? Why or why not?

4. **Analyze** In lines 5–10, why does the author of "Teens at Work" provide statistics about teen unemployment?

5. **Evaluate** Reread lines 26–34 of "Teens at Work." Are you convinced that early part-time work is important in developing a person's life-long career prospects?

6. **Evaluate** Briefly summarize the arguments made in each selection, making sure to include the main claim and support. Then tell which article you think presents the stronger argument and explain your opinion.

PERFORMANCE TASK

Speaking Activity: Oral Report In order to evaluate a claim made in an argument, you may need to do additional research. Prepare an oral report in which you present additional support that proves or disproves a claim made in one of the articles.

- Identify a claim that you will research.

- Use print and digital resources for your research.
- Display the results of your research in a graph or chart.
- Prepare an oral report about your findings and present it to the class. Be sure to use eye contact, appropriate volume, and clear pronunciation.

PERFORMANCE TASK

Speaking Activity: Oral Report See page 426a for instruction on presenting claims and findings. Students should review both arguments and

- identify a claim to research, using print and digital resources
- create a graph or chart to support their work
- present their report to the class

Analyzing the Text

Possible answers:

1. *The author's anecdote about her camp counselor experience is engaging and makes a good point. It creates a friendly, informal tone that makes what could be a complicated subject more accessible and understandable. It also suggests support for the claim that early work experiences can have a long-term impact on teens.*

2. *The opposing viewpoint is that parents believe it is more important for teens to study, pursue music or sports, or take college-level courses rather than work in menial jobs. The counterargument is that lower-income families whose teens need to work in order to help the family are hardest hit by teen unemployment.*

3. *The information is irrelevant to the topic of teen employment. It cites the extreme swings in business cycles inherent in capitalism as a reason for programs such as unemployment insurance, but it does not connect specifically to teen employment.*

4. *The author cites statistics compiled by the Bureau of Labor Statistics showing the highest unemployment rates since the bureau began keeping records in the late 1940s. These data make the point that the problem being discussed is extreme.*

5. *The author claims in a general way that the economy benefits from the skills teens acquire in part-time jobs. This claim would be better supported with additional evidence in the form of statistics on the number of businesses suffering from the lack of qualified candidates or with specific examples of skills teens acquire that help their professional development.*

6. *Both articles argue for legislation that will create more jobs for teens. They make similar claims, including the high teen unemployment rate, the negative effect of teen unemployment on family income, and the long-term benefits to the economy of workers who gain experience and skills as teens. "Teens at Work" presents the better argument. Although the support could be stronger, the evidence makes sense, is better organized, and includes a strong counterargument to an opposing viewpoint.*

TEACH

CLOSE READ

Critical Vocabulary

COMMON CORE L 4b, L 4d

Possible answers:

1. *Yes; a deficiency, or lack, of certain vitamins can be detrimental, or harmful, to the body or cause sickness.*

2. *No; if he or she were renowned, or well known, you would want to see the performance, not look away.*

3. *Because the law was your idea, stay in contact with lawmakers to encourage them to pass the law, or create advertisements to make the public aware of the law.*

4. *If one or two people do most of the work, the implication is that other team members are not working very much.*

Vocabulary Strategy: Using Greek Suffixes

Possible answers:

1. *Both socialism and communism refer to systems of government.*

2. *Impressionism is a style or practice of painting without elaborate details.*

3. *Realism is the practice of presenting realistic events and characters in literature.*

4. *Activism is the practice of taking action to oppose something.*

Critical Vocabulary

COMMON CORE L 4b, L 4d

sustain	borne	renowned	avert
initiative	detrimental	implication	deficiency

Practice and Apply Use what you know about the Vocabulary words to answer the following questions.

1. Is a vitamin **deficiency detrimental** to your health? Why or why not?

2. If a dancer were **renowned** for his or her performing style, would you **avert** you eyes during a performance? Why or why not?

3. If you create an **initiative** to pass a law, what might **sustain** interest in it?

4. If most of the work on a project is **borne** by one or two people, what is the **implication** about other members of that project's team?

Vocabulary Strategy: Using Greek Suffixes

Suffixes—word parts added to the end of a root or base word—provide clues about the meaning of a word. For example, knowing that the Greek suffix *-ism* means "a practice, doctrine, or system" helps you define words such as *capitalism*. Look at this example from "Teens Need Jobs, Not Just Cash":

> These structural problems with <u>capitalism</u>—the ups and downs of the business cycle—should not be borne by individuals, but collectively.

The context of the sentence and the meaning of the suffix *-ism* help you to understand that the author is referring to an economic system.

When you encounter a suffixed word, follow these steps:
- Identify the meaning of the suffix.
- Look at the base word or word root and think about its meaning.
- Apply the meanings to define the word. Confirm your definition in a dictionary.

Practice and Apply Identify the *-ism* word or words in each sentence. Use the suffix meaning to define the word. Confirm your definition in a dictionary.

1. Which form of government is more authoritarian, socialism or communism?

2. The French painter Claude Monet was a pioneer of impressionism.

3. Teens are attracted to the gritty realism of the writer S. E. Hinton's novels.

4. The students' activism led to the occupation of the administration building.

Strategies for Annotation ✎ 🖺 *Annotate it!*

Vocabulary Strategy: Using Greek Suffixes

COMMON CORE L 4b, L 4d

Have students use their eBook annotation tools to do the following:
- Highlight in yellow the word that includes the suffix *-ism*.
- Use the meaning of the suffix and the base word to determine meaning.
- Confirm the meaning in a dictionary.

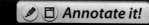

> These structural problems with <u>capitalism</u>—the ups and downs of the business cycle—should not be borne by i[ ] but collectively. That's why we have unemployment ins[ ]

an economic system.

Present Claims and Findings

TEACH

Before students work on the Performance Task, review that a **claim** is a statement of a position on an issue or problem. Explain that for an oral report a speaker's claim is the position or main idea that he or she wants to present.

Point out that after students identify text evidence and conduct research to support their claims, they need to present their findings by

- emphasizing their most important points and ideas
- stating ideas in a way that is easy for listeners to follow
- presenting relevant evidence, clear reasoning, and well-chosen details
- using appropriate eye contact, adequate volume, and clear pronunciation

Explain to students that evidence for a presentation might include photos and diagrams, information in charts or graphs, and film clips. Discuss why these forms of visual support help to make a speaker's ideas easier for listeners to follow.

Elicit or explain that most good presentations require rehearsal. Tell students to practice presentations for a friend, in front of a mirror, or by making a video of themselves.

PRACTICE AND APPLY

Have partners work together to plan a brief presentation on a topic of interest to them. Tell partners to incorporate some form of visual support and to practice the presentation to be sure they can maintain eye contact while speaking clearly with adequate volume.

Delineate and Evaluate an Argument

RETEACH

Review the terms *argument, claim, support, relevant,* and *evaluate.* Present simple arguments such as the following and have students identify the claim and its support:

> Any teenager who does not see this movie will have no friends. Every lunchtime conversation will be about this movie. Young people will talk about this movie for years to come. Teenagers who do not see this movie will try to pretend that they did.

Guide students to evaluate the relevance of the support in each argument presented.

 LEVEL UP TUTORIALS Assign the following *Level Up* tutorial: **Analyzing Arguments**

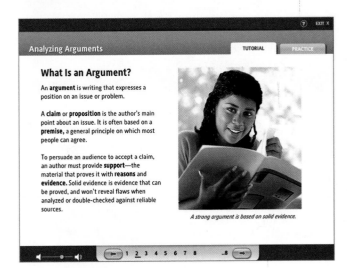

CLOSE READING APPLICATION

Have small groups of students work together to evaluate arguments presented in newspaper, magazine, or online editorials. Prompt students to identify each claim and its support and to evaluate the relevance of the support. Have groups present their findings to the class.

 **ANCHOR TEXT**

Chicago

Find Work

My Mother Enters the Work Force

Poem by Carl Sandburg   Poem by Rhina P. Espaillat   Poem by Rita Dove

Why These Texts?

Analyzing a poem's form deepens the reader's appreciation of that poem and is integral to understanding its meaning. This lesson focuses on poetic form and the different ways in which poets express thoughts and ideas.

Key Learning Objective: The student will be able to analyze a poem's form and understand how the use of figurative language emphasizes certain ideas.

For practice and application:

Background: *Regarding the topic of work, English humorist Jerome K. Jerome once wrote, "I like work: it fascinates me. I can sit and look at it for hours." As a testament to our frequent desire to avoid work, inventor Thomas Edison stated, "We often miss opportunity because it's dressed in overalls and looks like work." However, most people would agree that work adds value to our lives, and when we push ourselves to fulfill a particularly difficult task, we gain insight into what we can truly achieve.*

Poems About Work

Close Reader selection
from *Poems About Work*
"To be of use,"
Poem by Marge Piercy
"A Story of How a Wall Stands,"
Poem by Simon J. Ortiz

COMMON CORE Common Core Standards

RL 1 Cite textual evidence to support analysis.

RL 2 Determine a theme or central idea.

RL 4 Determine the meaning of words and phrases.

RL 5 Compare and contrast the structure of two or more texts.

W 4 Produce clear and coherent writing.

W 9a Apply grade 8 Reading standards to literature.

W 10 Write routinely over extended time frames and shorter time frames.

▲ Text Complexity Rubric

	Chicago	Find Work	My Mother Enters the Work Force
Quantitative Measures	**Lexile:** N/A	**Lexile:** N/A	**Lexile:** N/A
Qualitative Measures	**Levels of Meaning/Purpose** multiple levels of meaning (multiple themes)	**Levels of Meaning/Purpose** multiple levels of meaning (multiple themes)	**Levels of Meaning/Purpose** multiple levels of meaning (multiple themes)
	Structure free verse, no particular pattern	**Structure** complex structures, such as sonnets, villanelles, etc.	**Structure** free verse, no particular pattern
	Language Conventionality and Clarity figurative, symbolic language	**Language Conventionality and Clarity** figurative, less accessible language	**Language Conventionality and Clarity** figurative, symbolic language
	Knowledge Demands some cultural and literary knowledge useful	**Knowledge Demands** one or two references or allusions to other texts	**Knowledge Demands** increased amount of cultural and literary knowledge useful
Reader/Task Consideration	Teacher determined Vary by individual reader and type of text		

TEACH

CLOSE READ

Background Have students read the information about the poets. Explain to students that they will read three poems that reflect on different aspects of work and the role it plays in people's lives. The first poem celebrates the urbanization of the city of Chicago at the turn of the nineteenth century. The second poem reveals the purpose of work in a widow's life. The last poem describes the determination of a mother who used work to achieve a goal.

SETTING A PURPOSE Direct students to use the Setting a Purpose prompt to focus their reading. Remind students to generate questions of their own as they read.

CHICAGO
FIND WORK
MY MOTHER ENTERS THE WORK FORCE

Poem by Carl Sandburg   Poem by Rhina P. Espaillat   Poem by Rita Dove

Carl Sandburg (1878–1967) *was born in Galesburg, Illinois to Swedish immigrant parents. After the eighth grade, Sandburg quit school so he could help support his family. He worked a variety of jobs, from shining shoes to delivering milk. Later, he began hopping on freight trains to explore the West. Eventually, Sandburg settled in Chicago. With the publication of his poetry collections* Chicago Poems, Cornhuskers, *and* Smoke and Steel, *Sandburg gained a reputation as a poet of the workers and common people.*

Rhina P. Espaillat (b. 1932) *was born in the Dominican Republic, but had to leave when her family was exiled for opposing the dictatorship in that country. Espaillat's family settled in New York City, where as a young girl she began writing poetry. She wrote in both English and Spanish, and has been published in both languages. Espaillat's collections of poetry have won her many prestigious literary awards.*

Rita Dove (b. 1952) *was the first African American to be named Poet Laureate of the United States, one of the highest official honors for American poets. Born in Akron, Ohio, Dove was encouraged to read by her parents and excelled at school. She was named a Presidential Scholar, one of the top one hundred high-school graduates in the country. Dove has published short stories and novels, as well as her award-winning collections of poetry. She has also written the lyrics for the songs of many renowned musical composers.*

SETTING A PURPOSE All of the poems you are about to read share a view about workers. As you read, think about what each of the poets suggests about the impact of workers on those around them.

Compare Poems **427**

Close Read Screencasts   ▶ **View It!**

Modeled Discussions

Have students click the *Close Read* icons in their eBooks to access the screencasts in which readers discuss and annotate the following key lines from each poem:

- Sandburg's description of Chicago (lines 12–17)
- the epigraph at the beginning of "Find Work" (lines 1–5)
- the second stanza of "My Mother Enters the Work Force" (lines 8–15)

As a class, view and discuss at least one of these videos. Then, have students pair up to do an independent close read of these additional lines—lines 21–26 in "Chicago," lines 14–19 in "Find Work," or lines 16–23 in "My Mother Enters the Work Force."

Determine Meaning of Words and Phrases (LINES 1–5)

COMMON CORE RL 1, RL 4

Tell students that **figurative language** is language used imaginatively in ways that go beyond the literal meanings of the words. Explain that one type, called **personification,** is language that gives human qualities to an animal, object, or idea.

A **CITE TEXT EVIDENCE** Have students reread lines 1–5. Ask them to tell how the poet personifies the city of Chicago. Have students cite words and phrases that support their answers. *(In the first three lines, the poet describes the city as being many different kinds of workers. The poet also gives the city human physical characteristics, such as "husky" and "Big Shoulders.")* What impact do these descriptions have on the tone or feeling of the poem? *(Possible answer: The descriptions suggest feelings of admiration or awe.)*

Chicago
by Carl Sandburg

A
Hog Butcher for the World,
Tool Maker, Stacker of Wheat,
Player with Railroads and the Nation's Freight Handler;
Stormy, husky, brawling,
5   City of the Big Shoulders:

They tell me you are wicked and I believe them, for I
        have seen your painted women under the gas lamps
        luring the farm boys.
And they tell me you are crooked and I answer: Yes, it
        is true I have seen the gunman kill and go free to
        kill again.
And they tell me you are brutal and my reply is: On the faces
        of women and children I have seen the marks
        of wanton[1] hunger.
And having answered so I turn once more to those who
        sneer at this my city, and I give them back the sneer
        and say to them:
10   Come and show me another city with lifted head singing
        so proud to be alive and coarse and strong and cunning.
Flinging magnetic curses amid the toil of piling job on
        job, here is a tall bold slugger set vivid against the
        little soft cities;
Fierce as a dog with tongue lapping for action, cunning
        as a savage pitted against the wilderness,
            Bareheaded,
            Shoveling,
15   Wrecking,
            Planning,
            Building, breaking, rebuilding,

---
[1] **wanton:** without limitation.

SCAFFOLDING FOR ELL STUDENTS

Analyze Language Using a whiteboard, display lines 1–3. Draw attention to words ending with the suffix *-er,* explaining that it can mean "someone who." Have volunteers mark up the text.

- Highlight in blue words ending with the suffix *-er.*
- Underline the base word.
- Use the meanings of the base word and the suffix to infer the word's meaning.

ASK STUDENTS what these words ending in *-er* suggest about what the speaker finds interesting about Chicago. *(its workers)*

Tool Maker, Stacker of Wheat,

Player with Railroads and the Nation's Freight Handler;

Stormy, husky, brawling

> stacker = someone who stacks

Under the smoke, dust all over his mouth, laughing with
    white teeth,
Under the terrible burden of destiny laughing as a young
    man laughs,
20 Laughing even as an ignorant fighter laughs who has
    never lost a battle,
Bragging and laughing that under his wrist is the pulse, and
    under his ribs the heart of the people,
                                Laughing!
Laughing the stormy, husky, brawling laughter of
    Youth, half-naked, sweating, proud to be Hog
25   Butcher, Tool Maker, Stacker of Wheat, Player with
    Railroads and Freight Handler to the Nation.

A view of the Chicago stockyards, where animals were kept before slaugther

CLOSE READ

Determine Meaning of Words and Phrases

COMMON CORE **RL 4**

(LINES 23–26)

Review with students that poets use figurative language, such as personification, to create effects, emphasize feelings or ideas, and evoke emotion. Point out that the speaker also uses **epithets—** descriptive words and phrases that are sometimes added to or substituted for a name.

B **ASK STUDENTS** to reread lines 23–26. What do the epithets in these lines suggest about Chicago? *(Possible answer: The many different types of jobs they represent suggest that Chicago was a booming industrial city.)* What is the impact of the epithets at the end of the poem? *(Possible answer: Because the epithets were also used to begin the poem, they emphasize the importance of workers.)*

APPLYING ACADEMIC VOCABULARY

commentary	occupation

As you discuss the poem, incorporate the following Collection 6 academic vocabulary words: *commentary* and *occupation*. Point out that in this **commentary** on Chicago Sandburg describes the many different **occupations** that allowed people to earn a living at the turn of the nineteenth century. Discuss what it might have been like to work in Chicago at that time.

©Corbis

CLOSE READ

Determine Meaning of Words and Phrases
COMMON CORE RL 1, RL 4

Review the definition of *figurative language* and discuss the examples of personification and simile in "Chicago." Then, have students reread the poem. Discuss the impact that personification and simile have on meaning and emotion in the poem.

Analyzing the Text
COMMON CORE RL 1, RL 4

Possible answers:

1. *The names suggest that Chicago was a center for animal slaughterhouses, tool manufacturing, grain storage and distribution, and railroads.*

2. *The harsh adjectives* wicked, crooked, *and* brutal *are used to describe Chicago. Sandburg defends Chicago, saying there is no other city that is as "proud to be alive" or "coarse," "strong," and "cunning."*

3. *The positive adjectives* fierce, cunning, bareheaded, shoveling, wrecking, planning, building, breaking, *and* rebuilding *suggest that he admires the residents of Chicago for their determination and hard work.*

4. *Chicago is described as having a mouth and teeth and the ability to laugh. This suggests a sense of hope.*

5. *Similes: "laughing as a young man laughs," "Laughing as an ignorant fighter laughs"; Although the first comparison suggests the power of youth, the second tempers it with a nod to the need for experience.*

6. *Like a person, Chicago has a wrist, pulse, ribs, and heart and is able to brag and laugh.*

Determine Meaning of Words and Phrases
COMMON CORE RL 1, RL 4

Figurative language is language used in an imaginative way to communicate something beyond the literal meanings of the words. Poets use figurative language to create effects, to emphasize ideas, and to evoke emotions. Types of figurative language include the following.

- **Personification,** which gives human qualities to an animal, an object, or an idea. In the following lines from "Chicago," Sandburg personifies the city by giving it human characteristics, such as the ability to sing and feel pride.

  "Come and show me another city with lifted head singing
  so proud to be alive and coarse and strong and cunning."

- **Similes,** which compare things that are generally unlike by using the words *like* or *as*. In these lines, Sandburg uses similes to compare Chicago to a dog and to a savage:

  "Fierce as a dog with tongue lapping for action, cunning
  as a savage pitted against the wilderness"

  Think about the effects of personification and similes as you analyze "Chicago."

Analyzing the Text
COMMON CORE RL 1, RL 4

Cite Text Evidence Support your responses with evidence from the text.

1. **Infer** Reread lines 1–5. What do the different names for Chicago tell you about the city's economy at the time this poem was written?

2. **Analyze** Examine lines 6–8. What three adjectives are used to describe Chicago? How does the poet counter this negative view in lines 9–10?

3. **Infer** Reread lines 12–17. What adjectives used to describe Chicago reveal the poet's attitude toward the residents of the city? Describe his attitude.

4. **Analyze** Identify three examples of personification in line 18 of the poem. What is the effect of these personifications?

5. **Analyze** Identify two similes in lines 19–20. What is the effect of these comparisons?

6. **Analyze** How is Chicago personified in line 21 of the poem?

Strategies for Annotation
 Annotate it!

Determine Meaning of Words and Phrases
COMMON CORE RL 4

Share these strategies for guided or independent analysis:

- Highlight in yellow examples of personification.
- Underline examples of simile.
- On a note, record the meaning and effect of each example.

> Under the smoke, dust all over his mouth, laughing with white teeth,
>
> Under the terrible burden of destiny laughing as a young man laughs,

Effect: enjoying life

Determine Theme

COMMON CORE RL 2

(LINES 1–5)

Call students' attention to lines 1–5. Explain that this group of lines is an **epigraph,** a brief quotation at the beginning of a text. Tell students that an epigraph often suggests the theme of a literary work.

 ASK STUDENTS to reread lines 1–5. In what way might the epigraph suggest the theme for a poem with the title "Find Work"? *(Possible answer: Dickinson's poem suggests that everyday tasks can be important in someone's daily life. The need to "find work" can be of comparable importance.)*

Analyze Structure

COMMON CORE RL 1, RL 5

(LINES 6–19)

Tell students that the **form** of a poem is the way in which the words and lines are arranged on the page. Explain that form may also involve patterns of rhythm and rhyme.

 CITE TEXT EVIDENCE Ask students to reread lines 6–19, focusing on the pattern of rhyming words at the ends of lines. Have students describe the pattern and explain its effect. *(Lines 6 and 8 rhyme: young, tongue; Lines 7 and 9 rhyme: fruit, mute. The pattern is repeated in lines 10–13 and in lines 14–17. The pattern gives the poem a regular rhythm.)* How does the form of this poem differ from that of "Chicago"? *("Chicago" does not have a rhyme pattern.)* How does the form of each poem contribute to its meaning? *(Possible answer: The structured form of "Find Work" reinforces the idea that the speaker's grandmother gave structure to her life through work; the unstructured form of "Chicago" suggests that the city has a toughness that can adapt to any situation.)*

 Find Work

Poem by Rhina P. Espaillat

> *I tie my Hat—I crease my Shawl—*
> *Life's little duties do—precisely*
> *As the very least*
> *Were infinite—to me—*
> 5   *—Emily Dickinson, #443*

> My mother's mother, widowed very young
> of her first love, and of that love's first fruit,
> moved through her father's farm, her country tongue
> and country heart anaesthetized[1] and mute
> 10 with labor. So her kind was taught to do—
> "Find work," she would reply to every grief—
> and her one dictum,[2] whether false or true,
> tolled heavy with her passionate belief.
> Widowed again, with children, in her prime,
> 15 she spoke so little it was hard to bear
> so much composure, such a truce with time
> spent in the lifelong practice of despair.
> But I recall her floors, scrubbed white as bone,
> her dishes, and how painfully they shone.

---

[1] **anaesthetized:** made to feel numb or without feeling.
[2] **dictum:** saying or motto.

Find Work **431**

WHEN STUDENTS STRUGGLE...

Guide students in understanding the rhythm of the poem. Point out that some lines end with a period, some with a comma or dash, and some without any punctuation. Read lines 14–19 aloud, prompting students to notice that line breaks and punctuation affect rhythm as well as meaning. Then, reread the lines without attention to the line breaks. Discuss how reading the poem in this way changes the rhythm. Explain or elicit that reading lines aloud as the poet has written them can help to clarify meaning.

Analyze Structure

COMMON CORE RL 5

Review the meaning of the word *sonnet*. Discuss how the rhythm and rhyme in "Find Work" is similar to those in a song, and prompt students to describe how a sonnet's structure differs from that of other poems.

Then, review the information to help students analyze a poem's meter and rhyme scheme.

Have partners work together to note the meter and rhyme scheme in "Find Work." Discuss how these characteristics affect the poem's meaning.

Analyzing the Text

COMMON CORE RL 1, RL 2, RL 5

Possible answers:

1. ˘ ´ ˘ ´ ˘ ´ ˘ ˘ ´ ˘ ´

   with labor. So her kind was taught to do—

   ˘ ´ ˘ ´ ˘ ´ ˘ ˘ ´ ˘ ´

   "Find work," she would reply to every grief—

   ˘ ´ ˘ ´ ˘ ´ ˘ ´ ˘ ´

   and her one dictum, whether false or true,

   ˘ ´ ˘ ´ ˘ ´ ˘ ´ ˘ ´

   tolled heavy with her passionate belief.
   rhyme scheme: cdcd; meter: iambic pentameter

2. *The last two lines of "Find Work" are a couplet. They have a different rhyme scheme, and the meter in the last line changes. Also, the early lines describe the poet's grandmother, but these lines describe the poet's recollections of her house.*

3. *The speaker's grandmother was widowed twice, and work became a kind of medicine or therapy that helped her deal with her grief.*

---

eBook *Annotate It!*

Analyze Structure

COMMON CORE RL 5

"Find Work" is a sonnet, which means "little song." More specifically, a **sonnet** is a 14-line poem that has a specific pattern of rhythm and rhyme.

The rhythmic pattern in a poem is called the **meter**. It is determined by the stressed and unstressed syllables in the words.

- Each unit of meter, known as a **foot**, consists of one stressed syllable and one or two unstressed syllables. A foot that is made up of an unstressed syllable followed by a stressed syllable is an **iamb**.
- Sonnets are often written in **iambic pentameter**, a meter in which each line is made up of five (penta) feet of iambs.
- To show the meter in a line of poetry, a stressed syllable is indicated by the symbol ´ and an unstressed syllable by the symbol ˘.

˘ ´ ˘ ´ ˘ ´ ˘ ´ ˘ ´

My mother's mother, widowed very young

˘ ´ ˘ ´ ˘ ´ ˘ ´ ˘ ´

of her first love, and of that love's first fruit,

The **rhyme scheme** in a poem is the pattern of end rhymes. A rhyme scheme is noted by assigning a letter of the alphabet, beginning with *a*, to each line. Lines that rhyme are given the same letter.

My mother's mother, widowed very young	a
of her first love, and of that love's first fruit,	b
moved through her father's farm, her country tongue	a
and country heart anaesthetized and mute	b

Many sonnets follow the rhyme scheme *abab, cdcd, efef, gg.* The last two lines are a **couplet,** or rhyming pair of lines. Notice the characteristics of a sonnet as you analyze "Find Work."

Analyzing the Text

COMMON CORE RL 1, RL 2, RL 5

Cite Text Evidence Support your responses with evidence from the text.

1. **Identify Patterns** Use the symbols ´ and ˘ to mark the meter of lines 5–8 of the sonnet; use letters of the alphabet to identify the rhyme scheme. What type of rhythmic pattern, or meter, do these lines follow?

2. **Compare** How are the last two lines of "Find Work" different from the rest of the poem in form and content?

3. **Draw Conclusions** What role does work play in the life of the speaker's grandmother? Explain.

Strategies for Annotation ✏ 📋 *Annotate it!*

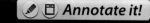

Analyze Structure

COMMON CORE RL 5

Have students use their eBook annotation tools to identify the poem's rhyme scheme:

- Highlight in yellow the last word of line 1 and any rhyming words.
- Highlight in green the last word of line 2 and any rhyming words.
- Continue for the remaining lines, using a different color for each new set of rhyming words.
- On a note, assign the lines that are highlighted in yellow the letter *a*, assign the lines highlighted in green the letter *b*, and so on.

My mother's mother, widowed very young

of her first love, and of that love's first fruit,

moved through her father's farm, her country tongue

and country heart anaesthetized and mute

abab, cdcd, efef, gg

Analyze Structure

COMMON CORE **RL 1, RL 5**

(LINES 1–23)

Review with students that the form of a poem is the way in which the words and lines are arranged on the page. Explain that some forms of poetry, such as a sonnet, follow fixed rules for number of lines, rhyme scheme, and meter. Tell them that other forms of poems do not follow any set rules. Explain that these poems are called **free verse.**

E CITE TEXT EVIDENCE Ask students to reread the poem. Have students analyze the lines, rhyme, and meter of the poem and tell what kind of poem it is. *(The lines of the poem are different lengths, and there are no set patterns of rhyme or rhythm. Therefore, the poem is free verse.)* How does the poem's form contribute to its style, or manner of writing? *(Possible answer: Free verse allows the poem to sound conversational, as if the speaker is directly addressing a friend.)*

COLLABORATIVE DISCUSSION Have students reread each poem independently before beginning their discussion. As students discuss their ideas, have them use evidence from the text to explain why they feel as they do. Then, have partners share their ideas with the larger group.

ASK STUDENTS to share any questions they generated in the course of reading and discussing this selection.

SCAFFOLDING FOR ELL STUDENTS

Use Cognates Point out that many Spanish and English words are similar. Help students from Spanish-speaking backgrounds access the text by using cognates to understand unfamiliar words. Display the poem and have volunteers identify cognates. Examples include

- perfect/perfecto (a) (line 7)
- locomotive/la locomotora (line 10)
- pair/el par (line 23)

ASK STUDENTS to explain how the sound of a sewing machine might be like the sound of a locomotive.

My Mother Enters the Work Force
Poem by Rita Dove

The path to ABC Business School
was paid for by a lucky sign:
ALTERATIONS, QUALIFIED SEAMSTRESS INQUIRE WITHIN.
Tested on sleeves, hers never puckered—puffed or sleek,
5   leg-o'-mutton or raglan—[1]
they barely needed the damp cloth
to steam them perfect.

Those were the afternoons. Evenings
she took in piecework,[2] the treadle machine
10 with its locomotive whir
traveling the lit path of the needle
through quicksand taffeta
or velvet deep as a forest.
And now and now sang the treadle,
15 *I know, I know. . . .*

And then it was day again, all morning
at the office machines, their clack and chatter
another journey—rougher,
that would go on forever
20 until she could break a hundred words
with no errors—ah, and then

no more postponed groceries,
and that blue pair of shoes!

COLLABORATIVE DISCUSSION With a partner, discuss which of the poems speaks to you most directly about the subject of work. Cite specific evidence from the text to support your ideas.

---

[1] **leg-o'-mutton or raglan:** types of sleeves. A leg-of-mutton sleeve is wide at the top and narrow at the bottom. A raglan sleeve is cut so that it continues up to the collar.

[2] **piecework:** work paid for according to the amount done, not the time it takes.

---

they barely needed the damp cloth

to steam them perfect.

Those were the afternoons. Evenings

she took in piecework, the treadle machine

with its locomotive whir

Analyze Structure COMMON CORE RL 5

Review the information about free verse, prompting students to identify how it differs from other poetic forms. Emphasize that although free verse poems do not follow any set structural rules the words and lines are carefully arranged to create a rhythm that emphasizes specific ideas and feelings. Ask students to tell how the poet's choice of line breaks, punctuation, and rhythm contributes to its meaning.

Analyzing the Text COMMON CORE RL 1, RL 2, RL 4, RL 5

Possible answers:

1. *The title indicates that the subject of the poem is the speaker's mother, and the speaker is the poet.*

2. *The speaker's mother worked as a seamstress to earn money to go to business school so she could earn money to provide food and clothes for the family.*

3. *One simile: "velvet deep as a forest." Velvet is compared to a forest. Two metaphors: "the treadle machine with its locomotive whir" and "quicksand taffeta." The sewing machine is compared to a locomotive. Taffeta cloth is compared to quicksand. These examples suggest the power of work.*

4. *The sewing machine singing suggests that work becomes a big part of a person's character.*

5. *The poem would sound less like someone talking directly to the reader; it may not have communicated the events and sounds as directly or authentically.*

---

 eBook *Annotate It!*

Analyze Structure COMMON CORE RL 5

Although sonnets and other types of poems follow an established structure, some poems have no special form at all. When a poem has no regular pattern of rhythm or rhyme, it is called **free verse**. The lines in a free verse poem flow more naturally and can create the effect of speech.

Just because a free verse poem doesn't have a set rhyme scheme or meter doesn't mean that the poem has no rhythm. Free verse poetry often

- achieves a rhythm that sounds more like everyday speech
- contains rhythmic sound effects, such as the repetition of sounds, words, or phrases

Look again at the first stanza of "My Mother Enters the Work Force." Notice whether the lines rhyme and whether they have a regular pattern of stressed and unstressed syllables. What is creating the rhythm in this stanza?

Analyzing the Text COMMON CORE RL 1, RL 2, RL 4, RL 5

 Cite Text Evidence Support your responses with evidence from the text.

1. **Infer** Who is the subject of this poem? Who is the speaker? Identify the lines that help you answer.

2. **Summarize** Give a brief summary of the events described in this poem.

3. **Analyze** A **metaphor** is a type of figurative language in which two things that are basically unlike one another are compared without using the words *like* or *as*. A **simile** is a comparison that uses like or as. Identify three examples of these types of figurative language in lines 9–16. In a chart like the one below, identify what is being compared in each. What is the impact of these metaphors?

Type of figurative language	What is being compared

4. **Evaluate** Look again at lines 9–16. What is the effect of the personification of the sewing machine?

5. **Analyze** How might the effect of this poem have been different if it had been written with a regular pattern of rhythm and rhyme rather than as free verse?

Strategies for Annotation  *Annotate it!*

Analyze Structure COMMON CORE RL 5

Share these strategies for guided or independent analysis:

- Highlight in yellow words that are emphasized.
- Underline words with repeating sounds.
- On a note, explain how the emphasis on these words affects the rhythm and meaning of the poem.

> And then it was day again, all morning
>
> at the office machines, their clack and chatter
>
> another journey—rougher,
>
> that would go on forever

Compare and Contrast Structure

COMMON CORE RL 5

As you've learned, some forms of poetry follow set rules of rhyme, length, or meter while others do not. Poems that follow a fixed set of rules are known as **traditional forms**. Sonnets, odes, and epic poems are all traditional forms. Free verse poems are known as open forms because they take their shape and pattern from the poem's content.

Usually a poet chooses a specific form in order to convey something unique about the subject. For example, rhyming lines with a sing-song nature might convey a playful approach to the subject. In free verse, the poet uses different line lengths to create slow or fast rhythms that may emphasize certain aspects of the topic.

Compare these lines from the sonnet "Find Work" and the free verse poem "My Mother Enters the Work Force." What do you notice about the different rhythms?

from "Find Work":

**Widowed again, with children, in her prime,
she spoke so little it was hard to bear
so much composure, such a truce with time
spent in the lifelong practice of despair.**

from "My Mother Enters the Work Force":

**And then it was day again, all morning
at the office machines, their clack and chatter
another journey—rougher,
that would go on forever**

The characteristics of a sonnet and of free verse are noted in the chart. Think about how they might affect the way a subject is presented.

	Sonnet	Free Verse
Number of Lines	• 14 lines	• any number of lines
Meter/Rhythm	• regular pattern of rhythm • usually written in iambic pentameter	• no regular rhythmic pattern
Rhyme Scheme	• rhyme scheme is *abab, cdcd, efef, gg*	• no established rhyme scheme

Continue to compare the structures of the poems as you analyze "Chicago," "Find Work," and "My Mother Enters the Work Force."

TEACH

CLOSE READ

Compare and Contrast Structure

COMMON CORE RL 5

Discuss the definitions of **traditional form** and **free verse** poetry, and review the features of each form. Emphasize that poets choose a rhythm for their poems that works best for the thoughts and ideas they want to express.

As they compare the lines of the two poems, have students tell how the different rhythms of the lines shown affect the meaning of each one. *(Possible answer: In the sonnet, the regular rhythm gives it a song-like feel. The pause at the end emphasizes the last word, conveying a more somber meaning. The longer lines of the free verse poem slow down the rhythm, while the shorter lines speed it up. The repeated consonant sound at the ends of the lines emphasizes the idea of repetitiveness in the work that the mother does.)*

Then, have partners use the chart to help them analyze the structure of each poem. Have students record on a Venn diagram how the characteristics of each poem are alike and different. Discuss how the different forms help each poet convey meaning.

Strategies for Annotation 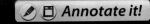 Annotate it!

Analyze Structure
COMMON CORE RL 5

Share these strategies for guided or independent analysis:

• Highlight in yellow words or syllables that are stressed.
• Underline rhyming words.
• On a note, describe how this rhythm affects meaning in the poem.

My mother's mother, widowed very young
of her first love, and of that love's first fruit,
moved through her father's farm, her country tongue
and country heart anaesthetized and mute

Analyzing the Text

 COMMON CORE RL 1, RL 2, RL 4, RL 5

Possible answers:

1. The poems "Chicago" and "My Mother Enters the Work Force" are both free verse. The lines of these poems don't rhyme, and there is no set meter/rhythmic pattern.

2. Both poems focus on the value of work. But in "Find Work," the value is primarily emotional/psychological. In "My Mother Enters the Work Force," the value is primarily economic.

3. The last two lines in both poems are the same in that the meter in each one changes, and the speaker makes a final statement that sums up the content of the poem. They are different in that "Find Work" ends with a serious, somber feel, and "My Mother Enters the Work Force" ends with an upbeat sense of achievement.

4. The tone of "Chicago" is proud and admiring. Text examples: "husky," "show me another city with lifted head singing so proud to be alive and coarse and strong and cunning," and "tall bold slugger." The tone of "Find Work" is sorrowful. Text examples: "heart anaesthetized and mute with labor," "grief," "lifelong practice of despair," and "how painfully they shone."

5. Both poems use simile and personification. "Chicago" personifies the city and uses simile to compare its personality to a fierce and cunning animal. "My Mother Enters the Work Force" personifies a sewing machine and compares the thickness of velvet to a deep forest.

Analyzing the Text

 COMMON CORE RL 1, RL 2, RL 4, RL 5, W 4, W 9a, W10

Cite Text Evidence   Support your responses with evidence from the texts.

1. **Identify Patterns** Of the three poems you just read, which two have the same form? Identify the characteristics that make these two poems similar in structure.

2. **Compare** Compare and contrast what the poems "Find Work" and "My Mother Enters the Work Force" have to say about the subject of work. What role does work serve for each of the mothers?

3. **Compare** In a Venn diagram like the one shown, compare and contrast the last two lines of "Find Work" with the last two lines of "My Mother Enters the Work Force."

"Find Work"   "My Mother Enters the Work Force"

4. **Analyze** The **tone** of a literary work expresses the writer's attitude toward his or her subject. Identify several examples of words and phrases that help establish the tone in the poems "Chicago" and "Find Work." Compare the tone in the two poems.

5. **Analyze** How is the kind of figurative language found in "Chicago" similar to that in "My Mother Enters the Work Force"? Give examples.

PERFORMANCE TASK

Writing Activity: Compare and Contrast Essay Write an essay in which you compare and contrast two of the poems you just read.

- Choose two of the three poems to write about.
- To help plan your essay, create a Venn diagram in which you compare and contrast the theme, tone, structure, and use of language in the two poems.
- Use the notes from your diagram to write a comparison of the poems.
- Be sure your essay includes evidence from both poems to support your conclusions.

PERFORMANCE TASK

COMMON CORE W 4, W 9a, W 10

Assign this performance task.

Writing Activity: Compare and Contrast Essay Have students work independently. Direct students to

- reread the poems before choosing two to compare
- create separate Venn diagrams for comparing theme, tone, and structure

- present each type of information in a separate paragraph
- include evidence from the poems that supports their ideas

Have students share their essays with the class.

INTERACTIVE WHITEBOARD LESSON
Tone

Learn the Skill ▸ How Do Writers Communicate Tone?

How Do Writers Communicate Tone?

Find Out

Writers can't rely on spoken language to communicate their attitude toward a subject. Rather, they create tone through their choice of words and details.

TEACH

Explain that **tone** is a writer's attitude toward or feelings about a subject. Words such as *angry, sad,* or *humorous* can be used to describe the tone of a text. Tell students that the tone of a poem can have a powerful impact on meaning. For example, a poet may create

- a somber tone, using words that create dark images to convey feelings of sadness or loss
- a cheerful tone, using positive words and images to celebrate a joyful event or experience

PRACTICE AND APPLY

Discuss with students how word choices in the three poems they have just read create different tones. For example, the phrases "Come and show me another city" and "coarse and strong and cunning" from "Chicago" suggest a tone of defiance and pride.

Have students identify details in "My Mother Enters the Work Force" that help them recognize its tone.

Compare and Contrast Structure

RETEACH

Review with students that the **form,** or structure, of a poem is the arrangement of the words and lines on the page.

Remind students that some forms, such as a **sonnet,** follow a set of rules that apply to its rhythm pattern, line length, or rhyme scheme. Other poems are considered **free verse,** in which the poet decides on the form. Review that poets choose a form of poetry that works best for the thoughts and ideas they want to express.

Guide students to use these steps for analyzing form, evaluating the role it plays in poetry, and comparing and contrasting different forms:

Step 1. Examine line length and stanza. Compare the number of lines per stanza and how the stanzas are organized. Note the emphasis created by the line breaks in each form.

Step 2. Look for a rhyme scheme. Look for patterns of rhyme, rhythm created by rhyming words, repetition, or alliteration, or regular patterns of stressed and unstressed syllables (meter).

Step 3. Analyze the effects of form. Compare the effects each form has on the meaning of the poem.

COLLABORATIVE DISCUSSION

Have students work in groups to apply the steps to "Chicago," "Find Work," "My Mother Enters the Work Force," or poems they are reading on their own. Have groups compare their results.

Poems About Work

To Be of Use

Poem by Marge Piercy

A Story of How a Wall Stands

Poem by Simon J. Ortiz

Why These Texts

Students may need practice analyzing free verse for style elements such as alliteration and rhythm. "To Be of Use" by Marge Piercy, and "A Story of How a Wall Stands" by Simon J. Ortiz are free-verse poems that students can compare and contrast to determine the effect of the free-verse structure. With the help of the close-reading questions, students will analyze the authors' choices. This close reading will lead students to deeper understanding of the effect free verse can have on a reader.

Background Have students read the background and the information about the authors. Introduce the selection by telling students that they will read two free-verse poems that have the same topic: work. Both authors have activist roots. Piercy's work frequently deals with feminism and social change. Ortiz's work brings attention to the American Indian voice, which he feels is unrepresented in American literature.

SETTING A PURPOSE Ask students to pay attention to the structure of the poems. How does the use of free verse support each author's purpose?

Common Core Support

- cite strong textual evidence
- determine a theme of a text
- determine the meaning of words as they are used in a text
- compare and contrast the structure of two texts

Text Complexity Rubric

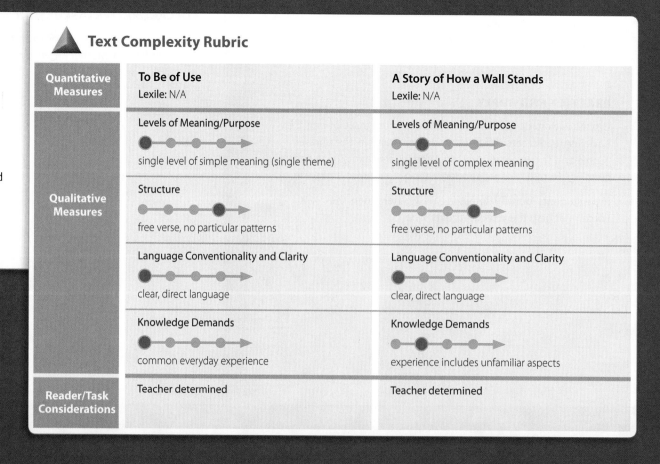

	To Be of Use Lexile: N/A	A Story of How a Wall Stands Lexile: N/A
Quantitative Measures		
Qualitative Measures	Levels of Meaning/Purpose single level of simple meaning (single theme)	Levels of Meaning/Purpose single level of complex meaning
	Structure free verse, no particular patterns	Structure free verse, no particular patterns
	Language Conventionality and Clarity clear, direct language	Language Conventionality and Clarity clear, direct language
	Knowledge Demands common everyday experience	Knowledge Demands experience includes unfamiliar aspects
Reader/Task Considerations	Teacher determined	Teacher determined

Strategies for CLOSE READING

Analyze Structure

Students should read the poems carefully all the way through. Close-reading questions at the bottom of the page will help them focus on a thorough analysis of the poems. As they read, students should jot down comments or questions about the poetry in the side margins.

WHEN STUDENTS STRUGGLE . . .

To help students analyze the structure of the poems, have them work in small groups to fill out a chart like the one shown below as they analyze the poems.

CITE TEXT EVIDENCE For practice in identifying and analyzing the characteristics of free verse, ask students to determine whether or not elements of style are present in each poem, and to cite examples of any style elements they might find.

	To Be of Use	A Story of How a Wall Stands
Regular Rhyme	No	No
Regular Rhythm	No	No
Rhythm of Everyday Speech	Yes "The people I love the best jump into work head first"	Yes "My father, who works with stone, says, 'That's just the part you see'"
Repetition of Sounds	Yes "and swim off with sure strokes almost out of sight"	Yes "'. . . there is stone woven together.' He ties one hand over the other, fitting like the bones of his hands and fingers." "hands"
Repetition of Words	Yes "people" "work"	Yes "stone" "mud" "fingers"
Repetition of Phrases	No	Yes "in the palm of his hand." "a long, long time."
Established Structure	No	No

Background *Regarding the topic of work, English humorist Jerome K. Jerome once wrote, "I like work: it fascinates me. I can sit and look at it for hours." As a testament to our frequent desire to avoid work, inventor Thomas Edison stated, "We often miss opportunity because it's dressed in overalls and looks like work." However, most people would agree that work adds value to our lives, and when we push ourselves to fulfill a particularly difficult task, we gain insight into what we can truly achieve.*

Poems About Work

To Be of Use . . . . Marge Piercy
A Story of How a Wall Stands . . . . . . Simon J. Ortiz

Marge Piercy *(b. 1936) was born into a family that struggled against the effects of the Great Depression. Her love of literature was instilled at a young age when she came down with rheumatic fever and was only able to read to entertain herself. The novels and poetry she writes frequently deal with the topics of feminism and social change. One of her most famous novels,* Women on the Edge of Time, *even incorporates elements of time travel.*

Simon J. Ortiz *(b. 1941) is one of the most influential and widely read American Indian writers. Ortiz was raised in Acoma Pueblo reservation as part of the Eagle Clan, where he spoke only his native language. When he was sent to boarding school, he was encouraged to speak English, and his struggle in transitioning between two different cultures led him to write about his experiences. Later, he would write as a means to bring attention to the American Indian voice, a voice he felt was unrepresented in American literature.*

131

1. **READ** ▶ As you read "To Be of Use," cite text evidence.

- Underline metaphors in lines 1–11.
- In the margin, summarize the people the speaker admires.

The speaker admires people who throw themselves into their work and don't give up on a job when it gets difficult. The speaker admires people who work together to get a job done, especially for the good of others.

To Be of Use
by Marge Piercy

(A) The people I love the best
jump into work head first
without dallying in the shallows
and swim off with sure strokes almost out of sight.
5 They seem to become natives of that element,
the black sleek heads of seals
bouncing like half-submerged balls.

I love people who harness themselves, an ox to a heavy cart,
who pull like water buffalo, with massive patience,
10 who strain in the mud and the muck to move things forward,
who do what has to be done, again and again.

I want to be with people who submerge
in the task, who go into the fields to harvest
and work in a row and pass the bags along,
15 who are not parlor generals and field deserters
but move in a common rhythm
when the food must come in or the fire be put out.

(B) The work of the world is common as mud.
Botched, it smears the hands, crumbles to dust.
20 But the thing worth doing well done
has a shape that satisfies, clean and evident.
Greek amphoras for wine or oil,
Hopi vases that held corn, are put in museums
but you know they were made to be used.
25 The pitcher cries for water to carry
and a person for work that is real.

2. ◀ **REREAD AND DISCUSS** Reread lines 18–26. In a small group, discuss what the author means by "The work of the world is common as mud." What idea does she emphasize by personifying the pitcher?

132

3. **READ** ▶ As you read "A Story of How a Wall Stands," begin to collect and cite text evidence.

- In the margin, explain what the speaker of "To Be of Use" would most likely admire about the father in this poem.
- Circle phrases that are repeated.

A Story of How a Wall Stands
by Simon J. Ortiz

My father, who works with stone,
says, "That's just the part you see,
the stones which seem to be
just packed in on the outside,"
5 and with his hands puts the stone and mud
in place. "Underneath what looks like loose stone,
there is stone woven together."
He ties one hand over the other,
fitting like the bones of his hands
10 and fingers. "That's what is
holding it together."

(C) "It is built that carefully,"
he says, "the mud mixed
to a certain texture," patiently
15 "with the fingers," worked
(D) in the palm of his hand. "So that
placed between the stones, they hold
together for a long, long time."

He tells me those things,
20 the story of them worked
with his fingers, in the palm
of his hands, working the stone
and the mud until they become
the wall that stands a long, long time.

The speaker of "To Be of Use" would admire the father's work with stone and mud to build the wall so carefully that it will stand for a long time.

133

---

1. **READ AND CITE TEXT EVIDENCE**

(A) **ASK STUDENTS** to cite text evidence to support their summary of the people the speaker admires. *Students should cite evidence from lines 1–4, lines 8–11, and lines 12–14, to show that the speaker admires people who throw themselves into their work and don't give up on a job when it gets difficult, and that she admires people who work together to get a job done, especially for the good of others.*

2. **REREAD AND DISCUSS USING TEXT EVIDENCE**

(B) **ASK STUDENTS** to delegate a reporter from each group to share the outcome of their discussion with the class. They will be asked to cite text evidence with line numbers to support their conclusions. *Students should recognize that "mud" is a metaphor for work done poorly, whereas clay that is shaped with positive intentions becomes the "Greek amphora" or the "Hopi vase."*

3. **READ AND CITE TEXT EVIDENCE**

(C) **ASK STUDENTS** to cite text evidence from both poems to support their explanation of what the speaker of "To Be of Use" would most likely admire about the father in this poem. *Students should cite evidence that the author of "To Be of Use" admires careful work, shown in lines 18–24. They should cite evidence from "A Story of How a Wall Stands" that shows that the father worked carefully, such as in lines 12–18, "they hold together for a long, long time."*

FOR ELL STUDENTS Explain that the adjective *certain* has several meanings. It can mean "definite, particular," "sure to happen," "unquestionable," or "dependable." Ask students which meaning the word had in this context. *"definite, particular"*

4. ◀ **REREAD** Reread lines 12–24. What is the effect of the author's use of repetition? Support your answer with explicit textual evidence.

The repetition of "a long, long time" not only gives a sense of rhythm, but also reinforces the idea that the wall will stay together for a very long time—"It is built that carefully." The repetition of the phrase "in the palm of his hand" reminds us how tedious and specific the work is, and why it needs to be performed "patiently."

SHORT RESPONSE

Cite Text Evidence Why do you think the poets chose to write these poems in free verse? What effect does the free verse structure have on the reader? Review your reading notes, and be sure to **cite evidence from the text** in your response.

In both "To Be of Use" and "A Story of How a Wall Stands," the free verse structure gives the poems a conversational quality. Ortiz's poem is structured as a dialogue between the author and his "father, who works with stone." In Piercy's poem, the free verse structure gives the feeling of the author speaking directly to the reader, providing personal insight into the people she "love[s] the best." In both poems, the free verse structure allows individual words and phrases to create a rhythmic feel, such as the repetition of "a long, long time" in "A Story of How a Wall Stands" and the declarative nature of the first line of each part of "To Be of Use."

134

---

4. **REREAD AND CITE TEXT EVIDENCE**

D **ASK STUDENTS** to cite specific text evidence to support their analysis of the author's use of repetition. *Students should cite the repeated phrases, "in the palm of his hand," and "a long, long time" (lines 16, 18, 21–22, and 24). They should explain that the phrase repetition provides a sense of rhythm, even though it is not a regular, repeated rhythm throughout the poem.*

SHORT RESPONSE

Cite Text Evidence Student responses will vary, but they should cite evidence from the poems to support their analysis. Students should:

- provide a text-based analysis of the effect of free verse in each poem.
- explain the effects of repetition.
- cite text evidence to support their analysis.

TO CHALLENGE STUDENTS . . .

For inspiration to write their own free verse about work, students can view the video *Mankind in 2 Minutes* in their eBooks.

ASK STUDENTS to write a free-verse poem on the subject of work. Encourage them to use repetition of sounds, words, or phrases in their poem. Have students peer review their poems with a partner before reading their poems aloud to the class. As a class, discuss the conversational rhythms of the free verse students wrote.

DIG DEEPER

With the class, return to Question 4, Reread. Have students share their responses.

ASK STUDENTS to cite the text evidence that supports their analysis of the effect of phrase repetition in Ortiz's poem.

- Ask students to state which phrases are repeated. *Students should notice that the phrases "in the palm of his hand" and "a long, long time" are repeated.*

- Point out the repetition of the words "hand/s" and "fingers," lines 5, 8, 9, 10, 15, 16, 21, and 22. Ask students to make an inference from this word repetition. *Students might infer that today, most walls are made by machines, so Ortiz emphasizes that this wall is made by hand.*

- Ask students to cite evidence of each step in building the wall. *Students should cite evidence from lines 13–18: first the mud is mixed to a certain texture with the fingers in the palm of the hand, and then the mud is "placed between the stones."*

- Discuss what is special about how this wall is made. How does the phrase repetition emphasize this? *Students should be able to explain that the wall is made "carefully" and "patiently." They may emphasize that today, things are sometimes made to last only a short time, to be replaced frequently.*

ASK STUDENTS to return to their Short Response answer and to revise it based on the class discussion.

COLLECTION 6
PERFORMANCE TASK A

Interactive Lessons
If you need help...
• **Writing Narratives**
• **Writing as a Process**

Write a Short Story

In this collection you read some different ideas about the value of work. For example, in the excerpt from *The Adventures of Tom Sawyer,* main character Tom finds a clever way to avoid work by turning it into play for his friends. In the following activity, you will write a realistic short story about a character who is working at an enjoyable job, or who has found a way to avoid doing work.

COMMON CORE

W 3a–e Write narratives.
W 4 Produce clear and coherent writing.
W 5 Develop and strengthen writing.
W 10 Write routinely over extended time frames and shorter time frames.

A successful short story

- establishes, develops, and resolves a conflict
- introduces and develops characters and a setting
- contains a plot with a well-structured event sequence
- uses dialogue, pacing, relevant descriptive details, and reflection to develop characters and events
- uses transitions to convey sequence
- provides a conclusion that flows from the story events and reflects a theme, or message, about life

PLAN

Establish Story Elements A realistic short story is a narrative that describes made-up characters, experiences, and events that seem as if they could exist or happen in real life. You can spark your imagination with ideas from stories and other texts you have read, from your own life, or from the world around you. The following steps will help you develop your ideas.

- Brainstorm ideas for your characters. What does your main character look like? How does the character act, speak, and relate to others? Who are the other characters in the story?
- Determine the setting—the time and place where the story occurs—and brainstorm ideas for events that will involve your character in an occupation or a type of work.

myNotebook

Use the annotation tools in your eBook to record text details that will help you generate ideas for your own story.

ACADEMIC VOCABULARY

As you write your narrative, be sure to use the academic vocabulary words.

commentary

minors

occupation

option

style

PERFORMANCE TASK A

WRITE A SHORT STORY

Introduce students to the Performance Task by reading the introductory paragraph with them and reviewing the criteria for what makes a good short story. Remind students that a story becomes more interesting when the characters seem real and when their problems are concerns with which readers can identify.

PLAN

ESTABLISH STORY ELEMENTS

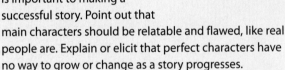

View It!

Professional Development Podcast:

Performance Tasks

Explain to students that creating realistic characters is important to making a successful story. Point out that main characters should be relatable and flawed, like real people are. Explain or elicit that perfect characters have no way to grow or change as a story progresses.

DECIDE ON A POINT OF VIEW

Discuss the advantages and disadvantages of each kind of narrator students may choose for their stories.

- A narrator who is part of the story gives the story a personal feel, but that narrator can only know what is going on in his or her mind.

- A narrator who is not one of the characters is impersonal but can tell about all of the characters' thoughts and feelings.

- Establish the conflict, or the struggle between opposing forces or ideas that the main character must overcome. Is there a particular job that your character wants to do or to avoid? What does he or she need to overcome to achieve that goal? What seems overwhelming about the challenge?

List the Events Complete a plot diagram to plan your story.

- Use the exposition to introduce your characters, setting, and conflict.

- Introduce obstacles that the characters have to overcome in the rising action. Think about how these obstacles help build tension or suspense. Use the main character's responses to these obstacles to draw out the story's action.

- At the climax, tell the most important or exciting event. Here the tension or suspense comes to a peak—your character is about to overcome the challenge or resolve the problem.

- Finally, end with the falling action and resolution to show how the conflict is resolved. Consider reflecting on the theme. What might you be saying about independence or resourcefulness?

- As you plan, keep pacing in mind. In a well-paced story, the action transitions smoothly from one event to the next.

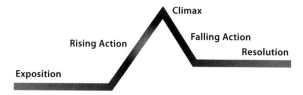

Decide on a Point of View Think about the point of view you want to use. Point of view refers to how a writer chooses to narrate a story.

- When a story is told from the first-person point of view, the narrator is a character in the story and uses first-person pronouns, such as *I, me,* and *we.*

- In a story told from the third-person point of view, the narrator is not a character in the story. The narrator tells the story using pronouns such as *he, she, it,* and *they.*

Consider Your Purpose and Audience Keep your audience in mind as you prepare to write. Decide which point of view and writing style best helps you achieve your purpose.

Write Your Short Story Review your plot diagram as you begin your draft.

- Introduce the main character and setting, engaging your audience with action and dialogue that sets up the conflict.
- Establish your point of view by introducing a narrator.
- Create the sequence of events, using transition words and phrases that clearly signal any shifts in setting.
- Use precise words and phrases and sensory language to create a vivid picture.
- Tell how the conflict is resolved. Clearly show how the character finally overcomes the challenge.
- Leave the audience with a theme on which to reflect.

myWriteSmart

Write your rough draft in *my*WriteSmart. Focus on getting your ideas down, rather than on perfecting your choice of language.

REVISE

Evaluate Your Draft Use the chart on the next page to evaluate the content and style of your story.

- Check that the introduction will grab your readers' attention.
- Examine the development of your characters. Are they believable, with speech and actions that seem authentic?
- How does the setting affect characters and help shape the plot? Add sensory details to clarify as necessary.
- Ensure that the conflict is clear and that plot events build to a climax.
- Examine the pacing to make sure it keeps the action moving in a smooth progression of events, building interest and suspense. Delete any unnecessary events.
- Be sure that the resolution reflects a theme, or life message.

myWriteSmart

Have a partner or a group of peers review your draft in *my*WriteSmart. Ask your reviewers to note whether your exposition, rising action, climax, falling action, and resolution are clearly written and easy to follow.

PRESENT

Create a Finished Copy Finalize your short story and choose a way to share it with your audience.

PRODUCE

WRITE YOUR SHORT STORY

Tell students that in their first draft they should concentrate on getting the action of the story plotted out. Remind students to use transition words, such as *then, later in the day,* and *the next week,* to help make the sequence of events easier for readers to follow.

REVISE

EVALUATE YOUR DRAFT

Explain to students that one of the ways to make a story more interesting is to include realistic dialogue. Have students review their drafts and think about places where they could add dialogue. Have students think about how the words that characters say let readers know what those characters are like.

PRESENT

CREATE A FINISHED COPY

Students can read their stories aloud to the class or publish them on a class or school website.

PERFORMANCE TASK A

IDEAS AND EVIDENCE

Have students use the chart to evaluate how they did on the Performance Task in each of the three main categories. You may want to provide examples of stories or passages that successfully execute these aspects of narrative writing. Have students compare their writing to the examples and identify improvements they could make.

COLLECTION 6 TASK A
SHORT STORY

	Ideas and Evidence	Organization	Language
ADVANCED	• The writer skillfully introduces, develops, and resolves a conflict. • The writer establishes a setting and effectively uses it to shape the plot. • Characters are well developed, compelling, and believable. • Dialogue and descriptions are used effectively.	• The event sequence is smooth and clearly structured, creating suspense and building to a strong, satisfying conclusion. • The writer uses effective pacing. • Transitions are successfully used to signal shifts in setting. • The conclusion clearly reflects a theme, or message, about life.	• The writer consistently maintains an effective point of view. • Vivid, precise words and phrases, as well as sensory language, are used to reveal the setting and characters. • Spelling, capitalization, and punctuation are correct. • Grammar and usage are correct.
COMPETENT	• The writer introduces, develops, and resolves a conflict. • The writer establishes a setting that somewhat shapes and affects the characters and conflict. • Characters are interesting and have some believable traits. • Dialogue and descriptions could be improved a bit.	• The event sequence is generally well structured but includes some extraneous events. • The story builds to a conclusion that could be more suspenseful and satisfying. • Pacing is somewhat uneven and confusing. • Transition words are used sporadically. • The conclusion touches on a theme or message but does not present it clearly.	• The writer mostly maintains a consistent point of view. • The writer generally uses descriptive words and phrases, but could include more sensory language. • Several spelling, capitalization, and punctuation errors occur. • Some grammatical and usage errors are repeated in the story.
LIMITED	• The writer introduces a conflict but does not develop or resolve it. • The setting is not clearly established and does not impact the story. • Characters are not adequately developed. • The story lacks sufficient dialogue and descriptions.	• Some of the story's events are structured unclearly and distract from the plot. • The story builds to a confusing or unsatisfying conclusion with little suspense. • Pacing is choppy or distracting. • Transition words are used incorrectly, if at all. • The conclusion does not reflect a theme, or message, about life.	• The point of view is inconsistent. • The story lacks precise words and phrases and sensory language. • Spelling, capitalization, and punctuation are often incorrect but do not make reading the story difficult. • Grammar and usage are incorrect in many places, but the writer's ideas are still clear.
EMERGING	• The story has no identifiable conflict. • The story lacks a setting. • Characters are underdeveloped or not believable. • Dialogue and descriptions are missing from the story.	• The story contains no clear sequence of events or plot. • There is no evidence of pacing. • The writer does not use transition words. • The conclusion is inappropriate to the story or is missing.	• The writer does not establish a clear point of view. • The story lacks precise language and sensory words. • Spelling, capitalization, and punctuation are incorrect and problematic throughout the story. • Many grammatical and usage errors obscure the meaning of the writer's ideas.

COLLECTION 6
PERFORMANCE TASK B

Interactive Lessons
If you need help...
• **Writing Arguments**
• **Writing as a Process**
• **Using Textual Evidence**

Write an Argument

A strong, well-constructed argument can convince readers to change their minds about an issue or to understand and accept an opposing view. In this activity, you will write an argument that justifies your views about whether it is important for teenagers to gain work experience during their school years. You will use evidence from the texts in the collection to support your position.

A successful argument

- contains an engaging introduction that clearly establishes the claim being made
- supports the claim with clear reasons and relevant evidence from a variety of credible sources
- establishes and maintains a formal style
- uses language that effectively conveys ideas and adds interest
- includes a conclusion that follows from the argument presented and leaves a lasting impression

COMMON CORE

RI 1 Cite textual evidence to support analysis and inferences.
W 1a–e Write arguments.
W 4 Produce clear and coherent writing.
W 5 Develop and strengthen writing.
W 8 Gather information from print/digital sources.
W 9b Apply grade 8 Reading standards to literary nonfiction.
W 10 Write routinely over extended time frames and shorter time frames.

> **PLAN**

Choose Your Position Revisit the texts you read in the collection and the points the writers made about the value of work. Consider whether teenagers need to gain work experience during their school years, and think about why or why not. Then, take a position you can argue effectively and write your claim.

Gather Information Focus on the selection(s) that have information you can cite to support your position.

- Make a list of reasons to explain why you have taken your position and jot down evidence that will support your reasons. Look for facts, quotations, and examples.
- Understand opposing views that might keep your audience from agreeing with you. Consider the counterclaims you will use to try to convince them to agree with your position.
- Emphasize the most important things you want your audience to understand about your position.

my **Notebook**

Use the annotation tools in your eBook to find evidence that supports your viewpoint. Save each piece of evidence to your notebook.

ACADEMIC VOCABULARY

As you plan and write your argument, be sure to use the academic vocabulary words.

commentary
minors
occupation
option
style

WRITE AN ARGUMENT

Introduce students to the Performance Task by reading the introductory paragraph with them and reviewing the criteria for what makes a good argument. Explain that a written argument is not a conflict or disagreement. Review that an argument is a carefully stated claim that is supported by reasons and evidence.

> **PLAN**

GATHER INFORMATION

Remind students that they should keep their audience in mind as they plan their arguments. Tell students that the reasons and evidence they use to support their claims may vary according to who that audience is. Point out that students should always take their audience into account when choosing the tone they will use in a piece of persuasive writing.

PERFORMANCE TASK B

Organize Your Ideas

Organize Your Ideas Think about how you will organize your argument. A graphic organizer, such as a hierarchy chart, can help you plan and present your ideas logically. Place your claim in the top box, your reasons in the next row of boxes, and your evidence in the bottom row.

Consider Your Purpose and Audience Think about your audience as you write. The development, organization, and style of your argument may be different for a group of classmates or friends than it would be for a group of adults.

> ## PRODUCE
>
> ### WRITE YOUR ARGUMENT
>
> Remind students that the purpose of an argument is to convince others that a claim is valid. Suggest that students deliver their arguments in their heads as they write to make sure that their points are logical and persuasive. Students should ask themselves if the points they are making would be convincing if presented to a member of the audience for which they are writing.

PRODUCE

Write Your Argument Use your notes and your graphic organizer as you begin your draft.

- Introduce your claim to your audience. Grab your readers' attention with a surprising or unexpected statistic, fact, or quotation.

- State your position clearly. Sequence your reasons and evidence logically. Decide whether it is more effective to begin or end with your strongest reason.

- Include relevant descriptions, facts, and details that emphasize your main points.

- Acknowledge counterclaims and include credible responses.

- Maintain a formal style, and use transition words and phrases such as *because, therefore,* and *for this reason* to clarify relationships between ideas. Vary the length and type of sentences as you write.

- Bring your argument to a conclusion. Summarize your viewpoint, repeating the most important reasons and evidence, and remind your audience why your position is the right one.

my **WriteSmart**

Write your rough draft in *my*WriteSmart. Focus on getting your ideas down, rather than on perfecting your choice of language.

REVISE

Evaluate Your Argument Use the chart on the next page to evaluate the substance and style of your argument.

- Check that your claim is clearly stated and logically supported by reasons and evidence.
- Examine your evidence to make sure it is relevant and based on accurate, credible sources.
- Combine short sentences into compound or complex sentences. Use transitions to connect your ideas.
- Ensure that your argument keeps your audience's attention and concludes with a statement that sums up your views and leaves a lasting impression.

*my*WriteSmart

Have a partner or a group of peers review your draft in *my*WriteSmart. Ask your reviewers to note any reasons that do not support the claim well or that lack sufficient evidence.

PRESENT

Create a Finished Copy Finalize your argument and choose a way to share it with your audience. Consider these options:

- Present your argument as an oral report.
- Post your argument as a blog on a classroom or school website.
- Present your ideas in a debate with someone who has taken an opposing position.

REVISE

EVALUATE YOUR ARGUMENT

Suggest that students read their drafts as if they were hearing the argument for the first time. They should ask themselves questions such as:

- Is my claim stated clearly?
- Are the reasons logical?
- Is the evidence persuasive?
- Is there anything I left out that would make my argument stronger?

PRESENT

CREATE A FINISHED COPY

Students can:

- present their argument orally. Remind students that their tone and delivery can help to make their arguments more persuasive.
- post their arguments as a blog on a school website. Encourage others to read the arguments and write comments about them. The authors can then respond to the comments.
- present their ideas in a debate with a classmate with a differing opinion. Students should review the counterclaims they considered while planning their arguments to help them prepare for the debate.

PERFORMANCE TASK B

IDEAS AND EVIDENCE

Have students use the chart to evaluate how they did on the Performance Task in each of the three main categories. Ask students to choose one category and think about how they could improve that aspect of their writing. For example, what would make their introduction more effective? Have students set goals for the next time they write an argument.

COLLECTION 6 TASK B
ARGUMENT

	Ideas and Evidence	Organization	Language
ADVANCED	• The introduction immediately grabs the audience's attention; the claim clearly states a position on a topic. • Logical reasons and relevant evidence convincingly support the writer's claim. • Opposing claims are anticipated and effectively addressed. • The concluding section effectively summarizes the claim.	• The reasons and evidence are organized logically and consistently throughout the argument. • Transitions effectively connect reasons and evidence to the writer's claim.	• The writer maintains a formal style. • Sentence beginnings, lengths, and structures vary and have a rhythmic flow. • Capitalization, punctuation, and other mechanics are correct. • Grammar and usage are correct.
COMPETENT	• The introduction could do more to grab the audience's attention; the claim states a position on an issue. • Most reasons and evidence support the writer's claim, but they could be more convincing. • Opposing claims are anticipated, but the responses need to be better developed. • The concluding section restates the claim.	• The organization of reasons and evidence is confusing in a few places. • A few more transitions are needed to connect reasons and evidence to the writer's claim.	• The style becomes informal in a few places. • Sentence beginnings, lengths, and structures vary somewhat. • Several capitalization and punctuation mistakes occur. • Some grammatical and usage errors are repeated in the argument.
LIMITED	• The introduction is ordinary; the claim identifies an issue, but the writer's position is not clearly stated. • The reasons and evidence are not always logical or relevant. • Opposing claims are anticipated but not addressed logically. • The concluding section includes an incomplete summary of the claim.	• The organization of reasons and evidence is logical in some places, but it often doesn't follow a pattern. • Many more transitions are needed to connect reasons and evidence to the writer's claim.	• The style becomes informal in many places. • Sentence structures barely vary, and some fragments or run-on sentences are present. • Several spelling and capitalization mistakes occur, and punctuation is inconsistent. • Grammar and usage are incorrect in many places.
EMERGING	• The introduction is missing. • Supporting reasons and evidence are missing. • Opposing claims are neither anticipated nor addressed. • The concluding section is missing.	• A logical organization is not used; reasons and evidence are presented randomly. • Transitions are not used, making the argument difficult to understand.	• The style is inappropriate for the argument. • Repetitive sentence structure, fragments, and run-on sentences make the speech hard to follow. • Spelling and capitalization are often incorrect, and punctuation is missing. • Many grammatical and usage errors obscure the meaning of ideas.

TEACHER NOTE:
The page numbers to the left indicate pages in the Student Edition. Except for the two entries below, the page numbers in the Student Edition and Teacher's Edition correspond.

Writing an Argument

COMMON CORE W 1a-e, W 4

Many of the Performance Tasks in this book ask you to craft an argument in which you support your ideas with text evidence. Any argument you write should include the following sections and characteristics.

Introduction

Clearly state your **claim**—the point your argument makes. As needed, provide context or background information to help readers understand your position. Note the most common opposing views as a way to distinguish and clarify your ideas. From the very beginning, make it clear for readers why your claim is strong; consider providing an overview of your reasons or a quotation that emphasizes your view in your introduction.

EXAMPLES

vague claim: We need fewer teenagers on the road.	**precise claim:** The state should raise the driving age to 18.
not distinguished from opposing view: There are plenty of people who don't want teenagers driving.	**distinguished from opposing view:** While some people think 16-year-olds are old enough to drive, the facts say otherwise.
confusing relationship of ideas: Teens want to drive. Many people drive cars.	**clear relationship of ideas:** By requiring teenagers to spend more time practicing their driving skills with their parents in the car, teenagers will be better prepared to get their licenses.

Development of Claims

The body of your argument must provide strong, logical reasons for your claim and must support those reasons with relevant evidence. A **reason** tells why your claim is valid; **evidence** provides specific examples that illustrate a reason. In the process of developing your claim you should also refute **counterclaims,** or opposing views, with equally strong reasons

and evidence. To demonstrate that you have thoroughly considered your view, provide a well-rounded look at both the strengths and limitations of your claim and opposing claims. The goal is not to undercut your argument, but rather to answer your readers' potential objections to it. Be sure, too, to consider how much your audience may already know about your topic in order to avoid boring or confusing readers.

EXAMPLES

claim lacking reasons: Teenagers are bad drivers because they are young and irresponsible.	**claim developed by reasons:** Among the reasons to raise the driving age to 18 is that more driving errors occur when teenagers lack practice behind the wheel.
omission of limitations: People opposed to this idea deny that there is any downside to this plan.	**fair discussion of limitations:** Raising the driving age to 18 might cause some opponents to request that we require less permitting time and eliminate driver's education.
inattention to audience's knowledge: Teenage driving errors can damage a car, creating imbalances in the car's engine that are emphasized at high rpm, which might result in throwing a connecting rod through the sump.	**awareness of audience's knowledge:** Those unfamiliar with the movement to raise the driving age from 16 to 18 might not be aware that even rural communities favor raising the driving age to prevent fatal car crashes involving teenagers.

Links Among Ideas

Even the strongest reasons and evidence will fail to sway readers if it is unclear how the reasons relate to the central claim of an argument. Make the connections clear for your readers, using not only transitional words and phrases, but also using clauses and even entire sentences as a bridge between ideas you have already discussed and ideas you are introducing.

EXAMPLES

transitional word linking claim and reason: The entire state will benefit from raising the driving age from 16 to 18 because teenagers will have more time to practice their driving.

transitional phrase linking reason and evidence: A higher driving age will reduce accidents on the road. In fact, safety experts say that, "One in five 16-year-olds will have a reportable car crash within the first year."

transitional clause linking claim and counter-claim: The safety benefits of raising the driving age are clear. Those opposed to such a measure might say that the inconvenience of driving 16-year-olds to after-school activities needs to be considered.

Appropriate Style and Tone

An effective argument is most often written in a direct and formal style. The style and tone you choose in an argument should not be an afterthought—the way you express your argument can either drive home your ideas or detract from them. Even as you argue in favor of your viewpoint, take care to remain objective in tone—avoid using loaded language when discussing opposing claims.

EXAMPLES

informal style: The new law would help all state residents so everyone should be in favor of the measure.

formal style: Because the law would help lower teenage driving accidents, making our roads safer, it is logical that state legislators would want to raise the driving age from 16 to 18.

biased tone: It doesn't make any sense to not raise the driving age.

objective tone: Arguments against this law have been refuted by statistics that show an increase in car accidents, many of which are fatal, among 16-year-olds.

inattention to conventions: We need to get this law passed!

attention to conventions: This law, which will greatly improve driving safety conditions in our state, needs to be considered by state lawmakers.

Conclusion

Your conclusion may range from a sentence to a full paragraph, but it must wrap up your argument in a satisfying way; a conclusion that sounds tacked-on helps your argument no more than providing no conclusion at all. A strong conclusion is a logical extension of the argument you have presented. It carries forth your ideas through an inference, question, quotation, or challenge.

EXAMPLES

inference: Support for safer roadways begins with our youth.

question: Who doesn't want to drive on roads that are safer?

quotation: As Jay Giedd, chief of brain imaging in the child psychiatric unit at the National Institute of Mental Health, explains regarding a study he led on brain research, "A crucial part of the teen's brain, the area that peers ahead and considers consequences, remains undeveloped. That means careless attitudes and rash emotions often drive teen decisions."

challenge: Laws of this type can be the difference between life and death.

Writing an Informative Essay

COMMON CORE W 2a–f, W 4

Most of the Performance Tasks in this book ask you to write informational or explanatory texts in which you present a topic and examine it thoughtfully, through a well-organized analysis of relevant content. Any informative or explanatory text that you create should include the following parts and features.

Introduction

Develop a strong **thesis statement.** That is, clearly state your **topic** and the **organizational framework** through which you will **connect** or **distinguish** elements of your topic. For example, you might state that your text will compare ideas, examine causes and effects, or explore a problem and its solutions.

EXAMPLE

Topic: Summer Jobs
Sample Thesis Statements
Compare-contrast: When deciding whether to take a summer job or not, consider the financial and career rewards or losses of working for a company or staying at home.
Cause-effect: While the causes of unemployment among teens, especially in a recession, aren't difficult to figure out, the consequences of not working might not be apparent right away.
Problem-solution: While our town faces a growing problem with joblessness among teenagers, we can get our youth back to work if businesses will step up and make a commitment to offer more apprenticeship programs.

Clarifying the organizational framework up front will help you organize the body of your text, suggest **headings** you can use to guide your readers, and help you identify **graphics** that you may need to clarify information. For example, if you compare and contrast the pros and cons of providing jobs for teens, you might create a chart like the one here to guide your writing. You could include the same chart in your paper as a graphic for readers. The row or column headings serve as natural paragraph headings.

	Working	Staying at Home
Finances	Earning income to save for college or a special purchase; ability to help their family pay bills, especially if mother or father is out of work	Missing out on income that could be used toward their college education or for discretionary purchases
Rewards	Learning a trade or skill that can be used in a future job; increased self confidence	Opportunity to take summer school classes or to volunteer for an important cause

Development of the Topic

In the body of your text, flesh out the organizational framework you established in your introduction with strong supporting paragraphs. Include only support directly relevant to your topic. Don't rely on a single source, and make sure the sources you do use are reputable and current. The table below illustrates types of support you might use to develop aspects of your topic. It also shows how transitions link text sections, create cohesion, and clarify the relationships among ideas.

Types of Support in Explanatory/ Informative Texts	Uses of Transitions in Explanatory/ Informative Texts
Facts and examples: One cause of unemployment among teens is a recession; *for example,* older workers might be willing to take part-time jobs that otherwise would have gone to teenagers.	*One cause* signals the shift from the introduction to the body text in a cause-and-effect essay. *For example* introduces the support for the cause being cited.
Concrete details: On the other hand, teens might have a better chance at getting a job than an older person might, since the teen might work for less money because career experience is as important to them as income is.	*On the other hand* transitions the reader from one point of comparison to another in a compare-contrast essay.
Statistics: Turn to the U.S. Bureau of Labor Statistics if you doubt the scope of America's unemployment problem. According to the bureau, in 2011, the unemployment rate for job aspirants 16 to 19 years old was 24.4 percent.	The entire transitional sentence introduces the part of a problem-solution essay that demonstrates the existence of a problem.

You can't always include all of the information you'd like to in a short essay, but you can plan to point readers directly to useful **multimedia links** either in the body of or at the end of your essay.

Style and Tone

Use formal English to establish your credibility as a source of information. To project authority, use the language of the domain, or field, that you are writing about. However, be sure to define unfamiliar terms to avoid using jargon your audience may not know. Provide extended definitions when your audience is likely to have limited knowledge of the topic.

Using quotations from reputable sources can also give your text authority; be sure to credit the source of quoted material. In general, keep the tone objective, avoiding slangy or biased expressions.

Informal, jargon-filled, biased language: Teenagers who do not try and find summer work are lazy and selfish, unwilling to take a job to help their families out in these hard economic times. These teens also have no regard for their future and don't take having a career seriously.

Extended definition in formal style and objective tone: Teenagers' employment statistics have worsened because more businesses, such as grocery stores, are using automated machines for low-level tasks, replacing the need to hire workers. An automated machine, as defined by the dictionary, "is the use of control systems and information technologies reducing the need for human intervention."

Conclusion

Wrap up your essay with a concluding statement or section that sums up or extends the information in your essay.

EXAMPLES

Articulate implications: Part-time jobs are where most teenagers will learn valuable workplace skills. Teens who don't have early job experience might miss out on crucial career and personal development and may never reach their full potential.

Emphasize significance: Without a talented young work force, our nation's future is in jeopardy. Businesses throughout the U.S. are already reporting deficiencies in quantities of candidates who can fill positions that require advanced capabilities.

Writing a Narrative

COMMON CORE W 3a-e, W 4

When you are writing a fictional tale, an autobiographical incident, or a firsthand biography, you write in the narrative mode. That means telling a story with a beginning, a climax, and a conclusion. Though there are important differences between fictional and nonfiction narratives, you use similar processes to develop them.

Identify a Problem, Situation, or Observation

For a nonfiction narrative, dig into your memory bank for a problem you dealt with or an observation you've made about your life. For fiction, try to invent a problem or situation that can unfold in interesting ways.

EXAMPLES

Problem (nonfiction)	Last summer, I wanted to work enough so I could save money to go to France this year and learn French.
Situation (fiction)	Mary's mom confiscated the girl's cell phone after she learned Mary had gotten a ticket for texting while driving.

Establish a Point of View

Decide who will tell your story. If you are writing a reflective essay about an important experience or person in your own life, you will be the narrator of the events you relate. If you are writing a work of fiction, you can choose to create a first-person narrator or tell the story from the third-person point of view. In that case, the narrator can focus on one character or reveal the thoughts and feelings of all the characters. The examples below show the differences between a first- and third-person narrator.

First-person narrator (nonfiction)	Several thousand dollars is what I needed to go to France for two months. But I couldn't earn that much working at a summer camp, and no other jobs were available.

Third-person narrator (fiction)	Mary didn't want to wait to reply to her boyfriend's text about going out to dinner that night, so she quickly replied while driving to the store. Just before she hit the send button, she noticed flashing lights behind her. She looked in the rearview mirror and saw that a cop was pulling her over.

Gather Details

To make real or imaginary experiences come alive on the page, you will need to use narrative techniques like description and dialogue. The questions in the left column in the chart below can help you search your memory or imagination for the details that will form the basis of your narrative. You don't have to respond in full sentences, but try to capture the sights, sounds, and feelings that bring your narrative to life.

Who, What, When, Where?	Narrative Techniques
People: Who are the people or characters involved in the experience? What did they look like? What did they do? What did they say?	**Description:** The cop, who was not smiling, had an ominous look on his face as he approached my car. "Do you know why I am pulling you over?" he asked sternly. "No, officer, was I speeding?" I replied. "You were texting while driving, which is against the law, and because you were not paying attention while you were typing, you almost hit the car next to you," he explained. "Please get our your driver's license, car registration, and insurance."

continued

Who, What, When, Where?	Narrative Techniques
Experience: What led up to or caused the event? What is the main event in the experience? What happened as a result of the event?	**Description:** I loved being a camp counselor, but I knew earning $8 an hour would not be enough to save the money I needed to go to France. I created my own business mowing lawns. Several people in my neighborhood needed help with their yard work and were willing to pay me $15 an hour!
Places: When and where did the events take place? What were the sights, sounds, and smells of this place?	**Description:** I remember how intense the humidity was while I was mowing Mrs. Anderson's lawn. The air felt thick, as if I were trying to breathe through a straw stuck in the mud. The sun's heat was so severe that my skin felt hot to the touch.

Sequence Events

Before you begin writing, list the key events of the experience or story in chronological, or time, order. Place a star next to the point of highest tension—for example, the point at which a key decision determines the outcome of events. In fiction, this point is called the climax, but a gripping nonfiction narrative will also have a climactic event.

To build suspense—the uncertainty a reader feels about what will happen next—you'll want to think about the pacing or rhythm of your narrative. Consider disrupting the chronological order of events by beginning at the end, then starting over. Or interrupt the forward flow of events with a flashback, which takes the reader to an earlier point in the narrative.

Another way to build suspense is with multiple plot lines. For example, the personal narrative about the trip to France involves a second plot line in which the narrator realizes she needs a second job to afford to go overseas. Both plot lines intersect when the narrator starts her own business in order to raise money to travel.

Use Vivid Language

As you revise, make an effort to use vivid language. Use precise words and phrases to describe feelings and action. Use telling details to show, rather than directly state, what a character is like. Use sensory language that lets readers see, feel, hear, smell, and taste what you or your characters experienced.

First Draft	Revision
My dad, who supported my trip to France, encouraged me to start my own business.	My dad raised my chin with his right hand so I could look him in the eye as he said, "Terri, I am proud of you for having the initiative to start your own business." [telling details]
The temperature was soaring past 100 degrees for the fifth day in a row.	The relentless sun scorched my skin, turning it into blisters of pain. The only relief I felt was when I soothed my skin with cool aloe vera lotion. [precise words and phrases]
Mary was furious with her mother for taking her cell phone.	Mary slammed her door, rattling the photos hanging on the walls. She turned the lock and collapsed onto her bed. [sensory details]

Conclusion

At the conclusion of the narrative, you or your narrator will reflect on the meaning of the events. The conclusion should follow logically from the climactic moment of the narrative. The narrator of a personal narrative usually reflects on the significance of the experience—the lessons learned or the legacy left.

EXAMPLE

As I stepped off the bus in Paris, all I could hear was the melody of French being spoken on the street. I looked left and saw a lovely outdoor cafe where people were reading and leisurely enjoying cafe au lait. In the distance was the majestic Eiffel Tower looking down on me as if to say, "You did it. You earned your way to France."

Conducting Research

 COMMON CORE W 7, W 8

The Performance Tasks in this book will require you to complete research projects related to the texts you've read in the collections. Whether the topic is stated in a Performance Task or is one you generate, the following information will guide you through your research project.

Focus Your Research and Formulate a Question

Some topics for a research project can be effectively covered in three pages; others require an entire book for a thorough treatment. Begin by developing a topic that is neither too narrow nor too broad for the time frame of the assignment. Also check your school and local libraries and databases to help you determine how to choose your topic. If there's too little information, you'll need to broaden your focus; if there's too much, you'll need to limit it.

With a topic in hand, formulate a research question; it will keep you on track as you conduct your research. A good research question cannot be answered in a single word. It should be open-ended. It should require investigation. You can also develop related research questions to explore your topic in more depth.

EXAMPLES

Possible topics for *The Diary of a Young Girl*	The Holocaust—too broad Holocaust victim Anne Frank—too narrow Anne's experience in the camps
Possible research question	To what degree are the settings and events in *The Diary of a Young Girl* based on fact?
Related questions	To what extent do historians agree or disagree on which aspects of *The Diary of a Young Girl* are real?

Locate and Evaluate Sources

To find answers to your research question, you'll need to investigate primary and secondary sources, whether in print or digital formats. **Primary sources** contain original, firsthand information, such as diaries, autobiographies, interviews, speeches, and eyewitness accounts. **Secondary sources** provide other people's versions of primary sources in encyclopedias, newspaper and magazine articles, biographies, and documentaries.

Your search for sources begins at the library and on the World Wide Web. Use **advanced search features** to help you find things quickly. Add a minus sign (–) before a word that should not appear in your results. Use an asterisk (*) in place of unknown words. List the name of and location of each possible source, adding comments about its potential usefulness. Assessing, or evaluating, your sources is an important step in the research process. Your goal is to use sources that are credible, or reliable and trustworthy.

Criteria for Assessing Sources	
Relevance: It covers the target aspect of my topic.	• How will the source be useful in answering my research question?
Accuracy: It includes information that can be verified by more than one authoritative source.	• Is the information up-to-date? Are the facts accurate? How can I verify them? • What qualifies the author to write about this topic? Is he or she an authority?
Objectivity: It presents multiple viewpoints on the topic.	• What, if any, biases can I detect? Does the writer favor one view of the topic?

Incorporating and Citing Source Material

When you draft your research project, you'll need to include material from your sources. This material can be **direct quotations, summaries,** or **paraphrases** of the original source material. Two well-known **style manuals** provide information on how to cite a range of print and digital sources: the *MLA Handbook for Writers of Research Papers* (published by the Modern Language Association) and Kate L. Turabian's *A Manual for Writers* (published by The University of Chicago Press). Both style manuals provide a wealth of information about conducting, formatting, drafting, and presenting your research, including guidelines for citing sources within the text (called parenthetical citations) and preparing the list of Works Cited, as well as correct use of the mechanics of writing. Your teacher will indicate which style manual you should use. The following examples use the format in the *MLA Handbook*.

Any material from sources must be completely documented, or you will be committing **plagiarism,** the unauthorized use of someone else's words or ideas. Plagiarism is not honest. As you take notes for your research project, be sure to keep complete information about your sources so that you can cite them correctly in the body of your paper. This applies to all sources, whether print or digital. Having complete information will also enable you to prepare the list of Works Cited. The list of Works Cited, which concludes your research project, provides author, title, and publication information for both print and digital sources. The following pages show the *MLA Handbook's* Works Cited citation formats for a variety of sources.

EXAMPLES

Direct quotation [The writer is citing comments made by eyewitnesses who had seen Anne Frank after she was apprehended by German police and transported to Auschwitz.]	In one interview with a friend of Anne Frank's, the friend states that, "...more often Anne displayed strength and courage. Her gregarious and confident nature allowed her to obtain extra bread rations for her mother, sister, and herself."
Summary [The writer is summarizing various accounts from prisoners that Anne Frank died of typhus while imprisoned at Bergen-Belsen.]	In the spring of 1945, nearly 20,000 prisoners, including Anne Frank, died after a typhus epidemic spread through the Bergen-Belsen concentration camp. A few weeks later, the camp was liberated by British troops.
Paraphrase [The writer is paraphrasing accounts from prisoners about Anne Frank's imprisonment, as well as interviews in the 1988 television documentary, *The Last Seven Months of Anne Frank*.]	Bloeme Evers-Emden, an Amsterdam native and schoolmate of Anne's, said she saw Anne while they were imprisoned in Auschwitz and confirmed that Anne had escaped being gassed because Anne had just turned 15. A majority of those gassed upon arriving at Auschwitz were younger than 15.

MLA Citation Guidelines

Today, you can find free websites that generate ready-made citations for research papers, using the information you provide. Such sites have some time-saving advantages when you're developing a Works Cited list. However, you should always check your citations carefully before you turn in your final paper. If you are following MLA style, use these guidelines to evaluate and finalize your work.

Books

One author

Lastname, Firstname. *Title of Book*. City of Publication: Publisher, Year of Publication. Medium of Publication.

Two authors or editors

Lastname, Firstname, and Firstname Lastname. *Title of Book*. City of Publication: Publisher, Year of Publication. Medium of Publication.

Three authors

Lastname, Firstname, Firstname Lastname, and Firstname Lastname. *Title of Book*. City of Publication: Publisher, Year of Publication. Medium of Publication.

Four or more authors

The abbreviation et al. means "and others." Use et al. instead of listing all the authors.

Lastname, Firstname, et al. *Title of Book*. City of Publication: Publisher, Year of Publication. Medium of Publication.

No author given

Title of Book. City of Publication: Publisher, Year of Publication. Medium of Publication.

An author and a translator

Lastname, Firstname. *Title of Book*. Trans. Firstname Lastname. City of Publication: Publisher, Year of Publication. Medium of Publication.

An author, a translator, and an editor

Lastname, Firstname. *Title of Book*. Trans. Firstname Lastname. Ed. Firstname Lastname. City of Publication: Publisher, Year of Publication. Medium of Publication.

Parts of Books

An introduction, a preface, a foreword, or an afterword written by someone other than the author(s) of a work

Lastname, Firstname. Part of Book. *Title of Book*. By Author of book's Firstname Lastname. City of Publication: Publisher, Year of Publication. Page span. Medium of Publication.

A poem, a short story, an essay, or a chapter in a collection of works by one author

Lastname, Firstname. "Title of Piece." *Title of Book*. Ed. Firstname Lastname. City of Publication: Publisher, Year of Publication. Page span. Medium of Publication.

A poem, a short story, an essay, or a chapter in an anthology of works by several authors

Lastname, Firstname. "Title of Piece." *Title of Book*. Ed. Firstname Lastname. City of Publication: Publisher, Year of Publication. Page range. Medium of Publication.

Magazines, Newspapers, and Encyclopedias

An article in a newspaper

Lastname, Firstname. "Title of Article." *Title of Book Periodical* Day Month Year: pages. Medium of Publication.

An article in a magazine

Lastname, Firstname. "Title of Article." *Title of Book Periodical* Day Month Year: pages. Medium of Publication.

An article in an encyclopedia

"Title of Article." *Title of Encyclopedia*. Year ed. Medium of Publication.

Miscellaneous Nonprint Sources

An interview

Lastname, Firstname. Personal interview. Day Month Year.

A video recording

Title of Recording. Producer, Year. Medium of Publication

Electronic Publications

A CD-ROM

"Title of Piece." *Title of CD*. Year ed. City of Publication: Publisher, Year of Publication. CD-ROM.

A document from an Internet site

Entries for online source should contain as much information as available.

Lastname, Firstname. "*Title of Piece*." Information on what the site is. Year. Web. Day Month Year (when accessed)

Participating in a Collaborative Discussion

 COMMON CORE SL 1a-d

Often, class activities, including the Performance Tasks in this book, will require you to work collaboratively with classmates. Whether your group will analyze a work of literature or try to solve a community problem, use the following guidelines to ensure a productive discussion.

Prepare for the Discussion

A productive discussion is one in which all the participants bring useful information and ideas to share. If your group will discuss a short story the class read, first re-read and annotate a copy of the story. Your annotations will help you quickly locate evidence to support your points. Participants in a discussion about an important issue should first research the issue and bring notes or information sources that will help guide the group. If you disagree with a point made by another group member, your case will be stronger if you back it up with specific evidence from your sources.

EXAMPLES

disagreeing without evidence: I don't think horror stories like "The Tell-Tale Heart" are relevant today because people prefer to go and see a scary movie rather than take the time to read a horror story.

providing evidence for disagreement: I disagree with Edgar Allan Poe's relevance today because I don't think students are inspired by horror tales in print. Students would rather watch a scary movie and enjoy the thrill of seeing and hearing the characters scream and run from whatever is chasing them. I think scary movies captivate people more than books from the 1800s do. I think books from that long ago are outdated when it comes to knowing what excites students and gets them scared. I mean how thrilling can an Edgar Allan Poe story be compared to seeing people running for their lives from decomposing zombies?

Set Ground Rules

The rules your group needs will depend on what your group is expected to accomplish. A discussion of themes in a poem will be unlikely to produce a single consensus; however, a discussion aimed at developing a solution to a problem should result in one strong proposal that all group members support. Answer the following questions to set ground rules that fit your group's purpose:

- What will this group produce? A range of ideas, a single decision, a plan of action, or something else? .

- How much time is available? How much of that time should be allotted to each part of our discussion (presenting ideas, summarizing or voting on final ideas, creating a product such as a written analysis or speech)?

- What roles need to be assigned within the group? Do we need a leader, a note-taker, a timekeeper, or other specific roles?

- What is the best way to synthesize our group's ideas? Should we take a vote, list group members as "for" or "against" in a chart, or use some other method to reach consensus or sum up the results of the discussion?

Move the Discussion Forward

Everyone in the group should be actively involved in synthesizing ideas. To make sure this happens, ask questions that draw out ideas, especially from less-talkative members of the group. If an idea or statement is confusing, try to paraphrase it, or ask the speaker to explain more about it. If you disagree with a statement, say so politely and explain in detail why you disagree.

SAMPLE DISCUSSION

MIKE: Cindy, what do you think about horror tales? Are they scarier in a book or a movie?	*Question draws out quiet member*
CINDY: I had a hard time reading Poe's "The Tell-Tale Heart." My attention span may be short, but I am most engrossed in a plot when I am in a movie theater. I love clenching my friend's hand and screaming together.	*Response relates discussion to larger ideas*
PETER: I think horror stories like "The Tell-Tale Heart" can be suspenseful. I don't need to be in a theater to visualize what is going to happen. Poe's writing brings the plot's tension to life for me.	*Question challenges Cindy's conclusion*
CINDY: Yes, there are elements of Poe's story that are suspenseful but I don't get the same reaction as I do when I am at the movies, too afraid to look. That is a sensory experience I don't think a book can replicate.	*Response elaborates on ideas*
MOLLY: I can see the pros of going to a theater and feeding off of the audience's energy, but I do think "The Tell-Tale Heart" is still relevant today. It allows you to create the tale in your head and form conclusions about what is going to happen.	*Paraphrases idea and challenges it further based on evidence*

Respond to Ideas

In a diverse group, everyone may have a different perspective on the topic of discussion, and that's a good thing. Consider what everyone has to say, and don't resist changing your view if other group members provide convincing evidence for theirs. If, instead, you feel more strongly than ever about your view, don't hesitate to say so and provide reasons related to what those with opposing views have said. Before wrapping up the discussion, try to sum up the points on which your group agrees and disagrees.

SAMPLE DISCUSSION

MOLLY: OK, we have just a few more minutes. Can we try to reach an agreement?	*Molly and Mike try to summarize points of agreement*
MIKE: I think there are two positions—1) those who think scary stories are best seen in a theater and 2) those who think written stories allow you to use your imagination more.	
PETER: Yes, I think "The Tell-Tale Heart" is relevant today. I like how the story is organized and I find it interesting that we don't know who the narrator is.	*Peter maintains his position*
CINDY: I can understand what Peter is saying. I think if I gave the book more of a chance, I could let my imagination help to create the suspense.	*Cindy and Mike qualify their views based on what they have heard*
MIKE: That makes sense. Sometimes we need to use our minds more and not be so dependent on a movie. Poe's words and themes are scary, and we just need to use our imagination.	
MOLLY: I'm with Peter. I like Poe's prose. His words build suspense and they take you back in time to a different era.	*Molly supports her position by making a new connection*

Debating an Issue

 COMMON CORE SL 3, SL 4

The selection and collection Performance Tasks in this text will direct you to engage in debates about issues relating to the selections you are reading. Use the guidelines that follow to have a productive and balanced argument about both sides of an issue.

The Structure of a Formal Debate

In a debate, two teams compete to win the support of the audience about an issue. In a **formal debate,** two teams, each with two members, present their arguments on a given proposition or policy statement. One team argues for the proposition or statement and the other team argues against it. Each debater must consider the proposition closely and must research both sides of it. To argue convincingly either for or against a proposition, a debater must be familiar with both sides of the issue.

Plan the Debate

The purpose of a debate is to allow participants and audience members to consider both sides of an issue. Use these planning suggestions to hold a balanced and productive debate:

- **Identify Debate Teams** Form groups of six members based on the issues that the Performance Tasks include. Three members of the team will argue for the affirmative side of the issue—that is, they support the issue. The other three members will argue for the negative side of the issue—that is, they do not support the issue.
- **Appoint a Moderator** The moderator will present the topic and goals of the debate, keep track of the time, and introduce and thank the participants.
- **Research and Prepare Notes** Search texts you've read as well as print and online sources for valid reasons and evidence to

support your team's claim. As with argument, be sure to anticipate possible opposing claims and compile evidence to counter those claims. You will use notes from your research during the debate.

- **Assign Debate Roles** One team member will introduce the team's claim and supporting evidence. Another team member will respond to questions and opposing claims in an exchange with a member of the opposing team. The last member will present a strong closing argument.

Hold the Debate

A formal debate is not a shouting match—rather, a well-run debate is an excellent forum for participants to express their viewpoints, build on others' ideas, and have a thoughtful, well-reasoned exchange of ideas. The moderator will begin by stating the topic or issue and introducing the participants. Participants should follow the moderator's instructions concerning whose turn it is to speak and how much time each speaker has.

- How effectively did the team rebut, or respond to, arguments made by the opposing team?
- Did the speakers maintain eye contact and speak at an appropriate rate and volume?
- Did the speakers observer proper debate etiquette—that is, did they follow the moderator's instructions, stay within their allotted time limits, and treat their opponents respectfully?

Formal Debate Format

Speaker	Role	Time
Affirmative Speaker 1	Present the claim and supporting evidence for the affirmative ("pro") side of the argument.	5 minutes
Negative Speaker 1	Ask probing questions that will prompt the other team to address flaws in the argument.	3 minutes
Affirmative Speaker 2	Respond to the questions posed by the opposing team and counter any concerns.	3 minutes
Speaker	Role	Time
Negative Speaker 2	Present the claim and supporting evidence for the negative ("con") side of the argument.	5 minutes
Affirmative Speaker 3	Summarize the claim and evidence for the affirmative side and explain why your reasoning is more valid.	3 minutes
Negative Speaker 3	Summarize the claim and evidence for the negative side and explain why your reasoning is more valid.	3 minutes

Evaluate the Debate

Use the following guidelines to evaluate a team in a debate:

- Did the team prove that the issue is significant? How thorough was the analysis?
- How did the team effectively argue that you should support their affirmative or negative side of the proposition or issue?
- How effectively did the team present reasons and evidence, including evidence from the texts, to support the proposition?

Reading Informational Texts: Patterns of Organization

Reading any type of writing is easier once you recognize how it is organized. Writers usually arrange ideas and information in ways that best help readers see how they are related. There are several common patterns of organization:

- main idea and supporting details
- chronological order
- cause-effect organization
- compare-and-contrast organization
- problem-solution organization

Writers also typically present arguments in ways that will help readers follow their reasoning.

1. Main Idea and Supporting Details

Main idea and supporting details is a basic pattern of organization in which a central idea about a topic is supported by details. The **main idea** is the most important idea about a topic that a particular text or paragraph conveys. **Supporting details** are words, phrases, or sentences that tell more about the main idea. The main idea may be directly stated at the beginning and then followed by supporting details, or it may be merely implied by the supporting details. It may also be stated after it has been implied by supporting details.

Strategies for Reading

- To find a stated main idea in a paragraph, identify the paragraph's topic. The topic is what the paragraph is about and can usually be summed up in one or two words. The word, or synonyms of it, will usually appear throughout the paragraph. Headings and subheadings are also clues to the topics of paragraphs.
- Look for the topic sentence, or the sentence that states the most important idea the paragraph conveys. It is often the first sentence in a paragraph; however, it may appear at the end.
- To find an implied main idea, ask yourself: Whom or what did I just read about? What do the details suggest about the topic?

- Formulate a sentence stating this idea and add it to the paragraph. Does your sentence convey the main idea?

Notice how the main idea is expressed in each of the following models.

Model:
Main Idea as the First Sentence

> On the second day of the heat wave, the temperature soared to a sweltering 110 degrees. The sun melted the tar of the newly paved driveway. It was almost impossible to escape the fumes, which caused him to hold his nose and breathe through his mouth. The air felt like a wet blanket smothering his lungs. Each breath was a struggle.

Main idea *(first sentence)*

Supporting details

Model:
Main Idea as the First Sentence

> His body tried to maintain a healthy temperature by producing large amounts of sweat. Because the air was so humid and there was no breeze, the sweat didn't evaporate and cool him at all. It just dripped unpleasantly, and he grew even hotter as he angrily tried to wipe it away. Despite losing all that water, he wasn't even thirsty. Though he didn't know it, he was in danger of becoming dehydrated.

Supporting details

Main idea

Model:
Implied Main Idea

As he walked along the street looking for something to drink, he began to feel light-headed. He ignored the feeling for a few minutes, but then became so dizzy that he had to sit down. Soon he started to feel sick to his stomach. As he stretched out, he began to shiver. "How can I be cold when it's 110 degrees?" he wondered before he fainted.

> **Implied main idea:** He was dehydrated, which was a serious problem.

Practice and Apply

Read each paragraph, and then do the following:

1. Identify the main idea in the paragraph, using one of the strategies discussed on the previous page. Tell whether it is stated or implied.
2. Evaluate the pattern of organization used in the paragraph. Does it express the main idea effectively?

Community service is an important part of our school life. Every student is encouraged to participate in one of the many school-approved service options. No grades are given for the service work, but students record their hours and what type of service they perform. We can also choose to be involved in more than one type of service. Whatever we choose, we learn how much the people of our community appreciate our help and how much we enjoy helping others.

They never saw him. Now and then they heard whispered rumors to the effect that he was in the neighborhood. The woods were searched. The roads were watched. There was never anything to indicate his whereabouts. But a few days afterward, a goodly number of slaves would be gone from the plantation. Neither the master nor the overseer had heard or seen anything unusual in the quarter. Sometimes one or the other would vaguely remember having heard a whippoorwill call somewhere in the woods, close by, late at night. Though it was the wrong season for whippoorwills.

—Ann Petry, *Harriet Tubman: Conductor on the Underground Railroad*

2. Chronological Order

Chronological order is the arrangement of events in the order in which they happen. This type of organization is used in many short stories and novels, historical writing, biographies, and autobiographies. To show the order of events, writers use order words such as *after, next,* and *later* and time words and phrases that identify specific times of day, days of the week, and dates, such as *the next morning, Tuesday, and March 13, 2007.*

Strategies for Reading

- Scan the text for headings and subheadings that may indicate a chronological pattern of organization.
- Look for words and phrases that identify times, such as *in a year, three hours earlier, in* AD *1066,* and *the next day.*
- Look for words that signal order, such as *first, afterward, then, during, later,* and *finally,* to see how events or steps are related.
- Note that a paragraph or passage in which ideas and information are arranged chronologically will have several words or phrases that indicate time order, not just one.
- Ask yourself: Are the events in the paragraph or passage presented in time order?

Notice the words and phrases that signal time order in the first two paragraphs of the following model.

Model:

Jackie Torrence, who was born in 1944, is the author of "Scary Stories." She spent much of her childhood on a North Carolina farm, where she grew up listening to traditional stories told by her grandfather. Years later, while working as a librarian, she was asked to read stories to some young children. She agreed, and the children were instantly captivated. Before long, Torrence was invited to tell stories in local and neighboring communities. Torrence, who was later dubbed "The Story Lady," went on to gain national prominence as a storyteller.

> **Time words and phrases**
>
> **Events**

COMMON CORE RI 2, RI 5

PRACTICE AND APPLY ANSWERS

1. *Community service is an important part of our school life—stated; A person helped slaves escape without being detected—unstated*
2. *main idea and supporting details; chronological order*

PRACTICE AND APPLY ANSWERS

1. *cause—cutting down trees; effect/ (cause)—destruction of rain forest; effect 1—extinction of plants and animals; effect 2—endangering Earth's well-being*

2. *cause, effects, due to, as a result of*

3. Cause-Effect Organization

Cause-effect organization is a pattern of organization that shows causal relationships between events, ideas, and trends. Cause-effect relationships may be directly stated or merely implied by the order in which the information is presented. Writers often use the cause-effect pattern in historical and scientific writing. Cause-effect relationships may have several forms.

One cause with one effect

One cause with multiple effects

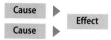

Multiple causes with a single effect

| Cause | ▶ | |
| Cause | ▶ | Effect |

A chain of causes and effects

Strategies for Reading

- Look for headings and subheadings that indicate a cause-effect pattern of organization, such as "Effects of Food Allergies."
- To find the effect or effects, read to answer the question "What happened?"
- To find the cause or causes, read to answer the question "Why did it happen?"
- Look for words and phrases that help you identify specific relationships between events, such as *because, since, had the effect of, led to, as a result, resulted in, for that reason, due to, therefore, if . . . then,* and *consequently.*
- Look closely at each cause-effect relationship. Do not assume that because one event happened before another, the first event caused the second event.
- Use graphic organizers like the diagrams shown to record cause-effect relationships as you read.

Notice the words that signal causes and effects in the following model.

Model:
We're Destroying Our Rain Forests

According to a study done by Brazilian scientists, nearly 5 million acres of rain forest are disappearing a year. That's equal to seven football fields a minute.

The cause of this destruction is simple—cutting down trees. Every minute, around 2,000 trees are felled to create highways, railroads, and farms. Some trees, such as mahogany and teak, are harvested for their beautiful hardwood.

This destruction of the rain forests has wide-ranging effects on living things. About 30,000 plant species live in the Amazon rain forest alone. These plants provide important foods such as bananas, coffee, chocolate, and nuts, as well as medicinal compounds found nowhere else. Just four square miles of a rain forest shelters more than 550 species of birds, reptiles, and amphibians. Almost 100 species worldwide face extinction every day, many due to habitat loss in rainforests.

Rain forests also act as climate regulators, balancing the exchange of oxygen and carbon dioxide in the atmosphere and helping to offset global warming. The earth's well-being will suffer as a result of the rain forests' destruction.

It is crucial that steps be taken immediately to reduce the number of trees being cut down. If this destruction is not reversed, within 50 years, thriving rain forests will be no more than a memory.

Effect

Signal words

Cause

Practice and Apply

Refer to the preceding model to do the following:

1. Use one of the graphic organizers on page R10 to show the multiple effects of cutting down trees described in the model.

2. List three words or phrases used to signal cause and effect in the last four paragraphs.

4. Compare-and-Contrast Organization

Compare-and-contrast organization is a pattern of organization that provides a way to look at similarities and differences in two or more subjects. A writer may use this pattern of organization to compare the important points or characteristics of two or more subjects. These points or characteristics are called **points of comparison.** There are two ways to develop compare-and-contrast organization:

Point-by-point organization—The writer discusses one point of comparison for both subjects, then goes on to the next point.

Subject-by-subject organization—The writer covers all points of comparison for one subject and then all points of comparison for the next subject.

Strategies for Reading

- Look in the text for headings, subheadings, and sentences that may suggest a compare-and-contrast pattern of organization, such as "Common Behaviors of Different Pets," to help you identify where similarities and differences are addressed.

- To find similarities, look for words and phrases such as *like, all, both, every,* and *in the same way.*

- To find differences, look for words and phrases such as *unlike, but, on the other hand, more, less, in contrast,* and *however.*

- Use a graphic organizer, such as a Venn diagram or a compare-and-contrast chart, to record points of comparison and similarities and differences.

	Subject 1	Subject 2
Point 1		
Point 2		
Point 3		

As you read the following models, use the signal words and phrases to identify the similarities and differences between the subjects and how the details are organized in each text.

Model 1

Mr. Frank and Mr. Van Daan

Moving into a tiny apartment with people you have never met is a sure way to discover your differences. In the play *The Diary of Anne Frank,* Mr. Frank and Mr. Van Daan are in a similar situation, but have very different personalities, behaviors, and relationships with their families.

> **Subjects**

Both men are Jews living in Nazi-occupied Amsterdam during World War II. Both have children: Mr. Frank, two daughters; and Mr. Van Daan, a son. They try to hide their families from the Nazis in the same apartment.

> **Comparison words and phrases**

Despite these similarities, there are many differences between the two men. First, they have nearly opposite personalities. Mr. Van Daan is very concerned with appearances and wears expensive clothes. He can be kind, but often loses his temper. He also has strong opinions about the roles of men and women. For example, he acts embarrassed that his son Peter likes his pet cat and disapproves of Anne's outspokenness. He tells her, "A man likes a girl who'll listen to him once in a while."

> **Comparison words and phrases**

> **Subjects**

In contrast, Mr. Frank doesn't seem to care about material things. He always stays calm and has compassion for other people. Even when Mr. Van Daan is caught stealing food, Mr. Frank tries to understand the man's behavior. Mr. Frank's attitude about women differs from Mr. Van Daan's as well. Mr. Frank never criticizes Anne for being unladylike; instead, he encourages her to be herself. He gives her a diary because he knows she loves to write, and he is proud of her creativity when she makes

> **Contrast words and phrases**

> **Subject**

PRACTICE AND APPLY POSSIBLE ANSWERS

1. *The models are similar in that they both use compare-and-contrast organization, but they differ in their specific arrangement of similarities and differences. The first model uses point-by-point organization, while the second uses subject-by-subject organization.*

2. *Model 1—both, same, similarities, differences, in contrast, on the other hand, differently; Model 2—and, on the other hand, unlike, like, also*

3. *Model 1—personalities, behavior, family relationships; Model 2—country of origin, leaves, brewing methods, methods for drinking, what's added*

4. *Answers will vary. Possible graphic:*

Characteristic	Yerba maté	Green tea
Country of origin	South America	China
Brewing method	brewed in gourd, absorbs boiling water twice	brewed in teapot for 2 minutes
Served in	bombilla	ceramic cup
What's added	milk, sugar, lemon juice	nothing
Health benefits	antioxidants, aids digestion	antioxidants, lowers cholesterol and blood sugar, relieves arthritis pain

Hanukkah presents for everyone. As Anne says about her father, "He's the only one who's ever given me the feeling that I have any sense."

The two men also respond differently to their situation. Mr. Van Daan is self-centered and believes he suffers more from hunger than the others. He even tries to take Anne's piece of cake. Mr. Frank, **on the other hand,** always puts the needs of others before his own. For example, he makes the newcomer, Dr. Dussel, feel welcome and gladly offers him food. He also risks his own safety to investigate when a robber enters the downstairs warehouse.

Contrast words and phrases

Mr. Frank and Mr. Van Daan relate differently with their families. Although Mr. and Mrs. Van Daan are close, they quarrel often. Mr. Van Daan criticizes his son's slowness and threatens to get rid of his beloved cat. In contrast, Mr. Frank shows only love and respect for his wife and daughters. Even when he scolds Anne, he does it privately and gently. After Anne hurts her mother's feelings, Mr. Frank tells her that parents "can only try to set a good example. The rest you must do yourself."

The differences between Mr. Frank and Mr. Van Daan in *The Diary of Anne Frank* far outnumber their similarities. Mr. Van Daan's selfishness endangers both families, while Mr. Frank's compassion and consideration help them all make the best of a terrible situation.

Model 2

Two for Tea

Next to water, tea is the most popular drink worldwide. Served hot or iced, it comes in a variety of flavors to suit every taste. **Yerba maté** and **green** tea are two varieties that seem to suit the tastes of increasing numbers of people of all ages and nationalities.

Subjects

Comparison words and phrases

Yerba maté is native to South America. Made from the dried leaves of the yerba maté tree, it is traditionally brewed in hollow gourds, which are themselves called *matés*. The gourd is filled three-quarters full with leaves, and they are then covered with hot water. When the leaves have completely absorbed the moisture, more water is added. The brewed tea is then drunk through a tube with a strainer at one end called a *bombilla*. Yerba maté is sometimes served with milk, sugar, or lemon juice to cut its slight bitterness.

Yerba maté is thought to offer many health benefits. It is loaded with antioxidants that may boost the immune system and help prevent cancer. It also seems to aid digestion.

Green tea, **on the other hand,** is native to China and was exported to Japan in about AD 800. **Unlike** yerba maté, green tea usually is brewed in teapots. Only about a teaspoonful of leaves is used per pot. The leaves are steeped for only around two minutes—much less than the soaking time for yerba maté. Green tea has a very mild taste and generally is served plain in ceramic cups so the delicate taste can be savored.

Contrast words and phrases

Like yerba maté, green tea **also** is beneficial to health. Similarly rich in antioxidants, it has been reputed to lower cholesterol and blood sugar and also to relieve the pain of arthritis. So, the next time you have tea for two, try one of these two popular drinks— yerba maté and green tea.

Comparison words and phrases

Practice and Apply

Refer to the preceding models to do the following:

1. Find one similarity and one difference in the organization of these two models.

2. For each model, list three words or phrases that signal comparisons or contrasts.

3. Identify two points in each model that the writer compares or contrasts.

4. Make a Venn diagram or compare-and-contrast graphic to show the similarities and differences in one of the models.

5. Problem-Solution Organization

Problem-solution organization is a pattern of organization in which a problem is stated and analyzed and then one or more solutions are proposed and examined. This pattern of organization is often used in persuasive writing, such as editorials or proposals.

Strategies for Reading

- Look for an explanation of the problem in the first or second paragraph.
- Look for words such as *problem* and *reason* that may signal an explanation of the problem.
- To find the solution, ask: What suggestion does the writer offer to solve the problem?
- Look for words such as *propose, conclude,* and *answer* that may signal a solution.

Model

Teachers, administrators, school board members, and parents have begun expressing concerns that the foreign language students aren't getting enough practice using their languages in conversation.

Students read dialogues from their textbooks and respond to questions. They also use the language lab to get more practice speaking the language. The facilities are limited, though, and have to be used after school, which conflicts with other activities. Also, the language lab doesn't give them real-life experience with using the new language to listen to others, either.

One solution to this problem would be to establish language tables in the lunchroom. Students taking a given language would eat lunch at a specific table one day a week. For that time, they would speak only the foreign language.

This plan has several advantages. First, it doesn't require any additional equipment, staff, or materials. Second, it wouldn't take time away from other classes or activities. Language students have to eat lunch just like everyone else, so why not make it an enjoyable learning experience?

Setting up language tables would let students supplement their language skills while nourishing their bodies. That's a recipe for success!

Practice and Apply

Reread the model and then answer the following questions:

1. According to the model, what is the cause of the problem?
2. What solution does the writer offer? What words are a clue?

 COMMON CORE **RI 5**

PRACTICE AND APPLY POSSIBLE ANSWERS

1. *Problem: Students have no opportunity to practice the foreign language they are studying. Cause: Facilities are limited and the language lab does not offer real-life experience using the new language.*

2. *Solution: Establish language tables in the lunchroom. Clues: "one solution to this problem," "several advantages"*

PRACTICE AND APPLY POSSIBLE ANSWERS

Claim: Hatchet is a good book to read.

Reason: It's an entertaining adventure story, teaches important survival skills, and shows how the main character changes.

Evidence: Brian learns to stay safe from wild animals, find food and water, build a fire without matches, and confront the dangers of the wilderness.

Counterargument: People may not like that the book is about an unusual and extreme situation, but it's really about facing and learning from whatever difficulties life brings.

Reading Persuasive Texts

1. Analyzing an Argument

An **argument** expresses a position on an issue or problem and supports it with reasons and evidence. Being able to analyze and evaluate arguments will help you distinguish between claims you should accept and those you should not. A sound argument should appeal strictly to reason. However, arguments are often used in texts that also contain other types of persuasive devices. An argument includes the following elements:

- A **claim** is the writer's position on an issue or problem.
- **Support** is any material that serves to prove a claim. In an argument, support usually consists of reasons and evidence.
- **Reasons** are declarations made to justify an action, decision, or belief. For example: "My reason for walking so quickly is that I'm afraid I'll be late for class."
- **Evidence** consists of the specific references, quotations, facts, examples, and opinions that support a claim. Evidence may also consist of statistics, reports of personal experience, or the views of experts.
- A **counterargument** is an argument made to oppose another argument. A good argument anticipates the opposition's objections and provides counterarguments to disprove or answer them.

Claim	I need a larger allowance.
Reason	I don't have enough money to pay for my school lunches, fees, and transportation.
Evidence	I had to borrow money from my friend two weeks in a row to buy lunch.
Counter-argument	My parents say I just need to budget my allowance better, but they don't realize what my expenses are.

Practice and Apply

Read the following book review and use a chart like the one shown to identify the claim, reason, evidence, and counterargument.

Hatchet
Reviewed by Kristen Loos

What would you do if you suddenly found yourself in the middle of a wilderness with no one else around and only a hatchet to help you survive? That's what happens to Brian Robeson, a boy about my age, in Gary Paulsen's book *Hatchet*. Even if this sounds like a situation you'll never be in, *Hatchet* is worth reading for what it says about facing your fears.

After his parents get a divorce, Brian heads up to northern Canada to spend the summer with his dad. But the pilot flying the airplane has a heart attack, and Brian is forced to crash-land it by himself. From then on, he has to handle everything by himself.

From the beginning all the way to the end of the book, Brian faces big problems just to survive. He's a city kid, so he's used to opening up the refrigerator any time he wants to eat. Now, at the edge of the woods, he has to figure out things like how to be safe from wild animals and how to make a fire without matches. At first, he panics. He doesn't even know what to drink or how to find and prepare food. Even so, he doesn't give up.

One of the things I like about the book is how Brian changes. At first, he hopes he will be rescued very soon. He thinks he can hold out for a few days until his parents or a search party finds him. Then, when a plane flies over without seeing him, he realizes that he is really on his own. He learns to make tools to fish and hunt with and to depend on himself for everything he needs.

Some readers may not like the book because they think this is an unusual situation that most people will never have to face. I don't agree, though, because I think the real message is not just about being lost in the wilderness, but about bravely dealing with whatever challenges we face in our lives.

I'm not going to spoil the book for you by saying how it ends or whether Brian gets rescued. Read it yourself for an exciting adventure and some good lessons about surviving in the wilderness. I hope you enjoy it as much as I did.

2. Recognizing Proposition and Support Patterns

To find an author's claim, support, and counterarguments, it's helpful to identify the author's method for making his or her case. Here are two ways writers often make their cases:

- **Proposition and Support** The writer presents a **proposition,** which is a claim that recommends a policy, and two or three reasons for accepting the policy. For example, "Cigarette smoking should be banned in public places because it's bad for people's health and smelly." Then the writer supports each reason with evidence.
- **Strawman** The writer presents a proposition. Instead of supporting it, though, he or she sums up the other side's position and disproves it. Once that "strawman" has been defeated, the writer declares his or her proposition the best or only option.

Writers usually reveal how they are going to present their cases in the first few paragraphs of their work. Study the following paragraph to see how it signals that the argument to come will use a proposition and support pattern.

Model

Have you wanted to ride your bike to school but been frightened off by the car traffic? If so, you're not alone. The city should create bike lanes on busy streets because it would make cycling safer and easier. | **Proposition** / **Support**

The next paragraph introduces an editorial in which the writer uses the strawman method.

Model

The city should create bike lanes on busy streets. Opponents of bike lanes will tell you that such lanes are a waste of money because drivers just ignore them, but that's not true. | **Proposition** / **Supposed argument against proposition**

Now use the preceding models and instruction to help you identify the way in which the author of this next introduction plans to persuade her readers to adopt her proposition. Explain how you arrived at your conclusion.

Every neighborhood should have a community garden. If the people in our neighborhood all had the chance to grow their own fruits, flowers, and vegetables in side-by-side garden plots, they would eat better, feel better, and get along better. Of course, not everyone would participate, but those who did would reap the benefits!

3. Recognizing Persuasive Techniques

Persuasive texts typically rely on more than just the **logical appeal** of an argument to be convincing. They also rely on ethical and emotional appeals and other **persuasive techniques**—devices that can convince you to adopt a position or take an action.

Ethical appeals establish a writer's credibility and trustworthiness with an audience. When a writer links a claim to to a widely accepted value, the writer not only gains moral support for that claim but also establishes himself or herself as a reputable, moral person readers can and should trust. For example, with the following appeal, the writer reminds readers of a value they should accept and suggests that if they share this value, then they should support the writer's position: "If you believe that all children deserve a good education, then vote for this legislation."

The chart shown here explains several other means by which a writer may attempt to sway you. Learn to recognize these techniques, and you are less likely to be influenced by them.

COMMON CORE   RI 1

PRACTICE AND APPLY POSSIBLE ANSWERS

The author uses a proposition and support method. The proposition is that every neighborhood should have a community garden. The support is that people who plant community gardens eat better, feel better, and get along better. Students will likely expect the author to continue by supporting these claims about people who plant community gardens.

PRACTICE AND APPLY POSSIBLE ANSWERS

Bandwagon appeal: "One of the most talked-about books"; "If you care about the planet, rush out and get a copy"
Testimonial/Appeal to authority: "Over 40 scientists have spoken in praise of the book"
Appeal to fear: "fresh drinking water may become more expensive and harder to find than gasoline!"; "competition for water will cause nations to go to war with each other"

Persuasive Technique	Example
Bandwagon appeal Taps into people's desire to belong	Join the millions of health-conscious people who drink Wonder Water!
Testimonial Relies on endorsements from well-known people or satisfied customers	Send your game over the top with Macon Ace—the racket designed and used by tennis legend Sonja Macon.
Snob appeal Taps into people's desire to be special or part of an elite group	The best deserve only the best—you deserve Beautiful Bubbles bath soap.
Appeals to pity, fear, or vanity Use strong feelings, rather than facts, to persuade	Why go unnoticed when Pretty Face can make you the center of attention?

Sometimes persuasive techniques are misused to create rhetorical fallacies. A **rhetorical fallacy** is writing or speech that is false or misleading. For example, an athlete who endorses a line of athletic shoes would be misleading the public if he or she wears a different kind of shoe in competitions.

Practice and Apply

Identify the persuasive techniques used in this model.

A Dry Future?

One of the most talked-about books published this year is *Glass Half Empty*. This informative book paints a frightening picture of our dwindling water resources. In the next few decades, fresh drinking water may become more expensive and harder to find than gasoline! The author warns that competition for water will cause nations to go to war with each other. Over 40 scientists have spoken in praise of the book. If you care about the planet, rush out and get a copy of *Glass Half Empty*.

4. Analyzing Logic and Reasoning

While persuasive techniques may sway you to side with a writer, they should not be enough to convince you that an argument is sound. To determine the soundness of an argument, examine the argument's claim and support and the logic or reasoning that links them. Identifying the writer's mode of reasoning can help.

The Inductive Mode of Reasoning

When a person uses specific evidence to arrive at a generalization, that person is using **inductive reasoning**. Similarly, when a writer presents specific evidence first and then offers a generalization drawn from that evidence, the writer is making an **inductive argument**. Here is an example of inductive reasoning.

Specific Evidence

Fact 1 Wind and water wear away rocks over time.

Fact 2 Earthquakes and volcanoes create immediate and drastic changes in the land.

Fact 3 The slow movement of the continents and spreading of the sea floor create new landforms.

Generalization

Natural forces continually change the surface of the earth.

Strategies for Determining the Soundness of Inductive Arguments

Ask yourself the following questions to evaluate an inductive argument:

- **Is the evidence valid and sufficient support for the conclusion?** Inaccurate facts lead to inaccurate conclusions.
- **Does the conclusion follow logically from the evidence?** From the facts listed, the conclusion that Earth's core as well as its surface are constantly changing would be too broad.
- **Is the evidence drawn from a large enough sample?** These three facts are enough to support the claim. If you wanted to claim that these are the *only* forces that cause change, you would need more facts.

The Deductive Mode of Reasoning

When a person uses a **premise**, or general principle, to form a conclusion about a particular situation or problem, that person is using **deductive reasoning**. For example,

| To drive a car well, all drivers must give driving their complete attention. | Premise, or general principle |

▼

| Talking on a cell phone takes some of a person's attention. | The situation being observed or considered |

▼

| Drivers shouldn't talk on cell phones while driving. | Conclusion (also considerd a deduction) |

Similarly, a writer is making a **deductive argument** when he or she begins the argument with a claim that is based on a premise and then presents evidence to support the claim. For example, a writer might begin a deductive argument with the claim "Drivers should not talk on cell phones while they are driving."

Strategies for Determining the Soundness of Deductive Arguments

Ask yourself the following questions to evaluate a deductive argument:

- **Is the premise actually stated, or is it implied?** Writers often present deductive arguments without stating the premises. They just assume that readers will recognize and agree with the premises. So you may want to identify the premise for yourself.

- **Is the premise correct?** Don't assume it is true. Ask yourself whether it is really true.

- **Is the conclusion valid?** To be valid, a conclusion in a deductive argument must follow logically from the premise and the specific situation.

The following chart shows two conclusions drawn from the same premise.

All spiders have eight legs.	
Accurate Deduction	**Inaccurate Deduction**
The black widow is a spider, therefore it has eight legs.	An octopus has eight legs, therefore it is a spider.

An octopus has eight legs, but it belongs to a different category of animals than the spider.

Now, as you read the following model, pay attention to how the author arrives at her conclusion.

> The other day when I was waiting at the stoplight on my bike, I noticed that the car in front of me was in the right lane and had its right turn signal on. Wouldn't you have assumed, just like I did, that the driver was going to turn right? Well, I was wrong, and you probably would've been, too. As soon as the light turned green, the car swerved across two lanes and turned left.
>
> Then there was the surprise birthday party the neighborhood kids and I had for one of our friends. We'd managed to keep it a secret, so we all expected her to be really surprised and pleased. Instead, she was upset and embarrassed because she wasn't dressed properly for a party.
>
> It's dangerous to make assumptions about how other people will act. I've learned that the hard way!

Practice and Apply

Refer to the preceding model and instruction to do the following:

1. Identify the mode of reasoning used in the model.
2. In your own words, explain the difference between inductively and deductively organizing ideas.

 COMMON CORE RI 3, RI 5

PRACTICE AND APPLY POSSIBLE ANSWERS

1. *Inductive reasoning: the writer presents two pieces of evidence—anecdotal examples about surprising reactions—and generalizes from them that it is unwise to assume how people will act.*

2. *When you arrange ideas inductively, you present each one and add them all up to reach a generalization or conclusion about them. When you arrange ideas deductively, you start with your generalization, or premise, make a claim based on that generalization, and then present your ideas.*

Identifying Faulty Reasoning

Sometimes an argument at first appears to make sense but isn't valid because it is based on a **fallacy.** A fallacy is an error in logic. Learn to recognize these common fallacies.

Type of Fallacy	Definition	Example
Circular reasoning	Supporting a statement by simply repeating it in different words.	My mother is always busy because **she has too much to do.**
Either/or fallacy	A statement that suggests that there are only two choices available in a situation that really offers more than two options.	**Either** I grow two inches this summer **or** I'll never make any friends at my new school.
Oversimplification	An explanation of a complex situation or problem as if it were much simpler than it is.	**All you have to do to get good grades** is listen carefully in class.
Overgeneralization	A generalization that is too broad. You can often recognize overgeneralizations by the use of words such as *all, everyone, every time, anything, no one,* and *none.*	**Nobody** has as many chores as I do.
Hasty generalization	A conclusion drawn from too little evidence or from evidence that is biased.	I sneezed after taking a bite of the salad, so **I must be allergic to something in it.**
Stereotyping	A dangerous type of overgeneralization. Stereotypes are broad statements about people on the basis of their gender, ethnicity, race, or political, social, professional, or religious group.	**Artists are emotional** and hard **to get along with.**
Attacking the person or name-calling	An attempt to discredit an idea by attacking the person or group associated with it. Candidates often engage in name-calling during political campaigns.	The senator only supports this bill because he is **corrupt.**
Evading the issue	Responding to an objection with arguments and evidence that do not address its central point.	I forgot to get the milk, **but dairy products are hard to digest anyway.**
False cause	The mistake of assuming that because one event occurred after another event, the first event caused the second one to occur.	It rained this afternoon **because I left my umbrella at home.**
Non sequitur	A conclusion that does not follow logically from the "proof" offered to support it.	Mrs. Lewis will make Steve the baseball team captain. **He is already the captain of the volleyball team.**

Look for examples of logical fallacies in the following argument. Identify each one and explain why you identified it as such.

Store clerks are so rude. A cashier was impatient with me in the supermarket the other day because I bought too much yogurt. They must train the employees to treat customers that way so more people will use the self-checkout lines. I need to budget more money for groceries.

5. Evaluating Persuasive Texts

Learning how to evaluate persuasive texts and identify bias will help you become more selective when doing research and also help you improve your own reasoning and arguing skills.

Strategies for Identifying Bias

Bias is an inclination for or against a particular opinion or viewpoint. A writer may reveal a strongly positive or negative bias on an issue by

- **presenting only one way** of looking at it
- **overlooking key information**
- **stacking more evidence on one side** of the argument than the other
- **using unfairly weighted evidence,** which is weak or unproven evidence that a writer treats as if it is more important than it really is
- **using loaded language,** which consists of words with strongly positive or negative connotations

EXAMPLE

At the Village Star, we bring you up-to-the-minute news. That's why so many people read our paper. (Someone who works for the paper is making the claim. *Up-to-the-minute* has very positive connotations. The writer also fails to mention important information: the paper is free.)

Strategies for Identifying Propaganda

Propaganda is any form of communication that is so distorted that it conveys false or misleading information. Logical fallacies such as name-calling, the either/or fallacy, and false causes are often used in propaganda. The following example shows false cause. The writer uses one fact to support a particular point of view but does not reveal another fact that does not support that viewpoint.

EXAMPLE

Since Jack Carter was elected mayor, unemployment has decreased by 25%. (The writer does not mention that it was the previous mayor, not Jack Carter, who was responsible for bringing in the new factory that provides the extra jobs.)

Strategies for Evaluating Evidence

It is important to have a set of standards by which you can evaluate persuasive texts. Use the questions below to help you critically assess facts and opinions that are presented as evidence.

- **Are the presented facts verifiable?** A **fact,** or **factual claim,** is a statement that can be proved by consulting a reliable source or doing research.
- **Are the presented opinions and commonplace assertions well informed?** An opinion is a statement of personal belief, feeling, or thought that does not require proof. A **commonplace assertion** is a statement that many people assume to be true but isn't necessarily so. When evaluating either type of statement, consider whether the author is knowledgeable about the topic and uses sound reasoning.
- **Is the evidence thorough and balanced?** Thorough evidence leaves no reasonable questions unanswered. Be alert to evidence that is weighted unfairly and contains loaded language or other signs of bias.
- **Is the evidence authoritative?** The people, groups, or organizations that provided the evidence should have credentials that support their authority.
- **Is it important that the evidence be current?** Where timeliness is crucial, as in the areas of medicine and technology, the evidence should reflect the latest developments in the areas.

PRACTICE AND APPLY ANSWERS

Stereotyping—the statement is too broad to possibly apply to such a large group: "Store clerks are so rude."

False cause—there's no proof or reason to believe that the quantity of the customer's yogurt was what caused the cashier's attitude: "A cashier was impatient with me in the supermarket the other day because I bought too much yogurt."

Hasty generalization—this one interaction provides too little evidence to draw a conclusion about how and why employees are trained: "They must train the employees to treat customers that way so more people will use the self-checkout lines."

Non sequitur—it doesn't follow logically from the previous statements: "I need to budget more money for groceries."

PRACTICE AND APPLY
POSSIBLE ANSWERS

Facts: "Our bodies need a well-balanced combination of protein, carbohydrates, fats, vitamins, minerals, and trace elements to function most effectively..."

Opinions: "Ultra Bars are the tastiest"; "they taste terrific"

Bias: "The ingredients in Ultra Bars have been chosen in the perfect proportion to ensure you get the maximum benefit."; "ordinary people should carry these bars with them"

PRACTICE AND APPLY
POSSIBLE ANSWERS

Possible evaluations: The writer's reasons make sense and are presented in logical order. The claim and reasons could be better supported (for example, he or she could provide figures on the exact costs of creating/maintaining the park, and the income from suggested activities).

The argument adequately addresses and counters opposing views, but exhibits faulty logic:

- *overgeneralization: "No one who cares..."*
- *either-or fallacy: "Without a park, we can't ensure..."*
- *circular reasoning: "parks are easier to supervise, too, because it isn't as hard to police them"*

Practice and Apply

Read the argument below. Identify the facts, opinions, and elements of bias.

> Ultra Bars are the tastiest and most efficient way to get your daily requirement of important nutrients. Our bodies need a well-balanced combination of protein, carbohydrates, fats, vitamins, minerals, and trace elements to function most effectively and make us feel our best. The ingredients in Ultra Bars have been chosen in the perfect proportion to ensure you get the maximum benefit. Best of all, they taste terrific. And they aren't just for athletes—ordinary people should carry these bars with them, too, for a quick boost throughout the day!

Strategies for Determining a Strong Argument

Make sure that all or most of the following statements are true:

- The argument presents a claim or controlling idea.
- The claim is connected to its support by a premise or generalization that most readers would readily agree with. Correct premise: *Doing your best will bring you personal pride.* Incorrect premise: *Doing your best will bring you success.*
- The reasons make sense.
- The reasons are presented in a logical and effective order.
- The claim and all reasons are adequately supported by sound evidence.
- The evidence is adequate, accurate, and appropriate.
- The logic is sound. There are no instances of faulty reasoning.
- The argument adequately anticipates and addresses readers' concerns and counterclaims with counterarguments.

Practice and Apply

Use the preceding criteria to evaluate the strength of the following proposal.

Model

Summary of Proposal

I propose that the city government create a park on the unused plot of land at the edge of town.

Need

We must preserve the natural beauty of the area for all to appreciate and enjoy.

Proposed Solution

The five-acre plot of land on the south side of town is now being considered for improvement.

Some people want to sell the land to a building developer. They say that doing this would be profitable for the town and also provide good housing for new residents.

It's true that the town could make money by developing the land. A park could also be a source of income, however.

The park would generate income in a number of ways. It could charge a small admission fee for summer concerts and other events. It also could lease the space to neighboring communities for their gatherings and to local food concessions and special-interest groups.

The cost of creating and maintaining a park is less than what it would bring in. Community groups already have agreed to donate plants, provide volunteers to landscape and take care of the grounds, create gazebos, and install benches, water fountains, and trashcans.

Without a park, we can't ensure the safety and health of our residents. It would have playgrounds and areas to bike, skate, picnic, and walk or jog. Unlike commercial and even residential buildings, parks do not encourage vandalism and graffiti. The chief of police has confirmed that parks are easier to supervise, too, because it isn't as hard to police them.

No one who cares about our community could fail to see how important it is to create this park.

Grammar

Writing that is full of mistakes can confuse or even annoy a reader. Punctuation errors in a letter might lead to a miscommunication and delay a reply. Sentence fragments might lower your grade on an essay. Paying attention to grammar, punctuation, and capitalization rules can make your writing clearer and easier to read.

Quick Reference: Parts of Speech

Part of Speech	Function	Examples
Noun	names a person, a place, a thing, an idea, a quality, or an action	
Common	serves as a general name, or a name common to an entire group	shadow, harmonica, paw, mistake
Proper	names a specific, one-of-a-kind person, place, or thing	Chinatown, Switzerland, Jupiter, Herbert
Singular	refers to a single person, place, thing, or idea	earthquake, laboratory, medication, outcome
Plural	refers to more than one person, place, thing, or idea	chemicals, splinters, geniuses, soldiers
Concrete	names something that can be perceived by the senses	calendar, basketball, ocean, snow
Abstract	names something that cannot be perceived by the senses	democracy, authority, beauty, fame
Compound	expresses a single idea through a combination of two or more words	self-esteem, mountaintop, firefighters, light bulb
Collective	refers to a group of people or things	team, family, class, choir
Possessive	shows who or what owns something	Pandora's, Strauss's, Franks', women's
Pronoun	takes the place of a noun or another pronoun	
Personal	refers to the person making a statement, the person(s) being addressed, or the person(s) or thing(s) the statement is about	I, me, my, mine, we, us, our, ours, you, your, yours, she, he, it, her, him, hers, his, its, they, them, their, theirs
Reflexive	follows a verb or preposition and refers to a preceding noun or pronoun	myself, yourself, herself, himself, itself, ourselves, yourselves, themselves
Intensive	emphasizes a noun or another pronoun	(same as reflexives)
Demonstrative	points to one or more specific persons or things	this, that, these, those

continued

Part of Speech	Function	Examples
Interrogative	signals a question	who, whom, whose, which, what
Indefinite	refers to one or more persons or things not specifically mentioned	both, all, most, many, anyone, everybody, several, none, some
Relative	introduces an adjective clause by relating it to a word in the clause	who, whom, whose, which, that
Verb	expresses an action, a condition, or a state of being	
Action	tells what the subject does or did, physically or mentally	find, know, clings, displayed, rises, crave
Linking	connects the subject to something that identifies or describes it	am, is, are, was, were, sound, taste, appear, feel, become, remain, seem
Auxiliary	precedes the main verb in a verb phrase	be, have, can, do, could, will, would, may, might
Transitive	directs the action toward someone or something; always has an object	She <u>opened</u> the **door.**
Intransitive	does not direct the action toward someone or something; does not have an object	The door **opened.**
Adjective	modifies a noun or pronoun	**slight** groan, **dying** gladiators, **ancient** sea, **two** pigtails
Adverb	modifies a verb, an adjective, or another adverb	**always** closed, **very** patiently, **more** pleasant, ran **quickly**
Preposition	relates one word to another word	at, by, for, from, in, of, on, to, with
Conjunction	joins words or word groups	
Coordinating	joins words or word groups used the same way	and, but, or, for, so, yet, nor
Correlative	used as a pair to join words or word groups used the same way	both . . . and, either . . . or, neither . . . nor
Subordinating	introduces a clause that cannot stand by itself as a complete sentence	although, after, as, before, because, when, if, unless
Interjection	expresses emotion	wow, ouch, hooray

Quick Reference: The Sentence and Its Parts

The diagrams that follow will give you a brief review of the essentials of a sentence and some of its parts.

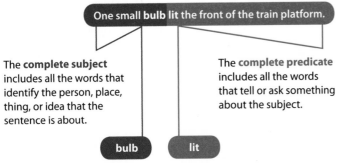

One small bulb lit the front of the train platform.

The **complete subject** includes all the words that identify the person, place, thing, or idea that the sentence is about.

bulb

The **simple subject** tells exactly whom or what the sentence is about. It may be one word or a group of words, but it does not include modifiers.

The **complete predicate** includes all the words that tell or ask something about the subject.

lit

The **simple predicate**, or **verb**, tells what the subject does or is. It may be one word or several, but it does not include modifiers.

Every word in a sentence is part of a complete subject or a complete predicate.

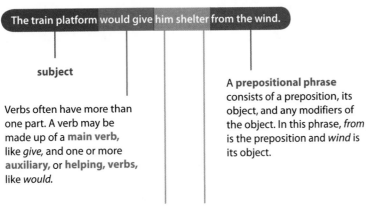

The train platform would give him shelter from the wind.

subject

Verbs often have more than one part. A verb may be made up of a **main verb**, like *give*, and one or more **auxiliary**, or **helping, verbs**, like *would*.

A **prepositional phrase** consists of a preposition, its object, and any modifiers of the object. In this phrase, *from* is the preposition and *wind* is its object.

An **indirect object** is a word or group of words that tells to whom or for whom or to what or for what the verb's action is performed. A sentence can have an indirect object only if it has a direct object. The indirect object always comes before the direct object.

A **direct object** is a word or group of words that tells who or what receives the action of the verb.

Quick Reference: Punctuation

Mark	Function	Examples
End Marks period, question mark, exclamation point	ends a sentence	We can start now**.** When would you like to leave**?** What a fantastic hit**!**
period	follows an initial or abbreviation **Exception:** postal abbreviations of states	Mrs. Dorothy Parker, Apple Inc., C. P. Cavafy, P.M., A.D., lb., oz., Blvd., Dr. NE (Nebraska), NV (Nevada)
period	follows a number or letter in an outline	I**.** Volcanoes A**.** Central-vent 1**.** Shield
Comma	separates part of a compound sentence	I had never disliked poetry, but now I really love it.
	separates items in a series	Her humor, grace, and kindness served her well.
	separates adjectives of equal rank that modify the same noun	The slow, easy route is best.
	sets off a term of address	Maria, how can I help you? You must do something, soldier.
	sets off a parenthetical expression	Hard workers, as you know, don't quit. I'm not a quitter, believe me.
	sets off an introductory word, phrase, or dependent clause	Yes, I forgot my key. At the beginning of the day, I feel fresh. While she was out, I was here. Having finished my chores, I went out.
	sets off a nonessential phrase or clause	Ed Pawn, the captain of the chess team, won. Ed Pawn, who is the captain, won. The two leading runners, sprinting toward the finish line, finished in a tie.
	sets off parts of dates and addresses	Mail it by May 14, 2010, to the Hauptman Company, 321 Market Street, Memphis, Tennessee.
	follows the salutation and closing of a letter	Dear Jim, Sincerely yours,
	separates words to avoid confusion	By noon, time had run out. What the minister does, does matter. While cooking, Jim burned his hand.

Mark	Function	Examples
Semicolon	separates items in a series that contain commas	We spent the first week of summer vacation in Chicago, Illinois; the second week in St. Louis, Missouri; and the third week in Albany, New York.
	separates parts of a compound sentence that are not joined by a coordinating conjunction	The last shall be first; the first shall be last. I read the Bible; however, I have not memorized it.
	separates parts of a compound sentence when the parts contain commas	After I ran out of money, I called my parents; but only my sister was home, unfortunately.
Colon	introduces a list	The names we wrote to were the following: Dana, John, and Will.
	introduces a long quotation	Abraham Lincoln wrote: "Four score and seven years ago, our fathers brought forth on this continent a new nation . . . ."
	follows the salutation of a business letter	To Whom It May Concern: Dear Leonard Atole:
	separates certain numbers	1:28 P.M., Genesis 2:5
Dash	indicates an abrupt break in thought	I was thinking of my mother—who is arriving tomorrow—just as you walked in.
Parentheses	enclose less important material	It was so unlike him (John is always on time) that I began to worry. The last World Series game (did you see it?) was fun.
Hyphen	joins parts of a compound adjective before a noun	The not-so-rich taxpayer won't stand for this!
	joins parts of a compound with *all-*, *ex-*, *self-*, or *-elect*	The ex-firefighter helped rescue him. Our president-elect is self-conscious.
	joins parts of a compound number (to ninety-nine)	Today is the twenty-fifth of November.
	joins parts of a fraction	My cup is one-third full.
	joins a prefix to a word beginning with a capital letter	I'm studying the U.S. presidents pre-1900. It snowed in mid-October.
	indicates that a word is divided at the end of a line	How could you have any reason-able expectations of getting a new computer?

continued

Mark	Function	Examples
Apostrophe	used with *s* to form the possessive of a noun or an indefinite pronoun	my friend's book, my friends' books, anyone's guess, somebody else's problem
	replaces one or more omitted letters in a contraction or numbers in a date	don't (omitted *o*), he'd (omitted *woul*), the class of '99 (omitted *19*)
	used with *s* to form the plural of a letter	I had two A's on my report card.
Quotation Marks	set off a speaker's exact words	"That, I'll do," Lemon said. "That," Lemon said, "I'll do." Did Lemon say, "That I'll do"? Lemon said, "That I'll do!"
	set off the title of a story, an article, a short poem, an essay, a song, or a chapter	I recited Wislawa Szymborska's "There But for the Grace" at the assembly. Poe's "The Tell-Tale Heart" and Sandburg's "Chicago" held my interest. I enjoyed Jean Davies Okimoto's "My Favorite Chaperone."
Ellipses	replace material omitted from a quotation	"Her diary tells us that she . . . thought of ordinary things, such as going to school with other kids. . . ."
Italics	indicate the title of a book, a play, a magazine, a long poem, an opera, a film, or a TV series, or the name of a ship	*Harriet Tubman: Conductor on the Underground Railroad*, *The Diary of Anne Frank*, *TIME*, *The Magic Flute*, the *Iliad*, *Star Wars*, *60 Minutes*, the *Mayflower*

Quick Reference: Capitalization

Category	Examples
People and Titles	
Names and initials of people	Jack London, T. S. Eliot
Titles used before a name	Professor Holmes, Senator Long
Deities and members of religious groups	Jesus, Allah, Buddha, Zeus, Baptists, Roman Catholics
Names of ethnic and national groups	Hispanics, Jews, African Americans
Geographical Names	
Cities, states, countries, continents	Philadelphia, Kansas, Japan, Europe
Regions, bodies of water, mountains	the South, Lake Baikal, Mount Everest
Geographic features, parks	Great Basin, Yellowstone National Park
Streets and roads, planets	318 East Sutton Drive, Charles Court, Jupiter, Mars
Organizations, Events, Etc.	
Companies, organizations, teams	Ford Motor Company, Boy Scouts of America, St. Louis Cardinals
Buildings, bridges, monuments	Empire State Building, Eads Bridge, Washington Monument
Documents, awards	Declaration of Independence, Stanley Cup
Special named events	Mardi Gras, World Series
Government bodies, historical periods and events	U.S. Senate, House of Representatives, Middle Ages, Vietnam War
Days and months, holidays	Thursday, March, Thanksgiving, Labor Day
Specific cars, boats, trains, planes	Porsche, Carpathia, Southwest Chief, Concorde
Proper Adjectives	
Adjectives formed from proper nouns	French cooking, Spanish omelet, Edwardian age, Western movie
First Words and the Pronoun *I*	
First word in a sentence or quotation	This is it. He said, "Let's go."
First word of sentence in parentheses that is not within another sentence	The spelling rules are covered in another section. (Consult that section for more information.)
First words in the salutation and closing of a letter	Dear Madam, Very truly yours,
First word in each line of most poetry Personal pronoun *I*	Then am I A happy fly If I live or if I die.
First word, last word, and all important words in a title	"The Powwow at the End of the World," "New Immigrants Share Their Stories," "What Is the Horror Genre?"

1 Nouns

A **noun** is a word used to name a person, a place, a thing, an idea, a quality, or an action. Nouns can be classified in several ways.

For more information on different types of nouns, see **Quick Reference: Parts of Speech,** page R29.

1.1 COMMON NOUNS

Common nouns are general names, common to entire groups.

1.2 PROPER NOUNS

Proper nouns name specific, one-of-a-kind people, places, and things.

Common	Proper
legend, canyon, girl, city	Pecos Bill, Canyon de Chelly, Anne, Amsterdam

For more information, see **Quick Reference: Capitalization,** page R35.

1.3 SINGULAR AND PLURAL NOUNS

A noun may take a singular or a plural form, depending on whether it names a single person, place, thing, or idea or more than one. Make sure you use appropriate spellings when forming plurals.

Common	Proper
diary, valley, revolution, calf	diaries, valleys, revolutions, calves

For more information, see **Forming Plural Nouns,** page R29.

1.4 POSSESSIVE NOUNS

A **possessive noun** shows who or what owns something.

For more information, see **Forming Possessives,** page R29.

2 Pronouns

A **pronoun** is a word that is used in place of a noun or another pronoun. The word or word group to which the pronoun refers is called its **antecedent.**

2.1 PERSONAL PRONOUNS

Personal pronouns change their form to express person, number, gender, and case. The forms of these pronouns are shown in the following chart.

	Nominative	Objective	Possessive
Singular			
First Person	I	me	my, mine
Second Person	you	you	your, yours
Third Person	she, he, it	her, him, it	her, hers, his, its
Plural			
First Person	we	us	our, ours
Second Person	you	you	your, yours
Third Person	they	them	their, theirs

2.2 AGREEMENT WITH ANTECEDENT

Pronouns should agree with their antecedents in number, gender, and person.

If an antecedent is singular, use a singular pronoun.

> EXAMPLE: *Rachel wrote a **detective story**. **It** has a surprise ending.*

If an antecedent is plural, use a plural pronoun.

> EXAMPLES: *The **characters** have **their** motives for murder.*
> *Javier loves **mysteries** and reads **them** all the time.*

The gender of a pronoun must be the same as the gender of its antecedent.

EXAMPLE: *The **man** has to use all **his** wits to stay alive and solve the crime.*

The person of the pronoun must be the same as the person of its antecedent. As the chart in Section 2.1 shows, a pronoun can be in first-person, second-person, or third-person form.

EXAMPLE: ***You** want a story to grab **your** attention.*

Grammar Practice

Rewrite each sentence so that the underlined pronoun agrees with its antecedent.

1. The story's suspense kept readers interested in <u>them</u>.
2. My dog Riley chews my tennis ball so I put <u>it</u> in the garage.
3. Many fans lost <u>them</u> voices during the final minutes of the basketball tournament.
4. I brought my favorite sandwich to school and kept <u>them</u> in my locker until lunchtime.
5. You and <u>her</u> friends should go to the amusement park this weekend.

2.3 PRONOUN FORMS

Personal pronouns change form to show how they function in sentences. The three forms are the subject form, the object form, and the possessive form. For examples of these pronouns, see the chart in Section 2.1.

A **subject pronoun** is used as a subject in a sentence.

EXAMPLE: *The poem "Chicago" is about the U.S. city Chicago. **It** was written by Carl Sandburg.*

Also use the subject form when the pronoun follows a linking verb.

EXAMPLE: *The city of Chicago is defended against accusations that **it** exploits the working class.*

An **object pronoun** is used as a direct object, an indirect object, or the object of a preposition.

SUBJECT   OBJECT
We will give them to her.
              OBJECT OF PREPOSITION

A **possessive pronoun** shows ownership. The pronouns *mine, yours, hers, his, its, ours,* and *theirs* can be used in place of nouns.

EXAMPLE: *The city's resilient spirit is **its** best asset.*

The pronouns *my, your, her, his, its, our,* and *their* are used before nouns.

EXAMPLE: *The poem changed **my** view about life in big cities.*

WATCH OUT! Many spelling errors can be avoided if you watch out for *its* and *their.* Don't confuse the possessive pronoun *its* with the contraction *it's,* meaning "it is" or "it has." The homonyms *they're* (a contraction of *they are*) and *there* ("in that place") are often mistakenly used for *their.*

TIP To decide which pronoun to use in a comparison such as "He tells better tales than (*I* or *me*)," fill in the missing word(s): *He tells better tales than I tell.*

Grammar Practice

Write the correct pronoun form to complete each sentence.

1. The scary movie frightened (him, he).
2. Michael emailed a copy of the book report to (she, her).
3. My brother's car is fast but (it, its) engine is too loud.
4. (Me, I) got in trouble with my parents for talking on my cell phone while I was driving to the grocery store.
5. (We, Us) need to attend the soccer game and root on our team to victory!

2.4 REFLEXIVE AND INTENSIVE PRONOUNS

These pronouns are formed by adding *-self* or *-selves* to certain personal pronouns. Their forms are the same, and they differ only in how they are used.

COMMON CORE **L 1**

GRAMMAR PRACTICE ANSWERS

1. *it*
2. *it*
3. *their*
4. *it*
5. *your*

COMMON CORE **L 1**

GRAMMAR PRACTICE ANSWERS

1. *him*
2. *her*
3. *its*
4. *I*
5. *We*

A **reflexive pronoun** follows a verb or preposition and reflects back on an earlier noun or pronoun.

> EXAMPLES: *He likes himself too much.*
> *She is now herself again.*

Intensive pronouns intensify or emphasize the nouns or pronouns to which they refer.

> EXAMPLES: *They themselves will educate their children.*
> *You did it yourself.*

WATCH OUT! Avoid using hisself or theirselves. Standard English does not include these forms.

> NONSTANDARD: *Colorful desert flowers offer theirselves to the poem's speaker.*

> STANDARD: *Colorful desert flowers offer themselves to the poem's speaker.*

2.5 DEMONSTRATIVE PRONOUNS

Demonstrative pronouns point out things and persons near and far.

	Singular	Plural
Near	this	these
Far	that	those

2.6 INDEFINITE PRONOUNS

Indefinite pronouns do not refer to specific persons or things and usually have no antecedents. The chart shows some commonly used indefinite pronouns.

Singular	Plural	Singular or Plural	
another	both	all	none
anybody	few	any	some
no one	many	more	most
neither			

TIP Indefinite pronouns that end in *-one, -body,* or *-thing* are always singular.

> INCORRECT: *Did everybody play their part well?*

If the indefinite pronoun might refer to either a male or a female, ***his or her*** may

be used to refer to it, or the sentence may be rewritten.

> CORRECT: *Did everybody play his or her part well?*
> *Did all the students play their parts well?*

2.7 INTERROGATIVE PRONOUNS

An **interrogative pronoun** tells a reader or listener that a question is coming. The interrogative pronouns are **who, whom, whose, which,** and **what.**

> EXAMPLES: *Who is going to rehearse with you?*
> *From whom did you receive the script?*

TIP *Who* is used as a subject; ***whom*** is used as an object. To find out which pronoun you need to use in a question, change the question to a statement.

> QUESTION: *(Who/Whom) did you meet there?*

> STATEMENT: *You met (?) there.*

Since the verb has a subject (***you***), the needed word must be the object form, ***whom.***

> EXAMPLE: *Whom did you meet there?*

WATCH OUT! A special problem arises when you use an interrupter, such as *do you think,* within a question.

> EXAMPLE: *(Who/Whom) do you think will win?*

If you eliminate the interrupter, it is clear that the word you need is ***who.***

2.8 RELATIVE PRONOUNS

Relative pronouns relate, or connect, adjective clauses to the words they modify in sentences. The noun or pronoun that a relative clause modifies is the antecedent of the relative pronoun. Here are the relative pronouns and their uses.

	Subject	Object	Possessive
Person	who	whom	whose
Thing	which	which	whose
Thing/Person	that	that	whose

Often, short sentences with related ideas can be combined by using a relative pronoun to create a more effective sentence.

SHORT SENTENCE: *Louisa May Alcott wrote* Hospital Sketches.

RELATED SENTENCE: Hospital Sketches *describes Alcott's experiences as a volunteer nurse.*

COMBINED SENTENCE: *Louisa May Alcott wrote* Hospital Sketches, *which describes her experiences as a volunteer nurse.*

Grammar Practice

Write the correct form of each incorrect pronoun.

1. Few would have volunteered her services like Alcott did.
2. For who did she risk her own life?
3. Everyone received their care from Alcott.
4. A wounded soldier proved hisself to be respectful.
5. Whom can read her diary without being moved?

2.9 PRONOUN REFERENCE PROBLEMS

The referent of a pronoun should always be clear. Avoid problems by rewriting sentences.

An **indefinite reference** occurs when the pronoun *it, you,* or *they* does not clearly refer to a specific antecedent.

UNCLEAR: *People appreciate it when they learn from an author's experiences.*

CLEAR: *People appreciate learning from an author's experiences.*

A **general reference** occurs when the pronoun *it, this, that, which,* or *such* is used to refer to a general idea rather than a specific antecedent.

UNCLEAR: *I picture myself in the author's situation. This helps me understand her reactions.*

CLEAR: *I picture myself in the author's situation. Putting myself in her position helps me understand her reactions.*

Ambiguous means "having more than one possible meaning." An **ambiguous reference** occurs when a pronoun could refer to two or more antecedents.

UNCLEAR: *Manuel urged Simon to edit his new film review.*

CLEAR: *Manuel urged Simon to edit Manuel's new film review.*

Grammar Practice

Rewrite the following sentences to correct indefinite, ambiguous, and general pronoun references.

1. Kerri told Kristen that she played well in the soccer game.
2. Everyone enjoyed the game and seeing their team win.
3. After the students left the locker rooms, the janitor cleaned them.
4. Before the game, the coach spoke to Kristen and she looked unhappy.

3 Verbs

A **verb** is a word that expresses an action, a condition, or a state of being.

For more information, see **Quick Reference: Parts of Speech,** page R29.

3.1 ACTION VERBS

Action verbs express mental or physical activity.

EXAMPLE: *Otto Frank comforted his family.*

3.2 LINKING VERBS

Linking verbs join subjects with words or phrases that rename or describe them.

EXAMPLE: *They were in hiding during the war.*

3.3 PRINCIPAL PARTS

Action and linking verbs typically have four principal parts, which are used to form verb tenses. The principal parts are the **present,** the **present participle,** the **past,** and the **past participle.**

COMMON CORE L1

GRAMMAR PRACTICE ANSWERS

1. *their*
2. *whom*
3. *his or her*
4. *himself*
5. *Who*

COMMON CORE L1

GRAMMAR PRACTICE ANSWERS

1. *Kerri told Kristen that Kristen played well in the soccer game.*
2. *Everyone enjoyed the game and seeing his or her team win.*
3. *After the students left the locker rooms, the janitor cleaned the premises.*
4. *Before the game, the coach spoke to Kristen and the coach looked unhappy.*

Action verbs and some linking verbs also fall into two categories: regular and irregular. A **regular verb** is a verb that forms its past and past participle by adding *-ed* or *-d* to the present form.

Present	Present Participle	Past	Past Participle
jump	(is) jumping	jumped	(has) jumped
solve	(is) solving	solved	(has) solved
grab	(is) grabbing	grabbed	(has) grabbed
carry	(is) carrying	carried	(has) carried

An **irregular verb** is a verb that forms its past and past participle in some other way than by adding *-ed* or *-d* to the present form.

Present	Present Participle	Past	Past Participle
begin	(is) beginning	began	(has) begun
solve	(is) breaking	broke	(has) broken
grab	(is) going	went	(has) gone

3.4 VERB TENSE

The **tense** of a verb indicates the time of the action or the state of being. An action or state of being can occur in the present, the past, or the future. There are six tenses, each expressing a different range of time.

The **present tense** expresses an action or state that is happening at the present time, occurs regularly, or is constant or generally true. Use the present participle.

　　NOW: *That snow looks deep.*

　　REGULAR: *It snows every day.*

　　GENERAL: *Snow falls.*

The **past tense** expresses an action that began and ended in the past. Use the past participle.

EXAMPLE: *The storyteller finished his tale.*

The **future tense** expresses an action or state that will occur. Use *shall* or *will* with the present participle.

　　EXAMPLE: *They will attend the next festival.*

The **present perfect tense** expresses an action or state that (1) was completed at an indefinite time in the past or (2) began in the past and continues into the present. Use *have* or *has* with the past participle.

　　EXAMPLE: *Poetry has inspired many readers.*

The **past perfect tense** expresses an action in the past that came before another action in the past. Use *had* with the past participle.

　　EXAMPLE: *He had built a fire before the dog ran away.*

The **future perfect tense** expresses an action in the future that will be completed before another action in the future. Use *shall have* or *will have* with the past participle.

　　EXAMPLE: *They will have read the novel before they see the movie version of the tale.*

TIP A past-tense form of an irregular verb is not used with an auxiliary verb, but a past-participle main irregular verb is always used with an auxiliary verb.

　　INCORRECT: *I have saw her somewhere before.* (*Saw* is the past-tense form of an irregular verb and shouldn't be used with *have*.)

　　CORRECT: *I have seen her somewhere before.*

　　INCORRECT: *I seen her somewhere before.* (*Seen* is the past participle of an irregular verb and shouldn't be used without an auxiliary verb.)

3.5 ROGRESSIVE FORMS

The progressive forms of the six tenses show ongoing actions. Use forms of be with the present participles of verbs.

　　PRESENT PROGRESSIVE: *Anne is arguing her case.*

PAST PROGRESSIVE: *Anne was arguing her case.*

FUTURE PROGRESSIVE: *Anne will be arguing her case.*

PRESENT PERFECT PROGRESSIVE: *Anne has been arguing her case.*

PAST PERFECT PROGRESSIVE: *Anne had been arguing her case.*

FUTURE PERFECT PROGRESSIVE: *Anne will have been arguing her case.*

WATCH OUT! Do not shift from tense to tense needlessly. Watch out for these special cases.

- In most compound sentences and in sentences with compound predicates, keep the tenses the same.

  INCORRECT: *She defied him, and he scolds her.*

  CORRECT: *She defied him, and he scolded her.*

- If one past action happens before another, do shift tenses.

  INCORRECT: *They wished they started earlier.*

  CORRECT: *They wished they had started earlier.*

Grammar Practice

Rewrite each sentence, using a form of the verb in parentheses. Identify each form that you use.

1. Frederick Douglass (write) a letter to Harriet Tubman in which he (praise) her.
2. He (say) that she (do) much to benefit enslaved people.
3. People (remember) her work with the Underground Railroad forever.
4. Both Douglass and Tubman (appear) in the history books that kids study.
5. They (inspire) seekers of justice for many years to come.

Rewrite each sentence to correct an error in tense.

1. When she went to the plantations, Tubman's signal has been the spiritual "Go Down Moses."

2. She is leading the slaves all the way from Maryland to Canada, and brought them to freedom.
3. Although she never will have been to Canada, she went bravely on.
4. They arrived safe and sound, but Tubman leaves for the South again.
5. Her life's work for the next six years had began.

3.6 ACTIVE AND PASSIVE VOICE

The voice of a verb tells whether its subject performs or receives the action expressed by the verb. When the subject performs the action, the verb is in the **active voice.** When the subject is the receiver of the action, the verb is in the **passive voice.**

Compare these two sentences:

ACTIVE: *Walt Whitman wrote "O Captain! My Captain!"*

PASSIVE: *"O Captain! My Captain!" was written by Walt Whitman.*

To form the passive voice, use a form of *be* with the past participle of the verb.

WATCH OUT! Use the passive voice sparingly. It can make writing awkward and less direct.

AWKWARD: *"The Monkey's Paw" is a short story that was written by W. W. Jacobs.*

BETTER: *W. W. Jacobs wrote the short story "The Monkey's Paw."*

There are occasions when you will choose to use the passive voice because

- you want to emphasize the receiver: ***The king was shot.***
- the doer is unknown: ***My books were stolen.***
- the doer is unimportant: ***French is spoken here.***

4 Modifiers

Modifiers are words or groups of words that change or limit the meanings of other words. Adjectives and adverbs are common modifiers.

GRAMMAR PRACTICE ANSWERS

1. *wrote—past; praised—past*
2. *said—past; had done—past perfect*
3. *will remember—future*
4. *appear—present*
5. *will inspire—future*

 COMMON CORE L1

GRAMMAR PRACTICE ANSWERS

1. *When she went to the plantations, Tubman's signal was the spiritual "Go Down Moses."*
2. *She led the slaves all the way from Maryland to Canada, and brought them to freedom.*
3. *Although she had never been to Canada, she went bravely on.*
4. *They arrived safe and sound, but Tubman left for the South again.*
5. *Her life's work for the next six years had begun.*

4.1 ADJECTIVES

Adjectives modify nouns and pronouns by telling which one, what kind, how many, or how much.

WHICH ONE: *this, that, these, those*

EXAMPLE: *This poem uses no capital letters.*

WHAT KIND: *electric, bright, small, open*

EXAMPLE: *An open flame would kill the moth.*

HOW MANY: *one, several, both, none, each*

EXAMPLE: *The moth wants one moment of beauty.*

HOW MUCH: *more, less, enough, as much*

EXAMPLE: *I think the cockroach has more sense than the moth.*

4.2 PREDICATE ADJECTIVES

Most adjectives come before the nouns they modify, as in the examples above. A **predicate adjective,** however, follows a linking verb and describes the subject.

EXAMPLE: *My friends are very intelligent.*

Be especially careful to use adjectives (not adverbs) after such linking verbs as *look, feel, grow, taste,* and *smell.*

EXAMPLE: *The bread smells wonderful.*

4.3 ADVERBS

Adverbs modify verbs, adjectives, and other adverbs by telling where, when, how, or to what extent.

WHERE: *The children played outside.*

WHEN: *The author spoke yesterday.*

HOW: *We walked slowly behind the leader.*

TO WHAT EXTENT: *He worked very hard.*

Adverbs may occur in many places in sentences, both before and after the words they modify.

EXAMPLES: *Suddenly the wind shifted.*
The wind suddenly shifted.
The wind shifted suddenly.

4.4 ADJECTIVE OR ADVERB?

Many adverbs are formed by adding **-ly** to adjectives.

EXAMPLES: *sweet, sweetly; gentle, gently*

However, **-ly** added to a noun will usually yield an adjective.

EXAMPLES: *friend, friendly; woman, womanly*

4.5 COMPARISON OF MODIFIERS

Modifiers can be used to compare two or more things. The form of a modifier shows the degree of comparison. Both adjectives and adverbs have **comparative** and **superlative** forms.

The **comparative form** is used to compare two things, groups, or actions.

EXAMPLES: *His father's hands were stronger than his own.*
My father was more courageous than I am.

The **superlative form** is used to compare more than two things, groups, or actions.

EXAMPLES: *His father's hands were the strongest in the family.*
My father was the most courageous of us all.

4.6 REGULAR COMPARISONS

Most one-syllable and some two-syllable adjectives and adverbs have comparatives and superlatives formed by adding **-er** and **-est.** All three-syllable and most two-syllable modifiers have comparatives and superlatives formed with **more** or **most.**

Modifier	Comparative	Superlative
small	smaller	smallest
thin	thinner	thinnest
sleepy	sleepier	sleepiest
useless	more useless	most useless
precisely	more precisely	most precisely

WATCH OUT! Note that spelling changes must sometimes be made to form the comparatives and superlatives of modifiers.

EXAMPLES: *friendly, friendlier* (Change *y* to *i* and add the ending.)
sad, sadder (Double the final consonant and add the ending.)

4.7 IRREGULAR COMPARISONS

Some commonly used modifiers have irregular comparative and superlative forms. They are listed in the chart. You may wish to memorize them.

Modifier	Comparative	Superlative
good	better	best
bad	worse	worst
far	farther or further	farthest or furthest
little	less or lesser	least
many	more	most
well	better	best
much	more	most

4.8 PROBLEMS WITH MODIFIERS

Study the tips that follow to avoid common mistakes:

Farther and Further Use *farther* for distances; use *further* for everything else.

Double Comparisons Make a comparison by using *-er/-est* or by using **more/most**. Using *-er* with **more** or using *-est* with **most** is incorrect.

> INCORRECT: *I like her more better than she likes me.*

> CORRECT: *I like her better than she likes me.*

Illogical Comparisons An illogical or confusing comparison results when two unrelated things are compared or when something is compared with itself. The word *other* or the word *else* should be used when comparing an individual member to the rest of a group.

> ILLOGICAL: *The cockroach is smarter than any insect.* (implies that the cockroach isn't an insect)

> LOGICAL: *The cockroach is smarter than any other insect.* (identifies that the cockroach is an insect)

Bad vs. Badly *Bad*, always an adjective, is used before a noun or after a linking verb. *Badly,* always an adverb, never modifies a noun. Be sure to use the right form after a linking verb.

> INCORRECT: *Ed felt badly after his team lost.*

> CORRECT: *Ed felt bad after his team lost.*

> DANGLING: *Looking out the window, his brother was seen driving by.*

> CLEARER: *Looking out the window, Josh saw his brother driving by.*

Grammar Practice

Choose the correct word or words from each pair in parentheses.

1. Mark Twain's attempt at studying the law did not go (good, well).
2. That wasn't the (worse, worst) of his many occupations, however.
3. He actually wasn't a (bad, badly) river-boat pilot.
4. He didn't have (no, any) confidence as a newspaper editor.
5. Still, that turned out to be the (more, most) satisfying job he ever had.

Grammar Practice

Rewrite each sentence that contains a misplaced or dangling modifier. Write "correct" if the sentence is written correctly.

1. Mark Twain discovered that he was a good storyteller working as an editor.
2. Twain often added exciting details to his stories.
3. It didn't matter to Twain whether all of the details were true in his articles.
4. He wrote 16 different articles about a single hay wagon in the paper.
5. When all else failed, he made up events.

5 The Sentence and Its Parts

A **sentence** is a group of words used to express a complete thought. A complete sentence has a subject and a predicate.

For more information, see **Quick Reference: The Sentence and Its Parts,** page R31.

COMMON CORE L1

GRAMMAR PRACTICE ANSWERS

1. *well*
2. *worst*
3. *bad*
4. *any*
5. *most*

COMMON CORE L1

GRAMMAR PRACTICE ANSWERS

1. *Working as an editor, Mark Twain discovered that he was a good storyteller.*
2. *correct*
3. *It didn't matter to Twain whether all of the details in his articles were true.*
4. *He wrote 16 different articles in the paper about a single hay wagon.*
5. *correct*

5.1 KINDS OF SENTENCES

There are four basic types of sentences.

Type	Definition	Example
Declarative	states a fact, a wish, an intent, or a feeling	This poem is about Abraham Lincoln.
Interrogative	asks a question	Did you understand the metaphor?
Imperative	gives a command or direction	Read it more closely.
Exclamatory	expresses strong feeling or excitement	Whitman really admired Lincoln!

5.2 COMPOUND SUBJECTS AND PREDICATES

A compound subject consists of two or more subjects that share the same verb. They are typically joined by the coordinating conjunctions *and* or *or.*

EXAMPLE: *A short story or novel will keep you engaged.*

A compound predicate consists of two or more predicates that share the same subject. They too are usually joined by a coordinating conjunction such as *and, but,* or *or.*

EXAMPLE: *The class finished all the poetry but did not read the short stories.*

5.3 COMPLEMENTS

A **complement** is a word or group of words that completes the meaning of the sentence. Some sentences contain only a subject and a verb. Most sentences, however, require additional words placed after the verb to complete the meaning of the sentence. There are three kinds of complements: direct objects, indirect objects, and subject complements.

Direct objects are words or word groups that receive the action of action verbs. A direct object answers the question *what* or *whom.*

EXAMPLES: *Ellis recited the poem.* (Recited what?)
His performance entertained the class. (Entertained whom?)

Indirect objects tell to whom or what or for whom or what the actions of verbs are performed. Indirect objects come before direct objects. In the following examples, the indirect objects are highlighted.

EXAMPLES: *The teacher gave the speech a good grade.* (Gave to what?)
He showed his father the teacher's comments. (Showed to whom?)

Subject complements come after linking verbs and identify or describe the subjects. A subject complement that names or identifies a subject is called a **predicate nominative.** Predicate nominatives include **predicate nouns** and **predicate pronouns.**

EXAMPLES: *My friends are very hard workers.*
The best writer in the class is she.

A subject complement that describes a subject is called a **predicate adjective.**

EXAMPLE: *The pianist appeared very energetic.*

6 Phrases

A **phrase** is a group of related words that does not contain a subject and a predicate but functions in a sentence as a single part of speech.

6.1 PREPOSITIONAL PHRASES

A **prepositional phrase** is a phrase that consists of a preposition, its object, and any modifiers of the object. Prepositional phrases that modify nouns or pronouns are called **adjective phrases.** Prepositional phrases that modify verbs, adjectives, or adverbs are **adverb phrases.**

ADJECTIVE PHRASE: *The central character of the story is a villain.*

ADVERB PHRASE: *He reveals his nature in the first scene.*

6.2 APPOSITIVES AND APPOSITIVE PHRASES

An **appositive** is a noun or pronoun that identifies or renames another noun or pronoun. An **appositive phrase** includes an appositive and modifiers of it. An appositive usually follows the noun or pronoun it identifies.

An appositive can be either **essential** or **nonessential.** An **essential appositive** provides information that is needed to identify what is referred to by the preceding noun or pronoun.

EXAMPLE: *The biography is about the courageous African American abolitionist Harriet Tubman.*

A **nonessential appositive** adds extra information about a noun or pronoun whose meaning is already clear. Nonessential appositives and appositive phrases are set off with commas.

EXAMPLE: *The story, a biography, describes how activists rescued people from slavery.*

7 Verbals and Verbal Phrases

A **verbal** is a verb form that is used as a noun, an adjective, or an adverb. A **verbal phrase** consists of a verbal along with its modifiers and complements. There are three kinds of verbals: **infinitives, participles,** and **gerunds.**

7.1 INFINITIVES AND INFINITIVE PHRASES

An **infinitive** is a verb form that usually begins with *to* and functions as a noun, an adjective, or an adverb. An **infinitive phrase** consists of an infinitive plus its modifiers and complements.

NOUN: *To show bravery is challenging.* (subject)
Harriet Tubman did not want to obey the laws of slavery. (direct object)

Her greatest trait was to become too courageous. (predicate nominative)

ADJECTIVE: *That was a trait to admire.* (adjective modifying *trait*)

ADVERB: *She joined the Underground Railroad to satisfy her anger.* (adverb modifying *created*)

Because *to* often precedes infinitives, it is usually easy to recognize them. However, sometimes *to* may be omitted.

EXAMPLE: *Her husband helped her [to] forgive herself.*

7.2 PARTICIPLES AND PARTICIPIAL PHRASES

A **participle** is a verb form that functions as an adjective. Like adjectives, participles modify nouns and pronouns. Most participles are present-participle forms, ending in *-ing,* or past-participle forms ending in *-ed* or *-en.* In the examples below, the participles are highlighted.

MODIFYING A NOUN: *The dying man had a smile on his face.*

MODIFYING A PRONOUN: *Frustrated, everyone abandoned the cause.*

Participial phrases are participles with all their modifiers and complements.

MODIFYING A NOUN: *The dogs searching for survivors are well trained.*

MODIFYING A PRONOUN: *Having approved your proposal, we are ready to act.*

7.3 DANGLING AND MISPLACED PARTICIPLES

A participle or participial phrase should be placed as close as possible to the word that it modifies. Otherwise the meaning of the sentence may not be clear.

MISPLACED: *The boys were looking for squirrels searching the trees.*

CLEARER: *The boys searching the trees were looking for squirrels.*

A participle or participial phrase that does not clearly modify anything in a sentence is called a **dangling participle.**

GRAMMAR PRACTICE ANSWERS

1. *I read an excerpt from Anne Frank's diary to learn more about her experiences.*

2. *Hiding from the Nazis, Anne was able to maintain her faith in other people.*

3. *Peter Van Daan, another person hiding in the Secret Annex, eventually became Anne's good friend.*

4. *The Nazis found the Franks' hiding place above the warehouse.*

5. *Having read this book, I know more about World War II.*

A dangling participle causes confusion because it appears to modify a word that it cannot sensibly modify. Correct a dangling participle by providing a word for the participle to modify.

> DANGLING: *Running like the wind, my hat fell off.* (The hat wasn't running.)

> CLEARER: *Running like the wind, I lost my hat.*

7.4 GERUNDS AND GERUND PHRASES

A **gerund** is a verb form ending in *-ing* that functions as a noun. Gerunds may perform any function nouns perform.

> SUBJECT: *Jogging is my favorite exercise.*

> DIRECT OBJECT: *My sister loves jogging.*

> INDIRECT OBJECT: *She gave jogging a try last year.*

> SUBJECT COMPLEMENT: *Their real passion is jogging.*

> OBJECT OF PREPOSITION: *The effects of jogging.*

Gerund phrases are gerunds with all their modifiers and complements.

> SUBJECT: *Using the Underground Railroad was Tubman's plan.*

> OBJECT OF PREPOSITION: *She flourished greatly after defying the slave owners.*

> APPOSITIVE: *Her family, remembering Tubman's courage and determination, admired her.*

Grammar Practice

Rewrite each sentence, adding the type of phrase shown in parentheses.

1. I read an excerpt from Anne Frank's diary. (infinitive phrase)
2. Anne was able to maintain her faith in other people. (gerund phrase)
3. Peter Van Daan eventually became Anne's good friend. (appositive phrase)
4. The Nazis found the Franks' hiding place. (prepositional phrase)
5. I know more about World War II. (participial phrase)

---

8 Clauses

A **clause** is a group of words that contains a subject and a predicate. There are two kinds of clauses: main and subordinate.

8.1 MAIN AND SUBORDINATE CLAUSES

A **main (independent) clause** can stand alone as a sentence.

> MAIN CLAUSE: *I enjoyed "Marigolds."*

A sentence may contain more than one main clause.

> EXAMPLE: *I read it twice, and I gave it to a friend.*

In the preceding example, the coordinating conjunction *and* joins two main clauses.

For more coordinating conjunctions, see **Quick Reference: Parts of Speech,** page R29.

A **subordinate (dependent) clause** cannot stand alone as a sentence. It is subordinate to, or dependent on, a main clause.

> EXAMPLE: *After I read it, I recommended it to my friends.*

The highlighted clause cannot stand by itself.

8.2 ADJECTIVE CLAUSES

An **adjective clause** is a subordinate clause used as an adjective. It usually follows the noun or pronoun it modifies.

> EXAMPLE: *The lesson that the story tells is about understanding the vulnerabilities of adulthood.*

Adjective clauses are typically introduced by the relative pronouns *who, whom, whose, which,* and *that.*

For more information, see **Relative Pronouns,** page R30.

> EXAMPLE: *Lizabeth, who was angered by her father's crying, tore up her neighbor's flowerbed.*

An adjective clause can be either essential or nonessential. An **essential adjective clause** provides information that is necessary to identify the preceding noun or pronoun.

> EXAMPLE: *She enjoyed disturbing John Burk who would curse at her.*

A **nonessential adjective clause** adds additional information about a noun or pronoun whose meaning is already clear. Nonessential clauses are set off with commas.

> EXAMPLE: *The marigolds, which were brilliant shades of yellow and gold, were destroyed by the children.*

8.3 ADVERB CLAUSES

An **adverb clause** is a subordinate clause that is used to modify a verb, an adjective, or an adverb. It is introduced by a subordinating conjunction.

For examples of subordinating conjunctions, see **Noun Clauses, page R47.**

Adverb clauses typically occur at the beginning or end of sentences.

> MODIFYING A VERB: *When he got bored, Nick told stories.*

> MODIFYING AN ADVERB: *Most people study more than Bob does.*

> MODIFYING AN ADJECTIVE: *He was excited because a cyclone was forming.*

TIP An adverb clause should be followed by a comma when it comes before a main clause. When an adverb clause comes after a main clause, a comma may not be needed.

8.4 NOUN CLAUSES

A **noun clause** is a subordinate clause that is used as a noun. A noun clause may be used as a subject, a direct object, an indirect object, a predicate nominative, or the object of a preposition. Noun clauses are introduced either by pronouns, such as *that, what, who, whoever, which,* and *whose,* or by subordinating conjunctions, such as *how, when, where, why,* and *whether.*

For more subordinating conjunctions, see **Quick Reference: Parts of Speech, page R29.**

TIP Because the same words may introduce adjective and noun clauses, you need to consider how a clause functions within its sentence. To determine if a clause is a noun clause, try substituting *something* or *someone* for the clause. If you can do it, it is probably a noun clause.

> EXAMPLES: *I know whose woods these are.* ("I know *something*." The clause is a noun clause, a direct object of the verb *know.*)
> *Give a copy to whoever wants one.* ("Give a copy to *someone*." The clause is a noun clause, an object of the preposition *to.*)

9 The Structure of Sentences

When classified by their structure, there are four kinds of sentences: simple, compound, complex, and compound-complex.

9.1 SIMPLE SENTENCES

A **simple sentence** is a sentence that has one main clause and no subordinate clauses.

> EXAMPLES: *Sam ran to the theater.*
> *Max waited in front of the theater.*

A simple sentence may contain a compound subject or a compound verb.

> EXAMPLES: *Sam and Max went to the movie.* (compound subject)
> *They clapped and cheered at their favorite parts.* (compound verb)

9.2 COMPOUND SENTENCES

A **compound sentence** consists of two or more main clauses. The clauses in compound sentences are joined with commas and coordinating conjunctions (*and, but, or, nor, yet, for, so*) or with semicolons. Like simple sentences, compound sentences do not contain any subordinate clauses.

GRAMMAR PRACTICE ANSWERS

1. *Jewell Parker Rhodes wrote "Block Party" to describe her old neighborhood and to publish a memoir of it.*

2. *In the story, she mentions many colorful characters, bike rides with her sister, and the world from her front stoop.*

3. *With her friends, Rhodes played hide and seek in the laundry hanging out to dry, slid down the banisters in the house, and rode a red tricycle through the kitchen.*

4. *A block party is when the street is closed off to traffic, hydrants are turned on by the fire department, and the neighbors gather for a picnic.*

5. *Rhodes went on to earn degrees in drama criticism, English, and creative writing.*

6. *She now writes novels, nonfiction, and articles for magazines.*

EXAMPLES: *Sam likes action movies, but Max prefers comedies.*
The actor jumped from one building to another; he barely made the final leap.

9.3 COMPLEX SENTENCES

A **complex sentence** consists of one main clause and one or more subordinate clauses.

> **EXAMPLES:** *One should not complain unless one has a better solution.*
> *Mr. Neiman, who is an artist, sketched pictures until the sun went down.*

9.4 COMPOUND-COMPLEX SENTENCES

A **compound-complex sentence** contains two or more main clauses and one or more subordinate clauses. Compound-complex sentences are both compound and complex.

> **COMPOUND:** *All the students knew the answer, yet they were too shy to volunteer.*

> **COMPOUND-COMPLEX:** *All the students knew the answer that their teacher expected, yet they were too shy to volunteer.*

9.5 PARALLEL STRUCTURE

When you write sentences, make sure that coordinate parts are equivalent, or **parallel,** in structure. For instance, be sure items you list in a series or contrast for emphasis are parallel.

> **NOT PARALLEL:** *I want to lose weight, becoming a musician, and good grades.* (*To lose weight* is an infinitive phrase, *becoming a musician* is a gerund phrase, and *grades* is a noun.)

> **PARALLEL:** *I want to lose weight, to become a musician, and to get good grades.* (*To lose, to become,* and *to get* are all infinitives.)

> **NOT PARALLEL:** *I not only want to lose weight, I'm keeping it off, too.* (*To lose weight* is an infinitive phrase; *keeping it off* is a gerund phrase.)

> **PARALLEL:** *I not only want to lose weight, I want to keep it off, too.* (*To lose weight* and *to keep it off* are both infinitive

---

phrases. To make them both infinitive, it is necessary to change *am* to an action verb. Now the contrast set up by *not only* adds emphasis to the second part of the statement.)

Grammar Practice

Revise each sentence to make its parts parallel.

1. Jewell Parker Rhodes wrote "Block Party" about her old neighborhood and to publish a memoir of it.

2. In the story, she mentions many colorful characters, riding her bike with her sister, and watching the world from her front stoop.

3. With her friends, Rhodes played hide and seek in the laundry hanging out to dry, would slide down the banisters in the house, and rode a red tricycle through the kitchen.

4. A block party is when the street is closed off to traffic, hydrants were turned on by the fire department, and the neighbors gather for a picnic.

5. Rhodes went on to earn degrees in drama criticism, English, and a third degree in creative writing.

6. She now writes novels, nonfiction, and even for magazines!

10 Writing Complete Sentences

Remember, a sentence is a group of words that expresses a complete thought. In writing that you wish to share with a reader, try to avoid both sentence fragments and run-on sentences.

10.1 CORRECTING FRAGMENTS

A **sentence fragment** is a group of words that is only part of a sentence. It does not express a complete thought and may be confusing to a reader or listener. A sentence fragment may be lacking a subject, a predicate, or both.

> **FRAGMENT:** *Worried about not doing well.* (no subject)

> **CORRECTED:** *Laura worried about not doing well.*

FRAGMENT: *Her mother and father.* (no predicate)

CORRECTED: *Her mother and father were both highly successful.*

FRAGMENT: *In a gentle way.* (neither subject nor predicate)

CORRECTED: *They tried to encourage her in a gentle way.*

In your writing, fragments may be a result of haste or incorrect punctuation. Sometimes fixing a fragment will be a matter of attaching it to a preceding or following sentence.

FRAGMENT: *Laura did her best. But never felt satisfied.*

CORRECTED: *Laura did her best but never felt satisfied.*

10.2 CORRECTING RUN-ON SENTENCES

A **run-on sentence** is made up of two or more sentences written as though they were one. Some run-ons have no punctuation within them. Others may have only commas where conjunctions or stronger punctuation marks are necessary.

Use your judgment in correcting run-on sentences, as you have choices. You can change a run-on to two sentences if the thoughts are not closely connected. If the thoughts are closely related, you can keep the run-on as one sentence by adding a semicolon or a conjunction.

RUN-ON: *She joined more clubs her friendships suffered.*

MAKE TWO SENTENCES: *She joined more clubs. Her friendships suffered.*

RUN-ON: *She joined more clubs they took up all her time.*

USE A SEMICOLON: *She joined more clubs; they took up all her time.*

ADD A CONJUNCTION: *She joined more clubs, but they took up all her time.*

WATCH OUT! When you form compound sentences, make sure you use appropriate punctuation: a comma before a coordinating conjunction, a semicolon when there is no coordinating conjunction. A very common mistake is to use a comma alone instead of a comma and a conjunction. This error is called a ***comma splice.***

INCORRECT: *He finished the job, he left the village.*

CORRECT: *He finished the job, and he left the village.*

11 Subject-Verb Agreement

The subject and verb in a clause must agree in number. Agreement means that if the subject is singular, the verb is also singular, and if the subject is plural, the verb is also plural.

11.1 BASIC AGREEMENT

Fortunately, agreement between subjects and verbs in English is simple. Most verbs show the difference between singular and plural only in the third person of the present tense. In the present tense, the third-person singular form ends in **-s.**

Present-Tense Verb Forms	
Singular	**Plural**
I sleep	we sleep
you sleep	you sleep
she he it sleeps	they sleep

11.2 AGREEMENT WITH *BE*

The verb ***be*** presents special problems in agreement, because this verb does not follow the usual verb patterns.

Forms of *Be*			
Present Tense		**Past Tense**	
Singular	**Plural**	**Singular**	**Plural**
I am	we are	I was	we were
you are	you are	you were	you were
she he it is	they are	she he it was	they were

11.3 WORDS BETWEEN SUBJECT AND VERB

A verb agrees only with its subject. When words come between a subject and a verb, ignore them when considering proper agreement. Identify the subject and make sure the verb agrees with it.

> EXAMPLES: *Whipped cream served with berries is my favorite sweet.*
>
> *A study by scientists recommends eating berries.*

11.4 AGREEMENT WITH COMPOUND SUBJECTS

Use plural verbs with most compound subjects joined by the word **and.**

> EXAMPLE: *My father and his friends play chess every day.*

To confirm that you need a plural verb, you could substitute the plural pronoun **they** for **my father and his friends.**

If a compound subject is thought of as a unit, use a singular verb. Test this by substituting the singular pronoun **it.**

> EXAMPLE: *Peanut butter and jelly [it] is my brother's favorite sandwich.*

Use a singular verb with a compound subject that is preceded by **each, every,** or **many a.**

> EXAMPLE: *Each novel and short story seems grounded in personal experience.*

When the parts of a compound subject are joined by **or, nor,** or the correlative conjunctions **either . . . or** or **neither . . . nor,** make the verb agree with the noun or pronoun nearest the verb.

> EXAMPLES: *Cookies or ice cream is my favorite dessert.*
> *Either Cheryl or her friends are being invited.*
> *Neither ice storms nor snow is predicted today.*

11.5 PERSONAL PRONOUNS AS SUBJECTS

When using a personal pronoun as a subject, make sure to match it with the correct form of the verb **be.** (See the chart in Section 11.2.) Note especially that the pronoun **you** takes the forms **are** and **were,** regardless of whether it is singular or plural.

WATCH OUT! *You is* and *you was* are nonstandard forms and should be avoided in writing and speaking. *We was* and *they was* are also forms to be avoided.

> INCORRECT: *You was a good student.*
> CORRECT: *You were a good student.*
> INCORRECT: *They was starting a new school.*
> CORRECT: *They were starting a new school.*

11.6 INDEFINITE PRONOUNS AS SUBJECTS

Some indefinite pronouns are always singular; some are always plural.

Singular Indefinite Pronouns			
another	either	neither	one
anybody	everybody	nobody	somebody
anyone	everyone	no one	someone
anything	everything	nothing	something
each	much		

> EXAMPLES: *Each of the writers was given an award. Somebody in the room upstairs is sleeping.*

Plural Indefinite Pronouns			
both	few	many	several

> EXAMPLES: *Many of the books in our library are not in circulation.*
> *Few have been returned recently.*

Still other indefinite pronouns may be either singular or plural.

Singular or Plural Indefinite Pronouns		
all	more	none
any	most	some

The number of the indefinite pronoun *any* or *none* often depends on the intended meaning.

> EXAMPLES: *Any of these topics has potential for a good article.* (any one topic)
> *Any of these topics have potential for good articles.* (all of the many topics)

The indefinite pronouns *all, some, more, most,* and *none* are singular when they refer to quantities or parts of things. They are plural when they refer to numbers of individual things. Context will usually provide a clue.

> EXAMPLES: *All of the flour is gone.* (referring to a quantity)
> *All of the flowers are gone.* (referring to individual items)

11.7 INVERTED SENTENCES

A sentence in which the subject follows the verb is called an **inverted sentence.** A subject can follow a verb or part of a verb phrase in a question, a sentence beginning with *here* or *there,* or a sentence in which an adjective, an adverb, or a phrase is placed first.

> EXAMPLES: *There clearly are far too many cooks in this kitchen.*
> *What is the correct ingredient for this stew?*
> *Far from the frazzled cooks stands the master chef.*

> **TIP** To check subject-verb agreement in some inverted sentences, place the subject before the verb. For example, change ***There are many people*** to ***Many people are there.***

11.8 SENTENCES WITH PREDICATE NOMINATIVES

In a sentence containing a predicate noun (nominative), the verb should agree with the subject, not the predicate noun.

> EXAMPLES: *The poems of Walt Whitman are a unique record of U.S. history.* (*Poems* is the subject—not *record*—and it takes the plural verb *are.*)

One unique record of U.S. history is the poems of Walt Whitman. (The subject is record—not poems—and it takes the singular verb is.)

11.9 *DON'T* AND *DOESN'T* AS AUXILIARY VERBS

The auxiliary verb *doesn't* is used with singular subjects and with the personal pronouns *she, he,* and *it.* The auxiliary verb *don't* is used with plural subjects and with the personal pronouns *I, we, you,* and *they.*

> SINGULAR: *Doesn't the poem "O Captain! My Captain!" sound almost like a news report?*
> *It doesn't sound like a poem, even though it rhymes.*

> PLURAL: *People don't know enough about United States President Abraham Lincoln. Don't they think history is important?*

11.10 COLLECTIVE NOUNS AS SUBJECTS

Collective nouns are singular nouns that name groups of persons or things. *Team,* for example, is the collective name of a group of individuals. A collective noun takes a singular verb when the group acts as a single unit. It takes a plural verb when the members of the group act separately.

> EXAMPLES: *Our team usually wins.* (The team as a whole wins.)
> *The faculty vote differently on most issues.* (The individual members of the faculty vote.)

11.11 RELATIVE PRONOUNS AS SUBJECTS

When the relative pronoun *who, which,* or *that* is used as a subject in an adjective clause, the verb in the clause must agree in number with the antecedent of the pronoun.

> SINGULAR: *The story that affects me the most is "The Diary of a Young Girl."*

The antecedent of the relative pronoun *that* is the singular *poem*; therefore, *that* is singular and must take the singular verb *affects.*

GRAMMAR PRACTICE ANSWERS

1. *describes*
2. *Doesn't*
3. *realizes*
4. *persuades*
5. *go*
6. *become*
7. *returns*
8. *begins*
9. *flees*
10. *find*

PLURAL: *Rita Dove and Audre Lorde are African-American poets* who write about life's issues.

The antecedent of the relative pronoun *who* is the plural compound subject *Rita Dove and Audre Lorde.* Therefore *who* is plural, and it takes the plural verb *write.*

Grammar Practice

Locate the subject in each sentence below. Then choose the correct verb form.

1. Mark Twain's novel *The Adventures of Tom Sawyer* (describes, describe) the escapades of a young boy growing up in a Mississippi River town.
2. (Doesn't, Don't) Tom have to white-wash a fence as punishment for playing hooky from school?
3. Nobody (realizes, realize) that Tom is tricking them into doing his work.
4. Tom falls in love with a new girl in town and (persuade, persuades) her to kiss him.
5. Huckleberry Finn and Tom (goes, go) to the graveyard and witness a murder.
6. Tom and his friend run away to an island to (become, becomes) pirates.
7. Tom (returns, return) home one night.
8. When Muff Potter's trial (begin, begins) Tom testifies.
9. Muff Potter is acquitted and the real murderer, Injun Joe, (flees, flee) the courtroom.
10. Tom and Huckleberry Finn (find, finds) buried treasure in a haunted house.

Vocabulary and Spelling

COMMON CORE L 2c, L 4, L 4a–d, L 5, L 5a–c, L 6

By learning and practicing vocabulary strategies, you'll know what to do when you encounter unfamiliar words while reading. You'll also know how to refine the words you use for different situations—personal, school, and work. Learning basic spelling rules and checking your spelling in a dictionary will help you spell words that you may not use frequently.

1 Using Context Clues

The context of a word is made up of the punctuation marks, words, sentences, and paragraphs that surround the word. A word's context can give you important clues about its meaning.

1.1 GENERAL CONTEXT

Sometimes you need to determine the meaning of an unfamiliar, ambiguous, or novel word by reading all the information in a passage.

Stop teasing me! Just because you are a better tennis player than I am doesn't mean you should belittle my abilities.

You can figure out from the context that belittle means "make something less than it is."

1.2 IDIOMS, SLANG, AND FIGURATIVE LANGUAGE

An **idiom** is an expression whose overall meaning differs from the meaning of the individual words.

A nasty case of the flu kept me under the weather. (Under the weather means "tired and sickly.")

Slang is informal language in which made-up words and ordinary words are used to mean something different from their meanings in formal English.

I'm going to jazz up this salad with some walnuts. (Jazz up means "make more interesting.")

Figurative language is language that communicates meaning beyond the literal meaning of the words.

The lone desert monument was like a sentinel standing guard. (Lone and standing guard help describe a sentinel.)

1.3 SPECIFIC CONTEXT CLUES

Sometimes writers help you understand the meanings of unfamiliar, ambiguous, or novel words by providing specific clues such as those shown in the chart.

Specific Context Clues		
Type of Clue	**Key Words/ Phrases**	**Example**
Definition or restatement of the meaning of the word	or, which is, that is, in other words, also known as, also called	Olympic gymnasts are very *limber,* or **flexible.**
Example following an unfamiliar word	such as, like, as if, for example, especially, including	We collected *kindling,* such as **dry twigs and branches,** to start the fire.
Comparison with a more familiar word or concept	as, like, also, similar to, in the same way, likewise	Kari's face was *luminous,* **like the rays of the sun.**
Contrast with a familiar word or experience	unlike, but, however, although, on the other hand, on the contrary	The summer was *sultry,* but the fall was **dry and cool.**
Cause-and-effect relationship in which one term is familiar	because, since, when, consequently, as a result, therefore	When the *tree fell across the road,* it **obstructed** traffic.

2 Analyzing Word Structure

Many words can be broken into smaller parts. These word parts include base words, roots, prefixes, and suffixes.

2.1 BASE WORDS

A **base word** is a word part that by itself is also a word. Other words or word parts can be added to base words to form new words.

2.2 ROOTS

A **root** is a word part that contains the core meaning of the word. Many English words contain roots that come from older languages such as Greek, Latin, Old English (Anglo-Saxon), and Norse. Knowing the meaning of the word's root can help you determine the word's meaning.

Root	Meaning	Example
aud (Latin)	hear	**aud**io, **aud**ition
voc (Latin)	voice	**voc**al, in**voc**e
mem, ment (Latin)	mind	**mem**ory, **ment**al, **ment**ion
chron (Greek)	time	**chron**ic, syn**chron**ize
gram (Greek)	something written	tele**gram**, **gram**mar
gen (Greek)	race, family	**gen**esis, **gen**re, **gen**ius
angr (Old Norse)	painfully constricted, sorrow	**ang**er, **ang**uish

2.3 PREFIXES

A **prefix** is a word part attached to the beginning of a word or word root. Most prefixes come from Greek, Latin, or Old English.

Prefix	Meaning	Example
mid-	middle, center	**mid**night
pro-	forward	**pro**ceed, **pro**cession
uni-	one	**uni**form, **uni**cycle
tele-	view	**tele**scope
multi-	many, much	**multi**media, **multi**vitamins

2.4 SUFFIXES

A **suffix** is a word part that appears at the end of a root or base word to form a new word. Some suffixes do not change word meaning. These suffixes are

- added to nouns to change the number of persons or objects
- added to verbs to change the tense
- added to modifiers to change the degree of comparison

Suffix	Meaning	Example
-s, -es	to change the number of a noun	lock + s = locks
-d, -ed, -ing	to change verb tense	stew + ed = stewed
-er, -est	to indicate comparison in modifiers	mild + er = milder soft + est = softest

Other suffixes can be added to the root or base to change the word's meaning. These suffixes can also determine a word's part of speech.

Suffix	Meaning	Example
-age	amount	foot**age**
-able, -ible	able, inclined to	read**able**, tang**ible**
-ant, -ent	a specific state or condition	pleas**ant**, differ**ent**

Strategies for Understanding Unfamiliar Words

- Look for any prefixes or suffixes. Remove them so that you can concentrate on the base word or the root.
- See if you recognize any elements—prefix, suffix, root, or base—of the word. You may be able to guess its meaning by analyzing one or two elements.
- Think about the way the word is used in the sentence. Use the context and the word parts to make a logical guess about the word's meaning.
- Look in a dictionary to see whether you are correct.

3 Understanding Word Origins

3.1 DEVELOPMENT OF THE ENGLISH LANGUAGE

During the past 2,000 years or so, English has developed from a language spoken by a few Germanic tribes into a language that is more widely spoken and written than any other in the world. Some experts, in fact, call today's English the first truly global language. Its most valuable characteristic is its ability to change and grow, adopting new words as the need arises. The history of the English language can be divided into three main periods.

Old English About the year AD 449, Germanic people who lived on the European continent along the North Sea began a series of invasions into Britain. At that time, Britain was inhabited by the Celts, whose native language was Gaelic. Over a period of years, the raiders conquered and settled in Britain. The conquerors, known today as the Anglo-Saxons, prospered in Britain. In time, Britain became "Engla land," and the Anglo-Saxon languages evolved into "Englisc," or what modern scholars call Old English.

Old English was very different from the English we speak today. It was harsher in sound, had no silent letters, and was written phonetically. Few examples of Old English remain in our current English vocabulary. Those that do exist, however, are common words for people, places, things, and actions.

man *(mann)*   wife *(wif)*   child *(cild)*

house *(hus)*   meat *(mete)*   drink *(drincan)*

sleep *(slæpan)*   live *(libban)*   fight *(feohtan)*

In the sixth and seventh centuries, missionaries from Rome and other Christian cities arrived in England, bringing with them their knowledge of religion and ancient languages. Among the most influential figures was St. Augustine, who converted thousands of Anglo-Saxons, including a king, to Christianity. As the Anglo-Saxons accepted this faith, they also accepted words from Latin and Greek.

Latin	Greek
candle	alphabet
cup	angel
priest	box
noon	demon
scripture	school

During the late eighth century, Viking invaders from Denmark and Norway settled in northeast England. As a result, Scandinavian words became part of Old English.

sky	knife	are
steak	leg	birth
they	skin	seat
window	them	their

Middle English The Norman Conquest brought great changes to England and its language. In 1066, England was defeated by the Normans, a people from an area in France. Their leader, William the Conqueror, staged a successful invasion of England and became the nation's new monarch. With William on the throne of England, Norman French became the language of the English court, government business, nobility, and scholars. Eventually, French words were adopted in everyday vocabulary as well.

The language that evolved is called Middle English. Middle English was not as harsh-sounding as Old English and borrowed many words from Norman French.

attorney	joint	mallet
baron	jolly	marriage
chivalry	laundry	merchandise
gown	lodge	petty

Norman French itself borrowed thousands of words from Latin and Greek, as well as from ancient Indian and Semitic languages. Consequently, Middle English also contained many of these foreign terms.

Latin	Greek	Indian	Semitic
language	circle	ginger	camel
library	hour	jungle	cinnamon
money	lantern	orange	coffee
serpent	leopard	sugar	lion
square	magnet	pepper	syrup

Modern English By the late 1400s, Middle English began to develop into Modern English. The various pronunciations, word forms, and spellings common to Middle English were becoming more uniform. One invention that aided this process was the printing press. Introduced to London around 1476, the printing press allowed printers to standardize the spellings of common English words. As a result, readers and writers of English became accustomed to following "rules" of spelling and grammar.

During this period, the English vocabulary also continued to grow as new ideas and discoveries demanded new words. As the English began to colonize and trade with other areas of the world, they borrowed foreign words. In time, the English vocabulary grew to include words from diverse languages, such as French, Dutch, Spanish, Italian, Portuguese, and Chinese. Many of these words stayed the way they were in their original languages.

French	Dutch	Spanish	Italian
ballet	boss	canyon	diva
beret	caboose	rodeo	carnival
mirage	dock	taco	spaghetti
vague	skate	tornado	studio

Portuguese	Chinese	Japanese	Native American
cashew	chow	kamikaze	caribou
mango	ginseng	karaoke	moccasin
jaguar	kung fu	sushi	papoose
yam	kow tow	tsunami	tomahawk

Today, the English language is still changing and absorbing new words. It is considered the international language of science and technology. It is also widely used in business and politics.

3.2 DICTIONARY AS A SOURCE OF WORD ORIGINS

Many dictionary entries provide information about a word's origin. This information often comes at the end of an entry, as in this example.

ge·om·e·try (jē-ŏm ĭ-trē) *n., pl.*-**tries 1.** The mathematics of the properties, measurement, and relationships of points, lines, angles, surfaces, and solids. **2.** Configuration; arrangement. **3.** A physical arrangement suggesting geometric forms or lines. [from Greek *geōmetriā,* from *geōmetrein,* to measure land].

3.3 WORD FAMILIES

Words that have the same root make up a word family and have related meanings. The charts below show some common Greek and Latin roots. Notice how the meanings of the example words are related to the meanings of their roots.

Latin Root	*circum,* around or about
English	**circumference** the boundary line of a circle
	circumnavigation the act of moving completely around
	circumstance a condition or fact surrounding an event

Greek Root	*monos,* single or alone
English	**monopoly** exclusive control by one group
	monologue a speech delivered by one person
	monotonous sounded or spoken in a single unvarying tone

French Root	*caval,* a horse
English	**calvary** troops trained to fight on horseback
	cavalcade a procession of riders or horsedrawn carriages

TIP Once you recognize a root in one English word, you will notice the same root in other words. Because these words develop from the same root, all words in the word family are similar in meaning.

4 Synonyms and Antonyms

4.1 SYNONYMS

Positive	Negative
slender	scrawny
thrifty	cheap
young	immature

A **synonym** is a word with a meaning similar to that of another word. You can find synonyms in a thesaurus or a dictionary. In a dictionary, synonyms are often given as part of the definition of the word. The following word pairs are synonyms:

satisfy/please   occasionally/sometimes

rob/steal   schedule/agenda

4.2 ANTONYMS

An **antonym** is a word with a meaning opposite that of another word. The following word pairs are antonyms:

accurate/incorrect   similar/different

fresh/stale   unusual/ordinary

5 Denotation and Connotation

5.1 DENOTATION

A word's dictionary meaning is called its **denotation.** For example, the denotation of the word *thin* is "having little flesh; spare; lean."

5.2 CONNOTATION

The images or feelings you connect to a word add a finer shade of meaning, called **connotation.** The connation of a word goes beyond its basic dictionary definition. Writers use connotations of words to communicate positive or negative feelings.

Make sure you understand the denotation and connotation of a word when you read it or use it in your writing.

6 Analogies

An **analogy** is a relationship between pairs of words. In an analogy question on a test, the words in one pair relate to each other the same way as the words in a second pair, one of which you have to choose. To complete an analogy, identify the relationship between the words in the first pair. Then choose the word that will cause the words in the second pair to relate to the other in the same way.

Analogies are often written as follows—

    cheap : expensive :: humid : dry

If the analogy is read out loud, you would say, "cheap is to expensive as humid is to dry."

There are various ways the word pairs in an analogy can be related.

- Words can be related because they are opposites, or antonyms, as in the example above.
- Words can be related because they are similar, or synonyms.

    tired : exhausted :: talkative : chatty

- Words can be related by function. If the first pair of words contains a noun and its function, the second pair should also.

    helmet : protection :: lamp : illumination

- Words can be related by description. If the first pair or words contains a noun and a word that describes it, the second pair should also.

    rain : wet :: lettuce : green

7 Homonyms, Homographs, and Homophones

7.1 HOMONYMS

Homonyms are words that have the same spelling and sound but have different meanings.

The snake shed its skin in the shed behind the house.

Shed can mean "to lose by natural process," but an identically spelled word means "a small structure."

Sometimes only one of the meanings of a homonym may be familiar to you. Use context clues to help you figure out the meaning of an unfamiliar word.

7.2 HOMOGRAPHS

Homographs are words that are spelled the same but have different meanings and origins. Some are also pronounced differently, as in these examples.

> *Please close the door. (klōz)*
>
> *That was a close call. (klōs)*

If you see a word used in a way that is unfamiliar to you, check a dictionary to see if it is a homograph.

7.3 HOMOPHONES

Homophones are words that sound alike but have different meanings and spellings. The following homophones are frequently misused:

it's/its	they're/their/there
to/too/two	stationary/stationery

Many misused homophones are pronouns and contractions. Whenever you are unsure whether to write *your* or *you're* and *who's* or *whose,* ask yourself if you mean *you are* and *who is/has.* If you do, write the contraction. For other homophones, such as *fair* and *fare,* use the meaning of the word to help you decide which one to use.

8 Words with Multiple Meanings

Some words have acquired additional meanings over time that are based on the original meaning.

> *I had to be replaced in the cast of the play because of the cast on my arm.*

These two uses of cast have different meanings, but both of them have the same origin. You will find all the meanings of cast listed in one entry in the dictionary.

9 Specialized Vocabulary

Specialized vocabulary is special terms suited to a particular field of study or work. For example, science, mathematics, and history all have their own technical or specialized vocabularies. To figure out specialized terms, you can use context clues and reference sources, such as dictionaries on specific subjects, atlases, or manuals.

10 Using Reference Sources

10.1 DICTIONARIES

A **general dictionary** will tell you not only a word's definitions but also its pronunciation, parts of speech, and history and origin, or etymology.

> ① **tan·gi·ble** (tăn´jə-bəl) *adj.*
> **1a.** Discernible by the touch; palpable. **b.** Possible to touch. **c.** Possible to be treated as fact; real or concrete. **2.** Possible to understand or realize. **3.** Relating to or being property of a physical nature, such as land, objects, and goods. [Late Latin *tangibilis,* from Latin *tangere,* to touch] ⑤

① Entry word
② Pronunciation
③ Part of speech
④ Definitions
⑤ Etymology

A **specialized dictionary** focuses on terms related to a particular field of study or work. Use a dictionary to check the spelling of any word you are unsure of in your English class and other classes as well.

10.2 THESAURI

A **thesaurus** (plural, *thesauri*) is a dictionary of synonyms. A thesaurus can be especially helpful when you find yourself using the same modifiers over and over again.

10.3 SYNONYM FINDERS

A **synonym finder** is often included in wordprocessing software. It enables you to highlight a word and be shown a display of its synonyms.

10.4 GLOSSARIES

A **glossary** is a list of specialized terms and their definitions. It is often found in the back of a book and sometimes includes pronunciations. Many textbooks contain glossaries. In fact, this textbook has three glossaries: the **Glossary of Literary and Informational Terms,** the **Glossary of Academic Vocabulary,** and the **Glossary of Critical Vocabulary.** Use these glossaries to help you understand how terms are used in this textbook.

11 Spelling Rules

11.1 WORDS ENDING IN A SILENT *E*

Before adding a suffix beginning with a vowel or *y* to a word ending in a silent *e,* drop the *e* (with some exceptions).

> amaze + -ing = amazing
>
> love + -able = lovable
>
> create + -ed = created
>
> nerve + -ous = nervous

Exceptions: *change + -able = changeable; courage + -ous = courageous*

When adding a suffix beginning with a consonant to a word ending in a silent *e,* keep the *e* (with some exceptions).

> late + -ly = lately
>
> spite + -ful = spiteful
>
> noise + -less = noiseless
>
> state + -ment = statement

Exceptions: *truly, argument, ninth, wholly, awful, and others*

When a suffix beginning with *a* or *o* is added to a word with a final silent *e,* the final *e* is usually retained if it is preceded by a soft *c* or a soft *g.*

> bridge + -able = bridgeable
>
> peace + -able = peaceable
>
> outrage + -ous = outrageous
>
> advantage + -ous = advantageous

When a suffix beginning with a vowel is added to words ending in *ee* or *oe,* the final, silent *e* is retained.

> agree + -ing = agreeing
>
> free + -ing = freeing
>
> hoe + -ing = hoeing
>
> see + -ing = seeing

11.2 WORDS ENDING IN *Y*

Before adding most suffixes to a word that ends in *y* preceded by a consonant, change the *y* to *i.*

> easy + -est = easiest
>
> crazy + -est = craziest
>
> silly + -ness = silliness
>
> marry + -age = marriage

Exceptions: *dryness, shyness,* and *slyness*

However, when you add *-ing,* the *y* does not change.

> empty + -ed = emptied   but
>
> empty + -ing = emptying

When adding a suffix to a word that ends in *y* preceded by a vowel, the *y* usually does not change.

> play + -er = player
>
> employ + -ed = employed
>
> coy + -ness = coyness
>
> pay + -able = payable

11.3 WORDS ENDING IN A CONSONANT

In one-syllable words that end in one consonant preceded by one short vowel, double the final consonant before adding a suffix beginning with a vowel, such as *-ed* or *-ing.* These are sometimes called 1+1+1 words.

> dip + -ed = dipped
>
> set + -ing = setting
>
> slim + -est = slimmest
>
> fit + -er = fitter

The rule does not apply to words of one syllable that end in a consonant preceded by two vowels.

> feel + -ing = feeling
>
> peel + -ed = peeled
>
> reap + -ed = reaped
>
> loot + -ed = looted

In words of more than one syllable, double the final consonant when (1) the word ends with one consonant preceded by one vowel and (2) when the word is accented on the last syllable.

be•gin′ per•mit′ re•fer′

In the following examples, note that in the new words formed with suffixes, the accent remains on the same syllable:

be•gin′ + -ing = be•gin′ning = beginning

per•mit′ + -ed = per•mit′ted = permitted

Exceptions: In some words with more than one syllable, though the accent remains on the same syllable when a suffix is added, the final consonant is nevertheless not doubled, as in the following examples:

tra′vel + er = tra′vel•er = traveler

mar′ket + er = mar′ket•er = marketer

In the following examples, the accent does not remain on the same syllable; thus, the final consonant is not doubled:

re•fer′ + -ence = ref′er•ence = reference

con•fer′ + -ence = con′fer•ence = conference

11.4 PREFIXES AND SUFFIXES

When adding a prefix to a word, do not change the spelling of the base word. When a prefix creates a double letter, keep both letters.

dis- + approve = disapprove

re- + build = rebuild

ir- + regular = irregular

mis- + spell = misspell

anti- + trust = antitrust

il- + logical = illogical

When adding **-ly** to a word ending in **l,** keep both **l's.** When adding **-ness** to a word ending in **n,** keep both **n's.**

careful + -ly = carefully

sudden + -ness = suddenness

final + -ly = finally

thin + -ness = thinness

11.5 FORMING PLURAL NOUNS

To form the plural of most nouns, just add **-s.**

prizes dreams circles stations

For most singular nouns ending in **o,** add **-s.**

solos halos studios photos pianos

For a few nouns ending in **o,** add **-es.**

heroes tomatoes potatoes echoes

When the singular noun ends in **s, sh, ch, x,** or **z,** add **-es.**

**waitresses brushes ditches
axes   buzzes**

When a singular noun ends in **y** with a consonant before it, change the **y** to **i** and add **-es.**

army—armies	candy—candies
baby—babies	diary—diaries
ferry—ferries	conspiracy—conspiracies

When a vowel (**a, e, i, o, u**) comes before the **y,** just add **-s.**

boy—boys	way—ways
array—arrays	alloy—alloys
weekday—weekdays	jockey—jockeys

For most nouns ending in **f** or **fe,** change the **f** to **v** and add **-es** or **-s.**

life—lives	shelf—shelves
thief—thieves	loaf—loaves
calf—calves	knife—knives

For some nouns ending in **f,** add **-s** to make the plural.

roofs chiefs reefs beliefs

Some nouns have the same form for both singular and plural.

deer sheep moose salmon trout

For some nouns, the plural is formed in a special way.

man—men	goose—geese
ox—oxen	woman—women
mouse—mice	child—children

For a compound noun written as one word, form the plural by changing the last word in the compound to its plural form.

stepchild—stepchildren

firefly—fireflies

If a compound noun is written as a hyphenated word or as two separate words, change the most important word to the plural form.

brother-in-law—brothers-in-law

life jacket—life jackets

11.6 FORMING POSSESSIVES

If a noun is singular, add **'s.**

mother—my mother's car

Ross—Ross's desk

Exception: The **s** after the apostrophe is dropped after *Jesus', Moses',* and certain names in classical mythology (*Zeus'*). These possessive forms can thus be pronounced easily.

If a noun is plural and ends with **s,** add an apostrophe.

parents—my parents' car

the Santinis—the Santinis' house

If a noun is plural but does not end in **s,** add **'s.**

people—the people's choice

women—the women's coats

11.7 SPECIAL SPELLING PROBLEMS

Only one English word ends in **-sede**: *supersede.* Three words end in **-ceed**: *exceed, proceed,* and *succeed.* All other verbs ending in the sound "seed" are spelled with **-cede**.

concede precede recede secede

In words with **ie** or **ei,** when the sound is long **e** (as in *she*), the word is spelled **ie** except after **c** (with some exceptions).

i before *e*	thief	relieve	field
	piece	grieve	pier
except after *c*	conceit	perceive	ceiling
	receive	receipt	
Exceptions:	either	neither	weird
	leisure	seize	

12 Commonly Confused Words

Words	Definitions	Examples
accept/ except	The verb *accept* means "to receive" or "to believe." *Except* is usually a preposition meaning "excluding."	Did the teacher **accept** your report? Everyone smiled for the photographer **except** Jody.
advice/ advise	*Advise* is a verb. *Advice* is a noun naming that which an *adviser* gives.	I **advise** you to take that job. Whom should I ask for **advice**?
affect/effect	As a verb, *affect* means "to influence." *Effect* as a verb means "to cause." If you want a noun, you will almost always want *effect*.	How deeply did the news **affect** him? The students tried to **effect** a change in school policy. What **effect** did the acidic soil produce in the plants?
all ready/ already	*All ready* is an adjective meaning "fully ready." *Already* is an adverb meaning "before" or "by this time."	He was **all ready** to go at noon. I have **already** seen that movie.
desert/ dessert	*Desert* (dĕz´ərt) means "a dry, sandy, barren region." *Desert* (dĭ-zûrt´) means "to abandon." *Dessert* (dĭ-zûrt´) is a sweet, such as cake.	The Sahara, in North Africa, is the world's largest **desert**. The night guard did not **desert** his post. Alison's favorite **dessert** is chocolate cake.
among/ between	*Between* is used when you are speaking of only two things. *Among* is used for three or more.	**Between** ice cream and sherbet, I prefer the latter. Gary Soto is **among** my favorite authors.
bring/take	*Bring* is used to denote motion toward a speaker or place. *Take* is used to denote motion away from such a person or place.	**Bring** the books over here, and I will **take** them to the library.
fewer/less	*Fewer* refers to the number of separate, countable units. *Less* refers to bulk quantity.	We have **less** literature and **fewer** selections in this year's curriculum.
leave/let	*Leave* means "to allow something to remain behind." *Let* means "to permit."	The librarian will **leave** some books on display but will not **let** us borrow any.
lie/lay	To *lie* is "to rest or recline." It does not take an object. *Lay* always takes an object.	Rover loves to **lie** in the sun. We always **lay** some bones next to him.
loose/lose	*Loose* (lo͞os) means "free, not restrained." *Lose* (lo͞oz) means "to misplace" or "to fail to find."	Who turned the horses **loose**? I hope we won't **lose** any of them.

passed/past	*Passed* is the past tense of pass and means "went by." *Past* is an adjective that means "of a former time." *Past* is also a noun that means "time gone by."	We **passed** through the Florida Keys during our vacation. My **past** experiences have taught me to set my alarm. Ebenezer Scrooge is a character who relives his **past.**
than/then	Use *than* in making comparisons. Use *then* on all other occasions.	Ramon is stronger **than** Mark. Cut the grass and **then** trim the hedges.
two/too/to	*Two* is the number. *Too* is an adverb meaning "also" or "very." Use *to* before a verb or as a preposition.	Meg had **to** go **to** town, **too.** We had **too** much reading **to** do. **Two** chapters is **too** many.
their/there/ they're	*Their* means "belonging to them." *There* means "in that place." *They're* is the contraction for "they are."	**There** is a movie playing at 9 P.M. **They're** going to see it with me. Sakara and Jessica drove away in **their** car after the movie.

Glossary of Literary and Informational Terms

Act An act is a major division within a play, similar to a chapter in a book. Each act may be further divided into smaller sections, called scenes. Plays can have as many as five acts. *The Diary of Anne Frank* has two acts.

Adventure Story An adventure story is a literary work in which action is the main element. An adventure novel usually focuses on a main character who is on a mission and is facing many challenges and choices.

Alliteration Alliteration is the repetition of consonant sounds at the beginning of words. Note the repetition of the *s* sound in this line: *S*uddenly *S*arah *s*ighed and *s*ank down on the *s*and.

See also Consonance.

Allusion An allusion is a reference to a famous person, place, event, or work of literature. In "The Drummer Boy of Shiloh" by Ray Bradbury, the general makes an allusion to the poet Henry Wadsworth Longfellow.

Analogy An analogy is a point-by-point comparison between two things that are alike in some respect. Often, writers use analogies in nonfiction to explain unfamiliar subjects or ideas in terms of familiar ones.

See also Extended Metaphor; Metaphor; Simile.

Anecdote An anecdote is a brief account of an interesting incident or event that is usually intended to entertain or make a point.

Antagonist The antagonist is a force working against the protagonist, or main character, in a story, play, or novel. The antagonist is usually another character but can be a force of nature, society itself, or an internal force within the main character.

See also Protagonist.

Appeal to Authority An appeal to authority is an attempt to persuade an audience by making reference to people who are experts on a subject.

Argument An argument is speaking or writing that expresses a position, or makes a claim, and supports it with reasons and evidence. An argument often takes into account other points of view, anticipating and answering objections that opponents might raise.

See also Claim; Counterargument; Evidence.

Assonance Assonance is the repetition of vowel sounds within nonrhyming words. An example of assonance is the repetition of the short *a* sound in the following line: The boy threw an apple at the animal.

Assumption An assumption is an opinion or belief that is taken for granted. It can be about a specific situation, a person, or the world in general. Assumptions are often unstated.

Author's Message An author's message is the main idea or theme of a particular work.

See also Main Idea; Theme.

Author's Perspective An author's perspective is the unique combination of ideas, values, feelings, and beliefs that influences the way the writer looks at a topic. Tone, or attitude, often reveals an author's perspective.

See also Author's Purpose; Tone.

Author's Position An author's position is his or her opinion on an issue or topic.

See also Claim.

Author's Purpose A writer usually writes for one or more of these purposes: to express thoughts or feelings, to inform or explain, to persuade, and to entertain.

See also Author's Perspective.

Autobiography An autobiography is a writer's account of his or her own life. In almost every case, it is told from the first-person point of view. Generally, an autobiography focuses on the most significant events and people in the writer's life over a period of time.

See also Memoir.

Ballad A ballad is a type of narrative poem that tells a story and was originally meant to be sung or recited. Because it tells a story, a ballad has a setting, a plot, and characters. Traditional ballads are written in four-line stanzas with regular rhythm and rhyme. Folk ballads were composed orally and handed down by word of mouth. These ballads usually tell about ordinary people who have unusual adventures or perform daring deeds. A literary ballad is a poem written by a poet in imitation of the form and content of a folk ballad.

Bias In a piece of writing, the author's bias is the side of an issue that he or she favors. Words with extremely positive or negative connotations are often a signal of an author's bias.

Bibliography A bibliography is a list of related books and other materials used to write a text. Bibliographies can be good sources for further study on a subject.

See also Works Consulted.

Biography A biography is the true account of a person's life, written by another person. As such, biographies are usually told from a third-person point of view. The writer of a biography usually researches his or her subject in order to present accurate information. The best biographers strive for honesty and balance in their accounts of their subjects' lives.

Blank Verse Blank verse is unrhymed poetry written in iambic pentameter. That is, each line of blank verse has five pairs of syllables. In most pairs, an unstressed syllable is followed by a stressed syllable. The most versatile of poetic forms, blank verse imitates the natural rhythms of English speech. Much of Shakespeare's drama is in blank verse.

Business Correspondence Business correspondence is written business communications such as business letters, e-mails, and memos. In general, business correspondence is brief, to the point, clear, courteous, and professional.

Cast of Characters In the script of a play, a cast of characters is a list of all the characters in the play, usually in order of appearance. It may include a brief description of each character.

Cause and Effect Two events are related by cause and effect when one event brings about, or causes, the other. The event that happens first is the **cause;** the one that follows

is the **effect**. Cause and effect is also a way of organizing an entire piece of writing. It helps writers show the relationships between events or ideas.

Character Characters are the people, animals, or imaginary creatures who take part in the action of a work of literature. Like real people, characters display certain qualities, or character traits, that develop and change over time, and they usually have motivations, or reasons, for their behaviors.

> **Central character:** Central or main characters are the most important characters in literary works. Generally, the plot of a short story focuses on one main character, but a novel may have several main characters.

> **Minor characters:** The less important characters in a literary work are known as minor characters. The story is not centered on them, but they help carry out the action of the story and help the reader learn more about the main character.

> **Dynamic character:** A dynamic character is one who undergoes important changes as a plot unfolds. The changes occur because of the character's actions and experiences in the story. The changes are usually internal and may be good or bad. Main characters are usually, though not always, dynamic.

> **Static character:** A static character is one who remains the same throughout a story. The character may experience events and have interactions with other characters, but he or she is not changed because of them.

See also Characterization; Character Traits.

Characterization The way a writer creates and develops characters is known as characterization. There are four basic methods of characterization:

- The writer may make direct comments about a character through the voice of the narrator.
- The writer may describe the character's physical appearance.
- The writer may present the character's own thoughts, speech, and actions.
- The writer may present thoughts, speech, and actions of other characters.

See also Character; Character Traits.

Character Traits Character traits are the qualities shown by a character. Traits may be physical (brown eyes) or expressions of personality (shyness). Writers reveal the traits of their characters through methods of characterization. Sometimes writers directly state a character's traits, but more often readers need to infer traits from a character's words, actions, thoughts, appearance, and relationships. Examples of words that describe traits include *courageous, humble, generous,* and *wild.*

Chronological Order Chronological order is the arrangement of events by their order of occurrence. This type of organization is used in fictional narratives and in historical writing, biography, and autobiography.

Claim In an argument, a claim is the writer's position on an issue or problem. Although an argument focuses on supporting one claim, a writer may make more than one claim in a text.

Clarify Clarifying is a strategy that helps readers understand or make clear what they are reading. Readers usually clarify by rereading, reading aloud, or discussing.

Classification Classification is a pattern of organization in which objects, ideas, and/or information are presented in groups, or classes, based on common characteristics.

Cliché A cliché is an overused expression. "Better late than never" and "hard as nails" are common examples. Good writers generally avoid clichés unless they are using them in dialogue to indicate something about a character's personality.

Climax The climax stage is the point of greatest interest in a story or play. The climax usually occurs toward the end of a story, after the reader has understood the conflict and become emotionally involved with the characters. At the climax, the conflict is resolved and the outcome of the plot usually becomes clear.

See also Plot.

Comedy A comedy is a dramatic work that is light and often humorous in tone, usually ending happily with a peaceful resolution of the main conflict.

Compare and Contrast To compare and contrast is to identify the similarities and differences of two or more subjects. Compare and contrast is also a pattern of organizing an entire piece of writing.

Conclusion A conclusion is a statement of belief based on evidence, experience, and reasoning. A valid conclusion is one that logically follows from the facts or statements upon which it is based.

Conflict A conflict is a struggle between opposing forces. Almost every story has a main conflict—a conflict that is the story's focus. An **external conflict** involves a character who struggles against a force outside him- or herself, such as nature, a physical obstacle, or another character. An **internal conflict** is one that occurs within a character. A **cultural conflict** is a struggle that arises because of differing values, customs, or circumstances between groups of people.

See also Plot.

Connect Connecting is a reader's process of relating the content of a text to his or her own knowledge and experience.

Connotation A word's connotations are the ideas and feelings associated with the word, as opposed to its dictionary definition. For example, the word *mother,* in addition to its basic meaning ("a female parent"), has connotations of love, warmth, and security.

Consonance Consonance is the repetition of consonant sounds within and at the end of words, as in "lonely afternoon." Consonance is unlike rhyme in that the vowel sounds preceding or following the repeated consonant sounds differ. Consonance is often used together with alliteration, assonance, and rhyme to create a musical quality, to emphasize certain words, or to unify a poem.

See also Alliteration.

Consumer Documents Consumer documents are printed materials that accompany products and services. They usually provide information about the use, care, operation, or assembly of the product or service they accompany. Some common consumer documents are applications, contracts, warranties, manuals, instructions, labels, brochures, and schedules.

Contemporary Literature Contemporary literature consists of works by authors who are currently writing today or who wrote in the recent past.

Context Clues When you encounter an unfamiliar word, you can often use context clues to understand it. Context clues are the words or phrases surrounding the word that provide hints about the word's meaning.

Counterargument A counterargument is an argument made to oppose another argument. A good argument anticipates opposing viewpoints and provides counterarguments to disprove them.

Couplet A couplet is a rhymed pair of lines. A couplet may be written in any rhythmic pattern.
See also Stanza.

Credibility Credibility is the believability or trustworthiness of a source and the information it provides.

Critical Essay *See* Essay.

Critical Review A critical review is an evaluation or critique by a reviewer, or critic. Types of reviews include film reviews, book reviews, music reviews, and art show reviews.

Database A database is a collection of information that can be quickly and easily accessed and searched and from which information can be easily retrieved. It is frequently presented in an electronic format.

Debate A debate is an organized exchange of opinions on an issue. In school settings, debate is usually a formal contest in which two opposing teams defend and attack a proposition.
See also Argument.

Deductive Reasoning Deductive reasoning is a way of thinking that begins with a generalization, presents a specific situation, and then moves forward with facts and evidence toward a logical conclusion. The following passage has a deductive argument embedded in it: "All students in the math class must take the quiz on Friday. Since Lana is in the class, she had better show up." This deductive argument can be broken down as follows: generalization—All students in the math class must take the quiz on Friday; specific situation—Lana is a student in the math class; conclusion—Therefore, Lana must take the math quiz.

Denotation A word's denotation is its dictionary definition.
See also Connotation.

Description Description is writing that helps a reader to picture events, objects, and characters. To create descriptions, writers often use imagery—words and phrases that appeal to the reader's senses.

Dialect A dialect is a form of a language that is spoken in a particular place or by a particular group of people. Dialects may feature unique pronunciations, vocabulary, and grammar.

Dialogue Dialogue is written conversation between two or more characters. Writers use dialogue to bring characters to life and to give readers insights into the characters' qualities, traits, and reactions to other characters. In fiction, dialogue is usually set off with quotation marks. In drama, stories are told primarily through dialogue.

Diary A diary is a daily record of a writer's thoughts, experiences, and feelings. As such, it is a type of autobiographical writing. The terms *diary* and *journal* are often used to mean the same thing.

Dictionary *See* Reference Works.

Drama A drama, or play, is a form of literature meant to be performed by actors in front of an audience. In a drama, the characters' dialogue and actions tell the story. The written form of a play is known as a script. A script usually includes dialogue, a cast of characters, and stage directions that give instructions about performing the drama. The person who writes the drama is known as the playwright or dramatist.

Dramatic Irony *See* Irony.

Draw Conclusions To draw a conclusion is to make a judgment or arrive at a belief based on evidence, experience, and reasoning.

Dynamic Character *See* Character.

Editorial An editorial is an opinion piece that usually appears on the editorial page of a newspaper or as part of a news broadcast. The editorial section of the newspaper presents opinions rather than objective news reports.

See also Op/Ed Piece.

Either/Or Fallacy An either/or fallacy is a statement that suggests that there are only two choices available in a situation when in fact there are more than two.

Elegy An elegy is an extended meditative poem in which the speaker reflects on death—often in tribute to a person who has died recently—or on an equally serious subject. Most elegies are written in formal, dignified language and are serious in tone.

Emotional Appeal An emotional appeal is a message that creates strong feelings in order to make a point. An appeal to fear is a message that taps into people's fear of losing their safety or security. An appeal to pity is a message that taps into people's sympathy and compassion for others to build support for an idea, a cause, or a proposed action. An appeal to vanity is a message that attempts to persuade by tapping into people's desire to feel good about themselves.

Encyclopedia *See* Reference Works.

Epic An epic is a long narrative poem on a serious subject, presented in an elevated or formal style. It traces the adventures of a great hero whose actions reflect the ideals and values of a nation or race. Epics address universal concerns, such as good and evil, life and death, and sin and redemption.

Essay An essay is a short work of nonfiction that deals with a single subject. There are many types of essays. An **expository essay** presents or explains information and ideas. A **personal essay** usually reflects the writer's experiences, feelings, and personality. A **persuasive essay** attempts to convince the reader to adopt a certain viewpoint. A **critical essay** evaluates a situation or a work of art.

Ethical Appeal In an ethical appeal, a writer links a claim to a widely accepted value in order to gain moral support for the claim. The appeal also creates an image of the writer as a trustworthy, moral person.

Evaluate To evaluate is to examine something carefully and to judge its value or worth. Evaluating is an important skill. A reader can evaluate the actions of a particular character, for example. A reader can also form opinions about the value of an entire work.

Evidence Evidence is a specific piece of information that is offered to support a claim. Evidence can take the form of a fact, a quotation, an example, a statistic, or a personal experience, among other things.

Exaggeration An extreme overstatement of an idea is called an exaggeration. It is often used for purposes of emphasis or humor.

Exposition Exposition is the first stage of a typical story plot. The exposition provides important background information and introduces the setting and the important characters. The conflict the characters face may also be introduced in the exposition, or it may be introduced later, in the rising action.

See also Plot.

Expository Essay *See* Essay.

Extended Metaphor An extended metaphor is a figure of speech that compares two essentially unlike things at some length and in several ways. It does not contain the words *like* or *as.*

See also Metaphor.

External Conflict *See* Conflict.

Fable A fable is a brief tale told to illustrate a moral or teach a lesson. Often the moral of a fable appears in a distinct and memorable statement near the tale's beginning or end.

See also Moral.

Fact Versus Opinion A fact is a statement that can be proved, or verified. An opinion, on the other hand, is a statement that cannot be proved because it expresses a person's beliefs, feelings, or thoughts.

See also Generalization; Inference.

Fallacy A fallacy is an error—usually in reasoning. Typically, a fallacy is based on an incorrect inference or a misuse of evidence.

See also Either/Or Fallacy; Logical Appeal; Overgeneralization.

Falling Action The falling action is the stage of the plot in which the story begins to draw to a close. The falling action comes after the climax and before the resolution. Events in the falling action show the results of the important decision or action that happened at the climax. Tension eases as the falling action begins; however, the final outcome of the story is not yet fully worked out at this stage.

See also Climax; Plot.

Fantasy Fantasy is a type of fiction that is highly imaginative and portrays events, settings, or characters that are unrealistic. The setting might be a nonexistent world, the plot might involve magic or the supernatural, and the characters might have superhuman powers.

Farce Farce is a type of exaggerated comedy that features an absurd plot, ridiculous situations, and humorous dialogue. The main purpose of a farce is to keep an audience laughing. Comic devices typically used in farces include mistaken identity, wordplay (such as puns and double meanings), and exaggeration.

Faulty Reasoning *See* Fallacy.

Feature Article A feature article is an article in a newspaper or magazine about a topic of human interest or lifestyles.

Fiction Fiction is prose writing that tells an imaginary story. The writer of a fictional work might invent all the events and characters or might base parts of the story on real people and events. The basic elements of fiction are plot, character, setting, and theme. Fiction includes both short stories and novels.

See also Novel; Short Story.

Figurative Language Figurative language is language that communicates meanings beyond the literal meanings of words. In figurative language, words are often used to symbolize ideas and concepts they would not otherwise be associated with. Writers use figurative language to create effects, to emphasize ideas, and to evoke emotions. Simile, metaphor, extended metaphor, hyperbole, and personification are examples of figurative language.

See also Hyperbole; Metaphor; Onomatopoeia; Personification; Simile.

First-Person Point of View *See* Point of View.

Flashback In a literary work, a flashback is an interruption of the action to present events that took place at an earlier time. A flashback provides information that can help a reader better understand a character's current situation.

Foil A foil is a character who provides a striking contrast to another character. By using a foil, a writer can call attention to certain traits possessed by a main character or simply enhance a character by contrast.

Folklore The traditions, customs, and stories that are passed down within a culture are known as its folklore. Folklore includes various types of literature, such as legends, folk tales, myths, trickster tales, and fables.

See also Fable; Folk Tale; Myth.

Folk Tale A folk tale is a story that has been passed from generation to generation by word of mouth. Folk tales may be set in the distant past and involve supernatural events. The characters in them may be animals, people, or superhuman beings.

Foreshadowing Foreshadowing occurs when a writer provides hints that suggest future events in a story. Foreshadowing creates suspense and makes readers eager to find out what will happen.

Form The structure or organization of a work of writing is often called its form. The form of a poem includes the arrangement of its words and lines on the page.

Free Verse Free verse is poetry that does not contain regular patterns of rhythm or rhyme.

The lines in free verse often flow more naturally than do rhymed, metrical lines and therefore achieve a rhythm more like that of everyday speech. Although free verse lacks conventional meter, it may contain various rhythmic and sound effects, such as repetitions of syllables or words. Free verse can be used for a variety of subjects.

See also Meter; Rhyme.

Generalization A generalization is a broad statement about a class or category of people, ideas, or things based on a study of, or a belief about, only some of its members.

See also Overgeneralization; Stereotyping.

Genre The term *genre* refers to a category in which a work of literature is classified. The major genres in literature are fiction, nonfiction, poetry, and drama.

Government Publications Government publications are documents produced by government organizations. Pamphlets, brochures, and reports are just some of the many forms these publications take. Government publications can be good resources for a wide variety of topics.

Graphic Aid A graphic aid is a visual tool that is printed, handwritten, or drawn. Charts, diagrams, graphs, photographs, and maps are examples of graphic aids.

Graphic Organizer A graphic organizer is a "word picture"—a visual illustration of a verbal statement—that helps a reader understand a text. Charts, tables, webs, and diagrams can all be graphic organizers. Graphic organizers and graphic aids can look the same. However, graphic organizers and graphic aids do differ in how they are used. Graphic aids help deliver important information to students using a text. Graphic organizers are actually created by students themselves. They help students understand the text or organize information.

Hero A hero is a main character or protagonist in a story. In older literary works, heroes tend to be better than ordinary humans. They are typically courageous, strong, honorable, and intelligent. They are protectors of society who hold back the forces of evil and fight to make the world a better place. In modern literature, a hero may simply be the most important character in a story. Such a hero is often an ordinary person with ordinary problems.

Historical Context The historical context of a literary work refers to the social conditions that inspired or influenced its creation. To understand and appreciate certain works, the reader must relate them to particular events in history.

Historical Document Historical documents are writings that have played a significant role in human events. The Declaration of Independence, for example, is a historical document.

Historical Dramas Historical dramas are plays that take place in the past and are based on real events. In many of these plays, the characters are also based on real historical figures. The dialogue and the action, however, are mostly created by the playwright.

Historical Fiction A short story or a novel can be called historical fiction when it is set in the past and includes real places and real events of historical importance.

How-To Book A how-to book explains how to do something—usually an activity, a sport, or a household project.

Humor Humor is a quality that provokes laughter or amusement. Writers create humor through exaggeration, amusing descriptions, irony, and witty and insightful dialogue.

Hyperbole Hyperbole is a figure of speech in which the truth is exaggerated for emphasis or humorous effect.

Idiom An idiom is an expression that has a meaning different from the meaning of its individual words. For example, "to go to the dogs" is an idiom meaning "to go to ruin."

Imagery Imagery consists of descriptive words and phrases that re-create sensory experiences for the reader. Imagery usually appeals to one or more of the five senses— sight, hearing, smell, taste, and touch—to help the reader imagine exactly what is being described. Note the appeals to sight, taste, and touch in the following lines: The aroma of popcorn drew me to the bright red concession stand.

Implied Main Idea *See* Main Idea.

Index The index of a book is an alphabetized list of important topics covered in the book and the page numbers on which they can be found. An index can be used to quickly find specific information about a topic.

Inductive Reasoning Inductive reasoning is the process of logical reasoning that starts with observations, examples, and facts and moves on to a general conclusion or principle.

Inference An inference is a logical guess that is made based on facts and one's own knowledge and experience.

Informational Text Informational text is writing that provides factual information. It often explains an idea or teaches a process. Examples include news reports, science textbooks, software instructions, and lab reports.

Internal Conflict *See* Conflict.

Internet The Internet is a global, interconnected system of computer networks that allows for communication through e-mail, listservs, and the World Wide Web. The Internet connects computers and computer users throughout the world.

Interview An interview is a conversation conducted by a writer or reporter in which facts or statements are elicited from another person, recorded, and then broadcast or published.

Irony Irony is a special kind of contrast between appearance and reality—usually one in which reality is the opposite of what it seems. One type of irony is **situational irony,** a contrast between what a reader or character expects and what actually exists or happens. Another type of irony is **dramatic irony,** where the reader or viewer knows something that a character does not know. **Verbal irony** exists when someone knowingly exaggerates or says one thing and means another.

Journal A journal is a periodical publication issued by a legal, medical, or other professional organization. The term may also be used to refer to a diary or daily record.

See also Diary.

Legend A legend is a story handed down from the past about a specific person, usually someone of heroic accomplishments. Legends usually have some basis in historical fact.

Limerick A limerick is a short, humorous poem composed of five lines. It usually has the rhyme scheme *aabba,* created by two rhyming couplets followed by a fifth line that rhymes with the first couplet. A limerick typically has a sing-song rhythm.

Limited Point of View *See* Point of View.

Line The line is the core unit of a poem. In poetry, line length is an essential element of the poem's meaning and rhythm. Line breaks, where a line of poetry ends, may coincide with grammatical units. However, a line break may also occur in the middle of a grammatical unit, therefore creating a meaningful pause or emphasis. Poets use a variety of line breaks to play with sense, grammar, and syntax and thereby create a wide range of effects.

Loaded Language Loaded language consists of words with strongly positive or negative connotations intended to influence a reader's or listener's attitude.

Logical Appeal A logical appeal is a way of writing or speaking that relies on logic and facts. It appeals to people's reasoning or intellect rather than to their values or emotions. Flawed logical appeals—that is, errors in reasoning—are called logical fallacies.

See also Fallacy.

Lyric Poetry A lyric poem is a short poem in which a single speaker expresses personal thoughts and feelings. Most poems other than dramatic and narrative poems are lyric poems. In ancient Greece, lyric poetry was meant to be sung. Modern lyrics are usually not intended for singing, but they are characterized by strong melodic rhythms. Lyric poetry has a variety of forms and covers many subjects, from love and death to everyday experiences.

Main Idea The main idea is the central or most important idea about a topic that a writer or speaker conveys. It can be the central idea of an entire work or of just a paragraph. Often, the main idea of a paragraph is expressed in a topic sentence. However, a main idea may just be implied, or suggested, by details. A main idea is typically supported by details.

Make Inferences *See* Inference.

Memoir A memoir is a form of autobiographical writing in which a writer shares his or her personal experiences and observations of significant events or people. Often informal or even intimate in tone, memoirs usually give readers insight into the impact of historical events on people's lives.

See also Autobiography.

Metaphor A metaphor is a comparison of two things that are basically unlike but have some qualities in common. Unlike a simile, a metaphor does not contain the words *like* or *as*.

See also Extended Metaphor; Figurative Language; Simile.

Meter Meter is a regular pattern of stressed and unstressed syllables in a poem. The meter of a poem emphasizes the musical quality of the language. Each unit of meter, known as a **foot**, consists of one stressed syllable and one or two unstressed syllables. In representations of meter, a stressed syllable is indicated by the symbol (ˊ); an unstressed syllable by the symbol (˘). The four basic types of metrical feet are the iamb, an unstressed syllable followed by a stressed syllable (˘ˊ); the trochee, a stressed syllable followed by an unstressed syllable (ˊ˘); the anapest, two unstressed syllables followed by a stressed syllable (˘˘ˊ); and the dactyl, a stressed syllable followed by two unstressed syllables (ˊ˘˘).

See also Rhythm.

Minor Character *See* Character.

Monitor Monitoring is the strategy of checking your comprehension as you read and modifying the strategies you are using to suit your needs. Monitoring often includes the following strategies: questioning, clarifying, visualizing, predicting, connecting, and rereading.

Mood Mood is the feeling or atmosphere that a writer creates for the reader. Descriptive words, imagery, and figurative language all influence the mood of a work.

See also Tone.

Moral A moral is a lesson that a story teaches. A moral is often stated at the end of a fable. Other times, the moral is implied.

See also Fable.

Motivation *See* Character.

Myth A myth is a traditional story, usually concerning some superhuman being or unlikely event, that was once widely believed to be true. Frequently, myths were attempts to explain natural phenomena, such as solar and lunar eclipses or the cycle of the seasons. For some peoples, myths were both a kind of science and a religion. In addition, myths served as literature and entertainment, just as they do for modern-day audiences.

Narrative Nonfiction Narrative nonfiction is writing that reads much like fiction, except that the characters, setting, and events are based on real life.

Narrative Poetry Poetry that tells a story is called narrative poetry. Like fiction, a narrative poem contains characters, a setting, and a plot. It might also contain such elements of poetry as rhyme, rhythm, imagery, and figurative language.

Narrator The narrator is the voice that tells a story. Sometimes the narrator is a character in the story. At other times, the narrator is an outside voice created by the writer. The narrator is not the same as the writer. An **unreliable narrator** is one who tells a story or interprets events in a way that makes readers doubt what he or she is saying. An unreliable narrator is usually a character in the story. The narrator may be unreliable for a number of different reasons. For example, the narrator may not have all the facts or may be too young to understand the situation.

See also Point of View.

News Article A news article is writing that reports on a recent event. In newspapers, news articles are usually brief and to the point, presenting the most important facts first, followed by more detailed information.

Nonfiction Nonfiction is writing that tells about real people, places, and events. Unlike fiction, nonfiction is mainly written to convey factual information. Nonfiction includes a wide range of writing—newspaper articles, letters, essays, biographies, movie reviews, speeches, true-life adventure stories, advertising, and more.

Novel A novel is a long work of fiction. Like a short story, a novel is the product of a writer's imagination. Because a novel is considerably longer than a short story, a novelist can develop the characters and story line more thoroughly.

See also Fiction.

Ode An ode is a type of lyric poem that deals with serious themes, such as justice, truth, or beauty. Odes appeal to both the imagination and the intellect, and many commemorate events or praise people or elements of nature.

Omniscient Point of View *See* Point of View.

Onomatopoeia Onomatopoeia is the use of words whose sounds echo their meanings, such as *buzz, whisper, gargle,* and *murmur.* As a literary technique, onomatopoeia goes beyond the use of simple echoing words. Skilled writers, especially poets, choose words whose sounds intensify images and suggest meaning.

Op/Ed Piece An op/ed piece is an opinion piece that typically appears opposite ("op") the editorial page of a newspaper. Unlike editorials, op/ed pieces are written and submitted by readers.

Oral Literature Oral literature consists of stories that have been passed down by word of mouth from generation to generation. Oral literature includes folk tales, legends, and myths. In more recent times, some examples of oral literature have been written down or recorded so that the stories can be preserved.

Organization *See* Pattern of Organization.

Overgeneralization An overgeneralization is a generalization that is too broad. You can often recognize overgeneralizations by the appearance of words and phrases such as *all,* *everyone, every time, any, anything, no one,* or *none.* An example is "None of the city's workers really cares about keeping the environment clean." In all probability, there are many exceptions. The writer can't possibly know the feelings of every city worker.

Overview An overview is a short summary of a story, a speech, or an essay.

Parallel Episodes Parallel episodes occur when elements of a plot are repeated several times in the course of a story. Fairy tales often employ parallel episodes, as in the examples of "Goldilocks and the Three Bears" and "The Three Little Pigs."

Paraphrase Paraphrasing is the restating of information in one's own words.

See also Summarize.

Part-by-Part Order Part-by-part order is a pattern of organization in which one idea or group of ideas suggests another, which suggests another, and so on until the end.

Pattern of Organization The term *pattern of organization* refers to the way ideas and information are arranged and organized. Patterns of organization include cause and effect, chronological, compare and contrast, classification, part-by-part, and problem-solution, among others.

See also Cause and Effect; Chronological Order; Classification; Compare and Contrast; Part-by-Part Order; Problem-Solution Order; Sequential Order.

Periodical A periodical is a magazine or other publication that is issued on a regular basis.

Personal Essay *See* Essay.

Personification The giving of human qualities to an animal, object, or idea is known as personification.

See also Figurative Language.

Persuasion Persuasion is the art of swaying others' feelings, beliefs, or actions. Persuasion normally appeals to both the mind and the emotions of the reader.

See also Appeal to Authority; Emotional Appeal; Ethical Appeal; Loaded Language;

Logical Appeal.

Persuasive Essay *See* Essay.

Play *See* Drama.

Playwright *See* Drama.

Plot The series of events in a story is called the plot. The plot usually centers on a **conflict,** or struggle, faced by the main character. The action that the characters take to solve the problem builds toward a **climax** in the story. At this point, or shortly afterward, the problem is solved and the story ends. Most story plots have five stages: exposition, rising action, climax, falling action, and resolution.

See also Climax; Conflict; Exposition; Falling Action; Rising Action.

Poetry Poetry is a type of literature in which words are carefully chosen and arranged to create certain effects. Poets use a variety of sound devices, imagery, and figurative language to express emotions and ideas.

See also Alliteration; Assonance; Ballad; Free Verse; Imagery; Meter; Narrative Poetry; Rhyme; Rhythm; Stanza.

Point of View Point of view refers to the method of narration used in a short story, novel, narrative poem, or work of nonfiction. In a work told from a **first-person** point of view, the narrator is a character in the story. In a work told from a **third-person** point of view, the narrative voice is outside the action, not one of the characters. If a story is told from a **third-person omniscient,** or all-knowing, point of view, the narrator sees into the minds of all the characters. If events are relayed from a **third-person limited** point of view, the narrator tells what only one character thinks, feels, and observes.

See also Narrator.

Predict Predicting is a reading strategy that involves using text clues to make a reasonable guess about what will happen next in a story.

Primary Source *See* Source.

Prior Knowledge Prior knowledge is the knowledge a reader already possesses about a topic. This information might come from personal experiences, expert accounts, books, films, or other sources.

Problem-Solution Order Problem-solution order is a pattern of organization in which a problem is stated and analyzed and then one or more solutions are proposed and examined.

Prop The word *prop,* originally an abbreviation of the word *property,* refers to any physical object that is used in a drama.

Propaganda Propaganda is any form of communication that is so distorted that it conveys false or misleading information to advance a specific belief or cause.

Prose The word *prose* refers to all forms of writing that are not in verse form. The term may be used to describe very different forms of writing—short stories as well as essays, for example.

Protagonist A protagonist is the main character in a story, play, or novel. The protagonist is involved in the main conflict of the story. Usually, the protagonist undergoes changes as the plot runs its course.

Public Document Public documents are documents that were written for the public to provide information that is of public interest or concern. They include government documents, speeches, signs, and rules and regulations.

See also Government Publications.

Radio Play A radio play is a drama that is written specifically to be broadcast over the radio. Because the audience is not meant to see a radio play, sound effects are often used to help listeners imagine the setting and the action. The stage directions in the play's script indicate the sound effects.

Recurring Theme *See* Theme.

Reference Works Reference works are sources that contain facts and background information on a wide range of subjects. Most reference works are good sources of reliable information because they have been reviewed by experts. The following are some common reference works: encyclopedias, dictionaries, thesauri, almanacs, atlases, and directories.

Repetition Repetition is a technique in which a sound, word, phrase, or line is repeated for emphasis or unity. Repetition often helps to reinforce meaning and create an appealing rhythm.

See also Alliteration; Sound Devices.

Resolution *See* Falling Action.

Review *See* Critical Review.

Rhetorical Question Rhetorical questions are those that have such obvious answers that they do not require a reply. Writers often use them to suggest that their claim is so obvious that everyone should agree with it.

Rhyme Rhyme is the occurrence of similar or identical sounds at the end of two or more words, such as *suite, heat,* and *complete.* Rhyme that occurs within a single line of poetry is internal rhyme. Rhyme that occurs at the ends of lines of poetry is called end rhyme. End rhyme that is not exact but approximate is called slant rhyme, or off rhyme.

Rhyme Scheme A rhyme scheme is a pattern of end rhymes in a poem. A rhyme scheme is noted by assigning a letter of the alphabet, beginning with *a,* to each line. Lines that rhyme are given the same letter.

Rhythm Rhythm is a pattern of stressed and unstressed syllables in a line of poetry. Poets use rhythm to bring out the musical quality of language, to emphasize ideas, and to create moods. Devices such as alliteration, rhyme, assonance, and consonance often contribute to creating rhythm.

See also Meter.

Rising Action The rising action is the stage of the plot that develops the conflict, or struggle. During this stage, events occur that make the conflict more complicated. The events in the rising action build toward a climax, or turning point.

See also Plot.

Scanning Scanning is the process used to search through a text for a particular fact or piece of information. When you scan, you sweep your eyes across a page, looking for key words that may lead you to the information you want.

Scene In a drama, the action is often divided into acts and scenes. Each scene presents an episode of the play's plot and typically occurs at a single place and time.

See also Act.

Scenery Scenery is a painted backdrop or other structures used to create the setting for a play.

Science Fiction Science fiction is fiction in which a writer explores unexpected possibilities of the past or the future, using known scientific data and theories as well as his or her creative imagination. Most science fiction writers create believable worlds, although some create fantasy worlds that have familiar elements.

See also Fantasy.

Scope Scope refers to a work's focus. For example, an article about Austin, Texas, that focuses on the city's history, economy, and residents has a broad scope. An article that focuses only on the restaurants in Austin has a narrower scope.

Screenplay A screenplay is a play written for film.

Script The text of a play, film, or broadcast is called a script.

Secondary Source *See* Source.

Sensory Details Sensory details are words and phrases that appeal to the reader's senses of sight, hearing, touch, smell, and taste.

See also Imagery.

Sequential Order Sequential order is a pattern of organization that shows the order of steps or stages in a process.

Setting The setting of a story, poem, or play is the time and place of the action. Sometimes the setting is clear and well-defined. At other times, it is left to the reader's imagination. Elements of setting include geographic location, historical period (past, present, or future), season, time of day, and culture.

Setting a Purpose The process of establishing specific reasons for reading a text is called setting a purpose.

Short Story A short story is a work of fiction that centers on a single idea and can be read in one sitting. Generally, a short story has one main conflict that involves the characters and keeps the story moving.

See also Fiction.

Sidebar A sidebar is additional information set in a box alongside or within a news or feature article. Popular magazines often make use of sidebars.

Signal Words In a text, signal words are words and phrases that help show how events or ideas are related. Some common examples of signal words are *and, but, however, nevertheless, therefore,* and *in addition.*

Simile A simile is a figure of speech that makes a comparison between two unlike things using the words *like* or *as*: My heart is pounding like a jackhammer.

See also Figurative Language; Metaphor.

Situational Irony *See* Irony.

Sonnet A sonnet is a poem that has a formal structure, containing 14 lines and a specific rhyme scheme and meter. A sonnet often consists of three quatrains, or four-line units, and a final couplet. The sonnet, which means "little song," can be used for a variety of subjects.

See also Couplet; Rhyme Scheme.

Sound Devices Sound devices, or uses of words for their connection to the sense of hearing, can convey meaning and mood or unify a work. Some common sound devices are **alliteration, assonance, consonance, meter, onomatopoeia, repetition, rhyme,** and **rhythm.**

See also Alliteration; Assonance; Consonance; Meter; Onomatopoeia; Repetition; Rhyme; Rhythm.

Source A source is anything that supplies information. **Primary sources** are materials created by people who witnessed or took part in the event they supply information about. Letters, diaries, autobiographies, and eyewitness accounts are primary sources. **Secondary sources** are those made by people who were not directly involved in the event or even present when it occurred. Encyclopedias, textbooks, biographies, and most news articles are examples of secondary sources.

Speaker In poetry, the speaker is the voice that "talks" to the reader, similar to the narrator in fiction. The speaker is not necessarily the poet.

Speech A speech is a talk or public address. The purpose of a speech may be to entertain, to explain, to persuade, to inspire, or any combination of these purposes.

Stage Directions In the script of a play, the instructions to the actors, director, and stage crew are called the stage directions. Stage directions might suggest scenery, lighting, sound effects, and ways for actors to move and speak. Stage directions often appear in parentheses and in italic type.

Stanza A stanza is a group of two or more lines that form a unit in a poem. Each stanza may have the same number of lines, or the number of lines may vary.

See also Couplet; Form; Poetry.

Static Character *See* Character.

Stereotype In literature, characters who are defined by a single trait are known as stereotypes. Such characters do not usually demonstrate the complexities of real people. Familiar stereotypes in popular literature include the absent-minded professor and the busybody.

Stereotyping Stereotyping is a dangerous type of overgeneralization. It can lead to unfair judgments of people based on their ethnic background, beliefs, practices, or physical appearance.

Structure The structure of a work of literature is the way in which it is put together. In poetry, structure involves the arrangement of words and lines to produce a desired effect. One structural unit in poetry is the stanza. In prose, structure involves the arrangement of such elements as sentences, paragraphs, and events.

Style A style is a manner of writing. It involves how something is said rather than what is said.

Subplot A subplot is an additional, or secondary, plot in a story. The subplot contains its own conflict, which is often separate from the main conflicts of the story.

Summarize To summarize is to briefly retell the main ideas of a piece of writing in one's own words.

See also Paraphrase.

Support Support is any information that helps to prove a claim.

Supporting Detail *See* Main Idea.

Surprise Ending A surprise ending is an unexpected plot twist at the end of a story. The surprise may be a sudden turn in the action or a piece of information that gives a different perspective to the entire story.

Suspense Suspense is a feeling of growing tension and excitement felt by a reader. Suspense makes a reader curious about the outcome of a story or an event within a story. A writer creates suspense by raising questions in the reader's mind. The use of foreshadowing is one way that writers create suspense.

See also Foreshadowing.

Symbol A symbol is a person, a place, an object, an animal, or an activity that stands for something beyond itself. For example, a flag is a colored piece of cloth that stands for a country. A white dove is a bird that represents peace.

Synthesize To synthesize information means to take individual pieces of information and combine them in order to gain a better understanding of a subject.

Tall Tale A tall tale is a humorously exaggerated story about impossible events, often involving the supernatural abilities of the main character.

Text Feature Text features are elements of a text, such as boldface type, headings, and subheadings, that help organize and call attention to important information. Italic type, bulleted or numbered lists, sidebars, and graphic aids such as charts, tables, timelines, illustrations, and photographs are also considered text features.

Theme A theme is a message about life or human nature that the writer shares with the reader. In many cases, readers must infer what the writer's message is. One way of figuring out a theme is to apply the lessons learned by the main characters to people in real life.

> **Recurring themes:** Themes found in a variety of works. For example, authors from different backgrounds might express similar themes having to do with the importance of family values.

> **Universal themes:** Themes that are found throughout the literature of all time periods.

See also Moral.

Thesaurus *See* Reference Works.

Thesis Statement A thesis statement is the main proposition that a writer attempts to support in a piece of writing. It serves as the controlling idea of the composition.

Third-Person Point of View *See* Point of View.

Title The title of a piece of writing is the name that is attached to it. A title often refers to an important aspect of the work.

Tone The tone of a literary work expresses the writer's attitude toward his or her subject. Words such as *angry, sad,* and *humorous* can be used to describe different tones.

See also Author's Perspective; Mood.

Topic Sentence The topic sentence of a paragraph states the paragraph's main idea. All other sentences in the paragraph provide supporting details.

Tragedy A tragedy is a dramatic work that presents the downfall of a dignified character or characters involved in historically or socially significant events. The events in a tragic plot are set in motion by a decision that is often an error in judgment on the part of the hero. Succeeding events are linked in a cause-and-effect relationship and lead inevitably to a disastrous conclusion, usually death.

Traits *See* Character Traits.

Treatment The way a topic is handled in a work is referred to as its treatment. Treatment includes the form the writing takes as well as the writer's purpose and tone.

Turning Point *See* Climax.

Understatement Understatement is a technique of creating emphasis by saying less than is actually or literally true. It is the opposite of **hyperbole,** or exaggeration. Understatement is often used to create a humorous effect.

Universal Theme *See* Theme.

Unreliable Narrator *See* Narrator.

Verbal Irony *See* Irony.

Visualize Visualizing is the process of forming a mental picture based on written or spoken information.

Voice The term *voice* refers to a writer's unique use of language that allows a reader to "hear" a human personality in the writer's work. Elements of style that contribute to a writer's voice can reveal much about the author's personality, beliefs, and attitudes.

Website A website is a collection of "pages" on the World Wide Web that is usually devoted to one specific subject. Pages are linked together and accessed by clicking hyperlinks or menus, which send the user from page to page within a website. Websites are created by companies, organizations, educational institutions, branches of the government, the military, and individuals.

Word Choice The success of any writing depends on the writer's choice of words. Words not only communicate ideas but also help describe events, characters, settings, and so on. Word choice can make a writer's work sound formal or informal, serious or humorous. A writer must choose words carefully depending on the goal of the piece of writing. For example, a writer working on a science article would probably use technical, formal words; a writer trying to establish the setting in a short story would probably use more descriptive words.

See also Style.

Workplace Document Workplace documents are materials that are produced or used within a work setting, usually to aid in the functioning of the workplace. They include job applications, office memos, training manuals, job descriptions, and sales reports.

Works Cited The term *works cited* refers to a list of all the works a writer has referred to in his or her text. This list often includes not only books and articles but also Internet sources.

Works Consulted The term *works consulted* refers to a list of all the works a writer consulted in order to create his or her text. It is not limited just to those works cited in the text.

See also Bibliography.

Using the Glossary

This glossary is an alphabetical list of vocabulary words found in the selections in this book. Use this glossary just as you would a dictionary—to determine the meanings, parts of speech, pronunciation, and syllabication of words. (Some technical, foreign, and more obscure words in this book are not listed here but are defined for you in the footnotes that accompany many of the selections.)

Many words in the English language have more than one meaning. This glossary gives the meanings that apply to the words as they are used in the selections in this book. Words closely related in form and meaning are listed together in one entry (for instance, *consumption* and *consume*), and the definition is given for the first form.

The following abbreviations are used to identify parts of speech of words:

adj. adjective   *adv.* adverb   *n.* noun   *v.* verb

Each word's pronunciation is given in parentheses. A guide to the pronunciation symbols appears in the Pronunciation Key below. The stress marks in the Pronunciation Key are used to indicate the force given to each syllable in a word. They can also help you determine where words are divided into syllables.

For more information about the words in this glossary or for information about words not listed here, consult a dictionary.

Pronunciation Key

Symbol	Examples	Symbol	Examples	Symbol	Examples
ă	pat	m	mum	v	valve
ā	pay	n	no, sudden	w	with
ä	father	ng	thing	y	yes
âr	care	ŏ	pot	z	zebra, xylem
b	bib	ō	toe	zh	vision, pleasure, garage
ch	church	ô	caught, paw		
d	deed, milled	oi	noise	ə	about, item, edible, gallop, circus
ĕ	pet	o͝o	took		
ē	bee	o͞o	boot	ər	butter
f	fife, phase, rough	ou	out		
g	gag	p	pop		
h	hit	r	roar	**Sounds in Foreign Words**	
hw	which	s	sauce	KH	*German* ich, ach; *Scottish* loch
ĭ	pit	sh	ship, dash	N	*French*, bon
ī	pie, by	t	tight, stopped	œ	*French* feu, œuf; *German* schön
îr	pier	th	thin		
j	judge	*th*	this	ü	*French* tu; *German* über
k	kick, cat, pique	ŭ	cut		
l	lid, needle*	ûr	urge, term, firm, word, heard		

* In English the consonants *l* and *n* often constitute complete syllables by themselves.

Stress Marks

The relevant emphasis with which the syllables of a word or phrase are spoken, called stress, is indicated in three different ways. The strongest, or primary, stress is marked with a bold mark (´). An intermediate, or secondary, level of stress is marked with a similar but lighter mark (´). The weakest stress is unmarked. Words of one syllable show no stress mark.

Glossary of Academic Vocabulary

access (ăkˊsĕs) *n.* a way of approaching or making use of

civil (sĭvˊəl) *adj.* of, or related to, citizens and their relations with each other and the state

commentary (kŏmˊən-tĕrˊē) *n.* explanation or interpretation in the form of comments or observations

communicate (kə-myōōˊnĭ-kātˊ) *v.* to convey information or exchange ideas

contribute (kən-trĭbˊyōōt) *v.* to give or supply for a common purpose

convention (kən-vĕnˊshən) *n.* a practice or procedure widely used by a group; a custom

debate (dĭ-bātˊ) *v.* to engage in arguments by discussing opposing points

deduce (dĭ-dōōsˊ) *v.* to reach a conclusion or decision through reasoning

demonstrate (dĕmˊən-stātˊ) *v.* to show clearly and deliberately

document (dŏcˊyə-mənt) *n.* written or printed paper that provides evidence or information

draft (drăft) *n.; v.* early versions or stages of a written document or plan; to write such a version

immigrate (ĭmˊĭ-grātˊ) *v.* to enter and settle in a new country

liberation (lĭbˊə-rāˊshən) *n.* the act of freeing or the state of being free

license (līˊsəns) *n.* a document that is issued as proof of legal permission to do something

minors (mīˊnərz) *n.* people who have not reached legal adulthood

occupation (ŏkˊyə-pāˊshən) *n.* an activity that serves as one's source of income

option (ŏpˊshən) *n.* something chosen or available as a choice

philosophy (fĭ-lŏsˊə-fē) *n.* the underlying theory or set of ideas related to life as a whole

predict (prĭ-dĭktˊ) *v.* to tell about in advance, especially on the basis of special knowledge

psychology (sī-kŏlˊə-jē) *n.* the study of mental processes and behaviors

publish (pŭbˊlĭsh) *v.* to prepare and issue a book or other material to the public

reaction (rē-ăkˊshən) *n.* a response to something

relocate (rē-lōˊkāt) *v.* to move to a new place

shifting (shĭftˊĭng) *adj.* changing attitudes, judgments, or emphases

style (stīl) *n.* the way in which something is said, done, expressed, or performed

sufficient (sə-fĭshˊənt) *adj.* being enough, or as much as needed

summary (sŭmˊə-rē) *n.* a condensed, or shorter, report that includes the main points of a text or event

symbolize (sĭmˊbə-līzˊ) *v.* to serve as a symbol of, or represent something else

technique (tĕk-nēkˊ) *n.* the systematic or orderly procedure by which a task is accomplished

trend (trĕnd) *n.* the general direction of something; a current style

Glossary of Critical Vocabulary

alacrity (ə-lăk´rĭ-tē) *n. Alacrity* is cheerful willingness or eagerness.

anecdote (ăn´ĭk-dōt´) *n.* An *anecdote* is a short account of an incident.

apprehension (ăp´rĭ-hĕn´shən) *n. Apprehension* is the fear or dread of the future.

arbitrary (är´bĭ-trĕr´ē) *adj.* If something is *arbitrary,* it is determined by chance or whim.

askew (ə-skyōō´) *adj.* When something is *askew,* it is off center.

attain (ə-tān´) *v.* If you *attain* something, you gain it or achieve it.

audacity (ô-dăs´ĭ-tē) *n. Audacity* is shameless daring or boldness.

autonomous (ô-tôn´ə-məs) *adj.* If someone is *autonomous,* the person is independent and not controlled by outside forces.

avert (ə-vûrt´) *v.* If you *avert* something, you prevent it from happening.

banal (bə-năl´) *adj.* If something is *banal,* it is very commonplace, dull, and unoriginal.

bane (bān) *n.* A *bane* is a cause of death, destruction, or ruin.

boon (bōōn) *n.* A *boon* is a gift or benefit.

borne (bôrn) *v.* If something is *borne,* it is carried or supported.

bravado (brə-vä´dō) *n. Bravado* is a false show of bravery.

cajole (kə-jōl´) *v.* When you *cajole,* you coax or urge gently.

chide (chīd) *v.* To *chide* is to scold or correct in some way.

cohort (kō´hôrt´) *n.* A *cohort* is a group or band of people.

commence (kə-mĕns´) *v.* When things *commence,* they begin or start.

compensation (kŏm´pən-sā´shən) *n. Compensation* is something, such as money, that is received as payment.

conceive (kən-sēv´) *v.* When you *conceive* an idea, you think of it.

condole (kən-dōl´) *v.* If you *condole* with someone, you express sympathy or sorrow.

confluence (kŏn´flōō-əns) *n.* A *confluence* is a gathering or joining together in one place.

conjecture (kən-jĕk´chər) *v.* If you *conjecture,* you guess or suppose.

contemplate (kŏn´təm-plāt´) *v.* When you *contemplate,* you look at something attentively and thoughtfully.

contractor (kŏn´trăk´tər) *n.* A *contractor* is a person who agrees to provide services for a specific price.

coup (kōō) *n.* A *coup* is the sudden overthrow of a government by a group of people.

covet (kŭv´ĭt) *v.* If you *covet* something, you strongly wish for it.

credulity (krĭ-dōō´lĭ-tē) *n. Credulity* is a tendency to believe too readily.

crevice (krĕv´ĭs) *n.* A *crevice* is a narrow crack.

deficiency (dĭ-fĭsh´ən-sē) *n.* A *deficiency* is a lack or shortage of something.

degradation (dĕg´rə-dā´shən) *n. Degradation* is the condition of being brought to a lower level or humiliated.

denunciation (dĭ-nŭn´sē-ā´shən) *n.* A *denunciation* is the public condemnation of something as wrong or evil.

derision (dĭ-rĭzh´ən) *n. Derision* is jeering laughter or ridicule.

despondent (dĭ-spŏn´dənt) *adj.* Someone who is *despondent* feels a loss of hope or confidence.

detrimental (dĕt´rə-mĕn´tl) *adj.* If something is *detrimental,* it causes damage or harm.

diffuse (dĭ-fyōōs´) *adj.* If something is *diffuse,* it is very spread out or scattered.

dilapidated (dĭ-lăp´ĭ-dā´tĭd) *adj.* If something is *dilapidated,* it is falling apart.

disheveled (dĭ-shĕv´əld) *adj.* When something is *disheveled*, it is messy or untidy.

dispatcher (dĭs-păch´ər) *n.* A *dispatcher* is a person who sends out vehicles according to a schedule.

dispel (dĭ-spĕl´) *v.* When you *dispel* something, you drive it away.

dispossess (dĭs´pə-zĕs´) *v.* To *dispossess* someone is to deny him or her possession of something.

egregious (ĭ-grē´jəs) *adj.* If something is *egregious*, it is very bad or offensive.

eloquence (ĕl´ə-kwəns) *n.* *Eloquence* is the ability to speak powerfully and persuasively.

emblematic (ĕm´blə măt´ĭk) *adj.* If something is *emblematic*, it is a symbol for something else.

evoke (ĭ-vōk´) *v.* When you *evoke* something, you summon it.

expiration (ĕk´spə-rā´shən) *n.* *Expiration* is the act of exhaling or breathing out.

exuberance (ĭg-zoō´bər-əns) *n.* *Exuberance* is a condition of unrestrained joy.

fate (fāt) *n.* *Fate* is a power that is thought to determine the course of events.

feeble (fē´bəl) *adj.* If someone is *feeble*, the person is very weak.

foreman (fôr´mən) *n.* A *foreman* is the leader of a work crew.

grimace (grĭm´ĭs) *n.* A *grimace* is a facial expression of pain or disgust.

grope (grōp) *v.* When you *grope*, you reach about in an uncertain way.

hypocritical (hĭp´ə-krĭt´-kəl) *adj.* If someone is *hypocritical*, the person is false or deceptive.

impervious (ĭm-pûr´vē-əs) *adj.* If something is *impervious*, it is impossible to penetrate.

impetuous (ĭm-pĕch´oō-əs) *adj.* If someone is *impetuous*, he or she acts without thinking things through.

implication (ĭm´plĭ-kā´shən) *n.* An *implication* is a connection or consequence.

impotent (ĭm´pə-tənt) *adj.* If someone is *impotent*, he or she is lacking strength or vigor.

inadequate (ĭn-ăd´ĭ-kwĭt) *adj.* If something is *inadequate*, it is insufficient or not enough.

incisive (ĭn-sī´sĭv) *adj.* If something is *incisive*, it is penetrating, clear, and sharp.

ineradicable (ĭn´ĭ răd´ĭ-kə-bəl) *adj.* If something is *ineradicable*, it is impossible to remove.

initiative (ĭ-nĭsh´ə-tĭv) *n.* An *initiative* is a beginning step in a plan.

insolent (ĭn´sə-lənt) *adj.* If someone is *insolent*, he or she is rude or disrespectful.

instill (ĭn-stĭl´) *v.* When you *instill* something, you supply it gradually.

intensify (ĭn-tĕn´sə-fī´) *v.* If you *intensify* something, you make it grow in strength.

intersperse (ĭn´tər-spûrs´) *adj.* If you *intersperse* something, you distribute it in different places.

irate (ī-rāt´) *adj.* If you are *irate*, you are very angry.

jubilation (joō´bə-lā´shən) *n.* *Jubilation* is the act of celebrating.

justify (jŭs´tə-fī´) *v.* If you *justify* something, you prove it is right or valid.

legitimately (lə-jĭt´ə-mĭt-lē) *adv.* When you do something *legitimately*, you do it lawfully.

linger (lĭng´gər) *v.* When you *linger*, you remain or stay longer.

looter (loōt´ər) *n.* A *looter* is someone who steals during a war or riot.

mediate (mē´dē-āt´) *v.* If you *mediate* a conflict, you try to settle the differences.

muted (myoō´tĭd) *adj.* When something is *muted*, it is softened or muffled.

natal (nāt´l) *adj.* If something is *natal*, it relates to birth.

naturalize (năch´ər-ə-līz´) *v.* When governments *naturalize* people, they grant them full citizenship.

nominal (nŏm´ə-nəl) *adj.* Something that is *nominal* is small or insignificant.

notion (nō´shən) *n.* A *notion* is a belief or opinion.

novice (nŏv´ĭs) *n.* A *novice* is a beginner.

oppress (ə-prĕs´) *v.* When you *oppress* someone, you overwhelm or crush them.

ostensible (ŏ-stĕn´sə-bəl) *adj.* If something is *ostensible*, it is apparent or supposed.

paradox (păr´ə-dŏks´) *n.* A *paradox* is a true statement that seems like it would not be true.

parallel (păr´ə-lĕl´) *adj.* If things are *parallel*, they have comparable or similar parts.

particular (pər-tĭk´yə-lər) *adj.* If you are *particular* about something, you are fussy about it and pay attention to its details.

peril (pĕr´əl) *n.* A *peril* is something that is dangerous.

pernicious (pər-nĭsh´əs) *adj.* If something is *pernicious*, it is very harmful or destructive.

perpetual (pər-pĕch´oo-əl) *adj.* If something is *perpetual*, it lasts for a very long time.

persecution (pûr´sĭ-kyoo´shən) *n. Persecution* is the harsh treatment of others, often due to race or religion.

perverse (pər-vûrs´) *adj.* If something is *perverse*, it is stubbornly contrary, wrong, or harmful.

poignant (poin´yənt) *adj.* If something is *poignant*, it is profoundly moving or touching.

precocious (prĭ-kō´shəs) *adj.* If someone is *precocious*, the person is mentally advanced for his or her age.

predicament (prĭ-dĭk´ə-mənt) *n.* A *predicament* is an unpleasant situation from which it is difficult to free oneself.

predominate (prĭ-dŏm´ə-nāt) *v.* If ideas or things *predominate*, they are the most common.

prosaic (prō-zā´ĭk) *adj.* If something is *prosaic*, it is dull or ordinary.

provisions (prə-vĭzh´ənz) *n. Provisions* are a stock of necessary supplies, such as food.

prudence (prood´ns) *n. Prudence* is the wise handling of practical matters.

quest (kwĕst) *n.* A *quest* is a search.

ramble (răm´bəl) *v.* When you *ramble*, you talk at length in an aimless way.

recap (rē-kăp´) *v.* To *recap* an event is to retell or summarize it.

refuge (rĕf´yooj) *n.* A *refuge* is a shelter from danger.

renowned (rĭ-nound´) *adj.* If something is *renowned*, it is famous.

repatriate (rē-pā´trē-āt´) *v.* To *repatriate* people is to return them to the country in which they were born.

reproach (rĭ-prōch´) *n.* A *reproach* is a scolding or blaming.

requisite (rĕk´wĭ-zĭt) *adj.* Something that is *requisite* is needed or essential.

resignation (rĕz´ĭg-nā´shən) *n. Resignation* is the acceptance of something that is inescapable.

resolute (rĕz´ə-loot´) *adj.* If you are *resolute*, you are firm or determined.

resonate (rĕz´ə-nāt´) *v.* When ideas *resonate*, they have a great effect or impact.

retribution (rĕt´rə-byoo´shən) *n. Retribution* is something given in repayment, usually as a punishment.

ruffian (rŭf´ē-ən) *n.* A *ruffian* is a thug or a gangster.

scuffle (skŭf´əl) *n.* A *scuffle* is a disorderly fight.

secede (sĭ-sēd´) *v.* When you *secede*, you formally withdraw from an organization or association.

solemn (sŏl´əm) *adj.* If an event is *solemn*, it is deeply serious.

splendid (splĕn´dĭd) *adj.* If something is *splendid*, it is magnificent or very good.

sponsor (spŏn´sər) v. If you *sponsor* someone, you support his or her admission into a group.

squalor (skwŏl´ər) n. *Squalor* is a filthy, shabby, and wretched condition, as from poverty.

stifle (stī´fəl) v. If you *stifle* something, you smother it.

stoicism (stō´ĭ-sĭz´ĕm) n. *Stoicism* is indifference to pleasure or pain, or a lack of visible emotion.

stoop (sto͞op) v. If you *stoop,* you bend forward and down from the waist.

strew (stro͞o) v. If you *strew* something, you spread it here and there, or scatter it.

stun (stŭn) v. To *stun* someone is to make him or her feel shocked or dazed.

succumb (sə-kŭm´) v. To *succumb* is to give in to an overwhelming force.

sullen (sŭl´ən) adj. *Sullen* people show silent resentment.

survey (sər-vā´) v. If you *survey* something, you inspect it.

sustain (sə-stān´) v. When you *sustain* something, you keep it in existence or continue it.

tangential (tăn-jĕn´shəl) adj. If something is *tangential,* it is only slightly connected.

telecommunications (tĕl´ĭ-kə-myo͞o´nĭ-kā´shəns) n. *Telecommunications* are the electronic systems that telephones and other electronic devices use to send information.

throng (thrông) n. A *throng* is a large group of people.

thwart (thwôrt) v. If you *thwart* something, you stop it from happening.

tranquil (trăng´kwəl) adj. If something is *tranquil,* it is calm.

tumult (to͞o´mŭlt´) n. A *tumult* is a disorderly disturbance.

unabated (ŭn´ə-bā´tĭd) adj. If something is *unabated,* it keeps its full force without decreasing.

unmoor (ŭn-mo͞or´) v. if you *unmoor* something, you release it from a place.

vehemently (vē´ə-mənt-lē) adv. If you do something *vehemently,* you do it with intense emotion.

vengeance (vĕn´jəns) n. *Vengeance* is a punishment given in return for a wrong.

vex (vĕks) v. If you *vex* someone, you annoy that person.

vindication (vĭn´dĭ-kā´shən) n. *Vindication* is the evidence or proof that someone's claim is correct.

whimper (hwĭm´pər) v. To *whimper* is to sob or let out a soft cry.

Index of Skills

Key:
Teacher's Edition page numbers and subject entries are printed in **boldface** type.
Subject entries and page references that apply to both the Student Edition and the Teacher's Edition appear in lightface type.
There is no content from the Close Reader in this index.

adjectives, R30, R42
adverbs, R30, R42
comparisons, R42
dangling, R43
misplaced, R43
problems with, R43
monitoring, R72
mood, of story, **78b, 168, 171,** 173, R72
mood, of verb
conditional, 166
imperative, 30, 176, 246, 404
indicative, 176, 246, 404
interrogative, 404
shifts in, 246
subjunctive, 120, 176
moral, R72
motivations, of characters, **9, 172, 215, 217, 221, 222,** 225, **228a, 303**
motives
commercial, 73
of documentary filmmaker, 73
political, 73
social, 73
multimedia campaign, 273–276
audience for, 273–274
developing argument for, 274
elements of successful, 273
gathering information for, 273
multiple formats for, 275
Performance Task Evaluation Chart, 276
planning, 273–274
presenting, 275
producing, 274–275
purpose of, 273–274
research for, 273
revising, 275
multimedia links, R5
multiple-meaning words, **121,** R58
multiple plot lines, R7
music, in film, 123
*my*Notebook, 79, 83, 133, 137, 203, 207, 269, 273, 389, 437, 441
myths, 117, R72
*my*WriteSmart, 28, 38, 51, 68, 74, 78, 80, 81, 84, 85, 96, 103, 118, 124, 130, 134, 135, 138, 139, 149, 164, 174, 196, 202, 204, 205, 208, 209, 226, 233, 268, 270, 274, 275, 354, 367, 376, 384, 388, 390, 391, 402, 416, 425, 436, 439, 443

N

narrative nonfiction, R72
narrative poetry, R72
narrative techniques, R6. *See also* literary techniques
narrator, R6, R72
analyzing, 96
as characters, 3, 5, 6, 89
in film, 265
first-person, **368a,** R6
omniscient, **397, 401**
in personal narratives, 83
and point of view, 95, **98a, 395,** 401, **404a**
third-person, R6
unreliable, **90, 92,** 95, R72
news article, R72
nonessential adjective clauses, R47

nonessential appositives, R45
nonfiction elements, **41, 42, 43, 44, 46, 49, 50**
noun clauses, R47
nouns, R29, R36
abstract, R29
collective, R29, R36
common, R29, R36
compound, R29
concrete, R29
infinitives as, 228
plural, 234, R29, R36, R60
possessive, R29, R36, R61
predicate, 198, R44
proper, R29, R36
singular, R29, R36
novels, R73

O

objective summary, 262a
objective tone, R3, R5
object of preposition, 198
object pronouns, R37
objects
direct, 198, R31, R44
indirect, R31, R44
observations, identifying, in writing narratives, R6
odes, 435, R73
omniscient narrators, **397,** 401
onomatopoeia, R73
op-ed pieces, R73
opinions, **246a,** R68
opinion writing activity, 260
oral information, 268, **268b**
oral literature, R73
oral reports, 425
organization
for arguments, 442
for informational texts, R16–R21
for persuasive speech, 134
organizational patterns, R16–R21, R73
cause and effect, 148, **418a,** R18
chronological order, **34,** 37, 38, **326, 335,** 353, **418a,** R17, R66
compare and contrast, **178, 179, 180, 185, 188, 190,** 195, **198a, 418a,** R16, R19–R20, R66
point-by-point, R19
problem-solution, **418a,** R21, R74
subject-by-subject, R19
outlines, creating, 80, 390
overgeneralization, R26, R73
oversimplification, R26
overview, R73

P

pacing, **78b,** 438, R7
paragraph structure, 418a
parallelism, **154,** 163, **381,** 383, 387, R48
paraphrasing, **388a,** R9, R73
parentheses, R33
parenthetical citations, R9
participle phrases, R45
participles, 40, 198, R45
dangling, R45
misplaced, R45

past, 40
present, 40
parts of speech, R29–R30
passive voice, 70, 246, R41
past participles, 40, R39
past perfect progressive tense, R40
past perfect tense, R39
past principal part, R39
past progressive tense, R40
past tense, R39
pattern of organization, R73. *See also* organizational patterns
patterns, identifying, 196, 324, 388, 436
Performance Assessment, 2c, 88c, 142c, 212c, 278c, 394c
Performance Task, end of collection
argument, 441–444
expository essay, 79–82, 389–392
literary analysis, 137–140, 207–210, 269–272
multimedia campaign, 273–276
personal narrative, 83–86
persuasive speech, 133–136
Plan, Produce, Revise, Present, 79–81, 83–85, 133–135, 137–139, 203–205, 207–209, 269–271, 273–275, 389–391, 437–439, 441–443
short story, 437–440
visual presentation, 203–206
Performance Task, selection
media activity, 38, 74, 124, 268
speaking activity, 78, 103, 130, 164, 174, 202, 244, 367, 384, 416, 425
writing activity, 28, 51, 68, 96, 118, 149, 196, 226, 233, 260, 354, 376, 388, 402, 436
Performance Task Evaluation Chart
argument, 444
expository essay, 82, 392
literary analysis, 140, 210, 272
multimedia campaign, 276
personal narrative, 86
persuasive speech, 136
short story, 440
visual presentation, 206
periodicals, R73
periods, R32
personal essays, 37, R73
audience for, 84
drafts of, 84
elements of successful, 83
images in, 84
organizational patterns in, 34
Performance Task Evaluation Chart, 86
personal narratives, 83–86
planning, 83–84
presenting, 85
purpose of, **31,** 84
revising, 85
sequence of events in, 83–84
situation, establishing, 83
personal pronouns, **127,** R29, R36, R50
personification, 233, **234a, 361, 428,** 430, 434, R73
persuasion, **384a,** R73
persuasive essays, R68
persuasive speeches, 133–136

audience for, 134
delivering, 135
drafts of, 134–135
elements of successful, 133
evaluating, 135
information gathering for, 133
organization for, 134
Performance Task Evaluation Chart, 136
planning, 133–134
position for, 133
practicing, 135
purpose of, 134
research for, 134
visuals for, 135
persuasive techniques, 265, 383, 384, **384a,** R23
persuasive texts
in advertising, 268a
analyzing, R22
evaluating, R27
reading, R22–R28
photographs, 50
phrases, R44
adjective, R44
adverb, R44
appositives, R45
gerund, R45
infinitive, 228, R45
participle, R45
prepositional, R31, R44
verbal, R45
pity, appeals to, 383, R24, R68
plagiarism, R9
Plan, Produce, Revise, Present. *See under* Performance Task, end of collection
plays. *See* drama
playwrights, **279, 296, 298,** 324
plot, 4, 27, 438, R74
conflict in, **17, 22,** 27, **98a,** 225, 438, R66, R74
elements of, 27, 438
falling action in, **25,** 27, **30a,** 438, R69
multiple plot lines, R7
narrator and, 5
resolution in, **26,** 27, **30a,** 438
rising action in, **8, 12,** 27, **30a**
stage directions and, 320
stages of, 30a, 98a
and theme, 225
plot diagram, 438
plural nouns, R29, R36, R60
poetic elements and devices. *See also* poetic form; poetry
alliteration, 387
allusions, 77, **78a, 78b**
consonance, 387
couplets, 432
imagery, 77, **388b**
line breaks, 78b
meter, **202b,** 432, 435, R72
mood, 78b
pace, 78b
parallelism, 387
personification, 233
repetition, 78, 387
rhyme, **202a,** R75
rhyme scheme, **202a,** 432, 435, R75

Index of Titles and Authors

Key:

Authors and titles that appear in the Student Edition are in lightface type.
Authors and titles that appear in the Close Reader are in **boldface** type.
Names of authors who appear in both the Student Edition and the Close Reader are lightface.
For these authors, Student Edition page references are lightface and Close Reader page references are **boldface.**

Student Edition Acknowledgments

"After Auschwitz" by Elie Wiesel. Text copyright © 1995 by Elie Wiesel. Reprinted by permission of Elie Wiesel.

The American Heritage Dictionary of the English Language, Fifth Edition. Text copyright © 2011 by Houghton Mifflin Harcourt. Adapted and reprinted by permission from *The American Heritage Dictionary of the English Language, Fifth Edition.*

Excerpt from *Anne Frank: The Book, the Life the Afterlife* by Francine Prose. Text copyright © 2009 by Francine Prose. Reprinted by permission of HarperCollins Publishers.

"Better Training for New Drivers" by Jamie Lincoln Kitman from *The New York Times*, May 28, 2012. Text copyright © 2012 by The New York Times. Reprinted by permission of PARS International on behalf of The New York Times.

Excerpt from *Bloody Times: The Funeral of Abraham Lincoln and the Manhunt for Jefferson Davis* by James L. Swanson. Text copyright © 2011 by James L. Swanson. Reprinted by permission of HarperCollins Publishers.

Excerpt from "Bonne Année" by Jean-Pierre Benoit from *The Butterfly's Way: Voices From the Haitian Dyaspora in the United States* edited by Edwidge Danticat. Text copyright © 2001 by Jean-Pierre Benoit. Reprinted by permission of Jean-Pierre Benoit.

"Chicago" from *Chicago Poems* by Carl Sandburg. Copyright © 1944 by Carl Sandburg. Reprinted by permission of Houghton Mifflin Harcourt.

Excerpt from *The Diary of a Young Girl: The Definitive Edition* by Anne Frank, edited by Otto H. Frank and Mirjam Pressler, translated by Susan Massotty. Text copyright © 1991, 2001 by The Anne Frank-Fonds, Basel, Switzerland. English translation copyright © 1995, 2001 by Doubleday, a division of Random House, Inc. and Penguin Group (UK) Inc.

The Diary of Anne Frank by Frances Goodrich and Albert Hackett. Text copyright © 1956 by Frances Goodrich, Albert Hackett and Otto Frank. Reprinted by permission of Random House, Inc. and Douglas & Kopelman Artists, Inc.

"The Drummer Boy of Shiloh" by Ray Bradbury. Text copyright © 1960 by Ray Bradbury. Originally published in *The Saturday Evening Post*. Reprinted by permission of Don Congdon Associates, Inc.

"Fatal Crashes Drop For 16-Year-Olds, Rise For Older Teens" by Allison Aubrey. Text copyright © 2011 by Allison Aubrey. Reprinted by permission of National Public Radio.

"Find Work" by Rhina P. Espaillat from *Poetry* magazine, February 1999. Text copyright © by Rhina P. Espaillat. Reprinted by permission of Rhina P. Espaillat.

"Hanging Fire" from *The Collected Poems of Audre Lorde* by Audre Lorde. Text copyright © 1997 by the Audre Lorde Estate. Reprinted by permission of W. W. Norton & Company, Inc.

Excerpts from *Harriet Tubman: Conductor on the Underground Railroad* by Ann Petry. Text copyright © 1955 by Ann Petry, renewed in 1983 by Ann Petry. Reprinted by permission of Russell & Volkening as agents for the author.

"Is 16 too young to drive a car?" by Robert Davis from *USA Today*, March 2, 2005. Text copyright © 2012 by USA Today. Reprinted by permission of PARS International on behalf of USA Today. All rights reserved.

Excerpt from *The Latehomecomer: A Hmong Family Memoir* by Kao Kalia Yang. Text copyright © 2008 by Kao Kalia Yang. Reprinted by permission of The Permissions Company on behalf of Coffee House Press.

"Leave the Voting Age Alone" by Jenny Diamond Cheng from *The New York Times*, May 28, 2012. Text copyright © 2012 by Jenny Diamond Cheng. Reprinted by permission of Jenny Diamond Cheng.

"Mandatory Service to Become an Adult" by Michael Thompson from *The New York Times*, May 28, 2012. Text copyright © 2012 by Michael Thompson. Reprinted by permission of Michael Thompson.

"Marigolds" by Eugenia Collier, originally published in *Negro Digest*, vol. XIX, no. 1, November 1969. Text copyright © 1969 by Eugenia Collier. Reprinted by permission of Eugenia Collier.

"My Favorite Chaperone" by Jean Davis Okimoto from *First Crossing: Stories About Teen Immigrants* edited by Donald R. Gallo. Text copyright © 2004 by Jean Davis Okimoto. Reprinted by permission of Jean Davis Okimoto.

"My Mother Enters the Work Force" from *On the Bus with Rosa Parks* by Rita Dove. Text copyright © 1999 by Rita Dove. Reprinted by permission of W. W. Norton & Company, Inc.

"One Last Time" from *Living Up the Street* by Gary Soto. Text copyright © 1985 by Gary Soto. Reprinted by permission of Gary Soto.

"A Parent's Role in the Path to Adulthood" by Barbara Hofer from *The New York Times*, May 28, 2012. Text copyright © 2012 by Barbara Hofer. Reprinted by permission of Barbara Hofer.

Excerpt adapted from *A Place to Call Home: What Immigrants Say Now About Life in America* by Scott Bittle and Jonathan Rochkind. Text copyright © 2009 by Public Agenda. Reprinted by permission of Public Agenda.

"The Powwow at the End of the World" from *The Summer of Black Widows* by Sherman Alexie. Text copyright © 1996 by Sherman Alexie. Reprinted by permission of Hanging Loose Press.

"Scary Tales" from *Jackie Torrence: The Magic of Creating Stories and the Art of Telling Them* by Jackie Torrence. Text copyright © 1998 by Jackie Torrence. Reprinted by permission of The Estate of Jackie Torrence.

"Teenagers" from *My Own True Name: New and Selected Poems for Young Adults* by Pat Mora. Text copyright © 2000 by Arte Público Press. Reprinted by permission of Arte Público Press.

"Teens at Work," by Kyle Swartz, from the *Record-Journal*, May 14, 2012. Text copyright © 2012 by the Record-Journal. Reprinted by permission of Record-Journal Publishing Co.

"Teens need jobs, not just cash" by Anne Michaud, originally published as "Summer jobs and the lost generation" in *Newsday*, July 11, 2012. Text copyright © 2012 by Newsday. Reprinted by permission of PARS International on behalf of Newsday.

"There But for the Grace" by Wislawa Szymborska from *Sounds, Feelings, Thoughts: Seventy Poems by Wislawa Szymborska* translated and introduced by Magnus J. Krynski and Robert A. Maguire. Text copyright © 1981 by Princeton University Press. Reprinted by permission of Princeton University Press.

Excerpt from "What is the Horror Genre?" by Stephen King from *Stephen King: a Critical Companion* by Sharon A. Russell. Text copyright © 1996 by Sharon A. Russell. Reprinted by permission of Copyright Clearance Center.

"What the Brain Says About Maturity" by Laurence Steinberg from *The New York Times*, May 28, 2012. Text copyright © 2012 by The New York Times. Reprinted by permission of PARS International on behalf of The New York Times.

Close Reader Acknowledgments

Excerpt from "Civil War Journal" from *The Journals of Louisa May Alcott* by Louisa May Alcott, edited by Joel Myerson, Daniel Shealy, and Madeleine B. Stern. Text copyright © 1989 by The Estate of Theresa W. Pratt. Reprinted by permission of Joel Myerson.

Excerpt from *The Diary of Anne Frank* by Frances Goodrich and Albert Hackett. Text copyright © 1956 by Frances Goodrich, Albert Hackett and Otto Frank. Reprinted by permission of Douglas & Kopelman Artists, Inc. and Random House, Inc.

"The Flying Machine" from *The Ray Bradbury Chronicles: Volume Two* by Ray Bradbury. Text copyright © 1992 by Ray Bradbury. Reprinted by permission of Don Congdon Associates, Inc.

"The Flying Machine" from *Golden Apples of the Sun* by Ray Bradbury. Text copyright © 1953, renewed 1986 by Ray Bradbury. Reprinted by permission of Don Congdon Associates, Inc.

"Frankenstein" from *Counting Myself Lucky* by Edward Field. Text copyright © 1963, 1967, 1973, 1977, 1978, 1987, 1992 by Edward Field. Reprinted by permission of Black Sparrow Press.

"Golden Glass" by Alma Luz Villanueva from *Hispanics in the U.S.: An Anthology of Creative Literature* edited by Francisco Jimenez and Gary D. Keller. Text copyright © 1981 by Alma Luz Villanueva. Reprinted by permission of Bilingual Press/Editorial Bilingue, Arizona State University.

"Hard on the Gas" from *Behind the Wheel: Poems About Driving* by Janet S. Wong. Text copyright © 1999 by Janet S. Wong. Reprinted by permission of Janet S. Wong.

"Identity" by Julio Noboa Polanco. Text copyright © 1962 by Julio Noboa Polanco. Reprinted by permission of Julio Noboa Polanco.

Excerpt from "Man-Made Monsters" from *A Natural History of Unnatural Things* by Daniel Cohen. Text copyright © 1971 by Daniel Cohen. Reprinted by permission of Henry Morrison, Inc.

"Museum Indians" from *Roofwalker* by Susan Power. Text copyright © 2002 by Susan Power. Reprinted by permission of Milkweed Editions.

"My Friend Douglass" from *Abraham Lincoln & Frederick Douglass* by Russell Freedman. Text copyright © 2012 by Russell Freedman. Reprinted by permission of Houghton Mifflin Harcourt Publishing Company.

"The Outsider" from *H.P. Lovecraft Tales* by H.P. Lovecraft. Text copyright © 2005 by H.P. Lovecraft. Reprinted by permission of Jabberwocky Literary Agency.

"The Real McCoy" from *Outward Dreams: Black Inventors and Their Inventions* by Jim Haskins. Text copyright © 1991 by Jim Haskins. Reprinted by permission of Walker and Company.

"A Story of How a Wall Stands" from *Woven Stone* by Simon J. Ortiz. Text copyright © 1992 by Simon J. Ortiz. Reprinted by permission of Simon J. Ortiz.

"To be of use" from *Circles on the Water: Selected Poems of Marge Piercy* by Marge Piercy. Text copyright © 1973, 1982 by Marge Piercy and Middlemarsh, Inc. Reprinted by permission of Random House, Inc. and Wallace Literary Agency, Inc.

"The Whistle" from *Down Garrapata Road* by Anne Estevis. Text copyright © 2003 by Anne Estevis. Reprinted by permission of Arte Público Press.